# Our Favorite Recipes

All the recipes that appear in *Cooking Light* meet high standards, but a few throughout the year are so incredibly good they become our staff's personal favorites. The dish pictured below and the recipes highlighted on the following pages are the ones that we whip up for our families and friends. We hope they'll become your favorites, too.

**Champion Chicken Parmesan** (*page 276*):
The zesty tomato sauce, with its sun-dried tomatoes, adds a new twist to this popular Italian recipe.

# More of
# Our Favorite Recipes

### Sour Cream-Lemon Pound Cake
*(page 88, cover photo):*

We measure pound cake not by the weight of its ingredients anymore, but by the depth of its flavors. This lemony variation was able to weaken knees staff-wide.

### ◄ Texas Sheet Cake *(page 56):*

Not even the Texas State Library and Archives Commission can tell us how Texas laid claim to this cake. It may have to do with the size of the chocolaty punch it packs: big—really big.

### Maple-Glazed Salmon *(page 69):*

You'll be gratefully amazed at how well the clean sweetness of pure maple syrup works with salmon—a perfect contrast for the fish's distinctive flavor.

### Creamy Gorgonzola Fettuccine *(page 144):*

Not only is pasta easy and fast to prepare, it's also a perfect blank canvas for flavor artistry. Especially this pasta, with its blend of asparagus, walnuts, and pungent Gorgonzola. This dish will be your masterpiece.

### ◄ Churrasco with Chimichurri
*(page 269):*

This beef-lover's delight drew applause in our Test Kitchens. Churrasco is a marinated steak that's grilled.

### ◄ Ooey-Gooey Peanut Butter-Chocolate Brownies
*(page 273):*

Marshmallow cream, peanut butter, and chocolate and just 5 grams of fat per serving— this recipe just might be heaven on earth.

### ◄ Golden Onion Strata with Gruyère and Prosciutto
*(page 113):*

We love the flavor and look of this strata, whose paper-thin prosciutto provides a welcome hint of salt.

### ◄ French Onion Soup with Beef and Barley
*(page 24):*

Chock-full of fiber-rich barley, this tasty variation on the classic will fill you with dang-that-was-good happiness any time of year.

### ◄ Squash-Rice Casserole
*(page 348):*

Don't let the simple name fool you: With its sour cream and Parmesan and Cheddar cheeses, this classic casserole is a taste sensation.

◀ **Monte Cristo Sandwiches** *(page 249)*:

Our lightened version of the classic sandwich takes just six minutes to cook. And with its trademark sweet-and-savory flavors, it's better for supper than it is for lunch.

◀ **Banana-Split Cheesecake** *(page 231)*:

Not many things go together better than cheesecake and chocolate. And this banana split-inspired blend of chocolate, banana, and strawberry flavors will delight dessert devotees to no end.

◀ **Wild Rice Crab Cakes** *(page 282)*:

The strong flavor and texture of wild rice, its nuttiness emphasized by the cumin in this recipe, make these crab cakes some of the heartiest and tastiest we've ever come across.

▲ **Pecan-Crusted Pork with Red Onion Marmalade and Roasted Sweet Potatoes** *(page 341)*:

This won highest marks from just about everyone who tasted it. Since it elicited raves in our Test Kitchens, we've no doubt it will do the same in your house.

◀ **Pecan Tassies in Cream Cheese Pastry** *(page 340)*:

Packed with pecans, these miniature tarts have all the taste of a big pecan pie, but their small size makes them ideal for parties and buffets.

◀ **Herb-Roasted Turkey with Cheese Grits** *(page 311)*:

Infused with garlic, rosemary, sage, and thyme, chef Jim Coleman's turkey is far more than just the usual holiday repeat. With cheese grits standing in for the stuffing, this dish is guaranteed to wow guests any time of year.

◀ **Spanish Toast** *(page 298)*:

Rubbing ripe tomatoes over garlic toast may seem a bit odd, but it's a tradition in Spain. The crisp toast practically melts the garlic and tomatoes. This is bound to become a tradition at your house, too.

**Peanutty Noodles** *(page 111):*

This Asian-inspired noodle dish balances fresh ginger, garlic, and cilantro with peanut butter. It's terrific as a side with pork, but it works just as well as a main dish if you toss in some cooked shrimp or chicken.

# Cooking Light®

## ANNUAL RECIPES 2001

Oxmoor House®

ISBN: 0-8487-1997-2
ISSN: 1091-3645

Printed in the United States of America
First printing 2000

Be sure to check with your health-care provider before making any changes in your diet.

Oxmoor House, Inc.

Editor-in-Chief: Nancy Fitzpatrick Wyatt
Senior Foods Editor: Katherine M. Eakin
Senior Editor, Copy and Homes: Olivia Kindig Wells
Art Director: James Boone

*Cooking Light*® *Annual Recipes* 2001

Editor: Adrienne S. Davis
Copy Editor: Jacqueline B. Giovanelli
Editorial Assistant: Heather Averett
Designer: Carol Damsky
Publishing Systems Administrator: Rick Tucker
Director, Production and Distribution: Phillip Lee
Books Production Manager: Larry Hunter
Production Assistant: Faye Porter Bonner
Contributing Indexer: Mary Ann Laurens

## *Cooking Light*®

Vice President, Editor: Doug Crichton
Executive Editors: Rod Davis, Billy R. Sims
Managing Editor: Hillari Dowdle
Senior Editors: Ellen Templeton Carroll, M.S., R.D. (Projects), Kelly P. Caudle (Articles), Jill G. Melton, M.S., R.D. (Food), Donna Raskin (Healthy Living)
Food Editor: Mary S. Creel, M.S., R.D.
Editorial Coordinator: Carol C. Noe
Assistant Food Editors: Krista Ackerbloom, M.S., R.D., Regan Miller Jones, R.D.
Assistant Fitness Editor: Melissa Ewey Johnson
Beauty Editor: Martha Schindler
Art Director: Susan Waldrip Dendy
Assistant Art Director: Lori Bianchi Nichols
Designers: Maya Metz Logue, Paul T. Marince
Assistant Designer: Brigette Mayer
Senior Photographer: Becky Luigart-Stayner
Photographer: Randy Mayor
Photo Stylists: Lydia E. DeGaris, Jan Gautro, Mary Catherine Muir
Test Kitchens Director: Rebecca J. Pate
Food Stylist: Kellie Gerber Kelley
Test Kitchens Staff: Sam Brannock, Martha Condra, Julie W. Cundiff, M. Kathleen Kanen, John Kirkpatrick, Mike Wilson
Copy Chief: Maria Parker Hopkins
Senior Copy Editor: Ritchey Halphen
Copy Editor: Ann Taylor
Production Editors: Hazel R. Eddins, Liz Rhoades
Copy/Production Assistant: Jennifer Southall
Editorial Assistants: Su Reid, Joyce McCann Swisdak
Office Manager: Mara Hamner
Research Assistant: Jason P. Mitchell
CookingLight.com
Editor: Lisa Delaney
Managing Editor: Maelynn Cheung
Assistant Editor: Stacey L. Strawn

### WE'RE HERE FOR YOU!

We at Oxmoor House are dedicated to serving you with reliable information that expands your imagination and enriches your life. We welcome your comments and suggestions. Please write us at:

Oxmoor House, Inc.
Editor, *Cooking Light*® *Annual Recipes*
2100 Lakeshore Drive
Birmingham, AL 35209

To order additional publications, call 1-205-877-6560.

Cover: *Sour Cream-Lemon Pound Cake* (page 88)

# contents

*continued*

# Our Year at *Cooking Light*®

Dear Readers,

With this comprehensive collection of the extraordinary recipes that have appeared in *Cooking Light* over the past year, we move into a new century and millennium. We can't help but be happy for ourselves and grateful to you for joining us as we take healthful cooking into a new era. We don't just like what we do, we love it. And we think you do, too. To make our common passion even more accessible, in this book we've presented all 906 of the recipes which appeared in *Cooking Light* in 2000. Each recipe is easy to find thanks to the easy-to-follow layouts, triple index system, and other features like "Our Favorite Recipes" (beginning on page 1).

Some of the highlights that made 2000, and thus this cookbook, outstanding are:

- We started strong and bold with our Taste of Trends 2000, surveying the top 12 flavor trends for the upcoming year. And we've recapped the top trends and recipes for you here (page 12).

- Our year-long Cooking Class 2000 series introduced a new generation (and some of the rest of us, too) to the basic techniques of healthful, low-fat cooking. From how to make pizza (page 52) to how to make great sauces (page 84), all the tips and techniques are gathered in this cookbook.

- We took our healthy lifestyle philosophy to the border cities of El Paso and Ciudad Juàrez to participate in a public health initiative to improve the diet and fitness habits of the area's 3 million residents. You'll see how traditional Tex-Mex favorites can be lightened with no loss of flavor (page 48).

- Throughout the year, we proved again that for the healthful cook, there really are no bad foods. Here, you find all the smart, tasty ways to use important ingredients such as whipping cream (page 81) and salt (page 297) to create healthful dishes.

- The holidays gave us the chance to create for you some of the best seasonal dining ideas around. Top chefs share their secrets for the turkey dinners they make at home (page 310), and we celebrate holiday simplicity—with great recipe and menu ideas for making it so (beginning on page 350).

- As *Cooking Light* continues to grow, we found that 10 issues a year just weren't enough, so in 2000 we brought out one more for a total of 11. Splitting our always popular July/August edition into all-new July and August issues gave you twice the selection for great summer eating. And every new recipe is in this cookbook (beginning on pages 188 and 218).

- Those with keen eyes noticed a brand-new look for *Cooking Light* in 2000, and thus for this book. With the help of the respected design firm WBGM, we spruced up our pages and added some great new sections, including the *Cooking Light* Profile, a monthly look at readers just like you whose lives are an inspiring balance of healthful eating and active and challenging interests.

As you use and enjoy all the great food ideas from this edition of the *Cooking Light Annual Recipes* series, try this tip to have even more fun: Pick out a combination of dishes you really like and invite some friends over for a special dinner. We've found it's a great way to socialize, and if you saw our special on the TVFN in May or review our story (page 110), you'll agree. All of this and more make this book one of the best—and certainly the tastiest—investments you'll find all year.

Best Regards,

Vice President/Editor

# january ◆ february

# Taste of Trends 2000

## Our pick of the top 12 flavor trends for the coming year.

What trends will the new year bring to your kitchen, your table, and your taste buds? We inquired within our ranks, asked the opinions of outside food experts, and peered into grocery stores and kitchens around the country. We found what we always do in the culinary world—lots of change, new ideas, brilliant flavors, and a considerable sense of adventure and exploration. This year, too, we found a strong current of tradition—whether in nostalgia for Mom's cooking, a renewed reverence for regional dishes, or just a simple acknowledgment, heightened by the change of millennia, that the future is always rooted in the past.

### Roasted Cabbage Rolls

We've revived a nearly forgotten comfort food—cabbage rolls. These are made in the Finnish style, with a corn syrup-bacon glaze that caramelizes during baking. (Recipe by Finnish-American Jim Fobel, a *Cooking Light* Contributor and the author of *Jim Fobel's Casseroles* and *Jim Fobel's Old-Fashioned Baking Book*.)

**CABBAGE ROLLS:**
- 1 (3-pound) head cabbage
- 2 tablespoons water
- Cooking spray
- 1 onion, slivered
- 1 cup water
- ⅓ cup uncooked long-grain rice
- 1 cup diced Granny Smith apple
- ⅔ cup chopped green onions
- ½ cup 2% reduced-fat milk
- 1¼ teaspoons garlic salt
- ¾ teaspoon dried rubbed sage
- ¼ teaspoon ground nutmeg
- ¼ teaspoon black pepper
- 1 large egg
- 1 pound ground turkey
- ¼ cup water

**BASTING GLAZE:**
- 4 bacon slices, chopped
- ⅓ cup dark corn syrup
- 3 tablespoons tomato paste
- 1½ tablespoons water
- ¾ teaspoon salt

**1.** To prepare cabbage rolls, core cabbage using a serrated knife. Place cabbage in an 8-inch square baking dish or 2-quart casserole; add 2 tablespoons water. Loosely cover with heavy-duty plastic wrap. Microwave at HIGH 9 minutes, rotating baking dish a half-turn after 5 minutes. Cover dish, and let stand 15 minutes. Discard any tough dark green leaves. Remove 8 light-colored cabbage leaves. Cut off raised portion of main vein of each leaf, and set leaves aside. Finely chop enough remaining cabbage to measure ½ cup, and set aside. Coarsely chop enough remaining cabbage to measure 2 cups; arrange in bottom of a 13 x 9-inch baking dish coated with cooking spray. Top with slivered onion.

**2.** Bring 1 cup water to a boil in a small saucepan. Add rice; reduce heat to medium-low, and cook 8 minutes. Drain well.

**3.** Preheat oven to 350°.

**4.** Combine ½ cup finely chopped cabbage, rice, apple, and next 7 ingredients. Crumble turkey over mixture; stir just until blended. Place about ½ cup turkey mixture in center of each cabbage leaf. Fold in edges of leaves, and roll up; place cabbage rolls on top of coarsely chopped cabbage. Cut several ¼-inch-deep slits across top of each roll. Pour ¼ cup water over rolls. Cover with foil, and bake at 350° for 30 minutes.

**5.** To prepare basting glaze, cook bacon in a small saucepan over medium heat 3 minutes or until lightly browned. Remove from heat. Remove bacon from pan; discard bacon drippings. Return bacon to pan; stir in corn syrup and remaining 3 ingredients. Uncover cabbage rolls; spoon one-third of basting glaze over cabbage rolls. Bake, uncovered, for 1 hour, basting with basting glaze every 20 minutes. Spoon about ¼ cup remaining cabbage on each of 8 plates; top each with 1 cabbage roll. Yield: 8 servings.

CALORIES 223 (20% from fat); FAT 4.9g (sat 1.7g, mono 1.6g, poly 1g); PROTEIN 17.4g; CARB 28.7g; FIBER 4.2g; CHOL 69mg; IRON 2.4mg; SODIUM 707mg; CALC 107mg

### Chocolate Espresso Pudding

Soy milk is as high in health-promoting isoflavones as tofu—1 cup contains 80 milligrams, an amount that's been shown to stave off osteoporosis. It is sold in cartons found on the baking aisle of the grocery store. (Recipe by Steven Petusevsky, Director of Creative Food Development for Whole Foods, a natural-foods chain.)

- ½ cup packed brown sugar
- ¼ cup cornstarch
- 3 tablespoons unsweetened cocoa
- 1 tablespoon instant coffee granules
- ⅛ teaspoon salt
- 2 cups fat-free soy milk
- 2 ounces bittersweet chocolate, chopped
- 1 teaspoon vanilla extract

**1.** Combine first 5 ingredients in a medium, heavy saucepan, and stir well with a whisk. Gradually stir in milk, and bring to a boil over medium heat. Reduce heat, and simmer 1 minute or until thick. Remove from heat, and add chocolate, stirring until melted. Stir in vanilla. Pour about ½ cup pudding into each of 4 dessert dishes; cover surface of pudding with plastic wrap. Chill at least 4 hours. Remove plastic wrap to serve. Yield: 4 servings.

CALORIES 281 (15% from fat); FAT 4.8g (sat 2.8g, mono 1.6g, poly 0.1g); PROTEIN 5.5g; CARB 56.2g; FIBER 0.6g; CHOL 0mg; IRON 2mg; SODIUM 134mg; CALC 237mg

## Soy
### 1

This powerhouse protein source seems to be the wonder food of our time. Researchers have discovered that it can fight cancer, menopausal symptoms, heart disease, and osteoporosis. Even the U.S. Food and Drug Administration is eating it up: The agency recently approved a health claim on food labels explaining soy protein's role in reducing heart-disease risk.

## Mangoes
### 2

Mangoes rate as the most-consumed fruit in the world. According to the Produce Marketing Association, U.S. consumption increased 20% from 1995 to an average 1.36 pounds per person (about 3 mangoes) in 1996, and it continues to rise. Besides their fabulous taste, these tropical goodies are packed with beta carotene, fiber, and vitamin C.

## Flaxseed
### 3

Flaxseed contains high amounts of phytoestrogens, as well as omega-3 fatty acids, which may help prevent heart disease. It also supplies iron, niacin, phosphorous, and vitamin E. Europeans have baked with this crunchy treasure for years. The Flax Council of Canada reports that U.S. consumption has jumped to an estimated 25,000 metric tons, up from 7,000 metric tons in 1994. The seed's nutty flavor lends itself to baked goods and grain dishes such as rice pilaf.

## Mom Food
### 4

Mashed potatoes don't hug you like Mom can, but they do lend comfort. Our affection for old-fashioned, homemade food isn't new, but it seems to rise as our lives grow more hectic.

## Homegrown Herbs
### 5

We are an herb-loving nation. Especially as our culinary repertoire increases, we use cupfuls of the flavorings. And there's a very healthful motive: The fresh, strong flavors of herbs let you rethink cooking that relies on salt, fat, sugar, and deep-frying as the summation of all culinary development.

## Sherry Vinegar
### 6

Among an expanding selection of vinegars—from pungent balsamics to those flavored with fruits or herbs—sherry vinegar stands out. This new Spanish import tastes nutty and mellow compared to its more piquant cousins. The flavor makes it ideal for a light salad dressing. Many grocery stores now carry the deep-red liquid, but the bottle may be a bit pricey (about $12 for 25 ounces). And you don't have to pour it on—a little goes a long way.

## New Regionalism
### 7

Multicultural cookbooks such as *The Basque Kitchen,* by Gerald and Cameron Hirigoyen (HarperCollins, 1999), and *Flavors of Puglia,* by Nancy Harmon Jenkins (Broadway Books, 1997), celebrate the recipes of a particular region, rather than an entire country. A variety of new books explore American locales: the Appalachian Mountains (*Smokehouse Ham, Spoon Bread, and Scuppernong Wine,* by Joseph Earl Dabney [Cumberland House, 1998]); the Heartland (*Prairie Home Cooking,* by Judith M. Fertig [The Harvard Common Press, 1999]); and the West (*The Wild West Cookbook,* by Cinda Chavich [Robert Rose Inc., 1998].

## Local Seasonal Fare
### 8

We used to take food's freshness for granted. But as the market's ability to ship increases, so does our interest in buying fruits and vegetables direct from the people who grow them. Across the country are nearly 1,000 farms known as CSAs (for "community-supported agriculture") where consumers buy in for a season's worth of fresh produce. The advantage to you: lower prices, fresher choices, and better flavors.

## Farm-Fresh Fish
### 9

The National Fisheries Institute reports that the worldwide production of farm-raised fish has more than doubled from approximately 10 million metric tons in 1984 to more than 27 million metric tons in 1995. Some say farm-raised fillets fall short on the flavor front, but they cost less and ensure a steady supply. Fish have omega-3s, polyunsaturated fatty acids that play a role in reducing the risk of heart disease.

## Latin Flair
### 10

South American steakhouses, Cuban cafés, empanada joints, and other Latin-influenced imports are popping up all over the United States. Places such as Las Tablas in Chicago, Cafe Habana in New York City, and Julia's Empanadas in Washington, D.C., have *Norte-americanos* learning a new lip-smacking vocabulary that includes *mojo,* a tropical fruit-based sauce; *chimichurri,* a tangy cross between vinaigrette and pesto made with lots of garlic; and *dulce de leche,* a creamy dessert.

## Indian Food
### 11

Food-trend watcher Art Siemering predicts Indian cuisine will become the next international culinary wave. Likewise, Linda Smithson and Eleanor Hanson of *Foodwatch Newsletter* call it "the fastest-growing ethnic cuisine." That's good news for the health-minded because the veggie-friendly food typically relies on bold, spicy flavors rather than fat.

## Asian Pantry
### 12

Notice more hoisin sauce, fish sauce, sesame oil, chile paste, or wasabi in grocery stores and restaurants? All of these once-exotic ingredients—whose robust flavors lend themselves to light cooking—are becoming as familiar as ketchup. Thai and Vietnamese food have grown more popular, perhaps made more accessible to Americans because of our long familiarity with Chinese cooking.

## Confetti Rice Pilaf with Toasted Flaxseed

To release the health benefits of flaxseed, the hard outer coating must be broken down. So we've toasted the seeds and chopped them in a blender before adding them to this pilaf. (Recipe by Patsey Jamieson, a recipe developer in Burlington, Vermont, and former food editor for *Eating Well* magazine.)

  ¼  cup flaxseed
  2  teaspoons olive oil
  1  cup chopped onion
  1  cup uncooked basmati or
     long-grain rice
  1  (16-ounce) can fat-free,
     less-sodium chicken broth
  ¼  cup chopped fresh parsley
  2  teaspoons grated lemon rind
  1  tablespoon fresh lemon juice
  ½  teaspoon salt
  ¼  teaspoon black pepper

**1.** Place flaxseed in a small nonstick skillet; cook over low heat 5 minutes or until toasted, stirring constantly. Place flaxseed in a blender; process just until chopped.
**2.** Heat oil in a saucepan over medium heat until hot. Add onion; cook over medium heat 3 minutes or until tender. Add rice. Cook 1 minute; stir constantly. Stir in broth; bring to a boil. Reduce heat; simmer 20 minutes or until rice is tender. Remove from heat; fluff with a fork. Stir in flaxseed, parsley and remaining ingredients. Yield: 4 servings (serving size: 1 cup).
**NOTE:** Flaxseed keeps best when stored in the refrigerator.

CALORIES 263 (25% from fat); FAT 7.2g (sat 0.7g, mono 4g, poly 2.1g); PROTEIN 7.5g; CARB 44.5g; FIBER 3.9g; CHOL 0mg; IRON 3.4mg; SODIUM 544mg; CALC 56mg

## Mango-Coconut Bread Pudding

Mangoes are now as common a fruit as oranges in your supermarket's produce section. (Recipe by Donna Shields, who lives in Key West, Florida, and is the author of *Caribbean Light*.)

**BREAD PUDDING:**
  1  cup fat-free milk
  ¼  cup honey
  1  teaspoon vanilla extract
  1  (14-ounce) can light coconut milk
  2  large eggs
  1  large egg white
  6  cups (1-inch) day-old cubed
     French bread (about 6 slices)
  2  cups diced peeled ripe mango
     (about ½ pound)
     Cooking spray
  ⅓  cup flaked sweetened coconut,
     toasted

**SAUCE:**
  ½  cup sugar
  ⅓  cup mango or apricot nectar
  1  tablespoon butter or stick margarine
  1  teaspoon cornstarch
  1  (5-ounce) can evaporated fat-free
     milk

**1.** Preheat oven to 350°.
**2.** To prepare bread pudding, combine first 6 ingredients in a large bowl. Stir in bread and mango. Let stand at room temperature 30 minutes. Pour mixture into an 11 x 7-inch baking dish coated with cooking spray. Bake at 350° for 1 hour. Sprinkle with coconut. Bake an additional 10 minutes or until set. Let stand 30 minutes before serving.
**3.** To prepare sauce, combine sugar and nectar in a small saucepan. Bring to a boil. Reduce heat, and simmer 10 minutes. Remove from heat; stir in butter. Combine cornstarch and evaporated milk in a small bowl. Add cornstarch mixture to nectar mixture. Bring to a boil over medium heat; cook 1 minute, stirring constantly. Serve warm over bread pudding. Yield: 8 servings.

CALORIES 285 (24% from fat); FAT 7.6g (sat 3g, mono 1.1g, poly 0.6g); PROTEIN 6.7g; CARB 48.4g; FIBER 1.5g; CHOL 61mg; IRON 1.3mg; SODIUM 234mg; CALC 118mg

## Churrasco with Pebre (Grilled Beef Tenderloin with Chilean Cilantro Sauce)

(pictured on page 40)

*Churrasco* means different things in different parts of Latin America: a particular cut of beef in Argentina, a general term for barbecue in Brazil, and a flat tenderloin in Nicaragua. For this dish, the steak is cut in the Nicaraguan style, seasoned with Salvadoran spices, and accented with a Chilean sauce called *pebre*. (Recipes by Steven Raichlen, award-winning author of *Healthy Latin Cooking*.)

     Cooking spray
  4  cups sliced onion
  ½  teaspoon sugar
  1  (1½-pound) center-cut beef
     tenderloin
  ½  teaspoon salt
  ½  teaspoon garlic powder
  ½  teaspoon dried oregano
  ½  teaspoon black pepper
  ¼  teaspoon ground cumin
     Pebre (Chilean Cilantro Sauce)

**1.** Place a large skillet coated with cooking spray over medium heat until hot. Add onion and sugar; cover and cook 10 minutes or until golden brown, stirring frequently. Keep warm.
**2.** Preheat broiler.
**3.** Cut tenderloin lengthwise with grain into 6 even steaks. Place 1 steak between 2 sheets of heavy-duty plastic wrap; flatten to an even thickness using a meat mallet or rolling pin. Repeat procedure with remaining steaks. Combine salt and next 4 ingredients. Rub salt mixture over both sides of steaks. Place steaks on a broiler pan coated with cooking spray. Broil 2 minutes on each side or until desired degree of doneness. Top each steak with onion mixture; drizzle each with 1 tablespoon Pebre. Yield: 6 servings (serving size: 3 ounces steak, ½ cup onion mixture, and 1 tablespoon Pebre).

(Totals include 1 tablespoon Pebre) CALORIES 167 (39% from fat); FAT 7.3g (sat 2.3g, mono 3.4g, poly 0.5g); PROTEIN 17.1g; CARB 8.2g; FIBER 1.7g; CHOL 48mg; IRON 2.5mg; SODIUM 329mg; CALC 27mg

**PEBRE (CHILEAN CILANTRO SAUCE):**

If you don't like cilantro, substitute parsley.

  ⅔  cup canned vegetable broth
  ½  cup minced fresh cilantro
  ½  cup minced onion
  ½  cup minced red bell pepper
  ¼  cup white vinegar
  ¼  cup extra-virgin olive oil
  1  teaspoon salt
  1  teaspoon dried oregano
  1  teaspoon crushed red pepper
  ½  teaspoon black pepper
  4  garlic cloves, minced

**1.** Combine all ingredients, stirring with a whisk until well-blended. Yield: 2 cups (serving size: 1 tablespoon).

**NOTE:** Store remaining sauce in an air-tight container in the refrigerator for up to 2 weeks.

CALORIES 18 (90% from fat); FAT 1.8g (sat 0.2g, mono 1.3g, poly 0.2g); PROTEIN 0.1g; CARB 0.8g; FIBER 0.2g; CHOL 0mg; IRON 0.1mg; SODIUM 95mg; CALC 4mg

## Garbanzo Stew

This vegetarian entrée is a great introduction to Indian food—spiced with garam masala, curry, and turmeric. *Garam masala*, a mixture of ground spices such as cloves, cinnamon, cardamom, coriander, cumin, nutmeg, and black peppercorns, is often found in gourmet grocery stores or in the Middle Eastern sections of supermarkets. (Recipes by Bharti Kirchner, the author of four cookbooks, including *The Healthy Cuisine of India*.)

  1  tablespoon olive oil
  1  cup finely chopped onion
  4  cups chopped seeded tomato
     (about 1½ pounds)
  1  teaspoon sugar
  1  teaspoon curry powder
  ½  teaspoon salt
  ¼  teaspoon ground turmeric
  ⅛  teaspoon ground red pepper
  2  (15½-ounce) cans chickpeas
     (garbanzo beans), drained
  ½  teaspoon garam masala
  ¼  cup chopped fresh cilantro
  Peanut Rice

**1.** Heat olive oil in a large saucepan over medium heat. Add onion, and sauté 5 minutes or until tender. Stir in tomato and next 5 ingredients. Cook 8 minutes or until thick, stirring occasionally. Stir in chickpeas and garam masala; cook 5 minutes or until thoroughly heated. Sprinkle each serving with 1 tablespoon cilantro. Serve over Peanut Rice. Yield: 4 servings (serving size: 1 cup stew and 1 cup rice).

(Totals include Peanut Rice) CALORIES 562 (21% from fat); FAT 17.1g (sat 1g, mono 3.5g, poly 2.3g); PROTEIN 24.4g; CARB 97.7g; FIBER 11.4g; CHOL 0mg; IRON 8.7mg; SODIUM 1,077mg; CALC 133mg

**PEANUT RICE:**

  2¼  cups water
   1  cup (uncooked) white basmati rice
   ½  teaspoon salt
   ¼  teaspoon ground turmeric
   ½  cup dry-roasted peanuts
   ½  cup frozen petite green peas,
      thawed

**1.** Bring water to a boil in a medium saucepan. Add rice, salt, and turmeric; cover, reduce heat, and simmer 20 minutes or until liquid is absorbed. Remove from heat; stir in peanuts and peas. Yield: 4 servings (serving size: 1 cup).

CALORIES 288 (29% from fat); FAT 9.3g (sat 1.3g, mono 4.5g, poly 2.9g); PROTEIN 9g; CARB 42.9g; FIBER 3g; CHOL 0mg; IRON 2.7mg; SODIUM 465mg; CALC 33mg

## Noodle Salad with Shrimp and Chile Dressing

The noodles in this dish—bean thread vermicelli—are also known as cellophane noodles. You can substitute 3 cups cooked angel hair pasta. Thai fish sauce and chile paste can be found bottled in the Asian food section of your grocery store. (Recipe by Theresa V. Laursen, coauthor of *True Thai: The Modern Art of Thai Cooking*.)

**DRESSING:**

  ¼  cup fresh lime juice (about 2 limes)
  1  tablespoon brown sugar
  1  tablespoon Thai fish sauce
  1  tablespoon chile paste

**SALAD:**

  2  cups boiling water
  3  ounces dried bean thread
     vermicelli
  ½  pound medium shrimp, cooked
     and peeled
  ½  cup torn mint leaves
  ¼  cup thinly sliced green onions
  ¼  cup sliced peeled fresh lemon
     grass
  1  Thai, hot red, or serrano chile,
     seeded and chopped
  4  romaine lettuce leaves
  ½  cup cilantro sprigs
  4  teaspoons finely chopped
     unsalted, dry-roasted peanuts

**1.** To prepare dressing, combine first 4 ingredients in a bowl, and stir well with a whisk.

**2.** To prepare salad, combine 2 cups boiling water and vermicelli in a bowl; cover and let stand 10 minutes. Drain noodles; rinse with cold water. Cut noodles into three pieces.

**3.** Combine noodles, shrimp, and next 4 ingredients in a large bowl. Pour dressing over noodle mixture, tossing gently to coat. Spoon 1 cup noodle salad onto each of 4 lettuce-lined plates. Sprinkle with cilantro and peanuts. Yield: 4 servings (serving size: 1 cup noodle salad, 2 tablespoons cilantro, and 1 teaspoon peanuts).

CALORIES 245 (12% from fat); FAT 3.2g (sat 0.6g, mono 0.9g, poly 0.8g); PROTEIN 10.4g; CARB 44.2g; FIBER 2g; CHOL 65mg; IRON 2mg; SODIUM 500mg; CALC 60mg

# Home Chip Advantage

*Invite your friends over for some casual fun, and surprise them with low-fat munchies of your own making.*

Go ahead. Ask your friends to come over for a cozy evening of some music, lively conversation, and happy grazing. The setup is minimal. The mood is casual, and the food should be, too. But not boring. Forget the usual stop 'n' grab party fare, and turn the evening into the real deal with your own—that's right, made by you, yourself—chips and dips.

## Hot Bean-and-Cheese Dip

- 1 (14.5-ounce) can diced tomatoes, drained and divided
- ½ teaspoon hot pepper sauce
- ¼ teaspoon salt
- ¼ teaspoon ground cumin
- ¼ teaspoon dried oregano
- 1 (16-ounce) can pinto beans, rinsed and drained
- 1 (16-ounce) can fat-free refried beans
- 1 (4.5-ounce) can chopped green chiles, drained
- Cooking spray
- ¾ cup (3 ounces) shredded sharp Cheddar cheese

**1.** Preheat oven to 350°.
**2.** Combine 1 cup tomatoes and next 7 ingredients. Spoon tomato mixture into a 1½-quart casserole dish coated with cooking spray. Top with cheese. Bake at 350° for 20 minutes or until cheese melts. Top with remaining tomatoes. Yield: 4½ cups (serving size: ¼ cup).

CALORIES 66 (23% from fat); FAT 1.7g (sat 1g, mono 0.5g, poly 0.1g); PROTEIN 3.8g; CARB 8.7g; FIBER 2g; CHOL 5mg; IRON 1mg; SODIUM 309mg; CALC 56mg

## Italian Baguette Chips

ITALIAN SEASONING:
- ¼ cup grated Parmesan cheese
- 1 teaspoon dried oregano
- 1 teaspoon dried basil
- ¼ teaspoon salt
- ¼ teaspoon garlic powder
- ¼ teaspoon black pepper

CHIPS:
- 40 (¼-inch-thick) slices diagonally cut French bread baguette
- Cooking spray

**1.** Preheat oven to 375°.
**2.** To prepare Italian seasoning, combine first 6 ingredients in a small bowl.
**3.** To prepare chips, arrange bread slices on 2 baking sheets coated with cooking spray. Coat bread with cooking spray. Sprinkle 4 teaspoons Italian seasoning over bread. Bake at 375° for 8 minutes or until crisp. Yield: 40 chips (serving size: 4 chips).
**NOTE:** Store remaining Italian seasoning in an airtight container in refrigerator.

CALORIES 89 (12% from fat); FAT 1.2g (sat 0.3g, mono 0.4g, poly 0.2g); PROTEIN 3g; CARB 16.3g; FIBER 0.9g; CHOL 0mg; IRON 0.8mg; SODIUM 216mg; CALC 32mg

## Creamy Feta-Spinach Dip

We've updated the classic spinach dip by adding tangy feta and omitting the artichokes and much of the fat.

- 1 (8-ounce) carton plain low-fat yogurt
- ¾ cup (3 ounces) crumbled feta cheese
- ¼ cup (2 ounces) ⅓-less-fat cream cheese, softened
- ¼ cup low-fat sour cream
- 1 garlic clove, crushed
- 1½ cups finely chopped spinach
- 1 tablespoon minced fresh or 1 teaspoon dried dill
- ⅛ teaspoon black pepper
- Fresh dill (optional)

**1.** Spoon yogurt onto several layers of heavy-duty paper towels; spread to ½-inch thickness. Cover with additional paper towels, and let stand 5 minutes. Scrape into a food processor using a rubber spatula. Add cheeses, sour cream, and garlic, and process until smooth, scraping sides of bowl once. Spoon yogurt mixture into a medium bowl, and stir in spinach, minced dill, and pepper. Cover and chill. Garnish with fresh dill, if desired. Yield: 2 cups (serving size: ¼ cup).

CALORIES 78 (62% from fat); FAT 5.4g (sat 3.4g, mono 1.4g, poly 0.2g); PROTEIN 4.2g; CARB 3.6g; FIBER 0.4g; CHOL 20mg; IRON 0.4mg; SODIUM 178mg; CALC 130mg

## Forest-Mushroom Dip

This is another dip that delivers great taste while keeping the fat in check. If you don't have a food processor, you can finely chop the mushrooms by hand.

- 2 (6-ounce) packages portobello mushroom caps, quartered
- 1 (8-ounce) package button mushrooms
- 1 garlic clove, halved
- ½ cup dry white wine
- 1 teaspoon dried thyme
- 2 tablespoons all-purpose flour
- ¼ cup (2 ounces) ⅓-less-fat cream cheese, softened
- 1 tablespoon lemon juice
- ¾ teaspoon salt
- ⅛ teaspoon black pepper
- ½ cup (2 ounces) finely shredded smoked gouda cheese
- ½ cup low-fat sour cream
- 3 tablespoons chopped fresh parsley
- 1 tablespoon green-onion tops (optional)

**1.** Place half of mushrooms in a food processor, and process until finely chopped. Spoon chopped mushrooms into a large skillet. Place remaining mushrooms and garlic in processor, and process until finely chopped. Spoon mushroom mixture into pan; add wine and thyme. Cook over medium-high heat 10 minutes or until liquid almost evaporates. Sprinkle mushroom mixture with flour, and stir well. Stir in cream cheese, lemon juice, salt, and pepper;

cook 1 minute. Spoon into a serving bowl; cover and cool.

**2.** Stir in gouda, sour cream, and parsley. Sprinkle with green-onion tops, if desired. Cover and chill. Yield: 3 cups (serving size: ¼ cup).

CALORIES 61 (56% from fat); FAT 3.8g (sat 2.3g, mono 1g, poly 0.2g); PROTEIN 3.1g; CARB 4.4g; FIBER 0.7g; CHOL 13mg; IRON 0.9mg; SODIUM 212mg; CALC 55mg

## Indian Egg-Roll Strips

Twenty won ton wrappers, each cut diagonally into quarters, can be substituted for the egg-roll wrappers.

**CURRY SEASONING:**
  1  tablespoon curry powder
  1  teaspoon paprika
  ½  teaspoon salt
  ½  teaspoon ground cumin
  ¼  teaspoon garlic powder
  ¼  teaspoon black pepper

**STRIPS:**
  10  egg-roll wrappers, each cut lengthwise into 8 strips
  Cooking spray

**1.** Preheat oven to 375°.
**2.** To prepare curry seasoning, combine first 6 ingredients in a small bowl.
**3.** To prepare strips, arrange egg-roll strips on 2 baking sheets coated with cooking spray. Coat strips with cooking spray, and sprinkle 2 teaspoons curry seasoning over strips. Bake strips at 375° for 8 minutes or until crisp. Yield: 80 strips (serving size: 8 strips).
**NOTE:** Store remaining curry seasoning in an airtight container.

CALORIES 49 (7% from fat); FAT 0.4g (sat 0g, mono 0.1g, poly 0.1g); PROTEIN 1.6g; CARB 9.5g; FIBER 0.1g; CHOL 1mg; IRON 1.2mg; SODIUM 139mg; CALC 9mg

## Thai Shrimp Dip

  1  pound medium shrimp, cooked and peeled
  ¼  cup (2 ounces) ⅓-less-fat cream cheese
  2  tablespoons light mayonnaise
  2  tablespoons fresh lime juice
  2  teaspoons Thai fish sauce or low-sodium soy sauce
  1  (12.3-ounce) package reduced-fat firm tofu, drained
  1  teaspoon dark sesame oil
  1  tablespoon minced peeled fresh ginger
  1  garlic clove, minced
  3  tablespoons minced green onions
  3  tablespoons chopped fresh cilantro
  Cooked and peeled shrimp (optional)
  Cilantro sprig (optional)

**1.** Place first 3 ingredients in a food processor, and process until minced. Add lime juice, fish sauce, and tofu; pulse until blended. Heat oil in a small skillet over medium heat; sauté ginger and garlic 2 minutes. Add to shrimp mixture, and pulse until combined. Add green onions and chopped cilantro, and pulse 3 or 4 times. Spoon into a bowl; cover and chill 1 hour. Garnish dip with additional shrimp and cilantro sprig, if desired. Yield: 3 cups (serving size: ¼ cup).

CALORIES 68 (40% from fat); FAT 3g (sat 1g, mono 0.8g, poly 0.8g); PROTEIN 8.6g; CARB 1.6g; FIBER 0g; CHOL 48mg; IRON 1mg; SODIUM 182mg; CALC 34mg

## Cajun Tortilla Chips

You can also make pita chips with this recipe. Start with five pitas, split in half, and cut each half into eight wedges. Then proceed with the recipe below.

**CAJUN SEASONING:**
  1½  teaspoons paprika
  1  teaspoon dried thyme
  ½  teaspoon garlic powder
  ½  teaspoon onion powder
  ½  teaspoon black pepper
  ¼  teaspoon salt
  ¼  teaspoon sugar
  ¼  teaspoon ground red pepper

**CHIPS:**
  10  (7-inch) flour tortillas, each cut into 8 wedges
  Cooking spray

**1.** Preheat oven to 375°.
**2.** To prepare Cajun seasoning, combine first 8 ingredients in a small bowl.
**3.** To prepare chips, arrange tortilla wedges on 2 baking sheets coated with cooking spray. Coat wedges with cooking spray. Sprinkle 2 teaspoons Cajun seasoning over wedges. Bake chips at 375° for 6 minutes or until crisp. Yield: 80 chips (serving size: 4 chips).
**NOTE:** Store remaining Cajun seasoning in an airtight container.

CALORIES 63 (20% from fat); FAT 1.4g (sat 0.2g, mono 0.6g, poly 0.5g); PROTEIN 1.7g; CARB 10.8g; FIBER 0.6g; CHOL 0mg; IRON 0.7mg; SODIUM 104mg; CALC 25mg

---

### Save 'N' Dip

Commercial dips are notoriously high in fat. And beyond spinach and French onion, there's simply not much variety available. That's why preparing our big-flavored, innovative dips makes sense.

For example, our Creamy Feta-Spinach Dip (recipe on page 16) is a zestier version of traditional spinach dip, and even with 62% of calories from fat, it's still far lighter.

And try comparing our Forest-Mushroom Dip (recipe on page 16) to commercial French onion dips—not only is it much more robust, but you'll see that with 56% of calories from fat as opposed to 82% of calories from fat in the store-bought version, it's a whole lot easier to swallow.

Add our easy-to-prepare and equally flavorful, low-fat chips to the mix, and you'll have an instant party without the extra fat.

# Pantry Raid

*No covert operation is necessary to turn pantry supplies into great last-minute dinners. Just get in there and grab something.*

When dinnertime approaches and you're at a loss for what to prepare, throw open the doors and raid your pantry. Let's assume it's well-stocked.

## Moroccan Chickpea-and-Vegetable Stew

**PREPARATION TIME: 15 MINUTES**

**COOKING TIME: 14 MINUTES**

    1   tablespoon vegetable oil
    2   cups (½-inch) cubed zucchini
    1   cup chopped onion
    ½   cup chopped carrot
    1   tablespoon bottled minced
        garlic
    1   cup fat-free, less-sodium chicken
        broth
    2   tablespoons raisins
  1¼   teaspoons ground ginger
  1¼   teaspoons ground cumin
    ¾   teaspoon ground coriander
    ½   teaspoon salt
    ¼   teaspoon ground cinnamon
    ¼   teaspoon black pepper
    2   (15½-ounce) cans chickpeas
        (garbanzo beans), drained
    1   (14.5-ounce) can no-salt-added
        stewed tomatoes, undrained
  1½   cups water
    1   cup uncooked couscous

**1.** Heat oil in a large nonstick skillet over medium-high heat. Add zucchini, onion, carrot, and garlic; sauté 5 minutes. Stir in broth and next 9 ingredients; bring to a boil. Cover, reduce heat, and simmer 8 minutes or until tender, stirring occasionally.
**2.** While chickpea mixture simmers, prepare couscous. Bring water to a boil in a medium saucepan; gradually stir in couscous. Remove from heat; cover and let stand 5 minutes. Fluff with a fork.

**3.** Serve stew over couscous. Yield: 6 servings (serving size: 1 cup stew and ½ cup couscous).

CALORIES 344 (14% from fat); FAT 5.4g (sat 0.7g, mono 1.5g, poly 2.4g); PROTEIN 15g; CARB 62.3g; FIBER 5.7g; CHOL 0mg; IRON 4.5mg; SODIUM 487mg; CALC 95mg

### menu
### Egg, Mushroom, and Roasted Red-Pepper Burritos
Maple-pecan grapefruit*

*Cut and section 2 grapefruit. Place, cut sides up, on a broiler pan. Combine 3 tablespoons maple syrup and ½ teaspoon vanilla extract; brush over grapefruit. Sprinkle evenly with 1 tablespoon chopped pecans; broil 5 minutes or until thoroughly heated. Serves 4.

## Egg, Mushroom, and Roasted Red-Pepper Burritos

**PREPARATION TIME: 10 MINUTES**

**COOKING TIME: 13 MINUTES**

    ¼   teaspoon salt
    3   large egg whites
    1   large egg
    ½   teaspoon butter or stick margarine
  1½   cups sliced mushrooms
    ½   cup chopped bottled roasted red
        bell peppers
    ¼   cup (1 ounce) diced sharp
        Cheddar cheese
    4   (8-inch) flour tortillas
    ½   cup bottled salsa

**1.** Combine first 3 ingredients in a bowl. Melt butter in a large nonstick skillet over medium heat. Add mushrooms; sauté 10 minutes. Add peppers; sauté 1 minute. Pour egg mixture into pan; cook until bottom begins to set, stirring to scramble. Remove from heat; stir in cheese.
**2.** Warm tortillas according to package directions. Spoon one-fourth of egg mixture down center of each tortilla; roll up. Serve with salsa. Yield: 4 servings (serving size: 1 burrito and 2 tablespoons salsa).

CALORIES 236 (29% from fat); FAT 7.6g (sat 2.7g, mono 2.7g, poly 1.6g); PROTEIN 10.9g; CARB 30.7g; FIBER 2.3g; CHOL 64mg; IRON 2.4mg; SODIUM 673mg; CALC 128mg

## Spicy Caribbean Black Beans and Rice

**PREPARATION TIME: 10 MINUTES**

**COOKING TIME: 20 MINUTES**

For the sake of efficiency, start cooking the rice first.

    1   teaspoon olive oil
  1¼   cups diced onion
    ¾   cup finely chopped carrot
    1   tablespoon bottled minced
        garlic
    2   cups cooked rice
    2   tablespoons dry sherry
    1   tablespoon balsamic vinegar
    1   teaspoon dried thyme
    ½   teaspoon black pepper
    ¼   teaspoon salt
    2   (15-ounce) cans black beans,
        rinsed and drained
    2   bay leaves

**1.** Heat oil in a large saucepan over medium heat. Add onion, carrot, and garlic; sauté 10 minutes. Add rice and remaining ingredients; cover, reduce heat, and simmer 5 minutes or until thoroughly heated. Discard bay leaves. Yield: 4 servings (serving size: 1¾ cups).

CALORIES 325 (6% from fat); FAT 2.3g (sat 0.4g, mono 0.9g, poly 0.5g); PROTEIN 13.9g; CARB 62.2g; FIBER 7.5g; CHOL 0mg; IRON 4.3mg; SODIUM 484mg; CALC 78mg

## Tuna-Pasta Puttanesca

**PREPARATION TIME: 12 MINUTES**

**COOKING TIME: 15 MINUTES**

    8   ounces uncooked gemelli or
        other short twisted spaghetti
    2   teaspoons olive oil
    ⅓   cup chopped pitted kalamata
        olives
    2   garlic cloves, crushed
    1   cup chopped seeded tomato
    ¼   teaspoon crushed red pepper
    1   (9-ounce) can solid white tuna
        in water, drained
    1   tablespoon chopped fresh
        parsley
    1   tablespoon fresh lemon juice

1. Cook pasta according to package directions, omitting salt and fat. Drain and keep warm.

2. While pasta cooks, heat oil in a large nonstick skillet over medium-high heat. Add olives and garlic, and sauté 2 minutes. Add tomato, pepper, and tuna; cook 3 minutes or until thoroughly heated.

3. Combine pasta, tuna mixture, parsley, and juice in a large bowl, and toss well. Yield: 4 servings (serving size: 1 cup).

CALORIES 324 (16% from fat); FAT 5.7g (sat 1g, mono 3g, poly 1.3g); PROTEIN 21.1g; CARB 46.1g; FIBER 2.3g; CHOL 21mg; IRON 3.2mg; SODIUM 300mg; CALC 27mg

## Linguine with Red Clam Sauce

(pictured on page 38)

**PREPARATION TIME: 12 MINUTES**

**COOKING TIME: 18 MINUTES**

- 12 ounces uncooked linguine
- 2 teaspoons olive oil
- 2 teaspoons bottled minced garlic
- 1 (25.5-ounce) bottle fat-free marinara pasta sauce (such as Muir Glen)
- 2 tablespoons sun-dried or regular tomato paste
- ¼ teaspoon crushed red pepper
- 3 (6½-ounce) cans chopped clams, undrained

1. Cook pasta according to package directions, omitting salt and fat. Drain, and keep warm.

2. Heat oil in a medium saucepan over medium heat. Add garlic; sauté 2 minutes. Stir in marinara sauce, tomato paste, and red pepper; bring to a simmer. Drain clams in a sieve over a bowl, reserving liquid; set clams aside. Stir reserved clam liquid into marinara-sauce mixture. Simmer 10 minutes. Stir in clams, and simmer 3 minutes. Serve pasta with sauce. Yield: 6 servings (serving size: 1 cup pasta and about 1 cup sauce).

CALORIES 330 (8% from fat); FAT 3.1g (sat 0.5g, mono 1.4g, poly 0.6); PROTEIN 16.9g; CARB 48.5g; FIBER 3.6g; CHOL 29mg; IRON 6.8mg; SODIUM 833mg; CALC 166mg

# A Day in the Healthy Life

Who has the time to eat well, exercise, and relax? You do! Stick with us for 24 hours, and this healthy living stuff might just stick with you forever.

## Tropical Tofu Smoothie

- ⅔ cup soft tofu, drained (about 3 ounces)
- 1 cup cubed pineapple, chilled
- 1 cup sliced strawberries, chilled
- ½ cup vanilla low-fat frozen yogurt
- ⅓ cup orange juice
- 1 teaspoon sugar
- Dash of ground nutmeg (optional)

1. Place tofu in a blender; process until smooth. Add pineapple and next 4 ingredients; process until smooth. Sprinkle with nutmeg, if desired. Serve immediately. Yield: 2 servings (serving size: 1 cup).

CALORIES 147 (15% from fat); FAT 2.5g (sat 0.6g, mono 0.1g, poly 0.5g); PROTEIN 4.8g; CARB 28.9g; FIBER 2.8g; CHOL 4mg; IRON 1.2mg; SODIUM 17mg; CALC 94mg

## Blueberry-Lemon Muffins

- 1½ cups all-purpose flour
- ½ cup yellow cornmeal
- ½ cup sugar
- 1½ teaspoons baking powder
- ½ teaspoon baking soda
- ¼ teaspoon salt
- 1 cup blueberries
- 1 cup low-fat buttermilk
- 3 tablespoons butter or stick margarine, melted
- 1 tablespoon grated lemon rind
- 1 large egg, lightly beaten
- Cooking spray
- 1 tablespoon sugar

1. Preheat oven to 400°.

2. Lightly spoon flour into dry measuring cups; level with a knife. Combine flour

and next 5 ingredients in a medium bowl. Stir in blueberries; make a well in center of mixture. Combine buttermilk, butter, rind, and egg; stir well with a whisk. Add to flour mixture; stir just until moist.

3. Spoon batter into 12 muffin cups coated with cooking spray; sprinkle evenly with 1 tablespoon sugar. Bake at 400° for 20 minutes or until a wooden pick inserted in center comes out clean. Remove muffins from pans immediately; place on a wire rack. Yield: 1 dozen (serving size: 1 muffin).

CALORIES 164 (22% from fat); FAT 4g (sat 2.2g, mono 1.1g, poly 0.3g); PROTEIN 3.5g; CARB 28.8g; FIBER 1.1g; CHOL 26mg; IRON 1.1mg; SODIUM 209mg; CALC 66mg

## Deluxe Roast Beef Sandwich

- 1 tablespoon light mayonnaise
- 2 teaspoons prepared horseradish
- 2 teaspoons chili sauce
- 2 (1-ounce) slices rye bread
- 1 romaine lettuce leaf
- 3 ounces thinly sliced deli roast beef
- 2 (¼-inch-thick) slices tomato
- 1 (⅛-inch-thick) slice red onion, separated into rings

1. Combine first 3 ingredients. Spread mayonnaise mixture on one bread slice. Top with lettuce leaf, roast beef, tomato slices, onion, and remaining bread slice. Yield: 1 serving.

CALORIES 412 (28% from fat); FAT 12.7g (sat 4.4g, mono 5.3g, poly 2.9g); PROTEIN 25g; CARB 51.2g; FIBER 5.6g; CHOL 5mg; IRON 4.2mg; SODIUM 1,122mg; CALC 86mg

# Day Planner for Healthy Eating

In this Day Planner, we give you a sample of how a moderately active, healthy woman dines on the 2,000 calories a day she needs to maintain her weight. As you can see, it's easy to get plenty of key nutrients, such as calcium, iron, and fiber, without overdoing it on fat and calories. We've kept the fat to less than 20% of calories, so there's room to juggle with some higher-fat fare (steak for dinner rather than chicken, for instance) and still remain under the 30% recommended by health organizations. Our suggested menu is not meant to be an exact prescription, but an example. Everyone's preferences and needs differ, so don't hesitate to tailor the menu.

If you're an "average" active man, you'll need to add about 700 calories to the lineup to keep you fueled for the day. Start by doubling up on nutrient-rich foods. Have two muffins at breakfast, or drink a double dose of the Tropical Tofu Smoothie (recipe on page 19). Add 2 ounces more of meat to your Deluxe Roast Beef Sandwich (recipe on page 19). Add a whole-grain roll with a pat of butter to your supper menu. And then indulge in two Butterscotch Bars (recipe on page 21) instead of just one.

If you're a woman who needs fewer calories, choose smaller portions (half a sandwich at lunch, half a container of yogurt for an afternoon snack), or try trimming a few of the snacks or the Butterscotch Bars (recipe on page 21) from the menu.

If one rule applies to everyone, it's this: Eat a balanced, varied, and moderate diet.

| | Calories | Fat | % Calories From Fat | Fiber | Iron | Calcium |
|---|---|---|---|---|---|---|
| **breakfast** | | | | | | |
| Tropical Tofu Smoothie (recipe on page 19) | 147 | 2.5 grams | 15% | 2.8 grams | 1.2 milligrams | 94 milligrams |
| Blueberry-Lemon Muffin (recipe on page 19) | 164 | 4 grams | 22% | 1.1 grams | 1.1 milligrams | 66 milligrams |
| Banana, 1 medium | 109 | 0.6 grams | 5% | 2.8 grams | 0.4 milligrams | 7 milligrams |
| **midmorning snack** | | | | | | |
| Apple, 1 medium | 81 | 0.5 grams | 6% | 3.7 grams | 0.2 milligrams | 10 milligrams |
| **lunch** | | | | | | |
| Deluxe Roast Beef Sandwich (recipe on page 19) | 412 | 12.7 grams | 28% | 5.6 grams | 4.2 milligrams | 86 milligrams |
| Carrot sticks, ½ cup | 23 | 0.3 grams | 12% | n/a | n/a | 14 milligrams |
| Pear, 1 medium | 98 | 0.7 grams | 6% | 4 grams | 0.4 milligrams | 18 milligrams |
| Fat-free milk, 8 ounces | 86 | 0.5 grams | 5% | 0 grams | 0 milligrams | 301 milligrams |
| **afternoon snack** | | | | | | |
| Chewy Coconut-Granola Bar (recipe on page 21) | 157 | 4.7 grams | 27% | 1.1 grams | 1 milligram | 34 milligrams |
| Fat-free milk, 4 ounces | 43 | 0.3 grams | 6% | 0 grams | 0 milligrams | 151 milligrams |
| **dinner** | | | | | | |
| Gingered Chicken with Noodles (recipe on page 21) | 341 | 9.2 grams | 24% | 4.6 grams | 4.4 milligrams | 81 milligrams |
| Fresh fruit salad, 1 cup (cantaloupe and grapes) | 85 | 0.7 grams | 7% | 1.4 grams | 0.4 milligrams | 18 milligrams |
| Butterscotch Bar (recipe on page 21) | 142 | 4.3 grams | 27% | 0.3 grams | 0.6 milligrams | 24 milligrams |
| **evening snack** | | | | | | |
| Air-popped popcorn, 3 cups | 92 | 1 gram | 10% | 3.6 grams | 0.6 milligrams | 2 milligrams |
| *Total* | 1,980 | 42 grams | 19% | 31 grams | 14.5 milligrams | 906 milligrams |

## Chewy Coconut-Granola Bars

Cooking spray
2 teaspoons all-purpose flour
⅔ cup all-purpose flour
⅓ cup whole-wheat flour
1 teaspoon baking powder
½ teaspoon salt
1¼ cups packed brown sugar
¼ cup vegetable oil
2 tablespoons fat-free milk
2 large eggs
1½ cups low-fat granola without raisins (such as Kellogg's)
¾ cup chopped dried mixed fruit (such as Marian Premium Tropical Medley)
½ cup flaked sweetened coconut

**1.** Preheat oven to 350°.
**2.** Coat a 13 x 9-inch baking pan with cooking spray; dust with 2 teaspoons all-purpose flour. Lightly spoon ⅔ cup all-purpose flour and whole-wheat flour into dry measuring cups; level with a knife. Combine flours, baking powder, and salt in a bowl; stir with a whisk. Combine sugar, oil, milk, and eggs in a large bowl; beat at high speed of a mixer until smooth. Add flour mixture, beating at low speed until blended. Fold in granola and fruit. Spoon into prepared pan. Sprinkle with coconut. Bake at 350° for 20 minutes or until golden. Cool on a wire rack. Yield: 20 servings (serving size: 1 bar).

CALORIES 157 (27% from fat); FAT 4.7g (sat 1.6g, mono 1.2g, poly 1.5g); PROTEIN 2.1g; CARB 27.8g; FIBER 1.1g; CHOL 22mg; IRON 1mg; SODIUM 122mg; CALC 34mg

## Butterscotch Bars

½ cup granulated sugar
½ cup packed brown sugar
¼ cup butter or stick margarine, softened
2 large egg whites
1 teaspoon vanilla extract
1¼ cups all-purpose flour
½ teaspoon baking powder
¼ teaspoon salt
Cooking spray
½ cup butterscotch morsels

**1.** Preheat oven to 350°.
**2.** Beat sugars and butter at medium speed of a mixer until well-blended (about 4 minutes). Add egg whites and vanilla; beat well. Lightly spoon flour into dry measuring cups, and level with a knife. Combine flour, baking powder, and salt; stir well with a whisk. Add flour mixture to sugar mixture; beat at low speed just until blended.
**3.** Spread batter evenly into an 8-inch square baking pan coated with cooking spray; sprinkle evenly with morsels. Bake at 350° for 28 minutes or until a wooden pick inserted in center comes out clean. Cool in pan on a wire rack. Yield: 16 servings (serving size: 1 bar).

CALORIES 142 (27% from fat); FAT 4.3g (sat 2.6g, mono 1.3g, poly 0.2g); PROTEIN 1.6g; CARB 24g; FIBER 0.3g; CHOL 8mg; IRON 0.6mg; SODIUM 95mg; CALC 24mg

## Gingered Chicken with Noodles

4 (4-ounce) skinned, boned chicken breast halves
¼ teaspoon salt
2 teaspoons dark sesame oil
1 tablespoon minced peeled fresh ginger
2 teaspoons minced seeded jalapeño pepper
2 garlic cloves, minced
2½ cups sugar snap peas, trimmed
¾ cup fat-free, less-sodium chicken broth
½ cup (2-inch) julienne-cut carrot
2 tablespoons low-sodium soy sauce
1 tablespoon cornstarch
1 tablespoon fat-free, less-sodium chicken broth
2 cups hot cooked Chinese-style egg noodles
¼ cup chopped fresh cilantro
¼ cup chopped dry-roasted peanuts

**1.** Sprinkle chicken with salt. Heat oil in a large nonstick skillet over medium-high heat. Add chicken. Sauté 3 minutes; turn chicken over. Add ginger, jalapeño, and garlic; cook 2 minutes, stirring often. Add peas, ¾ cup broth, carrot, and soy sauce; bring to a boil. Cover, reduce heat, and simmer 5 minutes or until chicken is done.
**2.** Remove chicken and vegetables from pan with a slotted spoon. Combine cornstarch and 1 tablespoon broth, and add to pan. Bring to a boil; cook 1 minute, stirring constantly.
**3.** Place ½ cup noodles on each of 4 serving plates; top with ½ cup vegetables, one breast half, and sauce. Sprinkle each serving with 1 tablespoon cilantro and 1 tablespoon peanuts. Yield: 4 servings.

CALORIES 341 (24% from fat); FAT 9.2g (sat 1.7g, mono 3.5g, poly 2.8g); PROTEIN 35g; CARB 28.7g; FIBER 4.6g; CHOL 86mg; IRON 4.4mg; SODIUM 573mg; CALC 81mg

## Greek Pasta Salad

6 cups water
1 pound large shrimp
½ cup low-fat Caesar dressing
2 teaspoons sun-dried tomato sprinkles
¾ teaspoon dried rosemary, crushed
5 cups cooked penne (about 10 ounces uncooked tube-shaped pasta)
¾ cup thinly sliced cucumber
⅓ cup chopped fresh basil
¼ cup chopped pitted kalamata olives
¼ cup sliced red onion, separated into rings
1 (7-ounce) bottle roasted red bell peppers, drained and cut into strips
¾ cup (3 ounces) crumbled feta cheese
¼ teaspoon freshly ground black pepper
Chopped fresh parsley (optional)

**1.** Bring 6 cups water to a boil in a large saucepan. Add shrimp; cook 3 minutes or until done. Drain and rinse with cold water. Peel and chill shrimp.
**2.** Combine shrimp, dressing, tomato sprinkles, and rosemary in a large bowl. Add pasta and next 5 ingredients; toss gently to coat. Cover; chill 1 hour. Sprinkle with cheese and black pepper. Garnish with chopped parsley, if desired. Yield: 6 servings (serving size: 1½ cups).

CALORIES 344 (27% from fat); FAT 10.2g (sat 3.2g, mono 3.3g, poly 2.9g); PROTEIN 20.7g; CARB 40g; FIBER 1.9g; CHOL 106mg; IRON 3.7mg; SODIUM 552mg; CALC 125mg

## Bueno Breakfast Burrito

2 tablespoons thinly sliced green onions
1 tablespoon finely chopped red bell pepper
2 teaspoons chopped fresh cilantro
1 large egg
1 large egg white
Dash of salt
Dash of black pepper
Cooking spray
1 (8-inch) fat-free flour tortilla
1 tablespoon tub-style fat-free cream cheese
2 tablespoons bottled salsa

**1.** Combine first 7 ingredients. Place a small nonstick skillet coated with cooking spray over medium-high heat until hot. Add egg mixture, and cook, without stirring, until egg mixture begins to set on bottom. Draw a spatula across bottom of pan to form large curds. Continue cooking until egg mixture is thick but still moist; do not stir constantly.
**2.** Place tortilla on a microwave-safe plate. Spread cream cheese over tortilla, and microwave at HIGH 15 seconds. Top with egg mixture and salsa, and roll up. Yield: 1 serving.

CALORIES 238 (23% from fat); FAT 6g (sat 1.6g, mono 2g, poly 0.8g); PROTEIN 15.7g; CARB 29.2g; FIBER 2.1g; CHOL 223mg; IRON 2.7mg; SODIUM 980mg; CALC 91mg

# Worth Pampering

*Temperamental pears require plenty of care getting from tree to table, but your cooking will love that extra attention.*

Treat a pear right, and you'll enjoy succulent taste and melt-in-your-mouth texture. Offend its sensitive nature, and you'll end up with bland mush. It seems that the only way to get a pear to give you what you want is to give it what it needs.

## Gingered Pear Sauce

Serve this as you would applesauce—with ham, pork, or by itself.

8 cups sliced peeled Anjou, Bartlett, or Bosc pear (about 8 large pears)
1 teaspoon grated lemon rind
¼ cup fresh lemon juice
¼ cup sugar
2 tablespoons chopped crystallized ginger
2 tablespoons brandy or apple juice

**1.** Combine first 3 ingredients in a bowl; toss well to coat. Place a large nonstick skillet over medium-high heat until hot. Add pear mixture; cook 2 minutes, stirring occasionally. Cover, reduce heat, and simmer 15 minutes. Increase heat to medium-high. Add sugar and crystallized ginger; cook 5 minutes or until liquid almost evaporates. Remove from heat, and stir in brandy. Yield: 3 cups (serving size: ½ cup).

CALORIES 182 (4% from fat); FAT 0.9g (sat 0g, mono 0.2g, poly 0.2g); PROTEIN 0.9g; CARB 44.1g; FIBER 3.5g; CHOL 0mg; IRON 0.9mg; SODIUM 1mg; CALC 30mg

## Jack Quesadillas with Pear Salsa

**PEAR SALSA:**
4 cups chopped peeled Anjou pear (about 2 pounds)
⅓ cup chopped red onion
2 tablespoons chopped fresh or 2 teaspoons dried mint
1 tablespoon grated lime rind
2 tablespoons fresh lime juice
1 teaspoon sugar
½ teaspoon freshly ground black pepper
1 jalapeño pepper, seeded and chopped

**QUESADILLAS:**
8 (8-inch) fat-free flour tortillas
2 cups (8 ounces) shredded Monterey Jack cheese
½ cup chopped green onions

**1.** To prepare salsa, combine first 8 ingredients in a bowl; cover and chill.
**2.** To prepare quesadillas, place 1 tortilla in a medium nonstick skillet over medium heat, and top with ½ cup cheese. Sprinkle with 2 tablespoons green onions; top with a tortilla. Cook 3 minutes, pressing down with a spatula until cheese melts. Turn carefully, and cook until thoroughly heated (about 1 minute). Repeat procedure with remaining tortillas, cheese, and green onions. Cut each quesadilla into sixths; serve with pear salsa. Yield: 6 servings (serving size: 4 quesadilla wedges and ½ cup salsa).

CALORIES 375 (29% from fat); FAT 12g (sat 7.2g, mono 3.4g, poly 0.5g); PROTEIN 14.1g; CARB 54.6g; FIBER 4.8g; CHOL 30mg; IRON 2.2mg; SODIUM 658mg; CALC 307mg

## Pork-and-Pear Sauté with Lemon-Vodka Sauce

You can put this simple dish together in a flash.

2 teaspoons olive oil, divided
2 (4-ounce) boned center-cut loin pork chops (about ¾ inch thick)
½ teaspoon salt, divided
½ teaspoon cracked black pepper, divided
2 peeled Anjou pears, cored and halved (about 1 pound)
¼ cup vodka or dry white wine
2 teaspoons grated lemon rind
1 tablespoon fresh lemon juice
1 tablespoon chopped fresh chives

**1.** Heat 1 teaspoon olive oil in a 10-inch skillet over medium heat. Sprinkle pork chops with ¼ teaspoon salt and ¼ teaspoon pepper. Add pork chops to skillet; sauté 3 minutes on each side or until pork is done. Remove pork from pan, and keep warm. Heat 1 teaspoon oil in pan over medium heat. Place pear in pan, cut sides down. Sauté 2 minutes on each side or until golden. Remove pear from pan, and keep warm. Stir in vodka, scraping pan to loosen browned bits. Stir in ¼ teaspoon salt, ¼ teaspoon pepper, rind, juice, and chives, and cook 1 minute. Yield: 2 servings (serving size: 1

pork chop, 2 pear halves, and 1 table-spoon sauce).

CALORIES 338 (36% from fat); FAT 13.3g (sat 3.2g, mono 5.5g, poly 1.2g); PROTEIN 25.9g; CARB 30.5g; FIBER 4.9g; CHOL 71mg; IRON 1.6mg; SODIUM 661mg; CALC 34mg

## Buttermilk Pancakes with Bourbon-Pear Sauce

    1  cup all-purpose flour
    1  teaspoon sugar
    ½  teaspoon baking soda
    ¼  teaspoon baking powder
    ¼  teaspoon salt
    1  cup low-fat buttermilk
    1  tablespoon butter or stick
       margarine, melted and cooled
    1  large egg, lightly beaten
  Bourbon-Pear Sauce

**1.** Lightly spoon flour into a dry measuring cup, and level with a knife. Combine flour and next 4 ingredients in a large bowl. Combine buttermilk, butter, and egg, and add to flour mixture, stirring with a whisk until smooth.
**2.** For each pancake, spoon about ¼ cup batter onto a hot nonstick griddle or nonstick skillet. Turn pancakes when tops are covered with bubbles and edges look cooked. Serve with Bourbon-Pear Sauce. Yield: 3 servings (serving size: 3 pancakes and ½ cup sauce).

(Totals include Bourbon-Pear Sauce) CALORIES 519 (19% from fat); FAT 10.7g (sat 5.4g, mono 3.1g, poly 0.9g); PROTEIN 10.4g; CARB 88g; FIBER 4.6g; CHOL 91mg; IRON 2.9mg; SODIUM 576mg; CALC 168mg

### BOURBON-PEAR SAUCE:
We liked Bosc pears best in this sauce, but most any kind will work.

    4  Bosc or Bartlett pears, peeled,
       cored, and thinly sliced
    1  teaspoon grated lemon rind
    2  teaspoons lemon juice
    2  teaspoons butter or stick margarine
    ¼  cup sugar
    ¼  cup bourbon
    ¼  teaspoon ground cinnamon

**1.** Combine first 3 ingredients; toss well. Melt butter in a large nonstick skillet over medium-high heat. Add pear mixture, and sauté 5 minutes or until pears are tender. Stir in sugar; cook 30 seconds. Add bourbon and cinnamon, and cook 1 minute. Yield: 1½ cups (serving size: ½ cup).
**NOTE:** Apple juice or pear nectar can be substituted for bourbon, if desired.

CALORIES 262 (12% from fat); FAT 3.4g (sat 1.6g, mono 0.9g, poly 0.3g); PROTEIN 0.9g; CARB 50.4g; FIBER 3.5g; CHOL 7mg; IRON 0.6mg; SODIUM 27mg; CALC 29mg

## Easy Pear Cobbler

The brandy imparts a great flavor to this dessert; substitute ¼ cup apple juice and 1 teaspoon vanilla extract if you prefer. Use ripe pears so you won't have crunchy or overly firm fruit in the cobbler.

    3  tablespoons butter, melted and
       divided
    6  very ripe Bartlett, Anjou, or
       Seckel pears, peeled, cored, and
       halved lengthwise (about 2¼
       pounds)
    1  cup all-purpose flour
    1  cup granulated sugar, divided
    1  teaspoon baking powder
    ½  teaspoon salt
    ¼  cup 2% reduced-fat milk
    ¼  cup brandy
    2  tablespoons brown sugar
    2  teaspoons grated lemon rind

**1.** Preheat oven to 400°.
**2.** Drizzle bottom of a 13 x 9-inch baking dish with 1½ tablespoons butter. Arrange pear halves in 3 rows, cut sides down, over butter. Lightly spoon flour into a dry measuring cup; level with a knife. Combine flour, ½ cup granulated sugar, baking powder, and salt in a small bowl. Add 1½ tablespoons butter, milk, and brandy; stir until well-blended. Spoon batter around pear halves. Combine ½ cup granulated sugar, brown sugar, and lemon rind; sprinkle over pear halves. Bake at 400° for 30 minutes or until bubbly. Yield: 9 servings.

CALORIES 250 (16% from fat); FAT 4.5g (sat 2.5g, mono 1.2g, poly 0.3g); PROTEIN 2g; CARB 52.9g; FIBER 1.9g; CHOL 10mg; IRON 1mg; SODIUM 229mg; CALC 55mg

## Pear Dutch Baby

It's best to serve this giant, soufflélike pancake immediately.

    4  Bartlett or Bosc pears, cored and
       thinly sliced (about 1 pound)
    ¼  cup packed brown sugar
    ¼  cup fresh lemon juice
    1  cup all-purpose flour
    1  cup 2% reduced-fat milk
    3  tablespoons granulated sugar
    ¼  teaspoon salt
    3  large eggs
    2  teaspoons butter or stick
       margarine
    1  tablespoon powdered sugar

**1.** Preheat oven to 425°.
**2.** Combine sliced pears, brown sugar, and lemon juice. Heat a 10-inch cast-iron or heavy ovenproof skillet over medium heat. Add pear mixture; sauté 5 minutes or until pears are golden. Remove pear mixture from pan, and keep warm.
**3.** Lightly spoon flour into a dry measuring cup, and level with a knife. Place flour in a large bowl. Combine milk, granulated sugar, salt, and eggs, stirring mixture well with a whisk. Add milk mixture to flour, stirring with a whisk until well-blended.
**4.** Melt butter in pan. Pour batter into pan. Bake at 425° for 25 minutes or until puffy and golden. Spoon pear mixture into center of pancake; sprinkle with powdered sugar. Cut into 6 wedges. Serve immediately. Yield: 6 servings.

CALORIES 253 (18% from fat); FAT 5.1g (sat 2.1g, mono 1.7g, poly 0.6g); PROTEIN 7.1g; CARB 46g; FIBER 2.3g; CHOL 117mg; IRON 1.7mg; SODIUM 168mg; CALC 82mg

# How to Make Super Soups

## Soup is the true melting pot of all good things to eat.

If there's one thing that will get you through multitudes of meals, taste even better as leftovers, and fill you with a dang-that-was-good happiness virtually any time of year, it has to be soup. Soup is also one of the best ways to introduce people to the genius and chemistry—what some say is the magic—of cooking.

Even though it's a type of cooking as basic as it is classic, and uses techniques such as caramelizing, deglazing, and thickening that can be applied to many other kinds of dishes, making soup isn't just a matter of tossing a few ingredients into a pot of hot water. Making soup teaches you how to think about the compatibility of ingredients, the roles of assembly and cooking times, and the blending of techniques—but without overwhelming or intimidating you.

### French Onion Soup with Beef and Barley

(pictured on page 38)

You can omit the sherry or replace it with white wine.

- 1 cup boiling water
- ½ ounce dried shiitake mushrooms
- 1 tablespoon dark sesame oil, divided
- 2 medium onions, each cut into 8 wedges (about 4 cups)
- ½ cup chopped shallots or onion
- 2 teaspoons chopped peeled fresh ginger
- 4 garlic cloves, minced
- 3 cups sliced button mushrooms
- 1 teaspoon brown sugar
- 1 (12-ounce) lean boneless sirloin steak, cut into 2-inch strips
- 4 cups water
- ⅔ cup uncooked pearl barley
- ¼ cup dry sherry
- 3 tablespoons low-sodium soy sauce
- 1 (10½-ounce) can beef consommé
- 12 (¼-inch-thick) slices diagonally cut French bread baguette
- ¾ cup (3 ounces) shredded Gruyère or Swiss cheese

1. Combine boiling water and shiitakes in a bowl; cover and let stand 30 minutes. Drain shiitakes in a colander over a bowl, reserving liquid. Slice shiitakes, discarding stems.
2. Heat 2 teaspoons oil in a large Dutch oven over medium-high heat. Add onion, shallots, ginger, and garlic; sauté 10 minutes or until lightly browned. Add shiitakes, button mushrooms, sugar, and beef. Sauté 10 minutes, scraping pan to loosen browned bits. Add reserved mushroom liquid, 4 cups water, and next 4 ingredients; bring to a boil. Cover, reduce heat, and simmer 50 minutes or until barley is tender. Stir in 1 teaspoon sesame oil.
3. Preheat broiler.
4. Ladle 1½ cups soup into each of 6 ovenproof soup bowls; top each serving with 2 bread slices and 2 tablespoons cheese. Broil 3 inches from heat 1 minute or until cheese melts. Serve immediately. Yield: 6 servings.

CALORIES 351 (27% from fat); FAT 10.7g (sat 4.3g, mono 3.8g, poly 1.7g); PROTEIN 24.6g; CARB 40g; FIBER 6.2g; CHOL 50mg; IRON 3.7mg; SODIUM 676mg; CALC 196mg

### Chile-Cheese Chowder

For a vegetarian soup, substitute 1 tablespoon oil for the bacon drippings and vegetable broth for the chicken broth.

- 2 bacon slices
- 1 cup chopped carrot
- 1 cup chopped seeded poblano chiles (about 3 large)
- 1 cup chopped onion
- 2 tablespoons minced seeded jalapeño peppers
- ½ teaspoon ground cumin
- 3 garlic cloves, minced
- 2 (16-ounce) cans fat-free, less-sodium chicken broth
- 5 cups diced peeled baking potato (about 1½ pounds)
- ½ teaspoon salt
- ⅓ cup all-purpose flour
- 2½ cups 1% low-fat milk
- ¾ cup (3 ounces) shredded Monterey Jack cheese with jalapeño peppers
- ½ cup (2 ounces) shredded reduced-fat sharp Cheddar cheese
- ⅔ cup sliced green onions

1. Cook bacon in a Dutch oven over medium-high heat until crisp. Remove bacon from pan, reserving 1 tablespoon drippings in pan. Crumble bacon; set aside.
2. Add carrot and next 5 ingredients to drippings in pan; sauté 10 minutes or until browned. Stir in broth, scraping pan to loosen browned bits. Add potato and salt. Bring to a boil; cover, reduce heat, and simmer 25 minutes or until potato is tender.
3. Lightly spoon flour into a dry measuring cup; level with a knife. Combine flour and milk in a small bowl, stirring with a whisk. Add to pan. Cook over medium heat until thick (about 12 minutes), stirring frequently. Remove from heat. Add cheeses, stirring until cheeses melt. Ladle into soup bowls; top with green onions and crumbled bacon. Yield: 10 servings (serving size: 1 cup soup, about 1 tablespoon green onions, and about 1 teaspoon bacon).

CALORIES 198 (30% from fat); FAT 6.7g (sat 3.9g, mono 2g, poly 0.4g); PROTEIN 9.7g; CARB 25.1g; FIBER 2.5g; CHOL 18mg; IRON 1.4mg; SODIUM 442mg; CALC 202mg

## Chile-Cheese Chowder Step-by-Steps

**1.** *Sauté vegetables in fat until well-browned, stirring occasionally. Deglaze pan by adding broth. This will loosen and dissolve flavorful bits stuck to pan.*

**2.** *Add potato and salt, bring to a boil, and simmer until potato is tender. A simmer is a very gentle boil whose bubbles should just barely break the surface.*

**3.** *Creamy soups are thickened with cream or a roux (a mixture of cooked butter and flour), but we're using a slurry (a mixture of milk and flour) to reduce fat. To make a slurry, gradually whisk milk into flour until smooth.*

**4.** *Then slowly add slurry to soup, bring to a boil, and cook until thick—at least 10 to 15 minutes, or the results may taste of flour and be too thin.*

and parsley. Yield: 8 servings (serving size: 1 cup).

CALORIES 267 (30% from fat); FAT 9g (sat 3.2g, mono 3.8g, poly 1.3g); PROTEIN 13.6g; CARB 33.8g; FIBER 5.9g; CHOL 9mg; IRON 3.6mg; SODIUM 479mg; CALC 87mg

## Chunky Chicken-and-Rice Soup with Turnips

Partially mashing the tender turnips gives this soup a homey, stewlike quality. The turnips impart an earthy sweetness to the soup that contrasts with the sharp cheese. You can use potatoes instead of turnips, if you prefer.

```
8   cups water
1   (3-pound) chicken
1   teaspoon vegetable oil
2   cups chopped leek (about 2 large)
½   teaspoon dried basil
½   teaspoon dried thyme
½   teaspoon dried oregano
3   cups coarsely chopped peeled
    turnips (about 1 pound)
½   cup uncooked long-grain or
    basmati rice
2   cups 2% reduced-fat milk
1   teaspoon salt
¾   cup (3 ounces) shredded reduced-
    fat extra-sharp Cheddar cheese
```

**1.** Combine water and chicken in a large Dutch oven; bring to a boil. Reduce heat to medium, and cook, uncovered, 1 hour. Remove from heat. Remove chicken from cooking liquid (broth); place chicken in a bowl, and chill 15 minutes. Remove skin from chicken, and remove meat from bones, discarding skin and bones. Chop chicken into bite-size pieces; cover and chill. Strain broth through a sieve into a large bowl; discard solids. Skim fat from surface; discard. Reserve 6 cups broth.

**2.** Heat oil in pan over medium-high heat. Add leek, basil, thyme, and oregano; sauté 5 minutes or until leek is browned. Add reserved broth, scraping pan to loosen browned bits. Stir in turnips and rice; bring to a boil. Reduce heat, and simmer 30 minutes or until
*Continued*

## White-Bean Soup with Peppers and Bacon

```
1½   cups dried navy beans
5    bacon slices
2    cups chopped red bell pepper
2    cups chopped onion
1    cup chopped carrot
1    teaspoon sugar
1    teaspoon onion powder
1    teaspoon garlic powder
¼    teaspoon black pepper
⅛    teaspoon ground red pepper
4    garlic cloves, minced
3    (16-ounce) cans fat-free,
     less-sodium chicken broth
½    cup chopped fresh parsley
```

**1.** Sort and wash beans; place in a large Dutch oven. Cover with water to 2 inches above beans; bring to a boil, and cook 2 minutes. Remove from heat; cover and let stand 1 hour. Drain beans.

**2.** Cook bacon in pan over medium heat until crisp. Remove bacon from pan; crumble and set aside. Add bell pepper and next 8 ingredients to drippings in pan; sauté 10 minutes or until browned. Stir in broth, scraping pan to loosen browned bits. Add beans. Bring to a boil; cover, reduce heat, and simmer 1 hour or until beans are tender.

**3.** Place 3 cups of bean mixture in a blender, and process until smooth. Return pureed mixture to pan. Stir in bacon

turnips are tender. Partially mash turnips with a potato masher. Add chicken, milk, and salt, and cook 5 minutes or until thoroughly heated. Remove from heat, and add cheese, stirring until it melts. Yield: 10 servings (serving size: 1 cup).

CALORIES 213 (30% from fat); FAT 7.1g (sat 2.7g, mono 2.3g, poly 1.3g); PROTEIN 20.9g; CARB 15.4g; FIBER 1.1g; CHOL 57mg; IRON 1.8mg; SODIUM 396mg; CALC 173mg

## Won Ton Soup

We've updated this classic by making the won tons with ground turkey and adding spinach and tomatoes to the broth.

**WON TONS:**
- 4 ounces ground turkey
- 2 tablespoons chopped green onions
- 1 tablespoon hoisin sauce
- 2 teaspoons low-sodium soy sauce
- 2 garlic cloves, peeled
- 16 won ton wrappers
- 2 teaspoons cornstarch

**SOUP:**
- 2 teaspoons olive oil
- ¼ cup diced carrot
- ¼ cup chopped green onions
- 3 cups water
- 2 tablespoons rice vinegar
- 1 teaspoon minced peeled fresh ginger
- ¼ teaspoon salt
- ¼ teaspoon black pepper
- 3 (16-ounce) cans fat-free, less-sodium chicken broth
- 2 cups sliced spinach
- 1 (14.5-ounce) can diced tomatoes, drained

**1.** To prepare won tons, place first 5 ingredients in a food processor. Process until well-combined, scraping sides of bowl once. Working with 1 won ton wrapper at a time (cover remaining wrappers with a damp towel to keep them from drying), spoon about 1 tablespoon turkey mixture into center of each wrapper. Moisten edges of dough with water; bring 2 opposite corners to center, pinching points to seal. Bring remaining 2 corners to center, pinching points to seal. Pinch 4 edges together to seal. Place won tons on a large baking sheet sprinkled with cornstarch (cover with a damp towel to keep them from drying).
**2.** To prepare soup, heat oil in a Dutch oven over medium-high heat until hot. Add carrot and ¼ cup green onions, and sauté 3 minutes or until tender. Add water and next 5 ingredients, and bring to a boil. Add won tons; reduce heat, and simmer 6 minutes. Stir in spinach and tomatoes. Serve immediately. Yield: 8 servings (serving size: 1¼ cups).

CALORIES 111 (15% from fat); FAT 1.9g (sat 0.3g, mono 1g, poly 0.3g); PROTEIN 7.9g; CARB 14.8g; FIBER 0.9g; CHOL 11mg; IRON 1.5mg; SODIUM 751mg; CALC 42mg

## Thai Shrimp Bisque

A *bisque* is a thickened soup that usually contains or is made from seafood. We've combined Thai seasonings with a classic French shrimp bisque for a creamy main-dish soup.

**MARINADE:**
- 1½ pounds medium shrimp
- 1½ tablespoons grated lime rind
- ⅓ cup fresh lime juice
- 1½ tablespoons ground coriander
- 1 tablespoon minced fresh cilantro
- 1 tablespoon minced peeled fresh ginger
- 1½ teaspoons sugar
- ¼ teaspoon ground red pepper
- 2 garlic cloves, crushed

**SHRIMP STOCK:**
- 2 cups water
- ¼ cup dry white wine
- 1 tablespoon tomato paste

**SOUP:**
- 1 teaspoon olive oil
- ½ cup chopped onion
- ⅓ cup chopped celery
- 1 (14-ounce) can light coconut milk
- 1 tablespoon tomato paste
- ¼ cup all-purpose flour
- 1 cup 2% reduced-fat milk
- 1 tablespoon grated lime rind
- 1 tablespoon minced fresh cilantro
- ½ teaspoon salt

**1.** To prepare marinade, peel shrimp, reserving shells. Combine shrimp and next 8 ingredients in a large zip-top plastic bag; seal and marinate in refrigerator 30 minutes.
**2.** To prepare shrimp stock, combine reserved shrimp shells, water, wine, and 1 tablespoon tomato paste in a large Dutch oven. Bring mixture to a boil. Reduce heat; simmer until liquid is reduced to 1 cup (about 10 minutes). Strain mixture through a sieve over a bowl, and discard solids.
**3.** To prepare soup, heat olive oil in a large Dutch oven over medium heat. Add onion and celery, and sauté 8 minutes or until browned. Add 1 cup shrimp stock, coconut milk, and 1 tablespoon tomato paste, scraping pan to loosen browned bits. Bring to a boil. Lightly spoon flour into a dry measuring cup, and level with a knife. Combine flour and reduced-fat milk in a small bowl, stirring with a whisk. Add to pan; reduce heat, and simmer until thick (about 5 minutes). Add shrimp and marinade, and cook 5 minutes. Stir in 1 tablespoon lime rind, 1 tablespoon cilantro, and salt. Yield: 4 servings (servings size: 1½ cups).

CALORIES 201 (30% from fat); FAT 6.7g (sat 3.2g, mono 1.7g, poly 1.2g); PROTEIN 19.9g; CARB 15.2g; FIBER 0.9g; CHOL 133mg; IRON 3.3mg; SODIUM 380mg; CALC 117mg

### Freezing Tips

All these soups will freeze well for up to two months. Pour into an airtight container, leaving enough room for expansion (usually an inch or two at top). To reheat, thaw completely in refrigerator; then place contents in a saucepan over low heat, adding some liquid if necessary.

## menu

**Creamy Wild-Rice Soup
with Smoked Turkey**

Ham-and-cheese grills*

*Combine 2 tablespoons apricot preserves
and 2 tablespoons light cream cheese.
Spread over each of 4 rye bread slices.
Top each with 2 ounces lean ham, 1 (¾-
ounce) slice fat-free Swiss cheese, and 1
bread slice. Melt 2 teaspoons butter in a
skillet; add sandwiches. Cook 2 minutes
on each side or until golden. Serves 4.

# The Truth about Casseroles

*These vegetable-rich hot dishes are easy to
put on your table all week.*

## Creamy Wild-Rice Soup with Smoked Turkey

2  teaspoons butter or stick
   margarine
1  cup chopped carrot
1  cup chopped onion
1  cup chopped green onions
1  teaspoon chopped fresh or
   ¼ teaspoon dried rosemary
¼  teaspoon black pepper
3  garlic cloves, minced
2  (16-ounce) cans fat-free,
   less-sodium chicken broth
1½  cups chopped smoked turkey
   breast (about ½ pound)
1  cup uncooked wild rice
⅓  cup all-purpose flour
2¾  cups 2% reduced-fat milk
2  tablespoons dry sherry
½  teaspoon salt

**1.** Melt butter in a Dutch oven over
medium-high heat. Add carrot and next
5 ingredients. Sauté 8 minutes or until
browned. Stir in broth, scraping pan to
loosen browned bits. Stir in turkey and
rice; bring to a boil. Cover, reduce heat,
and simmer 1 hour and 15 minutes or
until rice is tender.
**2.** Lightly spoon flour into a dry measuring cup; level with a knife. Combine flour
and milk in a small bowl, stirring with a
whisk. Add to pan. Cook over medium
heat until thick (about 8 minutes), stirring
frequently. Stir in sherry and salt. Yield: 8
servings (serving size: 1 cup).

CALORIES 203 (16% from fat); FAT 3.5g (sat 1.9g, mono 1g,
poly 0.5g); PROTEIN 15g; CARB 28.2g; FIBER 2.4g; CHOL 25mg;
IRON 1.1mg; SODIUM 540mg; CALC 129mg

## Cauliflower, Pasta, and Cheese Gratin

8  cups water
6  cups cauliflower florets (about
   1½ pounds)
¾  teaspoon salt, divided
8  ounces uncooked small seashell pasta
¼  cup all-purpose flour
3  cups 1% low-fat milk
2  teaspoons chopped fresh or
   ¾ teaspoon dried thyme
3  garlic cloves, crushed
1  cup (4 ounces) shredded reduced-
   fat sharp Cheddar cheese
½  cup (2 ounces) grated fresh
   Parmesan cheese
¾  cup finely chopped green onions
2  teaspoons Dijon mustard
¼  teaspoon black pepper
2  (1-ounce) slices white bread
2  teaspoons butter, melted

**1.** Preheat oven to 400°.
**2.** Bring water to a boil in a large
saucepan; add cauliflower and ½ teaspoon salt to boiling water, and cook 4
minutes or until tender. Remove cauliflower with a slotted spoon, reserving
cooking liquid; set cauliflower aside.
Bring cooking liquid to a rolling boil.
Add pasta, and cook 7 minutes or until
al dente; drain and set aside.
**3.** Lightly spoon flour into a dry measuring cup, and level with a knife. Combine
flour and milk in a saucepan, stirring well
with a whisk. Stir in thyme and garlic;
cook over medium heat until thick
(about 8 minutes), stirring constantly.
Remove from heat; stir in ¼ teaspoon
salt, cheeses, onions, mustard, and pepper.
Combine cauliflower, pasta, and cheese
sauce in a large bowl. Spoon cauliflower

mixture into a 13 x 9-inch baking dish.
Place bread in food processor; pulse 10
times or until coarse crumbs form to
measure 1 cup. Combine breadcrumbs
and butter; sprinkle evenly over cauliflower mixture. Bake at 400° for 20 minutes or until lightly browned. Yield: 6
servings (serving size: about 1½ cups).

CALORIES 375 (24% from fat); FAT 10g (sat 5.7g, mono 2.7g,
poly 0.7g); PROTEIN 21.2g; CARB 49.6g; FIBER 3.1g; CHOL 28mg;
IRON 1.5mg; SODIUM 788mg; CALC 476mg

## Polenta Casserole with Mushrooms, Tomatoes, and Ricotta

2  teaspoons olive oil, divided
2  cups chopped onion
3  cups coarsely chopped cremini
   mushrooms (about 12 ounces)
1½  teaspoons salt, divided
2  garlic cloves, chopped
⅓  cup dry red wine
1  tablespoon chopped fresh or
   1 teaspoon dried rosemary
1  tablespoon tomato paste
1  (14.5-ounce) can diced tomatoes,
   undrained
4  cups water
1  cup instant polenta (such as
   Contadina)
½  cup (2 ounces) grated fresh
   Parmesan cheese
¼  teaspoon black pepper
½  cup part-skim ricotta cheese
1½  teaspoons butter, cut into small
   pieces

**1.** Preheat oven to 400°.
**2.** Heat 1 teaspoon oil in a 10-inch cast-
iron skillet over medium-high heat. Add
onion; sauté 8 minutes. Add mushrooms,
½ teaspoon salt, and garlic, and cook 4
minutes, stirring frequently. Stir in wine,
rosemary, and tomato paste; reduce heat
to medium, and cook 3 minutes. Stir in
tomatoes, and cook until thick (about 10
minutes). Remove from heat.
**3.** Bring water to a boil in a saucepan;
stir in polenta and 1 teaspoon salt. Reduce heat to low; cook until thick (about
5 minutes), stirring frequently.

*Continued*

**4.** Spread one-third of polenta mixture into a 13 x 9-inch baking dish coated with 1 teaspoon oil. Spread half of tomato sauce over polenta, and top with 2 tablespoons Parmesan cheese and ⅛ teaspoon pepper. Drop half of ricotta cheese by spoonfuls onto Parmesan cheese. Repeat layers, ending with polenta. Top with ¼ cup Parmesan cheese and butter. Bake at 400° for 25 minutes or until bubbly. Yield: 6 servings (serving size: 1 [4½-inch] square).

CALORIES 235 (29% from fat); FAT 7.5g (sat 3.5g, mono 2.7g, poly 0.7g); PROTEIN 9.7g; CARB 35g; FIBER 2.2g; CHOL 15mg; IRON 1.4mg; SODIUM 891mg; CALC 206mg

## Navy Bean-and-Artichoke Casserole with Goat Cheese

- 2 (1-ounce) slices whole-wheat bread
- 2 (15-ounce) cans navy beans, undrained
- 2 teaspoons chopped fresh or ½ teaspoon dried thyme
- 2 teaspoons chopped fresh or ½ teaspoon dried rubbed sage
- ¼ teaspoon black pepper
- 4 garlic cloves, minced and divided
- 2 tablespoons olive oil, divided
- 3 cups chopped leek (about 3 large)
- 2 teaspoons chopped fresh or ½ teaspoon dried rosemary
- ⅛ teaspoon salt
- 1 (14-ounce) can artichoke bottoms, drained and each cut into 8 wedges
- Olive oil-flavored cooking spray
- 1¼ cups (5 ounces) crumbled goat cheese

**1.** Place bread in a food processor; pulse 10 times or until coarse crumbs form to measure 1 cup.
**2.** Preheat oven to 400°.
**3.** Drain beans in a colander over a bowl, reserving liquid. Add enough water to liquid to measure 1 cup. Combine beans, thyme, sage, pepper, and 1 garlic clove.
**4.** Heat 1 tablespoon oil in a large non-stick skillet over medium-high heat. Add 3 garlic cloves, leek, rosemary, salt, and artichokes; sauté 4 minutes. Stir in bean liquid mixture. Cover, reduce heat, and simmer 10 minutes, stirring occasionally.

Remove from heat. Spread half of bean mixture in an 11 x 7-inch baking dish coated with cooking spray, and top with half of goat cheese. Spread artichoke mixture over goat cheese; top with remaining bean mixture and remaining goat cheese. Combine breadcrumbs and 1 tablespoon oil; sprinkle over goat cheese. Bake at 400° for 25 minutes or until lightly browned. Yield: 6 servings (serving size: about 1 cup).

CALORIES 349 (28% from fat); FAT 10.8g (sat 4.4g, mono 4.7g, poly 1.1g); PROTEIN 17.3g; CARB 47.2g; FIBER 8.7g; CHOL 21mg; IRON 5.1mg; SODIUM 926mg; CALC 252mg

## Cabbage-and-Yukon Gold Potato Casserole

- 3 cups sliced peeled Yukon Gold or baking potato (about 1 pound)
- 8 cups (1-inch-thick) sliced green cabbage (about 1½ pounds)
- 1 tablespoon butter
- 2 tablespoons chopped fresh or 2 teaspoons dried rubbed sage
- 1 garlic clove, chopped
- 1 teaspoon salt
- ¼ teaspoon black pepper
- Cooking spray
- ⅓ cup all-purpose flour
- 1⅓ cups 1% low-fat milk
- ½ cup (2 ounces) shredded part-skim mozzarella cheese
- ¼ cup (1 ounce) grated fresh Parmesan cheese
- 2 large eggs
- 1 large egg white

**1.** Preheat oven to 350°.
**2.** Place potato in a large Dutch oven, and cover with water. Bring potato to a boil, and cook 6 minutes or until tender. Remove potato with a slotted spoon, reserving cooking liquid in pan. Place potato in a large bowl, and set aside. Add cabbage to cooking liquid in pan, and cook 5 minutes. Drain well. Add cabbage to potato.
**3.** Melt butter in a small skillet over medium heat; add sage and garlic. Cook 1 minute, stirring constantly. Stir sage mixture, salt, and pepper into potato mixture. Spoon potato mixture into a

2½-quart casserole dish coated with cooking spray.
**4.** Lightly spoon flour into a dry measuring cup; level with a knife. Combine flour, milk, and remaining 4 ingredients, and stir with a whisk. Pour milk mixture over potato mixture (do not stir). Bake at 350° for 50 minutes or until casserole is lightly browned. Yield: 6 servings (serving size: about 1½ cups).

CALORIES 225 (30% from fat); FAT 7.4g (sat 3.9g, mono 2.2g, poly 0.6g); PROTEIN 12.2g; CARB 28.5g; FIBER 4.2g; CHOL 90mg; IRON 1.9mg; SODIUM 613mg; CALC 256mg

### menu

#### Tortilla Casserole with Swiss Chard

Corn-and-black bean salad*

*Combine 1 (15-ounce) can black beans, drained and rinsed; 1 (11-ounce) can corn; and 1 (4-ounce) jar chopped pimentos, drained, in a bowl. Add ½ cup chopped green bell pepper, ¼ cup chopped purple onion, 1 tablespoon chopped fresh cilantro, 1 tablespoon cider vinegar, and 1 teaspoon sugar; stir well. Serves 6.

## Tortilla Casserole with Swiss Chard

Using slightly stale corn tortillas works best for this casserole. They should feel dry, but not hard or crisp.

- 2 teaspoons vegetable oil
- 2 cups thinly sliced onion, divided
- 3 garlic cloves, finely chopped
- ½ teaspoon salt
- 2 (8-ounce) packages button mushrooms, sliced
- 2 jalapeño peppers, seeded and chopped
- 4 cups finely chopped Swiss chard (about 1 bunch)
- ¼ cup chopped fresh parsley, divided
- ¼ cup water
- 1 (14.5-ounce) can diced tomatoes, undrained
- 12 (6-inch) corn tortillas, quartered
- 1 cup (4 ounces) shredded reduced-fat sharp Cheddar cheese
- ¼ cup low-fat sour cream

**1.** Preheat oven to 375°.

**2.** Heat oil in a large nonstick skillet over medium-high heat. Add 1 cup onion and garlic, and cook 1 minute, stirring constantly. Stir in salt, mushrooms, and jalapeños. Arrange chard over mushroom mixture. Cover, reduce heat, and cook 15 minutes or until tender. Stir in 2 tablespoons parsley.

**3.** Combine 1 cup onion, water, and tomatoes in a blender, and process until smooth. Pour tomato mixture into a saucepan. Bring to a boil; cook 4 minutes or until slightly thick. Arrange 16 tortilla quarters in a single layer in a 13 x 9-inch baking dish. Spread about 1 cup mushroom mixture over tortilla pieces. Top with ½ cup tomato mixture. Sprinkle with ⅓ cup cheese. Repeat layers twice, ending with ⅓ cup cheese. Bake at 375° for 20 minutes or until cheese melts. Top servings evenly with sour cream and 2 tablespoons parsley. Yield: 6 servings (serving size: 1 [4½-inch] square, 2 teaspoons sour cream, and 1 teaspoon parsley).

CALORIES 251 (29% from fat); FAT 8.1g (sat 3.4g, mono 2.2g, poly 1.7g); PROTEIN 12g; CARB 36.1g; FIBER 5.2g; CHOL 16mg; IRON 2.8mg; SODIUM 585mg; CALC 314mg

---

### Casserole or Not?

Cooks debate what constitutes an American casserole. But they agree that, at its most basic, it consists of an oven-baked dish containing two or more substantial elements. These vegetarian recipes qualify. They combine a vegetable, such as cauliflower or mushrooms, with a starch, such as polenta or potatoes. A small amount of cheese fills three functions: It tastes good, binds the ingredients, and provides protein.

---

# Getting Warmer

## Sure, everyone talks about cold weather; the trick is what to eat during it.

One of the greatest pleasures of winter is eating a big, warming meal on a frightfully frigid day. This kind of eating isn't just for pleasure, either. Central heating is great, but our bodies need internal fuel, too. And the best fuel is provided by the foods that have always been served when it's cold outside: soups, stews, casseroles, and roasts. These are big, rich, filling dishes, but they're not necessarily high in fat.

### Macaroni and Four Cheeses

- 1 pound uncooked medium elbow macaroni
- 1 (1-ounce) slice white bread
- 2½ cups 1% low-fat milk
- 2 bay leaves
- ¼ cup all-purpose flour
- 1 cup (4 ounces) shredded reduced-fat extra-sharp Cheddar cheese
- ½ cup (2 ounces) shredded Emmenthaler or Swiss cheese
- ½ cup (2 ounces) grated fresh Parmesan cheese
- ½ cup (2 ounces) crumbled Gorgonzola cheese
- ¾ teaspoon salt
- ¼ teaspoon black pepper
- Cooking spray
- 2 teaspoons minced fresh or ½ teaspoon dried rubbed sage
- 2 teaspoons butter or stick margarine, melted

**1.** Preheat oven to 400°.

**2.** Cook pasta in boiling water 5 minutes or until almost tender. Drain and rinse with cold water. Place pasta in a large bowl.

**3.** Place bread in a food processor; pulse 10 times or until coarse crumbs form. Set aside.

**4.** Bring milk and bay leaves to a simmer in a small saucepan. Remove from heat; cover and let stand 5 minutes. Discard bay leaves. Lightly spoon flour into a dry measuring cup; level with a knife. Place flour in a small bowl; gradually add milk, stirring with a whisk until well-blended. Return milk mixture to pan. Cook over medium heat until thick, stirring constantly with a whisk. Remove from heat. Add cheeses, salt, and pepper, stirring until cheeses melt. Pour cheese sauce over pasta; stir well. Spoon mixture into a 13 x 9-inch baking dish coated with cooking spray. Combine breadcrumbs, sage, and butter in a bowl; toss with a fork. Sprinkle breadcrumb mixture over pasta mixture.

**5.** Bake at 400° for 20 minutes or until thoroughly heated. Yield: 8 servings (serving size: 1¼ cups).

CALORIES 397 (26% from fat); FAT 11.3g (sat 6.6g, mono 3g, poly 0.7g); PROTEIN 20.7g; CARB 52g; FIBER 1.6g; CHOL 32mg; IRON 2.7mg; SODIUM 624mg; CALC 425mg

### Roast Chicken with Cumin, Honey, and Orange

- 1 (3-pound) roasting chicken
- ¼ cup honey
- 1½ tablespoons grated orange rind
- 1 tablespoon ground cumin
- ¼ teaspoon salt
- ⅛ teaspoon black pepper
- 1 garlic clove, minced

**1.** Preheat oven to 400°.

**2.** Remove and discard giblets from chicken. Rinse chicken with cold water; pat dry. Trim excess fat. Starting at neck cavity, loosen skin from breast and drumsticks by inserting fingers, gently pushing between skin and meat.

*Continued*

**3.** Combine honey and remaining 5 ingredients. Rub honey mixture under loosened skin and over breast and drumsticks. Lift wing tips up and over back; tuck under chicken.

**4.** Place chicken, breast side up, on a foil-lined broiler pan. Pierce skin several times with a meat fork. Insert meat thermometer into meaty part of thigh, making sure not to touch bone. Bake at 400° for 30 minutes; cover loosely with foil. Bake an additional 40 minutes or until thermometer registers 180°. Let stand 10 minutes. Discard skin. Yield: 4 servings (serving size: 3 ounces).

CALORIES 273 (27% from fat); FAT 8.2g (sat 2.2g, mono 3g, poly 1.9g); PROTEIN 31.2g; CARB 19g; FIBER 0.2g; CHOL 95mg; IRON 2.4mg; SODIUM 241mg; CALC 37mg

## Mashed Potatoes with Parsley-Shallot Butter

(pictured on page 39)

Serve these whipped potatoes with either the "Barbecued" Meat Loaf (recipe at right) or Roast Chicken with Cumin, Honey, and Orange (recipe on page 29).

1 teaspoon butter or stick margarine, softened
2 tablespoons diced shallots
3 tablespoons plus 2 teaspoons butter or stick margarine, softened
1 tablespoon minced fresh parsley
6½ cups cubed peeled Yukon gold or baking potato (about 2½ pounds)
2 garlic cloves, halved
½ cup 1% low-fat milk
3 tablespoons low-fat sour cream
¾ teaspoon salt
⅛ teaspoon black pepper

**1.** Melt 1 teaspoon butter in a small skillet over medium heat. Add shallots, and cook 3 minutes. Remove from heat, and cool to room temperature. Combine shallot mixture, 3 tablespoons plus 2 teaspoons butter, and parsley. Stir until mixture is well-blended; cover and chill.

**2.** Place potatoes and garlic in a saucepan, and cover with water; bring to a boil. Reduce heat, and simmer 25 minutes or until very tender; drain. Return potatoes to pan. Add milk and remaining 3 ingredients, and beat at medium speed of a mixer until smooth. Serve mashed potatoes with butter mixture. Yield: 8 servings (serving size: ¾ cup potatoes and 1½ teaspoons parsley-shallot butter).

CALORIES 207 (30% from fat); FAT 6.8g (sat 4.2g, mono 1.9g, poly 0.3g); PROTEIN 3.9g; CARB 32.6g; FIBER 2.2g; CHOL 19mg; IRON 0.6mg; SODIUM 300mg; CALC 46mg

## "Barbecued" Meat Loaf

(pictured on page 39)

1 cup ketchup
1 tablespoon Worcestershire sauce
1 tablespoon red wine vinegar
2 teaspoons chili powder
1 (½-ounce) slice white bread
½ cup 1% low-fat milk
1 cup minced fresh onion
½ cup (2 ounces) grated fresh Parmesan cheese
½ cup finely diced carrot
¼ cup minced fresh parsley
1 teaspoon chopped fresh or ¼ teaspoon dried rubbed sage
½ teaspoon black pepper
2 garlic cloves, minced
1½ pounds ground sirloin
½ pound lean ground pork
1 large egg, lightly beaten
Cooking spray

**1.** Preheat oven to 350°.
**2.** Combine first 4 ingredients in a small bowl.
**3.** Place bread in a food processor; process until finely ground. Combine bread and milk in a large bowl. Add ½ cup ketchup mixture, onion, and next 9 ingredients; stir until well-blended. Place beef mixture in an 8 x 4-inch loaf pan coated with cooking spray. Bake at 350° for 1 hour. Brush remaining ketchup mixture over top. Bake at 350° for 15 minutes. Let stand 10 minutes. Remove meat loaf from pan. Cut into 8 slices. Yield: 8 servings (serving size: 1 slice).

CALORIES 257 (33% from fat); FAT 9.5g (sat 3.8g, mono 3.7g, poly 0.7g); PROTEIN 28.9g; CARB 13.8g; FIBER 1.4g; CHOL 102mg; IRON 3.3mg; SODIUM 591mg; CALC 135mg

## Scotch Broth

1 (2-pound) boned leg of lamb
2 cups thinly sliced leek (about 2)
½ cup uncooked pearl barley
¼ cup yellow or green split peas
4 (16-ounce) cans fat-free, less-sodium chicken broth
4 cups (1-inch) cubed peeled turnips (about 1½ pounds)
1 cup chopped celery
1 cup (1-inch-thick) sliced carrot
½ teaspoon salt
¼ teaspoon black pepper

**1.** Trim fat from lamb, and cut lamb into 1-inch cubes. Combine lamb, leek, barley, peas, and broth in a large Dutch oven, and bring to a boil. Reduce heat, and simmer 45 minutes, stirring occasionally. Add turnips and remaining ingredients, and bring to a boil. Reduce heat, and simmer 40 minutes or until turnips are tender. Yield: 8 servings (serving size: 1½ cups).

CALORIES 218 (15% from fat); FAT 3.6g (sat 1.2g, mono 1.4g, poly 0.5g); PROTEIN 21.5g; CARB 24.1g; FIBER 4.5g; CHOL 45mg; IRON 2.7mg; SODIUM 740mg; CALC 56mg

## Jambalaya

1 teaspoon olive oil
1 cup chopped onion
½ cup chopped celery
1 tablespoon tomato paste
1 teaspoon dried basil
Dash of ground red pepper
3 garlic cloves, minced
1 bay leaf
2 (14.5-ounce) cans Cajun-recipe stewed tomatoes with pepper, garlic, and Cajun spices (such as Del Monte)
6 ounces andouille sausage, cut into ¼-inch-thick slices
1 (2-ounce) jar diced pimento, drained
3 cups cooked long-grain rice
½ pound peeled and deveined medium shrimp

**1.** Heat oil in a Dutch oven over medium-high heat. Add onion and next 9

ingredients; cook 7 minutes or until vegetables are tender, stirring frequently. Stir in rice and shrimp; cook 6 minutes or until shrimp are done. Yield: 4 servings (serving size: 2 cups).

CALORIES 317 (29% from fat); FAT 10.3g (sat 2.9g, mono 4g, poly 2.4g); PROTEIN 22.5g; CARB 34.7g; FIBER 2.2g; CHOL 116mg; IRON 4.3mg; SODIUM 1,247mg; CALC 135mg

## Roast Pork with Dried Fruits and Squash

The great thing about preparing a large roast is that you'll have pork left over for future meals. Wrap it in heavy-duty plastic wrap and aluminum foil; refrigerate for up to three days.

- ½ cup dried apricots
- ½ cup pitted prunes
- 2 cups hot water
- ½ teaspoon ground cinnamon
- 1 (5-pound) bone-in pork loin roast
- 1 tablespoon sugar
- 1 teaspoon grated peeled fresh ginger
- ¾ teaspoon salt
- ¼ teaspoon black pepper
- 5 cups cubed peeled butternut or acorn squash (about 1½ pounds)

**1.** Combine first 3 ingredients; cover and let stand 30 minutes or until soft. Drain in a colander over a bowl; reserve liquid. Combine fruit and cinnamon; set aside.
**2.** Preheat oven to 425°.
**3.** Trim fat from pork. Cut a 1½-inch-wide horizontal slit through center of pork to form a pocket using a long, thin knife. Stuff apricot mixture into pocket using handle of a wooden spoon to help push apricot mixture to center of pork.
**4.** Place pork on a broiler pan; insert meat thermometer into thickest portion of pork. Combine sugar, ginger, salt, and pepper. Pour ½ cup reserved liquid over pork; sprinkle with sugar mixture. Bake at 425° for 20 minutes. Reduce oven temperature to 325° (do not remove pork from oven); bake at 325° for 25 minutes. Arrange squash around pork. Bake at 325° an additional 45 minutes or until thermometer registers 160°

(slightly pink), basting pork with remaining liquid every 15 minutes.
**5.** Place pork on a serving platter; cover with foil. Let stand 15 minutes before slicing. Yield: 6 servings (serving size: 3 ounces pork and ⅓ cup squash).

CALORIES 336 (33% from fat); FAT 12.5g (sat 4.1g, mono 5.3g, poly 1.5g); PROTEIN 24.5g; CARB 33.3g; FIBER 2.1g; CHOL 77mg; IRON 2.8mg; SODIUM 373mg; CALC 63mg

## lighten up

# Hawaiian Delight

*Her favorite dessert was once "a bit of heaven on earth," but now this teen says it needs lightening.*

Sixteen-year-old Porsche Kakazu from Ewa Beach, Hawaii, is hooked on a dessert called Mandarin Cream Delight. "The recipe calls for a lot of butter, sour cream, and whipped topping," she says.

We tackled the crust first by cutting the amount of butter nearly in half. Then we switched to a mixture of low-fat and fat-free sour cream in the filling. And we topped it all off with a slightly smaller amount of reduced-calorie whipped topping.

That trio of changes helped shave off more than 150 calories and two-thirds of the fat.

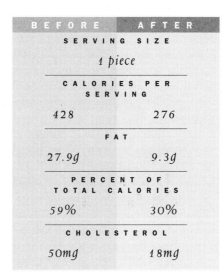

| BEFORE | AFTER |
|---|---|
| **SERVING SIZE** | |
| *1 piece* | |
| **CALORIES PER SERVING** | |
| 428 | 276 |
| **FAT** | |
| 27.9g | 9.3g |
| **PERCENT OF TOTAL CALORIES** | |
| 59% | 30% |
| **CHOLESTEROL** | |
| 50mg | 18mg |

## Mandarin Cream Delight

**CRUST:**
- 9 tablespoons butter or stick margarine, softened
- ½ cup sugar
- 1 teaspoon vanilla extract
- 1½ cups all-purpose flour
- ⅛ teaspoon salt
Cooking spray

**FILLING:**
- 2 (11-ounce) cans mandarin oranges in light syrup, undrained
- ¼ cup sugar
- 1 (16-ounce) carton fat-free sour cream
- 1 (8-ounce) carton low-fat sour cream
- 2 (3.4-ounce) packages vanilla instant pudding mix or 2 (1.4-ounce) packages sugar-free vanilla instant pudding mix
- 1 (8-ounce) container frozen reduced-calorie whipped topping, thawed
Mint sprigs (optional)

**1.** To prepare crust, combine butter, ½ cup sugar, and vanilla in a large bowl. Beat at medium speed of a mixer until light and fluffy (about 2 minutes). Lightly spoon flour into dry measuring cups; level with a knife. Add flour and salt to butter mixture, beating at low speed until well-blended.
**2.** Preheat oven to 400°.
**3.** Pat dough into a 13 x 9-inch baking dish coated with cooking spray, and pierce bottom of dough with a fork. Bake at 400° for 12 minutes or until lightly browned. Cool crust on a wire rack.
**4.** To prepare filling, drain mandarin oranges over a large bowl, reserving ½ cup juice. Combine juice, ¼ cup sugar, sour creams, and pudding mix in a large bowl. Stir in orange segments. Spoon orange mixture over crust, spreading evenly. Top with whipped topping. Chill 1 hour. Garnish with mint, if desired. Yield: 16 servings (serving size: 1 piece).

CALORIES 276 (30% from fat); FAT 9.3g (sat 6.4g, mono 2g, poly 0.4g); PROTEIN 4.2g; CARB 43g; FIBER 0.3g; CHOL 18mg; IRON 0.7mg; SODIUM 212mg; CALC 44mg

# Swiss Style

### Bored with your bread? The healthy Swiss way will put the party back in your baking and the yum in your slices.

The Swiss take their bread seriously. They prefer substantial loaves chock-full of fresh-ground grains, chewy seeds, and plump nuts. The Swiss eat the stuff up as fast as they can bake it, but are probably healthier for doing so, thanks to a reliance on natural ingredients, whole grains, and basic baking procedures.

Swiss bakers, who must pay craft dues based on how much yeast they buy, are notoriously frugal with the enzyme. They tend to add just enough yeast to allow the bread to rise, and when possible also employ a wild yeast sourdough. Eggs, sugar, and fats also are used sparingly, usually only for breads that are sweet. Swiss bakers tend to shun chemical additives, too; instead, they'll often add a touch of malt or levit (sourdough starter) to improve texture and fermentation. The characteristic flavors of Swiss breads are strong and bold. They're brought to full strength with the use of fresh cake yeast and—a special hallmark—a long, slow fermentation period.

We've tried to keep as many of these techniques as possible in translating these recipes for use at home, although in some cases we thought it best to work with ingredients more easily found in America. Still, you can get most of the ingredients the Swiss use. As for the leavening process, we've started with a water, flour, and yeast sponge. The base is slightly more liquid than the Swiss use because it's easier to leave unattended. Starting with a sponge also means that the first stage of the fermenting process is virtually foolproof. Because we're following the Swiss practice of using less yeast, we prefer the dried yeast sold in bulk rather than individual packets. If you live near a commercial bakery, ask if they'll sell you a pound of cake yeast, which you can divide into 16 portions and freeze.

## Two-Seed Potato Bread

Although it doesn't rise as tall as traditional American sandwich breads, this dense, flat-topped loaf is perfect for that lunchtime favorite.

    2   cups whole-wheat flour
  1½   cups bread flour, divided
    2   cups water
    ¾   cup diced peeled baking potato
    1   package dry yeast (about 2¼ teaspoons)
    3   tablespoons honey
    1   tablespoon vegetable oil
    1   teaspoon salt
        Cooking spray
    1   large egg white
    1   tablespoon unsalted pumpkinseed kernels
    1   tablespoon sunflower seed kernels

**1.** Lightly spoon flours into dry measuring cups; level with a knife. Combine water and potato in a saucepan; bring to a boil. Cook 15 minutes or until tender. Place potato mixture in a blender, and process until smooth. Reserve 1½ cups potato liquid; discard remaining potato liquid. Cool potato liquid to warm (100° to 110°). Combine 1 cup bread flour, potato liquid, and yeast in a large bowl. Cover and let stand at room temperature 1 hour.

**2.** Add whole-wheat flour, honey, oil, and salt to yeast mixture. Turn dough out onto a floured surface. Knead until smooth and elastic (about 5 minutes); add enough of remaining bread flour, 1 tablespoon at a time, to prevent dough from sticking to hands (dough will feel tacky). Place dough in a 9 x 5-inch loaf pan coated with cooking spray. Cover

and let rise in a warm place (85°), free from drafts, 30 minutes or until doubled in size. (Press two fingers into dough. If indentation remains, dough has risen enough.)

**3.** Preheat oven to 375°.

**4.** Uncover dough; brush egg white over loaf. Sprinkle dough with pumpkinseed and sunflower-seed kernels. Bake at 375° for 30 minutes or until loaf sounds hollow when tapped. Remove from pan; cool on a wire rack. Yield: 1 loaf, 12 servings (serving size: 1 slice).

CALORIES 175 (13% from fat); FAT 2.6g (sat 0.4g, mono 0.6g; poly 1.2g); PROTEIN 5.9g; CARB 33.5g; FIBER 2.9g; CHOL 0mg; IRON 1.9mg; SODIUM 202mg; CALC 12mg

## Wheat Berry-and-Walnut Bread

This dense, round loaf is great for sandwiches or as an accompaniment to a meal, soup, or stew. Wheat berries, which can be cooked and eaten as a cereal or softened and added to baked goods, are whole, unprocessed kernels of wheat. Look for them in health-food stores and some supermarkets.

  2½   cups whole-wheat flour, divided
    ½   cup rye flour
    ¼   cup all-purpose flour
  1½   cups warm 1% low-fat milk (100° to 110°)
    2   tablespoons shreds of wheat-bran cereal (such as All-Bran)
    1   package dry yeast (about 2¼ teaspoons)
    ½   cup water
    2   tablespoons uncooked wheat berries
    6   tablespoons chopped walnuts, divided
    3   tablespoons honey
    1   teaspoon salt
        Cooking spray
    1   teaspoon vegetable oil

**1.** Lightly spoon flours into dry measuring cups; level with a knife.

**2.** Combine ½ cup whole-wheat flour, warm milk, cereal, and yeast in a large bowl; stir well with a whisk. Cover and let stand at room temperature 1 hour.

**3.** Combine ½ cup water and wheat berries in a small microwave-safe bowl. Microwave at HIGH 1 minute or until mixture boils. Cover and let stand 1 hour. Drain.

**4.** Add wheat berries, 2 cups whole-wheat flour, rye flour, ¼ cup walnuts, honey, and salt to yeast mixture; stir until a soft dough forms (dough will feel tacky). Turn dough out onto a lightly floured surface. Knead until smooth and elastic (about 5 minutes); add enough of all-purpose flour, 1 tablespoon at a time, to prevent dough from sticking to hands. Place dough on a baking sheet coated with cooking spray. Shape into an 8-inch round loaf. Make a ¼-inch-deep "X" design in top of dough using a sharp knife. Brush dough with oil, and sprinkle with 2 tablespoons walnuts. Cover and let rise in a warm place (85°), free from drafts, 30 minutes or until doubled in size. (Press two fingers into dough. If indentation remains, dough has risen enough.)

**5.** Preheat oven to 375°.

**6.** Uncover dough. Bake at 375° for 25 minutes or until loaf sounds hollow when tapped. Remove from baking sheet; cool on a wire rack. Yield: 1 loaf, 12 servings (serving size: 1 slice).

CALORIES 177 (18% from fat); FAT 3.6g (sat 0.5g, mono 0.8g, poly 1.9g); PROTEIN 6.7g; CARB 32g; FIBER 4.6g; CHOL 1mg; IRON 1.6mg; SODIUM 220mg; CALC 53mg

## Flaxseed Bread

This small, dense, round loaf is made with flaxseed, a nutty-flavored grain that is rich in heart-healthy omega-3 fats. Slice some thick wedges of this hearty bread to go along with soup or stew.

```
1¼   cups whole-wheat flour
 1   cup bread flour
 1   cup warm water (100° to 110°)
 1   package dry yeast (about 2¼
     teaspoons)
 ½   cup flaxseed
 2   tablespoons flaxseed
 3   tablespoons nonfat dry milk
 2   tablespoons shreds of wheat-bran
     cereal (such as All-Bran)
 3   tablespoons honey
 1   tablespoon molasses
 1   teaspoon salt
 3   tablespoons bread flour
Cooking spray
 2   teaspoons cornmeal
 1   large egg white, lightly beaten
 1   teaspoon flaxseed
```

**1.** Lightly spoon whole-wheat flour and 1 cup bread flour into dry measuring cups, and level with a knife. Combine 1 cup bread flour, water, and yeast in a large bowl; stir well with a whisk. Cover yeast mixture, and let stand at room temperature 1 hour.

**2.** Place ½ cup flaxseed in a spice or coffee grinder; process until finely ground to measure ¾ cup. Add ground flaxseed, whole-wheat flour, 2 tablespoons whole flaxseed, and next 5 ingredients to yeast mixture, and stir until a soft dough forms (dough will feel tacky). Turn dough out onto a lightly floured surface. Knead until smooth and elastic (about 5 minutes); add enough of 3 tablespoons bread flour, 1 tablespoon at a time, to prevent dough from sticking to hands. Shape dough into a 5-inch round loaf; place onto a baking sheet coated with cooking spray and sprinkled with cornmeal. Brush loaf with egg white; sprinkle with 1 teaspoon flaxseed. Make 3 diagonal cuts ¼-inch-deep across top of loaf using a sharp knife. Cover and let rise in a warm place (85°), free from drafts, 1 hour or until doubled in size. (Press two fingers into dough. If indentation remains, dough has risen enough.)

**3.** Preheat oven to 375°.

**4.** Bake at 375° for 30 minutes or until bread sounds hollow when tapped. Remove from pan; cool on a wire rack. Yield: 1 loaf, 12 servings (serving slice: 1 slice).

**NOTE:** Flaxseed can be found in health-food stores and some supermarkets. Because it's rich in fat, you'll want to store flaxseed in the refrigerator or freezer. It will stay fresh for up to 6 months.

CALORIES 165 (26% from fat); FAT 4.7g (sat 0.4g, mono 3g, poly 0.7g); PROTEIN 6.4g; CARB 28.8g; FIBER 4.1g; CHOL 0mg; IRON 2.3mg; SODIUM 224mg; CALC 60mg

---

## Master Tips

Michael Kleinert, a master baker and director of the research laboratory at the Richemont Bakery and Confectionery Craft School in Lucerne, Switzerland, has taught countless aspiring bakers. Here are some of his suggestions for success with baking whole-grain breads at home.

• The flavor of bread can't develop properly unless you give the yeast enough time to interact with the flour. This fermentation period is also called a dough rest. Without it, bread has a one-dimensional flavor.

• When working with rye flour, remember that it is soft and sticky, and that working in additional flour doesn't help. The most important aspect is letting the dough rest for an hour after kneading and before shaping.

• If you have heavy ingredients such as seeds, put them into the dough toward the end of the kneading process so they don't interfere with the development of the gluten structure.

---

## Oatmeal-Raisin Bread

```
3¾   cups bread flour, divided
 ½   cup oat flour
 1   cup warm water (100° to 110°)
 1   package dry yeast (about 2¼
     teaspoons)
 ½   cup regular oats
 ¾   cup boiling water
 1   cup raisins
 3   tablespoons honey
 ½   teaspoon ground cinnamon
 2   tablespoons barley flour
 2   teaspoons salt
 1   teaspoon cider vinegar
Cooking spray
```

*Continued*

1. Lightly spoon bread and oat flours into dry measuring cups; level with a knife.

2. Combine ¾ cup bread flour, warm water, and yeast in a large bowl; stir well with a whisk. Cover and let stand at room temperature 1 hour.

3. Combine oats and boiling water in a small bowl. Stir in raisins, honey, and cinnamon. Set aside, and cool.

4. Add 2½ cups bread flour, oat flour, barley flour, salt, and vinegar to yeast mixture. Add oats mixture; stir until a soft dough forms (dough will feel tacky). Turn dough out onto a lightly floured surface. Knead dough until smooth and elastic (about 10 minutes); add enough of remaining bread flour, 1 tablespoon at a time, to prevent dough from sticking to hands. Shape into 2 (9-inch) oval loaves. Make 3 parallel cuts ¼-inch-deep across top of each loaf using a sharp knife. Place loaves on a baking sheet coated with cooking spray. Spray tops with cooking spray. Cover and let rise in a warm place (85°), free from drafts, 30 minutes or until doubled in size. (Press two fingers into dough. If indentation remains, dough has risen enough.)

5. Preheat oven to 375°.

6. Uncover dough. Bake at 375° for 30 minutes or until loaves sound hollow when tapped. Remove from baking sheet; cool on a wire rack. Yield: 2 loaves, 12 servings per loaf (serving size: 1 slice).

CALORIES 121 (5% from fat); FAT 0.7g (sat 0.1g, mono 0.1g, poly 0.2g); PROTEIN 3.5g; CARB 25.4g; FIBER 0.8g; CHOL 0mg; IRON 1.3mg; SODIUM 197mg; CALC 9mg

## Flour Finds

Although many supermarkets carry a wide array of flours, check your local health-food store for less commonly used flours such as rye and barley and grains such as flaxseed and wheat berries.

## Fruit-and-Nut Bread

(pictured on page 40)

This light-textured bread is inspired by an organic harvest bread baked at Bio Andreas on Andreasplatz, a lovely square in Basel's historic district. Whole red grapes are kneaded into the dough just before it is allowed to rise. We've replaced the chestnuts with easier-to-find hazelnuts.

- ⅔ cup hazelnuts
- 2½ cups all-purpose flour, divided
- 2 cups whole-wheat flour
- 1½ cups warm water (100° to 110°)
- 1 package dry yeast (about 2¼ teaspoons)
- 1 cup coarsely chopped dried mix fruit
- ⅓ cup packed brown sugar
- 2 tablespoons vegetable oil
- 1 teaspoon salt
- 1 large egg, beaten
- ½ cup seedless red grapes
- Cooking spray
- 2 teaspoons vegetable oil
- 1 tablespoon sunflower seed kernels

1. Preheat oven to 350°.

2. Place hazelnuts on a baking sheet. Bake nuts at 350° for 15 minutes, stirring once. Turn nuts out onto a towel. Roll up towel; rub off skins. Chop nuts.

3. Lightly spoon flours into dry measuring cups; level with a knife.

4. Combine 1 cup all-purpose flour, warm water, and yeast in a large bowl, and stir well with a whisk. Cover and let stand at room temperature 1 hour.

5. Add hazelnuts, 1 cup all-purpose flour, whole-wheat four, dried fruit, sugar, 2 tablespoons oil, salt, and egg to yeast mixture, and stir until a soft dough forms (dough will feel tacky). Turn dough out onto a lightly floured surface. Knead dough until smooth and elastic (about 5 minutes); add enough of remaining all-purpose flour, 1 tablespoon at a time, to prevent dough from sticking to hands. Arrange grapes over dough; gently knead on a lightly floured surface 4 or 5 times or just until grapes are incorporated into dough. Place dough on a baking sheet coated with cooking spray.

Shape into an 8-inch round loaf. Brush dough with 2 teaspoons oil. Sprinkle surface of dough with sunflower kernels, gently pressing kernels into dough. Cover and let rise in a warm place (85°), free from drafts, 45 minutes or until doubled in size. (Press two fingers into dough. If indentation remains, dough has risen enough.)

6. Preheat oven to 375°.

7. Uncover dough. Bake at 375° for 35 minutes or until loaf sounds hollow when tapped. Remove loaf from baking sheet; cool on a wire rack. Yield: 1 loaf, 18 servings (serving size: 1 slice).

CALORIES 200 (26% from fat); FAT 5.7g (sat 0.8g, mono 2.9g, poly 1.6g); PROTEIN 4.9g; CARB 33.8g; FIBER 2.5g; CHOL 12mg; IRON 1.9mg; SODIUM 138mg; CALC 24mg

## Swiss Strategies

Because American kitchens don't come equipped with the ultrahot steam ovens Swiss bakers use to put a beautiful brown crust on their typically oil- and sugar-free breads, we decided to take a small liberty. Adding a little honey (or any kind of sugar for that matter) to a bread dough can help promote browning.

We've also adapted the Swiss "sponge" method so that the yeast-and-flour mixture ferments in an hour instead of overnight. Swiss bakers prefer to use a little less yeast and allow the bubbly yeast-flour sponge to grow slowly. But we think our shorter method mimics the Swiss strategy with less fuss and with roughly the same end result.

# Time Well Spent

*Cutting business classes to watch cooking shows not only didn't hurt this California reader's grades, it inspired postgraduate studies in stir-fry.*

Audiotaped class lectures allowed Tuan Nguyen, University of California-Davis graduate, to stay at home, where he watched a daily lineup of cooking shows. His grades didn't suffer, though; he graduated with honors and got a good job at a computer-networking company.

With six years' experience preparing variations of Stir-Fried Vegetables and Tofu, the Redwood City, California, resident says the trick is to sauté the vegetables and the tofu in separate pans, and then combine.

## Stir-Fried Vegetables and Tofu

(pictured on page 37)

2 tablespoons olive oil, divided
⅔ cup julienne-cut carrot
2 garlic cloves, minced
¼ cup dry white wine, divided
2 cups julienne-cut zucchini
1½ cups julienne-cut yellow squash
1 (8-ounce) package button mushrooms, quartered
2½ cups quartered cremini mushrooms (about 8 ounces)
1 (12.3-ounce) package reduced-fat extra-firm tofu, drained and cut into cubes
3 tablespoons low-sodium soy sauce
2 cups fresh bean sprouts
¼ teaspoon salt
¼ teaspoon black pepper
3 cups hot cooked jasmine or other long-grain rice

**1.** Heat 1 tablespoon oil in a nonstick skillet over medium-high heat. Add carrot; stir-fry 4 minutes. Add garlic and 2 tablespoons wine; stir-fry 3 minutes. Add zucchini and squash; stir-fry 5 minutes.

Add mushrooms and 2 tablespoons wine; stir-fry 5 minutes. Remove from heat.
**2.** Heat 1 tablespoon oil in a medium nonstick skillet over medium-high heat. Add tofu; sauté 7 minutes, browning on all sides. Add soy sauce; cook 1 minute. Stir in sprouts, salt, and pepper. Add tofu mixture to vegetable mixture; heat thoroughly. Serve over rice. Yield: 6 servings (serving size: 1 cup stir-fry and ½ cup rice).

CALORIES 225 (22% from fat); FAT 5.5g (sat 0.8g, mono 3.4g, poly 0.9g); PROTEIN 10.1g; CARB 36g; FIBER 2.6g; CHOL 0mg; IRON 3.4mg; SODIUM 418mg; CALC 58mg

## Banana-Bran Soy Muffins

"I like to put new ingredients into old family recipes. When I started eating soy for health reasons, I added soy milk and soy flour to this favorite muffin recipe."
—Susan Boortz, Colfax, Wisconsin

1 cup wheat bran
1 cup mashed ripe banana
⅔ cup soy milk
¼ cup packed brown sugar
2 tablespoons prune baby food or prune butter (such as Lekvar)
1 large egg, lightly beaten
1¼ cups all-purpose flour
¼ cup soy flour
¼ cup finely chopped pecans
2 teaspoons baking powder
1 teaspoon ground cinnamon
½ teaspoon salt
Cooking spray

**1.** Preheat oven to 375°.
**2.** Combine first 3 ingredients; let stand 5 minutes. Add sugar, baby food, and egg; mix well. Lightly spoon flours into dry measuring cups; level with a knife. Combine flours and next 4 ingredients in a bowl; make a well in center of mixture. Add bran mixture to flour mixture, stirring just until moist.
**3.** Spoon batter into 12 muffin cups coated with cooking spray. Bake at 375° for 20 minutes or until muffins spring back when touched lightly in center. Remove muffins from pans immediately; cool muffins completely on a wire rack.

Yield: 1 dozen (serving size: 1 muffin).
**NOTE:** This muffin has a dense texture.

CALORIES 134 (21% from fat); FAT 3.2g (sat 0.5g, mono 1.4g, poly 1g); PROTEIN 4.3g; CARB 24.7g; FIBER 3.5g; CHOL 18mg; IRON 1.9mg; SODIUM 193mg; CALC 76mg

## Miso Chicken with Brown Rice

"I do a lot of Asian cooking, and I was looking for another use for miso. In this recipe, the sweetness in the miso blends well with the saltiness of the soy sauce."
—Michael Beets, Wichita, Kansas

2 tablespoons miso (soybean paste)
1½ tablespoons minced peeled fresh ginger
2 garlic cloves, minced
4 (4-ounce) skinned, boned chicken breast halves
Cooking spray
5 large egg whites, lightly beaten
1 cup finely chopped onion
1 cup thinly sliced carrot
1 tablespoon fish sauce
2½ cups cooked brown rice
1 cup diced shiitake mushroom caps (about 3 ounces)
2 tablespoons chopped fresh parsley
2 tablespoons chopped green onions
1 tablespoon low-sodium soy sauce
1½ cups chopped spinach

**1.** Combine first 3 ingredients in a small bowl. Rub miso mixture over both sides of chicken breast halves. Wrap each breast half securely in plastic wrap. Arrange packets in steamer rack; place rack in a Dutch oven. Steam packets, covered, 20 minutes or until done. Remove packets from steamer; let stand 5 minutes. Remove chicken from packets, reserving liquid from packets. Dice chicken; set aside. Discard water in pan; wipe pan dry with a paper towel.
**2.** Place a large nonstick skillet coated with cooking spray over medium-high heat until hot. Add egg whites, and cook 2 minutes or until done. Remove egg whites from skillet; coarsely chop.

*Continued*

**3.** Add reserved cooking liquid, chicken, onion, carrot, and fish sauce to Dutch oven; bring to a boil. Reduce heat to medium; cook 5 minutes or until liquid almost evaporates. Add rice, mushrooms, parsley, green onions, and soy sauce; cook 3 minutes. Stir in egg whites and spinach. Yield: 4 servings (serving size: 1½ cups).

CALORIES 344 (9% from fat); FAT 3.5g (sat 0.7g, mono 0.8g, poly 0.9g); PROTEIN 36.9g; CARB 40.5g; FIBER 5.6g; CHOL 66mg; IRON 3.3mg; SODIUM 998mg; CALC 83mg

### Piñata Pitas

"As a full-time college student with a full-time job, I need my meals to be fast and healthy. I created this recipe with both of those things in mind. It can be made in less than 30 minutes and is tasty served warm or cold."

—Jocelyn Robertson, Meridian, Idaho

Cooking spray
  1  cup chopped onion
  2  tablespoons balsamic vinegar
  1  (15.5-ounce) can golden hominy, drained
  1  (15-ounce) can black beans, rinsed and drained
  1  (12.3-ounce) package firm tofu, drained and cut into 1-inch cubes
  1  tablespoon dried parsley
  2  teaspoons ground coriander
  ½  teaspoon dried thyme
  ¼  teaspoon black pepper
  2  cups (8 ounces) crumbled feta cheese, divided
  4  (7-inch) pitas, cut in half
1½  cups chopped tomato
  ½  cup sliced green onions

**1.** Place a large nonstick skillet coated with cooking spray over medium-high heat. Add chopped onion; sauté 3 minutes. Add vinegar, hominy, beans, and tofu; sauté 10 minutes. Stir in parsley, coriander, thyme, and pepper; sauté 5 minutes. Remove from heat; stir in 1 cup cheese. Fill each pita half with ½ cup bean mixture; top each with 2 tablespoons cheese, 3 tablespoons tomato, and 1 tablespoon green onions. Yield: 8

servings (serving size: 1 pita half).

**NOTE:** 1 (15.25-ounce) can of whole-kernel corn, drained, may be substituted for hominy.

CALORIES 278 (30% from fat); FAT 9.3g (sat 4.7g, mono 1.9g, poly 1.8g); PROTEIN 14.4g; CARB 35.6g; FIBER 4.4g; CHOL 25mg; IRON 5.1mg; SODIUM 647mg; CALC 243mg

back to the best

# Cinnamon-Apple Cake

*When we first tasted this cake by Contributor Greg Patent for our October 1997 issue, we knew that we'd hit culinary gold. That's why we've chosen it to lead the "back to the best" honor roll of our all-time favorite* Cooking Light *recipes.*

### Cinnamon-Apple Cake

(pictured on page 37)

The cream cheese in the batter gives this cake lots of moisture. Because the cake is so tender, use a serrated knife to cut it.

1¾  cups sugar, divided
  ¾  cup (6 ounces) block-style fat-free cream cheese, softened
  ½  cup butter or stick margarine, softened
  1  teaspoon vanilla extract
  2  large eggs
1½  cups all-purpose flour
1½  teaspoons baking powder
  ¼  teaspoon salt
  2  teaspoons ground cinnamon
  3  cups chopped peeled Rome apple (about 2 large)
Cooking spray

**1.** Preheat oven to 350°.
**2.** Beat 1½ cups sugar, cream cheese, butter, and vanilla at medium speed of a mixer until well-blended (about 4 minutes). Add eggs, 1 at a time, beating well after each addition; set aside.

**3.** Lightly spoon flour into dry measuring cups; level with a knife. Combine flour, baking powder, and salt. Add flour mixture to sugar mixture; beat at low speed until blended. Combine ¼ cup sugar and cinnamon. Combine 2 tablespoons of cinnamon mixture and apple in a bowl; stir apple mixture into batter. Pour batter into an 8-inch springform pan coated with cooking spray, and sprinkle with remaining cinnamon mixture.

**4.** Bake at 350° for 1 hour and 15 minutes or until cake pulls away from sides of pan. Cool cake completely on a wire rack, and cut using a serrated knife. Yield: 12 servings.

**NOTE:** You can also make this cake in a 9-inch square cake pan or a 9-inch springform pan; just reduce baking time by 5 minutes.

CALORIES 281 (28% from fat); FAT 8.7g (sat 1.8g, mono 3.7g, poly 2.6g); PROTEIN 4.8g; CARB 46.3g; FIBER 1.2g; CHOL 39mg; IRON 1.1mg; SODIUM 234mg; CALC 89mg

---

### An Apple for Every Eye

From brilliant red Rome to butter-colored Golden Delicious, there are thousands of varieties of apples grown around the world. Only about 20 varieties are available in American markets.

For eating raw, try these apple varieties that are crisp, juicy, and have a balance of sugar and acid:
• Red Delicious
• Gala
• McIntosh
• Fuji
• Baldwin
• Empire

Texture and flavor are the key when choosing apples for cooking and baking. Choose apples that are ripe, so you don't end up with crunchy or over-ripe fruit after baking. Try these varieties for cooking:
• Rome
• Golden Delicious
• Braeburn
• Granny Smith
• Cortland
• Russet

Cinnamon-Apple Cake,
page 36

Stir-Fried Vegetables and Tofu,
page 35

**French Onion Soup with Beef and Barley, page 24**

**Linguine with Red Clam Sauce, page 19**

"Barbecued" Meat Loaf, Mashed Potatoes with Parsley-Shallot Butter, and green beans, page 30

**Fruit-and-Nut Bread, page 34**

**Churrasco with Pebre (Grilled Beef Tenderloin with Chilean Cilantro Sauce), page 14**

# march

# Blue Plate Specials

Did great home cooking beget the local diner—or the other way around? Doesn't matter. That big, friendly fare is a hit—and a healthy one, if done right—wherever it's served.

One of the great adventures of the road is the search for the modest diner or café that still serves up a great blue plate special—big, friendly helpings of casseroles, corn bread, coleslaw, steamed vegetables, meat loaf, onion rings, pork chops and applesauce, brisket, chicken—the kinds of simple, healthy foods that are also the staples of home cooking.

Diner food has a marked characteristic: It's real. Unlike the culinary fabrication, formatting, and assembling that goes on at the fast-food palaces, in a diner, someone is actually cooking the daily choices.

Perhaps it's our homes themselves that will be the guarantors of the blue plate's future. Diners don't specialize in home cooking by accident: We like what we find there because that's also what we cook up in our own kitchens. Even as our preferences evolve and we learn to make Beer-Battered Onion Rings (recipe on page 43) and Barbecued Pork Chops (recipe on page 45) that won't create instant love handles, we'll still want those tastes and flavors.

Indeed, as we make dishes like these better and better, keeping their inherent soundness while pepping them up with exciting new flavors, it's likely that we might even spur new interest in diner cuisine (yes, the words can be used together), kickstarting the tradition up yet another notch.

### Old-Fashioned Chicken Fricassee

A fricassee is usually made with chicken sautéed in butter and simmered with a chunky vegetable-wine sauce. Serve on a mound of mashed potatoes, grits, or rice.

- 3 tablespoons all-purpose flour
- 1 teaspoon paprika
- 1 teaspoon poultry seasoning
- ½ teaspoon salt
- ½ teaspoon black pepper
- 4 (6-ounce) skinned chicken breast halves
- 2 teaspoons butter or stick margarine
- 1½ cups chopped onion
- ½ cup chopped celery
- 3 garlic cloves, minced
- 1 cup fat-free, less-sodium chicken broth
- ¼ cup dry white wine
- 2 cups (3-inch) julienne-cut carrot
- ¼ cup chopped fresh parsley

**1.** Combine first 5 ingredients in a large zip-top plastic bag. Add chicken; toss well to coat. Remove chicken from bag; reserve flour mixture. Melt butter in a large nonstick skillet over medium heat. Add chicken, breast sides down; sauté 5 minutes or until chicken is browned. Remove chicken from pan; keep warm.
**2.** Add onion, celery, and garlic to pan; sauté 5 minutes, stirring occasionally. Stir in reserved flour mixture; cook 1 minute. Add broth and wine; bring to a boil. Add carrot. Return chicken to pan, breast sides up. Cover, reduce heat, and simmer 25 minutes or until chicken is done. Sprinkle with chopped parsley. Yield: 4 servings (serving size: 1 chicken breast half and ¾ cup sauce).

CALORIES 290 (14% from fat); FAT 4.4g (sat 1.8g, mono 1.1g, poly 0.7g); PROTEIN 42.5g; CARB 18.2g; FIBER 3.8g; CHOL 104mg; IRON 2.6mg; SODIUM 581mg; CALC 70mg

### Spicy Steak Fries

No respectable down-home diner would be complete without great fries. But by cutting down on the oil, we've kept these light enough not to bust your buttons.

- 1 tablespoon vegetable oil
- 2 large baking potatoes, each cut lengthwise into 12 wedges (about 1½ pounds)
- 2 teaspoons seasoning blend (such as Paul Prudhomme's Seafood Magic)
- ¼ teaspoon salt

**1.** Preheat oven to 400°.
**2.** Spread oil on a jelly-roll pan. Place potato wedges on pan. Sprinkle with seasoning blend; toss gently to coat. Bake at 400° for 40 minutes or until tender. Sprinkle with salt. Yield: 4 servings (serving size: 6 wedges).

CALORIES 216 (15% from fat); FAT 3.6g (sat 0.7g, mono 1g, poly 1.7g); PROTEIN 3.7g; CARB 42.9g; FIBER 3.1g; CHOL 0mg; IRON 2.3mg; SODIUM 275mg; CALC 17mg

### Grilled Sourdough Cheddar Melt

(pictured on page 59)

This is also called a patty melt: ground meat and cheese nestled between slices of bread and grilled. Prewrapped slices of processed Cheddar cheese are the only way to go, as they melt better. We do it here far lighter than you're likely to find it on the road.

- 2 teaspoons butter or stick margarine, divided
- Cooking spray
- 2 cups coarsely chopped onion
- 1 pound ground round
- ¼ teaspoon freshly ground black pepper
- ⅛ teaspoon salt
- 4 (¾-ounce) slices 2% reduced-fat processed sharp Cheddar cheese
- 8 (1½-ounce) slices sourdough or white bread

1. Melt 1 teaspoon butter in a large non-stick skillet coated with cooking spray over medium-high heat. Add onion, and cook 4 minutes or until golden brown, stirring frequently. Reduce heat; cook 10 minutes or until tender, stirring occasionally. Set aside.

2. Preheat broiler.

3. Combine beef, pepper, and salt in a medium bowl. Divide beef mixture into 4 equal portions, shaping each into a ¼-inch-thick oval patty. Place patties on a broiler pan coated with cooking spray; broil patties 4 minutes on each side or until done.

4. Place 1 cheese slice over each of 4 bread slices; top each slice with 1 patty and 3 tablespoons onion mixture. Cover with remaining bread slices. Melt ½ teaspoon butter in pan coated with cooking spray over medium heat; add 2 sandwiches to pan. Cook 4 minutes on each side or until browned and cheese melts. Repeat procedure with ½ teaspoon butter and remaining sandwiches. Yield: 4 servings (serving size: 1 sandwich).

CALORIES 462 (22% from fat); FAT 11.5g (sat 5.3g, mono 3.1g, poly 0.9g); PROTEIN 38.5g; CARB 49.3g; FIBER 3g; CHOL 80mg; IRON 5.2mg; SODIUM 909mg; CALC 357mg

## Baked Triple-Bean Pot

⅓ cup packed brown sugar
¼ cup ketchup
2 tablespoons Dijon mustard
⅛ teaspoon black pepper
1 (16-ounce) can baked beans
1 (16-ounce) can pinto beans, drained
1 (15.5-ounce) can butter or lima beans, drained

1. Preheat oven to 350°.

2. Combine first 4 ingredients in a 1½-quart casserole. Stir in beans. Cover casserole, and bake at 350° for 40 minutes or until thoroughly heated. Yield: 10 servings (serving size: ½ cup).

CALORIES 151 (8% from fat); FAT 1.4g (sat 0.4g, mono 0.5g, poly 0.2g); PROTEIN 6.5g; CARB 33.4g; FIBER 5.3g; CHOL 0mg; IRON 2.1mg; SODIUM 576mg; CALC 56mg

## Beer-Battered Onion Rings

(pictured on page 59)

Unless for some unknown reason you have an open can of beer in your refrigerator, try this simple way to flatten the suds you need for this batter. Measure ½ cup beer in a small bowl, and stir with a fork. You're left with about ⅓ cup flat beer.

2 large onions, peeled (about 1½ pounds)
⅔ cup all-purpose flour
½ teaspoon salt
¼ teaspoon paprika
¼ teaspoon freshly ground black pepper
⅓ cup flat beer
1 large egg white, lightly beaten
1½ tablespoons vegetable oil, divided
Cooking spray
¼ cup ketchup

1. Preheat oven to 400°.

2. Cut onions crosswise into ¾-inch-thick slices, and separate into rings. Use 16 largest rings; reserve remaining onion for another use. Lightly spoon flour into a dry measuring cup; level with a knife. Combine flour, salt, paprika, and pepper in a medium bowl. Stir in beer and egg white (batter will be thick). Heat 1½ teaspoons oil in a large nonstick skillet over medium-high heat. Dip 5 onion rings in batter, letting excess drip off. Add onion rings to pan; cook 2 minutes on each side or until golden. Place onion rings on a jelly-roll pan. Repeat procedure of dipping onion rings in batter and cooking in remaining oil, ending with 6 rings. Coat onion rings with cooking spray. Bake at 400° for 10 minutes or until crisp. Serve rings with ketchup. Yield: 4 servings (serving size: 4 onion rings and 1 tablespoon ketchup).

CALORIES 209 (25% from fat); FAT 5.8g (sat 1g, mono 1.6g, poly 2.7g); PROTEIN 5.1g; CARB 34.1g; FIBER 3.7g; CHOL 0mg; IRON 1.5mg; SODIUM 490mg; CALC 39mg

## Onion Rings Step-by-Steps

1. *Dip onion rings in batter, letting excess batter drip off.*

2. *Add onion rings to hot oil in pan; cook 2 minutes on each side or until golden.*

3. *Place onion rings on a jelly-roll pan; coat onion rings with cooking spray, and bake according to recipe.*

## Sautéed Apples

3 tablespoons butter or stick margarine
6 cups sliced peeled Granny Smith apple (about 2 pounds)
½ cup packed brown sugar
⅛ teaspoon ground cinnamon

**1.** Melt butter in a large skillet over medium-high heat. Add apple; sauté 6 minutes or until apple is just tender. Stir in sugar and cinnamon. Cook 1 minute or until sugar melts. Yield: 8 servings (serving size: ½ cup).

CALORIES 137 (30% from fat); FAT 4.6g (sat 2.7g, mono 1.3g, poly 0.2g); PROTEIN 0.2g; CARB 25.7g; FIBER 1.6g; CHOL 12mg; IRON 0.3mg; SODIUM 49mg; CALC 17mg

## Double Corn Bread

You can take the diner out of the country but not the country out of the diner. Our Double Corn Bread, though, won't burden your journey. It goes great with Hearty Navy Bean Soup (recipe at right).

1 cup all-purpose flour
1 cup yellow cornmeal
2 tablespoons sugar
2 teaspoons baking powder
½ teaspoon salt
½ teaspoon baking soda
1 cup low-fat buttermilk
½ cup frozen whole-kernel corn, thawed
½ cup diced red bell pepper
4 tablespoons butter or stick margarine, melted
1 large egg, lightly beaten
Cooking spray

**1.** Preheat oven to 425°.
**2.** Lightly spoon flour into a dry measuring cup, and level with a knife. Combine flour and next 5 ingredients in a large bowl, and make a well in center of mixture. Combine buttermilk and next 4 ingredients in a bowl; add buttermilk mixture to flour mixture. Stir just until dry ingredients are moist. Spoon batter into an 8-inch square baking pan coated with cooking spray. Bake at 425° for 20

minutes or until a wooden pick inserted in center comes out clean. Let corn bread stand 10 minutes. Yield: 9 servings (serving size: 1 [2½-inch] square).

CALORIES 202 (30% from fat); FAT 6.7g (sat 3.4g, mono 1.8g, poly 0.5g); PROTEIN 5.1g; CARB 31g; FIBER 1.7g; CHOL 38mg; IRON 1.7mg; SODIUM 384mg; CALC 102mg

### menu

**Hearty Navy Bean Soup**

Breadsticks

Strawberry-romaine salad*

*Combine 2 cups halved strawberries, 1 cup grapefruit sections, 1 tablespoon honey, 2 teaspoons vegetable oil, and ¼ teaspoon cinnamon in a bowl; let stand 30 minutes. Add 3 cups sliced romaine lettuce; toss well. Serves 4.

## Hearty Navy Bean Soup

1 pound dried navy beans (about 2 cups)
8 cups water
1 cup chopped onion
3 garlic cloves, chopped
2 smoked ham hocks (about 10 ounces)
2 bay leaves
2 cups thinly sliced carrot
¾ teaspoon salt
½ teaspoon black pepper

**1.** Sort and wash beans; place in a large Dutch oven. Cover with water to 2 inches above beans; cover and let stand 8 hours. Drain beans.
**2.** Combine beans, 8 cups water, and next 4 ingredients in pan, and bring to a boil. Cover, reduce heat, and simmer 2 hours. Stir in carrot, salt, and pepper. Simmer 40 minutes or until beans are tender. Discard bay leaves. Remove ham hocks, and shred meat, discarding fat and gristle. Return meat to pan. Yield: 8 servings (serving size: 1½ cups).
**NOTE:** To quick-soak beans, sort and wash beans, and place in a large Dutch oven. Cover with water to 2 inches above beans; bring to a boil, and cook

2 minutes. Remove from heat; cover and let stand 1 hour. Drain beans.

CALORIES 251 (9% from fat); FAT 2.6g (sat 0.9g, mono 0.9g, poly 0.6g); PROTEIN 17.8g; CARB 40.5g; FIBER 6.6g; CHOL 11mg; IRON 4.2mg; SODIUM 545mg; CALC 108mg

## Onion-Smothered Roast Brisket and Vegetables

A meat-and-three classic, this dish puts meat and potatoes squarely in the center of the plate, yet leaves room for more.

1 (2½-pound) beef brisket
6 cups thinly sliced onion, separated into rings
1 cup bottled chili sauce
½ cup beer
1 tablespoon brown sugar
1 tablespoon Worcestershire sauce
1 pound carrots, cut into 1½-inch-thick pieces (about 2 cups)
1½ pounds red potatoes (about 6), quartered
½ teaspoon seasoned salt
½ teaspoon garlic pepper (such as Lawry's)

**1.** Preheat oven to 325°.
**2.** Trim fat from brisket. Place brisket in a large roasting pan; top with onion. Combine chili sauce, beer, sugar, and Worcestershire sauce; pour over onion. Cover and bake at 325° for 1½ hours.
**3.** Stir onion into cooking liquid. Arrange carrot and potato around brisket; spoon cooking liquid over vegetables. Sprinkle seasoned salt and garlic pepper over meat and vegetables. Cover and bake an additional 1½ hours or until vegetables are tender.
**4.** Cut brisket diagonally across grain into thin slices. Arrange beef and vegetables in each of 8 shallow bowls, and serve with sauce. Yield: 8 servings (serving size: 3 ounces beef, 1 cup vegetables, and ⅓ cup sauce).
**NOTE:** If you don't have a large roasting pan, cut brisket in half, and place in a large Dutch oven.

CALORIES 361 (28% from fat); FAT 11.3g (sat 4.1g, mono 5g, poly 0.5g); PROTEIN 29.2g; CARB 35.8g; FIBER 4g; CHOL 79mg; IRON 4.2mg; SODIUM 682mg; CALC 55mg

## Barbecued Pork Chops

**SAUCE:**
- ¼ cup packed brown sugar
- ¼ cup ketchup
- 1 tablespoon Worcestershire sauce
- 1 tablespoon low-sodium soy sauce

**REMAINING INGREDIENTS:**
- 6 (6-ounce) bone-in center-cut pork chops (about ½ inch thick)
- 1 teaspoon dried thyme
- 1 teaspoon garlic salt
- ¼ teaspoon ground red pepper
- Cooking spray

**1.** Prepare grill or broiler.
**2.** To prepare sauce, combine first 4 ingredients in a small bowl. Place ¼ cup sauce in a small bowl, and set aside.
**3.** Trim fat from pork. Combine thyme, garlic salt, and pepper; sprinkle over pork. Place pork on a grill rack or broiler pan coated with cooking spray; cook 6 minutes on each side, basting with remaining sauce. Serve pork chops with reserved ¼ cup sauce. Yield: 6 servings (serving size: 1 pork chop and 2 teaspoons sauce).

CALORIES 244 (42% from fat); FAT 11.3g (sat 3.9g, mono 5g, poly 1.4g); PROTEIN 24.6g; CARB 9.9g; FIBER 0.2g; CHOL 77mg; IRON 1.5mg; SODIUM 649mg; CALC 22mg

## Sky-High Coconut Cream Pie

**FILLING:**
- ¾ cup sugar
- ¼ cup cornstarch
- ¼ teaspoon salt
- 2 cups 1% low-fat milk
- 2 large eggs, lightly beaten
- 2 tablespoons cream of coconut (such as Coco Lopez)
- ¼ teaspoon coconut extract
- ¼ teaspoon vanilla extract
- 1 (6-ounce) reduced-fat graham cracker crust

**MERINGUE:**
- 1 cup sugar
- ½ cup water
- 8 large egg whites
- 1 teaspoon cream of tartar

**1.** To prepare filling, combine first 3 ingredients in a heavy saucepan. Combine milk and eggs; gradually add to sugar mixture. Bring to a boil over medium heat; cook 1 minute or until thick, stirring constantly with a whisk. Remove from heat; stir in cream of coconut and extracts. Pour into pie crust. Cover with plastic wrap; chill until firm (about 2 hours).
**2.** Preheat broiler.
**3.** To prepare meringue, combine 1 cup sugar and water in a small saucepan; bring to a boil. Cook, without stirring, until candy thermometer registers 240°. Beat egg whites and cream of tartar at high speed of a mixer until foamy. Pour hot sugar syrup in a thin stream over egg white mixture, beating at high speed until stiff peaks form. Remove plastic wrap from filling. Spread meringue evenly over filling, sealing to edge of crust.
**4.** Broil 1 minute or until lightly browned; cool on a wire rack. Chill until set. Yield: 10 servings (serving size: 1 wedge).

CALORIES 288 (16% from fat); FAT 5g (sat 2.1g, mono 1.4g, poly 1.2g); PROTEIN 6.5g; CARB 53.8g; FIBER 0.1g; CHOL 46mg; IRON 0.6mg; SODIUM 215mg; CALC 67mg

**BANANA CREAM PIE VARIATION:**
Prepare recipe as directed above, but omit cream of coconut and coconut extract in filling. Arrange 1 cup sliced banana in bottom of graham cracker crust; pour filling over bananas, and top with meringue.

CALORIES 291 (16% from fat); FAT 5g (sat 2.1g, mono 1.4g, poly 1.2g); PROTEIN 6.5g; CARB 53.8g; FIBER 0.1g; CHOL 46mg; IRON 0.6mg; SODIUM 215mg; CALC 67mg

## Sky-High Chocolate Pie

**FILLING:**
- 2 cups fat-free milk, divided
- ⅔ cup sugar
- ⅓ cup unsweetened cocoa
- 3 tablespoons cornstarch
- ⅛ teaspoon salt
- 1 large egg
- 2 ounces semisweet chocolate, chopped
- 1 teaspoon vanilla extract
- 1 (6-ounce) reduced-fat graham cracker crust

**MERINGUE:**
- 1 cup sugar
- ½ cup water
- 8 large egg whites
- 1 teaspoon cream of tartar

**1.** To prepare filling, combine ½ cup milk, ⅔ cup sugar, and next 4 ingredients in a large bowl, stirring with a whisk.

*Continued*

---

### Sky-High or Not-so-High Meringues?

This Italian meringue may seem more involved, but following these steps will ensure that your egg whites are heated to a safe temperature.

**1.** Make a sugar syrup by heating sugar and water in a saucepan to 240°. Use a candy thermometer to get an exact temperature reading. If the mixture is overcooked, the syrup will harden like candy.

**2.** In a separate bowl, beat the egg whites and cream of tartar just until foamy. Then pour the sugar syrup into the egg whites in a slow, steady stream, beating continuously.

**3.** When the meringue mixture is glossy-looking with stiff peaks, it's ready to spoon onto the filling.

**4.** Preheat the broiler, place the pie in the oven, and broil for 1 minute or until lightly browned. The meringues on these pies are so tall you'll need to position your oven rack on the second shelf.

If you don't want as much meringue, use these amounts: ⅔ cup sugar, ¼ cup water, 3 egg whites, and ¼ teaspoon cream of tartar. The nutritional analysis is 24 fewer calories per wedge.

**2.** Heat 1½ cups milk in a heavy saucepan over medium-high heat to 180° or until tiny bubbles form around edge (do not boil). Remove from heat. Gradually add hot milk to sugar mixture, stirring constantly with a whisk. Return milk mixture to pan. Add chopped chocolate; cook over medium heat until thick and bubbly (about 5 minutes), stirring constantly. Reduce heat to low; cook 2 minutes, stirring constantly. Remove from heat; stir in vanilla. Pour into crust; cover surface of filling with plastic wrap. Chill 3 hours or until cold.

**3.** Preheat broiler.

**4.** To prepare meringue, combine 1 cup sugar and water in a small saucepan; bring to a boil. Cook, without stirring, until candy thermometer registers 240°. Beat egg whites and cream of tartar at high speed of a mixer until foamy. Pour hot sugar syrup in a thin stream over egg white mixture, beating at high speed until stiff peaks form. Remove plastic wrap from filling. Spread meringue evenly over filling; seal to edge of crust.

**5.** Broil 1 minute or until lightly browned; cool on a wire rack. Chill until set. Yield: 10 servings (serving size: 1 wedge).

CALORIES 297 (16% from fat); FAT 5.2g (sat 2.4g, mono 1.7g, poly 1.1g); PROTEIN 7g; CARB 56g; FIBER 0.1g; CHOL 23mg; IRON 1.1mg; SODIUM 182mg; CALC 72mg

inspired vegetarian

# Who's That Cute Legume?

*If lentils were a guy, he'd be the one you've been waiting for.*

Legumes are certainly a good-for-you food, but rarely do they inspire anything approaching passion. Lentils may be the exception: These are legumes you can learn to love, and for good reason. They cook quickly and don't require the planning of beans cooked from scratch.

Look for lentils in Indian or Middle Eastern markets, in specialty aisles at supermarkets, or via mail order sources.

## Lentils with Wine-Glazed Winter Vegetables

Winter vegetables are cooked separately, glazed with tomato paste and red wine, and then added to the lentils. Any lentils will work, but black or French green lentils make for the most dramatic presentation and have a great flavor.

```
   3   cups water
1½   cups dried lentils
   1   teaspoon salt, divided
   1   bay leaf
1½   teaspoons olive oil
   2   cups chopped onion
1½   cups chopped peeled celeriac
         (celery root)
   1   cup diced parsnip
   1   cup diced carrot
   1   tablespoon minced fresh or
         1 teaspoon dried tarragon, divided
   1   tablespoon tomato paste
   1   garlic clove, minced
⅔   cup dry red wine
   2   teaspoons Dijon mustard
   1   tablespoon butter
¼   teaspoon black pepper
```

**1.** Combine water, lentils, ½ teaspoon salt, and bay leaf in a medium saucepan; bring to a boil. Reduce heat, and simmer 25 minutes. Remove lentils from heat, and set aside.

**2.** Heat oil in a medium cast-iron or nonstick skillet over medium-high heat. Add onion, celeriac, parsnip, carrot, and 1½ teaspoons tarragon, and sauté 10 minutes or until browned. Stir in ½ teaspoon salt, tomato paste, and garlic; cook 1 minute. Stir in wine, scraping pan to loosen browned bits. Bring to a boil; cover, reduce heat, and simmer 10 minutes or until vegetables are tender. Stir in mustard. Add lentil mixture, and cook 2 minutes. Remove from heat; discard bay leaf, and stir in 1½ teaspoons tarragon, butter, and pepper. Yield: 4 servings (serving size: 1½ cups).

CALORIES 416 (13% from fat); FAT 6g (sat 2.2g, mono 2.4g, poly 0.8g); PROTEIN 23.2g; CARB 65.6g; FIBER 12.7g; CHOL 8mg; IRON 8mg; SODIUM 778mg; CALC 109mg

## Fragrant Red Lentils with Rice

Don't be put off by the long ingredient list. It calls for a lot of fragrant seasonings that either cook with the lentils or are used as a garnish. *Garam masala* is an Indian blend of dry-roasted, ground spices that includes up to a dozen different flavors ranging from cinnamon to fennel to black pepper; it can be found with other spices in many large supermarkets or specialty food shops.

```
   1   tablespoon vegetable oil
   1   cup diced onion
   1   teaspoon grated peeled fresh
         ginger
   1   teaspoon ground coriander
   1   teaspoon ground cumin
½   teaspoon ground turmeric
   2   garlic cloves, minced
   2   bay leaves
   3   cups water
1½   cups dried small red lentils
¾   teaspoon salt
   2   tablespoons butter or stick
         margarine
¾   cup chopped green onions
   1   tablespoon seeded minced
         jalapeño pepper
   3   tablespoons fresh lime juice
   2   tablespoons minced fresh
         cilantro
   1   teaspoon garam masala
2½   cups hot cooked brown basmati or
         brown rice
   5   tablespoons low-fat plain yogurt
```

**1.** Heat oil in a large saucepan over medium-high heat. Add diced onion, and sauté 6 minutes or until onion begins to brown. Add ginger and next 5 ingredients, and sauté 1 minute. Add 3 cups water, lentils, and salt, and bring to a boil. Cover, reduce heat, and simmer 20 minutes or until lentils are tender. Discard bay leaves.

**2.** Melt butter in a small skillet over medium heat. Add green onions and jalapeño; sauté 5 minutes. Add to lentil mixture; stir in juice, cilantro, and garam masala.

**3.** Place ½ cup rice into each of 5 shallow bowls; spoon ¾ cup lentil mixture over each serving. Top each with 1 tablespoon yogurt. Yield: 5 servings.

**NOTE:** Because jalapeño peppers can vary in heat intensity, you may wish to adjust the amount used based on your own preference for hot and spicy foods.

CALORIES 409 (20% from fat); FAT 9.3g (sat 3.8g, mono 2.7g, poly 2.1g); PROTEIN 20.6g; CARB 63.4g; FIBER 9.5g; CHOL 13mg; IRON 6.6mg; SODIUM 427mg; CALC 104mg

## Lentil-Vegetable Soup

This is one of those soups that tastes even better the next day. French dark green lentils make the most attractive and delicious soup, but any lentil will work.

  1½ tablespoons olive oil
  1⅓ cups finely diced onion
  ⅓ cup finely diced celery
  ⅓ cup finely diced carrot
  2 bay leaves
  2 tablespoons tomato paste
  1 teaspoon salt
  2 garlic cloves, minced
  6 cups water
  1 cup dried French dark green or other lentils
  6 cups chopped spinach
  ⅓ cup chopped fresh parsley
  2 teaspoons red wine vinegar
  2 teaspoons Dijon mustard
  ¼ teaspoon black pepper
  ¾ cup (3 ounces) shaved fresh Parmesan cheese

**1.** Heat oil in a large Dutch oven or stockpot over medium-high heat. Add onion, celery, carrot, and bay leaves; sauté 10 minutes. Add tomato paste, salt, and garlic; sauté 1 minute. Add 6 cups water and lentils; bring mixture to a boil. Partially cover, reduce heat, and simmer 25 minutes. Stir in spinach, parsley, vinegar, mustard, and pepper; cook 15 minutes. Discard bay leaves. Ladle soup into bowls; top with cheese. Yield: 6 servings (serving size: 1 cup soup and 2 tablespoons cheese).

CALORIES 234 (30% from fat); FAT 7.8g (sat 2.9g, mono 3.7g, poly 0.7g); PROTEIN 16.6g; CARB 26.6g; FIBER 7.3g; CHOL 10mg; IRON 5.1mg; SODIUM 729mg; CALC 260mg

## Pasta with Green Lentil Sauce and Chard

  ⅔ cup dried French dark green or other lentils
  ¾ teaspoon salt, divided
  2 bay leaves, divided
  3 tablespoons olive oil, divided
  1 cup finely diced onion
  1 cup finely diced red bell pepper
  ¾ cup finely diced carrot
  3 garlic cloves, minced
  ½ cup dry red wine
  1½ tablespoons tomato paste
  1 teaspoon Dijon mustard
  ¼ teaspoon black pepper
  4 quarts water
  6 cups chopped Swiss chard
  1 (12-ounce) package uncooked medium egg noodles
  6 tablespoons (1½ ounces) grated fresh Parmesan cheese

**1.** Combine lentils, ½ teaspoon salt, and 1 bay leaf in a medium saucepan. Cover with water to 3 inches above lentils; bring to a boil, reduce heat to medium-low, and simmer 25 minutes. Drain in a colander over a bowl, reserving 2 cups cooking liquid. Set aside.
**2.** Heat 1 tablespoon oil in a large cast-iron or nonstick skillet over medium heat. Add 1 bay leaf, onion, bell pepper, carrot, and garlic; sauté 12 minutes or until lightly browned. Stir in wine, tomato paste, and mustard, and cook 2 minutes or until vegetables are glazed. Add ¼ teaspoon salt and black pepper. Add lentils and reserved cooking liquid. Discard bay leaves.
**3.** Bring 4 quarts water to a boil in a large stockpot. Add chard, and cook 5 minutes. Remove chard with a slotted spoon. Stir chard into lentil mixture. Add pasta to boiling water; cook 6 minutes. Drain; toss pasta with 2 tablespoons oil. Place 1 cup pasta on each of 6 serving plates; top each serving with 1 cup lentil mixture. Sprinkle each serving with 1 tablespoon cheese. Yield: 6 servings.

CALORIES 426 (24% from fat); FAT 11.5g (sat 2.7g, mono 6.3g, poly 1.5g); PROTEIN 18.1g; CARB 60.7g; FIBER 5.8g; CHOL 59mg; IRON 6mg; SODIUM 533mg; CALC 148mg

## Lentil Potage with Spinach and Yogurt

A *potage* (poh-TAHZH) like this one is more than a soup; it's thick and hearty because of its mixture of chickpeas, barley, lentils, and bulgur (cracked wheat). The recipe calls for cooked pearl barley, so you'll need to prepare that first.

  2 tablespoons olive oil
  1½ cups diced onion
  2 teaspoons ground cumin
  1¼ teaspoons salt
  1 teaspoon paprika
  ½ teaspoon ground allspice
  ½ teaspoon ground turmeric
  ¼ teaspoon black pepper
  1 bay leaf
  6½ cups water
  1 cup dried petite black or other lentils
  14 cups chopped spinach (about 8 ounces)
  ½ cup uncooked bulgur or cracked wheat
  ½ cup cooked pearl barley
  1 (15½-ounce) can chickpeas (garbanzo beans), rinsed and drained
  1 (8-ounce) carton plain low-fat yogurt

**1.** Heat oil in a large Dutch oven over medium heat. Add onion and next 7 ingredients; cook 10 minutes. Add water and lentils, and bring to a boil. Reduce heat, and simmer 30 minutes. Add spinach, bulgur, barley, and chickpeas; cook 1 minute. Remove from heat, and discard bay leaf. Cover mixture, and let stand 15 minutes.
**2.** Spoon yogurt onto several layers of heavy-duty paper towels, spreading to ½-inch thickness. Cover yogurt with additional paper towels, and let stand 5 minutes. Scrape yogurt into a bowl using a rubber spatula. Serve drained yogurt with potage. Yield: 8 servings (serving size: 1 cup potage and 1 tablespoon drained yogurt).

CALORIES 251 (19% from fat); FAT 5.4g (sat 1g, mono 3g, poly 1g); PROTEIN 14g; CARB 39.2g; FIBER 7.9g; CHOL 2mg; IRON 4.9mg; SODIUM 486mg; CALC 127mg

# Living la Vida Sabrosa

## When the people of El Paso decided to shape up, they started walking—and cooking—like their lives depended on it. The results: very tasty.

Cooking Light was invited to El Paso, Texas, to help kick off the Qué Sabrosa Vida ("What a tasty life") campaign with our ideas on lightening traditional Tex-Mex restaurant favorites. At the program's heart is the simplest of theories: Lower the fat, reduce the calories, and make optimum use of local ingredients and any nutritious foods people already like.

If this could be done for signature dishes at local restaurants, it could be done for home cooking, too. Our four restaurant choices—Casa del Sol (from Ciudad Juárez, Mexico), L&J Cafe, Forti's Mexican Elder Restaurant, and La Norteña y Cafe Deluxe—turned eaters into believers. See page 51 for before-and-after details.

### Huevos Rancheros

This classic egg dish from La Norteña y Café Deluxe in El Paso makes one serving, but you can multiply the recipe accordingly. Make the salsa for the Ranchero Sauce first. It will keep in the refrigerator for up to five days. Rather than frying, we poached the eggs and dry-sautéed the tortillas.

    2  large eggs
    Cooking spray
    1  (6-inch) corn tortilla, cut into
       quarters
    Ranchero Sauce
    2  tablespoons (½ ounce) finely
       shredded reduced-fat sharp
       Cheddar cheese

1. Add water to a large skillet, filling two-thirds full. Bring to a boil; reduce heat, and simmer. Break each egg into a 6-ounce custard cup coated with cooking spray. Place custard cups in simmering water in skillet. Cover skillet; cook 6 minutes. Remove cups from water.
2. Place a large nonstick skillet coated with cooking spray over medium-high heat until hot. Add tortilla quarters; cook 2 minutes on each side or until browned.
3. Arrange tortilla quarters on a microwave-safe plate; top with eggs and Ranchero Sauce. Sprinkle with cheese. Microwave at HIGH 15 seconds or until cheese melts. Yield: 1 serving.

(Totals include Ranchero Sauce and La Norteña's Homemade Salsa) CALORIES 322 (43% from fat); FAT 15.4g (sat 4.9g, mono 4.1g, poly 1.8g); PROTEIN 20.8g; CARB 26.5g; FIBER 3.4g; CHOL 451mg; IRON 3mg; SODIUM 694mg; CALC 237mg

#### RANCHERO SAUCE:
    Cooking spray
    ⅓  cup chopped red onion
    ⅓  cup tomato juice
    ⅓  cup La Norteña's Homemade
       Salsa

1. Place a small saucepan coated with cooking spray over medium-high heat until hot. Add onion, and sauté 3 minutes. Add tomato juice and salsa; bring to a boil. Reduce heat to medium-low; simmer 4 minutes. Remove from heat; cool. Yield: ⅔ cup.

#### LA NORTEÑA'S HOMEMADE SALSA:
    1  whole garlic head
    6  ripe tomatoes (about 2½ pounds)
    6  jalapeño peppers, seeded
    Cooking spray
    3  cups tomato juice
    ¼  cup fresh lime juice

1. Preheat oven to 350°.
2. Remove white papery skin from garlic head (do not peel or separate cloves).

Wrap in foil. Bake at 350° for 1 hour; cool 10 minutes. Separate cloves; squeeze to extract garlic pulp. Discard skins.
3. Prepare grill or broiler.
4. Place tomatoes and peppers on a grill rack or broiler pan coated with cooking spray; grill or broil 15 minutes or until skins are blackened, turning occasionally. Peel tomatoes and peppers.
5. Place half of garlic pulp, half of tomatoes, and half of peppers in a blender, and process until coarsely chopped. Pour garlic mixture into a bowl. Repeat procedure with remaining garlic pulp, tomatoes, and peppers. Stir tomato juice and lime juice into garlic mixture. Yield: 7½ cups (serving size: ⅓ cup).

**NOTE:** Serve remaining salsa with baked tortilla chips or over grilled fish.

CALORIES 22 (8% from fat); FAT 0.2g (sat 0g, mono 0g, poly 0.1g); PROTEIN 0.9g; CARB 5.1g; FIBER 0.8g; CHOL 0mg; IRON 0.5mg; SODIUM 125mg; CALC 12mg

### Caldo de Res

This healthy, hearty main-dish soup is just one of the many caldos made fresh daily at the L&J Cafe. It's served with a side of rice and tortillas. The beef and the vegetables are cooked separately so that the vegetables don't soak up the fat from the beef. When in season, fresh corn on the cob is also added.

    1  (2-pound) beef shank
    12 cups water
    4  cups coarsely chopped green
       cabbage (about 10½ ounces)
    3  cups (½-inch-thick) slices zucchini
    2  cups vertically sliced onion
    1  cup (½-inch-thick) slices celery
    5  medium carrots, halved
       lengthwise and cut into 1-inch
       pieces
    5  garlic cloves, crushed
    3  chicken-flavored bouillon cubes
    Lime wedges
    Chopped fresh cilantro

1. Place beef shank in a large saucepan; cover with water to 2 inches above shank. Bring to a boil; cook 1 hour or until beef is tender. Drain beef shank.

Cool slightly; remove beef, discarding bone. Cut beef into large pieces; set aside.

**2.** While beef shank is cooking, combine 12 cups water and next 7 ingredients in a large Dutch oven. Bring to a boil; reduce heat, and simmer 30 minutes or until vegetables are crisp-tender. Ladle soup into large bowls, and top with beef. Serve with lime and cilantro. Yield: 8 servings (serving size: 2 cups soup and 2 ounces beef).

CALORIES 173 (22% from fat); FAT 4.2g (sat 1.4g, mono 1.7g, poly 0.4g); PROTEIN 21.4g; CARB 13g; FIBER 3.6g; CHOL 44mg; IRON 3mg; SODIUM 412mg; CALC 73mg

## Escabéche Casa del Sol (Marinated Vegetables)

*Escabéche* (es-keh-BENSH) is a marinated Spanish fish dish. Here, vegetables are marinated instead for a refreshing salsa that is served as an appetizer with chips. This recipe from Casa del Sol is inherently healthy—we simply decreased the oil.

    2  tablespoons black peppercorns
    1  tablespoon dried thyme
    1  tablespoon dried marjoram
 1½  teaspoons dried oregano
    4  bay leaves
    1  whole garlic head
 2½  cups (½-inch-thick) diagonally
        sliced carrot (about 1 pound)
    2  tablespoons vegetable oil
    2  onions, each cut into 12 wedges
    1  (12-ounce) jar sliced pickled
        jalapeño peppers, undrained
  ¾  cup cider vinegar
    1  cup water
    4  cups small cauliflower florets
    3  cups thinly sliced peeled jícama,
        cut into triangles
    6  cups (¼-inch-thick) diagonally
        sliced zucchini

**1.** Preheat oven to 400°.
**2.** Place first 5 ingredients on a triple layer of cheesecloth. Gather edges of cheesecloth together, and tie securely. Remove white papery skin from garlic head (do not peel or separate cloves); trim about ¼ inch from top of garlic.

Combine garlic, carrot, oil, and onion in an ovenproof Dutch oven. Bake, uncovered, at 400° for 30 minutes. Stir vegetables; add spice bag to vegetables. Bake an additional 25 minutes or until vegetables are tender. Peel garlic cloves; place garlic, carrot, onion, and spice bag in a large bowl.

**3.** Drain jalapeños over a bowl, reserving liquid. Place Dutch oven over medium-high heat; stir in reserved jalapeño juice and vinegar, scraping pan to loosen browned bits. Add 1 cup water, and bring to a boil. Add cauliflower and jícama; cover, reduce heat, and simmer 5 minutes. Remove from heat; add cauliflower mixture, jalapeños, and zucchini to carrot mixture. Let stand at room temperature 2 hours, stirring every 30 minutes. Discard spice bag; cover and store in refrigerator. Yield: 12 servings (serving size: 1 cup).

**NOTE:** Vegetable mixture can be stored up to 2 weeks in the refrigerator; serve at room temperature.

CALORIES 86 (29% from fat); FAT 2.8g (sat 0.6g, mono 0.8g, poly 1.4g); PROTEIN 2.8g; CARB 15g; FIBER 4.6g; CHOL 0mg; IRON 2.4mg; SODIUM 438mg; CALC 62mg

## Chicken Salpicón

(pictured on page 57)

*Salpicones*—refreshing mixtures of vegetables, fish, and/or chicken, served cold as appetizers—are popular in Latin America as well as Mexico. We lightened this one from Forti's Mexican Elder Restaurant in El Paso by decreasing the amount of oil and avocado.

    6  (4-ounce) skinned, boned
        chicken breast halves
    2  cups chopped seeded tomato
  ½  cup chopped onion
  ¼  cup chopped fresh cilantro
    6  jalapeño peppers, sliced
  ⅓  cup white vinegar
    1  teaspoon salt
    1  teaspoon vegetable oil
  ½  teaspoon black pepper
  ¾  cup diced peeled avocado
Iceberg lettuce leaves

**1.** Add water to a skillet, filling to a depth of 1 inch; bring to a boil. Add chicken; simmer 8 minutes or until done. Drain chicken. Cool and cut into thin strips.
**2.** Combine chicken strips, tomato, onion, cilantro, and jalapeño. Combine vinegar, salt, oil, and black pepper. Add vinegar mixture to chicken mixture; toss gently to coat. Add avocado just before serving; toss gently to coat. Serve chicken mixture over lettuce leaves. Yield: 6 servings (serving size: ½ cup).

CALORIES 194 (25% from fat); FAT 5.4g (sat 1g, mono 2.4g, poly 1.2g); PROTEIN 28.1g; CARB 8.6g; FIBER 2.3g; CHOL 66mg; IRON 1.9mg; SODIUM 479mg; CALC 37mg

## Green-Sauced Chicken Enchiladas

In this recipe from L&J Cafe in El Paso, we dry-sautéed the tortillas instead of frying them and decreased the cheese. Use corn tortillas; flour tortillas will turn gummy.

    8  (6-inch) corn tortillas
Green Enchilada Sauce (recipe on
        page 50)
    1  cup (4 ounces) shredded Wisconsin
        white Cheddar cheese, divided
Cooking spray
 2½  cups finely chopped cooked
        chicken breast (about 1 pound)

**1.** Preheat oven to 350°.
**2.** Heat a large nonstick skillet over medium-high heat until hot. Add tortillas; cook 1 minute on each side or until soft.
**3.** Spread 2 tablespoons Green Enchilada Sauce over each tortilla, spreading to edges; top each with 1 tablespoon cheese. Roll up, and place, seam sides down, in a 13 x 9-inch baking dish coated with cooking spray. Spoon chicken evenly over tortillas; top with remaining Green Enchilada Sauce. Sprinkle with ½ cup cheese. Cover and bake at 350° for 15 minutes. Yield: 4 servings (serving size: 2 enchiladas).

(Totals include Green Enchilada Sauce) CALORIES 390 (30% from fat); FAT 13g (sat 6.6g, mono 3.8g, poly 1.4g); PROTEIN 28.4g; CARB 41g; FIBER 5.2g; CHOL 74mg; IRON 1.6mg; SODIUM 1,123mg; CALC 358mg

*Continued*

**GREEN ENCHILADA SAUCE:**

L&J uses chiles called Big Jims—long, green chiles (also known as New Mexican chiles) that are very common in the Southwest. If you can't find them, use Anaheims or another mild chile such as a poblano. If you want the sauce spicier, add a diced jalapeño or serrano chile.

  12  long green chiles or Anaheim
       chiles (about 2 pounds)
   2  cups thinly sliced onion
   1  cup chopped tomato
  ½  cup water
  ¾  teaspoon salt
  ¼  teaspoon ground cumin
   6  garlic cloves, minced

**1.** Preheat oven to 450°.
**2.** Place chiles on a foil-lined baking sheet; bake at 450° for 20 minutes or until blackened, turning once. Place chiles in a zip-top plastic bag; seal and let stand 10 minutes. Peel; discard seeds and membranes. Cut chiles into thin strips. Place chiles, onion, and remaining ingredients in a medium saucepan. Bring to a boil; cover, reduce heat, and simmer 20 minutes. Yield: 3 cups (serving size: ¾ cup).

## Angela's Flan

Flan is a traditional dessert of Mexico. This one, created by Angela Garcia, a long-time cook at Forti's Mexican Elder Restaurant in El Paso, has some additional flavorings we really liked. The original recipe weighed in at less than 30% calories from fat, but we decreased it further by using low-fat milks in place of whole.

  ½  cup sugar
   1  tablespoon water
Cooking spray
   2  cups 2% reduced-fat milk
   1  tablespoon white rum
  ½  teaspoon vanilla extract
  ½  teaspoon almond extract
  ⅛  teaspoon ground cinnamon
   4  large eggs
   1  (14-ounce) can low-fat sweetened
       condensed milk

**1.** Preheat oven to 350°.
**2.** Combine sugar and water in a small, heavy saucepan, and cook over medium-high heat until sugar dissolves, stirring frequently. Continue cooking 3 minutes or until golden, stirring constantly. Immediately pour into 8 (6-ounce) custard cups coated with cooking spray, tipping quickly until caramelized sugar coats bottoms of cups.
**3.** Combine 2% reduced-fat milk and remaining 6 ingredients in a blender; process until smooth. Divide mixture evenly among prepared custard cups. Place cups in bottom of a broiler pan; add hot water to pan to a depth of 1 inch. Bake at 350° for 55 minutes or until a knife inserted in center comes out clean. Remove cups from pan; cool completely on a wire rack. Cover and chill at least 8 hours.
**4.** Loosen edges of custards with a knife or rubber spatula. Place a dessert plate, upside down, on top of each cup, and invert custards onto plates. Drizzle any remaining caramelized syrup over custards. Yield: 8 servings.

CALORIES 270 (19% from fat); FAT 5.7g (sat 2.8g, mono 1.9g, poly 0.5g); PROTEIN 9g; CARB 15.8g; FIBER 0g; CHOL 115mg; IRON 0.4mg; SODIUM 63mg; CALC 88mg

## Breast of Chicken Oaxaca

(pictured on page 59)

This decadent dish is from Casa del Sol in Ciudad Juárez, Mexico, just across the border from El Paso. We sautéed the chicken breasts in a small amount of oil instead of frying them and used low-fat sour cream in place of heavy cream in the chipotle sauce. Chipotle chiles are dry, smoked jalapeños found in the Mexican sections of most supermarkets.

**CHIPOTLE SAUCE:**
  ¼  cup hot water
  ½  teaspoon chicken-flavored
       bouillon granules
   4  canned chipotle chiles in adobo
       sauce
  ¾  cup low-fat sour cream
   1  tablespoon lime juice

**CHICKEN:**
   1  peeled avocado, cut into 6 wedges
   1  tablespoon lime juice
   6  (4-ounce) skinned, boned chicken
       breast halves
  ¾  cup (3 ounces) shredded asadero
       or Monterey Jack cheese
  ¼  teaspoon salt
  ⅛  teaspoon white pepper
   2  tablespoons all-purpose flour
   3  large egg whites, lightly beaten
   1  cup seasoned breadcrumbs
   1  tablespoon vegetable oil
Cooking spray
   8  cups hot cooked linguine (about
       1 pound uncooked pasta)
  ¼  cup sliced ripe olives
   2  tablespoons chopped parsley

**1.** To prepare chipotle sauce, combine first 3 ingredients in a blender; process until smooth. Pour sauce into a bowl; stir in sour cream and 1 tablespoon juice.
**2.** To prepare chicken, toss avocado with 1 tablespoon juice. Cut a horizontal slit through thickest portion of each breast half to form a pocket. Stuff 1 avocado slice and 2 tablespoons cheese into each pocket. Sprinkle chicken with salt and pepper, and dredge chicken in flour. Dip chicken in egg whites; dredge in breadcrumbs.
**3.** Heat oil in a large nonstick skillet coated with cooking spray over medium-high heat. Add chicken; sauté 6 minutes on each side or until chicken is done.
**4.** Toss pasta with olives and parsley. Place 1⅓ cups pasta on each of 6 plates. Arrange chicken on pasta; top each serving with about 3 tablespoons chipotle sauce. Yield: 6 servings.

CALORIES 674 (26% from fat); FAT 19.8g (sat 7.1g, mono 7.5g, poly 3.2g); PROTEIN 45.3g; CARB 77g; FIBER 3.8g; CHOL 88mg; IRON 5.7mg; SODIUM 570mg; CALC 216mg

### Border-Style Salsas

Traditional Mexican salsas (recipes at right) are thin and soupy, quite a contrast to some of the bottled varieties you find in the supermarket. Most salsas are low in fat, as were these—no lightening was required. Serve with baked tortilla chips.

## A Load Easily Lightened

In our testing of traditional and locally favorite recipes at nine popular El Paso/Ciudad Juárez restaurants, we found consistent evidence that just a few cooking changes dramatically lower the fat—at no flavor sacrifice—in dozens of Tex-Mex classics.

| | Original | Ours |
|---|---|---|
| **Chicken Salpicón** (recipe on page 49) | 264 calories, 20 grams fat (68% calories from fat) | 194 calories, 5.4 grams fat (25% calories from fat) |
| **Angela's Flan** (recipe on page 50) | 284 calories, 8.9 grams fat (28% calories from fat) | 270 calories, 5.7 grams fat (19% calories from fat) |
| **Green-Sauced Chicken Enchiladas** (recipe on page 49) | 686 calories, 40 grams fat (52% calories from fat) | 390 calories, 13 grams fat (30% calories from fat) |
| **Huevos Rancheros** (recipe on page 48) | 690 calories, 50 grams fat (65% calories from fat) | 322 calories, 15.4 grams fat (43% calories from fat) |
| **Breast of Chicken Oaxaca** (recipe on page 50) | 1,204 calories, 72 grams fat (54% calories from fat) | 674 calories, 19.8 grams fat (26% calories from fat) |
| **Escabéche Casa del Sol** (recipe on page 49) | 296 calories, 27.8 grams fat (85% calories from fat) | 86 calories, 2.8 grams fat (29% calories from fat) |
| **Caldo de Res** (recipe on page 48) | 290 calories, 8.1 grams fat (25% calories from fat) | 173 calories, 4.2 grams fat (22% calories from fat) |

### Salsa Manuela

This salsa from Casa del Sol in Ciudad Juárez, Mexico, is traditionally mashed by hand—if you do the same, remember to wear gloves, and don't wipe your eyes.

- 1 pound jalapeño peppers, halved and seeded
- 2 tomatoes, cut into ½-inch-thick slices (about 1 pound)
- 1 onion, cut into ½-inch-thick slices (about ½ pound)
- 2 cups water
- 1 teaspoon salt

**1.** Preheat broiler.

**2.** Place jalapeños, skin sides up, on a foil-lined baking sheet; broil 12 minutes or until blackened. Cut peppers in half lengthwise, discarding seeds and membranes. Cut into slices. Set peppers aside.

**3.** Place tomato slices on baking sheet; broil 10 minutes, turning after 5 minutes. Remove tomatoes. Place onion slices on baking sheet; broil 14 minutes, turning after 7 minutes.

**4.** Bring 2 cups water to a boil in a medium saucepan. Add peppers, tomato, onion, and salt; return to a boil. Reduce heat; simmer 30 minutes. Cool to room temperature. Mash mixture with hands or with a potato masher. Serve at room temperature or chilled. Store in an airtight container in refrigerator up to two weeks. Yield: 4 cups (serving size: ¼ cup).

CALORIES 17 (5% from fat); FAT 0.1g (sat 0g, mono 0g, poly 0.1g); PROTEIN 0.7g; CARB 4g; FIBER 0.8g; CHOL 0mg; IRON 0.4mg; SODIUM 150mg; CALC 8mg

### Four-Alarm Red Salsa

This is a fiery-hot salsa from L&J Cafe made from chile arbol, a dried chile.

- 1 ounce dried chile arbols, seeded
- ½ cup boiling water
- 3 cups chopped onion
- 1 cup water
- ½ cup chopped tomatillos (about 2)
- 2 teaspoons dried oregano
- 1½ teaspoons ground cumin
- ½ teaspoon salt
- 3 garlic cloves
- 1 (8-ounce) can tomato sauce

**1.** Combine chiles and boiling water; let stand 30 minutes. Drain.

**2.** Combine chiles, onion, and next 6 ingredients in a medium saucepan. Place over medium-high heat; bring to a boil. Reduce heat; simmer 20 minutes. Remove from heat; cool 15 minutes. Place onion mixture in a blender or food processor; process until blended (do not overblend). Add tomato sauce; stir well. Yield: 3 cups (serving size: 3 tablespoons).

CALORIES 26 (10% from fat); FAT 0.3g (sat 0g, mono 0g, poly 0.1g); PROTEIN 0.9g; CARB 5.5g; FIBER 1.3g; CHOL 0mg; IRON 0.5mg; SODIUM 167mg; CALC 17mg

### Green Salsa

This salsa from L&J Cafe is a good Mexican salsa—zesty, thin, and hot.

- 1 pound jalapeño peppers, stems removed
- 1½ cups chopped tomato
- 1½ cups chopped Vidalia or other sweet onion
- 1½ cups water
- 1 teaspoon salt
- ¾ teaspoon ground cumin
- 4 garlic cloves, chopped

**1.** Combine all ingredients in a Dutch oven over medium-high heat; bring to a boil. Cover, reduce heat, and simmer 20 minutes or until tender. Cool 10 minutes. Place in a blender or food processor; pulse 15 times or until coarsely chopped (do not overblend). Yield: 4 cups (serving size: 3 tablespoons).

CALORIES 15 (6% from fat); FAT 0.1g (sat 0g, mono 0g, poly 0.1g); PROTEIN 0.6g; CARB 3.4g; FIBER 0.7g; CHOL 0mg; IRON 0.3mg; SODIUM 114mg; CALC 8mg

# How to Make Lots of Dough

## For the best pizza you'll ever taste, make your own. And don't forget the calzone, focaccia, and bread.

With a few straightforward techniques, your kitchen can become your favorite pizzeria. All you need are the simplest of ingredients: flour, water, yeast, and salt—and your favorite toppings. Making pizza is really all about making dough, so that's where you'll start. Learning to make this dough will allow you to crank out an infinite number of calzones, focaccias, and even some rustic breads.

### All-Purpose Pizza Dough

This basic recipe, which can be used to make calzones, focaccia, or bread, can easily be doubled.

> 1 package dry yeast (about 2¼ teaspoons)
> 1¼ cups warm water (100° to 110°)
> 3¼ cups all-purpose flour, divided
> ½ teaspoon salt
> Cooking spray

**1.** Dissolve yeast in warm water in a large bowl, and let stand 5 minutes. Lightly spoon flour into dry measuring cups, and level with a knife. Add 1 cup flour and salt to yeast mixture, and stir well. Add 2 cups flour, 1 cup at a time, stirring well after each addition. Turn dough out onto a floured surface. Knead until smooth and elastic (about 10 minutes), adding enough of remaining flour, 1 tablespoon at a time, to prevent dough from sticking to hands (dough will feel tacky).

**2.** Place dough in a large bowl coated with cooking spray, turning to coat top. Cover and let rise in a warm place (85°), free from drafts, 1 hour or until doubled in size. (Press two fingers into dough. If indentation remains, dough has risen enough.) Punch dough down; cover and let rest 5 minutes. Shape dough according to recipe directions. Yield: dough for 1 pizza.

**NOTE:** To freeze, let dough rise once, punch down, and shape into a ball. Place in a heavy-duty zip-top plastic bag coated with cooking spray; squeeze out all air, and seal. Store in freezer for up to 1 month. To thaw, place dough in refrigerator 12 hours or overnight. With scissors, cut away plastic bag. Place dough on a floured surface, and shape according to recipe directions. Alternatively, for pizza, you can make dough, roll out, wrap in foil, and freeze. To bake, remove from freezer; top and bake according to recipe instructions (no need to thaw).

(Totals are for entire All-Purpose Pizza Dough) CALORIES 1,505 (3% from fat); FAT 5g (sat 0.8g, mono 0.7g, poly 2.1g); PROTEIN 44.6g; CARB 312.7g; FIBER 12.9g; CHOL 0mg; IRON 20mg; SODIUM 1,184mg; CALC 66mg

### Tomato-and-Basil Pizza

We love this pizza's flavor with Gruyère cheese, but you can use mozzarella if you prefer. Use fresh tomatoes if you have them in place of canned.

> All-Purpose Pizza Dough (recipe at left)
> 2 teaspoons yellow cornmeal
> 2 teaspoons olive oil
> 2 garlic cloves, minced
> 1 (14.5-ounce) can diced tomatoes, undrained
> Cooking spray
> ¾ cup (3 ounces) shredded Gruyère or Swiss cheese
> ¼ cup thinly sliced fresh basil
> ¼ cup (1 ounce) grated fresh Parmesan cheese

**1.** Roll prepared dough into a 15-inch circle on a floured surface. Place dough on a 15-inch round pizza pan sprinkled with cornmeal. Cover dough, and let rise in a warm place 20 minutes or until puffy.

**2.** Preheat oven to 450°.

**3.** Heat oil in a large nonstick skillet over medium-high heat. Add garlic; sauté 30 seconds. Add tomatoes; cook 5 minutes or until liquid almost evaporates.

**4.** Lightly coat dough with cooking spray. Spread tomato mixture over dough, leaving a 1-inch border, and top with Gruyère, basil, and Parmesan. Bake at 450° for 15 minutes or until golden. Yield: 4 servings (serving size: 2 slices).

CALORIES 547 (21% from fat); FAT 12.9g (sat 5.9g, mono 4.7g, poly 13g); PROTEIN 21.7g; CARB 84.6g; FIBER 4g; CHOL 29mg; IRON 5.8mg; SODIUM 668mg; CALC 363mg

---

### Dough Tips

• Making your own dough doesn't require precision timing. Make it in the morning and place it in the refrigerator until ready to use, or make it up to an hour before you rise it. You can also make it in a food processor or stand-up mixer with the kneading attachment.

• While kneading, massage the dough gently. If you overwork the dough, it will absorb too much flour, producing a dense, heavy bread or a dry, tough crust. Set your kitchen timer for 10 minutes so you won't over- or underknead.

• Make sure your oven is preheated. To produce a crunchy crust, you need to bake pizza, calzones, and focaccia in a very hot oven (from 450° to 550°).

• If you don't have a pizza pan, simply use a large baking sheet.

**1.** Once the yeast is dissolved, gradually add about 2 cups flour, stirring with a wooden spoon. You may need to add more or use less flour. A slightly sticky dough, though messy to handle, will make a more tender crust or bread.

**2.** Turn the dough out onto a floured surface, and knead until smooth and elastic (about 10 minutes). To knead, push out the mound of dough with the heels of your hands, fold it over, give it a quarter-turn, and repeat. If necessary, add slightly more flour while kneading.

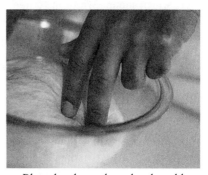

**3.** Place dough in a large bowl, and let rise in a warm place about 1 hour or until doubled in size. The dough is ready when you can press it with 2 fingers and the indentations remain. Just prior to shaping, punch down the dough, and let it rest for 5 minutes.

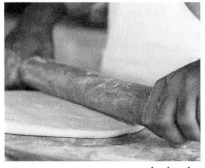

**To shape pizza crust,** pat the dough with floured hands, or stretch it with a rolling pin, starting at the center of the dough and moving toward the edge. Roll the dough into a 15-inch circle.

**To make calzones: 1.** Divide the dough into 6 equal portions; shape each into a ball. Roll each portion out to a 6-inch circle. Place filling mixture on half of dough, leaving a 1-inch border.

**2.** Fold dough over until edges almost meet; then fold bottom edge of dough over top edge, and crimp.

**To make focaccia,** roll out dough, let it rise, and then make indentations in top of dough with a wooden spoon or your fingers.

**To make bread,** sprinkle cheeses and herbs over dough, and roll up jelly-roll fashion. This makes a well-shaped loaf.

## Three-Cheese Pizza Bianca

*Bianca*, which means white in Italian, refers to a dish without tomato sauce. Infusing oil with the garlic in the microwave helps disperse the pungency of the garlic.

    All-Purpose Pizza Dough (recipe on page 52)
2  teaspoons yellow cornmeal
2  teaspoons olive oil
3  garlic cloves, minced
    Cooking spray
¾  cup fat-free ricotta cheese
¾  cup (3 ounces) finely shredded Gruyère cheese
2  tablespoons (½ ounce) grated fresh Parmesan cheese

**1.** Roll prepared dough into a 15-inch circle on a floured surface. Place dough on a 15-inch round pizza pan sprinkled with cornmeal. Cover dough, and let rise in a warm place 20 minutes or until puffy.

**2.** Preheat oven to 450°.

**3.** Combine oil and garlic in a small bowl. Cover and microwave at MEDIUM-HIGH (70% power) 1 minute or until bubbly. Cool 10 minutes.

**4.** Lightly coat dough with cooking spray. Combine garlic mixture and ricotta. Spread ricotta mixture over dough, leaving a 1-inch border. Sprinkle with Gruyère and Parmesan. Bake at 450° for 15 minutes or until golden. Yield: 4 servings (serving size: 2 slices).

CALORIES 541 (19% from fat); FAT 11.5g (sat 5.1g, mono 4.3g, poly 1.2g); PROTEIN 25.6g; CARB 83.5g; FIBER 3.3g; CHOL 31mg; IRON 5.1mg; SODIUM 449mg; CALC 356mg

### Pizza Points

Stretching the dough with your fists is a great way to shape the pizza because you get a more natural look, with bumps and blisters. The dough may tear slightly; just pinch it back together.

## Sausage, Fennel, and Provolone Calzones

The new low-fat chicken sausage will work great here, too. If you can't find fennel, increase the red bell pepper to 3 cups. Green bell peppers will also work. Add a tossed green salad to these calzones for a complete meal.

4  ounces sweet Italian sausage
2  cups thinly sliced fennel bulb (about 1 medium bulb)
1½  cups sliced red bell pepper
1  cup vertically sliced onion
    All-Purpose Pizza Dough (recipe on page 52)
1  large egg
1  tablespoon water
¾  cup (3 ounces) grated sharp provolone cheese
1  tablespoon yellow cornmeal

**1.** Remove casing from sausage. Cook sausage in a large nonstick skillet over medium-high heat until browned, stirring to crumble. Add fennel, bell pepper, and onion. Cover, reduce heat, and cook 9 minutes, stirring frequently. Cool slightly.

**2.** Preheat oven to 450°.

**3.** Divide prepared dough into 6 equal portions on a lightly floured surface; shape each piece into a ball. Roll each ball into a 6-inch circle. Combine egg and water with a whisk in a small bowl. Brush edge of each circle with egg mixture; reserve remaining egg mixture.

**4.** Place ⅔ cup sausage mixture on half of each circle, leaving a 1-inch border, and sprinkle each with 2 tablespoons cheese. Fold dough over sausage mixture until edges almost meet. Fold bottom edge over top edge; crimp edges of dough with fingers to form a rim. Place calzones on a baking sheet sprinkled with cornmeal. Brush tops with reserved egg mixture. Bake at 450° for 12 minutes or until golden brown. Yield: 6 servings (serving size: 1 calzone).

CALORIES 409 (26% from fat); FAT 11.7g (sat 4.9g, mono 4.2g, poly 1.4g); PROTEIN 16.3g; CARB 58.9g; FIBER 3.3g; CHOL 61mg; IRON 5.1mg; SODIUM 474mg; CALC 162mg

## Shrimp-and-Prosciutto Calzones

Fontina cheese works well in this calzone, but you can also use Swiss, Monterey Jack, or mozzarella. Make sure to finely chop the prosciutto so that its flavor disperses well. To save time, buy boiled or steamed shrimp from a local seafood market.

1  pound cooked medium shrimp, peeled and deveined
1  cup (4 ounces) shredded fontina cheese
1  ounce finely chopped prosciutto or ham
2  tablespoons thinly sliced fresh basil
1  tablespoon minced fresh chives
    All-Purpose Pizza Dough (recipe on page 52)
1  large egg
1  tablespoon water
1  tablespoon yellow cornmeal

**1.** Preheat oven to 450°.

**2.** Combine first 5 ingredients in a bowl.

**3.** Divide prepared dough into 6 equal portions on a lightly floured surface; shape each piece into a ball. Roll each ball into a 6-inch circle. Combine egg and water with a whisk in a small bowl. Brush edge of each circle with egg mixture; reserve remaining egg mixture.

**4.** Place ⅙ of shrimp mixture on half of each circle. Fold dough over shrimp mixture until edges almost meet. Fold bottom edge over top edge; crimp edges of dough with fingers to form a rim. Place calzones on a baking sheet sprinkled with cornmeal. Brush tops with reserved egg mixture. Bake calzones at 450° for 12 minutes or until golden brown. Yield: 6 servings (serving size: 1 calzone).

CALORIES 408 (19% from fat); FAT 8.6g (sat 4.3g, mono 2.4g, poly 1.1g); PROTEIN 26.4g; CARB 53.6g; FIBER 2.2g; CHOL 172mg; IRON 5.3mg; SODIUM 558mg; CALC 143mg

## Herbed Focaccia

All-Purpose Pizza Dough (recipe on
    page 52)
1  tablespoon chopped fresh flat-leaf
    parsley
1  teaspoon dried rubbed sage
1  teaspoon dried rosemary
1  teaspoon dried thyme
Cooking spray
1  tablespoon yellow cornmeal
1  tablespoon extra-virgin
    olive oil
½  teaspoon kosher salt

**1.** Roll prepared dough into a 12 x 8-
inch rectangle on a floured surface.
Sprinkle parsley, sage, rosemary, and
thyme over dough. Fold dough into
thirds. Knead lightly 1 minute or until
herbs are blended into dough. Cover
and let stand 10 minutes. Roll dough
into a 14 x 12-inch rectangle. Place
dough on a baking sheet coated with
cooking spray and sprinkled with cornmeal. Cover and let rise in a warm place
35 minutes or until doubled in size.
**2.** Preheat oven to 450°.
**3.** Uncover dough. Make indentations in
top of dough using handle of a wooden
spoon or your fingertips. Gently brush
dough with oil. Sprinkle with kosher
salt. Bake dough at 450° for 15 minutes
or until browned. Yield: 8 servings (serving size: 1 slice).

CALORIES 209 (11% from fat); FAT 2.5g (sat 0.4g, mono 1.4g,
poly 0.5g); PROTEIN 5.7g; CARB 40.2g; FIBER 1.8g; CHOL 0mg;
IRON 2.9mg; SODIUM 295mg; CALC 16mg

## Two-Cheese Oregano Bread

All-Purpose Pizza Dough (recipe
    on page 52)
½  cup (2 ounces) shredded
    provolone cheese
2  tablespoons (½ ounce) grated
    fresh Parmesan cheese
¼  teaspoon dried oregano
⅛  teaspoon crushed red pepper
1  tablespoon yellow cornmeal
1  teaspoon extra-virgin olive
    oil

**1.** Roll prepared dough into a 12 x 8-inch
rectangle. Combine cheeses, oregano,
and red pepper; sprinkle over dough,
leaving a ½-inch border. Beginning with
a long side, roll up jelly-roll fashion,
pressing firmly to eliminate air pockets;
pinch seam and ends to seal. Place roll,
seam side down, on a baking sheet sprinkled with cornmeal. Cut slits in top of
dough using a sharp knife. Cover and let
rise in a warm place 40 minutes or until
doubled in size.
**2.** Preheat oven to 450°.
**3.** Brush loaf with oil. Bake at 450° for
20 minutes or until loaf sounds hollow
when tapped. Yield: 8 servings (serving
size: 2 slices).

CALORIES 230 (14% from fat); FAT 3.6g (sat 1.7g, mono 1.2g,
poly 0.4g); PROTEIN 8.2g; CARB 40.2g; FIBER 1.7g; CHOL 6mg;
IRON 2.6mg; SODIUM 243mg; CALC 87mg

the cooking light
profile

# Healthy Is As Healthy Does

*From cycling mountain peaks to kayaking
raging rivers, the Keoghans are up for any
challenge. But their greatest feats are
keeping themselves, and 4-year-old Elle,
fit and eating smart.*

Phil Keoghan, host of The Travel
Channel's *Adventure Crazy*, and his wife,
Louise, have found "every weird way
imaginable" to stay fit and eat healthy
despite the pressures of parenthood and
careers—and to foster a healthy heritage
for their daughter, Elle. Here are some of
their secrets.

• To get Elle to eat more fruit, Louise
gives her a bowl of cut-up produce to
snack on while watching a video.

• Buy (or borrow) safe, sturdy child-
carrying equipment such as backpack-
style carriers and jogging strollers, so
children can join you on a hike or jog.

•The world is your gym. Playground
equipment, hotel stairs, even phone books
are workout tools for the Keoghans.

## Grilled Lemon-Basil Snapper with Roasted Peppers

The Keoghans prefer fresh and simple
meals such as this grilled-fish dish. While
the roasted red bell peppers are marinating, do as Phil, Louise, and Elle might do:
Enjoy yourselves by squeezing in a family
fun "workout" at a nearby playground.

3  large red bell peppers
2  tablespoons minced fresh basil
3  tablespoons water
2  tablespoons balsamic vinegar
1  tablespoon extra-virgin olive oil
2  teaspoons grated lemon rind
¼  teaspoon salt
¼  teaspoon freshly ground black
    pepper
4  (6-ounce) red snapper fillets or
    other firm white fish fillets
Cooking spray
Fresh chives (optional)

**1.** Preheat broiler.
**2.** Cut bell peppers in half lengthwise;
discard seeds and membranes. Place
pepper halves, skin sides up, on a foil-
lined baking sheet; flatten with hand.
Broil 12 minutes or until blackened.
Place in a zip-top plastic bag; seal. Let
stand 15 minutes. Peel and cut into ½-
inch-wide strips.
**3.** Combine basil and next 6 ingredients
in a medium bowl; stir well with a
whisk. Add pepper strips; toss well. Let
stand 1 hour. Drain peppers, reserving
marinade.
**4.** Prepare grill.
**5.** Brush both sides of fillets with reserved marinade. Place fish on a grill
rack coated with cooking spray. Grill 5
minutes on each side or until fish flakes
easily when tested with a fork, basting
frequently with remaining marinade.
**6.** Divide pepper strips evenly among 4
plates. Top each serving with a fillet.
Garnish with fresh chives, if desired.
Yield: 4 servings.

CALORIES 241 (24% from fat); FAT 6.5g (sat 1.1g, mono 3g,
poly 1.4g); PROTEIN 38.3g; CARB 6.5g; FIBER 1.8g; CHOL 67mg;
IRON 1.8mg; SODIUM 231mg; CALC 68mg

# That Old Texas Charm

*So many readers have fallen—heavily—for Texas Sheet Cake, we rushed to the rescue with a lighter version.*

From California to Virginia, the households of America have been quietly battling an addiction to Texas Sheet Cake. This continent-spanning charmer boasts a fudgelike icing that would melt in your mouth if not for its pecans.

Alas, our readers' passions were exceeded only by their alarm at the decidedly untamed levels of fat and calories. But we cut to the chase—or actually, the butter, which we reduced by half. We also took more butter out of the icing, along with some of the sugar, and stirred in far fewer pecans. We lowered the fat by more than half and dropped 157 calories per serving.

## Texas Sheet Cake

(pictured on page 57)

**CAKE:**

    Cooking spray
2  teaspoons all-purpose flour
2  cups all-purpose flour
2  cups granulated sugar
1  teaspoon baking soda
1  teaspoon ground cinnamon
¼  teaspoon salt
¾  cup water
½  cup butter or stick margarine
¼  cup unsweetened cocoa
½  cup low-fat buttermilk
1  teaspoon vanilla extract
2  large eggs

**ICING:**

6  tablespoons butter or stick margarine
⅓  cup fat-free milk
¼  cup unsweetened cocoa
3  cups powdered sugar
¼  cup chopped pecans, toasted
2  teaspoons vanilla extract

**1.** Preheat oven to 375°.

**2.** To prepare cake, coat a 15 x 10-inch jelly-roll pan with cooking spray, and dust with 2 teaspoons flour. Set prepared pan aside.

**3.** Lightly spoon 2 cups flour into dry measuring cups; level with a knife. Combine 2 cups flour and next 4 ingredients in a large bowl; stir well with a whisk. Combine water, ½ cup butter, and ¼ cup cocoa in a small saucepan; bring to a boil, stirring frequently. Remove from heat; pour into flour mixture. Beat at medium speed of a mixer until well-blended. Add buttermilk, 1 teaspoon vanilla, and eggs; beat well. Pour batter into prepared pan; bake at 375° for 17 minutes or until a wooden pick inserted in center comes out clean. Place on a wire rack.

**4.** To prepare icing, combine 6 tablespoons butter, milk, and ¼ cup cocoa in a medium saucepan; bring to a boil, stirring constantly. Remove from heat, and gradually stir in powdered sugar, pecans, and 2 teaspoons vanilla. Spread over hot cake. Cool completely on wire rack. Yield: 20 servings (serving size: 1 slice).

**NOTE:** You can also make this recipe in a 13 x 9-inch baking pan. Bake at 375° for 22 minutes.

CALORIES 298 (30% from fat); FAT 10g (sat 5.5g, mono 3.2g, poly 0.7g); PROTEIN 3.1g; CARB 49.8g; FIBER 0.5g; CHOL 44mg; IRON 1.1mg; SODIUM 188mg; CALC 25mg

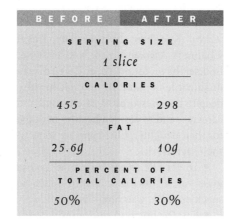

| BEFORE | AFTER |
|---|---|
| **SERVING SIZE** | |
| *1 slice* | |
| **CALORIES** | |
| 455 | 298 |
| **FAT** | |
| 25.6g | 10g |
| **PERCENT OF TOTAL CALORIES** | |
| 50% | 30% |

# Beef Carbonnade

*Try our Beef Carbonnade, which we've happily revisited from our January/February 1995 issue, and you'll understand how chuck roast can surpass filet mignon.*

## Beef Carbonnade

2  bacon slices, finely diced
2½  pounds boned chuck roast, cut into 1-inch cubes
½  teaspoon salt
½  teaspoon black pepper
1  garlic clove, minced
5  cups thinly sliced onion (about 4 medium)
3  tablespoons all-purpose flour
2  teaspoons white wine vinegar
½  teaspoon sugar
½  teaspoon dried thyme
1  (10½-ounce) can beef broth
1  (12-ounce) can light beer
1  bay leaf
6  cups hot cooked medium egg noodles (about 1 [12-ounce] package)

**1.** Preheat oven to 325°.

**2.** Cook bacon in a large Dutch oven over medium-high heat until crisp; remove bacon, reserving drippings in pan. Set bacon aside. Add beef, salt, and pepper to drippings in pan; cook 5 minutes, browning beef well on all sides. Add garlic; cook 30 seconds. Remove beef from pan with a slotted spoon; set aside.

**3.** Add onion to pan; cover and cook over medium heat 10 minutes, stirring occasionally. Stir in flour; cook 2 minutes. Add vinegar and next 5 ingredients; bring to a boil. Return bacon and beef to pan. Cover and bake at 325° for 2 hours or until beef is tender. Discard bay leaf. Serve over noodles. Yield: 6 servings (serving size: 1 cup beef mixture and 1 cup noodles).

CALORIES 540 (25% from fat); FAT 15.3g (sat 5.4g, mono 6.1g, poly 1.8g); PROTEIN 43.3g; CARB 52.1g; FIBER 5.5g; CHOL 147mg; IRON 7.1mg; SODIUM 636mg; CALC 60mg

Texas Sheet Cake,
page 56

Chicken Salpicón, page 49

Sweet Potato-Pecan Pancakes
with Vanilla-Maple Syrup,
pages 63 and 64

Grilled Sourdough
Cheddar Melt, page 42,
with Beer-Battered
Onion Rings, page 43

Breast of Chicken Oaxaca,
page 50

Mussel Saffron Soup, page 61

Asian Meatballs with Mushrooms
and Rice Noodles, page 74

# Sure and It's a Fine Catch

*A honeymoon in Ireland was the beginning of a love affair with one of the country's greatest cooking traditions—seafood.*

Growing up part of a second-generation Irish household in the United States, *Cooking Light's* Senior Healthy Living Editor Lisa Delaney thought Irish cuisine consisted solely of corned beef-and-cabbage.

But after honeymooning in the Connemara region of Ireland last June, she was surprised to find that the menus of the inns and centuries-old castles in Ireland's pastoral countryside read like a fishmonger's inventory list.

## Mussel Saffron Soup

(pictured on page 60)

*Chervil*, a delicate, anise-flavored herb, is sprinkled over the mussels just before serving.

    1   teaspoon butter or stick margarine
    ½   cup minced shallots
    1½  cups dry white wine
    ¼   cup minced fresh parsley
    ¼   teaspoon dried thyme
    ⅛   teaspoon saffron threads, crushed
    1   bay leaf
    1   garlic clove, minced
    50  mussels (about 2 pounds),
        scrubbed and debearded
    2   cups clam juice
    ¼   teaspoon freshly ground black
        pepper
    ⅛   teaspoon ground red pepper
    1   cup 2% reduced-fat milk
    ¼   cup chopped fresh chervil or
        parsley

**1.** Melt butter in a large Dutch oven over medium-high heat. Add minced shallots, and sauté 3 minutes. Add wine and next 5 ingredients; bring to a boil.

Add mussels. Cover and cook 5 minutes or until mussels open; discard any unopened shells. Strain mussel mixture through a cheesecloth-lined sieve into a medium bowl, reserving cooking liquid. Reserve 12 shells with meat intact.

**2.** Remove meat from remaining shells. Discard shells; chop meat and add to pan. Add reserved cooking liquid, clam juice, black pepper, and red pepper; bring to a boil. Reduce heat, and simmer 5 minutes. Stir in milk, and cook 1 minute or until soup is thoroughly heated. Pour soup into serving bowls. Top with reserved mussels and chervil. Yield: 4 servings (serving size: 1¼ cups soup, 3 mussels, and 1 tablespoon chervil).

CALORIES 205 (20% from fat); FAT 4.5g (sat 1.8g, mono 1.2g, poly 0.7g); PROTEIN 15.5g; CARB 11.3g; FIBER 0.2g; CHOL 40mg; IRON 5.2mg; SODIUM 598mg; CALC 133mg

## Prawns with Pernod

The licorice flavor of Pernod paired with shrimp is an unexpected combination, but one we found superlative. Some unique liqueurs such as Pernod are sold in small bottles; it's a convenient way to try unfamiliar varieties without investing in a large bottle.

    1   cup dry white wine
    ½   cup minced shallots
    2   tablespoons Pernod (licorice-
        flavored liqueur)
    2   tablespoons fresh lemon juice
    1   tablespoon butter or stick
        margarine
    2   tablespoons minced fresh or
        2 teaspoons dried parsley
    1   tablespoon minced fresh or
        1 teaspoon dried tarragon
    ½   teaspoon freshly ground black
        pepper
    2   garlic cloves, minced
    32  large shrimp, peeled and deveined
        (about 1½ pounds)
    Cooking spray
    1   cup minced seeded tomato
    8   (1-ounce) slices French bread,
        toasted

**1.** Combine wine and shallots in a small saucepan; bring to a boil, and cook until reduced to ½ cup (about 15 minutes). Remove from heat; stir in Pernod and next 6 ingredients.

**2.** Preheat broiler.

**3.** Arrange shrimp in a single layer on a jelly-roll pan coated with cooking spray, and pour Pernod mixture over shrimp. Broil 5 minutes or until shrimp are done. Sprinkle shrimp with tomato, and serve with French bread. Yield: 8 servings (serving size: 4 shrimp and 1 bread slice).

CALORIES 188 (17% from fat); FAT 3.6g (sat 1.3g, mono 1g, poly 0.7g); PROTEIN 16.1g; CARB 20.3g; FIBER 1.3g; CHOL 101mg; IRON 2.8mg; SODIUM 288mg; CALC 68mg

## Smoked Salmon with Hot Honey Mustard

The hot honey mustard will keep for up to two months when stored in a covered jar in the refrigerator.

    ½   cup dry mustard (1 [2-ounce] tin)
    ½   cup malt vinegar
    ¼   cup honey
    1   tablespoon orange juice
    1   large egg
    1   tablespoon chopped fresh or
        1 teaspoon dried dill
    1   pound smoked salmon fillet
    8   (1-ounce) slices whole-wheat
        bread, toasted and cut diagonally
        into fourths

**1.** Combine mustard and vinegar in a small saucepan, stirring with a whisk until smooth. Add honey, juice, and egg, and stir well with a whisk. Place over medium heat, and cook until thick (about 4 minutes), stirring constantly with a whisk. Cool. Stir in dill. Cover and chill. Serve with salmon and toast points. Yield: 16 servings (serving size: 1 ounce smoked salmon, 1 tablespoon mustard, and 2 toast points).

CALORIES 102 (26% from fat); FAT 3g (sat 0.4g, mono 1.6g, poly 0.8g); PROTEIN 7.4g; CARB 11.2g; FIBER 0.6g; CHOL 20mg; IRON 1mg; SODIUM 294mg; CALC 26mg

## Broiled Salmon with Sweet-and-Sour Cucumbers

   2 tablespoons Dijon mustard
   1 tablespoon brown sugar
   ½ teaspoon salt
   8 (6-ounce) salmon fillets (about 1 inch thick)
Cooking spray
Sweet-and-Sour Cucumbers

**1.** Preheat broiler.
**2.** Combine first 3 ingredients. Brush mustard mixture over fillets. Place fillets, skin sides down, on a broiler rack coated with cooking spray; broil 8 minutes or until fish flakes easily when tested with a fork. Serve fish with Sweet-and-Sour Cucumbers. Yield: 8 servings (serving size: 1 fillet and ⅓ cup cucumbers).

(Totals include Sweet-and-Sour Cucumbers) CALORIES 317 (41% from fat); FAT 14.5g (sat 2.5g, mono 6.8g, poly 3.2g); PROTEIN 35.4g; CARB 9.1g; FIBER 0.7g; CHOL 111mg; IRON 0.7mg; SODIUM 492mg; CALC 27mg

**SWEET-AND-SOUR CUCUMBERS:**
   4 cups thinly sliced peeled cucumber (about 3 large)
   3 tablespoons sugar
   ½ teaspoon salt
   ¼ cup cider vinegar
   1 tablespoon chopped fresh or 1 teaspoon dried dill

**1.** Place first 3 ingredients in a large bowl; toss gently to coat. Stir in vinegar and dill. Cover and chill 2 hours. Yield: 8 servings (serving size: ⅓ cup).

CALORIES 32 (4% from fat); FAT 0.2g (sat 0g, mono 0.1g, poly 0.1g); PROTEIN 0.6g; CARB 7.7g; FIBER 0.7g; CHOL 0mg; IRON 0.3mg; SODIUM 149mg; CALC 17mg

## Smoked Fish Spread

   ½ pound smoked whitefish
   ⅓ cup fat-free sour cream
   3 tablespoons (about 1½ ounces) ⅓-less-fat cream cheese
   2 teaspoons prepared horseradish
   1 teaspoon fresh lemon juice
   ⅛ teaspoon black pepper
Dash of Worcestershire sauce
  60 fat-free saltine crackers

**1.** Remove and discard skin and bones from fish. Flake fish into a bowl. Add remaining ingredients except crackers; stir with a fork until well-blended. Cover and chill. Serve with crackers. Yield: 20 servings (serving size: 1 tablespoon spread and 3 crackers).

CALORIES 57 (14% from fat); FAT 0.9g (sat 0.3g, mono 0.3g, poly 0.3g); PROTEIN 3.3g; CARB 7.5g; FIBER 0g; CHOL 6mg; IRON 0.5mg; SODIUM 126mg; CALC 3mg

## Creamed Cod with Ham and Potatoes

1½ pounds red potatoes
   1 pound skinned cod fillets, cut into 1-inch pieces
   2 cups 1% low-fat milk, divided
   1 bay leaf
   ⅛ teaspoon ground nutmeg
   ½ teaspoon salt
Dash of black pepper
   ⅓ cup all-purpose flour
   4 ounces smoked ham, cut into julienne strips
Cooking spray
   2 tablespoons grated Parmesan cheese
   1 teaspoon freshly ground black pepper

**1.** Place potatoes in a saucepan, and cover with water; bring to a boil. Reduce heat, and simmer 15 minutes or until tender; drain. Cool; peel and cut into 1-inch cubes. Set aside.
**2.** Place cod in a medium saucepan; add 1½ cups milk and bay leaf. Bring to a boil; reduce heat, and simmer 5 minutes or until fish flakes easily when tested with a fork. Remove from heat. Remove cod from pan using a slotted spoon, reserving milk mixture; discard bay leaf.
**3.** Preheat oven to 400°.
**4.** Combine reserved milk mixture, nutmeg, salt, and dash of pepper in a medium saucepan. Combine ½ cup milk and flour in a small bowl, and stir with a whisk; add flour mixture to saucepan. Cook over medium heat 1 minute or until slightly thick, stirring constantly. Cook 2 minutes. Add potato, cod, and ham; toss well. Pour mixture into an 11 x 7-inch baking dish coated with cooking spray. Sprinkle with cheese and freshly ground pepper. Bake at 400° for 30 minutes or until brown and bubbly. Let stand 10 minutes. Yield: 4 servings (serving size: 2 cups).

CALORIES 368 (15% from fat); FAT 6.2g (sat 2.8g, mono 1.2g, poly 1.5g); PROTEIN 34.8g; CARB 42.5g; FIBER 3.5g; CHOL 72mg; IRON 4mg; SODIUM 787mg; CALC 229mg

## Colcannon

Potatoes are a likely complement to an Irish seafood meal.

   5 cups cubed peeled baking potato (about 2½ pounds)
   1 tablespoon butter or stick margarine
   1 cup chopped onion
   2 cups chopped kale
   ½ cup 2% reduced-fat milk
   ⅓ cup low-fat sour cream
   ½ teaspoon salt
   ¼ teaspoon freshly ground black pepper

**1.** Place potato in a medium saucepan, and cover with water; bring to a boil. Reduce heat, and simmer potato 15 minutes or until tender; drain. Keep potatoes warm.
**2.** Melt butter in a large skillet over medium heat. Add onion; cook 5 minutes, stirring occasionally. Stir in kale, and cook 5 minutes. Remove from heat. Mash potato with a masher. Stir in kale mixture, milk, sour cream, salt, and pepper. Yield: 5 servings (serving size: 1 cup).

CALORIES 299 (16% from fat); FAT 5.2g (sat 3g, mono 1.4g, poly 0.4g); PROTEIN 7.1g; CARB 56.4g; FIBER 4.5g; CHOL 14mg; IRON 1.4mg; SODIUM 300mg; CALC 103mg

# Pancakes after Dark

## Mom treated you to them for breakfast, but now you're a grownup. Break the rules and have them for supper.

For supper, pancakes seem all the more indulgent. Many of us were taught as children—and now teach our children—that the evening meal is the one with the most rules. Having pancakes for supper doesn't just buck the custom of treating them as breakfast food; it suggests that maybe all those other dinner rules could be relaxed.

### Sweet Potato-Pecan Pancakes

(pictured on page 58)

These pancakes go best with our Vanilla-Maple Syrup (recipe on page 64).

1¼  cups all-purpose flour
¼  cup chopped pecans, toasted and divided
2¼  teaspoons baking powder
1  teaspoon pumpkin-pie spice
¼  teaspoon salt
1  cup fat-free milk
¼  cup packed dark brown sugar
1  tablespoon vegetable oil
1  teaspoon vanilla extract
2  large eggs, lightly beaten
1  (16-ounce) can sweet potatoes or yams, drained and mashed (about ¾ cup)

**1.** Lightly spoon flour into dry measuring cups; level with a knife. Combine flour, 2 tablespoons pecans, baking powder, pumpkin-pie spice, and salt in a large bowl. Combine milk and next 4 ingredients; add to flour mixture, stirring until smooth. Stir in sweet potatoes.
**2.** For each pancake, spoon about ¼ cup batter onto a hot nonstick griddle or large nonstick skillet. Turn pancakes when tops are covered with bubbles and edges look cooked. Sprinkle pancakes with 2 tablespoons pecans. Yield: 6 servings (serving size: 2 pancakes and 1 teaspoon pecans).

CALORIES 270 (26% from fat); FAT 7.9g (sat 1.4g, mono 3.5g, poly 2.3g); PROTEIN 7.3g; CARB 42.6g; FIBER 2.3g; CHOL 74mg; IRON 2.2mg; SODIUM 333mg; CALC 185mg

### Buckwheat-Honey Pancakes

Serve these pancakes with Vanilla-Maple Syrup (recipe on page 64).

⅔  cup buckwheat flour
½  cup all-purpose flour
1  teaspoon baking powder
¼  teaspoon baking soda
¼  teaspoon salt
⅛  teaspoon ground nutmeg
¾  cup plain fat-free yogurt
¼  cup honey
¼  cup fat-free milk
2  tablespoons vegetable oil
¾  teaspoon vanilla extract
3  large eggs, lightly beaten

**1.** Lightly spoon flours into dry measuring cups, and level with a knife. Combine flours and next 4 ingredients in a large bowl. Combine yogurt and remaining 5 ingredients; add to flour mixture, stirring until smooth.
**2.** Spoon about ¼ cup batter onto a hot nonstick griddle or large nonstick skillet. Turn pancakes when tops are covered with bubbles and edges look cooked. Yield: 4 servings (serving size: 3 pancakes).
**NOTE:** Store any leftover buckwheat flour in your refrigerator or freezer; whole-grain flours will spoil quickly at room temperature.

CALORIES 352 (29% from fat); FAT 11.5g (sat 2.7g, mono 3.7g, poly 4g); PROTEIN 13g; CARB 50.8g; FIBER 1.4g; CHOL 167mg; IRON 2.5mg; SODIUM 443mg; CALC 204mg

### Cheddar Pancakes with Sautéed Apples and Bacon

The sautéed apples make a savory-sweet topping for these pancakes. Pour Vanilla-Maple Syrup (recipe on page 64) over the apples if you like a saucier topping.

1⅓  cups all-purpose flour
1  tablespoon sugar
1¼  teaspoons baking powder
¼  teaspoon salt
¼  teaspoon baking soda
¼  teaspoon ground nutmeg
1⅓  cups plain low-fat yogurt
1¼  cups (5 ounces) shredded reduced-fat extra-sharp Cheddar cheese
2  tablespoons water
2  tablespoons Dijon mustard
2  teaspoons vegetable oil
1  large egg, lightly beaten
1  large egg white, lightly beaten
Sautéed Apples and Bacon

**1.** Lightly spoon flour into dry measuring cups, and level with a knife. Combine flour and next 5 ingredients in a large bowl. Combine yogurt and next 6 ingredients, and add to flour mixture, stirring until smooth.
**2.** Spoon about ¼ cup batter onto a hot nonstick griddle or large nonstick skillet. Turn pancakes when tops are covered with bubbles and edges looked cooked. Serve with Sautéed Apples and Bacon. Yield: 4 servings (serving size: 3 pancakes and ¾ cup topping).

(Totals include Sautéed Apples and Bacon) CALORIES 564 (25% from fat); FAT 15.4g (sat 6.8g, mono 4.7g, poly 2.3g); PROTEIN 25.2g; CARB 83.4g; FIBER 7.1g; CHOL 91mg; IRON 3mg; SODIUM 967mg; CALC 639mg

**SAUTÉED APPLES AND BACON:**
2  reduced-fat bacon slices
8  cups sliced peeled Granny Smith apple (about 2 pounds)
2  tablespoons sugar

**1.** Cook bacon in a large nonstick skillet over medium heat until crisp. Remove bacon from pan, reserving drippings in pan. Crumble bacon, and set aside. Add apple and sugar to drippings in pan.
*Continued*

Sauté 10 minutes or until apple is golden. Stir in bacon. Yield: 4 servings (serving size: ¾ cup).

CALORIES 167 (9% from fat); FAT 1.6g (sat 0.4g, mono 0.5g, poly 0.5g); PROTEIN 1.7g; CARB 39.8g; FIBER 5.9g; CHOL 3mg; IRON 0.5mg; SODIUM 73mg; CALC 15mg

## Peanut Butter Pancakes

Chunky peanut butter works best in this recipe. Serve these pancakes with Strawberry-Lemon Syrup (recipe at right), Raspberry-Honey Coulis (recipe at right), or jam.

1½  cups all-purpose flour
6  tablespoons sugar
2  teaspoons baking powder
¼  teaspoon salt
1¼  cups fat-free milk
¼  cup chunky peanut butter
1  tablespoon roasted peanut oil or vegetable oil
½  teaspoon vanilla extract
2  large eggs, lightly beaten

**1.** Lightly spoon flour into dry measuring cups; level with a knife. Combine flour, sugar, baking powder, and salt in a large bowl. Combine milk and remaining 4 ingredients; add to flour mixture, stirring until smooth.
**2.** Spoon about ¼ cup batter onto a hot nonstick griddle or large nonstick skillet. Turn pancakes when tops are covered with bubbles and edges look cooked. Yield: 5 servings (serving size: 2 pancakes).

CALORIES 349 (30% from fat); FAT 11.7g (sat 2.5g, mono 5.1g, poly 3.2g); PROTEIN 12.2g; CARB 49.4g; FIBER 1.2g; CHOL 90mg; IRON 2.5mg; SODIUM 432mg; CALC 204mg

## Vanilla-Maple Syrup

(pictured on page 58)

1½  cups maple syrup
1  (3-inch) piece vanilla bean, split lengthwise or ¼ teaspoon vanilla extract

**1.** Pour maple syrup into a medium saucepan. Scrape seeds from vanilla

bean; add seeds and bean to syrup. Bring to a simmer over medium heat, and cook 5 minutes. Remove from heat; discard bean. Yield: 1½ cups (serving size: 1 tablespoon).

CALORIES 52 (0% from fat); FAT 0g; PROTEIN 0g; CARB 13.2g; FIBER 0g; CHOL 0mg; IRON 0.2mg; SODIUM 2mg; CALC 13mg

## Raspberry-Honey Coulis

A *coulis* (koo-LEE) is a sauce made by pureeing fresh fruits. This recipe also makes a tasty topping for frozen yogurt or ice cream.

2  cups fresh raspberries
¾  cup orange juice
⅓  cup honey
2  tablespoons powdered sugar

**1.** Combine all ingredients in a blender, and process until smooth. Press mixture through a sieve over a bowl, reserving liquid; discard seeds. Yield: 2 cups (serving size: 1 tablespoon).

CALORIES 19 (0% from fat); FAT 0g; PROTEIN 0.1g; CARB 4.9g; FIBER 0.1g; CHOL 0mg; IRON 0.1mg; SODIUM 0mg; CALC 2mg

## Strawberry-Lemon Syrup

This syrup can be served hot or cold. You can also use it to top frozen yogurt or ice cream.

3  cups sliced strawberries, divided
1  cup sugar
¾  cup water
2  tablespoons fresh lemon juice
1  teaspoon grated lemon rind

**1.** Combine 2 cups strawberries, sugar, water, and lemon juice in a nonaluminum medium saucepan, and bring to a boil over medium-high heat. Cook until reduced to 1½ cups (about 20 minutes). Remove from heat, and let stand 10 minutes. Stir in 1 cup strawberries and rind. Yield: 2 cups (serving size: 1 tablespoon).

CALORIES 29 (3% from fat); FAT 0.1g (sat 0g, mono 0.1g, poly 0g); PROTEIN 0.1g; CARB 7.3g; FIBER 0.3g; CHOL 0mg; IRON 0.1mg; SODIUM 0mg; CALC 2mg

## Buttermilk-Pear Pancakes

1¼  cups all-purpose flour
¾  teaspoon baking powder
½  teaspoon ground cinnamon
¼  teaspoon baking soda
¼  teaspoon salt
1⅓  cups low-fat buttermilk
2  tablespoons maple syrup
1  tablespoon vegetable oil
1  large egg, lightly beaten
¾  cup finely chopped peeled ripe Bartlett or Anjou pear

**1.** Lightly spoon flour into dry measuring cups; level with a knife. Combine flour and next 4 ingredients in a large bowl. Combine buttermilk, syrup, oil, and egg; add to flour mixture, stirring until smooth. Fold in pear.
**2.** Spoon about ¼ cup batter onto a hot nonstick griddle or large nonstick skillet. Turn pancakes when tops are covered with bubbles and edges look cooked. Yield: 4 servings (serving size: 3 pancakes).

CALORIES 277 (21% from fat); FAT 6.6g (sat 1.9g, mono 1.9g, poly 2.1g); PROTEIN 8.8g; CARB 45.7g; FIBER 1.6g; CHOL 55mg; IRON 2.4mg; SODIUM 377mg; CALC 177mg

## Orange-Ricotta Pancakes

These pancakes will be small because the batter is thick and doesn't spread much. Serve them with Strawberry-Lemon Syrup (recipe at left), fresh sliced strawberries, or orange marmalade.

⅔  cup all-purpose flour
¼  cup sugar
½  teaspoon baking powder
¼  teaspoon baking soda
¼  teaspoon salt
¾  cup (3 ounces) part-skim ricotta cheese
¼  cup fat-free milk
¼  teaspoon grated orange rind
2  tablespoons fresh orange juice
3  large egg yolks, lightly beaten
3  large egg whites

**1.** Lightly spoon flour into a dry measuring cup, and level with a knife. Combine flour, sugar, baking powder, baking soda, and salt in a large bowl. Combine ricotta cheese and next 4 ingredients, and add to flour mixture, stirring until smooth. Beat egg whites at high speed of a mixer until stiff peaks form. Gently fold one-fourth of egg whites into cheese mixture; gently fold in remaining egg whites.

**2.** Spoon about ¼ cup batter onto a hot nonstick griddle or large nonstick skillet. Turn pancakes when tops are covered with bubbles and edges look cooked. Yield: 5 servings (serving size: 3 pancakes).

CALORIES 204 (28% from fat); FAT 6.3g (sat 2.8g, mono 2.1g, poly 0.6g); PROTEIN 10.1g; CARB 26.4g; FIBER 0.5g; CHOL 142mg; IRON 1.4mg; SODIUM 318mg; CALC 161mg

## Sausage Pancakes

1   tablespoon vegetable oil, divided
½   cup diced onion
1   (4-ounce) link hot Italian turkey sausage
1¼  cups all-purpose flour
1   teaspoon baking powder
¼   teaspoon baking soda
¼   teaspoon salt
⅛   teaspoon dried thyme
1¼  cups low-fat buttermilk
2   tablespoons apple butter
2   large eggs, lightly beaten

**1.** Heat 1 teaspoon oil in a large nonstick skillet over medium heat. Add onion; cook 5 minutes or until soft, stirring frequently. Remove casing from sausage. Add sausage to pan; cook until browned, stirring until finely crumbled. Remove sausage mixture from pan; set aside.

**2.** Lightly spoon flour into dry measuring cups, and level with a knife. Combine flour and next 4 ingredients in a large bowl. Combine 2 teaspoons oil, buttermilk, apple butter, and eggs, and add to flour mixture, stirring until smooth. Stir in sausage mixture.

**3.** Spoon about ¼ cup batter onto a hot nonstick griddle or large nonstick skillet. Turn pancakes when tops are covered with bubbles and edges look cooked. Yield: 4 servings (serving size: 3 pancakes).

CALORIES 316 (29% from fat); FAT 10.2g (sat 3.1g, mono 3.3g, poly 3g); PROTEIN 15.1g; CARB 40.3g; FIBER 1.5g; CHOL 133mg; IRON 2.8mg; SODIUM 581mg; CALC 186mg

## Potato, Zucchini, and Green Onion Pancakes

Shred the cooked potato after it has cooled; a warm potato will crumble if you try to shred it.

1   small baking potato, peeled (about 5 ounces)
1   cup grated zucchini
1   cup all-purpose flour
1   teaspoon baking powder
¾   teaspoon salt
½   teaspoon dried thyme
¼   teaspoon baking soda
¼   teaspoon ground nutmeg
¼   teaspoon black pepper
½   cup fat-free milk
¼   cup low-fat sour cream
1   tablespoon vegetable oil
¼   teaspoon hot sauce
3   large eggs, lightly beaten
½   cup chopped green onions
¼   cup low-fat sour cream
2   teaspoons chopped fresh chives

**1.** Place potato in a saucepan, and cover with water; bring to a boil. Reduce heat, and simmer 15 minutes or until tender; drain and cool. Shred potato.

**2.** Press zucchini on several layers of paper towels; cover with additional paper towels. Let stand 5 minutes, pressing down occasionally.

**3.** Lightly spoon flour into a dry measuring cup, and level with a knife. Combine flour and next 6 ingredients in a large bowl. Combine milk and next 4 ingredients; add to flour mixture, stirring until smooth. Fold in potato, zucchini, and onions.

**4.** Spoon about ¼ cup batter onto a hot nonstick griddle or large nonstick skillet. Turn pancakes when tops are covered with bubbles and edges look cooked. Top pancakes with sour cream and chives. Yield: 4 servings (serving size: 3 pancakes, 1 tablespoon sour cream, and ½ teaspoon chives).

CALORIES 292 (29% from fat); FAT 9.4g (sat 3g, mono 2.6g, poly 2.4g); PROTEIN 11.5g; CARB 40g; FIBER 2g; CHOL 171mg; IRON 2.7mg; SODIUM 733mg; CALC 208mg

# Ergo, Orzo

*A Virginia Latin teacher says her pasta salad is summa cum yummy.*

While studying classical architecture in Greece, Patty Lister of Falls Church, Virginia, picked up a lifelong craving for the country's cuisine. "Ever since, I have loved the combination of olives, lemons, and feta cheese," says the 30-year-old mother of two. She took a good hard look at the "same old pasta salad" she'd always eaten and redid it from the ground floor up.

## Lemony Orzo Salad

1   cup uncooked orzo (rice-shaped pasta)
1⅓  cups diced zucchini
⅓   cup diced red onion
⅓   cup minced fresh parsley
3   tablespoons fresh lemon juice
1   tablespoon minced fresh or 1 teaspoon dried basil
1   tablespoon olive oil
2   teaspoons minced fresh mint
½   teaspoon salt
¼   teaspoon black pepper
1   cup diced tomato
⅓   cup (1½ ounces) crumbled feta cheese
2   tablespoons chopped pitted kalamata olives

**1.** Cook orzo according to package directions, omitting salt and fat. Drain well. Combine orzo, zucchini, and onion in a large bowl; toss well. Combine parsley and next 6 ingredients; stir well with a whisk. Stir into orzo mixture; add tomato, cheese, and olives, tossing gently to coat. Yield: 6 servings (serving size: ¾ cup).

CALORIES 199 (22% from fat); FAT 4.8g (sat 1.5g, mono 2.3g, poly 0.6g); PROTEIN 6.7g; CARB 32.7g; FIBER 1.8g; CHOL 6mg; IRON 2.1mg; SODIUM 307mg; CALC 58mg

## "Honey Left Me in a Crunch" Chicken with Linguine

"My husband called and said that he was bringing home an associate for dinner. So, I made something with ingredients I had."

—Stefani X. Austin, Austin, Texas

  4 (4-ounce) skinned, boned chicken breast halves
1½ teaspoons dried Italian seasoning, divided
  1 tablespoon Dijon mustard
  ¼ teaspoon salt
  ¼ teaspoon black pepper
  4 garlic cloves, minced
  1 large egg, lightly beaten
  ½ cup all-purpose flour
  ⅓ cup honey-crunch toasted wheat germ
  1 tablespoon olive oil
  1 (26-ounce) bottle reduced-fat chunky pasta sauce (such as Muir Glen)
  3 cups hot cooked linguine (about 6 ounces uncooked pasta)

**1.** Place each chicken breast half between 2 sheets of heavy-duty plastic wrap, and flatten to ¼-inch thickness using a meat mallet or rolling pin. Combine 1 teaspoon Italian seasoning, mustard, and next 4 ingredients in a shallow dish; add chicken, turning to coat. Cover and marinate in refrigerator 15 minutes.
**2.** Combine ½ teaspoon Italian seasoning, flour, and wheat germ in a shallow dish. Remove chicken from egg mixture; dredge in flour mixture. Heat oil in a large nonstick skillet over medium-high heat. Add chicken, and cook 4 minutes on each side or until done. Keep warm.
**3.** Microwave sauce at MEDIUM-HIGH (70% power) 3 minutes or until hot, stirring after 2 minutes. Combine pasta with 1½ cups sauce. Spoon pasta mixture onto 4 plates. Arrange chicken over pasta, and top with remaining sauce. Yield: 4 servings (serving size: 1 cup pasta mixture, 1 chicken breast half, and ⅓ cup pasta sauce).

CALORIES 481 (19% from fat); FAT 9.9g (sat 1.9g, mono 3.7g, poly 2.7g); PROTEIN 37.7g; CARB 56.5g; FIBER 8.2g; CHOL 93mg; IRON 5.3mg; SODIUM 752mg; CALC 68mg

---

### menu
#### Veal Mediterranean
Italian vegetable salad*

*Combine 2 cups sliced zucchini, ½ cup sliced carrot, 1 tablespoon capers, and 1 (14-ounce) can drained quartered artichoke hearts. Add ¼ cup low-fat Italian dressing, tossing to coat. Serves 4.

## Veal Mediterranean

—Corinne Hickman, Santa Barbara, California

  4 (4-ounce) veal cutlets (about ¼ inch thick)
Cooking spray
  ¼ cup dry red wine
  1 teaspoon dried basil
  1 (14½-ounce) can Italian-style stewed tomatoes, undrained and chopped
  1 garlic clove, minced
  1 bay leaf
  1 tablespoon water
  1 teaspoon cornstarch
  4 cups hot cooked linguine (about 8 ounces uncooked pasta)
  ¼ cup sliced pimento-stuffed olives

**1.** Place veal between 2 sheets of heavy-duty plastic wrap; flatten to an even thickness using a meat mallet or rolling pin.
**2.** Heat a large nonstick skillet coated with cooking spray over medium heat. Add veal; cook 2½ minutes on each side. Add wine and next 4 ingredients; bring to a boil. Cover, reduce heat, and simmer 10 minutes or until veal is tender. Remove veal from pan; keep warm. Discard bay leaf.
**3.** Combine water and cornstarch; stir into tomato mixture. Cook until thick and bubbly (about 4 minutes), stirring constantly. Return veal to pan; cook 2 minutes. Serve over pasta; sprinkle with olives. Yield: 4 servings (serving size: 1 veal cutlet, ½ cup sauce, 1 cup pasta, and 1 tablespoon olives).

CALORIES 386 (13% from fat); FAT 5.6g (sat 1.4g, mono 1.8g, poly 0.9g); PROTEIN 31.3g; CARB 50.7g; FIBER 2g; CHOL 91mg; IRON 4mg; SODIUM 446mg; CALC 79mg

---

## Shrimp with Orzo

"I make this often because it's supereasy to throw together. It's also healthy and rich in flavor, and it always receives rave reviews. I usually serve it with a salad and focaccia."

—Erin Corry, Victoria, British Columbia

  1 (28-ounce) can diced tomatoes, undrained
1½ teaspoons olive oil
  1 cup diced onion
  3 garlic cloves, minced
  ¼ cup dry white wine
  3 tablespoons chopped fresh parsley, divided
  1 tablespoon capers
  ½ teaspoon dried oregano
  ½ teaspoon dried basil
  ¼ teaspoon black pepper
Dash of crushed red pepper
  1 pound medium shrimp, peeled and deveined
  2 cups hot cooked orzo (about 1 cup uncooked rice-shaped pasta)
Cooking spray
  ½ cup (2 ounces) crumbled feta cheese

**1.** Preheat oven to 450°.
**2.** Drain tomatoes through a sieve into a bowl, reserving tomatoes and ½ cup tomato liquid. Heat oil in a large nonstick skillet over medium heat. Add onion and garlic; sauté 3 minutes. Add wine; cook 1 minute. Add tomatoes, reserved tomato liquid, 1½ tablespoons parsley, capers, and next 4 ingredients to pan; cook 5 minutes. Add shrimp, and cook 2 minutes. Stir in pasta. Spoon shrimp mixture into an 11 x 7-inch baking dish coated with cooking spray. Top with feta cheese and 1½ tablespoons parsley. Bake at 450° for 10 minutes. Yield: 4 servings (serving size: 1½ cups).

CALORIES 424 (16% from fat); FAT 7.6g (sat 2.9g, mono 2.3g, poly 1.4g); PROTEIN 29.2g; CARB 57.1g; FIBER 3.8g; CHOL 142mg; IRON 6.1mg; SODIUM 671mg; CALC 200mg

## Cajun Chicken Pasta

"After my dad had a heart attack, I switched to a low-fat diet and started measuring ingredients. I looked at this recipe, and it was not low-fat at all. So I changed some things to make it more suitable. If you like spicy food, this is a good alternative to the same old red sauce."

—Tara B. Voskamp, Bryan, Texas

    1   pound skinned, boned chicken
        breast, cut into ½-inch strips
    1   tablespoon Cajun seasoning
  Cooking spray
    1   cup chopped green bell pepper
    1   cup chopped red bell pepper
    1   cup sliced mushrooms
    ½   cup sliced green onions
    4   cups hot cooked linguine (about
        8 ounces uncooked pasta)
    2   cups evaporated fat-free milk
    ¼   cup (1 ounce) grated fresh
        Parmesan cheese
    ½   teaspoon no-salt-added lemon
        pepper seasoning
    ½   teaspoon dried basil
    ¼   teaspoon salt
    ¼   teaspoon garlic powder
    ¼   teaspoon black pepper

**1.** Combine chicken and Cajun seasoning in a large zip-top plastic bag; seal and shake to coat. Heat a large nonstick skillet coated with cooking spray over medium heat. Add chicken mixture; sauté 7 minutes or until lightly browned. Add bell peppers, mushrooms, and onions; cook 3 minutes. Stir in pasta and remaining ingredients; bring to a boil. Cook 1 minute, stirring constantly. Serve immediately. Yield: 4 servings (serving size: 2 cups).

CALORIES 493 (9% from fat); FAT 5g (sat 1.9g, mono 1.1g, poly 1.1g); PROTEIN 46.9g; CARB 63.3g; FIBER 3.2g; CHOL 76mg; IRON 4.9mg; SODIUM 835mg; CALC 497mg

## Linguine with Clams and Artichokes in Red Sauce

"If you're entertaining, this is the perfect meal. It's fast, easy, and impressive."

—Rachael Rome, Dallas, Texas

    2   tablespoons olive oil
    2   tablespoons diced shallots
    2   garlic cloves, minced
    ⅓   cup dry white wine
    ¼   teaspoon black pepper
    1   (26-ounce) jar tomato-basil pasta
        sauce
    1   (14-ounce) can quartered
        artichoke hearts, drained
    1   (10-ounce) can baby clams,
        undrained
    2   tablespoons chopped fresh or
        2 teaspoons dried basil
    2   tablespoons finely chopped
        fresh parsley
    4   cups hot cooked linguine (about
        8 ounces uncooked pasta)

**1.** Heat oil in a large saucepan over medium-high heat. Add shallots and garlic, and sauté 2 minutes or until tender. Add wine and next 4 ingredients; reduce heat, and simmer 5 minutes. Stir in basil and parsley. Serve sauce over pasta. Yield: 4 servings (serving size: 1 cup sauce and 1 cup pasta).

CALORIES 434 (19% from fat); FAT 9.2g (sat 1.3g, mono 5.4g, poly 1.6g); PROTEIN 12.9g; CARB 65.6g; FIBER 6g; CHOL 31mg; IRON 6.4mg; SODIUM 957mg; CALC 297mg

## 30 minutes or less

# Uncannily Good Dinners

*Whip out your can opener for quick-and-easy weeknight meals.*

Don't think you're missing out just because dinner comes easy. You can create an almost endless variety of dishes with canned foods, given that there are more than 1,500 varieties. And they don't fall short on the nutrition front.

## Tuscan Chicken Stew

PREPARATION TIME: 12 MINUTES
COOKING TIME: 18 MINUTES

    ½   teaspoon dried rosemary, crushed
    ½   teaspoon salt
    ¼   teaspoon black pepper
    1   pound skinned, boned chicken
        breast, cut into (1-inch) pieces
    2   teaspoons olive oil
    2   teaspoons bottled minced garlic
    ½   cup fat-free, less-sodium chicken
        broth
    1   (15.5-ounce) can cannellini beans
        or other white beans, rinsed and
        drained
    1   (7-ounce) bottle roasted red bell
        peppers, drained and cut into
        ½-inch pieces
  3½   cups torn spinach

**1.** Combine first 4 ingredients; toss well. Heat oil in a nonstick skillet over medium-high heat. Add chicken; sauté 3 minutes. Add garlic; sauté 1 minute. Add broth, beans, and peppers; bring to a boil. Reduce heat; simmer 10 minutes or until chicken is done. Stir in spinach; simmer 1 minute. Yield: 4 servings (serving size: 1 cup).

CALORIES 290 (18% from fat); FAT 5.9g (sat 0.9g, mono 2.4g, poly 1.4g); PROTEIN 34.8g; CARB 25.1g; FIBER 5.1g; CHOL 66mg; IRON 4.5mg; SODIUM 612mg; CALC 110mg

## Red Potato-and-Salmon Chowder

PREPARATION TIME: 10 MINUTES
COOKING TIME: 20 MINUTES

    1   (14.5-ounce) can red salmon
    2   cups diced red potatoes
    2   bacon slices
    2   cups diced onion
    1   cup diced celery
    ½   teaspoon salt, divided
    ½   teaspoon bottled minced garlic
    1   tablespoon all-purpose flour
    3   cups 1% low-fat milk
    2   tablespoons chopped fresh chives
    2   tablespoons lemon juice
    ¼   teaspoon black pepper

*Continued*

1. Remove bones and skin from salmon.
2. Place potato in a saucepan. Cover with water; bring to a boil. Reduce heat. Simmer 12 minutes or until tender; drain.
3. While potato is cooking, sauté bacon in a large saucepan over medium heat until crisp. Remove bacon from saucepan; crumble. Add onion, celery, ¼ teaspoon salt, and garlic to bacon drippings in pan; sauté 4 minutes. Stir in flour; cook 30 seconds. Gradually stir in milk, and cook 3 minutes or until mixture begins to thicken. Stir in salmon, potato, bacon, ¼ teaspoon salt, chives, juice, and pepper; cook 3 minutes or until thoroughly heated. Yield: 5 servings (serving size: 1⅓ cups).

CALORIES 299 (36% from fat); FAT 11.8g (sat 4g, mono 4.7g, poly 2.3g); PROTEIN 21.5g; CARB 26.6g; FIBER 2.7g; CHOL 41mg; IRON 1.7mg; SODIUM 450mg; CALC 371mg

## Curried Chicken with Couscous

PREPARATION TIME: 8 MINUTES
COOKING TIME: 20 MINUTES

  1  cup water
  1  (14-ounce) can light coconut milk, divided
  1  teaspoon salt, divided
  1  cup uncooked couscous
  1  tablespoon all-purpose flour
  1  tablespoon curry powder
  1  pound skinned, boned chicken breast, cut into ½-inch strips
  2  teaspoons vegetable oil
  1  cup julienne-cut carrot
  ⅓  cup raisins
  ¼  cup chopped fresh cilantro

1. Combine water, ¾ cup coconut milk, and ½ teaspoon salt in a medium saucepan. Bring to a boil; gradually stir in couscous. Remove from heat; cover and let stand 5 minutes. Fluff with a fork.
2. Combine ½ teaspoon salt, flour, and curry powder. Add chicken, and toss gently to coat. Heat oil in a large non-stick skillet over medium-high heat. Add chicken, and stir-fry 5 minutes. Stir in remaining coconut milk, carrot, and

raisins; reduce heat, and simmer 7 minutes or until chicken is done, stirring occasionally. Serve over couscous. Sprinkle with cilantro. Yield: 4 servings (serving size: ¾ cup chicken mixture, ¾ cup couscous, and 1 tablespoon cilantro).

CALORIES 396 (22% from fat); FAT 9.6g (sat 5.6g, mono 1.3g, poly 1.6g); PROTEIN 32g; CARB 45.2g; FIBER 3.4g; CHOL 66mg; IRON 3.4mg; SODIUM 716mg; CALC 39mg

## Hominy Chili with Beans

Hominy is made of dried corn kernels from which the hulls and germs have been removed. You can find it in the canned-vegetable section of the supermarket near the corn.

PREPARATION TIME: 5 MINUTES
COOKING TIME: 18 MINUTES

  2  teaspoons vegetable oil
  2  teaspoons bottled minced garlic
  4  teaspoons chili powder
  1  teaspoon ground cumin
  1  (15.5-ounce) can white hominy, drained
  1  (15-ounce) can red beans, drained
  1  (14.5-ounce) can no-salt-added diced tomatoes, undrained
  1  (14.5-ounce) can no-salt-added stewed tomatoes, undrained and chopped
  ¼  cup low-fat sour cream
  ¼  cup (1 ounce) shredded reduced-fat sharp Cheddar cheese
  4  teaspoons minced fresh cilantro

1. Heat oil in a large saucepan over medium heat. Add garlic; sauté 1 minute. Stir in chili powder and next 5 ingredients; bring to a boil. Reduce heat; simmer, uncovered, 15 minutes. Spoon 1¼ cups chili into each of 4 bowls; top each serving with 1 tablespoon sour cream, 1 tablespoon cheese, and 1 teaspoon cilantro. Yield: 4 servings.
NOTE: If hominy is not available, you can substitute 1 (11-ounce) can vacuum-packed white corn or 1 (15.25-ounce) can whole-kernel corn, drained. Hominy imparts a distinctive flavor

remarkably different from that of corn, so if you use corn, know that the dish will be more like a basic chili with beans.

CALORIES 271 (23% from fat); FAT 6.8g (sat 2.6g, mono 2g, poly 1.8g); PROTEIN 11.7g; CARB 42.9g; FIBER 5.5g; CHOL 10mg; IRON 4.1mg; SODIUM 452mg; CALC 202mg

## Greek Shrimp and Spinach with Penne

PREPARATION TIME: 20 MINUTES
COOKING TIME: 8 MINUTES

  2  teaspoons olive oil, divided
     Cooking spray
  8  cups chopped spinach (about 10 ounces)
  1½  teaspoons bottled minced garlic
  1  pound large shrimp, peeled and deveined
  2  teaspoons lemon juice
  ½  teaspoon dried oregano
  ¼  teaspoon black pepper
  2  (14.5-ounce) cans diced tomatoes, undrained
  4  cups hot cooked penne (about 8 ounces uncooked tube-shaped pasta)
  ½  cup (2 ounces) crumbled feta cheese

1. Heat 1 teaspoon oil in a large nonstick skillet coated with cooking spray over medium-high heat. Add spinach; cook 2 minutes or just until spinach wilts. Spoon spinach mixture into a large bowl, and set aside. Add 1 teaspoon oil, garlic, and shrimp to pan; sauté 3 minutes. Stir in lemon juice, oregano, pepper, and tomatoes; cook 2 minutes or until thoroughly heated. Add shrimp mixture to spinach, and toss well. Serve over pasta, and sprinkle with cheese. Yield: 4 servings (serving size: 1¼ cups shrimp mixture, 1 cup pasta, and 2 tablespoons cheese).

CALORIES 421 (18% from fat); FAT 8.5g (sat 3g, mono 2.8g, poly 1.6g); PROTEIN 30.7g; CARB 56.1g; FIBER 5.7g; CHOL 142mg; IRON 7.7mg; SODIUM 680mg; CALC 256mg

## Pork-and-Pineapple Stir-Fry

PREPARATION TIME: 15 MINUTES
COOKING TIME: 15 MINUTES

1 cup beef broth
¼ cup tomato paste
1 tablespoon low-sodium soy sauce
2 teaspoons cornstarch
2 teaspoons brown sugar
2 teaspoons curry powder
¼ teaspoon chili powder
2 teaspoons vegetable oil, divided
Cooking spray
1 pound pork tenderloin, cut into short thin strips
1 cup sliced onion
1 cup sliced green bell pepper
2 teaspoons minced peeled fresh ginger
1½ teaspoons bottled minced garlic
1 (15¼-ounce) can light pineapple chunks, drained
4 cups hot cooked instant rice

1. Combine first 7 ingredients; set aside.
2. Heat 1 teaspoon oil in a large non-stick skillet coated with cooking spray over medium-high heat. Add pork, and stir-fry 4 minutes. Remove pork from pan, and set aside.
3. Heat 1 teaspoon oil in pan; add onion and bell pepper, and stir-fry 5 minutes or until vegetables are tender. Add ginger and garlic; cook 30 seconds. Return pork to pan; add broth mixture and pineapple. Stir-fry 3 minutes or until thoroughly heated. Serve over rice. Yield: 4 servings (serving size: 1 cup stir-fry and 1 cup rice).

CALORIES 417 (13% from fat); FAT 5.9g (sat 1.5g, mono 2.1g, poly 1.7g); PROTEIN 32.1g; CARB 57.8g; FIBER 3g; CHOL 74mg; IRON 5.4mg; SODIUM 515mg; CALC 56mg

## tastes of america

# The Maple Advantage

*Sure, maple syrup is great on pancakes. But invite it over for dinner tonight and watch it really shine.*

## Maple Chicken with Figs and Prunes

¼ cup dry vermouth or white wine
3 tablespoons maple syrup
3 tablespoons red wine vinegar
1 tablespoon capers
1 teaspoon fennel seeds
1 teaspoon dried oregano
¼ teaspoon salt
⅛ teaspoon black pepper
8 bite-size pitted prunes
8 dried Calimyrna figs
1 bay leaf
1 garlic clove, minced
4 (4-ounce) skinned, boned chicken breast halves
⅓ cup fat-free, less-sodium chicken broth
2 tablespoons chopped fresh parsley

1. Combine first 12 ingredients in a large zip-top plastic bag. Add chicken; seal bag, and marinate in refrigerator 2 hours, turning bag occasionally.
2. Preheat oven to 350°.
3. Arrange chicken mixture in a single layer in an 11 x 7-inch baking dish. Pour broth over chicken; cover with foil. Bake at 350° for 25 minutes. Uncover and increase oven temperature to 400° (do not remove from oven). Bake an additional 10 minutes or until done. Discard bay leaf. Sprinkle with parsley. Yield: 4 servings (serving size: 1 chicken breast half, 2 figs, 2 prunes, and ¼ cup sauce).

CALORIES 308 (6% from fat); FAT 2.1g (sat 0.5g, mono 0.6g, poly 0.6g); PROTEIN 28.3g; CARB 46.5g; FIBER 6g; CHOL 66mg; IRON 2.7mg; SODIUM 324mg; CALC 102mg

## Maple-Glazed Salmon

2 tablespoons maple syrup
1½ tablespoons apple juice
1½ tablespoons fresh lemon juice
2 teaspoons hoisin sauce
1½ teaspoons grated peeled fresh ginger
1½ teaspoons country-style Dijon mustard
¼ teaspoon five-spice powder
4 (6-ounce) salmon fillets (about 1 inch thick)
Cooking spray

1. Preheat broiler.
2. Combine first 7 ingredients in a large zip-top plastic bag. Add salmon to bag; seal. Marinate in refrigerator 15 minutes.
3. Remove salmon from bag, reserving marinade. Place salmon fillets, skin sides down, on a broiler rack coated with cooking spray. Broil 12 minutes or until fish flakes easily when tested with a fork, basting salmon with reserved marinade. Yield: 4 servings (serving size: 1 fillet).

CALORIES 316 (41% from fat); FAT 14.4g (sat 2.5g, mono 6.9g, poly 3.2g); PROTEIN 35g; CARB 9.3g; FIBER 0.1g; CHOL 111mg; IRON 0.9mg; SODIUM 184mg; CALC 18mg

## Prosciutto-Wrapped Shrimp with Lemon Couscous

3 tablespoons maple syrup
2 tablespoons bourbon
1 tablespoon teriyaki sauce
2 teaspoons Dijon mustard
½ teaspoon chili powder
24 jumbo shrimp (about 1½ pounds)
6 very thin slices prosciutto or ham (about 3½ ounces)
Cooking spray
Lemon Couscous

1. Preheat broiler.
2. Combine first 5 ingredients in a bowl, and stir with a whisk. Peel shrimp, leaving tails intact. Add shrimp to maple mixture, tossing to coat. Remove shrimp from bowl, and discard marinade. Cut each prosciutto slice lengthwise into 4 strips. Wrap 1 prosciutto strip around each shrimp. Thread shrimp onto 4

*Continued*

(8-inch) skewers. Place skewers on a broiler pan coated with cooking spray, and broil 3 minutes on each side or until done. Serve shrimp over Lemon Couscous. Yield: 4 servings (serving size: 6 shrimp and ½ cup couscous).

(Totals include Lemon Couscous) CALORIES 305 (12% from fat); FAT 4.2g (sat 1.2g, mono 1.4g, poly 0.9g); PROTEIN 36.1g; CARB 27.2g; FIBER 1.4g; CHOL 263mg; IRON 5.2mg; SODIUM 927mg; CALC 67mg

**LEMON COUSCOUS:**

1¼ cups water
¾ cup uncooked couscous
¼ cup sliced green onions
2 tablespoons finely chopped fresh parsley
2 tablespoons orange juice
1 teaspoon grated lemon rind
1 tablespoon fresh lemon juice
¼ teaspoon salt
⅛ teaspoon black pepper

**1.** Bring water to a boil in a medium saucepan; gradually stir in couscous. Remove from heat; cover and let stand 5 minutes. Fluff with a fork. Stir in onions and remaining ingredients. Yield: 4 servings (serving size: ½ cup).

CALORIES 102 (3% from fat); FAT 0.3g (sat 0g, mono 0g, poly 0g); PROTEIN 3.7g; CARB 21.8g; FIBER 1.3g; CHOL 0mg; IRON 0.8mg; SODIUM 151mg; CALC 9mg

## Pork Tenderloin with Maple Pan Juices

⅓ cup diced onion
¼ cup fresh orange juice, divided
¼ cup maple syrup, divided
2 tablespoons sake (rice wine)
2 tablespoons low-sodium soy sauce
⅛ teaspoon black pepper
2 garlic cloves, minced
1 (1-pound) pork tenderloin
Cooking spray
⅓ cup fat-free, less-sodium chicken broth

**1.** Combine onion, 2 tablespoons juice, 2 tablespoons syrup, sake, soy sauce, pepper, and garlic in a large zip-top plastic bag. Trim fat from pork. Add pork to bag; seal and marinate in refrigerator 2 hours.

**2.** Preheat oven to 400°.
**3.** Heat a 9-inch heavy ovenproof skillet coated with cooking spray over medium-high heat. Remove pork from bag, reserving marinade. Add pork to pan; cook 5 minutes, browning on all sides. Insert meat thermometer into thickest part of pork. Place pan in oven; bake at 400° for 30 minutes or until meat thermometer registers 160° (slightly pink). Remove pork from pan. Set aside, and keep warm.
**4.** Combine 2 tablespoons juice, 2 tablespoons syrup, reserved marinade, and broth in a small bowl. Add syrup mixture to pan, and place over medium-high heat, scraping pan to loosen browned bits. Bring to a boil; reduce heat, and simmer 5 minutes or until slightly thick. Serve sauce with pork. Yield: 4 servings (serving size: 3 ounces pork and 2 tablespoons sauce).

CALORIES 204 (13% from fat); FAT 3g (sat 1g, mono 1.3g, poly 0.4g); PROTEIN 24.4g; CARB 16.9g; FIBER 0.3g; CHOL 74mg; IRON 1.8mg; SODIUM 293mg; CALC 29mg

## Maple Pork-and-Vegetable Stew

1 tablespoon olive oil
1 (1½-pound) boned pork loin roast, cut into 1-inch cubes
2 cups diced onion
1 (8-ounce) package mushrooms, quartered
1¾ cups (⅛-inch) diagonally sliced carrot
¾ cup diced red bell pepper
2 tablespoons maple syrup
1 teaspoon dried rubbed sage
¼ teaspoon salt
¼ teaspoon black pepper
1 (16-ounce) can fat-free, less-sodium chicken broth
1 (12-ounce) bottle beer
2 tablespoons cornstarch
1 tablespoon red wine vinegar
1 tablespoon country-style Dijon mustard
8 cups hot cooked brown rice
Sage sprigs (optional)

**1.** Heat oil in a large Dutch oven over medium-high heat. Add half of pork; sauté 5 minutes or until browned. Remove from pan. Add remaining pork; sauté 5 minutes or until browned. Remove from pan. Add onion and mushrooms to pan; sauté 4 minutes. Return pork to pan; add carrot and next 7 ingredients. Bring to a boil; reduce heat, and simmer 1 hour or until pork is tender.
**2.** Combine cornstarch, vinegar, and mustard in a small bowl, and stir with a whisk. Add to pork mixture, and bring to a boil. Cook 3 minutes, stirring frequently. Serve with rice. Garnish with sage sprigs, if desired. Yield: 8 servings (serving size: 1 cup stew and 1 cup rice).

CALORIES 436 (21% from fat); FAT 10.3g (sat 2.9g, mono 4.9g, poly 1.6g); PROTEIN 24.9g; CARB 60.2g; FIBER 5.5g; CHOL 51mg; IRON 2.4mg; SODIUM 328mg; CALC 50mg

## Butternut Soup with Pears and Apples

1 tablespoon butter or stick margarine
1 cup chopped onion
¾ cup chopped celery
4 cups cubed peeled butternut squash (about 1¼ pounds)
1¾ cups water
1 cup chopped peeled Braeburn or other cooking apple
1 cup chopped peeled Anjou pear
½ cup apple juice
¼ teaspoon salt
⅛ teaspoon black pepper
1 (14½-ounce) can vegetable broth
1 bay leaf
3 tablespoons maple syrup

**1.** Melt butter in a Dutch oven over medium-high heat. Add onion and celery; sauté 4 minutes or until tender. Add squash and next 8 ingredients, and bring to a boil. Partially cover, reduce heat, and simmer 30 minutes or until tender. Discard bay leaf. Place half of squash mixture in a blender or food processor, and process until smooth. Pour pureed mixture into a bowl. Repeat procedure with remaining squash mixture. Return pureed mixture to pan, and stir in syrup. Cook over medium heat 5 minutes or until thoroughly heated. Yield: 7 servings (serving size: 1 cup).

CALORIES 117 (17% from fat); FAT 2.2g (sat 1.1g, mono 0.5g, poly 0.2g); PROTEIN 1.2g; CARB 25.5g; FIBER 2.3g; CHOL 4mg; IRON 0.8mg; SODIUM 402mg; CALC 48mg

# Green Light

*Mother Nature may have put on the brakes for many crops in this coldest of seasons, but it's full speed ahead for her nutritious and flavor-packed winter green vegetables.*

## Down-Home Chicken Stew

2 cups diced peeled baking potato, divided
1 cup diced peeled turnip (about 6 ounces)
2 (16-ounce) cans fat-free, less-sodium chicken broth, divided
3 tablespoons 2% reduced-fat milk
1 teaspoon butter or stick margarine
2 cups thinly sliced leek (about 2 large)
1 teaspoon dried thyme
4 garlic cloves, minced
1 cup sliced carrot
4 cups torn turnip greens
¾ pound skinned, boned chicken breast, cut into ½-inch pieces
1 teaspoon white vinegar
½ teaspoon hot pepper sauce
¼ teaspoon salt
⅛ teaspoon black pepper

**1.** Combine 1 cup potato, turnip, and 1 can broth in a small saucepan, and bring to a boil. Reduce heat; simmer 8 minutes or until tender. Combine potato mixture and milk in a blender or food processor; process until smooth.
**2.** Heat butter in a large, heavy saucepan over medium-low heat. Add leek, thyme, and garlic; sauté 12 minutes or until leek is tender. Add 1 cup potato, 1 can broth, and carrot. Cover and simmer 8 minutes. Stir in greens and chicken. Cover and simmer 12 minutes or until chicken is done. Stir in potato puree, vinegar, pepper sauce, salt, and pepper; simmer, uncovered, 6 minutes. Yield: 5 servings (serving size: 1½ cups).

CALORIES 208 (10% from fat); FAT 2.2g (sat 0.6g, mono 0.7g, poly 0.6g); PROTEIN 21.5g; CARB 25.3g; FIBER 3.8g; CHOL 40mg; IRON 2.9mg; SODIUM 618mg; CALC 155mg

## Cavatappi with Kale and Fava Beans

1 tablespoon olive oil
3 large garlic cloves, minced
1 cup fat-free, less-sodium chicken broth
¼ teaspoon salt
⅛ teaspoon black pepper
⅛ teaspoon crushed red pepper
28 cups torn fresh kale (about 1½ pounds)
6 cups hot cooked cavatappi (about 4 cups uncooked spiral-shaped pasta)
1 (19-ounce) can fava or kidney beans, drained
¾ cup (3 ounces) finely grated fresh Parmesan cheese

**1.** Heat oil in a large saucepan over medium-high heat. Add garlic; sauté 1 minute. Add broth, salt, and peppers; cook 2 minutes. Reduce heat to medium-low. Stir in kale, cavatappi, and beans; cook 2 minutes or until heated. Spoon into shallow bowls; top with cheese. Yield: 6 servings (serving size: 1½ cups pasta mixture and 2 tablespoons cheese).

CALORIES 359 (15% from fat); FAT 5.9g (sat 1.7g, mono 2.4g, poly 1.1g); PROTEIN 18.2g; CARB 60.6g; FIBER 5g; CHOL 5mg; IRON 5.3mg; SODIUM 465mg; CALC 267mg

## Wilted Beet Green-and-Escarole Salad with Pears

1 large beet
½ cup water
4 cups torn escarole
2 cups chopped beet greens
Cooking spray
1 cup chopped onion
¼ cup cranberry juice cocktail
3 tablespoons chopped sweetened dried cranberries (such as Craisins)
2 tablespoons red wine vinegar
1 teaspoon olive oil
3 cups thinly sliced pear (about 3 pears)
¼ cup (1 ounce) crumbled blue cheese

**1.** Preheat oven to 375°.
**2.** Scrub beet with a brush. Place beet in an 8-inch baking dish; add water to dish. Cover and bake at 375° for 45 minutes or until tender. Drain; cool slightly. Peel and cut into strips.
**3.** Combine escarole and beet greens in a large bowl. Place a small saucepan coated with cooking spray over medium heat. Add onion, and cook 5 minutes, stirring occasionally. Add cranberry juice, cranberries, vinegar, and oil; bring to a boil. Immediately pour mixture over salad. Cover for 5 minutes or until greens wilt. Add beet strips and pear, and toss gently to coat. Sprinkle salad with cheese. Serve immediately. Yield: 4 servings (serving size: 2 cups).

CALORIES 178 (20% from fat); FAT 4g (sat 1.6g, mono 1.5g, poly 0.4g); PROTEIN 4.8g; CARB 34.2g; FIBER 4.6g; CHOL 5mg; IRON 2.1mg; SODIUM 212mg; CALC 120mg

## Collard Greens with Lima Beans and Smoked Turkey

This one-pot meal can be made up to three days ahead and refrigerated.

1½ cups dried baby lima beans
1 tablespoon olive oil
2 cups vertically sliced red onion
3 cups fat-free, less-sodium chicken broth
1 cup diced smoked turkey breast (about 6 ounces)
½ teaspoon dried thyme
¼ teaspoon crushed red pepper
3 garlic cloves, minced
1 bay leaf
8 cups sliced collard greens (about ½ pound)
2 tablespoons red wine vinegar
1 (14.5-ounce) can diced tomatoes, undrained
¼ teaspoon salt
¼ teaspoon black pepper
Thyme sprigs (optional)

**1.** Sort and wash beans; place in an ovenproof Dutch oven. Cover with water to 2 inches above beans; bring to a
*Continued*

boil, and cook 20 minutes. Remove from heat; drain beans.

**2.** Preheat oven to 375°.

**3.** Heat oil in pan over medium-low heat. Add onion; sauté 10 minutes. Add beans, broth, and next 5 ingredients; bring to a boil. Cover and bake at 375° for 1 hour and 15 minutes. Stir in sliced collards, vinegar, and tomatoes. Cover and bake an additional 1 hour or until beans are tender, stirring occasionally. Stir in salt and pepper. Discard bay leaf. Garnish with thyme sprigs, if desired. Yield: 7 servings (serving size: 1 cup).

CALORIES 230 (13% from fat); FAT 3.3g (sat 0.7g, mono 1.7g, poly 0.7g); PROTEIN 17.4g; CARB 34.5g; FIBER 18.3g; CHOL 14mg; IRON 3.5mg; SODIUM 604mg; CALC 216mg

### Halibut Wrapped in Greens

The large turnip leaves are used as a wrapping for the fish; the turnip root is used for the sauce.

⅓  cup minced shallots
3  garlic cloves, minced
6  (6-ounce) halibut fillets or other lean white fish fillets
1  cup fat-free, less-sodium chicken broth
½  cup bottled clam juice
½  cup (¼-inch) cubed peeled turnips
⅓  cup dry white wine
1  tablespoon Dijon mustard
1½  teaspoons cornstarch
12  large turnip leaves
¼  teaspoon salt
⅛  teaspoon black pepper
Lemon slices (optional)

**1.** Combine shallots and garlic. Rub 1 teaspoon shallot mixture over each fillet; cover and chill. Place remaining shallot mixture, broth, clam juice, turnips, and wine in a small saucepan. Bring to a boil; cook until reduced to 1¼ cups (about 10 minutes). Stir in mustard and cornstarch; bring to a boil. Reduce heat; cook 1 minute or until thick. Keep warm.

**2.** Steam turnip leaves, covered, 30 seconds or until wilted. Rinse turnip leaves with cold water; drain well. Pat dry with paper towels. Remove stems; discard. Sprinkle fillets with salt and pepper. Place 1 fillet in center of 2 turnip leaves. Fold in 4 sides of leaves to cover fillet, forming a packet. Repeat procedure with remaining fillets and leaves. Steam packets, seam sides down, covered, 7 minutes or until fish is done. Drizzle sauce evenly over packets. Garnish with lemon slices, if desired. Yield: 6 servings (serving size: 1 packet and about 3 tablespoons sauce).

CALORIES 214 (18% from fat); FAT 4.2g (sat 0.6g, mono 1.1g, poly 1.5g); PROTEIN 36.8g; CARB 4.7g; FIBER 0.7g; CHOL 80mg; IRON 1.9mg; SODIUM 400mg; CALC 104mg

### Creamy Polenta and Sauté of Mixed Greens

1  ounce sun-dried tomatoes, packed without oil (about 8)
½  cup boiling water
1  cup yellow cornmeal
¼  teaspoon black pepper, divided
2  (16-ounce) cans fat-free, less-sodium chicken broth, divided
1  cup water
Olive oil-flavored cooking spray
2  cups vertically sliced onion
1  cup red bell pepper strips
4  garlic cloves, minced
5  cups torn mixed dark greens (such as beet, collard, mustard, turnip, and kale)
¼  cup (1 ounce) grated fresh Parmesan cheese

**1.** Combine tomatoes and boiling water; let stand 30 minutes. Drain and slice.

**2.** Combine cornmeal and ⅛ teaspoon black pepper in a large saucepan. Gradually add 3 cups broth and 1 cup water, stirring constantly with a whisk. Bring to a boil; reduce heat to medium, and cook 20 minutes, stirring frequently. Remove polenta from heat; keep warm.

**3.** Place a large nonstick skillet coated with cooking spray over medium heat until hot. Add onion and bell pepper; sauté 10 minutes or until tender. Add tomatoes and garlic; sauté 1 minute. Stir in 1 cup broth and greens; bring to a boil. Cover, reduce heat, and simmer 15 minutes or until greens are tender. Stir in ⅛ teaspoon black pepper. Spoon polenta evenly onto 4 plates, and top evenly with greens mixture. Sprinkle with cheese. Yield: 4 servings (serving size: 1 cup polenta, ¾ cup greens, and 1 tablespoon cheese).

CALORIES 245 (12% from fat); FAT 3.2g (sat 1.4g, mono 0.7g, poly 0.5g); PROTEIN 11.6g; CARB 43g; FIBER 5.9g; CHOL 5mg; IRON 3.4mg; SODIUM 774mg; CALC 243mg

### Pork, Kale, and Bok Choy Stir-Fry

1  (¾-pound) pork tenderloin
3  tablespoons low-sodium soy sauce, divided
2  tablespoons minced garlic, divided
2  teaspoons minced peeled fresh ginger, divided
½  cup fat-free, less-sodium chicken broth
3  tablespoons hoisin sauce
1  teaspoon cornstarch
1  tablespoon vegetable oil
¼  teaspoon crushed red pepper
2  cups sliced shiitake mushroom caps
1½  cups sliced green onions
4  cups sliced kale
4  cups sliced bok choy
5  cups hot cooked rice

**1.** Trim fat from pork; cut pork into 2 x ¼-inch strips. Combine pork, 2 tablespoons soy sauce, 2 teaspoons garlic, and 1 teaspoon ginger in a shallow bowl. Cover and marinate in refrigerator 2 hours.

**2.** Combine 1 tablespoon soy sauce, 2 teaspoons garlic, 1 teaspoon ginger, broth, hoisin sauce, and cornstarch in a small bowl; stir with a whisk. Heat oil in a large nonstick skillet over medium-high heat. Add 2 teaspoons garlic and crushed red pepper; stir-fry 30 seconds. Add mushrooms and onions; stir-fry 3 minutes. Add pork mixture and kale; stir-fry 3 minutes. Add broth mixture and bok choy; bring to a boil. Cook 1 minute or until mixture is thick. Serve over rice. Yield: 5 servings (serving size: 1 cup stir-fry and 1 cup rice).

CALORIES 407 (13% from fat); FAT 5.8g (sat 1.2g, mono 1.9g, poly 1.9g); PROTEIN 23.4g; CARB 66.1g; FIBER 3.6g; CHOL 44mg; IRON 5.2mg; SODIUM 543mg; CALC 189mg

# Express Package

## When great flavor absolutely positively has to be there, it's in the bag.

Old French chefs had two words for it: *en papillote*—in a paper bag. This wasn't a reference to where unsuccessful creations wound up; rather, it indicated a remarkably simple method that cooked foods in their own juices. While the traditional paper bag was actually parchment, the new, aluminum-foil packages or bags are bringing the joys of cooking *en papillote* back into the mainstream.

### Basil Shrimp with Feta and Orzo

    1  regular-size foil oven bag
    Cooking spray
    ½  cup uncooked orzo (rice-shaped pasta)
    2  teaspoons olive oil, divided
    1  cup diced tomato
    ¾  cup sliced green onions
    ½  cup (2 ounces) crumbled feta cheese
    ½  teaspoon grated lemon rind
    1  tablespoon fresh lemon juice
    ¼  teaspoon salt
    ¼  teaspoon black pepper
    ¾  pound large shrimp, peeled and deveined
    ¼  cup chopped fresh basil

**1.** Preheat oven to 450°.
**2.** Coat inside of oven bag with cooking spray. Place bag on a large shallow baking pan.
**3.** Cook pasta in boiling water 5 minutes, omitting salt and fat; drain. Place pasta in a large bowl. Stir in 1 teaspoon oil and next 7 ingredients. Place orzo mixture in prepared oven bag. Combine shrimp and basil. Arrange shrimp mixture on orzo mixture. Fold edge of bag over to seal. Bake at 450° for 25 minutes or until shrimp are done. Place bag on a platter. Cut open bag with a sharp knife, and peel back foil. Drizzle with 1 teaspoon oil. Yield: 2 servings (serving size: 1 cup orzo and about 5 ounces shrimp).

CALORIES 498 (26% from fat); FAT 14.4g (sat 5.5g, mono 5.1g, poly 1.9g); PROTEIN 38.8g; CARB 52.7g; FIBER 3.4g; CHOL 219mg; IRON 6.5mg; SODIUM 817mg; CALC 258mg

### Sicilian Tuna Steaks with Couscous

    1  regular-size foil oven bag
    Cooking spray
    ¼  cup fat-free, less-sodium chicken broth
    2  tablespoons chopped fresh parsley
    2  tablespoons chopped pitted green olives
    1  tablespoon raisins
    1  tablespoon capers
    2  tablespoons dry white wine
    1  tablespoon balsamic vinegar
    1  teaspoon sugar
    2  teaspoons olive oil
    ¼  teaspoon salt
    ⅛  teaspoon black pepper
    1  (14½-ounce) can Italian-style stewed tomatoes, undrained
    ½  cup uncooked couscous
    2  (5-ounce) tuna steaks (about ¾ inch thick)
    1  tablespoon pine nuts, toasted
    1  tablespoon chopped fresh parsley

**1.** Preheat oven to 450°.
**2.** Coat inside of oven bag with cooking spray. Place bag on a large shallow baking pan.
**3.** Combine broth and next 11 ingredients in a large bowl, and stir in couscous. Place couscous mixture in prepared oven bag. Place tuna on couscous mixture. Fold edge of bag over to seal. Bake at 450° for 20 minutes or until fish is medium-rare or desired degree of doneness. Place bag on a platter. Cut open bag with a sharp knife, and peel back foil. Sprinkle with toasted pine nuts and 1 tablespoon parsley. Yield: 2 servings (serving size: 1 tuna steak and 1 cup couscous).

CALORIES 492 (29% from fat); FAT 15.7g (sat 3.1g, mono 6.7g, poly 4.2g); PROTEIN 41.7g; CARB 47g; FIBER 3.3g; CHOL 54mg; IRON 4.5mg; SODIUM 834mg; CALC 87mg

### Paella Pouch

    1  large foil oven bag
    Cooking spray
    3  cups uncooked instant rice
    1  cup (½-inch) cut green beans
    ¾  cup chopped green bell pepper
    ¾  cup sliced green onions
    ¾  cup sliced bottled roasted red bell peppers
    ½  cup diced turkey kielbasa
    ½  cup water
    ¼  cup dry sherry
    1  tablespoon olive oil
    ¾  teaspoon salt
    ½  teaspoon ground turmeric
    ½  teaspoon dried thyme
    2  garlic cloves, minced
    1  (14.5-ounce) can diced tomatoes, undrained
    1  (14-ounce) can quartered artichoke hearts, drained
    1  (6½-ounce) can chopped clams, undrained
    1  pound medium shrimp, peeled and deveined
    1  pound sea scallops
    1  tablespoon olive oil
    3  tablespoons chopped fresh parsley

**1.** Preheat oven to 450°.
**2.** Coat inside of oven bag with cooking spray. Place bag on a large shallow baking pan.
**3.** Combine rice and next 15 ingredients in a large bowl. Add shrimp and scallops, and stir gently. Place mixture in prepared oven bag. Fold edge of bag over to seal. Bake at 450° for 40 minutes or until rice is cooked. Place bag on a platter. Cut open bag with a sharp knife, and peel back foil. Let stand 5 minutes. Drizzle with 1 tablespoon oil, and sprinkle with chopped parsley. Yield: 6 servings (serving size: 2 cups).

CALORIES 449 (17% from fat); FAT 8.3g (sat 1.4g, mono 4.2g, poly 1.6g); PROTEIN 35.5g; CARB 57.4g; FIBER 2.6g; CHOL 129mg; IRON 8.5mg; SODIUM 985mg; CALC 144mg

## Asian Meatballs with Mushrooms and Rice Noodles

(pictured on page 60)

1 regular-size foil oven bag
Cooking spray
½ pound ground turkey breast
¼ cup finely diced mushrooms
2 tablespoons thinly sliced green onions
1 tablespoon cornstarch, divided
1 tablespoon low-sodium soy sauce, divided
1 teaspoon dark sesame oil
4 cups hot water
4 ounces uncooked rice sticks (rice-flour noodles) or cooked vermicelli
¼ cup fat-free, less-sodium chicken broth
2 tablespoons dry sherry
1 tablespoon fresh lime juice
1½ cups sliced mushrooms
2 teaspoons minced peeled fresh ginger
1¼ teaspoons curry powder
1 garlic clove, minced
Cilantro sprigs

**1.** Preheat oven to 450°.
**2.** Coat inside of oven bag with cooking spray. Place bag on a large shallow baking pan.
**3.** Combine ground turkey, diced mushrooms, onions, 2 teaspoons cornstarch, 1 teaspoon soy sauce, and sesame oil in a bowl, and shape into 16 (1-inch) meatballs. Place meatballs on a single layer of wax paper.
**4.** Combine hot water and rice sticks in a bowl, and let stand 15 minutes. Drain well, and snip with scissors twice. Combine 1 teaspoon cornstarch and broth in a large bowl. Add 2 teaspoons soy sauce, sherry, and lime juice. Add rice sticks, sliced mushrooms, ginger, curry, and garlic, and toss well.
**5.** Place noodle mixture in prepared oven bag. Place meatballs on noodle mixture, and fold edge of bag over to seal. Bake at 450° for 20 minutes or until meatballs are done. Place bag on a platter; cut open with a sharp knife, and peel back foil. Garnish with cilantro sprigs. Yield: 2 servings (serving size: 8 meatballs, 1½ cups noodles, and 1 teaspoon cilantro).

CALORIES 383 (10% from fat); FAT 4.2g (sat 0.9g, mono 1.1g, poly 1.3g); PROTEIN 28g; CARB 59.5g; FIBER 1.8g; CHOL 60mg; IRON 2.2mg; SODIUM 630mg; CALC 23mg

## Miso Salmon with Asparagus

*Miso*, or soybean paste, is a mainstay of Japanese cuisine. You can find miso in many supermarkets, as well as in Asian groceries and health-food shops.

1 regular-size foil oven bag
Cooking spray
2½ cups (2-inch) diagonally sliced asparagus (about ¾ pound)
1 tablespoon minced peeled fresh ginger, divided
1 teaspoon dark sesame oil
¼ teaspoon salt
¼ cup sliced green onions
3 tablespoons sake (rice wine) or dry white wine
1 tablespoon miso (soybean paste)
1½ teaspoons sugar
1½ teaspoons lemon juice
2 (6-ounce) salmon fillets (about 1 inch thick)
4 lemon slices
2 teaspoons sesame seeds, toasted

**1.** Preheat oven to 450°.
**2.** Coat inside of bag with cooking spray. Place on a large shallow baking pan.
**3.** Combine asparagus, 2 teaspoons ginger, oil, and salt in a bowl. Place mixture in prepared oven bag. Combine 1 teaspoon ginger, onions, sake, miso, sugar, and lemon juice in a small bowl. Place fish over asparagus mixture; spoon miso mixture over fish. Top with lemon slices. Fold edge of bag over to seal. Bake at 450° for 20 minutes or until fish flakes easily when tested with a fork. Place bag on a platter. Cut open bag with a sharp knife, and fold back foil. Sprinkle with sesame seeds. Yield: 2 servings (serving size: 1 fillet and 1 cup asparagus).

CALORIES 393 (44% from fat); FAT 19g (sat 3.1g, mono 8.2g, poly 4.9g); PROTEIN 40.8g; CARB 17.8g; FIBER 4.6g; CHOL 111mg; IRON 3.7mg; SODIUM 786mg; CALC 106mg

## Chicken-and-Broccoli Teriyaki with Noodles

1 regular-size foil oven bag
Cooking spray
⅓ cup low-sodium teriyaki sauce
2 tablespoons minced peeled fresh ginger
1 tablespoon sugar
1 pound skinned, boned chicken thighs, cut into ½-inch bite-size pieces
1 cup fat-free, less-sodium chicken broth
2 teaspoons cornstarch
½ teaspoon dark sesame oil
2 (3-ounce) packages chicken-flavored ramen noodles
4 cups broccoli florets (about 11 ounces)
1 (8-ounce) package mushrooms, quartered
1 (8-ounce) can sliced water chestnuts, drained
⅓ cup chopped green onions

**1.** Coat inside of oven bag with cooking spray. Place bag on a large shallow baking pan.
**2.** Combine teriyaki sauce, ginger, and sugar in a zip-top plastic bag. Add chicken to bag; seal. Marinate in refrigerator 2 hours, turning occasionally. Remove chicken from bag, reserving marinade. Combine reserved marinade, broth, and cornstarch; stir with a whisk. Stir in oil and 1 flavor packet from noodles (discard remaining flavor packet). Set aside.
**3.** Preheat oven to 475°.
**4.** Break each noodle package into four pieces. Place noodles in prepared bag. Pour broth mixture over noodles. Add broccoli, mushrooms, and water chestnuts. Top with chicken. Fold edge of bag over to seal. Bake at 475° for 30 minutes or until chicken is done. Place bag on a platter. Cut open with a sharp knife, and peel back foil. Sprinkle with onions. Yield: 4 servings (serving size: 1¾ cups).

CALORIES 425 (29% from fat); FAT 13.7g (sat 5.3g, mono 4.8g, poly 2.3g); PROTEIN 32g; CARB 45.3g; FIBER 4.6g; CHOL 94mg; IRON 4.4mg; SODIUM 982mg; CALC 59mg

# april

# Shrimp: Always Liked It—Always Will

## America's favorite seafood finds 10 new reasons to join your table tonight.

From sea to shining sea, we are a nation of shrimp. Eaters, that is. Besides their succulent flavor, culinary versatility also plays a big role in shrimp's popularity, right along with its nationwide and largely year-round availability. Maybe that's why Americans put away more than 1 billion pounds of shrimp every year, fresh and frozen, from the most diminutive scampi to their gargantuan cousins known as prawns.

### Shrimp, Spinach, and Basil Pizza Bianca

1 (16-ounce) Italian cheese-flavored pizza crust (such as Boboli)
2 tablespoons cornstarch
1 (12-ounce) can evaporated fat-free milk
1 garlic clove, minced
¼ teaspoon salt
¼ teaspoon black pepper
Cooking spray
1 pound small shrimp, peeled and deveined
2½ cups sliced mushrooms
3 cups chopped spinach
½ teaspoon dried oregano
½ teaspoon dried basil
½ cup (2 ounces) shredded part-skim mozzarella cheese
½ cup (2 ounces) grated sharp provolone cheese

**1.** Preheat oven to 425°.
**2.** Place pizza crust on a baking sheet; set aside.
**3.** Combine cornstarch, milk, and garlic in a small saucepan, stirring well with a whisk. Bring to a boil over medium heat; cook 1 minute, stirring constantly. Stir in salt and pepper. Spread sauce over crust.
**4.** Heat a large nonstick skillet coated with cooking spray over medium-high heat; sauté shrimp 3 minutes. Add mushrooms; sauté 2 minutes. Stir in spinach; cook 1 minute or until spinach wilts. Drain. Spoon shrimp mixture over sauce.

Sprinkle with oregano and basil. Top with cheeses. Bake at 425° for 8 minutes or until cheese is melted. Yield: 8 servings (serving size: 1 wedge).

CALORIES 291 (22% from fat); FAT 7.1g (sat 3.2g, mono 2.3g, poly 1g); PROTEIN 22.5g; CARB 33.4g; FIBER 1.2g; CHOL 75mg; IRON 3.6mg; SODIUM 598mg; CALC 421mg

### Barbecue Shrimp

(pictured on page 95)

This signature Creole-Sicilian favorite from New Orleans is reborn with low-fat shortcuts. The peels are left on the shrimp to add flavor to the lush, buttery-peppery sauce. Serving this dish with bread for dipping means no sauce goes to waste.

½ cup fat-free Caesar dressing
⅓ cup Worcestershire sauce
2 tablespoons butter or stick margarine
1 tablespoon dried oregano
1 tablespoon paprika
1 tablespoon dried rosemary
1 tablespoon dried thyme
1½ teaspoons black pepper
1 teaspoon hot pepper sauce
5 bay leaves
3 garlic cloves, minced
2 pounds large shrimp
⅓ cup dry white wine
10 (1-ounce) slices French bread baguette
10 lemon wedges

**1.** Combine first 11 ingredients in a large nonstick skillet; bring to a boil. Add shrimp, and cook 7 minutes, stirring occasionally. Add wine, and cook 1 minute or until shrimp are done. Serve with bread and lemon wedges. Yield: 5 servings (serving size: 5 ounces shrimp with sauce and 2 bread slices).

CALORIES 403 (20% from fat); FAT 9.1g (sat 3.8g, mono 2.4g, poly 1.7g); PROTEIN 34.4g; CARB 41.7g; FIBER 2.8g; CHOL 219mg; IRON 7mg; SODIUM 1,021mg; CALC 211mg

### Broiled Shrimp over Black Bean-and-Corn Salad

**MARINATED SHRIMP:**
⅓ cup fresh lime juice
¼ cup thawed orange juice concentrate
2 tablespoons low-sodium soy sauce
2 tablespoons Worcestershire sauce
2 tablespoons honey
1 garlic clove, minced
2 pounds large shrimp, peeled and deveined
Cooking spray

**SALAD:**
2 cups coarsely chopped tomato
½ cup sliced green onions
⅓ cup chopped fresh cilantro
1 (15-ounce) can black beans, rinsed and drained
1 (15.25-ounce) can whole-kernel corn, drained
1 jalapeño pepper, seeded and chopped
¼ cup fresh lime juice
2 tablespoons olive oil
½ teaspoon ground cumin
¼ teaspoon salt
⅛ teaspoon black pepper

**1.** To prepare marinated shrimp, combine first 6 ingredients in a large zip-top plastic bag. Add shrimp to bag; seal. Marinate in refrigerator 1 hour, turning occasionally. Remove shrimp from bag; discard marinade.
**2.** Preheat broiler.
**3.** Place shrimp on a broiler pan coated with cooking spray. Broil 4 minutes or until shrimp are done.

**4.** To prepare salad, combine tomato and next 5 ingredients in a large bowl. Combine ¼ cup lime juice, oil, cumin, salt, and black pepper; stir with a whisk. Pour over bean mixture; toss well. Spoon salad onto each of 6 plates; top with shrimp. Yield: 6 servings (serving size: ¾ cup salad and 4 ounces shrimp).

CALORIES 343 (20% from fat); FAT 7.6g (sat 1.1g, mono 3.8g, poly 1.5g); PROTEIN 30.2g; CARB 42g; FIBER 3.6g; CHOL 172mg; IRON 4.9mg; SODIUM 782mg; CALC 104mg

## Shrimp, Peppers, and Cheese Grits

This is our version of a dish beloved throughout the coastal Carolinas' Low Country. Bacon kicks in added flavor; red and green peppers provide the technicolor.

- ½ cup chopped Canadian bacon
- 1 cup red bell pepper strips
- 1 cup green bell pepper strips
- 1 (10-ounce) can diced tomatoes and green chiles, drained
- 1½ pounds medium shrimp, peeled and deveined
- ½ cup chopped green onions
- 1⅔ cups fat-free milk
- 1 (16-ounce) can fat-free, less-sodium chicken broth
- 1 cup uncooked quick-cooking grits
- 1 cup (4 ounces) shredded reduced-fat sharp Cheddar cheese

**1.** Cook bacon in a skillet over medium heat 3 minutes or until lightly browned, stirring frequently. Add bell peppers; cook 10 minutes, stirring occasionally. Add tomatoes; cook 5 minutes. Add shrimp; cook 3 minutes. Stir in green onions; keep warm.

**2.** Combine milk and broth in a saucepan. Bring to a boil, and stir in grits. Bring to a boil; reduce heat, and cook 5 minutes or until thick, stirring occasionally. Stir in cheese. Serve shrimp mixture over grits. Yield: 4 servings (serving size: 1 cup grits and 1¼ cups shrimp mixture).

CALORIES 452 (19% from fat); FAT 9.4g (sat 4.1g, mono 2.5g, poly 1.4g); PROTEIN 46.5g; CARB 42.7g; FIBER 3.3g; CHOL 223mg; IRON 5.7mg; SODIUM 1,058mg; CALC 467mg

## Shrimp and Feta with Angel Hair

Cooking spray
- 2 pounds medium shrimp, peeled and deveined
- 2 cups chopped plum tomato (about ¾ pound)
- 1½ cups sliced green onions
- ½ cup sliced ripe olives
- 2 teaspoons dried dill
- 1 garlic clove, minced
- 4 cups hot cooked angel hair (about 8 ounces uncooked pasta)
- 1 cup (4 ounces) crumbled feta cheese

**1.** Heat a large nonstick skillet coated with cooking spray over medium-high heat. Add shrimp; cook 5 minutes, stirring frequently. Stir in tomato and next 4 ingredients; cook 4 minutes or until thoroughly heated. Combine shrimp mixture, pasta, and cheese in a large bowl; toss well. Yield: 6 servings (serving size: 1⅓ cups).

CALORIES 346 (21% from fat); FAT 8.2g (sat 3.5g, mono 2.2g, poly 1.4g); PROTEIN 31.7g; CARB 35.7g; FIBER 2.6g; CHOL 189mg; IRON 5.5mg; SODIUM 490mg; CALC 197mg

## Risotto with Snow Peas and Shrimp

- 2 (8-ounce) bottles clam juice
- 3 cups water
- 1 tablespoon olive oil
- ¼ cup minced shallots
- 1½ cups Arborio rice or other short-grain rice
- ⅓ cup dry white wine or dry vermouth
- ¾ pound medium shrimp, peeled and deveined
- 1 cup (½-inch) diagonally sliced snow peas
- 1 cup shelled green peas (about ¾ pound unshelled green peas)
- ¼ cup (1 ounce) grated fresh Parmesan cheese
- 1½ teaspoons chopped fresh or ½ teaspoon dried thyme
- 1 teaspoon grated lemon rind
- ¼ teaspoon black pepper

**1.** Bring clam juice and water to a simmer in a medium saucepan (do not boil). Keep warm over low heat.

**2.** Heat oil in a large saucepan over medium heat; add shallots, and cook 1 minute. Add rice; cook 1 minute, stirring constantly. Stir in wine; cook 1 minute. Stir in ½ cup juice mixture; cook 2 minutes or until liquid is nearly absorbed, stirring constantly. Add remaining juice mixture, ½ cup at a time, stirring constantly until each portion of juice mixture is absorbed before adding the next (about 20 minutes total). Stir in shrimp, snow peas, and green peas; cook 4 minutes or until shrimp are done, stirring constantly. Remove from heat; stir in cheese and remaining ingredients. Yield: 6 servings (serving size: 1 cup).

**NOTE:** Substitute frozen green peas for fresh, if desired.

CALORIES 302 (14% from fat); FAT 4.6g (sat 1.3g, mono 2.2g, poly 0.6g); PROTEIN 16.1g; CARB 47.3g; FIBER 2.3g; CHOL 68mg; IRON 4.2mg; SODIUM 306mg; CALC 111mg

## Shrimp-and-Squash Penne

- 2 tablespoons olive oil
- 4 cups thinly sliced yellow squash (about 4 small)
- 3 cups thinly sliced zucchini (about 2 medium)
- 1 pound medium shrimp, peeled and deveined
- ¼ cup fresh lemon juice
- 1 teaspoon dried basil
- 1 teaspoon dried oregano
- ½ teaspoon salt
- ¼ teaspoon black pepper
- 3 garlic cloves, minced
- 4 cups hot cooked penne (about ½ pound uncooked tube-shaped pasta)
- ½ cup thinly sliced fresh chives or green onions
- ¼ cup (1 ounce) grated fresh Parmesan cheese

**1.** Heat oil in a large nonstick skillet over medium-high heat. Add squash and zucchini, and sauté 10 minutes. Add
*Continued*

shrimp; sauté 3 minutes. Add juice and next 5 ingredients; cook 2 minutes or until shrimp are done. Combine shrimp mixture, pasta, chives, and cheese in a large bowl; toss gently. Yield: 5 servings (serving size: 2 cups).

CALORIES 351 (24% from fat); FAT 9.2g (sat 2.1g, mono 4.7g, poly 1.4g); PROTEIN 24.1g; CARB 43.7g; FIBER 3.6g; CHOL 107mg; IRON 4.6mg; SODIUM 434mg; CALC 162mg

## Shrimp and Asparagus with Ginger-Sesame Sauce

**MARINATED SHRIMP:**
¼ cup dry white wine
2 tablespoons chopped fresh parsley
2 tablespoons low-sodium soy sauce
2 teaspoons minced peeled fresh ginger
2 teaspoons dark sesame oil
¼ teaspoon salt
2 garlic cloves, minced
Dash of black pepper
1½ pounds medium shrimp, peeled and deveined

**REMAINING INGREDIENTS:**
2 teaspoons vegetable oil
2 cups (2-inch) diagonally sliced asparagus
1½ cups sliced shiitake mushroom caps (about 2 [3.5-ounce] packages)
1½ cups sliced button mushrooms
¼ cup water
2 teaspoons cornstarch
3 cups hot cooked long-grain rice
1 tablespoon sesame seeds

**1.** To prepare marinated shrimp, combine first 9 ingredients in a large zip-top plastic bag; seal and marinate in refrigerator 1 hour. Remove shrimp from bag, reserving marinade.
**2.** Heat vegetable oil in a large nonstick skillet over medium-high heat. Add asparagus and mushrooms; sauté 5 minutes. Add shrimp; cook 3 minutes or until shrimp are done.
**3.** Combine reserved marinade, water, and cornstarch. Add to skillet. Bring to a boil; cook 1 minute, stirring constantly.

Serve over rice. Sprinkle with sesame seeds. Yield: 4 servings (serving size: 1½ cups shrimp mixture and ¾ cup rice).

CALORIES 409 (19% from fat); FAT 8.5g (sat 1.4g, mono 2.3g, poly 3.6g); PROTEIN 32.5g; CARB 47.2g; FIBER 3.3g; CHOL 194mg; IRON 6.4mg; SODIUM 537mg; CALC 129mg

## Soft Shrimp Tacos with Tropical Salsa

**SALSA:**
¼ cup chopped green onions
1 tablespoon chopped fresh cilantro
1 tablespoon canned chopped green chiles
1 tablespoon lemon juice
1 (11-ounce) can mandarin oranges in light syrup, drained
1 (8-ounce) can pineapple tidbits in juice, drained

**TACOS:**
Cooking spray
1 cup yellow bell pepper strips
1 cup vertically sliced red onion
1 garlic clove, minced
1½ pounds medium shrimp, peeled and deveined
1 cup chopped tomato
½ teaspoon ground cumin
½ teaspoon chili powder
2 tablespoons chopped fresh cilantro
8 (6-inch) flour tortillas
1¼ cups (5 ounces) shredded reduced-fat Monterey Jack cheese

**1.** To prepare salsa, combine first 6 ingredients in a bowl. Cover and chill.
**2.** To prepare tacos, place a large nonstick skillet coated with cooking spray over medium-high heat until hot. Add bell pepper, sliced onion, and garlic; sauté 2 minutes. Add shrimp, tomato, cumin, and chili powder; sauté 3 minutes or until shrimp are done. Stir in 2 tablespoons cilantro. Spoon ½ cup shrimp mixture over one half of each tortilla, and top each with about 3 tablespoons cheese and 2 tablespoons salsa; fold tortillas in half. Yield: 8 servings.

CALORIES 276 (24% from fat); FAT 7.3g (sat 2.6g, mono 2.2g, poly 1.7g); PROTEIN 22g; CARB 30.4g; FIBER 2.3g; CHOL 109mg; IRON 3.4mg; SODIUM 395mg; CALC 233mg

## Quick Shrimp-and-Corn Soup

The velvety consistency and rich taste of this soup belie the speed with which it can be made.

Cooking spray
1 cup chopped onion
1 cup chopped green bell pepper
1 garlic clove, minced
¾ cup (6 ounces) ⅓-less-fat cream cheese, softened
2 cups fat-free milk
1 (15-ounce) can cream-style corn
1 (10¾-ounce) can condensed reduced-fat, reduced-sodium cream of mushroom soup, undiluted
1 (10-ounce) can diced tomatoes and green chiles, undrained
1¼ pounds medium shrimp, peeled and deveined
4 teaspoons sliced green onions

**1.** Heat a Dutch oven or large saucepan coated with cooking spray over medium-high heat. Add chopped onion, bell pepper, and garlic, and sauté 5 minutes. Stir in cream cheese; reduce heat, and cook until cheese is melted. Add milk, corn, soup, and tomatoes; cook 10 minutes, stirring occasionally. Bring milk mixture to a boil. Add shrimp; cook 5 minutes or until shrimp are done. Remove from heat. Sprinkle each serving with green onions. Yield: 8 servings (serving size: 1 cup soup and ½ teaspoon green onions).

CALORIES 228 (29% from fat); FAT 7.4g (sat 3.8g, mono 1.9g, poly 1.1g); PROTEIN 18.8g; CARB 20.8g; FIBER 1.5g; CHOL 118mg; IRON 2.4mg; SODIUM 663mg; CALC 176mg

### Shrimp Savvy

• Virtually all shrimp are quick-frozen at sea, and then defrosted for sale. And it's OK to refreeze them. We've done it for years without any problem. When you want to use refrozen shrimp, thaw them out in tap water.
• The only bad way to cook shrimp is too long. An overcooked shrimp is a rubbery shrimp or a mushy shrimp. Either way, it's a waste of taste.

# Supper under Pressure

*These dinnertime favorites taste even better—and come out faster—with a pressure cooker.*

Pressure cookers cut stovetop time significantly while producing some of the most succulent meals. And today's re-tooled versions can withstand human error without (literally) blowing their tops, thanks to special new safety devices.

This high-pressure cooking method works particularly well with meat. Inexpensive cuts such as chuck roast or lamb shanks come out in a fraction of the time because the pressure cooker keeps in steam while it heats. Neither the liquid nor the seasonings can escape; the meat is infused with moistness and rich flavor.

## Savory Braised-Pork Supper

1   (3-pound) Boston Butt pork roast
2   teaspoons Hungarian sweet paprika
1   teaspoon black pepper
¾   teaspoon salt
½   teaspoon dried rubbed sage
½   teaspoon dried thyme
½   teaspoon dry mustard
1   tablespoon vegetable oil
Cooking spray
2½   cups thinly sliced leek (about 2 large)
4   garlic cloves, minced
1   (16-ounce) can fat-free, less-sodium chicken broth
2   pounds red potatoes, quartered
2   cups (1-inch-thick) sliced carrot

**1.** Trim fat from pork. Combine paprika and next 5 ingredients; rub pork with paprika mixture. Heat oil in a 6-quart pressure cooker coated with cooking spray over medium-high heat. Add pork; brown on all sides. Remove from pan; set aside. Add leek and garlic to pan; sauté 2 minutes. Add broth; bring to a simmer. Return pork to pan; spoon leek mixture over pork. Close lid securely; bring to high pressure over high heat (about 3 minutes). Adjust heat to medium or level needed to maintain high pressure; cook 45 minutes.

**2.** Remove from heat; place pressure cooker under cold running water. Remove lid; stir in potato and carrot. Close lid securely; bring to high pressure over high heat. Adjust heat to medium or level needed to maintain high pressure; cook 15 minutes. Place pressure cooker under cold running water. Remove lid; remove vegetables and pork from pan. Cut pork into ¼-inch-thick slices; discard bone. Yield: 6 servings (serving size: 3 ounces pork and 1⅓ cups vegetables).

CALORIES 363 (30% from fat); FAT 11.8g (sat 3.6g, mono 4.8g, poly 2.3g); PROTEIN 27.6g; CARB 36.7g; FIBER 4.7g; CHOL 76mg; IRON 4.9mg; SODIUM 572mg; CALC 72mg

## Barbecue Brisket Sandwiches

1   cup sliced onion, separated into rings
¾   cup bottled chili sauce
½   cup beer
1   tablespoon Worcestershire sauce
1   (2½-pound) beef brisket
1   teaspoon black pepper
4   garlic cloves, minced
¼   cup packed brown sugar
8   (2½-ounce) submarine rolls

**1.** Combine first 4 ingredients in a 6-quart pressure cooker. Bring to a boil; reduce heat, and simmer 5 minutes. Remove ½ cup of chili sauce mixture from pressure cooker.

**2.** Trim fat from brisket. Cut brisket in half crosswise. Rub brisket with pepper and garlic. Place in pressure cooker. Spoon ½ cup chili sauce mixture over brisket. Close lid securely; bring to high pressure over high heat (about 5 minutes). Adjust heat to medium or level needed to maintain high pressure; cook 1 hour.

**3.** Remove from heat; place pressure cooker under cold running water. Remove lid. Remove brisket from pressure cooker, and set aside. Add brown sugar to chili sauce mixture in pressure cooker; bring to a boil. Reduce heat, and simmer, uncovered, 5 minutes, stirring frequently. Shred brisket using 2 forks. Return meat to sauce in pressure cooker; cook until thoroughly heated. Spoon 1 cup meat with sauce over bottom of each roll, and cover with tops of rolls. Yield: 8 servings.

CALORIES 494 (28% from fat); FAT 15.2g (sat 4g, mono 4.9g, poly 0.4g); PROTEIN 33.2g; CARB 54.2g; FIBER 0.9g; CHOL 79mg; IRON 5.9mg; SODIUM 886mg; CALC 43mg

## Osso Buco

We lightened up this Italian classic—made with veal shanks, white wine, olive oil, and spices—by reducing the oil and adding beef broth. The result is terrific.

2   pounds veal shanks (1½ inches thick)
¼   cup all-purpose flour
½   teaspoon salt
½   teaspoon freshly ground black pepper
1   tablespoon olive oil
2   cups (1-inch-thick) sliced carrot
4   garlic cloves, minced
2   medium onions, each cut into 8 wedges
¾   cup water, divided
¼   cup dry vermouth or white wine
1   tablespoon herbes de Provence
1   (10½-ounce) can beef broth
¼   cup chopped fresh flat-leaf parsley
1   teaspoon grated lemon rind
1   garlic clove, minced
4   cups hot cooked egg noodles (about 3 cups uncooked pasta)

**1.** Combine first 4 ingredients in a large zip-top plastic bag. Seal and shake to coat. Remove veal. Reserve remaining flour mixture in bag.

**2.** Heat oil in a 6-quart pressure cooker over medium heat until hot. Add shanks; cook 4 minutes on each side or until browned. Add carrot, 4 garlic cloves,
*Continued*

and onion; sauté 2 minutes. Stir in ½ cup water, vermouth, herbes de Provence, and broth; bring to a simmer. Close lid securely; bring to high pressure over high heat (about 6 minutes). Adjust heat to medium or level needed to maintain high pressure; cook 30 minutes. Remove from heat; place pressure cooker under cold running water. Remove lid.

**3.** Combine reserved flour mixture and ¼ cup water. Add to pan, and bring to a boil. Cook 5 minutes or until thick, stirring constantly. Combine parsley, rind, and minced garlic clove in a small bowl. Remove meat from bones, discarding bones and fat. Serve meat and vegetable mixture over egg noodles. Sprinkle with parsley mixture. Yield: 4 servings (serving size: 3 ounces veal, 1 cup vegetable mixture, 1 cup egg noodles, and 1 tablespoon parsley mixture).

CALORIES 488 (18% from fat); FAT 9.9g (sat 2.4g, mono 4.7g, poly 1.4g); PROTEIN 37.4g; CARB 61.2g; FIBER 7.3g; CHOL 131mg; IRON 6.4mg; SODIUM 807mg; CALC 92mg

## New Mexican Pork Chili

1 (2-pound) boned pork loin roast, cut into 1-inch cubes
2 teaspoons vegetable oil
2 tablespoons chili powder
1 tablespoon ground cumin
½ teaspoon salt
2 cups coarsely chopped onion
6 garlic cloves, chopped
1½ cups water
1 cup coarsely chopped seeded Anaheim chiles (about 3 chiles)
¾ cup dried pinto beans
1 tablespoon chopped drained canned chipotle chile in adobo sauce
1 (14.5-ounce) can no-salt-added stewed tomatoes, undrained
1 (10½-ounce) can beef broth
½ cup chopped fresh cilantro
½ cup fat-free sour cream
½ cup chopped tomato

**1.** Trim fat from pork.
**2.** Heat oil in a 6-quart pressure cooker over medium heat. Add pork; sprinkle with chili powder, cumin, and salt. Sauté

5 minutes. Add onion and garlic; sauté 2 minutes. Stir in water and next 5 ingredients. Close lid securely; bring to high pressure over high heat (about 3 minutes). Adjust heat to medium or level needed to maintain high pressure, and cook 40 minutes. Place pressure cooker under cold running water. Remove lid; skim fat from surface. Stir in cilantro. Ladle soup into each of 8 bowls; top each serving with sour cream and chopped tomato. Yield: 8 servings (serving size: 1 cup chili, 1 tablespoon sour cream, and 1 tablespoon chopped tomato).

CALORIES 308 (30% from fat); FAT 10g (sat 3.1g, mono 4.2g, poly 1.7g); PROTEIN 30.4g; CARB 24g; FIBER 4.1g; CHOL 64mg; IRON 3.7mg; SODIUM 471mg; CALC 80mg

## Tuscan Lamb Shanks

¾ cup dried Great Northern beans
3¼ cups water, divided
3 pounds lamb shanks (about 2 large shanks)
2 tablespoons all-purpose flour
½ teaspoon salt
½ teaspoon freshly ground black pepper
2 teaspoons olive oil, divided
½ cup sliced shallots
6 garlic cloves, sliced
1 cup dry red wine
¼ cup sun-dried tomato sprinkles
1 tablespoon chopped fresh or 1 teaspoon dried rosemary
1 tablespoon Worcestershire sauce
1 (14¼-ounce) can low-salt beef broth
5 cups hot cooked medium egg noodles (about 4 cups uncooked pasta)
2 tablespoons chopped fresh flat-leaf parsley

**1.** Sort and wash beans; combine with 3 cups water in a small saucepan. Bring to a boil; cook 1 minute. Remove from heat. Let stand 20 minutes. Drain; set aside.
**2.** Trim fat from lamb. Place flour, salt, and pepper in a large zip-top plastic bag; add lamb. Seal; shake to coat. Remove lamb from bag; shake off excess flour mixture. Reserve 1½ teaspoons flour

mixture. Heat 1 teaspoon oil in a 6-quart pressure cooker over medium heat. Add 1 lamb shank; cook 8 minutes on all sides or until browned. Remove lamb from pan. Repeat procedure with 1 teaspoon oil and 1 lamb shank. Add shallots and garlic, and sauté 2 minutes. Add beans, ¼ cup water, reserved 1½ teaspoons flour mixture, red wine, and next 4 ingredients. Return lamb to cooker. Close lid; bring to high pressure over high heat (about 7 minutes). Adjust heat to medium or level needed to maintain high pressure; cook 45 minutes.
**3.** Remove from heat; place pressure cooker under cold running water. Remove lid. Remove lamb from pan; cool completely. Remove meat from bones; discard bones, fat, and gristle. Skim fat from surface. Stir meat into bean mixture. Serve over noodles. Sprinkle with parsley. Yield: 5 servings (serving size: 1 cup stew and 1 cup noodles).

CALORIES 519 (17% from fat); FAT 10g (sat 3.4g, mono 5.1g, poly 1.5g); PROTEIN 38g; CARB 85g; FIBER 12.7g; CHOL 82mg; IRON 7mg; SODIUM 460mg; CALC 105mg

## Beef Bourguignonne

Red wine and mushrooms mark this dish as a classic from the Burgundy region of France.

1½ pounds boned chuck roast, cut into 1-inch cubes
¼ cup all-purpose flour
½ teaspoon salt
½ teaspoon black pepper
2 bacon slices, diced
½ cup dry red wine
1 (10½-ounce) can beef broth
3 cups baby carrots (about ¾ pound)
3 cups sliced shiitake mushroom caps (about ½ pound)
2 tablespoons chopped fresh or 2 teaspoons dried thyme
6 shallots, halved (about ½ pound)
4 garlic cloves, thinly sliced
7 cups hot cooked medium egg noodles (about 5 cups uncooked pasta)

**1.** Combine first 4 ingredients in a large zip-top plastic bag. Seal and shake to coat.

**2.** Cook half of bacon in a 6-quart pressure cooker over medium heat 30 seconds. Add half of beef mixture; cook 5 minutes or until browned. Remove beef from cooker. Repeat procedure with remaining bacon and beef mixture. Return beef to cooker. Stir in wine and broth, scraping pan to loosen browned bits. Add carrots, mushrooms, thyme, shallots, and garlic. Close lid securely; bring to high pressure over high heat (about 6 minutes). Adjust heat to medium or level needed to maintain high pressure; cook 20 minutes. Remove from heat; place pressure cooker under cold running water. Remove lid. Serve stew over noodles. Yield: 7 servings (serving size: 1 cup stew and 1 cup noodles).

CALORIES 376 (30% from fat); FAT 12.5g (sat 4.5g, mono 5.4g, poly 1.3g); PROTEIN 24.7g; CARB 40.9g; FIBER 3.3g; CHOL 44mg; IRON 5mg; SODIUM 525mg; CALC 53mg

# Putting Cream in Its Place

Cream makes its *Cooking Light* debut, reclaiming its rightful place in soups, sauces, pastas, and desserts.

Heavy cream isn't exactly common in a magazine dedicated to celebrating healthy lifestyles and lower-fat fare. In fact, *Cooking Light* launched in 1987 with whipping cream exiled from its pages. However, we routinely use other high-fat ingredients in the spirit of moderation, balance, and variety. Why not cream?

We began discussing ways to bring whipping cream into our fold in the same flavor-enhancing ways as other high-fat ingredients: in small amounts that are designed to enhance flavor, not add unnecessary fat and calories. We're here to report success, and to herald the first use of whipping cream in *Cooking Light* magazine. The bottom line with cooking has always been that *how* you use ingredients is just as important as which ones you use, and that's even more true with light cooking.

## Questions for Quick Cookers

**How do pressure cookers work so fast?**
You always have to put liquid in a pressure cooker—water, broth, or juices from foods. The liquid boils and turns to steam. The cooker locks in the steam, which allows the temperature inside to superheat very rapidly. A pressure cooker can reduce cooking times by about two-thirds.

**Why brown meats first?**
Browning produces a nice caramelized flavor in the meat. The caramelized, browned exterior then dissolves in the liquid in which it is cooked, adding to the overall flavor of the dish.

**Do they explode?**
New models have special safety devices that allow the steam to escape, even with the lid in place.

**Which foods work best?**
Most meats, especially tougher cuts, take very well to pressure cooking and become much more tender. Same with grains and with longer-cooking vegetables such as potatoes. Don't use your pressure cooker for anything that cooks really fast anyway, such as fish, or some vegetables. They'll turn mushy.

### Brown Sugar Pavlovas with Fruit

(pictured on page 93)

A *pavlova* is a crisp meringue shell piled with whipped cream and fresh berries. The meringues freeze for up to two months; remove them from the freezer before assembling the pavlovas—no reheating required.

   4   large egg whites
   2   teaspoons cornstarch
   ¼   teaspoon salt
   ¾   cup granulated sugar
   ¼   cup packed brown sugar
   1   teaspoon vanilla extract
   ¾   cup whipping cream
   2   tablespoons powdered sugar
   ¼   teaspoon ground cinnamon
   3   cups chopped fresh pineapple
   ¾   cup chopped peeled kiwi
   ¾   cup fresh blackberries or
        raspberries
   3   tablespoons fat-free caramel
        sundae syrup

**1.** Preheat oven to 350°.
**2.** Cover a large baking sheet with parchment paper. Draw 6 (4-inch) circles on paper. Turn paper over; secure with masking tape.

**3.** Beat egg whites, cornstarch, and salt at high speed of a mixer until foamy. Add granulated sugar and brown sugar, 1 tablespoon at a time, beating until thick and glossy. Add vanilla, beating well. Divide egg white mixture evenly among 6 drawn circles. Shape meringues into nests with 1-inch sides using back of a spoon. Place meringues in oven. Immediately reduce oven temperature to 300°; bake for 1 hour. Turn oven off, and cool meringues in closed oven at least 4 hours or until completely dry. (Meringues are done when surface is dry and meringues can be removed from paper without sticking to fingers.) Carefully remove meringue nests from paper.
**4.** Beat whipping cream, powdered sugar, and cinnamon at high speed of a mixer until stiff peaks form. Dollop ¼ cup whipped cream into each meringue nest. Top each with ½ cup pineapple, 2 tablespoons kiwi, and 2 tablespoons blackberries. Drizzle 1½ teaspoons caramel syrup over each serving. Serve immediately. Yield: 6 servings.
**NOTE:** Whipping cream whips better when the bowl and beaters are chilled.

CALORIES 356 (29% from fat); FAT 11.5g (sat 6.9g, mono 3.2g, poly 0.6g); PROTEIN 3.5g; CARB 61.9g; FIBER 2.8g; CHOL 41mg; IRON 0.7mg; SODIUM 178mg; CALC 53mg

## Creamy Lentil Soup

This is no ordinary lentil soup—half-and-half creates a satiny finish and creamy body, making typically watery lentils truly sublime. This is a great main-dish soup served with a green salad and rustic bread. It won't have the same smoky taste, but you can go vegetarian by substituting 2 tablespoons vegetable oil for the bacon drippings and vegetable broth for the chicken broth.

    3  bacon slices
    2  cups chopped leek
    1  cup chopped onion
    3  cups water
    2  cups chopped peeled baking
       potato (about 12 ounces)
    1  cup dried lentils
    ¾  cup chopped carrot
    ½  teaspoon salt
    1  (16-ounce) can fat-free,
       less-sodium chicken broth
    ½  cup half-and-half
    2  tablespoons dry sherry

**1.** Cook bacon in a Dutch oven over medium heat until crisp. Remove bacon from pan, reserving drippings in pan. Crumble bacon; set aside. Add leek and onion to pan; sauté 4 minutes. Add water, potato, lentils, carrot, salt, and broth; bring to a boil. Cover, reduce heat, and simmer 1 hour or until vegetables are tender. Place vegetable mixture in a blender or food processor; process until smooth. Return pureed mixture to pan; stir in half-and-half and sherry. Cook until thoroughly heated. Sprinkle with bacon. Yield: 6 servings (serving size: 1⅓ cups).

CALORIES 287 (29% from fat); FAT 9.4g (sat 4g, mono 3.7g, poly 1.1g); PROTEIN 13.6g; CARB 37.4g; FIBER 5.8g; CHOL 15mg; IRON 4.2mg; SODIUM 465mg; CALC 72mg

## Chicken Fricassee with Orzo

Cream is added to the vegetable mixture at the end to create a rich-tasting sauce that is soaked up by the orzo.

    4  (4-ounce) skinned, boned chicken
       breast halves
    ½  teaspoon salt
    ¼  teaspoon black pepper
    2  teaspoons butter or stick
       margarine
    ¾  cup chopped green onions
    ½  cup diced carrot
    ½  cup diced ham
    2  garlic cloves, minced
    1  cup fat-free, less-sodium chicken
       broth
    ½  cup Chardonnay or other dry
       white wine
    ⅓  cup whipping cream
    3  cups hot cooked orzo (about 1½
       cups uncooked rice-shaped pasta)
    ¼  cup chopped fresh parsley
    Parsley sprigs (optional)

**1.** Sprinkle chicken with salt and pepper. Melt butter in a large nonstick skillet over medium-high heat. Add chicken; cook 3 minutes on each side or until browned. Remove chicken from pan.
**2.** Add onions, carrot, ham, and garlic to pan; sauté 4 minutes or until lightly browned. Stir in broth and wine, scraping pan to loosen browned bits. Return chicken to pan; bring to a boil. Cover, reduce heat, and simmer 10 minutes or until chicken is done. Remove chicken from pan with a slotted spoon; keep warm. Add whipping cream to pan; cook, uncovered, over medium heat 8 minutes. Spoon ¾ cup orzo onto each of 4 plates. Top each with 1 chicken breast half, ⅓ cup sauce, and 1 tablespoon chopped parsley. Garnish with parsley sprigs, if desired. Yield: 4 servings.

CALORIES 527 (24% from fat); FAT 14.3g (sat 7.1g, mono 4.3g, poly 1.5g); PROTEIN 39.6g; CARB 57.7g; FIBER 2.8g; CHOL 105mg; IRON 4.4mg; SODIUM 726mg; CALC 68mg

## Parmesan-Crusted Chicken with Leeks and Apples

In keeping with a classic reduction sauce, whipping cream is added to a simmering broth mixture. Beware: Half-and-half or any kind of milk will curdle here.

    Cooking spray
    2½  cups coarsely chopped peeled
        Braeburn or Gala apple (about
        1 pound)
    1⅔  cups thinly sliced leek (about
        2 small)
    1   teaspoon sugar
    ¼   cup (1 ounce) grated fresh
        Parmesan cheese
    2   tablespoons all-purpose flour
    ½   teaspoon salt, divided
    ⅛   teaspoon black pepper
    4   (4-ounce) skinned, boned chicken
        breast halves
    1   teaspoon butter or stick margarine
    ¾   cup apple juice
    1   (16-ounce) can fat-free,
        less-sodium chicken broth
    ⅓   cup whipping cream
    ½   teaspoon chopped fresh or
        ⅛ teaspoon dried rosemary
    4   cups hot cooked wild rice mix
        (such as Uncle Ben's Long Grain
        & Wild Rice )

**1.** Heat a large nonstick skillet coated with cooking spray over medium-high heat until hot. Add apple, leek, and sugar; sauté 12 minutes or until browned. Remove from pan, and set aside.

**2.** Combine cheese, flour, ¼ teaspoon salt, and pepper in a shallow dish. Dredge chicken in cheese mixture. Melt butter in pan over medium-high heat. Add chicken to pan; sauté 4 minutes on each side or until chicken is done. Remove chicken from pan; keep warm. Add juice and broth to pan, scraping pan to loosen browned bits. Bring to a boil; cook broth mixture until reduced to 1½ cups (about 7 minutes).

**3.** Add cream; reduce heat, and cook 5 minutes. Stir in reserved apple mixture, rosemary, and ¼ teaspoon salt; cook 2 minutes. Spoon rice onto each of 4 plates; top with chicken and sauce. Yield: 4 servings (serving size: 1 chicken breast half, 1 cup rice, and about ½ cup sauce).

CALORIES 507 (22% from fat); FAT 12.6g (sat 6.8g, mono 3.4g, poly 1g); PROTEIN 35.8g; CARB 63.2g; FIBER 3.1g; CHOL 100mg; IRON 2.5mg; SODIUM 748mg; CALC 163mg

## Creamy Parmesan Pasta with Turkey Meatballs

**TURKEY MEATBALLS:**
½  pound ground turkey breast
¾  cup finely chopped onion
¾  cup fresh breadcrumbs
¼  cup chopped fresh parsley
½  teaspoon salt
⅛  teaspoon black pepper
2  garlic cloves, crushed
1  large egg white
Cooking spray

**REMAINING INGREDIENTS:**
½  cup dry white wine
½  cup chopped green onions
½  cup whipping cream
¼  cup (1 ounce) grated fresh Parmesan cheese
2  tablespoons water
5  cups hot cooked fettuccine (about 10 ounces uncooked pasta)

**1.** To prepare meatballs, combine first 8 ingredients in a bowl. Shape turkey mixture into 20 balls. Place a large nonstick skillet coated with cooking spray over medium-high heat until hot. Add meatballs;

brown on all sides. Remove meatballs from pan.

**2.** Add wine and green onions to pan, scraping pan to loosen browned bits; cook 2 minutes. Add whipping cream, cheese, and water; reduce heat to medium, and cook 3 minutes, stirring frequently. Add pasta, and cook 1 minute, tossing to coat. Place pasta on each of 4 plates; top with meatballs. Yield: 4 servings (serving size: 1¼ cups pasta and 5 meatballs).

CALORIES 499 (27% from fat); FAT 15.1g (sat 8.5g, mono 4.1g, poly 1g); PROTEIN 26.4g; CARB 62g; FIBER 4.1g; CHOL 76mg; IRON 3.6mg; SODIUM 595mg; CALC 151mg

## Pasta with Mussels and Monterey Jack

Jack cheese is added along with the half-and-half to temper the mixture and prevent curdling. Use only a top-quality Chardonnay or other wine you'd want to drink; it will make a big difference in the sauce.

2  teaspoons olive oil
1½  cups chopped red bell pepper
1  cup chopped green onions
3  garlic cloves, minced
1  cup Chardonnay or other dry white wine
2  pounds mussels, scrubbed and debearded
½  cup (2 ounces) shredded Monterey Jack cheese
¾  cup half-and-half
¼  teaspoon salt
⅛  teaspoon black pepper
3  cups chopped spinach
6  cups hot cooked capellini or angel hair (about 12 ounces uncooked pasta)

**1.** Heat oil in a Dutch oven over medium-high heat. Add bell pepper, onions, and garlic; sauté 5 minutes. Add wine and mussels; cover and cook 5 minutes or until mussels open. Discard any unopened shells. Remove mussels from pan with a slotted spoon; cool. Remove meat from mussels; set aside. Discard shells.

**2.** Add cheese, half-and-half, salt, and black pepper to pan; reduce heat, and

cook 5 minutes or until cheese melts. Stir in mussels, and cook 4 minutes or until thoroughly heated. Combine mussel mixture, chopped spinach, and pasta, tossing well. Yield: 5 servings (serving size: 1½ cups).

CALORIES 445 (25% from fat); FAT 12.3g (sat 5.5g, mono 4g, poly 1.4g); PROTEIN 22.3g; CARB 61.2g; FIBER 4.2g; CHOL 41mg; IRON 7.3mg; SODIUM 421mg; CALC 210mg

## Chunky Southwestern Clam Chowder

Traditional New England-style chowders are nothing more than cream, fish, and butter with a few crackers thrown in. Every ingredient imaginable has crept in and out of these chowders through the years, but one constant remains: cream.

2  red bell peppers (about ¾ pound)
1  jalapeño pepper
1  (10-ounce) can whole clams, undrained
1  bacon slice
1½  cups chopped onion
1½  tablespoons all-purpose flour
4  cups (½-inch) cubed peeled baking potato (about 2 pounds)
2  cups fresh corn kernels (about 4 ears)
1  cup Chardonnay or other dry white wine
2  (8-ounce) bottles clam juice
¾  cup half-and-half
½  cup chopped green onions
1  tablespoon chopped fresh basil
¼  teaspoon freshly ground black pepper

**1.** Preheat broiler. Cut bell peppers in half lengthwise; discard seeds and membranes. Place pepper halves, skin sides up, and jalapeño pepper on a foil-lined baking sheet; flatten bell peppers with hand. Broil 10 minutes or until blackened. Place peppers in a zip-top plastic bag; seal. Let stand 5 minutes. Discard seeds and membranes from jalapeño pepper. Peel and chop bell peppers and jalapeño pepper; set aside. Drain clams in a colander over a bowl, reserving liquid.
*Continued*

**2.** Cook bacon in a Dutch oven over medium heat until crisp. Remove bacon from pan, reserving drippings in pan. Crumble bacon; set aside. Add 1½ cups onion to pan; sauté 10 minutes. Add flour; cook 2 minutes, stirring constantly. Stir in reserved clam liquid, potato, corn, wine, and clam juice; bring to a boil. Partially cover, reduce heat, and simmer 25 minutes or until potato is tender. Stir in roasted peppers, clams, half-and-half, green onions, basil, and black pepper. Cook 5 minutes or until thoroughly heated. Sprinkle with crumbled bacon. Yield: 6 servings (serving size: 1½ cups).

CALORIES 241 (25% from fat); FAT 6.6g (sat 3.1g, mono 2.2g, poly 0.8g); PROTEIN 6.4g; CARB 37.8g; FIBER 4.7g; CHOL 37mg; IRON 3.2mg; SODIUM 339mg; CALC 154mg

# How to Make Great Sauces

## These four versatile sauces are your secret weapons in the quest for savvy cooking.

Nothing gives you more confidence as a cook than knowing how to make a great sauce. Learning to make a few of the classics—Tomato, Port-Wine Mushroom, Cheese, and Fudge—gives you carte blanche to almost unlimited dining pleasures.

In addition to being far lighter than those of yesterday, our four streamlined updates are easier to make, too.

### Caramelized Corn Sauté

It's hard to make fresh sweet corn taste better, but a splash of half-and-half does it by adding a nutty flavor. Milk would curdle here, but cream won't. Make sure to get all the pulp and milky juice when you cut the corn from the cob.

  1 teaspoon butter or stick margarine
  6 cups fresh corn kernels (about 5 ears)
  ½ cup chopped green onions
  ½ cup chopped red bell pepper
  ½ cup half-and-half
  ½ teaspoon salt
  ⅛ teaspoon black pepper

**1.** Heat butter in a large nonstick skillet over medium-high heat. Add corn, onions, and bell pepper; cook 10 minutes or until lightly browned, stirring frequently. Stir in half-and-half, salt, and black pepper; cook 2 minutes. Yield: 6 servings (serving size: about ¾ cup).

CALORIES 170 (25% from fat); FAT 4.8g (sat 2.1g, mono 1.4g, poly 1g); PROTEIN 5.8g; CARB 31.5g; FIBER 5.3g; CHOL 9mg; IRON 1.1mg; SODIUM 235mg; CALC 32mg

### Tomato Sauce

Canned tomatoes and other pantry ingredients team up for a tomato sauce that'll beat the jarred variety.

  1 tablespoon olive oil
  1½ cups chopped onion
  1 cup chopped green bell pepper
  1 teaspoon dried oregano
  4 garlic cloves, minced
  ½ cup dry red wine
  1 teaspoon dried basil
  ½ teaspoon salt
  ¼ teaspoon black pepper
  2 (28-ounce) cans whole plum tomatoes, undrained and chopped
  1 (6-ounce) can tomato paste
  2 bay leaves

**1.** Heat oil in a large saucepan over medium-high heat. Add onion, bell pepper, oregano, and garlic; cook 5 minutes or until vegetables are tender, stirring occasionally.
**2.** Add wine and remaining ingredients, and bring to a boil. Reduce heat, and simmer 30 minutes. Remove bay leaves. Yield: 8 cups (serving size: 1 cup).
**NOTE:** This sauce will freeze well for up to 3 months. Place it in an airtight container or zip-top plastic bag, and freeze.

CALORIES 93 (23% from fat); FAT 2.4g (sat 0.4g, mono 1.4g, poly 0.5g); PROTEIN 3.3g; CARB 17.1g; FIBER 3.3g; CHOL 0mg; IRON 2.4mg; SODIUM 487mg; CALC 77mg

### Port-Wine Mushroom Sauce

This sauce garnered our highest rating in the Test Kitchens. Try it with beef, lamb, venison, or pork. Use any kind of fresh mushroom in place of the shiitakes, but stick with port wine if possible.

  1½ cups sliced shiitake mushroom caps (about 3½ ounces)
  1 tablespoon all-purpose flour
  ⅓ cup port or other sweet red wine
  ¼ cup minced shallots
  1 tablespoon balsamic vinegar
  1 cup beef broth
  2 teaspoons Worcestershire sauce
  1 teaspoon tomato paste
  ⅛ teaspoon dried rosemary
  ½ teaspoon Dijon mustard

**1.** Combine mushrooms and flour in a bowl; toss well.
**2.** Combine wine, shallots, and vinegar in a medium skillet. Bring to a boil; cook until thick (about 3 minutes). Reduce heat to medium. Add broth, Worcestershire, tomato paste, and rosemary; cook 1 minute. Add mushroom mixture; cook 3 minutes, stirring constantly. Stir in mustard. Yield: 1 cup (serving size: ¼ cup).

CALORIES 69 (3% from fat); FAT 0.2g (sat 0.0g, mono 0.0g, poly 0.1g); PROTEIN 3.8g; CARB 8.4g; FIBER 0.5g; CHOL 0mg; IRON 1mg; SODIUM 367mg; CALC 14mg

## Cheese Sauce

Steeping the milk with peppercorns and a bay leaf infuses great flavor, but you can bypass that step if you choose.

1⅓ cups 1% low-fat milk
3 whole black peppercorns
1 bay leaf
3 tablespoons all-purpose flour
1 cup (4 ounces) finely shredded extra-sharp Cheddar cheese

**1.** Combine first 3 ingredients in a medium saucepan; cook over low heat 5 minutes. Remove from heat, and cool 5 minutes. Strain milk mixture through a sieve, discarding solids.
**2.** Place flour in pan; gradually add ¼ cup milk, stirring with a whisk until blended. Cook over low heat 1 minute, stirring constantly. Add remaining milk; cook until thick (about 5 minutes), stirring constantly. Remove from heat, and add cheese, stirring until melted. Yield: 1½ cups (serving size: about ¼ cup).

CALORIES 113 (55% from fat); FAT 6.8g (sat 4.3g, mono 1.9g, poly 0.2g); PROTEIN 6.8g; CARB 5.8g; FIBER 0.1g; CHOL 22mg; IRON 0.3mg; SODIUM 144mg; CALC 203mg

## Fudge Sauce

2 tablespoons butter or stick margarine
2 ounces unsweetened chocolate
½ cup sugar
6 tablespoons unsweetened cocoa
1 cup dark corn syrup
½ cup fat-free milk
2 teaspoons vanilla extract

**1.** Combine butter and chocolate in a saucepan; cook over low heat until chocolate melts, stirring occasionally. Combine sugar and cocoa in a medium bowl; add corn syrup and milk, stirring with a whisk until well-blended. Add cocoa mixture to saucepan. Bring to a boil over medium heat; cook 1 minute, stirring constantly. Remove from heat; stir in vanilla. Yield: 2 cups (serving size: 2 tablespoons).

CALORIES 125 (26% from fat); FAT 3.6g (sat 2.2g, mono 1g, poly 0.1g); PROTEIN 1.3g; CARB 24.4g; FIBER 0.1g; CHOL 4mg; IRON 0.6mg; SODIUM 45mg; CALC 17mg

## Sauce Step-by-Steps

### Tomato Sauce:

**1.** *Chop the tomatoes in the can with scissors or a sharp knife. This will cut down on your mess.*

**2.** *Sauté the vegetables. Add the chopped tomatoes and tomato paste. Simmer the sauce 30 minutes.*

### Port-Wine Mushroom Sauce:

**1.** *Combine the wine, shallots, and vinegar in a medium skillet. Bring to a boil; reduce the liquid by cooking about 3 minutes until thick and syrupy.*

**2.** *Lower heat to medium. Add the broth, Worcestershire, tomato paste, and rosemary; cook 1 minute. Add the mushroom mixture; cook 3 minutes, stirring constantly. Stir in the mustard.*

### Cheese Sauce:

**1.** *Steep the milk with peppercorns and bay leaf in a saucepan over low heat 5 minutes. Remove from heat; cool 5 minutes. Strain the milk mixture through a sieve; discard solids.*

**2.** *Make a slurry by gradually adding the aromatic milk mixture to the flour in a pan over low heat. Stirring constantly, cook 5 minutes. Remove from heat, and stir in the cheese.*

### Fudge Sauce:

**1.** *Over very low heat, cook the butter and chocolate together in a saucepan. Melting the chocolate with butter helps the chocolate melt evenly, but it can still scorch easily, so be sure to do it over the lowest heat. Add the remaining ingredients, and cook 1 minute.*

## Baked Rigatoni with Beef

Slightly undercook the pasta for this casserole; it cooks again in the oven.

 4 cups Tomato Sauce (recipe on page 84)
 1 pound ground round
 4 cups cooked rigatoni (about 2½ cups uncooked pasta)
 1½ cups (6 ounces) shredded part-skim mozzarella cheese, divided
 Cooking spray
 ¼ cup (1 ounce) grated fresh Parmesan cheese

**1.** Prepare Tomato Sauce.
**2.** Preheat oven to 350°.
**3.** Cook beef in a large nonstick skillet over medium-high heat until browned; stir to crumble. Drain well. Combine beef, Tomato Sauce, rigatoni, and 1 cup mozzarella in an 11 x 7-inch baking dish coated with cooking spray. Top with ½ cup mozzarella and Parmesan. Bake at 350° for 20 minutes or until thoroughly heated. Yield: 8 servings (serving size: 1 cup).

CALORIES 305 (28% from fat); FAT 9.6g (sat 4.3g, mono 3.5g, poly 0.7g); PROTEIN 24g; CARB 30.5g; FIBER 2.3g; CHOL 50mg; IRON 3.5mg; SODIUM 438mg; CALC 232mg

## Pepper Steak with Port-Wine Mushroom Sauce

Port-Wine Mushroom Sauce (recipe on page 84)
 4 (4-ounce) beef tenderloin steaks (about 1 inch thick)
 1 tablespoon black peppercorns, crushed
 ½ teaspoon kosher salt

**1.** Prepare Port-Wine Mushroom Sauce.
**2.** Sprinkle steaks with peppercorns and salt. Heat a nonstick skillet over medium-high heat. Add steaks; cook 3 minutes on each side or until desired degree of doneness. Serve steaks with warm Port-Wine Mushroom Sauce. Yield: 4 servings (serving size: 1 steak and ¼ cup sauce).

CALORIES 241 (29% from fat); FAT 7.7g (sat 3g, mono 2.9g, poly 0.4g); PROTEIN 27.5g; CARB 9.4g; FIBER 1g; CHOL 70mg; IRON 4.6mg; SODIUM 722mg; CALC 28mg

## Chocolate Turtle Brownie Sundaes

Fudge Sauce (recipe on page 85)

BROWNIES:
 Cooking spray
 3 tablespoons butter or stick margarine
 1 ounce unsweetened chocolate
 1 large egg
 1 large egg white
 2 tablespoons water
 1 teaspoon vanilla extract
 ⅔ cup all-purpose flour
 1 cup sugar
 ⅓ cup unsweetened cocoa
 ½ teaspoon baking powder
 1 tablespoon fat-free milk
 10 small soft caramel candies
 2 tablespoons coarsely chopped pecans

SUNDAES:
 4 cups vanilla low-fat frozen yogurt

**1.** Prepare Fudge Sauce.
**2.** Preheat oven to 350°.
**3.** To prepare brownies, coat bottom of an 8-inch square baking pan with cooking spray. Combine butter and chocolate in a large microwave-safe bowl. Microwave at HIGH 1 minute, and stir until melted. Add egg and egg white, stirring with a whisk. Stir in water and vanilla. Lightly spoon flour into dry measuring cups, and level with a knife. Combine flour, sugar, cocoa, and baking powder, and stir into chocolate mixture. Spread half of batter in bottom of prepared pan.
**4.** Combine milk and candies in a small microwave-safe bowl. Microwave at HIGH 1½ minutes, and stir until melted. Drizzle caramel mixture over batter in pan; sprinkle with pecans. Drop remaining batter by tablespoonfuls over pecans. Bake at 350° for 35 minutes or until a wooden pick inserted in center comes out almost clean. Cool completely on a wire rack. Cut into 16 squares.
**5.** To prepare sundaes, top each brownie with ¼ cup frozen yogurt and 2 tablespoons Fudge Sauce. Yield: 16 servings.

CALORIES 292 (28% from fat); FAT 9g (sat 5.1g, mono 2.6g, poly 0.7g); PROTEIN 4.4g; CARB 52.2g; FIBER 0.4g; CHOL 27mg; IRON 1.4mg; SODIUM 99mg; CALC 63mg

## Open-Faced Saucy Philly Cheesesteak Sandwich

(pictured on page 94)

The deli roast beef tastes terrific but bumps the sodium content up. Feel free to use a lower-sodium version.

 Cheese Sauce (recipe on page 85)
 1 teaspoon olive oil
 1½ cups red bell pepper strips
 1½ cups yellow bell pepper strips
 1½ cups vertically sliced onion
 1 tablespoon balsamic vinegar
 1 teaspoon sugar
 ¼ teaspoon dried oregano
 ¼ teaspoon garlic powder
 4 (2-ounce) slices bread, toasted
 ¾ pound thinly sliced deli roast beef
 2 tablespoons chopped fresh parsley

**1.** Prepare Cheese Sauce; keep warm.
**2.** Heat oil in a large nonstick skillet over medium-high heat. Add bell peppers and onion; sauté 8 minutes or until tender. Stir in vinegar, sugar, oregano, and garlic powder.
**3.** Preheat broiler.
**4.** Place toast slices on a baking sheet. Top each toast slice with 3 ounces roast beef, 6 tablespoons Cheese Sauce, and ¾ cup bell pepper mixture. Broil 1 minute or until sandwiches are thoroughly heated. Sprinkle sandwiches with chopped parsley. Yield: 4 servings.

CALORIES 447 (30% from fat); FAT 14.7g (sat 7.2g, mono 4.7g, poly 1.1g); PROTEIN 28.5g; CARB 49.2g; FIBER 3.9g; CHOL 41mg; IRON 4mg; SODIUM 1,307mg; CALC 388mg

# Speed to the Spud

*When microwave meets potato, dinner is served.*

Potatoes are famous for requiring minimal fuss—and they demand even less if you use your microwave. Most recent models can cook four average-size potatoes (about 1½ pounds) in around 16 minutes.

## Ham-and-Swiss-Loaded Potatoes

**PREPARATION TIME: 5 MINUTES**
**COOKING TIME: 25 MINUTES**

- 4 baking potatoes (about 1½ pounds)
- 1 cup diced 33%-less-sodium ham (about 6 ounces)
- 1 cup (4 ounces) shredded Swiss cheese, divided
- ½ cup thinly sliced green onions, divided
- ½ cup fat-free sour cream
- ¼ teaspoon freshly ground black pepper

**1.** Pierce potatoes with a fork; arrange in a circle on paper towels in microwave oven. Microwave at HIGH 16 minutes or until done, rearranging potatoes after 8 minutes. Let stand 5 minutes.
**2.** Preheat broiler.
**3.** Cut each potato in half lengthwise; scoop out pulp, leaving ¼-inch-thick shells. Combine potato pulp, ham, ½ cup cheese, ⅓ cup green onions, sour cream, and pepper.
**4.** Spoon potato mixture into shells. Combine ½ cup cheese and remaining green onions, and sprinkle over potatoes. Place potatoes on a baking sheet; broil 4 minutes or until golden. Yield: 4 servings (serving size: 2 potato halves).

CALORIES 376 (26% from fat); FAT 11g (sat 6.2g, mono 3.5g, poly 0.7g); PROTEIN 20.1g; CARB 47.9g; FIBER 3.4g; CHOL 51mg; IRON 2.9mg; SODIUM 540mg; CALC 359mg

## Cheesy Chicken-and-Broccoli-Topped Potatoes

**PREPARATION TIME: 10 MINUTES**
**COOKING TIME: 16 MINUTES**

- 4 baking potatoes (about 1½ pounds)
- ¾ pound skinned, boned chicken breast, cut into bite-size pieces
- 1 tablespoon all-purpose flour
- 1¼ teaspoons paprika, divided
- ½ teaspoon salt
- ¼ teaspoon freshly ground black pepper
- 1 tablespoon butter or stick margarine
- 2 cups small broccoli florets
- ⅔ cup fat-free, less-sodium chicken broth
- 1 cup (4 ounces) diced light processed cheese (such as Velveeta Light)

**1.** Pierce potatoes with a fork; arrange in a circle on paper towels in microwave oven. Microwave at HIGH 16 minutes or until done, rearranging potatoes after 8 minutes. Let stand 5 minutes.
**2.** While potatoes cook, combine chicken, flour, 1 teaspoon paprika, salt, and pepper in a large zip-top plastic bag; seal and shake to coat.
**3.** Melt butter in a large nonstick skillet over medium-high heat. Add chicken mixture and broccoli; sauté 5 minutes. Add broth; bring to a boil, and cook 3 minutes or until chicken is done. Add cheese, stirring just until melted.
**4.** Split potatoes open with fork, and fluff pulp. Spoon chicken mixture evenly over potatoes; sprinkle with ¼ teaspoon paprika. Yield: 4 servings (serving size: 1 potato and about ½ cup topping).

CALORIES 390 (17% from fat); FAT 7.4g (sat 4.2g, mono 1.9g, poly 0.7g); PROTEIN 31.6g; CARB 50.3g; FIBER 4.7g; CHOL 67mg; IRON 3.6mg; SODIUM 904mg; CALC 201mg

## Beef Bourguignonne-Topped Potatoes

**PREPARATION TIME: 14 MINUTES**
**COOKING TIME: 16 MINUTES**

- 4 baking potatoes (about 1½ pounds)
- 2 (6-ounce) beef tenderloin steaks, cut into 1-inch pieces
- 2 tablespoons all-purpose flour
- ¾ teaspoon salt
- ½ teaspoon black pepper
- 1 tablespoon butter or stick margarine
- 4 medium shallots, peeled and quartered
- 1 teaspoon dried thyme
- 1 teaspoon bottled minced garlic
- 1 (8-ounce) package presliced mushrooms
- ¾ cup beef broth
- ½ cup dry red wine
- Thyme sprigs (optional)

**1.** Pierce potatoes with a fork; arrange in a circle on paper towels in microwave oven. Microwave at HIGH 16 minutes or until done, rearranging potatoes after 8 minutes. Let stand 5 minutes.
**2.** While potatoes cook, combine beef, flour, salt, and pepper in a large zip-top plastic bag; seal and shake to coat.
**3.** Melt butter in a large nonstick skillet over medium-high heat. Add beef mixture and shallots; stir-fry 5 minutes. Add dried thyme, garlic, and mushrooms; stir-fry 3 minutes. Add broth and wine; cook 5 minutes or until shallots are tender and sauce thickens, stirring frequently. Remove from heat.
**4.** Split potatoes open with fork; fluff pulp. Spoon beef mixture evenly over potatoes. Garnish with thyme sprigs, if desired. Yield: 4 servings (serving size: 1 potato and 1 cup topping).

CALORIES 420 (20% from fat); FAT 8.9g (sat 4.1g, mono 3g, poly 0.6g); PROTEIN 26g; CARB 54.8g; FIBER 4.3g; CHOL 61mg; IRON 6.5mg; SODIUM 777mg; CALC 49mg

### Santa Fe Black Bean-Topped Potatoes

PREPARATION TIME: 10 MINUTES
COOKING TIME: 16 MINUTES

- 4 baking potatoes (about 1½ pounds)
- 2 teaspoons vegetable oil
- 1 cup diced yellow bell pepper
- ½ cup coarsely chopped onion
- 1 teaspoon bottled minced garlic
- ⅓ cup bottled salsa
- 1 teaspoon ground cumin
- 1 (15-ounce) can black beans, rinsed and drained
- 1 (14.5-ounce) can stewed tomatoes, coarsely chopped and drained
- 1 cup (4 ounces) shredded Monterey Jack cheese with jalapeño peppers
- ¼ cup low-fat sour cream
- ¼ cup chopped fresh cilantro

**1.** Pierce potatoes with a fork; arrange in a circle on paper towels in microwave oven. Microwave at HIGH 16 minutes or until done, rearranging potatoes after 8 minutes. Let stand 5 minutes.
**2.** While potatoes cook, heat oil in a large nonstick skillet over medium heat. Add bell pepper, onion, and garlic, and stir-fry 3 minutes. Stir in salsa, cumin, beans, and tomatoes, and cook 7 minutes or until thick.
**3.** Split potatoes open with fork, and fluff pulp. Spoon ¾ cup bean mixture over each potato. Top each with ¼ cup cheese, 1 tablespoon sour cream, and 1 tablespoon cilantro. Yield: 4 servings.

CALORIES 464 (27% from fat); FAT 13.8g (sat 7.1g, mono 3.8g, poly 1.8g); PROTEIN 18.6g; CARB 69.3g; FIBER 7.6g; CHOL 28mg; IRON 5.5mg; SODIUM 558mg; CALC 309mg

### Pepperoni Pizza-Topped Potatoes

PREPARATION TIME: 6 MINUTES
COOKING TIME: 16 MINUTES

- 4 baking potatoes (about 1½ pounds)
- 2 teaspoons olive oil
- 1 cup chopped onion
- 1 cup diced green bell pepper
- 1 teaspoon bottled minced garlic
- ⅔ cup bottled pizza sauce
- ½ cup turkey pepperoni slices, cut in half (about 2 ounces)
- ¼ teaspoon crushed red pepper
- 1 cup chopped tomato
- ¼ cup water
- 1 cup (4 ounces) preshredded part-skim mozzarella cheese

**1.** Pierce potatoes with a fork; arrange in a circle on paper towels in microwave oven. Microwave at HIGH 16 minutes or until done, rearranging potatoes after 8 minutes. Let stand 5 minutes.
**2.** While potatoes cook, heat oil in a large nonstick skillet over medium-high heat. Add onion, bell pepper, and garlic; stir-fry 5 minutes. Add pizza sauce, pepperoni, and red pepper; reduce heat, and simmer 3 minutes. Stir in tomato and water; simmer 3 minutes.
**3.** Split potatoes open with fork; fluff pulp. Spoon pepperoni mixture evenly over potatoes. Top with cheese. Yield: 4 servings (serving size: 1 potato, ½ cup topping, and ¼ cup cheese).

CALORIES 374 (24% from fat); FAT 9.9g (sat 4.1g, mono 3.8g, poly 1.3g); PROTEIN 17.1g; CARB 55.4g; FIBER 5.3g; CHOL 37mg; IRON 4.1mg; SODIUM 556mg; CALC 227mg

---

### Watt's Up?

Times in these recipes are based on our Test Kitchens' use of several microwave ovens ranging from 650 to 1,000 watts. All cooked the potatoes in 16 minutes and probably would not vary much from your own microwave, but be sure to consult the guide to your appliance for specific instructions. As with all microwave cooking, it's best to monitor for doneness.

---

classics

# A Few More Pounds

*We don't measure pound cake by the weight of its ingredients anymore—but by the depths of its flavors.*

### Sour Cream-Lemon Pound Cake

(pictured on front cover)

- Cooking spray
- 3 tablespoons dry breadcrumbs
- 3¼ cups all-purpose flour
- ½ teaspoon baking soda
- ¼ teaspoon salt
- ¾ cup butter or stick margarine, softened
- 2½ cups granulated sugar
- 2 teaspoons lemon extract
- 3 large eggs
- 1½ tablespoons grated lemon rind (about 2 lemons)
- ¼ cup fresh lemon juice, divided
- 1 (8-ounce) carton low-fat sour cream
- 1 cup powdered sugar

**1.** Preheat oven to 350°.
**2.** Coat a 10-inch tube pan with cooking spray; dust with breadcrumbs.
**3.** Lightly spoon flour into dry measuring cups; level with a knife. Combine flour, baking soda, and salt in a bowl; stir well with a whisk. Beat butter in a large bowl at medium speed of a mixer until light and fluffy. Gradually add granulated sugar and lemon extract, beating until well-blended. Add eggs, 1 at a time, beating well after each addition. Add grated lemon rind and 2 tablespoons lemon juice; beat 30 seconds. Add flour mixture to sugar mixture alternately with sour cream, beating at low speed, beginning and ending with flour mixture.
**4.** Spoon batter into prepared pan. Bake at 350° for 1 hour and 10 minutes or until a wooden pick inserted in center comes out clean. Cool in pan 10 minutes

on a wire rack; remove from pan. Cool completely on wire rack. Combine 2 tablespoons lemon juice and powdered sugar. Drizzle glaze over top of cake. Yield: 18 servings (serving size: 1 slice).

CALORIES 323 (29% from fat); FAT 10.4g (sat 6g, mono 3g, poly 0.6g); PROTEIN 4g; CARB 53.4g; FIBER 0.7g; CHOL 62mg; IRON 1.3mg; SODIUM 172mg; CALC 27mg

**SOUR CREAM POUND CAKE VARIATION:**
Substitute vanilla extract for lemon extract. Omit lemon juice and rind in cake. Substitute milk for lemon juice in glaze.

CALORIES 320 (29% from fat); FAT 10.4g (sat 6g, mono 3g, poly 0.6g); PROTEIN 4.1g; CARB 53.2g; FIBER 0.6g; CHOL 62mg; IRON 1.3mg; SODIUM 173mg; CALC 28mg

### Double-Banana Pound Cake

This cake packs a double punch of banana with the fruit and liqueur. The banana liqueur gives the cake a sweet, rich banana flavor.

Cooking spray
  3 tablespoons dry breadcrumbs
  3 cups all-purpose flour
  1 teaspoon baking powder
  ¼ teaspoon salt
  ¼ teaspoon ground mace
  1 cup mashed ripe banana
  ½ cup fat-free milk
  ½ cup banana liqueur or ½ cup fat-free milk and 1 tablespoon banana extract
  ¾ cup butter or stick margarine, softened
  2 cups granulated sugar
  1½ teaspoons vanilla extract
  3 large eggs
  1 tablespoon powdered sugar

**1.** Preheat oven to 350°.
**2.** Coat a 10-inch tube pan with cooking spray; dust with breadcrumbs.
**3.** Lightly spoon flour into dry measuring cups; level with a knife. Combine flour, baking powder, salt, and mace; stir well with a whisk. Combine mashed banana, milk, and banana liqueur in a bowl. Beat butter in a large bowl at medium speed of a mixer until light and fluffy. Gradually add granulated sugar and vanilla, and beat mixture until well-

blended. Add eggs, 1 at a time, beating well after each addition. Add flour mixture to sugar mixture alternately with banana mixture, beating at low speed, beginning and ending with flour mixture.
**4.** Spoon batter into prepared pan. Bake at 350° for 1 hour or until a wooden pick inserted in center comes out clean. Cool in pan 10 minutes on a wire rack; remove from pan. Cool completely on wire rack. Sift powdered sugar over top of cake. Yield: 18 servings (serving size: 1 slice).

CALORIES 286 (28% from fat); FAT 8.9g (sat 5.1g, mono 2.6g, poly 0.5g); PROTEIN 3.8g; CARB 44.8g; FIBER 0.9g; CHOL 58mg; IRON 1.3mg; SODIUM 163mg; CALC 37mg

### Brown Sugar Pound Cake

This was actually the most popular pound cake among our staff.

Cooking spray
  3 tablespoons dry breadcrumbs
  3 cups all-purpose flour
  1 teaspoon baking powder
  ¼ teaspoon salt
  ¾ cup butter or stick margarine, softened
  2 cups packed light brown sugar
  1 tablespoon vanilla extract
  3 large eggs
  1 cup fat-free milk
  1 tablespoon powdered sugar

**1.** Preheat oven to 350°.
**2.** Coat a 10-inch tube pan with cooking spray; dust with breadcrumbs.
**3.** Lightly spoon flour into dry measuring cups, and level with a knife. Combine flour, baking powder, and salt in a bowl; stir well with a whisk. Beat butter in a large bowl at medium speed of a mixer until light and fluffy. Gradually add brown sugar and vanilla, beating until well-blended. Add eggs, 1 at a time, beating well after each addition. Add flour mixture to sugar mixture alternately with milk, beating at low speed, beginning and ending with flour mixture.
**4.** Spoon batter into prepared pan. Bake at 350° for 1 hour and 5 minutes or until a wooden pick inserted in center comes out clean. Cool in pan 10 minutes on a

wire rack; remove from pan. Cool completely on wire rack. Sift powdered sugar over top of cake. Yield: 18 servings (serving size: 1 slice).

CALORIES 265 (30% from fat); FAT 8.9g (sat 5.1g, mono 2.6g, poly 0.5g); PROTEIN 3.9g; CARB 42.6g; FIBER 0.6g; CHOL 58mg; IRON 1.7mg; SODIUM 176mg; CALC 65mg

### Cornmeal Pound Cake

Cooking spray
  3 tablespoons dry breadcrumbs
  2 cups all-purpose flour
  1 cup cornmeal
  1 teaspoon baking powder
  1 teaspoon grated whole nutmeg
  ¼ teaspoon salt
  ¾ cup butter or stick margarine, softened
  1½ cups granulated sugar
  ⅔ cup packed brown sugar
  ½ teaspoon vanilla extract
  3 large eggs
  1 teaspoon grated orange rind
  1 cup fat-free milk
  1 tablespoon powdered sugar

**1.** Preheat oven to 350°.
**2.** Coat a 10-inch tube pan with cooking spray; dust with breadcrumbs.
**3.** Lightly spoon flour into dry measuring cups; level with a knife. Combine flour and next 4 ingredients in a bowl; stir well with a whisk. Beat butter in a large bowl at medium speed of a mixer until light and fluffy. Gradually add granulated and brown sugars and vanilla, beating until well-blended. Add eggs, 1 at a time, beating well after each addition. Add rind; beat 30 seconds. Add flour mixture to sugar mixture alternately with milk, beating at low speed, beginning and ending with flour mixture.
**4.** Spoon batter into prepared pan. Bake at 350° for 1 hour or until a wooden pick inserted in center comes out clean. Cool in pan 10 minutes on a wire rack; remove from pan. Cool completely on wire rack. Sift powdered sugar over top of cake. Yield: 18 servings (serving size: 1 slice).

CALORIES 267 (30% from fat); FAT 9g (sat 5.2g, mono 2.6g, poly 0.5g); PROTEIN 3.9g; CARB 43.3g; FIBER 0.8g; CHOL 58mg; IRON 1.4mg; SODIUM 169mg; CALC 51mg

## Spice Pound Cake

Cooking spray
- 3 tablespoons dry breadcrumbs
- 3 cups all-purpose flour
- 2 teaspoons ground cinnamon
- 1 teaspoon baking powder
- 1 teaspoon ground ginger
- ½ teaspoon grated whole nutmeg
- ½ teaspoon ground allspice
- ¼ teaspoon salt
- 10 tablespoons butter or stick margarine, softened
- 1⅓ cups granulated sugar
- 1 cup packed brown sugar
- 2 teaspoons vanilla extract
- 3 large eggs
- 1 cup fat-free milk
- 1 tablespoon powdered sugar

**1.** Preheat oven to 350°.

**2.** Coat a 10-inch tube pan with cooking spray; dust with breadcrumbs.

**3.** Lightly spoon flour into dry measuring cups; level with a knife. Combine flour and next 6 ingredients; stir well with a whisk. Beat butter in a large bowl at medium speed of a mixer until light and fluffy. Gradually add granulated and brown sugars and vanilla, beating until well-blended. Add eggs, 1 at a time, beating well after each addition. Add flour mixture to sugar mixture alternately with milk, beating at low speed, beginning and ending with flour mixture.

**4.** Spoon batter into prepared pan. Bake at 350° for 1 hour and 5 minutes or until a wooden pick inserted in center comes out clean. Cool in pan 10 minutes on a wire rack; remove from pan. Cool completely on wire rack. Sift powdered sugar over top of cake. Yield: 18 servings (serving size: 1 slice).

CALORIES 263 (26% from fat); FAT 7.6g (sat 4.3g, mono 2.2g, poly 0.5g); PROTEIN 3.9g; CARB 45g; FIBER 0.7g; CHOL 54mg; IRON 1.6mg; SODIUM 158mg; CALC 58mg

### Tube or Bundt Pan?

We preferred to bake these pound cakes in 10-inch tube pans, but you can also use a 12-cup Bundt pan. Just reduce the oven temperature to 325°.

## Black-and-White Pound Cake

(pictured on page 93)

The chocolate batter bakes into the vanilla batter, resulting in a contrasting swirl of black and white.

Cooking spray
- 3 tablespoons dry breadcrumbs
- 3 cups all-purpose flour
- 1 teaspoon baking powder
- ¼ teaspoon salt
- ¾ cup butter or stick margarine, softened
- 2 cups sugar
- 2 teaspoons vanilla extract
- 3 large eggs
- 1 cup 2% reduced-fat milk
- ¾ cup chocolate syrup
- ¼ teaspoon baking soda
- 1 tablespoon unsweetened cocoa

**1.** Preheat oven to 350°.

**2.** Coat a 10-inch tube pan with cooking spray; dust with breadcrumbs.

**3.** Lightly spoon flour into dry measuring cups, and level with a knife. Combine flour, baking powder, and salt in a bowl, and stir well with a whisk. Beat butter in a large bowl at medium speed of a mixer until light and fluffy. Gradually add sugar and vanilla, beating until well-blended. Add eggs, 1 at a time, beating well after each addition. Add flour mixture to sugar mixture alternately with milk, beating at low speed, beginning and ending with flour mixture.

**4.** Spoon two-thirds of batter (about 4 cups) into prepared pan. Add syrup and baking soda to remaining batter in bowl, stirring just until blended; spoon on top of batter in pan.

**5.** Bake at 350° for 1 hour and 15 minutes or until cake pulls away from sides of pan. Cool in pan 10 minutes on a wire rack; remove from pan. Cool completely on wire rack. Sift cocoa over top of cake. Yield: 18 servings (serving size: 1 slice).

CALORIES 289 (29% from fat); FAT 9.3g (sat 5.4g, mono 2.7g, poly 0.5g); PROTEIN 4.4g; CARB 47.3g; FIBER 0.6g; CHOL 59mg; IRON 1.5mg; SODIUM 192mg; CALC 46mg

## inspired vegetarian

# When Rice Is Nice

*Rice suits the shift into spring, when you hanker for fresh vegetables but still relish a warm, energizing meal.*

In the transitional months—April and its counterpart, September—white, basmati, or long-grain brown rice seems most appealing. These "transitional" rices are hearty but delicate enough to pair well with vegetables.

These rices are also quite versatile. They can be baked in a gratin, moistened with a creamy sauce, simmered into a robust pilaf, or tossed into a stir-fry. Clearly, rice can be much more than a side dish, especially for vegetarians looking for a meal that combines a grain with vegetables, herbs, dairy, and, most of all, good flavors.

### Creamy Rice with Asparagus

This is one of those quick, easy-to-prepare meals using ingredients that most folks have on hand. The egg, cooked by the heat of the rice, creates a creamy coating.

- 3 cups water
- ½ teaspoon salt, divided
- 3 cups (1-inch) sliced asparagus (about 12 ounces)
- 1½ cups uncooked long-grain rice
- 1 tablespoon butter
- 2 large eggs
- 1 cup grated Parmesan cheese, divided
- ¼ cup chopped fresh chives, divided
- 3 tablespoons chopped fresh basil
- 1 teaspoon grated lemon rind
- ¼ teaspoon black pepper

**1.** Bring 3 cups water and ¼ teaspoon salt to a boil in large saucepan. Add asparagus; cook 5 minutes or until crisp-tender. Remove asparagus with a slotted spoon; rinse with cold water, and set aside. Add rice and butter to cooking liquid; cover and simmer 15 to 20 minutes or until done. Set aside.

**2.** Combine ¼ teaspoon salt and eggs in a small bowl, stirring with a whisk until well-blended. Add ¾ cup cheese, 3 tablespoons chives, basil, lemon rind, and pepper; stir well. Stir egg mixture into hot rice. Stir in asparagus; cook rice mixture over low heat 1 minute or until rice mixture is thoroughly heated. Top with 1 tablespoon each of cheese and chives. Yield: 4 servings (serving size: 1 cup).

CALORIES 472 (28% from fat); FAT 14.7g (sat 8.2g, mono 4.5g, poly 0.9g); PROTEIN 22.5g; CARB 61.8g; FIBER 3.1g; CHOL 141mg; IRON 4.6mg; SODIUM 889mg; CALC 451mg

## Fried Rice with Pineapple and Tofu

(pictured on page 96)

The brown rice in this dish is nuttier-tasting and better for you than white. Long-grain brown rice tends to be a little milder than short-grain, but whichever you use, be sure to start this recipe using cold cooked rice.

    1   (14-ounce) package firm tofu,
        drained and cut into ½-inch cubes
    2   tablespoons roasted peanut oil or
        peanut oil, divided
    ¼   teaspoon salt
    1   cup (½-inch) pieces red bell
        pepper
    ¾   cup thinly sliced green onions
    1   cup shelled green peas
    ¼   pound snow peas, trimmed and cut
        lengthwise into thin strips
    4   cups cooked long-grain brown
        rice, chilled
    ¼   cup chopped fresh cilantro, divided
    1   (15¼-ounce) can pineapple
        chunks in juice, drained
    ¼   cup low-sodium soy sauce
    1   tablespoon chopped unsalted,
        dry-roasted peanuts

**1.** Place tofu between paper towels until barely moist. Heat 1 tablespoon oil in a large nonstick skillet or stir-fry pan over medium-high heat. Add tofu, and cook 8

minutes or until golden. Sprinkle with salt. Remove tofu from pan.

**2.** Heat 1 tablespoon oil in pan over medium-high heat. Add bell pepper and onions, and sauté 2 minutes. Add peas, and sauté 30 seconds. Stir in rice, and cook 2 minutes. Add tofu, 2 tablespoons cilantro, and pineapple; cook 1 minute, stirring gently. Remove from heat. Stir in soy sauce and peanuts. Sprinkle with 2 tablespoons cilantro. Yield: 7 servings (serving size: 1 cup).

CALORIES 256 (30% from fat); FAT 8.5g (sat 1.4g, mono 3.1g, poly 3.4g); PROTEIN 10.3g; CARB 36.5g; FIBER 4.5g; CHOL 0mg; IRON 4.9mg; SODIUM 375mg; CALC 102mg

## Rice-and-Noodle Pilaf

This unusual pilaf is made by first sautéing dry rice and noodles in butter and then boiling them. The result is a texture that is partially soft and partially crunchy. In countries such as Spain, this type of pilaf is typically made with *fideos* (fih-DAY-ohs), skinny egg noodles found in Latin and Middle Eastern markets. We've substituted easier-to-find spaghetti noodles.

    2   tablespoons butter
    3   ounces uncooked thin spaghetti,
        broken into 1-inch pieces, or fideo
        egg noodles
    1   cup uncooked long-grain rice
    2   cups boiling water
    ¼   teaspoon salt
    ¼   teaspoon black pepper

**1.** Melt butter in a large saucepan over medium heat, and add spaghetti. Sauté spaghetti 5 minutes or until lightly browned. Add rice, stirring to coat. Stir in water, salt, and pepper, and bring to a boil. Cover; reduce heat, and simmer 20 minutes or until liquid is absorbed. Remove pilaf from heat, and let stand 10 minutes. Fluff with a fork. Yield: 6 servings (serving size: ⅔ cup).

CALORIES 199 (19% from fat); FAT 4.3g (sat 2.5g, mono 1.2g, poly 0.3g); PROTEIN 4.1g; CARB 35.3g; FIBER 0.8g; CHOL 10mg; IRON 1.9mg; SODIUM 139mg; CALC 13mg

**menu**

### Rice-and-Spinach Gratin with Dill

Maple-orange sweet potatoes*

*Arrange 2 cups sliced peeled sweet potatoes in a 1-quart baking dish. Combine 2 tablespoons brown sugar, 1 tablespoon maple syrup, 1 teaspoon grated orange rind, 2 tablespoons orange juice, and 2 tablespoons melted butter; spoon over sweet potatoes. Cover and bake at 400° for 35 minutes. Stir; bake, uncovered, 30 minutes. Serves 4.

## Rice-and-Spinach Gratin with Dill

This simple gratin can be assembled ahead and baked later. Combining rice and spinach and binding them with a sauce makes for a substantial main dish.

SPINACH:

    1   (10-ounce) package fresh spinach,
        chopped (about 4 cups)
    2   teaspoons butter
    1   cup finely chopped green onions
    2   tablespoons chopped fresh parsley
    1   tablespoon chopped fresh dill
    2   garlic cloves, minced

SAUCE:

    1   tablespoon butter
    ¼   cup minced fresh onion
    2½  tablespoons all-purpose flour
    2   cups 2% reduced-fat milk
    ¾   teaspoon salt
    ¾   teaspoon freshly ground black
        pepper
    ¼   teaspoon grated whole nutmeg

REMAINING INGREDIENTS:

    3   cups hot cooked long-grain rice
    ½   cup part-skim ricotta cheese
        Cooking spray

**1.** Preheat oven to 400°.

**2.** To prepare spinach, heat a large nonstick skillet over medium heat. Add spinach, and cook 5 minutes or until slightly wilted, stirring frequently. Stir in 2 teaspoons butter and next 4 ingredients;
*Continued*

sauté 3 minutes. Spoon spinach mixture into a large bowl; set aside.

**3.** To prepare sauce, melt 1 tablespoon butter in a small saucepan over medium heat. Add minced onion, and cook 3 minutes. Stir in flour. Add milk; stir with a whisk. Bring to a boil; reduce heat, and simmer 20 minutes, stirring frequently. Stir in salt, pepper, and nutmeg. Add sauce to spinach mixture. Stir in rice and ricotta cheese. Spoon rice mixture into an 11 x 7-inch baking dish coated with cooking spray. Bake at 400° for 15 minutes. Yield: 4 servings (serving size: about 1¼ cups).

CALORIES 365 (25% from fat); FAT 10.3g (sat 6.1g, mono 2.9g, poly 0.6g); PROTEIN 14.1g; CARB 54.7g; FIBER 4.8g; CHOL 32mg; IRON 4.5mg; SODIUM 650mg; CALC 353mg

### Leek-and-Mascarpone Cheese Risotto

Leeks, golden saffron, a touch of lemon, and basil leaves make this a cheerful risotto. *Mascarpone* (mas-kar-POHN) is a buttery Italian triple-cream cheese found in many supermarkets and gourmet food shops. Regular cream cheese makes an acceptable, though not as rich, substitute.

    8   cups water
    6   cups chopped leek (about 6 large),
        divided
    2   cups chopped fresh flat-leaf
        parsley, divided
    1   cup chopped fresh basil, divided
    ½   teaspoon salt
    6   thyme sprigs
    2   carrots, cut into 1-inch-thick pieces
    2   garlic cloves, crushed
    1   large onion, cut into 1-inch pieces
    1   celery stalk, cut into 1-inch pieces
    ¼   teaspoon saffron threads
    2   tablespoons butter
    2   cups uncooked Arborio rice
        or other short-grain rice
    ½   cup dry white wine
    ⅓   cup (3 ounces) mascarpone cheese
    1   teaspoon grated lemon rind
    1   teaspoon salt
    ½   teaspoon black pepper
    ⅓   cup (1½ ounces) grated fresh
        Parmesan cheese

**1.** Combine water, 2 cups chopped leek, 1 cup parsley, ½ cup basil, ½ teaspoon salt, and next 5 ingredients in a large Dutch oven. Bring to a boil over medium heat. Reduce heat; simmer, uncovered, 35 minutes. Strain broth through a sieve into a large bowl; discard solids. Reserve 5½ cups broth; reserve remaining broth for another use.

**2.** Bring 5½ cups broth and saffron to a simmer in a small saucepan (do not boil). Keep warm over low heat. Melt butter in a large saucepan over medium-high heat. Add 4 cups chopped leek; sauté 5 minutes. Add rice; cook 2 minutes. Add wine; cook 1 minute or until liquid is nearly absorbed. Stir in 2 cups broth; cook 5 minutes or until liquid is nearly absorbed, stirring constantly. Add remaining broth, ½ cup at a time, stirring constantly until each portion of broth is absorbed before adding the next (about 15 minutes total). Add 1 cup parsley, ½ cup basil, mascarpone, lemon rind, salt, and pepper; cook 1 minute or until mascarpone melts. Sprinkle with Parmesan. Yield: 8 servings (serving size: 1 cup).

CALORIES 323 (27% from fat); FAT 9.8g (sat 5.4g, mono 3.1g, poly 0.8g); PROTEIN 7g; CARB 48.7g; FIBER 1.8g; CHOL 21mg; IRON 4.1mg; SODIUM 589mg; CALC 135mg

### The Long and Short

**Long-grain rice** has firm, separate grains that work well in salads, casseroles, and side dishes.
**Medium- and short-grain** rices are plumper when cooked, and tend to cling together. These are useful in dishes needing a creamy consistency, such as rice puddings, croquettes, and meat loaf. Sometimes short-grain rice is called pearl or short rice.

# Dualing Kitchens

*Two cooks won't necessarily spoil the broth—not with a little creative separation.*

Mark and Annette Shideler love to cook so much that while renovating their home in Mount Sinai, Long Island, New York, they customized the kitchen with his-and-hers work stations.

### Sweet Potato-Wild Rice Salad

    3   cups fat-free, less-sodium chicken
        broth
    1   cup uncooked wild rice
    2   cups (½-inch) cubed peeled sweet
        potato
    1   tablespoon plus ½ teaspoon olive
        oil, divided
    ⅓   cup diced Red Delicious apple
    ¼   cup thawed orange juice
        concentrate, undiluted
    ¼   cup chopped green onions
    ¼   cup raisins
    Mint sprigs (optional)

**1.** Bring chicken broth to a boil in a medium saucepan. Add rice; cover, reduce heat, and simmer 45 minutes or until liquid is absorbed.

**2.** Preheat oven to 400°.

**3.** Combine sweet potato and ½ teaspoon oil; toss well to coat. Arrange sweet potato in a single layer on a jelly-roll pan. Bake at 400° for 30 minutes, turning once.

**4.** Combine diced apple and orange juice concentrate in a small bowl. Drain, reserving concentrate. Combine 1 tablespoon oil and reserved concentrate; stir well with a whisk.

**5.** Combine rice, apple concentrate mixture, green onions, and raisins; gently stir in potato. Cover and chill 1 hour. Garnish with mint sprigs, if desired. Yield: 6 servings (serving: ⅔ cup).

CALORIES 217 (13% from fat); FAT 3.1g (sat 0.4g, mono 2g, poly 0.5g); PROTEIN 6.7g; CARB 41.8g; FIBER 3.3g; CHOL 0mg; IRON 1mg; SODIUM 249mg; CALC 25mg

**Black-and-White Pound Cake, page 90**

**Brown Sugar Pavlovas with Fruit, page 81**

Open-Faced Saucy
Philly Cheesesteak
Sandwich, page 86

Potatoes Primavera,
page 105

Barbecue Shrimp,
page 76

Warm Scallop Salad
with Lime and Cilantro,
page 102

Fried Rice with
Pineapple and Tofu,
page 91

# Supper and the Single Parent

*Feeding you and yours after a long day should be fast, fun, and an oasis of togetherness.*

## Chile-Cheese Rice Burritos

Cooking spray
½ cup shredded zucchini
½ cup thinly sliced green onions
1 cup hot cooked rice
¼ cup (1 ounce) shredded Monterey Jack cheese with jalapeño peppers
1 tablespoon canned chopped green chiles
¼ teaspoon salt
⅛ teaspoon black pepper
¼ cup fat-free sour cream
2 (8-inch) flour tortillas
½ cup shredded iceberg lettuce
½ cup diced tomato
2 tablespoons bottled salsa

**1.** Place a nonstick skillet coated with cooking spray over medium-high heat until hot. Add zucchini and onions; sauté 3 minutes or until tender. Stir in rice and next 4 ingredients; cook 1 minute, stirring constantly. Remove from heat; stir in sour cream.
**2.** Warm tortillas according to package directions. Spoon half of rice mixture down center of each tortilla. Top each with half of lettuce and tomato; roll up. Serve with salsa. Yield: 2 servings (serving size: 1 burrito and 1 tablespoon salsa).

CALORIES 358 (20% from fat); FAT 8.1g (sat 3.3g, mono 2.6g, poly 1.7g); PROTEIN 13g; CARB 57.4g; FIBER 3.6g; CHOL 11mg; IRON 3.4mg; SODIUM 726mg; CALC 244mg

## Zesty Cheese Ravioli

Ravioli, one of the kid-friendliest Italian meals, gets a quick boost with spinach.

½ cup water
1 (14.5-ounce) can no-salt-added diced tomatoes, undrained
1 garlic clove, minced
1 (9-ounce) package fresh cheese ravioli (such as Contadina)
2 cups finely chopped spinach (5 ounces)
⅛ teaspoon sugar
⅛ teaspoon coarsely ground black pepper
1 tablespoon grated Parmesan cheese

**1.** Combine first 3 ingredients in a large saucepan; bring to a boil. Add ravioli; cover and cook 5 minutes. Uncover and cook an additional 5 minutes or until done.
**2.** Stir in spinach, sugar, and pepper; cover and cook 2 minutes. Remove from heat, and let stand 5 minutes. Sprinkle with Parmesan cheese. Yield: 2 servings (serving size: 2 cups).

CALORIES 505 (26% from fat); FAT 14.5g (sat 8g, mono 4.1g, poly 0.4g); PROTEIN 25.8g; CARB 69.7g; FIBER 7.4g; CHOL 107mg; IRON 5.6mg; SODIUM 640mg; CALC 476mg

## Crispy Sesame Shrimp

¾ cup herb-seasoned stuffing mix (such as Pepperidge Farm), crushed
1 teaspoon sesame seeds
¼ teaspoon paprika
⅛ teaspoon salt
⅛ teaspoon garlic powder
⅛ teaspoon black pepper
1 large egg white, lightly beaten
10 large shrimp, peeled and deveined (about ¾ pound)
Cooking spray

**1.** Preheat oven to 425°.
**2.** Combine first 6 ingredients in a small bowl. Place beaten egg white in a small shallow bowl. Dip shrimp in egg white; dredge in stuffing mixture. Place shrimp on a large baking sheet coated with cooking spray. Lightly coat shrimp with cooking spray. Bake at 425° for 15 minutes or until golden. Yield: 2 servings (serving size: 5 shrimp).

CALORIES 242 (15% from fat); FAT 4.1g (sat 0.6g, mono 0.7g, poly 1.9g); PROTEIN 30.5g; CARB 18.6g; FIBER 1.7g; CHOL 194mg; IRON 4.3mg; SODIUM 656mg; CALC 104mg

## Meat Sauce Macaroni

½ pound ground round
½ cup commercial pizza sauce
⅛ teaspoon salt
⅛ teaspoon black pepper
1 cup hot cooked elbow macaroni (about 2 ounces uncooked)
2 tablespoons (about ½ ounce) shredded reduced-fat sharp Cheddar cheese

**1.** Cook meat in a nonstick skillet over medium-high heat until browned, stirring to crumble. Drain. Wipe drippings from pan with a paper towel; return meat to pan. Add sauce, salt, and pepper; cook 2 minutes. Add pasta; cook 2 minutes or until thoroughly heated. Sprinkle each serving with 1 tablespoon cheese. Yield: 2 servings (serving size: 1¼ cups).

CALORIES 310 (28% from fat); FAT 9.6g (sat 3.4g, mono 3.9g, poly 0.7g); PROTEIN 30.5g; CARB 24.5g; FIBER 1.5g; CHOL 74mg; IRON 4.1mg; SODIUM 445mg; CALC 90mg

## Spaghetti with Broccoli and Ham

3 ounces uncooked spaghetti
1 cup small broccoli florets
½ cup light Alfredo sauce (such as Contadina)
½ cup diced low-sodium ham (about 2½ ounces)
⅛ teaspoon black pepper
2 teaspoons grated Parmesan cheese

**1.** Cook spaghetti in boiling water 9 minutes, omitting salt and fat. Add broccoli; cook 1 minute. Drain well.
**2.** Combine Alfredo sauce and ham in a small saucepan. Cook 2 minutes or until
*Continued*

hot. Add spaghetti mixture and pepper, and cook until thoroughly heated. Sprinkle each serving with 1 teaspoon cheese. Yield: 2 servings (serving size: 1 cup).

CALORIES 327 (30% from fat); FAT 11g (sat 5.2g, mono 3.9g, poly 1g); PROTEIN 17g; CARB 40.1g; FIBER 2.4g; CHOL 42mg; IRON 2.4mg; SODIUM 740mg; CALC 158mg

## Poached Pears and Vanilla Ice Cream

2 cups water
1 tablespoon fresh lemon juice
½ teaspoon vanilla extract
1 (3-inch) cinnamon stick
1 (3-inch) piece lemon rind
1 large pear, peeled, halved and cored
1 cup vanilla low-fat ice cream
¼ teaspoon ground cinnamon (optional)

**1.** Combine first 5 ingredients in a large saucepan; bring to a boil. Add pear halves; cover, reduce heat, and simmer 8 minutes or until tender. Remove pear halves with a slotted spoon; discard liquid. Place pears in a large shallow dish; cover and chill. Serve pear halves with ice cream. Sprinkle with cinnamon, if desired. Yield: 2 servings (serving size: 1 pear half and ½ cup ice cream).

CALORIES 141 (20% from fat); FAT 3.2g (sat 1.8g, mono 0.9g, poly 0.2g); PROTEIN 2.8g; CARB 27.5g; FIBER 1.3g; CHOL 9mg; IRON 0.3mg; SODIUM 56mg; CALC 101mg

## Couscous and Glazed Chicken

½ pound chicken breast tenders (about 6 tenders)
⅛ teaspoon salt
¼ teaspoon black pepper
½ teaspoon olive oil
Cooking spray
2 tablespoons apricot preserves
1 teaspoon balsamic vinegar
1 cup fat-free, less-sodium chicken broth
⅓ cup finely chopped dried apricots
½ cup uncooked couscous

**1.** Sprinkle chicken with salt and pepper. Heat oil in a small nonstick skillet coated with cooking spray over medium-high heat. Add chicken, and cook 4 minutes or until done, turning after 2 minutes.
**2.** Combine preserves and vinegar in a bowl; add chicken. Keep warm. Add broth to pan, scraping pan to loosen browned bits; add apricots. Bring to a boil; cover, reduce heat, and simmer 2 minutes. Gradually stir in couscous; top with chicken mixture. Remove from heat; cover and let stand 5 minutes. Fluff couscous with a fork. Yield: 2 servings (serving size: 3 chicken tenders and 1 cup couscous).

CALORIES 374 (8% from fat); FAT 3.3g (sat 0.6g, mono 1.3g, poly 0.6g); PROTEIN 33.3g; CARB 53.2g; FIBER 3.5g; CHOL 66mg; IRON 2.7mg; SODIUM 474mg; CALC 27mg

## in season

# Avanti, Arugula

*This eternal favorite of Italian cuisine is never better than in the spring, when the green, peppery leaves are at their best.*

## White Bean Salad with Shrimp and Arugula

4 cups trimmed arugula (about 4 ounces)
2 tablespoons fresh lemon juice
¼ teaspoon salt
⅛ teaspoon black pepper
1 (15.5-ounce) can Great Northern beans, rinsed and drained
1 tablespoon olive oil
⅓ cup diced red onion
1 pound medium shrimp, cooked and peeled
1 large garlic clove, minced

**1.** Combine all ingredients in a large bowl; toss well. Yield: 4 servings (serving size: about 1¼ cups).

CALORIES 215 (22% from fat); FAT 5.3g (sat 0.7g, mono 2.5g, poly 0.9g); PROTEIN 24g; CARB 18.4g; FIBER 3.3g; CHOL 129mg; IRON 4mg; SODIUM 466mg; CALC 140mg

## Tabbouleh with Arugula and Chicken

You'll find bulgur in most supermarkets next to the pasta and rice.

1 cup uncooked bulgur or cracked wheat
1 cup boiling water
1½ cups chopped ready-to-eat roasted skinned, boned chicken breasts (about 2 breasts)
1 cup diced tomato
½ cup chopped arugula (about ½ ounce)
⅓ cup diced red onion
¼ cup finely chopped fresh parsley
2 tablespoons finely chopped fresh mint
2 tablespoons fresh lemon juice
1 tablespoon olive oil
¼ teaspoon salt
⅛ teaspoon black pepper
24 arugula leaves

**1.** Combine bulgur and water in a large bowl. Cover and let stand 25 minutes. Stir in chicken and next 9 ingredients; cover and chill. Serve on arugula-lined plates. Yield: 4 servings (serving size: 1½ cups).

CALORIES 218 (21% from fat); FAT 5g (sat 0.9g, mono 2.9g, poly 0.8g); PROTEIN 14.9g; CARB 31g; FIBER 7.5g; CHOL 26mg; IRON 1.5mg; SODIUM 379mg; CALC 43mg

## Arugula-Cheese Grinder with Basil Mayonnaise

This vegetarian sandwich can be made with almost any kind of cheese or bread.

3 tablespoons light mayonnaise
1 tablespoon minced fresh basil
¼ teaspoon salt
⅛ teaspoon black pepper
4 (3-ounce) loaves French bread
8 (½-inch-thick) slices tomato
¾ cup alfalfa sprouts
4 (½-ounce) slices reduced-fat Havarti cheese
20 arugula leaves

**1.** Combine first 4 ingredients. Cut loaves in half horizontally; spread mayonnaise mixture evenly over cut sides of bread. Arrange 2 tomato slices over bottom half of each loaf; top each with 3 tablespoons sprouts, 1 cheese slice, and 5 arugula leaves. Top with remaining bread halves; serve immediately. Yield: 4 servings.

CALORIES 315 (27% from fat); FAT 9.3g (sat 2.9g, mono 3.3g, poly 2.4g); PROTEIN 12g; CARB 45.3g; FIBER 3.3g; CHOL 9mg; IRON 2.6mg; SODIUM 832mg; CALC 188mg

---

**menu**

**Field Salad with Roasted Leeks, Mushrooms, and Feta**

Broiled scallops with gremolata*

*Place 1½ pounds sea scallops in a large shallow baking dish. Combine 3 tablespoons lemon juice, 2 tablespoons water, 1½ tablespoons olive oil, 1 tablespoon minced fresh parsley, and 2 teaspoons grated lemon rind; pour over scallops. Broil 12 minutes or until done, stirring after 6 minutes. Serves 4.

---

## Field Salad with Roasted Leeks, Mushrooms, and Feta

 1  cup thinly sliced leek
 1  teaspoon olive oil
Cooking spray
 3  cups trimmed arugula (about 3 ounces)
 3  cups fresh spinach leaves
 1  cup sliced mushrooms
 ¼  cup (1 ounce) crumbled feta cheese
 3  tablespoons bottled light dill-mustard dressing (such as Maple Grove Farms of Vermont)

**1.** Preheat oven to 450°.
**2.** Combine sliced leek and oil. Spread leek mixture in a jelly-roll pan coated with cooking spray. Bake at 450° for 10 minutes or until browned. Combine leek mixture, arugula, spinach, mushrooms, and cheese in a large bowl. Drizzle with dressing, and toss gently to coat. Yield: 4 servings (serving size: 1¾ cups).

CALORIES 88 (51% from fat); FAT 5g (sat 1.6g, mono 1.7g, poly 1.4g); PROTEIN 2.6g; CARB 8.6g; FIBER 1.4g; CHOL 6mg; IRON 1.4mg; SODIUM 197mg; CALC 103mg

---

## Rice Pilaf with Arugula and Pistachios

A cup of chopped onion and two garlic cloves can be used in place of the shallots in this flavorful side dish. The hot rice wilts the arugula, which is stirred in at the end. Any kind of white rice will work in this pilaf, but we liked aromatic basmati best.

 1  tablespoon olive oil
 1  cup finely chopped shallots (about 5 shallots)
 1½  cups uncooked basmati rice
 3  cups canned vegetable broth
 ⅓  cup dry white wine
 ⅛  teaspoon salt
 ¼  teaspoon black pepper
 4  cups trimmed arugula (about 4 ounces)
 ¼  cup coarsely chopped pistachios

**1.** Heat olive oil in a large saucepan over medium heat. Add shallots, and cook 4 minutes. Stir in rice, and sauté 2 minutes. Add broth, wine, salt, and pepper, and bring to a boil. Cover, reduce heat, and simmer 20 minutes. Stir in arugula and pistachios. Yield: 5 servings (serving size: 1 cup).

CALORIES 331 (23% from fat); FAT 8.4g (sat 1g, mono 5.1g, poly 1.1g); PROTEIN 7.2g; CARB 54.8g; FIBER 2.4g; CHOL 0mg; IRON 3.9mg; SODIUM 672mg; CALC 78mg

---

## Potato Salad with Arugula Pesto, Peas, and Zucchini

PESTO:
 2  cups trimmed arugula (about 2 ounces)
 2  cups torn spinach
 ¼  cup basil leaves
 ¼  cup (1 ounce) grated fresh Parmesan cheese
 3  tablespoons sliced green onions
 1½  tablespoons fresh lemon juice
 1  tablespoon olive oil
 1  tablespoon water
 ½  teaspoon salt
 ⅛  teaspoon black pepper

REMAINING INGREDIENTS:
 4  cups (½-inch) cubed red potato (about 1¼ pounds)
 ½  cup shelled green peas (about 2½ ounces)
 1  cup diced zucchini

**1.** To prepare pesto, combine first 5 ingredients in a food processor; process until minced. Add lemon juice and next 4 ingredients; process until well-blended.
**2.** Place potato in a large saucepan, and cover with water; bring to a boil. Reduce heat, and simmer 9 minutes. Add peas, and cook 1 minute or until tender. Drain. Combine potato mixture, pesto, and zucchini in a bowl; toss well. Yield: 5 servings (serving size: 1 cup).

CALORIES 158 (26% from fat); FAT 4.5g (sat 1.4g, mono 2.4g, poly 0.4g); PROTEIN 6g; CARB 24.8g; FIBER 3g; CHOL 4mg; IRON 1.6mg; SODIUM 342mg; CALC 113mg

---

## Creamy Potato-Arugula Soup

 1  tablespoon olive oil
 1½  cups sliced leek or onion
 ¾  cup sliced celery
 1¾  cups diced peeled baking potato (about ¾ pound)
 1  cup water
 ½  cup diced zucchini
 ⅛  teaspoon salt
 ⅛  teaspoon black pepper
 1  (14½-ounce) can vegetable broth
 4  cups trimmed arugula (about 4 ounces)
 2  cups torn spinach
 2  cups 2% reduced-fat milk
 1  tablespoon sherry

**1.** Heat olive oil in a Dutch oven over medium heat. Add leek and celery, and cook 7 minutes or until leek is wilted, stirring occasionally. Add potato and next 5 ingredients, and bring to a boil. Cover, reduce heat, and simmer 15 minutes or until vegetables are tender. Stir in arugula and spinach, and cook 2 minutes or until wilted. Cool slightly. Place half of mixture in a food processor or blender, and process until smooth. Pour

*Continued*

puree into a large bowl. Repeat procedure with remaining mixture. Return pureed mixture to pan. Stir in milk and sherry, and cook 5 minutes or until thoroughly heated. Yield: 7 servings (serving size: 1 cup).

CALORIES 112 (31% from fat); FAT 3.8g (sat 1.1g, mono 1.8g, poly 0.3g); PROTEIN 4.2g; CARB 15.7g; FIBER 16g; CHOL 6mg; IRON 1.2mg; SODIUM 387mg; CALC 138mg

## reader recipes

# Preserving Tradition

*A lawyer keeps to precedent in a family curry recipe.*

When native Floridian Mikey Thomas married her high-school sweetheart, Adrian, she inherited a Thomas family tradition: Indian Chicken Curry. An attorney, Mikey wanted to keep to precedent.

### Indian Chicken Curry

 2 teaspoons curry powder
 2 teaspoons chili powder
 2 teaspoons ground red pepper
 1 teaspoon salt
 1 teaspoon ground coriander
 1 teaspoon ground ginger
 1 teaspoon ground cumin
 1 teaspoon ground cinnamon
 3 tablespoons butter or stick margarine
 1 cup chopped onion
 2 garlic cloves, minced
 1 pound skinned, boned chicken breast, cut into 1-inch cubes
 1 (8-ounce) carton plain fat-free yogurt
 1 (6-ounce) can tomato paste
 5 cups cubed peeled baking potato (about 2½ pounds)
 4 cups water
 4½ cups hot cooked basmati rice
 ⅔ cup chopped tomato

**1.** Combine first 8 ingredients. Melt butter in a Dutch oven over medium

heat; sauté onion and garlic 5 minutes. Stir in spice mixture; sauté 5 minutes. Add chicken; sauté 10 minutes. Combine yogurt and tomato paste; stir with a whisk. Add yogurt mixture, potato, and water to pan. Bring to a boil; cover, reduce heat, and simmer 1 hour, stirring occasionally. Serve chicken mixture over rice, and top with chopped tomato. Yield: 9 servings (serving size: 1 cup curry mixture, ½ cup rice, and about 1 tablespoon tomato).

CALORIES 315 (15% from fat); FAT 5.2g (sat 2.7g, mono 1.4g, poly 0.5g); PROTEIN 18.2g; CARB 49g; FIBER 3g; CHOL 40mg; IRON 3.1mg; SODIUM 377mg; CALC 96mg

### Jewish Apple Cake

"This recipe has been in my family since I was a child. I was appalled by all the eggs and oil that were in the classic recipe, so I made it as light as possible without destroying it. Now when people ask if this cake is high in fat, I can tell them 'no.'"
—Vivian Jones, Landenberg, Pennsylvania

 Cooking spray
 2 teaspoons all-purpose flour
 1 cup granulated sugar
 1 cup packed brown sugar
 ½ cup sweetened applesauce
 ½ cup orange juice
 ⅓ cup vegetable oil
 2 tablespoons (1 ounce) ⅓-less-fat cream cheese
 2½ teaspoons vanilla extract
 3 large egg whites
 2 large eggs
 3 cups all-purpose flour
 1 tablespoon baking powder
 ½ teaspoon salt
 3½ cups sliced peeled apple (about 1 pound)
 3 tablespoons granulated sugar
 2 tablespoons ground cinnamon
 2 tablespoons chopped walnuts

**1.** Preheat oven to 350°.
**2.** Coat a 10-inch tube pan with cooking spray, and dust with 2 teaspoons flour. Set prepared pan aside.
**3.** Beat 1 cup granulated sugar and next 8 ingredients at medium speed of a

mixer until blended. Lightly spoon flour into dry measuring cups; level with a knife. Combine flour, baking powder, and salt. Add flour mixture to sugar mixture, beating at low speed just until blended. Combine apple and remaining 3 ingredients. Spoon half of batter into prepared pan. Top with half of apple mixture. Repeat with remaining batter and apple mixture. Bake at 350° for 1 hour and 15 minutes. Cool 10 minutes in pan on a wire rack; remove from pan. Cool completely on wire rack. Yield: 16 servings.

CALORIES 287 (21% from fat); FAT 6.6g (sat 1.4g, mono 1.9g, poly 2.8g); PROTEIN 4.4g; CARB 53.6g; FIBER 1.5g; CHOL 29mg; IRON 2mg; SODIUM 196mg; CALC 84mg

### Champagne-Feta Risotto

"One time when I was making risotto, I had leftover champagne, so I tossed it in. Now I'm famous for this dish."
—James Kempf, Riverbank, California

 ⅓ cup water
 ½ teaspoon dried basil
 2 (16-ounce) cans fat-free, less-sodium chicken broth
 1 tablespoon olive oil
 1 cup chopped onion
 1 cup Arborio rice or other short-grain rice
 ½ cup champagne or white wine
 ⅔ cup (about 2½ ounces) crumbled feta cheese
 ¼ cup (1 ounce) grated fresh Parmesan cheese

**1.** Bring first 3 ingredients to a simmer in a medium saucepan (do not boil). Keep warm over low heat.
**2.** Heat oil in a large saucepan over medium-high heat. Add onion, and sauté 3 minutes. Add rice; sauté 2 minutes. Stir in champagne; cook 1 minute or until liquid is absorbed. Stir in 1 cup broth mixture; cook 5 minutes or until liquid is nearly absorbed, stirring constantly. Reduce heat to medium. Add remaining broth mixture, ½ cup at a time, stirring constantly until each portion of broth is absorbed before adding the next (about

25 minutes total). Stir in feta. Sprinkle each serving with Parmesan cheese. Yield: 4 servings (serving size: 1 cup risotto and 1 tablespoon Parmesan).

CALORIES 331 (27% from fat); FAT 10.1g (sat 4.9g, mono 4.1g, poly 0.6g); PROTEIN 12.4g; CARB 45.8g; FIBER 1.5g; CHOL 24mg; IRON 2.6mg; SODIUM 835mg; CALC 204mg

## Savory Roasted-Vegetable Pitas

"A friend of mine made something similar to this, and I nearly fell out of my chair when I saw how much fat was in the recipe. I came up with a lower-fat marinade so close to the original that my friend can't tell the difference."

—Charlotte Gaston, Macon, Georgia

**MARINATED VEGETABLES:**
3 tablespoons water
2 tablespoons olive oil
1½ tablespoons minced fresh or 1½ teaspoons dried oregano
2 teaspoons balsamic vinegar
2 teaspoons Dijon mustard
1½ teaspoons fresh lemon juice
¼ teaspoon salt
¼ teaspoon freshly ground black pepper
2 garlic cloves, minced
8 whole mushrooms (about 4 ounces)
6 (½-inch-thick) slices eggplant (about ½ pound)
3 (½-inch-thick) slices onion
1 medium yellow squash, halved lengthwise
1 medium zucchini, halved lengthwise

**REMAINING INGREDIENTS:**
Cooking spray
⅔ cup diced tomato
¼ cup chopped bottled roasted red bell peppers
4 (6-inch) whole-wheat pitas, cut in half and toasted
8 (½-ounce) slices part-skim mozzarella cheese

**1.** To prepare marinated vegetables, combine first 9 ingredients in a large zip-top plastic bag; add mushrooms and next 4 ingredients to bag. Seal and marinate at room temperature 2 hours, turning bag occasionally. Remove vegetables from bag; discard marinade.
**2.** Preheat oven to 400°.
**3.** Arrange marinated vegetables in a single layer in a shallow roasting pan coated with cooking spray. Bake at 400° for 25 minutes or until tender, stirring occasionally. Remove from pan; cool. Chop vegetables, and place in a large bowl; stir in tomato and bell peppers. Line each pita half with a cheese slice; fill each with ½ cup vegetable mixture. Yield: 4 servings (serving size: 2 pita halves).

CALORIES 335 (28% from fat); FAT 10.5g (sat 3.8g, mono 4.1g, poly 1.5g); PROTEIN 16.3g; CARB 49.3g; FIBER 8.7g; CHOL 16mg; IRON 3.3mg; SODIUM 593mg; CALC 231mg

## Grilled Asparagus

"My mom made this asparagus when Dad was barbecuing steaks, and it made all of the kids run to the table. Try this recipe with someone who says they don't like this vegetable, and you may have a convert on your hands."

—Ken Adams, Marysville, Michigan

1 pound asparagus
3 tablespoons balsamic vinegar
2 tablespoons fresh lemon juice
1 tablespoon olive oil
1 tablespoon low-sodium soy sauce
⅛ teaspoon black pepper
Cooking spray

**1.** Prepare grill.
**2.** Snap off tough ends of asparagus. Combine all ingredients except cooking spray in a large zip-top plastic bag; seal and marinate 30 minutes. Remove asparagus from bag, and discard marinade. Place asparagus on grill rack coated with cooking spray; grill 5 minutes on each side or until asparagus is done. Yield: 4 servings.

CALORIES 36 (50% from fat); FAT 2g (sat 0.3g, mono 1.3g, poly 0.3g); PROTEIN 1.8g; CARB 4g; FIBER 1.6g; CHOL 0mg; IRON 0.8mg; SODIUM 62mg; CALC 17mg

## Applesauce, Bran, and Oatmeal Muffins

"This is a low-fat, high-fiber muffin that I modified from a basic muffin recipe. You can customize it to your own taste by adding nuts. These muffins freeze extremely well."

—Tom Wells, West Mifflin, Pennsylvania

1¼ cups all-purpose flour
1 cup quick-cooking oats
¾ cup wheat bran
½ cup packed brown sugar
1 teaspoon baking powder
1 teaspoon ground cinnamon
¾ teaspoon baking soda
¼ teaspoon salt
½ cup raisins
1 cup applesauce
½ cup fat-free milk
1 tablespoon vegetable oil
1 tablespoon light-colored corn syrup
1 large egg
Cooking spray

**1.** Preheat oven to 375°.
**2.** Lightly spoon flour into dry measuring cups; level with a knife. Combine flour and next 7 ingredients in a medium bowl. Stir in raisins; make a well in center of mixture. Combine applesauce and next 4 ingredients; stir well with a whisk. Add to flour mixture, stirring just until moist. Spoon batter into 12 muffin cups coated with cooking spray. Bake at 375° for 18 minutes or until muffins spring back when touched lightly in center. Remove muffins from pans immediately; cool on a wire rack. Yield: 1 dozen (serving size: 1 muffin).
**NOTE:** Before freezing, let muffins cool completely on a wire rack. Store them in a heavy-duty zip-top plastic bag in your freezer for up to 1 month.

CALORIES 169 (13% from fat); FAT 2.4g (sat 0.5g, mono 0.7g, poly 0.9g); PROTEIN 4.1g; CARB 34.9g; FIBER 3.2g; CHOL 19mg; IRON 1.8mg; SODIUM 186mg; CALC 59mg

# Oldways and Your Ways

If you've ever wondered how some of the world's healthiest and best-tasting foods seem to wind up in your favorite home recipes and restaurants these days, you'll be glad to know it's not by accident. You have friends in the business.

Ever heard of a Boston-based nonprofit educational group known as the Oldways Preservation & Exchange Trust? Since its founding in 1990, the much-acclaimed organization has profoundly changed how Americans think about health, food, and the practical wisdom of tradition. Oldways' goal is to help people adopt healthful diets based on traditional healthy cuisines from around the world and use foods grown in environmentally sustainable ways.

### Warm Scallop Salad with Lime and Cilantro

(pictured on page 95)

This salad takes its flavors from the popular Latin American appetizer *ceviche*, a dish made with fish "cooked" in a marinade of lime juice, onions, tomatoes, and peppers.

- 2 teaspoons olive oil, divided
- ¼ cup minced red onion
- 1 to 2 tablespoons minced seeded jalapeño pepper
- 1 pound sea scallops
- 1½ cups diced plum tomato
- 1 cup chopped yellow bell pepper
- ½ cup diced peeled avocado
- ¼ cup chopped fresh cilantro
- 1 tablespoon fresh lime juice
- ¼ teaspoon salt
- 1 garlic clove, minced
- 6 cups trimmed watercress (about 1 bunch)
- 4 (6-inch) pitas, quartered and toasted

**1.** Heat 1 teaspoon olive oil in a large nonstick skillet over medium heat. Add onion and jalapeño; sauté 2 minutes. Add scallops; sauté 3 minutes or until done. Stir in 1 teaspoon oil, tomato, and next 6 ingredients. Remove from heat.

**2.** Arrange watercress on each of 4 plates; top with scallop salad, and serve with pitas. Yield: 4 servings (serving size: 1½ cups watercress, 1 cup scallop salad, and 1 pita).

CALORIES 307 (21% from fat); FAT 7g (sat 1g, mono 3.6g, poly 1.3g); PROTEIN 25.8g; CARB 36.1g; FIBER 4.9g; CHOL 37mg; IRON 2.9mg; SODIUM 590mg; CALC 143mg

### Sweet Orange Couscous with Dried Fruit

The traditional version of this Mediterranean dessert is often sweetened with sugarcane. We've used honey and granulated sugar to achieve the same end result.

- 3 cups water, divided
- 3 tablespoons sugar
- 3 tablespoons honey
- 32 dried apricot halves (about 5½ ounces)
- 2½ teaspoons grated orange rind
- 1 teaspoon fresh lemon juice
- 1 (3-inch) cinnamon stick
- 1 cardamom pod (optional)
- ⅓ cup fresh orange juice
- 2 tablespoons chopped pitted dates
- ½ cup uncooked couscous
- ⅛ teaspoon salt
- 2 tablespoons chopped fresh mint

**1.** Combine 2 cups water, sugar, and honey in a medium saucepan. Bring to a boil. Stir in apricots, rind, lemon juice, cinnamon, and cardamom, if desired. Reduce heat, and simmer 25 minutes. Cool. Remove apricots with a slotted spoon; set aside. Strain syrup through a sieve into a large bowl; discard solids. Add orange juice and dates to syrup; cover and chill.

**2.** Bring 1 cup water to a boil in pan; gradually stir in couscous and salt. Remove from heat; cover and let stand 5 minutes. Fluff with a fork. Cool completely. Spoon ½ cup couscous into each of 4 bowls. Arrange 8 apricot halves over each serving; sprinkle each with 1½ teaspoons mint. Spoon ½ cup date mixture over each serving. Yield: 4 servings.

CALORIES 266 (1% from fat); FAT 0.4g (sat 0.1g, mono 0.1g, poly 0.1g); PROTEIN 4g; CARB 66.3g; FIBER 4.6g; CHOL 0mg; IRON 2.4mg; SODIUM 80mg; CALC 25mg

### Suquet of Cod

In the rugged seacoast areas near Barcelona, Spain, Catalan cooks make this very soupy fish-and-potato stew with the catch of the day, usually some kind of white fish. Roughly translated, *suquet* means "juice" or "juicy."

- 1 teaspoon olive oil
- 2 cups chopped onion
- 3½ cups water
- ⅓ cup dry white wine
- ½ teaspoon saffron threads
- 2 (8-ounce) bottles clam juice
- 1 lemon slice
- ¼ cup fresh parsley leaves
- ¼ cup slivered almonds, toasted
- 1 tablespoon all-purpose flour
- 1 teaspoon sweet paprika
- 5 garlic cloves
- 1 pound diced peeled Yukon gold potatoes
- 1 pound cod or other lean white fish fillets
- 1 (10-ounce) package frozen baby peas
- ¼ teaspoon freshly ground black pepper
- ⅛ teaspoon salt

1. Heat oil in a large nonstick skillet over medium heat. Add onion; sauté 5 minutes or until tender. Add water and next 4 ingredients; bring to a boil. Reduce heat; simmer 10 minutes.

2. Place parsley and next 4 ingredients in a food processor; process until smooth. Add parsley mixture to pan; stir well. Add potato; simmer 20 minutes or until almost tender. Add cod and peas; simmer 10 minutes or until fish flakes easily when tested with a fork. Break up fish into bite-size pieces. Remove and discard lemon; sprinkle stew with pepper and salt. Ladle into soup bowls. Yield: 4 servings (serving size: 2 cups).

CALORIES 333 (15% from fat); FAT 5.7g (sat 0.7g, mono 3g, poly 1.3g); PROTEIN 29.5g; CARB 42.3g; FIBER 7.6g; CHOL 52mg; IRON 3.6mg; SODIUM 721mg; CALC 102mg

## Greek Phyllo Pie with Garlicky Greens and Feta

In Greece, feta-and-spinach pies like this one are made with lots of olive oil and are usually served as small appetizers. We've added rice to the traditional filling mixture and baked the popular dish as a whole pie rather than individual triangles.

- 2 cups water
- 11 cups chopped kale (about 1 pound)
- 10 cups chopped Swiss chard (about 1½ pounds)
- 1 tablespoon olive oil, divided
- 2 cups chopped onion
- 1 cup chopped fennel bulb
- ⅔ cup hot cooked long-grain rice
- 1 to 2 tablespoons chopped fresh or 1 teaspoon dried mint
- ½ teaspoon salt
- ¼ teaspoon ground nutmeg
- ⅛ teaspoon ground red pepper
- 4 garlic cloves, minced
- 3 large egg whites
- 1 (12-ounce) carton 1% low-fat cottage cheese
- 1 (4-ounce) package crumbled feta cheese
- 11 sheets frozen phyllo dough, thawed
- Cooking spray

1. Bring 2 cups water to a boil in a Dutch oven. Add kale; cover and cook 4 minutes. Stir in Swiss chard; cover and cook 3 minutes. Drain well, and cool. Place greens on paper towels, and squeeze until barely moist. Place greens in a large bowl; set aside.

2. Heat 2 teaspoons olive oil in pan over medium heat. Add onion and fennel; sauté 10 minutes or until soft. Stir onion mixture, rice, and next 8 ingredients into greens. Set aside.

3. Preheat oven to 350°.

4. Gently press 1 sheet of phyllo into an 11-inch round removable-bottom tart pan coated with cooking spray, allowing ends to extend over edges of pan; lightly coat with cooking spray. Place second sheet of phyllo over first sheet to form a crisscross design; lightly coat phyllo with cooking spray. Repeat procedure with 5 sheets of phyllo and cooking spray, pressing sheets down into pan. Spoon greens mixture over phyllo in pan. Cover greens mixture with 1 sheet of phyllo, continuing crisscross design; lightly coat phyllo with cooking spray. Repeat procedure with 2 sheets of phyllo and cooking spray, continuing crisscross design. Cover with remaining sheet of phyllo. Fold in edges of phyllo to fit pan and form a rim. Brush with 1 teaspoon oil. Cut 5 slits in top of dough to allow steam to escape. Bake at 350° for 50 minutes or until golden brown. Let stand 5 minutes. Yield: 10 servings (serving size: 1 wedge).

NOTE: If you can find packages of fresh phyllo dough, the delicate sheets will be easier to work with (they separate more readily) than the frozen variety. Look for fresh phyllo dough in ethnic markets or specialty-food shops.

CALORIES 209 (29% from fat); FAT 6.7g (sat 2.5g, mono 2.1g, poly 1.6g); PROTEIN 12g; CARB 26.8g; FIBER 2g; CHOL 12mg; IRON 3.2mg; SODIUM 665mg; CALC 195mg

## Sesame Barbecued Tofu over Noodles and Greens

Tofu is popular throughout Asia. Here it's cooked with hoisin sauce, a Chinese condiment made from soybeans, garlic, and spices, and served over *udon* (OO-dohn) noodles, thick spaghetti-like noodles made from whole wheat.

- 2½ tablespoons hoisin sauce, divided
- 1½ tablespoons low-sodium soy sauce, divided
- 1 tablespoon ketchup
- 1 tablespoon Dijon mustard
- 1 teaspoon sesame seeds, toasted
- ½ teaspoon dark sesame oil
- ½ teaspoon chile paste, divided
- 1 pound firm or extra-firm tofu, drained and cut into 12 slices
- Cooking spray
- 2 (16-ounce) cans fat-free, less-sodium chicken broth
- 3 garlic cloves, minced
- 1 (10-ounce) package fresh spinach
- 4 cups hot cooked udon noodles (thick, round fresh Japanese wheat noodles) or spaghetti

1. Preheat broiler.

2. Combine 1½ teaspoons hoisin, 1½ teaspoons soy sauce, ketchup, mustard, sesame seeds, oil, and ¼ teaspoon chile paste in a small bowl.

3. Place tofu on a foil-lined baking sheet coated with cooking spray. Brush tofu with half of hoisin mixture; broil 6 minutes or until browned. Turn tofu over; brush with remaining hoisin mixture. Broil 6 minutes or until browned. Cover; keep warm.

4. Combine 2 tablespoons hoisin, 1 tablespoon soy sauce, ¼ teaspoon chile paste, broth, and garlic in a Dutch oven. Bring to a boil; cook 2 minutes. Add spinach; cook until wilted. Stir in noodles. Spoon 1½ cups noodle mixture into each of 4 large bowls; top each serving with 3 tofu slices. Yield: 4 servings.

NOTE: Look for chile paste and udon noodles in the Asian section of supermarkets or at specialty Asian markets.

CALORIES 366 (20% from fat); FAT 8.3g (sat 1.2g, mono 2g, poly 4.3g); PROTEIN 21.5g; CARB 52g; FIBER 6.8g; CHOL 0mg; IRON 10.2mg; SODIUM 975mg; CALC 215mg

## Vegetable Donburi over Seasoned Rice

*Donburi* (dohn-boo-REE) is "fast food" in Japan—boiled rice topped with broth and either vegetables, meat, fish, or eggs. We combine shiitake mushroom caps, carrots, and green onions, and flavor it with *miso*, a slightly sweet paste made from ground soybeans. Find miso in large supermarkets, Asian markets, or health-food stores.

- 5 cups water, divided
- 2½ cups uncooked sushi rice or other short-grain rice
- 1 (14½-ounce) can vegetable broth
- 2½ tablespoons miso (soybean paste)
- 2½ tablespoons low-sodium soy sauce
- 1½ tablespoons sugar
- 6 cups thinly sliced shiitake mushroom caps (about 1 pound mushrooms)
- 1 tablespoon minced peeled fresh ginger
- 2 garlic cloves, minced
- 1 cup shredded carrot
- ¾ cup (1-inch) sliced green onions
- 2 large egg whites
- 1 large egg

**1.** Bring 3 cups water to a boil in a medium saucepan; add rice. Cover, reduce heat, and simmer 12 minutes. Remove from heat; let stand.

**2.** Bring 2 cups water and broth to a boil in a large saucepan. Stir in miso, soy sauce, and sugar. Add mushrooms, ginger, and garlic; reduce heat, and simmer 2 minutes. Stir in carrot and onions; cook 2 minutes.

**3.** Whisk egg whites and egg in a small bowl. Gently pour egg mixture into broth mixture (do not stir); cook 1 minute. Remove from heat; gently stir.

**4.** Spoon 1 cup rice into each of 6 large soup bowls. Ladle 1 cup broth mixture evenly over each serving. Yield: 6 servings.

**NOTE:** Sushi rice, a sticky rice that's available in many large supermarkets, holds together well when topped with vegetables and broth. But any rice will work in this dish.

CALORIES 315 (6% from fat); FAT 2.2g (sat 0.5g, mono 0.5g, poly 0.5g); PROTEIN 8.8g; CARB 64.4g; FIBER 2.8g; CHOL 44mg; IRON 4.4mg; SODIUM 869mg; CALC 33mg

## Cuban Chicken-and-Plantain Stew

In Latin American countries, the *plantain*, or cooking banana, is a common ingredient in stews, soups, or casseroles. It's used much as the potato is in the United States and has a mild squashlike flavor. Look for firm plantains; overripe fruit will become mushy during cooking.

- 1 tablespoon olive oil
- ¾ pound skinned, boned chicken breast, cut into bite-size pieces
- 1 cup chopped onion
- ½ cup chopped green bell pepper
- 1½ cups chopped plum tomato
- 1 cup dry sherry
- 1½ teaspoons paprika
- 1 teaspoon ground cumin
- 1 teaspoon dried oregano
- ¼ teaspoon salt
- ¼ teaspoon freshly ground black pepper
- 2 garlic cloves, minced
- 1 (14¼-ounce) can low-salt beef or chicken broth
- 2 cups sliced plantains (about ¾ pound)
- 2 tablespoons chopped fresh parsley

**1.** Heat oil in a Dutch oven over medium-high heat. Add chicken, onion, and bell pepper; sauté 5 minutes, stirring frequently. Stir in tomato and next 8 ingredients. Bring to a boil; reduce heat, and simmer 15 minutes. Stir in plantains; cook 10 minutes or until tender. Sprinkle with parsley. Yield: 4 servings (serving size: 1¼ cups).

**NOTE:** Beef broth is used to help deepen the flavor in this stew, but chicken broth is a fine substitute.

CALORIES 283 (17% from fat); FAT 5.4g (sat 0.9g, mono 2.9g, poly 0.9g); PROTEIN 22.7g; CARB 38.2g; FIBER 2.7g; CHOL 49mg; IRON 2.9mg; SODIUM 223mg; CALC 48mg

## Spring Posole

This hearty soup has its roots in Mexico's Pacific Coast region. A combination of pork, hominy (dried corn), spices, and broth, it's usually a popular holiday meal. Our spring version contains spinach and is topped with the traditional garnishes of chopped lettuce, radishes, and cheese.

- 2 teaspoons olive oil
- 1 cup chopped onion
- 2 teaspoons ground cumin
- 1½ teaspoons ground coriander
- ¼ teaspoon salt
- 1 minced drained canned chipotle chile in adobo sauce
- 2½ cups diced plum tomato
- 3 garlic cloves, minced
- 2 (15.5-ounce) cans golden hominy, drained and rinsed
- 2 (16-ounce) cans fat-free, less-sodium chicken broth
- 1 (1-pound) pork tenderloin
- 6 cups chopped spinach
- 1 cup cilantro sprigs
- 1½ cups thinly sliced romaine lettuce
- ¾ cup thinly sliced radishes
- ¾ cup (3 ounces) shredded manchego cheese or Monterey Jack cheese
- ¼ cup thinly sliced green onions

**1.** Heat olive oil in a Dutch oven over medium heat. Add onion and next 4 ingredients; cook 4 minutes, stirring frequently. Stir in tomato, garlic, hominy, and broth. Reduce heat, and simmer 20 minutes.

**2.** Trim fat from pork. Cut pork into bite-size pieces. Add pork, spinach, and cilantro to pan. Cook 7 minutes or until pork is done. Ladle 1½ cups soup into each of 6 bowls; top each with ¼ cup lettuce, 2 tablespoons radishes, 2 tablespoons cheese, and 2 teaspoons green onions. Yield: 6 servings.

CALORIES 287 (28% from fat); FAT 9g (sat 3.7g, mono 3.5g, poly 0.9g); PROTEIN 26g; CARB 25.9g; FIBER 6.8g; CHOL 60mg; IRON 5mg; SODIUM 814mg; CALC 223mg

# Primavera Everywhere

## Spring isn't a season. It's an attitude—especially in your cooking.

Mention "primavera," and most people think of a creamy, vegetable-topped pasta. But *primavera* (Italian for "spring," literally "first green") is more than an adjective for noodles. It's a spirit. It's the time of year when life is creative, fresh.

A quarter-century ago, the legendary culinary showman Sirio Maccioni—owner of the famed Manhattan restaurant Le Cirque—improvised with a few ingredients while vacationing in Nova Scotia. A little pasta, some fresh vegetables, a simple white cream sauce, and pasta primavera was born.

### Potatoes Primavera

(pictured on page 94)

2 pounds small red potatoes, quartered
1½ cups fat-free, less-sodium chicken broth
½ cup dry white wine
2 tablespoons fresh lemon juice
2 garlic cloves, minced
½ teaspoon salt, divided
3 cups sugar snap peas, trimmed (about 8 ounces)
3 cups (1½-inch) diagonally sliced asparagus (about 1 pound)
2 cups baby carrots, halved lengthwise (about 8 ounces)
1 tablespoon olive oil
2 teaspoons grated lemon rind
⅛ teaspoon black pepper
1 cup radishes, quartered lengthwise
⅓ cup small fresh mint leaves
⅓ cup fresh cilantro leaves
⅓ cup fresh flat-leaf parsley leaves
2 cups trimmed watercress (about 1 bunch)

**1.** Combine first 5 ingredients in a large saucepan, and bring to a boil. Reduce heat, and simmer 15 minutes. Remove potatoes with a slotted spoon. Bring broth mixture to a boil; cook until reduced to ½ cup (about 8 minutes). Combine broth mixture, potatoes, and ¼ teaspoon salt in a bowl; set aside.
**2.** Steam peas, covered, 2 minutes or until crisp-tender. Rinse peas with cold water, and drain. Steam asparagus, covered, 2 minutes or until crisp-tender. Rinse asparagus with cold water; drain. Steam carrots, covered, 4 minutes or until crisp-tender. Rinse carrots with cold water; drain. Combine ¼ teaspoon salt, peas, asparagus, carrots, oil, rind, and pepper in a large bowl. Combine potato mixture, vegetable mixture, radishes, mint, cilantro, and parsley, tossing well to coat. Arrange watercress on each of 8 plates; divide potato mixture evenly among plates. Yield: 8 servings (serving size: 1¾ cups potato mixture and ¼ cup watercress).

CALORIES 157 (13% from fat); FAT 2.2g (sat 0.3g, mono 1.3g, poly 0.3g); PROTEIN 6.5g; CARB 30g; FIBER 5.9g; CHOL 0mg; IRON 3.6mg; SODIUM 268mg; CALC 81mg

### Fresh Rhubarb Cake

4 cups sliced fresh rhubarb (about 1½ pounds)
1⅓ cups sugar, divided
Cooking spray
⅓ cup butter or stick margarine, softened
1 large egg
2 teaspoons grated orange rind
1 teaspoon vanilla extract
1¼ cups all-purpose flour
1 teaspoon baking powder
½ teaspoon baking soda
⅛ teaspoon salt
¾ cup low-fat buttermilk

**1.** Preheat oven to 350°.
**2.** Combine rhubarb and ⅔ cup sugar in a bowl. Spoon rhubarb mixture into an 8-inch square baking dish coated with cooking spray. Beat ⅔ cup sugar and butter at medium speed of a mixer until well-blended (about 5 minutes). Add egg, beating well. Beat in orange rind and vanilla. Lightly spoon flour into dry measuring cups; level with a knife. Combine flour, baking powder, baking soda, and salt; stir well with a whisk. Add flour mixture to sugar mixture alternately with buttermilk, beginning and ending with flour mixture. Spoon batter over rhubarb mixture. Bake at 350° for 55 minutes or until a wooden pick inserted in center comes out clean. Yield: 9 servings.

CALORIES 270 (27% from fat); FAT 8.1g (sat 4.7g, mono 2.3g, poly 0.5g); PROTEIN 3.8g; CARB 46.6g; FIBER 0.8g; CHOL 43mg; IRON 1.1mg; SODIUM 247mg; CALC 110mg

### Risotto with Asparagus, Fennel, and Leeks

Risotto primavera is popular throughout Italy—Venice in particular. Fennel, asparagus, and leeks—all harbingers of spring—team up in this creamy rice dish.

5 cups fat-free, less-sodium chicken broth
1 tablespoon olive oil
2 cups thinly sliced leek (about 2 large)
¾ cup thinly sliced fennel bulb (about 1 small bulb)
1½ cups uncooked Arborio rice or other short-grain rice
¼ cup dry white wine
1½ cups (½-inch) diagonally cut asparagus
½ teaspoon chopped fresh or ⅛ teaspoon dried rosemary
⅛ teaspoon black pepper
¼ cup (1 ounce) grated fresh Parmesan cheese

**1.** Bring broth to a simmer in a saucepan (do not boil). Keep warm over low heat.
**2.** Heat olive oil in a large saucepan over medium-high heat; add leek and fennel,

*Continued*

and sauté 5 minutes or until tender. Add rice, and cook 1 minute, stirring constantly. Stir in wine, and cook 1 minute or until liquid is nearly absorbed, stirring constantly. Stir in 1 cup broth, and cook until liquid is nearly absorbed, stirring constantly. Add asparagus, rosemary, black pepper, and remaining broth, ½ cup at a time, stirring constantly until each portion of broth is absorbed before adding the next (about 15 minutes total). Stir in grated cheese. Yield: 6 servings (serving size: 1 cup).

CALORIES 267 (13% from fat); FAT 4g (sat 1.2g, mono 2.1g, poly 0.4g); PROTEIN 9.1g; CARB 47.7g; FIBER 1.9g; CHOL 3mg; IRON 3.5mg; SODIUM 486mg; CALC 98mg

## Tortellini Primavera

You can use regular-size varieties of squash—just cut them into smaller pieces.

    4   quarts water
    1   (9-ounce) package fresh
        three-cheese tortellini (such as
        Contadina), uncooked
    1   cup vertically sliced baby carrots
 1½   cups fresh shelled green peas
        (about 1½ pounds unshelled)
    2   teaspoons olive oil
   ⅓   cup thinly sliced green onions
    1   garlic clove, minced
   ½   cup canned vegetable broth
    2   cups quartered baby pattypan
        squash
    1   cup vertically sliced baby zucchini
    2   cups torn arugula
    2   tablespoons finely chopped fresh
        parsley
    1   tablespoon minced fresh chives
    1   tablespoon fresh lemon juice
   ¼   teaspoon salt
   ⅛   teaspoon black pepper

**1.** Bring 4 quarts water to a boil in a large Dutch oven. Add pasta; cook 5 minutes. Add carrots; cook 2 minutes. Add peas; cook 30 seconds. Drain and rinse with cold water; drain well.
**2.** Heat oil in a large nonstick skillet over medium-high heat. Add green onions and garlic, and sauté 2 minutes.

Add pasta mixture, broth, pattypan squash, and zucchini, and bring to a boil. Cover, reduce heat, and simmer until thoroughly heated. Stir in arugula and remaining ingredients. Yield: 6 servings (serving size: 1½ cups).

CALORIES 206 (21% from fat); FAT 7.8g (sat 2.1g, mono 2g, poly 0.3g); PROTEIN 9.6g; CARB 30.2g; FIBER 3.9g; CHOL 20mg; IRON 1.7mg; SODIUM 389mg; CALC 143mg

## Pasta Primavera with Shrimp

    3   cups uncooked cavatappi (spiral
        tube-shaped pasta) or other
        short tube-shaped pasta
    2   cups sugar snap peas, trimmed
    1   tablespoon olive oil
    1   pound medium shrimp, peeled and
        deveined
    1   tablespoon chopped fresh oregano
   ¼   teaspoon salt
   ¼   teaspoon black pepper
    2   garlic cloves, minced
    4   cups torn spinach
 1½   cups cherry tomatoes, halved
    1   cup (4 ounces) crumbled feta
        cheese

**1.** Cook pasta in boiling water 6 minutes, omitting salt and fat. Add peas, and cook 2 minutes; drain. Heat oil in a medium nonstick skillet over medium-high heat. Add shrimp, oregano, salt, pepper, and garlic; sauté 3 minutes or until shrimp are done. Combine pasta mixture, shrimp mixture, and remaining ingredients in a large bowl; toss well. Yield: 6 servings (serving size: about 1½ cups).

CALORIES 329 (23% from fat); FAT 8.5g (sat 3.5g, mono 2.8g, poly 1.2g); PROTEIN 25.6g; CARB 36.9g; FIBER 4.1g; CHOL 131mg; IRON 5.7mg; SODIUM 458mg; CALC 204mg

## Frittata with Swiss Chard, Potatoes, and Fontina

Swiss chard is a beautiful, although overlooked, vegetable at its best in spring. It tastes like a combination of spinach and beets (its cousins), but with a meatier texture. Use both the leaves and stems after cleaning thoroughly.

    2   cups diced baking potato (about ¾
        pound)
   ½   teaspoon salt, divided
    6   cups coarsely chopped Swiss chard
        (about 8 ounces)
   ⅓   cup water
   ⅓   cup fat-free milk
   ¼   cup chopped fresh parsley
   ¼   teaspoon black pepper
    4   large egg whites
    3   large eggs
 1½   teaspoons butter or stick
        margarine
        Cooking spray
   ½   cup (2 ounces) shredded fontina or
        Swiss cheese

**1.** Place potato in a saucepan; cover with water. Bring to a boil; cook 8 minutes or until tender. Drain and cool. Toss potato with ¼ teaspoon salt. Set aside.
**2.** Combine Swiss chard and water in a large saucepan over medium heat. Cover and cook 10 minutes or until Swiss chard is tender. Drain.
**3.** Combine ¼ teaspoon salt, milk, and next 4 ingredients in a large bowl; stir with a whisk. Stir in potato and Swiss chard. Melt butter in a medium nonstick skillet coated with cooking spray over medium heat. Pour egg mixture into pan. Cover, reduce heat, and cook 10 minutes or until almost set. Sprinkle with cheese.
**4.** Preheat broiler.
**5.** Wrap handle of skillet with foil. Broil 5 minutes or until golden brown. Yield: 4 servings (serving size: 1 wedge).

CALORIES 257 (36% from fat); FAT 10.2g (sat 4.9g, mono 3.2g, poly 0.9g); PROTEIN 15.7g; CARB 26.2g; FIBER 2.2g; CHOL 186mg; IRON 3.1mg; SODIUM 565mg; CALC 172mg

## Fresh Strawberry Pie

This is an easy recipe to make when you have a bucket of freshly picked berries. And it seems that this pie tastes more like a strawberry than the berry itself. The berries used to make the glaze can be any size, as they're macerated and pureed. But the berries piled in the pie should be small—the smaller the better, in fact.

**CRUST:**

    50  reduced-calorie vanilla wafers
    ¼  cup butter or stick margarine, melted
    2  tablespoons sugar
    1  teaspoon grated orange rind
       Cooking spray

**FILLING:**

    2  cups ripe strawberries
    ½  cup water
    ⅔  cup sugar
    2  tablespoons cornstarch
    1  tablespoon fresh lemon juice
    6  cups small ripe strawberries
    ½  cup frozen reduced-calorie whipped topping, thawed and divided

**1.** Preheat oven to 350°.

**2.** To prepare crust, place wafers in a food processor, and process until finely ground. Add butter, 2 tablespoons sugar, and orange rind, and pulse 10 times or just until wafers are moist. Press into bottom and up sides of a 9-inch pie plate coated with cooking spray. Bake at 350° for 15 minutes; cool on a wire rack.

**3.** To prepare filling, mash 2 cups strawberries with a potato masher. Combine mashed strawberries and water in a small saucepan; bring to a boil, and cook 5 minutes, stirring occasionally. Press strawberry mixture through a sieve into a bowl, and reserve 1 cup strawberry liquid (add enough water to measure 1 cup, if necessary). Discard pulp.

**4.** Combine ⅔ cup sugar and cornstarch in a pan; add strawberry liquid, stirring well with a whisk. Bring to a boil; cook 1 minute, stirring constantly. Reduce heat, and cook 2 minutes. Remove from heat; stir in lemon juice.

**5.** Arrange a layer of small strawberries, stem sides down, in crust. Spoon about one-third of sauce over strawberries. Arrange remaining strawberries on top, and spoon remaining sauce over strawberries. Chill at least 3 hours. Serve with whipped topping. Yield: 8 servings (serving size: 1 wedge and 1 tablespoon whipped topping).

CALORIES 285 (27% from fat); FAT 8.5g (sat 4.6g, mono 2.5g, poly 0.9g); PROTEIN 1.9g; CARB 52.2g; FIBER 3.5g; CHOL 16mg; IRON 1.2mg; SODIUM 146mg; CALC 42mg

## White Bean Salad with Asparagus and Artichokes

If you run into baby artichokes in your market, be sure to grab them. Although a little labor-intensive to prepare, they are delicious in this vegetarian bean salad. If you don't have baby artichokes, you can use fresh artichoke bottoms or, in a real pinch, canned artichoke hearts.

    10  fresh baby artichokes, peeled and quartered
    2  cups (1-inch) diagonally cut asparagus
    ⅓  cup thinly sliced radishes
    3  tablespoons thinly sliced green onions
    2  tablespoons thinly sliced fresh basil
    2  tablespoons fresh lemon juice
    1  tablespoon extra-virgin olive oil
    ¼  teaspoon salt
    ⅛  teaspoon black pepper
    1  (19-ounce) can Great Northern beans or other white beans, rinsed and drained

**1.** Steam artichokes, covered, 10 minutes or until tender. Steam asparagus, covered, 2 minutes. Combine radishes and remaining 7 ingredients in a bowl; gently stir in artichokes and asparagus. Yield: 4 servings (serving size: 1 cup).

CALORIES 170 (22% from fat); FAT 4.2g (sat 0.7g, mono 2.5g, poly 0.6g); PROTEIN 10.3g; CARB 26.7g; FIBER 5g; CHOL 0mg; IRON 2.7mg; SODIUM 400mg; CALC 89mg

## Chunky Minestrone Primavera with Clams

This stew is a wonderful mélange of spring vegetables, but it will take to almost any variation.

    1  tablespoon olive oil
    1½  cups diced fennel bulb (about 1 large bulb)
    1  cup chopped onion
    2½  cups diced zucchini
    2  cups diced baking potato (about 8 ounces)
    1½  cups water
    ¾  cup diced carrot
    ½  cup uncooked long-grain rice
    1  teaspoon dried oregano
    ¼  teaspoon salt
    ¼  teaspoon black pepper
    2  (16-ounce) cans fat-free, less-sodium chicken broth
    1  (15.5-ounce) can Great Northern beans or other white beans, rinsed and drained
    2  garlic cloves, minced
    1  cup shelled green peas (about 1 pound unshelled)
    ⅓  cup chopped fresh flat-leaf parsley
    ¼  cup chopped fresh basil
    1  (6½-ounce) can chopped clams, undrained
    ½  cup (2 ounces) grated Asiago or fresh Parmesan cheese

**1.** Heat oil in a large Dutch oven over medium-high heat. Add fennel and onion, and sauté 5 minutes. Add zucchini and next 10 ingredients; bring to a boil. Cover, reduce heat, and simmer 30 minutes. Add peas, parsley, basil, and clams, and cook, uncovered, 5 minutes. Ladle soup into each of 8 bowls; sprinkle with cheese. Yield: 8 servings (serving size: 1½ cups soup and 1 tablespoon cheese).

CALORIES 230 (16% from fat); FAT 4.2g (sat 1.6g, mono 1.9g, poly 0.4g); PROTEIN 12.2g; CARB 33.5g; FIBER 4.2g; CHOL 15mg; IRON 3.8mg; SODIUM 653mg; CALC 158mg

# Jamaican Banana Bread

*Feast your eyes on our favorite banana bread, and you'll see at once why we chose it to be a part of our tribute to Cooking Light's best all-time recipes.*

One bite of the island-inspired flavors—lime, rum, coconut, and pecans—will convince you that this is a quick bread with a personality. Has been since it first appeared in our March 1997 issue.

### Jamaican Banana Bread

**BREAD:**

- 2 tablespoons butter or stick margarine, softened
- 2 tablespoons (1 ounce) ⅓-less-fat cream cheese, softened
- 1 cup granulated sugar
- 1 large egg
- 2 cups all-purpose flour
- 2 teaspoons baking powder
- ½ teaspoon baking soda
- ⅛ teaspoon salt
- 1 cup mashed ripe banana
- ½ cup fat-free milk
- 2 tablespoons dark rum or ¼ teaspoon imitation rum extract and 2 tablespoons water
- ½ teaspoon grated lime rind
- 2 teaspoons lime juice
- 1 teaspoon vanilla extract
- ¼ cup chopped pecans, toasted
- ¼ cup flaked sweetened coconut
- Cooking spray

**TOPPING:**

- ¼ cup packed brown sugar
- 2 teaspoons butter or stick margarine
- 2 teaspoons lime juice
- 2 teaspoons dark rum or ⅛ teaspoon imitation rum extract and 2 teaspoons water
- 2 tablespoons chopped pecans, toasted
- 2 tablespoons flaked sweetened coconut

**1.** Preheat oven to 375°.

**2.** To prepare bread, beat 2 tablespoons butter and cream cheese at medium speed of a mixer; add 1 cup sugar, beating well. Add egg; beat well.

**3.** Lightly spoon flour into dry measuring cups; level with a knife. Combine flour, baking powder, baking soda, and salt, stirring well. Combine banana and next 5 ingredients, stirring well. Add flour mixture to sugar mixture alternately with banana mixture, beginning and ending with flour mixture; mix after each addition. Stir in ¼ cup chopped pecans and ¼ cup coconut.

**4.** Pour batter into an 8 x 4-inch loaf pan coated with cooking spray; bake at 375° for 1 hour. Cool in pan 10 minutes; remove from pan. Cool on a wire rack.

**5.** To prepare topping, combine brown sugar and next 3 ingredients in a saucepan; bring to a simmer. Cook 1 minute, stirring constantly. Remove from heat. Stir in 2 tablespoons each pecans and coconut; spoon over loaf. Yield: 16 servings (serving size: 1 slice).

CALORIES 193 (26% from fat); FAT 5.5g (sat 2.4g, mono 1.9g, poly 0.7g); PROTEIN 2.9g; CARB 32.2g; FIBER 1.1g; CHOL 20mg; IRON 1mg; SODIUM 163mg; CALC 55mg

# Touché, Soufflé!

*When a Knightdale, North Carolina, reader asked us to lighten this recipe, a whole neighborhood kicked up its heels.*

Lisa Noto vividly recalls when her neighborhood chum Leslie Ambrose invited their group of buddies over for breakfast and served a French Toast Soufflé. "Then Leslie nonchalantly told us that it had about a dozen eggs, some cream cheese, and whipping cream. I nearly died," Noto says.

We did a little juggling with the ingredients by replacing the whipping cream with a mixture of 2% reduced-fat milk and half-and-half, cutting out four eggs, and switching to ⅓-less-fat cream cheese. That's 127 fewer calories, 16.4 fewer grams of fat, and a lot less cholesterol.

### French Toast Soufflé

- 10 cups (1-inch) cubed sturdy white bread (such as Pepperidge Farm Hearty White, about 16 [1-ounce] slices)
- Cooking spray
- 1 (8-ounce) block ⅓-less-fat cream cheese, softened
- 8 large eggs
- 1½ cups 2% reduced-fat milk
- ⅔ cup half-and-half
- ½ cup maple syrup
- ½ teaspoon vanilla extract
- 2 tablespoons powdered sugar
- ¾ cup maple syrup

**1.** Place bread cubes in a 13 x 9-inch baking dish coated with cooking spray. Beat cream cheese at medium speed of a mixer until smooth. Add eggs, 1 at a time, mixing well after each addition. Add milk, half-and-half, ½ cup maple syrup, and vanilla, and mix until smooth. Pour cream cheese mixture over top of bread; cover and refrigerate overnight.

**2.** Preheat oven to 375°.

**3.** Remove bread mixture from refrigerator; let stand on counter 30 minutes. Bake at 375° for 50 minutes or until set. Sprinkle soufflé with powdered sugar, and serve with maple syrup. Yield: 12 servings (serving size: 1 slice soufflé and 1 tablespoon maple syrup).

CALORIES 346 (30% from fat); FAT 11.5g (sat 5.5g, mono 3.8g, poly 1g); PROTEIN 11.6g; CARB 51.7g; FIBER 2.7g; CHOL 169mg; IRON 1.9mg; SODIUM 396mg; CALC 131mg

| BEFORE | AFTER |
|---|---|
| **SERVING SIZE** | |
| *1 slice* | |
| **CALORIES PER SERVING** | |
| 473 | 346 |
| **FAT** | |
| 27.9g | 11.5g |
| **PERCENT OF TOTAL CALORIES** | |
| 53% | 30% |
| **CHOLESTEROL** | |
| 297mg | 169mg |

# may

# Come on Over and Cook

## Join readers from around the country in a fresh and friendly new approach to dinner.

When Amy Fong decided to create a dinner with other *Cooking Light* readers from the San Francisco Bay area, she unwittingly was taking a tasty leap aboard a national trend. Connected as never before via the *Cooking Light* Web site (CookingLight.com), readers from around the country are seeking each other out. Dinner parties featuring *Cooking Light* recipes are perfect for freshening up get-togethers with a familiar circle of friends or, as Amy learned, for meeting new ones.

### menu

**White-Bean Hummus Dip**

**Shrimp with Roasted Pepper-Horseradish Dip**

**Chive-and-Garlic Knots**

**Peanutty Noodles**

**Spinach Salad with Pomegranate Dressing and Crispy Won Ton "Croutons"**

**Apricot-Stuffed Spice-Rubbed Pork Loin**

**White Chocolate-Raspberry Cheesecake**

## White-Bean Hummus Dip

¼ cup chopped green onions
2 tablespoons fresh lemon juice
2 tablespoons tahini (sesame-seed paste)
½ teaspoon dried oregano
¼ teaspoon ground cumin
⅛ teaspoon salt
⅛ teaspoon black pepper
1 (19-ounce) can cannellini beans or other white beans, rinsed and drained
1 garlic clove, peeled

**1.** Combine all ingredients in a food processor, and process until smooth. Yield: 1¾ cups (serving size: ¼ cup).

CALORIES 108 (30% from fat); FAT 3.6g (sat 0.4g, mono 1.2g, poly 1.6g); PROTEIN 5g; CARB 15g; FIBER 2.2g; CHOL 0mg; IRON 2mg; SODIUM 144mg; CALC 48mg

## Shrimp with Roasted Pepper-Horseradish Dip

To help keep cooks happy before dinner is served, offer this appetizer. Make the sauce up to three days in advance and refrigerate. To save time, you can use four bottled roasted bell peppers instead of roasting your own. Prepare the shrimp—or buy precooked—the day of the party.

4 large red bell peppers (about 2 pounds)
3 tablespoons low-fat sour cream
3 tablespoons prepared horseradish
1 tablespoon olive oil
2 teaspoons fresh lemon juice
½ teaspoon salt
¼ teaspoon black pepper
2 garlic cloves, chopped
6 cups water
2 pounds large shrimp

**1.** Preheat broiler.
**2.** Cut bell peppers in half lengthwise; discard seeds and membranes. Place pepper halves, skin sides up, on a foil-lined baking sheet; flatten with hand. Broil 15 minutes or until blackened. Place in a zip-top plastic bag; seal. Let stand 15 minutes. Peel peppers. Place bell peppers, sour cream, and next 6 ingredients in a food processor; process until smooth, scraping sides of bowl occasionally. Place bell pepper mixture in a small bowl. Cover and chill.

**3.** Bring 6 cups water to a boil in a Dutch oven. Add shrimp; cook 3 minutes or until done. Drain and rinse with cold water; peel. Cover and chill shrimp. Serve shrimp with sauce. Yield: 8 servings (serving size: 3 ounces shrimp and ¼ cup sauce).

CALORIES 137 (28% from fat); FAT 4.2g (sat 1g, mono 1.7g, poly 1g); PROTEIN 18.3g; CARB 6.4g; FIBER 1.5g; CHOL 131mg; IRON 3.1mg; SODIUM 295mg; CALC 60mg

## Chive-and-Garlic Knots

Refrigerated bread dough makes these knots quick and easy. Your guests may enjoy shaping them for you the night of your party. Or you can make these rolls a day ahead, wrap them in foil, and reheat them in the oven at 350° for 10 minutes.

1½ tablespoons butter or stick margarine
2 garlic cloves, minced
½ teaspoon garlic powder
1 (11-ounce) can refrigerated French bread dough
2 tablespoons chopped fresh chives or green onions
2 tablespoons grated Parmesan cheese
Cooking spray

**1.** Preheat oven to 350°.
**2.** Melt butter in a small skillet over medium heat. Add minced garlic; sauté 30 seconds or until lightly browned. Remove from heat; stir in garlic powder.
**3.** Unroll French bread dough onto a lightly floured surface; brush dough with garlic mixture. Sprinkle dough with chives and cheese. Cut dough crosswise into 12 strips. Shape each strip into a knot. Place knots onto a baking sheet coated with cooking spray. Bake at 350° for 17 minutes or until lightly browned. Serve warm. Yield: 12 servings (serving size: 1 roll).

CALORIES 81 (29% from fat); FAT 2.6g (sat 1.3g, mono 0.8g, poly 0.4g); PROTEIN 2.5g; CARB 11.6g; FIBER 0g; CHOL 5mg; IRON 0.6mg; SODIUM 185mg; CALC 13mg

## Peanutty Noodles

(pictured on page 4)

This dish comes together quickly when one person prepares the sauce while another sautés the vegetables. Break the pasta in half before cooking to make serving easier. These noodles also become their own main dish when you add cooked shrimp or chicken.

- 2 carrots, peeled
- 1 tablespoon vegetable oil, divided
- 2 teaspoons grated peeled fresh ginger
- 3 garlic cloves, minced
- 1 cup fat-free, less-sodium chicken broth
- ½ cup natural-style peanut butter (such as Smucker's)
- ¼ cup low-sodium soy sauce
- 3 tablespoons rice or white wine vinegar
- 1 teaspoon chili garlic sauce (such as Lee Kum Kee)
- ¼ teaspoon salt
- Cooking spray
- 2 cups red bell pepper strips
- 1 pound snow peas, trimmed
- 8 cups hot cooked linguine (about 1 pound uncooked pasta)
- ½ cup chopped fresh cilantro

**1.** Shave carrots lengthwise into thin strips using a vegetable peeler, and set aside.
**2.** Heat 1 teaspoon oil in a small saucepan over medium heat. Add ginger and minced garlic; sauté 30 seconds. Add chicken broth and next 5 ingredients; stir until well-blended. Reduce heat, and simmer 7 minutes, stirring occasionally. Remove from heat, and keep warm.
**3.** Heat 2 teaspoons oil in a large nonstick skillet coated with cooking spray over medium-high heat. Add bell peppers and snow peas; sauté 5 minutes or until tender. Remove from heat. Combine carrot, peanut butter mixture, bell pepper mixture, and linguine in a large bowl; toss well. Sprinkle with cilantro. Serve warm or at room temperature. Yield: 10 servings (serving size: 1 cup).

CALORIES 296 (27% from fat); FAT 8.8g (sat 1.7g, mono 3.8g, poly 2.7g); PROTEIN 11.7g; CARB 43.1g; FIBER 3.4g; CHOL 1mg; IRON 3.6mg; SODIUM 400mg; CALC 44mg

## Spinach Salad with Pomegranate Dressing and Crispy Won Ton "Croutons"

Make the "croutons" ahead of time. Won ton wrappers are found in the refrigerated case of the supermarket, usually in the produce section or next to the tofu. Pomegranate molasses is in Middle Eastern markets, but you can substitute 2 tablespoons honey and 1 tablespoon lime juice.

**CROUTONS:**

- 2 teaspoons ground cumin
- 2 teaspoons ground coriander
- ½ teaspoon salt
- 12 ounces won ton wrappers, cut into ¼-inch strips
- 2 teaspoons vegetable oil

**SALAD:**

- ⅓ cup fresh orange juice
- 2 tablespoons pomegranate molasses
- 2 tablespoons extra-virgin olive oil
- ½ teaspoon salt
- ⅛ teaspoon black pepper
- 12 cups torn spinach (about 6 ounces)
- 1 cup thinly sliced red onion
- 2 (11-ounce) cans mandarin oranges in light syrup, drained

**1.** Preheat oven to 400°.
**2.** To prepare croutons, combine first 3 ingredients in a bowl. Place won ton strips and vegetable oil in a large zip-top plastic bag; seal and toss to coat. Open bag. Sprinkle with cumin mixture; seal and toss to coat. Place won ton strips in a single layer on 2 baking sheets. Bake at 400° for 8 minutes or until crisp; turn strips once. Cool.
**3.** To prepare salad, combine juice, molasses, olive oil, salt, and pepper in a small bowl, stirring with a whisk. Combine croutons, juice mixture, spinach, onion, and oranges; toss well to coat. Serve immediately. Yield: 8 servings (serving size: 1¼ cups).
**NOTE:** To disperse oil over won ton wrappers, shake them vigorously in a bag. They tend to clump together, but be patient. They will eventually separate.

CALORIES 219 (25% from fat); FAT 6g (sat 0.8g, mono 3.9g, poly 0.9g); PROTEIN 4.2g; CARB 38g; FIBER 2.2g; CHOL 3mg; IRON 2.3mg; SODIUM 485mg; CALC 58mg

## Apricot-Stuffed Spice-Rubbed Pork Loin

Make this among your first projects for the evening because the pork loin bakes for nearly two hours. You can also stuff it a day ahead, refrigerate it, and then pop it in the oven just before your guests arrive.

- 1 tablespoon ground cumin
- 1 tablespoon brown sugar
- 1 teaspoon salt
- 1 teaspoon ground ginger
- 1 teaspoon garlic powder
- ½ teaspoon five-spice powder
- ½ teaspoon ground red pepper
- 1⅓ cups finely chopped dried apricots (1 [6-ounce] package)
- 2 tablespoons capers
- 1 (3-pound) boned pork loin roast
- Cooking spray

**1.** Preheat oven to 350°.
**2.** Combine first 7 ingredients in a small bowl.
**3.** Combine apricots and capers; set aside. Trim fat from pork. Cut a 1½-inch-wide horizontal slit into end of pork; cut through to other end of pork to form a deep pocket using a long, thin knife. Spoon apricot mixture into pocket; pack using handle of a wooden spoon. Rub surface of pork with cumin mixture. Place pork on a broiler pan coated with cooking spray. Insert meat thermometer into thickest portion of pork. Bake at 350° for 1 hour and 55 minutes or until thermometer registers 160° (slightly pink). Yield: 12 servings (serving size: 3 ounces stuffed pork).

CALORIES 256 (44% from fat); FAT 12.6g (sat 4.3g, mono 5.7g, poly 1.6g); PROTEIN 24.6g; CARB 10.1g; FIBER 1.4g; CHOL 81mg; IRON 2.1mg; SODIUM 297mg; CALC 21mg

## White Chocolate-Raspberry Cheesecake

Prepare this cheesecake ahead of time because it needs time to chill. Baking it in a water bath keeps it moist and creamy.

**CRUST:**

1⅓ cups graham cracker crumbs
¼ cup sugar
1 tablespoon butter or stick margarine, melted
Cooking spray
3 cups fresh raspberries

**FILLING:**

2 (8-ounce) blocks fat-free cream cheese, softened
1 (8-ounce) block ⅓-less-fat cream cheese, softened
1 cup sugar
¼ cup amaretto (almond-flavored liqueur)
2 tablespoons flour
2 teaspoons vanilla extract
¼ teaspoon salt
3 ounces white chocolate, melted
3 large eggs
Fresh raspberries (optional)

**1.** Preheat oven to 325°.
**2.** Combine first 3 ingredients in a small bowl. Firmly press mixture into bottom and 1 inch up sides of a 9-inch springform pan coated with cooking spray. Wrap outside of pan with foil. Arrange 3 cups berries in crust; set aside.
**3.** Place cheeses in a large bowl; beat at medium speed of a mixer until smooth. Add 1 cup sugar and next 5 ingredients; beat until smooth. Add eggs, 1 at a time, beating well after each addition. Pour cheese mixture into prepared pan. Place cheesecake in a large shallow pan; add hot water to pan to a depth of 1 inch. Bake at 325° for 1 hour and 10 minutes or until almost set. Remove cheesecake from oven; cool to room temperature. Cover and chill at least 4 hours. Garnish with additional raspberries, if desired. Yield: 12 servings (serving size: 1 wedge).

CALORIES 315 (29% from fat); FAT 10.3g (sat 5.6g, mono 3.4g, poly 0.7g); PROTEIN 10.4g; CARB 41.5g; FIBER 2.4g; CHOL 82mg; IRON 0.9mg; SODIUM 454mg; CALC 149mg

## taste of america

# Georgia's Other Peaches

*They only grow in a small corner of Georgia, but Vidalia onions are famous around the country for their subtle sweetness.*

In Toombs County, Georgia, Vidalias are juicy, mild, and very sweet—sweeter, they say, than Walla Wallas from Washington, 1015 Sweets from Texas, and Imperial Sweets from California—due to the area's unique combination of soils and climate. Onions from those other states share with Vidalias the high sugar and water content that is their delicious signature. But to onion connoisseurs, the pale yellow bulbs from Georgia are the cream of the crop. Vidalias shine in recipes that let them steal the show—mixed into a tangy relish for fish, baked whole with rosemary, or caramelized to the fullest extent of their generous sugar.

## Sweet-and-Hot Onion Salsa

For a tropical twist, try ripe mango in place of the red plum. Serve this salsa with baked tortilla chips, or grilled chicken, fish, or pork.

1 cup chopped Vidalia or other sweet onion
¼ cup orange juice
2 tablespoons water
1 teaspoon sugar
1¼ cups diced red plum
1 cup diced Granny Smith apple
1 tablespoon chopped seeded jalapeño pepper
1 tablespoon white wine vinegar
2 teaspoons lime juice
⅛ teaspoon salt
⅛ teaspoon black pepper
1 garlic clove, minced

**1.** Combine first 4 ingredients in a small saucepan. Bring to a boil; cover, reduce heat, and simmer 10 minutes. Uncover and cook 3 minutes or until liquid almost evaporates, stirring frequently.
**2.** Place onion mixture in a bowl, and cool to room temperature. Stir in plum and remaining ingredients. Cover and chill. Yield: 2½ cups (serving size: ¼ cup).

CALORIES 30 (6% from fat); FAT 0.2g (sat 0g, mono 0.1g, poly 0.1g); PROTEIN 0.5g; CARB 7.3g; FIBER 1.1g; CHOL 0mg; IRON 0.1mg; SODIUM 30mg; CALC 7mg

## Rosemary-Glazed Vidalia Onions

1 cup dry red wine
2 tablespoons sugar
1 tablespoon chopped fresh or 1 teaspoon dried rosemary
1 tablespoon fresh lemon juice
⅛ teaspoon ground cloves
⅛ teaspoon ground black pepper
2 medium Vidalia or other sweet onions, unpeeled (about 1¼ pounds)
Cooking spray
2 teaspoons olive oil

**1.** Preheat oven to 400°.
**2.** Combine first 6 ingredients in a small saucepan; bring to a boil. Reduce heat to medium; cook, uncovered, until reduced to ½ cup (about 10 minutes). Set aside.
**3.** Cut onions lengthwise in half. Place onions, cut sides down, in a small baking dish coated with cooking spray. Drizzle olive oil over onions. Cover onions, and bake at 400° for 25 minutes. Uncover and bake 20 minutes. Remove onions from oven. Turn onions over, and pour wine mixture over onions. Bake for an additional 20 minutes or until onions are tender, basting every 5 minutes. Serve onions with wine mixture. Yield: 4 servings (serving size: 1 onion half and about 1 tablespoon glaze).

CALORIES 105 (23% from fat); FAT 2.7g (sat 0.4g, mono 1.7g, poly 0.4g); PROTEIN 1.8g; CARB 19.9g; FIBER 2.8g; CHOL 0mg; IRON 0.7mg; SODIUM 9mg; CALC 37mg

## Golden Onion Strata with Gruyère and Prosciutto

(pictured on page 2)

We love the flavor and layered look of this strata, with paper-thin prosciutto providing a mere but welcome hint of salt. It's a perfect make-ahead dish for brunch.

    4  cups chopped Vidalia or other
       sweet onion
    1  cup (4 ounces) very thin slices
       prosciutto or ham, chopped
   ⅓  cup water
  2½  cups fat-free milk
   ¼  teaspoon dry mustard
   ⅛  teaspoon black pepper
    1  (8-ounce) carton egg substitute
    8  cups (½-inch) cubed French bread
       (about 9 ounces)
    1  cup (4 ounces) shredded Gruyère,
       Jarlsberg, or Swiss cheese, divided

**1.** Heat a large nonstick skillet over medium-high heat. Add onion and prosciutto, and sauté 5 minutes or until onion begins to brown. Add water; cover, reduce heat to low, and simmer 30 minutes. Uncover and simmer 30 minutes or until liquid almost evaporates. Cool.

**2.** Combine milk, mustard, pepper, and egg substitute in a large bowl, and stir with a whisk until mixture is well-blended. Stir in onion mixture. Add bread, tossing gently to coat.

**3.** Arrange half of bread mixture in a single layer in an 11 x 7-inch baking dish. Sprinkle with ½ cup cheese, and top with remaining bread mixture. Cover strata, and chill 8 hours or overnight.

**4.** Preheat oven to 350°.

**5.** Uncover strata. Bake at 350° for 25 minutes. Sprinkle with ½ cup cheese; bake an additional 20 minutes or until set. Yield: 8 servings.

CALORIES 245 (26% from fat); FAT 7.1g (sat 3.4g, mono 2.5g, poly 0.7g); PROTEIN 16.7g; CARB 28.1g; FIBER 2.5g; CHOL 25mg; IRON 1.8mg; SODIUM 539mg; CALC 289mg

## Potato, Caramelized Onion, and Feta Pizza

The sweetness of Vidalias counterpoints the saltiness of feta cheese as the potato stakes out a mild, middle ground.

   ⅓  cup sun-dried tomatoes, packed
       without oil
    1  cup boiling water
    1  tablespoon olive oil
    3  cups thinly sliced Vidalia or other
       sweet onion
    1  (11-ounce) package refrigerated
       French bread dough
    1  tablespoon cornmeal
    2  cups thinly sliced small red
       potatoes
    1  tablespoon olive oil
    2  teaspoons minced fresh or
       ½ teaspoon dried thyme
    1  teaspoon minced fresh or
       ¼ teaspoon dried rosemary
   ¼  teaspoon black pepper
   ⅛  teaspoon salt
       Cooking spray
   ¼  cup tomato puree
   ½  cup (2 ounces) crumbled feta
       cheese

**1.** Preheat oven to 425°.

**2.** Combine tomatoes and water; let stand, covered, 30 minutes. Drain tomatoes; coarsely chop.

**3.** Heat 1 tablespoon olive oil in a large nonstick skillet over medium-high heat. Add onion; sauté 5 minutes. Cook 15 minutes or until golden brown, stirring frequently.

**4.** Unroll bread dough, and flatten into a 13-inch circle on a lightly floured surface. Place dough on a 12-inch pizza pan sprinkled with cornmeal. Crimp edges of dough with fingers to form a rim. Pierce dough with a fork. Bake at 425° for 10 minutes, and set aside.

**5.** Combine potatoes and next 5 ingredients in a bowl. Coat a jelly-roll pan with cooking spray; arrange potatoes in a single layer in prepared pan. Bake at 425° for 20 minutes or until potatoes are lightly browned, stirring once.

**6.** Spread tomato puree over crust. Top with potatoes, caramelized onions, and sun-dried tomatoes; sprinkle with

cheese. Bake at 425° for 15 minutes or until crust is browned. Yield: 8 servings (serving size: 1 wedge).

CALORIES 208 (28% from fat); FAT 6.5g (sat 1.9g, mono 3.3g, poly 1g); PROTEIN 6.3g; CARB 31.9g; FIBER 2.3g; CHOL 6mg; IRON 1.9mg; SODIUM 479mg; CALC 54mg

## Spicy Chicken Breasts with Caramelized Onion-Red Pepper Relish

  1½  teaspoons olive oil
    1  teaspoon ground coriander
    1  teaspoon chili powder
   ½  teaspoon salt
   ½  teaspoon garlic powder
   ½  teaspoon ground cinnamon
   ¼  teaspoon ground red pepper
    4  (4-ounce) skinned, boned chicken
       breast halves
    2  cups sliced Vidalia or other sweet
       onion
    2  red bell peppers, each cut into 4
       wedges
   ¼  cup chopped fresh basil
    2  tablespoons pine nuts, toasted
    1  tablespoon balsamic vinegar

**1.** Preheat oven to 450°.

**2.** Combine first 7 ingredients in a small bowl. Rub both sides of chicken with spice mixture. Arrange onion and bell peppers in a 13 x 9-inch baking dish, and top with chicken. Bake at 450° for 20 minutes. Reduce oven temperature to 375° (do not remove chicken from oven), and bake an additional 15 minutes or until chicken is done. Remove chicken from dish, and keep warm. Remove onion mixture from dish, and chop. Combine onion mixture, basil, nuts, and vinegar. Serve with chicken. Yield: 4 servings (serving size: 1 chicken breast half and about ½ cup relish).

CALORIES 212 (26% from fat); FAT 6.1g (sat 1.1g, mono 2.6g, poly 1.7g); PROTEIN 28.9g; CARB 11.1g; FIBER 2.7g; CHOL 66mg; IRON 2.2mg; SODIUM 377mg; CALC 45mg

## Creole Catfish with Vidalia-Olive Relish

An intriguing blend of spices adds character to these catfish fillets, while the relish—a balance of tangy olives and sweet onions—makes the perfect finishing touch.

- 2 teaspoons olive oil, divided
- 1 cup chopped Vidalia or other sweet onion
- ⅓ cup chopped red bell pepper
- 2 tablespoons chopped pitted green olives
- 2 tablespoons chopped pitted kalamata olives
- 2 tablespoons water
- 1 tablespoon dried thyme, divided
- 1 tablespoon paprika
- ¼ teaspoon salt
- ¼ teaspoon garlic powder
- ⅛ teaspoon ground red pepper
- 4 (6-ounce) farm-raised catfish fillets
- Cooking spray

**1.** Heat 1 teaspoon oil in a large nonstick skillet over medium-high heat. Add onion; sauté 5 minutes. Spoon onion into a bowl. Stir in bell pepper, olives, water, and 1 teaspoon thyme. Stir well. Cover and refrigerate at least 2 hours.
**2.** Prepare grill.
**3.** Combine 1 teaspoon olive oil, 2 teaspoons dried thyme, paprika, salt, garlic powder, and ground red pepper. Rub paprika mixture over both sides of fillets. Place fillets on a grill rack coated with cooking spray; grill 5 minutes on each side or until fish flakes easily when tested with a fork. Serve with relish. Yield: 4 servings (serving size: 1 fillet and about ⅓ cup relish).

CALORIES 211 (39% from fat); FAT 9.2g (sat 1.8g, mono 4.4g, poly 1.8g); PROTEIN 25.2g; CARB 6.6g; FIBER 1.8g; CHOL 77mg; IRON 3.5mg; SODIUM 308mg; CALC 93mg

# Not Your Grandma's Potpies

## Tasty ideas from around the world give an old comfort food a new—and lighter—lease on life.

Right up there with meat loaf and mashed potatoes, potpies deliver exactly what people have in mind when they dream of comfort food. Part of that comfort, alas, has been eating as though there is no tomorrow when it comes to fat. That's where we stepped in. Loving potpies does not have to mean leaving them behind, just giving them a leaner, but no less flavorful, upgrade. We started by rethinking both pastry and filling, and then moved on to bring in great ideas from cooking around the world. The old potpies say mom, while the new ones offer us a reminder that moms are global.

### Curried-Chicken Potpie

This recipe combines the highlights of Indian food with a legendary Carolina chicken casserole called country captain.

**CRUST:**
- 1 cup all-purpose flour, divided
- 3 tablespoons ice water
- 1 tablespoon cider vinegar
- ¼ teaspoon salt
- ¼ cup vegetable shortening

**FILLING:**
- 1 teaspoon olive oil
- 2 tablespoons curry powder
- 2 cups diced peeled baking potato (about 12 ounces)
- ¾ cup chopped onion
- ¾ cup chopped red bell pepper
- 2 garlic cloves, minced
- 1½ pounds skinned, boned chicken breasts, cut into bite-size pieces
- 1½ cups fat-free, less-sodium chicken broth
- 1 cup sliced fresh mushrooms
- ¾ cup frozen green peas, thawed
- ½ cup golden raisins
- 1 teaspoon salt
- ½ teaspoon black pepper
- 2 tablespoons cornstarch
- 1 tablespoon water
- ½ cup (4 ounces) ⅓-less-fat cream cheese
- Cooking spray

**1.** To prepare crust, lightly spoon flour into a dry measuring cup, and level with a knife. Combine ¼ cup flour, ice water, and vinegar in a small bowl, and stir with a whisk until well-blended to create a slurry. Set aside. Combine ¾ cup flour and salt in a large bowl, and cut in shortening with a pastry blender or 2 knives until mixture resembles coarse meal. Add slurry to flour mixture, and toss with a fork until moist. Press mixture gently into a 4-inch circle on heavy-duty plastic wrap; cover with additional plastic wrap. Chill 15 minutes.
**2.** Preheat oven to 400°.
**3.** To prepare filling, heat oil in a large nonstick skillet over medium-high heat. Add curry; cook 2 minutes. Add potato, onion, bell pepper, garlic, and chicken; stir-fry 3 minutes. Add broth and next 5 ingredients; bring to a boil. Cover, reduce heat, and simmer 5 minutes or until chicken is done. Combine cornstarch and 1 tablespoon water in a small bowl. Stir cornstarch mixture and cream cheese into chicken mixture; cook 1 minute or until cream cheese is melted.
**4.** Spoon filling into a round 2-quart casserole coated with cooking spray. Roll crust into an 11-inch circle, and place over mixture. Cut 6 slits in top of dough to allow steam to escape. Bake at 400° for 30 minutes or until golden brown and bubbly around edges. Let stand 10 minutes. Yield: 6 servings.

**NOTE:** You can also make this in an 11 x 7-inch baking dish. When you prepare the crust, press dough into a 6 x 4-inch rectangle, and chill. Roll dough into an 11 x 7-inch rectangle and place over the filling.

CALORIES 454 (29% from fat); FAT 14.5g (sat 5.2g, mono 4.7g, poly 2.9g); PROTEIN 34.1g; CARB 46.1g; FIBER 4.1g; CHOL 80mg; IRON 3.6mg; SODIUM 786mg; CALC 62mg

## Cheddar-Asparagus Potpie

If you prefer, the microwave works great for cooking the asparagus and potato, giving you a potless head start on this recipe.

    4  cups (1-inch) sliced asparagus
         (about 1 pound)
    2  cups (½-inch) diced red potato
    ½  cup all-purpose flour
  1½  teaspoons paprika
    ¾  teaspoon salt
    ⅛  teaspoon ground red pepper
    1  garlic clove, minced
  2½  cups fat-free milk
    1  cup (4 ounces) shredded reduced-
         fat sharp Cheddar cheese (such as
         Cracker Barrel)
    ¾  cup (½-inch) diced lean smoked
         ham
    ½  cup sliced green onions
       Cooking spray
    4  sheets frozen phyllo dough,
         thawed
    1  tablespoon butter or stick
         margarine, melted

**1.** Preheat oven to 350°.
**2.** Cook asparagus in boiling water 2 minutes or until crisp-tender. Remove from pan with a slotted spoon. Place asparagus in a bowl; set aside. Add potato to pan; cook in boiling water 5 minutes or until tender. Drain. Add to asparagus.
**3.** Lightly spoon flour into a dry measuring cup; level with a knife. Place flour and next 4 ingredients in a large saucepan. Gradually add milk, stirring with a whisk until blended. Cook over medium heat until thick (about 10 minutes), stirring constantly. Add cheese, stirring until cheese melts. Remove from heat; stir in asparagus, potato, ham, and onions. Spoon asparagus mixture into an 11 x 7-inch baking dish coated with cooking spray.
**4.** Place 1 phyllo sheet on a large cutting board or work surface (cover remaining dough to keep from drying), and gently brush 1 side of phyllo with about 1 teaspoon melted butter. Fold phyllo in half crosswise, and place over filling. Repeat procedure with remaining phyllo and butter. Trim excess phyllo from edges of dish, and discard. Lightly coat phyllo with cooking spray.
**5.** Bake at 350° for 25 minutes or until crust is golden brown and bubbly around edges. Let potpie stand 10 minutes. Yield: 6 servings.

CALORIES 266 (25% from fat); FAT 7.3g (sat 3.6g, mono 2.1g, poly 1g); PROTEIN 18g; CARB 33.5g; FIBER 3.4g; CHOL 27mg; IRON 2.8mg; SODIUM 827mg; CALC 331mg

## Beef Empanada Potpie

In Latin America, *empanadas* (em-pah-NAH-das) are small, fried turnovers or pies that are usually built around seasoned meat. We have taken the terrific flavors but abandoned the frying to create a soul-warming potpie.

       Cooking spray
  3½  cups diced baking potato (about
         1¼ pounds)
    1  cup chopped onion
  1¼  pounds ground sirloin
  1½  teaspoons dried oregano
  1½  teaspoons chili powder
    1  teaspoon ground cumin
    ½  teaspoon salt
       Dash of black pepper
    2  large garlic cloves, minced
    ⅓  cup all-purpose flour
    ½  cup beer
    1  (14.5-ounce) can diced tomatoes
         with green pepper and onion,
         drained
    1  (10.5-ounce) can beef consomme
    2  tablespoons chopped pitted green
         olives
    1  tablespoon cider vinegar
    1  (10.6-ounce) box refrigerated
         garlic breadsticks

**1.** Preheat oven to 350°.
**2.** To prepare filling, heat a large Dutch oven coated with cooking spray over medium heat. Add potato and onion; cover and cook 7 minutes, stirring occasionally. Add beef and next 6 ingredients; cook, uncovered, 7 minutes or until browned, stirring to crumble. Lightly spoon flour into a dry measuring cup; level with a knife. Add flour to pan; cook 1 minute. Gradually add beer, tomatoes, and consomme; bring to a boil. Remove from heat, and stir in olives and vinegar.
**3.** Spoon mixture into an 11 x 7-inch baking dish coated with cooking spray. Unroll both dough portions (do not separate dough into breadsticks); roll dough together, forming a 12 x 10-inch rectangle. Place dough on top of beef mixture, pressing to edge of dish. Cut 5 slits in top of crust to allow steam to escape. Gently brush 1 tablespoon garlic spread that is packaged with breadsticks over crust; reserve remaining spread for another use.
**4.** Bake at 350° for 25 minutes or until golden brown and bubbly around edges. Let stand 10 minutes before serving. Yield: 6 servings.

CALORIES 432 (20% from fat); FAT 9.6g (sat 2.8g, mono 3.5g, poly 1.6g); PROTEIN 28.1g; CARB 56.4g; FIBER 3.1g; CHOL 58mg; IRON 6.3mg; SODIUM 966mg; CALC 49mg

## Southwestern Chicken Potpie

The key to the bright flavors of this potpie may well be the spiced-up crust. A little chili powder and cumin go a long way toward making this a southwestern treat.

**CHICKEN:**
    ¼  cup plain low-fat yogurt
    2  tablespoons minced fresh
         cilantro
    2  tablespoons lime juice
    ½  teaspoon ground cumin
    1  large garlic clove, minced
  1½  pounds skinned, boned
         chicken breast, cut into
         bite-size pieces

*Continued*

## CRUST:

- 1 cup all-purpose flour, divided
- 3 tablespoons ice water
- 1 teaspoon cider vinegar
- ½ teaspoon chili powder
- ½ teaspoon ground cumin
- ¼ teaspoon salt
- ¼ cup vegetable shortening

### REMAINING INGREDIENTS:

- 1 teaspoon olive oil, divided
- 2 cups frozen whole-kernel corn, thawed
- 2¼ cups fat-free, less-sodium chicken broth, divided
- 1 medium zucchini, halved lengthwise and thinly sliced (about 2 cups)
- 1 (4.5-ounce) can chopped green chiles, rinsed and drained
- ⅓ cup all-purpose flour
- ¾ teaspoon salt
- ½ teaspoon chili powder
- ¼ teaspoon ground cumin
- ⅛ teaspoon black pepper
- Cooking spray

**1.** To prepare chicken, combine first 5 ingredients in a large zip-top plastic bag; add chicken to bag. Seal and marinate in refrigerator at least 4 hours or overnight.

**2.** To prepare crust, lightly spoon 1 cup flour into a dry measuring cup; level with a knife. Combine ¼ cup flour, water, and vinegar in a small bowl; stir with a whisk to create a slurry. Set aside. Combine ¾ cup flour, ½ teaspoon chili powder, ½ teaspoon cumin, and ¼ teaspoon salt in a large bowl; cut in shortening with a pastry blender or 2 knives until mixture resembles coarse meal. Add slurry to flour mixture; toss with a fork until moist. Press mixture gently into a 6 x 4-inch rectangle on heavy-duty plastic wrap; cover with additional plastic wrap. Roll dough, still covered, into a 12 x 7-inch rectangle; freeze 10 minutes.

**3.** Preheat oven to 400°.

**4.** Remove chicken from bag; discard marinade. Heat ½ teaspoon oil in a large nonstick skillet over medium-high heat. Add chicken to pan; cook 5 minutes or until browned. Remove chicken from pan, and place in a large bowl. Add corn to pan; sauté 6 minutes or until browned.

Add ¼ cup broth, scraping pan to loosen browned bits. Add corn mixture to chicken. Add ½ teaspoon oil to pan. Add zucchini; cook 6 minutes or until brown. Add zucchini and green chiles to corn mixture; toss well.

**5.** Lightly spoon ⅓ cup flour into a dry measuring cup; level with a knife. Combine flour and ½ cup broth in a small bowl; stir with a whisk. Place flour mixture in a saucepan; gradually add 1½ cups broth, ¾ teaspoon salt, ½ teaspoon chili powder, ¼ teaspoon cumin, and black pepper. Bring to a boil over medium heat; cook 5 minutes or until thick, stirring constantly. Pour over chicken mixture; toss to coat. Spoon mixture into an 11 x 7-inch baking dish coated with cooking spray.

**6.** Remove 1 sheet of plastic wrap from dough; let stand 1 minute or until pliable. Fit dough over chicken mixture. Remove top sheet of plastic wrap, pressing dough to edge of dish. Cut 5 slits in crust to allow steam to escape. Bake at 400° for 35 minutes or until golden brown and bubbly around edges. Let stand on a wire rack 10 minutes. Yield: 6 servings.

CALORIES 361 (25% from fat); FAT 10.1g (sat 2.4g, mono 3.4g, poly 2.9g); PROTEIN 32.5g; CARB 34.9g; FIBER 2.6g; CHOL 66mg; IRON 2.8mg; SODIUM 730mg; CALC 38mg

# Roasted-Vegetable Potpie with Feta

For this potpie, prepare the crust while the vegetables are roasting.

### ROASTED VEGETABLES:

- 6 cups (1-inch) cubed peeled eggplant (about 1¼ pounds)
- 2 cups (1-inch) cubed zucchini
- 2 cups (1-inch) pieces red bell pepper
- 2 cups (1-inch) pieces yellow bell pepper
- 2 cups (½-inch-thick) sliced carrot
- 1 large Vidalia or other sweet onion, cut into 8 wedges
- Cooking spray
- 20 (½-inch-thick) slices portobello mushrooms (about 2 large)
- 4 plum tomatoes, halved lengthwise
- 1 large garlic clove, minced

### BUTTERMILK PASTRY:

- 1 cup all-purpose flour
- ¼ teaspoon baking powder
- ¼ teaspoon salt
- ¼ cup low-fat buttermilk
- 2 tablespoons butter or stick margarine, melted and cooled
- 1 teaspoon cider vinegar

### REMAINING INGREDIENTS:

- ½ cup (2 ounces) finely crumbled feta cheese
- ⅓ cup thinly sliced fresh basil
- ¼ cup fat-free, less-sodium chicken broth
- 1 tablespoon balsamic vinegar
- ½ teaspoon dried rosemary
- ½ teaspoon salt
- ⅛ teaspoon black pepper
- 1 large egg white, lightly beaten
- 1½ teaspoons sesame seeds

**1.** Preheat oven to 450°.

**2.** To prepare roasted vegetables, combine first 6 ingredients in a large bowl. Place on a jelly-roll pan coated with cooking spray. Bake at 450° for 40 minutes, stirring once. Add mushrooms, tomatoes, and garlic; bake an additional 30 minutes or until vegetables are tender. Remove roasted vegetables from oven. Reduce oven temperature to 400°.

**3.** To prepare buttermilk pastry, lightly spoon flour into a dry measuring cup; level with a knife. Combine flour, baking powder, and ¼ teaspoon salt in a small bowl. Add buttermilk, butter, and cider vinegar; toss with a fork until moist. Gently press mixture into a 6 x 4-inch rectangle on heavy-duty plastic wrap; cover with additional plastic wrap. Roll dough, still covered, into a 12 x 7-inch rectangle; freeze 10 minutes. Remove 1 sheet of plastic wrap; let stand 1 minute or until pliable.

**4.** Combine roasted vegetables, feta, and next 6 ingredients in an 11 x 7-inch baking dish coated with cooking spray. Fit dough over filling. Remove top sheet of plastic wrap. Brush with egg white; sprinkle with sesame seeds. Cut 6 slits in top of dough to allow steam to escape.

**5.** Bake at 400° for 35 minutes or until potpie is golden brown and bubbly around edges. Let stand 10 minutes. Yield: 6 servings.

CALORIES 234 (29% from fat); FAT 7.5g (sat 4.1g, mono 1.8g, poly 0.9g); PROTEIN 8.3g; CARB 36.2g; FIBER 6.5g; CHOL 19mg; IRON 3.3mg; SODIUM 517mg; CALC 122mg

## Shrimp Creole Potpie

1 teaspoon olive oil
2 cups chopped onion
1 cup diced celery
1 cup chopped green bell pepper
1 teaspoon dried basil
½ teaspoon dried thyme
2 garlic cloves, minced
2 tablespoons all-purpose flour
⅓ cup water
1 tablespoon tomato paste
1 teaspoon lemon juice
1 teaspoon Worcestershire sauce
1 teaspoon sugar
½ teaspoon salt
½ teaspoon black pepper
½ teaspoon hot sauce
2 pounds large shrimp, peeled and deveined
1 (14.5-ounce) can diced tomatoes, drained
½ cup uncooked instant rice
½ cup sliced green onions
½ cup chopped fresh parsley
Cooking spray
1 (10.6-ounce) box refrigerated garlic breadsticks

**1.** Preheat oven to 350°.
**2.** Heat olive oil in a large nonstick skillet over medium-high heat. Add chopped onion, and sauté 5 minutes. Add celery and bell pepper, and sauté 5 minutes. Stir in basil, thyme, and garlic, and sauté 2 minutes. Stir in flour, and cook 1 minute. Gradually stir in water and next 9 ingredients, and cook 1 minute. Remove from heat, and stir in rice, green onions, and parsley. Spoon shrimp mixture into an 11 x 7-inch baking dish coated with cooking spray.
**3.** Unroll both dough portions (do not separate dough into breadsticks); roll dough together, forming a 12 x 10-inch rectangle. Place dough on top of shrimp mixture, pressing to edge of dish. Cut 5 slits in top of crust to allow steam to escape. Gently brush 1 tablespoon garlic spread that is packaged with breadsticks over crust; reserve remaining spread for another use. Bake at 350° for 30 minutes or until golden brown and bubbly around edges. Let stand 10 minutes. Yield: 6 servings.

CALORIES 353 (19% from fat); FAT 7.3g (sat 1.5g, mono 2.2g, poly 2.2g); PROTEIN 29.2g; CARB 42.2g; FIBER 2.9g; CHOL 172mg; IRON 6mg; SODIUM 934mg; CALC 116mg

---

### Why, Oh Why, Did We Make This Pie?

Our goal was not only to incorporate bigger, bolder flavors than those in commercial potpies but also to create a healthier alternative. We shopped our way through the frozen-food aisles to see just what we were up against and found some of the store-boughts to be pretty tasty. But we also found they give fast food a good run for its fat grams.

The list led off with Marie Callender's Beef Pot Pie and Chicken and Broccoli Pot Pie. The beef weighed in at 550 calories per serving, with 32 grams of fat (52% of its calories). The chicken-and-broccoli potpie was even higher, with 620 calories and 45 grams of fat (65% of its calories). Others we sampled—Swanson Hungry-Man, Swanson PotatoTopped, and Banquet, for instance—ranged from 400 to 440 calories per serving, with between 20 and 23 grams of fat.

Those numbers are based on the manufacturers' assertion that one potpie equals two servings. But for many folks we know, one potpie equals one serving—and that approach brings a Marie Callender's Chicken and Broccoli Pot Pie in at 1,240 calories and 90 grams of fat.

---

## Clam Chowder-Spinach Potpie

As in several of our potpies, the crust plays a major role in the pleasure—in this case cornmeal adds appeal. The diced potatoes help thicken the filling.

**CRUST:**
¾ cup all-purpose flour
3 tablespoons yellow cornmeal
1½ teaspoons sugar
¼ teaspoon salt
3 tablespoons vegetable shortening
3 tablespoons ice water
1 teaspoon cider vinegar

**FILLING:**
2 (6½-ounce) cans chopped clams, undrained
2 cups 1% low-fat milk, divided
½ teaspoon dried thyme
3 cups diced peeled baking potato (about 1¼ pounds)
1 cup chopped onion
⅓ cup all-purpose flour
¼ cup dry white wine
1 bacon slice, cooked and crumbled
¼ teaspoon celery salt
¼ teaspoon hot sauce
¼ teaspoon Worcestershire sauce
⅛ teaspoon black pepper
1 (10-ounce) package frozen chopped spinach, thawed, drained, and squeezed dry
Cooking spray

**1.** To prepare crust, lightly spoon ¾ cup flour into dry measuring cups; level with a knife. Combine ¾ cup flour, cornmeal, sugar, and salt in a large bowl; cut in shortening with a pastry blender or 2 knives until mixture resembles coarse meal. Sprinkle surface with ice water and vinegar; toss with a fork until moist and crumbly (do not form a ball). Press mixture gently into a 6 x 4-inch rectangle on heavy-duty plastic wrap; cover with additional plastic wrap. Chill 15 minutes.
**2.** Preheat oven to 400°.
**3.** To prepare filling, drain clams in a colander over a bowl, reserving juice. Set clams aside. Combine reserved clam juice, 1½ cups milk, and thyme in a
*Continued*

large saucepan; bring to a boil. Add potato and onion. Bring to a boil; cook 2 minutes. Drain potato mixture in a colander over a bowl, reserving cooking liquid. Set potato mixture aside. Return cooking liquid to pan over medium heat. Lightly spoon ⅓ cup flour into a dry measuring cup; level with a knife. Combine ½ cup milk and ⅓ cup flour in a small bowl; stir with a whisk. Stir flour mixture into cooking liquid in pan. Stir in wine and bacon. Bring to a boil; cook 5 minutes, stirring frequently.

**4.** Remove from heat; add potato mixture. Partially mash with a potato masher. Stir in clams, celery salt, and next 4 ingredients. Spoon mixture into an 11 x 7-inch baking dish coated with cooking spray. Roll dough into a 12 x 8-inch rectangle. Remove 1 sheet of plastic wrap; fit dough on top of clam mixture, pressing to edge of dish. Remove top sheet of plastic wrap. Cut 5 slits in top of crust to allow steam to escape. Bake at 400° for 30 minutes or until golden brown and bubbly around edges. Let stand 10 minutes. Yield: 6 servings.

CALORIES 306 (23% from fat); FAT 7.8g (sat 2.3g, mono 2.5g, poly 2.1g); PROTEIN 13.9g; CARB 45.4g; FIBER 3.4g; CHOL 24mg; IRON 5.6mg; SODIUM 641mg; CALC 206mg

---

### Pies on Ice Can Be Twice as Nice

You can freeze any extra pies you make from these recipes.

Prepare the filling and pastry crust, and assemble the potpies as directed. Cover the dish with plastic wrap, then aluminum foil, and freeze. Or divide the recipe, and freeze two smaller versions in 8-inch-square baking dishes. That nets you two meals for the effort of one. When it's time to bake, thaw the potpie in the refrigerator overnight, then bake at the called-for temperature. (Starting with a chilled product means adding 10 to 15 minutes to the total baking time, though.)

If you plan to freeze your potpies, use our pastry crust as opposed to phyllo, breadsticks, or any other prepared product.

---

reader recipes

# Katie's Goal

*A soccer-playing chef wraps her Mother's Day present in flour tortillas.*

As a halfback for the Ocala (Florida) Lightning all-star soccer team, 12-year-old Katie Crouch doesn't like to sit on the bench. So when her mom was too tired to cook dinner one evening, it didn't take long to find a substitute. Or, as it turned out, a game-winning recipe: Baked Chicken Tortillas. "I was mixing stuff together from the refrigerator and thought about a chicken tortilla and just came up with it," Katie says. Her mom, Karen, liked it so much that Katie put the dish in play again for Mother's Day.

## Baked Chicken Tortillas

- 1 cup bottled salsa, divided
- 1 (8-ounce) carton low-fat sour cream
- 6 (10-inch) flour tortillas
- 1½ cups chopped cooked chicken breast (about ¾ pound)
- ⅓ cup chopped tomato
- ⅓ cup chopped green or red bell pepper
- ¼ cup chopped onion
- Cooking spray
- ¾ cup (3 ounces) shredded reduced-fat Cheddar cheese

**1.** Preheat oven to 350°.
**2.** Combine ½ cup salsa and sour cream in a small bowl, and spread evenly over tortillas. Divide chicken, tomato, bell pepper, and onion evenly down centers of tortillas, and roll up. Place rolls, seam sides down, in an 11 x 7-inch baking dish coated with cooking spray. Top with ½ cup salsa. Bake at 350° for 15 minutes. Sprinkle with cheese; bake an additional 5 minutes or until cheese melts. Yield: 6 servings (serving size: 1 roll).

CALORIES 379 (26% from fat); FAT 10.8g (sat 4.1g, mono 3.7g, poly 2.5g); PROTEIN 28.7g; CARB 38.9g; FIBER 2.8g; CHOL 64mg; IRON 3mg; SODIUM 623mg; CALC 284mg

---

### Pepper Slaw

"Thirty years ago, I married a wonderful man from Pennsylvania. His mother cooked a lot of traditional Pennsylvania Dutch-type meals, and this was one of the recipes that was handed down to her by her mother."
—Barb Bressi-Donohue, Las Vegas, Nevada

- 3 cups thinly sliced green cabbage
- 3 cups thinly sliced red cabbage
- ½ cup grated carrot
- ⅓ cup chopped green bell pepper
- ½ cup sugar
- ½ cup red wine vinegar
- ¼ cup water
- ⅛ teaspoon salt

**1.** Combine first 4 ingredients in a large bowl. Combine sugar, vinegar, water, and salt; stir well with a whisk. Pour over cabbage mixture, tossing to coat. Cover and chill 1 hour. Yield: 7 servings (serving size: 1 cup).

CALORIES 78 (2% from fat); FAT 0.2g (sat 0g, mono 0g, poly 0.1g); PROTEIN 0.9g; CARB 19.4g; FIBER 1.7g; CHOL 0mg; IRON 0.5mg; SODIUM 54mg; CALC 32mg

---

### Quick-and-Easy Turkey Burgers

"My daughters were interested in low-fat alternatives to their favorite foods. The first time I made turkey burgers, they tasted bland. Teriyaki sauce and onions added just the right pizzazz, and we made this quick meal a weekly habit."
—Judi Lehrian, Hummelstown, Pennsylvania

- 1 pound ground turkey breast
- 2 teaspoons garlic powder
- 1 teaspoon Cajun seasoning
- ¼ teaspoon black pepper
- 3 tablespoons light teriyaki sauce
- 1 tablespoon water
- Cooking spray
- 1 large onion, cut into ¼-inch-thick slices (about 2 cups)
- 1 teaspoon olive oil
- 4 (1½-ounce) hamburger buns
- 8 (¼-inch-thick) slices tomato
- 4 curly leaf lettuce leaves

1. Combine first 4 ingredients in a large bowl. Divide turkey mixture into 4 equal portions, shaping each portion into a ½-inch-thick patty. Combine teriyaki sauce and water in a small bowl.

2. Place a large nonstick skillet coated with cooking spray over medium heat until hot. Add onion slices; cover and cook 10 minutes or until onion is golden brown, stirring frequently. Stir in 1 tablespoon teriyaki mixture. Remove onion from pan, and keep warm. Add olive oil to pan. Add patties, and cook 5 minutes over medium heat. Add 3 tablespoons teriyaki mixture to pan. Carefully turn patties over, and cook 3 minutes or until golden. Place 1 patty on bottom half of each bun, and top each patty with ¼ cup onion, 2 tomato slices, and 1 lettuce leaf. Top with remaining bun halves. Yield: 4 servings.

**NOTE:** You can freeze any uncooked turkey patties for up to 1 month. To freeze, separate patties with wax paper; place them in a heavy-duty zip-top plastic bag, remove excess air, seal, and freeze. Thaw in refrigerator.

CALORIES 278 (15% from fat); FAT 4.7g (sat 1.2g, mono 1.3g, poly 1.4g); PROTEIN 30g; CARB 28.9g; FIBER 2.4g; CHOL 60mg; IRON 2.1mg; SODIUM 949mg; CALC 73mg

## White Gazpacho

"My mom served this long before we ever started counting fat grams. I lightened the recipe by using fat-free sour cream and fat-free chicken broth. The wonderful taste stayed the same."

—Fredye Factor, Dallas, Texas

2 cups chopped seeded peeled cucumber (about 2 medium)
1 cup fat-free, less-sodium chicken broth
1½ tablespoons white wine vinegar
⅛ teaspoon salt
1 (16-ounce) container fat-free sour cream
1 garlic clove, crushed
1 cup diced tomato (about 1 medium)
½ cup chopped green onions

1. Place first 6 ingredients in a blender, and pulse 3 or 4 times or until coarsely chopped. Cover soup, and chill 3 hours or overnight. Ladle soup into bowls, and top with tomato and onions. Yield: 4 servings (serving size: 1 cup soup, ¼ cup tomato, and 2 tablespoons onions).

CALORIES 108 (3% from fat); FAT 0.3g (sat 0.1g, mono 0g, poly 0.1g); PROTEIN 9.8g; CARB 13.2g; FIBER 1.3g; CHOL 0mg; IRON 0.5mg; SODIUM 281mg; CALC 142mg

## Darcy's Veggie Chili

"The first time I had this chili, I'd just gotten off the plane from boarding school. Mom and I went straight to the kitchen to catch up, dance to Bonnie Raitt, and cook. After I went away to college, my friends and I would gather for the night, and I would make this chili. It's warm, inviting, and perfect for cozy times at home."

—Darcy Donald, Falmouth, Maine

2 teaspoons olive oil
1½ cups chopped onion (about 1 large)
3 garlic cloves, chopped
5 teaspoons chili powder
1 tablespoon brown sugar
1 tablespoon ground cumin
1 tablespoon dried oregano
½ teaspoon dried coriander
⅛ teaspoon ground allspice
⅛ teaspoon ground cloves
1 jalapeño pepper, seeded and diced
1½ cups water
1 cup diced red bell pepper (about 1 medium)
1 cup diced green bell pepper (about 1 medium)
3 tablespoons tomato paste
1 (16-ounce) can kidney beans, drained and rinsed
1 (14.5-ounce) can diced tomatoes, undrained
½ cup (2 ounces) shredded reduced-fat sharp Cheddar cheese

1. Heat olive oil in a Dutch oven over medium-high heat. Add onion and garlic, and sauté 5 minutes. Add chili powder and next 7 ingredients, and cook 1 minute. Add water and next 5 ingredients, and cook over medium heat 15 minutes. Ladle chili into bowls, and top each serving with cheese. Yield: 4 servings (serving size: 1½ cups chili and 2 tablespoons cheese).

**NOTE:** This chili can be made ahead and frozen for up to 3 months. To freeze, let chili cool completely in refrigerator; place chili in heavy-duty zip-top plastic bags, remove excess air, seal, and freeze. Thaw chili in refrigerator. Cook over medium heat or in microwave until thoroughly heated.

CALORIES 246 (25% from fat); FAT 6.9g (sat 2.2g, mono 2.9g, poly 1.2g); PROTEIN 13.2g; CARB 37g; FIBER 7.3g; CHOL 10mg; IRON 5.9mg; SODIUM 437mg; CALC 239mg

## Mary's Salsa

"My mom has always made the best salsa. About three or four years ago, she decided to make a batch with leftover tomatoes we'd picked from the garden; this recipe just grew from there. Now I make it for my family and friends at work, and they love it."

—Julia Staley, Franklinville, North Carolina

2 cups diced tomato (about 2 medium)
⅔ cup diced onion
3 tablespoons minced fresh cilantro
1 tablespoon fresh lime juice
1 garlic clove, minced
1 jalapeño pepper, seeded and chopped

1. Combine all ingredients in a bowl; cover and chill 1 hour. Yield: 2½ cups (serving size: ¼ cup).

**NOTE:** Serve with baked tortilla chips or as a topping for grilled chicken, fish, or hamburgers.

CALORIES 14 (13% from fat); FAT 0.2g (sat 0g, mono 0g, poly 0.1g); PROTEIN 0.5g; CARB 3.1g; FIBER 0.7g; CHOL 0mg; IRON 0.3mg; SODIUM 4mg; CALC 6mg

### "Mom's Best" Noodle Kugel

"I've been making this, or helping my mother make this, for as long as I can remember. She served it to our family at special gatherings, so whenever I make it, I always remember the good times I had growing up. I lightened it by using fat-free and low-fat cheeses, and egg substitute."

—Kerri Levine, Longwood, Florida

> 1 cup raisins
> 1 cup fat-free cottage cheese
> ⅓ cup (3 ounces) ⅓-less-fat cream cheese
> ¼ cup sugar
> 1 (8-ounce) carton fat-free sour cream
> 1 (4-ounce) carton egg substitute
> 8 cups cooked yolk-free egg noodles (about 12 ounces uncooked)
> Cooking spray
> 2 tablespoons sugar
> 1 teaspoon ground cinnamon

**1.** Preheat oven to 350°.
**2.** Combine first 6 ingredients in a large bowl. Add noodles, tossing gently to coat. Spoon mixture into an 11 x 7-inch baking dish coated with cooking spray. Combine 2 tablespoons sugar and cinnamon; sprinkle over noodle mixture. Bake at 350° for 45 minutes or until set. Yield: 8 servings (serving size: 1 cup).

CALORIES 319 (9% from fat); FAT 3.2g (sat 1.5g, mono 0.7g, poly 0.5g); PROTEIN 14.7g; CARB 58.7g; FIBER 1.6g; CHOL 9mg; IRON 2.1mg; SODIUM 194mg; CALC 39mg

### Creole Macaroni

"When I was a young bride and my daughter was a newborn, a neighbor brought me a dish that she called Creole. I doctored a few things, added mushrooms and macaroni, and have been making it for 24 years. When my daughter got married, this is the first recipe I passed on in a recipe file I made for her."

—Debbie Mander, Pittsburgh, Pennsylvania

> 1 pound ground round
> 1 cup chopped onion (about 1 medium)
> 1 cup sliced mushrooms
> 1 cup cooked medium elbow macaroni
> 1 tablespoon sugar
> ½ teaspoon dried Italian seasoning
> ¼ teaspoon garlic salt
> ¼ teaspoon black pepper
> 1 (14.5-ounce) can stewed tomatoes, undrained
> 1 (10¾-ounce) can condensed reduced-fat, reduced-sodium tomato soup, undiluted
> Cooking spray
> ¾ cup (3 ounces) shredded reduced-fat sharp Cheddar cheese, divided

**1.** Preheat oven to 350°.
**2.** Cook ground beef, onion, and mushrooms in a large nonstick skillet over medium-high heat until beef is browned, stirring to crumble. Drain.
**3.** Combine beef mixture, macaroni, and next 6 ingredients in a 2-quart casserole dish coated with cooking spray. Stir in ½ cup cheese; sprinkle ¼ cup cheese over top. Bake at 350° for 30 minutes or until bubbly. Yield: 4 servings (serving size: 1¾ cups).
**NOTE:** This dish reheats well. Store it in refrigerator for up to 3 days or in freezer for up to 1 month.

CALORIES 388 (30% from fat); FAT 12.9g (sat 5.3g, mono 4.6g, poly 0.8g); PROTEIN 35.2g; CARB 33.4g; FIBER 3g; CHOL 83mg; IRON 4.2mg; SODIUM 800mg; CALC 230mg

## lighten up

# News You Can Use

*Two reporters fell in love over a plate of Spaghetti Pie, but their recipe won't make more romantic headlines without some healthy editing.*

"The way to a man's heart is through his stomach" might seem an unsupported rumor, but it is a verifiable fact for journalist Elaine Finn. "I made Spaghetti Pie for my husband on one of our very first dates," says the 36-year-old native Ohioan, now a desktop publisher who lives in New Jersey. "He swears when he tasted it, he decided right then that he wanted to marry me."

Eight years of marriage and uncounted casseroles later, Finn was having qualms about serving the fat-laden casserole to her family anymore, particularly to the three newest devotees: Matthew, 7; Ginny, 6; and the most enthusiastic fan, 3-year-old Sarah.

We took Finn's original recipe and worked it over, switching from ground beef to lean ground round and halving the amount. We deleted some of the Cheddar cheese and the full-fat versions of sour cream and cream cheese, replacing each with lighter versions. We cut nearly 40 grams of fat, 100 grams of cholesterol, and 367 calories.

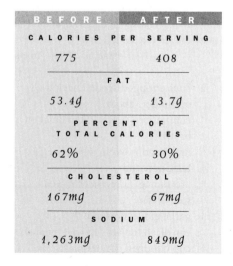

| BEFORE | AFTER |
|---|---|
| **CALORIES PER SERVING** | |
| 775 | 408 |
| **FAT** | |
| 53.4g | 13.7g |
| **PERCENT OF TOTAL CALORIES** | |
| 62% | 30% |
| **CHOLESTEROL** | |
| 167mg | 67mg |
| **SODIUM** | |
| 1,263mg | 849mg |

## Spaghetti Pie

Though it's really a deep-dish casserole, many Midwesterners lovingly refer to this recipe as Spaghetti Pie. You can substitute plain tomato sauce and add ¼ teaspoon of garlic powder, if desired.

    1  pound ground round
    ¼  teaspoon salt
    ¼  teaspoon black pepper
    2  (8-ounce) cans tomato sauce
       with garlic
 1½  cups low-fat sour cream
    ½  cup chopped green onions
    ¼  cup (2 ounces) ⅓-less-fat cream
       cheese, softened
    4  cups hot cooked spaghetti (about
       8 ounces uncooked pasta)
Cooking spray
 1⅓  cups (about 5 ounces) shredded
       reduced-fat extra-sharp Cheddar
       cheese

**1.** Preheat oven to 350°.
**2.** Cook meat in a large nonstick skillet over medium heat until browned, stirring to crumble. Drain well, and return meat to pan. Stir in salt, pepper, and tomato sauce. Bring to a boil; reduce heat, and simmer 20 minutes.
**3.** Combine sour cream, green onions, and cream cheese in a small bowl, and set aside. Place spaghetti noodles in a 2-quart casserole dish coated with cooking spray. Spread sour cream mixture over spaghetti noodles. Top with meat mixture. Sprinkle with Cheddar cheese. Cover and bake at 350° for 25 minutes. Uncover; bake an additional 5 minutes or until cheese is bubbly. Yield: 6 servings.

CALORIES 408 (30% from fat); FAT 13.7g (sat 7.3g, mono 4.2g, poly 0.8g); PROTEIN 28.4g; CARB 39.9g; FIBER 2.9g; CHOL 67mg; IRON 3.4mg; SODIUM 849mg; CALC 376mg

# Hola, Paella

## Could this Spanish classic be the perfect one-pan meal for America?

Among all of Spain's classic meals, none is more festive than *paella* (pie-AY-yuh), the most soul-satisfying rice dish of Europe. The basic ingredients in paella are simple—even humble: rice, peppers, tomatoes, garlic, and peas, as well as chicken and sausages or, for a seafood paella, fish and shellfish.

### Traditional Spanish Paella

(pictured on page 130)

For this meal, choose a good Spanish red wine from the Rioja region.

**HERB BLEND:**
    1  cup chopped fresh parsley
    ¼  cup fresh lemon juice
    1  tablespoon olive oil
    2  large garlic cloves, minced

**PAELLA:**
    1  cup water
    1  teaspoon saffron threads
    3  (16-ounce) cans fat-free, less-
       sodium chicken broth
    8  unpeeled jumbo shrimp (about ½
       pound)
    1  tablespoon olive oil
    4  skinned, boned chicken thighs, cut
       in half
    2  links Spanish chorizo sausage (about
       6½ ounces) or turkey kielbasa, cut
       into ½-inch-thick slices
    1  (4-ounce) slice prosciutto or
       33%-less-sodium ham, cut into
       1-inch pieces
    2  cups finely chopped onion
    1  cup finely chopped red bell pepper
    1  cup canned diced tomatoes,
       undrained
    1  teaspoon sweet paprika
    3  large garlic cloves, minced
    3  cups uncooked Arborio rice or
       other short-grain rice
    1  cup frozen green peas
    8  mussels, scrubbed and debearded
    ¼  cup fresh lemon juice
Lemon wedges (optional)

**1.** To prepare herb blend, combine first 4 ingredients, and set aside.
**2.** To prepare paella, combine water, saffron, and broth in a large saucepan. Bring to a simmer (do not boil). Keep warm over low heat. Peel and devein shrimp, leaving tails intact; set aside.
**3.** Heat 1 tablespoon oil in a large paella pan or large skillet over medium-high heat. Add chicken; sauté 2 minutes on each side. Remove from pan. Add sausage and prosciutto to pan; sauté 2 minutes. Remove from pan. Add shrimp to pan, and sauté 2 minutes. Remove from pan. Reduce heat to medium-low. Add onion and bell pepper to pan; sauté 15 minutes, stirring occasionally. Add tomatoes, paprika, and 3 garlic cloves; cook 5 minutes. Add rice; cook 1 minute, stirring constantly. Stir in herb blend, broth mixture, chicken, sausage mixture, and peas. Bring to a low boil; cook 10 minutes, stirring frequently. Add mussels to pan, nestling them into rice mixture. Cook 5 minutes or until shells open; discard any unopened shells. Arrange shrimp, heads down, in rice mixture, and cook 5 minutes or until shrimp are done. Sprinkle with ¼ cup lemon juice. Remove from heat; cover with a towel, and let stand 10 minutes. Serve with lemon wedges, if desired. Yield: 8 servings (serving size: 1½ cups paella, 1 shrimp, and 1 mussel).

CALORIES 521 (23% from fat); FAT 13.3g (sat 3.7g, mono 6.8g, poly 2g); PROTEIN 25.5g; CARB 72.1g; FIBER 3.6g; CHOL 80mg; IRON 6mg; SODIUM 871mg; CALC 60mg

## Spicy Paella with Chile, Lime, and Cilantro

Although traditional paellas aren't spicy, you can incorporate bolder seasonings. A bit of chile, lime, and cilantro in place of traditional saffron creates robust flavors. Look for a red wine from the Ribera del Duero region of Spain to go with this recipe. Ribera del Duero reds are bolder than other Spanish wines, so they go well with spicy flavors.

**BROTH:**

1 dried New Mexican or Anaheim chile
1 teaspoon ground cumin
½ teaspoon ground cinnamon
2 garlic cloves, peeled
2 (16-ounce) cans fat-free, less-sodium chicken broth

**HERB BLEND:**

½ cup chopped fresh cilantro
¼ cup fresh lime juice
1 tablespoon olive oil
2 garlic cloves, minced

**PAELLA:**

24 unpeeled large shrimp (about 2 pounds)
1 teaspoon olive oil
2 (3.5-ounce) andouille sausages or chicken sausages with habanero chiles and tequila (such as Gerhard's), cut into ½-inch pieces
2½ cups finely chopped red bell pepper
2 cups finely chopped onion
2 cups sliced zucchini
1 cup canned diced tomatoes, undrained
1 teaspoon hot paprika
¼ teaspoon salt
3 garlic cloves, minced
2 cups uncooked Arborio rice or other short-grain rice
1 cup frozen whole-kernel corn
8 lime wedges

**1.** To prepare broth, remove stem and seeds from chile. Combine chile, cumin, cinnamon, and 2 garlic cloves in a food processor; process until minced. Combine chile mixture and broth in a saucepan. Bring to a simmer (do not boil). Keep warm over low heat.

**2.** To prepare herb blend, combine cilantro, lime juice, 1 tablespoon oil, and 2 garlic cloves; set aside.

**3.** To prepare paella, peel and devein shrimp, leaving tails intact; set aside. Heat 1 teaspoon oil in large paella pan or large skillet over medium heat. Add sausages; sauté 3 minutes. Remove from pan. Add shrimp to pan; sauté 2 minutes. Remove from pan. Add bell pepper and onion to pan, and sauté 5 minutes, stirring occasionally. Add zucchini; sauté 5 minutes. Add tomatoes, paprika, salt, and 3 garlic cloves; cook 5 minutes, scraping pan to loosen browned bits. Add rice; cook 1 minute, stirring constantly. Stir in broth mixture, herb blend, sausages, and corn; cook 10 minutes, stirring frequently.

**4.** Arrange shrimp, heads down, in rice mixture; cook 10 minutes. Remove from heat. Cover with a towel, and let stand 10 minutes. Serve with lime wedges. Yield: 8 servings (serving size: 1½ cups paella and 3 shrimp).

CALORIES 383 (20% from fat); FAT 8.4g (sat 2.4g, mono 4.2g, poly 1.3g); PROTEIN 22.1g; CARB 54.5g; FIBER 3g; CHOL 100mg; IRON 5.2mg; SODIUM 574mg; CALC 68mg

## Seafood Paella

Seafood paellas should be made with a variety of fish and shellfish, each adding its own flavor and texture. Always include jumbo shrimp, mussels or clams, and a firm white fish such as monkfish, halibut, or sea bass. Seafood paellas are often served with a cold, fresh, dry fino sherry; however, a zesty, dry California Sauvignon Blanc works well, too.

**BROTH:**

3 cups water
1 cup dry white wine
1 teaspoon saffron threads
2 (8-ounce) bottles clam juice

**HERB BLEND:**

1 cup chopped fresh parsley
⅓ cup fresh lemon juice
1 tablespoon olive oil
1 teaspoon dried tarragon
2 large garlic cloves, minced

**PAELLA:**

1 pound monkfish or other firm white fish fillets
16 unpeeled jumbo shrimp (about 1 pound)
1 tablespoon olive oil
2 cups finely chopped onion
1 cup finely chopped red bell pepper
1 cup canned diced tomatoes, undrained
1 teaspoon sweet paprika
½ teaspoon crushed red pepper
3 garlic cloves, minced
3 cups uncooked Arborio rice or other short-grain rice
1 cup frozen green peas
16 littleneck clams
1 (7-ounce) jar sliced pimento, drained
2 tablespoons fresh lemon juice

**1.** To prepare broth, combine first 4 ingredients in a saucepan. Bring to a simmer (do not boil). Keep warm over low heat.

**2.** To prepare herb blend, combine parsley and next 4 ingredients; set aside.

**3.** To prepare paella, trim connective tissue from monkfish; cut into 1-inch pieces. Peel and devein shrimp, leaving tails intact. Heat 1 tablespoon oil in a large paella pan or large skillet over medium-high heat. Add fish and shrimp; sauté 1 minute (seafood mixture will not be cooked through). Remove seafood mixture from pan, and keep warm. Add onion and bell pepper to pan, and sauté 5 minutes. Add tomatoes, paprika, crushed red pepper, and 3 garlic cloves; cook 5 minutes. Add rice, and cook 1 minute, stirring constantly. Stir in broth, herb blend, and peas. Bring to a low boil, and cook 10 minutes, stirring frequently.

**4.** Add clams to pan, nestling them into rice mixture. Cook 5 minutes or until shells open; discard any unopened shells. Stir in seafood mixture, and arrange shrimp, heads down, in rice mixture. Arrange pimento slices spokelike on top of rice mixture; cook 5 minutes. Sprinkle with lemon juice. Remove from heat; cover with a towel, and let stand 10 minutes. Yield: 8 servings (serving size: 1¾ cups paella, 2 shrimp, and 2 clams).

CALORIES 445 (12% from fat); FAT 5.8g (sat 1g, mono 3g, poly 1.2g); PROTEIN 24.6g; CARB 72.1g; FIBER 3.7g; CHOL 75mg; IRON 7.6mg; SODIUM 273mg; CALC 79mg

# How to Stir-Fry with Style

Chop, sauté, sizzle, and stir your way to more hot tasty fun than your kitchen should allow.

The art of stir-frying, so grounded in ancient ways yet so thoroughly adaptable to the modern, is a perfect way to make healthy cooking handy to those new to the kitchen. It also gives more seasoned veterans a valuable refresher. The classic starting point is the wok—that deep, concave pan you've seen in Asian restaurants and that can be found these days in kitchenware aisles of many major supermarkets. But for a modern touch, we like a newer piece of equipment, the Western-influenced stir-fry pan, a cross between a wok and a skillet.

The other simple requirements of stir-frying come down to preparation and timing. That means a little advance chopping, mixing, and measuring.

These recipes will guide you through it all, from choosing the best ingredients to scooping it all onto the plate.

## Pad Thai

This is one of the most famous stir-fry dishes ever, and Thailand's most well-known noodle dish. It's fairly high in sodium due to the flavor-adding fish sauce and soy sauce, but lower than you'll find at most restaurants.

6¾ cups water, divided
½ pound uncooked rice sticks (rice-flour noodles) or vermicelli
2 tablespoons vegetable oil, divided
¼ cup low-sodium soy sauce
¼ cup Thai fish sauce
2 tablespoons brown sugar
2 large eggs, lightly beaten
¾ pound skinned, boned chicken breast, cut into 1-inch strips
2 garlic cloves, minced
½ pound medium shrimp, peeled and deveined
½ cup (1-inch) sliced green onions
2 teaspoons paprika
2 cups fresh bean sprouts
½ cup chopped fresh cilantro
2 tablespoons chopped peanuts
6 lime wedges

1. Place 6 cups water in a stir-fry pan or wok; bring to a boil. Add noodles; cook 4 minutes. Drain and rinse with cold water; drain well. Place cooked noodles in a large bowl. Add 1 teaspoon oil; toss well. Set aside.
2. Combine ¾ cup water, soy sauce, fish sauce, and brown sugar in a small bowl; set aside.
3. Heat 1 teaspoon oil in a stir-fry pan or wok over medium heat. Add eggs; stir-fry 1 minute. Add eggs to noodle mixture. Heat 1 teaspoon oil in pan over medium-high heat. Add chicken and garlic; stir-fry 5 minutes. Add to noodle mixture. Heat 1 tablespoon oil in pan. Add shrimp, onions, and paprika; stir-fry 3 minutes. Add soy sauce mixture and noodle mixture to pan; cook 3 minutes or until thoroughly heated. Remove from heat; toss with sprouts and cilantro. Sprinkle with peanuts. Serve with lime wedges. Yield: 6 servings (serving size: 1 cup noodle mixture and 1 lime wedge).

CALORIES 347 (24% from fat); FAT 9.3g (sat 1.4g, mono 4.3g, poly 2.5g); PROTEIN 24.5g; CARB 41.6g; FIBER 1.2g; CHOL 150mg; IRON 2.6mg; SODIUM 1,364mg; CALC 57mg

## Shrimp and Broccoli in Chili Sauce

Chili sauce comes in a 12-ounce bottle next to the ketchup in the supermarket.

1½ pounds medium shrimp, peeled and deveined
2 tablespoons minced seeded jalapeño pepper (about 2 peppers)
2 tablespoons dry sherry
1½ teaspoons paprika
½ teaspoon ground red pepper
4 garlic cloves, crushed
⅓ cup water
¼ cup chili sauce (such as Heinz)
2 teaspoons cornstarch
2 teaspoons sugar
½ teaspoon salt
1 tablespoon vegetable oil
3 cups broccoli florets
4 cups cooked soba (about 8 ounces uncooked buckwheat noodles) or vermicelli

1. Combine first 6 ingredients in a medium bowl; cover and chill 1 hour.
2. Combine water and next 4 ingredients in a small bowl; set aside.
3. Heat oil in a stir-fry pan or wok over medium-high heat. Add broccoli; stir-fry 2 minutes. Add shrimp mixture; stir-fry 5 minutes or until shrimp are done. Add cornstarch mixture, and bring to a boil. Cook 1 minute or until sauce thickens. Serve over soba noodles. Yield: 4 servings (serving size: about 1 cup stir-fry and 1 cup noodles).

CALORIES 441 (14% from fat); FAT 7g (sat 1.3g, mono 2g, poly 2.6g); PROTEIN 35.7g; CARB 54.2g; FIBER 5.6g; CHOL 194mg; IRON 5.1mg; SODIUM 1,219mg; CALC 130mg

### Stir, Not Shake

For actually stirring and tossing ingredients, a long-handled stir-fry spatula is perfect, but we've also used a long-handled wooden spoon and a heat-resistant rubber spatula. Stir-fry utensils are available in stainless steel, wood, and heat-resistant nylon, which are safe to use on nonstick cooking surfaces.

## Chicken-Cashew Stir-Fry Step-by-Steps

**1.** *Prepare all your ingredients in advance. This is helpful due to the frenzied pace of stir-frying. Start with the sauce, even though it's added at the very end. Combine the chicken broth, oyster sauce, honey, and other ingredients in a medium bowl with a whisk. Set aside.*

**2.** *Chop all the vegetables, and arrange in separate bowls or small piles so that they're ready to be scooped up and tossed into the pan. Chopping them ahead also allows them some time to dry out, which is good because lots of moisture will make the vegetables steam or braise rather than stir-fry.*

**3.** *Heat the oil in a stir-fry pan or wok over medium-high heat for 2 minutes. You want the oil very hot so the vegetables will cook quickly. Add the onions, and stir-fry 1 minute. Add the remaining vegetables, stir-frying 2 minutes for each. Remove the vegetables from the pan. Keep warm.*

**4.** *Add the sauce, vegetables, pineapple, cashews, and crushed red pepper to the pan after you've stir-fried the chicken. Then bring mixture to a boil. Cornstarch-thickened sauces must be brought to a boil for the cornstarch to activate and not taste starchy. Cook 1 minute or until thick.*

### Woks Are Great, But Stir-Fry Pans Are Even Better

Stir-fry cooking has long been associated with the traditional carbon-steel wok. But the relatively new stir-fry pan with a nonreactive stainless-steel or anodized-aluminum surface is a terrific alternative, and one we preferred. For all these recipes we used a 12-inch Joyce Chen or Calphalon nonstick stir-fry pan.

Unlike the round-bottom woks, which require a ring on which the vessel can sit, the stir-fry pan has a wide, flat bottom that rests evenly on a smooth-top cooking surface. Both the stainless-steel and anodized-aluminum surfaces distribute heat evenly. The stick-resistant surfaces are easy to maintain and will not rust, so there's no need for time-consuming seasoning.

## Chicken-Cashew Stir-Fry

We just couldn't resist this classic dish, which combines both sweet and hot Asian flavors. It is a basic recipe from which you can vary the ingredients as you like.

- ½ cup fat-free, less-sodium chicken broth
- 3 tablespoons oyster sauce (such as Kame)
- 1½ tablespoons cornstarch
- 1½ tablespoons honey
- 1 tablespoon low-sodium soy sauce
- 2 teaspoons rice or white wine vinegar
- ½ teaspoon salt
- 2 tablespoons vegetable oil, divided
- 1 cup chopped green onions, divided
- 1 small onion, cut into 8 wedges
- 1 cup (3 x ¼-inch) julienne-cut red bell pepper
- ½ cup diagonally sliced carrot
- 1 cup sliced mushrooms
- 1 cup snow peas
- 1 pound skinned, boned chicken thighs, cut into bite-size pieces
- ¼ cup canned pineapple chunks in juice, drained
- ⅓ cup cashews
- ½ to 1 teaspoon crushed red pepper
- 6 cups hot cooked long-grain rice

**1.** Combine first 7 ingredients in a small bowl; set aside.
**2.** Heat 1 tablespoon oil in a stir-fry pan or wok over medium-high heat. Add ½ cup green onions and onion wedges; stir-fry 1 minute. Add bell pepper and carrot; stir-fry 2 minutes. Add mushrooms and peas; stir-fry 2 minutes. Remove vegetable mixture from pan. Keep warm.
**3.** Heat 1 tablespoon oil in pan over medium-high heat. Add chicken; stir-fry 5 minutes. Add broth mixture, vegetable mixture, pineapple, cashews, and crushed red pepper; bring to a boil, and cook 1 minute or until thick. Stir in ½ cup green onions. Serve with rice. Yield: 6 servings (serving size: 1⅓ cups stir-fry and 1 cup rice).

CALORIES 474 (22% from fat); FAT 11.8g (sat 2.4g, mono 4.5g, poly 3.8g); PROTEIN 22.5g; CARB 68.5g; FIBER 3.8g; CHOL 60mg; IRON 4.3mg; SODIUM 553mg; CALC 67mg

## Asian Vegetable Stir-Fry

This is a particularly light, vegetarian stir-fry dish. To make it a more substantial main dish, add tofu or chicken. You can use regular green cabbage in place of the napa.

  2  tablespoons tomato paste
  1  tablespoon rice vinegar
  1  tablespoon low-sodium soy sauce
  1  teaspoon curry powder
  ½  teaspoon salt
  ⅛  teaspoon black pepper
  2  tablespoons vegetable oil
  1  Vidalia or other sweet onion, cut into 8 wedges
  1  medium zucchini, quartered lengthwise and cut into 1-inch-thick slices (about 2 cups)
  1  medium yellow squash, quartered lengthwise and cut into 1-inch-thick slices (about 2 cups)
  1  cup chopped celery
  2  cups (¼-inch-thick) sliced green bell pepper
  ½  cup water
  ¼  cup drained, sliced water chestnuts
  2  cups thinly sliced napa (Chinese) cabbage
  1  tablespoon pine nuts

**1.** Combine first 6 ingredients in a small bowl; set aside.
**2.** Heat oil in a stir-fry pan or wok over medium heat. Add onion; stir-fry 1 minute. Increase heat to medium-high. Add zucchini, yellow squash, and celery; stir-fry 5 minutes. Add bell pepper, water, and water chestnuts; stir-fry 3 minutes.
**3.** Add tomato paste mixture; bring to a boil, and cook 1 minute. Stir in cabbage and pine nuts. Yield: 6 servings (serving size: 1 cup).

CALORIES 102 (57% from fat); FAT 6.5g (sat 1.1g, mono 2.7g, poly 2.3g); PROTEIN 2.5g; CARB 10.8g; FIBER 3.1g; CHOL 0mg; IRON 1.6mg; SODIUM 303mg; CALC 56mg

## Fried Rice with Smoked Ham

  2  tablespoons vegetable oil, divided
  1  large egg, lightly beaten
  6  cups vertically sliced onion (about 2 large onions)
  2  garlic cloves, minced
  1  cup lean julienne-cut smoked ham (about ½ pound)
  7  cups cooked brown or white basmati rice
  1  cup frozen green peas, thawed
  ½  cup whole baby corn
  ¼  cup low-sodium soy sauce
  1  tablespoon dark sesame oil
  ¼  teaspoon salt
  ¼  teaspoon ground white pepper
     Cilantro sprigs (optional)

**1.** Heat 1 tablespoon oil in a stir-fry pan or wok over medium heat. Add egg; stir-fry 30 seconds or until egg is done. Remove egg mixture from skillet.
**2.** Add 1 tablespoon oil to pan. Add onion; stir-fry 3 minutes. Add garlic; stir-fry 1 minute. Increase heat to medium-high; add ham, and stir-fry 3 minutes. Add rice, peas, and corn; stir-fry 3 minutes. Add egg mixture, soy sauce, sesame oil, salt, and pepper; stir-fry 1 minute or until thoroughly heated. Garnish with cilantro, if desired. Yield: 6 servings (serving size: 1⅓ cups).

CALORIES 459 (24% from fat); FAT 12.1g (sat 2.1g, mono 4.3g, poly 4.7g); PROTEIN 18.1g; CARB 67.8g; FIBER 8g; CHOL 57mg; IRON 2.4mg; SODIUM 784mg; CALC 60mg

## Stir-Fried Orange-Ginger Tofu

  3  tablespoons thawed orange juice concentrate
  1  tablespoon dry sherry
  1½ teaspoons cornstarch
  1  teaspoon brown sugar
  2  teaspoons dark sesame oil
  ½  teaspoon salt
  1  tablespoon vegetable oil
  1  tablespoon minced peeled fresh ginger
  3  garlic cloves, crushed
  1⅔ cups sliced shiitake mushrooms, caps and stems (about 1 [3½-ounce] package)
  1¼ cups (1-inch) sliced asparagus (about ½ pound)
  1¼ cups thinly sliced leek (about 2 large)
  ½  pound firm tofu, drained and cubed

**1.** Combine first 6 ingredients in a small bowl, and set cornstarch mixture aside.
**2.** Heat 1 tablespoon oil in a stir-fry pan or wok over medium heat. Add minced ginger and crushed garlic; stir-fry 30 seconds. Add sliced mushrooms, asparagus, and leek; stir-fry 3 minutes. Add cubed tofu; stir-fry 4 minutes. Stir in cornstarch mixture. Bring to a boil; cook 1 minute. Yield: 3 servings (serving size: 1 cup).

CALORIES 218 (49% from fat); FAT 11.8g (sat 1.4g, mono 4.8g, poly 4.8g); PROTEIN 9.2g; CARB 21.6g; FIBER 3.2g; CHOL 0mg; IRON 6mg; SODIUM 408mg; CALC 130mg

---

### Keep It Clean

Take care maintaining your cutting board for food safety's sake. Chop vegetables before meats or seafoods to avoid contamination, and hand-wash your cutting board after each use with mild soap and warm water. Rinse and dry the board immediately, treating wooden ones with a food-safe oil. Periodically sponge the board with cold water and mild household bleach, rinsing and drying it thoroughly.

# Just the Flax, Ma'am

*Its nutty flavor is temptation enough, but flaxseed is also a health powerhouse.*

Not only does its nutty flavor transform cooking, but the tiny, reddish-brown flaxseed is also a minibastion of nutrition and other healthy properties.

**Omega-3 fats:** More than 70% of the fat in flaxseed comes from alpha-linolenic acid (ALA), a member of the omega-3 family and cousin to the heart-healthy fats found in fish such as salmon and mackerel.

**Lignans:** Estrogens found in plants (phytoestrogens), these compounds are similar to isoflavones, the potent disease-fighters in soybeans. And like isoflavones, they may play a role in warding off hormone-dependent cancers such as those found in breasts and prostates.

**Fiber:** Because flaxseed contains both soluble and insoluble fiber, it packs a dual healthy punch. The soluble fiber helps lower cholesterol levels and keep blood sugar steady, while the insoluble fiber helps ward off constipation.

## Crusty Whole-Grain Flaxseed Rolls

Use kitchen scissors to quickly cut an "X" in the top of each roll.

　⅓ cup flaxseed
　1 cup warm water (100° to 110°)
　1 cup warm 2% reduced-fat milk (100° to 110°)
　3 tablespoons brown sugar
　1 package dry yeast (about 2¼ teaspoons)
　2 cups whole-wheat flour
　2 cups all-purpose flour, divided
　2 teaspoons salt
　2 teaspoons vegetable oil
Cooking spray
　1 tablespoon water
　1 large egg white
　2 tablespoons flaxseed

**1.** Place ⅓ cup flaxseed in a blender or clean coffee grinder, and process until ground to measure ½ cup flaxseed meal; set aside.

**2.** Combine warm water and warm milk in a large bowl. Dissolve sugar and yeast in milk mixture; let stand 5 minutes. Lightly spoon flours into dry measuring cups; level with a knife. Add flaxseed meal, whole-wheat flour, 1½ cups all-purpose flour, salt, and oil to yeast mixture; stir to form a soft dough. Turn dough out onto a floured surface. Knead until smooth and elastic (about 10 minutes); add enough of remaining all-purpose flour, 1 tablespoon at a time, to prevent dough from sticking to hands (dough will feel tacky).

**3.** Place dough in a large bowl coated with cooking spray, turning to coat top. Cover and let rise in a warm place (85°), free from drafts, 1 hour or until doubled in size. (Press two fingers into dough. If indentation remains, dough has risen enough.) Punch dough down; cover and let rest 5 minutes.

**4.** Divide dough into 18 equal portions, shaping each portion into a ball (cover remaining dough while working to prevent it from drying). Place balls 2 inches apart on a large baking sheet coated with cooking spray. Cover and let rise 45 minutes or until dough is doubled in size.

**5.** Preheat oven to 425°.

**6.** Uncover rolls; cut a ¼-inch-deep "X" in top of each roll. Combine 1 tablespoon water and egg white, and brush over rolls. Sprinkle rolls with 2 tablespoons flaxseed. Bake at 425° for 15 minutes or until rolls are browned on bottom and sound hollow when tapped. Remove rolls from pan. Yield: 18 servings (serving size: 1 roll).

**NOTE:** These rolls freeze well. To freeze, cool rolls completely, and store in a zip-top plastic freezer bag. When ready to use, remove rolls from bag, and thaw completely. Preheat oven to 350°. Place rolls on a baking sheet; cover with foil, and bake until rolls are heated, about 8 minutes.

CALORIES 136 (20% from fat); FAT 3g (sat 0.5g, mono 0.6g, poly 1.7g); PROTEIN 4.9g; CARB 24.3g; FIBER 3.1g; CHOL 1mg; IRON 1.7mg; SODIUM 274mg; CALC 36mg

## Flaxseed Falafel Sandwich

　⅓ cup flaxseed
　1 (19-ounce) can chickpeas (garbanzo beans), undrained
　2 garlic cloves, crushed
　¼ cup chopped fresh parsley
　2 tablespoons fresh lemon juice
　1 teaspoon ground cumin
　½ teaspoon salt
　¼ teaspoon ground coriander
　¼ teaspoon ground red pepper
　¼ cup dry breadcrumbs
　1 tablespoon flaxseed
　1 large egg white, lightly beaten
　1 teaspoon olive oil
Cooking spray
　4 (6-inch) pitas, cut in half
　8 curly leaf lettuce leaves
Mediterranean Chopped Salad
　½ cup plain fat-free yogurt

**1.** Place ⅓ cup flaxseed in a blender or clean coffee grinder, and process until ground to measure ½ cup flaxseed meal; set flaxseed meal aside.

**2.** Drain chickpeas over a bowl, reserving 1 tablespoon liquid. Place chickpeas, garlic, and 1 tablespoon reserved liquid in blender; pulse 5 times or until coarsely chopped. Add flaxseed meal, parsley, and next 5 ingredients; pulse just until mixture is combined. Divide chickpea mixture into 8 equal portions, shaping each into a ½-inch-thick patty. Combine breadcrumbs and 1 tablespoon flaxseed in a shallow dish. Dip patties in egg white; dredge in breadcrumb mixture.

**3.** Heat oil in a large nonstick skillet coated with cooking spray over medium-high heat. Add patties; cook 5 minutes on each side or until browned.

**4.** Line each pita half with a lettuce leaf; fill each pita half with 1 patty and 2½ tablespoons Mediterranean Chopped Salad. Top each with 1 tablespoon yogurt. Yield: 4 servings (serving size: 2 pita halves).

(Totals include Mediterranean Chopped Salad) CALORIES 507 (26% from fat); FAT 14.4g (sat 1.7g, mono 4.8g, poly 7g); PROTEIN 21.7g; CARB 79.3g; FIBER 9.9g; CHOL 1mg; IRON 7.5mg; SODIUM 1,100mg; CALC 248mg

**MEDITERRANEAN CHOPPED SALAD:**

1 cup diced tomato
½ cup diced peeled English cucumber
2 tablespoons chopped green onions
2 tablespoons chopped fresh cilantro
2 teaspoons minced seeded jalapeño pepper
2 teaspoons fresh lemon juice
2 teaspoons olive oil
¼ teaspoon salt
⅛ teaspoon black pepper

**1.** Combine all ingredients in a medium bowl; toss gently. Let stand for up to 2 hours. Yield: 4 servings (serving size: about ⅓ cup).

CALORIES 34 (66% from fat); FAT 2.5g (sat 0.3g, mono 1.7g, poly 0.3g); PROTEIN 0.6g; CARB 3.3g; FIBER 0.8g; CHOL 0mg; IRON 0.4mg; SODIUM 153mg; CALC 10mg

## Molasses Crackle Cookies

⅓ cup flaxseed
2 cups all-purpose flour
2 teaspoons baking soda
1¼ teaspoons ground cinnamon
½ teaspoon salt
½ teaspoon ground cloves
½ teaspoon ground ginger
1⅓ cups sugar, divided
½ cup unsweetened apple butter spread (such as Tap 'n Apple)
¼ cup molasses
2 tablespoons vegetable oil
1 large egg white
Cooking spray
1 tablespoon flaxseed

**1.** Place ⅓ cup flaxseed in a blender or clean coffee grinder, and process until ground to measure ½ cup meal. Lightly spoon flour into dry measuring cups, and level with a knife. Combine flaxseed meal, flour, and next 5 ingredients; stir with a whisk. Combine 1 cup sugar, apple butter, molasses, oil, and egg white, and stir with a whisk. Add to flour mixture, stirring just until moist. Cover bowl with a sheet of heavy-duty plastic wrap; place bowl in freezer 1 hour.
**2.** Preheat oven to 350°.

**3.** Lightly coat hands with cooking spray. Shape dough into 36 balls, about 1 tablespoon each. Combine ⅓ cup sugar and 1 tablespoon flaxseed in a small bowl; roll balls in sugar mixture. Place 2 inches apart on baking sheets coated with cooking spray. Bake at 350° for 13 minutes or until golden. Cool 5 minutes on pans. Remove cookies from pans, and cool completely on wire racks. Yield: 3 dozen (serving size: 1 cookie).
**NOTE:** This cookie dough freezes well. Make dough and shape into a large ball; freeze ball in a zip-top plastic freezer bag. When ready to use, thaw dough completely in refrigerator. Shape, coat, and bake as instructed.

CALORIES 80 (19% from fat); FAT 1.7g (sat 0.2g, mono 0.4g, poly 1g); PROTEIN 1.2g; CARB 15.9g; FIBER 0.6g; CHOL 0mg; IRON 0.7mg; SODIUM 106mg; CALC 12mg

## Lemon-Flaxseed Loaf Cake

Cooking spray
1 tablespoon granulated sugar
¼ cup flaxseed
1 cup granulated sugar
2 large eggs
2 cups all-purpose flour
1½ teaspoons baking powder
½ teaspoon baking soda
½ teaspoon salt
¾ cup low-fat buttermilk
¼ cup vegetable oil
2 teaspoons grated lemon rind
1 teaspoon vanilla extract
½ cup powdered sugar
1 tablespoon fresh lemon juice

**1.** Preheat oven to 350°.
**2.** Coat an 8 x 4-inch loaf pan with cooking spray; sprinkle with 1 tablespoon granulated sugar. Set pan aside. Place flaxseed in a blender or clean coffee grinder, and process until ground to measure about 6 tablespoons flaxseed meal; set aside.
**3.** Combine 1 cup granulated sugar and eggs in a large bowl; beat at high speed of a mixer 3 minutes or until mixture is thick and pale. Lightly spoon flour into dry measuring cups; level with a knife.

Combine flaxseed meal, flour, baking powder, baking soda, and salt in a large bowl; stir well with a whisk. Combine buttermilk, oil, lemon rind, and vanilla in a bowl. Add flour mixture to egg mixture alternately with buttermilk mixture, beginning and ending with flour mixture.
**4.** Spoon batter into prepared pan. Bake at 350° for 55 minutes or until a wooden pick inserted in center comes out clean. Cool in pan 5 minutes on a wire rack; remove from pan. Cool completely on wire rack.
**5.** Combine powdered sugar and lemon juice; drizzle over top of loaf. Yield: 12 servings (serving size: 1 slice).

CALORIES 242 (28% from fat); FAT 7.4g (sat 1.4g, mono 2.1g, poly 3.5g); PROTEIN 4.5g; CARB 40.7g; FIBER 1.4g; CHOL 37mg; IRON 4.6mg; SODIUM 232mg; CALC 70mg

---

### The Real Meaning of Flour Power

To glean the most flaxseed benefit, you'll need to grind the seeds. That breaks through the tough outer hull (which might otherwise pass through your body undigested) and unleashes all the heart- and health-beneficial compounds. Either a blender or a clean coffee grinder does the job neatly. Just pulse until the seeds form a flourlike powder.

Keep in mind that once you grind flaxseed, the delicate oil in the seed is exposed to air and light, and can therefore spoil and produce off flavors.

To prolong their shelf life, store ground seeds (or flaxseed meal) in the refrigerator in an airtight, opaque container. Stored carefully, ground seeds will stay fresh for up to 90 days. Left whole, flaxseed can be stored at room temperature for up to a year.

# Reaching Out to Touch Everyone

*From the vast Texas Panhandle, Becky McKinley spreads her inspiration about healthy living and low-fat cooking as a caterer, columnist, and mother.*

We've all heard about community involvement. Becky McKinley, a 45-year-old mother of three, has made it her business and her mission to tell everyone in the Texas Panhandle region who can read, watch TV, attend a cooking class, or come to a party that a healthy lifestyle is just too easy, happy, and energizing to pass up.

### Green Chile-Chicken Stew

This low-fat version of a popular Texas stew is a favorite among Becky McKinley's family and friends. For added panache, serve it in bread bowls, as Becky does.

    8    cups water
    ½    teaspoon salt
    ½    teaspoon black pepper
    2    (6-ounce) skinned chicken breast halves
    2    bay leaves
    4    cups (½-inch) cubed red potato (about 1½ pounds)
    1½   cups chopped onion (about 1 large)
    ½    cup thinly sliced carrot
    2    teaspoons minced fresh cilantro
    2    teaspoons paprika
    ½    teaspoon garlic salt
    ¼    teaspoon ground cumin
    3    (4.5-ounce) cans chopped green chiles
    1    (14.5-ounce) can no-salt-added diced tomatoes, undrained
    1    (10-ounce) can diced tomatoes and green chiles (such as Ro•Tel), undrained
    ½    cup evaporated fat-free milk
    6    tablespoons (1½ ounces) shredded reduced-fat sharp Cheddar cheese

**1.** Combine first 5 ingredients in a Dutch oven. Bring to a boil; cook 10 minutes. Remove from heat. Remove chicken from broth; remove chicken from bones, discarding bones. Cut meat into bite-size pieces; return to broth. Discard bay leaves.
**2.** Add potato and next 9 ingredients to broth. Bring to a boil; reduce heat, and simmer 50 minutes or until potato is done. Remove from heat; stir in milk. Ladle stew into individual bowls, and sprinkle with cheese. Yield: 6 servings (serving size: 1⅔ cups stew and 1 tablespoon cheese).

CALORIES 239 (9% from fat); FAT 2.3g (sat 1g, mono 0.6g, poly 0.4g); PROTEIN 18.4g; CARB 36.3g; FIBER 4g; CHOL 32mg; IRON 2.3mg; SODIUM 914mg; CALC 180mg

---

### What's the Secret?

The message in Becky McKinley's classes, columns, clinics, and catering is familiar: Healthy living is no more complicated than eating delicious, well-balanced meals and getting some exercise. Her own tips:

**Keep it simple.** Keep family meals as uncomplicated as possible. "I try to get everything organized in advance using recipes that don't require dozens of ingredients," she says. "It's easier than most people think."

**Stay balanced.** "What's the point of eating something if it doesn't taste good?" Becky asks. "When I learned how to cook low-fat, great-tasting meals, I felt healthier and didn't miss the fat at all. But keeping a balance is important, too." That's why, for example, she uses reduced-fat instead of fat-free products and thinks that for some flavors, there are no substitutes. "I like my real butter," she says. "I just use it in smaller amounts."

**Find exercise that works for you.** Stick with activities you enjoy. "It's easier for me to stick with an exercise routine because it's fun and uncomplicated."

---

# Creamy Caesar Salad with Spicy Croutons

*This salad is a top choice from the July/August 1995 issue.*

### Creamy Caesar Salad with Spicy Croutons

(pictured on page 129)

    1    garlic clove, halved
    ½    cup fat-free mayonnaise
    2    tablespoons red wine vinegar
    2    teaspoons Dijon mustard
    2    teaspoons white wine Worcestershire sauce
    1    teaspoon anchovy paste
    ¼    teaspoon black pepper
    2    teaspoons olive oil
    ¾    teaspoon Cajun seasoning
    1    garlic clove, minced
    2    cups (¾-inch) sourdough bread cubes
    18   cups torn romaine lettuce
    ⅓    cup (1½ ounces) grated fresh Parmesan cheese

**1.** Drop garlic halves through opening in a blender lid with blender on; process until minced. Add mayonnaise and next 5 ingredients; process until well-blended. Cover and chill at least 1 hour.
**2.** Preheat oven to 400°.
**3.** Combine olive oil, Cajun seasoning, and minced garlic in a medium microwave-safe bowl. Microwave at HIGH 20 seconds. Add bread cubes; toss gently to coat. Spread bread cubes in a single layer on a baking sheet; bake at 400° for 15 minutes or until golden brown.
**4.** Place lettuce in a large bowl. Add dressing; toss gently to coat. Sprinkle with cheese; top with croutons. Yield: 6 servings (serving size: 2 cups).

CALORIES 137 (27% from fat); FAT 4.1g (sat 1.3g, mono 1.6g, poly 0.4g); PROTEIN 7.7g; CARB 18.2g; FIBER 4.1g; CHOL 4mg; IRON 3mg; SODIUM 836mg; CALC 176mg

Roasted Chicken with Lemon Curd, page 138

Creamy Caesar Salad with Spicy Croutons, page 128

Traditional Spanish Paella,
page 121

Wine Coolers,
page 137

Broiled Salmon with Honey
and Vermouth, Spring Salad
with Asparagus and Radishes,
and Skillet-Roasted Potatoes
with Lemon and Mint,
pages 136 and 137

Lemon-Swirled Cheesecake,
page 138

# Power of Positive Eating

## Just say "yes" to healthy foods—and "yum" to lifelong pleasures.

T ired of being told what not to eat? These days, every other new book on the market contains its own special proscription, some hitherto undiscovered "secret" about which foods to deep-six. Not from us, though. *Cooking Light* has always stuck with one simple message: Choose a balanced diet in combination with sensible exercise.

It's worth noting that there's been an important shift in proactive advice from five of the nation's leading health organizations: the American Academy of Pediatrics, the American Dietetic Association, the American Heart Association, the American Institute for Cancer Research, and the National Institutes of Health.

Within the past year, all have endorsed a new dietary position that emphasizes what might be called the power of positive eating: concentrating on what foods are good for you, rather than worrying about the ones that aren't.

### menu

**Orange-Wild Rice Salad with Smoked Turkey**

Asiago-herb loaf*

*Combine ¼ cup melted butter, ¼ cup minced green onions, ½ teaspoon each dried basil and oregano. Split a 1-pound loaf Italian bread; spread butter mixture over cut sides, and sprinkle with ½ cup shredded Asiago cheese. Broil 1 minute or until lightly browned. Serves 12.

## Orange-Wild Rice Salad with Smoked Turkey

You'll love the contrast of textures—crunchy wild rice, crispy celery, chewy dried cherries, and soft, juicy oranges. And their combined flavors make this summer salad the life of picnics, potlucks, or just the office lunch.

- 6 cups water
- 1 cup uncooked wild rice
- 1 cup orange sections (about 4 oranges)
- ½ cup diced celery
- ⅓ cup dried sweet cherries or sweetened dried cranberries (such as Craisins)
- ½ pound smoked turkey breast, diced
- ¼ cup thawed orange juice concentrate, undiluted
- 2 tablespoons fresh lemon juice
- 2 tablespoons water
- 1 tablespoon Dijon mustard
- 1½ teaspoons olive oil
- ½ teaspoon salt
- ¼ teaspoon freshly ground black pepper

**1.** Bring water to a boil in a medium saucepan; stir in rice. Partially cover, reduce heat, and simmer 1 hour or until tender. Drain; cool. Place rice, oranges, celery, cherries, and turkey in a bowl.
**2.** Combine orange juice concentrate and remaining 6 ingredients; stir well with a whisk. Pour over rice mixture; toss well. Cover and chill. Yield: 7 servings (serving size: 1 cup).

CALORIES 192 (15% from fat); FAT 3.3g (sat 0.8g, mono 1.6g, poly 0.8g); PROTEIN 11.9g; CARB 30.4g; FIBER 2.9g; CHOL 18mg; IRON 1.6mg; SODIUM 465mg; CALC 29mg

## Lemon-Basil Bean Bowl

Lima beans go upscale in this main-dish salad. Paired with green beans, tomatoes, and bacon, and then dressed with a lemon-basil vinaigrette, the result is so tasty our Test Kitchens gave it a near-perfect rating.

- ⅓ cup chopped fresh basil
- 1 teaspoon grated lemon rind
- 2 tablespoons fresh lemon juice
- 1 tablespoon olive oil
- 2½ teaspoons Dijon mustard
- ½ teaspoon sugar
- ¼ teaspoon salt
- ¼ teaspoon freshly ground black pepper
- 1 garlic clove, minced
- 4 cups (1-inch) cut green beans (about 1 pound)
- 1½ cups chopped plum tomato
- 1 (10-ounce) package frozen baby lima beans, cooked and drained
- 4 low-fat bacon slices, cooked and crumbled (drained)

**1.** Combine first 9 ingredients in a bowl; stir with a whisk.
**2.** Steam green beans, covered, 8 minutes or until tender. Combine green beans, tomato, and lima beans in a large bowl. Pour basil mixture over bean mixture, and toss well. Sprinkle with bacon. Yield: 6 servings (serving size: 1 cup).

CALORIES 133 (25% from fat); FAT 3.7g (sat 0.7g, mono 2.1g, poly 1g); PROTEIN 7.1g; CARB 19.4g; FIBER 3g; CHOL 3mg; IRON 2.4mg; SODIUM 334mg; CALC 53mg

## Super-Duper Sunrise Shake

Four different fruits gives this smoothie sweet, tart, tropical flavors—not to mention a thick, milkshakelike texture.

- 1½ cups orange juice
- ½ cup frozen unsweetened raspberries
- 2 tablespoons toasted wheat germ
- 1 (16-ounce) can apricot halves in light syrup, drained
- 1 large ripe banana, peeled

**1.** Combine all ingredients in a blender; process until smooth. Yield: 3 servings (serving size: 1 cup).

CALORIES 183 (4% from fat); FAT 0.9g (sat 0.2g, mono 0.1g, poly 0.4g); PROTEIN 3.1g; CARB 43.7g; FIBER 3.7g; CHOL 0mg; IRON 1mg; SODIUM 3mg; CALC 31mg

## Greek-Style Burgers with Feta Aïoli

This burger—stuffed with roasted bell peppers and spinach—carries Greek flavors in every bite. We've topped it with a tomato slice, lettuce leaves, and our low-fat version of the garlicky French mayonnaise *aïoli* (ay-OH-lee)—made more flavorful by adding feta cheese.

**AÏOLI:**

- ½ cup (2 ounces) crumbled feta cheese
- 2 tablespoons light mayonnaise
- 2 tablespoons plain fat-free yogurt
- ¼ teaspoon coarsely ground black pepper
- 1 garlic clove, minced

**BURGERS:**

- 5 (½-inch-thick) slices red onion
- Cooking spray
- 1 pound lean ground round
- ⅔ cup fresh breadcrumbs
- ⅓ cup chopped bottled roasted red bell peppers
- ¼ cup chopped fresh parsley
- 1 teaspoon dried oregano
- ¼ teaspoon salt
- ¼ teaspoon coarsely ground black pepper
- 1 (10-ounce) package frozen chopped spinach, thawed, drained, and squeezed dry
- 1 large egg, lightly beaten
- 2 garlic cloves, crushed
- 5 (1½-ounce) sourdough sandwich buns

**1.** To prepare aïoli, combine first 5 ingredients in a food processor; pulse 1 minute or until smooth. Cover and chill.
**2.** Prepare grill or broiler.
**3.** To prepare burgers, place onion slices on a grill rack or broiler pan coated with cooking spray, and cook 2 minutes on each side. Set aside.
**4.** Combine beef and next 9 ingredients in a large bowl. Divide beef mixture into 5 equal portions, shaping each portion into a ½-inch-thick patty. Place patties on grill rack or broiler pan coated with cooking spray, and cook 6 minutes on each side or until burgers are done.

Spread 1½ tablespoons aïoli over top half of each bun. Place patties on bottom halves of buns, and top each with 1 onion slice and top half of bun. Yield: 5 sandwiches (serving size: 1 sandwich).

CALORIES 385 (28% from fat); FAT 12.1g (sat 4.4g, mono 4.4g, poly 1.8g); PROTEIN 30.5g; CARB 38g; FIBER 4.3g; CHOL 110mg; IRON 5.7mg; SODIUM 712mg; CALC 225mg; ZINC 4.4mg

## Loaded Macaroni and Cheese

Macaroni made with two different Italian cheeses seems pretty decadent on its own. But we've added red peppers, carrots, peas, and broccoli to give this old favorite a new twist and a lot more flavor.

- ¼ cup all-purpose flour
- 2 cups 2% reduced-fat milk
- 3 garlic cloves, minced
- 1 cup (4 ounces) shredded fontina cheese
- 1 cup (4 ounces) grated Asiago cheese
- ¼ cup chopped fresh basil
- 1 tablespoon spicy brown mustard
- ¾ teaspoon salt
- ½ teaspoon freshly ground black pepper
- ¼ teaspoon garlic powder
- 8 cups water
- 5 cups uncooked macaroni or cavatappi pasta (about 12 ounces)
- 2 cups broccoli florets
- 1 cup diced carrot
- 1 cup (2-inch) julienne-cut red bell pepper
- 1 cup frozen petite green peas, thawed

**1.** Lightly spoon flour into a dry measuring cup; level with a knife. Place in a medium saucepan; gradually add milk, stirring with a whisk until blended. Stir in minced garlic. Place over medium heat, and cook until thick (about 5 minutes); stir constantly. Stir in fontina and next 6 ingredients, and cook 1 minute. Stir constantly until cheese melts.
**2.** Bring water to a boil. Add pasta, and cook 6 minutes. Add broccoli and carrot, and cook 6 minutes. Stir in bell pepper

and peas; cook 1 minute. Drain. Combine pasta mixture and cheese mixture. Serve immediately. Yield: 6 servings (serving size: 1½ cups).

CALORIES 461 (27% from fat); FAT 13.8g (sat 8g, mono 3.8g, poly 1g); PROTEIN 24g; CARB 59.4g; FIBER 4.4g; CHOL 48mg; IRON 3.6mg; SODIUM 640mg; CALC 449mg

## Waffles with Two-Berry Syrup

Wheat germ and flaxseed are the ingredients that give these waffles a wonderfully nutty flavor and crunchy texture. But it's the syrup, laced with maple and two kinds of berries, that elevates this breakfast to the sublime.

**WAFFLES:**

- 2 tablespoons flaxseed
- 1 cup all-purpose flour
- ½ cup whole-wheat flour
- ¼ cup toasted wheat germ
- 2 tablespoons sugar
- 1½ teaspoons baking powder
- ½ teaspoon salt
- 1½ cups fat-free milk
- ¾ cup egg substitute
- 1½ tablespoons canola oil
- 1 teaspoon vanilla extract
- Cooking spray

**SYRUP:**

- 1½ cups frozen blueberries
- 1½ cups frozen unsweetened raspberries
- ½ cup maple syrup
- ¼ teaspoon ground cinnamon

**1.** To prepare waffles, place flaxseed in a clean coffee grinder or blender; process until ground to measure ¼ cup flaxseed meal. Set flaxseed meal aside. Lightly spoon flours into dry measuring cups; level with a knife. Combine flaxseed meal, flours, wheat germ, sugar, baking powder, and salt in a large bowl; make a well in center of mixture. Combine milk, egg substitute, oil, and vanilla; add to flour mixture, stirring just until moist.
**2.** Coat a waffle iron with cooking spray; preheat. Spoon about ¼ cup of batter per 4-inch waffle onto hot waffle iron, spreading batter to edges. Cook 5

to 6 minutes or until steaming stops; repeat procedure with remaining batter.

**3.** To prepare syrup, combine berries, maple syrup, and ground cinnamon in a saucepan. Cook over medium heat until thoroughly heated. Serve warm over waffles. Yield: 6 servings (serving size: 2 waffles and ⅓ cup syrup).

**NOTE:** Look for flaxseed, a grain rich in heart-healthy omega-3 fats, in health-food stores or large supermarkets. Freeze leftover waffles individually on a cookie sheet and then transfer to a zip-top plastic freezer bag for storage. To reheat, place frozen waffles in toaster.

CALORIES 332 (18% from fat); FAT 6.6g (sat 0.7g, mono 2.5g, poly 2.8g); PROTEIN 10.8g; CARB 60.5g; FIBER 6.5g; CHOL 1mg; IRON 3.3mg; SODIUM 400mg; CALC 199mg

## Pan-Seared Cod over Vegetable Ragoût

This easy-to-fix skillet dinner elevates plain white fish to the height of good taste as the fish is incorporated into a Mediterranean-style ragoût chock-full of tasty ingredients such as prosciutto and shiitake mushrooms.

2½  teaspoons olive oil, divided
 ½  cup diced prosciutto (about 2 ounces)
  3  garlic cloves, minced
  4  cups thinly sliced shiitake mushroom caps (about 10 ounces)
1½  cups chopped leek
  3  cups diced plum tomato (about 1 pound)
 ¼  teaspoon salt
 ¼  teaspoon freshly ground black pepper
  1  (10-ounce) package fresh spinach, coarsely chopped
  1  cup torn fresh basil leaves
  4  (6-ounce) cod or other firm white fish fillets (1 inch thick)
  1  tablespoon all-purpose flour

**1.** Heat ½ teaspoon olive oil in a large nonstick skillet over low heat. Add prosciutto; sauté 5 minutes. Stir in garlic; remove from pan. Set aside.

**2.** Heat 1 teaspoon olive oil in pan over medium-high heat. Add mushrooms and leek; sauté 8 minutes. Stir in tomato, salt, and pepper. Gradually add spinach to pan, and stir until spinach is wilted (about 3 minutes). Stir in prosciutto mixture and basil. Remove from pan; cover and keep warm.

**3.** Heat 1 teaspoon olive oil in pan over medium-high heat. Dredge fillets in flour. Add fillets to pan; sauté 3 minutes on each side. Cover and cook 2 minutes or until fish flakes easily when tested with a fork. Divide spinach mixture among 4 plates; top with fillets. Yield: 4 servings (serving size: 1 fillet and about 1 cup ragoût).

CALORIES 287 (20% from fat); FAT 6.4g (sat 1.2g, mono 3g, poly 1.4g); PROTEIN 39.1g; CARB 20g; FIBER 5.9g; CHOL 82mg; IRON 5.3mg; SODIUM 525mg; CALC 146mg

## Cheesy Broccoli and Roasted Bell Pepper Strata

This can also be made in two 8-inch square baking dishes. Freeze one for later.

  1  teaspoon olive oil
1½  cups chopped onion
1½  teaspoons dried fines herbes
 ½  teaspoon black pepper
 ¼  teaspoon salt
  5  garlic cloves, minced
  1  cup evaporated fat-free milk
  1  tablespoon Dijon mustard
  2  (8-ounce) cartons egg substitute
  4  cups coarsely chopped broccoli florets (about 1 bunch)
  2  (7-ounce) bottles roasted red bell peppers, drained
 12  (1-ounce) slices hearty white bread
Cooking spray
  1  cup (4 ounces) shredded reduced-fat sharp Cheddar cheese, divided
 ⅓  cup (about 1½ ounces) grated fresh Romano or Parmesan cheese

**1.** Heat oil in a medium nonstick skillet over medium-high heat. Add onion, fines herbes, black pepper, and salt; sauté 5 minutes. Stir in garlic; remove from heat.

**2.** Combine milk, mustard, and egg substitute. Stir in onion mixture. Steam broccoli, covered, 5 minutes. Slice bell pepper into strips.

**3.** Arrange half of bread slices in a single layer in a 13 x 9-inch baking dish coated with cooking spray. Spoon 2 cups broccoli and 1 cup bell pepper evenly over bread slices; sprinkle with ½ cup Cheddar cheese. Repeat procedure with remaining bread, broccoli, and bell pepper. Top with Romano cheese.

**4.** Pour milk mixture over bread mixture. Cover; chill 8 hours or overnight.

**5.** Preheat oven to 325°.

**6.** Uncover strata; bake at 325° for 45 minutes or until set. Sprinkle with ½ cup Cheddar cheese; bake an additional 5 minutes. Yield: 9 servings.

CALORIES 245 (22% from fat); FAT 6g (sat 2.7g, mono 2.2g, poly 0.6g); PROTEIN 17.4g; CARB 30.5g; FIBER 3g; CHOL 15mg; IRON 2.8mg; SODIUM 614mg; CALC 335mg

## Fresh Fruit Compote with Orange-Lime Drizzle

  2  cups sliced strawberries
  1  cup cubed peeled kiwifruit (about 4)
  1  cup sliced banana (about 2)
  1  cup cubed peeled ripe mango
  1  cup cubed peeled papaya
  2  tablespoons thawed orange juice concentrate, undiluted
  2  teaspoons lime juice
  3  tablespoons chopped fresh mint

**1.** Combine first 5 ingredients in a large bowl, and set aside. Combine juices and mint, and drizzle over fruit mixture. Toss gently to coat. Yield: 6 servings (serving size: 1 cup).

CALORIES 106 (6% from fat); FAT 0.7g (sat 0.1g, mono 0.1g, poly 0.3g); PROTEIN 1.5g; CARB 26.3g; FIBER 4.4g; CHOL 0mg; IRON 0.6mg; SODIUM 5mg; CALC 33mg

# Spring Companions

*Cooking for two comes naturally when the season's produce is at its tasty best.*

## Chicken with Mushrooms and Leeks

Wash the leeks thoroughly to rid them of any dirt and sand.

- ⅔ cup fat-free, less-sodium chicken broth
- 1½ tablespoons tomato paste
- ⅛ teaspoon salt
- ⅛ teaspoon dried thyme
- ⅛ teaspoon black pepper
- 1 garlic clove, minced
- 1 tablespoon Italian-seasoned breadcrumbs
- 2 (4-ounce) skinned, boned chicken breast halves
- 1 teaspoon olive oil
- 1 cup thinly sliced leek (about 1 large)
- 1 cup thinly sliced mushrooms

**1.** Combine first 6 ingredients in a bowl; stir with a whisk. Set aside.
**2.** Place breadcrumbs in a shallow dish. Dredge chicken in breadcrumbs. Heat olive oil in a large nonstick skillet over medium-high heat. Add chicken, and sauté 3 minutes on each side or until chicken is golden brown. Remove chicken from pan, and keep warm. Add leek and mushrooms to pan, and sauté 2 minutes or until mushrooms are lightly browned. Return chicken to pan, and stir in broth mixture. Cover mixture, and simmer 10 minutes or until chicken is done. Yield: 2 servings (serving size: 1 chicken breast half and ⅓ cup topping).

CALORIES 218 (17% from fat); FAT 4.2g (sat 0.8g, mono 2.1g, poly 0.7g); PROTEIN 29.8g; CARB 14.9g; FIBER 1.7g; CHOL 66mg; IRON 3mg; SODIUM 495mg; CALC 58mg

## Broiled Salmon with Honey and Vermouth

(pictured on page 131)

Leave the skin on the salmon while it cooks, and then remove it to serve.

- 2 tablespoons honey
- 2 tablespoons dry vermouth or white wine
- 1½ teaspoons grated peeled fresh ginger
- 1½ teaspoons country-style Dijon mustard
- ⅛ teaspoon salt
- ⅛ teaspoon black pepper
- 2 (6-ounce) salmon fillets (about 1 inch thick)
- Cooking spray

**1.** Preheat broiler.
**2.** Combine first 6 ingredients in a small bowl; stir with a whisk. Place salmon on a broiler pan coated with cooking spray; brush with half of honey mixture. Broil 8 minutes or until fish flakes easily when tested with a fork, basting frequently with remaining honey mixture Yield: 2 servings (serving size: 1 fillet).

CALORIES 366 (36% from fat); FAT 14.6g (sat 2.5g, mono 7g, poly 3.3g); PROTEIN 35g; CARB 18.8g; FIBER 0g; CHOL 111mg; IRON 0.9mg; SODIUM 346mg; CALC 12mg

## Spring Salad with Asparagus and Radishes

(pictured on page 131)

Use asparagus stalks of approximately the same size so that they cook evenly.

- 1 cup (1-inch) diagonally sliced asparagus (about 6 ounces)
- 3 cups gourmet salad greens
- 3 thinly sliced radishes
- 1½ tablespoons fat-free red wine vinaigrette (such as Girard's)
- ½ teaspoon country-style Dijon mustard
- 1½ tablespoons (about ½ ounce) finely crumbled feta cheese

**1.** Steam asparagus, covered, 3 minutes or until tender. Rinse asparagus with cold water, and pat dry. Combine asparagus, greens, and radishes in a large bowl. Combine vinaigrette and mustard in a small bowl, and stir well with a whisk. Add vinaigrette mixture and feta to salad, tossing gently to coat. Yield: 2 servings (serving size: 1½ cups).
**NOTE:** You can prepare greens, asparagus, and radishes up to an hour ahead. Combine them in a large bowl; cover with a paper towel and chill.

CALORIES 58 (29% from fat); FAT 1.9g (sat 1.1g, mono 0.3g, poly 0.2g); PROTEIN 3.9g; CARB 7.6g; FIBER 2.9g; CHOL 6mg; IRON 1.6mg; SODIUM 348mg; CALC 81mg

## Skillet-Roasted Potatoes with Lemon and Mint

(pictured on page 131)

Lemon rind and mint give these potatoes a zesty, springtime flavor. You'll be able to find mint in the grocery store, if not in your own garden.

      2  cups (½-inch) diced baking potato
      1  teaspoon butter or stick margarine
      1  teaspoon olive oil
      2  teaspoons chopped fresh mint
      1  teaspoon grated lemon rind
     ⅛  teaspoon salt
        Dash of black pepper

**1.** Place diced potato in a medium saucepan, and cover with water; bring to a boil. Reduce heat, and simmer 5 minutes; drain and cool.
**2.** Heat butter and olive oil in a large nonstick skillet over medium-high heat. Add potatoes, and cook 10 minutes or until potatoes are golden brown. Add chopped mint and remaining ingredients, and toss to coat. Yield: 2 servings (serving size: about 1 cup).

CALORIES 223 (17% from fat); FAT 4.3g (sat 1.6g, mono 2.2g, poly 0.3g); PROTEIN 3.8g; CARB 43.1g; FIBER 3.1g; CHOL 5mg; IRON 2.4mg; SODIUM 180mg; CALC 20mg

## Strawberries with Orange-Ricotta Cream

Prepare the orange-ricotta cream early in the day. You'll have a half cup of the cheese mixture left over. Store it in an airtight container in the refrigerator for up to one week.

     ½  cup part-skim ricotta cheese
     ½  cup vanilla low-fat yogurt
      1  tablespoon sugar
     ½  teaspoon grated orange rind
     ½  teaspoon vanilla extract
      1  cup quartered strawberries
      2  whole strawberries (optional)

**1.** Combine first 5 ingredients in a blender; process until smooth. Spoon cheese mixture into a small bowl; cover and chill mixture 3 hours. Spoon ½ cup

quartered strawberries into each of 2 small bowls, and top each with 2 tablespoons cheese mixture. Garnish each serving with a whole strawberry, if desired. Yield: 2 servings.

CALORIES 76 (25% from fat); FAT 2.1g (sat 1.2g, mono 0.6g, poly 0.2g); PROTEIN 3.7g; CARB 11.2g; FIBER 1.7g; CHOL 7mg; IRON 0.4mg; SODIUM 39mg; CALC 99mg

## Wine Coolers

(pictured on page 131)

     ½  cup cranberry-mango juice (such as Ocean Spray) or any cranberry juice
     ½  cup orange juice
     ½  cup Merlot or other dry red wine
     ⅔  cup seltzer water
      2  lime slices
      2  orange slices

**1.** Combine first 4 ingredients in a pitcher; serve over ice. Garnish with lime and orange slices. Yield: 2 servings (serving size: 1 cup).

CALORIES 101 (0% from fat); FAT 0g; PROTEIN 0.5g; CARB 16g; FIBER 0.1g; CHOL 0mg; IRON 0.3mg; SODIUM 46mg; CALC 18mg

## classics

# New Lease on Lemon

*The only way to put the creamy smoothness of lemon curd in your cooking more often is to make it lower in fat. We did.*

Lemon curd—a creamy mixture made from lemon juice, sugar, butter, and egg yolks—is delightful by itself. Its real calling is what it adds to your cooking. But we're not crazy about two other things it adds: high fat and cholesterol counts. We've created a reduced-fat lemon curd.

To cut the fat, we used fewer eggs and less butter. And we skipped the traditional double boiler in favor of a good heavy saucepan. Be attentive, use medium (not high) heat, and don't stop whisking.

## Lemon Curd

For a lime-curd variation, substitute lime rind and juice for the lemon rind and juice.

     ¾  cup sugar
      1  tablespoon grated lemon rind
      2  large eggs
     ⅔  cup fresh lemon juice (about 3 large lemons)
      2  tablespoons butter or stick margarine

**1.** Combine first 3 ingredients in a saucepan over medium heat, stirring with a whisk. Cook until sugar dissolves and mixture is light in color (about 3 minutes). Stir in lemon juice and butter; cook 5 minutes or until mixture thinly coats back of a spoon, stirring constantly with a whisk. Cool. Cover and chill (mixture will thicken as it cools). Yield: 1⅓ cups (serving size: 1 tablespoon).
**NOTE:** Lemon Curd can be stored in refrigerator for up to 1 week. You can easily double the recipe and freeze half of it in a heavy-duty zip-top plastic bag. Thaw in refrigerator, and use within 1 week of thawing.

CALORIES 47 (31% from fat); FAT 1.6g (sat 0.8g, mono 0.5g, poly 0.1g); PROTEIN 0.7g; CARB 7.9g; FIBER 0g; CHOL 24mg; IRON 0.1mg; SODIUM 18mg; CALC 4mg

## Fresh-Fruit Pizza with Lemon Curd

The Lemon Curd not only holds the fruit in place, it serves as an exquisite anchor for all the flavors. It's best served the day it's made.

      1  (18-ounce) package refrigerated sugar cookie dough
        Cooking spray
      2  tablespoons seedless raspberry jam, melted
     ¾  cup Lemon Curd (recipe above)
      2  cups fresh raspberries
      2  cups fresh blackberries
      1  cup sliced fresh strawberries
      1  plum, sliced
      2  teaspoons sugar

*Continued*

1. Preheat oven to 350°.
2. Press dough into a 12-inch pizza pan coated with cooking spray. Bake at 350° for 12 minutes or until golden brown. Cool completely on a wire rack.
3. Preheat broiler.
4. Spread jam over crust. Spread Lemon Curd over jam; arrange raspberries, blackberries, strawberry slices, and plum slices on top. Sprinkle sugar over fruit; broil 3 minutes. Yield: 12 servings (serving size: 1 wedge).

CALORIES 261 (30% from fat); FAT 8.6g (sat 2.3g, mono 2.8g, poly 3g); PROTEIN 2.5g; CARB 43.1g; FIBER 3.1g; CHOL 37mg; IRON 1.4mg; SODIUM 173mg; CALC 19mg

## Lemon-Swirled Cheesecake

(pictured on page 132)

Herb lovers: Try adding 1 tablespoon finely chopped fresh rosemary to the crust. If your springform pan is made of dark metal, cook the cheesecake 5 to 10 minutes less.

CRUST:
⅔ cup all-purpose flour
2 tablespoons sugar
2 tablespoons chilled butter or stick margarine, cut into small pieces
1 tablespoon ice water
Cooking spray

FILLING:
3 (8-ounce) blocks fat-free cream cheese, softened
2 (8-ounce) blocks ⅓-less-fat cream cheese, softened
1¾ cups sugar
3 tablespoons all-purpose flour
2½ teaspoons grated lemon rind
2 teaspoons vanilla extract
¼ teaspoon salt
5 large eggs
1 cup Lemon Curd (recipe on page 137)

1. Preheat oven to 400°.
2. To prepare crust, lightly spoon ⅔ cup flour into a dry measuring cup, and level with a knife. Place ⅔ cup flour and 2 tablespoons sugar in a food processor;

pulse 2 times or until combined. Add chilled butter; pulse 6 times or until mixture resembles coarse meal. With processor on, slowly pour ice water through food chute, processing just until blended (do not allow dough to form a ball). Firmly press mixture into bottom of a 9-inch springform pan coated with cooking spray. Bake at 400° for 10 minutes; cool on a wire rack.
3. Reduce oven temperature to 325°.
4. To prepare filling, beat cheeses at high speed of a mixer until smooth. Add 1¾ cups sugar and next 4 ingredients; beat well. Add eggs, 1 at a time, beating well after each addition.
5. Pour cheese mixture into prepared crust. Spoon mounds of Lemon Curd over filling, and swirl together using tip of a knife. Bake at 325° for 1 hour and 15 minutes or until cheesecake is almost set. Remove cheesecake from oven, and cool to room temperature. Cover and chill at least 8 hours. Yield: 16 servings (serving size: 1 slice).

CALORIES 310 (33% from fat); FAT 11.4g (sat 6.4g, mono 3.5g, poly 0.6g); PROTEIN 12.2g; CARB 39g; FIBER 0.2g; CHOL 126mg; IRON 0.7mg; SODIUM 458mg; CALC 155mg

## Spring for a Pan

To make a cheesecake, you'll need a springform pan. What is it?

It's a round metal pan with high, straight sides encircled by a metal belt, or spring (hence the name), that clamps tight, molding the shape of the cake.

When baking is finished, you can unclamp the spring and remove the sides. The bottom of the pan holds the finished cheesecake and can be used for serving.

If you don't have a springform pan, you might like the new model made by Frieling (800-827-2582). Made with heavy-duty coated metal, it won't react with the acids in lemon juice, as will some older aluminum pans. It's also nonstick and has a glass bottom. Springform pans come in 8-, 9-, and 10-inch sizes, with 9 inches the most common.

## Roasted Chicken with Lemon Curd

(pictured on page 129)

From Europe to Asia, chicken and lemon are natural flavor partners. In this recipe, the Lemon Curd acts as a tangy glaze.

1 (3½-pound) chicken
1 tablespoon chopped fresh rosemary
2 teaspoons chopped fresh thyme
½ teaspoon salt
¼ teaspoon freshly ground black pepper
4 garlic cloves, crushed
Cooking spray
½ cup Lemon Curd (recipe on page 137)
3 large lemons, halved
Fresh rosemary sprigs (optional)

1. Preheat oven to 450°.
2. Remove and discard giblets and neck from chicken. Rinse chicken with cold water; pat dry. Trim excess fat. Starting at neck cavity, loosen skin from breast and drumsticks by inserting fingers, gently pushing between skin and meat.
3. Combine chopped rosemary and next 4 ingredients. Rub mixture under loosened skin, and rub over breast and drumsticks. Lift wing tips up and over back; tuck under chicken.
4. Place chicken, breast side up, on a broiler pan coated with cooking spray. Pierce skin several times with a meat fork. Insert a meat thermometer into meaty part of thigh, making sure not to touch bone; brush chicken with Lemon Curd. Arrange lemons around chicken. Bake at 450° for 30 minutes. Reduce oven temperature to 350° (do not remove chicken from oven), and bake an additional 1 hour or until thermometer registers 180°. (Cover chicken loosely with foil if it gets too brown.) Remove chicken from oven. Cover chicken loosely with foil, and let stand 10 minutes. Discard skin. Serve with lemon halves, and garnish with rosemary sprigs, if desired. Yield: 5 servings (serving size: 3 ounces chicken and 1 lemon half).

CALORIES 269 (33% from fat); FAT 10g (sat 3.4g, mono 3.5g, poly 1.9g); PROTEIN 29.8g; CARB 13.7g; FIBER 0.2g; CHOL 126mg; IRON 1.5mg; SODIUM 349mg; CALC 30mg

## Brown Sugar Shortcakes with Berries and Lemon Curd

1 cup sliced strawberries
½ cup blackberries
½ cup blueberries
2 Brown Sugar Shortcakes
¾ cup Lemon Curd (recipe on page 137)

**1.** Combine strawberries, blackberries, and blueberries in a bowl. Split shortcakes in half horizontally using a serrated knife, and place each half on a dessert plate. Spoon ½ cup berry mixture over each shortcake half, and spoon 3 tablespoons Lemon Curd over each serving. Yield: 4 servings.

(Totals include Brown Sugar Shortcakes) CALORIES 305 (30% from fat); FAT 10.1g (sat 5.1g, mono 3.3g, poly 0.9g); PROTEIN 5.2g; CARB 50.9g; FIBER 3g; CHOL 83mg; IRON 1.6mg; SODIUM 257mg; CALC 84mg

**BROWN SUGAR SHORTCAKES:**

2¼ cups all-purpose flour
⅓ cup packed light brown sugar
¼ cup slivered almonds, toasted and finely chopped
2 teaspoons baking powder
½ teaspoon salt
¼ teaspoon baking soda
⅓ cup chilled butter or stick margarine, cut into small pieces
¾ cup low-fat buttermilk
Cooking spray
1 tablespoon turbinado or granulated sugar

**1.** Preheat oven to 450°.
**2.** Lightly spoon flour into dry measuring cups, and level with a knife. Combine flour and next 5 ingredients in a bowl, and cut in butter with a pastry blender or 2 knives until mixture resembles coarse meal. Add buttermilk, and stir just until moist.
**3.** Turn dough out onto a lightly floured surface, and knead lightly 5 or 6 times. Roll dough to a ½-inch thickness, and cut with a 2½-inch biscuit cutter into 8 shortcakes. Place shortcakes on a baking sheet coated with cooking spray, and sprinkle with turbinado sugar. Bake at 450° for 10 minutes or until golden.

Remove shortcakes from baking sheet; cool on a wire rack. Yield: 8 servings.
**NOTE:** Place remaining shortcakes in an airtight container, and freeze for up to 2 weeks. Thaw at room temperature.

CALORIES 266 (34% from fat); FAT 10g (sat 5.2g, mono 3.4g, poly 0.8g); PROTEIN 5.2g; CARB 39.4g; FIBER 1.3g; CHOL 21mg; IRON 2.1mg; SODIUM 402mg; CALC 119mg

## Double-Lemon Soufflés

Cooking spray
2 tablespoons granulated sugar
¼ cup all-purpose flour
1½ cups 2% reduced-fat milk
1½ teaspoons grated lemon rind
⅓ cup fresh lemon juice
¼ cup granulated sugar
3 large egg yolks
5 large egg whites
¼ teaspoon cream of tartar
Dash of salt
⅓ cup granulated sugar
½ cup Lemon Curd (recipe on page 137)
⅓ cup powdered sugar

**1.** Coat 8 (6-ounce) ramekins or custard cups with cooking spray; sprinkle with 2 tablespoons granulated sugar. Place prepared ramekins on a baking sheet.
**2.** Lightly spoon flour into a dry measuring cup, and level with a knife. Place flour in a small saucepan. Gradually add milk, stirring with a whisk until well-blended. Stir in lemon rind, lemon juice, and ¼ cup granulated sugar. Cook lemon mixture over medium heat until thick and bubbly (about 5 minutes), stirring constantly. Gradually add hot lemon mixture to egg yolks, stirring constantly with a whisk. Return lemon mixture to pan, and cook over medium heat until thick (about 3 minutes), stirring constantly. Remove from heat. Place pan in a large ice-filled bowl for 25 minutes or until custard comes to room temperature, stirring occasionally.
**3.** Preheat oven to 400°.
**4.** Beat egg whites, cream of tartar, and salt at high speed of a mixer until soft peaks form. Gradually add ⅓ cup granulated sugar, 1 tablespoon at a time,

beating egg white mixture until stiff peaks form. Gently fold one-fourth of egg white mixture into lemon mixture, and gently fold in remaining egg white mixture. Spoon mixture into prepared ramekins.
**5.** Bake at 400° for 20 minutes or until soufflés are puffy and set. Heat Lemon Curd in a small saucepan over low heat until warm. Spoon 1 tablespoon Lemon Curd onto each soufflé, and sprinkle each with 2 teaspoons powdered sugar. Serve immediately. Yield: 8 servings.

CALORIES 209 (20% from fat); FAT 4.6g (sat 2g, mono 1.5g, poly 0.5g); PROTEIN 5.8g; CARB 37.1g; FIBER 0.1g; CHOL 109mg; IRON 0.6mg; SODIUM 101mg; CALC 72mg

### Best Way to Grate a Lemon

You may have heard of a new tool that grates lemon rind with ease—it's called a **rasp.** It's not really new, actually; it's been a standard woodworking implement for years. We love it because it's quick and produces lighter, drier flakes as opposed to the wetter zest produced by a box or handheld grater. You can find rasps at most hardware stores.

# The Flavor of Memories

*Shelling just-picked peas may tempt you to pop them into your mouth. But it's worth the wait to cook them in dishes like these.*

Although most of the peas in this country are sold frozen, fresh ones are worth the search, and the shelling. From purees to primavera with pasta, from braised to the classic Southern approach—as a side dish—fresh-from-the-pod peas provide a healthful boost and an eye-pleasing addition to any plate.

Choose young pods that are well-filled and velvety soft to the touch. Those that look as if they are about to explode because they're too mature will taste tough and mealy when cooked. To prevent the sugar in the peas from converting to starch, store the peas uncovered in the refrigerator while they are still in their pods.

### Risi e Bisi

This classic Venetian dish of rice and peas is for the lazy—no monotonous stirring.

```
 2   teaspoons butter or stick
     margarine
 ½   cup chopped onion
 ⅓   cup finely chopped smoked ham
1½   cups shelled green peas (about
     1½ pounds unshelled green peas)
 1   cup uncooked Arborio rice or
     other short-grain rice
 3   cups fat-free, less-sodium chicken
     broth
 ½   cup dry white wine
 ⅓   cup (1½ ounces) grated fresh
     Parmesan cheese
 2   tablespoons chopped fresh parsley
 ⅛   teaspoon black pepper
```

**1.** Melt butter in a large saucepan over medium-high heat. Add onion and ham; sauté 3 minutes. Add peas and rice; cook

2 minutes. Add broth and wine; bring to a boil. Cover, reduce heat, and simmer 20 minutes, stirring occasionally. Stir in cheese, parsley, and pepper. Yield: 4 servings (serving size: 1¼ cups).

CALORIES 335 (17% from fat); FAT 6.2g (sat 3.4g, mono 2g, poly 0.4g); PROTEIN 16.8g; CARB 51.2g; FIBER 3.1g; CHOL 22mg; IRON 3.5mg; SODIUM 860mg; CALC 153mg

### Pasta Primavera

To keep the prosciutto from sticking together in the pasta, lay it out on a plate to dry after you chop it. The rich, nutty flavor of the Asiago complements the saltiness of the prosciutto, but Parmesan can be substituted if necessary.

```
12   ounces uncooked spaghettini or
     vermicelli
2½   cups (3-inch) diagonally sliced
     asparagus (about 1 pound)
1½   cups shelled green peas
     (about 1½ pounds unshelled)
 1   tablespoon olive oil, divided
 2   cups diced zucchini
 ½   cup sliced green onions
 1   cup fat-free, less-sodium chicken
     broth
 ⅓   cup dry white wine
 2   tablespoons minced fresh basil
 2   tablespoons minced fresh oregano
 ½   teaspoon kosher salt
 ¼   teaspoon black pepper
 2   ounces thinly sliced prosciutto or
     ham, chopped
 ¾   cup (3 ounces) grated Asiago or
     fresh Parmesan cheese
```

**1.** Bring water to a boil in a large Dutch oven, and add pasta. Cook pasta 5 minutes. Add asparagus, and cook 2 minutes. Add peas, and cook 1 minute. Drain well, and set aside.
**2.** Heat 2 teaspoons oil in a large nonstick skillet over medium-high heat. Add zucchini; sauté 5 minutes. Add onions; sauté 1 minute. Add broth and wine; bring to a boil. Stir in pasta mixture, basil, and oregano; cook 1 minute. Remove from heat; stir in 1 teaspoon oil, salt, pepper, and prosciutto. Spoon 1¼ cups primavera into each of 8 shallow

bowls; top each serving with 1½ tablespoons cheese. Yield: 8 servings.

CALORIES 269 (21% from fat); FAT 6.2g (sat 2.4g, mono 2.5g, poly 0.7g); PROTEIN 13.8g; CARB 40g; FIBER 3.2g; CHOL 15mg; IRON 3.1mg; SODIUM 448mg; CALC 154mg

---

### menu

**Fresh Peas with Lettuce**

Parslied boiled potatoes

Peppered filet mignon*

*Firmly press 2 tablespoons crushed black pepper into 6 (4-ounce) beef tenderloin steaks. Cook steaks in a nonstick skillet over medium-high heat 4 minutes on each side or to desired doneness. Remove from pan; add ½ cup beef broth, ⅓ cup balsamic vinegar, and 3 tablespoons red currant jelly to pan; cook 5 minutes or until thickened. Spoon over steaks. Serves 6.

---

### Fresh Peas with Lettuce

To shred the romaine, stack the leaves; then roll up lengthwise and slice crosswise. This is known as a *chiffonade*. Serve with ham, pork, or chicken.

```
1½   teaspoons butter or stick
     margarine, divided
 1   cup chopped Vidalia or other
     sweet onion
 ½   cup coarsely chopped celery
 1   teaspoon chopped fresh or ¼
     teaspoon dried thyme
 2   cups shelled green peas (about
     2 pounds unshelled green peas)
 1   cup fat-free, less-sodium chicken
     broth
 1   teaspoon sugar
 ¼   teaspoon salt
 1   cup shredded romaine lettuce
 2   tablespoons chopped fresh parsley
 ¼   teaspoon coarsely ground black
     pepper
```

**1.** Melt 1 teaspoon butter in a medium nonstick skillet over medium-high heat. Add onion, celery, and thyme; sauté 5 minutes or until tender. Add peas, broth, sugar, and salt, and bring to a boil.

Reduce heat, and simmer 15 minutes or until peas are tender.

**2.** Stir in ½ teaspoon butter, lettuce, and parsley. Remove from heat, and sprinkle with pepper. Yield: 6 servings (serving size: ½ cup).

CALORIES 69 (16% from fat); FAT 1.2g (sat 0.7g, mono 0.3g, poly 0.2g); PROTEIN 3.8g; CARB 11.1g; FIBER 2.6g; CHOL 3mg; IRON 1.1mg; SODIUM 201mg; CALC 29mg

## Curried Chicken with Spring Peas

Serve this dish with any combination of these toppings: diced fresh mango, mango chutney, chopped fresh cilantro, or some chopped peanuts.

  2  teaspoons vegetable oil
  3  cups chopped onion
  ¼  cup minced peeled fresh ginger
1½  tablespoons curry powder
  ½  teaspoon ground cumin
  ¼  teaspoon ground cinnamon
  2  garlic cloves, minced
  2  tablespoons all-purpose flour
  2  tablespoons tomato paste
  2  teaspoons sugar
  1  teaspoon salt
  ¼  teaspoon black pepper
  1  (16-ounce) can fat-free, less-sodium chicken broth
  3  cups (1-inch) cubed peeled red potato (about 1 pound)
  1  cup diced peeled Granny Smith apple (about 8 ounces)
1½  cups shelled green peas (about 1½ pounds unshelled green peas)
  1  pound skinned, boned chicken breast, cut crosswise into ¼-inch strips
  ⅓  cup low-fat sour cream
  6  cups hot cooked basmati rice

**1.** Heat oil in a large nonstick saucepan over medium-high heat. Add onion, and sauté 10 minutes or until browned, stirring frequently. Add minced ginger, curry, cumin, cinnamon, and garlic; sauté 1 minute. Add flour, tomato paste, sugar, salt, and pepper; cook 1 minute, stirring constantly (mixture will have a thick, pasty consistency).

**2.** Gradually add chicken broth, scraping pan to loosen browned bits; bring to a boil. Add cubed potato and diced apple; bring mixture to a boil. Cover, reduce heat, and simmer 10 minutes. Add peas; bring to a boil. Cover, reduce heat, and simmer 10 minutes or until peas and potatoes are tender. Add chicken to pan, and simmer, uncovered, 6 minutes or until chicken is done. Remove from heat, and stir in sour cream. Serve with rice. Yield: 6 servings (serving size: 1⅓ cups chicken mixture and 1 cup rice).

CALORIES 499 (9% from fat); FAT 5g (sat 1.7g, mono 1.4g, poly 1.3g); PROTEIN 28.1g; CARB 84g; FIBER 6.2g; CHOL 49mg; IRON 4.5mg; SODIUM 619mg; CALC 90mg

## Spring Pea Soup with Crab Flan

This recipe was adapted from a memorable meal served by Brooke Vosika, executive chef at the Four Seasons Hotel in Atlanta. Prepare the soup while the flans bake.

**FLAN:**
  ¼  cup 2% reduced-fat milk
  1  large egg
  2  large egg whites
  ¾  cup lump crabmeat, drained and shell pieces removed (about 4 ounces)
  ¼  cup sliced green onions
  ¼  teaspoon salt
  ⅛  teaspoon black pepper
Cooking spray

**SOUP:**
  1  teaspoon olive oil
  ½  cup chopped onion
  1  garlic clove, minced
3½  cups fat-free, less-sodium chicken broth
2½  cups shelled green peas, divided (about 2½ pounds unshelled green peas)
  ¼  teaspoon salt
  1  cup torn spinach
  ½  cup water
  2  cups chopped tomato

**1.** Preheat oven to 325°.
**2.** To prepare flan, combine first 3 ingredients in a bowl, and stir with a whisk.

Stir in crabmeat, green onions, ¼ teaspoon salt, and pepper. Divide mixture evenly among 4 (6-ounce) custard cups or ramekins coated with cooking spray. Place cups on a baking sheet. Bake at 325° for 50 minutes or until a knife inserted in center comes out clean. Remove cups from baking sheet. Loosen edges of custards with a knife or rubber spatula. Place a small plate, upside down, on top of each cup; invert onto plates. Keep warm.

**3.** To prepare soup, heat oil in a Dutch oven over medium heat. Add chopped onion and garlic; sauté 5 minutes. Stir in broth, 2 cups peas, and ¼ teaspoon salt. Bring to a boil; reduce heat, and simmer 20 minutes or until peas are tender. Cool slightly. Place soup and spinach in a blender, and process until smooth. Set aside, and keep warm. Add ½ cup peas and ½ cup water to pan, and cook, covered, 4 minutes or until just tender.

**4.** Place ½ cup chopped tomato into each of 4 soup bowls. Arrange flans on top of tomato, and ladle 1 cup soup around each flan. Top each serving with 2 tablespoons steamed peas. Yield: 4 servings.

CALORIES 195 (19% from fat); FAT 4.1g (sat 0.9g, mono 1.6g, poly 0.9g); PROTEIN 17.8g; CARB 22g; FIBER 4.8g; CHOL 82mg; IRON 2.5mg; SODIUM 851mg; CALC 94mg

### Finding Fresh Peas

Fresh green peas are rarely seen in the supermarket these days because few people care to shell them. But as we've mentioned, their flavor is worth the searching and the shelling.

High-quality fresh peas must be young, cooled quickly after harvest, and kept cold until they are eaten. If allowed to warm, the peas will lose sugar—and tenderness— quickly. Be sure to choose pea pods that are uniformly green and well filled.

# The Truth about Tofu

*Tofu isn't too good to be true, but it is too good—and tasty—to overlook.*

### Tofu with Red Curry Paste, Peas, and Yellow Tomatoes

Red curry paste can be found in the ethnic or gourmet sections of most large supermarkets. The paste is a blend of clarified butter (ghee), curry powder, vinegar, and other seasonings. Use either Indian or Asian curry paste; it comes in mild and hot versions, so adjust the heat to suit your preference.

1 (14-ounce) package firm tofu, drained and cut into 1-inch cubes
2 tablespoons fresh lime juice
1 teaspoon ground turmeric
¼ teaspoon salt
⅛ teaspoon black pepper
2 teaspoons olive oil
2 cups thinly sliced onion
1 cup light coconut milk
1 to 2 tablespoons red curry paste
1 cup shelled green peas (about 1 pound unshelled) or frozen green peas, thawed
½ cup chopped yellow tomato
4 cups hot cooked long-grain rice

**1.** Place a large nonstick skillet over medium-high heat. Add tofu; cook until liquid from tofu is evaporated (about 3 minutes). Remove tofu from pan; sprinkle with lime juice, turmeric, salt, and pepper.
**2.** Heat oil in pan over medium-high heat. Add onion; sauté 5 minutes. Add tofu, and cook 7 minutes or until golden. Combine milk and curry paste; add to pan. Reduce heat, and simmer 3 minutes. Add peas and tomato; cook 2 minutes. Serve over rice. Yield: 4

servings (serving size: 1 cup tofu mixture and 1 cup rice).

CALORIES 421 (23% from fat); FAT 10.6g (sat 3.1g, mono 2.9g, poly 3.1g); PROTEIN 15.5g; CARB 66.9g; FIBER 5.3g; CHOL 0mg; IRON 8.7mg; SODIUM 344mg; CALC 154mg

### Tofu Triangles with Spicy Onion Sauce

You can substitute canned diced tomatoes for the plum tomatoes. Look for chickpea flour in health-food stores.

1 (14-ounce) package firm tofu, drained and cut into 6 (¾-inch-thick) slices
¼ cup chickpea flour or all-purpose flour
2 teaspoons canola oil
2 cups thinly sliced onion, separated into rings (about 1 large onion)
1 teaspoon curry powder
½ teaspoon salt
¼ teaspoon ground cumin
¼ teaspoon ground turmeric
¼ teaspoon black pepper
1 cup diced plum tomato (about 3 medium)
2 tablespoons chopped fresh cilantro
1 tablespoon brown sugar
½ cup water
3 tablespoons red wine vinegar
4 cups hot cooked long-grain rice

**1.** Place tofu slices on several layers of paper towels; cover with additional paper towels. Let stand 5 minutes, pressing down occasionally. Cut each tofu slice diagonally into 2 triangles. Place flour in a shallow dish, and dredge tofu triangles in flour. Heat oil in a large nonstick skillet over medium-high heat. Add tofu; sauté 3 minutes on each side. Set aside; keep warm.
**2.** Add onion to pan, and stir-fry 4 minutes. Add curry, salt, cumin, turmeric, and pepper, and stir-fry 1 minute. Add tomato, cilantro, and sugar, and stir-fry 2 minutes. Add water and vinegar; bring to a boil, scraping pan to loosen browned bits. Cook 2 minutes. Spoon onion sauce over tofu. Serve with rice.

Yield: 4 servings (serving size: 3 tofu triangles, about ½ cup onion sauce, and 1 cup rice).

CALORIES 382 (19% from fat); FAT 8g (sat 1g, mono 2.6g, poly 3.7g); PROTEIN 14.6g; CARB 66.5g; FIBER 6.3g; CHOL 0mg; IRON 8.3mg; SODIUM 313mg; CALC 158mg

### Creamy Potato-and-Leek Soup

Pureed tofu provides this soup with its creamy background. Serve this soup with crisp whole-wheat toast, either to eat alongside or break into the bowl.

1 tablespoon canola oil
6 cups thinly sliced leek (about 3 large)
8 ounces peeled Yukon gold or red potato, quartered and thinly sliced (about 1½ cups)
1 cup chopped fresh parsley, divided
1 teaspoon chopped fresh thyme
¾ teaspoon salt
1 bay leaf
4 cups water
1 cup reduced-fat firm tofu (about 6 ounces)
⅛ teaspoon black pepper

**1.** Heat oil in a large Dutch oven over medium-high heat. Add leek, and sauté 5 minutes. Reduce heat to medium; add potato, ½ cup parsley, thyme, salt, and bay leaf. Cook 15 minutes, stirring occasionally. Add water, and bring to a boil. Cover, reduce heat, and simmer 20 minutes. Discard bay leaf.
**2.** Combine 2 cups potato mixture and tofu in a blender or food processor, and process until smooth. Return pureed potato mixture to pan. Stir in ½ cup parsley and pepper. Cook 5 minutes or until thoroughly heated. Yield: 6 servings (serving size: 1 cup).

CALORIES 130 (21% from fat); FAT 3g (sat 0.3g, mono 1.5g, poly 1.1g); PROTEIN 4.8g; CARB 22.6g; FIBER 2.3g; CHOL 0mg; IRON 3.3mg; SODIUM 350mg; CALC 91mg

## Glazed-Tofu Sandwich

1 (14-ounce) package firm tofu, drained and cut into 8 (½-inch-thick) slices
1 teaspoon olive oil
¼ teaspoon salt
¼ teaspoon black pepper
¼ cup Worcestershire sauce
⅓ cup low-fat mayonnaise
⅓ cup chopped fresh basil
1 garlic clove, minced
8 (1½-ounce) slices whole-wheat bread, toasted
8 (¼-inch-thick) slices tomato (about 8 ounces)

**1.** Place tofu slices on several layers of paper towels; cover with additional paper towels. Let stand 5 minutes, pressing down occasionally. Heat oil in a large nonstick skillet over medium-high heat. Add tofu, and sauté 4 minutes. Turn slices over, and sprinkle with salt and pepper; sauté 4 minutes. Spoon Worcestershire sauce over tofu; cook 30 seconds or until browned, turning once.
**2.** Combine mayonnaise, basil, and garlic. Spread mayonnaise mixture evenly over each of 4 bread slices, layering each slice with 2 tofu slices and 2 tomato slices. Cover tofu and tomato with remaining bread slices. Yield: 4 servings.

CALORIES 360 (27% from fat); FAT 10.8g (sat 1.8g, mono 3.7g, poly 4.4g); PROTEIN 16.5g; CARB 51.9g; FIBER 5.4g; CHOL 0mg; IRON 8.4mg; SODIUM 939mg; CALC 217mg

## Barbecued-Tofu Sandwich

Think what you will about barbecue's affinity for tofu, this match-up makes a wonderful hot sandwich. Put a little Tofu Coleslaw (recipe at right) next to it for an extra kick.

1 (14-ounce) package firm tofu, drained and cut into 8 (½-inch-thick) slices
⅛ teaspoon salt
⅓ cup all-purpose flour
1 teaspoon vegetable oil
1 cup commercial barbecue sauce
4 (2-ounce) hamburger buns

**1.** Place tofu on several layers of paper towels; cover with additional paper towels. Let stand 1 hour, pressing down occasionally. Sprinkle slices with salt.
**2.** Place flour in a shallow dish; dredge tofu slices in flour. Heat oil in a large nonstick skillet over medium-high heat. Add tofu; brush half of barbecue sauce over tofu, and cook 2 minutes. Turn slices over; brush with remaining barbecue sauce, and cook 3 minutes or until tofu is glazed. Place 2 tofu slices on bottom half of each bun; cover with tops of buns. Yield: 4 servings.

CALORIES 332 (27% from fat); FAT 10g (sat 1.8g, mono 2.4g, poly 5.1g); PROTEIN 15g; CARB 46.3g; FIBER 3.4g; CHOL 0mg; IRON 8.2mg; SODIUM 907mg; CALC 196mg

## Tofu Coleslaw

Firm tofu forms the creamy base of the coleslaw dressing.

4 cups thinly sliced green cabbage
¾ cup grated carrot
¾ cup finely diced celery
1 cup reduced-fat firm tofu, drained (about 6 ounces)
¼ cup low-fat mayonnaise
4 teaspoons rice vinegar
2 teaspoons prepared mustard
1 teaspoon sugar
½ teaspoon salt
⅛ teaspoon ground red pepper
2 garlic cloves
¼ cup chopped fresh parsley

**1.** Combine cabbage, carrot, and celery in a large bowl.
**2.** Combine tofu and next 7 ingredients in a blender or food processor; process until smooth, scraping sides of bowl occasionally. Add parsley, pulsing once. Pour over cabbage mixture, tossing to coat. Cover and chill. Yield: 8 servings (serving size: ½ cup).

CALORIES 42 (19% from fat); FAT 0.9g (sat 0.1g, mono 0.2g, poly 0.5g); PROTEIN 2.4g; CARB 6.6g; FIBER 1.5g; CHOL 0mg; IRON 0.6mg; SODIUM 275mg; CALC 38mg

## 30 minutes or less

# Pasta Pronto

*Use your noodles for fast meals and friendly flavors. Pasta may be the time-stressed cook's ultimate secret weapon.*

## Lamb-and-Caponata Pasta Toss

**PREPARATION TIME: 10 MINUTES**
**COOKING TIME: 20 MINUTES**

8 ounces uncooked ziti (short tube-shaped pasta)
Cooking spray
½ pound lean ground lamb or ground round
1 tablespoon olive oil
3 cups diced peeled eggplant (about 8 ounces)
1 cup chopped onion
4 garlic cloves, minced
1 tablespoon balsamic vinegar
¼ teaspoon crushed red pepper
2 (14.5-ounce) cans diced tomatoes with basil, garlic, and oregano, undrained
¼ cup chopped fresh or 4 teaspoons dried basil
¼ cup grated Parmesan cheese

**1.** Cook pasta according to package directions, omitting salt and fat.
**2.** While pasta cooks, place a large nonstick skillet coated with cooking spray over medium-high heat. Add lamb; cook until browned, stirring to crumble. Remove lamb from pan. Add oil, eggplant, onion, and garlic to pan; sauté 8 minutes. Add vinegar, red pepper, and tomatoes, and bring to a boil. Cover, reduce heat, and simmer 10 minutes. Return lamb to pan; cook 2 minutes or until thoroughly heated.
**3.** Drain pasta; place in a bowl. Add lamb mixture and basil; toss well. Serve with cheese. Yield: 6 servings (serving size: 1⅓ cups pasta and 2 teaspoons cheese).

CALORIES 303 (18% from fat); FAT 6.1g (sat 1.9g, mono 2.8g, poly 1g); PROTEIN 15.5g; CARB 47g; FIBER 2.6g; CHOL 21mg; IRON 4.4mg; SODIUM 869mg; CALC 183mg

## Southwestern Roasted-Vegetable Couscous

PREPARATION TIME: 10 MINUTES
COOKING TIME: 20 MINUTES

    1  cup uncooked couscous
   ¼  cup water
    1  (16-ounce) can fat-free,
       less-sodium chicken broth
    1  cup diced red bell pepper
    1  cup presliced mushrooms
   ½  cup diced carrots
    1  tablespoon vegetable oil
    1  teaspoon chili powder
   ½  teaspoon salt
   ½  teaspoon black pepper
   ¼  teaspoon ground cumin
    1  (11-ounce) can no-salt-added
       whole-kernel corn, drained
    1  teaspoon bottled minced garlic
   ⅓  cup chopped green onions
    1  (15-ounce) can black beans,
       rinsed and drained

**1.** Preheat oven to 425°.
**2.** Place couscous on a jelly-roll pan, and bake at 425° for 5 minutes or until lightly browned. Bring water and broth to a boil in a saucepan, and gradually stir in couscous. Remove from heat; cover and let stand 5 minutes. Fluff with a fork, and set aside.
**3.** While couscous stands, combine bell pepper and next 9 ingredients in a large bowl, and stir well. Arrange vegetable mixture on jelly-roll pan; bake at 425° for 12 minutes. Combine couscous, roasted vegetables, onions, and beans in a large bowl, and stir well. Yield: 4 servings (serving size: 1½ cups).

CALORIES 322 (15% from fat); FAT 5.2g (sat 1g, mono 1.3g, poly 2.4g); PROTEIN 14.1g; CARB 56.6g; FIBER 6.1g; CHOL 0mg; IRON 3.4mg; SODIUM 857mg; CALC 38mg

## Tortellini-and-Spinach Toss

PREPARATION TIME: 15 MINUTES
COOKING TIME: 12 MINUTES

    2  (9-ounce) packages fresh chicken
       or cheese tortellini, uncooked
    2  teaspoons olive oil
    4  garlic cloves, minced
    1  cup fat-free, less-sodium chicken broth
   ¼  teaspoon crushed red pepper
    2  (14.5-ounce) cans diced tomatoes,
       undrained
    2  cups torn spinach
   ½  cup (2 ounces) grated fresh
       Romano or Parmesan cheese
    2  tablespoons chopped fresh or
       2 teaspoons dried basil

**1.** Cook pasta according to package directions, omitting salt and fat.
**2.** Heat oil in a saucepan over medium-high heat. Add garlic; cook 3 minutes. Add broth, pepper, and tomatoes; bring to a boil. Reduce heat; simmer 6 minutes, stirring occasionally. Remove from heat; stir in spinach.
**3.** Drain pasta; place in a bowl. Add tomato mixture; toss well. Serve with cheese and basil. Yield: 6 servings (serving size: 1⅓ cups pasta, 4 teaspoons cheese, and 1 teaspoon basil).

CALORIES 317 (21% from fat); FAT 7.3g (sat 2.3g, mono 3.1g, poly 1.3g); PROTEIN 15.2g; CARB 47.8g; FIBER 2.9g; CHOL 38mg; IRON 3.3mg; SODIUM 856mg; CALC 161mg

## Italian-Style Mussels and Spaghettini

PREPARATION TIME: 7 MINUTES
COOKING TIME: 21 MINUTES

    8  ounces uncooked spaghettini
    2  tablespoons olive oil
    4  garlic cloves, minced
   ½  cup clam juice
   ¼  teaspoon crushed red pepper
    1  (14½-ounce) can Italian-style
       diced tomatoes, undrained
   20  mussels (about 1 pound), rinsed
       and debearded
    1  (6-ounce) can no-salt-added
       tomato paste
   ¼  cup chopped fresh flat-leaf parsley

**1.** Cook pasta according to package directions, omitting salt and fat.
**2.** Heat oil in a Dutch oven over medium heat. Add garlic; sauté 4 minutes. Add clam juice, red pepper, and tomatoes. Bring to a boil. Reduce heat; simmer, uncovered, 5 minutes.
**3.** Add mussels; cover and cook 3 minutes or until shells open. Discard any unopened shells. Stir in tomato paste, and cook uncovered, 2 minutes, or until sauce thickens.
**4.** Drain pasta, and place in 4 bowls. Top with mussels and sauce. Serve with parsley. Yield: 4 servings (serving size: 1 cup pasta, 5 mussels, 1 tablespoon parsley, and ½ cup sauce).

CALORIES 384 (20% from fat); FAT 8.7g (sat 1.2g, mono 5.3g, poly 1.2g); PROTEIN 14.9g; CARB 61.6g; FIBER 1.6g; CHOL 12mg; IRON 5.5mg; SODIUM 470mg; CALC 101mg

## Creamy Gorgonzola Fettuccine

PREPARATION TIME: 10 MINUTES
COOKING TIME: 15 MINUTES

    8  ounces uncooked fettuccine
    3  cups (1-inch) diagonally sliced
       asparagus (about 10 ounces)
    2  teaspoons butter or stick
       margarine
    4  garlic cloves, minced
    1  tablespoon all-purpose flour
   1¼  cups fat-free milk
   ¼  cup (2 ounces) ⅓-less-fat cream
       cheese
   ¼  teaspoon salt
   ½  cup (2 ounces) Gorgonzola or
       other blue cheese, crumbled
    2  tablespoons chopped walnuts,
       toasted
Freshly ground black pepper (optional)

**1.** Cook pasta in boiling water 6 minutes, omitting salt and fat. Add asparagus, and cook 2 minutes or until tender.
**2.** While pasta is cooking, melt butter in a medium saucepan over medium-high heat. Add garlic, and cook 3 minutes. Add flour; cook 30 seconds, stirring constantly. Gradually add milk, stirring well with a whisk. Stir in cream cheese and

salt; cook 3 minutes or until thick, stirring constantly.

**3.** Drain pasta and asparagus; place in a large bowl. Add sauce; tossing to coat. Serve with Gorgonzola and walnuts, and sprinkle with pepper, if desired. Yield: 4 servings (serving size: 1¼ cups pasta, 2 tablespoons Gorgonzola, and 1½ teaspoons walnuts).

CALORIES 399 (29% from fat); FAT 12.8g (sat 6.4g, mono 3.3g, poly 2.2g); PROTEIN 18g; CARB 54.3g; FIBER 3.8g; CHOL 28mg; IRON 3.4mg; SODIUM 467mg; CALC 220mg

### North African Chicken and Couscous

PREPARATION TIME: 20 MINUTES
COOKING TIME: 8 MINUTES

    2   cups water
1½   cups uncooked couscous
    ½   cup golden raisins
    ½   cup thawed orange juice
        concentrate, undiluted
    ⅓   cup lemon juice
    2   tablespoons water
    2   tablespoons olive oil
    2   teaspoons ground cumin
    ½   teaspoon salt
    ¼   teaspoon black pepper
    3   cups chopped ready-to-eat roasted
        skinned, boned chicken breast
        (about 3 breasts)
    2   cups chopped peeled cucumber
    1   cup chopped red bell pepper
    ¼   cup thinly sliced green onions
    ½   cup chopped fresh cilantro
        Sliced green onions (optional)

**1.** Bring water to a boil in a medium saucepan, and gradually stir in couscous and raisins. Remove from heat. Cover; let stand 5 minutes. Fluff with a fork.
**2.** Combine orange juice and next 6 ingredients; stir well with a whisk.
**3.** Combine couscous mixture, juice mixture, chicken, and next 4 ingredients in a large bowl, and toss well. Garnish with green onions, if desired. Yield: 6 servings (serving size: 2 cups).

CALORIES 332 (18% from fat); FAT 6.6g (sat 1.2g, mono 3.9g, poly 0.9g); PROTEIN 19.6g; CARB 51.2g; FIBER 3.3g; CHOL 35mg; IRON 2.8mg; SODIUM 498mg; CALC 51mg

### Warm Bow-Tie Pasta Salad

PREPARATION TIME: 18 MINUTES
COOKING TIME: 12 MINUTES

    8   ounces uncooked farfalle (bow-tie
        pasta)
    2   tablespoons olive oil, divided
1⅓   cups julienne-cut red bell pepper
        (about 1 large pepper)
    1   cup sliced cremini mushrooms
        (about 2 ounces)
    1   cup thinly sliced shiitake
        mushroom caps (about 2 ounces)
    3   garlic cloves, minced
    3   tablespoons balsamic vinegar
    1   tablespoon Dijon mustard
    ¼   teaspoon salt
    6   cups gourmet salad greens
    ½   cup (2 ounces) finely grated
        Asiago cheese
        Freshly ground black pepper (optional)

**1.** Cook pasta according to package directions, omitting salt and fat.
**2.** While pasta is cooking, heat 1 tablespoon oil in a large nonstick skillet over medium heat. Add bell pepper, mushrooms, and garlic, and sauté 10 minutes. Combine 1 tablespoon oil, vinegar, mustard, and salt in a large bowl.
**3.** Drain pasta. Add pasta, mushroom mixture, and salad greens, to bowl; toss gently. Serve with cheese and black pepper, if desired. Yield: 4 servings (serving size: 2 cups pasta and 2 tablespoons cheese).

CALORIES 360 (30% from fat); FAT 12.1g (sat 3.5g, mono 6.4g, poly 1.3g); PROTEIN 14.1g; CARB 48.6g; FIBER 3.6g; CHOL 15mg; IRON 4mg; SODIUM 441mg; CALC 198mg

dinner tonight

# Salads in the Round

*With these savvy spins, main-dish salads aren't just for squares.*

There's more than one way to fill a soup bowl—with a handy main-dish salad.

### Confetti Pasta Salad with Chicken

Draining plain yogurt on paper towels for just five minutes gives it a thick consistency that's almost like sour cream.

    ½   cup water
    ¼   cup dry white wine
    3   (4-ounce) skinned, boned chicken
        breast halves
    1   large garlic clove, sliced
1½   cups plain low-fat yogurt
    ¼   cup light mayonnaise
2½   tablespoons fresh lemon juice
    1   tablespoon cider vinegar
    2   teaspoons spicy brown mustard
    ¾   teaspoon salt
    ½   teaspoon dried oregano
    ¼   teaspoon garlic powder
    ¼   teaspoon black pepper
    4   cups cooked tubetti or ditalini
        (very short tube-shaped pasta)
        (about 1⅓ cups uncooked pasta)
    ½   cup chopped celery
    ½   cup finely chopped red bell
        pepper
    ½   cup finely chopped green bell
        pepper
    ½   cup finely chopped carrot
    ¼   cup chopped fresh parsley

**1.** Combine first 4 ingredients in a saucepan; bring to a simmer. Cover and simmer 15 minutes or until chicken is done. Remove chicken pieces from broth; cool and coarsely chop. Bring broth to a boil over high heat; cook until reduced to ¼ cup (about 5 minutes). Cool.
**2.** Spoon yogurt onto several layers of heavy-duty paper towels, and spread to ½-inch thickness. Cover with additional paper towels, and let stand 5 minutes. Scrape into a bowl using a rubber spatula.
**3.** Combine reduced broth, yogurt, mayonnaise, and next 7 ingredients in a large bowl. Stir in chicken, pasta, and remaining ingredients. Cover and chill thoroughly. Yield: 8 servings (serving size: 1 cup).

CALORIES 209 (17% from fat); FAT 3.9g (sat 1.1g, mono 1g, poly 1.4g); PROTEIN 16g; CARB 25.7g; FIBER 1.9g; CHOL 30mg; IRON 1.8mg; SODIUM 359mg; CALC 106mg

## Monterey Pasta Salad with Almonds

¼ cup minced green onions
1 tablespoon sugar
2 tablespoons fresh lime juice
2 tablespoons white wine vinegar
1 tablespoon vegetable oil
2 teaspoons Dijon mustard
½ teaspoon cracked black pepper
¼ teaspoon salt
2 cups cooked rotini (corkscrew pasta) (about 4 ounces uncooked)
½ cup (2 ounces) shredded reduced-fat Monterey Jack cheese
2 tablespoons finely chopped almonds, toasted
2 tablespoons minced fresh cilantro
1 (15-ounce) can black beans, rinsed and drained

**1.** Combine first 8 ingredients. Add pasta and remaining ingredients; toss. Cover; chill thoroughly. Yield: 4 servings (serving size: 1 cup).

CALORIES 295 (27% from fat); FAT 8.7g (sat 2.5g, mono 3g, poly 2.4g); PROTEIN 13.9g; CARB 41g; FIBER 3.9g; CHOL 9mg; IRON 2.8mg; SODIUM 480mg; CALC 152mg

## Tangy Lentil Salad

Serve this high-fiber meatless salad with crisp breadsticks and fresh fruit. It also doubles as a sandwich filling for lunch the next day. Transport it in a zip-top plastic bag, and then spoon it into a pita pocket.

2 cups water
1 cup dried lentils
½ teaspoon salt
1 bay leaf
1 cup diced seeded peeled cucumber
½ cup diced celery
¼ cup diced red onion
¼ cup orange juice
2 tablespoons white wine vinegar
4 teaspoons Dijon mustard
½ cup (2 ounces) crumbled feta cheese

**1.** Combine first 4 ingredients in a medium saucepan. Bring to a boil; cover, reduce heat, and simmer 25 minutes or until tender. Drain well; discard bay leaf.
**2.** Combine lentils, cucumber, celery, and onion in a medium bowl. Combine orange juice, vinegar, and mustard; stir with a whisk. Add to lentil mixture. Stir in cheese. Cover; chill thoroughly. Yield: 4 servings (serving size: 1 cup).

CALORIES 225 (16% from fat); FAT 3.9g (sat 2.2g, mono 0.7g, poly 0.3g); PROTEIN 16.0g; CARB 32.6g; FIBER 6.1g; CHOL 13mg; IRON 4.6mg; SODIUM 621mg; CALC 110mg

## Shrimp, Avocado, and Farfalle Salad

Make this salad up to one day ahead. Add the avocado just before serving.

2 teaspoons ground cumin
½ teaspoon salt
¼ teaspoon ground red pepper
⅓ cup tomato juice
2 tablespoons red wine vinegar
1 tablespoon fresh lime juice
1 tablespoon olive oil
1 pound medium shrimp, cooked and peeled
4½ cups cooked farfalle (about 3½ cups uncooked bow tie pasta)
1½ cups halved cherry tomatoes
1 cup fresh corn kernels (about 2 ears)
½ cup diced red bell pepper
½ cup chopped fresh cilantro
⅓ cup thinly sliced green onions
½ cup diced peeled avocado

**1.** Combine first 7 ingredients; stir well with a whisk. Add shrimp and remaining ingredients; toss gently. Yield: 5 servings (serving size: 2 cups).

CALORIES 345 (21% from fat); FAT 8g (sat 1.2g, mono 4g, poly 1.6g); PROTEIN 22g; CARB 47.5g; FIBER 5.1g; CHOL 103mg; IRON 5.2mg; SODIUM 412mg; CALC 72mg

## Nomad Salad

1½ cups uncooked bulgur or cracked wheat
1½ cups boiling water
1 cup dried figs, halved
1 cup chopped fresh parsley
½ cup chopped fresh mint
½ cup sweetened dried cranberries (such as Craisins)
½ cup lemon juice
2 tablespoons olive oil
½ teaspoon salt
½ teaspoon black pepper
1 (15½-ounce) can chickpeas (garbanzo beans), drained

**1.** Combine bulgur and boiling water in a large bowl. Cover and let stand 30 minutes. Stir in figs and remaining ingredients; cover salad and chill thoroughly. Yield: 5 servings (serving size: 1½ cups).

CALORIES 390 (18% from fat); FAT 7.7g (sat 1.1g, mono 4.5g, poly 1.5g); PROTEIN 11.3g; CARB 75g; FIBER 14.7g; CHOL 0mg; IRON 4mg; SODIUM 363mg; CALC 96mg

## Tomato Panzanella with Provolone and Ham

3½ cups diced tomato (about 1½ pounds)
1 tablespoon capers
⅛ teaspoon salt
¼ teaspoon freshly ground black pepper
1 garlic clove, minced
2 tablespoons balsamic vinegar
4 cups (1-inch) cubed day-old rosemary bread (about 8 ounces)
½ cup (3 ounces) diced 33%-less-sodium ham
½ cup (2 ounces) diced sharp provolone cheese
½ cup chopped fresh basil

**1.** Combine first 5 ingredients; cover and marinate in refrigerator 8 hours. Stir in vinegar.
**2.** Add bread and remaining ingredients just before serving; toss gently. Yield: 4 servings (serving size: 1¾ cups).

CALORIES 272 (25% from fat); FAT 7.6g (sat 3.4g, mono 2.4g, poly 1g); PROTEIN 13.8g; CARB 38.3g; FIBER 3.5g; CHOL 22mg; IRON 2.5mg; SODIUM 940mg; CALC 168mg

# june

# Weeknight Wraps

## If you make it, it can be wrapped—a good mantra for busy weeknights and hungry families.

You know what a wrap is: a burrito that's been to California. But the sojourn was a success, because now that their celebrity has mellowed, wraps can be seen for what they really are—perfect delivery packages for flavor and nutrition.

And wraps don't require much infrastructure. A tortilla. Fillings. That, plus a quick roll, fold, and tuck, and you've got a meal. Just about anything goes inside, from pepper steak with blue cheese to kale and cannellini beans.

### Cajun Catfish Wraps with Slaw

This crispy, spicy catfish makes the perfect companion to the vegetable crunch of the mellow cabbage slaw.

**SLAW:**
- 3½ cups thinly sliced red or green cabbage
- ¼ cup light mayonnaise
- 1½ tablespoons cider vinegar
- ½ teaspoon sugar

**WRAPS:**
- 1 tablespoon all-purpose flour
- 1 tablespoon paprika
- 1½ teaspoons dried thyme
- 1½ teaspoons dried oregano
- 1 teaspoon garlic powder
- 1 teaspoon black pepper
- ½ teaspoon salt
- ¼ teaspoon ground red pepper
- 4 (6-ounce) farm-raised catfish fillets
- 1 tablespoon butter or stick margarine
- 4 (8-inch) fat-free flour tortillas

**1.** To prepare slaw, combine first 4 ingredients in a bowl; cover and chill.
**2.** To prepare wraps, combine flour and next 7 ingredients in a shallow dish. Dredge fillets in flour mixture. Melt butter in a large nonstick skillet over medium-high heat. Add fillets; sauté 5 minutes. Turn fillets over; cook 4 minutes or until fish flakes easily when tested with a fork.

**3.** Warm tortillas according to package directions. Cut each catfish fillet lengthwise into 4 pieces. Arrange 4 fillet pieces on each tortilla; top each serving with about ¾ cup slaw, and roll up. Yield: 4 servings (serving size: 1 wrap).

CALORIES 397 (27% from fat); FAT 11.7g (sat 3.7g, mono 3.9g, poly 2.7g); PROTEIN 35.6g; CARB 36.6g; FIBER 3g; CHOL 106mg; IRON 4.7mg; SODIUM 918mg; CALC 126mg

### Ginger-Peanut Chicken-Salad Wraps

To make preparation easier, substitute slices of breast meat from prepackaged rotisserie chicken; the dish will be a little higher in fat and sodium.

- 1 teaspoon olive oil
- 6 (4-ounce) skinned, boned chicken breast halves
- 1 cup chopped seeded peeled cucumber
- ¾ cup chopped red bell pepper
- 1½ tablespoons sugar
- 1 tablespoon minced peeled fresh ginger
- 3 tablespoons fresh lime juice
- 1 tablespoon low-sodium soy sauce
- ¼ teaspoon salt
- ¼ teaspoon ground red pepper
- 1 garlic clove, crushed
- ¼ cup creamy peanut butter
- 2 tablespoons water
- 3 tablespoons chopped fresh cilantro
- 8 (8-inch) fat-free flour tortillas
- 4 cups chopped romaine lettuce

**1.** Heat oil in a large nonstick skillet over medium-high heat. Add chicken; cook 5 minutes on each side or until done. Remove chicken from pan; cool. Shred chicken into bite-size pieces. Place chicken, cucumber, and bell pepper in a large bowl; set aside.
**2.** Place sugar and next 6 ingredients in a blender, and process until smooth. Add peanut butter and water; process until smooth, scraping sides. Add peanut butter mixture to chicken mixture; stir well. Add cilantro, and toss well. Warm tortillas according to package directions. Spoon ½ cup chicken mixture onto each tortilla; top each serving with ½ cup lettuce, and roll up. Yield: 8 servings (serving size: 1 wrap).

CALORIES 280 (19% from fat); FAT 5.9g (sat 1.1g, mono 2.7g, poly 1.6g); PROTEIN 25.8g; CARB 30.5g; FIBER 2.4g; CHOL 49mg; IRON 2.5mg; SODIUM 572mg; CALC 29mg

### Blue Cheese-Pepper Steak Wraps

- 12 ounces boned top round steak
- 2 teaspoons dry mustard
- ½ teaspoon black pepper
- ¼ teaspoon garlic powder
- ¼ teaspoon salt
- Cooking spray
- 2 cups sliced mushrooms
- 1 onion, cut into ¼-inch-thick wedges
- 1 medium red bell pepper, seeded and cut into ¼-inch strips
- 2 tablespoons water
- 1½ tablespoons red wine vinegar
- ½ cup (2 ounces) crumbled blue cheese or feta cheese
- 4 (8-inch) fat-free flour tortillas
- 2 cups chopped romaine lettuce

**1.** Trim fat from beef; slice beef into ¼-inch strips. Set aside.
**2.** Combine mustard, black pepper, garlic powder, and salt in a large bowl. Add beef, tossing to coat.
**3.** Place a large nonstick skillet coated with cooking spray over medium-high heat until hot. Add beef mixture; sauté 4 minutes or until done. Remove from pan; keep warm. Add mushrooms, onion

wedges, and bell pepper to pan, and sauté 2 minutes. Add water; cover and cook 5 minutes, stirring occasionally. Stir in beef mixture and vinegar. Remove from heat; stir in cheese.

**4.** Warm tortillas according to package directions. Spoon 1 cup beef mixture onto each tortilla; top each serving with ½ cup lettuce, and roll up. Yield: 4 servings (serving size: 1 wrap).

CALORIES 310 (24% from fat); FAT 8.1g (sat 3.9g, mono 2.5g, poly 0.5g); PROTEIN 26.3g; CARB 32.4g; FIBER 3.3g; CHOL 56mg; IRON 4.1mg; SODIUM 732mg; CALC 103mg

### Kale-and-Cannellini Wrapinis

Twelve cups of kale may seem too much, but it cooks down to only about 2 cups.

  3  bacon slices
 12  cups water
 12  cups chopped kale (about 1¼ pounds)
  1  (19-ounce) can cannellini beans or other white beans, undrained
  1  teaspoon crushed red pepper
  1  garlic clove, minced
  1  cup diced carrot
  1  teaspoon dried rubbed sage
 ¼  teaspoon salt
  4  (8-inch) fat-free flour tortillas
 ¼  cup (1 ounce) finely grated fresh Romano cheese

**1.** Cook bacon in a large nonstick skillet over medium heat until crisp. Remove bacon from pan, reserving 1 tablespoon drippings in pan. Crumble bacon, and set aside. Bring water to a boil in a large stockpot; add kale. Cook 6 minutes or until tender; drain and set aside. Drain beans in a colander over a bowl, reserving ⅓ cup liquid.

**2.** Heat drippings in pan over medium-high heat. Add red pepper and garlic, and sauté 3 minutes. Add crumbled bacon, reserved bean liquid, carrot, sage, and salt; bring to a boil. Cover, reduce heat, and simmer 5 minutes or until carrot is crisp-tender. Uncover and cook 3 minutes or until liquid almost evaporates. Stir in beans and kale; cook 2 minutes.

**3.** Warm tortillas according to package directions. Spoon 1 cup kale mixture onto each tortilla; top each serving with 1 tablespoon cheese, and roll up. Yield: 4 servings (serving size: 1 wrap).

CALORIES 422 (24% from fat); FAT 11.3g (sat 3.3g, mono 4.7g, poly 2.2g); PROTEIN 19.2g; CARB 64.4g; FIBER 6.9g; CHOL 13mg; IRON 5.8mg; SODIUM 862mg; CALC 255mg

### Spicy Ranch Chicken Wraps

  2  teaspoons chili powder
  2  teaspoons vegetable oil
 1½  teaspoons ground cumin
 ½  teaspoon salt
 1¼  pounds skinned, boned chicken breast, cut into ½-inch strips
 ½  cup low-fat buttermilk
 ¼  cup light mayonnaise
  2  tablespoons minced fresh parsley
  2  tablespoons fresh lime juice
  2  jalapeño peppers, seeded and diced
  2  garlic cloves, crushed
  4  (8-inch) fat-free flour tortillas
  3  cups chopped romaine lettuce
 1⅓  cups chopped seeded tomato

**1.** Combine first 4 ingredients in a heavy-duty, zip-top plastic bag. Add chicken; seal and shake to coat. Remove chicken from bag. Combine buttermilk and next 5 ingredients in a small bowl, and stir well with a whisk.

**2.** Place a large nonstick skillet over medium-high heat until hot. Add chicken, and sauté 2 minutes or until chicken is done. Add buttermilk mixture; cover and cook 1 minute. Remove from heat.

**3.** Warm tortillas according to package directions. Spoon about ¾ cup chicken mixture onto each tortilla, and top each serving with ¾ cup chopped lettuce and ⅓ cup chopped tomato. Roll up. Yield: 4 servings (serving size: 1 wrap).

CALORIES 362 (20% from fat); FAT 7.9g (sat 1.8g, mono 2.2g, poly 3.2g); PROTEIN 38.7g; CARB 32.9g; FIBER 2.9g; CHOL 87mg; IRON 3.4mg; SODIUM 724mg; CALC 84mg

### Cheddar-Succotash Wraps

  2  cups cubed baking potato (about ½ pound)
  2  cups frozen baby lima beans, thawed
 ¼  cup water
  1  teaspoon olive oil
Cooking spray
  2  cups fresh corn kernels (about 4 ears)
 ½  cup chopped green bell pepper
  3  garlic cloves, minced
 ½  cup 2% reduced-fat milk
 ½  teaspoon salt
 ½  cup (2 ounces) shredded sharp Cheddar cheese
 ½  cup (2 ounces) shredded Monterey Jack cheese with jalapeño peppers
  6  (8-inch) fat-free flour tortillas
 ¾  cup sliced green onions
 ¾  cup salsa

**1.** Combine first 3 ingredients in a bowl. Cover; microwave at HIGH 3 minutes or until tender. Stir after 1½ minutes. Drain.

**2.** Heat oil in a large nonstick skillet coated with cooking spray over medium-high heat. Add corn, bell pepper, and garlic; sauté 5 minutes or until tender. Stir in potato mixture, milk, and salt. Add cheeses, stirring until cheeses melt.

**3.** Warm tortillas according to package directions. Spoon corn mixture evenly down centers of tortillas; roll up. Serve wraps with onions and salsa. Serve immediately. Yield: 6 servings (serving size: 1 wrap, 2 tablespoons onions, and 2 tablespoons salsa).

CALORIES 376 (20% from fat); FAT 8.2g (sat 4.3g, mono 2.6g, poly 0.7g); PROTEIN 16.4g; CARB 61.7g; FIBER 5.6g; CHOL 19mg; IRON 4.2mg; SODIUM 897mg; CALC 213mg

# The Bamboo Bonus

*Put a bamboo steamer to work in your kitchen for some of the fastest and best dinners this side of Asia.*

Steaming, one of the oldest cooking techniques, requires no added fat, and foods already low in fat can be steamed to perfection without drying out.

Bamboo steamers—two or three 10- to 12-inch thatched, stackable trays, plus a lid to hold in the steam—are sold in Asian markets and in many mainstream cookware shops. Inexpensive, at about $10 for a steamer with two racks, they're also simple to use. Designed to keep stir-fried items safe from overexposure to heat, the bamboo latticework lets the steam in but also out so that no water drips back onto the food to dilute its flavors or turn it soggy.

## Steamed Vegetables with Cantonese Dipping Sauce

This easy all-vegetable side dish gets an intense flavor boost from the soy-sesame dipping sauce.

- 6 cups torn bok choy
- 1 cup broccoli florets
- 1 cup cauliflower florets
- ¼ cup Cantonese Dipping Sauce (recipe at right)

**1.** Arrange bok choy, broccoli, and cauliflower in a single layer on bamboo steamer racks. Add water to a wok to a depth of 1 inch; bring to a boil. Cover and place steamer in wok. Steam 5 minutes or until vegetables are crisp-tender.
**2.** Combine vegetables and ¼ cup Cantonese Dipping Sauce in a bowl, and toss gently to coat. Yield: 4 servings (serving size: 1½ cups).

CALORIES 73 (11% from fat); FAT 0.9g (sat 0.2g, mono 0.2g, poly 0.4g); PROTEIN 3.7g; CARB 14.5g; FIBER 2.4g; CHOL 0mg; IRON 1.5mg; SODIUM 726mg; CALC 130mg

## Steamed Dumplings with Spicy Turkey Filling

Dramatic good taste goes into the filling, but you'll also love our soy-sesame Cantonese Dipping Sauce (recipe at right). Or, for additional convenience, you can use your favorite commercial Asian sauce.

- 1 pound ground turkey
- ¼ cup minced celery
- ¼ cup minced red bell pepper
- ¼ cup low-sodium soy sauce
- 2 tablespoons minced green onions
- 1 tablespoon dry sherry
- 1 tablespoon cornstarch
- 1 teaspoon minced peeled fresh ginger
- ½ teaspoon dark sesame oil
- ¼ teaspoon Thai chile paste
- 2 garlic cloves, minced
- 35 won ton wrappers
- 2 teaspoons cornstarch
- 12 large napa (Chinese) cabbage leaves
- Cantonese Dipping Sauce (recipe at right)

**1.** Combine first 11 ingredients in a large bowl. Working with 1 won ton wrapper at a time (cover remaining wrappers with a damp towel to keep them from drying out), spoon about 1 tablespoon turkey mixture into center of each. Moisten edges of wrapper with water; bring 2 opposite corners together. Press edges together with a fork to seal, forming a triangle. Place dumplings on a large baking sheet sprinkled with 2 teaspoons cornstarch.
**2.** Line bottom of each rack of a bamboo steamer with half of cabbage leaves. Place dumplings ½ inch apart on steamer racks (about 6 or 7 per rack), and cover with steamer lid. Add water to a wok to a depth of 1 inch, and bring to a boil. Place steamer in wok, and steam 20 minutes. Carefully remove dumplings and cabbage from steamer. Repeat with remaining cabbage leaves and dumplings. Serve with Cantonese Dipping Sauce. Yield: 7 servings (serving size: 5 dumplings and 1 tablespoon sauce).

CALORIES 247 (25% from fat); FAT 6.9g (sat 2.2g, mono 2.6g, poly 2.2g); PROTEIN 15.8g; CARB 28.1g; FIBER 0.2g; CHOL 57mg; IRON 2.3mg; SODIUM 894mg; CALC 35mg

## Steamed Lemon Grass Shrimp

- 1½ pounds unpeeled medium shrimp
- 2 stalks lemon grass, split lengthwise
- 2 cups yellow bell pepper strips
- ½ cup (1-inch) diagonally sliced green onions
- 1 tablespoon chopped peeled fresh ginger
- 1 tablespoon chopped seeded serrano chile
- 6 cilantro sprigs
- 2 limes, sliced (about 10 slices)
- 4 lime wedges

**1.** Peel shrimp, leaving tails intact. Cut 2 pieces of parchment paper to fit into racks of a bamboo steamer. Top with lemon grass. Divide shrimp, bell pepper, and next 5 ingredients between racks; cover with steamer lid.
**2.** Add water to a wok to a depth of 1 inch, and bring to a boil. Place steamer in wok; steam 7 minutes or until shrimp are done. Remove shrimp mixture from steamer; discard parchment paper. Serve shrimp mixture with lime wedges. Yield: 4 servings (serving size: 5 ounces shrimp).

CALORIES 154 (15% from fat); FAT 2.5g (sat 0.5g, mono 0.3g, poly 1g); PROTEIN 26.6g; CARB 5.2g; FIBER 1.2g; CHOL 194mg; IRON 3.9mg; SODIUM 193mg; CALC 79mg

## Cantonese Dipping Sauce

- ⅓ cup low-sodium soy sauce
- ½ teaspoon dry sherry
- ½ teaspoon dark sesame oil
- 2 tablespoons sugar
- 1 tablespoon cornstarch
- 2 tablespoons water

**1.** Combine first 4 ingredients in a small saucepan; bring to a boil over medium heat. Dissolve cornstarch in water, and slowly add to soy mixture, stirring constantly. Bring to a boil; cook 1 minute or until sauce thickens. Yield: ½ cup (serving size: 1 tablespoon).

CALORIES 24 (11% from fat); FAT 0.3g (sat 0g, mono 0.1g, poly 0.1g); PROTEIN 0.5g; CARB 4.9g; FIBER 0g; CHOL 0mg; IRON 0.2mg; SODIUM 322mg; CALC 2mg

## Steamed Snapper with Tomatoes and Feta

3 cups chopped tomato
½ cup diced onion
¼ cup dry white wine
1 tablespoon dried oregano
1 tablespoon chopped fresh or
  1 teaspoon dried parsley
1 teaspoon fresh lemon juice
½ teaspoon freshly ground black
  pepper
¼ teaspoon salt
¼ teaspoon crushed red pepper
2 garlic cloves, minced
4 (6-ounce) red snapper or other
  firm white fish fillets
2 cups cooked couscous
½ cup (2 ounces) finely crumbled
  feta cheese

**1.** Combine first 10 ingredients in a medium bowl. Spoon 2 cups of tomato mixture into each of 2 rimmed salad dishes; arrange 2 fillets on top of tomato mixture in each dish, and set each dish in a bamboo steamer basket. Stack baskets, and cover with steamer lid. Add water to a wok to a depth of 1 inch, and bring to a boil.
**2.** Place steamer in wok; steam fillets 10 minutes or until fish flakes easily when tested with a fork. Serve fish and tomato mixture over couscous; sprinkle with cheese. Yield: 4 servings (serving size: 1 fillet, 1 cup tomato mixture, ½ cup couscous, and 2 tablespoons cheese).

CALORIES 356 (16% from fat); FAT 6.2g (sat 2.7g, mono 1.3g, poly 1.2g); PROTEIN 42.1g; CARB 30.4g; FIBER 3.2g; CHOL 76mg; IRON 2.3mg; SODIUM 431mg; CALC 160mg

## Steamed Chicken with Black Bean Salsa

Don't write this dish off as plain steamed chicken breast until you've tasted it with the crisp, cool salsa on top.

4 (4-ounce) skinned, boned chicken
  breast halves
2 garlic cloves, minced
1 cup thinly sliced onion
1 cup chopped tomato
2 tablespoons red wine vinegar
1 tablespoon fresh lime juice
1 tablespoon olive oil
1 teaspoon chopped fresh cilantro
½ teaspoon freshly ground black
  pepper
¼ teaspoon salt
1 (15-ounce) can black beans, rinsed
  and drained
1 jalapeño pepper, seeded and minced

**1.** Cut 2 pieces of parchment paper to fit into racks of a bamboo steamer. Rub chicken with garlic; arrange in steamer. Top chicken with onion, and cover with steamer lid. Add water to a wok to a depth of 1 inch, and bring to a boil. Place steamer basket in wok; steam chicken 20 minutes or until chicken is done. Cut chicken into slices.
**2.** While chicken cooks, combine tomato and remaining 8 ingredients in a large bowl. Divide onion evenly among 4 plates, and top with chicken. Serve with salsa. Yield: 4 servings (serving size: 1 chicken breast half and 1 cup salsa).

CALORIES 264 (19% from fat); FAT 5.5g (sat 1g, mono 2.9g, poly 0.9g); PROTEIN 32.7g; CARB 21.2g; FIBER 3.9g; CHOL 66mg; IRON 2.6mg; SODIUM 356mg; CALC 44mg

inspired vegetarian

# Four Easy Pizzas

*Forget the delivery guy: For the best pizza in town, roll your own dough and add your own toppings.*

Stop thinking of pizza as fast food. The point of making and eating a good pizza, or any other food worth passing over your tongue, isn't to get in and out of the kitchen in a hurry. It's to cook something really good and enjoy eating it—preferably with someone else.

## Whole-Wheat Pizza Dough

1 package dry yeast (about 2¼
  teaspoons)
¼ teaspoon sugar
1½ cups warm water (100° to 110°)
2½ to 2¾ cups all-purpose flour,
  divided
1 cup whole-wheat flour
1 tablespoon olive oil
1½ teaspoons salt
Cooking spray

**1.** Dissolve yeast and sugar in warm water in a large bowl; let stand 5 minutes. Lightly spoon flour into dry measuring cups; level with a knife. Add 2¼ cups all-purpose flour, whole-wheat flour, oil, and salt to yeast mixture, stirring until well-blended. Turn dough out onto a floured surface. Knead until smooth and elastic (about 10 minutes); add enough of remaining flour, 1 tablespoon at a time, to prevent dough from sticking to hands (dough will feel tacky).
**2.** Place dough in a large bowl coated with cooking spray, turning to coat top. Cover and let rise in a warm place (85°), free from drafts, 45 minutes or until doubled in size. (Press two fingers into dough. If indentation remains, dough has risen enough.) Punch dough down; cover and let rest 5 minutes. Divide dough in half; roll each half into a
*Continued*

---

### Steaming Tips—Wok Optional

Steaming promises perfect taste and texture, but you need to make sure you don't overcook anything. The water has to be boiling before you set the steamer racks over it.

You should set something—aluminum foil or a heatproof dish—in the bottom of the steamer rack to hold the food. This makes cleanup easier, and some foods give off juices in cooking

that make a fine sauce.

If you don't have a wok, you can use any kind of pot or pan that accommodates your steamer. You'll need one that keeps food out of the water but doesn't prevent steam from rising up through your food. Inexpensive metal rings that fit in the bottoms of larger pots to keep steamers above the water are sold in cookware shops.

12-inch circle on a floured surface. Top and bake according to recipe directions. Yield: 2 (12-inch) pizza crusts.

**NOTE:** This dough may be frozen. Follow directions for kneading dough, and shape dough into 2 balls. Coat balls with cooking spray, and place into a zip-top plastic freezer bag. Thaw overnight in refrigerator. Cover and let rise in a warm place (85°), free from drafts, 1½ hours or until doubled in size. (Press two fingers into dough. If indentation remains, dough has risen enough.) Shape as instructed.

(Totals are for 1 [12-inch] Pizza Crust) CALORIES 847 (11% from fat); FAT 9.9g (sat 1.4g, mono 5.4g, poly 1.9g); PROTEIN 25.7g; CARB 164.6g; FIBER 12.7g; CHOL 0mg; IRON 10.2mg; SODIUM 1,764mg; CALC 47mg

**PLAIN PIZZA DOUGH VARIATION:**

Whole-wheat flour may be omitted; replace it with 1 cup all-purpose flour.

(Totals are for 1 [12-inch] Pizza Crust) CALORIES 871 (10% from fat); FAT 9.4g (sat 1.3g, mono 5.3g, poly 1.7g); PROTEIN 23.9g; CARB 168.8g; FIBER 6.9g; CHOL 0mg; IRON 10.8mg; SODIUM 1,762mg; CALC 36mg

## Tomato Pizza with Capers, Basil, and Garlic

Use a mixture of tomatoes for this pizza—red plum, yellow, or any kind of heirloom tomato. The Plain Pizza Dough variation (recipe above), made with all-purpose flour, tastes best for a tomato pizza.

½ recipe Plain Pizza Dough (recipe above)
Cooking spray
1 tablespoon yellow cornmeal
½ cup (2 ounces) shredded part-skim mozzarella cheese
4 tomatoes, cut into ½-inch-thick slices (about 1 pound)
2 tablespoons capers
¼ cup chopped fresh basil
½ teaspoon black pepper
¼ teaspoon salt
2 garlic cloves, minced
1 teaspoon extra-virgin olive oil

**1.** Preheat oven to 500°.
**2.** Roll dough into a 12-inch circle on a lightly floured surface. Place dough on a 12-inch pizza pan or baking sheet coated with cooking spray and sprinkled with cornmeal. Crimp edges of dough with fingers to form a rim. Sprinkle cheese on crust. Arrange sliced tomato on cheese; sprinkle with capers.
**3.** Bake at 500° for 15 minutes or until crust is golden. Remove from oven; sprinkle with basil, pepper, salt, and garlic. Drizzle with oil. Cool slightly (tomatoes will be hot). Cut pizza into 4 wedges. Yield: 4 servings (serving size: 1 wedge).

CALORIES 303 (19% from fat); FAT 6.4g (sat 2g, mono 2.9g, poly 0.9g); PROTEIN 10.8g; CARB 50.8g; FIBER 3.4g; CHOL 8mg; IRON 3.6mg; SODIUM 775mg; CALC 115mg

## Mushroom Pizza with Thyme

¼ cup chopped fresh parsley
2 teaspoons chopped fresh or ½ teaspoon dried thyme
2 garlic cloves, minced
2 teaspoons olive oil
4 cups sliced cremini mushrooms (about 10 ounces)
3 tablespoons fresh lemon juice
½ teaspoon salt
¼ teaspoon black pepper
½ recipe Whole-Wheat Pizza Dough (recipe on page 151)
Cooking spray
1 tablespoon yellow cornmeal
¼ cup (1 ounce) grated fresh Parmesan cheese

**1.** Preheat oven to 500°.
**2.** Combine first 3 ingredients in a small bowl. Set aside.
**3.** Heat oil in a large nonstick skillet over medium-high heat. Add mushrooms and juice, and sauté 5 minutes. Stir in 2 tablespoons parsley mixture, salt, and pepper.
**4.** Roll dough into a 12-inch circle on a floured surface. Place dough on a 12-inch pizza pan or baking sheet coated with cooking spray and sprinkled with cornmeal. Crimp edges of dough with fingers to form a rim. Top with mushroom mixture.
**5.** Bake at 500° for 12 minutes or until browned. Remove from oven; top with 2 tablespoons parsley mixture and cheese. Cut pizza into 4 wedges. Yield: 4 servings (serving size: 1 wedge).

CALORIES 294 (22% from fat); FAT 7.1g (sat 1.9g, mono 3.6g, poly 1g); PROTEIN 10.9g; CARB 48.2g; FIBER 4.5g; CHOL 5mg; IRON 4mg; SODIUM 853mg; CALC 110mg

## Caramelized Onion Pizza with Gorgonzola and Arugula

2 teaspoons olive oil
12 cups thinly sliced onion (about 3 pounds)
2 teaspoons chopped fresh or ½ teaspoon dried rosemary, divided
½ teaspoon salt
¼ teaspoon black pepper
½ recipe Whole-Wheat Pizza Dough (recipe on page 151)
Cooking spray
1 tablespoon yellow cornmeal
½ cup (2 ounces) crumbled Gorgonzola, blue, or feta cheese
2 tablespoons coarsely chopped walnuts
1 cup trimmed arugula

**1.** Heat oil in a large cast-iron or non-stick skillet over medium-high heat. Add onion, and sauté 5 minutes, stirring frequently. Stir in 1 teaspoon rosemary, salt, and pepper. Cook 15 to 20 minutes or until onion is a deep golden brown, stirring frequently.
**2.** Preheat oven to 500°.
**3.** Roll dough into a 12-inch circle on a lightly floured surface. Place dough on a 12-inch pizza pan or baking sheet coated with cooking spray and sprinkled with cornmeal. Crimp edges of dough with fingers to form a rim. Top with onion. Bake at 500° for 10 minutes. Add cheese and walnuts; bake an additional 3 minutes or until cheese melts. Remove from oven; top with 1 teaspoon rosemary and arugula. Cut pizza into 4 wedges. Yield: 4 servings (serving size: 1 wedge).

CALORIES 449 (24% from fat); FAT 11.8g (sat 3.6g, mono 4.7g, poly 2.6g); PROTEIN 14.8g; CARB 73.8g; FIBER 10.1g; CHOL 11mg; IRON 3.7mg; SODIUM 944mg; CALC 172mg

## Pizza with Sautéed Radicchio

This pizza is for people who love the bitter, nutty taste of radicchio (rah-DEE-kee-oh), a red-leafed Italian chicory. The two cheeses, mozzarella and ricotta, help temper radicchio's natural edge.

    2   teaspoons olive oil
    3   cups thinly sliced Vidalia or other
        sweet onion (about 12 ounces)
    6   cups coarsely chopped radicchio
        (about 8 ounces) or escarole
    ½   teaspoon salt
    2   garlic cloves, minced
    1   tablespoon balsamic vinegar
    ¼   teaspoon black pepper
    ½   recipe Whole-Wheat Pizza Dough
        (recipe on page 151)
    Cooking spray
    1   tablespoon yellow cornmeal
    ½   cup (2 ounces) shredded
        part-skim mozzarella cheese
    ¼   cup part-skim ricotta cheese

**1.** Heat oil in a large cast-iron or non-stick skillet over medium-high heat. Add onion, and sauté 5 minutes, stirring frequently. Cook 10 to 15 minutes or until deep golden brown, stirring frequently. Add radicchio and salt; sauté 5 minutes or until wilted. Add garlic; cook 1 minute. Remove from heat; stir in vinegar. Sprinkle with black pepper.
**2.** Preheat oven to 500°.
**3.** Roll dough into a 12-inch circle on a lightly floured surface. Place pizza dough on a 12-inch pizza pan or baking sheet coated with cooking spray and sprinkled with cornmeal. Crimp edges of pizza dough with fingers to form a rim. Sprinkle mozzarella cheese on crust. Top with radicchio mixture. Drop ricotta by teaspoonfuls onto radicchio mixture.
**4.** Bake pizza at 500° for 15 minutes or until browned. Cut pizza into 4 wedges. Yield: 4 servings (serving size: 1 wedge).

CALORIES 347 (23% from fat); FAT 8.7g (sat 2.9g, mono 4.1g, poly 1g); PROTEIN 13.7g; CARB 54.6g; FIBER 5.5g; CHOL 13mg; IRON 3.4mg; SODIUM 835mg; CALC 177mg

# The Wisdom of Salmon

### New tactics have saved this prized fish from extinction—just in time to make health headlines and amazing new dishes.

Fresh salmon, formerly threatened by extinction, has come full circle back to its heyday as one of the nation's most plentiful fish. As the wild supply has diminished, salmon entrepreneurs have picked up the slack, converting coastal fjords in Norway, lochs in Scotland, and coves in Maine into sea farms.

## Indian-Spiced Roast Salmon

    1   teaspoon ground cumin
    1   teaspoon ground coriander
    ½   teaspoon ground turmeric
    ½   teaspoon dried thyme
    ½   teaspoon fennel seeds, crushed
    ½   teaspoon black pepper
    ¼   teaspoon ground cinnamon
    ⅛   teaspoon ground cloves
    4   (6-ounce) salmon fillets (about
        1¼-inches thick)
    ½   teaspoon salt
    1   teaspoon olive oil
    ¼   cup plain fat-free yogurt
    4   lemon wedges

**1.** Preheat oven to 400°.
**2.** Combine first 8 ingredients in a shallow dish. Sprinkle fillets with salt; dredge fillets in spice mixture. Heat oil in a large ovenproof skillet over medium-high heat. Add fillets, skin sides up; cook 5 minutes or until bottoms are golden. Turn fillets over. Wrap handle of skillet with foil; bake at 400° for 10 minutes or until fish flakes easily when tested with a fork. Remove skin from fillets; discard skin. Serve with yogurt and lemon wedges. Yield: 4 servings (serving size: 1 fillet, 1 tablespoon yogurt, and 1 lemon wedge).

CALORIES 301 (46% from fat); FAT 15.4g (sat 2.7g, mono 7.7g, poly 3.2g); PROTEIN 35.9g; CARB 2.6g; FIBER 0.3g; CHOL 111mg; IRON 1.6mg; SODIUM 390mg; CALC 54mg

## Broiled Salmon over Parmesan Grits

    ¾   cup fat-free, less-sodium chicken
        broth
    ½   teaspoon salt
    2   tablespoons minced fresh onion
    1   garlic clove, minced
    1½  cups water
    ½   cup regular grits
    1   teaspoon olive oil
    ⅔   cup sliced mushrooms
    2   tablespoons grated Parmigiano-
        Reggiano or fresh Parmesan
        cheese
    4   (6-ounce) salmon fillets
        (about 1 inch thick)
    ¼   teaspoon salt
    ¼   teaspoon dried thyme
    ¼   teaspoon black pepper
    Cooking spray
    2   teaspoons finely chopped fresh
        parsley

**1.** Combine first 4 ingredients in a small saucepan. Bring to a boil; reduce heat, and simmer 5 minutes or until onion is tender. Add water; bring to a boil. Gradually add grits, stirring with a whisk until blended. Cover, reduce heat, and simmer 10 minutes or until done.
**2.** Preheat broiler.
**3.** Heat oil in a small nonstick skillet over medium-high heat. Add mushrooms,
*Continued*

and sauté 5 minutes or until golden. Stir mushrooms and cheese into grits. Set aside.

**4.** Sprinkle fillets with ¼ teaspoon salt, thyme, and pepper; place fillets, skin sides down, on a broiler pan coated with cooking spray. Broil 10 minutes or until fish flakes easily when tested with a fork. Remove skin from fillets; discard skin. Spoon ½ cup grits on each of 4 plates; top each serving with a fillet. Sprinkle with parsley. Yield: 4 servings.

CALORIES 379 (39% from fat); FAT 16.4g (sat 3.2g, mono 7.9g, poly 3.3g); PROTEIN 38.8g; CARB 16.7g; FIBER 1.3g; CHOL 113mg; IRON 1.8mg; SODIUM 672mg; CALC 57mg

## Grilled-Salmon Salad

    ¾ cup chopped seeded peeled
       cucumber
    3 tablespoons plain low-fat
       yogurt
    2 tablespoons lemon juice
  1½ teaspoons chopped fresh parsley
  1½ teaspoons chopped fresh chives
  1¼ teaspoons grated lemon rind
    ¼ teaspoon black pepper
    1 garlic clove, sliced
    4 (6-ounce) salmon fillets (about
       1 inch thick)
    1 teaspoon black pepper
    ½ teaspoon salt
  Cooking spray
    4 cups gourmet salad greens (about
       4 ounces)
    ¾ cup basil leaves
    ½ cup cubed peeled ripe mango

**1.** Prepare grill.
**2.** Place first 8 ingredients in a blender or food processor; process until almost smooth.
**3.** Sprinkle fish with 1 teaspoon pepper and salt. Place fish, skin sides up, on a grill rack coated with cooking spray, and grill 5 minutes on each side or until fish flakes easily when tested with a fork. Remove skin from fillets; discard skin. Break fish into chunks.
**4.** Place greens and basil in a large bowl; add ¼ cup cucumber dressing, tossing well. Arrange salad on 4 plates. Divide salmon chunks evenly among salads; top

each serving with 2 tablespoons cucumber dressing and 2 tablespoons mango. Yield: 4 servings.

CALORIES 317 (41% from fat); FAT 14.6g (sat 2.6g, mono 6.9g, poly 3.3g); PROTEIN 37g; CARB 8.1g; FIBER 2g; CHOL 112mg; IRON 1.9mg; SODIUM 392mg; CALC 75mg

## Sesame-Crusted Salmon Sandwich

This updated version of a fish sandwich is full of peppery watercress sprigs and crispy sprouts. A drizzle of hoisin sauce, a sweet-and-spicy Asian condiment made with soybeans, garlic, and spices, adds a vibrant accent. You can find the sauce in the Asian section of your supermarket.

    2 tablespoons hoisin sauce
    4 teaspoons low-sodium soy sauce
    ½ teaspoon dark sesame oil
    4 (6-ounce) skinned tail-end salmon
       fillets (½ inch thick)
    4 teaspoons sesame seeds
    ¼ teaspoon salt
    ¼ teaspoon black pepper
  Cooking spray
    4 (3-ounce) submarine rolls, split
    2 cups trimmed watercress (about 1
       bunch)
    8 (¼-inch-thick) slices tomato
    1 cup alfalfa sprouts

**1.** Combine first 3 ingredients in a small bowl; set aside. Sprinkle fillets with sesame seeds, salt, and pepper, pressing mixture gently into fillets. Heat a large nonstick skillet coated with cooking spray over medium-high heat. Add fillets; sauté 4 minutes on each side or until fish flakes easily when tested with a fork.
**2.** Spread hoisin mixture evenly on top halves of rolls. Arrange ½ cup watercress and 2 tomato slices over bottom half of each roll; top each with a fillet and ¼ cup sprouts. Cover with tops of rolls. Yield: 4 servings (serving size: 1 sandwich).

CALORIES 565 (28% from fat); FAT 17.4g (sat 3g, mono 7.8g, poly 4.5g); PROTEIN 44.4g; CARB 54.2g; FIBER 3.6g; CHOL 112mg; IRON 3.4mg; SODIUM 998mg; CALC 80mg

**menu**

**Spicy Herb-Grilled Salmon Steaks**

Mandarin salad*

*Combine 6 cups sliced romaine lettuce; 1 (11-ounce) can mandarin oranges, drained; and 1 (8-ounce) can sliced water chestnuts, drained, in a large bowl. Combine ¼ cup rice vinegar and 1 teaspoon dark sesame oil in a small bowl; add to salad, tossing well. Serves 4.

## Spicy Herb-Grilled Salmon Steaks

Smoky-rich salmon is balanced by a sauce of fresh herbs, ginger, and jalapeño peppers in this grilled dish. To cut down on the amount of jalapeño pepper, substitute a milder chile (such as Anaheim).

    ½ cup basil leaves
    ⅓ cup mint leaves
    3 tablespoons minced seeded
       jalapeño pepper
    2 tablespoons white vinegar
  2½ teaspoons minced peeled fresh ginger
    1 teaspoon sugar
    2 teaspoons fish sauce
    2 garlic cloves, chopped
    4 (6-ounce) salmon steaks (about 1
       inch thick)
    ½ teaspoon salt
    ⅛ teaspoon black pepper
  Cooking spray
    ¼ cup finely chopped fresh basil
    4 lime wedges

**1.** Prepare grill.
**2.** Combine first 8 ingredients in a blender or food processor, and process until smooth. Set aside. Sprinkle salmon steaks with salt and black pepper. Place fish on a grill rack coated with cooking spray, and grill 5 minutes on each side or until fish flakes easily when tested with a fork. Spoon sauce over fish, and garnish with chopped basil and lime wedges. Yield: 4 servings (serving size: 1 steak and 2 tablespoons sauce).

CALORIES 293 (44% from fat); FAT 14.2g (sat 2.5g, mono 6.8g, poly 3.2g); PROTEIN 35.5g; CARB 3.7g; FIBER 0.3g; CHOL 111mg; IRON 0.9mg; SODIUM 596mg; CALC 27mg

## Roast Salmon with Tomatoes and Tarragon

(pictured on page 165)

These fillets are cooked skin side up to prevent them from drying out as they roast. Once they're cooked, the skin comes off easily, and the fillets can be flipped right side up.

- 4 (6-ounce) salmon fillets (about 1½ inches thick)
- ¼ teaspoon salt
- ¼ teaspoon black pepper
- 1½ cups chopped seeded peeled tomato (about 1 pound)
- 2 teaspoons low-sodium soy sauce
- 2½ teaspoons coarsely chopped fresh or ¾ teaspoon dried tarragon
- 2 teaspoons Dijon mustard
- Tarragon sprigs (optional)

**1.** Preheat oven to 425°.
**2.** Sprinkle salmon fillets with salt and pepper. Place fillets, skin sides up, in a large ovenproof skillet or small roasting pan. Spoon chopped tomato around fillets, and drizzle fillets with soy sauce. Wrap handle of skillet with foil, and bake fillets at 425° for 12 minutes or until fish flakes easily when tested with a fork. Remove skin from fillets, and discard skin. Remove fillets from pan, and keep warm. Add chopped tarragon and mustard to tomato, stirring well. Spoon tomato mixture over fillets. Garnish with tarragon sprigs, if desired. Yield: 4 servings (serving size: 1 fillet and 1½ tablespoons topping).

CALORIES 295 (44% from fat); FAT 14.4g (sat 2.5g, mono 6.9g, poly 3.2g); PROTEIN 35.5g; CARB 3.5g; FIBER 0.8g; CHOL 111mg; IRON 1.1mg; SODIUM 376mg; CALC 15mg

## Salmon with Dill-Citrus Sauce

Salmon fillets, because of their naturally high fat content, brown beautifully in a hot nonstick pan without added oil. Here, they're simmered in a tangy mixture of lemon, lime, and orange juices, and finished with a bracing hit of fresh dill.

- 4 (6-ounce) skinned salmon fillets (about 1½ inches thick)
- ½ teaspoon salt
- ¼ teaspoon black pepper
- ⅔ cup julienne-cut red bell pepper
- ½ cup thinly sliced shallots
- ½ cup fresh orange juice (about 2 oranges)
- 2 teaspoons fresh lime juice
- 2 teaspoons fresh lemon juice
- 2 teaspoons chopped fresh or ½ teaspoon dried dill
- 4 lemon wedges

**1.** Sprinkle fillets with salt and black pepper. Heat a large nonstick skillet over medium-high heat. Place fillets, flat sides up, in pan; cook 2 minutes on each side or until browned. Add bell pepper and shallots; reduce heat, and cook 2 minutes. Add juices; cover and simmer 8 minutes or until fish flakes easily when tested with a fork. Remove fish from pan; keep warm. Bring vegetable mixture to a boil; cook, uncovered, 3 minutes or until slightly thick. Place a fillet on each of 4 plates; top each serving with 3 tablespoons vegetable mixture. Sprinkle with dill; serve with lemon wedges. Yield: 4 servings.

CALORIES 312 (41% from fat); FAT 14.1g (sat 2.5g, mono 6.8g, poly 3.1g); PROTEIN 35.8g; CARB 8.7g; FIBER 0.6g; CHOL 111mg; IRON 1.3mg; SODIUM 381mg; CALC 24mg

## Oven-Poached Salmon with Vegetables

- ⅔ cup fat-free, less-sodium chicken broth
- ½ cup thinly sliced fennel bulb (about 1 small bulb)
- ¼ cup julienne-cut carrot
- 6 thyme sprigs
- 1 garlic clove, minced
- ⅔ cup dry white wine
- ½ cup diced green bell pepper
- ½ cup diced red bell pepper
- 4 (6-ounce) salmon fillets (about 1 inch thick)
- ½ teaspoon salt
- ¼ teaspoon freshly ground black pepper

**1.** Preheat oven to 325°.
**2.** Combine first 5 ingredients in a large ovenproof skillet; bring to a simmer over low heat. Cover and cook 5 minutes. Stir in wine and bell peppers. Cook 1 minute; remove from heat. Sprinkle fillets with salt and black pepper. Place fillets, skin sides up, over vegetable mixture in pan. Cover with lid; wrap handle with foil. Bake at 325° for 15 minutes or until fish flakes easily when tested with a fork. Discard skin and thyme sprigs. Arrange fillets and fennel mixture on each of 4 plates; drizzle with cooking liquid. Yield: 4 servings (serving size: 1 fillet, ⅓ cup fennel mixture, and 3 tablespoons cooking liquid).

CALORIES 298 (43% from fat); FAT 14.2g (sat 2.5g, mono 6.8g, poly 3.2g); PROTEIN 36.2g; CARB 4.3g; FIBER 0.9g; CHOL 111mg; IRON 1.7mg; SODIUM 466mg; CALC 30mg

## Wild or Farmed?

- If a salmon is filleted, it's difficult to distinguish wild from farmed. Some farmed salmon are fed carotene pigments to deepen their color, creating an orange hue. Wild-salmon flesh ranges from a light pink to a deep red.
- A whole Atlantic salmon (the farmed choice) has a sloping head and spots on its back resembling Xs. Wild king salmon has round spots on its skin, a somewhat squat head, and a black mouth. When sold whole, wild salmon is usually labeled as such.
- Wild salmon has a greater range of flavors, from rich, distinctive king salmon to delicately flavored pink. Farmed salmon's flavors vary depending on the feed mixture each farm uses, but the end result is usually a midrange mild taste.
- Farmed salmon dominates today's markets, but you can still find wild salmon if you're willing to pay more for it. Much of the wild catch ends up on the West Coast, where many favor it for philosophical as well as culinary reasons. The peak season for wild salmon is April to October; farmed salmon, which is harvested upon demand, is available fresh year-round.

cooking class

# How to Master a Grill

*Get hot. Get primal. Put the fire to great burgers, chicken, pork chops, and fajitas.*

Grilling is simplicity in action: cooking your food—from meats to veggies—directly over hot coals (or a gas flame) for a short time. There's also an indirect form of grilling that takes a little longer. Both are different from barbecuing, which involves cooking for a long time over low heat.

Grilling puts the emphasis on planning, and then on close attention during the rapid cooking. That's why it's important to choose high-quality ingredients.

As for equipment, anything from a converted 55-gallon drum to a discount-store special will work fine. Beyond that, you need only the most basic of gear: flame-proof mitts, an instant-read thermometer, and sturdy tongs.

We'd be remiss if we didn't point out that because much of the fat sizzles right off the meat or seafood, grilling is one of the most healthful techniques around.

### Teriyaki Burgers

- 1 pound ground round
- ¼ cup low-sodium soy sauce
- ¼ cup chopped green onions
- 1 teaspoon grated peeled fresh ginger
- ¼ teaspoon black pepper
- 1 garlic clove, minced

**1.** Combine all ingredients in a bowl. Divide beef mixture into 4 equal portions, shaping each into a ½-inch-thick patty.
**2.** Prepare grill.
**3.** Place patties on grill rack; grill 4 minutes on each side or until desired degree of doneness. Yield: 4 servings (serving size: 1 burger).

CALORIES 175 (35% from fat); FAT 6.9g (sat 2.5g, mono 2.9g, poly 0.3g); PROTEIN 24.4g; CARB 0.9g; FIBER 0.2g; CHOL 70mg; IRON 2.4mg; SODIUM 445mg; CALC 11mg

## Grilling Tips

Grill **vegetables** for 10 minutes, and then cut them accordingly. To make sure your vegetables are smoky-tasting, place them directly on the grill, as opposed to using a grill basket.

For slow-grilled **turkey,** use wood chips to impart a subtle flavor. Any kind of chips can be used. Sprinkle them on the hot coals just before placing the turkey on the grill. Place the drip pan on the side of the grill where the heat has been turned off. Place the turkey on the rack over the drip pan.

Thread **shrimp** on metal or bamboo skewers to save time when turning them on the grill. Instead of flipping one at a time, just flip an entire skewerful. If using bamboo skewers, be sure to soak them in water for 30 minutes so they don't burn.

Place flattened **chicken** on the grill, and turn halfway through cooking. If you don't want to use a whole bird, use chicken pieces, and grill for a shorter amount of time.

Grill **salmon,** skin side down, without turning, for about 10 minutes per inch of thickness. To remove from the grill, slide a spatula between the salmon and the skin. The salmon will lift right off, leaving the skin behind.

## Grilled Italian Vegetables with Pasta

These smoky vegetables are also great as an appetizer with goat cheese and baguette slices. Salting the eggplant pulls out some of the bitter flavor, but you can skip that step if you prefer. To create tasty variations on this pasta, add different greens or fresh herbs, such as arugula or mint, along with another cheese such as Romano or feta.

     1   (1¼-pound) eggplant, cut into
         ½-inch-thick slices
     1   teaspoon salt, divided
     ¾   pound zucchini, quartered
         lengthwise and cut into
         1-inch-thick slices
     1   red bell pepper, seeded and
         quartered
         Cooking spray
     4   plum tomatoes, halved
     4   cups (3-inch) sliced green onions
         (about 2 bunches)
     2   tablespoons extra-virgin olive oil
     1   tablespoon grated lemon rind
     ½   cup thinly sliced fresh basil
     6   cups hot cooked penne (about 12
         ounces uncooked tube-shaped
         pasta)
     ¼   cup (1 ounce) grated fresh
         Parmesan cheese

**1.** Place eggplant in a colander; sprinkle with ¾ teaspoon salt. Toss gently to coat. Cover and let stand 30 minutes. Rinse eggplant with cold water, and drain well.
**2.** Prepare grill.
**3.** Place eggplant, zucchini, and bell pepper on grill rack coated with cooking spray. Grill 10 minutes, turning once. Add tomatoes and onions; cook 5 minutes, turning often. Remove vegetables from grill; cut all except tomato into 1-inch pieces. Cut tomato halves in half lengthwise.
**4.** Combine ¼ teaspoon salt, oil, rind, and basil in a large bowl. Add vegetable mixture, pasta, and cheese; toss well. Yield: 6 servings (serving size: 2 cups).

CALORIES 333 (20% from fat); FAT 7.3g (sat 1.6g, mono 3.9g, poly 1.1g); PROTEIN 12.2g; CARB 57g; FIBER 6.1g; CHOL 3mg; IRON 4.2mg; SODIUM 295mg; CALC 138mg

## Indonesian Shrimp Saté with Creamy Peanut Sauce

If you can't get jumbo shrimp, get the largest ones possible as they're best for grilling. Thread the shrimp and peppers on two parallel skewers to make them easier to turn. Butterflying the shrimp makes them more attractive. Cut to, but not all the way through, the back sides of the shrimp.

**MARINADE:**
     3   tablespoons water
     2   tablespoons low-sodium soy sauce
     1   tablespoon minced peeled fresh
         ginger
     1   serrano chile, seeded and minced
     1   garlic clove, minced
     1½  pounds jumbo shrimp, peeled and
         deveined
     1   red bell pepper, cut into 1½-inch
         pieces

**SAUCE:**
     ⅓   cup light coconut milk
     3   tablespoons reduced-fat peanut
         butter
     1   tablespoon fresh lime juice
     2   teaspoons sugar
     ¼   cup chopped fresh cilantro
         Cooking spray
     4   lime wedges

**1.** To prepare marinade, combine first 7 ingredients in a zip-top plastic bag; seal and marinate in refrigerator 1 hour, turning bag occasionally. Remove shrimp and bell pepper from bag; discard marinade.
**2.** To prepare sauce, combine coconut milk, peanut butter, lime juice, and sugar in a blender, and process until smooth. Stir in cilantro; set aside.
**3.** Prepare grill.
**4.** Thread shrimp and bell pepper onto each of 4 (12-inch) skewers. Place kebabs on grill rack coated with cooking spray; grill 8 minutes or until done, turning once. Remove from heat; drizzle each serving with 1 tablespoon peanut sauce. Serve with remaining peanut sauce and lime wedges. Yield: 4 servings.

CALORIES 234 (30% from fat); FAT 7.9g (sat 2g, mono 2.7g, poly 2.4g); PROTEIN 29.1g; CARB 10.8g; FIBER 1g; CHOL 194mg; IRON 3.7mg; SODIUM 390mg; CALC 73mg

## Beef-and-Chicken Fajitas with Peppers and Onions

(pictured on page 166)

The meat and vegetables for these colorful wraps are marinated in a zesty mixture of lime, garlic, and other seasonings.

**MARINADE:**
     ¼   cup olive oil
     1   teaspoon grated lime rind
     2½  tablespoons fresh lime juice
     2   tablespoons Worcestershire
         sauce
     1½  teaspoons ground cumin
     1   teaspoon salt
     ½   teaspoon dried oregano
     ½   teaspoon coarsely ground black
         pepper
     2   garlic cloves, minced
     1   (14.25-ounce) can low-salt beef
         broth

**FAJITAS:**
     1   (1-pound) flank steak
     1   pound skinned, boned chicken
         breast
     2   red bell peppers, each cut into
         12 wedges
     2   green bell peppers, each cut into
         12 wedges
     1   large Vidalia or other sweet onion,
         cut into 16 wedges
         Cooking spray
    16   (6-inch) fat-free flour tortillas
     1   cup bottled salsa
     ¼   cup low-fat sour cream
     ½   cup chopped fresh cilantro
         Fresh cilantro sprigs (optional)

**1.** To prepare marinade, combine first 10 ingredients in a large bowl; set aside.
**2.** To prepare fajitas, trim fat from steak. Score a diamond pattern on both sides of steak. Combine 1½ cups marinade, steak, and chicken in a large zip-top plastic bag. Seal and marinate in refrigerator 4 hours or overnight, turning occasionally. Combine remaining marinade, bell peppers, and onion in a zip-top plastic bag. Seal and marinate in refrigerator 4 hours or overnight, turning occasionally.
**3.** Prepare grill.

*Continued*

**4.** Remove steak and chicken from bag; discard marinade. Remove vegetables from bag; reserve marinade. Place reserved marinade in a small saucepan; set aside. Place steak, chicken, and vegetables on grill rack coated with cooking spray; cook 8 minutes on each side or until desired degree of doneness.

**5.** Wrap tortillas tightly in foil; place tortilla packet on grill rack last 2 minutes of grilling time. Bring reserved marinade to a boil. Cut steak and chicken diagonally across grain into thin slices. Place steak, chicken, and vegetables on a serving platter; drizzle with reserved marinade.

**6.** Arrange about 1 ounce steak, about 1 ounce chicken, 3 bell pepper wedges, and 1 onion wedge in each tortilla; top with 1 tablespoon salsa, about 1 teaspoon sour cream, and ½ tablespoon chopped cilantro. Fold sides of tortillas over filling. Garnish with cilantro sprigs, if desired. Serve immediately. Yield: 8 servings (serving size: 2 fajitas).

CALORIES 407 (31% from fat); FAT 14.2g (sat 4.3g, mono 7.1g, poly 1.4g); PROTEIN 31.1g; CARB 40.6g; FIBER 5.3g; CHOL 64mg; IRON 3.9mg; SODIUM 841mg; CALC 79mg

## Texas Dry-Rub Slow-Grilled Turkey Breast

Any kind of wood chips will work here. Serve this moist turkey breast with sweet potato wedges: Cut potatoes into 6 wedges; toss with oil, salt, and pepper, and bake at 400° for 35 minutes or until done.

    1   cup hickory wood chips
    1   tablespoon Hungarian sweet
        paprika or paprika
    1   tablespoon brown sugar
    1   teaspoon salt
    ¾   teaspoon garlic powder
    ¾   teaspoon onion powder
    ¾   teaspoon black pepper
    ½   teaspoon ground red pepper
    ¼   teaspoon ground cloves
    1   (2-pound) skinned, boned turkey
        breast half
    Cooking spray

**1.** Soak wood chips in water 1 hour. Drain well.

**2.** Combine paprika and next 7 ingredients; rub turkey with spice mixture.

**3.** To prepare turkey for indirect grilling, preheat grill to medium-hot using both burners. After preheating, turn left burner off (leave right burner on). Place wood chips on hot coals. Place a disposable foil pan on briquettes on left side. Pour 2 cups water in pan. Coat grill rack with cooking spray, and place on grill. Place turkey on grill rack covering left burner. Cover and grill 1 hour and 50 minutes or until a meat thermometer registers 180°, turning halfway through cooking time. Yield: 8 servings (serving size: 3 ounces turkey).

CALORIES 139 (19% from fat); FAT 2.9g (sat 0.9g, mono 0.5g, poly 0.9g); PROTEIN 24.8g; CARB 1.8g; FIBER 0.3g; CHOL 57mg; IRON 1.4mg; SODIUM 347mg; CALC 21mg

## Honey Mustard-Glazed Salmon with Sweet-and-Sour Relish

Don't forget to keep the skin on the salmon fillets while they grill. It holds the fish together, making the fillets easier to remove from the grill; it also protects them from the heat, ensuring that they don't overcook.

**RELISH:**
    1   tablespoon white wine vinegar
    1   tablespoon water
    2   teaspoons sugar
    ¼   teaspoon salt
    ½   cup chopped red onion
    1   tablespoon minced fresh parsley
    ½   cup chopped yellow squash

**SALMON:**
    6   (6-ounce) salmon fillets, skin on
        (1 inch thick)
    ¼   teaspoon salt
    Cooking spray
    2   tablespoons Dijon mustard
    2   tablespoons honey

**1.** To prepare relish, combine first 4 ingredients in a medium glass bowl. Microwave at HIGH 30 seconds or until sugar dissolves. Cool. Stir in onion, parsley, and squash. Cover and refrigerate 1 to 4 hours.

**2.** Prepare grill.

**3.** To prepare salmon, sprinkle fillets with ¼ teaspoon salt. Place fillets, skin sides down, on grill rack coated with cooking spray; cover and cook 9 minutes. Combine mustard and honey in a small bowl; brush over fillets. Cover and cook 2 minutes or until fish flakes easily when tested with a fork. Serve with relish. Yield: 6 servings (serving size: 1 fillet and ⅓ cup relish).

CALORIES 323 (40% from fat); FAT 14.5g (sat 2.5g, mono 7g, poly 3.2g); PROTEIN 35.5g; CARB 10.4g; FIBER 0.9g; CHOL 111mg; IRON 1mg; SODIUM 430mg; CALC 21mg

## Grilled Split Chicken with Rosemary and Garlic

In this recipe, the chicken is first split and then flattened (butterflied), a technique that allows for quicker and more uniform cooking. This is easier than you might think—use a sharp chef's knife or kitchen shears to cut along the backbone, and then lay out flat. The chicken needs to marinate for 24 hours, so be sure to start a day ahead.

    1   (3½-pound) chicken
    ½   cup low-fat buttermilk
    1   tablespoon chopped fresh rosemary
    ½   teaspoon salt
    ½   teaspoon hot pepper sauce
    2   garlic cloves, minced
    Cooking spray

**1.** Remove and discard giblets and neck from chicken. Rinse chicken with cold water; pat dry. Trim excess fat. Place chicken, breast side down, on a cutting surface. Cut chicken in half lengthwise along backbone, cutting to, but not through, other side. Turn chicken over. Starting at neck cavity, loosen skin from breast and drumsticks by inserting fingers, gently pushing between skin and meat. Place chicken, breast side up, in a large shallow dish. Combine buttermilk and remaining ingredients except cooking spray; pour under skin and over surface of chicken. Cut a 1-inch slit in skin at bottom of each breast half. Insert tip of a drumstick into each slit. Cover and marinate in refrigerator 24 hours.

**2.** To prepare for indirect grilling, pre-heat grill to medium-hot using both burners. After preheating, turn left burner off (leave right burner on). Place a disposable foil pan on briquettes on left side. Pour 2 cups water in pan. Coat grill rack with cooking spray; place on grill. Place chicken, skin side down, on grill rack covering left burner. Cover and grill 1½ hours or until a meat thermometer registers 180°, turning halfway through cooking time. Discard skin before serving. Yield: 5 servings (serving size: 3 ounces).

CALORIES 196 (35% from fat); FAT 7.6g (sat 2.1g, mono 2.7g, poly 1.8g); PROTEIN 29g; CARB 0.9g; FIBER 0.1g; CHOL 88mg; IRON 1.3mg; SODIUM 210mg; CALC 32mg

## Herb-and-Citrus Turkey Burgers

1 pound ground turkey
2 tablespoons minced fresh basil
1 tablespoon minced fresh sage
1 tablespoon thawed orange juice concentrate, undiluted
1 teaspoon grated orange rind
½ teaspoon salt
¼ teaspoon black pepper

**1.** Combine all ingredients in a bowl. Divide turkey mixture into 4 equal portions, shaping each into a ½-inch-thick patty.
**2.** Prepare grill.
**3.** Place patties on grill rack; grill 7 minutes on each side or until done. Yield: 4 servings (serving size: 1 burger).

CALORIES 188 (48% from fat); FAT 10.1g (sat 3.5g, mono 3.9g, poly 3g); PROTEIN 20.2g; CARB 2.1g; FIBER 0.2g; CHOL 95mg; IRON 1.2mg; SODIUM 383mg; CALC 28mg

### Quick Grilling How-tos

• Marinate food in the refrigerator.
• Before you place the rack on the grill, coat it with cooking spray so the food has less chance of sticking.
• Use medium fire for seafood, more intense fire for meats.
• Always place grilled foods on a clean platter or cutting board.

## Chipotle-Marinated Pork Chops with Chimichurri Sauce

Chimichurri—an Argentine condiment—is a thick herb sauce packed with flavor. Roasted potatoes are the perfect accompaniment. You can also prepare this recipe with a pork tenderloin or pork loin. If you don't have time to marinate your pork chops, just skip that step and serve them with the Chimichurri Sauce.

**PORK CHOPS:**

¾ cup fat-free, low-sodium chicken broth
1 drained canned chipotle chile in adobo sauce
4 (6-ounce) center-cut pork chops (about ¾ inch thick)

**CHIMICHURRI SAUCE:**

1 cup fresh flat-leaf parsley leaves
¼ cup fat-free, low-sodium chicken broth
2 tablespoons extra-virgin olive oil
2 tablespoons white wine vinegar
½ teaspoon dried oregano
¼ teaspoon salt
⅛ teaspoon freshly ground black pepper
2 garlic cloves
½ cup shredded carrot
½ cup minced fresh onion
Cooking spray

**1.** To prepare pork chops, combine ¾ cup chicken broth and chipotle chile in a blender; process until smooth.

Combine chile mixture and pork chops in a large zip-top plastic bag. Seal and marinate in refrigerator 2 hours. Remove chops from bag; discard marinade.
**2.** To prepare Chimichurri Sauce, combine parsley and next 7 ingredients in a blender; process until smooth. Pour into a bowl; stir in carrot and onion. Set aside.
**3.** Prepare grill.
**4.** Place chops on grill rack coated with cooking spray; cook 5 minutes on each side or until done. Serve with Chimichurri Sauce. Yield: 4 servings (serving size: 1 pork chop and ¼ cup sauce).

(Totals include Chimichurri Sauce) CALORIES 311 (56% from fat); FAT 19.2g (sat 5.1g, mono 10.5g, poly 2.2g); PROTEIN 27.6g; CARB 5.4g; FIBER 1.6g; CHOL 84mg; IRON 2.2mg; SODIUM 321mg; CALC 42mg

## Hot-and-Spicy Asian-Rubbed Chicken

For a main-dish salad, you can slice the chicken into thin strips and pile on top of greens; then toss with low-fat dressing.

2 teaspoons five-spice powder
1 teaspoon sugar
½ teaspoon salt
½ teaspoon garlic powder
¼ teaspoon ground red pepper
4 (4-ounce) skinned, boned chicken breast halves
Cooking spray

**1.** Prepare grill.
**2.** Combine first 5 ingredients in a large bowl. Rub chicken with spice mixture. Place chicken on grill rack coated with cooking spray; grill 5 minutes on each side or until done. Yield: 4 servings (serving size: 1 chicken breast half).

CALORIES 133 (11% from fat); FAT 1.6g (sat 0.4g, mono 0.4g, poly 0.4g); PROTEIN 26.3g; CARB 1.5g; FIBER 0.1g; CHOL 66mg; IRON 1mg; SODIUM 367mg; CALC 17mg

# Falling for Couscous

## If you were slow to the charms of this popular North African staple, now you'll be in love for life.

Has couscous' newfound celebrity caused you to take another look at this ancient yet thoroughly modern culinary chameleon? It's still a favorite at Middle Eastern restaurants, of course, where it's commonly flavored with saffron. Naturally low in fat, it's also making the scene these days at some of America's trendiest restaurants. The discovery isn't limited to restaurateurs. Use among home cooks is skyrocketing. Sales of couscous have more than doubled in the last five years.

### Picnic Couscous Salad

This piquant, lemony salad also makes a light lunch by itself.

1¼ cups fat-free, less-sodium chicken broth or water
1 cup uncooked couscous
1 teaspoon grated lemon rind
2 tablespoons fresh lemon juice
1 tablespoon olive oil
¾ teaspoon Dijon mustard
1 cup quartered cherry tomatoes
½ cup chopped pimento-stuffed olives
¼ cup chopped red onion
¼ cup chopped fresh parsley
¼ teaspoon salt
¼ teaspoon freshly ground black pepper
1 (15.8-ounce) can Great Northern beans, rinsed and drained

1. Bring broth to a boil in a medium saucepan; gradually stir in couscous. Remove from heat; cover and let stand 5 minutes. Fluff with a fork; cool.
2. Combine lemon rind, juice, oil, and mustard in a large bowl; stir well with a whisk. Add couscous, tomatoes, and remaining ingredients; toss well. Yield: 5 servings (serving size: 1 cup).

CALORIES 236 (19% from fat); FAT 4.9g (sat 0.7g, mono 2.8g, poly 0.5g); PROTEIN 10.4g; CARB 40.7g; FIBER 5.4g; CHOL 1mg; IRON 4.1mg; SODIUM 449mg; CALC 85mg

### Couscous-and-Cucumber Salad with Buttermilk-Dill Dressing

Try this salad with barbecued chicken or grilled salmon.

1¼ cups water
1 cup uncooked couscous
½ cup low-fat buttermilk
¼ cup plain low-fat yogurt
2 tablespoons chopped fresh dill
2 tablespoons white vinegar
1 tablespoon olive oil
½ teaspoon salt
¼ teaspoon black pepper
1 cup chopped red bell pepper
¼ cup thinly sliced green onions
2 cucumbers, peeled, quartered lengthwise, and sliced (about ¾ pound)

1. Bring water to a boil in a medium saucepan; gradually stir in couscous. Remove from heat; cover and let stand 5 minutes. Fluff with a fork; cool.
2. Combine buttermilk and next 6 ingredients in a large bowl; stir well with a whisk. Add couscous, bell pepper, onions, and cucumbers; toss gently. Yield: 6 servings (serving size: 1 cup).

CALORIES 140 (21% from fat); FAT 3.2g (sat 0.7g, mono 1.8g, poly 0.3g); PROTEIN 5.2g; CARB 24g; FIBER 1.8g; CHOL 1mg; IRON 1.3mg; SODIUM 221mg; CALC 67mg

### Niçoise-Style Couscous Salad

Our version uses components of the classic salade niçoise—tuna, olives, and green beans.

1¼ cups water
1 cup uncooked couscous
1½ cups (2-inch) sliced green beans
¼ teaspoon salt, divided
1 (8-ounce) tuna steak (1 inch thick)
Cooking spray
3 tablespoons fresh lemon juice
1 tablespoon extra-virgin olive oil
1½ teaspoons anchovy paste
¼ teaspoon black pepper
2 garlic cloves, crushed
1 cup chopped tomato
⅓ cup coarsely chopped pitted kalamata olives
¼ cup chopped red onion
¼ cup chopped fresh parsley
1 hard-cooked large egg, cut into 4 wedges

1. Bring water to a boil in a medium saucepan; gradually stir in couscous. Remove from heat; cover and let stand 5 minutes. Fluff with a fork; cool.
2. Steam beans, covered, 7 minutes.
3. Sprinkle ⅛ teaspoon salt over tuna. Heat a medium nonstick skillet coated with cooking spray over medium-high heat until hot. Add tuna; cook 3 minutes on each side or until medium-rare or desired degree of doneness. Break tuna into chunks.
4. Combine ⅛ teaspoon salt, lemon juice, oil, anchovy paste, pepper, and garlic in a large bowl; stir well with a whisk. Add couscous, beans, tuna, tomato, olives, onion, and parsley; toss gently. Top each serving with an egg wedge. Yield: 4 servings (serving size: 1½ cups).

CALORIES 310 (28% from fat); FAT 9.7g (sat 1.8g, mono 4.7g, poly 1.7g); PROTEIN 21.6g; CARB 35.4g; FIBER 3.6g; CHOL 75mg; IRON 2.8mg; SODIUM 552mg; CALC 46mg

## Sesame Shrimp-and-Couscous Salad

3¼ cups water, divided
½ pound medium shrimp, peeled and deveined
1 cup uncooked couscous
¼ cup seasoned rice vinegar
2 teaspoons vegetable oil
1½ teaspoons low-sodium soy sauce
½ teaspoon dark sesame oil
1 garlic clove, crushed
1½ cups thinly sliced romaine lettuce
1 cup chopped red bell pepper
¾ cup frozen green peas, thawed
¼ cup chopped fresh cilantro
2 tablespoons finely chopped unsalted, dry-roasted peanuts

**1.** Bring 2 cups water to a boil in a medium saucepan. Add shrimp; cook 3 minutes or until done. Drain and rinse with cold water; cut shrimp in half. Bring 1¼ cups water to a boil in saucepan; gradually stir in couscous. Remove from heat; cover and let stand 5 minutes. Fluff with a fork; cool.
**2.** Combine vinegar, vegetable oil, soy sauce, sesame oil, and garlic in a large bowl; stir well with a whisk. Add shrimp, couscous, lettuce, bell pepper, peas, and cilantro; toss well. Sprinkle with peanuts. Yield: 4 servings (serving size: 1½ cups).

CALORIES 276 (21% from fat); FAT 6.5g (sat 1g, mono 2.1g, poly 2.5g); PROTEIN 16.8g; CARB 35.6g; FIBER 4.1g; CHOL 65mg; IRON 3.2mg; SODIUM 164mg; CALC 49mg

## Fresh Mozzarella, Tomato, and Basil Couscous Salad

2 cups diced tomato
¾ cup (3 ounces) diced fresh mozzarella cheese
3 tablespoons minced shallots
2 teaspoons extra-virgin olive oil
½ teaspoon salt
½ teaspoon black pepper
1 garlic clove, crushed
1¼ cups water
1 cup uncooked couscous
¼ cup chopped fresh basil
Basil leaves (optional)

**1.** Combine first 7 ingredients in a large bowl; cover and marinate in refrigerator 30 minutes.
**2.** Bring water to a boil in a medium saucepan; gradually stir in couscous. Remove from heat; cover and let stand 5 minutes. Fluff with a fork; cool. Add couscous and chopped basil to tomato mixture; toss gently. Garnish with basil leaves, if desired. Yield: 5 servings (serving size: 1 cup).

CALORIES 186 (29% from fat); FAT 6g (sat 2.5g, mono 2.5g, poly 0.4g); PROTEIN 7.9g; CARB 26.5g; FIBER 2.1g; CHOL 13mg; IRON 1.1mg; SODIUM 308mg; CALC 99mg

## Chicken-Avocado Couscous Salad with Tomatillo Dressing

Tomatillos look like small green tomatoes but taste tart and tangy. Remove the papery husks, and wash the tomatillos well before using. Serve this as a main dish with flour tortillas and a green salad.

1¼ cups water
1 cup uncooked couscous
5 medium tomatillos, quartered (about 6 ounces)
3 tablespoons fresh lime juice
1 tablespoon olive oil
1 teaspoon sugar
1½ cups cubed ready-to-eat roasted skinned, boned chicken breasts (about 2 breasts)
1 cup chopped peeled avocado
¾ cup fresh corn kernels (about 1 ear)
¾ cup rinsed drained canned black beans
¼ cup chopped fresh cilantro
2 tablespoons thinly sliced green onions
1 tablespoon finely chopped seeded jalapeño pepper
½ teaspoon salt
¼ teaspoon ground cumin
Cilantro sprigs (optional)

**1.** Bring water to a boil in a medium saucepan; gradually stir in couscous. Remove from heat; cover and let stand 5 minutes. Fluff with a fork; cool.
**2.** Place tomatillos in a food processor; process until chopped. Add juice, oil, and sugar; process until smooth.
**3.** Combine couscous, tomatillo dressing, chicken, and remaining ingredients except cilantro sprigs in a large bowl; toss gently. Garnish with cilantro sprigs, if desired. Yield: 5 servings (serving size: 1½ cups).

CALORIES 299 (28% from fat); FAT 9.4g (sat 1.6g, mono 5.4g, poly 1.2g); PROTEIN 18.3g; CARB 38.2g; FIBER 3.8g; CHOL 28mg; IRON 1.9mg; SODIUM 549mg; CALC 30mg

## Nectarine-and-Chickpea Couscous Salad with Honey-Cumin Dressing

Try this as a light summer lunch or as a side dish for pork or ham.

1¼ cups water
1 cup uncooked couscous
2 tablespoons fresh lime juice
1 tablespoon olive oil
1 tablespoon honey
½ teaspoon salt
½ teaspoon ground cumin
½ teaspoon ground coriander
1½ cups coarsely chopped nectarines (about 3 medium)
½ cup coarsely chopped spinach
¼ cup thinly sliced green onions
1 (15½-ounce) can chickpeas (garbanzo beans), drained
Nectarine slices (optional)

**1.** Bring water to a boil in a medium saucepan; gradually stir in couscous. Remove from heat; cover and let stand 5 minutes. Fluff with a fork; cool.
**2.** Combine lime juice and next 5 ingredients in a large bowl; stir well with a whisk. Add couscous, chopped nectarines, spinach, onions, and chickpeas; toss well. Garnish with nectarine slices, if desired. Yield: 6 servings (serving size: 1 cup).

CALORIES 213 (16% from fat); FAT 3.9g (sat 0.5g, mono 2g, poly 0.8g); PROTEIN 7.8g; CARB 38.8g; FIBER 3.6g; CHOL 0mg; IRON 2.2mg; SODIUM 297mg; CALC 36mg

# Odd Couples

*Sometimes matching unlikely flavors creates surprisingly perfect unions.*

Often the best collaborations result from what may seem the most unlikely of matches. Oddball flavor combinations can rev up old standbys such as chocolate cake; "weird" alliances can generate a brand new union. All you have to do is open your mind—or at least your refrigerator and pantry.

## Peppercorn Ice Cream with Rum-Glazed Pineapple

2   cups 1% low-fat milk, divided
1   teaspoon black peppercorns, coarsely crushed
2   large egg yolks
2   tablespoons granulated sugar
1   tablespoon vanilla extract
¼   teaspoon grated lime rind
1   tablespoon fresh lime juice
1   (14-ounce) can fat-free sweetened condensed milk
¼   cup packed brown sugar
¼   cup dark rum
7   (½-inch-thick) slices pineapple
Cooking spray
Lime slices (optional)

**1.** Combine 1¼ cups low-fat milk and peppercorns in a medium heavy saucepan; bring to a simmer. Remove from heat. Let stand, covered, 10 minutes. Strain milk through a cheesecloth-lined sieve into a bowl; discard solids.
**2.** Place egg yolks in a bowl. Gradually add hot milk to egg yolks, stirring constantly with a whisk. Return milk mixture to pan. Add granulated sugar; cook over medium heat until milk mixture coats a metal spoon (about 3 minutes), stirring constantly. Combine ¾ cup low-fat milk, vanilla, lime rind, lime juice, and condensed milk in a medium bowl. Gradually add custard, stirring with a whisk. Cover and chill completely.

**3.** Pour mixture into freezer can of an ice-cream freezer; freeze according to manufacturer's instructions. Spoon ice cream into a freezer-safe container; cover and freeze 1 hour or until firm.
**4.** Combine brown sugar and rum in a small microwave-safe bowl; microwave at HIGH 1½ minutes or until sugar dissolves, stirring after 45 seconds.
**5.** Prepare grill or broiler.
**6.** Place pineapple on grill rack or broiler pan coated with cooking spray, and cook 2 minutes on each side or until lightly browned, basting occasionally with rum mixture. Place 1 pineapple slice on each of 7 dessert plates; top each serving with ½ cup ice cream. Garnish with lime slices, if desired. Yield: 7 servings.

CALORIES 266 (8% from fat); FAT 2.4g (sat 0.9g, mono 0.8g, poly 0.2g); PROTEIN 7.6g; CARB 52.5g; FIBER 0.2g; CHOL 71mg; IRON 0.6mg; SODIUM 98mg; CALC 249mg

## Java-Crusted Chicken and Mushrooms

Ground coffee meets chicken in the form of an interesting, tasty rub. Make sure you use finely ground coffee such as the kind sold for automatic coffee makers; anything coarser could be gritty.

½   cup ground coffee
¼   cup all-purpose flour
2   tablespoons brown sugar
1   tablespoon coarsely ground black pepper
2   chicken breast halves (about 1 pound), skinned
2   chicken drumsticks (about ½ pound), skinned
2   chicken thighs (about ½ pound), skinned
2   teaspoons vegetable oil
3   cups quartered mushrooms (about 8 ounces)
1   (16-ounce) can fat-free, less-sodium chicken broth, divided
1   onion, quartered
1   cup pineapple juice
1   tablespoon all-purpose flour
½   teaspoon salt
6   cups hot cooked long-grain rice

**1.** Combine first 4 ingredients in a large zip-top plastic bag. Add chicken; seal and shake well. Heat oil in a large non-stick skillet over medium-high heat. Add chicken; sauté 5 minutes on each side. Remove chicken from pan.
**2.** Add mushrooms, 1½ cups broth, and onion to pan, scraping pan to loosen browned bits. Bring to a boil, and cook 5 minutes. Return chicken to pan. Add juice; bring to a boil. Cover; reduce heat, and simmer 45 minutes or until tender.
**3.** Combine ½ cup broth and 1 tablespoon flour in a small bowl. Stir broth mixture and salt into pan; cook, uncovered, 3 minutes or until thick and bubbly. Serve with rice. Yield: 6 servings (serving size: 1 chicken piece, about ½ cup sauce, and 1 cup rice).

CALORIES 462 (11% from fat); FAT 5.4g (sat 1.2g, mono 1.6g, poly 1.6g); PROTEIN 31.2g; CARB 69.3g; FIBER 2.7g; CHOL 76mg; IRON 4.1mg; SODIUM 434mg; CALC 58mg

## Chocolate Fire Cake

Hot and sweet merge in this dark chocolate cake that gets a hint of spice from ground red pepper.

1   cup sugar
⅓   cup butter or stick margarine, softened
1   large egg
1¼   cups all-purpose flour
6   tablespoons unsweetened cocoa
1½   teaspoons baking powder
1   teaspoon ground cinnamon
½   teaspoon ground red pepper
¼   teaspoon salt
¾   cup 1% low-fat milk
2   teaspoons vanilla extract
Baking spray with flour
2   tablespoons semisweet chocolate chips

**1.** Preheat oven to 350°.
**2.** Beat sugar and butter at medium speed of a mixer until well-blended (about 5 minutes). Add egg, beating well. Lightly spoon flour into dry measuring cups; level with a knife. Combine flour and next 5 ingredients, stirring well with a whisk. Combine milk and vanilla. Add

flour mixture to sugar mixture alternately with milk mixture, beginning and ending with flour mixture.

**3.** Pour batter into a 9-inch round cake pan coated with baking spray. Bake at 350° for 35 minutes or until a wooden pick inserted in center comes out clean. Cool in pan 10 minutes on a wire rack; remove from pan. Cool cake completely on wire rack.

**4.** Place chips in a small heavy-duty zip-top plastic bag, and seal. Submerge bag in very hot water until chips melt, or microwave at HIGH 1 minute or until melted. Snip a tiny hole in 1 corner of bag; drizzle chocolate over cake. Yield: 10 servings (serving size: 1 wedge).

CALORIES 233 (32% from fat); FAT 8.3g (sat 4.8g, mono 2.3g, poly 0.4g); PROTEIN 4g; CARB 36.2g; FIBER 0.5g; CHOL 40mg; IRON 1.6mg; SODIUM 212mg; CALC 79mg

## Navy Bean-and-Peanut Butter Soup

Cooking spray
1½ cups chopped onion
1 cup finely chopped celery
½ cup finely diced smoked ham
1 garlic clove, minced
3 cups fat-free, less-sodium chicken broth
⅛ teaspoon ground red pepper
1 (16-ounce) can navy beans, drained
1 (14.5-ounce) can diced tomatoes, drained
3 tablespoons creamy peanut butter
1 tablespoon chopped fresh parsley

**1.** Place a large saucepan coated with cooking spray over medium-high heat until hot. Add onion, celery, ham, and garlic; sauté 8 minutes. Add broth and next 3 ingredients; bring to a boil. Reduce heat, and simmer 15 minutes. Add peanut butter, stirring with a whisk. Cook 5 minutes, stirring occasionally. Sprinkle each serving with parsley. Yield: 6 servings (serving size: 1 cup).

CALORIES 168 (28% from fat); FAT 5.2g (sat 1g, mono 2.1g, poly 1.4g); PROTEIN 11.2g; CARB 20g; FIBER 3.4g; CHOL 6mg; IRON 1.7mg; SODIUM 778mg; CALC 58mg

## Vanilla-Glazed Pork Chops with Cipollini Onions

These pork chops benefit from the sweet surprise of vanilla. Don't substitute vanilla extract for the beans; the flavor won't be the same.

4 (4-ounce) boned center-cut loin pork chops (about ½ inch thick)
½ teaspoon salt
½ teaspoon black pepper
1 teaspoon vegetable oil
Cooking spray
12 cipollini onions or small boiling onions, peeled (about ¾ pound)
1 (3-inch) piece vanilla bean, split lengthwise
¾ cup Madeira wine
1 tablespoon brown sugar
2 tablespoons balsamic vinegar
1 teaspoon cornstarch

**1.** Sprinkle chops with salt and pepper. Heat oil in a large nonstick skillet coated with cooking spray over medium-high heat until hot. Add chops and onions; cook 4 minutes on each side or until lightly browned. Scrape seeds from vanilla bean; add seeds, bean, and wine to pan, scraping pan to loosen browned bits. Cover, reduce heat, and simmer 20 minutes or until pork and onions are tender. Remove pork and onions from pan with a slotted spoon; keep warm.

**2.** Combine brown sugar, balsamic vinegar, and cornstarch in a small bowl. Add to wine mixture in pan, and bring mixture to a boil. Cook mixture 1 minute, stirring constantly. Discard vanilla bean. Serve vanilla sauce with pork chops and onions. Yield: 4 servings (serving size: 1 chop, 3 onions, and about 2 tablespoons sauce).

CALORIES 232 (36% from fat); FAT 9.4g (sat 3g, mono 4g, poly 1.4g); PROTEIN 25.6g; CARB 9.8g; FIBER 0.4g; CHOL 71mg; IRON 1.4mg; SODIUM 378mg; CALC 32mg

the cooking light profile

# Takes One to Know One

*Alabamian Peggy Heal's passion for staying fit and eating healthfully unites a full circle of friends who all want the best out of life.*

As an active professional, Peggy fits friends, fitness, and good food into her life. Here are her tips on how you can do it, too.
•**Meet people through athletics.** You're bound to gain friends and improve your fitness. "If you enjoy the same sport, right away you'll have something in common," Peggy says.
•**Get a dog.** They're not only good friends, they'll keep you in shape. Peggy runs, hikes, and plays fetch with her two dogs regularly.
•**Eat with friends.** You'll find that you have so much to talk about, you won't notice that you're skipping dessert.
•**Make the important things routine.** Peggy has standing dates for running, tennis, and dinner parties with friends.

## Barbecued-Chicken Quesadillas

Peggy received this south-of-the-border-inspired recipe from a former roommate who whipped it up one night. It has been one of Peggy's favorites for quick weeknight dinners ever since.

Cooking spray
2 (4-ounce) skinned, boned chicken breast halves
¼ cup honey barbecue sauce (such as Kraft)
½ cup chopped tomato
¼ cup chopped onion
2 tablespoons minced fresh cilantro
2 (8-inch) flour tortillas
¼ cup (1 ounce) shredded reduced-fat sharp Cheddar cheese
2 cilantro sprigs (optional)

*Continued*

1. Preheat oven to 400°.
2. Place a medium nonstick skillet coated with cooking spray over medium heat until hot. Add chicken; sauté 6 minutes on each side. Remove from skillet; shred. Add barbecue sauce; toss.
3. Combine tomato, onion, and minced cilantro in a small bowl. Spoon half of chicken mixture down center of each tortilla. Top with tomato mixture, and sprinkle with cheese. Fold over; secure with a wooden pick. Place on a baking sheet. Bake at 400° for 4 minutes or until cheese melts. Garnish quesadillas with cilantro sprigs, if desired. Yield: 2 servings (serving size: 1 quesadilla).

CALORIES 353 (21% from fat); FAT 8.3g (sat 2.6g, mono 2.7g, poly 2.1g); PROTEIN 35.4g; CARB 32.7g; FIBER 2.6g; CHOL 75mg; IRON 3mg; SODIUM 643mg; CALC 209mg

# How Much Is That in "Skoshes"?

*Getting the true measure of her grandmother's Poppy-Seed Cake was an act of tasty translation for a New York City reader.*

Jennifer Bell learned almost everything she knows about baking from her grandmother, Ruby Hosimer. Jennifer came to understand that a "skosh" is slightly less than a pinch and that a "tad" is a bit more than a dash. But getting the right quantities to maintain the quality of her grandmother's rich Poppy-Seed Cake, smothered in creamy frosting, was a particular challenge.

To standardize the recipe, Jennifer translated loose descriptive amounts into teaspoons, tablespoons, and cups. But the cake presented far too much fat for the health-minded 29-year-old. So we crunched a few numbers of our own. First we subtracted two eggs, half the butter, and all the sour cream; then we switched regular cream cheese in the icing for fat-free. We trimmed more than a third of the calories and almost 19 grams of fat.

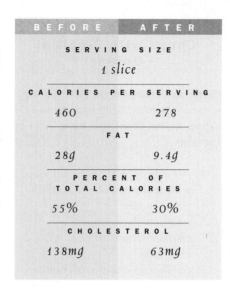

| BEFORE | AFTER |
|---|---|
| **SERVING SIZE** | |
| *1 slice* | |
| **CALORIES PER SERVING** | |
| 460 | 278 |
| **FAT** | |
| 28g | 9.4g |
| **PERCENT OF TOTAL CALORIES** | |
| 55% | 30% |
| **CHOLESTEROL** | |
| 138mg | 63mg |

## Poppy-Seed Cake

**CAKE:**

  2 cups all-purpose flour
1½ teaspoons baking powder
 ⅛ teaspoon salt
1½ cups granulated sugar
 ¾ cup (6 ounces) block-style fat-free cream cheese
 ½ cup butter or stick margarine, softened
  3 large eggs
 ¼ cup poppy seeds
  1 tablespoon grated lemon rind
1½ teaspoons vanilla extract
   Cooking spray

**FROSTING:**

 ¼ cup (2 ounces) block-style fat-free cream cheese, chilled
  2 tablespoons butter or stick margarine, chilled
  1 teaspoon grated lemon rind
1½ cups powdered sugar

1. Preheat oven to 325°.
2. To prepare cake, lightly spoon flour into dry measuring cups, and level with a knife. Combine flour, baking powder, and salt in a bowl, stirring well with a whisk. Beat 1½ cups granulated sugar, ¾ cup cream cheese, and ½ cup softened butter at medium speed of a mixer until well-blended. Add eggs, 1 at a time, beating mixture well after each addition. Add flour mixture, and beat at low speed just until blended. Stir in poppy seeds, 1 tablespoon lemon rind, and vanilla.
3. Spoon batter into a 9-inch tube pan coated with cooking spray. Bake at 325° for 40 minutes or until a wooden pick inserted near center comes out clean. Cool in pan 10 minutes on a wire rack; remove cake from pan. Cool completely on wire rack.
4. To prepare frosting, beat ¼ cup cream cheese, 2 tablespoons butter, and 1 teaspoon lemon rind until light and fluffy. Gradually add powdered sugar, beating just until blended (do not overbeat). Spread frosting over top of cake. Yield: 16 servings (serving size: 1 slice).
**NOTE:** The cake can be made using a 10-inch tube pan; bake at 325° for 30 minutes or until a wooden pick inserted near center of cake comes out clean. You can also bake the cake in a 9 x 5-inch loaf pan; bake at 325° for 1 hour or until a wooden pick inserted near center comes out clean.

CALORIES 278 (30% from fat); FAT 9.4g (sat 4.9g, mono 2.6g, poly 1.2g); PROTEIN 5.3g; CARB 43.5g; FIBER 0.6g; CHOL 63mg; IRON 1.2mg; SODIUM 236mg; CALC 107mg

---

### Sizing Up the Pan

Tube pans come in a variety of sizes, typically 9- or 10-inch. Because each holds batter differently, baking times vary. In this recipe, we call for a 9-inch tube pan. If yours is 10 inches, decrease the baking time by about 10 minutes.

---

Roast Salmon with Tomatoes
and Tarragon, page 155

Beef-and-Chicken Fajitas
with Peppers and Onions,
page 157

Open-Faced Burgers
with Onion-Mushroom
Topping, page 181

Jägerschnitzel,
page 169

Chipotle-Black
Bean Soup,
page 176

Raspberry-Cream
Cheese Brownies,
page 180

English Summer
Pudding, page 171

# Land Without Drive-Ins

*In the Austrian Alps, the best way to find great food is with your own two feet.*

## Jägerschnitzel

(pictured on page 167)

Pork tenderloin slices are pounded into thin cutlets (or *schnitzel*) and served with a vegetable stew in this homage to Alpine hunters.

  2 teaspoons vegetable oil
  3 cups thinly sliced mushrooms
  3 cups coarsely chopped red bell pepper
  2 cups coarsely chopped onion
  1 cup thinly sliced carrot
  2 garlic cloves, minced
  1 (14.5-ounce) can diced tomatoes, undrained
  1 tablespoon all-purpose flour
  1 teaspoon paprika
  2 tablespoons water
  1 pound pork tenderloin
  ½ teaspoon coarsely ground black pepper
  ¼ teaspoon salt
Cooking spray
  3 cups hot cooked yolk-free noodles (about 6 ounces uncooked pasta)
Chopped fresh parsley (optional)

**1.** Heat oil in a large Dutch oven over medium-high heat. Add mushrooms, bell pepper, onion, carrot, and garlic; sauté 10 minutes. Add tomatoes; cover, reduce heat, and simmer 20 minutes or until vegetables are tender. Combine flour, paprika, and water in a small bowl. Stir into tomato mixture; cook 3 minutes or until slightly thick. Keep warm.
**2.** Trim fat from pork; cut pork crosswise into 16 pieces. Place each piece between 2 sheets of heavy-duty plastic wrap, and flatten each piece to ¼-inch thickness using a meat mallet or rolling pin. Sprinkle both sides of pork with black pepper and salt. Place a large nonstick skillet coated with cooking spray over medium-high heat until hot. Add pork; cook 4 minutes on each side or until done.
**3.** Serve vegetable mixture over noodles; top with pork slices. Garnish with parsley, if desired. Yield: 4 servings (serving size: 1¼ cups sauce, ¾ cup noodles, and 4 pork slices).

CALORIES 438 (19% from fat); FAT 9.2g (sat 2g, mono 3.6g, poly 2.7g); PROTEIN 35.2g; CARB 55.4g; FIBER 5.9g; CHOL 79mg; IRON 4.7mg; SODIUM 419mg; CALC 73mg

## Linzertorte

Named for Linz, Austria, the town where it originated, this lattice-topped tart features an almond pastry and blackberry-jam filling.

1½ cups all-purpose flour
  ½ cup ground blanched almonds
  ½ teaspoon ground cinnamon
  ¼ teaspoon salt
  ¼ teaspoon baking powder
  ½ cup granulated sugar
  ¼ cup tub-style light cream cheese
  ½ teaspoon vanilla extract
  1 large egg
Cooking spray
1¼ cups seedless blackberry jam
  1 teaspoon sifted powdered sugar

**1.** Lightly spoon flour into dry measuring cups, and level with a knife. Combine flour, almonds, cinnamon, salt, and baking powder in a bowl.
**2.** Combine granulated sugar and cream cheese in a food processor; pulse 4 times. Add vanilla and egg, and pulse 3 times. Add flour mixture; pulse 10 times or until combined. Gently press two-thirds of dough into a 4-inch circle on heavy-duty plastic wrap; cover with additional plastic wrap. Chill 30 minutes. Gently press remaining one-third of dough into a 4-inch circle on heavy-duty plastic wrap; cover with additional plastic wrap. Roll into a 9-inch circle. Chill 30 minutes. Roll larger portion of dough, still covered, into an 11-inch circle. Chill 10 minutes or until plastic wrap can be easily removed.
**3.** Preheat oven to 325°.
**4.** Working with larger portion of dough, remove 1 sheet of plastic wrap; fit dough into a 9-inch round removable-bottom tart pan coated with cooking spray. Remove top sheet of plastic wrap; fold edges under. Spoon blackberry jam into prepared crust.
**5.** Working with smaller portion of dough, remove 1 sheet of plastic wrap. Cut dough into ½-inch strips. Gently remove dough strips from bottom sheet of plastic wrap; arrange in a lattice design over preserves. Seal dough strips to edge of crust. Place tart on a baking sheet.
**6.** Bake at 325° for 50 minutes or until crust is browned and filling is bubbly. Cool on a wire rack. Sprinkle with powdered sugar. Yield: 9 servings.

CALORIES 236 (20% from fat); FAT 5.2g (sat 1.2g, mono 2.4g, poly 0.9g); PROTEIN 5.1g; CARB 44.4g; FIBER 3.7g; CHOL 28mg; IRON 1.3mg; SODIUM 106mg; CALC 39mg

## Marinated Tomatoes and Green Beans

The vinegar-style dressing is typical of an Austrian vegetable salad.

  ¾ cup white wine vinegar
  2 tablespoons minced fresh parsley
  1 tablespoon vegetable oil
  2 teaspoons Dijon mustard
  1 teaspoon sugar
  ½ teaspoon salt
  ¼ teaspoon pepper
  6 cups (2-inch) cut green beans (about 1½ pounds)
  6 small tomatoes, each cut into 8 wedges (about 1½ pounds)
 16 Boston lettuce leaves
  4 (¼-inch-thick) slices onion, separated into rings

**1.** Combine first 7 ingredients in a jar; cover tightly, and shake vigorously.
**2.** Steam beans, covered, 7 minutes or until crisp-tender. Rinse beans under cold water, and drain. Place beans and tomato
*Continued*

wedges in a shallow bowl, and pour vinaigrette over vegetables, tossing gently to coat. Cover and marinate in refrigerator 1 to 2 hours, stirring occasionally.

**3.** Place 2 lettuce leaves on each of 8 salad plates. Arrange ¾ cup beans on one half of each plate; arrange 6 tomato wedges on other half of plate. Top each serving with onion rings, and drizzle each serving with 1 tablespoon vinaigrette. Yield: 8 servings.

CALORIES 71 (28% from fat); FAT 2.2g (sat 0.4g, mono 0.6g, poly 1g); PROTEIN 2.6g; CARB 11.4g; FIBER 3.2g; CHOL 0mg; IRON 1.4mg; SODIUM 201mg; CALC 43mg

# Berries Do It Better

Beauties of the fruit world and best friends of the dessert table, berries are also some of the best bodyguards you'll ever taste.

New studies keep cropping up to herald the powerful nutritional punch of fresh-picked summer berries. Beneath their beauty and flavor lurk legions of antioxidants—damage-control warriors that attack the free radicals that contribute to aging, heart disease, and other human woes. Berries are also high in fiber, low in calories, and virtually fat-free.

## Viennese Potato-Cucumber Salad

Pungent celeriac (celery root) is a common ingredient in soups, salads, and stuffings in Austria, France, and Scandinavia.

    1  cup diced peeled red potato
    ⅓  cup low-fat sour cream
    1½ tablespoons white wine vinegar
    ¾  teaspoon sugar
    ¼  teaspoon salt
    ¼  teaspoon pepper
    ¼  teaspoon dry mustard
    ½  cup shredded peeled celeriac
       (celery root)
    ½  small cucumber, peeled, halved
       lengthwise, seeded, and thinly
       sliced (about ½ cup)
    4  cups torn Boston lettuce
    1  hard-cooked large egg, diced
    Minced fresh chives (optional)

**1.** Place potato in a small saucepan; cover with water. Bring to a boil; cook 10 minutes or until tender. Drain; cool.
**2.** Combine sour cream and next 5 ingredients in a large bowl. Stir in celeriac and cucumber. Add potato, lettuce, and egg; toss gently to coat. Garnish with chives, if desired. Yield: 5 servings (serving size: 1 cup).

CALORIES 71 (34% from fat); FAT 2.7g (sat 1.3g, mono 0.8g, poly 0.3g); PROTEIN 3g; CARB 9.4g; FIBER 1g; CHOL 47mg; IRON 0.6mg; SODIUM 155mg; CALC 29mg

## Blackberry-Cream Cheese Crêpes

    8  Blender Crêpes
    5  cups fresh blackberries, divided
    ¾  cup water, divided
    ⅓  cup granulated sugar
    1  tablespoon lemon juice
    1  tablespoon brandy
    2  teaspoons cornstarch
    ¼  teaspoon ground cinnamon
    1  tablespoon butter or stick margarine
    ½  cup (4 ounces) ⅓-less-fat cream
       cheese, softened
    1  teaspoon powdered sugar

**1.** Prepare Blender Crêpes; set aside.
**2.** Combine 1 cup blackberries and ½ cup water in a blender. Process about 1 minute or until smooth. Strain blackberry mixture through a sieve.
**3.** Combine blackberry puree, ¼ cup water, granulated sugar, lemon juice, brandy, cornstarch, and cinnamon in a small saucepan; bring to a boil. Cook 1 minute over medium heat, stirring constantly. Remove from heat; stir in butter.
**4.** Spread 1 tablespoon cream cheese over each crêpe, and top each with 2 teaspoons sauce and ¼ cup blackberries. Fold each crêpe in half, then in quarters. Spoon 2 tablespoons sauce on each of 8 dessert plates; top each with 1 crêpe and ¼ cup blackberries. Sift powdered sugar evenly over crêpes. Yield: 8 servings.

(Totals include Blender Crêpes) CALORIES 188 (29% from fat); FAT 6g (sat 3.2g, mono 1.7g, poly 0.5g); PROTEIN 4.6g; CARB 30.3g; FIBER 5.1g; CHOL 42mg; IRON 1.1mg; SODIUM 91mg; CALC 74mg

**BLENDER CRÊPES:**
    ⅔  cup all-purpose flour
    ¾  cup fat-free milk
    1  teaspoon granulated sugar
    1  large egg
    Cooking spray

**1.** Lightly spoon flour into dry measuring cups, and level with a knife. Combine flour, milk, sugar, and egg in a blender; cover and process until smooth. Pour batter into a bowl; cover and chill 30 minutes.
**2.** Place an 8-inch crêpe pan or nonstick skillet coated with cooking spray over medium heat until hot. Remove from heat. Pour a scant ¼ cup batter into pan; quickly tilt in all directions so batter covers pan with a thin film. Cook about 1 minute.
**3.** Carefully lift edge of crêpe with a spatula to test for doneness. The crêpe is ready to turn when it can be shaken loose from pan and underside is lightly browned. Turn crêpe over; cook 10 seconds on other side.
**4.** Place crêpe on a towel; cool. Repeat procedure until all batter is used, stirring batter before each repetition. Stack crêpes between layers of wax paper or paper towels to prevent sticking. Yield: 8 servings (serving size: 1 crêpe).
**NOTE:** Coat pan with cooking spray only as needed while cooking crêpes. To make ahead, layer crêpes between sheets of wax paper, and store in a zip-top plastic bag in refrigerator.

CALORIES 55 (13% from fat); FAT 0.8g (sat 0.2g, mono 0.3g, poly 0.1g); PROTEIN 2.6g; CARB 9g; FIBER 0.3g; CHOL 27mg; IRON 0.5mg; SODIUM 20mg; CALC 33mg

## Berries Jubilee

This is a berry version of the famous flaming cherries jubilee. Skip the alcohol and flaming step if you prefer; no additional liquid needs to be substituted for the brandy.

    2   tablespoons sugar
    1   tablespoon cornstarch
  ⅛   teaspoon salt
  ½   teaspoon grated orange rind
  1¼  cups orange juice
  1½  cups fresh blueberries
  1½  cups fresh raspberries
  ¼   cup brandy
    4   cups vanilla low-fat ice cream

**1.** Combine first 3 ingredients in a large skillet. Stir in rind and juice; bring to a boil. Cook 1 minute or until slightly thick. Add berries; cook 3 minutes or until thoroughly heated. Pour brandy into one side of skillet. Ignite brandy with a long match; let flames die down. Spoon berry sauce over ice cream. Yield: 8 servings (serving size: ½ cup ice cream and ⅓ cup sauce).

CALORIES 152 (18% from fat); FAT 3.1g (sat 1.8g, mono 0.8g, poly 0.2g); PROTEIN 3.2g; CARB 29.8g; FIBER 2.4g; CHOL 9mg; IRON 0.3mg; SODIUM 95mg; CALC 102mg

## Cornmeal Pancakes with Poached Spring Berries

    1   cup all-purpose flour
  ⅔   cup yellow cornmeal
    3   tablespoons sugar
    1   teaspoon baking powder
  ¼   teaspoon baking soda
  ¼   teaspoon salt
  1½  cups low-fat buttermilk
    2   tablespoons vegetable oil
    2   large egg whites
  Cooking spray
  Poached Spring Berries

**1.** Lightly spoon flour into a dry measuring cup; level with a knife. Combine flour and next 5 ingredients. Combine buttermilk and oil. Add to flour mixture, stirring until smooth. Beat egg whites at high speed of a mixer until stiff peaks form. Gently fold into flour mixture.

**2.** Spoon about ¼ cup batter for each pancake onto a hot nonstick griddle or nonstick skillet coated with cooking spray. Turn pancakes when tops are covered with bubbles and edges look cooked. Serve pancakes with Poached Spring Berries. Yield: 6 servings (serving size: 2 pancakes and ¼ cup berries).

(Totals include Poached Spring Berries) CALORIES 308 (18% from fat); FAT 6.3g (sat 0.9g, mono 1.4g, poly 2.5g); PROTEIN 7.2g; CARB 55.3g; FIBER 3.3g; CHOL 0mg; IRON 1.9mg; SODIUM 283mg; CALC 132mg

**POACHED SPRING BERRIES:**

  ⅓   cup sugar
  ⅓   cup orange juice
    1   cup fresh raspberries
  ¾   cup fresh blueberries
    2   teaspoons Grand Marnier or
        other orange-flavored liqueur
        or orange juice

**1.** Combine sugar and orange juice in a small saucepan, and bring to a boil over medium heat. Reduce heat, and simmer, uncovered, 10 minutes, stirring occasionally. Stir in raspberries and blueberries; cook 2 minutes or just until warm, stirring occasionally. Remove mixture from heat, and stir in liqueur. Serve warm. Yield: 6 servings (serving size: ¼ cup).

CALORIES 75 (2% from fat); FAT 0.2g (sat 0g, mono 0g, poly 0.1g); PROTEIN 0.4g; CARB 17.9g; FIBER 1.9g; CHOL 0mg; IRON 0.2mg; SODIUM 2mg; CALC 7mg

## Blackberry-Lemon Upside-Down Cake

    2   teaspoons butter or stick
        margarine, melted
  ⅓   cup packed brown sugar
  1½  teaspoons grated lemon
        rind
    2   cups fresh blackberries
  1¼  cups all-purpose flour
  1½  teaspoons baking powder
  ¼   teaspoon salt
  ⅔   cup granulated sugar
    2   tablespoons butter or stick
        margarine, softened
    1   large egg
  ¾   teaspoon vanilla extract
  ½   cup fat-free milk

**1.** Preheat oven to 350°.

**2.** Place 2 teaspoons melted butter in bottom of a 9-inch round cake pan; sprinkle with brown sugar and lemon rind. Top with blackberries; set aside.

**3.** Lightly spoon flour into dry measuring cups; level with a knife. Combine flour, baking powder, and salt in a small bowl.

**4.** Beat granulated sugar and 2 tablespoons butter in a large bowl at medium speed of a mixer until well-blended. Add egg and vanilla; beat well. Add flour mixture to egg mixture alternately with milk, beginning and ending with flour mixture; mix after each addition. Spoon batter over blackberries.

**5.** Bake at 350° for 40 minutes or until a wooden pick inserted in center comes out clean. Cool in pan 5 minutes on a wire rack. Loosen edges of cake with a knife. Place a plate upside down on top of cake pan; invert onto plate. Yield: 8 servings.

CALORIES 239 (18% from fat); FAT 4.8g (sat 2.7g, mono 1.4g, poly 0.4g); PROTEIN 3.7g; CARB 46.2g; FIBER 2.4g; CHOL 38mg; IRON 1.5mg; SODIUM 224mg; CALC 97mg

## English Summer Pudding

(pictured on page 168)

This is a low-fat version of the classic English molded desserts that alternate layers of cake or bread, fruit, and custard. We've left out the custard here.

  4½  cups coarsely chopped peeled ripe
        fresh peaches (about 1¾ pounds)
    2   cups fresh raspberries
    2   cups fresh blackberries
  ⅓   cup orange juice
  ¼   cup sugar
    3   tablespoons Triple Sec or other
        orange-flavored liqueur or orange
        juice
    1   teaspoon grated lemon rind
    1   (10-inch) round angel food cake
  Fresh raspberries or blackberries
        (optional)

*Continued*

**1.** Combine first 7 ingredients in a large saucepan; bring to a boil. Reduce heat; simmer 10 minutes, stirring occasionally. Set aside.

**2.** Cut cake into 1-inch-thick slices; cut each slice in half diagonally to make 2 triangles. Line bottom and sides of a 3-quart straight-sided glass bowl or trifle bowl with half of cake pieces; spoon half of peach mixture into cake-lined bowl. Arrange half of remaining cake pieces over peach mixture, and spoon remaining peach mixture over cake. Top with remaining cake pieces.

**3.** Place plastic wrap on surface of cake pieces, and place a small plate on top of plastic wrap; place a 1-pound can on plate to firmly press mixture. Chill 8 hours. Remove plate and plastic wrap. Garnish with additional fresh berries, if desired. Yield: 8 servings (serving size: 1 cup).

CALORIES 221 (2% from fat); FAT 0.5g (sat 0.1g, mono 0.1g, poly 0.3g); PROTEIN 3.6g; CARB 50.6g; FIBER 6.1g; CHOL 0mg; IRON 0.6mg; SODIUM 190mg; CALC 56mg

### Cool Summer-Berry Soup

**SOUP:**

- 2 cups fresh raspberries
- 2 cups halved fresh strawberries
- ½ cup cranberry-raspberry juice drink
- ½ cup dry white wine
- ¼ cup sugar
- ⅛ teaspoon ground cinnamon
- 1 (8-ounce) carton strawberry low-fat yogurt

**GARNISH:**

- 1 cup fresh blueberries
- 2 teaspoons sugar
- 2 teaspoons cranberry-raspberry juice drink

**1.** To prepare soup, place first 3 ingredients in a blender, and process until smooth. Strain raspberry mixture through a sieve into a medium saucepan. Stir in wine, ¼ cup sugar, and cinnamon. Bring to a boil over medium heat; cook 2 minutes. Remove from heat. Place in a large bowl; cover and chill 3 hours. Stir in yogurt.

**2.** To prepare garnish, place blueberries, 2 teaspoons sugar, and 2 teaspoons juice drink in a blender; process until smooth. Strain blueberry mixture through a sieve.

**3.** Spoon 1 cup soup into each of 4 bowls. Drizzle each serving with 1 tablespoon garnish. Yield: 4 servings.

CALORIES 208 (6% from fat); FAT 1.4g (sat 0.5g, mono 0.3g, poly 0.4g); PROTEIN 3.6g; CARB 48.4g; FIBER 7g; CHOL 2mg; IRON 0.9mg; SODIUM 37mg; CALC 109mg

### Blueberry-Almond Coffeecake

- 1 cup all-purpose flour
- ½ cup granulated sugar
- ¾ teaspoon baking powder
- ½ teaspoon salt
- ¼ teaspoon baking soda
- 1 cup fresh blueberries, divided
- ⅔ cup low-fat buttermilk
- 2 tablespoons butter or stick margarine, melted
- 1 teaspoon vanilla extract
- ¼ teaspoon almond extract
- 1 large egg
- Cooking spray
- ¼ cup sliced almonds
- 1 tablespoon brown sugar
- ¼ teaspoon ground cinnamon

**1.** Preheat oven to 350°.

**2.** Lightly spoon flour into a dry measuring cup; level with a knife. Combine flour and next 4 ingredients in a large bowl; add ⅔ cup blueberries, and toss well. Combine buttermilk, butter, extracts, and egg; stir well with a whisk. Add to flour mixture, stirring just until flour mixture is moist.

**3.** Spoon batter into an 8-inch square baking pan coated with cooking spray, spreading evenly. Top with ⅓ cup blueberries.

**4.** Combine almonds, brown sugar, and cinnamon, and sprinkle over blueberries. Bake at 350° for 35 minutes or until a wooden pick inserted in center comes out clean. Yield: 8 servings (serving size: 1 [4 x 2-inch] square).

CALORIES 188 (27% from fat); FAT 5.7g (sat 2.4g, mono 2.2g, poly 0.6g); PROTEIN 3.9g; CARB 30.6g; FIBER 1.3g; CHOL 35mg; IRON 1.1mg; SODIUM 282mg; CALC 69mg

### Raspberry-Champagne Granita

This frozen dessert, similar to sorbet, is easy to prepare and almost entirely fat-free. Much of the alcohol evaporates during cooking, but the flavor of champagne remains.

- 2 cups fresh raspberries
- 2 tablespoons fresh lime juice
- 1½ cups water
- 1 cup sugar
- ¾ cup champagne

**1.** Place raspberries and lime juice in a blender; process until smooth.

**2.** Combine water, sugar, and champagne in a medium saucepan; bring to a boil. Reduce heat; simmer 1 minute or until sugar melts. Remove from heat; stir in raspberry puree. Pour mixture into a large, shallow baking dish. Cover and freeze 8 hours.

**3.** Remove dish from freezer, and let stand 5 minutes. Scrape entire mixture with a fork until fluffy. Yield: 6 servings (serving size: 1 cup).

CALORIES 152 (1% from fat); FAT 0.2g (sat 0g, mono 0g, poly 0.1g); PROTEIN 0.5g; CARB 38.9g; FIBER 2.8g; CHOL 0mg; IRON 0.4mg; SODIUM 3mg; CALC 12mg

sound bites

# Sowing Your Oats

*The cozy oats that caught your fancy in the '80s are still around—but the ways to cook with them have moved uptown.*

In the late 1980s, nutritionists announced a remarkable find: The soluble fiber so plentiful in oatmeal and oat bran could help lower cholesterol and reduce the risk of heart disease. Oats also have plenty of vitamins $B_1$, $B_2$, and E. Riding on such a healthy spin, oats began showing up on tables across America. The fad faded, but the health benefits remained—and so did some of the better ideas for cooking with this wonderful grain.

## Mushroom-and-Spinach Quiche in an Oat Crust

Oats lend a crunchy contrast to the creamy filling of this quiche.

**CRUST:**

    1   cup regular oats
    ⅓   cup oat bran
    2   tablespoons chilled butter or stick
        margarine, cut into small pieces
    3   tablespoons cold water
        Cooking spray

**FILLING:**

    1   cup chopped leek
    1¼  cups sliced mushrooms
    1   cup evaporated fat-free milk
    ¼   cup (1 ounce) grated fresh
        Parmesan cheese
    ½   teaspoon salt
    ¼   teaspoon dried dill
    ¼   teaspoon dried thyme
    ¼   teaspoon black pepper
    3   large egg whites
    2   large eggs
    1   (10-ounce) package frozen
        chopped spinach, thawed,
        drained, and squeezed dry
    ¼   cup (1 ounce) finely shredded
        Gruyère or Swiss cheese

**1.** Preheat oven to 375°.
**2.** To prepare crust, combine oats and oat bran; cut in butter with a pastry blender or 2 knives until mixture resembles coarse meal. Add water; stir just until moist. Press mixture gently into a ball on wax paper, and cover with additional wax paper. Roll dough, still covered, into a 10-inch circle.
**3.** Remove 1 sheet of wax paper, and fit dough into a 9-inch pie plate coated with cooking spray. Remove top sheet of wax paper. Bake at 375° for 7 minutes. Cool on a wire rack.
**4.** To prepare filling, place a medium nonstick skillet coated with cooking spray over medium-high heat until hot. Add leek; sauté 2 minutes. Add mushrooms; sauté 5 minutes. Remove from heat; spoon into a bowl.
**5.** Combine milk and next 8 ingredients in a blender, and process until smooth. Add to mushroom mixture, and stir well.

Pour into prepared crust, and sprinkle with Gruyère cheese. Bake at 375° for 35 minutes or until a knife inserted near center comes out clean. Let stand 5 minutes. Yield: 6 servings (serving size: 1 wedge).

CALORIES 235 (38% from fat); FAT 10g (sat 4.9g, mono 3g, poly 1g); PROTEIN 15.2g; CARB 22.2g; FIBER 3.9g; CHOL 94mg; IRON 2.9mg; SODIUM 463mg; CALC 314mg

## Apple-Oat Upside-Down Cake

    ¾   cup quick-cooking oats
    ¾   cup warm apple juice
    2   tablespoons vegetable oil
    ¼   cup egg substitute or 2 large
        egg whites
    2   teaspoons vanilla extract
    1   tablespoon butter or stick
        margarine, melted
        Cooking spray
    1   cup packed brown sugar, divided
    1   large Granny Smith apple, peeled
        and thinly sliced (about 1½ cups)
    1¼  cups all-purpose flour
    1   teaspoon baking soda
    1   teaspoon ground cinnamon
    ½   teaspoon salt
    ¼   teaspoon ground nutmeg

**1.** Preheat oven to 350°.
**2.** Combine first 3 ingredients; let stand 10 minutes. Stir in egg substitute and vanilla.
**3.** Pour butter in bottom of a 9-inch cake pan coated with cooking spray. Sprinkle with ¼ cup sugar. Arrange apple slices spokelike on top of sugar, working from center of pan to edge.
**4.** Lightly spoon flour into dry measuring cups; level with a knife. Combine ¾ cup sugar, flour, baking soda, cinnamon, salt, and nutmeg in a large bowl; stir with a whisk. Add oat mixture; stir just until moist. Pour batter into prepared pan.
**5.** Bake at 350° for 40 minutes or until a wooden pick inserted in center comes out clean. Cool in pan 10 minutes. Place a plate upside down on top of cake; invert onto plate. Cut into wedges. Yield: 8 servings (serving size: 1 wedge).

CALORIES 278 (18% from fat); FAT 5.7g (sat 1.7g, mono 1.6g, poly 2g); PROTEIN 4.1g; CARB 53.1g; FIBER 1.8g; CHOL 4mg; IRON 2.1mg; SODIUM 342mg; CALC 39mg

## Spiced Fruity Oatmeal

    1½  cups apple juice
    ½   cup water
    ⅛   teaspoon salt
    1⅓  cups regular oats
    ¼   cup sweetened dried cranberries
        (such as Craisins) or raisins
    ¼   cup 1% low-fat milk
    1   tablespoon brown sugar
    ¾   teaspoon ground cinnamon
    ⅛   teaspoon ground nutmeg
    2   tablespoons chopped walnuts

**1.** Combine first 3 ingredients in a medium saucepan; bring to a boil. Stir in oats and cranberries; reduce heat, and simmer 4 minutes, stirring occasionally. Stir in milk, sugar, cinnamon, and nutmeg; cook 1 minute. Spoon into bowls; sprinkle with walnuts. Yield: 4 servings (serving size: ¾ cup oatmeal and 1½ teaspoons walnuts).

CALORIES 212 (18% from fat); FAT 4.2g (sat 0.6g, mono 1.1g, poly 2.1g); PROTEIN 5.8g; CARB 38.9g; FIBER 3.7g; CHOL 1mg; IRON 1.8mg; SODIUM 86mg; CALC 49mg

**MICROWAVE VARIATION:**
Combine first 5 ingredients in a 2-quart glass measure or medium bowl, and microwave at HIGH 4 minutes or until slightly thick, stirring after 2 minutes. Stir in milk, sugar, cinnamon, and nutmeg; let stand, covered, 1 minute. Spoon into bowls; sprinkle with walnuts.

## Herb-Oat Crusted Chicken

    1   cup regular oats
    ½   teaspoon salt
    ¼   teaspoon dried rubbed sage
    ¼   teaspoon dried summer savory
        or parsley
    ¼   teaspoon dried thyme
    ¼   teaspoon black pepper
    ⅓   cup egg substitute
    6   (4-ounce) skinned, boned chicken
        breast halves
        Cooking spray
    2   tablespoons butter or stick
        margarine, melted

*Continued*

1. Preheat oven to 400°.

2. Arrange oats in a single layer on a jelly-roll pan; bake at 400° for 5 minutes or until golden. Combine oats, salt, and next 4 ingredients in a food processor; process until oats are finely chopped. Place oat mixture in a shallow dish; place egg substitute in a medium bowl. Dip chicken in egg substitute, and dredge in oat mixture. Place chicken on a baking sheet coated with cooking spray, and drizzle butter over chicken. Bake at 400° for 20 minutes or until done. Yield: 6 servings (serving size: 1 chicken breast half).

CALORIES 219 (25% from fat); FAT 6.2g (sat 2.9g, mono 1.7g, poly 0.8g); PROTEIN 29.7g; CARB 9.4g; FIBER 1.5g; CHOL 76mg; IRON 1.8mg; SODIUM 329mg; CALC 28mg

## Oatmeal Cookies with A-Peel

1 cup sweetened dried cranberries (such as Craisins) or raisins
½ cup orange juice
½ cup granulated sugar
½ cup packed brown sugar
¼ cup butter or stick margarine, softened
2 tablespoons light-colored corn syrup
1 large egg
1½ cups all-purpose flour
1 teaspoon baking soda
½ teaspoon baking powder
½ teaspoon salt
3 cups regular oats
⅓ cup coarsely chopped walnuts
1 tablespoon grated orange rind
Cooking spray

1. Preheat oven to 375°.

2. Combine cranberries and orange juice in a bowl; cover and let stand 10 minutes.

3. Beat sugars and butter at medium speed of a mixer until light and fluffy. Add corn syrup and egg; beat well. Stir in cranberry mixture.

4. Lightly spoon flour into dry measuring cups, and level with a knife. Combine flour, baking soda, baking powder, and salt in a bowl, stirring well with a whisk. Add oats, walnuts, and orange rind; stir well. Add to sugar mixture; stir until well-blended.

5. Drop by level tablespoons 2 inches apart onto baking sheets coated with cooking spray. Bake at 375° for 8 minutes or until almost set. Cool on a wire rack. Yield: 4 dozen (serving size: 1 cookie).

CALORIES 78 (22% from fat); FAT 1.9g (sat 0.7g, mono 0.5g, poly 0.5g); PROTEIN 1.6g; CARB 13.8g; FIBER 0.8g; CHOL 7mg; IRON 0.5mg; SODIUM 69mg; CALC 10mg

## Honey Twists

¾ cup regular oats
¾ cup boiling water
½ cup 1% low-fat milk
¼ cup honey
1 teaspoon salt
2 teaspoons olive oil
1 package dry yeast (about 2¼ teaspoons)
1 teaspoon sugar
¼ cup warm water (100° to 110°)
2¾ cups bread flour, divided
½ cup whole-wheat flour
¼ cup yellow cornmeal
Cooking spray
1 tablespoon water
1 large egg white

1. Combine oats and boiling water in a bowl; let stand 5 minutes. Stir in milk, honey, salt, and oil.

2. Dissolve yeast and sugar in warm water in a large bowl; let stand 5 minutes. Stir in oat mixture. Lightly spoon flours into dry measuring cups; level with a knife. Combine 2½ cups bread flour, whole-wheat flour, and cornmeal, and gradually add to yeast mixture, stirring until a soft dough forms. Turn dough out onto a lightly floured surface. Knead until smooth and elastic (about 8 minutes); add enough of remaining flour, 1 tablespoon at a time, to prevent dough from sticking to hands.

3. Place dough in a bowl coated with cooking spray, turning to coat top. Cover; let rise in a warm place (85°), free from drafts, 1 hour or until doubled in size. (Press two fingers into dough. If indentation remains, dough has risen enough.) Punch dough down; let rest 10 minutes.

4. Preheat oven to 375°.

5. Divide dough into 18 equal portions. Roll into 18 (10-inch-long) strips; fold each in half from end to end. Pick up both ends of each strip; twist. Pinch ends together to seal. Place twists ½ inch apart on a baking sheet coated with cooking spray; let rise 30 minutes. Combine 1 tablespoon water and egg white; brush over twists. Bake at 375° for 12 minutes. Serve warm. Yield: 1½ dozen (serving size: 1 twist).

CALORIES 132 (9% from fat); FAT 1.3g (sat 0.2g, mono 0.5g, poly 0.3g); PROTEIN 4.2g; CARB 25.9g; FIBER 1g; CHOL 0mg; IRON 1.4mg; SODIUM 138mg; CALC 15mg

## Garlic-Herb Meat Loaf

7 tablespoons ketchup, divided
1 cup quick-cooking oats
½ cup finely chopped onion
2 tablespoons dried parsley
1 tablespoon dried basil
¾ teaspoon salt
½ teaspoon black pepper
1 pound ground sirloin
1 pound ground turkey
2 large eggs, lightly beaten
2 large egg whites, lightly beaten
2 garlic cloves, minced
Cooking spray

1. Preheat oven to 375°.

2. Combine 3 tablespoons ketchup, oats, and next 10 ingredients in a large bowl; stir mixture until well-blended.

3. Shape meat mixture into a 9 x 5-inch loaf on a broiler pan coated with cooking spray; spoon 4 tablespoons ketchup over meat loaf. Insert a meat thermometer into loaf. Bake at 375° for 1 hour and 10 minutes or until thermometer registers 160°. Let stand 10 minutes. Remove meat loaf from pan; cut into 16 slices. Yield: 8 servings (serving size: 2 slices).

CALORIES 230 (25% from fat); FAT 6.5g (sat 2.1g, mono 2.3g, poly 1g); PROTEIN 29.5g; CARB 12.3g; FIBER 1.6g; CHOL 125mg; IRON 3.2mg; SODIUM 479mg; CALC 38mg

## Banana-Oat Quick Bread

1½ cups all-purpose flour
1 cup quick-cooking oats
¾ cup packed brown sugar
2½ teaspoons baking powder
¼ teaspoon salt
1 cup mashed ripe banana
½ cup low-fat buttermilk
¼ cup vegetable oil
¼ cup egg substitute or 2 large egg
whites
Cooking spray
¼ cup quick-cooking oats
2 tablespoons coarsely chopped
walnuts
2 tablespoons brown sugar
2 teaspoons butter or stick margarine

**1.** Preheat oven to 350°.
**2.** Lightly spoon flour into dry measuring cups, and level with a knife. Combine flour and next 4 ingredients in a large bowl; make a well in center of mixture. Combine banana, buttermilk, oil, and egg substitute in a bowl; add to flour mixture. Stir just until moist. Spoon batter into an 8 x 4-inch loaf pan coated with cooking spray.
**3.** Combine ¼ cup oats, walnuts, 2 tablespoons brown sugar, and butter, and sprinkle over batter. Bake at 350° for 1 hour or until a wooden pick inserted in center comes out clean. Cool 5 minutes in pan on a wire rack; remove from pan. Cool completely on wire rack. Yield: 16 servings (serving size: 1 slice).

CALORIES 170 (28% from fat); FAT 5.2g (sat 1.1g, mono 1.4g, poly 2.2g); PROTEIN 3.3g; CARB 28.4g; FIBER 1.4g; CHOL 1mg; IRON 1.3mg; SODIUM 132mg; CALC 69mg

### Know Your Oats

Oats usually come in three forms: **Regular** (or "old-fashioned"), **quick-cooking,** and **instant.** The first two can be used interchangeably in our recipes, although we have specified in each the kind that works best. Instant oats—to which you only add hot water—aren't recommended in these recipes because they are pre-processed and too finely cut to provide enough substance and texture.

# Doctor Delicious

*A North Carolina physician kept his word to his wife and also gave new life to his mom's Greek-style casserole.*

When Wendel Naumann, M.D., returns home from the Carolinas Medical Center in Charlotte, North Carolina, he trades in his scrubs for jeans and an apron. "I promised my wife, Jan, that I would take over the cooking after I passed my gynecologic-oncology board examination," says the busy 38-year-old.

"Once I learned some of the easy tricks to light cooking by reading your magazine," the doc-in-the-kitchen says, "I started lightening my old recipes and realized that they still tasted great." Naumann has created a leaner version of his mother's Baked Shrimp with Feta Cheese.

### Baked Shrimp with Feta Cheese

1 teaspoon olive oil
¾ teaspoon dried oregano
½ teaspoon salt
¼ teaspoon crushed red pepper
1 pound medium shrimp, peeled and deveined
3 garlic cloves, minced
Cooking spray
½ cup dry white wine
3 cups diced plum tomato (about ¾ pound)
¾ cup (3 ounces) finely crumbled feta cheese
4 cups hot cooked linguine (about 8 ounces uncooked pasta)
¼ cup minced fresh parsley

**1.** Preheat oven to 350°.
**2.** Heat oil in a large nonstick skillet over medium-high heat. Add oregano and next 4 ingredients; sauté 3 minutes. Spoon shrimp mixture into an 11 x 7-inch baking dish coated with cooking spray.
**3.** Add wine to skillet; cook over low heat until reduced to ¼ cup (about 3 minutes). Stir in tomato, and pour over shrimp mixture. Sprinkle with cheese, and bake at 350° for 10 minutes. Serve mixture over pasta, and sprinkle with parsley. Yield: 4 servings (serving size: 1 cup shrimp mixture, 1 cup pasta, and 1 tablespoon parsley).

CALORIES 404 (19% from fat); FAT 8.7g (sat 3.8g, mono 2.3g, poly 1.5g); PROTEIN 29g; CARB 51.8g; FIBER 3.1g; CHOL 148mg; IRON 5.5mg; SODIUM 677mg; CALC 182mg

### Chicken Marsala Casserole

—Jenny D. Arey, Columbus, Georgia

¾ cup all-purpose flour
1 (8-ounce) carton low-fat sour cream
1 cup fat-free milk
¼ teaspoon salt
¼ teaspoon coarsely ground black pepper
1 (16-ounce) can fat-free, less-sodium chicken broth
½ cup Marsala wine
⅓ cup chopped celery
⅛ teaspoon ground cardamom
1 pound skinned, boned chicken breast, cut into bite-size pieces
1 (8-ounce) package presliced mushrooms
2 cups hot cooked angel hair (about 4 ounces uncooked pasta)
Cooking spray
½ cup (2 ounces) shredded Cheddar cheese

**1.** Preheat oven to 350°.
**2.** Lightly spoon flour into dry measuring cups; level with a knife. Combine flour and sour cream in a medium saucepan, stirring with a whisk. Add milk, salt, black pepper, and chicken broth. Bring to a boil; reduce heat, and simmer 2 minutes, stirring constantly. Remove from heat.
**3.** Place a large nonstick skillet over medium-high heat until hot. Add wine and next 4 ingredients, and cook 10 minutes or until liquid almost evaporates.
**4.** Combine cream sauce, chicken mixture, and pasta; spoon into a 13 x 9-inch
*Continued*

baking dish coated with cooking spray. Sprinkle with cheese; bake at 350° for 30 minutes. Yield: 6 servings (serving size: 1 cup).

CALORIES 336 (25% from fat); FAT 9.4g (sat 5.2g, mono 2.5g, poly 0.8g); PROTEIN 28.2g; CARB 32.9g; FIBER 1.5g; CHOL 69mg; IRON 2.7mg; SODIUM 413mg; CALC 178mg

## Roasted Eggplant-and-Onion Pasta

—Christine Frisco,
Provincetown, Massachusetts

1  eggplant, cut into ¾-inch-thick slices (about 1 pound)
1  medium onion, sliced and separated into rings (about 1 cup)
Cooking spray
8  ounces uncooked penne (tube-shaped pasta)
1  tablespoon olive oil
3  garlic cloves, minced
2  cups diced plum tomato (about ½ pound)
2  tablespoons chopped fresh or 2 teaspoons dried basil
¼  teaspoon salt
¼  teaspoon black pepper
¾  cup (3 ounces) finely crumbled feta cheese
¼  cup (1 ounce) grated fresh Parmesan cheese
4  teaspoons pine nuts, toasted

**1.** Preheat broiler.
**2.** Place eggplant slices and onion on a baking sheet coated with cooking spray, and broil 20 minutes, turning once. Remove from oven; cool. Cut into bite-size pieces.
**3.** While eggplant and onion broil, cook pasta according to package directions, omitting salt and fat.
**4.** Heat olive oil in a large nonstick skillet over medium heat. Add garlic, and sauté 1 minute. Add tomato, basil, salt, and pepper; cook over low heat 10 minutes. Stir in eggplant and onion, and cook 5 minutes. Add pasta, stirring well. Divide pasta mixture evenly among 4 plates, and top with cheeses and pine nuts. Yield: 4 servings (serving size: 1½

cups pasta mixture, 3 tablespoons feta, 1 tablespoon Parmesan, and 1 teaspoon pine nuts).

CALORIES 405 (30% from fat); FAT 13.3g (sat 5.5g, mono 4.9g, poly 1.8g); PROTEIN 16.2g; CARB 56.9g; FIBER 5.3g; CHOL 25mg; IRON 3.5mg; SODIUM 532mg; CALC 237mg

## Chipotle-Black Bean Soup

(pictured on page 167)

"The chipotle chile gives this soup a smoky flavor that makes it different from other black bean soups."

—Nancy Niemeyer, Cincinnati, Ohio

**SOUP:**

1  cup dried black beans (about 6 ounces)
½  cup boiling water
1  dried chipotle chile
1  teaspoon olive oil
¼  cup chopped onion
1  garlic clove, minced
2  cups water
¼  teaspoon dried oregano
⅛  teaspoon ground cumin
1  (16-ounce) can fat-free, less-sodium chicken broth
¼  teaspoon ground red pepper
1  (14.5-ounce) can diced tomatoes and green chiles, undrained

**TOPPINGS:**

2  (6-inch) corn tortillas, cut into ¼-inch strips
Cooking spray
½  cup plain fat-free yogurt
¼  cup (1 ounce) finely shredded reduced-fat sharp Cheddar cheese

**1.** To prepare soup, sort and wash beans; place in a large Dutch oven. Cover with water to 2 inches above beans; bring to a boil, and cook 2 minutes. Remove from heat; cover and let stand 1 hour. Drain.
**2.** Combine boiling water and chipotle chile in a bowl; let stand 15 minutes or until soft. Drain, seed, and chop.
**3.** Heat oil in a large Dutch oven over medium-high heat. Add onion; sauté 2 minutes or until tender. Add garlic; sauté 1 minute. Add beans, chipotle chile, 2

cups water, oregano, cumin, and broth; bring to a boil. Cover, reduce heat, and simmer 3 hours or until beans are soft. Place 1 cup soup in a blender; process until smooth. Return to pan. Stir in pepper and tomatoes; cook until thoroughly heated.
**4.** Preheat oven to 350°.
**5.** To prepare toppings, place tortilla strips in a single layer on a baking sheet. Lightly coat tortilla strips with cooking spray. Bake at 350° for 12 minutes or until toasted.
**6.** Ladle soup into each of 4 bowls; top with tortilla strips, yogurt, and cheese. Yield: 4 servings (serving size: 1¼ cups soup, 2 tablespoons yogurt, 1 tablespoon cheese, and ¼ cup tortilla strips).

CALORIES 276 (12% from fat); FAT 3.7g (sat 1.2g, mono 1.4g, poly 0.7g); PROTEIN 15.8g; CARB 42.7g; FIBER 7.9g; CHOL 5mg; IRON 3.4mg; SODIUM 769mg; CALC 222mg

## Creamy Asparagus Soup

—Rofina Silverman,
San Anselmo, California

2  pounds asparagus spears
1  (14½-ounce) can vegetable broth
1  teaspoon olive oil
1  cup chopped onion
2  garlic cloves, minced
1  cup soy milk or 1% low-fat milk
1  cup reduced-fat firm tofu, drained and cut into 1-inch cubes (about 6 ounces)
1  tablespoon grated lemon rind
¼  teaspoon black pepper

**1.** Snap off tough ends of asparagus. Cut a 1-inch tip from each asparagus spear; set aside. Reserve stalks. Bring broth to a boil in a medium saucepan; add asparagus stalks. Cook 5 minutes; strain through a sieve into a bowl, reserving ¾ cup broth.
**2.** Heat oil in pan over medium heat. Add onion and garlic, and sauté 5 minutes. Add asparagus stalks and milk; simmer 8 minutes or until tender. Combine asparagus mixture, reserved broth, and tofu in a blender; process until smooth. Strain mixture through a sieve over a bowl; discard solids. Combine asparagus

puree, asparagus tips, lemon rind, and pepper in pan; simmer over low heat 5 minutes or until asparagus is tender. Yield: 4 servings (serving size: ¾ cup).

CALORIES 144 (24% from fat); FAT 3.8g (sat 0.5g, mono 1.1g, poly 1.1g); PROTEIN 12.2g; CARB 19.4g; FIBER 3.1g; CHOL 0mg; IRON 2.7mg; SODIUM 596mg; CALC 127mg

## Marinated-Vegetable Salad

"This is so basic and versatile that you can use whatever vegetables are in season. It is excellent with grilled meat."
—Dorothy R. Duder, Burbank, California

    3   cups diagonally sliced carrot
        (about 1 pound)
    2   cups (2-inch) julienne-cut
        zucchini
    1   cup vertically sliced red onion
    ½   cup (2-inch) julienne-cut red bell
        pepper
    ¼   cup red wine vinegar
    2   tablespoons (½ ounce) finely
        grated fresh Parmesan cheese
    1   tablespoon chopped fresh parsley
    1   tablespoon olive oil
    1   tablespoon water
    ¼   teaspoon dried basil
    ¼   teaspoon dried oregano
    ¼   teaspoon salt
    ⅛   teaspoon black pepper

**1.** Place carrot in a microwave-safe dish; cover with plastic wrap. Microwave at HIGH 4 minutes or until crisp-tender; cool.
**2.** Place zucchini in a microwave-safe dish; cover with plastic wrap. Microwave at HIGH 1½ minutes or until crisp-tender; cool.
**3.** Combine sliced carrot, zucchini pieces, sliced onion, and bell pepper pieces in a large bowl. Combine vinegar and remaining 8 ingredients in a small bowl, stirring with a whisk. Pour vinegar mixture over vegetables, tossing to coat. Cover vegetables, and marinate in refrigerator 2 hours. Yield: 7 servings (serving size: 1 cup).

CALORIES 59 (40% from fat); FAT 2.6g (sat 0.6g, mono 1.6g, poly 0.3g); PROTEIN 1.8g; CARB 8.1g; FIBER 2.2g; CHOL 1mg; IRON 0.6mg; SODIUM 129mg; CALC 44mg

## in season

# Sister Squash

*From Native American cooking to supermarket aisle, summer squash is an abundant national treasure.*

Summer squash's mild taste and cool flavor make it perfect for blending with other ingredients or in simple preparations highlighting the taste of fresh herbs.

## Crispy Zucchini Sticks with Creamy Salsa Dip

    ½   cup bottled salsa
    ¼   cup fat-free sour cream
    2   zucchini (about ¾ pound)
    ⅔   cup Italian-seasoned breadcrumbs
    ½   cup yellow cornmeal
    2   tablespoons (½ ounce) grated
        fresh Parmesan cheese
    2   tablespoons minced fresh parsley
    ¼   teaspoon salt
    ⅓   cup all-purpose flour
    3   large egg whites, lightly beaten
    Cooking spray

**1.** Preheat oven to 450°.
**2.** Combine salsa and sour cream; set aside.
**3.** Cut each zucchini lengthwise into quarters; cut each quarter crosswise into 3 pieces.
**4.** Combine breadcrumbs and next 4 ingredients in a shallow dish. Dredge 6 zucchini pieces in flour. Dip in egg whites, and dredge in breadcrumb mixture. Repeat procedure with remaining zucchini, flour, egg whites, and breadcrumb mixture. Place zucchini on a large baking sheet coated with cooking spray. Lightly coat zucchini with cooking spray. Bake at 450° for 25 minutes or until lightly browned and crisp, carefully turning after 12 minutes. Serve zucchini immediately with salsa dip. Yield: 6 servings (serving size: 4 zucchini pieces and 2 tablespoons dip).

CALORIES 153 (9% from fat); FAT 1.6g (sat 0.6g, mono 0.4g, poly 0.2g); PROTEIN 7.6g; CARB 27g; FIBER 1.5g; CHOL 2mg; IRON 1.7mg; SODIUM 620mg; CALC 71mg

## Summer-Squash Gratin with Gruyère

    1¾  pounds Yukon gold or red potatoes
        (about 9 potatoes)
    ⅓   cup all-purpose flour
    ½   cup fat-free, less-sodium chicken
        broth
    1½  cups 1% low-fat milk
    ¼   cup dry white wine
    ½   teaspoon salt
    ¼   teaspoon black pepper
    ¼   teaspoon ground nutmeg
    2   garlic cloves, minced
    1   cup (4 ounces) grated Gruyère
        cheese
    Cooking spray
    1   cup thinly sliced onion
    2   tablespoons chopped fresh
        oregano
    2   cups thinly sliced zucchini
        (about 1 pound)
    2   cups thinly sliced yellow squash
        (about 1 pound)
    ⅓   cup Italian-seasoned breadcrumbs
    2   teaspoons olive oil

**1.** Preheat oven to 375°.
**2.** Pierce potatoes with a fork. Arrange in a circle on paper towels in microwave oven; cover with wax paper. Microwave at HIGH 5 minutes or until crisp-tender; cool. Thinly slice potatoes.
**3.** Lightly spoon flour into a dry measuring cup; level with a knife. Combine flour and broth in a medium saucepan; stir with a whisk. Stir in milk and next 5 ingredients. Bring mixture to a boil over medium heat, and cook until thick (about 10 minutes), stirring constantly with a whisk. Remove from heat; add cheese, stirring until cheese melts.
**4.** Arrange half of potato slices in bottom of a 13 x 9-inch baking dish coated with cooking spray. Top with half of onion, oregano, zucchini, yellow squash, and cheese sauce. Repeat procedure with remaining potato, onion, oregano, zucchini, yellow squash, and cheese sauce.
**5.** Bake at 375° for 1 hour or until gratin is tender. Combine breadcrumbs and oil in a small bowl; toss well. Sprinkle breadcrumb mixture over gratin.
**6.** Preheat broiler.

*Continued*

**7.** Broil gratin 30 seconds or until bread-crumbs are lightly browned. Let stand 10 minutes. Yield: 8 servings.

CALORIES 222 (28% from fat); FAT 6.8g (sat 3.3g, mono 2.5g, poly 0.6g); PROTEIN 10.4g; CARB 30.9g; FIBER 3g; CHOL 17mg; IRON 2.3mg; SODIUM 388mg; CALC 241mg

## Summer Squash-and-Corn Sauté

This makes a terrific side to just about any entrée—particularly roast chicken, grilled steak, or ham.

 1 teaspoon olive oil
 2 teaspoons cumin seeds
 2 cups fresh corn kernels (about 4 ears)
 1 cup sliced onion
 3 garlic cloves, minced
 2 cups (¼-inch-thick) diagonally sliced zucchini (about ¾ pound)
 2 cups (¼-inch-thick) diagonally sliced yellow squash (about ¾ pound)
 ½ teaspoon salt
 1 (4.5-ounce) can chopped green chiles
 2 tablespoons chopped fresh cilantro
 ½ cup (2 ounces) shredded reduced-fat Monterey Jack cheese

**1.** Heat oil in a large nonstick skillet over medium-high heat; cook cumin seeds 30 seconds or until toasted, stirring frequently. Add corn, onion, and garlic; sauté 5 minutes or until lightly browned. Add zucchini, yellow squash, salt, and chiles, and sauté 6 minutes or until tender. Stir in cilantro. Remove from heat; sprinkle with cheese. Cover and let stand 5 minutes or until cheese melts. Yield: 6 servings (serving size: 1 cup).

CALORIES 109 (29% from fat); FAT 3.5g (sat 1.4g, mono 1.5g, poly 0.6g); PROTEIN 6.1g; CARB 16.7g; FIBER 3.4g; CHOL 6mg; IRON 1.3mg; SODIUM 517mg; CALC 108mg

## Chilled Summer-Squash Soup with Curry

 2 teaspoons curry powder
 1¼ pounds yellow squash, cubed
 ½ cup chopped onion
 1 (14½-ounce) can vegetable broth
 1¾ cups low-fat buttermilk
 1 tablespoon chopped fresh mint
 ½ teaspoon salt

**1.** Cook curry powder in a large saucepan over medium heat 1 minute or until toasted. Add squash, onion, and broth. Bring to a boil; cover, reduce heat, and simmer 25 minutes or until tender. Place squash mixture in a blender; process until smooth. Pour mixture into a bowl; cover and chill. Stir in buttermilk, mint, and salt. Yield: 5 servings (serving size: 1 cup).

CALORIES 82 (24% from fat); FAT 2.2g (sat 1g, mono 0.6g, poly 0.4g); PROTEIN 4.8g; CARB 12.3g; FIBER 2.5g; CHOL 0mg; IRON 0.8mg; SODIUM 681mg; CALC 136mg

## Lemon-Glazed Zucchini Quick Bread

 2⅓ cups all-purpose flour
 ¾ cup granulated sugar
 2 teaspoons baking powder
 1 teaspoon ground cinnamon
 ½ teaspoon baking soda
 ½ teaspoon salt
 ¼ teaspoon ground nutmeg
 1 cup finely shredded zucchini
 ½ cup 1% low-fat milk
 ¼ cup vegetable oil
 2 tablespoons grated lemon rind
 1 large egg
 Cooking spray
 1 cup sifted powdered sugar
 2 tablespoons fresh lemon juice

**1.** Preheat oven to 350°.
**2.** Lightly spoon flour into dry measuring cups; level with a knife. Combine flour and next 6 ingredients in a large bowl; make a well in center of mixture. Combine zucchini, milk, oil, rind, and egg in a bowl; add to flour mixture. Stir just until moist.
**3.** Spoon batter into an 8 x 4-inch loaf pan coated with cooking spray. Bake at

350° for 1 hour or until a wooden pick inserted in center comes out clean. Cool 10 minutes in pan on a wire rack; remove from pan. Cool completely on wire rack.
**4.** Combine powdered sugar and lemon juice; stir with a whisk. Drizzle over loaf. Yield: 12 servings (serving size: 1 slice).

CALORIES 230 (21% from fat); FAT 5.4g (sat 1.1g, mono 1.6g, poly 2.4g); PROTEIN 3.5g; CARB 42.6g; FIBER 0.8g; CHOL 19mg; IRON 1.4mg; SODIUM 243mg; CALC 69mg

## Cheesy Squash-and-Rice Pie

Instead of fried rice, try making this light vegetarian entrée with your leftover rice. The yellow and green squash are colorful, but it's fine to use all of one or the other.

 1 teaspoon olive oil
 3 cups (¼-inch-thick) sliced yellow squash (about ½ pound)
 2 cups (¼-inch-thick) sliced zucchini (about ½ pound)
 1 cup chopped onion
 1½ teaspoons chopped fresh or ½ teaspoon dried rosemary
 1½ cups cooked rice
 3 tablespoons minced fresh chives or green onions
 Cooking spray
 ½ cup 1% low-fat milk
 ½ cup (4 ounces) garlic and herbs reduced-fat soft spreadable cheese (such as rondelé)
 ¾ teaspoon salt
 ¼ teaspoon black pepper
 2 large eggs, lightly beaten
 2 large egg whites, lightly beaten

**1.** Preheat oven to 350°.
**2.** Heat oil in a large nonstick skillet over medium heat until hot. Add yellow squash, zucchini, onion, and rosemary; cook 20 minutes or until vegetables are tender, stirring occasionally. Cool.
**3.** Combine squash mixture, rice, and chives in a large bowl; spoon into a 9-inch pie plate coated with cooking spray. Combine milk and remaining 5 ingredients; stir well with a whisk. Pour over squash mixture. Bake at 350° for 45

minutes or until center is set. Yield: 4
servings (serving size: 1 wedge).

CALORIES 262 (30% from fat); FAT 8.6g (sat 3.8g, mono 3.2g,
poly 0.8g); PROTEIN 14g; CARB 32.6g; FIBER 3.4g; CHOL 122mg;
IRON 2mg; SODIUM 710mg; CALC 142mg

### Grilled Zucchini-and-Summer Squash Salad with Citrus Splash Dressing

2 tablespoons grated orange rind
¾ cup fresh orange juice
(about 3 oranges)
½ cup fresh lime juice (about 3
limes)
3 tablespoons honey
2 teaspoons olive oil
½ teaspoon salt
¼ teaspoon crushed red pepper
2 red onions
4 zucchini, each halved lengthwise
(about 1¼ pounds)
4 yellow squash, each halved
lengthwise (about 1 pound)
Cooking spray
3 tablespoons thinly sliced fresh
basil

1. Combine first 7 ingredients in a large
zip-top plastic bag. Peel onions, leaving
root intact; cut each onion into 4
wedges. Add onion, zucchini, and yellow squash to bag. Seal and marinate in
refrigerator 1 hour, turning bag occasionally.
2. Prepare grill.
3. Drain vegetables in a colander over a
bowl, reserving marinade. Place vegetables on a grill rack coated with cooking
spray, and grill 8 minutes or until tender;
turn and baste occasionally with ¾ cup
marinade. Place vegetables on a serving
platter; sprinkle with basil. Serve vegetables with remaining marinade. Yield: 4
servings (serving size: 2 zucchini halves,
2 squash halves, 2 onion wedges, and 3
tablespoons citrus dressing).

CALORIES 168 (16% from fat); FAT 3g (sat 0.4g, mono 1.8g,
poly 0.5g); PROTEIN 4g; CARB 36.1g; FIBER 4g; CHOL 0mg;
IRON 1.3mg; SODIUM 302mg; CALC 70mg

classics

# Boy-Oh-Boy Brownies!

*Snacks so super, there's really only one
response.*

We all know brownies are among the
top 10 snacks in recorded time. You can
prepare all these mouthwatering recipes
ahead and freeze them. So you can make
a lot of them pretty much whenever you
want and never, ever run out.

### Peanut Butter-Chocolate Chip Brownies

Cooking spray
1 cup all-purpose flour
¼ cup semisweet chocolate
minichips
¼ teaspoon baking soda
⅛ teaspoon salt
¾ cup granulated sugar
¼ cup packed dark brown sugar
¼ cup creamy peanut butter
1 tablespoon vegetable oil
1 teaspoon vanilla extract
1 large egg
1 large egg white

1. Preheat oven to 350°.
2. Coat bottom of an 8-inch square baking pan with cooking spray (do not coat
sides of pan).
3. Lightly spoon flour into a dry measuring cup; level with a knife. Combine
flour, chocolate chips, soda, and salt in a
bowl.
4. Combine sugars and remaining 5 ingredients in a bowl; stir until well-
blended. Add flour mixture, stirring just
until blended. Spread batter in bottom
of prepared pan. Bake at 350° for 25
minutes or until a wooden pick inserted
in center comes out almost clean. Cool
on a wire rack. Yield: 16 servings (serving size: 1 brownie).

CALORIES 125 (30% from fat); FAT 4.2g (sat 1.1g, mono 1.7g,
poly 1.1g); PROTEIN 2.7g; CARB 19.8g; FIBER 0.5g; CHOL 14mg;
IRON 0.6mg; SODIUM 66mg; CALC 7mg

### Black-Forest Brownies

Instead of candied cherries, you can substitute dried sweetened cherries softened
in boiling water about 5 minutes, drained,
and chopped.

**BROWNIES:**
Cooking spray
¾ cup plus 2 tablespoons
all-purpose flour
¼ teaspoon baking powder
¼ teaspoon baking soda
⅛ teaspoon salt
1 cup granulated sugar
⅔ cup unsweetened cocoa
¼ cup butter or stick margarine,
melted
2 tablespoons water
1 teaspoon vanilla extract
1 large egg
1 large egg white
¼ cup coarsely chopped candied
cherries
3 tablespoons coarsely chopped walnuts

**GLAZE:**
½ cup sifted powdered sugar
¼ teaspoon almond extract
1¾ teaspoons hot water

1. Preheat oven to 350°.
2. To prepare brownies, coat bottom of
an 8-inch square baking pan with cooking spray (do not coat sides of pan).
3. Lightly spoon flour into dry measuring
cups; level with a knife. Combine flour,
baking powder, baking soda, and salt in a
medium bowl. Combine granulated sugar
and next 6 ingredients; stir well with a
whisk. Add to flour mixture; stir just until
moist. Stir in cherries and walnuts.
Spread batter in bottom of prepared pan.
4. Bake at 350° for 35 minutes or until a
wooden pick inserted in center of
brownies comes out almost clean. Cool
on a wire rack.
5. To prepare glaze, combine powdered
sugar, almond extract, and 1¾ teaspoons
water in a small bowl. Drizzle glaze over
brownies, and let stand 15 minutes. Yield:
16 servings (serving size: 1 brownie).

CALORIES 153 (27% from fat); FAT 4.6g (sat 2.3g, mono 1.2g,
poly 0.8g); PROTEIN 2.8g; CARB 25.6g; FIBER 0.3g; CHOL 22mg;
IRON 1.1mg; SODIUM 83mg; CALC 15mg

## Raspberry-Cream Cheese Brownies

(pictured on page 168)

FILLING:
- ⅓ cup sugar
- ⅓ cup (3 ounces) ⅓-less-fat cream cheese, softened
- 2 teaspoons all-purpose flour
- ½ teaspoon vanilla extract
- 1 large egg white

BROWNIES:
- Cooking spray
- ¾ cup all-purpose flour
- ¼ teaspoon baking powder
- ¼ teaspoon baking soda
- ⅛ teaspoon salt
- 1 cup sugar
- ⅔ cup unsweetened cocoa
- ¼ cup butter or stick margarine, melted
- 1 tablespoon water
- 1 teaspoon vanilla extract
- 1 large egg
- 2 large egg whites
- 3 tablespoons raspberry preserves

**1.** Preheat oven to 350°.
**2.** To prepare filling, beat first 5 ingredients at medium speed of a mixer until well-blended, and set aside.
**3.** To prepare brownies, coat bottom of an 8-inch square baking pan with cooking spray (do not coat sides of pan). Lightly spoon ¾ cup flour into dry measuring cups, and level with a knife. Combine flour, baking powder, baking soda, and salt in a medium bowl. Combine 1 cup sugar and next 6 ingredients, stirring well with a whisk. Add to flour mixture, stirring just until moist. Spread two-thirds of batter in bottom of prepared pan. Pour filling over batter, spreading evenly. Carefully drop remaining batter and preserves by spoonfuls over filling; swirl together using tip of a knife to marble. Bake at 350° for 40 minutes or until a wooden pick inserted in center comes out almost clean. Cool on a wire rack. Yield: 16 servings (serving size: 1 brownie).

CALORIES 161 (28% from fat); FAT 5g (sat 3g, mono 1.4g, poly 0.2g); PROTEIN 3.3g; CARB 25.9g; FIBER 0.2g; CHOL 26mg; IRON 1mg; SODIUM 113mg; CALC 18mg

## Mocha Double-Fudge Brownies

- Cooking spray
- ⅔ cup all-purpose flour
- 1 cup sugar
- ½ cup unsweetened cocoa
- ¼ cup butter or stick margarine, melted
- 2 tablespoons water
- 1 tablespoon instant coffee granules
- 1 teaspoon vanilla extract
- ½ teaspoon baking powder
- 1 large egg
- 1 large egg white
- ¼ cup semisweet chocolate minichips
- ¼ cup fat-free hot fudge chocolate topping

**1.** Preheat oven to 350°.
**2.** Coat bottom of an 8-inch square baking pan with cooking spray (do not coat sides of pan).
**3.** Lightly spoon flour into dry measuring cups, and level with a knife. Combine sugar and next 8 ingredients in a bowl. Add flour and minichips, stirring just until blended. Spread half of batter in bottom of prepared pan. Spread chocolate topping over batter (topping will not completely cover batter). Spread remaining batter over topping. Bake at 350° for 35 minutes or until a wooden pick inserted in center comes out almost clean. Cool on a wire rack. Yield: 16 servings (serving size: 1 brownie).

CALORIES 138 (30% from fat); FAT 4.6g (sat 2.7g, mono 1.3g, poly 0.2g); PROTEIN 2.3g; CARB 22.4g; FIBER 0.3g; CHOL 22mg; IRON 0.8mg; SODIUM 55mg; CALC 12mg

## Butter Pecan-Toffee Brownies

BROWNIES:
- Cooking spray
- 1 cup packed brown sugar
- 3 tablespoons butter or stick margarine, melted
- 1 teaspoon vanilla extract
- 1 large egg
- ¾ cup all-purpose flour
- 2 tablespoons chopped pecans
- ½ teaspoon baking powder
- ⅛ teaspoon salt

TOPPING:
- ⅔ cup powdered sugar
- 2 tablespoons semisweet chocolate minichips, melted
- 1 tablespoon hot water
- 2 tablespoons almond brickle chips (such as Heath)

**1.** Preheat oven to 350°.
**2.** To prepare brownies, coat bottom of an 8-inch square baking pan with cooking spray (do not coat sides of pan).
**3.** Combine brown sugar and next 3 ingredients; stir well with a whisk. Lightly spoon flour into dry measuring cups; level with a knife. Combine flour, pecans, baking powder, and salt; stir into brown sugar mixture. Spread in bottom of prepared pan. Bake at 350° for 22 minutes or until a wooden pick inserted in center comes out almost clean. Cool on a wire rack.
**4.** To prepare topping, combine powdered sugar, minichips, and hot water; stir until smooth. Spread over brownies; sprinkle with brickle chips. Chill 30 minutes or until topping is set. Yield: 16 servings (serving size: 1 brownie).

CALORIES 141 (27% from fat); FAT 4.3g (sat 2g, mono 1.4g, poly 0.4g); PROTEIN 1.2g; CARB 25g; FIBER 0.2g; CHOL 20mg; IRON 0.7mg; SODIUM 75mg; CALC 24mg

## Chewy Coconut-Butterscotch Bars

- Cooking spray
- 1¼ cups all-purpose flour
- 1¼ teaspoons baking powder
- ⅛ teaspoon salt
- 1 cup packed dark brown sugar
- 3 tablespoons vegetable oil
- 1 teaspoon vanilla extract
- 1 large egg
- 1 large egg white
- ⅓ cup chopped pitted dates
- ¼ cup flaked sweetened coconut
- 2 tablespoons semisweet chocolate minichips
- 2 tablespoons butterscotch morsels

**1.** Preheat oven to 350°.
**2.** Coat bottom of an 8-inch square baking pan with cooking spray (do not coat sides of pan).

**3.** Lightly spoon flour into dry measuring cups, and level with a knife. Combine flour, baking powder, and salt in a bowl. Combine sugar, oil, vanilla, egg, and egg white in a large bowl; stir with a whisk until well-blended. Add flour mixture and dates; stir just until blended. Spread in bottom of prepared pan. Bake at 350° for 15 minutes; remove from oven. Combine coconut, minichips, and butterscotch morsels; sprinkle over brownies. Bake an additional 10 minutes or until a wooden pick inserted in center comes out almost clean; cool on a wire rack. Yield: 16 servings (serving size: 1 brownie).

CALORIES 131 (30% from fat); FAT 4.3g (sat 1.6g, mono 1g, poly 1.3g); PROTEIN 1.8g; CARB 21.5g; FIBER 0.6g; CHOL 14mg; IRON 0.8mg; SODIUM 73mg; CALC 36mg

## 30 minutes or less

# Round Advice

*Sensational, speedy meals start with ground round, a great lean version of America's favorite meat.*

### Open-Faced Burgers with Onion-Mushroom Topping

(pictured on page 166)

**PREPARATION TIME: 10 MINUTES**
**COOKING TIME: 18 MINUTES**

2   teaspoons olive oil
1   medium sweet onion, sliced and
      separated into rings
2   (8-ounce) packages presliced
      mushrooms
½   teaspoon salt
2   teaspoons balsamic vinegar
1½  tablespoons paprika
½   teaspoon salt
½   teaspoon dried thyme
¼   teaspoon ground red pepper
¼   teaspoon freshly ground black pepper
1   pound ground round
2   English muffins, split and toasted

**1.** Prepare grill.
**2.** Heat oil in a large nonstick skillet over medium-high heat. Add onion, and cook 5 minutes or until golden. Add mushrooms and salt; cook 5 minutes, stirring constantly. Add vinegar; remove mixture from pan. Set aside.
**3.** Combine paprika and next 4 ingredients. Divide ground round into 4 equal portions, shaping each into a ½-inch-thick patty. Coat patties with spice mixture. Grill patties 4 minutes on each side or until done. Place burgers on muffin halves, and top each burger with ¼ cup onion mixture. Yield: 4 servings (serving size: 1 sandwich).

CALORIES 320 (30% from fat); FAT 10.5g (sat 3g, mono 4.8g, poly 1.2g); PROTEIN 29.4g; CARB 27.3g; FIBER 4.6g; CHOL 70mg; IRON 5.1mg; SODIUM 813mg; CALC 82mg

### Curried Beef with Potatoes and Peas

**PREPARATION TIME: 10 MINUTES**
**COOKING TIME: 10 MINUTES**

1   pound ground round
1   cup chopped onion
1   cup frozen green peas
2   teaspoons olive oil
2   cups (½-inch) cubed
      peeled red potatoes
      (about ¾ pound)
1   cup fat-free, less-sodium
      chicken broth
2½  teaspoons curry powder
1   tablespoon mango chutney
      (such as Sharwood's Major Grey)
½   teaspoon salt
¼   teaspoon freshly ground
      black pepper
Chopped fresh cilantro (optional)

**1.** Cook beef and onion in a large nonstick skillet over medium-high heat until browned; stir to crumble. Stir in peas.
**2.** While meat mixture is cooking, heat oil in a large nonstick skillet over medium-high heat. Add potato; cook 8 minutes or until lightly browned. Add broth and curry; cook 2 minutes. Add potato mixture, chutney, salt, and pepper to meat mixture; simmer 1 minute.

Sprinkle with cilantro, if desired. Yield: 4 servings (serving size: 1 cup).

CALORIES 310 (27% from fat); FAT 9.4g (sat 2.8g, mono 4.7g, poly 0.6g); PROTEIN 29.1g; CARB 25.7g; FIBER 4.7g; CHOL 70mg; IRON 4mg; SODIUM 579mg; CALC 34mg

### Shortcut Lasagna

This dish has all the flavor of lasagna, but takes a fraction of the time to prepare and serves up like a casserole.

**PREPARATION TIME: 8 MINUTES**
**COOKING TIME: 21 MINUTES**

8   ounces uncooked medium egg
      noodles
1¼  cups fat-free ricotta cheese
1½  cups (6 ounces) shredded sharp
      provolone cheese, divided
1   teaspoon dried basil
½   teaspoon dried oregano
¼   teaspoon salt
¼   teaspoon black pepper
1   pound ground round
2   cups tomato sauce
Cooking spray

**1.** Preheat oven to 375°.
**2.** Cook noodles in boiling water 5 minutes, omitting salt and fat.
**3.** While noodles are cooking, combine ricotta, 1 cup provolone cheese, basil, oregano, salt, and pepper in a small bowl; set aside. Cook beef in a large nonstick skillet over medium-high heat until browned, stirring to crumble. Stir in tomato sauce; remove from heat.
**4.** Drain noodles. Combine noodles and meat mixture in large bowl. Place 3 cups noodle mixture in an 11 x 7-inch baking dish coated with cooking spray. Spread ricotta mixture over noodle mixture. Top with remaining noodle mixture, and sprinkle with ½ cup provolone cheese. Bake at 375° for 15 minutes or until cheese melts. Yield: 6 servings.

CALORIES 416 (30% from fat); FAT 14g (sat 6.8g, mono 4.5g, poly 0.9g); PROTEIN 37g; CARB 37.2g; FIBER 2.3g; CHOL 107mg; IRON 4.1mg; SODIUM 912mg; CALC 333mg

## Meatballs and Peppers

**PREPARATION TIME: 10 MINUTES**
**COOKING TIME: 20 MINUTES**

  1  cup thinly sliced green bell
      pepper
  1  cup thinly sliced red bell pepper
  1  cup thinly sliced yellow bell
      pepper
1⅓  cups water
  1  (10½-ounce) can beef consommé
  1  bay leaf
  1  (1-ounce) slice whole-wheat bread
  1  pound ground round
  1  tablespoon finely chopped onion
  ½  teaspoon dried oregano
  ½  teaspoon salt
  ½  teaspoon freshly ground black
      pepper
  1  large egg white
  1  garlic clove, crushed
  2  teaspoons olive oil
  2  tablespoons all-purpose flour
  ¼  cup water
  ⅓  cup finely chopped fresh or
      1½ teaspoons dried basil
  2  teaspoons white wine vinegar

**1.** Combine first 6 ingredients in a large saucepan. Bring to a boil; cover, reduce heat, and simmer 20 minutes.
**2.** While peppers are cooking, place bread in a food processor; pulse 10 times or until coarse crumbs form to measure ½ cup. Combine breadcrumbs, beef, and next 6 ingredients in a bowl; shape mixture into 36 (1-inch) meatballs. Heat olive oil in a large nonstick skillet over medium-high heat. Add meatballs; cook 10 minutes, browning on all sides.
**3.** Combine flour and ¼ cup water in a small bowl; stir with a whisk. Add to bell pepper mixture in saucepan. Add meatballs; cook 3 minutes, stirring constantly. Stir in basil and vinegar. Remove bay leaf. Yield: 4 servings (serving size: 1 cup bell pepper mixture and 9 meatballs).

CALORIES 263 (34% from fat); FAT 9.8g (sat 2.9g, mono 4.7g, poly 0.8g); PROTEIN 30.2g; CARB 12.4g; FIBER 1.9g; CHOL 70mg; IRON 4.3mg; SODIUM 788mg; CALC 34mg

## Quick Chili Con Carne

**PREPARATION TIME: 5 MINUTES**
**COOKING TIME: 24 MINUTES**

  1  pound ground round
  1  cup coarsely chopped onion
  1  chopped red bell pepper
  2  tablespoons ground red pepper
1½  cups spicy-hot vegetable juice
  1  cup frozen whole-kernel corn
  1  cup beef broth
  1  (15-ounce) can black beans, rinsed
      and drained
  6  tablespoons minced fresh cilantro
  6  tablespoons (1½ ounces) shredded
      reduced-fat sharp Cheddar cheese
  6  tablespoons fat-free sour cream

**1.** Cook beef in a large nonstick skillet over medium-high heat until browned, stirring to crumble. Add onion, bell pepper, and red pepper; sauté 10 minutes or until vegetables are tender. Add juice, corn, broth, and beans; bring to a boil. Reduce heat, and simmer 10 minutes. Spoon into each of 6 soup bowls, and top each serving with cilantro, shredded cheese, and sour cream. Yield: 6 servings (serving size: 1 cup chili, 1 tablespoon cilantro, 1 tablespoon cheese, and 1 tablespoon sour cream).

CALORIES 269 (23% from fat); FAT 6.9g (sat 2.6g, mono 2.5g, poly 0.7g); PROTEIN 26.9g; CARB 25.2g; FIBER 4.4g; CHOL 51mg; IRON 3.7mg; SODIUM 600mg; CALC 120mg

## Caribbean-Style Beef Soft Tacos

Look for plantains that are just beginning to turn black.

**PREPARATION TIME: 15 MINUTES**
**COOKING TIME: 15 MINUTES**

  1  pound ground round
  2  garlic cloves, minced
  1  diced green bell pepper
  1  plantain, peeled and diced
  1  (14.5-ounce) can diced tomatoes,
      undrained
  ½  cup pimento-stuffed olives,
      chopped
  ½  teaspoon salt
  ½  teaspoon ground cumin
  ½  teaspoon black pepper
  8  (6-inch) corn tortillas
  2  cups chopped romaine lettuce

**1.** Cook beef in a large nonstick skillet over medium-high heat until browned, stirring to crumble. Add garlic, bell pepper, and plantain; cook 3 minutes. Add tomatoes and next 4 ingredients; cook 5 minutes, stirring occasionally.
**2.** Heat tortillas according to package directions. Spoon ½ cup meat mixture onto each tortilla; top each with ¼ cup lettuce, and roll up. Yield: 4 servings (serving size: 2 tacos).

CALORIES 419 (24% from fat); FAT 11.4g (sat 3.1g, mono 5.4g, poly 1.4g); PROTEIN 30.1g; CARB 52.4g; FIBER 5.9g; CHOL 70mg; IRON 6.1mg; SODIUM 874mg; CALC 166mg

---

### Beef Tips

Ground beef gets dinner on the table in a hurry, but some people wonder if the speed brings too much fat. It doesn't have to if you use the right cut.

Regular ground beef contains no more than 30% fat, while ground chuck drops to about 20%. Our choice is ground round, with no more than 15% fat. It's juicy, not greasy.

# Instant Indulgences

*Fresh fruit and convenience products mix it up to give you superfast seasonal desserts.*

Short on time and long in the sweet tooth? Not a problem if you remember two high-speed tips for indulgent urgencies: fresh, seasonal fruits and convenience products from your supermarket.

However you use them, they're so ready-to-eat that prep time seems meaningless. They're also low in fat—thanks to a new line of remarkably useful dessert sauces—and full of refreshing flavors.

What could be easier than grabbing some bananas, low-fat ice cream, and a little fudge sauce to make our instant-hit Banana-Chocolate Parfait?

## Banana-Chocolate Parfait

2  (1-ounce) hazelnut biscotti (such as La Tempesta) or plain biscotti
6  tablespoons fat-free hot fudge sauce (such as Hershey's)
4  cups low-fat coffee ice cream (such as Starbuck's Latte)
4  cups thinly sliced ripe banana (about 4 large)
1  cup canned refrigerated light whipped cream (such as Lucerne or Redi-Whip)

**1.** Place biscotti in a large zip-top plastic bag, coarsely crushing with a meat mallet or rolling pin to yield ½ cup; set aside.
**2.** Place fudge sauce in a microwave-safe bowl. Cover and microwave at HIGH 45 seconds or until melted.
**3.** Spoon ¼ cup ice cream into each of 8 parfait glasses. Top each with ¼ cup banana and 1 tablespoon whipped cream; repeat layers, ending with whipped cream. Sprinkle each parfait with about 1 tablespoon biscotti crumbs, and top

with about 1½ teaspoons fudge sauce. Yield: 8 servings.

CALORIES 324 (14% from fat); FAT 5.1g (sat 2.8g, mono 1.3g, poly 0.3g); PROTEIN 6.9g; CARB 63g; FIBER 2.4g; CHOL 15mg; IRON 0.5mg; SODIUM 134mg; CALC 117mg

## Instant Tiramisu

The Italian pop classic pick-me-up (that's what *tira mi su* means) is terrific even without the fat of the usual mascarpone-rich restaurant version. You can find ladyfingers in the bakery section of your supermarket near the packaged angel food cake.

1  cup part-skim ricotta cheese
¾  cup (6 ounces) ⅓-less-fat cream cheese
½  cup sugar
24  ladyfingers (2 [3-ounce] packages)
½  cup Kahlúa (coffee-flavored liqueur)
1  tablespoon unsweetened cocoa

**1.** Combine ricotta, cream cheese, and sugar in a food processor; process until smooth.
**2.** Split ladyfingers in half lengthwise. Arrange 24 halves in a single layer in an 11 x 7-inch baking dish. Drizzle with ¼ cup Kahlúa, and let stand 5 minutes. Spread half of cheese mixture evenly over ladyfingers. Repeat procedure with remaining ladyfingers, Kahlúa, and cheese mixture. Sprinkle with cocoa. Yield: 10 servings.

CALORIES 216 (29% from fat); FAT 6.9g (sat 5g, mono 2.5g, poly 0.3g); PROTEIN 6.8g; CARB 27g; FIBER 0.2g; CHOL 55mg; IRON 0.7mg; SODIUM 244mg; CALC 106mg

## Fast Fruit Tarts

6  tablespoons apricot preserves
1  (3.5-ounce) fat-free, commercial vanilla pudding cup (such as Hunt's)
6  mini graham cracker pie crusts (such as Keebler)
1  cup sliced strawberries
1  cup blackberries

**1.** Place preserves in a small microwave-safe bowl, and microwave at HIGH 1 minute or until melted.
**2.** Spoon 2 tablespoons pudding onto each crust; top each serving evenly with fruit. Spoon 1 tablespoon preserves over each tart. Yield: 6 servings.

CALORIES 211 (26% from fat); FAT 6.2g (sat 1g, mono 2g, poly 1.9g); PROTEIN 2g; CARB 37.9g; FIBER 2.1g; CHOL 0mg; IRON 0.7mg; SODIUM 201mg; CALC 27mg

## Tortilla Cinnamon Crisp Sundae

An entire package of 10 tortillas may be prepared and stored in an airtight container for future use; if using all 10, then triple the amounts of butter, cinnamon, and sugar.

2  tablespoons sugar
1½  teaspoons ground cinnamon
3  (8-inch) fat-free flour tortillas, each cut into 6 wedges
1  tablespoon butter or stick margarine, melted
⅓  cup fat-free caramel topping
3  cups vanilla low-fat ice cream

**1.** Preheat broiler.
**2.** Combine sugar and cinnamon. Arrange tortilla wedges on a baking sheet. Brush both sides of tortilla wedges with butter; sprinkle both sides with cinnamon-sugar mixture. Broil 1 minute on each side or until lightly browned. Place caramel topping in a small microwave-safe bowl, and microwave at HIGH 45 seconds or until melted. Place ½ cup ice cream into each of 6 bowls. Drizzle about 1 tablespoon caramel topping over each serving. Serve each sundae with 3 tortilla wedges. Yield: 6 servings.

CALORIES 239 (18% from fat); FAT 4.8g (sat 2.9g, mono 1.4g, poly 0.2g); PROTEIN 4.1g; CARB 45.4g; FIBER 0.6g; CHOL 14mg; IRON 0.8mg; SODIUM 295mg; CALC 108mg

## Peach Delight

Fresh peaches take on a caramelized sweetness under the broiler.

    2   cups fresh raspberries
    3   tablespoons sugar
    2   tablespoons water
    4   peeled peaches, halved and pitted
    2   cups vanilla low-fat ice cream
    ¼   cup chopped fresh mint

**1.** Preheat broiler.
**2.** Combine first 3 ingredients in a blender, and process until smooth. Set aside. Broil peach halves, cut sides up, 2 minutes or until lightly browned.
**3.** Place peach halves into each of 8 dessert bowls; spoon ¼ cup ice cream into each peach half. Drizzle raspberry mixture evenly over ice cream. Sprinkle each serving with 1½ teaspoons chopped mint. Yield: 8 servings.

CALORIES 100 (14% from fat); FAT 1.6g (sat 0.9g, mono 0.4g, poly 0.2g); PROTEIN 1.9g; CARB 21.2g; FIBER 3.1g; CHOL 5mg; IRON 0.3mg; SODIUM 28mg; CALC 56mg

## Spicy Melon Salad

You can usually find precut melon at your supermarket; cantaloupe and honeydew are our favorites. Ground cumin and jalapeño pepper add unexpected flavors.

    ⅔   cup water
    ½   cup minced fresh mint
    ¼   cup sugar
    1   jalapeño pepper, seeded and minced
    8   cups chopped melon (such as cantaloupe and honeydew) (about 1½ pounds)
    ½   teaspoon ground cumin

**1.** Combine first 4 ingredients in a small saucepan. Bring mixture to a boil; reduce heat, and simmer 5 minutes. Combine melon and cumin in a large bowl; drizzle with mint mixture. Toss well to combine. Yield: 8 servings (serving size: 1 cup).

CALORIES 83 (3% from fat); FAT 0.3g (sat 0.1g, mono 0g, poly 0.1g); PROTEIN 1.2g; CARB 20.9g; FIBER 1.3g; CHOL 0mg; IRON 0.3mg; SODIUM 16mg; CALC 16mg

# Balsamic Vinegar Chicken with Almond Peppers

*No chicken entrée captures our taste buds quite like this one, styled after classic Italian trattoria fare.*

Plump, sweet raisins offset tart balsamic vinegar in the bell pepper sauce. Toasted almonds lend a lively crunch. The zesty, colorful mixture tops chicken breasts bursting with juices, which are sealed in during cooking by a coating of flour, egg whites, and a breadcrumb mixture. Because it was developed with Rozanne Gold's penchant for extracting the most flavor from simple dishes, this recipe, which first appeared in our September 1994 issue, takes a mere half-hour to prepare. But the result is a dish of complex flavors worth savoring slowly, and one we knew belonged in our yearlong lineup of all-time *Cooking Light* favorites.

### Balsamic Vinegar Chicken with Almond Peppers

    2   large red bell peppers (about ¾ pound)
    2   large green bell peppers (about ¾ pound)
    2   teaspoons olive oil
    ⅓   cup raisins
    ¼   cup balsamic vinegar
    1½  teaspoons sugar
    ¼   teaspoon salt
    ⅛   teaspoon black pepper
    ¼   cup slivered almonds, toasted
    6   (4-ounce) skinned, boned chicken breast halves
    3   tablespoons dry breadcrumbs
    3   tablespoons grated Parmesan cheese
    ¼   cup all-purpose flour
    2   egg whites
    2   teaspoons olive oil
    2   tablespoons balsamic vinegar
    2   tablespoons water

**1.** Cut bell peppers into 2 x 2½-inch strips. Heat 2 teaspoons olive oil in a large nonstick skillet over medium-high heat. Add pepper strips; sauté 8 minutes. Add raisins; sauté 1 minute. Add ¼ cup vinegar, sugar, salt, and black pepper; cook 1 minute. Remove from heat; stir in almonds. Set aside, and keep warm.
**2.** Place each piece of chicken between 2 sheets of heavy-duty plastic wrap; flatten to ¼-inch thickness using a meat mallet or rolling pin. Combine breadcrumbs and cheese in a shallow dish. Place flour in a shallow dish; dredge each chicken piece in flour, and dip in egg whites. Dredge chicken in breadcrumb mixture.
**3.** Heat 2 teaspoons olive oil in a large nonstick skillet over medium-high heat. Add chicken, and cook 3 minutes on each side or until done. Remove from heat. Place chicken and bell pepper mixture on a serving platter; set aside, and keep warm.
**4.** Add 2 tablespoons vinegar and water to pan; stir with a wooden spoon to loosen browned bits. Spoon mixture over chicken and bell pepper mixture. Yield: 6 servings (serving size: 1 chicken breast half and ½ cup bell peppers).

CALORIES 288 (30% from fat); FAT 9.5g (sat 2g, mono 4.9g, poly 1.7g); PROTEIN 31.3g; CARB 19.4g; FIBER 2.6g; CHOL 74mg; IRON 2.8mg; SODIUM 253mg; CALC 73mg

# Colorfully Cookable

*Pretty lavender's subtle but distinctive flavor deserves a brighter place in your cooking.*

Fresh lavender brings a delicate, unique quality to certain foods—particularly baked goods such as biscotti, tea cakes, and rolls. While some people use the plant's blossoms and even the stems, we think the leaves deliver more and better flavors. You'll only need a little each time; the leaves are relatively potent—too much may result in a perfumy, soapy taste.

## Lavender-Honey Loaf

1 teaspoon water
1 large egg
3 tablespoons honey
1 package dry yeast (about 2¼ teaspoons)
¾ cup warm water (100° to 110°)
3½ cups all-purpose flour, divided
3 tablespoons finely chopped fresh lavender leaves
3 tablespoons butter or stick margarine, melted
1 teaspoon salt
Cooking spray

**1.** Combine 1 teaspoon water and egg in a small bowl, stirring with a whisk. Reserve 1 tablespoon egg mixture.

**2.** Dissolve honey and yeast in warm water in a large bowl; let stand 5 minutes. Lightly spoon flour into dry measuring cups; level with a knife. Add 2 cups flour, remaining egg mixture, lavender, butter, and salt to yeast mixture; stir well. Stir in 1¼ cups flour to form a stiff dough.

**3.** Turn dough out onto a lightly floured surface. Knead until smooth and elastic (about 10 minutes); add enough of remaining flour, 1 tablespoon at a time, to prevent dough from sticking to hands (dough will feel tacky).

**4.** Place dough in a large bowl coated with cooking spray, turning to coat top. Cover and let rise in a warm place (85°), free from drafts, 45 minutes or until doubled in size. (Press two fingers into dough. If indentation remains, dough has risen enough.) Punch dough down; cover and let rest 5 minutes. Divide in half. Working with one portion at a time (cover remaining dough to keep from drying), roll each portion into a 12-inch rope on a floured surface. Twist ropes together, pinching ends to seal. Place dough in an 8 x 4-inch loaf pan coated with cooking spray. Cover and let rise 45 minutes or until doubled in size.

**5.** Preheat oven to 375°.

**6.** Uncover dough. Gently brush reserved egg mixture over loaf. Bake loaf at 375° for 35 minutes or until browned on bottom and loaf sounds hollow when tapped. Remove loaf from pan; cool

completely on a wire rack. Yield: 14 servings (serving size: 1 slice).

**NOTE:** To freeze for up to 1 month, place in an airtight container, or wrap in heavy-duty plastic wrap or foil. Unwrap loaf, and thaw at room temperature 2 hours before serving.

CALORIES 157 (18% from fat); FAT 3.2g (sat 1.7g, mono 0.9g, poly 0.3g); PROTEIN 3.9g; CARB 27.8g; FIBER 1g; CHOL 22mg; IRON 1.6mg; SODIUM 198mg; CALC 8mg

## Biscotti with Lavender and Orange

½ cup sugar
3 tablespoons butter or stick margarine, softened
1½ tablespoons chopped fresh lavender leaves
½ teaspoon grated orange rind
½ teaspoon vanilla extract
2 large egg whites
1½ cups all-purpose flour
¾ teaspoon baking powder
⅛ teaspoon salt
2 tablespoons sliced almonds, toasted
Cooking spray

**1.** Preheat oven to 325°.

**2.** Beat first 5 ingredients at medium speed of a mixer until well-blended. Beat in egg whites. Lightly spoon flour into dry measuring cups, and level with a knife. Combine flour, baking powder, and salt; gradually add flour mixture to sugar mixture, beating until blended. Stir in almonds.

**3.** Turn biscotti dough out onto a baking sheet coated with cooking spray. With lightly floured hands, shape dough into a 10-inch-long roll; flatten roll to a 1-inch thickness. Bake roll at 325° for 30 minutes. Remove roll from baking sheet, and cool 10 minutes on a wire rack.

**4.** Cut roll diagonally into 14 (½-inch) slices using a serrated knife. Place slices, upright, on baking sheet. Bake slices at 325° for 15 minutes (cookies will be slightly soft in center but will harden as they cool).

**5.** Remove from baking sheet; cool completely on wire rack. Yield: 14 servings (serving size: 1 biscotto).

**NOTE:** Store in an airtight container. To freeze up to 6 months, place biscotti in an airtight container.

CALORIES 106 (26% from fat); FAT 3.1g (sat 1.6g, mono 1g, poly 0.2g); PROTEIN 2.1g; CARB 17.7g; FIBER 0.5g; CHOL 7mg; IRON 0.7mg; SODIUM 80mg; CALC 20mg

## Glazed Lavender Tea Cake

A perfect vehicle for the beginner lavender cook, this subtly sweet, delicate tea cake is great for breakfast, dessert, or a snack.

**CAKE:**

1 cup granulated sugar
5 tablespoons butter or stick margarine, softened
½ teaspoon vanilla extract
1 large egg
1 large egg white
1¾ cups all-purpose flour
1 teaspoon baking powder
¼ teaspoon baking soda
¼ teaspoon salt
1 cup plain fat-free yogurt
2 tablespoons finely chopped fresh lavender leaves
Cooking spray

**GLAZE:**

⅓ cup sifted powdered sugar
1 teaspoon water
¼ teaspoon vanilla extract

**1.** Preheat oven to 350°.

**2.** To prepare cake, beat granulated sugar, butter, and ½ teaspoon vanilla at medium speed of a mixer until well-blended (about 5 minutes). Add egg and egg white, 1 at a time; beat well after each addition. Lightly spoon flour into dry measuring cups; level with a knife. Combine flour, baking powder, baking soda, and salt. Add flour mixture to sugar mixture alternately with yogurt, beginning and ending with flour mixture. Stir in lavender.

*Continued*

**3.** Pour batter into an 8-inch loaf pan coated with cooking spray. Bake at 350° for 1 hour or until a wooden pick inserted in center comes out clean.

**4.** To prepare glaze, combine powdered sugar, water, and ¼ teaspoon vanilla. Spread over hot cake. Cool in pan 20 minutes on a wire rack; remove from pan. Cool completely on wire rack. Yield: 10 servings (serving size: 1 slice).

**NOTE**: To freeze up to 1 month without glaze, place in an airtight container, or wrap in heavy-duty plastic wrap or foil. Unwrap and thaw at room temperature 2 hours before serving. Prepare glaze, and spread over cake.

CALORIES 247 (24% from fat); FAT 6.6g (sat 3.8g, mono 1.9g, poly 0.4g); PROTEIN 4.6g; CARB 42.7g; FIBER 0.6g; CHOL 38mg; IRON 1.2mg; SODIUM 227mg; CALC 80mg

## Lavender-Apricot Swirls

Instead of the usual cinnamon rolls, try this brightly flavored alternative.

    2¼   cups all-purpose flour
    ¼    cup sugar
    2½   teaspoons baking powder
    ½    teaspoon salt
    3    tablespoons chilled butter or stick
         margarine, cut into small pieces
    2    tablespoons chopped fresh
         lavender leaves
    ½    cup 1% low-fat milk
    1    large egg, lightly beaten
    2    tablespoons apricot preserves
    Cooking spray
    1½   teaspoons sugar

**1.** Preheat oven to 375°.
**2.** Lightly spoon flour into dry measuring cups, and level with a knife. Combine flour, ¼ cup sugar, baking powder, and salt in a bowl; cut in butter with a pastry blender or 2 knives until mixture resembles coarse meal. Stir in lavender. Add milk and egg, stirring just until moist.
**3.** Turn dough out onto a lightly floured surface. Knead 5 times. Roll into a 9 x 7-inch rectangle. Spread apricot preserves over dough, leaving a ½-inch border. Beginning with long side, roll up jelly-roll

fashion; pinch seam to seal (do not seal ends of roll). Cut roll into 9 (1-inch) slices. Place slices, cut sides up, in an 8-inch round cake pan coated with cooking spray. Sprinkle slices with 1½ teaspoons sugar. Bake at 375° for 35 minutes or until golden brown and a wooden pick inserted in center comes out clean. Yield: 9 servings.

**NOTE**: To freeze for up to 1 month, place swirls in an airtight container, or wrap in heavy-duty plastic wrap or foil. Unwrap and thaw at room temperature 2 hours before serving.

CALORIES 198 (22% from fat); FAT 4.9g (sat 2.7g, mono 1.4g, poly 0.4g); PROTEIN 4.5g; CARB 34g; FIBER 0.9g; CHOL 35mg; IRON 1.7mg; SODIUM 321mg; CALC 102mg

## Lavender Lemonade

Lavender adds a delightfully different dimension to this refreshing summer favorite.

    4    cups water, divided
    ¼    cup chopped fresh lavender leaves
    ⅔    cup sugar
    1    cup fresh lemon juice (about 6
         lemons)
    Lavender stems (optional)

**1.** Bring 1 cup water to a boil in a medium saucepan. Combine boiling water and lavender in a medium bowl; cover and steep 30 minutes. Strain lavender mixture through a fine sieve into a bowl; discard lavender leaves.
**2.** Combine 3 cups water and sugar in saucepan. Bring mixture to a boil, and cook 1 minute or until sugar is dissolved. Combine lavender water, sugar syrup, and lemon juice in a pitcher. Cover and chill. Serve over ice. Garnish lemonade with lavender stems, if desired. Yield: 5 servings (serving size: 1 cup).

CALORIES 115 (0% from fat); FAT 0g; PROTEIN 0.2g; CARB 30.9g; FIBER 0.2g; CHOL 0mg; IRON 0mg; SODIUM 1mg; CALC 4mg

## Lavender-Pineapple Granita

    1    cup water
    ¾    cup pineapple juice
    ⅓    cup sugar
    3    tablespoons chopped fresh
         lavender leaves
    Lavender blooms (optional)

**1.** Combine first 4 ingredients in a medium saucepan. Bring to a boil, stirring occasionally; remove from heat. Let stand 30 minutes.
**2.** Strain lavender mixture through a fine sieve over a bowl, discarding solids. Pour mixture into a 13 x 9-inch baking dish. Cover and freeze 8 hours or until firm.
**3.** Remove lavender mixture from freezer, and scrape entire mixture with a fork until fluffy. Garnish with lavender blooms, if desired. Yield: 6 servings (serving size: ½ cup).

CALORIES 61 (0% from fat); FAT 0g; PROTEIN 0.1g; CARB 15.4g; FIBER 0g; CHOL 0mg; IRON 0.1mg; SODIUM 0mg; CALC 5mg

### Cooking with Lavender

Cooking with lavender is actually pretty straightforward. In most cases, you simply pull the leaves from the stem (toward the flowers, not the roots), then chop the leaves and add them directly to the recipe.

In some uses, such as for our lemonade and granita, you'll steep the leaves in water, and then strain out the leaves—similar to brewing a cup of tea. And don't forget the blossoms. Put them in a vase on the table, and let their fragrance fill the room.

# july

# Corn to Be Wild

## Hey, this was the food of the gods. Cook it with attitude.

Corn brings more to the table than we of recent generations may have been lulled into believing. Call it a resurgence, call it a reawakening, or call it revenge—the latest chapter in the corn chronicles is all about popping back.

### Roasted Corn, Black Bean, and Mango Salad

(pictured on page 203)

Browning corn in a skillet gives it a nutty, caramelized flavor that contrasts with the tartness of the mango. But brown it well—corn likes it that way.

- 1 tablespoon vegetable oil
- 2 garlic cloves, minced
- 3 cups fresh corn kernels (about 6 ears)
- 2 cups diced peeled ripe mango (about 2 pounds)
- 1 cup chopped red onion
- 1 cup chopped red bell pepper
- ⅓ cup fresh lime juice
- 3 tablespoons chopped fresh cilantro
- ½ teaspoon salt
- ½ teaspoon ground cumin
- 1 drained canned chipotle chile in adobo sauce, chopped
- 2 (15-ounce) cans black beans, rinsed and drained
- 8 cups gourmet salad greens

**1.** Heat oil in a large nonstick skillet over medium-high heat. Add garlic; cook 30 seconds. Stir in corn; cook 8 minutes or until browned, stirring occasionally. Place corn mixture in a large bowl. Add mango and next 8 ingredients; stir well. Arrange 1 cup greens on each of 8 plates. Spoon 1 cup corn mixture over each serving. Yield: 8 servings.

CALORIES 204 (15% from fat); FAT 3.3g (sat 0.6g, mono 0.8g, poly 1.5g); PROTEIN 9.2g; CARB 39g; FIBER 6.9g; CHOL 0mg; IRON 2.8mg; SODIUM 315mg; CALC 56mg

---

**menu**

**Corn-and-Shrimp Tortilla Soup**

**Grilled mangoes with cilantro vinaigrette***

*Peel and cut 2 mangoes into ¼-inch slices. Grill or broil 2 minutes on each side or until golden. Combine 2 tablespoons fresh lime juice, 1 tablespoon chopped fresh cilantro, 1 teaspoon minced jalapeño pepper, and 1 teaspoon olive oil. Brush over mango slices. Serves 4.

### Corn-and-Shrimp Tortilla Soup

- 1½ tablespoons vegetable oil, divided
- 4 (6-inch) corn tortillas, cut into ¼-inch strips
- 1 cup chopped red bell pepper
- 1 teaspoon ground cumin
- 1 teaspoon dried oregano
- 2 garlic cloves, minced
- 2 jalapeño peppers, seeded and minced
- 1 (14.5-ounce) can diced tomatoes, drained
- 1 (16-ounce) can fat-free, less-sodium chicken broth
- 1 (8-ounce) bottle clam juice
- 2 cups fresh corn kernels (about 4 ears)
- 1½ pounds medium shrimp, peeled and deveined
- ½ cup chopped green onions
- ¼ cup chopped fresh cilantro
- ¼ cup lime juice
- ¼ teaspoon black pepper

**1.** Heat 1 tablespoon oil in a Dutch oven over medium-high heat. Add tortilla strips, and sauté 4 minutes or until crisp. Remove strips, and drain on paper towels.

**2.** Add 1½ teaspoons oil to pan. Add bell pepper and next 5 ingredients; sauté 4 minutes. Stir in broth and clam juice; bring to a boil. Reduce heat, and simmer 5 minutes. Add corn and shrimp; cook 3 minutes or until shrimp are done. Remove from heat; stir in onions, cilantro, lime juice, and black pepper. Ladle soup into bowls. Divide tortilla strips evenly over servings. Yield: 4 servings (serving size: 1¾ cups).

**NOTE:** To freeze up to 1 month, place cooled soup in an airtight container. Thaw in refrigerator.

CALORIES 353 (24% from fat); FAT 9.3g (sat 1.6g, mono 2.4g, poly 4.2g); PROTEIN 33.2g; CARB 36.9g; FIBER 5.6g; CHOL 196mg; IRON 5.9mg; SODIUM 719mg; CALC 169mg

### Cajun-Grilled Corn on the Cob

- 1 teaspoon dried oregano
- 1 teaspoon paprika
- ¾ teaspoon garlic powder
- ¾ teaspoon onion powder
- ½ teaspoon salt
- ¼ teaspoon dried thyme
- ¼ teaspoon black pepper
- ⅛ teaspoon ground red pepper
- 4 ears corn with husks
- 2 teaspoons butter or stick margarine, melted

**1.** Prepare grill.

**2.** Combine first 8 ingredients in a small bowl; set aside.

**3.** Pull husks back from corn, and scrub silks. Brush butter over corn; sprinkle with spice mixture. Place corn on grill rack; grill 12 minutes or until done, turning occasionally. Yield: 4 servings (serving size: 1 ear of corn).

CALORIES 105 (26% from fat); FAT 3g (sat 1.4g, mono 0.9g, poly 0.6g); PROTEIN 2.7g; CARB 20.3g; FIBER 3.1g; CHOL 5mg; IRON 0.9mg; SODIUM 326mg; CALC 13mg

## North African-Grilled Corn on the Cob

2 teaspoons ground cumin
2 teaspoons ground coriander
1 teaspoon dried oregano
½ teaspoon ground ginger
½ teaspoon salt
¼ teaspoon ground cinnamon
¼ teaspoon black pepper
Dash of ground cloves
4 ears corn with husks
2 teaspoons butter or stick margarine, melted

**1.** Prepare grill.
**2.** Combine first 8 ingredients in a small bowl; set aside.
**3.** Pull husks back from corn; scrub silks. Brush butter over corn; sprinkle with spice mixture. Place corn on grill rack; grill 12 minutes or until done, turning occasionally. Yield: 4 servings (serving size: 1 ear of corn).

CALORIES 105 (27% from fat); FAT 3.2g (sat 1.4g, mono 1.0g, poly 0.6g); PROTEIN 2.7g; CARB 20.1g; FIBER 3.1g; CHOL 5mg; IRON 1.5mg; SODIUM 328mg; CALC 24mg

## Jerk-Grilled Corn on the Cob

¾ teaspoon ground allspice
½ teaspoon dried thyme
½ teaspoon ground cinnamon
½ teaspoon salt
½ teaspoon black pepper
¼ teaspoon ground nutmeg
⅛ teaspoon ground red pepper
4 ears corn with husks
2 teaspoons butter or stick margarine, melted

**1.** Prepare grill.
**2.** Combine first 7 ingredients; set aside.
**3.** Pull husks back from corn, and scrub silks. Brush butter over corn; sprinkle with spice mixture. Place corn on grill rack; grill 12 minutes or until done, turning occasionally. Yield: 4 servings (serving size: 1 ear of corn).

CALORIES 102 (26% from fat); FAT 3g (sat 1.4g, mono 0.9g, poly 0.5g); PROTEIN 2.5g; CARB 19.7g; FIBER 3g; CHOL 5mg; IRON 0.9mg; SODIUM 326mg; CALC 13mg

## Curried Corn-Crab Cakes

¾ cup fresh corn kernels (about 2 ears)
¼ cup finely chopped onion
¼ cup diced red bell pepper
½ teaspoon curry powder
1 garlic clove, minced
1 pound lump crabmeat, shells removed
⅓ cup low-fat mayonnaise
3 tablespoons minced fresh cilantro
2 tablespoons chopped fresh mint
2 tablespoons fresh lime juice
1 tablespoon low-sodium soy sauce
2 large egg whites
10 tablespoons dry breadcrumbs, divided
4 teaspoons vegetable oil
Lime wedges

**1.** Heat a large nonstick skillet over medium-high heat. Add first 5 ingredients; sauté 4 minutes or until vegetables are soft. Place corn mixture in a large bowl; cool completely. Stir in crabmeat; set aside.
**2.** Combine mayonnaise and next 5 ingredients in a small bowl. Gently fold mayonnaise mixture into crab mixture. Stir in 7 tablespoons breadcrumbs. Divide mixture into 8 equal portions, shaping each into a ¾-inch-thick patty. Dredge patties in 3 tablespoons breadcrumbs.
**3.** Heat oil in pan over medium-high heat. Place patties in pan; cook 4 minutes. Turn patties, and cover pan; cook 4 minutes or until done. Serve with lime wedges. Yield: 8 servings (serving size: 1 patty).

CALORIES 151 (27% from fat); FAT 4.6g (sat 0.8g, mono 1.3g, poly 2.1g); PROTEIN 14.1g; CARB 13.1g; FIBER 0.9g; CHOL 57mg; IRON 1.4mg; SODIUM 400mg; CALC 84mg

## Buttermilk-Apricot-Corn Sherbet

At first glance, corn may seem odd in a dessert. But its sweet flavor and juicy texture make it all that a sherbet could ever dream of.

1¼ cups fresh corn kernels (about 2 ears)
½ cup sugar
⅓ cup fresh lemon juice
¼ cup honey
1 (15¼-ounce) can apricot halves in heavy syrup, drained
2 cups low-fat buttermilk

**1.** Place first 5 ingredients in a blender or food processor; process until smooth. Combine corn mixture and buttermilk in a large bowl; cover and chill 20 minutes.
**2.** Pour buttermilk mixture into freezer can of an ice-cream freezer; freeze according to manufacturer's instructions. Spoon ice cream into a freezer-safe container; cover and freeze 1 hour or until firm. Yield: 10 servings (serving size: ½ cup).

CALORIES 125 (7% from fat); FAT 1g (sat 0.5g, mono 0.3g, poly 0.1g); PROTEIN 2.5g; CARB 28.3g; FIBER 1g; CHOL 2mg; IRON 0.3mg; SODIUM 29mg; CALC 62mg

## Cumin-Spiked Popcorn

So what if it's not fresh corn? We couldn't resist throwing in a popcorn recipe.

¾ cup popcorn kernels
1 tablespoon olive oil
1½ teaspoons ground cumin
1 teaspoon ground coriander
1 teaspoon salt
⅛ teaspoon ground red pepper

**1.** Combine all ingredients in a Dutch oven. Cover and shake vigorously 7 minutes over medium-high heat or until all kernels are popped. Yield: 4 quarts (serving size: 2 cups).
**NOTE:** Store in an airtight container.

CALORIES 86 (28% from fat); FAT 2.7g (sat 0.4g, mono 1.5g, poly 0.5g); PROTEIN 2.4g; CARB 14.1g; FIBER 3g; CHOL 0mg; IRON 0.8mg; SODIUM 294mg; CALC 7mg

## Strawberry Shortcakes with Corn

The classic is reinvented with sweet corn tucked inside the shortcakes.

**SHORTCAKES:**

1¾ cups all-purpose flour
¼ cup yellow cornmeal
1½ teaspoons baking powder
½ teaspoon salt
¼ teaspoon baking soda
6 tablespoons chilled butter or stick margarine, cut into small pieces
1 cup fresh corn kernels (about 2 ears)
¾ cup low-fat buttermilk
5 tablespoons plus 2 teaspoons brown sugar, divided

**STRAWBERRIES:**

5 cups quartered strawberries
1 tablespoon brown sugar

**REMAINING INGREDIENT:**

2½ cups vanilla low-fat yogurt

**1.** Preheat oven to 425°.
**2.** To prepare shortcakes, lightly spoon flour into dry measuring cups, and level with a knife. Combine flour and next 4 ingredients in a bowl; cut in butter with a pastry blender or 2 knives until mixture resembles coarse meal. Stir in corn.
**3.** Combine buttermilk and ¼ cup brown sugar in a small bowl. Add to flour mixture; stir until a soft dough forms (dough may be sticky). Turn dough out onto a floured surface; shape into a 9 x 7-inch rectangle, and flatten to ½-inch thickness. Cut dough into 10 rectangles.
**4.** Line a baking sheet with parchment paper. Place shortcakes on pan; top each shortcake with ½ teaspoon brown sugar. Bake at 425° for 15 minutes or until done. Cool.
**5.** Combine strawberries and 1 table-spoon brown sugar in a large bowl. Let stand 15 minutes.
**6.** Spoon yogurt onto several layers of heavy-duty paper towels; spread to ½-inch thickness. Cover with additional paper towels; let stand 5 minutes. Scrape into a bowl using a rubber spatula; cover and refrigerate.
**7.** To serve, split each shortcake in half horizontally. Fill each with ½ cup strawberries and 1 tablespoon yogurt. Yield: 10 servings.

**NOTE:** To freeze shortcakes up to 1 month, wrap cooled shortcakes in heavy-duty plastic wrap and foil. Thaw at room temperature.

CALORIES 281 (28% from fat); FAT 8.7g (sat 5g, mono 2.4g, poly 0.6g); PROTEIN 7.1g; CARB 45.5g; FIBER 3g; CHOL 22mg; IRON 1.8mg; SODIUM 346mg; CALC 185mg

## passport

# Market Inspiration

*For fresh food ideas in Paris or Peoria, explore the local market.*

It's been more than 70 years since Papa Hemingway shopped the Left Bank markets along the Rue de Mouffetard, but not much has changed. Sure, Parisians have succumbed to the convenience of supermarkets for staples such as canned foods. But most still trek to neighborhood markets for fresh produce, cheese, seafood, pâté, and flowers or a bottle of wine.

On the Rue de Mouffetard, seasoned merchants line the busy cobblestone lane, proudly displaying their assortments of domestic and imported fare. You can survey vine-ripe tomatoes from Provence, pungent goat cheese from Sancerre, fresh shellfish from the coast—even sweet Florida corn and Chilean peaches.

## Mussels Steamed in White Wine

1 tablespoon olive oil
1½ cups finely chopped onion
1½ cups dry white wine
3 pounds mussels, scrubbed and debearded (about 60 mussels)
¼ cup finely chopped fresh parsley
½ teaspoon black pepper

**1.** Heat olive oil in a large stockpot over medium heat. Add onion, and sauté 4 minutes or until tender. Add wine, and bring to a simmer. Add mussels; cover and cook 5 minutes or until shells open. Remove from heat, and discard any unopened shells. Divide mussels and broth evenly among 4 shallow bowls; sprinkle with parsley and pepper. Yield: 4 servings (serving size: about 15 mussels and ⅓ cup broth).

CALORIES 220 (26% from fat); FAT 6.3g (sat 1g, mono 3.1g, poly 1.1g); PROTEIN 15.6g; CARB 11g; FIBER 1.4g; CHOL 35mg; IRON 5.8mg; SODIUM 360mg; CALC 59mg

### Sorting and Cleaning Mussels

• Make sure the mussels are alive. Thump an opened shell; if it closes, the mussel is alive and fine to use. Discard any that refuse to close.
• Scrub the shells with a stiff brush to remove any debris.
• Remove the byssus, or "beard," that hangs out of the shell. Simply pull it off with your fingers. Mussels spoil quickly after debearding, so prepare them immediately.

## Home-Style Parisian Potato Salad

The vinegar and anchovies give this dish a fresh, seasonal flavor you don't find in most mayonnaise-based potato salads.

1½ pounds small red potatoes (about 15 potatoes)
3 tablespoons sherry vinegar or red wine vinegar, divided
¼ teaspoon salt
¼ teaspoon black pepper
3 tablespoons finely chopped bottled roasted red bell peppers
2 tablespoons minced fresh parsley
1 tablespoon extra-virgin olive oil
8 chopped pitted kalamata olives
4 canned anchovy fillets, finely chopped (about 1 ounce)
2 garlic cloves, minced
Flat-leaf parsley sprigs (optional)
Whole anchovy fillets (optional)

1. Place potatoes in a large saucepan, and cover with water; bring to a boil. Reduce heat, and simmer 15 minutes or until tender; drain and cool slightly. Cut potatoes into ¼-inch-thick slices. Combine potatoes, 2 tablespoons vinegar, salt, and pepper; toss gently. Let stand 5 minutes.
2. Combine 1 tablespoon vinegar, bell pepper, and next 5 ingredients in a bowl; stir with a whisk. Pour over potatoes; toss gently to coat. Garnish with parsley sprigs and whole anchovy fillets, if desired. Serve at room temperature. Yield: 4 servings (serving size: 1 cup).

CALORIES 192 (23% from fat); FAT 4.9g (sat 0.8g, mono 3.3g, poly 0.6g); PROTEIN 5.3g; CARB 30.7g; FIBER 3.6g; CHOL 4mg; IRON 2.9mg; SODIUM 444mg; CALC 46mg

## Salad with Goat Cheese Croutons

Briefly freezing the goat cheese will help prevent it from crumbling when you slice it. Pureed chickpeas add body to the light, flavorful vinaigrette.

    1   (4-ounce) package goat cheese
    1   (15½-ounce) can chickpeas
        (garbanzo beans), undrained
    2   tablespoons white wine vinegar
    1   tablespoon finely chopped shallots
    1   tablespoon chopped fresh chives
    2   teaspoons Dijon mustard
    1   teaspoon fresh lemon juice
    ½   teaspoon extra-virgin olive oil
    ¼   teaspoon salt
    ¼   teaspoon black pepper
    6   (½-inch-thick) slices French bread
        baguette
   12   cups gourmet salad greens

1. Place goat cheese in freezer 10 minutes or until firm.
2. Drain chickpeas in a colander over a bowl; reserve ½ cup liquid. Combine 2 tablespoons chickpeas, liquid, vinegar, and next 7 ingredients in a blender; process until smooth. Reserve remaining chickpeas for salad.
3. Preheat broiler.
4. Cut goat cheese into 6 rounds. Place bread slices on a baking sheet; broil 2 minutes or until toasted. Top each bread slice with a goat cheese round; broil 1 minute or until lightly browned.
5. Combine chickpea vinaigrette, remaining chickpeas, and salad greens in a bowl, and toss well. Serve with goat cheese croutons. Yield: 6 servings (serving size: 1⅔ cups salad and 1 crouton).

CALORIES 202 (27% from fat); FAT 6g (sat 3.1g, mono 1.6g, poly 0.8g); PROTEIN 9.4g; CARB 27.9g; FIBER 7.1g; CHOL 17mg; IRON 2.8mg; SODIUM 509mg; CALC 169mg

## Country Chicken Pâté

We kept the creamy texture of this lightened classic by using low-fat sour cream and fat-free cream cheese instead of butter and heavy cream. Serve this rich appetizer with a French bread baguette, coarse-grained mustard, and gherkins.

    1   teaspoon butter or stick
        margarine
    ½   cup finely chopped onion
    2   garlic cloves, chopped
    4   ounces chicken livers
    2   tablespoons port or other
        sweet red wine
    ½   teaspoon salt
    ½   teaspoon black pepper
    ¼   teaspoon dried thyme
    ¼   teaspoon ground nutmeg
Dash of ground cinnamon
Dash of ground allspice
    1   tablespoon low-fat sour cream
    1   pound boned, skinned chicken
        breast, cut into ½-inch pieces
    1   (8-ounce) block fat-free cream
        cheese, cubed and softened
Cooking spray

1. Preheat oven to 325°.
2. Melt butter in a small nonstick skillet over medium heat. Add onion and garlic, and sauté 4 minutes. Add chicken livers; cook 2 minutes or until livers lose their pink color. Add port, and cook 3 minutes or until most of liquid evaporates. Cool.
3. Place chicken liver mixture, salt, and next 5 ingredients in a food processor or blender; process until smooth, scraping sides of bowl occasionally. Add sour cream, chicken breast, and cream cheese; process until smooth, scraping sides of bowl occasionally. Spread chicken mixture into an 8 x 4-inch loaf pan coated with cooking spray. Bake at 325° for 1 hour or until a thermometer registers 170°. Cool; cover and chill 8 hours. Serve at room temperature. Yield: 10 servings.

CALORIES 95 (16% from fat); FAT 1.7g (sat 0.7g, mono 0.4g, poly 0.3g); PROTEIN 15.9g; CARB 2.4g; FIBER 0.2g; CHOL 82mg; IRON 1.4mg; SODIUM 297mg; CALC 76mg

## Steamed Salmon with Watercress Sauce

As many seafood-loving French cooks know, there's no better way to retain the flavor and succulence of a fresh fish fillet than by steaming it in the microwave. Peppery watercress in the creamy sauce balances the sharpness of the lemon juice-steamed salmon.

    1   cup fat-free, less-sodium chicken
        broth
    ½   cup Chardonnay or other dry
        white wine
    ¼   cup minced shallots
    1   bay leaf
    ¼   cup 1% low-fat milk
    2   teaspoons cornstarch
    ½   cup finely chopped trimmed
        watercress
    4   (6-ounce) salmon fillets
        (about 1 inch thick)
    2   tablespoons fresh lemon juice
        (about 1 medium lemon)
    ¼   teaspoon salt
    ¼   teaspoon freshly ground black
        pepper
Watercress sprigs (optional)
Lemon wedges (optional)

1. Combine first 4 ingredients in a small saucepan; bring to a boil. Reduce heat, and simmer, uncovered, until reduced to ¾ cup (about 20 minutes). Discard bay leaf. Combine milk and cornstarch, stirring with a whisk. Add to broth mixture; bring to a boil. Cook 1 minute, stirring constantly. Stir in chopped watercress; cook 30 seconds. Keep warm.

*Continued*

**2.** Arrange salmon fillets in a single layer in an 11 x 7-inch baking dish, and sprinkle with lemon juice, salt, and pepper. Cover with plastic wrap, and vent. Microwave at HIGH 4½ minutes or until fish flakes easily when tested with a fork. Place 1 fillet on each of 4 plates; top each serving with ¼ cup sauce. Garnish with watercress sprigs and lemon wedges, if desired. Yield: 4 servings.

CALORIES 304 (42% from fat); FAT 14.2g (sat 2.6g, mono 6.8g, poly 3.1g); PROTEIN 36.5g; CARB 5.1g; FIBER 0.2g; CHOL 112mg; IRON 1mg; SODIUM 364mg; CALC 40mg

inspired vegetarian

# Greatest-Hit Medleys

*Stir-fry doesn't have to be your final answer in uniting the flavors of fresh vegetables and spices.*

If you're not a stir-fry kind of cook, you may like these medleys—combinations of a variety of vegetables seasoned with a sauce or distinctive flavorings. That's essentially what stir-frying does, too, but there's a difference.

With a stir-fry, most of the prep work of paring, trimming, and cutting is done up-front; then the vegetables are cooked quickly over high heat.

Medleys break it down in staggered layers. Onions and hard vegetables, for instance, get a head start in the pot; other faster-cooking ingredients can be prepared closer to the finale. And the cooking is gentler throughout.

Medleys let you meld the many options into even bigger and more interesting combinations.

## Eggplant, Potato, and Chickpea Casserole

1 large red or yellow bell pepper
¾ pound peeled Yukon gold or red potato, cut into 2-inch cubes
1 cup basil leaves
1 cup cilantro sprigs
1 tablespoon olive oil
¼ teaspoon ground cumin
2 garlic cloves
2 cups chopped seeded tomato (about 1 pound)
½ cup water
½ teaspoon salt
¼ teaspoon freshly ground black pepper
1 (1-pound) eggplant, cut into 2-inch pieces
1 large onion, cut into 8 wedges (about ½ pound)
1 (15½-ounce) can chickpeas (garbanzo beans), drained
6 lemon wedges (optional)

**1.** Preheat broiler.
**2.** Cut bell pepper in half lengthwise, and discard seeds and membranes. Place pepper halves, skin sides up, on a foil-lined baking sheet; flatten with hand. Broil 10 minutes or until blackened. Place in a zip-top plastic bag, and seal. Let stand 10 minutes. Peel and cut into large strips.
**3.** Place potato in a medium saucepan, and cover with water; bring to a boil. Reduce heat, and simmer 5 minutes; drain potato.
**4.** Preheat oven to 375°.
**5.** Combine basil and next 4 ingredients in a food processor; process until finely minced. Combine bell pepper, cooked potato, basil mixture, tomato, and next 6 ingredients in a 13 x 9-inch baking dish; cover with foil. Bake at 375° for 1 hour. Uncover, stir, and bake an additional 20 minutes or until vegetables are tender. Serve with lemon wedges, if desired. Yield: 4 servings (serving size: 2 cups).

CALORIES 324 (18% from fat); FAT 6.6g (sat 0.9g, mono 3.1g, poly 1.7g); PROTEIN 12.8g; CARB 58.5g; FIBER 11g; CHOL 0mg; IRON 5.8mg; SODIUM 446mg; CALC 115mg

## Summer Squash, Carrot, and Green Pea Ragoût over Polenta

This light-and-simple ragoût made with fresh produce is the essence of summer. Make the polenta first, and keep it warm while you prepare the vegetables.

POLENTA:
4 cups water
1 cup instant polenta
½ teaspoon salt

RAGOÛT:
2 cups thinly sliced carrot
2 teaspoons olive oil
1 cup diced onion
1 garlic clove, minced
3 cups diced yellow squash (about 1 pound)
1¼ cups water, divided
2 tablespoons chopped fresh flat-leaf parsley, divided
½ teaspoon salt
¼ teaspoon freshly ground black pepper
2 cups shelled green peas (about 2 pounds unshelled green peas)
¼ cup thinly sliced fresh basil
2 tablespoons fresh lemon juice
1½ tablespoons butter or stick margarine
5 tablespoons (about 1 ounce) grated Asiago cheese

**1.** To prepare polenta, bring 4 cups water to a boil in a saucepan; stir in polenta and ½ teaspoon salt. Reduce heat, and cook until thick (about 5 minutes), stirring frequently. Keep warm.
**2.** To prepare ragoût, cook carrot in boiling water 5 minutes or until crisp-tender; drain. Rinse with cold water; drain well.
**3.** Heat oil in a Dutch oven over medium heat. Add onion and garlic; cook 5 minutes or until soft. Stir in squash, ½ cup water, 1 tablespoon parsley, ½ teaspoon salt, and pepper; cover, reduce heat, and simmer 8 minutes or until squash is tender. Stir in carrot, ¾ cup water, and peas. Bring to a simmer; cook 10 minutes. Stir in 1 tablespoon parsley, basil, lemon juice, and butter. Serve ragoût with

polenta. Sprinkle with cheese. Yield: 5 servings (serving size: 1 cup ragoût, ¾ cup polenta, and 1 tablespoon cheese).

CALORIES 294 (25% from fat); FAT 8.3g (sat 3.7g, mono 2.9g, poly 0.6g); PROTEIN 9.6g; CARB 49.4g; FIBER 5.8g; CHOL 17mg; IRON 1.7mg; SODIUM 615mg; CALC 136mg

## Thai Summer Squash and Tofu with Fresh Corn

This dish is rich and soupy; the basmati rice makes a flavorful base. Fresh corn adds a natural sweetness.

 1   teaspoon roasted peanut oil or vegetable oil
 1   cup diced yellow squash
 1   cup diced zucchini
 1   (12.3-ounce) package reduced-fat extra-firm tofu, drained and cut into ½-inch cubes
 ½   teaspoon salt, divided
 3   cups fresh corn kernels (about 4 ears)
 1   cup light coconut milk
 ¾   cup (½-inch) sliced green onions
 ⅓   cup water
 1   tablespoon chopped fresh basil
 1   tablespoon chopped fresh cilantro
 1   teaspoon low-sodium soy sauce
 ¼   teaspoon freshly ground black pepper
 1   jalapeño pepper, seeded and chopped
 2   cups hot cooked basmati rice
 2   tablespoons chopped unsalted cashews, toasted

**1.** Heat oil in a large nonstick skillet over medium-high heat. Add yellow squash, zucchini, and tofu; sprinkle with ¼ teaspoon salt. Stir-fry 8 minutes or until lightly browned. Stir in ¼ teaspoon salt, corn, and next 8 ingredients. Reduce heat, and simmer 8 minutes or until corn is tender. Serve with rice. Sprinkle with cashews. Yield: 4 servings (serving size: 1¼ cups vegetables, ½ cup rice, and 1½ teaspoons nuts).

CALORIES 283 (28% from fat); FAT 8.7g (sat 3g, mono 2.4g, poly 2.1g); PROTEIN 12.9g; CARB 43.4g; FIBER 5.5g; CHOL 0mg; IRON 3.1mg; SODIUM 462mg; CALC 78mg

## Summer Vegetable Stew with Basil Puree

**BASIL PUREE:**
 1   cup basil leaves
 1   garlic clove
 3   tablespoons water
 2   tablespoons olive oil
 ⅛   teaspoon salt

**VEGETABLES:**
 1   tablespoon olive oil
 2   bay leaves
 1   onion, cut into ¼-inch-thick wedges
 6   garlic cloves, halved
 2   thyme sprigs
 1½  cups (2-inch-thick) sliced carrot
 1   pound small red potatoes, halved
 ½   teaspoon salt
 ½   teaspoon black pepper
 3   cups (1-inch) cubed yellow squash (about ¾ pound)
 1   cup yellow bell pepper strips
 ½   pound green beans, trimmed and cut into 3-inch pieces
 2   tomatoes, peeled and cut into 1-inch pieces
 2   tablespoons (½ ounce) grated fresh Parmesan cheese

**1.** To prepare basil puree, combine basil and 1 garlic clove in a blender; process until smooth. Add water, 2 tablespoons oil, and ⅛ teaspoon salt; process until blended. Set aside.
**2.** To prepare vegetables, heat 1 tablespoon oil in a large Dutch oven over low heat. Add bay leaves; cook 1 minute. Add onion, 6 garlic cloves, and thyme; cover and cook 10 minutes. Add carrot, potatoes, ½ teaspoon salt, and black pepper; cover and cook 20 minutes. Add squash, bell pepper, and beans; cover and cook 15 minutes. Add tomatoes; cover and cook 10 minutes. Discard bay leaves and thyme. Spoon stew into individual bowls; drizzle with basil puree, and sprinkle with Parmesan. Yield: 5 servings (serving size: 2 cups stew, about 1 tablespoon basil puree, and about 1 teaspoon cheese).

CALORIES 240 (36% from fat); FAT 9.7g (sat 1.7g, mono 6.3g, poly 1.1g); PROTEIN 6.8g; CARB 35.4g; FIBER 7.5g; CHOL 2mg; IRON 3.3mg; SODIUM 373mg; CALC 123mg

## Bell Pepper-and-Potato Tagine over Couscous

Harissa is a fiery-hot condiment available in Middle Eastern markets.

 2   teaspoons olive oil
 1¾  cups diced onion
 2   tablespoons tomato paste
 1½  teaspoons dried mint flakes
 ½   teaspoon crushed red pepper
 6   garlic cloves, crushed
 2   peeled baking potatoes, each cut into 6 wedges (about 1 pound)
 2   cups (1-inch) red bell pepper strips
 2   cups (1-inch) green bell pepper strips
 1   teaspoon salt
 1   (15½-ounce) can chickpeas (garbanzo beans), drained
 3   cups chopped seeded tomato (about 2 pounds)
 3   cups water
 1   teaspoon harissa (optional)
 ¾   cup uncooked couscous
 3   tablespoons chopped fresh parsley

**1.** Heat olive oil in a Dutch oven over medium-high heat. Add onion and next 5 ingredients; cook 10 minutes, stirring occasionally. Add bell peppers, salt, and chickpeas; sauté 5 minutes. Stir in tomato and water. Bring to a boil; partially cover, reduce heat, and simmer 25 minutes or until potato is tender. Remove vegetables with a slotted spoon. Set aside; keep warm. Reserve 1 cup cooking liquid.
**2.** Bring reserved cooking liquid to a boil in a medium saucepan; stir in harissa, if desired. Gradually stir in couscous. Remove from heat; cover and let stand 5 minutes. Fluff with a fork. Serve with vegetables; sprinkle with chopped parsley. Yield: 5 servings (serving size: about 1⅓ cups tagine and ½ cup couscous).

CALORIES 382 (11% from fat); FAT 4.6g (sat 0.7g, mono 1.9g, poly 1.5g); PROTEIN 13.6g; CARB 74.3g; FIBER 9g; CHOL 0mg; IRON 4.5mg; SODIUM 596mg; CALC 77mg

# How to Bake a Pie to Die For

## They just don't get any better than the ones you make at home.

Nothing's better than homemade pie. That's why we're devoted to showing you the simple secrets of matching tender, flaky piecrusts with luscious, melt-in-your-mouth fillings.

### Coconut Cream Pie with Pineapple

(pictured on page 203)

The cream of the cream of coconut enhances the flavor, but you can leave it out.

**CRUST:**

  1  cup all-purpose flour, divided
  3  tablespoons ice water
  2  tablespoons sugar
  ⅛  teaspoon salt
  ¼  cup vegetable shortening
Cooking spray

**FILLING:**

  1  (8¼-ounce) can crushed pineapple in heavy syrup
  ¾  cup sugar
  ¼  cup cornstarch
  ¼  teaspoon salt
1½  cups 1% low-fat milk
  2  large eggs, lightly beaten
  2  tablespoons cream of coconut (such as Coco Lopez)
  ¼  teaspoon coconut extract
  ¼  teaspoon vanilla extract
1½  cups frozen fat-free whipped topping, thawed
  ¼  cup flaked sweetened coconut, toasted

**1.** Preheat oven to 425°.
**2.** To prepare crust, lightly spoon flour into dry measuring cups; level with a knife.

Combine ¼ cup flour and water; stir with a whisk until slurry is well-blended.
**3.** Combine ¾ cup flour, 2 tablespoons sugar, and ⅛ teaspoon salt in a bowl; cut in shortening with a pastry blender or 2 knives until mixture resembles coarse meal. Add slurry; mix with a fork until flour mixture is moist.
**4.** Press mixture gently into a 4-inch circle on heavy-duty plastic wrap, and cover with additional plastic wrap. Roll dough, still covered, into a 12-inch circle. Freeze 10 minutes.
**5.** Remove 1 sheet of plastic wrap, and fit dough into a 9-inch pie plate coated with cooking spray. Remove top sheet of plastic wrap. Fold edges under, and flute. Line dough with a piece of foil, and arrange pie weights or dried beans on foil. Bake at 425° for 20 minutes or until edge is lightly browned. Remove pie weights and foil from crust; cool crust on a wire rack.
**6.** To prepare filling, drain pineapple in a colander, and spoon into prepared crust. Combine ¾ cup sugar, cornstarch, and ¼ teaspoon salt in a saucepan, and stir in milk. Bring to a boil; cook 1 minute, stirring with a whisk. Gradually add about ⅓ cup hot custard to beaten eggs, stirring constantly with a whisk. Return egg mixture to pan. Cook 2 minutes or until thick, stirring constantly. Remove mixture from heat; stir in cream of coconut and extracts. Spoon mixture into prepared crust. Cover surface of

filling with plastic wrap; chill until set (about 2 hours).
**7.** Remove plastic wrap, and spread whipped topping evenly over filling. Sprinkle with coconut. Yield: 8 servings.

CALORIES 319 (28% from fat); FAT 10g (sat 6.4g, mono 2.4g, poly 0.5g); PROTEIN 5g; CARB 51.9g; FIBER 0.9g; CHOL 73mg; IRON 1.2mg; SODIUM 226mg; CALC 68mg

### Brown Sugar-Peach Pie with Coconut Streusel

There are two good ways to peel peaches: with a potato peeler if they're not too ripe or, if they are, by plunging them in boiling water for about 30 seconds, making the skin a cinch to peel off with a paring knife.

  ½  (15-ounce) package refrigerated pie crust dough (such as Pillsbury)
  ⅔  cup packed brown sugar, divided
  ¼  cup uncooked quick-cooking tapioca
  ½  teaspoon ground cinnamon
  6  cups sliced peeled ripe peaches, divided (about 3 pounds)
  ⅓  cup regular oats
  ¼  cup flaked sweetened coconut
1½  tablespoons butter or stick margarine, melted

**1.** Preheat oven to 425°.
**2.** Fit dough into a 9-inch pie plate. Fold edges under; flute. Line dough with a piece of foil, and arrange pie weights or dried beans on foil. Bake at 425° for 12 minutes. Remove pie weights and foil. Cool crust on a wire rack.
**3.** Combine ⅓ cup sugar, tapioca, and cinnamon in a bowl; sprinkle over 4½ cups peaches. Toss gently, and let stand 15 minutes. Spoon into prepared crust. Top with 1½ cups peaches. Place pie in a 425° oven. Immediately reduce oven temperature to 350° (do not remove pie from oven); bake 30 minutes. Combine ⅓ cup sugar, oats, coconut, and butter; sprinkle over peach mixture. Shield edges of crust with foil. Bake an additional 30 minutes or until mixture is bubbly. Cool on a wire rack. Yield: 8 servings.

CALORIES 309 (31% from fat); FAT 10.6g (sat 5.1g, mono 3.9g, poly 1g); PROTEIN 2.1g; CARB 53g; FIBER 3.1g; CHOL 11mg; IRON 0.8mg; SODIUM 138mg; CALC 27mg

# Five Steps to Perfect Pastry

**1.** *Lower-fat pastry is more difficult to manage than traditional higher-fat pastry. A slurry—a flour-and-water mixture—makes the pastry easier to handle. To make the slurry, stir flour and water together with a whisk until smooth.*

**2.** *Cut the shortening into the flour. We've used vegetable shortening (such as Crisco) in our crust, but butter works just as well. To cut in the shortening, combine the flour and shortening until pebble-size crumbs form. This may take as long as 5 minutes. This technique disperses the fat into the flour, which creates pockets when heated that make the pastry flaky. You can use a traditional pastry blender or your food processor for this—simply pulse until pebble-size crumbs form.*

**3.** *Add the slurry to the crumbs, stirring until moist. Gently press the flour mixture into a 4-inch circle on plastic wrap.*

**4.** *Roll the dough into a 12-inch circle. If you don't have a rolling pin, you can use a straight-sided jar or glass. To get an even thickness, think of rolling north, south, east, and west. Lift up the rolling pin as you near the edges so they won't get too thin.*

**5.** *For refrigerated pies, the pastry is baked without the filling; this is called blind baking. Line the pastry with foil or wax paper, and fill it with pie weights or uncooked dried beans. (The beans can't be cooked afterward.) This weighs down the pastry and prevents it from bubbling up as it bakes in the oven.*

## Peanut Butter-Banana Pie

Bananas that are firm rather than extra-ripe work best in this pie. Pulsing cookies in a food processor will give you the best cookie crumbs.

**CRUST:**

- 1 cup reduced-calorie vanilla wafer crumbs (about 30 cookies)
- 2 tablespoons butter or stick margarine, melted and cooled
- 1 large egg white, lightly beaten
- Cooking spray

**FILLING:**

- ⅔ cup sugar
- 3½ tablespoons cornstarch
- ¼ teaspoon salt
- 1⅓ cups 1% low-fat milk
- 2 large eggs, lightly beaten
- 2 tablespoons creamy peanut butter
- 1 teaspoon vanilla extract
- 2½ cups sliced banana
- 1½ cups frozen reduced-calorie whipped topping, thawed

**1.** Preheat oven to 350°.

**2.** To prepare crust, combine first 3 ingredients in a bowl, tossing with a fork until moist. Press into bottom and up sides of a 9-inch pie plate coated with cooking spray. Bake at 350° for 12 minutes; cool crust on a wire rack.

**3.** To prepare filling, combine sugar, cornstarch, and salt in a small heavy saucepan. Gradually add milk, stirring with a whisk until well-blended. Cook over medium heat until mixture comes to a boil; cook 1 minute, stirring with a whisk. Gradually add about ⅓ cup hot

*Continued*

custard to beaten eggs, stirring constantly with a whisk. Return egg mixture to pan. Cook over medium heat until thick (about 1 minute); stir constantly. Remove from heat, and stir in peanut butter and vanilla. Cool slightly.

**4.** Arrange banana slices in bottom of prepared crust; spoon filling over bananas. Press plastic wrap onto surface of filling; chill 4 hours. Remove plastic wrap. Spread whipped topping evenly over filling. Chill. Yield: 8 servings.

CALORIES 294 (29% from fat); FAT 9.5g (sat 4.7g, mono 2.8g, poly 1.4g); PROTEIN 5.9g; CARB 47.8g; FIBER 1.4g; CHOL 65mg; IRON 0.8mg; SODIUM 225mg; CALC 80mg

## Double-Chocolate Cream Pie

Use the cookie crust from the Peanut Butter-Banana Pie (recipe on page 195) if you don't want to make this homemade pastry crust. For a lower-fat pie, use fat-free milk in place of the 1% low-fat milk. For a richer pie (albeit higher in fat), use 2% reduced-fat milk.

**CRUST:**
1 cup all-purpose flour, divided
3 tablespoons ice water
2 tablespoons sugar
⅛ teaspoon salt
¼ cup vegetable shortening
Cooking spray

**FILLING:**
¾ cup sugar
¼ cup unsweetened cocoa
3 tablespoons cornstarch
⅛ teaspoon salt
2 cups 1% low-fat milk
1 large egg, lightly beaten
1½ ounces semisweet chocolate, grated
1 teaspoon vanilla extract
1½ cups frozen fat-free whipped topping, thawed

**1.** Preheat oven to 425°.
**2.** To prepare crust, lightly spoon flour into dry measuring cups, and level with a knife. Combine ¼ cup flour and water, stirring with a whisk until slurry is well-blended.

**3.** Combine ¾ cup flour, 2 tablespoons sugar, and ⅛ teaspoon salt in a bowl; cut in shortening with a pastry blender or 2 knives until mixture resembles coarse meal. Add slurry; mix with a fork until flour mixture is moist.
**4.** Press mixture gently into a 4-inch circle on heavy-duty plastic wrap; cover with additional plastic wrap. Roll dough, still covered, into a 12-inch circle. Freeze 10 minutes.
**5.** Remove 1 sheet of plastic wrap; fit dough into a 9-inch pie plate coated with cooking spray. Remove top sheet of plastic wrap. Fold edges under; flute. Line dough with a piece of foil; arrange pie weights or dried beans on foil. Bake at 425° for 20 minutes or until edge is lightly browned. Remove pie weights and foil. Reduce temperature to 350°. Bake an additional 5 minutes; cool on a wire rack.
**6.** To prepare filling, combine ¾ cup sugar, cocoa, cornstarch, ⅛ teaspoon salt, and milk in a medium saucepan; stir well with a whisk. Cook, stirring constantly, 1 minute or until mixture comes to a full boil. Gradually add ⅓ cup hot milk mixture to beaten egg; stir well. Return egg mixture to pan. Cook 2 minutes or until mixture thickens, stirring constantly. Remove from heat; add grated chocolate, stirring until chocolate melts and mixture is smooth. Stir in vanilla. Spoon into pastry crust. Cover surface of filling with plastic wrap. Chill until set (about 2 hours). Remove plastic wrap; spread whipped topping evenly over filling. Yield: 8 servings.

CALORIES 301 (28% from fat); FAT 9.3g (sat 5.5g, mono 2.7g, poly 0.5g); PROTEIN 5.6g; CARB 48.5g; FIBER 0.5g; CHOL 46mg; IRON 1.5mg; SODIUM 180mg; CALC 89mg

## Lattice-Topped Blueberry Pie

**CRUST:**
1½ cups all-purpose flour, divided
½ cup ice water
1½ teaspoons sugar
¼ teaspoon salt
4½ tablespoons vegetable shortening
Cooking spray

**FILLING:**
1 cup sugar, divided
3½ tablespoons cornstarch
⅛ teaspoon salt
6 cups fresh blueberries
1½ tablespoons butter or stick margarine, melted
¾ teaspoon vanilla extract

**1.** To prepare crust, lightly spoon flour into dry measuring cups; level with a knife. Combine ¼ cup flour and ice water, stirring with a whisk until slurry is well-blended. Combine 1¼ cups flour, 1½ teaspoons sugar, and ¼ teaspoon salt in a bowl; cut in shortening with a pastry blender or 2 knives until mixture resembles coarse meal. Add slurry; mix with a fork until flour mixture is moist.
**2.** Gently press two-thirds of mixture into a 4-inch circle on heavy-duty plastic wrap; cover with additional plastic wrap. Roll dough into a 12-inch circle. Press remaining mixture into a 4-inch circle on heavy-duty plastic wrap; cover with additional plastic wrap. Roll dough into a 9-inch circle. Freeze both portions of dough 10 minutes. Working with larger portion of dough, remove 1 sheet of plastic wrap; fit dough into a 9-inch pie plate coated with cooking spray. Remove top sheet of plastic wrap.
**3.** To prepare filling, combine ¾ cup plus 3 tablespoons sugar, cornstarch, and ⅛ teaspoon salt in a bowl, and sprinkle over blueberries. Toss gently. Stir in butter and vanilla. Spoon blueberry mixture into crust.
**4.** Preheat oven to 375°.
**5.** Remove top sheet of plastic wrap from remaining dough. Cut dough into 6 (1½-inch) strips. Gently remove dough strips from bottom sheet of plastic wrap; arrange in a lattice design over blueberry mixture. Seal dough strips to edge of crust. Place pie on a baking sheet covered with foil. Sprinkle lattice with 1 tablespoon sugar.
**6.** Bake at 375° for 1 hour and 15 minutes or until crust is browned and filling is bubbly. Cool on a wire rack. Yield: 8 servings.

CALORIES 333 (24% from fat); FAT 8.9g (sat 2.9g, mono 2.7g, poly 2.2g); PROTEIN 3.2g; CARB 62.3g; FIBER 3.6g; CHOL 6mg; IRON 1.3mg; SODIUM 139mg; CALC 11mg

## Brown Sugar-Peach Pie with Coconut Streusel:

**1.** Peel the peaches; toss with sugar, tapioca, and cinnamon. If the peaches are very juicy, add 1 to 2 tablespoons tapioca to thicken the filling.

**2.** To make the streusel, combine sugar, oats, coconut, and butter with a fork until crumbly and all the dry ingredients are moist. This may take 2 to 3 minutes.

## Peanut Butter-Banana Pie:

**1.** Use wax paper coated with cooking spray to press the cookie-crumb mixture into the pie plate. This keeps the crumbs from sticking to your hands.

**2.** The custard is gradually added to the eggs (called tempering). The mixture is returned to the pan and cooked until thick. If the eggs were added directly to the hot custard, they could curdle.

## Double-Chocolate Cream Pie:

**1.** Place the rolled-out pastry in the freezer for 10 minutes. This makes it easier to work with. Fit the dough into a 9-inch pie plate by inverting the dough over the plate. Peel off the plastic wrap. If the dough tears, just press it back together.

**2.** Grating the chocolate helps it melt faster, but you can chop it into small pieces, too. Grate the chocolate with a handheld grater or zester, or use the smallest holes on your box grater.

## Coconut Cream Pie with Pineapple:

**1.** For cornstarch to thicken properly for the filling, the mixture must come to a full boil. Stirring constantly at this stage is crucial to prevent lumps.

## Lattice-Topped Blueberry Pie:

**1.** Cut the dough into six large strips (12 thin strips are typical) so they're easier to work with. For the lattice top, alternate the horizontal and vertical strips.

# When You Dish Upon a Star

Put a fresh touch on your summertime parties with a lively alfresco buffet under the best light show around—the universe.

You don't have to be an astronomer to appreciate the beauty of the night sky. Could there be anything on earth more worthy of celebration? In recent years an especially easy and spontaneous way to hang out under the heavens has evolved: the star party. No, not the kind in Hollywood, the kind in your own backyard.

---

### Stargazing Menu For 8

**Cosmic Crab Salad with Corn Chips**

**Stellar Sesame Shrimp with Miso Dipping Sauce**

**Celestial Chicken, Mint, and Cucumber Skewers with Spring Onion Sauce**

**Spiced Pork-and-Red Pepper Skewers with Meteoric Mango Sauce**

**Out-of-This-World Pizza with Goat Cheese and Fig Tapenade**

**Watermelon-and-Kiwi Skewers with Starry Strawberry Cream**

**Heavenly Apricot Cobbler Bars**

---

## Cosmic Crab Salad with Corn Chips

The homemade corn chips can be made several days in advance; store them in a zip-top plastic bag to keep them crisp. It's best to make the crab salad the afternoon of the party.

    6   (6-inch) corn tortillas
    1   teaspoon vegetable oil
    ¼   teaspoon kosher salt
    ¼   cup (2 ounces) ⅓-less-fat cream
        cheese
    2   tablespoons sliced green onions
    2   tablespoons low-fat mayonnaise
    1½  tablespoons fresh lime juice
    1   teaspoon taco seasoning
    1¾  cups lump crabmeat, shell pieces
        removed (about 6 ounces)
    ½   cup fresh corn kernels
        Cilantro leaves (optional)

**1.** Preheat oven to 400°.
**2.** Brush 1 side of each tortilla with oil; cut each tortilla into 8 wedges. Place wedges on a large baking sheet; sprinkle with salt. Bake at 400° for 6 minutes or until lightly browned. Cool.
**3.** Combine cream cheese and next 4 ingredients in a bowl. Add crab and corn; stir gently. Cover and chill up to 4 hours. Serve with corn chips; garnish with cilantro leaves, if desired. Yield: 8 servings (serving size: 6 corn chips and ¼ cup crab salad).

CALORIES 103 (30% from fat); FAT 3.4g (sat 1.2g, mono 0.9g, poly 0.9g); PROTEIN 6.4g; CARB 12.3g; FIBER 1.2g; CHOL 27mg; IRON 0.6mg; SODIUM 252mg; CALC 60mg

## Stellar Sesame Shrimp with Miso Dipping Sauce

The shrimp are best prepared the day of the party and refrigerated up to eight hours. Make the miso dipping sauce up to three days in advance, and chill. Kosher salt gives an added crunch to the shrimp.

    ¼   cup orange-pineapple juice
        concentrate, thawed and undiluted
    1   tablespoon water
    1   tablespoon red miso (soybean
        paste)
    2   teaspoons finely chopped peeled
        fresh ginger
    2   teaspoons dark sesame oil
    1   garlic clove, minced
    24  unpeeled large shrimp (about 1
        pound)
    2   teaspoons vegetable oil
    ¼   teaspoon kosher salt
    ⅛   teaspoon freshly ground black
        pepper
    1   tablespoon sesame seeds, toasted

**1.** Combine first 6 ingredients in a bowl; stir well with a whisk.
**2.** Preheat oven to 450°.
**3.** Peel and devein shrimp, leaving tails intact. Combine shrimp, vegetable oil, salt, and pepper in a bowl; toss gently. Place shrimp on a foil-lined baking sheet; sprinkle with sesame seeds. Bake at 450° for 7 minutes or until shrimp are done. Serve with sauce. Yield: 12 servings (serving size: 2 shrimp and 2 teaspoons sauce).

CALORIES 61 (37% from fat); FAT 2.5g (sat 0.4g, mono 0.8g, poly 1.1g); PROTEIN 6.2g; CARB 5.1g; FIBER 0.1g; CHOL 43mg; IRON 1mg; SODIUM 159mg; CALC 26mg

## Celestial Chicken, Mint, and Cucumber Skewers with Spring Onion Sauce

You can assemble these skewers one day in advance. Cover them with a damp paper towel; then cover them with plastic wrap. Keep refrigerated, and serve chilled. You can also make the onion sauce up to 24 hours in advance.

- ¾ cup low-fat mayonnaise
- ⅓ cup low-fat buttermilk
- 3 tablespoons chopped green onion tops
- 1 tablespoon chopped fresh or 1 teaspoon dried tarragon
- 1 tablespoon chopped fresh or 1 teaspoon dried dill
- 2 teaspoons white wine vinegar
- ½ small cucumber (about 2 ounces)
- 3 cups water
- ½ pound skinned, boned chicken breast, cut into 24 (¾-inch) pieces
- 24 small mint leaves
- Cucumber slices (optional)

**1.** Place first 6 ingredients in a blender; process until smooth. Cover and chill.
**2.** Cut cucumber half lengthwise into 4 pieces; cut each piece crosswise into 6 (¼-inch) slices. Bring water to a boil in a medium saucepan. Add chicken; cook 4 minutes or until done. Drain well, and cool. Thread 1 chicken piece, 1 cucumber piece, and 1 mint leaf onto each of 24 (6-inch) skewers. Cover and chill. Serve with sauce; garnish with cucumber slices, if desired. Yield: 8 servings (serving size: 3 skewers and 2 tablespoons sauce).

CALORIES 76 (25% from fat); FAT 2.1g (sat 0.4g, mono 0.5g, poly 1g); PROTEIN 7.1g; CARB 7.1g; FIBER 0.2g; CHOL 17mg; IRON 0.4mg; SODIUM 235mg; CALC 22mg

## Spiced Pork-and-Red Pepper Skewers with Meteoric Mango Sauce

Make the sauce in advance; cover and chill. The skewers can be assembled a day in advance and put on the grill just before serving.

- 1 cup cubed peeled ripe mango
- 2 tablespoons fresh orange juice
- 1 teaspoon fresh lime juice
- ¼ teaspoon salt
- 1 small garlic clove, minced
- 1 tablespoon chopped green onion tops
- 1 tablespoon finely chopped fresh basil
- 1 teaspoon finely chopped jalapeño pepper
- 1 (1-pound) pork tenderloin
- 32 (¾-inch) pieces red bell pepper (about 1 large)
- 2 teaspoons olive oil
- 2 teaspoons Old Bay seasoning
- Cooking spray

**1.** Place first 5 ingredients in a food processor or blender; process until smooth. Spoon into a bowl; stir in onions, basil, and jalapeño. Cover mixture, and chill.
**2.** Preheat oven to 450°.
**3.** Trim fat from pork; cut into 32 (¾-inch) cubes. Place pork and bell pepper in a medium bowl. Drizzle with oil, and sprinkle with seasoning, tossing well to coat. Thread 1 bell pepper piece and 1 pork cube onto each of 32 (6-inch) skewers. Place kebabs on a broiler pan coated with cooking spray; bake at 450° for 10 minutes or until pork is done. Serve kebabs with mango sauce. Yield: 8 servings (serving size: 4 kebabs and 4 teaspoons sauce).

CALORIES 104 (30% from fat); FAT 3.5g (sat 0.9g, mono 1.8g, poly 0.4g); PROTEIN 13.2g; CARB 4.8g; FIBER 0.6g; CHOL 42mg; IRON 0.9mg; SODIUM 269mg; CALC 9mg

## Out-of-This-World Pizza with Goat Cheese and Fig Tapenade

A *tapenade* is a condiment from the Provence region of France typically made with olives, capers, and other seasonings. Ours contains figs, which gives it its thick consistency. It can be made several days in advance and refrigerated. On the day of the party, assemble the pizzas up to one hour in advance, cover, and leave at room temperature until ready to bake.

- ⅔ cup chopped dried figs (about 4 ounces)
- 3 tablespoons water
- 3 tablespoons chopped pitted kalamata olives
- 1 tablespoon balsamic vinegar
- 1 teaspoon olive oil
- 1 teaspoon chopped fresh thyme
- ⅛ teaspoon freshly ground black pepper
- 4 whole-wheat English muffins, split
- 1 cup (4 ounces) crumbled soft goat cheese
- Thyme sprigs (optional)

**1.** Preheat oven to 375°.
**2.** Combine figs and water in a small saucepan over medium heat. Cook 5 minutes until liquid is absorbed, stirring frequently. Place figs in a small bowl. Stir in olives, vinegar, oil, chopped thyme, and pepper. Top each muffin half with 2 tablespoons cheese and 2 tablespoons fig mixture. Place muffin halves on a foil-lined baking sheet. Bake at 375° for 15 minutes or until cheese melts. Cut each muffin half in half. Garnish with thyme sprigs, if desired. Yield: 8 servings (serving size: 2 pieces).

CALORIES 175 (28% from fat); FAT 5.5g (sat 2.5g, mono 2g, poly 0.6g); PROTEIN 5.7g; CARB 26.8g; FIBER 3.4g; CHOL 13mg; IRON 1.7mg; SODIUM 290mg; CALC 131mg

## Watermelon-and-Kiwi Skewers with Starry Strawberry Cream

(pictured on page 201)

The watermelon and kiwifruit can be cut up one day in advance. Thread the fruit onto skewers a few hours before the party. The strawberry cream is best when prepared only a few hours prior to serving.

- ¾ cup sliced strawberries
- ½ cup vanilla low-fat yogurt
- 1 tablespoon ⅓-less-fat cream cheese
- 1 teaspoon fresh lemon juice
- ½ teaspoon powdered sugar
- 24 (½-inch) watermelon balls
- 2 kiwifruit, each peeled and cut into 12 pieces

**1.** Place first 5 ingredients in a blender; process until smooth. Cover and chill.
**2.** Thread 1 watermelon ball and 1 kiwifruit piece onto each of 24 skewers. Serve with sauce. Yield: 8 servings (serving size: 3 skewers and 2 tablespoons sauce).
**NOTE:** To shape kiwifruit, cut a thin vertical slice off both ends of fruit, revealing flesh. Peel by cutting vertical strips from one end to the other. Cut each kiwifruit lengthwise into quarters. Cut each quarter crosswise into thirds.

CALORIES 40 (18% from fat); FAT 0.8g (sat 0.4g, mono 0.2g, poly 0.1g); PROTEIN 1.3g; CARB 7.6g; FIBER 1.1g; CHOL 2mg; IRON 0.2mg; SODIUM 18mg; CALC 34mg

## Heavenly Apricot Cobbler Bars

(pictured on page 201)

These bar cookies can be made several days in advance; store in an airtight container with wax paper between layers to prevent sticking.

- 5 tablespoons butter or stick margarine, softened
- ¼ cup powdered sugar
- ¼ cup packed brown sugar
- ¼ teaspoon salt
- ⅛ teaspoon almond extract
- 1¼ cups all-purpose flour
- ¾ cup apricot preserves
- ½ cup low-fat granola without raisins, crushed (such as Kellogg's Low-fat Granola without Raisins)

**1.** Preheat oven to 350°.
**2.** Beat butter at medium speed of a mixer until light and fluffy. Add sugars, salt, and extract, beating well. Lightly spoon flour into dry measuring cups, and level with a knife. Gradually add flour to butter mixture, beating until moist. Remove ⅓ cup flour mixture, and set aside.
**3.** Press remaining flour mixture into bottom of an 8-inch square baking dish. Bake at 350° for 15 minutes or until lightly golden. Gently spread preserves over warm shortbread. Combine ⅓ cup flour mixture with granola; sprinkle over preserves. Bake at 350° for an additional 20 minutes or until golden brown. Cool. Yield: 2 dozen bars (serving size: 1 [2 x 1⅓-inch] piece).

CALORIES 91 (26% from fat); FAT 2.6g (sat 1.5g, mono 0.8g, poly 0.1g); PROTEIN 0.9g; CARB 16.5g; FIBER 0.4g; CHOL 6mg; IRON 0.5mg; SODIUM 59mg; CALC 7mg

---

### Best Bets on Earth

How do you pick the best time for a "star party?" According to Deborah Byrd, amateur astronomer and producer of the syndicated radio program *Earth and Sky*, summer months are best: Not only are the nights warmer, but you can see the summer Milky Way—an edgewise view of our galaxy, which looks like a hazy pathway in the sky.

You also get meteor showers. Of the dozen or so that occur each year, Byrd says two converge in late July and early August. Those can provide glimpses of meteors almost every hour, especially after midnight.

---

## back to the best

# Vidalia Onion Risotto with Feta Cheese

*You never forget your first love; we feel the same way about Vidalia Onion Risotto with Feta Cheese.*

We'd toyed with other risottos before, but this one came along in our June 1995 issue and sent our senses soaring. As it should be with all risottos, serve it immediately.

### Vidalia Onion Risotto with Feta Cheese

- 2 teaspoons vegetable oil
- 2 cups chopped Vidalia or other sweet onion
- 2 large garlic cloves, minced
- 1½ cups uncooked Arborio rice or other short-grain rice
- 2 (14½-ounce) cans vegetable broth
- ½ cup (2 ounces) crumbled feta cheese, divided
- ⅓ cup chopped fresh flat-leaf parsley
- ¼ cup (1 ounce) grated fresh Parmesan cheese
- Freshly ground black pepper
- Flat-leaf parsley sprigs (optional)

**1.** Heat oil in a saucepan over medium heat. Add onion and garlic; sauté 1 minute. Stir in rice. Add ½ cup broth; cook until liquid is nearly absorbed, stirring constantly. Add remaining broth, ½ cup at a time, stirring constantly until each portion of broth is nearly absorbed before adding the next (about 20 minutes total). Remove from heat; stir in ¼ cup feta, chopped parsley, and Parmesan. Spoon into a serving bowl; top with ¼ cup feta and pepper. Garnish with parsley sprigs, if desired. Yield: 5 servings (serving size: 1 cup).

CALORIES 321 (18% from fat); FAT 6.5g (sat 2.8g, mono 1.5g, poly 1.1g); PROTEIN 8.5g; CARB 56.1g; FIBER 2.3g; CHOL 13mg; IRON 3mg; SODIUM 670mg; CALCIUM 135mg

Watermelon-and-Kiwi Skewers
with Starry Strawberry Cream
and Heavenly Apricot Cobbler
Bars, page 200

Malaysian Lime-Coconut
Swordfish, page 209

Roasted Corn, Black Bean, and Mango Salad, page 188

Coconut Cream Pie with Pineapple, page 194

Blueberry Crisp à la Mode,
page 212

Tabbouleh with Beans
and Feta, page 211

# Choose Your Cherries

*This is the big time for Bings, Rainiers, and Sweethearts—and they'll take top billing in your cooking, too.*

From late June through the dwindling days of August, fresh cherries fill grocery stores in bin-busting seasonal abundance. You'll mostly find the Bing, rotund and ranging from fire-engine red to mahogany.

But other varieties also appear and are generally interchangeable, such as the Sweetheart, named for its shape; the Rainier, golden with a pinkish blush; or the Lapin, a large, red variety.

## Chilled Cherry Soup

This dessert soup is perfect for a summer meal. We liked Riesling the best, but any sweet white wine will work well.

    4   cups pitted sweet cherries
    2   tablespoons sugar
    1   teaspoon grated lemon rind
    ¼   teaspoon ground ginger
    ⅛   teaspoon ground allspice
    ⅓   cup Riesling or other slightly
        sweet white wine
    2   tablespoons low-fat sour cream
    2   tablespoons fresh lemon juice
    1   (8-ounce) carton vanilla low-fat
        yogurt

**1.** Combine first 5 ingredients in a blender or food processor, and process until cherries are finely chopped. Add wine, sour cream, and lemon juice; process until smooth. Add yogurt, and pulse 3 or 4 times or until blended. Pour into a bowl, and cover surface of soup with plastic wrap. Chill thoroughly. Yield: 7 servings (serving size: ½ cup).

CALORIES 116 (13% from fat); FAT 1.7g (sat 0.8g, mono 0.5g, poly 0.3g); PROTEIN 2.8g; CARB 22.6g; FIBER 1.9g; CHOL 3mg; IRON 0.4mg; SODIUM 24mg; CALC 74mg

## Black Forest Cherry Cheesecake

Dark, sweet cherries offset the filling and crust for a dramatic look and the best taste.

**CHERRY TOPPING:**

    2   cups pitted dark sweet cherries
    ¼   cup sugar
    1   tablespoon fresh lemon juice
    2   teaspoons cornstarch

**CRUST:**

    1⅓ cups chocolate graham cracker
        crumbs (about 9½ cookie sheets)
    ¼   cup sugar
    1   tablespoon butter or stick
        margarine, melted
    1   large egg white
    Cooking spray

**FILLING:**

    1   cup fat-free sour cream
    ½   cup fat-free sweetened condensed
        milk
    1   (8-ounce) block ⅓-less-fat cream
        cheese, softened
    1   (8-ounce) block fat-free cream
        cheese, softened
    1¼ cups sugar
    3   tablespoons unsweetened cocoa
    2   teaspoons vanilla extract
    2   large eggs
    ½   cup semisweet chocolate minichips
    36  dark sweet cherries, pitted and halved

**1.** To prepare cherry topping, place 2 cups cherries in a blender or food processor, and process until smooth. Combine pureed cherries, ¼ cup sugar, lemon juice, and cornstarch in a small saucepan. Bring to a boil, and cook 1 minute, stirring constantly. Pour cherry topping into a bowl; cover and chill.
**2.** Preheat oven to 350°.
**3.** To prepare crust, combine crumbs, ¼ cup sugar, butter, and egg white in a bowl; toss with a fork until well-blended. Press crumb mixture into bottom of a 10-inch springform pan coated with cooking spray. Bake at 350° for 10 minutes; cool on a wire rack. Reduce oven temperature to 300°.
**4.** To prepare filling, combine sour cream, milk, and cheeses in a large

bowl. Beat at medium speed of a mixer until well-blended. Add 1¼ cups sugar, cocoa, vanilla, and eggs; beat well. Stir in minichips. Pour cheese mixture into prepared crust. Bake at 300° for 50 minutes or until almost set (center will not be firm, but will set up as it chills). Turn oven off; cool cheesecake in closed oven 40 minutes. Remove from oven; cool on a wire rack. Spread cherry topping over cheesecake. Top with cherry halves. Cover and chill 8 hours. Yield: 16 servings.

CALORIES 292 (25% from fat); FAT 8.1g (sat 4.3g, mono 2.5g, poly 0.7g); PROTEIN 7.6g; CARB 47.5g; FIBER 1.1g; CHOL 43mg; IRON 0.8mg; SODIUM 233mg; CALC 106mg

## Salad with Fresh Cherries, Prosciutto, and Cheese

    1   tablespoon olive oil
    Cooking spray
    2   ounces thinly sliced prosciutto or
        ham, chopped
    3   garlic cloves, crushed
    ⅓   cup champagne vinegar or white
        wine vinegar
    ¼   cup water
    1   tablespoon finely chopped fresh or
        1 teaspoon dried basil
    1   tablespoon fresh lemon juice
    2   teaspoons Dijon mustard
    ½   teaspoon sugar
    ⅛   teaspoon black pepper
    8   cups gourmet salad greens
    1   cup sweet cherries, pitted and
        quartered
    ½   cup (2 ounces) crumbled goat or
        feta cheese

**1.** Heat oil in a large nonstick skillet coated with cooking spray over medium heat. Add prosciutto; sauté 5 minutes or until lightly browned. Add garlic; sauté 1 minute. Remove from heat; stir in vinegar and next 6 ingredients. Combine greens, cherries, and cheese in a large bowl, and add vinaigrette, tossing well. Yield: 4 servings (serving size: 2 cups).

CALORIES 150 (52% from fat); FAT 8.6g (sat 3.2g, mono 4.1g, poly 0.9g); PROTEIN 7.7g; CARB 11.1g; FIBER 2.8g; CHOL 21mg; IRON 1.7mg; SODIUM 317mg; CALC 122mg

## Grilled Chicken Salad with Cherries

Golden-red Rainier cherries look prettiest in this salad, but any fresh sweet cherries will do.

CHICKEN:

    2  teaspoons olive oil
    6  (4-ounce) skinned, boned chicken breast halves
    ¼  teaspoon salt
    ¼  teaspoon black pepper
       Cooking spray

VINAIGRETTE:

    ⅓  cup water
    ¼  cup red wine vinegar
    2  tablespoons minced shallots
    1  tablespoon olive oil
    2  teaspoons Dijon mustard
    1½ teaspoons minced fresh or
    ½  teaspoon dried thyme
    ½  teaspoon sugar
    ¼  teaspoon salt
    ⅛  teaspoon black pepper

SALAD:

    6  cups gourmet salad greens
    1½ cups coarsely chopped pitted sweet cherries
    6  whole cherries (optional)

**1.** To prepare chicken, rub 2 teaspoons oil over chicken. Sprinkle chicken with ¼ teaspoon salt and ¼ teaspoon pepper.
**2.** Prepare grill.
**3.** Place chicken on grill rack coated with cooking spray; grill 6 minutes on each side or until chicken is done. Cut into ¼-inch-thick slices.
**4.** To prepare vinaigrette, combine water and next 8 ingredients in a small bowl; stir with a whisk.
**5.** Arrange salad greens on plates, and top with sliced chicken, chopped cherries, and vinaigrette. Garnish with whole cherries, if desired. Yield: 6 servings (serving size: 1 cup salad greens, 3 ounces chicken, ¼ cup chopped cherries, and 2 tablespoons vinaigrette).

CALORIES 217 (31% from fat); FAT 7.5g (sat 1.5g, mono 4g, poly 1.2g); PROTEIN 27.8g; CARB 8.8g; FIBER 1.9g; CHOL 72mg; IRON 1.7mg; SODIUM 290mg; CALC 41mg

## Cherry-Almond Coffeecake

TOPPING:

    ¼  cup all-purpose flour
    ⅓  cup packed brown sugar
    ¼  cup regular oats
    1  teaspoon ground cinnamon
    1  tablespoon chilled butter or stick margarine, cut into small pieces

CAKE:

    1½ cups all-purpose flour
    1  teaspoon baking powder
    ½  teaspoon baking soda
    ¼  teaspoon salt
    ½  cup granulated sugar
    1½ tablespoons butter or stick margarine, softened
    1  cup plain low-fat yogurt
    1½ teaspoons vanilla extract
    ¾  teaspoon almond extract
    1  large egg
       Cooking spray
    1½ cups pitted sweet cherries, quartered
    2  tablespoons slivered almonds

**1.** Preheat oven to 350°.
**2.** To prepare topping, lightly spoon ¼ cup flour into a dry measuring cup, and level with a knife. Combine ¼ cup flour, brown sugar, oats, and cinnamon in a small bowl; cut in 1 tablespoon butter with a pastry blender or 2 knives until mixture resembles coarse meal. Set aside.
**3.** To prepare cake, lightly spoon 1½ cups flour into dry measuring cups; level with a knife. Combine 1½ cups flour, baking powder, baking soda, and salt; set aside. Beat granulated sugar and 1½ tablespoons butter at medium speed of a mixer. Add yogurt, extracts, and egg; beat well. Add flour mixture; beat at low speed until well-blended (batter will be thick). Spread half of batter in bottom of an 8-inch square baking pan coated with cooking spray; top with cherries. Sprinkle with 3 tablespoons topping. Repeat procedure with remaining batter and topping. Sprinkle with almonds. Bake at 350° for 45 minutes. Cool completely on a wire rack. Yield: 9 servings.

CALORIES 254 (20% from fat); FAT 5.6g (sat 2.6g, mono 1.9g, poly 0.6g); PROTEIN 5.6g; CARB 45.7g; FIBER 1.7g; CHOL 35mg; IRON 1.8mg; SODIUM 252mg; CALC 106mg

## the cooking light profile

# Jump-Starting Healthy Habits

*Sheila Agnew Burke walked her way into a better life nine years ago and has never looked back.*

Nine years ago, stress from her workload caused Sheila Agnew Burke to take on some bad habits—poor eating and little exercise. She put on 25 pounds.

Sheila resolved to change her ways. She began walking three miles a day. She continued to eat healthy foods, but scaled back on what had become supersize portions. Within months, Sheila was back to her old "perfect size 10" self, and felt perfect, too.

### Southwestern Lasagna

Make this dish 24 hours ahead so the juices from the sauce and ricotta mixture have time to soften the precooked lasagna noodles. Or you can use regular cooked lasagna noodles and proceed with the recipe immediately.

       Cooking spray
    1  cup chopped onion
    ½  pound ground turkey
    4  cups bottled salsa
    2  teaspoons ground cumin
    8  garlic cloves, minced and divided
    1  (15-ounce) can pinto beans, rinsed and drained
    1  (15-ounce) carton part-skim ricotta cheese
    ½  cup (4 ounces) ⅓-less-fat cream cheese
    ½  cup (2 ounces) grated fresh Parmesan cheese, divided
    1  large egg white
    1  (10-ounce) package frozen chopped spinach, thawed, drained, and squeezed dry
   15  precooked lasagna noodles
    1  cup (4 ounces) preshredded reduced-fat Mexican blend or Cheddar cheese
       Oregano sprigs (optional)

1. Place a large nonstick skillet coated with cooking spray over medium-high heat until hot. Add onion, and cook 3 minutes. Add turkey, and cook until browned, stirring to crumble. Add salsa, cumin, half of the garlic, and beans.

2. Place ricotta in a food processor, and process 1 minute or until smooth. Add remaining garlic, cream cheese, ¼ cup Parmesan, and egg white; pulse 2 or 3 times. Add spinach, and pulse 2 or 3 times.

3. Spread ¾ cup turkey mixture in bottom of a 13 x 9-inch baking dish coated with cooking spray. Arrange 3 noodles over turkey mixture, and top with 1 cup ricotta mixture, ¾ cup turkey mixture, and ¼ cup Mexican cheese. Repeat layers, ending with noodles. Spread remaining turkey mixture over noodles. Cover with foil; store in refrigerator up to 24 hours.

4. Preheat oven to 375°.

5. Bake, covered, at 375° for 30 minutes. Uncover and sprinkle with ¼ cup Parmesan cheese, and bake, uncovered, 10 minutes. Let stand 10 minutes. Garnish with oregano sprigs, if desired. Yield: 9 servings.

CALORIES 400 (28% from fat); FAT 12.5g (sat 7g, mono 3.6g, poly 0.9g); PROTEIN 26.7g; CARB 45g; FIBER 5g; CHOL 53mg; IRON 4.7mg; SODIUM 994mg; CALC 414mg

## lighten up

# Garden Recital

*A piano teacher gets new inspiration from her garden—without weighty notes from too much fat.*

As a piano instructor, Lisa McGinness knows the appeal of a popular repertoire. Thanks to a bumper crop of tomatoes and basil from her garden, she's been happy to perform her rendition of Tomato-Basil Soup about every other week in her Houston, Texas, home.

Lisa's composition bottoms out the scales with 1 cup of heavy cream and ¼ pound of butter. We cut out all the butter and substituted ⅓ cup half-and-half for the heavy cream. Then, we made an inspired leap to ⅓-less-fat cream cheese.

## Tomato-Basil Soup

4  cups chopped seeded peeled tomato (about 4 large)
4  cups low-sodium tomato juice
⅓  cup fresh basil leaves
1  cup 1% low-fat milk
¼  teaspoon salt
¼  teaspoon cracked black pepper
½  cup (4 ounces) ⅓-less-fat cream cheese, softened
Basil leaves, thinly sliced (optional)
8  (½-inch-thick) slices diagonally cut French bread baguette

1. Bring tomato and juice to a boil in a large saucepan. Reduce heat; simmer, uncovered, 30 minutes.

2. Place tomato mixture and ⅓ cup basil in a blender or food processor; process until smooth. Return pureed mixture to pan; stir in milk, salt, and pepper. Add cream cheese, stirring well with a whisk, and cook over medium heat until thick (about 5 minutes). Ladle soup into individual bowls; garnish with sliced basil, if desired. Serve with bread. Yield: 8 servings (serving size: 1 cup soup and 1 bread slice).

NOTE: Refrigerate remaining soup in an airtight container up to 1 week.

CALORIES 133 (30% from fat); FAT 4.4g (sat 2.4g, mono 1.3g, poly 0.4g); PROTEIN 5.4g; CARB 18.7g; FIBER 1.9g; CHOL 12mg; IRON 1.5mg; SODIUM 310mg; CALC 77mg

| BEFORE | AFTER |
|---|---|
| SERVING SIZE | |
| *1 cup soup and 1 bread slice* | |
| CALORIES PER SERVING | |
| 318 | 133 |
| FAT | |
| 26.6g | 4.4g |
| PERCENT OF TOTAL CALORIES | |
| 75% | 30% |
| CHOLESTEROL | |
| 82mg | 12mg |
| SODIUM | |
| 696mg | 310mg |

# Access Asia

*Flavor-packed cuisines from the far side of the Pacific provide a link to quick world-class dinners.*

Asian cuisines lure with their exotic flair, lively flavors, and healthy ingredients. Look to the East for cooking inspiration, and you'll get a speedy meal that's lower in salt and calories and tastes terrific.

## Thai Steak Salad with Basil and Mint

PREPARATION TIME: 10 MINUTES
COOKING TIME: 8 MINUTES

If you're unfamiliar with fish sauce, you may want to use the lesser amount.

DRESSING:
2  tablespoons sugar
2  tablespoons lime juice
1  to 2 tablespoons fish sauce
1  tablespoon water
1  teaspoon Thai chili paste

SALAD:
1  (1-pound) flank steak
⅛  teaspoon salt
⅛  teaspoon freshly ground black pepper
Cooking spray
3  cups sliced romaine lettuce
1  cup diced cucumber
1  cup red bell pepper strips (about 1 medium)
¾  cup thinly sliced red onion
½  cup sliced fresh basil
¼  cup sliced fresh mint
12  cherry tomatoes, halved

1. To prepare dressing, combine first 5 ingredients; set aside.

2. To prepare salad, sprinkle both sides of steak with salt and black pepper. Heat a large nonstick skillet coated with cooking spray over medium-high

*Continued*

heat. Add steak; cook 8 minutes or until desired degree of doneness, turning after 4 minutes. Remove steak from pan; cover and set aside. Combine lettuce and remaining 6 ingredients in a large bowl; drizzle with 3 tablespoons dressing. Arrange 1¼ cups salad on each of 4 plates. Cut steak diagonally across grain into thin slices. Divide steak evenly among salads; drizzle with remaining dressing. Yield: 4 servings.

CALORIES 260 (39% from fat); FAT 11.3g (sat 4.7g, mono 4.4g, poly 0.8g); PROTEIN 24.8g; CARB 15.1g; FIBER 2.5g; CHOL 57mg; IRON 3.6mg; SODIUM 524mg; CALC 44mg

## Indonesian Coriander-Honey Chicken

PREPARATION TIME: 18 MINUTES
COOKING TIME: 12 MINUTES

 2 tablespoons peanuts
 2 teaspoons bottled minced fresh ginger
 3 garlic cloves, peeled
 ⅓ cup low-sodium soy sauce
 1 tablespoon ground coriander
 1 tablespoon honey
 ½ tablespoon Thai chili paste
 12 skinned, boned chicken thighs (about 1½ pounds)

**1.** Place first 3 ingredients in a food processor; pulse 2 or 3 times or until minced. Add soy sauce, coriander, honey, and chili paste, and process until smooth. Place marinade in a large bowl; add chicken, and toss to coat. Chill 10 minutes.
**2.** Preheat broiler.
**3.** Remove chicken from bowl; discard marinade. Place chicken on a foil-lined baking sheet; broil 6 minutes on each side or until done. Yield: 6 servings (serving size: 2 thighs).

CALORIES 154 (30% from fat); FAT 5.2g (sat 1.2g, mono 1.8g, poly 1.3g); PROTEIN 23.1g; CARB 2.8g; FIBER 0.2g; CHOL 94mg; IRON 1.4mg; SODIUM 330mg; CALC 17mg

**menu**

**Steamed Bali-Style Sea Bass**

Roasted fingerling potatoes*

*Combine 16 fingerling potatoes, cut in half lengthwise; 1 tablespoon olive oil; 2 garlic cloves, minced; ¼ teaspoon salt; and pepper. Arrange potatoes on a jelly-roll pan; bake at 425° for 20 minutes or until tender, stirring occasionally. Serves 4.

## Steamed Bali-Style Sea Bass

PREPARATION TIME: 15 MINUTES
COOKING TIME: 15 MINUTES

 2 teaspoons vegetable oil
 1⅔ cups diced shallots (about 4 large shallots)
 1 tablespoon bottled minced fresh ginger
 ½ teaspoon Thai chili paste
 ¼ teaspoon salt
 10 macadamia nuts (about ¾ ounce)
 1 plum tomato, quartered
 1 garlic clove, peeled
 2 cups trimmed watercress, coarsely chopped
 4 (6-ounce) sea bass fillets (about 1 inch thick)

**1.** Heat oil in a medium nonstick skillet over medium-high heat. Add shallots; sauté 3 minutes. Remove from heat.
**2.** Place shallot mixture, ginger, and next 5 ingredients in a food processor; pulse until coarsely blended. Set aside.
**3.** Arrange watercress on a large sheet of foil. Arrange fillets on top of watercress; spread shallot mixture over fillets. Fold foil over fish to form a packet; loosely seal. Place packet in bottom of a bamboo steamer. Cover with steamer lid. Add water to a large skillet to a depth of 1 inch; bring to a boil. Place steamer in pan; steam fillets 15 minutes or until fish flakes easily when tested with a fork. Yield: 4 servings (serving size: 1 fillet).

CALORIES 310 (37% from fat); FAT 12.8g (sat 2.4g, mono 6.3g, poly 3g); PROTEIN 34.8g; CARB 14g; FIBER 1.3g; CHOL 116mg; IRON 3.6mg; SODIUM 300mg; CALC 187mg

## Curried Noodles with Scallops

PREPARATION TIME: 15 MINUTES
COOKING TIME: 11 MINUTES

 ½ pound uncooked rice sticks (rice-flour noodles) or vermicelli
 1 cup fat-free, less-sodium chicken broth
 2 teaspoons curry powder
 ¼ teaspoon salt
 ¼ teaspoon ground red pepper
 2 large egg whites
 1 large egg
 1 tablespoon vegetable oil
 1 cup (1-inch) sliced green onions
 1 tablespoon bottled minced fresh ginger
 1½ teaspoons bottled minced garlic
 1½ pounds bay scallops
 ½ cup frozen green peas, thawed
 6 tablespoons mango chutney
 2 tablespoons chopped fresh cilantro

**1.** Cook noodles according to package directions, omitting salt and fat. Drain and rinse with cold water; drain well.
**2.** Combine broth, curry, salt, pepper, egg whites, and egg in a medium bowl; stir well with a whisk. Set aside.
**3.** Heat oil in a large nonstick skillet over medium-high heat. Add onions, ginger, and garlic; stir-fry 30 seconds. Add scallops and peas; stir-fry 3 minutes. Reduce heat to medium-low. Stir in noodles; toss well. Stir in egg mixture; cover and cook 5 minutes. Divide noodle mixture evenly among 6 plates. Spoon 1 tablespoon chutney over each serving, and sprinkle evenly with cilantro. Yield: 6 servings (serving size: about 1 cup).

CALORIES 332 (11% from fat); FAT 4.2g (sat 0.8g, mono 1.1g, poly 1.5g); PROTEIN 23.1g; CARB 49.6g; FIBER 1.5g; CHOL 74mg; IRON 1.4mg; SODIUM 508mg; CALC 60mg

## Malaysian Lime-Coconut Swordfish

(pictured on page 202)

PREPARATION TIME: 12 MINUTES

COOKING TIME: 15 MINUTES

Lemon grass gives a characteristic citrus flavor and fragrance to many Asian dishes. You'll find this herb with long, thin, gray-green leaves in the produce section of many supermarkets. You can substitute grated lemon peel, but cut the amount you use by half.

 ⅓ cup light coconut milk
 ¼ cup chopped fresh cilantro
 2 tablespoons thinly sliced peeled fresh lemon grass (about 1 stalk) or 1 tablespoon grated lemon peel
 2 tablespoons fish sauce
 1 tablespoon brown sugar
 1 teaspoon lime juice
 ½ teaspoon Thai chili paste (such as Dynasty)
 2 shallots, peeled
 1 garlic clove, peeled
 1 (1½-pound) swordfish steak (about 1 inch thick)
 Cooking spray
 Cilantro sprigs (optional)
 Lemon wedges (optional)

**1.** Preheat broiler.
**2.** Combine first 9 ingredients in a food processor; pulse 3 times or until coarsely chopped. Place fish on a broiler pan coated with cooking spray; spread ½ cup shallot mixture evenly over fish. Broil 15 minutes or until fish flakes easily when tested with a fork. Serve fish with remaining shallot mixture, and garnish with cilantro sprigs and lemon wedges, if desired. Yield: 4 servings (serving size: 5 ounces fish and 2 tablespoons sauce).

CALORIES 255 (30% from fat); FAT 8.5g (sat 2.7g, mono 2.9g, poly 1.8g); PROTEIN 36.8g; CARB 5.4g; FIBER 0.2g; CHOL 71mg; IRON 2mg; SODIUM 840mg; CALC 18mg

## Soba Noodles with Tofu

PREPARATION TIME: 15 MINUTES

COOKING TIME: 8 MINUTES

*Nori*—roasted seaweed in paper-thin sheets—is most frequently used to wrap sushi. *Mirin*, also called rice wine, is sweet and low in alcohol. Look for both in Asian markets or large supermarkets.

 1 (8-ounce) package soba (buckwheat noodles), uncooked
 ¼ cup low-sodium soy sauce
 2 teaspoons sugar
 3 tablespoons mirin (sweet rice wine)
 1 (16-ounce) can fat-free, less-sodium chicken broth
 1 pound soft tofu, drained and cut into ½-inch cubes
 ¼ cup finely chopped nori (roasted seaweed; about 1 sheet)
 ¼ cup thinly sliced green onions
 2 teaspoons toasted sesame seeds

**1.** Cook noodles according to package directions, omitting salt and fat. Drain noodles well.
**2.** While noodles cook, combine soy sauce, sugar, mirin, and broth in a medium saucepan; bring to a boil. Pour into a bowl; cover and place in freezer about 8 minutes to cool slightly.
**3.** Place ¾ cup noodles in each of 4 shallow bowls; divide tofu evenly among bowls. Ladle ½ cup broth mixture into each bowl; sprinkle each serving with 1 tablespoon nori, 1 tablespoon onions, and ½ teaspoon sesame seeds. Yield: 4 servings.

CALORIES 322 (13% from fat); FAT 4.7g (sat 0.7g, mono 0.9g, poly 2.5g); PROTEIN 16.9g; CARB 47.3g; FIBER 3.3g; CHOL 0mg; IRON 3.8mg; SODIUM 811mg; CALC 146mg

## menu

### Chinese-Barbecued Pork Tenderloin

Egg fried rice*

*Heat 1 teaspoon vegetable oil in a large nonstick skillet over medium-high heat. Add ½ cup egg substitute and 1 teaspoon dark sesame oil; stir-fry 2 minutes. Add 3 cups cold cooked rice; stir-fry 3 minutes. Add ½ cup fresh peas and ¼ cup diced carrot; stir-fry 5 minutes. Add ¼ teaspoon salt and pepper. Serves 4.

## Chinese-Barbecued Pork Tenderloin

PREPARATION TIME: 5 MINUTES

COOKING TIME: 25 MINUTES

 1 (1-pound) pork tenderloin
 2 teaspoons brown sugar
 ½ teaspoon five-spice powder
 ¼ teaspoon salt
 ⅛ teaspoon ground red pepper
 Cooking spray
 1 tablespoon hoisin sauce
 1 tablespoon orange juice
 ½ teaspoon dark sesame oil

**1.** Preheat oven to 400°.
**2.** Trim fat from pork. Combine sugar and next 3 ingredients. Rub pork with spice mixture.
**3.** Place pork on a broiler pan coated with cooking spray; insert a meat thermometer into thickest portion of tenderloin. Bake at 400° for 10 minutes. Combine hoisin, orange juice, and oil in a small bowl; brush over tenderloin. Bake an additional 15 minutes or until thermometer registers 160° (slightly pink). Yield: 4 servings (serving size: 3 ounces).

CALORIES 165 (27% from fat); FAT 5g (sat 1.5g, mono 2.1g, poly 0.9g); PROTEIN 24.7g; CARB 3.9g; FIBER 0.2g; CHOL 79mg; IRON 1.5mg; SODIUM 269mg; CALC 14mg

## Singapore Spicy Shrimp over Spinach

PREPARATION TIME: 15 MINUTES
COOKING TIME: 6 MINUTES

    1  tablespoon vegetable oil, divided
    1  (10-ounce) bag spinach, coarsely
       chopped
 1½  pounds peeled and deveined
       medium shrimp
    1  cup red bell pepper strips (about 1
       medium)
  ¼  cup sake (rice wine) or sweet
       white wine
  ¼  cup oyster sauce
    2  teaspoons bottled minced garlic
    1  teaspoon brown sugar
    1  teaspoon Thai chili paste

**1.** Heat 1 teaspoon vegetable oil in a large nonstick skillet over medium heat. Add chopped spinach, and stir-fry 1 minute or until wilted. Remove from pan, and keep warm.
**2.** Heat 2 teaspoons oil in pan over medium-high heat. Add shrimp and bell pepper; stir-fry 2 minutes. Combine sake and next 4 ingredients. Add sake mixture to shrimp mixture. Bring to a boil; cook 1 minute. Serve shrimp mixture over spinach. Yield: 4 servings (serving size: about 1 cup shrimp mixture and ½ cup spinach).

CALORIES 257 (24% from fat); FAT 6.8g (sat 1.2g, mono 1.5g, poly 3g); PROTEIN 37.2g; CARB 9.1g; FIBER 3.3g; CHOL 259mg; IRON 6.5mg; SODIUM 730mg; CALC 172mg

# No-Heat Eats

## Six main-dish salads that fill up your table without heating up your kitchen.

Everyday salad is a modest affair: lettuce, tomato, a radish here, a carrot there, and dressing. Simplicity prevails, and actual cooking never enters the picture. Not so with the main-dish salad. Fully accessorized with proteins and starches from tasty companions such as chicken, tuna, or cannellini beans, the salad becomes the point, rather than the prelude, of a meal. Does that role mean extra stove time? Not at all.

Nutritious, meal-making salads don't have to get anywhere near those verbs most summertime cooks would sooner avoid: bake, boil, simmer, and steam. Home gardens, roadside produce stands, and farmers' markets are brimming with seasonal pickings: succulent tomatoes, sweet bell peppers, crunchy cucumbers, tender summer squashes, fragrant herbs, and much more to make your salads sparkle without any addition to your utility bill.

### Chicken Caesar Salad

Using a precooked rotisserie chicken makes this salad extra easy and fast, although any leftover cooked chicken will work.

SALAD:

    1  (2-pound) whole roasted chicken,
       skinned
  11  cups torn romaine lettuce (about
       1¼ pounds)
    1  cup red bell pepper strips

VINAIGRETTE:

    3  tablespoons olive oil
 1½  tablespoons fresh lemon juice
    2  teaspoons Worcestershire sauce
    2  teaspoons Dijon mustard
  ¼  teaspoon sugar
  ¼  teaspoon salt
  ¼  teaspoon black pepper
    1  garlic clove, crushed
 1½  cups plain croutons
  ½  cup (2 ounces) grated fresh
       Parmesan cheese

**1.** To prepare salad, remove chicken from bones; shred with 2 forks to measure 3 cups meat. Combine chicken, lettuce, and bell pepper in a large bowl.
**2.** To prepare vinaigrette, combine oil and next 7 ingredients in a bowl, stirring

well with a whisk. Pour over salad, and toss well. Sprinkle with croutons and cheese; toss gently to combine. Yield: 6 servings (serving size: 2 cups).

CALORIES 306 (47% from fat); FAT 16g (sat 4.3g, mono 8.2g, poly 2.2g); PROTEIN 29.4g; CARB 10.3g; FIBER 2.4g; CHOL 78mg; IRON 2.8mg; SODIUM 445mg; CALC 171mg

### Mediterranean Shrimp Salad

  ½  cup chopped pitted green olives
  ¼  cup basil leaves
    3  tablespoons finely chopped
       red onion
    3  tablespoons fresh lemon juice
 1½  tablespoons olive oil
    1  pound small shrimp, cooked
       and peeled
    8  cups mixed salad greens
    1  cup diced plum tomato
  ¼  cup chopped fresh flat-leaf parsley
    1  teaspoon freshly ground black pepper
    1  (8-ounce) loaf French bread, sliced

**1.** Place first 5 ingredients in a blender or food processor, and pulse until well-blended. Place ½ cup olive mixture in a large bowl; add shrimp, and toss to coat. Add remaining olive mixture to salad greens; toss to coat. Divide greens evenly among 4 plates, and top with shrimp mixture and tomato. Sprinkle with parsley and pepper. Serve with bread. Yield: 4 servings (serving size: 2 cups greens, ¾ cup shrimp mixture, ¼ cup tomato, 1 tablespoon parsley, and 2 ounces bread).

CALORIES 363 (24% from fat); FAT 9.6g (sat 1.6g, mono 5.6g, poly 1.6g); PROTEIN 31.5g; CARB 37.5g; FIBER 5.2g; CHOL 221mg; IRON 7.5mg; SODIUM 767mg; CALC 160mg

## Italian White Bean-and-Artichoke Salad

Try to handle this salad as gently as possible so the canned beans will hold their shape.

VINAIGRETTE:
2½ tablespoons red wine vinegar
2 tablespoons olive oil
1 teaspoon tomato paste
¼ teaspoon salt
⅛ teaspoon black pepper
1 garlic clove, minced

SALAD:
6 cups thinly sliced spinach (about 5 ounces)
2 cups green bell pepper strips
¾ cup (3 ounces) diced sharp provolone cheese
½ cup diagonally sliced celery
½ cup vertically sliced red onion
2 tablespoons chopped fresh basil
1 tablespoon chopped fresh parsley
1 (19-ounce) can cannellini beans or other white beans, drained
1 (14-ounce) can artichoke hearts, drained and quartered

1. To prepare vinaigrette, combine first 6 ingredients in a small bowl; stir with a whisk.
2. To prepare salad, combine spinach and remaining 8 ingredients. Drizzle with vinaigrette, and toss gently. Yield: 4 servings (serving size: 2 cups).

CALORIES 343 (36% from fat); FAT 13.5g (sat 5.2g, mono 6.5g, poly 1.5g); PROTEIN 17.4g; CARB 38.6g; FIBER 6.1g; CHOL 15mg; IRON 5.3mg; SODIUM 727mg; CALC 285mg

## Black Bean-Taco Salad with Lime Vinaigrette

With chicken, Cheddar cheese, and black beans, this southwestern-influenced salad needs nothing on the side except some iced tea. Fresh lime gives it a citrusy counterpunch.

VINAIGRETTE:
¼ cup chopped seeded tomato
¼ cup chopped fresh cilantro
2 tablespoons olive oil
1 tablespoon cider vinegar
1 teaspoon grated lime rind
1 tablespoon fresh lime juice
¼ teaspoon salt
¼ teaspoon ground cumin
¼ teaspoon chili powder
¼ teaspoon black pepper
1 garlic clove, peeled

SALAD:
8 cups thinly sliced iceberg lettuce
1½ cups chopped ready-to-eat roasted skinned, boned chicken breast (about 2 breasts)
1 cup chopped tomato
1 cup chopped green bell pepper
1 cup finely diced red onion
½ cup (2 ounces) shredded reduced-fat sharp Cheddar cheese
1 (15-ounce) can black beans, rinsed and drained
4 cups fat-free baked tortilla chips (about 4 ounces)

1. To prepare vinaigrette, combine first 11 ingredients in a blender or food processor; process until smooth.
2. To prepare salad, combine lettuce and next 6 ingredients in a large bowl. Add vinaigrette; toss well to coat. Serve with chips. Yield: 4 servings (serving size: about 2 cups salad and 1 cup chips).

CALORIES 402 (28% from fat); FAT 12.6g (sat 3.2g, mono 6.5g, poly 1.9g); PROTEIN 24.5g; CARB 51.6g; FIBER 8g; CHOL 35mg; IRON 3.6mg; SODIUM 861mg; CALC 236mg

## Tabbouleh with Beans and Feta

(pictured on page 204)

1¼ cups uncooked bulgur or cracked wheat
2 cups boiling water
¼ cup commercial pesto
3 tablespoons fresh lemon juice
2 cups cherry tomatoes, halved
¾ cup (3 ounces) crumbled feta cheese
⅓ cup thinly sliced green onions
2 tablespoons minced fresh parsley
¼ teaspoon freshly ground black pepper
1 (19-ounce) can chickpeas (garbanzo beans), rinsed and drained
4 (7-inch) pitas, cut in half

1. Combine bulgur and boiling water in a large bowl. Cover and let stand 30 minutes, and drain. Combine pesto and lemon juice; stir with a whisk. Combine bulgur, pesto mixture, tomatoes, and next 5 ingredients in a large bowl; toss gently to combine. Serve with pita halves. Yield: 4 servings (serving size: 1½ cups salad and 2 pita halves).

CALORIES 599 (26% from fat); FAT 17.4g (sat 5.4g, mono 7.5g, poly 2.9g); PROTEIN 23.3g; CARB 93.3g; FIBER 14.2g; CHOL 21mg; IRON 7.8mg; SODIUM 856mg; CALC 352mg

## Vegetable Panzanella with Tuna

Be sure your bread is dry so the croutons won't get soggy when tossed with the dressing. If you're using fresh bread, bake the bread cubes at 350° for 5 minutes. Serve this salad immediately, while the bread is crunchy.

VINAIGRETTE:
2 tablespoons chopped fresh parsley
2 tablespoons chopped fresh basil
2 tablespoons olive oil
2 tablespoons red wine vinegar
¼ teaspoon freshly ground black pepper
1 garlic clove, minced

*Continued*

2½  pounds cucumber, peeled, halved lengthwise, seeded, and sliced (about 4 cups)
1¼  cups diced zucchini
1  cup diced red bell pepper
¾  cup halved pitted kalamata olives
½  cup thinly sliced red onion
¼  teaspoon salt
3  tomatoes, each cut into 8 wedges (about 1½ pounds)
1  (6-ounce) can albacore tuna in water, drained and flaked
4  cups (½-inch) cubed day-old whole-wheat bread (about 13 [1-ounce] slices)

**1.** To prepare vinaigrette, combine first 6 ingredients; stir with a whisk.
**2.** To prepare salad, combine cucumber and next 7 ingredients in a large bowl. Add bread. Drizzle with vinaigrette; toss gently to combine. Yield: 6 servings (serving size: 2 cups).

CALORIES 298 (30% from fat); FAT 10g (sat 1.7g, mono 6g, poly 1.8g); PROTEIN 13.6g; CARB 41.1g; FIBER 5.9g; CHOL 9mg; IRON 4mg; SODIUM 668mg; CALC 109mg

happy endings

# Too Sweet Not to Eat

*Fresh fruits and warm times can add up to some very tempting desserts.*

Fresh strawberries, plums, cantaloupe—the flavors of the season practically invite you to eat the very words.

But put these great fruits to better use in desserts that ease you into the warm months to come with sweetness that's neither heavy nor yawn-inducing.

The best part is that because we offer seven tempting recipes, you can have a different dessert every night of the week. Only question: Which dessert for which evening?

## Blueberry Crisp à la Mode

(pictured on page 204)

6  cups blueberries
2  tablespoons brown sugar
1  tablespoon all-purpose flour
1  tablespoon fresh lemon juice
⅔  cup all-purpose flour
½  cup packed brown sugar
½  cup regular oats
¾  teaspoon ground cinnamon
4½  tablespoons chilled butter or stick margarine, cut into small pieces
2  cups vanilla low-fat frozen yogurt

**1.** Preheat oven to 375°.
**2.** Combine first 4 ingredients in a medium bowl; spoon into an 11 x 7-inch baking dish. Lightly spoon ⅔ cup flour into a dry measuring cup, and level with a knife. Combine ⅔ cup flour, ½ cup brown sugar, oats, and cinnamon, and cut in butter with a pastry blender or 2 knives until mixture resembles coarse meal. Sprinkle over blueberry mixture. Bake at 375° for 30 minutes or until bubbly. Top each serving with ¼ cup frozen yogurt. Yield: 8 servings.
**NOTE:** The topping may also be made in a food processor. Place ⅔ cup flour, ½ cup brown sugar, oats, and cinnamon in a food processor, and pulse 2 times or until combined. Add butter; pulse 4 times or until mixture resembles coarse meal.

CALORIES 288 (26% from fat); FAT 8.3g (sat 4.8g, mono 2g, poly 0.9g); PROTEIN 4.2g; CARB 52g; FIBER 3.8g; CHOL 22mg; IRON 1.3mg; SODIUM 96mg; CALC 77mg

## Peach Cobbler

FILLING:
6  cups diced peeled peaches (about 2¾ pounds)
¼  cup granulated sugar
1  tablespoon cornstarch
1  tablespoon peach schnapps (optional)
½  teaspoon ground cinnamon
½  teaspoon grated lemon rind
2  tablespoons fresh lemon juice

TOPPING:
½  cup all-purpose flour
½  cup regular oats
½  cup packed brown sugar
2  tablespoons butter or stick margarine, melted
2  tablespoons vegetable oil
1  teaspoon ground cinnamon

**1.** Preheat oven to 350°.
**2.** To prepare filling, combine first 7 ingredients in a bowl; spoon into a 10-inch cast-iron skillet.
**3.** To prepare topping, lightly spoon flour into a dry measuring cup, and level with a knife. Combine flour and remaining 5 ingredients in a small bowl, and toss with a fork until well-blended. Sprinkle topping evenly over peach mixture. Bake at 350° for 40 minutes or until bubbly. Yield: 8 servings.
**NOTE:** Cobbler can also be made in an 11 x 7-inch baking dish.

CALORIES 234 (26% from fat); FAT 6.8g (sat 2.5g, mono 2g, poly 2g); PROTEIN 2.5g; CARB 43.2g; FIBER 2.7g; CHOL 8mg; IRON 1.1mg; SODIUM 35mg; CALC 28mg

## Triple-Layer Strawberry Cake

With the help of a prepared cake, this dessert is a snap to assemble; be sure to allow enough time for it to firm up in the freezer.

1  (10½-ounce) loaf angel food cake
2  cups sliced strawberries, divided
3  cups strawberry fat-free frozen yogurt, softened
1  tablespoon sugar
1  tablespoon orange juice

**1.** Split cake in thirds horizontally using a serrated knife; place bottom cake layer, cut side up, on a platter. Arrange ½ cup strawberries on cake; spread with 1½ cups yogurt, and top with middle cake layer. Repeat procedure with ½ cup strawberries and 1½ cups yogurt. Top with remaining cake layer; freeze 2 hours.
**2.** Combine 1 cup strawberries, sugar, and orange juice in a blender, and process until smooth. Cover and chill. Serve sauce with cake. Yield: 8 servings

(serving size: 1 cake slice and 1½ tablespoons sauce).

CALORIES 182 (1% from fat); FAT 0.3g (sat 0g, mono 0g, poly 0.1g); PROTEIN 5.4g; CARB 41.4g; FIBER 0.9g; CHOL 0mg; IRON 0.2mg; SODIUM 240mg; CALC 144mg

## Ricotta Cheesecake with Fresh-Plum Sauce

⅓  cup vanilla wafer crumbs (about 8 cookies)
Cooking spray
  1  (15-ounce) carton fat-free ricotta cheese
  1  (8-ounce) block ⅓-less-fat cream cheese, softened
¼  cup all-purpose flour
⅔  cup sugar
½  cup plain fat-free yogurt
1½  teaspoons vanilla extract
  1  teaspoon grated lemon rind
  2  large egg whites
  2  large eggs
Fresh-Plum Sauce

**1.** Preheat oven to 325°.
**2.** Sprinkle wafer crumbs over bottom and halfway up sides of a 9-inch springform pan coated with cooking spray.
**3.** Place ricotta in a food processor, and process until smooth. Add cream cheese, and process until smooth. Lightly spoon flour into a dry measuring cup; level with a knife. Add flour and next 6 ingredients to cheese mixture; pulse until well-blended. Pour into prepared pan; bake at 325° for 55 minutes or until almost set. Turn oven off; let stand in closed oven 30 minutes. Remove from oven, and cool on a wire rack. Cover and chill at least 8 hours. Serve with Fresh-Plum Sauce. Yield: 10 servings (serving size: 1 wedge and about 2 tablespoons sauce).

(Totals include Fresh-Plum Sauce) CALORIES 244 (27% from fat); FAT 7.4g (sat 3.9g, mono 2.3g, poly 0.4g); PROTEIN 11.7g; CARB 34.7g; FIBER 1g; CHOL 66mg; IRON 0.5mg; SODIUM 159mg; CALC 121mg

### FRESH-PLUM SAUCE:
2½  cups sliced plums (about ¾ pound)
⅓  cup sugar
  2  tablespoons water

**1.** Combine all ingredients in a saucepan. Cover; bring to a simmer over medium-low heat. Reduce heat to low; cook 15 minutes or until plums are tender. Cool slightly. Place in a food processor, and pulse 6 times or until chunky. Yield: 1½ cups (serving size: about 2 tablespoons).

CALORIES 49 (6% from fat); FAT 0.3g (sat 0g, mono 0.2g, poly 0.1g); PROTEIN 0.3g; CARB 12.1g; FIBER 0.9g; CHOL 0mg; IRON 0mg; SODIUM 0mg; CALC 2mg

## Plum Strudel

This Austrian favorite reaches across international waters to provide a great setting for peak-season California plums.

  1  tablespoon vegetable oil
  1  tablespoon butter or stick margarine, melted
  3  tablespoons dark brown sugar
  3  tablespoons dry breadcrumbs
  1  teaspoon ground cinnamon
  4  cups thinly sliced plums (about 1 pound)
¼  cup packed dark brown sugar
¼  cup diced pitted prunes
½  teaspoon grated lemon rind
  8  sheets frozen phyllo pastry, thawed
Cooking spray
½  teaspoon cinnamon-sugar or granulated sugar

**1.** Preheat oven to 350°.
**2.** Combine vegetable oil and butter in a custard cup or small bowl.
**3.** Combine 3 tablespoons brown sugar, breadcrumbs, and ground cinnamon in a small bowl.
**4.** Toss plums, ¼ cup brown sugar, prunes, and rind in a large bowl.
**5.** Place 2 phyllo sheets on a large cutting board or work surface (cover remaining dough to keep from drying), and lightly brush with oil mixture. Sprinkle with 2 tablespoons breadcrumb mixture. Repeat layers with remaining phyllo, oil mixture, and breadcrumb mixture, ending with phyllo. Lightly coat top phyllo sheet with cooking spray. Arrange plum mixture over phyllo, leaving a 2-inch border. Starting at short edge, roll up phyllo jelly-roll fashion. (Do not roll tightly, or strudel may split.) Place strudel, seam side down, on a baking sheet coated with cooking spray. Lightly coat strudel with cooking spray; sprinkle with cinnamon-sugar.
**6.** Bake at 350° for 30 minutes or until golden. Cool 10 minutes, and remove from pan. Cut with a serrated knife. Yield: 8 servings.

CALORIES 184 (25% from fat); FAT 5.1g (sat 1.5g, mono 1.6g, poly 1.8g); PROTEIN 2.3g; CARB 33.6g; FIBER 1.8g; CHOL 4mg; IRON 1.3mg; SODIUM 133mg; CALC 27mg

## Minted Strawberries and Bananas in Cantaloupe Cups

You can skip making the cantaloupe cups and simply serve the fruit mixture in dessert bowls. You could also make cantaloupe balls and toss all the ingredients together.

  2  cantaloupes (about 2½ pounds)
  3  cups sliced strawberries
½  cup orange juice
¼  cup sugar
¼  cup chopped fresh mint
  1  tablespoon lemon juice
  2  teaspoons vanilla extract
1½  cups sliced banana

**1.** Cut cantaloupes in half crosswise; discard seeds. Cover and chill.
**2.** Combine strawberries and next 5 ingredients in a bowl. Cover and chill 30 minutes. Stir in banana; spoon 1 cup strawberry mixture into each cantaloupe half. Yield: 4 servings.

CALORIES 248 (5% from fat); FAT 1.4g (sat 0.5g, mono 0.2g, poly 0.3g); PROTEIN 3.8g; CARB 59.8g; FIBER 7.7g; CHOL 0mg; IRON 1.2mg; SODIUM 26mg; CALC 53mg

## Peach Melba Crisp

To take advantage of another fruit in peak season, substitute unpeeled nectarines for the peaches.

- ½ cup all-purpose flour
- ¼ cup granulated sugar
- ¼ cup packed brown sugar
- 3 tablespoons chilled butter or stick margarine, cut into small pieces
- 6 cups sliced peeled peaches (about 2¾ pounds)
- 2 teaspoons lemon juice
- 1 cup fresh raspberries
- 1 tablespoon granulated sugar
- 1 tablespoon cornstarch
- Cooking spray
- 1 tablespoon seedless raspberry jam, melted

**1.** Preheat oven to 375°.
**2.** Lightly spoon flour into a dry measuring cup, and level with a knife. Combine flour, ¼ cup granulated sugar, and ¼ cup brown sugar in a bowl; cut in butter with a pastry blender or 2 knives until mixture resembles coarse meal.
**3.** Combine peaches and juice in a large bowl; toss gently to coat. Add raspberries, 1 tablespoon granulated sugar, and cornstarch; toss gently. Spoon fruit mixture into an 8-inch square baking dish coated with cooking spray; drizzle jam evenly over fruit. Sprinkle with flour mixture. Bake at 375° for 45 minutes or until browned. Yield: 6 servings.

CALORIES 261 (21% from fat); FAT 6.2g (sat 3.6g, mono 1.8g, poly 0.5g); PROTEIN 2.5g; CARB 52g; FIBER 5.1g; CHOL 16mg; IRON 1mg; SODIUM 64mg; CALC 25mg

## resources

# Take Back the Freezer

*Grocery stores don't have a monopoly on frozen dinners. Here's how to make your own.*

Short on time and tired of store-bought frozen meals? Can't remember the last time you enjoyed a sit-down dinner? How about this for a solution: Cook several meals from scratch on the weekend, and then freeze the results for the hurried pace of the week. It's the ultimate make-ahead strategy—all the convenience of quick-and-easy meals but with the flavor of your own healthy home cooking.

From lasagna to pork chops, you'll move your entrées from freezer to oven to table with minimal effort.

## Tomato-Basil Lasagna with Prosciutto

Freezing instructions: After assembling lasagna, cover and freeze up to 1 month. Thaw in refrigerator; bake as directed.

- 5 garlic cloves
- 1 (16-ounce) carton 1% low-fat cottage cheese
- ½ cup (4 ounces) block-style fat-free cream cheese
- ¼ cup (1 ounce) grated fresh Romano cheese, divided
- 2½ teaspoons dried basil
- ½ teaspoon crushed red pepper
- 1 large egg
- 1 (26-ounce) bottle fat-free tomato-basil pasta sauce (such as Muir Glen)
- Cooking spray
- 12 cooked lasagna noodles
- 1 cup (4 ounces) chopped prosciutto or ham
- 1 cup (4 ounces) shredded part-skim mozzarella cheese

**1.** Preheat oven to 375°.
**2.** Drop garlic through food chute with food processor on, and process until minced. Add cottage cheese; process 2 minutes or until smooth. Add cream cheese, 2 tablespoons Romano, basil, pepper, and egg; process until well-blended.
**3.** Spread ½ cup pasta sauce in bottom of a 13 x 9-inch baking dish coated with cooking spray. Arrange 3 noodles over pasta sauce; top with 1 cup cheese mixture, ⅓ cup prosciutto, and ¾ cup pasta sauce. Repeat layers two times, ending with noodles. Spread remaining pasta sauce over noodles. Sprinkle with 2 tablespoons Romano and mozzarella.
**4.** Cover and bake at 375° for 45 minutes or until sauce is bubbly. Uncover and bake an additional 15 minutes. Let lasagna stand 5 minutes. Yield: 9 servings.

CALORIES 272 (19% from fat); FAT 5.6g (sat 2.8g, mono 1.8g, poly 0.6g); PROTEIN 20.8g; CARB 33g; FIBER 2.1g; CHOL 47mg; IRON 2.3mg; SODIUM 775mg; CALC 213mg

## Sweet-and-Spicy Barbecued Beans

Freezing instructions: After spooning into casserole dish, cover and freeze up to 3 months. Thaw in refrigerator; bake as directed.

- 2 teaspoons olive oil
- 1 cup chopped onion
- 4 garlic cloves, minced
- 8 cups chopped kale (about ¾ pound)
- ½ cup water
- ½ cup hickory barbecue sauce (such as Kraft)
- 2 tablespoons Dijon mustard
- 1 tablespoon cider vinegar
- 1 teaspoon hot sauce
- 2 (16-ounce) cans kidney beans, rinsed and drained

**1.** Preheat oven to 350°.
**2.** Heat oil in a large nonstick skillet over medium heat. Add onion and garlic; sauté 5 minutes or until onion is tender. Stir in remaining ingredients; spoon into a 2-quart casserole. Cover and bake at

350° for 45 minutes or until thoroughly heated. Yield: 6 servings (serving size: about ¾ cup).

CALORIES 191 (14% from fat); FAT 3g (sat 0.4g, mono 1.6g, poly 0.8g); PROTEIN 10.6g; CARB 32.6g; FIBER 4.7g; CHOL 0mg; IRON 3.8mg; SODIUM 414mg; CALC 115mg

## Pork Ragoût

Freezing instructions: After cooking ragoût, place in a large heavy-duty zip-top plastic bag. Cool completely in refrigerator; freeze up to 1 month. To reheat, place bag in a large pot of boiling water (do not unseal bag). Cook 15 minutes or until thoroughly heated. Remove bag from water using tongs. While ragoût is reheating, grate cheese, and cook pasta according to package instructions, omitting salt and fat.

   1   pound boned pork loin
   1   (4-ounce) link hot turkey
       Italian sausage
   1   cup chopped onion
   1   tablespoon chopped fresh or
       1 teaspoon dried rosemary
   ¼   teaspoon salt
   ¼   teaspoon black pepper
   ¾   cup fat-free, less-sodium chicken
       broth
   ¾   cup Zinfandel or other dry red
       wine
   1   (28-ounce) can Italian-style
       whole tomatoes, undrained and
       chopped
   4   cups hot cooked penne (about
       8 ounces uncooked tube-shaped
       pasta)
   ¼   cup (1 ounce) grated fresh
       Romano cheese
   Fresh rosemary sprigs (optional)

**1.** Trim fat from pork; cut pork into ¼-inch cubes.
**2.** Remove casing from sausage. Cook sausage in a Dutch oven over medium-high heat until browned; stir to crumble. Remove sausage from pan with a slotted spoon. Add onion to pan; sauté 4 minutes or until lightly browned. Add pork, and sauté 5 minutes. Add sausage, chopped rosemary, salt, and pepper. Stir in broth and wine, scraping pan to loosen browned bits. Bring to a boil; cook 5 minutes. Add tomatoes, and bring to a boil. Reduce heat, and simmer 30 minutes. Serve over pasta, and sprinkle with cheese. Garnish with rosemary sprigs, if desired. Yield: 4 servings (serving size: 1 cup ragoût, 1 cup pasta, and 1 tablespoon cheese).

CALORIES 490 (24% from fat); FAT 12.9g (sat 4.7g, mono 4.9g, poly 2.1g); PROTEIN 36.7g; CARB 55.8g; FIBER 3.7g; CHOL 86mg; IRON 4.9mg; SODIUM 874mg; CALC 160mg

## Short Sharp Chops

Freezing instructions: Combine pork and marinade in a large heavy-duty zip-top plastic bag, and place in freezer up to 2 months. Thaw in refrigerator; cook as directed.

   8   (2-ounce) boned center-cut loin
       pork chops (¼ inch thick)
   ¼   cup low-sodium soy sauce
   ¼   cup thawed orange juice
       concentrate, undiluted
   ¼   cup chopped green onions
   2   teaspoons grated peeled fresh
       ginger
   ½   teaspoon black pepper
   2   garlic cloves, minced
   1   teaspoon olive oil

**1.** Trim fat from pork. Combine soy sauce and next 5 ingredients in a large zip-top plastic bag. Add pork to bag; seal and marinate in refrigerator 1 hour, turning bag occasionally. Remove pork from bag; discard marinade.
**2.** Heat oil in a large nonstick skillet over medium-high heat. Add chops; sauté 3 minutes on each side. Yield: 4 servings (serving size: 2 chops).

CALORIES 177 (42% from fat); FAT 8.2g (sat 2.6g, mono 4.1g, poly 0.9g); PROTEIN 19.8g; CARB 4g; FIBER 0.2g; CHOL 56mg; IRON 0.9mg; SODIUM 256mg; CALC 14mg

## Greek Lamb Burgers with Cucumber Sauce

Freezing instructions: After forming patties, wrap each individually in heavy-duty aluminum foil, and freeze up to 2 months. Thaw in refrigerator; cook as directed.

   2   (1-ounce) slices day-old white
       bread
   ⅓   cup chopped red onion
   ⅓   cup chopped fresh mint
   2   tablespoons grated lemon rind
       (about 2 lemons)
   ½   teaspoon salt
   ¼   teaspoon ground red pepper
   1   pound lean ground lamb
   1   (10-ounce) package frozen
       chopped spinach, thawed,
       drained, and squeezed dry
   3   garlic cloves, minced
   Cooking spray
   Cucumber Sauce

**1.** Prepare grill.
**2.** Place bread in food processor; pulse until coarsely ground. Combine breadcrumbs, onion, and next 7 ingredients in a bowl. Divide mixture into 4 equal portions, shaping each into a ½-inch-thick patty.
**3.** Place patties on grill rack coated with cooking spray, and grill 7 minutes on each side or until done. Serve with Cucumber Sauce. Yield: 4 servings (serving size: 1 burger and 2 tablespoons sauce).

(Totals include Cucumber Sauce) CALORIES 234 (30% from fat); FAT 7.8g (sat 2.7g, mono 3.1g, poly 2g); PROTEIN 27.6g; CARB 13.1g; FIBER 2.4g; CHOL 76mg; IRON 3.9mg; SODIUM 498mg; CALC 129mg

**CUCUMBER SAUCE:**
   ¼   cup diced seeded peeled
       cucumber
   ¼   cup plain low-fat yogurt
   1   teaspoon chopped fresh
       parsley
   1   garlic clove, minced

**1.** Combine all ingredients in a bowl; cover and chill. Yield: ½ cup (serving size: 2 tablespoons).

CALORIES 11 (16% from fat); FAT 0.2g (sat 0.1g, mono 0.1g, poly 0g); PROTEIN 0.8g; CARB 1.4g; FIBER 0.1g; CHOL 1mg; IRON 0.1mg; SODIUM 11mg; CALC 29mg

## Chunky Chipotle-
## Chicken Chili

Freezing instructions: After adding chicken and bacon to corn mixture, spoon into a freezer-safe container. Cool mixture completely in refrigerator; cover and freeze up to 3 months. Thaw in refrigerator. Place in a large skillet; cook over medium-low heat until thoroughly heated, stirring occasionally.

    3   bacon slices
    1   pound skinned, boned chicken
        breast, cut into 1-inch pieces
    ½   cup chopped red onion
    1   teaspoon ground coriander
    5   garlic cloves, minced
    1   drained canned chipotle chile in
        adobo sauce, seeded and minced
    1   cup frozen whole-kernel corn,
        thawed
    1   (16-ounce) bottle salsa
    1   (15-ounce) can pinto beans, rinsed
        and drained
    1   (7-ounce) bottle roasted red bell
        peppers, drained and sliced

**1.** Cook bacon in a large nonstick skillet over medium heat until crisp. Remove bacon from pan; crumble. Add chicken to drippings in pan; sauté 4 minutes. Remove from pan; keep warm.
**2.** Add onion, coriander, garlic, and chile to pan; sauté 3 minutes. Add corn, salsa, beans, and bell peppers; cover and cook 5 minutes. Return chicken and bacon to pan; cook 5 minutes or until thoroughly heated. Yield: 6 servings (serving size: 1 cup).

CALORIES 293 (30% from fat); FAT 9.8g (sat 3.4g, mono 4.1g, poly 1.5g); PROTEIN 24.7g; CARB 26g; FIBER 4.2g; CHOL 53mg; IRON 2.9mg; SODIUM 686mg; CALC 69mg

## Moroccan Chicken
## with Green Olives

Freezing instructions: After adding chicken to broth mixture, simmer 5 minutes. Place in a freezer-safe container; cool completely in refrigerator. Freeze up to 2 months. Thaw overnight in refrigerator. Heat a large skillet over medium heat; add chicken mixture, and cook 10 minutes or until thoroughly heated.

    1   teaspoon ground coriander
    ½   teaspoon dried mint flakes
    ½   teaspoon ground cinnamon
    ¼   teaspoon salt
    ¼   teaspoon black pepper
    4   (4-ounce) skinned, boned
        chicken breast halves
    2   teaspoons olive oil, divided
    2   cups sliced onion
    1   cup fat-free, less-sodium chicken
        broth
    1   (6-ounce) can thawed orange juice
        concentrate, undiluted
   10   green olives, sliced

**1.** Combine first 5 ingredients; rub chicken with spice mixture.
**2.** Heat 1 teaspoon oil in a large nonstick skillet over medium-high heat; add chicken. Cook 2 minutes on each side, and set aside.
**3.** Heat 1 teaspoon olive oil in pan. Add sliced onion, and cook 8 minutes or until golden. Stir in chicken broth, orange juice concentrate, and olives; bring to a boil. Return chicken to pan; reduce heat, and simmer mixture 15 minutes or until chicken is done. Yield: 4 servings (serving size: 1 chicken breast half and ½ cup sauce).

CALORIES 253 (17% from fat); FAT 4.7g (sat 0.9g, mono 2.7g, poly 0.6g); PROTEIN 28.9g; CARB 23.1g; FIBER 2g; CHOL 66mg; IRON 1.8mg; SODIUM 456mg; CALC 57mg

## Tips for a Cold World

• Don't overcook food items that are intended for the freezer, and be particularly careful to slightly undercook pasta, rice, and vegetables.
• Cool all foods completely by setting meals in the refrigerator for at least one hour before freezing.
• Allow adequate time for your frozen foods to thaw before reheating. About 24 to 48 hours in the refrigerator will completely thaw most freezer items.
• Store foods in any kind of airtight container, such as heavy-duty plastic containers or heavy-duty zip-top plastic bags. For dishes that go from freezer to oven, cover containers with heavy-duty aluminum foil.
• Make certain that all freezer containers are sealed completely and that you've removed excess air before sealing.
• Don't forget to label (we use a permanent ink marker) with reheating instructions before freezing. This will streamline your preparation. Include the name of the meal, date frozen, number of servings, temperature and length of time it bakes, and any other necessary information.

# august

# Summer's Simplest 6

## You've got fresh veggies. You've got an hour. You've got dinner.

You don't have to be a vegetarian to get some of the best eating pleasures of the year from summer's peak load of produce. Dinnertime favorites rise to hitherto unforeseen heights of lip-smacking delight when matched with fresh vegetables. With these recipes (none with cooking times of more than an hour), you can do dinner six ways from Sunday.

### Gazpacho Shrimp Salad

We've combined the classic components of Spanish-inspired gazpacho with shrimp and salad greens in this refreshing entrée that's perfect for American summers. Make it truly multinational by serving crusty French bread so you can soak up every last drop.

1½  cups (1½-inch) diagonally sliced green beans (about ½ pound)
1  pound large shrimp, cooked and peeled
2  cups cubed seeded cucumber
2  cups chopped tomato
⅓  cup diced green bell pepper
¼  cup diagonally sliced green onions
¼  cup thinly sliced fresh basil
¼  cup tomato juice
3  tablespoons red wine vinegar
4  teaspoons extra-virgin olive oil
¼  teaspoon sugar
¼  teaspoon salt
⅛  teaspoon black pepper
⅛  teaspoon hot sauce
2  garlic cloves, minced
8  cups gourmet salad greens

**1.** Steam beans, covered, 4 minutes or until crisp-tender. Drain and rinse with cold water; drain well.
**2.** Combine beans, shrimp, and next 5 ingredients in a large bowl. Combine juice and next 7 ingredients in a small bowl; stir well with a whisk. Pour over shrimp mixture; toss well. Serve over greens. Yield: 4 servings (serving size: 2 cups shrimp mixture and 2 cups greens).

**NOTE:** Serve at room temperature or chilled.

CALORIES 200 (28% from fat); FAT 6.2g (sat 1g, mono 3.6g, poly 1.1g); PROTEIN 22.3g; CARB 15.6g; FIBER 5g; CHOL 166mg; IRON 5.3mg; SODIUM 417mg; CALC 122mg

### Grilled Tuna Niçoise

Cherry tomatoes are plentiful right now, so use a variety of them—red, yellow pear-shaped, or orange—in this classic salad.

4  cups cubed red potato (about 1¼ pounds)
½  pound green beans, trimmed
1  (8-ounce) tuna steak (about ¾ inch thick)
Cooking spray
½  cup vertically sliced red onion
½  cup chopped fresh parsley
1  tablespoon chopped fresh or 1 teaspoon dried tarragon
½  cup fat-free, less-sodium chicken broth
3  tablespoons white wine vinegar
1  tablespoon extra-virgin olive oil
1  tablespoon Dijon mustard
¼  teaspoon salt
¼  teaspoon freshly ground black pepper
8  cups gourmet salad greens
1  cup cherry tomatoes, halved
¼  cup niçoise olives

**1.** Cook potato in boiling water 6 minutes or until tender; remove with a slotted spoon. Add green beans to boiling water, and cook 3 minutes or until crisp-tender. Drain.
**2.** Prepare grill or broiler.
**3.** Place fish on a grill rack or broiler pan coated with cooking spray; cook 3 minutes on each side or until desired degree of doneness. Cut fish into 1-inch chunks.
**4.** Combine potato, fish, onion, parsley, and tarragon in a large bowl. Combine broth and next 5 ingredients; stir well with a whisk. Pour ½ cup broth mixture over potato mixture, and toss well.
**5.** Divide beans, greens, and tomatoes evenly among 4 plates. Top each serving with 1½ cups potato mixture and 1 tablespoon olives. Drizzle 1 tablespoon of remaining broth mixture over each serving. Yield: 4 servings.

CALORIES 299 (26% from fat); FAT 8.6g (sat 1.6g, mono 4.8g, poly 1.8g); PROTEIN 19.8g; CARB 37.2g; FIBER 6.9g; CHOL 21mg; IRON 4.7mg; SODIUM 458mg; CALC 104mg

### Lemon-Dill Couscous with Chicken and Vegetables

(pictured on page 222)

1½  cups water
1  cup uncooked couscous
2  cups chopped ready-to-eat roasted skinned, boned chicken breast (about 2 breasts)
1½  cups diced yellow squash (about ½ pound)
1  cup diced red bell pepper
½  cup chopped fresh flat-leaf parsley
¼  cup fat-free, less-sodium chicken broth
3  tablespoons fresh lemon juice
2  tablespoons chopped fresh or 2 teaspoons dried dill
1  tablespoon extra-virgin olive oil
½  teaspoon salt
⅛  teaspoon black pepper

**1.** Bring water to a boil in a medium saucepan; gradually stir in couscous. Remove from heat; cover and let stand 5 minutes. Fluff with a fork. Spoon couscous into a large bowl. Add chicken and remaining ingredients; toss well. Yield: 4 servings (serving size: 2 cups).

CALORIES 246 (19% from fat); FAT 5.3g (sat 1.1g, mono 3g, poly 0.8g); PROTEIN 19g; CARB 31.9g; FIBER 3.2g; CHOL 35mg; IRON 2.1mg; SODIUM 624mg; CALC 43mg

## Flank Steak with Corn-Tomato Relish and Grilled Garlic Bread

(pictured on page 221)

Chop all the onions needed for the marinade and relish at the same time, and make the relish while the steak is marinating.

    1  (1-pound) flank steak
    ⅓  cup dry red wine
    ¼  cup chopped Vidalia or other sweet onion
    2  teaspoons low-sodium soy sauce
    2  garlic cloves, minced
    ¼  teaspoon salt
    ¼  teaspoon black pepper
       Cooking spray
    4  (2-ounce) slices Italian bread
    2  garlic cloves, halved
       Corn-Tomato Relish
       Basil sprigs (optional)

**1.** Trim fat from steak. Combine wine, onion, soy sauce, and garlic in a large zip-top plastic bag; add steak to bag. Seal and marinate in refrigerator 30 minutes, turning occasionally.
**2.** Prepare grill.
**3.** Remove steak from bag; discard marinade. Sprinkle steak with salt and pepper. Place on grill rack coated with cooking spray; grill 5 minutes on each side or until desired degree of doneness. Cut diagonally across grain into thin slices. Place bread slices on grill rack; grill 2 minutes on each side or until lightly browned. Rub 1 side of each bread slice with 1 garlic clove half. Serve with steak and Corn-Tomato Relish. Garnish with basil, if desired. Yield: 4 servings (serving size: 3 ounces steak, 1 bread slice, and ¾ cup relish).

(Totals include Corn-Tomato Relish) CALORIES 473 (29% from fat); FAT 15.5g (sat 5.9g, mono 6.5g, poly 1.2g); PROTEIN 30.1g; CARB 52.6g; FIBER 5.2g; CHOL 60mg; IRON 4.4mg; SODIUM 753mg; CALC 39mg

### CORN-TOMATO RELISH:

    1  teaspoon olive oil
    1  cup chopped Vidalia or other sweet onion
    1½  cups fresh corn kernels (about 3 ears)
    1½  cups diced tomato (about ¾ pound)
    ⅓  cup thinly sliced fresh basil
    1  tablespoon fresh lime juice
    1  teaspoon sugar
    ¼  teaspoon salt
    ¼  teaspoon crushed red pepper
    ⅛  teaspoon black pepper

**1.** Heat oil in a large nonstick skillet over medium heat. Add onion, and sauté 5 minutes or until tender. Add corn; cook 8 minutes or until tender, stirring frequently. Remove from heat, and cool slightly. Combine corn mixture, tomato, and remaining ingredients in a large bowl; toss gently. Yield: 4 servings (serving size: ¾ cup).

CALORIES 96 (20% from fat); FAT 2.1g (sat 0.3g, mono 1.1g, poly 0.6g); PROTEIN 3g; CARB 19.4g; FIBER 3.5g; CHOL 0mg; IRON 0.8mg; SODIUM 163mg; CALC 19mg

## Keeping Your Veggies Fresh

Here's how to keep your produce at its peak of freshness.

• Store summer squash and bell peppers in plastic bags in the refrigerator up to 7 days.

• Green beans keep better in an airtight container, so refrigerate them up to 4 days in a zip-top plastic bag.

• Because the sugar in corn starts to convert to starch immediately after picking, it's best to use corn the same day you buy it.

• Herbs like a little moisture to keep from wilting and drying out. Wrap herbs in a damp paper towel, place in a plastic bag, and refrigerate 5 to 7 days.

• Never refrigerate tomatoes; it destroys the flavor and texture of the pulp. Instead, keep tomatoes at room temperature, stem sides down and away from direct sunlight, for a few days.

## Garden Vegetable Stir-Fry with Tofu and Brown Rice

(pictured on page 224)

    2  tablespoons water
    1½  tablespoons cornstarch
    1  cup canned vegetable broth
    2  tablespoons oyster sauce
    2  tablespoons low-sodium soy sauce
    1  tablespoon rice vinegar
    1  teaspoon sugar
    1  teaspoon dark sesame oil
    ½  teaspoon crushed red pepper
    3  teaspoons vegetable oil, divided
    1  (12.3-ounce) package reduced-fat firm tofu, drained and cut into ½-inch cubes
    1  cup thinly sliced onion
    1  cup red bell pepper strips
    3  cups sliced zucchini (about ¾ pound)
    1  cup snow peas, trimmed
    ½  cup diagonally sliced carrot
    1  (8-ounce) can sliced water chestnuts, drained
    1  cup cilantro sprigs
    3  cups hot cooked long-grain brown rice

**1.** Combine water and cornstarch in a bowl; stir with a whisk. Stir in broth and next 6 ingredients.
**2.** Heat 2 teaspoons vegetable oil in a large nonstick skillet over medium-high heat. Add tofu; stir-fry 8 minutes or until golden brown, stirring occasionally. Remove tofu from pan. Place tofu on several layers of paper towels.
**3.** Add 1 teaspoon vegetable oil to pan. Add onion and bell pepper, and stir-fry 2 minutes. Add zucchini, snow peas, carrot, and water chestnuts; stir-fry 1 minute. Add tofu and broth mixture. Bring to a boil, and cook 2 minutes. Stir in cilantro. Serve with rice. Yield: 4 servings (serving size: 1¼ cups stir-fry and ¾ cup rice).

CALORIES 365 (18% from fat); FAT 7.4g (sat 1.3g, mono 2.2g, poly 3.2g); PROTEIN 15.1g; CARB 60.8g; FIBER 6.3g; CHOL 0mg; IRON 4.3mg; SODIUM 827mg; CALC 129mg

## Mexican Bulgur Salad with Citrus-Jalapeño Vinaigrette

1 cup uncooked bulgur or cracked wheat
1 cup boiling water
1½ cups diced zucchini
1 cup fresh corn kernels (about 2 ears)
¾ cup (3 ounces) diced Monterey Jack cheese with jalapeño peppers
3 tablespoons minced fresh cilantro
1 (15-ounce) can black beans, rinsed and drained
¼ cup fresh orange juice
¼ cup fresh lime juice
2 tablespoons minced seeded jalapeño pepper
1 tablespoon extra-virgin olive oil
¼ teaspoon salt
¼ teaspoon ground cumin
Lime wedges (optional)

**1.** Combine bulgur and boiling water in a large bowl. Cover; let stand 30 minutes or until liquid is absorbed. Add zucchini and next 4 ingredients; stir gently. Combine orange juice and next 5 ingredients; stir with a whisk. Pour juice mixture over bulgur mixture; toss gently. Serve salad at room temperature or chilled. Garnish with lime wedges, if desired. Yield: 4 servings (serving size: 1½ cups).

CALORIES 371 (28% from fat); FAT 11.4g (sat 4.8g, mono 4.6g, poly 1.1g); PROTEIN 17.6g; CARB 55.1g; FIBER 11g; CHOL 17mg; IRON 3.2mg; SODIUM 413mg; CALC 207mg

# How Their Garden Grows

*For Anne and Hillary LeClaire, gardening became the first step in a healthy lifetime of harmony with the ebb and flow of the seasons.*

When the sun is barely up in Chatham, Massachusetts—a seaside town of 7,000 people on the eastern tip of Cape Cod—Anne LeClaire is already making rounds in her garden. Later in the day, she'll be working on her current novel and later still sharing a seasonal feast with husband Hillary, a retired military pilot turned commercial fisherman. Over the years, Anne's garden, combined with Hillary's new life on the seas, has meant that the LeClaires have learned to eat not just well, but healthfully.

### Making Your Garden Grow

Anne LeClaire began her gardening life as a way to relax but quickly saw that the fresh produce gave her the means—and the motive—for healthier meals, too. With more than two decades' experience growing her dinners, she has a few tips on how to get started.

**Plant what you love.** "If you love herbs, start with herbs," Anne says. "If you're insane for radishes, start with a little radish bed."

**Tend your plants according to the season.** "Prepare the ground properly in the spring, stay one step ahead of the weeds in the early summer, and water at least twice a week as the temperature rises."

**Location is important.** "Don't try to grow tomatoes in a shady area. And never plant mint, which spreads rapidly, in the center of your garden."

**Be bossy.** "Gardening requires a certain ruthlessness," she says. "You can't let the weeds or the mint have their own way."

## Fish Soup Provençale

This recipe from Anne LeClaire makes good use of the green and red bell peppers that become plentiful in gardens and farmers' markets this time of year. Ask for the freshest fish available at your supermarket or favorite seafood market.

1 tablespoon olive oil
2 cups chopped onion
1 cup chopped green bell pepper
¾ cup chopped red bell pepper
1 garlic clove, minced
¼ teaspoon crushed red pepper
¼ teaspoon grated orange rind
¼ teaspoon dried thyme
⅛ teaspoon fennel seeds
1 (14.5-ounce) can Italian-style whole tomatoes, undrained and chopped
1 bay leaf
2 cups cubed peeled baking potato (about 8 ounces)
1½ cups water
½ cup dry white wine
1 pound grouper or other firm white fish fillets, cut into 1-inch pieces
2 tablespoons chopped fresh parsley
¼ cup half-and-half
¾ teaspoon salt
¼ teaspoon black pepper

**1.** Heat oil in a stockpot over medium-high heat. Add onion, bell peppers, and garlic; sauté 5 minutes. Add crushed red pepper and next 5 ingredients, and bring to a boil. Add potato; cover and cook 10 minutes, stirring occasionally. Add water and wine; bring to a boil, and cook 5 minutes. Add fish and parsley; bring to a boil. Cover and cook 2 minutes or until fish is done. Remove from heat; discard bay leaf. Stir in half-and-half, salt, and black pepper. Yield: 6 servings (serving size: about 1⅓ cups).

CALORIES 188 (23% from fat); FAT 4.7g (sat 1.3g, mono 2.2g, poly 0.7g); PROTEIN 17.5g; CARB 19.4g; FIBER 2.9g; CHOL 32mg; IRON 2.2mg; SODIUM 456mg; CALC 71mg

Almond Angel Food Cake with Crème Anglaise and Macerated Strawberries, page 240

Flank Steak with Corn-Tomato Relish and Grilled Garlic Bread, page 219

Banana-Split Cheesecake,
page 231

Lemon-Dill Couscous with
Chicken and Vegetables,
page 218

Oriental Salad, page 229

Garden Vegetable Stir-Fry
with Tofu and Brown Rice,
page 219

Fragrant Chicken in
Creamy Almond Sauce
and Kale-Cabbage Sauté,
page 225

# The Essence of Indian

## At the heart of the latest American passion for Indian cooking lies a very simple secret: spice.

Exciting flavors and variety are the essence of Indian cooking, and at the heart of that essence are spices—and the combining of techniques that give them such presence and power. For example, Indian cooks sizzle whole mustard seeds in oil at the beginning of cooking to draw out the flavor. They grind turmeric, mix it with water, and use the resulting paste as a sauce base. They dry-roast cinnamon, cloves, and cardamom seeds and grind them together—*garam masala* being the result—sprinkling the powder over a cooked dish for a final finish.

Indian cooking techniques are easy to master, the ingredients are a snap to purchase, and most dishes can be made ahead of time. American kitchens can adapt to Indian fare on their own terms. For example, you don't always need to prepare an elaborate, multicourse Indian meal. One spicy dish can serve as a complement to the kind of dinner you'd ordinarily prepare. And shopping for an Indian dinner does not have to be an extra burden. If you accumulate a basic set of spices such as cumin, coriander, turmeric, and *garam masala*, along with some staples, you're all set.

## Tomato Chutney

This condiment is great served warm or chilled with fish, chicken, or rice.

    2   teaspoons vegetable oil
    1   tablespoon minced peeled fresh
        ginger
    3   garlic cloves, minced
    5   cups chopped seeded tomato
        (about 2 pounds)
    2   tablespoons sugar
    1   teaspoon ground cumin
    ½   teaspoon salt
    ¼   teaspoon ground turmeric

**1.** Heat oil in a large nonstick skillet over medium heat. Add ginger and garlic; sauté 1 minute. Add tomato and remaining ingredients; bring to a boil. Cover and cook 5 minutes, stirring occasionally. Uncover and cook 15 minutes, stirring frequently. Yield: 1½ cups (serving size: 2 tablespoons).

CALORIES 32 (28% from fat); FAT 1g (sat 0.2g, mono 0.2g, poly 0.4g); PROTEIN 0.8g; CARB 6g; FIBER 0.8g; CHOL 0mg; IRON 0.4mg; SODIUM 104mg; CALC 6mg

## Kale-Cabbage Sauté

(pictured on page 224)

    2   teaspoons vegetable oil
    ½   teaspoon cumin seeds
    2   teaspoons minced peeled fresh
        ginger
    2   cups vertically sliced onion
    1   tablespoon chopped seeded
        jalapeño pepper
    1   teaspoon sugar
    ½   teaspoon salt
    ½   teaspoon ground turmeric
    5   cups chopped kale
    2   cups presliced green cabbage
    2   tablespoons water

**1.** Heat oil in a large nonstick skillet over medium heat. Add cumin seeds; cook 1 minute. Add ginger; cook 1 minute, stirring frequently. Add onion; cook 5 minutes. Stir in jalapeño and remaining ingredients. Cover and cook 15 minutes or until kale is tender; stir occasionally. Yield: 6 servings (serving size: ½ cup).

CALORIES 67 (28% from fat); FAT 2.1g (sat 0.4g, mono 0.5g, poly 1g); PROTEIN 2.7g; CARB 11.4g; FIBER 2.2g; CHOL 0mg; IRON 1.4mg; SODIUM 226mg; CALC 98mg

## Fragrant Chicken in Creamy Almond Sauce

(pictured on page 224)

    1    tablespoon olive oil
    6    (3-inch) cinnamon sticks
    5    bay leaves
    1½   cups finely chopped onion
    6    garlic cloves, minced
    2    teaspoons curry powder
    ½    teaspoon ground turmeric
    ½    teaspoon salt
    ¼    teaspoon ground cardamom
    2½   pounds skinned, boned chicken
         breast, cut into 1-inch pieces
    1    cup fat-free, less-sodium chicken
         broth
    ¼    cup fat-free sour cream
    1    teaspoon all-purpose flour
    ½    teaspoon sugar
    ¼    cup slivered almonds, toasted and
         ground
    ⅓    cup chopped red bell pepper
    2    tablespoons slivered almonds,
         toasted
    Cinnamon sticks (optional)

**1.** Heat oil in a large nonstick skillet over medium heat. Add 6 cinnamon sticks and bay leaves. Cook 2 minutes or until fragrant. Add onion and garlic; sauté 5 minutes or until tender. Add curry powder, turmeric, salt, and cardamom. Add chicken and broth; bring to a boil. Cover, reduce heat, and simmer 35 minutes or until chicken is tender.

**2.** Remove chicken from pan with a slotted spoon. Cook liquid remaining in pan over low heat 5 minutes. Combine sour cream, flour, and sugar in a small bowl; stir in ½ cup hot liquid. Add sour cream mixture to pan, stirring until smooth. Return chicken to pan; stir in ground almonds. Cook 5 minutes or until thick, stirring frequently. Sprinkle with bell pepper. Remove and discard cinnamon sticks and bay leaves. Sprinkle with slivered almonds; garnish with cinnamon sticks, if desired. Yield: 6 servings (serving size: about 1 cup chicken mixture and 1 teaspoon almonds).

CALORIES 304 (23% from fat); FAT 7.9g (sat 1.3g, mono 4.2g, poly 1.3g); PROTEIN 46.9g; CARB 8.7g; FIBER 2.1g; CHOL 110mg; IRON 2.4mg; SODIUM 410mg; CALC 60mg

## Hearty Kidney Beans and Spinach

2   (15-ounce) cans kidney beans, undrained
1   tablespoon vegetable oil
1   cup minced fresh onion
3   garlic cloves, minced
2   teaspoons ground coriander
1   teaspoon ground cumin
½   teaspoon ground turmeric
1   jalapeño pepper, seeded and minced
4   cups chopped spinach
½   teaspoon garam masala
¼   teaspoon salt
    Lemon slices (optional)
    Cilantro sprigs (optional)

**1.** Drain beans through a sieve into a bowl, reserving ½ cup liquid. Discard remaining bean liquid. Place reserved ½ cup liquid and ½ cup beans in a blender or food processor; process until smooth.
**2.** Heat oil in a large nonstick skillet over medium-high heat. Add onion and garlic; sauté 3 minutes. Add coriander, cumin, turmeric, and jalapeño; sauté 1 minute. Add pureed bean mixture; cover, reduce heat, and cook 5 minutes. Add remaining beans; cover and cook until thoroughly heated. Stir in spinach, garam masala, and salt; cook 3 minutes or until spinach is wilted. Garnish each serving with a lemon slice and cilantro sprigs, if desired. Yield: 4 servings (serving size: ¾ cup).

CALORIES 188 (21% from fat); FAT 4.3g (sat 0.7g, mono 1.1g, poly 2g); PROTEIN 10.2g; CARB 29.6g; FIBER 12.6g; CHOL 0mg; IRON 4.2mg; SODIUM 711mg; CALC 121mg

## Spicy Garlic-Roasted Potatoes

4   teaspoons vegetable oil
5   garlic cloves, minced
2   teaspoons ground cumin
¼   teaspoon ground red pepper
1½  pounds red potatoes, cut into 1½-inch pieces
½   teaspoon salt
    Cooking spray

**1.** Preheat oven to 400°.

**2.** Heat oil in a large skillet over medium-high heat. Add garlic; cook until golden (about 30 seconds), stirring constantly. Add cumin and red pepper. Add potato and salt; toss well. Place potato mixture in a roasting pan coated with cooking spray. Bake at 400° for 25 minutes or until tender. Yield: 4 servings (serving size: 1 cup).

CALORIES 176 (26% from fat); FAT 5.1g (sat 0.6g, mono 1.2g, poly 1.8g); PROTEIN 4.2g; CARB 30g; FIBER 3.3g; CHOL 0mg; IRON 3mg; SODIUM 307mg; CALC 39mg

## Potatoes, Green Beans, and Carrots with Cashews

2   teaspoons vegetable oil
2   cups vertically sliced onion
2   tablespoons minced peeled fresh ginger
½   teaspoon ground turmeric
8   cups (¾-inch) cubed yellow Finnish or Yukon gold potatoes (about 1½ pounds)
3   cups (2½-inch) julienne-cut carrot (about 1 pound)
⅓   cup finely chopped seeded jalapeño pepper (about 2 large)
1½  cups canned vegetable broth, divided
2½  cups (2-inch) cut green beans (about ½ pound)
2   teaspoons sugar
¼   cup chopped unsalted cashews (about 1 ounce), ground
⅓   cup very thinly sliced red onion, separated into rings
2   tablespoons minced fresh cilantro
¼   cup chopped unsalted cashews (about 1 ounce), toasted

**1.** Heat oil in a Dutch oven over medium-high heat. Add 2 cups onion, ginger, and turmeric; sauté 2 minutes. Add potatoes, carrot, jalapeño, and 1 cup broth; bring to a boil. Cover, reduce heat, and simmer 25 minutes. Add ½ cup broth, beans, and sugar; cook 12 minutes, stirring occasionally. Stir in ground cashews. Top each serving with red onion, cilantro, and toasted cashews. Yield: 6 servings (servings size: 1½ cups potato mixture, 1 tablespoon onion,

1 teaspoon cilantro, and 2 teaspoons cashews).

CALORIES 296 (21% from fat); FAT 7g (sat 1.4g, mono 3.3g, poly 1.9g); PROTEIN 7.7g; CARB 56.2g; FIBER 7.6g; CHOL 0mg; IRON 3.2mg; SODIUM 313mg; CALC 64mg

---

### menu

#### Red-Lentil Soup

#### Spinach-mushroom salad*

*Heat 1 teaspoon vegetable oil in a large skillet; add 1 cup thinly sliced onion. Sauté 10 minutes or until golden. Combine onion mixture, 6 cups fresh spinach, 1 cup sliced mushrooms, and 3 tablespoons light red wine vinegar salad dressing in a large bowl; toss well. Serves 4.

---

## Red-Lentil Soup

2⅓  cups water, divided
1½  cups dried small red lentils
1   teaspoon sugar
¼   teaspoon ground turmeric
1   (14½-ounce) can vegetable broth
1   tablespoon vegetable oil
½   teaspoon cumin seeds
1½  cups minced onion
3   garlic cloves, minced
2   tablespoons fresh lime juice
⅛   teaspoon salt
⅛   teaspoon ground red pepper
    Cilantro sprigs (optional)

**1.** Combine 1⅓ cups water, lentils, sugar, turmeric, and broth in a medium saucepan; bring to a boil. Cover, reduce heat, and simmer 10 minutes or until lentils are very tender. Cool slightly. Place lentil mixture in a food processor or blender; process until smooth. Set aside.
**2.** Heat oil in a large nonstick skillet over medium heat. Add cumin seeds; cook 30 seconds or until toasted. Add onion and garlic; sauté 10 minutes or until lightly browned. Stir in lentil mixture, 1 cup water, juice, salt, and red pepper; cook until thoroughly heated. Garnish with cilantro sprigs, if desired. Yield: 5 servings (serving size: 1 cup).

CALORIES 255 (13% from fat); FAT 3.8g (sat 0.7g, mono 1g, poly 1.8g); PROTEIN 16.9g; CARB 40.6g; FIBER 7.6g; CHOL 0mg; IRON 5.5mg; SODIUM 466mg; CALC 45mg

## Garlic Shrimp in Yogurt Sauce

1½ tablespoons vegetable oil
8 garlic cloves, minced
¾ cup water
2 teaspoons ground cumin
1 teaspoon ground coriander
½ teaspoon ground turmeric
1½ pounds large shrimp, peeled and deveined
2 teaspoons all-purpose flour
2 teaspoons sugar
½ teaspoon salt
1 (8-ounce) carton plain fat-free yogurt
¾ cup (1-inch) sliced green onions

**1.** Heat oil in a large nonstick skillet over medium-high heat. Add garlic; cook until golden (about 30 seconds), stirring constantly. Stir in water, cumin, coriander, and turmeric. Cover, reduce heat, and simmer 7 minutes. Add shrimp; cook 3 minutes.
**2.** Combine flour, sugar, salt, and yogurt; stir with a whisk. Stir yogurt mixture into shrimp mixture. Cover and cook 4 minutes or until shrimp are done. Stir in onions. Yield: 4 servings (serving size: about 1 cup).

CALORIES 245 (28% from fat); FAT 7.8g (sat 1.4g, mono 2g, poly 3.4g); PROTEIN 30.3g; CARB 12.7g; FIBER 0.7g; CHOL 195mg; IRON 4.4mg; SODIUM 531mg; CALC 216mg

## Cashew "Fudge"

1 cup unsalted cashews (about 4 ounces)
1 (15-ounce) carton fat-free ricotta cheese
1½ cups nonfat dry milk
6 tablespoons sugar
1 teaspoon ground cardamom
2 tablespoons chopped pistachios (about 8)

**1.** Place cashews in a food processor or blender; process until coarsely ground.
**2.** Combine cashews, ricotta, dry milk, sugar, and cardamom in a large saucepan over medium heat; cook 8 minutes, stirring well until mixture is smooth and

pulls away from sides of pan. Spoon mixture into an 8-inch square baking dish; spread evenly. Sprinkle with pistachios. Cool completely. Yield: 2 dozen (serving size: 1 [2 x 1¼-inch] piece).

CALORIES 80 (26% from fat); FAT 2.3g (sat 0.5g, mono 1.4g, poly 0.4g); PROTEIN 6g; CARB 9.9g; FIBER 0.3g; CHOL 3mg; IRON 0.3mg; SODIUM 50mg; CALC 127mg

---

### Indian Essentials

Numerous spice bowls fill the cupboards of Indian cooks, but you can create many of their delicious dishes with only a few basics.

**Cardamom:** Small green or white pods enclose fragrant seeds. Use either the whole pod or the ground seeds to add a warm, spicy-sweet flavor to foods.

**Cilantro:** This annual herb with green, lacy leaves looks like parsley but has a pungent odor and flavor.

**Coriander:** The dried, round fruit of the cilantro herb, about the size of a black peppercorn, is most often used in the ground form. It has a warm, fruity aroma.

**Cumin:** The bitter taste of this crescent-shaped seed mellows to a nutty flavor during cooking. Use whole or ground.

**Curry:** This mixture of spices comes in varying degrees of heat—mild, medium, or hot. It may contain as many as 20 spices, including cardamom, chiles, cumin, and red and black pepper. The longer the list of ingredients, the more complex the flavor.

**Garam masala:** Meaning "hot spices," this is so named because it is believed to raise body temperature. Although not spicy, the mixture adds a fragrant warmth to dishes. It's readily available from Indian grocers, but you can make this mix at home. Grind three 4-inch cinnamon sticks, the seeds of 12 cardamom pods, and six cloves in a spice grinder, sieving any large pieces. Yields 1 tablespoon.

**Turmeric:** This bright-yellow powder adds both color and a slight bitter flavor to dishes.

---

# Fruit in Your Soup

*That's right—put it in a bowl and eat it with a spoon, just as Mother Nature intended.*

Succulent peaches, tender strawberries, fragrant cantaloupes, juicy blackberries—Mother Nature's offerings seem perfect in pies, cobblers, and sorbets; in jams and cakes; or even straight off the vine or tree. But as soup?

Absolutely. Naturally low in fat and calories, fruit soups make an excellent appetizer, light lunch, snack, or dessert.

## Cantaloupe Soup with Port Syrup and Pancetta

1 cup port wine
1½ tablespoons sugar
2 ounces pancetta or lean ham, cut into thin strips
6 cups cubed seeded peeled cantaloupe, chilled (about 1 [3-pound] melon)
1½ tablespoons honey
⅛ teaspoon salt

**1.** Combine wine and sugar in a small saucepan over medium-high heat; cook 18 minutes or until reduced to ¼ cup. Remove syrup from heat. Pour into a bowl; cover and chill.
**2.** Cook pancetta in a medium nonstick skillet over medium heat 10 minutes or until crisp. Remove from pan, and drain on paper towels.
**3.** Place cantaloupe, honey, and salt in a blender, and process until smooth. Ladle soup into shallow bowls; dollop syrup over soup, and sprinkle with pancetta. Serve immediately. Yield: 4 servings (serving size: 1 cup soup, 1 tablespoon syrup, and 1 tablespoon pancetta).

CALORIES 243 (9% from fat); FAT 2.5g (sat 0.8g, mono 0.9g, poly 0.5g); PROTEIN 3.3g; CARB 38.6g; FIBER 1.9g; CHOL 3mg; IRON 0.8mg; SODIUM 157mg; CALC 30mg

## Orange-Buttermilk Soup with Blackberry Puree

This tangy soup is balanced by the sweet blackberry puree. Serving the soup over vanilla ice cream turns this dish into an exhilarating dessert.

- 1 cup fresh blackberries
- 1 teaspoon sugar
- 1¾ cups low-fat buttermilk
- 1¾ cups fresh orange juice (about 4 oranges)
- 3 tablespoons sugar
- 1 tablespoon chopped crystallized ginger
- 1 cup vanilla low-fat ice cream

**1.** Place blackberries and 1 teaspoon sugar in a blender; process until smooth. Strain mixture through a sieve into a bowl, and set aside; discard solids.
**2.** Place buttermilk, orange juice, 3 tablespoons sugar, and ginger in a blender; process 30 seconds or until smooth. Cover and chill.
**3.** Spoon ¼ cup ice cream into each of 4 soup bowls; pour 1 cup soup over each serving. Drizzle each serving with 1 tablespoon blackberry puree. Serve immediately. Yield: 4 servings.

CALORIES 200 (15% from fat); FAT 3.3g (sat 1.9g, mono 0.9g, poly 0.2g); PROTEIN 6g; CARB 37.9g; FIBER 0.7g; CHOL 5mg; IRON 0.7mg; SODIUM 85mg; CALC 195mg

## Strawberry-Champagne Soup

Try serving this simple soup with a light herb cheese (such as Boursin) and crackers. The freshest strawberries you can get will enhance the effect.

- 5 cups quartered strawberries (about 2 pounds)
- ¼ cup sugar
- ⅛ teaspoon salt
- 1 cup champagne
- Cracked black pepper (optional)

**1.** Place strawberries in a medium bowl. Sprinkle with sugar and salt; toss well. Place strawberry mixture in a blender or food processor, and process until smooth. Cover mixture and chill 2 hours. Stir in champagne. Serve soup immediately. Sprinkle with black pepper, if desired. Yield: 4 servings (serving size: 1 cup).

CALORIES 161 (4% from fat); FAT 0.8g (sat 0.1g, mono 0.1g, poly 0.4g); PROTEIN 1.6g; CARB 29.1g; FIBER 5.2g; CHOL 0mg; IRON 1.2mg; SODIUM 78mg; CALC 34mg

## Tropical Fruit Soup with Pineapple Salsa

If you don't have papaya, you can substitute mango or just use all pineapple for the salsa. You can find passionfruit nectar in the Latin-food sections of most large supermarkets.

**SALSA:**
- ½ cup diced peeled pineapple
- ½ cup diced peeled papaya
- 2 tablespoons dark rum
- 2 teaspoons sugar

**SOUP:**
- 3 cups vanilla low-fat yogurt
- 1 cup passionfruit nectar
- ⅓ cup pineapple juice
- ¼ teaspoon coconut extract
- ⅛ teaspoon salt
- ¼ cup flaked sweetened coconut, toasted

**1.** To prepare salsa, combine first 4 ingredients in a small bowl; set aside.
**2.** To prepare soup, combine yogurt and next 4 ingredients in a medium bowl, and stir well with a whisk. Cover and chill. Ladle soup into shallow bowls, and top with salsa. Sprinkle each serving with toasted coconut. Yield: 4 servings (serving size: 1 cup soup, ¼ cup salsa, and 1 tablespoon coconut).

CALORIES 264 (15% from fat); FAT 4.3g (sat 3.2g, mono 0.7g, poly 0.1g); PROTEIN 8.8g; CARB 43.3g; FIBER 0.9g; CHOL 9mg; IRON 0.4mg; SODIUM 204mg; CALC 301mg

## Fresh Cherry-Orange Soup

- 3 cups sweet cherries, pitted
- ½ cup bottled cherry juice (such as Juicy Juice)
- 1 teaspoon grated orange rind
- ½ cup fresh orange juice (about 1 orange)
- ⅓ cup low-fat sour cream
- ⅓ cup plain fat-free yogurt
- ¼ cup sugar
- 3 sweet cherries (optional)

**1.** Place first 7 ingredients in a blender; process until smooth. Cover and chill.
**2.** Ladle soup into individual shallow bowls, and garnish each serving with a cherry, if desired. Yield: 3 servings (serving size: 1 cup).

CALORIES 260 (16% from fat); FAT 4.6g (sat 2.4g, mono 1.4g, poly 0.6g); PROTEIN 4.2g; CARB 53.8g; FIBER 3.4g; CHOL 10mg; IRON 0.6mg; SODIUM 32mg; CALC 104mg

## Vanilla-Roasted Peach Soup with Cardamom Cream

Roasting the peaches brings out their natural sweetness and makes them soft and easy to peel. But if you want to bypass that step, just use very ripe peeled peaches, and puree them with the honey.

- 3 peaches, halved and pitted (about 2 pounds)
- 2 tablespoons sugar
- 1 (4-inch) piece vanilla bean, split lengthwise
- 1½ tablespoons honey
- 1½ cups orange juice
- ⅛ teaspoon salt
- ⅛ teaspoon vanilla extract
- ¼ cup low-fat sour cream
- ⅛ teaspoon ground cardamom
- Sliced peeled peaches (optional)

**1.** Preheat oven to 350°.
**2.** Combine peach halves and sugar in a large bowl. Scrape seeds from vanilla bean, and add seeds to bowl; discard bean. Toss peach mixture well. Place peach halves, cut sides down, on a baking sheet

lined with parchment paper. Bake at 350° for 25 minutes or until tender; cool. Peel and discard skins. Place peach halves and honey in a blender or food processor, and process until smooth. Add juice, salt, and vanilla; process until well-blended. Pour into a bowl; cover and chill 2 hours.

**3.** Combine sour cream and cardamom. Ladle soup into bowls; top with cardamom cream. Garnish with sliced peaches, if desired. Yield: 4 servings (serving size: 1 cup soup and 1 tablespoon cardamom cream).

CALORIES 143 (12% from fat); FAT 1.9g (sat 1.1g, mono 0.6g, poly 0.1g); PROTEIN 1.6g; CARB 31.7g; FIBER 1.7g; CHOL 6mg; IRON 0.2mg; SODIUM 81mg; CALC 29mg

## lighten up

# A League of Their Own

*We nailed a culinary hole in one for a Wisconsin reader and her golfing gang.*

Susie Ziegler enjoys food as much as a round of golf, which may help explain why she's a member of the Crystal Lake Ladies Wednesday Afternoon Golf League in Plymouth, Wisconsin. The league's 80 players gather weekly during the summer to whack the back nine, and then revive themselves with refreshments. In fact, it's the postgame spread, not the pursuit of par, that has led to a multiyear waiting list to join the league.

Susie got in early enough, though, to taste a slightly sweet but tangy Oriental Salad another golfer brought to a league meeting three years ago. Susie adored the crunchy mouthful of flavors, but not the triple bogey of fat.

We lightened the dressing and the Japanese curly noodles. Susie called her sisters of the swing together to set up a playoff between the new recipe and the old. The scoreboard was conclusive: 183 calories and 30% from fat in the light versus 249 calories and 70% from fat in the heavy.

## Oriental Salad

(pictured on page 223)

⅓ cup rice or cider vinegar
¼ cup sugar
2½ tablespoons vegetable oil
2 tablespoons honey
2 tablespoons low-sodium soy sauce
1 tablespoon butter or stick margarine
¼ cup slivered almonds, toasted
2 tablespoons sunflower seed kernels
2 (5-ounce) packages Japanese curly noodles (*chuka soba*), crumbled
8 cups shredded napa (Chinese) cabbage
2 cups shredded carrot
1 cup thinly sliced green onions

**1.** Combine first 5 ingredients in a small saucepan. Bring to a boil, and cook 1 minute, stirring constantly. Spoon mixture into a bowl; cover and chill.
**2.** Melt butter in a large nonstick skillet over medium-high heat. Add almonds, sunflower kernels, and noodles; cook 3 minutes or until lightly toasted, tossing occasionally. Spoon mixture into a large bowl; cover and chill. Add vinegar mixture to noodle mixture; let stand 15 minutes. Add cabbage, carrot, and onions, tossing to coat. Yield: 12 servings (serving size: ¾ cup).

CALORIES 183 (30% from fat); FAT 6.1g (sat 1.4g, mono 2g, poly 2.4g); PROTEIN 4.4g; CARB 29g; FIBER 2g; CHOL 3mg; IRON 1.1mg; SODIUM 259mg; CALC 68mg

| BEFORE | AFTER |
|---|---|
| **SERVING SIZE** | |
| ¾ cup | |
| **CALORIES PER SERVING** | |
| 249 | 183 |
| **FAT** | |
| 19.4g | 6.1g |
| **PERCENT OF TOTAL CALORIES** | |
| 70% | 30% |

## inspired vegetarian

# Perfect for Pasta

*Put your bumper crops into warm main-dish pasta salads for the kinds of flavors that come but once a year.*

All these dishes are most enjoyable hot, out of the pot. You can turn up the flavor on any of them by seasoning them with good vinegars such as aged red wine, champagne, or balsamic. Just remember that their textures and flavors will be better if you serve them warm, even tepid, rather than cold.

## Whole-Wheat Spaghetti with Arugula

As they mature, arugula leaves get hot and spicy as well as plentiful and cheap. Even when cooked, they have an assertive personality.

2 tablespoons olive oil, divided
¼ teaspoon crushed red pepper
2 garlic cloves, minced
1 cup chopped tomato
1 pound arugula, trimmed and torn (about 16 cups)
4 cups hot cooked whole-wheat spaghetti (about 8 ounces uncooked pasta)
1½ tablespoons red wine vinegar
¾ teaspoon salt
½ teaspoon freshly ground black pepper
½ cup (2 ounces) grated fresh Parmesan cheese

**1.** Heat 1 tablespoon oil over medium-high heat in a Dutch oven. Add red pepper and garlic; sauté 20 seconds. Add tomato and arugula; sauté 2 minutes or until arugula is wilted. Spoon into a large bowl. Add 1 tablespoon oil, spaghetti, vinegar, salt, and black pepper; toss well. Sprinkle with cheese. Yield: 4 servings (serving size: 1½ cups pasta and 2 tablespoons cheese).

CALORIES 347 (30% from fat); FAT 11.6g (sat 4.3g, mono 6.1g, poly 0.7g); PROTEIN 17.5g; CARB 41.6g; FIBER 8.2g; CHOL 10mg; IRON 4.4mg; SODIUM 705mg; CALC 322mg

## Summer Garden Pasta

1 (16-ounce) package fusilli (short twisted spaghetti)
2 tablespoons olive oil
3 cups diced yellow squash (about 1 pound)
1 cup thinly sliced red onion
1 cup diced red bell pepper
1 cup thinly sliced carrot
2 garlic cloves, minced
2 cups diced seeded tomato
⅓ cup chopped fresh parsley
2 tablespoons chopped fresh mint
1 tablespoon chopped fresh or 1 teaspoon dried thyme
¾ teaspoon salt
½ teaspoon black pepper

**1.** Cook pasta in boiling water 8 minutes. Drain in a colander over a bowl, reserving ½ cup cooking liquid.
**2.** Heat oil in a large nonstick skillet over medium heat. Add squash, onion, bell pepper, carrot, and garlic; sauté 8 minutes. Stir in pasta, reserved cooking liquid, tomato, and remaining ingredients, and cook until thoroughly heated. Yield: 6 servings (serving size: 2 cups).

CALORIES 373 (15% from fat); FAT 6.3g (sat 0.9g, mono 3.5g, poly 1.1g); PROTEIN 11.9g; CARB 68.1g; FIBER 5.4g; CHOL 0mg; IRON 4.3mg; SODIUM 315mg; CALC 51mg

## Soba with Sesame and Tofu

If you cook these noodles ahead of time, make sure you rinse them well.

⅓ cup low-sodium soy sauce
2 tablespoons rice vinegar
1 tablespoon minced peeled fresh ginger
1 teaspoon sugar
1½ teaspoons dark sesame oil
½ teaspoon chili oil or vegetable oil
1½ tablespoons sesame seeds
4 cups cooked soba (about 8 ounces uncooked buckwheat noodles)
2 cups sliced peeled cucumber
1 cup thinly sliced green onions
2 cups cubed firm tofu (about 12 ounces)

**1.** Combine first 6 ingredients in a small bowl; set aside.
**2.** Cook sesame seeds in a small saucepan over medium heat 1 minute or until toasted.
**3.** Combine sesame seeds, noodles, cucumber, and onions in a large bowl; toss mixture gently.
**4.** Divide noodle mixture evenly among 4 bowls; top with tofu and sauce. Yield: 4 servings (servings size: 1 cup noodles, ½ cup tofu, and 2 tablespoons sauce).

CALORIES 310 (24% from fat); FAT 8.4g (sat 1.2g, mono 2.4g, poly 4.2g); PROTEIN 18.3g; CARB 46.3g; FIBER 2.2g; CHOL 0mg; IRON 6.8mg; SODIUM 844mg; CALC 159mg

## Penne with Zucchini and Ricotta

Zucchini is cut in the same shape as the pasta; ricotta cheese is dabbed onto the hot pasta, and then melted into it. You can substitute oregano for the marjoram.

1 (16-ounce) package penne (tube-shaped pasta)
3 garlic cloves, peeled
2 pounds small zucchini, halved lengthwise and cut diagonally into ½-inch slices (about 7 cups)
¼ cup (1 ounce) grated fresh Parmesan cheese, divided
2 tablespoons extra-virgin olive oil
1 tablespoon chopped fresh or 1 teaspoon dried marjoram
¾ teaspoon salt
¼ teaspoon black pepper
1 cup part-skim ricotta cheese

**1.** Cook pasta and garlic in boiling water 7 minutes; add zucchini, and cook 3 minutes. Drain well; discard garlic cloves. Place pasta mixture in a large bowl. Add 2 tablespoons Parmesan, oil, marjoram, salt, and pepper; toss well to coat. Drop ricotta by tablespoonfuls into pasta mixture; toss well. Sprinkle each serving with Parmesan. Yield: 6 servings (serving size: 1⅔ cups pasta and 1 teaspoon Parmesan).

CALORIES 417 (22% from fat); FAT 10.4g (sat 3.6g, mono 4.8g, poly 1.1g); PROTEIN 17.8g; CARB 63.2g; FIBER 2.6g; CHOL 16mg; IRON 3.9mg; SODIUM 430mg; CALC 206mg

## Fusilli with Green Beans and Oregano

August is a great time to find all kinds of fresh beans, from wide Romanos to skinny French filets. This dish is best with the thinnest green beans you can find.

3 cups water
½ pound (2-inch) cut green beans
4 cups hot cooked fusilli (about 8 ounces uncooked pasta)
½ cup chopped fresh flat-leaf parsley
½ cup thinly sliced green onions
2 tablespoons chopped fresh or 2 teaspoons dried oregano
1 tablespoon extra-virgin olive oil
½ teaspoon salt
¼ teaspoon freshly ground black pepper
1 garlic clove, minced
¼ cup (1 ounce) grated fresh Parmesan cheese

**1.** Bring 3 cups water to a boil in a large saucepan; add beans. Cook 4 minutes or until tender; drain. Combine beans, pasta, and next 7 ingredients in a large bowl; toss well. Sprinkle with cheese. Yield: 4 servings (serving size: 1½ cups pasta and 1 tablespoon cheese).

CALORIES 295 (19% from fat); FAT 6.3g (sat 1.8g, mono 3.2g, poly 0.8g); PROTEIN 11.4g; CARB 48.7g; FIBER 3.3g; CHOL 5mg; IRON 3.8mg; SODIUM 420mg; CALC 145mg

## Bow Tie Pasta with Cherry Tomatoes, Capers, and Basil

4 cups hot cooked bow tie pasta
4 cups halved cherry tomatoes (about 2 pints)
⅓ cup thinly sliced fresh basil
¼ cup chopped pitted niçoise olives
2 tablespoons capers
2 tablespoons extra-virgin olive oil
¾ teaspoon salt
½ teaspoon crushed red pepper
½ teaspoon freshly ground black pepper
2 garlic cloves, minced
Red wine vinegar (optional)

1. Combine first 10 ingredients in a large bowl, and toss well. Sprinkle vinegar over each serving, if desired. Yield: 4 servings (serving size: 2 cups).

CALORIES 315 (26% from fat); FAT 9.1g (sat 1.3g, mono 5.9g, poly 1.3g); PROTEIN 8.8g; CARB 50.7g; FIBER 3.5g; CHOL 0mg; IRON 3.4mg; SODIUM 641mg; CALC 35mg

## happy endings

# Cool Chocolate Cheesecakes

*What's better than your favorite dessert? Two of them.*

Even in the dog days of summer, a cheesecake will delight dessert devotees with its deliciously dense texture. So why leave it without a perfect mate? Add some chocolate, and you've got a match made in, well, your mouth. With our low-fat recipes, you have plenty of wiggle room for toppings and mixtures.

### Chocolate-Mint Cheesecake

CRUST:
- 1 cup packaged chocolate cookie crumbs (such as Oreo)
- 2 tablespoons sugar
- 1 tablespoon butter or stick margarine, melted
- Cooking spray

FILLING:
- 3 (8-ounce) blocks fat-free cream cheese, softened
- 1 (8-ounce) block 1/3-less-fat cream cheese, softened
- 1 cup sugar
- 3 tablespoons all-purpose flour
- 2 teaspoons vanilla extract
- 4 large eggs
- 10 crème de menthe chocolaty mint thins, chopped

1. Preheat oven to 300°.

2. To prepare crust, combine first 3 ingredients; toss with a fork until moist. Press mixture into bottom of a 9-inch springform pan coated with cooking spray.

3. To prepare filling, beat cheeses at high speed of a mixer until smooth. Add 1 cup sugar, flour, and vanilla; beat well. Add eggs, 1 at a time, beating well after each addition. Stir in chopped mints.

4. Pour cheese mixture into prepared pan; bake at 300° for 1 hour or until almost set. Cheesecake is done when center barely moves when pan is touched. Remove cheesecake from oven; run a knife around outside edge. Cool to room temperature. Cover and chill at least 8 hours. Yield: 16 servings (serving size: 1 wedge).

CALORIES 222 (34% from fat); FAT 8.4g (sat 4.3g, mono 2.4g, poly 1.1g); PROTEIN 9.9g; CARB 25.5g; FIBER 0.4g; CHOL 75mg; IRON 0.9mg; SODIUM 385mg; CALC 141mg

### Banana-Split Cheesecake

(pictured on page 222)

CRUST:
- 1 cup packaged chocolate cookie crumbs (such as Oreo)
- 2 tablespoons sugar
- 1 tablespoon butter or stick margarine, melted
- Cooking spray

FILLING:
- 3 (8-ounce) blocks fat-free cream cheese, softened
- 1 (8-ounce) block 1/3-less-fat cream cheese, softened
- 1 (8-ounce) carton low-fat sour cream
- 1 1/2 cups sugar
- 1 1/2 cups mashed ripe banana
- 3 tablespoons all-purpose flour
- 2 teaspoons vanilla extract
- 4 large eggs

TOPPINGS:
- 1/3 cup canned crushed pineapple in juice, drained
- 1/3 cup strawberry sundae syrup
- 1/3 cup chocolate syrup
- 1/4 cup chopped pecans, toasted
- 16 maraschino cherries, drained

1. Preheat oven to 325°.

2. To prepare crust, combine first 3 ingredients in a bowl; toss with a fork until moist. Press into bottom of a 9-inch springform pan coated with cooking spray.

3. To prepare filling, beat cheeses and sour cream at high speed of a mixer until smooth. Add 1 1/2 cups sugar, banana, flour, and vanilla; beat well. Add eggs, 1 at a time; beat well after each addition.

4. Pour cheese mixture into prepared pan; bake at 325° for 1 hour and 10 minutes or until almost set. Cheesecake is done when center barely moves when pan is touched. Remove cheesecake from oven; run a knife around outside edge. Cool cheesecake to room temperature. Cover and chill at least 8 hours. Top each serving with 1 teaspoon pineapple, 1 teaspoon strawberry syrup, 1 teaspoon chocolate syrup, 3/4 teaspoon pecans, and 1 cherry. Yield: 16 servings (serving size: 1 wedge with toppings).

CALORIES 317 (30% from fat); FAT 10.6g (sat 4.6g, mono 3.7g, poly 1.5g); PROTEIN 10.7g; CARB 45g; FIBER 1g; CHOL 81mg; IRON 1.2mg; SODIUM 393mg; CALC 158mg

### Chocolate Cheesecake

CRUST:
- 1 cup packaged chocolate cookie crumbs (such as Oreo)
- 2 tablespoons sugar
- 1 tablespoon butter or stick margarine, melted
- Cooking spray

FILLING:
- 1/2 cup Dutch process cocoa
- 1/4 cup 1% low-fat milk
- 3 ounces semisweet chocolate, melted
- 4 (8-ounce) blocks fat-free cream cheese, softened
- 1 (8-ounce) block 1/3-less-fat cream cheese, softened
- 1 1/2 cups sugar
- 3 tablespoons all-purpose flour
- 2 teaspoons vanilla extract
- 4 large eggs
- 2 tablespoons sliced almonds, toasted

*Continued*

1. Preheat oven to 325°.

2. To prepare crust, combine first 3 ingredients; toss with a fork until moist. Press into bottom of a 9-inch springform pan coated with cooking spray.

3. To prepare filling, combine cocoa, milk, and chocolate, and stir well with a whisk. Beat cheeses at high speed of a mixer until smooth. Add 1½ cups sugar, flour, and vanilla; beat well. Add chocolate mixture; beat well. Add eggs, 1 at a time, beating well after each addition.

4. Pour cheese mixture into prepared pan; bake at 325° for 1 hour and 10 minutes or until almost set. Cheesecake is done when center barely moves when pan is touched. Remove cheesecake from oven, and run a knife around outside edge. Cool to room temperature. Cover and chill at least 8 hours. Sprinkle with almonds. Yield: 16 servings (serving size: 1 wedge).

CALORIES 284 (31% from fat); FAT 9.9g (sat 4.7g, mono 3.3g, poly 1.2g); PROTEIN 13.1g; CARB 35.3g; FIBER 0.4g; CHOL 78mg; IRON 1.5mg; SODIUM 471mg; CALC 191mg

## Mocha-Chocolate Cheesecake

CRUST:

- 1 cup packaged chocolate cookie crumbs (such as Oreo)
- 2 tablespoons sugar
- 1 tablespoon butter or stick margarine, melted
- Cooking spray

FILLING:

- ½ cup Dutch process cocoa
- ⅓ cup Kahlúa (coffee-flavored liqueur)
- 3 (8-ounce) blocks fat-free cream cheese, softened
- 1 (8-ounce) block ⅓-less-fat cream cheese, softened
- ½ cup low-fat sour cream
- 1¼ cups sugar
- 3 tablespoons all-purpose flour
- 2 teaspoons vanilla extract
- 2 large eggs
- 2 large egg whites
- 16 chocolate-coated coffee beans (optional)

1. Preheat oven to 325°.

2. To prepare crust, combine first 3 ingredients in a bowl; toss with a fork until moist. Press mixture into bottom of a 9-inch springform pan coated with cooking spray.

3. To prepare filling, combine cocoa and Kahlúa, and stir well with a whisk. Beat cheeses and sour cream at high speed of a mixer until smooth. Add 1¼ cups sugar, flour, and vanilla; beat well. Add eggs and egg whites, 1 at a time, beating well after each addition. Stir in cocoa mixture.

4. Pour mixture into prepared pan; bake at 325° for 1 hour and 5 minutes or until almost set. Cheesecake is done when center barely moves when pan is touched. Remove from oven; run a knife around outside edge. Cool to room temperature. Cover and chill at least 8 hours. Garnish with coffee beans, if desired. Yield: 16 servings (serving size: 1 wedge).

CALORIES 241 (30% from fat); FAT 8g (sat 3.9g, mono 2.4g, poly 1.1g); PROTEIN 10.3g; CARB 30.8g; FIBER 0.3g; CHOL 51mg; IRON 1.2mg; SODIUM 386mg; CALC 147mg

## German Chocolate Cheesecake

CRUST:

- ⅔ cup all-purpose flour
- 2 tablespoons sugar
- 2 tablespoons chilled butter or stick margarine, cut into small pieces
- 1 tablespoon ice water
- Cooking spray

FILLING:

- ½ cup Dutch process cocoa
- ½ cup fat-free hot fudge topping
- ¼ cup 2% reduced-fat milk
- 2 (8-ounce) blocks fat-free cream cheese, softened
- 1½ cups (12 ounces) ⅓-less-fat cream cheese, softened
- 1½ cups sugar
- 3 tablespoons all-purpose flour
- 2 teaspoons vanilla extract
- ¼ teaspoon coconut extract
- 2 large eggs
- 2 large egg whites

TOPPING:

- ⅔ cup fat-free caramel sundae topping
- ⅓ cup chopped pecans, toasted
- ⅓ cup flaked sweetened coconut, toasted

1. Preheat oven to 400°.

2. To prepare crust, lightly spoon ⅔ cup flour into dry measuring cups; level with a knife. Place ⅔ cup flour and 2 tablespoons sugar in a food processor; pulse until combined. Add butter; pulse 3 times or until mixture resembles coarse meal. With processor on, pour ice water through chute, processing just until blended (do not form a ball). Press into bottom of a 9-inch springform pan coated with cooking spray. Bake at 400° for 8 minutes or until lightly browned. Cool on a wire rack. Reduce oven temperature to 325°.

3. To prepare filling, combine cocoa, fudge topping, and milk in a small bowl. Beat cheeses at high speed of a mixer until smooth. Add 1½ cups sugar, 3 tablespoons flour, and extracts. Add eggs and egg whites, 1 at a time, beating well after each addition. Add cocoa mixture; beat well.

4. Pour cheese mixture into prepared pan. Bake at 325° for 1 hour and 5 minutes or until almost set. Cheesecake is done when center barely moves when pan is touched. Remove cheesecake from oven; run a knife around outside edge. Cool to room temperature.

5. To prepare topping, combine caramel sundae topping, chopped pecans, and toasted coconut; spread over cheesecake. Cover cheesecake, and chill at least 8 hours. Yield: 16 servings (serving size: 1 wedge).

CALORIES 314 (29% from fat); FAT 10g (sat 5.3g, mono 3.2g, poly 0.8g); PROTEIN 9.7g; CARB 46.1g; FIBER 1.1g; CHOL 53mg; IRON 1.2mg; SODIUM 352mg; CALC 128mg

# Five Steps to Earning Your Stripes

*Getting zebra stripes in your cheesecake is a cinch, and kind of fun. Just follow these easy procedures.*

**1.** *Pour one-third of white batter into prepared pan.*

**2.** *Pour one-half of chocolate batter in center of white batter; spread to within 1 inch of edge of white batter.*

**3.** *Pour one-third of white batter in center of chocolate batter; spread to within 1 inch of edge of chocolate batter.*

**4.** *Pour remaining chocolate batter in center of white batter; spread to within 1 inch of edge of white batter.*

**5.** *Pour remaining white batter in center of chocolate batter; spread to within 1 inch of edge of chocolate batter.*

## Zebra-Stripe Cheesecake

The stripe design can be achieved simply—just layer dark- and light-colored batters. There's no swirling involved.

**CRUST:**

- 1 cup graham cracker crumbs (about 8 cookie sheets)
- 2 tablespoons butter or stick margarine, melted

Cooking spray

**FILLING:**

- 3 (8-ounce) blocks fat-free cream cheese, softened
- 1 (8-ounce) block ⅓-less-fat cream cheese, softened
- 1 cup sugar
- ½ cup 1% low-fat milk
- 2 teaspoons vanilla extract
- 2 large eggs
- 2 large egg whites
- 4 ounces semisweet chocolate, melted

**1.** Preheat oven to 325°.

**2.** To prepare crust, combine cracker crumbs and butter in a bowl; toss with a fork until moist. Press into bottom of a 9-inch springform pan coated with cooking spray.

**3.** To prepare filling, beat cheeses at high speed of a mixer until smooth. Add sugar, milk, and vanilla, beating well. Add eggs and egg whites, 1 at a time, beating well after each addition. Pour half of cheese mixture into another bowl. Add chocolate to remaining batter. Pour one-third of white batter into prepared pan. Pour one-half of chocolate batter in center of white batter in pan; spread to within 1 inch of edge of white batter. Pour one-third of white batter in center of chocolate batter; spread to within 1 inch of edge of chocolate batter. Pour remaining chocolate batter in center of white batter; spread to within 1 inch of edge of white batter. Pour remaining white batter in center of chocolate batter; spread to within 1 inch of edge of chocolate batter. (Design on top should look like a target.)

*Continued*

**4.** Bake at 325° for 1 hour and 10 minutes or until almost set. Cheesecake is done when center barely moves when pan is touched. Remove cheesecake from oven; run a knife around outside edge. Cool to room temperature. Cover and chill at least 8 hours. Yield: 16 servings (serving size: 1 wedge).

CALORIES 210 (36% from fat); FAT 8.4g (sat 4.7g, mono 2.7g, poly 0.5g); PROTEIN 9.7g; CARB 23.8g; FIBER 0.1g; CHOL 50mg; IRON 0.6mg; SODIUM 385mg; CALC 147mg

---

### Fail-Safe Cheesecakes

Sometimes cheesecake can turn out too dry or totally soupy. Here's how to prevent that from happening to yours.

• When your cheesecake is done, the center will jiggle slightly; this part should be about 3 inches in diameter. Place the pan on a wire rack, run a knife around the outside edge, and let it cool completely to room temperature.

• Some cracking on the top is normal in a cheesecake and can even make it look prettier. Generally, the slower the cheesecake is cooked, the less chance of cracking. So that your cheesecake cooks slowly and evenly, use an oven thermometer to make sure your oven stays at the correct temperature.

• Our cheesecakes were prepared in two types of springform pans: shiny aluminum and those with a dark, almost black surface. If you use a dark pan, decrease baking time by 10 minutes.

• The best way to cut a cheesecake is with a skinny knife—the thinner the better.

---

# A Small-Kitchen Survival Guide

## From the teeniest of kitchens can come the tastiest of meals.

New York is a city made for cooks. There's a grocery on every corner, a greenmarket every day, and stores specializing in every kind of ethnic cuisine. What more could a cook ask for? A kitchen that's bigger than a breadbox, that's what.

### Teeny-Kitchen-Maximizing Menu 1
**Easy Greek Chicken Casserole**

**Swiss Chard with Onions**

**Nutty Graham Cake**

About 786 calories (25% from fat) per serving.

### Easy Greek Chicken Casserole

This easy one-dish meal is prepared and cooked in only one pot, saving you space and cleanup. You can decrease the sodium by using less anchovy paste or by replacing it with the olives.

   1   tablespoon olive oil
   2   cups chopped onion (about 1 large)
   2   tablespoons dried thyme
   1   to 2 teaspoons black pepper
 10   garlic cloves, minced
   6   cups (½-inch) cubed red potato (about 2 pounds)
   2   cups (1-inch) cut green beans (about ½ pound)
   ¼   cup water
   2   tablespoons anchovy paste or finely chopped olives
   2   (14.5-ounce) cans no-salt-added diced tomatoes, undrained
   8   skinned, boned chicken thighs (about 1 pound)
   ½   cup (2 ounces) crumbled feta cheese

**1.** Preheat oven to 375°.
**2.** Heat oil in a large ovenproof Dutch oven over medium heat. Add onion; sauté 3 minutes. Add thyme, pepper, and garlic; sauté 1 minute. Increase heat to medium-high. Add potato; sauté 8 minutes or until potato begins to brown. Stir in beans, water, anchovy paste, and tomatoes. Remove mixture from heat. Nestle chicken thighs into potato mixture. Top with feta. Cover and bake at 375° for 45 minutes. Yield: 4 servings (serving size: 2 thighs and 2 cups potato mixture).

CALORIES 488 (23% from fat); FAT 12.6g (sat 4.2g, mono 4.9g, poly 2.1g); PROTEIN 34.5g; CARB 62g; FIBER 7.3g; CHOL 134mg; IRON 7.8mg; SODIUM 775mg; CALC 250mg

### Swiss Chard with Onions

   2   teaspoons olive oil
   2   cups thinly sliced onion
   8   cups torn Swiss chard (about 12 ounces)
   1   teaspoon Worcestershire sauce
   ¼   teaspoon salt
   ⅛   teaspoon black pepper

**1.** Heat oil in a large nonstick skillet over medium-high heat. Add onion; sauté 5 minutes or until lightly browned. Add chard; stir-fry 10 minutes or until wilted. Stir in Worcestershire, salt, and pepper. Yield: 4 servings (serving size: ½ cup).

CALORIES 59 (38% from fat); FAT 2.5g (sat 0.4g, mono 1.7g, poly 0.3g); PROTEIN 2.1g; CARB 8.4g; FIBER 1.8g; CHOL 0mg; IRON 1.6mg; SODIUM 342mg; CALC 57mg

## Space Challenge

If space is still your final culinary frontier, try these succinct strategies for making the dinner that doesn't need more room than you've got.

• **Use your stovetop and oven concurrently.** Your stove, like your computer, can multitask, so slate the oven for a main dish and the stovetop for a side—or vice versa.

• **Stagger start times.** For your meal, include one long-cooking dish and a second that you can prepare while the first cooks.

• **Make it ahead.** Be sure to include in your dinner menu at least one dish that you can complete hours or even days in advance, then serve cold or warm to room temperature.

• **Partially precook.** Many dishes can be partially prepared ahead of time and put on hold while you work on other parts of the meal.

• **Chop as you go.** Pre-prep chopping makes assembly easier but has the counterproductive side effect of crowding your surface space. Better to chop as the need arises, then clean up and move on to the next thing.

• **Minimize pots.** Try to cook all of a dish's ingredients in a single pot, even if it means sautéing in shifts or pushing ingredients to the side of the pan to clear a space in the middle.

• **Keep it clean rather than compulsive.** Unless you're cooking with raw meat, poultry, or seafood, you can stay sanitary without getting fanatical. For example, there's no need to wash knives, bowls, food processor parts, or cutting surfaces in between vegetables. For those, a quick rinse or wipe as you work is just fine.

**Teeny-Kitchen-Maximizing Menu 2**

**Chop-As-You-Go Pasta with Mushrooms and Ham**

**Sesame Asparagus with Garlic**

**Ginger Meringue Cookies**

About 493 calories (17% from fat) per serving.

## Chop-As-You-Go Pasta with Mushrooms and Ham

Unlike most recipes, which recommend assembling your ingredients before you begin, here you simply chop as you go—minimizing the need for lots of space.

1½   teaspoons olive oil
1   cup chopped onion
½   cup chopped red bell pepper
2   garlic cloves, crushed
1   (3½-ounce) package shiitake mushrooms, sliced
1   cup sliced button mushrooms
¾   cup dry white wine
½   cup diced smoked ham (about 3 ounces)
3   tablespoons all-purpose flour
¾   cup 2% reduced-fat milk
4   cups hot cooked farfalle (about 3 cups uncooked bow tie pasta) or penne or fusilli
½   cup frozen green peas, thawed
¼   cup chopped fresh basil
¼   teaspoon salt
¼   teaspoon black pepper

**1.** Heat oil in a large nonstick skillet over medium heat. Add onion, bell pepper, and garlic; cook 10 minutes, stirring frequently. Stir in mushrooms; cook 5 minutes. Stir in wine and ham. Bring to a boil; cook 4 minutes. Place flour in a bowl; gradually add milk, stirring with a whisk until blended. Add to vegetables; cook until thick (about 3 minutes), stirring frequently. Stir in hot pasta and remaining ingredients. Yield: 4 servings (serving size: 1½ cups).

CALORIES 361 (16% from fat); FAT 6.6g (sat 2g, mono 2.9g, poly 1g); PROTEIN 15.3g; CARB 59.7g; FIBER 4.4g; CHOL 16mg; IRON 4.1mg; SODIUM 417mg; CALC 93mg

## Nutty Graham Cake

2   cups all-purpose flour
1   cup low-fat graham cracker crumbs (about 6 cookie sheets)
1   cup packed brown sugar
½   cup granulated sugar
½   cup (4 ounces) block-style fat-free cream cheese
6   tablespoons butter or stick margarine, softened
1   teaspoon baking powder
1   teaspoon baking soda
1   teaspoon salt
½   teaspoon ground cinnamon
1   tablespoon grated orange rind
1   cup orange juice
2   large eggs
1   large egg white
⅓   cup chopped nuts (pecans and walnuts)
Cooking spray
1   cup frozen fat-free whipped topping, thawed
Powdered sugar (optional)

**1.** Preheat oven to 350°.

**2.** Lightly spoon flour into dry measuring cups, and level with a knife. Combine flour, crumbs, and next 12 ingredients; beat mixture at medium speed of a mixer 2 minutes. Stir in nuts. Spoon batter into a 12-cup Bundt pan coated with cooking spray. Bake at 350° for 50 minutes or until a wooden pick inserted in center comes out clean. Cool on a wire rack 5 minutes. Remove cake from pan; cool completely on wire rack. Serve cake with whipped topping. Sprinkle with powdered sugar, if desired. Yield: 16 servings (serving size: 1 cake slice and 1 tablespoon whipped topping).

CALORIES 239 (27% from fat); FAT 7.1g (sat 3.1g, mono 2.6g, poly 0.7g); PROTEIN 4.4g; CARB 40.1g; FIBER 0.7g; CHOL 41mg; IRON 1.4mg; SODIUM 400mg; CALC 59mg

## Sesame Asparagus with Garlic

So you can cook the pasta dish on the stove-top, make this side dish ahead and chill it.

- ¼ cup rice vinegar
- 3 tablespoons low-sodium soy sauce
- 2 teaspoons dark sesame oil
- 2 garlic cloves, crushed
- 1 pound asparagus
- ¼ cup water
- Sesame seeds (optional)

**1.** Combine first 4 ingredients in a small bowl; set aside. Snap off tough ends of asparagus. Place asparagus and water in an 11 x 7-inch baking dish. Microwave at HIGH 3 minutes or until tender; drain. Pour vinegar mixture over asparagus, and toss well. Chill at least 1 hour or overnight. Serve cold or at room temperature. Sprinkle asparagus with sesame seeds, if desired. Yield: 4 servings.

CALORIES 51 (44% from fat); FAT 2.5g (sat 0.4g, mono 0.9g, poly 1g); PROTEIN 2.7g; CARB 5.5g; FIBER 1.9g; CHOL 0mg; IRON 1mg; SODIUM 366mg; CALC 24mg

## Ginger Meringue Cookies

The only real space these cookies take up is inside your oven—where they sit for 2 hours. Store them in a zip-top plastic bag.

- 2 large egg whites
- ⅛ teaspoon cream of tartar
- ⅓ cup sugar
- 1 tablespoon finely chopped crystallized ginger
- ¼ teaspoon almond extract

**1.** Preheat oven to 300°.
**2.** Beat egg whites and cream of tartar at high speed of a mixer until soft peaks form. Add sugar, 1 tablespoon at a time, beating until stiff peaks form. Fold in crystallized ginger and almond extract. Cover a baking sheet with parchment paper, and secure to baking sheet with masking tape. Drop cookie batter by 2 tablespoonfuls onto prepared baking sheet. Bake at 300° for 40 minutes or until dry and crisp. Turn oven off, and cool meringues in closed oven at least 2 hours. Carefully remove meringues from parchment paper. Store in an airtight container. Yield: 1 dozen (serving size: 3 cookies).

**NOTE:** Leaving the cookies in the turned-off oven at least 2 hours makes them very dry and crisp. If you prefer a chewier cookie, you can remove them from the oven after they're done baking. You can also freeze them in a heavy-duty zip-top plastic bag up to 6 weeks.

CALORIES 81 (0% from fat); FAT 0g; PROTEIN 1.7g; CARB 18.7g; FIBER 0g; CHOL 0mg; IRON 0.5mg; SODIUM 28mg; CALC 6mg

---

### Must-Haves for the Small Kitchen

**Food processor:** Veggie prep takes much less space and time when you let electricity do the work.

**Really big skillet:** A one-pan dish requires a serious pan—at least a foot in diameter, big enough to hold a meal for four.

**Dutch oven:** Casseroles and roasts are great small-kitchen solutions; a 6-quart ovenproof Dutch oven goes from stovetop to oven and can handle just about anything you bake.

**Immersion blender:** Minimize messes by pureeing your soups, sauces, salad dressings, and desserts in their pot or bowl of origin.

**"No Trespassing" sign:** If you let friends and family come into your tiny kitchen, they're invariably going to end up between you and the wine when you have to deglaze the pan.

---

# Figidaboudit

*You gotta love these sunny wonders. And this is the time of year to do it.*

Those who don't love fresh figs probably know this sweet, succulent fruit only in the dried form because it grows in just a few warm parts of the country. Dried figs compare to fresh ones as raisins do to grapes, or prunes to plums. To taste figs fresh and cook with them seasonally—well, not much can compare.

## Fig-and-Ginger Chutney

This is a rather piquant jam; the ginger gives it heat. Serve it with grilled meats (especially pork) or curried dishes. Store it in an airtight container in the refrigerator up to 2 weeks.

- ⅓ cup raisins
- ⅓ cup red wine vinegar
- ¼ cup honey
- 2 teaspoons slivered crystallized ginger
- 10 ounces fresh figs, trimmed and quartered (about 2 cups)
- ½ teaspoon mustard seeds
- 3 whole cloves
- 1 teaspoon balsamic vinegar

**1.** Combine first 4 ingredients in a nonaluminum saucepan; bring to a boil. Reduce heat; simmer 5 minutes or until syrupy. Add figs, mustard seeds, and cloves. Cover, reduce heat, and simmer 10 minutes or until figs are just tender. Remove from heat; discard cloves, and add balsamic vinegar. Serve warm, at room temperature, or chilled. Yield: 1½ cups (serving size: 1 tablespoon).

CALORIES 27 (4% from fat); FAT 0.1g (sat 0g, mono 0g, poly 0.1g); PROTEIN 0.2g; CARB 7.2g; FIBER 0.5g; CHOL 0mg; IRON 0.2mg; SODIUM 1mg; CALC 6mg

## Fig-and-Arugula Salad with Parmesan

The combination of flavors in this recipe—sweet figs, sharp cheese, and peppery arugula—couldn't be better; it received the highest rating in our Test Kitchens.

- 2 tablespoons minced shallots
- 1½ tablespoons balsamic vinegar
- 1 tablespoon extra-virgin olive oil
- ¼ teaspoon salt
- 16 fresh figs, each cut in half lengthwise
- 6 cups trimmed arugula (about 6 ounces)
- ¼ teaspoon freshly ground black pepper
- ¼ cup (1 ounce) shaved fresh Parmesan cheese

**1.** Combine first 4 ingredients in a large bowl; stir well with a whisk. Add figs; cover and let stand 20 minutes. Add arugula and pepper; toss well. Top with cheese. Serve immediately. Yield: 4 servings (serving size: 1½ cups).

CALORIES 156 (33% from fat); FAT 5.8g (sat 1.7g, mono 3.1g, poly 0.5g); PROTEIN 4.6g; CARB 25.1g; FIBER 4.9g; CHOL 5mg; IRON 1.1mg; SODIUM 273mg; CALC 194mg

## Fig Clafouti

Clafouti (kla-foo-TEE) is one of the easiest French desserts to prepare. Make it by topping a layer of fresh fruit with batter, and then baking; the resulting texture is between that of a pudding and a cake.

- ½ pound small fresh figs (about 18), quartered
- Cooking spray
- ¾ cup all-purpose flour
- ⅓ cup sugar
- ¼ teaspoon salt
- ⅛ teaspoon ground cloves
- 2 cups 2% reduced-fat milk
- ½ teaspoon grated orange rind
- 3 large eggs, lightly beaten

**1.** Preheat oven to 375°.
**2.** Place figs in a 10-inch deep-dish pie plate coated with cooking spray. Lightly spoon flour into dry measuring cups; level with a knife. Combine flour, sugar, salt, and cloves. Gradually add half of milk, stirring with a whisk. Stir in remaining milk, rind, and eggs. Pour batter over figs. Bake at 375° for 1 hour or until set; cool. Yield: 6 servings (serving size: 1 wedge).

CALORIES 208 (19% from fat); FAT 4.5g (sat 1.8g, mono 1.5g, poly 0.6g); PROTEIN 7.9g; CARB 34.8g; FIBER 1.8g; CHOL 117mg; IRON 1.3mg; SODIUM 172mg; CALC 128mg

## Poached Pears with Raspberries and Figs

Late summer and early fall are boom times for raspberries and figs, as well as the beginning of the season for pears. The three make a delicious compote.

- 4 ripe Bartlett pears
- 4 cups water
- ½ cup sugar
- ½ cup orange honey or regular honey
- 3 (3-inch) lemon rind strips
- 3 whole cloves
- 1 (1½-inch) piece vanilla bean, split lengthwise
- 1 cup fresh raspberries
- 12 fresh figs, each cut in half lengthwise
- 8 mint sprigs (optional)

**1.** Peel and core pears. Cut each pear in half lengthwise. Combine water and next 4 ingredients in a large nonaluminum saucepan. Scrape seeds from vanilla bean, and add to sugar mixture; discard bean. Bring sugar mixture to a simmer over medium heat, stirring occasionally. Place pears, cut sides up, in pan; simmer 25 minutes or until tender. Remove pear halves with a slotted spoon, reserving sugar mixture; place pear halves in a large shallow dish. Cover and chill.
**2.** Bring sugar mixture to a boil; cook until reduced to 1 cup (about 30 minutes). Cool. Serve each pear half with 2 tablespoons sauce, 2 tablespoons raspberries, and 3 fig halves; garnish with a mint sprig, if desired. Yield: 8 servings.

CALORIES 225 (2% from fat); FAT 0.6g (sat 0.1g, mono 0.1g, poly 0.2g); PROTEIN 1.1g; CARB 59g; FIBER 5.1g; CHOL 0mg; IRON 0.7mg; SODIUM 2mg; CALC 40mg

## menu

### Fresh Fig Focaccia

Italian salad*

*Cut 2 tomatoes into ½-inch-thick slices; cut slices in half. Arrange tomatoes, 4 ounces cubed sharp provolone cheese, and ½ cup thinly sliced red onion in a shallow dish. Pour ¼ cup light Italian dressing over vegetables; cover and chill. Serve over gourmet salad greens. Serves 4.

## Fresh Fig Focaccia

Some focaccias are made with grapes, but figs make a delightful alternative. Serve plain, with thin slices of Parmesan, or toasted for breakfast.

- 1 package dry yeast (about 2¼ teaspoons)
- 1 cup warm water (100° to 110°)
- 2 tablespoons olive oil, divided
- 1 tablespoon honey
- 1 teaspoon grated orange rind
- ½ teaspoon salt
- 2¾ cups all-purpose flour, divided
- Cooking spray
- 9 fresh figs (about 10 ounces), each cut into eighths (about 2 cups), divided
- 1 tablespoon turbinado sugar or granulated sugar
- ½ teaspoon aniseed

**1.** Dissolve yeast in warm water in a large bowl; let stand 5 minutes. Stir in 1½ tablespoons oil, honey, rind, and salt. Lightly spoon flour into dry measuring cups; level with a knife. Stir 2½ cups flour into yeast mixture. Turn dough out onto a floured surface. Knead until smooth and elastic (about 10 minutes); add enough of remaining flour, 1 tablespoon at a time, to prevent dough from sticking to hands (dough will feel tacky).
**2.** Place dough in a large bowl coated with cooking spray, turning to coat top. Cover dough, and let rise in a warm place (85°), free from drafts, 45 minutes *Continued*

or until doubled in size. (Press two fingers into dough. If indentation remains, dough has risen enough.) Punch dough down, and turn out onto a lightly floured surface. Arrange ⅔ cup figs over dough; gently knead 4 or 5 times or just until figs are incorporated into dough. Press into a 15 x 10-inch rectangle. Place on a large baking sheet coated with cooking spray. Cover and let rise 30 minutes or until doubled in size.

**3.** Preheat oven to 400°.

**4.** Uncover dough. Make indentations in top of dough using handle of a wooden spoon or your fingertips. Gently brush dough with 1½ teaspoons oil. Sprinkle surface of dough with remaining figs, gently pressing figs into dough. Sprinkle with sugar and aniseed. Bake at 400° for 25 minutes or until golden. Yield: 9 servings.

CALORIES 205 (16% from fat); FAT 3.6g (sat 0.5g, mono 2.3g, poly 0.5g); PROTEIN 4.5g; CARB 39.1g; FIBER 2.4g; CHOL 0mg; IRON 2.1mg; SODIUM 131mg; CALC 19mg

### Braised Chicken Thighs with Figs and Bay Leaves

Chicken thighs are more succulent than breasts, but you can use the latter if you prefer. You can also use dried figs in place of the fresh. Serve this entrée with couscous to capture the tangy sauce.

    8   chicken thighs (about 2¼ pounds),
        skinned
    ½   teaspoon salt
    ¼   teaspoon black pepper
    8   bay leaves
    2   teaspoons olive oil
    3   tablespoons water
    ½   cup sliced shallots
    ⅓   cup dry red wine
    1   tablespoon red wine vinegar
    1   teaspoon honey
    16  fresh figs, each cut in half
        lengthwise

**1.** Sprinkle chicken with salt and pepper. Place 1 bay leaf on each chicken thigh. Heat oil in a heavy 10-inch skillet over medium-high heat. Place chicken, bay leaf sides down, in pan. Cook 5 minutes

or until browned. Turn chicken over; cook 3 minutes. Add water; cover, reduce heat, and simmer 5 minutes. Remove chicken from pan. Add shallots; cook 2 minutes. Add chicken, wine, vinegar, and honey to pan; bring to a boil. Cook 1 minute. Cover, reduce heat, and simmer 5 minutes or until chicken is done. Add figs; cover and simmer 5 minutes or until figs are tender. Discard bay leaves. Yield: 4 servings (serving size: 2 chicken thighs, 8 fig halves, and ¼ cup sauce).

CALORIES 393 (26% from fat); FAT 11.4g (sat 2.6g, mono 4.5g, poly 2.5g); PROTEIN 42.4g; CARB 27.4g; FIBER 4.4g; CHOL 163mg; IRON 2.9mg; SODIUM 472mg; CALC 74mg

### Fig Facts

If you live in California, you are among the lucky fig-rich few. Most of the figs harvested in the United States are grown in California's Central Valley. Although there are hundreds of fig varieties, only about a half dozen types are grown commercially in California.

The most popular varieties are:

**Calimyrna:** With its delicious nut-like flavor and tender, golden skin, this fig is great for eating out of hand.

**Adriatic:** The most prolific of all the varieties, the Adriatic fig has red flesh and golden skin. Its high sugar content, retained as the fruit dries, makes this fig the best choice for fig bars and desserts.

**Kadota:** This fig is thick-skinned and has a creamy amber color when ripe. Practically seedless, it's ideal for canning, preserving, and drying.

**Mission:** Named for the mission fathers who planted it as they traveled along the California coast, this dark-purple fig is known for its intense flavor. It darkens to a rich black when dried.

back to the best

# Filet Mignon with Mushroom-Wine Sauce

*Dabble a robust sauce on filet mignon, one of the most tender cuts of meat, and dinner can be downright sublime.*

That's why we've included Filet Mignon with Mushroom-Wine Sauce, from our March 1995 issue, in our tribute to our all-time favorite recipes.

Dry Cabernet Sauvignon enhances the earthiness of shiitakes in the sauce; thyme adds depth.

Preparation is simple and quick, which is good because you'll want to make this impressive recipe again and again.

While its 39% fat content might seem high, the 10.7 gram total is less than you'd get with a tablespoon of oil or butter.

For an elegant and well-balanced meal, serve this with a vegetable and wild rice or some other delicious, carbohydrate-rich side dish.

And don't forget to pour yourself a glass of the remaining wine.

### Filet Mignon with Mushroom-Wine Sauce

    1    tablespoon butter or stick
         margarine, divided
    ⅓    cup finely chopped shallots
    ½    pound fresh shiitake mushrooms,
         stems removed
    1½   cups Cabernet Sauvignon or other
         dry red wine, divided
    1    (10½-ounce) can beef consommé,
         undiluted and divided
    Cracked black pepper
    4    (4-ounce) filet mignon steaks
         (about 1 inch thick)
    1    tablespoon low-sodium soy
         sauce
    2    teaspoons cornstarch
    1    teaspoon dried thyme
    Thyme sprigs (optional)

**1.** Melt 1½ teaspoons butter in a nonstick skillet over medium heat. Add shallots and mushrooms; sauté 4 minutes. Add 1 cup wine and ¾ cup consommé; cook 5 minutes, stirring frequently. Remove mushrooms with a slotted spoon; place in a bowl. Increase heat to high; cook wine mixture until reduced to ½ cup (about 5 minutes). Add to mushrooms in bowl; set aside. Wipe pan with a paper towel.

**2.** Sprinkle pepper over steaks. Melt 1½ teaspoons butter in pan over medium heat. Add steaks; cook 3 minutes on each side. Reduce heat to medium-low; cook 1½ minutes on each side or until desired degree of doneness. Place on a platter; keep warm.

**3.** Combine soy sauce and cornstarch. Add ½ cup wine and remaining consommé to skillet; scrape skillet to loosen browned bits. Bring to a boil; cook 1 minute. Add mushroom mixture, cornstarch mixture, and dried thyme; bring to a boil, and cook 1 minute, stirring constantly. Serve sauce with steaks. Garnish with thyme sprigs, if desired. Yield: 4 servings (serving size: 1 steak and ½ cup sauce).

CALORIES 250 (39% from fat); FAT 10.7g (sat 3.6g, mono 4.1g, poly 1.4g); PROTEIN 28.5g; CARB 9.4g; FIBER 0.9g; CHOL 84mg; IRON 5.1mg; SODIUM 712mg; CALC 30mg

# How to Cook Eggs-tatically

## Do you really know how indispensable eggs are to cooking?

Most cooks need eggs. It's not necessarily their flavor that makes eggs so hard to do without. It's the cooking chemistry. The strong binding power of the proteins, as well as the ability to induce either expansion or thickening, is critical in perhaps thousands of recipes and has been for centuries. Eggs are also divisible—white and yolk—which allows you to draw on the strengths of whichever component you happen to need. And, of course, you can use these components together.

Mastery of the egg ensures success in almost any culinary inclination.

### Spinach, Caramelized Onion, and Feta Quiche

To decrease fat, we've used 2 egg yolks and 5 egg whites. Some egg yolks are necessary to produce a creamy filling. You can refrigerate the leftover yolks up to 3 days in an airtight container (add a tablespoon of water so the yolks don't develop a film).

> 2  teaspoons olive oil
> 3  cups chopped onion
> 1  teaspoon sugar
> ½  teaspoon salt
> 2  cups frozen Southern-style hash brown potatoes, thawed
> 1  (11-ounce) can refrigerated soft breadstick dough
> Cooking spray
> 1  (10-ounce) package frozen chopped spinach, thawed, drained, and squeezed dry
> 1  cup fat-free milk
> 5  large egg whites
> 2  large egg yolks
> 1¼  cups (5 ounces) crumbled feta cheese

**1.** Preheat oven to 350°.

**2.** Heat olive oil in a large nonstick skillet over medium heat. Add onion, sugar, and salt; cook 30 minutes or until golden brown, stirring occasionally. Stir in potatoes, and cook 5 minutes or until lightly browned. Remove from heat.

**3.** Unroll dough, separating into strips. Working on a flat surface, coil one strip of dough around itself in a spiral pattern. Add second strip of dough to end of first strip, pinching ends together to seal; continue coiling dough. Repeat procedure with remaining dough strips. Cover and let dough rest 10 minutes. Roll dough into a 12-inch circle, and fit into a 10-inch deep-dish pie plate coated with cooking spray.

**4.** Spread potato mixture in bottom of prepared crust, and top with spinach. Combine milk, egg whites, egg yolks, and cheese; pour milk mixture over spinach. Bake at 350° for 1 hour or until set, shielding crust with foil after 50 minutes. Let stand 10 minutes before serving. Yield: 8 servings.

CALORIES 262 (29% from fat); FAT 8.4g (sat 3.7g, mono 2.8g, poly 1.3g); PROTEIN 11.7g; CARB 35.3g; FIBER 2.4g; CHOL 72mg; IRON 2.5mg; SODIUM 713mg; CALC 188mg

## Almond Angel Food Cake Step-by-Steps

### Almond Angel Food Cake:

*Folding gently incorporates the beaten egg whites into the dry ingredients, which gives angel food cake its light, airy texture. To fold, "cut" down the center and up the sides of the bowl with a rubber spatula, gently combining the two mixtures.*

### Crème Anglaise:

*Crème anglaise is a custard sauce thick-ened solely with egg yolks (no starch), giving it a silky, smooth texture. The trick with egg yolks is to get them to thicken without turning into scrambled eggs. To do this, cook the sauce over low to medium heat, stirring constantly. When the sauce is thick enough to coat the back of a spoon, remove from heat. It's done.*

## Almond Angel Food Cake with Crème Anglaise and Macerated Strawberries

(pictured on page 221)

This recipe highlights eggs at their very best—the cake gets its regal airiness from beaten egg whites, and the crème anglaise gets its silky-smooth consistency from egg yolks. This cake doesn't rise as much as a traditional angel food cake does because of the almonds, which weigh it down slightly. Macerated strawberries (berries that have been soaked or marinated in a liquid) add color and a fruity burst. You can also try this with blueberries or raspberries.

**STRAWBERRIES:**

  8  cups sliced strawberries
  2  tablespoons granulated sugar
  2  tablespoons orange juice
  1  teaspoon grated orange rind

**CAKE:**

  ¾  cup slivered almonds
  2  tablespoons granulated sugar
  1  cup sifted cake flour
  ½  cup powdered sugar
  ½  teaspoon salt
 10  large egg whites
1¼  teaspoons cream of tartar
  ¾  cup granulated sugar
1½  teaspoons almond extract

**CRÈME ANGLAISE:**

 ⅔  cup granulated sugar
  8  large egg yolks
3½  cups 1% low-fat milk
  1  tablespoon vanilla extract

**1.** Preheat oven to 325°.
**2.** To prepare strawberries, combine first 4 ingredients in a bowl. Cover and chill 3 hours.
**3.** To prepare cake, place almonds and 2 tablespoons granulated sugar in a food processor; pulse until finely chopped. Sift together flour, powdered sugar, and salt into a bowl. Combine almond mix-ture with flour mixture, and set aside. Beat egg whites in a large bowl at high speed of a mixer until foamy. Add cream of tartar; beat until soft peaks form. Add

¾ cup granulated sugar, 1 tablespoon at a time, beating until stiff peaks form. Sprinkle flour mixture over egg white mixture, ¼ cup at a time; fold in. Fold in almond extract. Spoon batter into an un-greased 10-inch tube pan, and spread evenly. Bake at 325° for 1 hour or until cake springs back when lightly touched.
**4.** While cake is baking, prepare crème anglaise. Combine ⅔ cup sugar and yolks in a large saucepan, stirring with a whisk until blended. Gradually add milk to pan, stirring constantly with a whisk. Cook over medium heat until mixture coats back of a spoon (about 8 minutes), stirring constantly. Immediately pour mix-ture into a bowl; stir in vanilla. Cover and chill (mixture will thicken as it cools).
**5.** Invert cake pan, and cool 40 minutes. Loosen cake from sides of pan using a narrow metal spatula. Invert cake onto plate. Serve with strawberries and crème anglaise. Yield: 16 servings (serving size: 1 slice cake, ⅓ cup strawberries, and ¼ cup crème anglaise).

CALORIES 237 (22% from fat); FAT 5.8g (sat 1.4g, mono 2.7g, poly 1.0g); PROTEIN 7.2g; CARB 39.6g; FIBER 2.3g; CHOL 111mg; IRON 1.3mg; SODIUM 138mg; CALC 103mg

### No More Separation Anxiety

Egg whites beat up to a higher vol-ume when at room temperature, but it's definitely easier to sepa-rate eggs when they're cold. If you're like most people, you sepa-rate an egg by pouring the yolk back and forth from one half of the eggshell to the other so that the white slides off into a bowl. But neither we nor the American Egg Board recommend this for two reasons: It can introduce bacteria from the eggshell pores into the egg, and there's a greater chance of the shell breaking the yolk.

It's fine to use your hands. Your fingers are softer and don't bring in bacteria. Just crack the egg, and let the the white run through your fingers into a bowl. Of course, wash your hands be-fore and after.

## Roasted Garlic-and-Rosemary Soufflé

In this recipe, the eggs do double duty—the whites inflate the soufflé, and the yolks thicken the sauce that forms the base. To get a jump on this soufflé, you can roast the garlic up to 2 days ahead. Then extract the pulp, and store in an airtight container in the refrigerator. Serve with pork, lamb, chicken, or beef.

1 whole garlic head
Cooking spray
1 tablespoon dry breadcrumbs
¼ cup all-purpose flour
¼ teaspoon salt
1 cup fat-free milk
⅓ cup (about 1½ ounces) grated fresh Parmesan cheese
½ teaspoon dried rosemary, crushed
2 large egg yolks, lightly beaten
4 large egg whites
½ teaspoon cream of tartar

**1.** Preheat oven to 350°.
**2.** Remove white papery skin from garlic head (do not peel or separate cloves). Wrap garlic head in foil. Bake at 350° for 1 hour; cool 10 minutes. Separate cloves, and squeeze to extract garlic pulp. Discard skins.
**3.** Coat a 1-quart soufflé dish with cooking spray; sprinkle bottom of dish with breadcrumbs.
**4.** Lightly spoon flour into a dry measuring cup, and level with a knife. Spoon flour and salt into a large saucepan, and gradually add milk, stirring with a whisk. Cook milk mixture over medium heat until thick (about 6 minutes), stirring constantly. Remove from heat. Stir in garlic pulp, cheese, rosemary, and egg yolks.
**5.** Beat egg whites and cream of tartar at high speed of a mixer until soft peaks form. Gently fold one-fourth of egg white mixture into garlic mixture; gently fold in remaining egg white mixture. Spoon into prepared soufflé dish. Bake at 350° for 50 minutes or until puffy and set. Yield: 6 servings.

CALORIES 111 (30% from fat); FAT 3.7g (sat 1.7g, mono 1.2g, poly 0.4g); PROTEIN 8.2g; CARB 11g; FIBER 0.4g; CHOL 78mg; IRON 0.8mg; SODIUM 268mg; CALC 157mg

## Double-Vanilla Meringue Cookies

Add the vanilla bean seeds at the end of the beating process, as their natural oils can prevent the egg whites from beating to stiff peaks. If you don't have a vanilla bean, use 2 teaspoons vanilla extract instead of 1. When baked slowly for a long time, stiffly beaten egg whites turn crisp, as they do in these cookies. Bake them 10 minutes less for a cookie that's slightly chewy on the inside. Store cookies in an airtight container up to 1 week or freeze up to 3 months.

1 cup sugar, divided
1 vanilla bean
3 large egg whites (at room temperature)
¼ teaspoon cream of tartar
¼ teaspoon salt
1 teaspoon vanilla extract

**1.** Preheat oven to 325°.
**2.** Place ¼ cup sugar in a small bowl. Scrape seeds from vanilla bean, and add seeds to sugar; discard bean. Stir well with a whisk.
**3.** Beat egg whites, cream of tartar, and salt at high speed of a mixer until foamy. Gradually add ¾ cup sugar, 1 tablespoon at a time, beating mixture until stiff peaks form. Gradually add vanilla bean mixture and extract; beat until just combined. (Stiff peaks will take on consistency of marshmallow cream.)
**4.** Cover a baking sheet with parchment paper; secure to baking sheet with masking tape. Drop batter by level tablespoonfuls onto prepared baking sheet. Bake at 325° for 35 minutes or until crisp. Cool on pan on a wire rack. Repeat procedure with remaining batter, reusing parchment paper. Store in an airtight container. Yield: 2½ dozen (serving size: 1 cookie).

CALORIES 28 (0% from fat); FAT 0g; PROTEIN 0.3g; CARB 6.7g; FIBER 0g; CHOL 0mg; IRON 0mg; SODIUM 25mg; CALC 0mg

## Perfect Peaks

### Soft:

**Roasted Garlic-and-Rosemary Soufflé:** *For soufflés, you'll want soft peaks—the stage before stiff peaks form. When you lift the beaters from the mixture, the peaks should curve like waves. For a puffed soufflé, beat egg whites separately and then fold them into the base thickened with the yolks.*

### Stiff:

**Double-Vanilla Meringue Cookies:** *Beat room-temperature egg whites with cream of tartar (which helps stabilize them) and salt until foamy. Then add the sugar, beating until stiff peaks form. When you lift the beaters from the mixture, stiff peaks will stand up.*

### Overbeaten:

**Mocha Mousse:** *Overbeaten egg whites won't fold in smoothly. Watch carefully, because egg whites can go from stiff to dry and overbeaten in as little as 30 seconds.*

## Ins and Outs of Eggs

- Eggs are easier to separate when they're cold.
- Egg whites beat up to a higher volume when left at room temperature for 15 minutes.
- It's estimated that 1 out of 20,000 eggs is infected with salmonella; because of this risk (albeit small), we don't recommend eating raw eggs. They're safe if brought to a temperature of 160°.
- The condition and type of bowl in which you beat egg whites really does matter. Keep it dry and clean; if it's wet or harbors any residual oil, the whites won't whip properly. Glass, ceramic, or metal bowls are best.
- Brown and white eggs are alike inside.
- A large egg has 76 calories: 17 from the white and 59 from the yolk. The whites are generally more health-friendly, containing more than half the total protein of a whole egg and none of the fat. The yolk is tasty, nutrient-rich, and useful in cooking but carries 213 milligrams of cholesterol and 5 grams of fat, 1.6 of which are saturated.
- It is nearly impossible to hard-cook an egg at an altitude of more than 10,000 feet (in case you're planning a trek).
- The white ropelike strands in the egg white, called the chalazae (kuh-LAY-zee), hold the yolk in place and are not, contrary to popular belief, the beginnings of an embryo. In fact, the more prominent the chalazae are, the fresher the egg.
- Eggs keep for three to five weeks in your refrigerator. It's best to keep them in the carton (whether made of foam or pulp) because it insulates the eggs and helps maintain moisture.
- Egg substitutes are simply egg whites combined with corn oil, water, flavorings, and preservatives. Because of these additives, they can't be beaten to peak stage. Egg whites work the same, if not better, in most applications.

## Italian Meat Loaf with Fresh Basil and Provolone

In addition to providing the lift in cakes, egg whites act as a binder for dishes such as crab cakes, salmon patties, and meat loaf. Serve this dish with your favorite mashed-potato recipe.

      1  cup boiling water
    ½  cup sun-dried tomatoes, packed without oil
    ½  cup ketchup
      1  cup seasoned breadcrumbs
    ¾  cup finely chopped onion
    ¾  cup chopped fresh basil
    ½  cup (2 ounces) shredded sharp provolone cheese
      2  large egg whites
      2  garlic cloves, minced
      1  pound ground round
      Cooking spray
    ⅓  cup ketchup

**1.** Combine boiling water and tomatoes in a bowl; let stand 30 minutes or until soft. Drain tomatoes; finely chop.
**2.** Preheat oven to 350°.
**3.** Combine ½ cup ketchup and next 7 ingredients in a large bowl. Add tomatoes to meat mixture. Shape meat mixture into a 9 x 5-inch loaf on a broiler pan coated with cooking spray. Spread ⅓ cup ketchup over meat loaf. Bake at 350° for 1 hour or until a meat thermometer inserted in center of loaf registers 160°. Let stand 10 minutes before slicing. Cut into 12 slices. Yield: 6 servings (serving size: 2 slices).

CALORIES 294 (27% from fat); FAT 8.7g (sat 3.6g, mono 3.2g, poly 0.7g); PROTEIN 24.3g; CARB 30.8g; FIBER 2.5g; CHOL 53mg; IRON 3.9mg; SODIUM 893mg; CALC 149mg

## Mocha Mousse

Egg whites must be brought to a temperature of 160° to be safe (we don't recommend eating raw eggs due to the risk of salmonella). This can be done without coagulating or cooking the whites (a no-no in a mousse) by combining them with sugar and beating over simmering water as we do here. The result is called an Italian meringue. If you don't have a double boiler, a bowl that fits over a saucepan will work fine.

      2  ounces semisweet chocolate, chopped
      1  tablespoon instant espresso granules or 2 tablespoons instant coffee granules
      1  tablespoon unsweetened cocoa
      2  tablespoons hot water
    ⅔  cup sugar
      2  tablespoons water
    ¼  teaspoon cream of tartar
      3  large egg whites
    ⅓  cup frozen reduced-calorie whipped topping, thawed
      2  teaspoons grated semisweet chocolate

**1.** Combine first 4 ingredients in a small saucepan. Cook over low heat until chocolate melts and mixture is smooth, stirring constantly. Remove from heat.
**2.** Combine sugar, 2 tablespoons water, cream of tartar, and egg whites in top of a double boiler. Place over simmering water; beat mixture at high speed of a mixer until stiff peaks form (about 4 minutes). Gently stir one-fourth of egg white mixture into chocolate mixture; gently fold in remaining egg white mixture and whipped topping. Divide mixture evenly among 4 dessert dishes. Cover and chill. Sprinkle each serving with ½ teaspoon grated chocolate. Yield: 4 servings.

**NOTE:** To freeze, cool completely; cover and freeze. Thaw in refrigerator.

CALORIES 238 (23% from fat); FAT 6g (sat 3.9g, mono 1.8g, poly 0.2g); PROTEIN 4.1g; CARB 45.6g; FIBER 0.2g; CHOL 0mg; IRON 0.9mg; SODIUM 45mg; CALC 16mg

## reader recipes

# Art You Can Eat

*An artist creates a colorful kitchen masterpiece that tastes as good as it looks.*

When we first tasted reader Carolyn Cary's colorful and piquant Chicken-Pasta Salad, we knew we'd uncovered a real culinary artist. But we weren't the first to discover her talents of the palate—or palette. This 38-year-old painter works out of a 150-year-old log cabin nestled in the Carrollton, Georgia, woods that she shares with her husband, Greg, and 2½-year-old son, Emmery. She sometimes swaps her paintbrush for a spoon or a hoe to engage in her other favorite creative pursuits: cooking and gardening.

### Chicken-Pasta Salad

    2  cups cooked small seashell pasta
       (about 1 cup uncooked pasta)
 1 ½  cups cubed cooked chicken breast
       (about 6 ounces)
    1  cup diced red bell pepper
    1  cup shredded yellow squash
       (about 1 medium)
    ½  cup sliced carrot
    ½  cup sliced green onions
    ½  cup fresh corn kernels (about 1 ear)
    ½  cup frozen green peas, thawed
    1  (15-ounce) can black beans, rinsed
       and drained
    ¼  cup rice vinegar
    3  tablespoons olive oil
    2  teaspoons Dijon mustard
    ½  teaspoon ground cumin
    ¼  teaspoon salt
    ¼  teaspoon hot sauce

**1.** Combine first 9 ingredients in a large bowl. Combine rice vinegar and remaining 5 ingredients in a small bowl; stir well with a whisk. Pour vinegar mixture over chicken mixture, and toss gently to coat. Serve at room temperature or chilled. Yield: 7 servings (serving size: 1 cup).

CALORIES 229 (29% from fat); FAT 7.5g (sat 1.2g, mono 4.7g, poly 1g); PROTEIN 14.1g; CARB 26.6g; FIBER 3.5g; CHOL 21mg; IRON 2.4mg; SODIUM 219mg; CALC 33mg

## Chicken Bruschetta

"Every time I make this recipe, I get rave reviews. I like it because it has the typical bruschetta toppings and is light and kind of tangy. You can serve it with a salad, but it's a healthy meal by itself."

—Erika Cross MacDonald,
Nashua, New Hampshire

    1  teaspoon garlic powder
    ½  teaspoon salt, divided
    ¼  teaspoon black pepper, divided
    4  (4-ounce) skinned, boned chicken
       breast halves
Cooking spray
    1  tablespoon olive oil
    1  (8-ounce) package presliced
       mushrooms
    1  small zucchini, quartered
       lengthwise and sliced (about 5
       ounces)
    4  garlic cloves, minced
    1  cup chopped plum tomato
    ½  cup chopped red onion
    ½  cup chopped fresh basil
    4  teaspoons balsamic vinegar
    ¼  cup (1 ounce) grated fresh
       Parmesan cheese

**1.** Preheat broiler.
**2.** Combine garlic powder, ¼ teaspoon salt, and ⅛ teaspoon pepper in a small bowl; sprinkle chicken with garlic powder mixture. Place chicken on a broiler pan coated with cooking spray, and broil 6 minutes on each side or until chicken is done. Remove chicken from pan, and keep warm.
**3.** Heat olive oil in a large nonstick skillet over medium-high heat. Add ¼ teaspoon salt, mushrooms, zucchini, and minced garlic; sauté 2 minutes. Add ⅛ teaspoon black pepper, tomato, onion, basil, and vinegar; sauté 3 minutes. Serve vegetable mixture over chicken; sprinkle with cheese. Yield: 4 servings (serving size: 1 chicken breast half, ½ cup vegetables, and 1 tablespoon cheese).

CALORIES 229 (29% from fat); FAT 7.3g (sat 2.1g, mono 3.5g, poly 1g); PROTEIN 31.4g; CARB 9.7g; FIBER 2.1g; CHOL 71mg; IRON 2.3mg; SODIUM 489mg; CALC 126mg

## Marsala Shrimp

"My husband and I were trying to lose some weight, so when I made this dish, I tried to use ingredients that we liked and were also low in calories. I tried several versions, and the one with Marsala wine is by far the best."

—Cheryl Snell, Gresham, Oregon

    ¼  cup all-purpose flour
    ½  teaspoon salt
    ½  teaspoon black pepper
    1  pound large shrimp, peeled and
       deveined
    1  tablespoon vegetable oil, divided
    2  garlic cloves, minced
    1  (8-ounce) package presliced
       mushrooms
    1  cup diced plum tomato
    ½  cup Marsala
    ¼  cup water
    4  cups hot cooked linguine (about 8
       ounces uncooked pasta)

**1.** Lightly spoon flour into a dry measuring cup; level with a knife. Combine flour, salt, and pepper in a shallow dish. Dredge shrimp in flour mixture.
**2.** Heat 2 teaspoons oil in a large nonstick skillet over medium-high heat. Add shrimp to pan; sauté 5 minutes or until golden. Remove shrimp from pan. Add 1 teaspoon oil to pan. Add garlic and mushrooms; sauté 3 minutes. Add tomato; cook 1 minute. Stir in shrimp, wine, and water; bring to boil. Reduce heat, and simmer 2 minutes or until sauce thickens. Serve over pasta. Yield: 4 servings (serving size: 3 ounces shrimp, ¼ cup sauce, and 1 cup pasta).

CALORIES 420 (13% from fat); FAT 6.2g (sat 1.1g, mono 1.4g, poly 2.8g); PROTEIN 27g; CARB 55.5g; FIBER 2.9g; CHOL 129mg; IRON 5.8mg; SODIUM 431mg; CALC 67mg

## Chicken Scampi

"My father loves the garlic flavor of scampi, so over the years I've tried various recipes to find one that tastes as good as the one from his favorite Italian restaurant. After many attempts, this one seems to capture the flavor best, and without all the butter."

—Kellie Mulleavy, Lambertville, Michigan

    1  pound skinned, boned chicken
       breast, cut into 1-inch-wide strips
    ¼  cup egg substitute
    ⅓  cup Italian-seasoned breadcrumbs
       Cooking spray
    2  tablespoons butter or stick
       margarine
    3  garlic cloves, minced
    1  cup fat-free, less-sodium chicken
       broth
    ⅔  cup dry white wine
    1½ tablespoons chopped fresh or
       1½ teaspoons dried parsley
    1½ teaspoons salt-free seasoning
       (such as Mrs. Dash)
    ¼  teaspoon dried oregano
    ⅛  teaspoon salt
    3  cups hot cooked linguine (about
       6 ounces uncooked pasta)
    ¼  cup (1 ounce) grated fresh
       Parmesan cheese

**1.** Dip chicken in egg substitute; dredge in breadcrumbs.
**2.** Place a large nonstick skillet coated with cooking spray over medium-high heat until hot. Add chicken, and sauté 6 minutes or until browned. Remove chicken from pan.
**3.** Melt butter in pan over medium-high heat. Add garlic, and sauté 1 minute. Add broth and next 5 ingredients, and bring to a boil. Add chicken; reduce heat, and simmer 20 minutes. Place ¾ cup pasta on each of 4 plates; top each serving with ¾ cup chicken mixture, and sprinkle with 1 tablespoon cheese. Yield: 4 servings.

CALORIES 419 (22% from fat); FAT 10.2g (sat 5.3g, mono 2.8g, poly 1g); PROTEIN 37.6g; CARB 41.9g; FIBER 1.2g; CHOL 86mg; IRON 3.3mg; SODIUM 721mg; CALC 129mg

### menu

#### Molasses-Barbecued Chicken Drumsticks

#### Green bean sauté*

*Steam 1 pound green beans over boiling water until crisp-tender. Heat 2 teaspoons vegetable oil in a skillet. Add beans and 3 minced garlic cloves; sauté 1 minute. Add 2 tablespoons lemon juice, ⅛ teaspoon salt, and ⅛ teaspoon pepper. Serves 4.

## Molasses-Barbecued Chicken Drumsticks

"I've been providing home health care for 21 years, and I am always trying to work out lighter recipes for my patients. My husband likes to grill, and I love molasses, so I came up with this sauce for chicken. It tastes great."

—Charlotte Bryant, Greensburg, Kentucky

    ¼  cup spicy-hot vegetable juice
    2  tablespoons chili sauce (such as
       Heinz)
    1  tablespoon molasses
    2  teaspoons red wine vinegar
    1  teaspoon Dijon mustard
    1½ teaspoons prepared horseradish
    1  garlic clove, crushed
    8  chicken drumsticks, skinned (about
       1½ pounds)
       Cooking spray

**1.** Prepare grill.
**2.** Combine first 7 ingredients in a small saucepan; bring to a boil. Reduce heat, and simmer 5 minutes, stirring constantly. Remove from heat.
**3.** Place chicken on a grill rack coated with cooking spray. Grill 30 minutes or until done, turning frequently. Baste chicken frequently with sauce after 15 minutes. Yield: 4 servings (serving size: 2 drumsticks).

CALORIES 142 (25% from fat); FAT 3.9g (sat 1g, mono 1.3g, poly 1g); PROTEIN 18.6g; CARB 6.8g; FIBER 0.2g; CHOL 60mg; IRON 1.2mg; SODIUM 249mg; CALC 24mg

# september

# What's In a Name?

## Sometimes dishes with foreign names are closer to home than you think.

Does it matter if some of our favorite foreign foods really aren't? Spaghetti and meatballs, chop suey, and English muffins—these foods may lack "authenticity," but they've compensated with something we like even better. By taking liberties with Old World traditions and techniques, and adapting them to the New World, they've become true American originals. We've given these famous dishes a healthy spin.

### German Chocolate Bundt Cake

The cake takes its name from Samuel German, an American who created a baking-chocolate bar for Walter Baker & Co. The bar was named "Baker's German's Sweet Chocolate" in his honor. Today, the apostrophe and the "s" have been dropped, thus giving a false impression of the chocolate's origin.

**STREUSEL:**

¼ cup all-purpose flour
½ cup packed brown sugar
2 tablespoons chilled butter or stick margarine, cut into small pieces
⅓ cup flaked sweetened coconut
⅓ cup chopped pecans

**CAKE:**

Cooking spray
1 tablespoon granulated sugar
½ cup unsweetened cocoa
1 ounce sweet baking chocolate
½ cup boiling water
1½ cups granulated sugar
⅓ cup butter or stick margarine, softened
2 teaspoons vanilla extract
2 large egg whites
2 cups all-purpose flour
2 teaspoons baking powder
½ teaspoon baking soda
½ teaspoon salt
1 cup low-fat buttermilk

**GLAZE:**

1 cup powdered sugar
1 tablespoon butter or stick margarine, melted
4 teaspoons fat-free milk

**1.** Preheat oven to 325°.

**2.** To prepare streusel, lightly spoon ¼ cup flour into a dry measuring cup; level with a knife. Combine ¼ cup flour and brown sugar in a small bowl; cut in 2 tablespoons butter with a pastry blender or 2 knives until mixture resembles coarse meal. Stir in coconut and pecans.

**3.** To prepare cake, coat a 12-cup Bundt pan with cooking spray; sprinkle with 1 tablespoon granulated sugar. Set aside. Combine cocoa and baking chocolate in a small bowl; add boiling water, stirring until chocolate melts. Set aside.

**4.** Beat 1½ cups granulated sugar and ⅓ cup butter at medium speed of a mixer until well-blended (about 5 minutes). Add vanilla and egg whites, 1 at a time, beating well after each addition. Lightly spoon 2 cups flour into dry measuring cups; level with a knife. Combine 2 cups flour, baking powder, baking soda, and salt, stirring well with a whisk. Add flour mixture to sugar mixture alternately with buttermilk, beginning and ending with flour mixture. Stir in cocoa mixture. Spoon half of batter into prepared pan; top with streusel. Spoon remaining batter over streusel. Bake at 325° for 1 hour or until a wooden pick inserted in center comes out clean. Cool in pan on a wire rack 10 minutes; remove from pan. Cool completely.

**5.** To prepare glaze, combine powdered sugar and 1 tablespoon butter. Add milk; stir with a whisk. Drizzle over cake. Yield: 16 servings (serving size: 1 wedge).

CALORIES 302 (29% from fat); FAT 9.8g (sat 5.3g, mono 3.2g, poly 0.8g); PROTEIN 3.8g; CARB 58g; FIBER 0.7g; CHOL 16mg; IRON 1.6mg; SODIUM 224mg; CALC 58mg

### English Muffins

Similar tea muffins may exist in Great Britain, but none that go by the name "English Muffin." The version we know and love today was created by Samuel Bath Thomas, an English immigrant who opened a bakery in New York City in 1880. These muffins freeze well or can be stored for a day at room temperature in an airtight container.

1 cup 2% reduced-fat milk
3 tablespoons vegetable oil
2 tablespoons sugar
1¼ teaspoons salt
1 package dry yeast
¼ cup warm water (100° to 110°)
3½ cups all-purpose flour, divided
1 large egg, lightly beaten
Cooking spray

**1.** Cook milk in a heavy saucepan over medium-high heat to 180° or until tiny bubbles form around edge (do not boil). Remove from heat. Pour milk into a large bowl. Stir in oil, sugar, and salt. Cool to about 90°.

**2.** Dissolve yeast in warm water in a small bowl; let stand 5 minutes. Lightly spoon flour into dry measuring cups; level with a knife. Stir yeast mixture, 3 cups flour, and egg into milk mixture. Turn dough out onto a lightly floured surface. Knead until smooth and elastic (about 10 minutes); add enough of remaining flour, 1 tablespoon at a time, to prevent dough from sticking to hands (dough will feel tacky). Place dough in a large bowl coated with cooking spray, turning to coat top. Cover and let rise in a warm place (85°), free from drafts, 45 minutes or until doubled in size. (Press two fingers into dough. If indentation remains, dough has risen enough.)

**3.** Punch dough down. Divide in half. Working with one portion at a time (cover remaining dough to keep from drying), roll each portion to ¼-inch thickness. Let dough rest about 5 minutes. Cut each portion with a 4-inch biscuit cutter into 8 muffins. Place muffins on a large baking sheet. Cover and let rise 30 minutes or until doubled in size.

**4.** Preheat oven to 350°.

**5.** Bake muffins at 350° for 7 minutes. Turn muffins over; bake an additional 7 minutes or until lightly browned. Cool. Yield: 16 servings (serving size: 1 muffin).

CALORIES 142 (22% from fat); FAT 3.5g (sat 0.8g, mono 1g, poly 1.4g); PROTEIN 3.9g; CARB 23.4g; FIBER 0.9g; CHOL 15mg; IRON 1.4mg; SODIUM 195mg; CALC 25mg

## Spaghetti and Meatballs

Each is a classic Italian dish, but pairing them didn't start in the Old Country. Italian-American immigrants were the first to top spaghetti with meatballs in the early 1900s.

⅓ cup Italian-seasoned breadcrumbs
¼ cup (1 ounce) grated fresh Parmesan cheese
¼ cup chopped fresh parsley
½ teaspoon dried basil
1 pound ground turkey
2 large egg whites
1 teaspoon olive oil
3 cups Tomato Sauce (recipe at right)
3 cups hot cooked spaghetti (about 6 ounces uncooked pasta)

**1.** Combine first 6 ingredients in a bowl; shape mixture into 16 (1½-inch) meatballs. Heat olive oil in a large nonstick skillet over medium-high heat. Add meatballs; cook 5 minutes, browning on all sides. Add Tomato Sauce, and bring to a boil. Cover, reduce heat, and simmer 15 minutes. Serve over spaghetti. Yield: 4 servings (serving size: 4 meatballs, about ¾ cup sauce, and ¾ cup noodles).

CALORIES 437 (17% from fat); FAT 8.4g (sat 2.7g, mono 2.9g, poly 1.7g); PROTEIN 37.9g; CARB 51.2g; FIBER 3.4g; CHOL 79mg; IRON 5.6mg; SODIUM 600mg; CALC 195mg

## Tomato Sauce

1 teaspoon olive oil
1 cup chopped onion
2 garlic cloves, minced
½ cup dry white wine
2 tablespoons tomato paste
2 teaspoons dried basil
2 teaspoons dried oregano
¼ teaspoon black pepper
1 (14.5-ounce) can diced tomatoes with basil, garlic, and oregano, undrained
1 (8-ounce) can no-salt-added tomato sauce

**1.** Heat oil in a large nonstick skillet over medium-high heat. Add onion and garlic, and sauté 5 minutes. Stir in wine and remaining ingredients; bring to a boil. Reduce heat; simmer 15 minutes. Yield: 4 cups (serving size: ½ cup).

CALORIES 41 (18% from fat); FAT 0.8g (sat 0.1g, mono 0.4g, poly 0.2g); PROTEIN 1.4g; CARB 8g; FIBER 1.4g; CHOL 0mg; IRON 1.1mg; SODIUM 78mg; CALC 46mg

## Veal Parmesan

This is another dish created by Italian-American restaurateurs. It takes its name from the Parmesan cheese used to coat the veal. The cheese, in turn, is named after the Italian city of Parma.

4 (4-ounce) veal cutlets (about ½ inch thick)
¼ cup all-purpose flour
⅛ teaspoon black pepper
2 large egg whites, lightly beaten
½ cup Italian-seasoned breadcrumbs
¼ cup (1 ounce) grated fresh Parmesan cheese
2 teaspoons olive oil
2 cups Tomato Sauce (recipe above)
Cooking spray
¾ cup (3 ounces) shredded part-skim mozzarella cheese

**1.** Preheat oven to 350°.
**2.** Place each cutlet between 2 sheets of heavy-duty plastic wrap; flatten to ¼-inch thickness using a meat mallet or rolling pin.

**3.** Lightly spoon flour into a dry measuring cup; level with a knife. Combine flour and pepper in a large bowl. Place egg whites in a shallow dish. Combine breadcrumbs and Parmesan in a shallow dish.

**4.** Dredge veal in flour mixture. Dip each cutlet in egg whites; dredge in breadcrumb mixture.

**5.** Heat oil in a large nonstick skillet over medium-high heat. Add veal, and sauté 1 minute on each side or until browned. Remove from heat.

**6.** Spread 1 cup Tomato Sauce in an 11 x 7-inch baking dish coated with cooking spray. Arrange cutlets in a single layer on top of sauce; spoon remaining Tomato Sauce over veal. Sprinkle veal with mozzarella. Bake at 350° for 10 minutes. Yield: 4 servings (serving size: 1 veal cutlet and about ½ cup sauce).

CALORIES 362 (30% from fat); FAT 12.2g (sat 5.6g, mono 5.2g, poly 1.1g); PROTEIN 36.6g; CARB 25.4g; FIBER 1.7g; CHOL 111mg; IRON 3mg; SODIUM 812mg; CALC 301mg

### menu
### Swiss Steak
### Mashed potatoes
Glazed carrots*

*Melt 2 teaspoons butter in a large skillet over medium heat; stir in 2 tablespoons honey. Add 2 cups (¼-inch) diagonally sliced carrots, ⅛ teaspoon salt, and ⅛ teaspoon pepper. Cover and cook 10 minutes or until carrots are tender. Garnish with chopped fresh parsley. Serves 4.

## Swiss Steak

This name comes from the English term "swissing," a method of smoothing cloth between a set of rollers. Swiss steaks are flattened with a rolling pin or mallet before cooking.

4 (4-ounce) boned chuck steaks
2 garlic cloves, chopped
¼ cup all-purpose flour
½ teaspoon salt
½ teaspoon black pepper
1 tablespoon vegetable oil
5 cups sliced onion
1¼ cups water

*Continued*

1. Trim fat from steaks. Place each steak between 2 sheets of heavy-duty plastic wrap; flatten each piece to ¼-inch thickness using a meat mallet or rolling pin. Rub steaks with garlic. Lightly spoon flour into a dry measuring cup, and level with a knife. Combine flour, salt, and pepper. Sprinkle steaks with flour mixture.

2. Heat oil in a large cast-iron skillet over medium-high heat. Add steaks, and cook 4 minutes or until brown. Turn steaks over. Add onion, and cook 4 minutes. Add water. Cover, reduce heat, and simmer 1½ hours or until meat is tender. Yield: 4 servings (serving size: 1 steak and about ½ cup onions).

CALORIES 267 (32% from fat); FAT 9.4g (sat 2.8g, mono 3.3g, poly 2.1g); PROTEIN 26.6g; CARB 18.6g; FIBER 2.9g; CHOL 68mg; IRON 3.6mg; SODIUM 374mg; CALC 41mg

## Vichyssoise

Formally known as *crème vichyssoise glacée*, this cold potato-and-leek soup was created by Louis Diat, a chef at the Ritz-Carlton Hotel in New York City. The name, translated literally, means "coming from Vichy," a French city near Diat's childhood home. This version of the classic cold potato-leek soup is also good warm.

    1   tablespoon vegetable oil
    3   cups diced leek (about 3 large)
    3   cups diced peeled baking potato
        (about 1¼ pounds)
    1   (16-ounce) can fat-free,
        less-sodium chicken broth
    ⅔   cup half-and-half
    ¼   teaspoon salt
    ⅛   teaspoon black pepper
    1   tablespoon minced fresh chives

1. Heat vegetable oil in a large saucepan over medium-low heat. Add diced leek; cover and cook 10 minutes or until soft. Stir in diced potato and chicken broth, and bring to a boil. Cover potato mixture, reduce heat, and simmer 15 minutes or until potato is tender. Place potato mixture in a blender or food processor, and process until smooth. Place potato mixture in a large bowl, and cool to

room temperature. Stir in half-and-half, salt, and black pepper. Cover and chill. Sprinkle soup with minced chives. Yield: 5 servings (serving size: 1 cup).

CALORIES 221 (27% from fat); FAT 6.7g (sat 2.9g, mono 1.9g, poly 1.6g); PROTEIN 5.3g; CARB 35.1g; FIBER 2.5g; CHOL 12mg; IRON 1.7mg; SODIUM 340mg; CALC 77mg

## Chicken Tetrazzini

Named after Luisa Tetrazzini, an Italian opera singer who toured America in the early 1900s, this dish is believed to have been created in San Francisco, the soprano's favorite American city. Instead of folding chunks of cooked chicken into cooked spaghetti, arrange the sliced chicken atop the casserole, add more sauce, and top it with breadcrumbs and cheese.

SAUCE:
    2   tablespoons olive oil
    ¾   cup diced carrot
    ⅓   cup diced onion
    2   tablespoons all-purpose flour
    2   cups 1% low-fat milk
    1   (16-ounce) can fat-free,
        less-sodium chicken broth
    2   cups sliced mushrooms
    ¼   cup dry sherry
    ½   teaspoon salt
    ½   teaspoon black pepper

REMAINING INGREDIENTS:
    Cooking spray
    6   (4-ounce) skinned, boned chicken
        breast halves
    6   cups hot cooked spaghetti (about
        12 ounces uncooked pasta)
    ¼   cup chopped fresh parsley
    ½   cup dry breadcrumbs
    ⅓   cup grated Parmesan cheese

1. To prepare sauce, heat oil in a medium saucepan over medium heat. Add carrot and onion; sauté 10 minutes or until soft. Add flour; cook 1 minute. Combine carrot mixture, milk, and broth in a blender; process until smooth. Return mixture to pan, and add mushrooms, sherry, salt, and pepper. Cook until reduced to 3½ cups (about 30 minutes), stirring occasionally.

2. Preheat oven to 350°.

3. Place a large nonstick skillet coated with cooking spray over medium-high heat. Add chicken; cook 5 minutes on each side or until done. Cut chicken into thin slices; keep warm.

4. Combine 2 cups sauce, spaghetti, and chopped parsley in a large bowl. Spoon into a 13 x 9-inch baking dish coated with cooking spray. Arrange chicken on top of spaghetti mixture; spoon remaining sauce over chicken. Sprinkle with breadcrumbs and cheese. Bake at 350° for 15 minutes or until lightly browned. Yield: 8 servings.

CALORIES 373 (18% from fat); FAT 7.3g (sat 2g, mono 3.5g, poly 1g); PROTEIN 30.8g; CARB 43.9g; FIBER 2g; CHOL 54mg; IRON 3.3mg; SODIUM 477mg; CALC 161mg

## Pork Chop Suey

This dish is believed to have originated among Chinese immigrants working on the Pacific railroad lines in the 1850s. The name is supposedly derived from the Mandarin Chinese phrase *tsa tsui*, meaning "a little of this and that."

    1   (1-pound) pork tenderloin
    ¼   cup all-purpose flour
    2   tablespoons vegetable oil,
        divided
    2   cups thinly sliced bok choy
    1   cup sliced celery
    1   cup red bell pepper strips
    1   cup sliced mushrooms
    1   (8-ounce) can sliced water
        chestnuts, drained
    2   garlic cloves, minced
    ¼   cup fat-free, less-sodium
        chicken broth
    ¼   cup low-sodium soy sauce
    1   tablespoon cornstarch
    1   tablespoon dry sherry
    ½   teaspoon ground ginger
    2   cups hot cooked long-grain rice
    ¼   cup sliced green onions

1. Trim fat from pork; cut pork into 1-inch pieces. Lightly spoon flour into a dry measuring cup; level with a knife. Combine flour and pork in a zip-top plastic bag; seal and shake well.

**2.** Heat 1 tablespoon oil in a large non-stick skillet over medium-high heat. Add pork; cook 3 minutes or until browned. Remove from pan; keep warm.

**3.** Add 1 tablespoon oil to pan. Add bok choy and next 5 ingredients; stir-fry 3 minutes. Combine broth, soy sauce, cornstarch, sherry, and ginger; stir well with a whisk. Add pork and broth mixture to pan; cook 1 minute or until thick. Serve over rice; sprinkle with onions. Yield: 4 servings (serving size: 1½ cups chop suey, ½ cup rice, and 1 tablespoon onions).

CALORIES 406 (23% from fat); FAT 10.2g (sat 2.3g, mono 3.4g, poly 3.8g); PROTEIN 28.9g; CARB 46.4g; FIBER 2.7g; CHOL 74mg; IRON 4.1mg; SODIUM 532mg; CALC 83mg

## 30 minutes or less

# Hot for Supper

*Sandwiches used to be the gambler's friend, but luckily for us they've moved to the dinner table.*

Legend has it that the Fourth Earl of Sandwich concocted the first meat-on-bread meal in the mid-1700s so he could eat without having to leave the gambling table. Sandwiches are still quick to make, but there's no need to limit them to the noon hour. Serve them hot and full of goodies, and you've hit the jackpot for dinner.

## Monte Cristo Sandwiches

(pictured on page 3)

**PREPARATION TIME: 5 MINUTES**
**COOKING TIME: 6 MINUTES**

  3   tablespoons honey mustard
  8   (1-ounce) slices white bread
  4   (1-ounce) slices Swiss cheese
  ¼   pound thinly sliced smoked ham
  ⅓   cup fat-free milk
  2   large egg whites
  Cooking spray
  2   teaspoons powdered sugar
  ¼   cup seedless raspberry jam

**1.** Spread about 1 teaspoon mustard over each bread slice. Place 1 cheese slice on each of 4 bread slices. Divide ham evenly over cheese. Cover with remaining 4 bread slices, mustard sides down. Combine milk and egg whites in a shallow dish. Dip both sides of each sandwich into milk mixture.

**2.** Heat a large nonstick skillet coated with cooking spray over medium heat. Cook sandwiches 3 minutes on each side or until lightly browned. Sprinkle each sandwich with ½ teaspoon sugar; top each with 1 tablespoon jam. Yield: 4 servings.

CALORIES 387 (27% from fat); FAT 11.5g (sat 6g, mono 3.7g, poly 0.9g); PROTEIN 20.7g; CARB 49.1g; FIBER 1.6g; CHOL 40mg; IRON 2.1mg; SODIUM 840mg; CALC 366mg

## Tuna Melt

**PREPARATION TIME: 15 MINUTES**
**COOKING TIME: 4 MINUTES**

  2   English muffins, split
  ¼   cup chopped green onions
  ¼   cup light mayonnaise
  2   teaspoons Worcestershire sauce
  2   teaspoons prepared horseradish
  1   teaspoon prepared mustard
  ⅛   teaspoon ground red pepper
  1   (9-ounce) can solid white tuna in water, drained
  4   (¼-inch-thick) slices tomato
  ½   cup (2 ounces) shredded reduced-fat sharp Cheddar cheese

**1.** Preheat broiler.

**2.** Place muffin halves on a baking sheet, and broil 3 minutes or until lightly toasted.

**3.** Combine green onions and next 6 ingredients in a medium bowl. Divide evenly among muffin halves. Top each muffin half with a tomato slice, and sprinkle with 2 tablespoons cheese. Broil 4 minutes or until golden brown. Yield: 2 servings (serving size: 2 muffin halves).

CALORIES 411 (24% from fat); FAT 10.9g (sat 4.1g, mono 2.9g, poly 2.8g); PROTEIN 37.3g; CARB 39.4g; FIBER 2.4g; CHOL 57mg; IRON 2.5mg; SODIUM 1,114mg; CALC 371mg

## Tuscan Seared-Tuna Sandwiches

**PREPARATION TIME: 10 MINUTES**
**COOKING TIME: 6 MINUTES**

Cook the tuna in two batches.

  1   (6-ounce) jar marinated artichoke hearts, undrained
  1   (2-ounce) jar diced pimento, drained
  1   teaspoon dried rosemary, divided
  1   teaspoon bottled minced garlic
  4   (4-ounce) tuna steaks (about ½ inch thick)
  ½   teaspoon freshly ground black pepper
  Cooking spray
  4   (2½-ounce) Kaiser rolls or hamburger buns
  2   tablespoons fat-free mayonnaise

**1.** Drain artichokes over a bowl, reserving 3 tablespoons marinade. Chop artichokes, and combine with 1 tablespoon reserved marinade, pimento, and ½ teaspoon rosemary; set aside.

**2.** Combine 2 tablespoons reserved marinade, ½ teaspoon rosemary, and garlic in a small bowl; brush over fish, and sprinkle with pepper.

**3.** Place a grill pan coated with cooking spray over medium-high heat. Add fish, and cook 2 minutes on each side or until fish is medium-rare or desired degree of doneness; keep warm.

**4.** Preheat broiler.

**5.** Place rolls, cut sides up, on a baking sheet; broil 2 minutes or until toasted. Spread mayonnaise evenly over bottom halves of rolls. Top each with a tuna steak and ¼ cup artichoke mixture; cover with roll tops. Yield: 4 servings.

CALORIES 421 (30% from fat); FAT 14g (sat 3.4g, mono 4.1g, poly 5.8g); PROTEIN 35g; CARB 38.9g; FIBER 1.9g; CHOL 43mg; IRON 2.7mg; SODIUM 604mg; CALC 91mg

## Onion-Smothered Chicken Sandwiches

PREPARATION TIME: 5 MINUTES
COOKING TIME: 25 MINUTES

    1   teaspoon olive oil
    2   cups thinly sliced onion
    ¼   cup honey
    ¼   cup cider vinegar
    4   (4-ounce) skinned, boned chicken
        breast halves
    2   tablespoons Dijon mustard
    1   tablespoon honey
    ½   teaspoon paprika
    ⅛   teaspoon salt
        Cooking spray
    4   (1¼-ounce) slices rye bread,
        toasted

**1.** Heat oil in a large nonstick skillet over medium-high heat. Add onion; cook 1 minute. Cover, reduce heat to medium, and cook 6 minutes or until soft. Stir in ¼ cup honey and vinegar. Cook, uncovered, 10 minutes, stirring occasionally. Set aside.

**2.** While onions are cooking, place each chicken breast half between 2 sheets of heavy-duty plastic wrap, and flatten to ½-inch thickness using a meat mallet or rolling pin. Combine mustard, 1 tablespoon honey, paprika, and salt in a small bowl. Brush half of mustard mixture over one side of chicken. Heat a large grill pan or skillet coated with cooking spray over medium-high heat. Place chicken, coated side down, in pan; cook 4 minutes. Brush chicken with remaining mustard mixture. Turn chicken over; cook 4 minutes or until done. Place 1 chicken breast half on each toast slice, and top each with 2 tablespoons onion mixture. Yield: 4 servings.

CALORIES 351 (12% from fat); FAT 4.6g (sat 0.8g, mono 2.1g, poly 0.9g); PROTEIN 30.3g; CARB 47.1g; FIBER 3.4g; CHOL 66mg; IRON 2.3mg; SODIUM 630mg; CALC 55mg

## Italian Beef Subs

PREPARATION TIME: 14 MINUTES
COOKING TIME: 10 MINUTES

Giardiniera is a combination of spicy pickled vegetables; the heat varies depending on the amount of hot peppers in the product.

    2   teaspoons olive oil
    1½  cups green bell pepper strips
    2   teaspoons bottled minced garlic
    1   teaspoon dried oregano
    1   (14¼-ounce) can low-salt beef broth
    1   pound thinly sliced deli roast beef
    4   (3-ounce) submarine rolls, toasted
    ½   cup bottled giardiniera (such as
        Cento), drained

**1.** Heat oil in a large nonstick skillet over medium heat. Add bell pepper and garlic; sauté 2 minutes. Stir in oregano and broth. Bring mixture to a boil; reduce heat, and simmer 10 minutes. Remove bell pepper mixture from pan. Add beef to pan, and cook 45 seconds. Divide beef evenly among bottom halves of rolls; top each with ¼ cup bell pepper mixture and 2 tablespoons giardiniera. Cover with roll tops. Yield: 4 servings.

CALORIES 399 (20% from fat); FAT 8.7g (sat 2.1g, mono 2.2g, poly 0.3g); PROTEIN 32.3g; CARB 48.5g; FIBER 3.2g; CHOL 63mg; IRON 7mg; SODIUM 1,310mg; CALC 114mg

## Greek Meatball Pitas

PREPARATION TIME: 15 MINUTES
COOKING TIME: 12 MINUTES

    ½   pound lean ground lamb
    2   tablespoons finely chopped onion
    ¾   teaspoon salt
    ½   teaspoon dried oregano
    ½   teaspoon bottled minced garlic
    ¼   teaspoon black pepper
    ½   cup plain low-fat yogurt
    ½   cup diced cucumber
    2   teaspoons finely chopped onion
    1   teaspoon dried dill
    ½   teaspoon sugar
    2   cups gourmet salad greens .
    8   (¼-inch-thick) slices plum tomato
    2   (6-inch) pitas, cut in half

**1.** Preheat oven to 450°.

**2.** Combine first 6 ingredients. Shape mixture into 16 (1-inch) meatballs; place on a broiler pan. Bake at 450° for 12 minutes or until done. Combine yogurt and next 4 ingredients in a bowl. Arrange 4 meatballs, ½ cup greens, and 2 tomato slices in each pita half. Drizzle each pita half with ¼ cup yogurt dressing. Yield: 4 servings.

CALORIES 237 (17% from fat); FAT 4.6g (sat 1.6g, mono 1.6g, poly 1.2g); PROTEIN 18.3g; CARB 30g; FIBER 2.1g; CHOL 39mg; IRON 3mg; SODIUM 587mg; CALC 124mg

## Barbecue Pork-and-Coleslaw Hoagies

PREPARATION TIME: 10 MINUTES
COOKING TIME: 15 MINUTES

    1   (1-pound) pork tenderloin
    ½   cup spicy barbecue sauce (such as
        Kraft Spicy Cajun), divided
        Cooking spray
    2½  cups packaged cabbage-and-carrot
        coleslaw
    2½  tablespoons low-fat sour cream
    1½  tablespoons light mayonnaise
    1½  teaspoons sugar
    2½  teaspoons prepared horseradish
    4   (2½-ounce) hoagie rolls with
        sesame seeds
        Dill pickle slices (optional)

**1.** Preheat broiler.

**2.** Trim fat from pork; cut pork in half lengthwise. Brush pork with 3 tablespoons barbecue sauce. Place pork on a broiler pan coated with cooking spray, and broil 15 minutes or until a meat thermometer registers 155° (slightly pink); turn pork occasionally. Cut into ¼-inch-thick slices.

**3.** While pork is cooking, combine coleslaw and next 4 ingredients in a medium bowl; set aside.

**4.** Combine pork and 3 tablespoons barbecue sauce. Brush cut sides of bread with 2 tablespoons barbecue sauce. Divide pork evenly among bottom halves of rolls. Top each with about ½ cup coleslaw and pickles (if desired); cover with roll tops. Yield: 4 servings.

**NOTE:** You can also grill the pork. Place pork on a grill rack coated with cooking spray, and grill 15 minutes or until thermometer registers 155° (slightly pink), turning pork occasionally.

CALORIES 398 (23% from fat); FAT 10.2g (sat 3.6g, mono 4g, poly 1.7g); PROTEIN 34g; CARB 45g; FIBER 3.4g; CHOL 88mg; IRON 4.6mg; SODIUM 717mg; CALC 106mg

## Eggplant-and-Portobello Mushroom Melts

**PREPARATION TIME: 10 MINUTES**
**COOKING TIME: 12 MINUTES**

    4   portobello mushrooms (about
        10 ounces)
    4   (½-inch-thick) slices peeled
        eggplant (about 8 ounces)
    ¼   cup balsamic vinaigrette (such as
        Wish-Bone), divided
    ¼   cup chopped bottled roasted red
        bell peppers
    2   tablespoons chopped fresh basil
    4   (½-ounce) slices provolone cheese
    4   (2-ounce) onion rolls, halved
    ½   cup spinach leaves

**1.** Preheat broiler.
**2.** Remove stems from mushrooms; discard stems. Remove brown gills from undersides of mushrooms using a sharp knife; discard gills. Place mushrooms and eggplant on a broiler pan; brush vegetables with 1 tablespoon vinaigrette. Broil 6 minutes. Turn vegetables over; brush with 1 tablespoon vinaigrette. Broil 5 minutes or until tender.
**3.** Combine bell peppers and basil. Spoon 1 tablespoon pepper mixture over each eggplant slice. Top each mushroom with 1 cheese slice. Broil 1 minute or until cheese melts. Brush 2 tablespoons vinaigrette evenly over cut sides of rolls. Arrange spinach evenly on bottom halves of rolls. Top each with 1 mushroom and 1 eggplant slice; cover with roll tops. Yield: 4 servings.

CALORIES 276 (30% from fat); FAT 9.3g (sat 3.5g, mono 2.5g, poly 2.5g); PROTEIN 12g; CARB 39.6g; FIBER 3.9g; CHOL 15mg; IRON 2.9mg; SODIUM 564mg; CALC 205mg

# Desserts à Deux

*Sweet treats don't have to be the troublesome twos.*

Dinner for two, whether for romance or just you and your 8-year-old, is easy. Even if the meal for you and your companion comes from a recipe intended for eight, no biggie: Downsizing a recipe is fairly easy. Not so with dessert.

The best bet is to plan dessert for two from the start, and that's what we've done here with four recipes perfect for you and anyone else you think is worth it.

## Chocolate Chip Meringues with Strawberries

You can double the recipe for the meringues and save some for a later date; they freeze beautifully up to two months. Just remove them from the freezer and top them with the strawberry mixture—no thawing required. You can also substitute raspberries for the strawberries, if you prefer.

    1   large egg white
    ⅛   teaspoon cream of tartar
        Dash of salt
    ¼   cup powdered sugar
    1   tablespoon semisweet chocolate
        chips
    ¼   teaspoon vanilla extract
    ½   cup sliced strawberries
    ½   teaspoon granulated sugar

**1.** Preheat oven to 250°.
**2.** Cover a baking sheet with parchment paper. Draw 2 (3-inch) circles on paper. Turn paper over, and secure with masking tape. Beat egg white, cream of tartar, and salt at high speed of a mixer until foamy. Gradually add powdered sugar, 1 tablespoon at a time, beating until stiff peaks form (do not underbeat). Fold in chocolate chips and vanilla.
**3.** Divide egg white mixture evenly between 2 drawn circles. Shape meringues into nests using back of a spoon. Bake at

250° for 1 to 1½ hours or until dry. Turn oven off, and cool meringue nests in closed oven for at least 3 hours. Carefully remove meringue nests from paper. Combine strawberries and granulated sugar. Spoon strawberry mixture evenly over meringues. Yield: 2 servings.

CALORIES 113 (17% from fat); FAT 2.1g (sat 1.1g, mono 0.6g, poly 0.1g); PROTEIN 2.2g; CARB 22.4g; FIBER 1g; CHOL 0mg; IRON 0.3mg; SODIUM 98mg; CALC 9mg

## Banana Bread Pudding with Caramel Sauce

Try this recipe the next time you have a leftover French loaf; the texture of bread pudding is better with day-old bread. You can also use fat-free fudge topping in place of the caramel topping.

    ⅓   cup 1% low-fat milk
    1   tablespoon dark brown sugar
    ⅛   teaspoon ground cinnamon
    1   large egg
    2   cups (½-inch) cubed French bread
        (about 2 [1-ounce] slices)
        Cooking spray
    ½   cup mashed ripe banana (about
        1 banana)
    1   tablespoon granulated sugar
    2   tablespoons fat-free caramel
        topping
        Powdered sugar (optional)

**1.** Combine first 4 ingredients in a small bowl, and stir with a whisk. Place ½ cup bread cubes into each of 2 (8-ounce) ramekins coated with cooking spray. Spoon 2 tablespoons milk mixture over each serving, and top each with ¼ cup banana. Sprinkle each serving with 1½ teaspoons granulated sugar. Repeat procedure with remaining bread and milk mixture. Chill 30 minutes.
**2.** Preheat oven to 350°.
**3.** Bake puddings at 350° for 50 minutes or until done. Spoon 1 tablespoon caramel sauce over each serving. Sprinkle with powdered sugar, if desired. Yield: 2 servings.

CALORIES 297 (14% from fat); FAT 4.5g (sat 1.4g, mono 1.6g, poly 0.9g); PROTEIN 8g; CARB 57.2g; FIBER 2.3g; CHOL 108mg; IRON 1.4mg; SODIUM 265mg; CALC 92mg

### Toasted-Coconut Tapioca

¾ cup light coconut milk
¾ cup fat-free milk
3 tablespoons sugar
4 teaspoons uncooked quick-cooking tapioca
2 tablespoons egg substitute
Dash of salt
¼ teaspoon vanilla extract
2 tablespoons flaked sweetened coconut, toasted

**1.** Combine first 6 ingredients in a medium saucepan, and let stand 5 minutes. Bring mixture to a boil over medium-high heat, stirring constantly. Remove from heat, and stir in vanilla. Divide mixture evenly between 2 dessert bowls. Cover and chill until thick. Sprinkle each serving with 1 tablespoon toasted coconut. Yield: 2 servings.

CALORIES 222 (28% from fat); FAT 6.9g (sat 6g, mono 0.3g, poly 0.1g); PROTEIN 4.8g; CARB 35g; FIBER 0.3g; CHOL 2mg; IRON 1mg; SODIUM 194mg; CALC 120mg

### Individual Chocolate Soufflés

(pictured on page 260)

Cooking spray
2 teaspoons granulated sugar
½ cup water
¼ cup powdered sugar
2 tablespoons unsweetened cocoa
2 tablespoons 1% low-fat milk
1½ teaspoons all-purpose flour
1 large egg yolk
⅛ teaspoon vanilla extract
1 large egg white
⅛ teaspoon cream of tartar
1 tablespoon granulated sugar
2 teaspoons powdered sugar

**1.** Preheat oven to 350°.
**2.** Coat 2 (8-ounce) ramekins with cooking spray, and sprinkle with 2 teaspoons granulated sugar. Place ramekins on a baking sheet; set aside.
**3.** Combine water and next 5 ingredients in top of a double boiler. Cook over simmering water until thick (about 10 minutes), stirring constantly with a whisk. Remove from heat; add vanilla.
**4.** Beat egg white and cream of tartar at high speed of a mixer until soft peaks form. Gradually add 1 tablespoon granulated sugar, beating until stiff peaks form. Gently fold one-fourth of egg white mixture into chocolate mixture; gently fold in remaining egg white mixture. Spoon evenly into prepared ramekins. Bake at 350° for 20 minutes or until puffy and set. Sprinkle each soufflé with 1 teaspoon powdered sugar. Serve immediately. Yield: 2 servings.

CALORIES 188 (19% from fat); FAT 3.9g (sat 1.4g, mono 1.4g, poly 0.6g); PROTEIN 5.4g; CARB 33g; FIBER 0g; CHOL 110mg; IRON 1.4mg; SODIUM 41mg; CALC 40mg

# I Scream, You Scream

*Today's fast-and-easy ice-cream makers will have you shouting from delight, not frustration.*

Grocery stores stock ice cream in all sorts of gourmet flavors, but most are full of fat. The solution is to make your own, and it's easier than you think.

### Banana-Maple Ice Cream

It's important to make sure eggs are safe, which means bringing them to a temperature of at least 160°. Be sure to do this slowly over heat no higher than medium so you don't curdle the yolks. Using your heaviest saucepan will disperse the heat better than a thinner pan.

1½ cups 2% reduced-fat milk, divided
¼ cup sugar
2 large egg yolks
¼ cup nonfat dry milk
1 teaspoon vanilla extract
1 cup mashed ripe banana (about 2 medium)
½ cup maple syrup

**1.** Combine 1 cup milk, sugar, and egg yolks in a small heavy saucepan; stir well with a whisk. Place over medium heat, stirring constantly. Cook 8 minutes or until mixture reaches 180° and is slightly thickened (do not boil). Remove from heat. Pour custard into a cool bowl; place over ice water to cool completely. Combine ½ cup milk, dry milk, and vanilla. Stir in custard, banana, and syrup. Cover and chill.
**2.** Pour mixture into freezer can of an ice-cream freezer; freeze according to manufacturer's instructions. Spoon ice cream into a freezer-safe container; cover and freeze 1 hour or until firm. Yield: 3½ cups (serving size: ½ cup).

CALORIES 177 (14% from fat); FAT 2.7g (sat 1.2g, mono 0.9g, poly 0.3g); PROTEIN 4.4g; CARB 34.7g; FIBER 0.8g; CHOL 67mg; IRON 0.6mg; SODIUM 54mg; CALC 141mg

### Banana-Maple Ice-Cream Pie

1 cup graham cracker crumbs
3 tablespoons sugar
2 tablespoons butter or stick margarine, melted
2 teaspoons water
1 teaspoon vanilla extract
3½ cups Banana-Maple Ice Cream (recipe at left)
1 cup reduced-calorie whipped topping, thawed (optional)
½ cup sliced banana (optional)

**1.** Preheat oven to 350°.
**2.** Combine first 5 ingredients; toss with a fork until moist. Press into bottom and up sides of a 9-inch pie plate. Bake at 350° for 10 minutes or until lightly browned. Cool on a wire rack.
**3.** Spoon ice cream into prepared crust, spreading evenly. Cover with plastic wrap, and freeze until firm. Top with whipped topping and banana, if desired. Yield: 8 servings (serving size: 1 wedge).

CALORIES 279 (25% from fat); FAT 7.6g (sat 4.1g, mono 2g, poly 0.5g); PROTEIN 5g; CARB 48.5g; FIBER 1.2g; CHOL 67mg; IRON 1mg; SODIUM 161mg; CALC 135mg

## Ice-Cream Sandwiches

You can use any kind of low-fat ice cream in these sandwiches, even store-bought, but we loved the combination of Banana-Maple Ice Cream (recipe on page 252) with the chocolate-chip cookies.

**CHOCOLATE-CHIP COOKIES:**
- 1 cup all-purpose flour
- ½ teaspoon baking soda
- ⅛ teaspoon salt
- ½ cup packed brown sugar
- ¼ cup granulated sugar
- 2½ tablespoons butter or stick margarine
- 2 teaspoons water
- 1 teaspoon vanilla extract
- 2 large egg whites
- Cooking spray
- 2 tablespoons semisweet chocolate minichips

**FILLING:**
- 2½ cups Banana-Maple Ice Cream (recipe on page 252)

**1.** Preheat oven to 375°.
**2.** To prepare chocolate-chip cookies, lightly spoon flour into a dry measuring cup; level with a knife. Combine flour, soda, and salt in a small bowl; set aside. Beat sugars and butter at medium speed of a mixer in a large bowl until well-blended. Add water, vanilla, and egg whites; beat well. Add flour mixture; beat until well-blended. Drop by level tablespoons 2 inches apart onto baking sheets coated with cooking spray (you should get 20 cookies). Sprinkle chips evenly over dough. Bake at 375° for 8 minutes or until lightly browned. Cool 2 minutes or until cookies can be easily removed from pan; cool cookies on wire racks.
**3.** Spoon ¼ cup Banana-Maple Ice Cream onto each of 10 cookies. Top with remaining cookies, pressing gently. Wrap sandwiches tightly in plastic wrap, and freeze until firm. Yield: 10 servings (serving size: 1 sandwich).

CALORIES 236 (19% from fat); FAT 5g (sat 2.8g, mono 1.5g, poly 0.4g); PROTEIN 4.3g; CARB 44g; FIBER 1g; CHOL 41mg; IRON 1.4mg; SODIUM 164mg; CALC 85mg

## Pineapple-Brown Sugar Frozen Yogurt

This recipe makes 9 cups but you can easily half it if you have an ice-cream maker that doesn't accommodate that much.

- 1½ cups packed light brown sugar
- 2 (15¼-ounce) cans crushed pineapple in juice, undrained
- 4 cups vanilla low-fat yogurt
- 2 teaspoons vanilla extract

**1.** Combine sugar and pineapple in a medium saucepan over medium heat, and cook until sugar dissolves, stirring occasionally. Remove from heat, and cool slightly. Chill.
**2.** Combine pineapple mixture, yogurt, and vanilla in a large bowl. Pour mixture into freezer can of an ice-cream freezer; and freeze according to manufacturer's instructions. Spoon yogurt into a freezer-safe container; cover and freeze 1 hour or until firm. Yield: 9 cups (serving size: ½ cup).

CALORIES 142 (4% from fat); FAT 0.7g (sat 0.4g, mono 0.2g, poly 0.1g); PROTEIN 2.7g; CARB 32.4g; FIBER 0.4g; CHOL 3mg; IRON 0.5mg; SODIUM 41mg; CALC 109mg

## Watermelon-Cantaloupe Sorbet

Fragrant and refreshing, this sorbet is wonderful by itself. But we discovered it's also perfect in the Frozen Cardamom Bombe with Watermelon-Cantaloupe Center (recipe at right).

- ½ cup sugar
- ⅓ cup water
- 1½ cups cubed peeled cantaloupe
- 1½ cups cubed seeded watermelon
- 3 tablespoons fresh lime juice

**1.** Combine sugar and water in a small saucepan. Bring to a boil; cook 1 minute or until sugar dissolves. Cool completely. Place cantaloupe and watermelon in a blender or food processor, and process until smooth.
**2.** Combine sugar syrup, melon mixture, and lime juice. Pour sorbet mixture into freezer can of an ice-cream freezer, and freeze according to manufacturer's instructions. Spoon sorbet into a freezer-safe container; cover and freeze 1 hour or until firm. Yield: 3 cups (serving size: ½ cup).

CALORIES 93 (3% from fat); FAT 0.3g (sat 0.1g, mono 0g, poly 0.1g); PROTEIN 0.6g; CARB 23.4g; FIBER 0.5g; CHOL 0mg; IRON 0.2mg; SODIUM 5mg; CALC 8mg

## Frozen Cardamom Bombe with Watermelon-Cantaloupe Center

A bombe is simply molded ice cream and cake. You can use a special 4- or 6-cup bombe mold, or a Pyrex bowl as we did. Combining commercial low-fat ice cream with the spices makes this an easy recipe.

**ICE CREAM:**
- 3 cups low-fat vanilla ice cream, softened
- ½ teaspoon ground cinnamon
- ¼ teaspoon ground cardamom
- ½ teaspoon almond extract

**CAKE:**
- Cooking spray
- ⅓ cup sugar
- 1 large egg
- ½ cup all-purpose flour
- ½ teaspoon baking soda
- ⅛ teaspoon salt
- ¼ cup 2% reduced-fat milk
- 1 tablespoon butter or stick margarine, melted
- 1 teaspoon vanilla extract

**REMAINING INGREDIENTS:**
- ¼ cup apricot all-fruit spread (such as St. Dalfour)
- 3 cups Watermelon-Cantaloupe Sorbet (recipe at left)

**1.** To prepare ice cream, combine first 4 ingredients in a bowl; freeze until firm.
**2.** Preheat oven to 350°.
**3.** To prepare cake, coat bottom of an 8-inch round cake pan with cooking spray; line bottom with wax paper. Coat wax
*Continued*

paper with cooking spray. Combine sugar and egg in a medium bowl; beat at medium speed of a mixer 1 minute or until well-blended. Lightly spoon flour into a dry measuring cup; level with a knife. Combine flour, soda, and salt; stir well with a whisk. Add flour mixture to sugar mixture; stir well. Stir in milk, butter, and vanilla. Pour into prepared pan. Bake at 350° for 15 minutes or until a wooden pick inserted in center comes out clean. Cool in pan 10 minutes on a wire rack, and remove from pan. Cool cake completely on wire rack. Spread apricot spread over bottom of cake layer, and set aside.

**4.** Line a 6-cup glass bowl with heavy-duty plastic wrap, allowing wrap to extend over edge of bowl; place in freezer 10 minutes. Press ice cream into bottom and up sides of bowl; freeze 30 minutes or until firm. Spoon Watermelon-Cantaloupe Sorbet into center of bowl, pressing firmly. Press cake layer firmly onto top of ice cream and sorbet, apricot spread side down. Cover and freeze until firm.

**5.** Dip bowl into hot water for a few seconds. Place a plate upside down on top of bowl; invert bombe onto plate. Remove plastic wrap, and cut into wedges. Yield: 12 servings (serving size: 1 wedge).

CALORIES 173 (17% from fat); FAT 3.2g (sat 1.7g, mono 0.9g, poly 0.3g); PROTEIN 2.8g; CARB 32.8g; FIBER 0.4g; CHOL 26mg; IRON 0.5mg; SODIUM 125mg; CALC 61mg

### Tequila-Lime Sorbet

1½  cups water
¾  cup sugar
2  teaspoons grated lime rind
½  cup fresh lime juice (about 3 limes)
2  tablespoons tequila

**1.** Combine water and sugar in a small saucepan. Bring to a boil; cook 1 minute or until sugar dissolves. Cool completely.
**2.** Combine sugar syrup, rind, juice, and tequila. Pour mixture into freezer can of an ice-cream freezer; freeze according to manufacturer's instructions. Spoon sorbet into a freezer-safe container;

cover and freeze 1 hour or until firm. Yield: 2½ cups (serving size: ½ cup).

CALORIES 136 (0% from fat); FAT 0g; PROTEIN 0.1g; CARB 32.3g; FIBER 0g; CHOL 0mg; IRON 0mg; SODIUM 1mg; CALC 4mg

---

### Cylinder or Bucket?

Ice-cream makers come in two basic types: cylinder and bucket. Each is available in manual or electric models; prices vary.

**Cylinder freezers:** These makers require no salt or ice; you simply place the cylinder bowl, which contains a liquid coolant, in your freezer for six to 24 hours. When the coolant is completely frozen, attach the cylinder to the base of the machine; then pour in your ice-cream mixture and turn on the machine.

*Pros:* Because there's no ice or salt, this is a convenient, neat way to make frozen treats. It's also quiet and quick.

*Cons:* You need to think ahead with this kind, being sure to freeze the cylinder for the appropriate amount of time. If you have the freezer space, though, it's great to just leave it there so you can make ice cream on a whim. You can only make up to 1½ quarts each cycle, so you might need to halve some recipes.

**Bucket freezers:** These are generally larger than the cylinder freezers and require ice and salt (which lowers the temperature by melting the ice and absorbing heat from the ice-cream mixture).

*Pros:* You can make up to 6 quarts of ice cream in this type of freezer, so it's the one to go with for family reunions. And many folks prefer the nostalgia of a hand-cranked bucket freezer.

*Cons:* You have to fuss with ice and salt, which can get messy. Sometimes the ice can jam in electric models, so you need to pay attention.

---

# Peanuts or True Love?

*When her fiancé is out of town, this Seattle reader carries on an affair with peanut-sauced chicken.*

Kate Sackett, a 32-year-old executive assistant in Seattle, likes to keep in shape and favors a gym about a block away from the office. One day while lunching at one of her favorite casual eateries—the gym's café—she tried a dish she loved so much that she decided to learn how to make it herself. Thus was born Spicy Soba Noodles with Chicken in Peanut Sauce.

The only holdout is her fiancé, Andy, who's not fond of peanut sauce. Not a problem. "I make it for my friends every time he goes out of town," she admits.

### Spicy Soba Noodles with Chicken in Peanut Sauce

(pictured on page 257)

1  carrot, peeled
⅓  cup reduced-fat peanut butter
2  tablespoons honey
1  tablespoon chopped peeled fresh ginger
1  tablespoon low-sodium soy sauce
1  to 2 teaspoons crushed red pepper
1  garlic clove, minced
1  (16-ounce) can fat-free, less-sodium chicken broth, divided
1  pound skinned, boned chicken breast
5  cups cooked soba (buckwheat noodles)
6  tablespoons sliced green onions
6  tablespoons chopped unsalted, dry-roasted peanuts

**1.** Shave carrot lengthwise into thin strips using a vegetable peeler; set aside.
**2.** Combine peanut butter, honey, ginger, soy sauce, pepper, garlic, and ⅓ cup chicken broth in a small bowl; stir with a whisk until smooth.

**3.** Place chicken in a large saucepan; add 1⅔ cups broth. Bring to a boil; reduce heat, and simmer 4 minutes or until done. Remove from heat; let stand 20 minutes. Drain and cut chicken into 2-inch pieces. Combine carrot, peanut sauce, chicken, and noodles in a large bowl; toss to coat. Sprinkle with onions and peanuts. Yield: 6 servings (serving size: 1 cup).

CALORIES 398 (26% from fat); FAT 11.4g (sat 2.1g, mono 5.2g, poly 3.6g); PROTEIN 29.5g; CARB 43.4g; FIBER 4.3g; CHOL 44mg; IRON 1.9mg; SODIUM 477mg; CALC 40mg

## Mango Chicken

"During the summer, I always make this recipe when my friends and I get together. The mango makes it seem so festive during the warm-weather months."

—Mindy Shouse, Columbia, Missouri

    3 tablespoons low-sodium soy sauce
    1 tablespoon honey
    ¾ teaspoon ground ginger
    ¾ teaspoon cornstarch
    ¼ teaspoon paprika
    ¼ teaspoon black pepper, divided
    12 ounces skinned, boned chicken
       breast, cut into ½-inch strips
    Cooking spray
    3 cups chopped bok choy
    1 cup sliced mushrooms
    1 cup chopped peeled mango
       (about 1 medium)
    4 cups hot cooked rice

**1.** Combine first 5 ingredients and ⅛ teaspoon pepper in a small bowl, stirring well with a whisk. Sprinkle chicken with ⅛ teaspoon pepper.
**2.** Place a large skillet coated with cooking spray over medium-high heat until hot. Add chicken; sauté 5 minutes or until done. Add bok choy, mushrooms, and mango; sauté 2 minutes. Stir in soy sauce mixture. Bring to a boil; cook 1 minute or until slightly thick. Serve over rice. Yield: 4 servings (serving size: 1¼ cups chicken mixture and 1 cup rice).

CALORIES 382 (4% from fat); FAT 1.8g (sat 0.4g, mono 0.4g, poly 0.5g); PROTEIN 25.7g; CARB 64.7g; FIBER 2.5g; CHOL 49mg; IRON 3.5mg; SODIUM 454mg; CALC 94mg

## Chicken-Orange Stir-Fry

"About 15 years ago, I ordered a Chinese hand-hammered wok while watching an infomercial in the middle of the night. It turned out to be the best piece of cookware I've ever owned. This is a variation of the first chicken stir-fry I made in the wok."

—Neil J. Bindelglass, Brooklyn, New York

    1 (11-ounce) can mandarin oranges
       in light syrup, undrained
    ⅓ cup thawed orange juice
       concentrate, undiluted
    2 tablespoons low-sodium soy sauce
    1 tablespoon minced peeled fresh
       ginger
    1½ teaspoons apricot preserves
    ½ teaspoon dark sesame oil
    ⅛ teaspoon chili oil (optional)
    1 garlic clove, minced
    ½ pound skinned, boned chicken
       breast, cut into bite-size pieces
    1½ teaspoons canola or vegetable oil
    1 cup (1-inch) diagonally sliced
       asparagus (about 4 ounces)
    ½ cup (3-inch) julienne-cut red bell
       pepper
    ½ cup (3-inch) julienne-cut zucchini
       (about 1 small)
    ½ cup (3-inch) julienne-cut carrot
       (about 1 medium)
    ½ cup snow peas
    ½ cup diagonally sliced celery
    ½ pound green beans, trimmed and
       diagonally sliced
    1 (8-ounce) package presliced
       mushrooms
    1½ teaspoons cornstarch
    3 cups hot cooked rice
    2 tablespoons slivered almonds,
       toasted

**1.** Drain oranges in a colander over a bowl, reserving syrup.
**2.** Combine juice concentrate and next 6 ingredients in a bowl, stirring with a whisk. Add chicken; cover and marinate in refrigerator 1 hour.
**3.** Heat canola oil in a stir-fry pan or wok over medium-high heat. Add asparagus and next 6 ingredients; stir-fry 6 minutes or until crisp-tender. Add mushrooms, and stir-fry 2 minutes. Remove

vegetable mixture from pan. Add chicken mixture to pan, and stir-fry 4 minutes or until chicken is done. Return vegetable mixture to pan. Combine reserved syrup and cornstarch in a small bowl, stirring well with a whisk. Add syrup mixture to pan, and cook 1 minute or until slightly thick. Stir in oranges. Serve over rice, and sprinkle with almonds. Yield: 4 servings (serving size: 1½ cups chicken mixture, ¾ cup rice, and 1½ teaspoons almonds).

CALORIES 434 (11% from fat); FAT 5.5g (sat 0.7g, mono 2g, poly 2.1g); PROTEIN 21.9g; CARB 76g; FIBER 5.5g; CHOL 33mg; IRON 4.6mg; SODIUM 313mg; CALC 94mg

## Hot-and-Spicy Philippine Salad

"The flavors of this dish reminded my sister, Sandy, and me of a friend's cooking. She is from the Philippines, so we named it in her honor. The cilantro, lime, and jalapeño give this light salad so much flavor you won't even miss the oil."

—Debbie Gale, Chandler, Arizona

**DRESSING:**
    ½ cup chopped fresh cilantro
    ½ cup fresh lime juice (about 6 limes)
    ½ cup rice vinegar
    1 tablespoon brown sugar
    ½ teaspoon grated peeled fresh
       ginger
    1 jalapeño pepper, seeded and
       chopped

**SALAD:**
    4 cups torn romaine lettuce
    2 cups cubed cooked chicken breast
       (about ¾ pound)
    1½ cups chopped tomato
    1 cup chopped red bell pepper
       (about 1 medium)
    ½ cup chopped green bell pepper
    ½ cup julienne-cut carrot (about
       1 medium)
    ¼ cup chopped green onions

**1.** To prepare dressing, combine first 6 ingredients in a bowl; stir with a whisk. Cover and chill 2 hours.

*Continued*

**2.** To prepare salad, combine lettuce and remaining 6 ingredients in a large bowl. Pour dressing over salad, tossing gently to coat. Yield: 4 servings (serving size: 1¾ cups).

CALORIES 203 (26% from fat); FAT 5.9g (sat 1.5g, mono 2g, poly 1.5g); PROTEIN 22.9g; CARB 15g; FIBER 3.6g; CHOL 62mg; IRON 3.2mg; SODIUM 87mg; CALC 61mg

### Grilled Chicken and Portobellos

"My cousin Dan and I both live in apartments, and we're not allowed to have grills. Whenever we go to other people's houses, we offer to cook so we can use their grills. Last summer we had some portobello mushrooms on hand, and we came up with this great recipe."

—Amy E. Rhoad, Mount Laurel, New Jersey

2¼ cups Marsala wine, divided
2 tablespoons Worcestershire sauce
4 (4-ounce) skinned, boned chicken breast halves
4 portobello mushroom caps (about 1 pound)
Cooking spray
¼ cup diced shallots

**1.** Combine 2 cups wine, Worcestershire sauce, and chicken in a large zip-top plastic bag; seal and marinate in refrigerator 1 hour. Remove chicken from bag, reserving marinade.
**2.** Prepare grill.
**3.** Lightly coat mushrooms with cooking spray. Place mushrooms, top sides down, on grill rack coated with cooking spray; spoon 1 tablespoon wine into each cap. Add chicken to grill rack; grill mushrooms and chicken 6 minutes on each side or until chicken is done. Cut mushrooms into ½-inch-thick slices.
**4.** While chicken and mushrooms are grilling, place a medium skillet coated with cooking spray over medium-high heat until hot. Add shallots; sauté 1 minute. Add reserved marinade, and bring to a boil. Reduce heat, and simmer until reduced to ½ cup (about 15 minutes). Serve chicken and mushrooms with sauce. Yield: 4 servings (serving

size: 1 chicken breast half, 1 mushroom cap, and 2 tablespoons sauce).

CALORIES 193 (9% from fat); FAT 2g (sat 0.5g, mono 0.4g, poly 0.6g); PROTEIN 29.2g; CARB 13.5g; FIBER 1.5g; CHOL 66mg; IRON 2.6mg; SODIUM 165mg; CALC 40mg

lighten up

# Putting the Dip in Diploma

*A nutrition expert can't give up an old college habit—finding the perfect low-fat snack dip.*

While Randy Hecht was studying for her nutrition degree at Syracuse University, she developed a singular obsession: spinach-and-artichoke dip. The pursuit of the cheese-laden appetizer continues in New York City, where she writes promotional copy for a pharmaceutical company.

Deep down, though, Randy knows what she really ought to be writing is a confessional, and it would begin: "I know this just has way too much fat." After seeing the recipe she uses at home, we concur. The marinated artichokes alone fattened the dip by 50 grams. So that's where we started: A switch to canned artichoke hearts got rid of 15% of the fat. Our next move was to substitute lower fat sour cream and cheeses for the full-fat varieties used in the original. When we totaled it up, we'd given Randy a new 148-calorie-per-serving dip, compared with 223 in the old version. More notable, we all but banished the fat, dropping it to 5 grams per serving, a nearly two-thirds reduction from the original.

### Spinach-and-Artichoke Dip

(pictured on page 257)

2 cups (8 ounces) shredded part-skim mozzarella cheese, divided
½ cup fat-free sour cream
¼ cup (1 ounce) grated fresh Parmesan cheese, divided
¼ teaspoon black pepper
3 garlic cloves, crushed
1 (14-ounce) can artichoke hearts, drained and chopped
1 (8-ounce) block ⅓-less-fat cream cheese, softened
1 (8-ounce) block fat-free cream cheese, softened
½ (10-ounce) package frozen chopped spinach, thawed, drained, and squeezed dry
1 (13.5-ounce) package baked tortilla chips (about 16 cups)

**1.** Preheat oven to 350°.
**2.** Combine 1½ cups mozzarella, sour cream, 2 tablespoons Parmesan, pepper, and next 5 ingredients in a large bowl, and stir until well-blended. Spoon mixture into a 1½-quart baking dish. Sprinkle with ½ cup mozzarella and 2 tablespoons Parmesan. Bake at 350° for 30 minutes or until bubbly and golden brown. Serve with tortilla chips. Yield: 5½ cups (serving size: ¼ cup dip and about 6 chips).

CALORIES 148 (30% from fat); FAT 5g (sat 2.9g, mono 1.5g, poly 0.5g); PROTEIN 7.7g; CARB 18.3g; FIBER 1.5g; CHOL 17mg; IRON 0.6mg; SODIUM 318mg; CALC 164mg

| BEFORE | AFTER |
|---|---|
| **SERVING SIZE** | |
| ¼ cup dip & about 6 chips | |
| **CALORIES PER SERVING** | |
| 223 | 148 |
| **FAT** | |
| 14.1g | 5g |
| **PERCENT OF TOTAL CALORIES** | |
| 57% | 30% |
| **SODIUM** | |
| 379mg | 318mg |

Spinach-and-Artichoke Dip,
page 256

Spicy Soba Noodles with
Chicken in Peanut Sauce,
page 254

Feta Omelet with Breadcrumbs, page 271,
and Greens with Garlic and Lemon, page 272

Ooey-Gooey Peanut
Butter-Chocolate
Brownies, page 273

Grilled Sweet Potatoes with
Orange-Chipotle Glaze, page 269,
and Pork Tenderloin with
Costa Rican Coffee Glaze, page 270

Individual Chocolate Soufflés,
page 252

Greek-Style Scampi,
page 267

# How to Make Great Pasta Dishes

*There's no magic required, just loving attention.*

Pasta tastes so good in Italy because it's cooked with care and attention to detail. That's why we're teaching you about the cooking of pasta dishes—Italian ones, specifically. Not to exclude the pasta traditions from elsewhere around the world, but for a beginning cook, chances are that Italian dishes are very familiar already and thus ideal teaching tools. Learning to take noodles and combine them with flavors and techniques full of both Italian and Italian-American influences will give you a tremendous inventory of tastes and traditions for more meals than you can count.

## Farfalle Carbonara

This dish needs to go straight from the stove-top to the table; after sitting for just a few minutes, it loses its creaminess. If it's a little thick when done, add some low-fat milk to thin it out. Use a good Romano cheese (such as Locatelli) for the most flavor. The garlic procedure here may strike you as unorthodox, but we think it works very well.

2 tablespoons water
2 garlic cloves, minced
4 quarts water
3 cups uncooked farfalle (about 8 ounces bow tie pasta) or other short pasta
2 large eggs, lightly beaten
½ cup (2 ounces) grated fresh pecorino Romano cheese or Parmesan cheese
4 bacon slices, cooked and crumbled

**1.** Heat a large nonstick skillet over medium heat. Add 2 tablespoons water and garlic; remove from heat.

**2.** Bring 4 quarts water to a boil in a large stockpot. Add farfalle; return to a boil. Cook, uncovered, 10 minutes or until al dente, stirring occasionally. Remove ½ cup pasta cooking water, and whisk into eggs, stirring vigorously. Drain farfalle; add to garlic mixture in skillet. Stir well. Add egg mixture to farfalle. Cook mixture over medium-low heat until thick (about 4 minutes), stirring constantly. Remove from heat; stir in cheese and bacon. Serve immediately. Yield: 4 servings (serving size: 1 cup).

CALORIES 348 (28% from fat); FAT 10.8g (sat 4.3g, mono 3.8g, poly 1.2g); PROTEIN 17g; CARB 43.6g; FIBER 1.4g; CHOL 123mg; IRON 2.8mg; SODIUM 333mg; CALC 167mg

## Penne with Green Beans, Sun-Dried Tomatoes, and Toasted Breadcrumbs

Any tube-shaped or short pasta such as ziti, rigatoni, or mostaccioli will stand in for the penne just fine.

½ cup boiling water
½ cup (1 ounce) sun-dried tomatoes, packed without oil (about 12)
4 quarts water
3 cups uncooked penne (about 12 ounces uncooked tube-shaped pasta) or other short pasta
2 tablespoons olive oil, divided
4 cups (2-inch) cut green beans (about 12 ounces)
2 garlic cloves, minced
2 tablespoons Italian-seasoned breadcrumbs
½ teaspoon salt
¼ cup (1 ounce) grated fresh pecorino Romano or Parmesan cheese
2 tablespoons capers
1 teaspoon red wine vinegar
¼ teaspoon black pepper

**1.** Combine boiling water and tomatoes in a bowl; let stand 30 minutes or until soft. Drain over a bowl, reserving ¼ cup liquid; slice tomatoes lengthwise.
**2.** Bring 4 quarts water to a boil in a large stockpot. Add penne; return to a boil. Cook, uncovered, 10 minutes or until al dente, stirring occasionally. Drain.

**3.** Heat 1 tablespoon oil in a large non-stick skillet over medium-high heat. Add green beans; cover and cook 3 minutes, stirring occasionally. Reduce heat to medium; add reserved tomato liquid, tomatoes, and garlic; cover and cook 2 minutes, stirring occasionally. Stir in breadcrumbs and salt; sauté 2 minutes. Stir in penne, 1 tablespoon oil, cheese, capers, vinegar, and pepper. Toss well. Yield: 4 servings (serving size: 2 cups).

CALORIES 360 (25% from fat); FAT 10g (sat 2.4g, mono 5.7g, poly 1.1g); PROTEIN 12.9g; CARB 56.1g; FIBER 4.1g; CHOL 7mg; IRON 3.9mg; SODIUM 745mg; CALC 132mg

## Spaghetti Aglio e Olio

In Italian, aglio e olio (AH-lyoh ay OH-lyoh) means "garlic and oil." Typically, the garlic is fried in olive oil on the stovetop, but we've cooked it with olive oil in the microwave, which is easier and eliminates the risk of burning the garlic. You can add some crushed red pepper flakes for a spicier version.

2 tablespoons extra-virgin olive oil
¼ teaspoon dried oregano
4 large garlic cloves, minced
4 quarts water
8 ounces uncooked spaghetti
½ cup fat-free, less-sodium chicken broth
2 tablespoons minced fresh parsley

**1.** Combine olive oil, oregano, and minced garlic in a small microwave-safe bowl. Cover with wax paper, and microwave at HIGH 1 minute.
**2.** Bring water to a boil in a large stockpot. Add spaghetti; return to a boil. Cook, uncovered, 10 minutes or until al dente, stirring occasionally. Drain. Return to pot. Stir in garlic mixture and broth. Cook over medium heat 4 minutes or until broth is absorbed, stirring constantly. Stir in parsley. Yield: 4 servings (serving size: 1 cup).

CALORIES 278 (25% from fat); FAT 7.7g (sat 1.0g, mono 5.1g, poly 1.0g); PROTEIN 7.9g; CARB 43.7g; FIBER 1.5g; CHOL 0mg; IRON 2.4mg; SODIUM 66mg; CALC 20mg

## Pasta Tips

Pasta needs lots of water to roll around in—this dilutes the starch the pasta releases. Too little water makes the pasta starchy or gummy. Four quarts for 8 ounces of pasta is ample. Bring the water to a boil, add the pasta, and stir to separate the strands.

Pasta can be tricky to serve because it has a tendency to slip and slide. The best serving utensil, especially for longer pasta, is a metal or wooden pasta fork or tongs. For short pasta, a large spoon works fine.

While layering **lasagna** isn't an exact science, it helps to follow a few rules. Always spread a little sauce on the bottom of your lasagna dish so the pasta doesn't stick. And always end with sauce on top; if the noodles are exposed at the top while lasagna bakes, they'll turn dry and hard.

In classic **carbonara**, the heat of the pasta actually cooks the eggs. But for safety's sake, we've cooked them on top of the stove. Once the egg mixture is added to the pasta and cooked over low heat, it's important to stir constantly. This ensures that the eggs get creamy instead of scrambled.

### A Note on Salting

We agree with most cooks that adding salt to the cooking water helps bring out the flavor of the pasta. While we didn't find that salted water changed the pasta's consistency (as some folks assert), it certainly makes the pasta taste better on its own.

But when tossing the pasta with flavorful sauces, as we've done in these recipes, salting the water is far less critical. So to avoid adding unnecessary sodium, we chose not to salt the water in these recipes, and our nutritional analyses reflect that. If you're not watching your sodium intake, you can salt as you prefer.

## Grilled Summer Vegetable Lasagna

You can substitute 3 (8-ounce) cans of tomato puree for the homemade tomato puree. Using a grill pan makes it easy to prepare the vegetables indoors. To make the recipe ahead, assemble this lasagna and refrigerate it up to eight hours. Let stand at room temperature for 30 minutes; then bake as directed.

**GRILLED VEGETABLES:**
- 3 large red or yellow bell peppers, seeded and cut lengthwise into quarters
- Cooking spray
- 3 medium yellow squash, cut lengthwise into ¼-inch-thick slices
- 1 large red onion, cut into ¼-inch-thick slices

**TOMATO PUREE:**
- 4 pounds tomatoes, cut lengthwise into quarters
- ⅓ cup vodka
- 1½ teaspoons salt

**WHITE SAUCE:**
- 2½ tablespoons all-purpose flour
- ¼ teaspoon salt
- ¼ teaspoon ground nutmeg
- 2 cups fat-free milk

**REMAINING INGREDIENTS:**
- 4 quarts water
- 12 uncooked lasagna noodles
- 1 cup chopped fresh basil
- ¾ teaspoon freshly ground black pepper
- 1 cup (4 ounces) finely shredded Gruyère cheese
- ½ cup (2 ounces) grated fresh Parmesan cheese

**1.** Prepare grill.
**2.** To prepare grilled vegetables, place bell peppers, skin sides down, on a grill rack coated with cooking spray; cook 15 minutes or until blackened. Place in a zip-top plastic bag; seal. Let stand 15 minutes. Peel and cut into strips.
**3.** Place squash and onion on grill; cook 5 minutes on each side or until tender.
**4.** To prepare tomato puree, place tomatoes

in a large Dutch oven. Cover and cook over medium heat 30 minutes or until tender, stirring occasionally. Place tomatoes in a blender or food processor; process until smooth. Return to pan. Stir in vodka; bring to a boil. Reduce heat, and simmer 10 minutes, stirring occasionally. Stir in 1½ teaspoons salt. (You will have 5 cups puree.)

**5.** To prepare white sauce, combine flour, ¼ teaspoon salt, and nutmeg in a medium saucepan, and gradually add milk, stirring with a whisk. Cook over medium-high heat until thick (about 7 minutes), stirring constantly. Set aside.

**6.** Bring water to a boil in a large stockpot. Add noodles; return to a boil. Cook, uncovered, 10 minutes or until noodles are done, stirring occasionally. Drain.

**7.** Preheat oven to 375°.

**8.** Spread ⅓ cup white sauce in a 13 x 9-inch baking dish coated with cooking spray. Arrange 3 noodles over white sauce; top with one-third of grilled vegetables, ⅓ cup basil, ⅓ cup white sauce, and ½ cup tomato puree. Sprinkle with ¼ teaspoon black pepper, ¼ cup Gruyère, and 2 tablespoons Parmesan. Repeat layers twice, ending with noodles. Spread remaining white sauce, 1½ cups tomato puree, remaining Gruyère, and remaining Parmesan over noodles. Bake at 375° for 45 minutes or until bubbly and top is browned. Remove from oven; let stand 15 minutes. Yield: 8 servings (serving size: 1 piece).

**NOTE:** You will have 2 cups of leftover tomato puree. Cover and refrigerate 1 week, or freeze up to 3 months.

CALORIES 347 (22% from fat); FAT 8.4g (sat 4.3g, mono 2.3g, poly 1g); PROTEIN 17.4g; CARB 51.8g; FIBER 4.7g; CHOL 22mg; IRON 3.3mg; SODIUM 567mg; CALC 358mg

## Ziti with Tuscan Porcini Mushroom Sauce

Intensely flavored dried porcini, along with fresh button mushrooms, give this dish a real Tuscan touch. Any dried mushroom will work well in this recipe, but authentic Italian porcini are worth the extra cost.

- ¾ cup fat-free, less-sodium chicken broth
- ¼ cup chopped dried porcini mushrooms (about ¼ ounce)
- 1 tablespoon olive oil
- 3 cups sliced button mushrooms (8 ounces)
- 1 teaspoon minced fresh or ¼ teaspoon dried rosemary
- ⅛ teaspoon salt
- 2 garlic cloves, minced
- 4 quarts water
- 3 cups uncooked ziti (about 8 ounces short tube-shaped pasta) or other short pasta
- ¼ cup (1 ounce) grated fresh Parmesan cheese
- 1 tablespoon finely chopped parsley
- ¼ teaspoon black pepper

**1.** Combine broth and porcini mushrooms in a small microwave-safe bowl. Cover with wax paper; microwave at HIGH 2 minutes. Let stand 10 minutes.

**2.** Heat olive oil in a large nonstick skillet over medium-high heat. Add button mushrooms, rosemary, salt, and garlic; sauté 3 minutes. Add broth and porcini mushrooms to pan; remove from heat.

**3.** Bring water to a boil in a large stockpot. Add ziti; return to a boil. Cook, uncovered, 10 minutes or until al dente, stirring occasionally. Drain. Stir ziti into mushroom mixture; cook 3 minutes or until thoroughly heated. Stir in cheese, parsley, and pepper. Yield: 4 servings (serving size: 1½ cups).

CALORIES 295 (20% from fat); FAT 6.4g (sat 1.8g, mono 3.1g, poly 0.8g); PROTEIN 11.8g; CARB 47.6g; FIBER 2.5g; CHOL 5mg; IRON 3.2mg; SODIUM 284mg; CALC 105mg

## Putting Pasta in the Pot

Cooking the pasta itself is fairly simple, and most packages give directions. But make sure to follow these procedures:

1. Use a large pot as full of water as possible. For 8 ounces of dried pasta, you'll want to fill a 4-quart pot with water.
2. Cover pot, and bring water to a full rolling boil over high heat before adding pasta.
3. Add pasta, and stir with a pasta fork or large tongs to separate strands.
4. Start timing cooking when water returns to a boil. If you use fresh pasta, remember that it cooks more quickly than dried.
5. Always cook pasta uncovered over high heat.
6. Start testing for doneness a few minutes before indicated cooking time. Pasta that offers resistance to the bite but has no trace of brittleness is al dente. This is how you want it. If an undercooked piece of pasta is cut in half, a white dot or line is clearly visible in the center. Al dente pasta has only a speck of white remaining, meaning the pasta has absorbed just enough water to hydrate it.
7. Set a large colander in the sink so water drains quickly. Do not rinse.
8. Return pasta to the warm cooking pot or add to the skillet with sauce, and toss immediately with large tongs or a pasta fork.

## Fettuccine with Ragù Sauce

Ragù, or meat sauce, is as varied as the regions in Italy. This version is loosely based on a traditional ragù Bolognese. With thawed ragù from the freezer and refrigerated fresh fettuccine, this homemade dish comes together in less than 15 minutes. You can also use fresh spinach fettuccine or dried fettuccine.

    4   quarts water
    1   (9-ounce) package fresh fettuccine, uncooked
    2   teaspoons butter or stick margarine
    2   cups hot Ragù Sauce
    2   teaspoons grated fresh Parmesan cheese

**1.** Bring water to a boil in a large stockpot. Add fettuccine, stirring to separate noodles; return to a boil. Cook, uncovered, 3 minutes or until done, stirring occasionally. Drain and return pasta to pan; stir in butter. Add 2 cups Ragù Sauce; cook 1 minute or until thoroughly heated. Sprinkle with cheese. Yield: 4 servings (serving size: 1¼ cups pasta and ½ teaspoon cheese).

(Totals include Ragù Sauce) CALORIES 343 (30% from fat); FAT 11.4g (sat 4.7g, mono 4.6g, poly 1.1g); PROTEIN 17.2g; CARB 42.9g; FIBER 1.7g; CHOL 82mg; IRON 3.6mg; SODIUM 384mg; CALC 59mg

RAGÙ SAUCE:
    1    teaspoon olive oil
    1½   cups finely chopped onion
    1    cup finely chopped celery
    1    cup finely chopped carrot
    3½   cups finely chopped portobello mushrooms
    1    pound ground round
    ¾    cup dry white wine (such as Orvieto or Pinot Grigio)
    1    cup whole milk
    2    bay leaves
    1    (16-ounce) can fat-free, less-sodium chicken broth
    1    (10¾-ounce) can tomato puree
    ½    teaspoon salt
    ½    teaspoon black pepper

**1.** Heat olive oil in a large nonstick saucepan over medium-high heat. Add onion, celery, and carrot; cover and cook 7 minutes. Reduce heat to medium. Add mushrooms; cover and cook 5 minutes. Remove mushroom mixture with a slotted spoon; set aside.

**2.** Add beef to pan; cook over medium-high heat until browned, stirring to crumble. Add wine; bring to a boil, and cook 5 minutes. Add mushroom mixture, milk, bay leaves, broth, and puree. Heat mixture to 180° or until tiny bubbles form around edge of pan, stirring frequently (do not boil). Reduce heat to medium-low, and simmer 2 hours. Add salt and pepper; discard bay leaves. Yield: 6 cups (serving size: ½ cup).

**NOTE:** Cool remaining Ragù Sauce to room temperature. Cover and refrigerate 1 week, or freeze up to 3 months.

CALORIES 137 (50% from fat); FAT 7.7g (sat 3.1g, mono 3.3g, poly 0.4g); PROTEIN 9.5g; CARB 7.7g; FIBER 1.7g; CHOL 29mg; IRON 1.4mg; SODIUM 328mg; CALC 44mg

## Spicy Seafood Fusilli

Fusilli is one of the few pastas that comes both long and short. Either will work in this dish, but we prefer the long. You can use canned clams in place of fresh, if you prefer. Just make sure to drain them first.

    4    quarts water
    8    ounces uncooked long fusilli or 3 cups uncooked short fusilli (twisted spaghetti)
    2    tablespoons olive oil
    ⅓    cup minced shallots
    ½    teaspoon fennel seeds, crushed
    Dash of powdered saffron (optional)
    ⅛    teaspoon salt
    1    (14.5-ounce) can diced tomatoes, undrained
    16   littleneck clams, scrubbed
    ¾    pound large shrimp, peeled and deveined
    2    teaspoons grated lemon rind
    1    teaspoon minced seeded jalapeño pepper

**1.** Bring water to a boil in a large stockpot. Add fusilli; return to a boil. Cook, uncovered, 10 minutes or until fusilli is al dente, stirring occasionally. Drain.

**2.** Heat olive oil in a large skillet over medium-low heat. Add shallots, fennel seeds, and saffron (if desired). Cover and cook 4 minutes or until shallots are tender, stirring occasionally. Stir in salt and tomatoes. Increase heat to medium; cover and cook 5 minutes. Add clams. Increase heat to high; cover and cook 6 minutes or until clams open. Add shrimp, rind, and jalapeño. Stir gently. Cover and cook 3 minutes or until shrimp are done. Discard any unopened clamshells. Stir in fusilli. Yield: 4 servings (serving size: 2 cups).

CALORIES 396 (21% from fat); FAT 9.4g (sat 1.3g, mono 5.3g, poly 1.6g); PROTEIN 26.2g; CARB 50.8g; FIBER 2.2g; CHOL 109mg; IRON 9.6mg; SODIUM 358mg; CALC 96mg

## Choosing Your Pasta

We think there's actually very little practical cooking difference among the brands of pasta available at the supermarket. Once they're incorporated into a recipe, they all taste about the same, so we don't recommend paying more for a fancy name, domestic or imported. In fact, some independent studies have shown that many people find American-made pasta just as good as Italian.

**What about dried versus fresh?** It's pretty much up to you. In our recipes, we use mostly dried, which is basically a mixture of semolina flour—ground from durum wheat—and water. In commercial factories, the mix is made into a paste that is turned into different shapes by passing through dies, or large metal discs filled with holes. The pasta is then dried and packaged.

Fresh pasta, which can be substituted in any of the recipes, is perishable, so it's generally pricier than dried. It also takes almost no time to cook—two to three minutes on average. In Italy, fresh pasta is traditionally made from soft wheat flour and eggs (so it has more cholesterol than dried). But some American fresh pasta producers use semolina flour to make a refrigerated fresh pasta that's sturdier than the Italian kind.

# Land of Lentils

The whole world loves the tasty little legume grown right here in America. It's time we got in on our own act.

On gently rolling hills within a 5,000-square-mile area of eastern Washington and northern Idaho, farmers will spend the day harvesting lentils. Much of their bounty, which totals more than 100 million pounds of lentils each year, winds up in countries such as Ethiopia, Haiti, and Japan. In those places, as well as in much of Europe, and even more so in India and parts of the Middle East, lentils rank as anything from favorites to staples. While the United States ranks sixth in worldwide production, it consumes less than one-quarter of its crop. About the only place lentils aren't on the dinner table week in and week out is right here where they come from.

## Curried Lentil-Spinach Salad with Shrimp

You can use brown or red lentils in this salad, but the brown hold their shape better. For an interesting variation, try substituting seared scallops and fresh cilantro for the shrimp and mint.

    3   cups water
    ¾   cup dried brown or red lentils
    ½   teaspoon salt, divided
    ¼   cup chopped fresh mint
    ¼   cup fresh lemon juice (about 2
        lemons)
    2   tablespoons honey
    2   tablespoons Dijon mustard
    2   tablespoons extra-virgin olive oil
    1½  teaspoons curry powder
    8   cups torn spinach
    2   cups sliced mushrooms
    1   red bell pepper, cut into ¼-inch
        strips
    ½   pound medium shrimp, cooked
        and peeled

**1.** Combine water, red lentils, and ¼ teaspoon salt in a medium saucepan. Bring to a boil; cover, reduce heat to medium-low, and simmer 20 minutes. Drain and set aside.
**2.** Combine ¼ teaspoon salt, mint, and next 5 ingredients. Combine ¼ cup mint dressing, spinach, mushrooms, and pepper; toss well to coat. Combine lentils and ¼ cup mint dressing; toss well.

**3.** Arrange 2 cups spinach mixture on each of 4 plates; top each serving with ½ cup lentil mixture. Divide shrimp evenly among salads; drizzle with remaining dressing. Yield: 4 servings.

CALORIES 312 (26% from fat); FAT 9.1g (sat 1.2g, mono 5.6g, poly 1.4g); PROTEIN 23g; CARB 38.5g; FIBER 9.7g; CHOL 65mg; IRON 8.3mg; SODIUM 573mg; CALC 161mg

## Barbecue Baked Lentils

    3   cups water
    2   cups dried brown lentils
    ½   teaspoon salt, divided
    1   cup diced onion
    ⅔   cup ketchup
    ⅓   cup maple syrup
    ¼   cup prepared mustard
    ½   teaspoon ground ginger
    ½   teaspoon vanilla extract
    ¼   teaspoon ground allspice
    ¼   teaspoon black pepper

**1.** Preheat oven to 350°.
**2.** Combine water, lentils, and ¼ teaspoon salt in a large saucepan. Bring to a boil; cover, reduce heat to medium-low, and simmer 20 minutes. Drain lentils in a colander over a bowl, reserving 1 cup cooking liquid.
**3.** Combine lentils and diced onion in an 11 x 7-inch baking dish. Combine ¼ teaspoon salt, reserved cooking liquid, ketchup, and remaining 6 ingredients.

Pour ketchup mixture over lentil mixture, stirring to combine. Bake at 350° for 1 hour. Yield: 8 servings (serving size: ¾ cup).

CALORIES 233 (4% from fat); FAT 1g (sat 0.1g, mono 0.4g, poly 0.3g); PROTEIN 14.4g; CARB 44.2g; FIBER 6.2g; CHOL 0mg; IRON 4.9mg; SODIUM 488mg; CALC 49mg

## Lentil-and-Sausage-Stuffed Peppers

    3   red bell peppers
    3   yellow bell peppers
    3   cups water, divided
    ½   cup dried brown lentils
    ¼   teaspoon salt
    ½   cup uncooked long-grain rice
    1   cup diced onion
    8   ounces basil, pine nut, and chicken
        sausage, chopped (such as
        Gerhard's)
    1   cup (4 ounces) shredded part-skim
        mozzarella cheese
    ¼   cup dried currants or raisins
    ¼   cup chopped fresh parsley
    2   tablespoons balsamic vinegar
    1   tablespoon capers
    2   tablespoons chopped fresh basil
    ¼   teaspoon black pepper
    ¼   cup (1 ounce) grated fresh
        Parmesan cheese

**1.** Cut bell peppers in half, keeping stems intact. Discard seeds and membranes. Cook bell peppers in boiling water 5 minutes; drain and set aside.
**2.** Combine 2 cups water, lentils, and salt in a saucepan. Bring to a boil; cover, reduce heat to medium-low, and simmer 20 minutes. Drain and set aside.
**3.** Bring 1 cup water to a boil in a medium saucepan; add rice and onion. Cover, reduce heat, and simmer 20 minutes or until liquid is absorbed. Remove from heat. Set aside. Place sausage in a small nonstick skillet over medium-high heat; sauté until browned.
**4.** Preheat oven to 350°.
**5.** Combine lentils, rice mixture, sausage, mozzarella, and next 6 ingredients in a large bowl. Divide lentil mixture evenly among bell peppers; sprinkle with
*Continued*

Parmesan. Place stuffed peppers in an 11 x 7-inch baking dish; cover and bake at 350° for 15 minutes. Uncover and bake an additional 15 minutes. Yield: 6 servings (serving size: 2 pepper halves).

CALORIES 292 (30% from fat); FAT 9.7g (sat 4.2g, mono 2.4g, poly 2.7g); PROTEIN 19.2g; CARB 33.7g; FIBER 4.3g; CHOL 48mg; IRON 4mg; SODIUM 541mg; CALC 211mg

## Red-Lentil Burgers with Aïoli

These burgers are very soft before cooking, so let them cook on the first side for at least 5 minutes before flipping. Aïoli is a strong garlic mayonnaise that hails from southern France.

AÏOLI:
¼ cup light mayonnaise
½ teaspoon fresh lemon juice
1 garlic clove, minced

BURGERS:
2 cups water
¾ cup dried red lentils
¾ teaspoon salt, divided
Cooking spray
1 cup diced onion
½ cup finely diced carrot
3 garlic cloves, chopped
2 cups chopped mushrooms
1 teaspoon dried marjoram
¼ teaspoon black pepper
3 tablespoons Madeira (optional)
⅓ cup dry breadcrumbs
1 tablespoon fresh lemon juice
2 large egg whites
1 tablespoon vegetable oil

REMAINING INGREDIENTS:
6 (1½-ounce) hamburger buns
Arugula or curly lettuce leaves
6 (¼-inch-thick) slices tomato
6 (⅛-inch-thick) slices onion

**1.** To prepare aïoli, combine first 3 ingredients; cover and refrigerate.
**2.** To prepare burgers, combine water, lentils, and ¼ teaspoon salt in a medium saucepan; bring to a boil. Cover, reduce heat to medium-low, and simmer 20 minutes. Drain; set aside.

**3.** Heat a large nonstick skillet coated with cooking spray over medium-high heat. Add onion, carrot, and 3 garlic cloves; sauté 3 minutes. Add ½ teaspoon salt, mushrooms, marjoram, and pepper; cook 3 minutes, stirring occasionally. Add wine, if desired; cook 1 minute or until liquid almost evaporates. Place onion mixture in a large bowl; let stand 5 minutes. Stir in lentils, breadcrumbs, 1 tablespoon lemon juice, and egg whites. Cover and chill 30 minutes (to help firm up mixture).
**4.** Divide lentil mixture into 6 equal portions, shaping each portion into a ½-inch-thick patty. Heat vegetable oil in a nonstick skillet over medium heat. Add lentil patties, and cook 5 minutes on each side.
**5.** Line bottom half of each hamburger bun with an arugula or lettuce leaf, and top each bun half with a burger, 2 teaspoons aïoli, 1 tomato slice, 1 onion slice, and top half of bun. Yield: 6 servings.

CALORIES 324 (23% from fat); FAT 8.1g (sat 1.6g, mono 2g, poly 3.9g); PROTEIN 13.9g; CARB 48.3g; FIBER 5.8g; CHOL 3mg; IRON 4.6mg; SODIUM 688mg; CALC 109mg

## Roasted Red Potato-and-Lentil Salad with Dijon Dressing

2 pounds medium red potatoes, cut into wedges
3 tablespoons olive oil, divided
¾ teaspoon salt, divided
2 cups water
½ cup dried brown lentils
⅓ cup plain fat-free yogurt
3 tablespoons Dijon mustard
3 tablespoons cider vinegar
2 teaspoons sugar
1 cup chopped red bell pepper
½ cup chopped green onions
Cracked black pepper (optional)

**1.** Preheat oven to 425°.
**2.** Combine potatoes, 1 tablespoon oil, and ¼ teaspoon salt in a 13 x 9-inch baking dish; toss well. Bake at 425° for 35 minutes or until tender, stirring occasionally.

**3.** While potatoes are cooking, combine ¼ teaspoon salt, water, and lentils in a medium saucepan. Bring to a boil; cover, reduce heat to medium-low, and simmer 20 minutes. Drain well, and set aside.
**4.** Combine 2 tablespoons oil, ¼ teaspoon salt, yogurt, mustard, vinegar, and sugar in a small bowl, stirring with a whisk. Combine potatoes, lentils, bell pepper, and onions in a large bowl. Drizzle with dressing, and toss gently to combine. Sprinkle with black pepper, if desired. Yield: 9 servings (serving size: ⅔ cup).

CALORIES 185 (25% from fat); FAT 5.1g (sat 0.7g, mono 3.6g, poly 0.6g); PROTEIN 5.6g; CARB 29.9g; FIBER 3.1g; CHOL 0mg; IRON 1.6mg; SODIUM 289mg; CALC 33mg

## Spanish Lentil Soup

Onions, bell peppers, garlic, and sherry vinegar lend this soup a Spanish flair.

1 tablespoon olive oil
1 cup diced onion
4 garlic cloves, minced
¾ cup chopped red bell pepper
¾ cup chopped green bell pepper
2 tablespoons sherry vinegar or red wine vinegar
1½ teaspoons ground cumin
¼ teaspoon crushed red pepper
1½ cups chopped plum tomato (about ¾ pound)
1 teaspoon salt
6 cups water
2 cups dried red lentils
1 teaspoon Hungarian sweet paprika

**1.** Heat olive oil in a large saucepan over medium-high heat. Add onion and garlic, and sauté 2 minutes. Add bell peppers, vinegar, cumin, and crushed red pepper, and sauté 3 minutes. Add chopped tomato and salt, and cook 2 minutes. Add water, lentils, and paprika; bring to a boil. Partially cover, reduce heat, and simmer 25 minutes or until lentils are tender. Yield: 9 servings (serving size: 1 cup).

CALORIES 185 (11% from fat); FAT 2.3g (sat 0.3g, mono 1.3g, poly 0.5g); PROTEIN 12.9g; CARB 29.6g; FIBER 6.1g; CHOL 0mg; IRON 4.7mg; SODIUM 289mg; CALC 35mg

## Seared Salmon and Warm Lentils

**LENTILS:**

3 cups water
¾ cup dried brown lentils
½ teaspoon salt, divided
½ teaspoon olive oil
1 cup chopped onion
1 cup chopped seeded tomato
2½ tablespoons red wine vinegar
2 tablespoons chopped fresh basil
¼ teaspoon black pepper
2 garlic cloves, minced

**SALMON:**

2 tablespoons all-purpose flour
¼ teaspoon salt
¼ teaspoon black pepper
¼ teaspoon dried thyme
4 (6-ounce) salmon fillets (about 2 inches thick), skin removed
1 teaspoon olive oil

**1.** To prepare lentils, combine water, lentils, and ¼ teaspoon salt in a medium saucepan. Bring to a boil; cover, reduce heat to medium-low, and simmer 20 minutes. Drain; set aside.

**2.** Heat ½ teaspoon oil in a large non-stick skillet over medium-high heat. Add onion; sauté 5 minutes or until lightly browned. Add lentils, ¼ teaspoon salt, tomato, vinegar, basil, ¼ teaspoon pepper, and garlic; toss gently.

**3.** To prepare salmon, combine flour, ¼ teaspoon salt, ¼ teaspoon pepper, and thyme. Sprinkle fillets with flour mixture. Heat 1 teaspoon oil in pan over medium-high heat. Add fillets, and sauté 6 minutes on each side or until fish flakes easily when tested with a fork.

**4.** Divide lentils evenly among 4 plates, and top each serving with a salmon fillet. Yield: 4 servings (servings size: ¾ cup lentils and 1 salmon fillet).

CALORIES 457 (32% from fat); FAT 16.3g (sat 2.8g, mono 8.1g, poly 3.5g); PROTEIN 46.4g; CARB 30.4g; FIBER 5.6g; CHOL 111mg; IRON 4.6mg; SODIUM 533mg; CALC 47mg

---

### Take Your Pick

Most grocery stores stock brown lentils. But there are many other kinds. Try any of these.

**U.S. Regular or Brewer (brown lentils):** This is the most common variety sold at American supermarkets. They're a bit larger than the Pardina and Red Chief.

**Red Chief:** These colorful lentils are split in two, making them smaller and also quicker to cook. Because they're more likely than other types to turn mushy, they're best mixed in burgers, meat loaves, or soups.

**Pardina:** This smallest of lentils is favored because it holds its shape during cooking and has an earthy, nutty flavor. Terrific for pilafs and salads.

**De Puy:** Sometimes called French green lentils, this tasty variety is mostly grown in Canada.

You can find a variety of lentils in specialty stores or at these Web sites: www.mountoosoorganics.com, www.legumesplus.com, or www.healthyflavors.com. For more sources, call the USA Dry Pea & Lentil Council at 208-882-3023, or visit its Web site (www.pea-lentil.com).

**Caution:** Because lentils can overcook quickly, especially the smaller ones, you should always start checking for doneness before the specified time.

---

# Greek-Style Scampi

*To call Greek-Style Scampi one of our favorite recipes, and therefore worthy of a place in* Cooking Light's *list of all-time best recipes, is an understatement.*

This marks the third appearance of the must-have-more dish in our magazine. It debuted in our April 1996 issue, and then starred in our 10-year anniversary issue (April 1997). Our staff can't resist these zingy Mediterranean flavors.

### Greek-Style Scampi

(pictured on page 260)

1 teaspoon olive oil
5 garlic cloves, minced
½ cup chopped fresh parsley, divided
2 (28-ounce) cans whole tomatoes, drained and coarsely chopped
1¼ pounds large shrimp, peeled and deveined
1 cup (4 ounces) crumbled feta cheese
2 tablespoons fresh lemon juice
¼ teaspoon freshly ground black pepper
4 cups hot cooked spaghetti (about 8 ounces uncooked pasta)

**1.** Preheat oven to 400°.

**2.** Heat oil in a large Dutch oven over medium heat. Add garlic; sauté 30 seconds. Add ¼ cup parsley and tomatoes. Reduce heat, and simmer 10 minutes. Add shrimp; cook 5 minutes. Pour mixture into a 13 x 9-inch baking dish; sprinkle with cheese. Bake at 400° for 10 minutes. Sprinkle with ¼ cup parsley, lemon juice, and pepper; serve over pasta. Yield: 6 servings (serving size: 1 cup scampi and ¾ cup pasta).

CALORIES 321 (20% from fat); FAT 7.3g (sat 3.4g, mono 1.8g, poly 1.2g); PROTEIN 26.5g; CARB 37.1g; FIBER 3g; CHOL 147mg; IRON 4.9mg; SODIUM 630mg; CALC 202mg

# North of South America

## Latin cooking's upbeat flavors are making new waves in kitchens and on grills across the United States.

From New York City to Miami to Los Angeles, with stop-offs in almost any city with a booming Hispanic population, grocery stores and restaurants offer the lively Latin dishes and ingredients of the fastest-growing demographic group in the United States. Dubbed Nuevo Latino, this new cuisine can be found around kitchens and backyard grills in just about any neighborhood within the sound of a salsa beat.

### Grilled Cornish Hens with Honey Mustard-Cilantro Glaze

3 (1¼-pound) Cornish hens
3 tablespoons mustard seeds
2 tablespoons celery seeds
2 cups honey
1 cup cilantro leaves
3 tablespoons dry mustard
3 tablespoons cracked black pepper
3 tablespoons white vinegar
2 tablespoons olive oil
2 teaspoons salt
6 garlic cloves, chopped (about ¼ cup)
Cooking spray

**1.** Remove and discard giblets and necks from hens. Rinse hens with cold water; pat dry. Remove skin; trim excess fat. Split hens in half lengthwise.
**2.** Combine mustard seeds and celery seeds in a small skillet; cook over medium heat 1 minute or until toasted. Place seeds in a blender, and process until ground. Add honey and next 7 ingredients; process mixture until well-blended. Place hens and 1 cup honey mixture in a shallow dish; cover and marinate in refrigerator 8 hours, reserving remaining honey mixture.
**3.** Prepare grill.
**4.** Remove hens from dish; discard marinade. Place hens on grill rack coated with cooking spray; grill 25 minutes or until juices run clear, turning and basting frequently with reserved honey mixture. Yield: 6 servings (serving size: 1 hen half).

CALORIES 403 (24% from fat); FAT 10.9g (sat 2.3g, mono 4.9g, poly 2g); PROTEIN 28.9g; CARB 50.2g; FIBER 1g; CHOL 83mg; IRON 3mg; SODIUM 479mg; CALC 71mg

### Grilled Sea Scallops with Pine Nut-Raisin Compote

Dry sherry can replace the cream sherry, but the dish won't be as sweet. Make sure that your grill rack is clean and well-coated with cooking spray, because scallops are delicate and can stick and tear very easily. For a subtle rosemary flavor, try threading the scallops on large, sturdy rosemary sprigs.

2¼ pounds sea scallops
¼ cup fresh lemon juice
1½ teaspoons olive oil
⅛ teaspoon salt
⅛ teaspoon black pepper
¼ cup pine nuts
1½ cups cream sherry
1 cup raisins
Cooking spray

**1.** Combine first 5 ingredients in a large shallow dish; cover and marinate in refrigerator 20 minutes.
**2.** Cook pine nuts in a large skillet over medium-high heat 1 minute or until lightly browned, stirring frequently. Remove pine nuts from pan. Add sherry and raisins to pan. Bring to a boil; cook 8 minutes or until raisins are plump and sherry is slightly syrupy. Remove from heat; stir in pine nuts.
**3.** Prepare grill.
**4.** Remove scallops from dish, and discard marinade. Thread scallops onto 6 (12-inch) skewers. Place skewers on grill rack coated with cooking spray. Grill 2 minutes on each side or until done. Serve with raisin compote. Yield: 6 servings (serving size: 1 kebab and about 2 tablespoons raisin compote).

CALORIES 291 (26% from fat); FAT 8.3g (sat 1.2g, mono 3.1g, poly 3g); PROTEIN 30.5g; CARB 26.2g; FIBER 1.4g; CHOL 56mg; IRON 1.5mg; SODIUM 313mg; CALC 58mg

### Plantains with Balsamic-Basil Glaze

When shopping for plantains for this side dish, be sure to pick ripe ones with black skin and just a touch of firmness. These go very well with the Churrasco with Chimichurri Sauce (recipe on page 269) or the Grilled Cornish Hens with Honey Mustard-Cilantro Glaze (recipe at left). A grill basket makes grilling the plantains a breeze.

1 cup balsamic vinegar
2 tablespoons butter or stick margarine, melted
2 tablespoons honey
2 tablespoons chopped fresh basil
½ teaspoon salt
4 soft black plantains, peeled (about 2 pounds)
Cooking spray

**1.** Prepare grill.
**2.** Place vinegar in a small saucepan. Bring to a boil; cook until reduced to ¼ cup (about 7 minutes). Combine vinegar, butter, honey, basil, and salt in a small bowl. Place plantains on grill rack coated with cooking spray; grill 10 minutes or until tender, turning and basting frequently with vinegar mixture. Cut plantains in half diagonally. Yield: 8 servings (serving size: ½ plantain).

CALORIES 203 (15% from fat); FAT 3.5g (sat 2g, mono 0.9g, poly 0.3g); PROTEIN 1.7g; CARB 46.7g; FIBER 0.7g; CHOL 8mg; IRON 1.1mg; SODIUM 182mg; CALC 7mg

## Churrasco with Chimichurri Sauce

(pictured on page 2)

The sauce alone is high in fat, but ours is still much lower than traditional versions, which contain more than 1 cup of oil.

- 1 (1½-pound) boned sirloin steak
- 1½ cups cilantro sprigs
- 1 cup white vinegar
- ¾ cup chopped onion
- 2 teaspoons ground cumin
- 2 teaspoons dried oregano
- 2 teaspoons dried thyme
- 2 teaspoons black pepper
- 1 teaspoon salt
- 6 garlic cloves, chopped (about ¼ cup)
- 3 bay leaves
- Cooking spray
- Chimichurri Sauce

**1.** Trim fat from steak; set steak aside. Combine cilantro and next 9 ingredients in a large zip-top plastic bag. Add steak to bag; seal. Marinate in refrigerator 3 hours, turning occasionally. Remove steak from bag; discard marinade.
**2.** Prepare grill.
**3.** Place steak on grill rack coated with cooking spray; grill steak 8 minutes on each side or until desired degree of doneness. Let stand 3 minutes. Cut steak diagonally across grain into thin slices. Serve with Chimichurri Sauce. Yield: 6 servings (serving size: 3 ounces steak and about 2½ tablespoons sauce).

(Totals include Chimichurri Sauce) CALORIES 239 (43% from fat); FAT 11.5g (sat 3.3g, mono 6.2g, poly 0.8g); PROTEIN 26.6g; CARB 7.5g; FIBER 1.7g; CHOL 76mg; IRON 5.4mg; SODIUM 459mg; CALC 79mg

### CHIMICHURRI SAUCE:

- ¼ cup white vinegar
- 2 tablespoons extra-virgin olive oil
- ½ teaspoon salt
- 6 garlic cloves
- 3 bay leaves
- 2 jalapeño peppers, stems removed
- 1 cup minced fresh parsley
- ¼ cup minced fresh oregano

**1.** Place first 6 ingredients in a blender; process until smooth. Add parsley and oregano, and stir well. Yield: 1 cup (serving size: about 2½ tablespoons).

CALORIES 55 (77% from fat); FAT 4.7g (sat 0.7g, mono 3.4g, poly 0.5g); PROTEIN 0.7g; CARB 3.5g; FIBER 0.8g; CHOL 0mg; IRON 1.4mg; SODIUM 202mg; CALC 40mg

---

## Latino Cooking Lexicon

You'll encounter new names as well as flavors when you journey into the culinary traditions from way south of the border.

**Adobo** (ah-DOH-boh): A spiced marinade.

**Chimichurri** (chee-mee-CHUR-ee): The perfect condiment for beefy churrasco. Made with parsley, garlic, and olive oil, it's like a pesto reinvented in Argentina.

**Chipotle** (chih-POHT-lay): Smoked jalapeño, both dried or canned in adobo sauce.

**Churrasco** (choor-AS-koh): In Argentina (and now Brazil), marinated and grilled skirt steak. In Nicaragua, the same treatment is given to filet mignon. We call for sirloin.

**Empanada** (em-pah-NAH-dah): Spanish-inspired pastry turnover, stuffed with spiced meat or seafood.

**Mojo** (MO-ho): This spicy Caribbean sauce is a mixture of garlic, citrus juice, oil, and fresh herbs.

**Picadillo** (pee-kah-DEE-yoh): Spicy ground beef, usually cooked with olives and capers, served with rice, black beans, and fried plantains.

**Poblano** (poh-BLAH-noh): Fresh green chile used in Mexico and Central America. When dried, it's called *ancho.*

**Sofrito** (soh-FREE-toh): The foundation of many stews and meat dishes, a sauté of onion, garlic, bell pepper, tomato, herbs, and spices.

**Tamal** (tah-MAHL): As in "tamale," a cornmeal-based appetizer or snack, usually steamed in a corn husk.

**Yuca** (YUHK-uh): African root vegetable. Also known as *cassava* and *manioc.* Different from yucca, a plant belonging to the agave family, which gives the world tequila.

---

## Peruvian Sarsa Salad

This chopped salad from Peru is robust and full of texture. While there are many versions, nearly all include radishes, mint, onions, and cheese.

- 1 cup thinly sliced red onion
- ½ cup sliced radishes
- ½ cup frozen lima beans, thawed
- ½ cup canned white hominy, drained
- ¼ cup (1 ounce) crumbled feta cheese
- ¼ cup chopped bottled roasted red bell peppers
- 2 tablespoons chopped fresh mint
- 2 tablespoons chopped fresh cilantro
- 3 tablespoons fresh lemon juice
- 1 tablespoon olive oil
- ¼ teaspoon salt
- ¼ teaspoon freshly ground black pepper
- 3 garlic cloves, minced

**1.** Combine first 8 ingredients in a large bowl. Combine lemon juice and remaining 4 ingredients; stir with a whisk. Drizzle dressing over salad, and toss gently to combine. Yield: 6 servings (serving size: ½ cup).

CALORIES 77 (42% from fat); FAT 3.6g (sat 1.1g, mono 1.9g, poly 0.3g); PROTEIN 2.6g; CARB 9.5g; FIBER 1.3g; CHOL 4mg; IRON 0.8mg; SODIUM 198mg; CALC 44mg

---

## Grilled Sweet Potatoes with Orange-Chipotle Glaze

(pictured on page 259)

Sweet potatoes pair perfectly with grilled chicken and make a great home for bold and spicy glazes.

- 4 large sweet potatoes (about 2 pounds)
- 1 can chipotle chiles in adobo sauce
- 2 tablespoons butter or stick margarine, melted
- 1 tablespoon chopped fresh cilantro
- ½ teaspoon salt
- 1 (6-ounce) can thawed orange juice concentrate, undiluted
- Cooking spray

*Continued*

**1.** Prepare grill.

**2.** Cut potatoes in half lengthwise. Cook potato halves in boiling water 5 minutes or until crisp-tender; drain. Rinse with cold water; drain well. While potatoes are cooking, remove 3 tablespoons adobo sauce from canned chiles. Place remaining sauce and chiles in a zip-top plastic bag; freeze for another use. Combine 3 tablespoons adobo sauce, butter, cilantro, salt, and juice in a small bowl. Place potatoes on grill rack coated with cooking spray, and grill 4 minutes on each side or until potatoes are done, basting frequently with orange juice mixture. Yield: 8 servings (serving size: 1 potato half).

CALORIES 185 (17% from fat); FAT 3.5g (sat 1.9g, mono 1g, poly 0.4g); PROTEIN 2.4g; CARB 36.6g; FIBER 3.6g; CHOL 8mg; IRON 0.8mg; SODIUM 240mg; CALC 37mg

## Grilled Tuna with Rain Forest Glaze

Tuna is one of the best fish to choose for your grill. Here it works to unite the sweet-tart tropical fruit juice with the heat of the chiles. Any kind of hot pepper, such as jalapeño or serrano, will work in place of the habanero.

- 1 cup pineapple juice
- 1 cup cranberry juice cocktail
- 1 cup mango or apricot nectar
- 1 tablespoon sugar
- 2 tablespoons lime juice
- 1 tablespoon grated peeled fresh ginger
- 1 teaspoon chopped seeded habanero pepper
- ½ teaspoon salt
- ½ teaspoon grated lemon rind
- ½ teaspoon grated orange rind
- 1 tablespoon cornstarch
- 1 tablespoon water
- 1 cup thinly sliced green onions
- 6 (6-ounce) tuna steaks (about ¾ inch thick)
- Cooking spray

**1.** Combine first 10 ingredients in a large saucepan. Bring to a boil, and cook until reduced to 1½ cups (about 15 minutes); remove from heat. Combine cornstarch and water in a small bowl; stir well with a whisk. Add to pan. Bring to a boil; cook 1 minute, stirring constantly. Remove from heat; stir in onions.

**2.** Prepare grill.

**3.** Place tuna on grill rack coated with cooking spray; grill 3 minutes on each side or until medium-rare or desired degree of doneness, basting frequently with glaze. Yield: 6 servings.

CALORIES 328 (23% from fat); FAT 8.3g (sat 2.1g, mono 2.7g, poly 2.4g); PROTEIN 38.8g; CARB 23.4g; FIBER 0.7g; CHOL 63mg; IRON 2.3mg; SODIUM 266mg; CALC 25mg

## Barbecue Black Beans with Rum

Rum has always been a major part of the Caribbean's history and personality, but these beans are also good without it.

- 5 ounces chorizo
- 1 cup diced onion
- 4 garlic cloves, finely chopped
- 2 jalapeño peppers, seeded and chopped
- ½ cup ketchup
- ½ cup molasses
- ½ cup dark rum
- ¼ cup prepared mustard
- 2 tablespoons brown sugar
- 2 tablespoons Worcestershire sauce
- 1 tablespoon hot sauce
- ½ teaspoon ground ginger
- 3 (15-ounce) cans black beans, drained

**1.** Cook chorizo in a large saucepan over medium heat until browned, stirring to crumble; drain and set aside. Add onion, garlic, and jalapeños to pan; cook 5 minutes or until onion is tender. Stir in ketchup and next 7 ingredients; bring to a boil. Reduce heat, and simmer 5 minutes, stirring occasionally. Stir in chorizo and beans; simmer over low heat 1 hour, stirring occasionally. Yield: 9 servings (serving size: ½ cup).

CALORIES 241 (19% from fat); FAT 5.1g (sat 1.7g, mono 2.2g, poly 0.6g); PROTEIN 10.4g; CARB 41.3g; FIBER 4.2g; CHOL 9.2mg; IRON 3.1mg; SODIUM 562mg; CALC 83mg

## Pork Tenderloin with Costa Rican Coffee Glaze

(pictured on page 259)

Because coffee works as a savory underpinning for bright, tropical flavors, it has become a time-honored New World tradition in soups, stews, chilis, and sauces.

- 1 tablespoon olive oil
- ½ cup chopped onion
- 1 tablespoon grated peeled fresh ginger
- 2 garlic cloves, chopped
- 1 serrano chile, chopped
- 1½ tablespoons molasses
- ½ cup dark rum
- 4 cups hot brewed coffee
- 1 tablespoon ground coffee
- 1½ teaspoons ground cinnamon
- 1½ teaspoons unsweetened cocoa
- 1 tablespoon butter or stick margarine, softened
- ½ teaspoon salt
- 2 pounds pork tenderloin
- Cooking spray

**1.** Heat oil in a large skillet over medium-high heat. Add onion; sauté 5 minutes. Add ginger, garlic, and serrano; sauté 2 minutes. Stir in molasses. Remove from heat; carefully stir in rum. Cook mixture 2 minutes. Stir in brewed coffee, ground coffee, cinnamon, and cocoa. Bring to a boil; cook until reduced to 1½ cups (about 20 minutes). Remove from heat; cool. Place mixture in a blender; process until smooth. Stir in butter and salt.

**2.** Trim fat from pork. Cut pork lengthwise into 8 (½-inch-wide) strips. Thread pork strips onto 8 (10-inch) skewers.

**3.** Prepare grill.

**4.** Place kebabs on grill rack coated with cooking spray; grill 4 minutes on each side or until desired degree of doneness, turning and basting frequently with coffee mixture. Yield: 8 servings (serving size: 1 kebab).

CALORIES 197 (35% from fat); FAT 7.6g (sat 2.7g, mono 2.9g, poly 1.5g); PROTEIN 26.2g; CARB 4.5g; FIBER 0.2g; CHOL 87mg; IRON 2.1mg; SODIUM 226mg; CALC 23mg

# Where Appetizers Make a Meal

*Take a lesson from the sunny Mediterranean and turn a collection of bold, healthy appetizers into a robust meal.*

In the Mediterranean, dinner is started with a number of little appetizers, or *meze* (pronounced meh-ZAY), which are so delicious that you're often happily satisfied before the main course arrives. If you're looking for a fun approach to dinner, you can make a meal of meze. Many are simple and familiar.

## Braised Eggplants and Potatoes with Tomatoes, Capers, and Olives

Instead of Japanese eggplants, you can substitute 2 (1-pound) regular eggplants, halved and sliced.

```
  6  Japanese eggplants, cut diagonally
       into 1½-inch-thick slices (about
       2 pounds)
2½  teaspoons salt, divided
  2  red bell peppers
 12  small red potatoes (about 1½ pounds)
  6  large tomatoes, cored (about
       4 pounds)
  2  tablespoons olive oil, divided
  5  cups thinly sliced onion
1¼  cups julienne-cut celery
  2  tablespoons tomato paste
1½  teaspoons dried oregano
  1  teaspoon honey
  2  garlic cloves, chopped
  ½  teaspoon black pepper
  1  cup water
  ½  cup chopped fresh parsley
  ⅓  cup pitted kalamata olives
  ¼  cup capers
  8  lemon wedges
```

**1.** Place eggplant slices in a colander, and sprinkle with 2 teaspoons salt. Toss well, and drain 1 hour. Place eggplant slices on several layers of paper towels; cover with additional paper towels. Let stand 5 minutes, pressing down occasionally.

**2.** Preheat broiler.

**3.** Cut bell peppers in half lengthwise; discard seeds and membranes. Place pepper halves, skin sides up, on a foil-lined baking sheet; flatten with hand. Broil 15 minutes or until blackened. Place in a zip-top plastic bag; seal. Let stand 15 minutes. Peel and cut into 1-inch strips.

**4.** Place potatoes in a medium saucepan, and cover with water. Bring to a boil; reduce heat, and simmer 15 minutes or until almost tender. Remove potatoes with a slotted spoon; set aside.

**5.** Return water to a boil. Add 3 tomatoes to pan; reduce heat, and simmer 1 minute or until tomato skins begin to curl. Remove tomatoes with a slotted spoon, and plunge tomatoes into ice water. Slip skins off tomatoes using a paring knife. Repeat procedure with remaining tomatoes. Cut tomatoes in half. Seed tomatoes in a sieve over a bowl, reserving juice; discard seeds. Chop tomato pulp. Combine reserved tomato juice and chopped tomatoes. Discard water.

**6.** Heat 1 tablespoon olive oil in pan over medium-low heat. Add sliced onion, and cook 15 minutes, stirring occasionally. Stir in tomato mixture, celery, tomato paste, oregano, honey, and garlic; bring to a boil. Reduce heat to medium, and cook 25 minutes, stirring occasionally. Sprinkle with ½ teaspoon salt and black pepper.

**7.** Rinse eggplant, and pat dry on paper towels. Heat 1 tablespoon oil in a large Dutch oven or stockpot over medium heat. Add eggplant, and sauté 15 minutes or until tender. Add bell pepper, potatoes, tomato mixture, 1 cup water, parsley, olives, and capers, and bring to a boil. Reduce heat, and simmer 20 minutes or until potatoes are very tender. Serve with lemon wedges. Yield: 8 servings (serving size: 1½ cups).

CALORIES 210 (24% from fat); FAT 5.5g (sat 0.8g, mono 3.4g, poly 0.9g); PROTEIN 6g; CARB 38.8g; FIBER 8.5g; CHOL 0mg; IRON 3.4mg; SODIUM 673mg; CALC 69mg

## Feta Omelet with Breadcrumbs

(pictured on page 258)

Tiny folded omelets are often part of the *meze* course. Feta is a traditional stuffing. We've simplified the cooking by making one large omelet and cutting it into wedges; plan to make it at the last minute if you prefer your eggs warm.

```
  5  tablespoons water
  ¼  teaspoon salt
  4  large eggs
  4  large egg whites
  1  tablespoon olive oil
  ¾  cup dry breadcrumbs
  ½  cup (2 ounces) crumbled feta
       cheese
  ¼  cup thinly sliced green onions
  2  tablespoons chopped fresh parsley
  1  tablespoon chopped fresh or
       1 teaspoon dried oregano
```

**1.** Preheat broiler.

**2.** Combine first 4 ingredients in a bowl; stir well with a whisk. Heat oil in a 9-inch cast-iron skillet over medium heat. Add breadcrumbs; cook 1 minute or until lightly browned. Spread egg mixture evenly in pan; top with cheese. Broil 15 minutes or until omelet is firm. Sprinkle with onions, parsley, and oregano. Cut into wedges. Yield: 6 servings (serving size: 1 wedge).

CALORIES 163 (47% from fat); FAT 8.5g (sat 3g, mono 3.8g, poly 0.9g); PROTEIN 9.7g; CARB 11.4g; FIBER 0.5g; CHOL 156mg; IRON 1.6mg; SODIUM 400mg; CALC 104mg

## Beet-and-Onion Salad

```
  1  pound beets
  1  bay leaf
  1  cup thinly sliced onion
  2  tablespoons chopped fresh
       parsley
  1  tablespoon chopped fresh oregano
  2  tablespoons red wine vinegar
  1  tablespoon olive oil
  ½  teaspoon salt
```
Freshly ground black pepper (optional)

*Continued*

1. Leave root and 1 inch of stem on beets; scrub with a brush. Steam beets and bay leaf, covered, 30 minutes or until tender. Discard bay leaf. Drain and rinse beets with cold water. Drain beets. Trim off beet roots, and rub off skins. Cut beets into ¼-inch slices. Combine beet slices and onion slices; arrange on a serving platter.

2. Combine parsley and next 4 ingredients, stirring with a whisk. Pour dressing over beet mixture. Sprinkle with pepper, if desired. Yield: 6 servings (serving size: ⅔ cup).

CALORIES 62 (35% from fat); FAT 2.4g (sat 0.3g, mono 1.7g, poly 0.3g); PROTEIN 1.5g; CARB 9.3g; FIBER 1.1g; CHOL 0mg; IRON 0.8mg; SODIUM 256mg; CALC 22mg

## Okra Stewed with Tomatoes

This recipe uses a simple trick to keep the texture of the okra firm: Coat with vinegar and salt before cooking. Even those who claim to dislike okra will be swayed by this stew, which is especially well liked in the Mediterranean.

    1  pound small okra pods
    1½ tablespoons white vinegar
    ¼  teaspoon salt, divided
    2  teaspoons olive oil
    1½ cups chopped onion
    1  cup chopped tomato
    ⅛  teaspoon sugar
    ⅛  teaspoon black pepper
    ¼  cup chopped fresh parsley

1. Combine okra, vinegar, and ⅛ teaspoon salt in a bowl. Let stand 1 hour, stirring occasionally.

2. Heat oil in a medium nonstick skillet over medium-high heat. Add onion, and sauté 7 minutes or until tender. Stir in ⅛ teaspoon salt, tomato, sugar, and pepper. Reduce heat, and simmer 15 minutes. Add okra mixture, and cook 40 minutes or until tender, stirring occasionally. Stir in parsley. Yield: 8 servings (serving size: ¾ cup).

CALORIES 50 (23% from fat); FAT 1.3g (sat 0.2g, mono 0.9g, poly 0.2g); PROTEIN 1.8g; CARB 8.5g; FIBER 1.5g; CHOL 0mg; IRON 0.8mg; SODIUM 82mg; CALC 56mg

## Greens with Garlic and Lemon

(pictured on page 258)

    4  quarts water
    6  cups torn turnip greens
    6  cups torn collard greens
    1½ teaspoons olive oil
    2  garlic cloves, finely chopped
    ⅛  teaspoon salt
    4  lemon wedges

1. Bring 4 quarts water to a boil in an 8-quart stockpot. Add greens; cover and cook 20 minutes. Drain well. Heat oil in a small skillet over medium-high heat. Add garlic, and sauté 30 seconds or until lightly browned. Combine greens, garlic mixture, and salt in a medium bowl; toss well. Serve with lemon wedges. Yield: 4 servings (serving size: ½ cup).

CALORIES 63 (31% from fat); FAT 2.2g (sat 0.3g, mono 1.3g, poly 0.3g); PROTEIN 2.6g; CARB 10.3g; FIBER 4g; CHOL 0mg; IRON 1.8mg; SODIUM 140mg; CALC 317mg

## Warm Potato Salad

    3  Yukon gold or red potatoes, cut into ¼-inch-thick slices (about 1 pound)
    ¼  cup sliced onion, separated into rings
    2  tablespoons quartered pitted kalamata olives
    3  tablespoons red wine vinegar
    1  tablespoon olive oil
    2  tablespoons chopped fresh parsley
    1  teaspoon chopped fresh or ¼ teaspoon dried thyme
    ½  teaspoon salt
    ¼  teaspoon pepper

1. Cook potato in boiling water 5 minutes or until tender; drain well. Combine potato, onion, and olives in a bowl. Combine vinegar and remaining 5 ingredients, stirring well with a whisk. Pour over potato mixture; toss gently. Serve warm. Yield: 6 servings (serving size: ½ cup).

CALORIES 85 (30% from fat); FAT 2.8g (sat 0.4g, mono 2g, poly 0.3g); PROTEIN 1.8g; CARB 13.7g; FIBER 1.7g; CHOL 0mg; IRON 1.3mg; SODIUM 242mg; CALC 18mg

# Lowbrow Chow We Love

*You can call it trite, but you know it's true: Sometimes only iceberg and Velveeta will do.*

These old-time culinary favorites simplify cooking and add texture and flavor to meals. And in some cases they just plain work better than the more highfalutin alternatives.

## Peanut Butter-Crispy Rice Bars

This s'more-ish mixture is very sticky, so try coating your hands with cooking spray before pressing it into the pan.

    ⅓  cup creamy peanut butter
    1  tablespoon butter or stick margarine
    1  (10½-ounce) bag miniature marshmallows
    6  cups oven-toasted rice cereal (such as Rice Krispies)
    Cooking spray
    ¾  cup peanut butter chips

1. Combine peanut butter and butter in a large microwave-safe bowl. Microwave at HIGH 45 seconds or until mixture melts. Add marshmallows; microwave at HIGH 1½ minutes or until smooth, stirring every 30 seconds. Add cereal to peanut butter mixture; toss until well-combined. Pat cereal mixture into a 13 x 9-inch baking pan coated with cooking spray.

2. Place peanut butter chips in a small microwave-safe bowl. Microwave at HIGH 30 seconds or until chips melt. Spoon melted chips into a small heavy-duty zip-top plastic bag; seal. Snip a tiny hole in 1 corner of bag; drizzle melted chips over cereal mixture. Cool slightly; cut into 24 bars. Yield: 2 dozen (serving size: 1 bar).

CALORIES 118 (30% from fat); FAT 3.9g (sat 1.3g, mono 1.5g, poly 0.8g); PROTEIN 2.6g; CARB 19g; FIBER 0.7g; CHOL 1mg; IRON 0.4mg; SODIUM 93mg; CALC 9mg

## Two-Step Macaroni and Cheese

Processed cheese is a must in this quintessential quick-and-easy dish. It melts easily and gets smooth and creamy without help from flour, eggs, or other ingredients used in fancier counterparts. You can make prep even simpler by heating the first four ingredients in the microwave for about 3 minutes in a covered dish instead of cooking them on the stovetop.

½ cup 1% low-fat milk
¼ teaspoon dry mustard
¼ teaspoon black pepper
6 ounces processed cheese (such as Velveeta), cubed
4 cups hot cooked elbow macaroni (about 8 ounces uncooked pasta)

**1.** Combine first 4 ingredients in a large saucepan over medium heat; cook until smooth, stirring frequently. Remove from heat; stir in macaroni. Serve immediately. Yield: 4 servings (serving size: 1 cup).

CALORIES 327 (28% from fat); FAT 10.3g (sat 5.5g, mono 2.9g, poly 0.6g); PROTEIN 14.8g; CARB 43g; FIBER 2.2g; CHOL 29mg; IRON 2mg; SODIUM 659mg; CALC 277mg

## Classic Layered Salad

This salad wouldn't be the same without iceberg lettuce, which contrasts perfectly with the creamy mix of ingredients.

½ cup light mayonnaise
2 tablespoons grated Parmesan cheese
2 teaspoons sugar
⅛ teaspoon salt
⅛ teaspoon black pepper
1 large ripe tomato, cut into 8 wedges
4 cups torn iceberg lettuce
2 cups small cauliflower florets
½ cup thinly sliced red onion
1 tablespoon bottled real bacon bits

**1.** Combine first 5 ingredients; stir well with a whisk. Arrange tomato wedges in bottom of a 2-quart serving bowl. Top with lettuce and cauliflower. Spread

mayonnaise mixture over cauliflower. Top with onion and bacon bits. Cover with plastic wrap, and chill 8 hours or overnight. Toss gently before serving. Yield: 7 servings (serving size: 1 cup).

CALORIES 65 (33% from fat); FAT 2.4g (sat 0.8g, mono 0.7g, poly 0.8g); PROTEIN 2.1g; CARB 9.5g; FIBER 1.3g; CHOL 2mg; IRON 0.4mg; SODIUM 261mg; CALC 36mg

## Ooey-Gooey Peanut Butter-Chocolate Brownies

(pictured on page 258)

¾ cup fat-free sweetened condensed milk, divided
¼ cup butter or stick margarine, melted and cooled
¼ cup fat-free milk
1 (18.25-ounce) package devil's food cake mix
1 large egg white, lightly beaten
Cooking spray
1 (7-ounce) jar marshmallow creme (about 1¾ cups)
½ cup peanut butter morsels

**1.** Preheat oven to 350°.
**2.** Combine ¼ cup condensed milk, butter, and next 3 ingredients in a bowl (batter will be very stiff). Coat bottom of a 13 x 9-inch baking pan with cooking spray. Press two-thirds of batter into prepared pan using floured hands; pat evenly (layer will be thin).
**3.** Bake at 350° for 10 minutes. Combine ½ cup condensed milk and marshmallow creme in a bowl; stir in morsels. Spread marshmallow mixture evenly over brownie layer. Carefully drop remaining batter by spoonfuls over marshmallow mixture. Bake at 350° for 30 minutes. Cool completely in pan on a wire rack. Yield: 2 dozen (serving size: 1 brownie).

CALORIES 176 (25% from fat); FAT 5g (sat 2.1g, mono 1.6g, poly 1.1g); PROTEIN 2.6g; CARB 29.9g; FIBER 0.8g; CHOL 6mg; IRON 0.8mg; SODIUM 212mg; CALC 30mg

### menu
### Grilled Turkey Club
Broccoli slaw*

*Combine 4 cups broccoli, carrot, and red cabbage mix; ½ cup chopped red bell pepper; ¼ cup red wine vinegar; 1 tablespoon olive oil; ⅛ teaspoon salt; and ⅛ teaspoon pepper in a large bowl. Toss well. Cover and chill. Serves 4.

## Grilled Turkey Club

We've dressed up the humble grilled cheese by adding turkey, mustard, tomato, and bacon bits. But it still depends on the melting wizardry of processed cheese. We used regular processed cheese, but if you want to cut more calories and fat, try the fat-free version, which also melts well.

¼ cup spicy brown mustard
8 (2-ounce) slices Texas toast
4 ounces thinly sliced cooked turkey breast
8 (¼-inch-thick) slices tomato
4 (¾-ounce) slices American processed cheese
¼ cup bottled real bacon bits
Black pepper
Cooking spray

**1.** Spread 1½ teaspoons mustard over each bread slice. Layer each of 4 slices with 1 ounce turkey, 2 tomato slices, 1 cheese slice, 1 tablespoon bacon bits, and a dash of pepper. Top with remaining bread slices. Heat a large nonstick skillet coated with cooking spray over medium heat. Place 2 sandwiches in pan; cook 2 minutes on each side or until toasted. Repeat procedure with remaining sandwiches. Cut each sandwich in half. Yield: 4 servings.

CALORIES 498 (30% from fat); FAT 16.8g (sat 6.8g, mono 6.7g, poly 2g); PROTEIN 26.5g; CARB 58.8g; FIBER 3g; CHOL 52mg; IRON 4.2mg; SODIUM 1,220mg; CALC 260mg

## Chicken Taco Salad

Taco salad was made for the crunch and texture of iceberg lettuce—or maybe vice versa—but in a pinch, romaine could stand in.

- ¾ cup bottled salsa
- 3 tablespoons white wine vinegar
- 1 teaspoon sugar
- ½ teaspoon ground cumin
- ¼ teaspoon dried thyme
- ¼ teaspoon bottled minced garlic
- Dash of ground red pepper
- ½ pound skinned, boned chicken breast, cut into 1-inch strips
- 1 cup halved cherry tomatoes (about 12 tomatoes)
- 1 cup canned kidney beans, rinsed and drained
- ¼ cup minced fresh cilantro
- 1 tablespoon olive oil
- Cooking spray
- 4 cups coarsely chopped iceberg lettuce
- 1 cup (4 ounces) shredded reduced-fat Cheddar cheese
- 32 low-fat baked tortilla chips

**1.** Combine first 7 ingredients in a bowl. Combine ½ cup of salsa mixture and chicken in a zip-top plastic bag; seal bag, and marinate in refrigerator 30 minutes. Add tomatoes, beans, cilantro, and oil to remaining salsa mixture; cover and marinate in refrigerator 30 minutes.
**2.** Place a medium nonstick skillet coated with cooking spray over medium-high heat until hot. Add chicken mixture; sauté 5 minutes or until chicken is done.
**3.** Place 1 cup lettuce on each of 4 plates; top each serving with ½ cup bean mixture and one-fourth of chicken mixture. Sprinkle each serving with ¼ cup cheese. Serve each salad with 8 tortilla chips. Yield: 4 servings.

CALORIES 391 (25% from fat); FAT 11g (sat 3.9g, mono 2.8g, poly 1g); PROTEIN 30.4g; CARB 43.8g; FIBER 6g; CHOL 51mg; IRON 4mg; SODIUM 767mg; CALC 320mg

---

# A Winning Game Plan

*For Shanelle Porter, vying for the Olympics is just one part of a strategy to stay fit, eat smart, and sing to the music.*

Every morning, Shanelle Porter knocks out 250 crunches and 100 calf raises, plus 15 minutes of ab work on the Torso Track in a corner of her Denver bedroom. And then there are the two to four hours every afternoon at the track and gym at the University of Colorado in Boulder—a 40-minute drive from Qwest, where she has a full-time job writing articles for the telecommunications company's newsletter.

In her steady and constant drive to train for a spot as a sprinter on the U.S. Olympic team, Shanelle, 28, sees her life evolving toward true wholeness. Shanelle has found a way to pull it together, thanks to the help that she's received in the process.

Over the past four years, the U.S. Olympic Committee's Job Opportunities Program has enlisted 55 American companies to provide support for Olympic hopefuls, and another three corporations—Qwest, JCPenney, and Home Depot—have joined in with extensive programs. For Shanelle, as well as the six other track-and-field athletes who constitute "Team Qwest," the support has made the difference between being able to compete and wondering what it would have been like.

---

## Fruity Tuna-Salad Pita Sandwiches

Shanelle loves easy-to-make recipes like this one. These sandwiches taste great and pair protein with carbohydrates to keep your energy level up. You can substitute one (9-ounce) can of solid white tuna in water, drained, for the tuna steak.

- 1 hard-cooked egg
- 1 teaspoon lemon juice
- Dash of black pepper
- 1 (8-ounce) tuna steak
- Cooking spray
- ¼ cup diced celery
- ¼ cup raisins
- 2 tablespoons minced green onions
- 3 tablespoons reduced-fat mayonnaise
- 1 teaspoon Dijon mustard
- 1 (8-ounce) can unsweetened pineapple tidbits, drained
- 2 (5-inch) whole-wheat pitas, cut in half
- 1⅓ cups torn Bibb lettuce
- 8 (¼-inch-thick) slices tomato

**1.** Slice egg in half lengthwise, and remove yolk; reserve egg yolk for another use. Dice egg white halves; set aside.
**2.** Prepare grill or broiler.
**3.** Sprinkle lemon juice and pepper over tuna. Place tuna on a grill or broiler rack coated with cooking spray; cook 4 minutes on each side or until tuna is medium-rare or desired degree of doneness. Coarsely chop tuna.
**4.** Combine tuna, diced egg white, celery, and next 5 ingredients in a bowl. Line each pita half with ⅓ cup lettuce and 2 tomato slices. Divide tuna mixture evenly among pita halves. Yield: 4 servings (serving size: 1 pita half).

CALORIES 227 (22% from fat); FAT 5.5g (sat 1.4g, mono 1.7g, poly 1.4g); PROTEIN 17.9g; CARB 26.6g; FIBER 1.9g; CHOL 75mg; IRON 2.1mg; SODIUM 218mg; CALC 47mg

# october

# Too Two

## What to do if one cook too many is spoiling your broth—and you're married to him.

Carmen Cook has taught hundreds of couples how to cook together in the past 12 years through her course called Romantic Dinners: Cooking for Couples at Manhattan's culinary center of the New School for Social Research. According to Cook, "It's a rare couple that effortlessly cooks together—it takes skill. And experience. You've got to laugh, cede territory, really support each other's efforts, be diplomatic, and cherish the defining moments of your successes—and flops." Cook believes that for couples, the shared experience exceeds the value of the product. "You can always order out if a quality kitchen experience seems out of the question. Tuck something homemade in the freezer for such times—a quart of soup, perhaps," she suggests.

### Champion Chicken Parmesan

(pictured on page 1)

TOMATO SAUCE:
- 1 ounce sun-dried tomatoes, packed without oil (about ¼ cup)
- 1 cup boiling water
- 1 teaspoon olive oil
- 2 cups chopped red bell pepper
- 1 cup chopped onion
- 2 (14.5-ounce) cans diced tomatoes, undrained
- ¼ cup chopped fresh parsley
- 2 tablespoons chopped fresh basil
- 1 tablespoon balsamic vinegar
- ¼ teaspoon black pepper
- 2 garlic cloves, minced

CHICKEN:
- ¼ cup all-purpose flour
- ¼ cup grated Parmesan cheese
- ¼ teaspoon black pepper
- 4 (4-ounce) skinned, boned chicken breast halves
- 1 large egg white, lightly beaten
- 1 tablespoon olive oil
- Cooking spray
- 1 cup (4 ounces) shredded part-skim mozzarella cheese
- 3 cups hot cooked linguine (about 6 ounces uncooked pasta)

**1.** To prepare tomato sauce, combine sun-dried tomatoes and water in a bowl; cover and let stand 30 minutes or until soft. Drain and finely chop tomatoes.

**2.** Heat 1 teaspoon olive oil in a large saucepan over medium-high heat. Add sun-dried tomatoes, bell pepper, and onion; sauté 7 minutes. Stir in canned tomatoes; bring to a boil. Cover, reduce heat, and simmer 10 minutes. Remove from heat; stir in parsley, basil, vinegar, ¼ teaspoon black pepper, and garlic.

**3.** Preheat oven to 350°.

**4.** To prepare chicken, lightly spoon flour into a dry measuring cup; level with a knife. Combine flour, Parmesan, and ¼ teaspoon black pepper in a shallow dish. Place each breast half between 2 sheets of heavy-duty plastic wrap; flatten to ¼-inch thickness using a meat mallet or rolling pin. Dip each breast half in egg white; dredge in flour mixture. Heat 1 tablespoon oil in a large nonstick skillet over medium-high heat. Add chicken; cook 5 minutes on each side or until golden. Arrange in a 13 x 9-inch baking dish coated with cooking spray. Pour tomato sauce over chicken. Sprinkle with mozzarella. Bake at 350° for 15 minutes. Serve over linguine. Yield: 4 servings (serving size: 1 chicken breast half, 1 cup sauce, ¼ cup cheese, and ¾ cup pasta).

CALORIES 559 (26% from fat); FAT 15.9g (sat 5.6g, mono 6.3g, poly 2g); PROTEIN 46.3g; CARB 58.1g; FIBER 6.4g; CHOL 93mg; IRON 6.1mg; SODIUM 792mg; CALC 359mg

### Gingered Pear Tart

Let the more experienced cook tackle the pastry; though it's not difficult, the novice may be better off making the pear filling.

PASTRY:
- 1¼ cups all-purpose flour
- 2 tablespoons sugar
- ¼ teaspoon salt
- 5 tablespoons chilled butter or stick margarine, cut into small pieces
- 5 tablespoons ice water

FILLING:
- 3 Bartlett pears, peeled, cored, and cut lengthwise into ¼-inch-thick slices (about 1½ pounds)
- ⅓ cup sugar
- 2 tablespoons finely chopped crystallized ginger
- 1½ tablespoons cornstarch
- 1 teaspoon ground cinnamon

**1.** Preheat oven to 375°.

**2.** To prepare pastry, lightly spoon flour into dry measuring cups, and level with a knife. Combine flour, 2 tablespoons sugar, and salt in a bowl; cut in butter with a pastry blender or 2 knives until mixture resembles coarse meal. Sprinkle surface with ice water, 1 tablespoon at a time; toss with a fork until moist and crumbly (do not form a ball).

**3.** Press mixture gently into a 4-inch circle on heavy-duty plastic wrap, and cover with additional plastic wrap. Chill 15 minutes. Roll dough, still covered, into an 11-inch circle. Place dough in freezer 5 minutes or until plastic wrap can be easily removed. Remove 1 sheet of plastic wrap; fit dough into a 9-inch round removable-bottom tart pan. Remove top sheet of plastic wrap. Press dough against bottom and sides of pan. Trim excess dough.

**4.** To prepare filling, combine pears and remaining 4 ingredients; toss gently. Spoon filling into prepared crust. Bake at 375° for 45 minutes or until crust is browned and filling is bubbly. Cool on a wire rack 20 minutes. Yield: 8 servings.

CALORIES 228 (30% from fat); FAT 7.6g (sat 4.8g, mono 2.3g, poly 0.4g); PROTEIN 2.4g; CARB 39.1g; FIBER 2.1g; CHOL 21mg; IRON 1.6mg; SODIUM 153mg; CALC 21mg

## Spinach Ravioli with Tomato Sauce

(pictured on page 295)

This is an easy recipe to divvy up: The boss gets the fun part of making the ravioli while the sous-chef stands guard over the sauce.

**RAVIOLI:**

- ½  cup part-skim ricotta cheese
- ⅓  cup (1⅓ ounces) grated fresh Romano cheese
- ¼  teaspoon salt
- ⅛  teaspoon ground nutmeg
- 1  (10-ounce) package frozen chopped spinach, thawed, drained, and squeezed dry
- 1  large egg white, lightly beaten
- 32  won ton wrappers
- 1  large egg white, lightly beaten
- 1  tablespoon cornstarch

**SAUCE:**

- 2  teaspoons olive oil
- 4  garlic cloves, chopped
- 1  teaspoon sugar
- ¼  teaspoon salt
- ¼  teaspoon crushed red pepper
- 2  (14.5-ounce) cans no-salt-added diced tomatoes, drained
- ¼  cup chopped fresh basil
- ¼  cup (1 ounce) grated fresh Romano cheese

**1.** To prepare ravioli, combine first 6 ingredients in a bowl.
**2.** Working with 1 won ton wrapper at a time (cover remaining wrappers with a damp towel to keep them from drying), spoon about 1 level tablespoon spinach mixture into center of each wrapper. Brush edges of wrapper with egg white, and top with another wrapper, stretching top slightly to meet edges of bottom wrapper. Press edges together firmly with fingers. Cut ravioli into rounds with a 3-inch biscuit cutter; discard edges. Place ravioli on a large baking sheet sprinkled with cornstarch. Fill a large Dutch oven with water, and bring to a simmer; add half of ravioli (cover remaining ravioli with a damp towel to keep them from drying). Cook 4 to 5 minutes or until done (do not boil). Remove ravioli with a slotted spoon. Keep warm. Repeat procedure with remaining ravioli.
**3.** To prepare sauce, heat oil in a saucepan over medium heat. Add garlic; sauté 1 minute. Stir in sugar, ¼ teaspoon salt, pepper, and tomatoes; bring to a boil. Reduce heat, and simmer 2 minutes. Remove from heat; stir in basil. Spoon sauce over ravioli, and top with ¼ cup Romano. Yield: 4 servings (serving size: 4 ravioli, ½ cup sauce, and 1 tablespoon cheese).

CALORIES 298 (30% from fat); FAT 9.9g (sat 4.8g, mono 3.7g, poly 0.7g); PROTEIN 17.3g; CARB 35.9g; FIBER 2.2g; CHOL 30mg; IRON 3.4mg; SODIUM 830mg; CALC 406mg

## Spanish-Style Salad

The cook making the vinaigrette will be done before the salad maker. That will give the lead chef a chance to lend a hand with the salad.

**SALAD:**

- 2  cups (½-inch) cubed French bread
- 6  cups torn Bibb lettuce
- 1  cup torn radicchio
- 1  cup chopped oranges
- 14  pitted kalamata olives, halved

**VINAIGRETTE:**

- 2  tablespoons fresh orange juice
- 2  tablespoons sherry vinegar or red wine vinegar
- 1  tablespoon capers
- 2  teaspoons extra-virgin olive oil
- 1  teaspoon Dijon mustard
- ½  teaspoon sugar
- ¼  teaspoon freshly ground black pepper
- 1  garlic clove, minced

**1.** Preheat oven to 350°.
**2.** To prepare salad, place bread cubes in a single layer on a jelly-roll pan. Bake at 350° for 12 minutes or until toasted. Cool.
**3.** Combine bread cubes, lettuce, radicchio, oranges, and olives in a large bowl.
**4.** To prepare vinaigrette, combine orange juice and remaining 7 ingredients; stir well with a whisk. Pour over salad; toss well. Yield: 5 servings (serving size: 2 cups).

CALORIES 115 (30% from fat); FAT 3.8g (sat 0.6g, mono 2.5g, poly 0.6g); PROTEIN 3g; CARB 17.1g; FIBER 2.9g; CHOL 0mg; IRON 1.1mg; SODIUM 406mg; CALC 39mg

## Colorful Vegetable Medley with Chive Aïoli

The head cook will likely opt to make the aïoli and relax while the assistant slaves away prepping the vegetables. You can serve the vegetables warm as a side dish with a roast, at room temperature as an appetizer, or even as a first-course salad.

**VEGETABLES:**

- 4  beets (about 2 pounds)
- 3½  cups broccoli florets (about 10 ounces)
- 1½  cups (¾-inch) diagonally sliced carrot
- 2  tablespoons water
- ¼  teaspoon salt

**AÏOLI:**

- ½  cup low-fat sour cream
- ¼  cup fat-free mayonnaise
- 2  tablespoons fresh lemon juice
- 2  teaspoons olive oil
- ¼  teaspoon salt
- 4  garlic cloves, peeled
- 3  tablespoons chopped fresh chives

**1.** To prepare vegetables, trim off beet roots; peel beets. Cut each beet into 6 wedges. Place beet wedges in an 11 x 7-inch baking dish. Cover and microwave at HIGH 5 minutes; cool slightly. Add broccoli florets and carrot slices; sprinkle with water and ¼ teaspoon salt. Cover and microwave at HIGH 10 minutes or until tender. Remove vegetables with a slotted spoon, and place in a shallow serving dish.
**2.** To prepare aïoli, place sour cream and next 5 ingredients in a blender or food processor; process until smooth, scraping sides of bowl once. Place garlic mixture in a small bowl; stir in chives. Serve with vegetables. Yield: 6 servings (serving size: 1 cup vegetables and 2 tablespoons aïoli).

CALORIES 143 (28% from fat); FAT 4.4g (sat 1.8g, mono 1.9g, poly 0.4g); PROTEIN 4.9g; CARB 23.8g; FIBER 3.7g; CHOL 8mg; IRON 1.8mg; SODIUM 476mg; CALC 81mg

## Albóndigas Soup

This classic Spanish soup combines meat-balls—*albóndigas* (ahl-BON-dee-gahs)—and a spicy broth. Cook One makes the meatballs while Cook Two preps the rest.

**MEATBALLS:**
- ¾ pound ground round
- ¼ cup Italian-seasoned breadcrumbs
- ¼ cup minced fresh onion
- ¼ cup bottled salsa
- ½ teaspoon ground cumin

Cooking spray

**SOUP:**
- 2 (6-inch) corn tortillas, cut into ¼-inch strips
- 1 teaspoon vegetable oil
- 1 cup chopped onion
- 1 cup chopped seeded poblano chile or 1 (4.5-ounce) can chopped green chiles
- 4 garlic cloves, minced
- ½ cup bottled salsa
- ½ cup water
- 1 teaspoon ground cumin
- 1 (16-ounce) can fat-free, less-sodium chicken broth
- 1 (14.5-ounce) can no-salt-added diced tomatoes, undrained
- ¼ cup diced peeled avocado
- ¼ cup chopped fresh cilantro

**1.** Preheat oven to 450°.
**2.** To prepare meatballs, combine first 5 ingredients. Shape mixture into 32 (¾-inch) meatballs; place on a broiler pan coated with cooking spray. Bake at 450° 12 minutes or until done. Set aside.
**3.** To prepare soup, place tortilla strips in a single layer on a jelly-roll pan coated with cooking spray. Bake at 450° for 5 minutes or until lightly browned. Set aside. Heat oil in a large sauce-pan over medium heat. Add 1 cup onion, poblano, and garlic; cook 5 minutes, stir-ring occasionally. Stir in ½ cup salsa and next 4 ingredients; reduce heat, and sim-mer 10 minutes. Stir in meatballs; cook 5 minutes or until thoroughly heated. Ladle soup into individual bowls, and top with tortilla strips, diced avocado, and chopped cilantro. Yield: 4 servings (serving size: 1¾ cups soup, about 12 tortilla strips, 1 tablespoon avocado, and 1 tablespoon cilantro).

CALORIES 297 (28% from fat); FAT 9.3g (sat 2.6g, mono 4.1g, poly 1.5g); PROTEIN 24.9g; CARB 29.8g; FIBER 4.5g; CHOL 52mg; IRON 4.5mg; SODIUM 733mg; CALC 118mg

## Chicken-and-Oyster Mushroom Crêpes

Crêpes are fun to make with a partner. The person in charge can make the crêpes and let the helper work on the filling. When the crêpes are ready to fill, both can pitch in. These feature oyster mushrooms, which are pale gray to dark brown and have a meatier texture than button mush-rooms. Raw, they have a robust, slightly peppery flavor that mellows when cooked.

**CRÊPES:**
- ¾ cup all-purpose flour
- ⅛ teaspoon salt
- 1 cup fat-free milk
- 1 large egg
- 1 large egg white

Cooking spray

**FILLING:**
- 1 tablespoon butter or stick margarine
- ½ cup sliced shallots
- 4 cups diced oyster mushroom caps (about 9 ounces)
- ½ teaspoon dried thyme
- 3 garlic cloves, chopped
- 3 tablespoons all-purpose flour
- 1½ cups fat-free, less-sodium chicken broth
- 2 tablespoons dry sherry
- ¼ teaspoon salt
- ¼ teaspoon black pepper
- 2 cups shredded ready-to-eat roasted skinned, boned chicken breast (about 2 breasts)
- ¼ cup (1 ounce) grated Asiago cheese

**1.** To prepare crêpes, lightly spoon ¾ cup flour into dry measuring cups, and level with a knife. Combine flour and ⅛ teaspoon salt in a bowl. Add milk, egg, and egg white, stirring with a whisk until almost smooth. Cover batter; chill 1 hour.
**2.** Place an 8-inch crêpe pan or nonstick skillet coated with cooking spray over medium-high heat until hot. Remove pan from heat. Pour a scant ¼ cup batter into pan; quickly tilt pan in all directions so batter covers pan with a thin film. Cook about 1 minute.
**3.** Carefully lift edge of crêpe with a spatula to test for doneness. Crêpe is ready to turn when it can be shaken loose from pan and underside is lightly browned. Turn crêpe over; cook 30 sec-onds on other side.
**4.** Place crêpe on a towel; cool. Repeat procedure with remaining batter. Stack crêpes between single layers of wax paper or paper towels to prevent sticking.
**5.** Preheat oven to 350°.
**6.** To prepare filling, melt butter in a large nonstick skillet over medium heat. Add shallots, and sauté 3 minutes. Add mushrooms, thyme, and garlic; sauté 5 minutes. Sprinkle mushroom mixture with 3 tablespoons flour; cook 1 minute. Gradually stir in broth, sherry, ¼ tea-spoon salt, and pepper. Bring mixture to a boil; reduce heat, and simmer until thick (about 2 minutes). Remove from heat, and reserve ½ cup mushroom mix-ture. Stir chicken into remaining mush-room mixture.
**7.** Spoon about ⅓ cup chicken mixture onto center of each crêpe. Bring 2 oppo-site sides to center; fold over filling. Place filled crêpes, seam sides down, in a 13 x 9-inch baking dish coated with cooking spray. Spoon reserved ½ cup mushroom mixture over crêpes, and sprinkle with cheese. Bake at 350° for 15 minutes or until thoroughly heated. Yield: 6 servings (serving size: 1 crêpe with sauce).

CALORIES 217 (23% from fat); FAT 5.6g (sat 2.7g, mono 1.6g, poly 0.7g); PROTEIN 18.6g; CARB 22.9g; FIBER 1.2g; CHOL 74mg; IRON 2mg; SODIUM 612mg; CALC 121mg

## Garlic Mashed Potatoes with Pepper-Cream Gravy

Boiling potatoes is definitely a task for a subordinate. But be sure to allow for a head start since the head cook will need only 10 minutes to make the gravy. Try this with a simple entrée such as a pot roast, baked chicken, or pork loin.

**POTATOES:**

- 6 cups cubed red potato (about 2 pounds)
- 6 garlic cloves, peeled
- ¾ cup 1% low-fat milk
- 1 tablespoon butter or stick margarine
- ½ teaspoon salt
- ¼ teaspoon freshly ground black pepper

**GRAVY:**

- 1 tablespoon butter or stick margarine
- 2 tablespoons all-purpose flour
- 1 cup 1% low-fat milk
- ½ teaspoon freshly ground black pepper
- ¼ teaspoon salt
- 2 tablespoons chopped fresh chives

**1.** To prepare potatoes, place potato and garlic in a Dutch oven; cover with water. Bring to a boil, and cook 20 minutes or until very tender. Drain well; return to pan, and place over medium heat. Stir in ¾ cup milk, 1 tablespoon butter, ½ teaspoon salt, and ¼ teaspoon pepper. Mash potato mixture with a potato masher. Cook 5 minutes or until thoroughly heated. Keep warm.

**2.** To prepare gravy, melt 1 tablespoon butter in a saucepan over medium heat. Add flour, and cook 1 minute, stirring constantly. Gradually add 1 cup milk, ½ teaspoon pepper, and ¼ teaspoon salt; stir with a whisk. Bring to a boil; stir constantly. Reduce heat, and cook 5 minutes, stirring occasionally. Serve gravy with potatoes; sprinkle with chives. Yield: 5 servings (serving size: 1 cup potatoes and about 2 tablespoons gravy).

CALORIES 229 (22% from fat); FAT 5.7g (sat 3.5g, mono 1.6g, poly 0.3g); PROTEIN 7.5g; CARB 38g; FIBER 3.5g; CHOL 16mg; IRON 2.7mg; SODIUM 455mg; CALC 140mg

## Partner Paella

One person can be in charge of cleaning and peeling the seafood while the other chops the vegetables and gathers the rest of the ingredients.

- ⅓ cup vermouth or dry white wine
- ½ teaspoon saffron threads
- 1 tablespoon olive oil
- 2¼ cups chopped onion
- 4 garlic cloves, minced
- 1 cup uncooked Arborio rice
- 6 ounces chorizo, cut into ¼-inch-thick slices
- ½ teaspoon salt
- ¼ teaspoon ground red pepper
- 1½ cups fat-free, less-sodium chicken broth
- 1½ cups chopped seeded tomato (about 1 large)
- 1¼ cups chopped yellow bell pepper
- ½ cup frozen green peas
- 12 large shrimp, peeled and deveined (about ½ pound)
- 12 mussels, scrubbed and debearded

**1.** Preheat oven to 400°.

**2.** Combine vermouth and saffron in a small bowl; set aside. Heat oil in a large nonstick skillet over medium heat. Add onion and garlic; sauté 5 minutes or until tender. Add rice and chorizo; cook 1 minute, stirring frequently. Stir in vermouth mixture, salt, red pepper, and broth; bring to a boil. Reduce heat; simmer 8 minutes, stirring constantly. Stir in tomato, bell pepper, and peas. Remove from heat; nestle shrimp and mussels into rice mixture. Cover with lid or foil; bake at 400° for 35 minutes or until all liquid is absorbed. Discard any unopened shells. Yield: 6 servings (serving size: 1⅓ cups).

CALORIES 331 (30% from fat); FAT 11g (sat 3.5g, mono 5.8g, poly 1.5g); PROTEIN 18.1g; CARB 40.2g; FIBER 3.2g; CHOL 79mg; IRON 4mg; SODIUM 518mg; CALC 54mg

# Sweet Two-Timer

*Newlyweds discover a lightened apple dessert that's so good, they can't help eating it twice as often.*

When Christine O'Such's fiancé, Rob, announced to his coworkers that he was going to get married, they teased him about all the extra weight he would surely gain by wedding a woman who loves to cook. But knowing that Christine always cooked light, he wasn't too concerned. Then he tasted her family's Apple Torte—a gooey, fruit-topped, cream-cheese concoction that's more like a cheesecake. He knew he was in trouble.

His bride-to-be wanted no strife—or excess fat—in paradise. The 26-year-old telecommunications specialist from Sterling, Virginia, likes to play around with variations on her mother's recipes and had already lightened the dessert.

## Christine's Apple Torte

Christine O'Such calls this a torte, but it's actually similar to a cheesecake.

**CRUST:**

- ½ cup sugar
- ¼ cup butter or stick margarine, softened
- 4 teaspoons water
- ¼ teaspoon vanilla extract
- 1 cup all-purpose flour
- Cooking spray

**FILLING:**

- ¼ cup sugar
- ½ teaspoon vanilla extract
- 1 (8-ounce) block fat-free cream cheese
- 1 large egg
- 4 cups diced peeled Rome apple (about 1½ pounds)
- ½ cup sugar
- ½ teaspoon ground cinnamon
- ½ cup coarsely chopped walnuts
- Cinnamon sticks (optional)

*Continued*

**1.** Preheat oven to 450°.

**2.** To prepare crust, beat first 4 ingredients until well-blended at medium speed of a mixer. Lightly spoon flour into a dry measuring cup, and level with a knife. Add flour to sugar mixture, beating at medium-low speed until mixture is well-blended. Press crust into bottom and ¾ inch up sides of a 9-inch springform pan coated with cooking spray.

**3.** To prepare filling, beat ¼ cup sugar, ½ teaspoon vanilla, cream cheese, and egg at low speed until smooth. Pour cream cheese mixture into prepared crust. Combine apple, ½ cup sugar, and ground cinnamon in a bowl. Spread apple mixture evenly over cream cheese mixture; sprinkle with nuts.

**4.** Bake at 450° for 10 minutes. Reduce oven temperature to 400° (do not remove torte from oven); bake an additional 25 minutes or until lightly browned and filling is set. Cool on a wire rack. Garnish with cinnamon sticks, if desired. Yield: 10 servings.

CALORIES 275 (29% from fat); FAT 9g (sat 3.3g, mono 2.4g, poly 2.7g); PROTEIN 6.8g; CARB 42.8g; FIBER 1.6g; CHOL 39mg; IRON 0.9mg; SODIUM 190mg; CALC 77mg

## Toni's Banana Bread

"My mom, Toni, has been making this banana bread for what seems like forever. We're nuts about all kinds of bread, and this is a family favorite—even the dog loves it. While it may seem odd not to add spices, the pure banana flavor is what makes it so delicious."

—Anita Epler, San Francisco, California

  1  cup mashed ripe banana (about 2 medium)
 ⅔  cup sugar
 ¼  cup vegetable oil
 ¼  cup egg substitute or 1 large egg white
  1  large egg
1¾  cups all-purpose flour
1¼  teaspoons cream of tartar
 ¾  teaspoon baking soda
 ½  teaspoon salt
    Cooking spray

**1.** Preheat oven to 350°.

**2.** Combine first 5 ingredients in a large bowl; beat at medium speed of a mixer until smooth.

**3.** Lightly spoon flour into dry measuring cups, and level with a knife. Combine flour, cream of tartar, baking soda, and salt in a bowl, stirring with a whisk. Add flour mixture to banana mixture, stirring just until moist. Spoon batter into an 8 x 4-inch loaf pan coated with cooking spray.

**4.** Bake at 350° for 40 minutes or until a wooden pick inserted in center comes out clean. Cool 10 minutes in pan on a wire rack; remove from pan. Cool completely on rack. Yield: 12 servings (serving size: 1 slice).

**NOTE:** To freeze individual slices, place in heavy-duty zip-top plastic bags. Remove excess air from bags; seal and freeze up to 1 month. To thaw, let stand at room temperature.

CALORIES 174 (27% from fat); FAT 5.3g (sat 1g, mono 1.5g, poly 2.4g); PROTEIN 3.1g; CARB 29.1g; FIBER 0.9g; CHOL 18mg; IRON 1.1mg; SODIUM 190mg; CALC 8mg

## Cocoa-Banana Cake

"I love that no one can even tell this cake is low-fat. I usually make it when I'm headed to a gathering, and it's always a big hit."

—Mary Pat Baldauf,
Columbia, South Carolina

**CAKE:**

 ⅔  cup fat-free fruit puree (such as Sunsweet Lighter Bake)
 ½  cup water
 ½  cup low-fat buttermilk
  2  tablespoons vegetable oil
  2  teaspoons instant coffee granules
 ¼  teaspoon banana extract
  2  large egg yolks
  1  cup all-purpose flour
1½  cups granulated sugar, divided
 ¾  cup unsweetened cocoa
  2  teaspoons baking powder
  1  teaspoon baking soda
 ¼  teaspoon salt
  6  large egg whites
    Cooking spray

**ICING:**

  1  cup powdered sugar
  2  tablespoons fat-free milk
 ⅛  teaspoon banana extract (optional)
  1  (8-ounce) container frozen fat-free whipped topping, thawed
  1  cup sliced banana
 ⅛  teaspoon unsweetened cocoa (optional)

**1.** Preheat oven to 350°.

**2.** To prepare cake, combine first 7 ingredients; stir well with a whisk. Lightly spoon flour into a dry measuring cup, and level with a knife. Combine flour, 1 cup granulated sugar, and next 4 ingredients in a large bowl. Add buttermilk mixture to flour mixture, stirring just until blended.

**3.** Beat egg whites at high speed of a mixer until soft peaks form. Add ½ cup granulated sugar, 1 tablespoon at a time, beating until stiff peaks form. Fold beaten egg whites into batter; pour batter into a 13 x 9-inch baking pan coated with cooking spray.

**4.** Bake at 350° for 35 minutes or until a wooden pick inserted in center comes out clean. Cool completely on a wire rack.

**5.** To prepare icing, combine powdered sugar, fat-free milk, and ⅛ teaspoon banana extract (if desired). Fold in whipped topping. Spread icing over cake; cover and chill at least 1 hour. Top with banana slices, and sprinkle with cocoa, if desired. Yield: 12 servings.

CALORIES 318 (12% from fat); FAT 4.3g (sat 1.2g, mono 1.3g, poly 1.3g); PROTEIN 5.4g; CARB 64g; FIBER 0.6g; CHOL 37mg; IRON 1.7mg; SODIUM 287mg; CALC 77mg

## Microwave Vanilla Pudding

"This pudding takes about 10 minutes to make and can be the foundation for every custard dessert you prepare."

—Nancy Large, Clinton, Tennessee

 ⅓  cup all-purpose flour
 ½  cup sugar
 ⅛  teaspoon salt
  2  cups fat-free milk, divided
 ¼  cup egg substitute
  1  teaspoon vanilla extract

1. Lightly spoon flour into a dry measuring cup; level with a knife. Combine flour, sugar, and salt in a medium microwave-safe bowl; gradually add 1¾ cups milk, stirring well with a whisk. Microwave at HIGH 4 to 5 minutes or until thick, stirring after every minute.

2. Combine ¼ cup milk and egg substitute in a large bowl. Gently stir one-fourth of hot milk mixture into egg substitute mixture; add to remaining hot milk mixture. Microwave at HIGH 1 minute; stir well. Stir in vanilla. Pour into a bowl; cover surface of pudding with plastic wrap. Chill. Yield: 5 servings (serving size: ½ cup).

CALORIES 151 (1% from fat); FAT 0.2g (sat 0.1g, mono 0.1g, poly 0g); PROTEIN 5.4g; CARB 31.4g; FIBER 0.2g; CHOL 2mg; IRON 0.6mg; SODIUM 128mg; CALC 126mg

## Sundae Pudding Cake

"My mother began making this cake 35 years ago. And even though I've lightened it, the dessert is still easy to make and tastes fabulous—I'd make it more often if I weren't tempted to eat the whole thing."

—Jane M. Perkinson, White Plains, New York

| 1¼ | cups all-purpose flour |
| ½ | cup granulated sugar |
| 3 | tablespoons unsweetened cocoa |
| 2 | teaspoons baking powder |
| ½ | teaspoon salt |
| ¾ | cup fat-free milk |
| 2 | tablespoons fat-free fruit puree (such as Sunsweet Lighter Bake) |
| 1 | teaspoon vanilla extract |
| ¼ | cup chopped walnuts |
| | Cooking spray |
| ⅓ | cup packed brown sugar |
| 2 | tablespoons granulated sugar |
| 2 | tablespoons unsweetened cocoa |
| 1½ | cups boiling water |
| 1½ | teaspoons instant coffee granules |

1. Preheat oven to 350°.
2. Lightly spoon flour into dry measuring cups; level with a knife. Combine flour and next 4 ingredients in a medium bowl. Add milk, fruit puree, and vanilla; stir well. Stir in nuts.

3. Spoon batter into an 8-inch square baking pan coated with cooking spray. Combine brown sugar, 2 tablespoons granulated sugar, and 2 tablespoons cocoa; sprinkle over batter. Combine boiling water and coffee, stirring to dissolve. Pour coffee mixture over batter. (Do not stir.) Bake at 350° for 50 minutes or until cake springs back when touched lightly in center. Serve warm. Yield: 9 servings.

CALORIES 194 (12% from fat); FAT 2.6g (sat 0.4g, mono 0.8g, poly 1.4g); PROTEIN 4.1g; CARB 39.1g; FIBER 0.7g; CHOL 1mg; IRON 1.6mg; SODIUM 147mg; CALC 81mg

## Granny Smith Apple Cake

"This is one of my favorite recipes ever. I got it from a friend and lightened it by replacing the oil with applesauce, which makes the cake really moist. My friends and family rave about it—they can't believe it's low-fat—and the whole thing is gone in no time. This is an anytime kind of recipe, but I think the cake tastes best when you just open the refrigerator and take a bite."

—Suzy Gilbert, Mt. Vernon, Washington

**CAKE:**

| 3 | cups all-purpose flour |
| 1 | teaspoon salt |
| 1 | teaspoon baking soda |
| 1 | teaspoon ground cinnamon |
| 1 | teaspoon ground nutmeg |
| 2 | cups diced Granny Smith apple (about 12 ounces) |
| ¼ | cup chopped pecans |
| 2 | cups granulated sugar |
| 1 | cup applesauce |
| 1 | teaspoon vanilla extract |
| 3 | large eggs |
| | Cooking spray |

**ICING:**

| ½ | cup butter or stick margarine, softened |
| 1 | (8-ounce) block fat-free cream cheese, softened |
| 1⅓ | cups powdered sugar |
| 1 | teaspoon vanilla extract |

1. Preheat oven to 325°.

2. To prepare cake, lightly spoon flour into dry measuring cups; level with a knife. Combine flour and next 4 ingredients in a large bowl; stir with a whisk. Add apple and pecans; toss gently to combine. Make a well in center of mixture. Combine granulated sugar, applesauce, 1 teaspoon vanilla, and eggs in a bowl; beat at medium speed of a mixer until well-blended. Add to flour mixture. Stir just until moist. Spoon batter into a 13 x 9-inch baking pan coated with cooking spray. Bake at 325° for 55 minutes or until a wooden pick inserted in center comes out clean. Cool completely on a wire rack.

3. To prepare icing, beat butter and cream cheese with a mixer at medium speed until smooth. Add powdered sugar and 1 teaspoon vanilla; beat just until blended. Spread icing over cake. Yield: 16 servings.

CALORIES 329 (23% from fat); FAT 8.4g (sat 4.1g, mono 2.9g, poly 0.8g); PROTEIN 5.9g; CARB 57.9g; FIBER 1.4g; CHOL 59mg; IRON 1.4mg; SODIUM 382mg; CALC 55mg

## Kim's Best Pumpkin Bread

"I came up with this recipe because I wanted a healthier alternative to the sweet breads my family loves to eat. My children think it's fantastic—I make the bread a lot for their play groups, and it's always a hit."

—Kim Metz, Ellicott City, Maryland

| ⅓ | cup fat-free milk |
| 2½ | tablespoons vegetable oil |
| 2 | large eggs |
| 2 | large egg whites |
| 1 | (15-ounce) can pumpkin |
| 2 | cups all-purpose flour |
| 1 | cup quick-cooking oats |
| 1 | cup sugar |
| 2 | teaspoons baking powder |
| 2 | teaspoons ground cinnamon |
| ½ | teaspoon baking soda |
| ½ | teaspoon salt |
| 1 | cup raisins |
| ¼ | cup chopped pecans |
| | Cooking spray |

*Continued*

**1.** Preheat oven to 350°.

**2.** Combine first 5 ingredients in a medium bowl; stir well with a whisk.

**3.** Lightly spoon flour into dry measuring cups; level with a knife. Combine flour and next 6 ingredients in a large bowl; make a well in center of mixture. Add pumpkin mixture to flour mixture, stirring just until moist. Fold in raisins and pecans.

**4.** Spoon batter into 2 (8 x 4-inch) loaf pans coated with cooking spray. Bake at 350° for 50 minutes or until a wooden pick inserted in center comes out clean. Cool 10 minutes in pans on a wire rack; remove from pans. Cool completely on rack. Yield: 2 loaves, 12 servings per loaf (serving size: 1 slice).

**NOTE:** To freeze individual slices, place in heavy-duty zip-top plastic bags. Remove excess air from bags; seal and freeze up to 4 months. To thaw, let stand at room temperature.

CALORIES 134 (19% from fat); FAT 2.8g (sat 0.5g, mono 1.1g, poly 1g); PROTEIN 2.9g; CARB 25.2g; FIBER 1.7g; CHOL 18mg; IRON 1.2mg; SODIUM 103mg; CALC 39mg

### Cherry Salad

"This dish is a great combination of sweet and tart with the pineapple and cherries—a really vibrant taste."

—Mary L. Dubler, Fort Collins, Colorado

- 1 (20-ounce) can light cherry pie filling
- 1 (14-ounce) can fat-free sweetened condensed milk
- 1 (8-ounce) can crushed pineapple in juice, drained
- 1 (12-ounce) tub frozen fat-free whipped topping, thawed

**1.** Combine first 3 ingredients in a large bowl; stir until well-blended. Gently fold in whipped topping. Yield: 6 servings (serving size: 1⅓ cups).

**NOTE:** You can also serve this as a frozen dessert. Spoon into a 13 x 9-inch baking dish; cover with plastic wrap and freeze.

CALORIES 338 (1% from fat); FAT 0.2g (sat 0g, mono 0g, poly 0.1g); PROTEIN 5.7g; CARB 73.4g; FIBER 0.2g; CHOL 9mg; IRON 0.4mg; SODIUM 382mg; CALC 179mg

# Wild as It Gets

*Wild, strong, unflinching in flavor and texture, this is "rice" with an attitude.*

Wild rice. It's an evocative name, but don't let the imagery fool you. Wild rice isn't rice at all—it's the seed of an annual water grass, *Zizania aquatica*, which is natural to the cold waters of Minnesota and Canada.

Wild rice serves as a perfect accent to both savory and sweet ingredients. It can not only mingle in a meat dish, adding an undercurrent of gaminess, but it also can cozy up well with fruit.

Savvy cooks know that rice and wild rice are not the same thing, and while the former is perfect as the base of many a dish, wild rice is more wisely used as a flavoring mixed with other ingredients.

### Minnesota Wild Rice Pilaf

The wild rice and mushrooms give this pilaf an earthy flavor that pairs well with duck or pork.

- 1¼ cups water
- 2 (16-ounce) cans fat-free, less-sodium chicken broth
- 1½ cups uncooked wild rice (Gourmet Grains Minnesota Cultivated Wild Rice)
- 1 tablespoon butter or stick margarine
- 3 cups sliced mushrooms
- 1 cup chopped onion
- ½ cup finely chopped fresh parsley
- ⅓ cup chopped pecans, toasted
- ¾ teaspoon poultry seasoning
- ½ teaspoon salt
- ¼ teaspoon black pepper
- Cooking spray

**1.** Bring water and broth to a boil in a medium saucepan. Add wild rice; cover, reduce heat, and simmer 1 hour or until tender. Drain.

**2.** Preheat oven to 325°.

**3.** Melt butter in a large nonstick skillet over medium-high heat. Add mushrooms and onion; sauté 6 minutes. Remove from heat; stir in parsley and next 4 ingredients. Combine rice and mushroom mixture in a 2-quart casserole coated with cooking spray. Cover and bake at 325° for 25 minutes. Yield: 8 servings (serving size: 1 cup).

CALORIES 177 (27% from fat); FAT 5.4g (sat 1.2g, mono 2.6g, poly 1.1g); PROTEIN 6.9g; CARB 27.2g; FIBER 2.8g; CHOL 4mg; IRON 1.4mg; SODIUM 347mg; CALC 21mg

### Wild Rice Crab Cakes

(pictured on page 296)

The addition of cumin to these hearty crab cakes enhances the nuttiness of the wild rice. If you want to top them with a sauce, combine light mayonnaise with lemon juice and a pinch of curry powder. Serve these with lemon wedges.

- 1½ cups water
- ½ cup uncooked wild rice (Gourmet Grains Minnesota Cultivated Wild Rice)
- 1 pound lump crabmeat, drained and shell pieces removed
- ¾ cup dry breadcrumbs
- ½ cup finely chopped red bell pepper
- ¼ cup minced shallots
- ¼ cup light mayonnaise
- 2 tablespoons Dijon mustard
- 1½ tablespoons fresh lemon juice
- ½ teaspoon salt
- ½ teaspoon ground cumin
- ⅛ teaspoon ground red pepper
- ⅛ teaspoon black pepper
- 2 large egg whites, lightly beaten
- 4 teaspoons olive oil, divided

**1.** Bring water to a boil in a medium saucepan. Add wild rice; cover, reduce heat, and simmer 1 hour or until tender. Combine cooked wild rice, crab, and next 11 ingredients in a large bowl. Divide mixture into 8 equal portions, shaping each into a 1-inch-thick patty.

**2.** Heat 2 teaspoons oil in a large nonstick skillet over medium heat. Add 4 patties, and cook 4 minutes. Carefully turn patties over; cook 4 minutes or until golden. Repeat procedure with remaining oil and patties. Yield: 8 servings (serving size: 1 crab cake).

CALORIES 186 (31% from fat); FAT 6.4g (sat 1g, mono 2.9g, poly 2g); PROTEIN 15.1g; CARB 16.4g; FIBER 1g; CHOL 59mg; IRON 1.6mg; SODIUM 524mg; CALC 87mg

## Wild Rice-Oatmeal Bread

    2   cups water, divided
    ⅓   cup uncooked wild rice (Gourmet
        Grains Minnesota Cultivated Wild
        Rice)
    1   cup regular oats
    1   teaspoon sugar
    2   packages dry yeast (about 4½
        teaspoons)
    ½   cup warm water (100° to 110°)
    1   cup warm 1% low-fat milk (100°
        to 110°)
    ¼   cup sugar
    3   tablespoons molasses
    2   teaspoons salt
    5   cups all-purpose flour, divided
    Cooking spray

1. Bring 1 cup water to a boil in a medium saucepan. Add wild rice; cover, reduce heat, and simmer 1 hour or until tender. Drain if necessary. Set wild rice aside.
2. Bring 1 cup water to a boil in a medium saucepan. Add oats, and cook over medium-high heat 2½ minutes or until thick, stirring mixture constantly. Pour oatmeal into a large bowl. Dissolve 1 teaspoon sugar and yeast in ½ cup warm water in a small bowl; let stand 5 minutes. Add cooked wild rice, yeast mixture, warm milk, ¼ cup sugar, molasses, and salt to oatmeal; stir well.
3. Lightly spoon flour into dry measuring cups; level with a knife. Add 4½ cups flour to oatmeal mixture; stir until blended. Turn dough out onto a floured surface. Knead until smooth and elastic (about 5 minutes); add enough of remaining flour, 1 tablespoon at a time, to prevent dough from sticking to hands (dough will feel tacky).

4. Place dough in a large bowl coated with cooking spray, turning to coat top. Cover and let rise in a warm place (85°), free from drafts, 1 hour or until doubled in size. (Press two fingers into dough. If indentation remains, dough has risen enough.) Punch dough down, and let rest 5 minutes. Roll dough into a 14 x 7-inch rectangle on a floured surface. Roll up rectangle tightly, starting with a short edge, pressing firmly to eliminate air pockets; pinch seam and ends to seal. Place roll, seam side down, in a 9 x 5-inch loaf pan coated with cooking spray. Cover and let rise 45 minutes or until doubled in size.
5. Preheat oven to 375°.
6. Uncover dough. Bake at 375° for 35 minutes or until loaf is browned on bottom and sounds hollow when tapped. Remove loaf from pan, and cool on a wire rack. Yield: 1 loaf, 16 servings (serving size: 1 slice).

CALORIES 204 (4% from fat); FAT 1g (sat 0.2g, mono 0.2g, poly 0.3g); PROTEIN 6.1g; CARB 42.4g; FIBER 2g; CHOL 1mg; IRON 2.4mg; SODIUM 303mg; CALC 36mg

## Wild Rice-Squash Risotto

This creamy dish has all the taste and texture of risotto without the time-consuming stirring procedure. The recipe is from Kevin Cullen, chef at Goodfellow's restaurant in Minneapolis.

    ⅔   cup water
    ⅓   cup uncooked wild rice (Gourmet
        Grains Minnesota Cultivated Wild
        Rice)
    1¼  cups diced peeled acorn squash or
        butternut squash
    2   poblano chiles (about ¼ pound)
    1   cup fat-free, less-sodium chicken
        broth
    1½  cups cooked Arborio rice
    ½   cup (2 ounces) grated fresh
        Romano cheese
    2   tablespoons butter or stick
        margarine
    1   tablespoon chopped fresh or
        1 teaspoon dried thyme
    ¼   teaspoon salt
    ¼   teaspoon black pepper

1. Bring water to a boil in a medium saucepan. Add wild rice; cover, reduce heat, and simmer 1 hour or until tender. Set aside.
2. Cook squash in boiling water 4 minutes or until tender. Rinse squash with cold water; drain.
3. Preheat broiler.
4. Cut poblanos in half lengthwise; discard seeds and membranes. Place pepper halves, skin sides up, on a foil-lined baking sheet; flatten with hand. Broil 10 minutes or until blackened, turning occasionally. Place in a zip-top plastic bag; seal. Let stand 15 minutes. Peel and chop poblanos. Set aside.
5. Bring broth to a boil in a large saucepan. Add cooked wild rice and Arborio rice; cook 2 minutes, stirring constantly. Reduce heat to medium, and add cheese and butter, stirring until cheese melts. Add squash, poblanos, thyme, salt, and pepper; cook 2 minutes or until thoroughly heated. Yield: 4 servings (serving size: 1 cup).

CALORIES 322 (28% from fat); FAT 10g (sat 6.1g, mono 2.9g, poly 0.5g); PROTEIN 10.7g; CARB 47.8g; FIBER 2.4g; CHOL 30mg; IRON 2.6mg; SODIUM 500mg; CALC 179mg

## Wild Ways

Wild rice certainly can live up to its free-spirited image. For a start, it sometimes takes over an hour to cook fully. The best way to tell when it's done is to notice when the grains start to split. Sometimes you have to drain off excess water, sometimes you don't.

Results depend on the variety you use. In these recipes, we call for 100% wild rice. We used the Gourmet Grains Minnesota Cultivated Wild Rice brand that comes in a 6-ounce box and is available nationally. If you have wild rice blends, save them for another use—they won't work in these recipes.

## Sausage Soup with Spinach and Wild Rice

This soup freezes well. Store it in the freezer in an airtight container up to 2 months.

1½ cups water
½ cup uncooked wild rice (Gourmet Grains Minnesota Cultivated Wild Rice)
1 pound turkey Italian sausage
1 teaspoon olive oil
1 cup chopped onion
3 garlic cloves, crushed
3 cups water
3 tablespoons tomato paste
1 teaspoon dried oregano
1 teaspoon dried basil
3 (16-ounce) cans fat-free, less-sodium chicken broth
1 (14.5-ounce) can diced tomatoes, undrained
3 cups torn spinach
¼ teaspoon salt
¼ teaspoon black pepper
3 tablespoons grated fresh Parmesan cheese

**1.** Bring 1½ cups water to a boil in a medium saucepan. Add wild rice; cover, reduce heat, and simmer 1 hour or until tender. Set aside.
**2.** Cook sausage in a Dutch oven over medium-high heat until browned; stir to crumble. Drain sausage; set aside.
**3.** Heat oil in Dutch oven over medium-high heat. Add onion, and sauté 3 minutes. Add garlic, and sauté 1 minute. Add sausage, 3 cups water, and next 5 ingredients; bring to a boil. Reduce heat; simmer 20 minutes. Stir in cooked wild rice, spinach, salt, and pepper. Ladle soup into bowls; sprinkle with cheese. Yield: 9 servings (serving size: 1⅓ cups soup and 1 teaspoon cheese).

CALORIES 161 (33% from fat); FAT 5.9g (sat 2.1g, mono 2.8g, poly 1.6g); PROTEIN 13.8g; CARB 13.4g; FIBER 2.3g; CHOL 40mg; IRON 2mg; SODIUM 797mg; CALC 82mg

## Chicken Breasts with Wild Rice-and-Fig Pilaf

¼ cup water
1 (16-ounce) can fat-free, less-sodium chicken broth
¾ cup uncooked wild rice (Gourmet Grains Minnesota Cultivated Wild Rice)
1 tablespoon butter or stick margarine
1 cup finely chopped onion
½ cup finely chopped celery
1 cup chopped dried figs
2 ounces prosciutto or ham, thinly sliced (about ½ cup)
¾ teaspoon dried thyme
½ teaspoon salt, divided
½ teaspoon black pepper, divided
¼ teaspoon paprika
4 (4-ounce) skinned, boned chicken breast halves
1 teaspoon vegetable oil
Thyme sprigs (optional)

**1.** Bring water and broth to a boil in a medium saucepan. Add wild rice; cover, reduce heat, and simmer 1 hour or until rice is tender.
**2.** Melt butter in a large nonstick skillet over medium-high heat. Add onion and celery; sauté 5 minutes or until tender. Stir in rice, figs, prosciutto, dried thyme, ¼ teaspoon salt, ¼ teaspoon black pepper, and paprika. Remove from heat, and keep warm.
**3.** Sprinkle chicken with ¼ teaspoon salt and ¼ teaspoon pepper.
**4.** Heat vegetable oil in a large nonstick skillet over medium heat. Add chicken breasts, and cook 7 minutes on each side or until done. Serve chicken with wild rice pilaf, and garnish with thyme sprigs, if desired. Yield: 4 servings (serving size: 1 chicken breast half and 1 cup rice).

CALORIES 414 (16% from fat); FAT 7.6g (sat 3g, mono 2.3g, poly 1.6g); PROTEIN 37.1g; CARB 51g; FIBER 7.1g; CHOL 82mg; IRON 3.1mg; SODIUM 869mg; CALC 94mg

## Wild Rice-Sweet Potato Salad with Pears

An innovative match-up of unexpected ingredients, this salad is even more terrific served with ham or pork. The recipe is courtesy of Kevin Cullen, chef at Goodfellow's restaurant in Minneapolis—true wild rice country.

SALAD:
2 cups water
1 cup uncooked wild rice (Gourmet Grains Minnesota Cultivated Wild Rice)
1 cup diced peeled sweet potato
1⅓ cups peeled Bartlett pear, cored and diced (about 2 pears)
½ teaspoon fresh lemon juice
1 cup diced yellow bell pepper (about 1 pepper)
¼ cup sliced green onions
1 tablespoon toasted sesame seeds
1 teaspoon salt

VINAIGRETTE:
3 tablespoons cider vinegar
3 tablespoons apple cider
2 tablespoons dark sesame oil
1 tablespoon thawed orange juice concentrate
½ teaspoon dried rubbed sage
1 garlic clove, minced

**1.** To prepare salad, bring water to a boil in a medium saucepan. Add wild rice; cover, reduce heat, and simmer 1 hour or until tender. Set aside.
**2.** Cook diced sweet potato in boiling water 5 minutes or until tender. Drain and rinse with cold water; drain well. Set aside.
**3.** Combine pear and lemon juice in a large bowl, and toss to coat. Add cooked wild rice, sweet potato, bell pepper, green onions, sesame seeds, and salt; toss well.
**4.** To prepare vinaigrette, combine vinegar and remaining 5 ingredients; stir well with a whisk. Pour over rice mixture, tossing to coat. Yield: 8 servings (serving size: ½ cup).

CALORIES 153 (26% from fat); FAT 4.4g (sat 0.6g, mono 1.6g, poly 1.9g); PROTEIN 3.7g; CARB 26.2g; FIBER 2.5g; CHOL 0mg; IRON 1mg; SODIUM 298mg; CALC 28mg

## Chicken, Arugula, and Wild Rice Salad with Sautéed Apples

**VINAIGRETTE:**

¼ cup champagne vinegar or white wine vinegar
1½ tablespoons extra-virgin olive oil
1 tablespoon sugar
1 tablespoon fresh lemon juice
1 teaspoon Dijon mustard
½ teaspoon dried basil
⅛ teaspoon salt
⅛ teaspoon black pepper

**SALAD:**

1¾ cups water
⅔ cup uncooked wild rice (Gourmet Grains Minnesota Cultivated Wild Rice)
2 Granny Smith apples, each cut into 8 wedges
1½ tablespoons fresh lemon juice
3 cups trimmed arugula or spinach
2 cups chopped ready-to-eat roasted skinned, boned chicken breast (about 2 breasts)
1 cup seedless red grapes, halved
¼ cup (1 ounce) crumbled Gorgonzola or blue cheese

**1.** To prepare vinaigrette, combine first 8 ingredients in a jar. Cover jar tightly, and shake vigorously; set aside.

**2.** To prepare salad, bring water to a boil in a medium saucepan. Add wild rice; cover, reduce heat, and simmer 1 hour or until tender.

**3.** Combine apple wedges and 1½ tablespoons lemon juice in a small bowl, and toss well. Heat a nonstick skillet over medium-high heat; add apple mixture. Cook 6 minutes or until tender, stirring frequently.

**4.** Combine cooked wild rice, arugula, chicken, grapes, and cheese in a large bowl. Add vinaigrette, and toss well. Place 1½ cups salad on each of 4 serving plates, and top each serving with 4 apple wedges. Yield: 4 servings.

CALORIES 308 (27% from fat); FAT 9.3g (sat 2.6g, mono 4.8g, poly 1g); PROTEIN 20.6g; CARB 37.6g; FIBER 4g; CHOL 45mg; IRON 1.1mg; SODIUM 555mg; CALC 86mg

## lighten up

# Dracula's Revenge

*The trick is the scary name; the treat is a tasty Halloween favorite.*

Vampires, take note. Elaine Breeding's creamy, cheesy pasta dish is so loaded with garlic that her husband, Bob, dubbed it "Dracula's Revenge" when she served it to guests in her Sykesville, Maryland, home several years ago.

This Baked Penne with Sausage and Garlic is delicious, but the fat is monstrously high. With its whole milk, Italian sausage, and almost a cup of butter, one serving weighed in at about 30 grams of fat.

We switched to low-fat milk and turkey sausage, and we reduced the butter to about a sixth of that in the original. We were able to cut the fat grams in half, slicing the percentage to 30%—down from a scary 49%. And we roasted the garlic, which mellows the dish's distinctive bite without killing it.

### Dracula's Revenge (Baked Penne with Sausage and Garlic)

2 whole garlic heads
1 pound sweet turkey Italian sausage
1 teaspoon chopped fresh or
¼ teaspoon dried sage
1 teaspoon chopped fresh or
¼ teaspoon dried rosemary
2 tablespoons butter or stick margarine
⅓ cup all-purpose flour
6 cups 1% low-fat milk
1 cup (4 ounces) grated fresh Parmesan cheese
⅔ cup (about 2½ ounces) shredded Gruyère or Swiss cheese
½ teaspoon salt
⅛ teaspoon black pepper
8 cups hot cooked penne (about 1 pound uncooked tube-shaped pasta) or rigatoni
Cooking spray

**1.** Preheat oven to 350°.

**2.** Remove white papery skin from garlic heads (do not peel or separate cloves). Wrap each head separately in foil. Bake at 350° for 1 hour; cool 10 minutes. Separate cloves; squeeze to extract garlic pulp. Discard skins. Set garlic aside.

**3.** Increase oven temperature to 400°.

**4.** Remove casings from sausage. Cook sausage in a large nonstick skillet over medium heat until browned, stirring to crumble. Remove from pan with a slotted spoon. Place sausage in a large bowl; stir in sage and rosemary.

**5.** Melt butter in a large saucepan over medium heat. Lightly spoon flour into a dry measuring cup; level with a knife. Add flour to melted butter, stirring with a whisk. Gradually add milk; cook until slightly thick, stirring constantly with a whisk (about 10 minutes). Stir in roasted garlic, cheeses, salt, and pepper. Remove mixture from heat. Add 5½ cups cheese sauce and cooked pasta to sausage, stirring to coat. Spoon pasta mixture into a 13 x 9-inch baking dish coated with cooking spray. Top with remaining sauce. Bake at 400° for 15 minutes or until thoroughly heated. Yield: 10 servings.

CALORIES 434 (30% from fat); FAT 14.4g (sat 7.2g, mono 4.5g, poly 2g); PROTEIN 26.3g; CARB 48.7g; FIBER 1.4g; CHOL 57mg; IRON 3mg; SODIUM 700mg; CALC 425mg

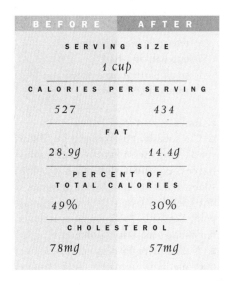

| BEFORE | AFTER |
|---|---|
| **SERVING SIZE** | |
| *1 cup* | |
| **CALORIES PER SERVING** | |
| 527 | 434 |
| **FAT** | |
| 28.9g | 14.4g |
| **PERCENT OF TOTAL CALORIES** | |
| 49% | 30% |
| **CHOLESTEROL** | |
| 78mg | 57mg |

# Playing Squash

*Don't wait until its namesake season to dig into winter squash.*

Winter squash—a collection of thick-skinned, vine-grown gourds—usually makes its cold-weather debut at Thanksgiving. But why wait? Hubbards, buttercups, and butternuts are harvested at summer's end and are much more tender and juicy then than they will be deep into winter. There's no reason you shouldn't get a head start: Winter squashes not only taste delicious, but they're also very easy to prepare.

### Curried Squash-and-Pear Bisque

    1  butternut squash (about 2¾ pounds)
    1  tablespoon butter
    2  cups chopped peeled Bartlett pear (about 1 pound)
 1½  cups thinly sliced onion
 2⅓  cups water
    1  cup pear nectar
    2  (14½-ounce) cans vegetable broth
 2½  teaspoons curry powder
  ½  teaspoon salt
  ⅛  teaspoon black pepper
  ½  cup half-and-half
    1  small Bartlett pear, cored and thinly sliced

**1.** Preheat oven to 375°.
**2.** Cut squash in half lengthwise; discard seeds and membrane. Place squash halves, cut sides down, on a baking sheet; bake at 375° for 45 minutes or until tender. Cool. Peel squash; mash pulp. Set aside 3½ cups pulp, reserving remaining squash for another use.
**3.** Melt butter in a large Dutch oven over medium-high heat. Add chopped pear and onion; sauté 10 minutes or until lightly browned. Add squash pulp, water, and next 5 ingredients. Bring to a boil; partially cover, reduce heat, and simmer 40 minutes. Place one-third of squash mixture in a blender; process until smooth. Pour pureed mixture into a large bowl; repeat procedure with remaining squash mixture. Return squash mixture to pan; stir in half-and-half. Cook over low heat 3 minutes or until thoroughly heated. Ladle soup into bowls, and garnish with pear slices. Yield: 8 servings (serving size: 1¼ cups).

CALORIES 149 (25% from fat); FAT 4.2g (sat 2g, mono 1g, poly 0.2g); PROTEIN 1.9g; CARB 29.4g; FIBER 3.7g; CHOL 10mg; IRON 1mg; SODIUM 622mg; CALC 70mg

### Winter Squash Risotto with Radicchio

The natural sweetness of blue hubbard squash offsets the slightly bitter flavor of radicchio. Half-and-half adds to the creaminess of this main-dish risotto, but you can use milk instead. If you can't find blue hubbard, buttercup or butternut squash will work fine.

    1  blue hubbard squash (about 4 pounds)
    2  cups water
    1  (14½-ounce) can vegetable broth
      Cooking spray
 2½  cups sliced radicchio
  ¼  teaspoon freshly ground black pepper, divided
 1½  teaspoons butter
  ½  cup finely diced onion
    1  cup uncooked Arborio rice or other short-grain rice
  ¼  cup dry white wine
    2  tablespoons half-and-half or whole milk
  ½  cup (2 ounces) grated fresh Parmesan cheese

**1.** Preheat oven to 375°.
**2.** Cut squash in half lengthwise; discard seeds and membrane. Place squash halves, cut sides down, on a baking sheet; bake at 375° for 50 minutes or until squash is tender. Cool. Peel squash; mash pulp. Set aside 1 cup pulp, reserving remaining pulp for another use.
**3.** Bring water and broth to a simmer in a large saucepan. Keep warm over low heat. Place a Dutch oven coated with cooking spray over medium-high heat until hot. Add radicchio to Dutch oven; sauté 2 minutes or until wilted. Place radicchio in a bowl. Sprinkle with ⅛ teaspoon pepper. Melt butter in Dutch oven. Add onion; sauté 3 minutes or until lightly browned. Add rice; sauté 1 minute. Stir in wine and ½ cup broth mixture; cook 3 minutes or until liquid is nearly absorbed, stirring constantly. Add 2 cups broth mixture, ½ cup at a time, stirring constantly until each portion of liquid is absorbed before adding next (about 15 minutes total). Stir in 1 cup squash pulp. Repeat procedure with remaining 1¼ cups broth mixture (about 9 minutes total). Stir in radicchio mixture and half-and-half. Remove from heat; stir in cheese. Sprinkle risotto with ⅛ teaspoon pepper. Yield: 4 servings (serving size: 1 cup).

CALORIES 333 (23% from fat); FAT 7.6g (sat 4.2g, mono 2g, poly 0.3g); PROTEIN 10.5g; CARB 50.5g; FIBER 2g; CHOL 18mg; IRON 2.9mg; SODIUM 889mg; CALC 238mg

### Winter Squash and Savoy Cabbage with Toasted Sesame Seeds

The naturally sweet flavors of the squash, cabbage, and onion are rounded out by the nuttiness of toasted sesame seeds and dark sesame oil.

    2  teaspoons vegetable oil
    1  teaspoon dark sesame oil
    5  cups (½-inch) cubed peeled butternut squash (about 2 pounds)
    1  cup diced onion
    8  cups coarsely chopped Savoy or green cabbage
  ½  cup water
  ¾  teaspoon salt
    2  tablespoons sesame seeds, toasted
    1  tablespoon low-sodium soy sauce

**1.** Heat oils in a large nonstick skillet over medium-high heat. Add squash and onion; sauté 7 minutes or until lightly browned. Stir in cabbage, water, and salt; cover and cook 5 minutes or until tender. Stir in sesame seeds and soy sauce. Serve immediately. Yield: 6 servings (serving size: 1 cup).

CALORIES 128 (29% from fat); FAT 4g (sat 0.6g, mono 1.4g, poly 1.8g); PROTEIN 4.1g; CARB 22.6g; FIBER 2.9g; CHOL 0mg; IRON 1.6mg; SODIUM 406mg; CALC 125mg

## Baked Spaghetti Squash with Tomato Sauce and Olives

Spaghetti squash has flesh so stringy that it resembles spaghetti when you scrape it out. So why not serve it with a tomato sauce?

    1   spaghetti squash (about 3¼
        pounds)
    1½  tablespoons olive oil
    1   cup minced fresh onion
    1   teaspoon dried oregano
    ½   teaspoon dried thyme
    2   bay leaves
    Dash of crushed red pepper
    3   garlic cloves, minced and divided
    1   cup dry red wine
    ½   cup water
    ⅓   cup coarsely chopped pitted
        kalamata olives
    1   tablespoon capers
    ¼   teaspoon freshly ground black
        pepper
    ⅛   teaspoon salt
    1   (28-ounce) can crushed tomatoes,
        undrained
    ¼   cup (1 ounce) grated fresh
        Parmesan cheese
    ¼   cup chopped fresh parsley

**1.** Preheat oven to 375°.
**2.** Pierce squash with a fork. Place squash on a baking sheet; bake at 375° for 1½ hours or until tender. Cool. Cut squash in half lengthwise; discard seeds. Scrape inside of squash with a fork to remove spaghetti-like strands to measure 6 cups. Keep warm.
**3.** While squash is baking, heat oil in a large nonstick skillet over medium heat. Add onion, oregano, thyme, bay leaves, and red pepper; sauté 5 minutes. Add 2 minced garlic cloves, wine, and next 6 ingredients; bring to a boil. Reduce heat, and simmer until thick (about 30

minutes). Discard bay leaves. Serve sauce over squash.
**4.** Combine 1 minced garlic clove, Parmesan cheese, and parsley. Sprinkle over each serving. Yield: 6 servings (serving size: 1 cup squash, ¾ cup sauce, and 1 tablespoon cheese mixture).

CALORIES 128 (28% from fat); FAT 3.9g (sat 1.2g, mono 1.9g, poly 0.6g); PROTEIN 4.8g; CARB 20.4g; FIBER 3.5g; CHOL 3mg; IRON 2.2mg; SODIUM 505mg; CALC 159mg

## Winter Squash Soufflé and Greens

The big, bold flavor of Swiss chard contrasts superbly with the creamy, buttery taste of the squash soufflé.

    1   butternut squash (about 2¾
        pounds)
    ½   cup 1% low-fat milk
    ⅓   cup (1⅓ ounces) shredded
        fontina cheese
    ¼   teaspoon salt
    1   large egg
    1   large egg white
    Cooking spray
    2   quarts water
    ½   teaspoon salt
    8   cups finely chopped Swiss chard
        or collard greens
    1   teaspoon butter

**1.** Preheat oven to 375°.
**2.** Cut squash in half lengthwise; discard seeds and membrane. Place squash halves, cut sides down, on a baking sheet; bake at 375° for 45 minutes or until tender. Cool. Peel squash. Mash pulp. Set aside 2 cups pulp, reserving remaining pulp for another use.
**3.** Combine 2 cups squash pulp, milk, and next 4 ingredients in a food processor; process until smooth. Pour into a 1-quart soufflé dish coated with cooking spray. Place soufflé dish in a 9-inch square baking pan; add hot water to pan to a depth of 1 inch. Bake at 375° for 40 minutes or until puffy and set.
**4.** While squash is baking, bring 2 quarts water and ½ teaspoon salt to a boil in an 8-quart stockpot or Dutch oven. Add Swiss chard; cover and cook 8 minutes.

Drain well; toss with butter. Serve immediately with squash soufflé. Yield: 6 servings (serving size: ½ cup soufflé and ¼ cup greens).

CALORIES 138 (29% from fat); FAT 4.5g (sat 2.1g, mono 1.2g, poly 0.6g); PROTEIN 7.6g; CARB 20.2g; FIBER 2.2g; CHOL 47mg; IRON 2.3mg; SODIUM 370mg; CALC 215mg

### menu

#### Winter Squash Stew with Pinto Beans and Corn

Spicy cumin chips*

*Cut each of 3 (5-inch) pitas into 6 wedges; place on a baking sheet. Lightly coat with cooking spray. Sprinkle with a mixture of ¼ teaspoon each of salt, garlic powder, ground cumin, and chili powder. Bake at 350° for 15 minutes or until crisp. Serves 6.

## Winter Squash Stew with Pinto Beans and Corn

    2   tablespoons vegetable oil
    3   cups (¾-inch) cubed peeled
        buttercup or butternut squash
        (about 1¼ pounds)
    1   cup diced onion
    2½  cups water, divided
    2   teaspoons paprika
    1   teaspoon ground cumin
    ¼   teaspoon ground coriander
    1   dried New Mexican chile, seeded
    ¼   teaspoon salt
    1   (14.5-ounce) can diced tomatoes,
        undrained
    1   cup frozen whole-kernel corn
    1   (15-ounce) can pinto beans, rinsed
        and drained

**1.** Heat vegetable oil in a large Dutch oven over medium-high heat. Add squash and onion, and sauté 5 minutes. Add 1 cup water and next 4 ingredients; cover and cook 5 minutes. Add 1½ cups water, salt, and tomatoes; cover, reduce heat, and simmer 20 minutes. Add corn and beans; cover and cook 15 minutes. Discard chile. Yield: 4 servings (serving size: 1½ cups).

CALORIES 281 (25% from fat); FAT 7.9g (sat 1.4g, mono 2.3g, poly 3.8g); PROTEIN 9.6g; CARB 48g; FIBER 6.9g; CHOL 0mg; IRON 3.9mg; SODIUM 511mg; CALC 133mg

# Fondue 4-Ever

*It's back, baby. But better.*

It still means "melted" in French, and it still seems ever-so-'70s, but these days fondue—its renaissance duly proclaimed by the *Wall Street Journal*, *New York* magazine, and even the food industry's *Trend/Wire*—is a whole new ballgame. The drippy cheeses and artery-clogging oils no longer reign; today's fondue is lighter, healthier, and more eclectic. According to *Foodwatch*, only about 15% of the new fondue recipes are entrées. That means more choices and less need to rely on just one pot to make an entire meal.

### Shrimp Bouillabaisse Fondue

This fondue contains ingredients that are typically found in bouillabaisse, a seafood stew from Provence.

- ½ teaspoon garlic powder
- ¼ teaspoon salt
- ¼ teaspoon black pepper
- ⅛ teaspoon ground red pepper
- 2¼ pounds large shrimp, peeled and deveined
- 1 tablespoon olive oil
- 2 cups diced fennel bulb (about 1 bulb)
- 3 garlic cloves, minced
- 1 cup dry white wine
- 1 teaspoon grated orange rind
- ¼ teaspoon saffron threads
- 2 (8-ounce) bottles clam juice
- 1 (14.5-ounce) can diced tomatoes, undrained
- 9 ounces French bread, toasted and cut into 1-inch cubes

**1.** Combine first 5 ingredients in a bowl; toss gently to coat. Heat oil in a large skillet over medium-high heat. Add shrimp mixture, and sauté 3 minutes or until shrimp are done. Remove shrimp from pan; set aside. Add fennel and minced garlic to pan; sauté 3 minutes or until tender. Add wine and next 4 ingredients. Bring to a boil; reduce heat, and simmer 5 minutes. Place mixture in a blender; process until smooth. Pour into a fondue pot; keep warm over medium flame. Serve with shrimp and bread. Yield: 6 servings (serving size: 5 ounces shrimp, 1½ ounces bread, and about ¾ cup fondue).

CALORIES 345 (17% from fat); FAT 6.6g (sat 1.1g, mono 2.6g, poly 1.6g); PROTEIN 40.2g; CARB 29.7g; FIBER 1.5g; CHOL 261mg; IRON 6.7mg; SODIUM 994mg; CALC 190mg

### Sweet-and-Spicy Peanut Fondue

To save a little preparation time, buy pre-cooked chicken or cubed deli ham or turkey.

- 1 teaspoon peanut oil
- 1½ tablespoons grated peeled fresh ginger
- 4 garlic cloves, minced
- 1¼ cups fat-free, less-sodium chicken broth
- ½ cup creamy reduced-fat peanut butter
- ¼ cup rice vinegar
- ¼ cup low-sodium soy sauce
- 3 tablespoons hoisin sauce
- ¼ teaspoon chile paste with garlic
- 4 cups cubed cooked chicken breast (about 1½ pounds)
- 2 cups (1-inch-square) cut red bell pepper
- 2 cups snow peas, halved crosswise
- 2 (8-ounce) cans pineapple chunks in juice, drained
- 1 (8-ounce) can water chestnuts, drained

**1.** Heat oil in a medium saucepan over medium heat. Add ginger and garlic; sauté 1 minute. Add broth and next 5 ingredients; stir with a whisk. Bring to a boil. Reduce heat, and simmer 7 minutes or until sauce is smooth and thick, stirring occasionally. Pour into a fondue pot; keep warm over low flame. Serve with chicken, bell pepper, snow peas, pineapple, and water chestnuts. Yield: 8 servings (serving size: ½ cup chicken, ¼ cup bell pepper, ¼ cup snow peas, about ¼ cup pineapple, 2 tablespoons water chestnuts, and about ⅓ cup fondue).

CALORIES 280 (30% from fat); FAT 9.2g (sat 2g, mono 4.1g, poly 2.6g); PROTEIN 26.5g; CARB 22.7g; FIBER 2.7g; CHOL 54mg; IRON 2.5mg; SODIUM 596mg; CALC 40mg

### Lamb Skewers with Yogurt Sauce

In the style of Asian hot pot dishes, the lamb in this recipe developed by Chef Terrance Brennan is cooked at the table in a pot of simmering broth.

- 1 medium cucumber, peeled, seeded, and chopped (about 8 ounces)
- ⅛ teaspoon salt
- 1½ cups plain fat-free yogurt
- 1 tablespoon chopped fresh or 1 teaspoon dried dill
- 1 tablespoon dried oregano
- ⅛ teaspoon ground red pepper
- ⅛ teaspoon black pepper
- 1 garlic clove, minced
- 2 pounds boned leg of lamb
- 2 (16-ounce) cans fat-free, less-sodium chicken broth
- ¼ teaspoon salt
- ¼ teaspoon black pepper

**1.** Place cucumber in a blender; process until smooth. Place cucumber in a sieve; sprinkle with ⅛ teaspoon salt. Drain 1 hour. Combine cucumber, yogurt, and next 5 ingredients in a small bowl; stir until well-blended.

**2.** Trim fat from lamb; cut lamb into 1-inch cubes. Combine broth, ¼ teaspoon salt, and ¼ teaspoon pepper in a medium saucepan. Bring to a boil; cook 2 minutes. Pour into fondue pot; simmer over medium flame. Pierce lamb cubes with skewers; cook in broth mixture until desired degree of doneness is reached. Serve with yogurt sauce. Yield: 8 servings (serving size: about 3 ounces lamb and 3 tablespoons sauce).

CALORIES 149 (24% from fat); FAT 4g (sat 1.5g, mono 1.6g, poly 0.4g); PROTEIN 21.7g; CARB 5g; FIBER 0.3g; CHOL 55mg; IRON 2mg; SODIUM 436mg; CALC 106mg

## Thai Coconut-Lime Fondue

This fondue is really a two-course meal. After you've dipped all the pork and snap peas, add rice to the pot. It will soak up the flavor of the seasoned pork and create a delicious, soupy side dish.

**DIPPERS:**

1½  pounds pork tenderloin
    Cooking spray
  1  tablespoon water
  1  tablespoon rice vinegar
  1  tablespoon low-sodium soy sauce
  1  tablespoon honey
  2  cups sugar snap peas, trimmed

**FONDUE:**

  1  teaspoon sesame oil
  1  tablespoon minced peeled fresh
     ginger
  3  garlic cloves, minced
  1  (16-ounce) can fat-free, less-sodium
     chicken broth
  ¼  cup all-purpose flour
  ¼  cup water
  1  cup light coconut milk
  1  teaspoon grated lime rind
  ¼  cup fresh lime juice
1½  tablespoons brown sugar
  ⅛  teaspoon salt
  ⅛  teaspoon crushed red pepper

**REMAINING INGREDIENT:**

  3  cups hot cooked rice

**1.** Preheat oven to 425°.
**2.** To prepare dippers, trim fat from pork. Place pork on a rack coated with cooking spray. Line bottom of a shallow roasting pan with foil; place rack in pan. Combine water, vinegar, soy sauce, and honey in a small bowl; brush mixture over pork. Insert a meat thermometer into thickest part of pork. Bake at 425° for 30 minutes or until thermometer registers 160°. Cut pork into bite-size pieces.
**3.** Cook peas in boiling water 1 minute or until crisp-tender. Drain and rinse with cold water.
**4.** To prepare fondue, heat oil in a medium saucepan over medium-high heat. Add ginger and garlic; sauté 30 seconds. Stir in broth. Bring to a boil; cook 2

minutes. Remove from heat. Lightly spoon flour into a dry measuring cup; level with a knife. Combine flour and water, stirring well with a whisk. Add flour mixture, coconut milk, and next 5 ingredients to broth mixture; cook over medium heat 8 minutes or until slightly thick and bubbly, stirring frequently. Pour into a fondue pot. Keep warm over low flame. Dip pork and peas into fondue.
**5.** Spoon rice into fondue pot after dippers are eaten. Heat 1 minute, and ladle into soup bowls. Yield: 6 servings (serving size: 3 ounces pork, ⅓ cup peas, ½ cup rice, and ½ cup fondue).

CALORIES 357 (18% from fat); FAT 7.2g (sat 2.9g, mono 2.3g, poly 1g); PROTEIN 29.7g; CARB 41.1g; FIBER 1.9g; CHOL 79mg; IRON 3.8mg; SODIUM 365mg; CALC 47mg

## Caramel Apple Fondue

This cider-spiced caramel fondue with apples is a perfect treat for a Halloween party. If you don't have many guests, this recipe is easy to cut in half. You can also make the entire caramel fondue and store half in the refrigerator to use later as a topping for ice cream.

 82  small soft caramel candies
     (about 1½ pounds)
  ¾  cup apple cider
  ½  cup half-and-half
  1  tablespoon brandy (optional)
     Dash of ground nutmeg
  2  whole cloves
  1  (3-inch) cinnamon stick
  9  Granny Smith apples, each cut
     into 8 wedges (about 4½ pounds)

**1.** Place candies and cider in a medium heavy saucepan over medium heat; cook 12 minutes or until candies melt, stirring frequently. Stir in half-and-half and next 4 ingredients. Reduce heat, and cook 15 minutes, stirring occasionally. Discard cloves and cinnamon stick. Pour into a fondue pot. Keep warm over low flame. Serve with apple wedges. Yield: 12 servings (serving size: 6 apple wedges and ¼ cup caramel fondue).

CALORIES 298 (18% from fat); FAT 6.1g (sat 4.5g, mono 0.8g, poly 0.3g); PROTEIN 3.1g; CARB 61.7g; FIBER 3.5g; CHOL 8mg; IRON 0.3mg; SODIUM 144mg; CALC 97mg

## Buffalo Chicken with Blue Cheese Fondue

To keep the cheese creamy and smooth, stir the dippers in a figure-eight movement. A heavy enamel fondue pot helps prevent the cheese from burning on the bottom. Wing sauce can be found with other hot sauces in the condiment section of your grocery store.

**DIPPERS:**

  4  (4-ounce) skinned, boned chicken
     breast halves
     Cooking spray
  ¼  cup bottled wing sauce
     (such as Crystal), divided
  2  cups green beans, trimmed
     (about 8 ounces)
  2  cups (3 x ½-inch) carrot sticks
  2  cups (3-inch) celery sticks
  2  cups red bell pepper strips
 12  ounces French bread, toasted and
     cut into 1-inch cubes

**FONDUE:**

  2  cups (8 ounces) crumbled blue
     cheese
  1  tablespoon cornstarch
  1  cup dry white wine
  ⅔  cup 1% low-fat milk
  1  (8-ounce) block fat-free cream
     cheese, softened

**1.** Preheat oven to 400°.
**2.** To prepare dippers, place each chicken breast half between 2 sheets of heavy-duty plastic wrap, and flatten to ½-inch thickness using a meat mallet or rolling pin. Place chicken on a baking sheet coated with cooking spray. Brush with 2 tablespoons wing sauce. Bake at 400° for 5 minutes. Turn chicken over, and brush with 2 tablespoons wing sauce. Bake an additional 5 minutes or until done. Cut chicken into 1-inch pieces.
**3.** Cook beans in boiling water 1 minute or until crisp-tender; drain. Rinse with cold water; drain well. Place beans on a platter with carrot, celery, bell pepper, and bread; set aside.
**4.** To prepare fondue, combine blue cheese and cornstarch in a large
*Continued*

saucepan. Stir in wine, milk, and cream cheese. Bring to a boil over medium heat; cook 1 minute, stirring constantly. Reduce heat to medium-low; cook 8 minutes or until mixture is smooth, stirring frequently. Pour into a fondue pot. Keep warm over low flame. Serve with dippers. Yield: 8 servings (serving size: 1½ ounces chicken, ¼ cup beans, ¼ cup carrots, ¼ cup celery, ¼ cup bell pepper, 1½ ounces bread, and about ⅓ cup fondue).

CALORIES 352 (27% from fat); FAT 10.5g (sat 5.9g, mono 3g, poly 0.8g); PROTEIN 28.7g; CARB 34.1g; FIBER 3.3g; CHOL 60mg; IRON 2.5mg; SODIUM 991mg; CALC 319mg

### Chocolate-Frangelico Fondue

This creamy chocolate fondue will coat best if the banana and strawberries are briefly chilled before serving. You can substitute your favorite liqueur for the Frangelico.

⅓ cup half-and-half
¼ cup fat-free milk
8 ounces semisweet chocolate, chopped
1¼ cups sifted powdered sugar
¼ cup water
2 tablespoons Frangelico (hazelnut-flavored liqueur)
2 tablespoons dark corn syrup
4 cups (1-inch) cubed angel food cake (about 3 ounces)
2 cups sliced banana
2 cups quartered small strawberries

**1.** Combine first 3 ingredients in a medium saucepan; cook over medium-low heat 5 minutes or until smooth, stirring constantly. Stir in sugar, water, liqueur, and syrup. Cook 10 minutes or until mixture is smooth, stirring constantly. Pour into a fondue pot. Keep warm over low flame. Serve with cake, banana, and strawberries. Yield: 8 servings (serving size: ½ cup cake, ¼ cup banana, ¼ cup strawberries, and ¼ cup fondue).

CALORIES 322 (30% from fat); FAT 10.6g (sat 6.4g, mono 3.5g, poly 0.5g); PROTEIN 3.4g; CARB 58.9g; FIBER 2.1g; CHOL 4mg; IRON 1.3mg; SODIUM 70mg; CALC 48mg

### The Means to the Melting

Which pot is best for making which type of fondue?

**For carnivores:** You'll need a steel or aluminum pot to withstand the heat it takes to properly cook meat and seafood (ceramic cracks at high temperatures). Choose pots that have bases that can burn either alcohol fuel or fuel paste (considered safer since it doesn't splash).

**For chocoholics:** Chocolate fondue must be kept over very low heat so it doesn't scorch. A ceramic pot heated with a candle is your best bet.

**For cheese lovers:** Cheese fondue is heated at a much lower temperature. Your best choice is a ceramic pot—preferably one with a wide base for even heating—which may be kept warm by either fuel, fuel paste, or a small candle.

**Dipper's delight:** If you're a fondue fanatic, you can get away with just one pot, if it's electric. Although this type must be near an outlet, the various temperature settings allow cooking virtually any type of fondue.

the cooking light profile

# From the Heart of Cuba

*For Adelita Silva-Lopez, the way to keep a culinary tradition alive is to make it better.*

Twenty-two years ago, Adelita Silva-Lopez's brother-in-law Gus, who was only 39, suffered a heart attack. Adelita stepped in to care for him, following to the letter the cardiologist's special diet of low-calorie, low-fat dishes. And Adelita gained a passion for healthful eating. Now 46 and living in Tampa, Florida, the Cuba native has relentlessly decreased the fatty meat and full-fat dairy products in her family's favorite traditional dishes.

### Healthy Picadillo

This is one of Adelita's favorite recipes. She serves it with white rice or baked plantains.

2 pounds ground round
1 tablespoon olive oil
1½ cups thinly sliced onion
1 garlic clove, minced
1½ cups (¼-inch-thick) slices yellow bell pepper, each slice cut in half
1½ cups (¼-inch-thick) slices red bell pepper, each slice cut in half
1 cup finely chopped carrot
¾ cup golden raisins
½ cup dry white wine
¼ cup sliced pimento-stuffed manzanilla or green olives (about 15 olives)
2 tablespoons balsamic vinegar
1½ teaspoons salt
⅛ teaspoon black pepper
2 bay leaves
1 (14.5-ounce) can no-salt-added stewed tomatoes, undrained
1 (8-ounce) can no-salt-added tomato sauce

**1.** Cook beef in a large nonstick skillet over medium-high heat until browned; stir to crumble. Remove from pan; drain well.
**2.** Add oil to pan. Add onion and garlic; sauté 3 minutes. Add bell peppers and carrot; sauté 3 minutes. Return beef to pan. Stir in raisins and remaining ingredients; bring to a boil. Reduce heat; simmer 15 minutes, stirring occasionally. Discard bay leaves. Yield: 8 servings (serving size: 1 cup).

CALORIES 280 (29% from fat); FAT 9.1g (sat 2.8g, mono 4.4g, poly 0.6g); PROTEIN 26.4g; CARB 24g; FIBER 2.2g; CHOL 70mg; IRON 3.8mg; SODIUM 557mg; CALC 46mg

# History in the Baking

America can trace its love affair with apple crisp back to colonial days—but this old favorite continues to change with the times.

Crisps (or crumbles, as they're sometimes called) and their cousin the cobbler are among America's oldest fruit desserts. They became popular back in colonial days, when brick ovens offered folks a new alternative to the open fires over which the crisps' ancestors, plainly named grunts and slumps, were steamed. Ovens allowed cooks to substitute pastry crusts and sweet, crumbly toppings for the soft dumplings that grunted or slumped as they cooked.

One of the best things about crisps is that even though the fundamentals never really change, the adaptations and variations can be great fun. Right down to the choice of apples. Using fresh, high-quality fruit is more important than the variety chosen (we've used Granny Smiths and Rome apples). These recipes specify cold butter, but as long as the butter isn't too soft, its temperature isn't really all that important.

## Maple-Walnut Apple Crisp

- ⅓ cup all-purpose flour
- ½ cup packed light brown sugar
- ⅓ cup regular oats
- ¼ teaspoon ground cinnamon
- ¼ cup chilled butter or stick margarine, cut into small pieces
- 3 tablespoons chopped walnuts
- 7 cups sliced peeled Rome apple (about 3 pounds)
- ¼ cup maple syrup
- ½ teaspoon ground cinnamon

**1.** Preheat oven to 375°.
**2.** Lightly spoon flour into a dry measuring cup; level with a knife. Combine flour, sugar, oats, and ¼ teaspoon cinnamon in a medium bowl; cut in butter with a pastry blender or 2 knives until mixture is crumbly. Stir in walnuts.
**3.** Combine apple, maple syrup, and ½ teaspoon ground cinnamon in a large bowl; toss well. Spoon apple mixture into an 8-inch square baking dish or 1½-quart casserole. Sprinkle with crumb mixture. Bake at 375° for 45 minutes or until golden brown. Serve warm. Yield: 9 servings.

CALORIES 208 (31% from fat); FAT 7.1g (sat 3.4g, mono 1.9g, poly 1.3g); PROTEIN 1.8g; CARB 36.5g; FIBER 2.3g; CHOL 14mg; IRON 0.9mg; SODIUM 58mg; CALC 27mg

## Cranberry-Orange Apple Crisp

- ¼ cup all-purpose flour
- ¼ cup cornmeal
- ¼ cup granulated sugar
- ¼ cup packed light brown sugar
- ¼ cup chilled butter or stick margarine, cut into small pieces
- 7 cups diced peeled Rome apple (about 3 pounds)
- 1 cup fresh or frozen cranberries
- 2 tablespoons granulated sugar
- 2 teaspoons grated orange rind
- 3 tablespoons orange juice

**1.** Preheat oven to 375°.
**2.** Lightly spoon flour into a dry measuring cup; level with a knife. Combine flour, cornmeal, ¼ cup granulated sugar, and brown sugar in a bowl; cut in butter with a pastry blender or 2 knives until mixture is crumbly.
**3.** Combine apple and remaining 4 ingredients; toss well. Spoon into an 8-inch square baking dish or 1½-quart casserole. Sprinkle with crumb mixture. Bake at 375° for 45 minutes or until golden brown. Yield: 9 servings.

CALORIES 183 (27% from fat); FAT 5.5g (sat 3.2g, mono 1.5g, poly 0.3g); PROTEIN 0.9g; CARB 34.6g; FIBER 2.1g; CHOL 14mg; IRON 0.5mg; SODIUM 55mg; CALC 13mg

## Amaretto Apple Crisp

- ½ cup all-purpose flour
- ¼ cup granulated sugar
- ¼ cup packed light brown sugar
- ¼ cup chilled butter or stick margarine, cut into small pieces
- 3 tablespoons slivered almonds, toasted
- 7 cups sliced peeled Granny Smith apple (about 3 pounds)
- ⅓ cup amaretto (almond-flavored liqueur) or apple juice

**1.** Preheat oven to 375°.
**2.** Lightly spoon flour into a dry measuring cup; level with a knife. Combine flour and sugars in a bowl; cut in butter with a pastry blender or 2 knives until mixture is crumbly. Add toasted almonds, and toss well.
**3.** Combine apple and amaretto in a bowl; toss well. Spoon apple mixture into an 8-inch square baking dish or 1½-quart casserole. Sprinkle with crumb mixture. Bake at 375° for 45 minutes or until golden brown. Yield: 9 servings.

CALORIES 204 (29% from fat); FAT 6.5g (sat 3.4g, mono 2.2g, poly 0.5g); PROTEIN 1.3g; CARB 32.5g; FIBER 2g; CHOL 14mg; IRON 0.6mg; SODIUM 55mg; CALC 16mg

## Caramel Apple Crisp

- ½ cup all-purpose flour
- ¼ cup granulated sugar
- ¼ cup packed light brown sugar
- ¼ cup chilled butter or stick margarine, cut into small pieces
- ½ cup coarsely broken peanut brittle (such as Planters)
- 3½ cups sliced peeled Granny Smith apple (about 1½ pounds)
- 3½ cups sliced peeled Rome apple (about 1½ pounds)
- ⅓ cup fat-free caramel sundae syrup

**1.** Preheat oven to 375°.
**2.** Lightly spoon flour into a dry measuring cup; level with a knife. Combine flour and sugars in a bowl; cut in butter with a pastry blender or 2 knives until

*Continued*

mixture is crumbly. Add peanut brittle; toss well.

**3.** Combine apple and syrup in a bowl; toss well. Spoon apple mixture into an 8-inch square baking dish or 1½-quart casserole. Sprinkle with crumb mixture. Bake at 375° for 45 minutes or until golden brown. Yield: 9 servings.

CALORIES 222 (25% from fat); FAT 6.2g (sat 3.4g, mono 1.9g, poly 0.5g); PROTEIN 1.2g; CARB 41.8g; FIBER 1.9g; CHOL 14mg; IRON 0.6mg; SODIUM 100mg; CALC 17mg

## Banana-Coconut Apple Crisp

½ cup all-purpose flour
¼ cup granulated sugar
¼ cup packed light brown sugar
¼ cup chilled butter or stick margarine, cut into small pieces
⅓ cup flaked sweetened coconut
7 cups sliced peeled Rome apple (about 3 pounds)
¾ cup diced ripe banana
¼ cup apricot preserves
3 tablespoons orange juice

**1.** Preheat oven to 375°.
**2.** Lightly spoon flour into a dry measuring cup; level with a knife. Combine flour and sugars in a bowl; cut in butter with a pastry blender or 2 knives until mixture is crumbly. Stir in coconut.
**3.** Combine apple and remaining 3 ingredients in a bowl; toss well. Spoon apple mixture into an 8-inch square baking dish or 1½-quart casserole. Sprinkle with crumb mixture. Bake at 375° for 45 minutes or until golden brown. Yield: 9 servings.

CALORIES 216 (28% from fat); FAT 6.7g (sat 4.3g, mono 1.6g, poly 0.3g); PROTEIN 1.2g; CARB 40.3g; FIBER 2.4g; CHOL 14mg; IRON 0.7mg; SODIUM 67mg; CALC 15mg

## Tropical Pineapple-Apple Crisp

½ cup all-purpose flour
¼ cup granulated sugar
¼ cup packed light brown sugar
3 tablespoons chilled butter or stick margarine, cut into small pieces
¼ cup chopped macadamia nuts
7 cups sliced peeled Rome apple (about 3 pounds)
1 (8-ounce) can pineapple tidbits in juice, drained
⅓ cup diced dried tropical fruit (such as Mariani)
1 tablespoon granulated sugar
1½ teaspoons grated peeled fresh ginger

**1.** Preheat oven to 375°.
**2.** Lightly spoon flour into a dry measuring cup; level with a knife. Combine flour, ¼ cup granulated sugar, and brown sugar in a bowl; cut in butter with a pastry blender or 2 knives until mixture is crumbly. Add nuts; toss well.
**3.** Combine apple and remaining 4 ingredients in a large bowl; toss well. Spoon apple mixture into an 8-inch square baking dish or 1½-quart casserole. Sprinkle with crumb mixture. Bake at 375° for 45 minutes or until golden brown. Yield: 9 servings.

CALORIES 208 (31% from fat); FAT 7.2g (sat 3g, mono 3.4g, poly 0.3g); PROTEIN 1.2g; CARB 37.1g; FIBER 2.4g; CHOL 10mg; IRON 0.7mg; SODIUM 46mg; CALC 14mg

## Spicy Autumn Crisp

(pictured on page 293)

Tart apple contrasts with the sweet, deep flavors of spices and molasses. Try it with vanilla frozen yogurt.

**TOPPING:**

9 gingersnap cookies (such as Nabisco)
¼ cup granulated sugar
¼ cup packed light brown sugar
2 tablespoons all-purpose flour
¼ cup chilled butter or stick margarine, cut into small pieces

**FILLING:**

3½ cups chopped peeled Granny Smith apple (about 1½ pounds)
3½ cups coarsely chopped peeled Bartlett pear (about 1½ pounds)
½ cup chopped pitted dates or golden raisins
¼ cup molasses
¾ teaspoon ground cinnamon
½ teaspoon ground ginger
⅛ teaspoon ground nutmeg
⅛ teaspoon ground cloves

**1.** Preheat oven to 375°.
**2.** To prepare topping, place cookies in a food processor; pulse 10 times or until coarse crumbs form to measure ½ cup. Combine cookie crumbs, sugars, and flour in a medium bowl; cut in butter with a pastry blender or 2 knives until mixture is crumbly.
**3.** To prepare filling, combine apple and remaining 7 ingredients in a large bowl; toss well. Spoon apple mixture into an 8-inch square baking dish or 1½-quart casserole. Sprinkle with topping. Bake at 375° for 45 minutes or until bubbly. Yield: 9 servings.

CALORIES 246 (25% from fat); FAT 6.9g (sat 3.6g, mono 2.1g, poly 0.6g); PROTEIN 1.3g; CARB 47.9g; FIBER 2.7g; CHOL 17mg; IRON 1.4mg; SODIUM 69mg; CALC 54mg

Spicy Autumn Crisp,
page 292

Roasted Pepper Pesto-
Tomato Pizza, page 302

Spanish Toast, page 298

Creamy Four-Cheese
Macaroni, page 308

Spinach Ravioli with
Tomato Sauce, page 277

Fattoosh (Mixed Herb and Toasted Pita Salad), page 303

Wild Rice Crab Cakes, page 282

# Salt Uncensored

### By land or by sea, shaken or stirred, crystals or grains, salt is indispensable to life—and to good cooking.

Salt is arguably the most important ingredient in our pantries. Without salt as a seasoning, most cooked foods and many fresh ones just don't reach their full potential. With it—and that can often mean nothing more than the classic pinch—flavors blossom. And although some people must closely monitor their sodium intake, for most of us, the moderate use of salt in cooking presents no health risks.

Mastering salt is probably one of the easiest and fastest ways to improve your cooking. A little salt at the right time is infinitely more flavor-enhancing than a downpour at the wrong time. This is how professional chefs make food taste so good; they know that salt added after cooking cannot make up for a lack of it during the process.

## Trout Baked in a Salt Crust

Don't let this title mislead you. The salt crust actually functions like a blanket that prevents steam and juices from escaping. The result is moist, flavorful fish—not an overly salty taste. The crust also captures the aromas of the ginger, garlic, and lime and forces them into the fish. Grape leaves can be found in the ethnic sections of most supermarkets.

  1   (16-ounce) jar large grape leaves (about 40 leaves)
  8   (¼-inch) slices peeled fresh ginger
  4   garlic cloves, thinly sliced
  8   lime slices
  4   (8-ounce) cleaned whole brook trout
  6   pounds rock salt
  2   tablespoons fresh lime juice (about 2 limes)
  2   teaspoons sugar
  1½  teaspoons fish sauce
  3   garlic cloves, minced
  2   serrano chiles, seeded and minced
  2   tablespoons minced fresh cilantro

**1.** Preheat oven to 350°.
**2.** Drain and rinse grape leaves; set aside.
**3.** Divide ginger, garlic slices, and lime slices evenly among cavities of fish; set aside.

**4.** Cover a baking sheet or jelly-roll pan with rock salt to a depth of ½ inch. Arrange half of grape leaves on salt, leaving a 1½-inch border. Place fish on leaves. Cover fish with 10 leaves, tucking leaves around fish. Place remaining leaves loosely over fish. Cover fish and leaves with a ½-inch layer of rock salt. Bake at 350° for 35 minutes. Remove fish from oven; let stand 10 minutes.
**5.** Combine lime juice and next 4 ingredients. Set aside.
**6.** Cover a large work surface with newspaper. Tip baking sheet gently over newspaper to remove loose salt. Use a small spatula to gently remove fish, still in grape leaves. Remove any salt from outside of leaves; peel away leaves, and discard. Arrange fish on individual plates; serve with sauce. Sprinkle fish with cilantro. Yield: 4 servings (serving size: 1 trout and 1 tablespoon sauce).
**NOTE:** You can use this technique with most any fish, including fillets and steaks. If you use these cuts, place ginger, lime slices, and garlic slices on top of fish.

CALORIES 223 (24% from fat); FAT 5.9g (sat 1.1g, mono 1.8g, poly 2.1g); PROTEIN 36.3g; CARB 4.2g; FIBER 0.2g; CHOL 99mg; IRON 3.5mg; SODIUM 211mg; CALC 125mg

## Salt vs. Sodium

Taste and texture, not nutrition, are the main reasons to use the salt you prefer.

**Sodium can vary significantly:** It ranges from 230 milligrams in ¼ teaspoon Celtic Sea Salt to 490 milligrams in Baleine Coarse Crystals Sea Salt. The same amount of kosher salt varies from 280 milligrams in Diamond Crystal to 480 in Morton's; it's 580 milligrams in most iodized table salts.

**It's all a matter of density:** Some salts are fluffed so that the crystals contain more air; others are created as hollow pyramids to increase their flavor surfaces. Lower sodium generally indicates less density in the crystals, but it doesn't necessarily have anything to do with flavor.

That's for you to decide, and you may want to adjust accordingly the amount of salt used in these recipes. Just know that kosher and sea salts actually taste saltier than the same amount of table salt—so you get more flavor with less sodium.

**What about salt and your health?** The value of a lower-sodium diet in preventing or treating hypertension has been controversial. But a new study reaffirms the importance of restricting sodium, especially if your blood pressure is high or high-normal. Participants in the DASH (Dietary Approaches to Stop Hypertension) Sodium study with high (above 140/90) and high-normal (120/80 to 139/89) blood pressures lowered them significantly on a diet containing 1,500 milligrams of sodium a day—less than half of what the average American eats. Their diets were also high in fruits, vegetables, and low-fat dairy products.

Experts aren't yet recommending that people with normal blood pressure go easy on salt, but this study indicates it may be of some benefit. **Questions? Ask your doctor.**

## Spanish Toast

(pictured on page 294)

Rubbing ripe tomatoes over garlic toast is a tradition in Spain, where it's common to find a plate of tomatoes and garlic on the table, waiting for the toast to arrive. The crisp toast almost melts the garlic and the tomatoes. Very ripe tomatoes and a hearty, dense bread work best. If firing up the grill to toast the bread seems daunting, you can broil or bake it in the oven.

    8   (2-ounce) slices sourdough bread
    4   garlic cloves, halved
    4   small tomatoes, each cut in half
        crosswise (about ¾ pound)
    4   teaspoons extra-virgin olive oil
    ¼   teaspoon kosher salt or sea salt
    ¼   teaspoon freshly ground black
        pepper

**1.** Prepare grill.
**2.** Place bread slices on grill rack; grill 2 minutes on each side or until lightly browned. Rub 1 side of each bread slice with 1 garlic clove half and 1 tomato half (tomato pulp will rub off onto bread). Discard tomato peels. Drizzle ½ teaspoon olive oil over each bread slice; sprinkle evenly with salt and pepper. Yield: 8 servings.

CALORIES 168 (19% from fat); FAT 3.5g (sat 0.6g, mono 2.1g, poly 0.5g); PROTEIN 5.5g; CARB 29.3g; FIBER 1.4g; CHOL 0mg; IRON 1.6mg; SODIUM 351mg; CALC 60mg

## Summer Jewel Salad

The pleasure of this dish comes from the salt's crunchy texture against the juicy cherry tomatoes. This recipe showcases the distinctive taste of sea salt, but kosher salt will work, too. Add the salt just before serving.

    4   cups cherry tomatoes, halved
    2   tablespoons chopped fresh
        chives
    1   tablespoon extra-virgin olive oil
    ¼   teaspoon freshly ground black
        pepper
    1   teaspoon sea salt

**1.** Combine first 4 ingredients; toss gently. Divide evenly among 4 plates; sprinkle with salt. Serve at room temperature. Yield: 7 servings (serving size: ½ cup).

CALORIES 36 (55% from fat); FAT 2.2g (sat 0.3g, mono 1.5g, poly 0.3g); PROTEIN 0.8g; CARB 4.1g; FIBER 1g; CHOL 0mg; IRON 0.4mg; SODIUM 271mg; CALC 5mg

## Roasted Shrimp with Honey-Pepper Vinaigrette

Shrimp roasted on a bed of hot rock salt are succulent, tender, fragrant, and not at all salty. The salt helps transfer heat efficiently and evenly rather than flavor the shrimp, though it does seem to accent their naturally briny character.

    3   tablespoons sherry vinegar
    2   tablespoons honey
    1   tablespoon minced shallots
    1   tablespoon extra-virgin olive oil
    1   teaspoon freshly ground black
        pepper
    ½   teaspoon kosher salt
    2   garlic cloves, minced
    3   pounds rock salt
    12  unpeeled jumbo shrimp (about ¾
        pound)

**1.** Preheat oven to 400°.
**2.** Combine first 7 ingredients in a bowl; stir well with a whisk.
**3.** Place a 1-inch-thick layer of rock salt (about 3 pounds) in bottom of an oven-proof Dutch oven. Place pan in oven at 400° for 30 minutes or until rock salt is very hot. Arrange shrimp in a single layer over rock salt. Cover and bake at 400° for 2 minutes. Turn shrimp over, and bake for an additional 2 minutes or until done. Serve shrimp with vinaigrette. Yield: 4 appetizer servings (serving size: 3 shrimp and 1½ tablespoons vinaigrette).

CALORIES 170 (25% from fat); FAT 4.8g (sat 0.5g, mono 1.7g, poly 0.7g); PROTEIN 17.4g; CARB 11.2g; FIBER 0.1g; CHOL 129mg; IRON 2.3mg; SODIUM 267mg; CALC 48mg

## Brined Chicken with Lemon

Brining, or soaking food in a salt solution, can improve the flavor of chicken. Soaking the chicken in brine overnight allows for uniform salting and produces a very moist chicken.

    4   quarts water
    ⅔   cup kosher salt
    1   (4- to 5-pound) roasting chicken
    4   (⅛-inch-thick) slices lemon
    ¼   teaspoon black pepper
    4   lemon wedges
    4   flat-leaf parsley sprigs
    2   garlic cloves, cut in half
    1   shallot, peeled and quartered

**1.** Combine 4 quarts water and salt in a Dutch oven, stirring until salt dissolves. Remove and discard giblets and neck from chicken. Rinse chicken with cold water; pat dry. Trim excess fat. Add chicken to salt mixture; cover and refrigerate 8 hours or overnight.
**2.** Preheat oven to 400°.
**3.** Remove chicken from brine; discard brine. Pat chicken dry with paper towels. Starting at neck cavity, loosen skin from breast and drumsticks by inserting fingers, gently pushing between skin and meat. Place lemon slices under loosened skin. Sprinkle cavity with pepper; place lemon wedges, parsley, garlic, and shallot into cavity. Lift wing tips up and over back; tuck under chicken. Place on rack of a broiler pan. Bake at 400° for 1 hour and 10 minutes or until thermometer registers 180°. Discard skin. Yield: 8 servings (serving size: 3 ounces chicken).

CALORIES 164 (35% from fat); FAT 6.3g (sat 1.7g, mono 2.3g, poly 1.5g); PROTEIN 24.7g; CARB 1g; FIBER 0.1g; CHOL 76mg; IRON 1.1mg; SODIUM 494mg; CALC 18mg

# Salt, Salt, Salt

It's not all the same. Salt comes in dozens of textures, colors, and tastes. In our recipes, we generally use the three most popular varieties—kosher, sea, and table. But you might be interested in some of the other choices you may have encountered.

| Type | Qualities | Recommended Uses | Availability and Price |
|---|---|---|---|
| Table salt (Plain) | Small, hard, dry cubes; pours easily; dissolves slowly; sharp-tasting on front of palate, otherwise mild | General cooking, household cleaner | Widely available; cheap |
| Table salt (Iodized) | Same as plain table salt, with iodine added | Prevents goiter (an iodine-deficiency disease common where seafood is not available) | Widely available; cheap |
| Kosher (Diamond Crystal) | Dry, hollow pyramids; dissolves quickly; moderately salty; delicate | General cooking, baking, brining, preserving, finishing; all-purpose | Regional; cheap |
| Kosher (Other brands) | Flattened cubes and fused flattened cubes; very dry and hard; dissolves slowly; mild | General cooking except baking; salt crusts and salt doughs | Generally available; cheap |
| Sea salt | Any salt from sea water; often the same as table salt | Finishing | Types and prices vary widely |
| *Sel gris* | Hard, moist gray crystals of solar-evaporated salt from the northern Atlantic coast of France; briny; sweet; delicate; dissolves slowly | Baking and roasting; finishing | Mail-order, gourmet shops; expensive |
| *Fleur de sel* | Hard, slightly moist white crystals of solar-evaporated salt from the northern Atlantic coast of France; briny; sweet; delicate; dissolves slowly | Finishing (condiment) | Mail-order, gourmet shops; expensive |
| Hawaiian Alae | Pale-orange crystals; hard, dry; slight taste of iron; silky from natural clay | Finishing | Regional, mail-order; cheap |
| Black Salt (*Kala namak*) | Large rocks or fine powder; pale violet to purple-black; strong sulfuric aroma; earthy | Indian cuisine | Mail-order, ethnic markets; moderate |

## Slow-Roasted Pork Tacos

This simple recipe was inspired by the traditional *kalua* pork of Hawaii, for which a whole pig is rubbed thoroughly with salt and baked in an underground pit. In this dish, the salt combines with the slow cooking to make the pork incredibly tender and flavorful. Don't use a leaner cut of pork, such as pork loin or tenderloin, or the meat will be dry. These tacos are also terrific with a mango or other fruit salsa.

3½ pounds Boston Butt pork roast
3 tablespoons kosher salt
20 (6-inch) corn tortillas
¼ cup minced fresh cilantro
10 lime wedges

**1.** Preheat oven to 275°.
**2.** Trim fat from roast; rub surface of roast with salt. Place meat in a large Dutch oven; cover and place in oven. Cook 3 hours or until pork falls apart when pressed with back of a fork. Remove from oven; let stand, covered, 15 minutes. Remove meat from bones, and shred with 2 forks. Set aside.
**3.** Warm tortillas according to package directions. Fill each tortilla with about 1½ ounces pork; serve with cilantro and lime wedges. Yield: 10 servings (serving size: 2 tacos).

CALORIES 333 (40% from fat); FAT 14.9g (sat 4.9g, mono 6.4g, poly 2.2g); PROTEIN 25.9g; CARB 23.4g; FIBER 2.7g; CHOL 88mg; IRON 2.2mg; SODIUM 486mg; CALC 97mg

## The Simplest Green Salad

This recipe for the most basic of all salads begins with the Italian tradition of putting salt directly on the greens, before the olive oil or anything else. You'll be surprised at how much flavor just ¼ teaspoon kosher salt can impart when tossed with greens in this way.

10 cups mixed salad greens
¼ teaspoon kosher salt
5 teaspoons extra-virgin olive oil
2 teaspoons fresh lemon juice
⅛ teaspoon freshly ground black pepper

*Continued*

**1.** Place greens in a large bowl; sprinkle with salt, tossing gently. Add remaining ingredients, tossing to coat. Serve immediately. Yield: 5 servings (serving size: 2 cups).

CALORIES 58 (73% from fat); FAT 4.7g (sat 0.6g, mono 3.3g, poly 0.5g); PROTEIN 1.8g; CARB 2.9g; FIBER 1.9g; CHOL 0mg; IRON 1.3mg; SODIUM 65mg; CALC 41mg

## Potatoes Roasted on Salt, Caraway, and Cumin

1¼ teaspoons caraway seeds, divided
  1 tablespoon butter or stick margarine
1½ cups rock salt
  ½ teaspoon cumin seeds
  ½ teaspoon black pepper
  1 pound small red potatoes, quartered

**1.** Preheat oven to 425°.
**2.** Cook ¼ teaspoon caraway seeds in a small saucepan over low heat 1 minute or until toasted. Add butter, and cook until melted; set aside.
**3.** Spread rock salt evenly in bottom of a shallow 3-quart casserole. Sprinkle 1 teaspoon caraway seeds, cumin seeds, and pepper over rock salt. Arrange potatoes over salt mixture. Bake at 425° for 35 minutes or until tender. Remove potatoes from salt mixture; discard salt mixture. Combine butter mixture and potatoes; toss to coat. Yield: 5 servings (serving size: ½ cup).

CALORIES 91 (25% from fat); FAT 2.5g (sat 1.5g, mono 0.7g, poly 0.2g); PROTEIN 2.2g; CARB 15.6g; FIBER 1.8g; CHOL 6mg; IRON 1.5mg; SODIUM 265mg; CALC 19mg

# Mangia, Presto

*Take a lesson from Italians with these speedy weeknight dinners.*

Can a culture that relishes 12-course meals also inspire quick and simple cooking? Ask the Italians, whose culinary ingenuity helped not only to perfect pasta, but also to tailor it perfectly for modern needs in fast-cooking entrées. These flavorful entrées come together so quickly and taste so great, you may decide to dine like an Italian, lingering over your meal to savor the flavors.

## Penne with Ricotta and Mint

**PREPARATION TIME: 10 MINUTES**
**COOKING TIME: 14 MINUTES**

  1 cup part-skim ricotta cheese
  2 tablespoons minced fresh parsley
  2 tablespoons thinly sliced green onions
  1 tablespoon minced fresh mint
  1 tablespoon butter or stick margarine, melted
  1 tablespoon lemon juice
  1 teaspoon salt
  1 teaspoon freshly ground black pepper
  1 pound uncooked penne (tube-shaped pasta)
  2 tablespoons grated Parmesan cheese

**1.** Combine first 8 ingredients in a large bowl; set aside.
**2.** Cook pasta according to package directions, omitting salt and fat. Drain pasta in a colander over a bowl, reserving ½ cup cooking liquid. Add ½ cup cooking liquid to ricotta mixture; stir until mixture is well-blended.
**3.** Add pasta to ricotta mixture; toss well. Sprinkle with Parmesan. Yield: 6 servings (serving size: 1⅓ cups).

CALORIES 364 (17% from fat); FAT 6.9g (sat 3.7g, mono 1.8g, poly 0.7g); PROTEIN 15.2g; CARB 59.3g; FIBER 2g; CHOL 19mg; IRON 3.3mg; SODIUM 499mg; CALC 154mg

## Baked Fish with Olive-Crumb Coating

**PREPARATION TIME: 10 MINUTES**
**COOKING TIME: 12 MINUTES**

2¼ pounds red snapper or other lean white fish fillets
  Cooking spray
  3 tablespoons lemon juice
  ⅓ cup dry breadcrumbs
  ⅓ cup chopped green olives
  1 tablespoon olive oil
  2 teaspoons dried oregano
  1 teaspoon bottled minced garlic
  ¼ teaspoon white pepper
  1 (2.25-ounce) can chopped ripe olives, drained
  6 lemon wedges

**1.** Preheat oven to 450°.
**2.** Arrange fish in a 13 x 9-inch baking dish coated with cooking spray; sprinkle with lemon juice.
**3.** Combine breadcrumbs and next 6 ingredients; stir until moist. Spread olive mixture evenly over fillets, pressing firmly to coat. Bake at 450° for 12 minutes or until fish flakes easily when tested with a fork. Serve fish with lemon wedges. Yield: 6 servings (serving size: 5 ounces fish).

CALORIES 239 (25% from fat); FAT 6.7g (sat 1.2g, mono 3.6g, poly 1.4g); PROTEIN 36g; CARB 6.9g; FIBER 0.8g; CHOL 63mg; IRON 1.6mg; SODIUM 326mg; CALC 95mg

## Raisin-and-Pine Nut Stuffed Peppers

PREPARATION TIME: 10 MINUTES
COOKING TIME: 18 MINUTES

This recipe conveniently uses the microwave to cook the peppers and heat the sauce, a blend of pureed canned chickpeas and commercial pasta sauce.

2 cups fat-free Italian herb pasta sauce, divided (such as Muir Glen)
¾ pound ground turkey
½ cup uncooked instant rice
¼ cup raisins
2 tablespoons grated Romano cheese
2 tablespoons pine nuts
1 teaspoon dried basil
1 teaspoon black pepper
½ teaspoon salt
1 teaspoon bottled minced garlic
4 large red bell peppers (about 1½ pounds)
1 (15½-ounce) can chickpeas (garbanzo beans), undrained
1 teaspoon olive oil

**1.** Combine 1 cup pasta sauce, turkey, and next 8 ingredients in a bowl. Cut tops off bell peppers; reserve tops. Discard seeds and membranes.
**2.** Divide turkey mixture evenly among peppers, and cover with reserved tops. Place peppers in an 8-inch square baking dish. Microwave at HIGH 14 minutes or until tender.
**3.** While peppers are cooking, drain chickpeas in a colander over a bowl, reserving ⅔ cup chickpeas and ¼ cup liquid. Reserve remaining chickpeas for another use. Place 1 cup pasta sauce, ⅔ cup chickpeas, ¼ cup chickpea liquid, and olive oil in a blender or food processor; process until well-blended. Place chickpea mixture in a 2-cup glass measure. Microwave at HIGH 2 minutes or until thoroughly heated, stirring after 1 minute. Serve stuffed bell peppers with sauce. Yield: 4 servings (serving size: 1 stuffed pepper and ⅓ cup sauce).

CALORIES 450 (30% from fat); FAT 15.2g (sat 4.1g, mono 5.9g, poly 4.9g); PROTEIN 24.7g; CARB 55.2g; FIBER 9.6g; CHOL 75mg; IRON 5.9mg; SODIUM 898mg; CALC 115mg

---

## menu

### Pork Medallions with Orange-Rosemary Sauce

Steamed Brussels sprouts

Roasted onion wedges*

*Peel 2 large sweet onions; cut each into 6 wedges, and place in a baking dish. Combine 2 tablespoons balsamic vinegar, 2 tablespoons honey, 1 tablespoon olive oil, and ¼ teaspoon salt. Drizzle over onions; toss well. Cover and bake at 450° for 25 minutes; uncover and bake 25 minutes or until tender. Serves 4.

---

## Pork Medallions with Orange-Rosemary Sauce

PREPARATION TIME: 10 MINUTES
COOKING TIME: 17 MINUTES

1 pound pork tenderloin
½ teaspoon black pepper
¼ teaspoon salt
2 teaspoons olive oil, divided
Cooking spray
1 tablespoon bottled minced garlic
½ cup dry red wine
½ teaspoon dried rosemary, crumbled
2 tablespoons tomato paste
¾ cup fat-free, less-sodium chicken broth
¼ cup orange juice

**1.** Trim fat from pork, and cut pork crosswise into 1-inch-thick pieces. Place each piece between 2 sheets of heavy-duty plastic wrap; flatten each piece to ½-inch thickness using a meat mallet or rolling pin. Sprinkle both sides of pork with pepper and salt.
**2.** Heat 1 teaspoon oil in a 9-inch cast-iron skillet coated with cooking spray over medium-high heat. Add pork; cook 3 minutes on each side or until done. Remove pork from pan; set aside.
**3.** Heat 1 teaspoon oil in pan. Add garlic; sauté 45 seconds. Stir in wine and rosemary, scraping pan to loosen browned bits. Add tomato paste; cook 2 minutes. Stir in broth and orange juice; cook until thick (about 6 minutes). Serve pork with sauce. Yield: 4 servings (serving size: 3 ounces pork and ¼ cup sauce).

CALORIES 195 (25% from fat); FAT 5.4g (sat 1.3g, mono 3g, poly 0.6g); PROTEIN 25.2g; CARB 5.4g; FIBER 0.6g; CHOL 74mg; IRON 2.2mg; SODIUM 302mg; CALC 27mg

---

## Pasta e Fagioli

PREPARATION TIME: 6 MINUTES
COOKING TIME: 20 MINUTES

*Fagioli* (fa-ZHOH-lee) is Italian for "beans"; in cooking, it refers primarily to white beans.

1 tablespoon olive oil
6 ounces hot turkey Italian sausage
1½ tablespoons bottled minced garlic
1 cup water
1 (16-ounce) can fat-free, less-sodium chicken broth
1 (8-ounce) can no-salt-added tomato sauce
1 cup uncooked small seashell pasta (about 4 ounces)
½ cup grated Romano cheese, divided
1½ teaspoons dried oregano
¼ teaspoon salt
¼ teaspoon white pepper
2 (15-ounce) cans cannellini beans or other white beans, drained
Minced fresh parsley (optional)
Crushed red pepper (optional)

**1.** Heat oil in a large saucepan over medium-high heat. Add sausage and garlic; sauté 2 minutes or until browned, stirring to crumble. Add water, broth, and tomato sauce; bring to a boil. Stir in pasta, ¼ cup cheese, oregano, salt, white pepper, and beans; bring to a boil. Cover, reduce heat, and simmer 8 minutes or until pasta is done. Let stand 5 minutes; sprinkle with ¼ cup cheese. Garnish each serving with parsley and red pepper, if desired. Yield: 6 servings (serving size: 1 cup).

CALORIES 353 (26% from fat); FAT 10.2g (sat 3.1g, mono 4.1g, poly 2.3g); PROTEIN 20.5g; CARB 45.6g; FIBER 4.5g; CHOL 34mg; IRON 4.5mg; SODIUM 742mg; CALC 177mg

## Quick Mozzarella Chicken

PREPARATION TIME: 10 MINUTES
COOKING TIME: 18 MINUTES

     4   ounces uncooked spaghetti
     ½   cup Italian-seasoned breadcrumbs
     3   tablespoons grated Parmesan cheese
     4   (4-ounce) skinned, boned chicken
         breast halves
     ¼   cup egg substitute
     1   tablespoon olive oil
     4   (¾-ounce) slices part-skim
         mozzarella cheese
    2½   cups fat-free Italian herb pasta
         sauce (such as Muir Glen)
     2   tablespoons chopped fresh parsley

**1.** Preheat oven to 425°.
**2.** Cook pasta according to package directions, omitting salt and fat. Drain well.
**3.** While pasta is cooking, prepare chicken. Combine breadcrumbs and Parmesan cheese in a shallow dish. Dip chicken in egg substitute, and dredge in breadcrumb mixture.
**4.** Heat olive oil in a 9-inch cast-iron skillet over medium-high heat. Add chicken to pan, and cook 2 minutes on each side. Top chicken with mozzarella slices, and place pan in oven. Bake at 425° for 14 minutes or until chicken is done.
**5.** While chicken is cooking, heat pasta sauce in a medium saucepan over medium-low heat.
**6.** Place ½ cup pasta on each of 4 plates; top each serving with a chicken breast half and ⅔ cup sauce. Sprinkle with parsley. Yield: 4 servings.

CALORIES 429 (17% from fat); FAT 9.4g (sat 3.5g, mono 4.1g, poly 1.1g); PROTEIN 40.1g; CARB 43.5g; FIBER 3.3g; CHOL 80mg; IRON 3.8mg; SODIUM 796mg; CALC 218mg

## Parmesan Polenta with Sausage and Mushrooms

PREPARATION TIME: 5 MINUTES
COOKING TIME: 24 MINUTES

     3   (3-ounce) links hot turkey Italian
         sausage
     1   teaspoon olive oil
     ⅓   cup dry white wine
     2   (8-ounce) packages presliced
         mushrooms
     2   tablespoons chopped fresh or
         2 teaspoons dried basil
     1   (14.5-ounce) can diced tomatoes,
         drained
     4   cups water
     1   cup instant polenta (such as
         Contadina)
     ¾   teaspoon garlic powder
     ½   teaspoon sugar
     ¼   teaspoon salt
     ⅓   cup grated Parmesan cheese

**1.** Pierce sausages; cut each diagonally into 1-inch pieces. Heat oil in a large nonstick skillet over medium-high heat. Add sausage; cook 3 minutes or until browned. Add wine and mushrooms; cover, reduce heat, and cook 10 minutes. Stir occasionally. Remove sausage from pan. Cook mushroom mixture over medium-high heat 5 minutes or until liquid almost evaporates. Stir in basil and tomatoes; cook 1 minute or until heated. Return sausage to pan; keep warm.
**2.** While sauce is simmering, prepare polenta. Bring water to a boil in a medium saucepan; stir in polenta, garlic powder, sugar, and salt. Reduce heat to low; cook until thick (about 5 minutes), stirring frequently. Stir in cheese. Serve with sausage mixture. Yield: 5 servings (serving size: about ¾ cup sausage mixture and ¾ cup polenta).

CALORIES 288 (30% from fat); FAT 9.5g (sat 3.3g, mono 3.6g, poly 2.4g); PROTEIN 18.2g; CARB 35.1g; FIBER 1.6g; CHOL 58mg; IRON 2.5mg; SODIUM 689mg; CALC 95mg

## Roasted Pepper Pesto-Tomato Pizza

(pictured on page 293)

PREPARATION TIME: 10 MINUTES
COOKING TIME: 10 MINUTES

     1   large garlic clove, peeled
     1   cup basil leaves
     ¼   cup (1 ounce) grated fresh Parmesan
         cheese
     2   tablespoons tomato paste
    1½   tablespoons water
     1   teaspoon sugar
     1   teaspoon extra-virgin olive oil
     1   (5.2-ounce) bottle roasted red bell
         peppers, drained
     1   (1-pound) Italian cheese-flavored
         pizza crust (such as Boboli)
     ¾   cup (3 ounces) shredded part-skim
         mozzarella cheese
     3   plum tomatoes, thinly sliced
         (about 6 ounces)
     ½   teaspoon dried oregano

**1.** Preheat oven to 450°.
**2.** Drop garlic through food chute with food processor on; process until minced. Add basil and next 6 ingredients, and process until smooth, scraping sides of bowl once.
**3.** Place pizza crust on a baking sheet. Spread pepper mixture over pizza crust, leaving a ½-inch border; sprinkle with mozzarella. Arrange tomato slices in a single layer on top of cheese. Bake at 450° for 10 minutes. Sprinkle pizza with oregano. Yield: 6 servings (serving size: 1 slice).

CALORIES 285 (28% from fat); FAT 8.7g (sat 3.9g, mono 3.4g, poly 0.9g); PROTEIN 14.2g; CARB 37.2g; FIBER 1g; CHOL 12mg; IRON 2.7mg; SODIUM 611mg; CALC 376mg

# Learning Lebanese

A little of this, a little of that, some dancing, some music—in Lebanon, that's the recipe for healthy meals and lasting friendships.

A combination of tastiness and healthfulness is a persistent theme in Lebanese food. With the usual benefits of the Mediterranean diet, Lebanese cooking emphasizes such ingredients as olive oil, onions, garlic, nuts, lemons, oranges, and fresh vegetables (raw and pickled carrot and cucumber slices are especially popular in Lebanon) rather than butter and red meat.

More intriguing is the Lebanese habit of grazing on various little dishes throughout the day. Breakfast might be a *manouchi*, a heated burrito-like sandwich featuring goat cheese or thyme filling, tomatoes, and pickles. Lunch would likely feature another sandwich of some sort—kebabs, *shawarma* (spit-roasted lamb or chicken slices stuffed in a pita with onions, tomatoes, pickles, and garlic sauce), and *falafel* being the most popular. Dinner would be *mezze*, a variety of appetizers shared with a group of friends. (For Greek and vegetarian versions of *mezze*, see "Where Appetizers Make a Meal" on page 271.)

## Falafel

1½ cups dried chickpeas (garbanzo beans; about 12 ounces)
2 cups chopped fresh cilantro
1 teaspoon ground cumin
1 teaspoon ground allspice
¼ teaspoon salt
¼ teaspoon black pepper
⅛ teaspoon ground red pepper
5 garlic cloves, peeled
1 onion, quartered
1 leek, trimmed and cut into 3 pieces
6 tablespoons olive oil, divided
Yogurt-Tahini Dip (recipe at right)
8 (6-inch) pitas, cut in half

**1.** Sort and wash chickpeas; place in a large bowl. Cover with water to 2 inches above beans. Cover; let stand 8 hours. Drain.
**2.** Combine chickpeas, cilantro, and next 8 ingredients in a food processor; process until mixture resembles coarse meal. Divide chickpea mixture into 16 equal portions, shaping each into a ½-inch-thick patty.
**3.** Heat 2 tablespoons oil in a large non-stick skillet. Add 5 patties; cook 3 minutes on each side or until golden. Repeat procedure twice with remaining oil and patties.
**4.** Spread 1 tablespoon Yogurt-Tahini Dip in each pita half; fill with 1 patty. Yield: 8 servings (serving size: 2 pita halves).

CALORIES 430 (29% from fat); FAT 13.9g (sat 1.8g, mono 8.3g, poly 2.5g); PROTEIN 14.6g; CARB 63.3g; FIBER 5.3g; CHOL 0mg; IRON 5.7mg; SODIUM 398mg; CALC 140mg

## Yogurt-Tahini Dip

1 cup plain low-fat yogurt
3 tablespoons tahini (sesame-seed paste)
2 tablespoons fresh lemon juice
1 tablespoon chopped fresh flat-leaf parsley
½ teaspoon salt
1 garlic clove, crushed

**1.** Combine all ingredients in a large bowl; cover and refrigerate 30 minutes. Yield: 1 cup (serving size: 1 tablespoon).

CALORIES 27 (60% from fat); FAT 1.8g (sat 0.4g, mono 0.6g, poly 0.6g); PROTEIN 1.3g; CARB 1.9g; FIBER 0.3g; CHOL 1mg; IRON 0.3mg; SODIUM 87mg; CALC 41mg

## Fool (or Fül) Medammes
*Fava Bean Salad*

1⅓ cups dried fava beans (about 9 ounces)
¼ cup chopped fresh flat-leaf parsley
2½ tablespoons extra-virgin olive oil
2 tablespoons fresh lemon juice
½ teaspoon kosher salt
½ teaspoon ground cumin
3 garlic cloves, crushed
1 hard-cooked large egg, finely chopped

**1.** Sort and wash beans; place in a large saucepan. Cover with water to 2 inches above beans; cover and let stand 8 hours. Drain beans.
**2.** Return beans to pan. Cover with water to 2 inches above beans. Bring to a boil; cover, reduce heat, and simmer 45 minutes or until tender. Drain well. Place beans in a medium bowl. Stir in parsley and next 5 ingredients; toss gently. Sprinkle with egg. Yield: 8 servings (serving size: ½ cup).

CALORIES 160 (30% from fat); FAT 5.4g (sat 0.9g, mono 3.5g, poly 0.7g); PROTEIN 9.3g; CARB 19.5g; FIBER 4.8g; CHOL 28mg; IRON 2.5mg; SODIUM 134mg; CALC 42mg

## Fattoosh
*Mixed Herb and Toasted Pita Salad*

(pictured on page 296)

2 (6-inch) pitas
3 tablespoons ground sumac or 2 tablespoons grated lemon rind
1 tablespoon extra-virgin olive oil
8 cups thinly sliced romaine lettuce
2 cups chopped tomato
1½ cups chopped fresh parsley
1 cup thinly sliced green onions
½ cup chopped fresh mint
½ teaspoon salt
1 cucumber, quartered lengthwise and thinly sliced (about 2 cups)

**1.** Preheat oven to 400°.
**2.** Place pitas in a single layer on a baking sheet. Bake at 400° for 6 minutes or
*Continued*

until toasted; break into bite-size pieces. Combine pita pieces, sumac, and oil, tossing well to coat. Add lettuce and remaining ingredients; toss well. Yield: 4 servings (serving size: 2 cups).

**NOTE:** Ground sumac is available at Middle Eastern markets.

CALORIES 169 (24% from fat); FAT 4.6g (sat 0.6g, mono 2.7g, poly 0.8g); PROTEIN 6.8g; CARB 28.1g; FIBER 5.7g; CHOL 0mg; IRON 4.4mg; SODIUM 480mg; CALC 133mg

## Shawarma
*Lamb Pitas*

Often sold by street vendors, this Lebanese favorite is a large lamb kebab that is marinated overnight, threaded onto a long skewer, and placed in front of a vertical grill. The meat rotates and cooks, allowing the shawarma seller to slice it and make sandwiches. Although our lighter homemade version is baked rather than skewered and grilled, the flavor is very close to that of the real thing.

1½  pounds boned leg of lamb
2  cups thinly sliced onion
⅓  cup fresh lemon juice
½  teaspoon ground cinnamon
½  teaspoon ground allspice
½  teaspoon black pepper
¼  teaspoon salt
5  thyme sprigs
6  (7-inch) pitas
Yogurt-Tahini Dip (recipe on page 303)
½  cup red onion slices, separated into rings
¼  cup chopped fresh mint
12  (¼-inch-thick) slices tomato, halved
3  gherkin pickles, thinly sliced lengthwise

**1.** Trim fat from lamb. Combine 2 cups onion and next 6 ingredients in a large zip-top plastic bag. Add lamb to bag; seal. Marinate in refrigerator 2 hours, turning occasionally. Remove lamb from bag; discard marinade.
**2.** Preheat oven to 350°.
**3.** Place lamb on a broiler pan; insert meat thermometer into thickest portion of lamb. Bake at 350° for 1 hour or until thermometer registers 145° (medium-rare) to 160° (medium). Let stand 15 minutes. Cut lengthwise into thin strips.
**4.** Spread each pita with about 2½ tablespoons Yogurt-Tahini Dip. Divide lamb, red onion, mint, tomato, and pickles evenly among pitas; roll up. Serve immediately. Yield: 6 servings (serving size: 1 sandwich).

CALORIES 397 (24% from fat); FAT 10.7g (sat 2.9g, mono 3.8g, poly 2.5g); PROTEIN 32.8g; CARB 42.1g; FIBER 3.3g; CHOL 75mg; IRON 4.9mg; SODIUM 1,117mg; CALC 183mg

## Marinated Roast Chicken with Garlic Dip

**GARLIC DIP:**
½  cup plain fat-free yogurt
¼  teaspoon kosher salt
4  garlic cloves, crushed
1  tablespoon extra-virgin olive oil
1  tablespoon fresh lemon juice

**CHICKEN:**
1  (3½-pound) roasting chicken
2  tablespoons fresh lemon juice
1  tablespoon extra-virgin olive oil
½  teaspoon kosher salt
½  teaspoon ground allspice
¼  teaspoon black pepper
⅛  teaspoon ground cinnamon
6  garlic cloves, crushed
Dash of ground red pepper

**1.** To prepare garlic dip, spoon yogurt onto several layers of heavy-duty paper towels; spread to ½-inch thickness. Cover with additional paper towels; let stand 5 minutes. Scrape into a bowl using a rubber spatula. Place salt and garlic in a mortar; crush with a pestle until smooth. Drizzle with 1 tablespoon oil; stir with a small whisk. Add garlic mixture and 1 tablespoon juice to yogurt. Cover and chill.
**2.** To prepare chicken, remove and discard giblets and neck from chicken. Rinse chicken with cold water, and pat dry. Trim excess fat. Starting at neck cavity, loosen skin from breast and drumsticks by inserting fingers, gently pushing between skin and meat. Combine 2 tablespoons juice and remaining 7 ingredients. Rub juice mixture under loosened skin and inside body cavity. Place chicken in a large zip-top plastic bag; seal and marinate in refrigerator 1 hour.
**3.** Preheat oven to 350°.
**4.** Remove chicken from bag; place chicken, breast side up, on a broiler pan. Insert meat thermometer into meaty part of thigh, making sure not to touch bone. Bake at 350° for 1 hour and 10 minutes or until thermometer registers 180°. Cover chicken loosely with foil, and let stand 10 minutes. Discard skin. Serve with garlic dip. Yield: 4 servings (serving size: 1 chicken quarter and 2 tablespoons dip).

CALORIES 326 (44% from fat); FAT 16g (sat 3.5g, mono 8.3g, poly 2.7g); PROTEIN 38g; CARB 6g; FIBER 0.3g; CHOL 111mg; IRON 1.8mg; SODIUM 569mg; CALC 93mg

## Tabbouleh
*Parsley, Tomato, and Bulgur Salad*

The amount of bulgur used varies according to family tradition. We've included less here to allow the flavors of the tomato and parsley to come through.

4  cups diced tomato
⅔  cup chopped fresh flat-leaf parsley
⅓  cup thinly sliced green onions
¼  cup uncooked bulgur
¼  cup chopped fresh mint
2½  teaspoons extra-virgin olive oil
2  tablespoons fresh lemon juice
½  teaspoon kosher salt
½  teaspoon ground allspice
¼  teaspoon ground cinnamon
¼  teaspoon freshly ground black pepper
5  large iceberg lettuce leaves

**1.** Combine first 5 ingredients in a large bowl. Cover and let stand 30 minutes. Stir in oil and next 5 ingredients; toss well. Serve with lettuce leaves. Yield: 5 servings (serving size: 1 cup salad and 1 lettuce leaf).

CALORIES 83 (31% from fat); FAT 2.9g (sat 0.4g, mono 1.8g, poly 0.5g); PROTEIN 2.6g; CARB 14g; FIBER 3.6g; CHOL 0mg; IRON 1.6mg; SODIUM 255mg; CALC 31mg

## Baked Kibbeh

Moistening your fingers will help you assemble this layered meat pie. Pomegranate molasses is available in Middle Eastern markets or in a supermarket's international-food section.

**STUFFING:**

- 1 teaspoon butter or stick margarine
- 3 cups chopped onion
- ½ pound lean ground lamb
- ⅓ cup pine nuts, toasted
- 2 teaspoons ground cinnamon
- 2 teaspoons ground allspice
- ½ teaspoon salt
- ½ teaspoon black pepper
- 1 teaspoon pomegranate molasses (optional)

**KIBBEH:**

- 2 cups uncooked bulgur
- 2 cups minced fresh onion
- 2 teaspoons ground cinnamon
- 2 teaspoons ground allspice
- ½ teaspoon salt
- ½ teaspoon black pepper
- 1 pound lean ground lamb
- Cooking spray
- 2 teaspoons butter or stick margarine

**1.** Preheat oven to 350°.

**2.** To prepare stuffing, melt 1 teaspoon butter in a large nonstick skillet over medium-high heat. Add 3 cups onion; sauté 3 minutes. Add ½ pound lamb, and cook until browned, stirring to crumble. Remove from heat. Stir in pine nuts, next 4 ingredients, and pomegranate molasses, if desired. Set stuffing aside.

**3.** To prepare kibbeh, combine bulgur and next 6 ingredients in a large bowl. Press half of kibbeh into bottom of an 11 x 7-inch baking dish coated with cooking spray. Spread stuffing over kibbeh. Press remaining kibbeh over stuffing. Cut kibbeh into quarters. Press thumb into center of each quarter, leaving an indentation. Place ½ teaspoon butter into each indentation. Bake at 350° for 20 minutes. Let stand 5 minutes. Cut each quarter in half. Yield: 8 servings.

CALORIES 335 (29% from fat); FAT 10.7g (sat 3.4g, mono 3.8g, poly 3.1g); PROTEIN 25g; CARB 38.4g; FIBER 9.1g; CHOL 60mg; IRON 3.9mg; SODIUM 376mg; CALC 68mg

## cooking class

# How to Roast a Chicken and Rave

*Of all cooking techniques, roasting has to be one of the easiest because you do almost none of the work.*

Roasting follows basic science: As intense dry heat penetrates the chicken or meat inside the oven, the juices bubble to the surface. The liquid evaporates, leaving proteins and sugars that caramelize the meat to create the characteristic roasted color, aroma, and flavor.

A few words of advice: Roasting generally requires tender cuts, which are usually higher in fat. We've used beef tenderloin, pork loin, leg of lamb, and whole chicken—all moderately lean.

## Sunday Roasted Chicken with Giblet Gravy

To save time, we made the broth for the gravy by simmering canned chicken broth with vegetables, the giblets, and the neck. Make this while the chicken roasts. To make stock for soups and sauces, place the bones and discarded skin from a roasted chicken in a Dutch oven. Cover with water, and simmer for 1 to 3 hours. Strain before using.

- 1 (6-pound) roasting chicken
- 2 (16-ounce) cans fat-free, less-sodium chicken broth, divided
- 1 carrot, cut into 2-inch pieces
- 1 celery stalk, cut into 2-inch pieces
- 1 onion, quartered
- 2 large garlic cloves, unpeeled and halved
- 2 bay leaves
- 1 teaspoon kosher salt
- 1 tablespoon dried thyme
- 1 tablespoon dried rubbed sage
- ¼ cup all-purpose flour
- ¼ teaspoon black pepper

**1.** Remove giblets and neck from chicken, discarding liver. Cut off wing tips, and combine with giblets, neck, 3 cups broth, carrot, celery, onion, garlic, and bay leaves in a saucepan. Bring to a boil; partially cover, reduce heat, and simmer 45 minutes. Strain broth mixture through a sieve into a bowl, reserving broth and giblets. Mince giblets; add to strained broth, and set aside. Discard remaining solids.

**2.** Preheat oven to 375°.

**3.** Rinse chicken with cold water; pat dry. Trim excess fat. Starting at neck cavity, loosen skin from breast and drumsticks by inserting fingers, gently pushing between skin and meat. Combine salt, thyme, and sage in a small bowl. Rub thyme mixture under loosened skin and over breast and drumsticks. Gently press skin to secure. Tie legs with string.

**4.** Place chicken, breast side up, on rack of a broiler pan or roasting pan. Insert a meat thermometer into meaty part of thigh, making sure not to touch bone. Bake at 375° for 1 hour and 30 minutes or until thermometer registers 180° and juices run clear. Cover chicken loosely with foil, and let stand 10 minutes for chicken to reabsorb juices. Discard skin. Remove rack from pan. Add ½ cup broth to drippings in pan (you'll have about ¾ cup drippings), scraping pan to loosen browned bits. Pour drippings into a zip-top plastic bag. Snip off a corner of bag; drain liquid into saucepan, stopping before fat layer reaches opening. Discard fat.

**5.** Add reserved giblet mixture to broth mixture in saucepan.

**6.** Combine remaining ½ cup broth and flour in a bowl. Add flour mixture to saucepan; bring to a boil. Reduce heat, and cook 10 minutes, stirring constantly. Stir in pepper. Serve with chicken. Yield: 10 servings (serving size: 3 ounces chicken and ¼ cup gravy).

CALORIES 202 (32% from fat); FAT 7.1g (sat 2g, mono 2.4g, poly 1.6g); PROTEIN 28.8g; CARB 3.5g; FIBER 0.2g; CHOL 115mg; IRON 2.6mg; SODIUM 469mg; CALC 26mg

## Roasting Step-by-Steps

### Pepper-Crusted Beef Tenderloin:

**1.** *Trim any excess fat from the tenderloin. You'll notice that the end is tapered and much thinner than the middle section, so fold the end under enough to approximate the thickness of the middle. This encourages even cooking and prevents the end from overcooking.*

**2.** *Rub beef with a mixture of breadcrumbs, parsley, pepper, and salt. This creates a flavorful crust.*

### Mediterranean Roasted Leg of Lamb:

**1.** *Unroll the roast, and trim the fat. To infuse the roast with flavor, spread with rosemary, salt, and minced garlic.*

**2.** *Reroll roast, and secure at 3-inch intervals with string. Tuck rosemary sprigs under string.*

### Honey-Cumin Roasted Pork:

**1.** *The drippings from the roast make the base for a flavorful sauce or gravy. To deglaze the pan, add broth to the drippings, scraping to loosen the browned bits.*

**2.** *Then combine the drippings and additional broth in a saucepan, and simmer for 5 minutes. This reduces the sauce and concentrates its flavor.*

### Pepper-Crusted Beef Tenderloin with Horseradish Sauce

1    (4-pound) beef tenderloin
1½  teaspoons olive oil
3    tablespoons dry breadcrumbs
3    tablespoons minced fresh flat-leaf parsley
1½  teaspoons coarsely ground black pepper
¾   teaspoon kosher salt, divided
Cooking spray
1    cup fat-free sour cream
2    tablespoons prepared horseradish
1    teaspoon grated lemon rind
½   teaspoon Worcestershire sauce
¼   teaspoon hot pepper sauce

**1.** Preheat oven to 400°.
**2.** Trim fat from tenderloin; fold under 3 inches of small end. Rub tenderloin with oil. Combine breadcrumbs, parsley, pepper, and ½ teaspoon salt. Rub tenderloin with crumb mixture; coat with cooking spray. Place tenderloin on rack of a broiler pan or roasting pan. Insert a meat thermometer into thickest portion of tenderloin. Bake at 400° for 30 minutes. Increase oven temperature to 425° (do not remove roast from oven). Bake an additional 10 minutes or until thermometer registers 140° (medium-rare) to 155° (medium). Place tenderloin on a platter, and cover with foil. Let stand 10 minutes for tenderloin to reabsorb juices. (Temperature of roast will increase 5° upon standing.)
**3.** Combine ¼ teaspoon salt, sour cream, and remaining 4 ingredients in a small bowl. Serve with beef. Yield: 16 servings (serving size: 3 ounces beef and 1 tablespoon horseradish sauce).

CALORIES 195 (39% from fat); FAT 8.4g (sat 3.2g, mono 3.4g, poly 0.4g); PROTEIN 25.3g; CARB 2.4g; FIBER 0.2g; CHOL 71mg; IRON 3.2mg; SODIUM 193mg; CALC 12mg

## Mediterranean Roasted Leg of Lamb with Red Wine Sauce

Because heat draws moisture to the surface of the roast, cover it and let it stand for 10 minutes before carving. This helps the roast reabsorb the juices. The drippings from the roast are combined with red wine to make a flavorful sauce. Use a full-bodied, dry red wine such as Cabernet Sauvignon, Merlot, or Cabernet Franc. Increasing the oven temperature for the last 20 minutes browns the lamb.

  1  (5½- to 6-pound) rolled boned leg of lamb
  1  teaspoon minced fresh rosemary
  ¾  teaspoon kosher salt, divided
  2  garlic cloves, minced
  ⅛  teaspoon black pepper
  1  tablespoon olive oil
  6  rosemary sprigs
  2  cups dry red wine, divided
  1½  tablespoons cornstarch

**1.** Preheat oven to 400°.
**2.** Unroll roast; trim fat. Spread minced rosemary, ¼ teaspoon salt, and garlic into folds of roast. Reroll roast; secure at 3-inch intervals with heavy string. Sprinkle with ¼ teaspoon salt and pepper. Drizzle with oil. Secure rosemary sprigs under strings on roast. Place roast on rack of a broiler pan or roasting pan; insert meat thermometer into thickest portion of roast. Bake at 400° for 1 hour. Increase oven temperature to 425° (do not remove roast from oven). Bake an additional 20 minutes or until thermometer registers 140° (medium-rare) to 155° (medium). Place roast on a platter; cover with foil. Let stand 10 minutes for roast to reabsorb juices. (Temperature of roast will increase 5° upon standing.) Remove string and rosemary sprigs before slicing.
**3.** Remove rack from pan. Combine ½ cup wine and cornstarch; set aside. Add ½ cup wine to drippings in pan; scrape pan to loosen browned bits. Combine drippings mixture and 1 cup wine in a saucepan; bring to a boil. Cook 5 minutes. Add ¼ teaspoon salt and cornstarch mixture; return to a boil. Cook 1 minute or until thick, stirring constantly.

Serve with lamb. Yield: 19 servings (serving size: 3 ounces lamb and about 1½ tablespoons sauce).

CALORIES 175 (38% from fat); FAT 7.4g (sat 2.5g, mono 3.4g, poly 0.5g); PROTEIN 24.4g; CARB 1.1g; FIBER 0g; CHOL 76mg; IRON 1.9mg; SODIUM 153mg; CALC 10mg

---

## Equipment for Roasting

You need only a few essentials for roasting: an oven; a heavy, shallow roasting pan; and a thermometer to determine doneness.

**Oven:** Position the rack in the center—usually the second level from the bottom—so hot air can evenly surround the roast.

**Pan:** Most roasting pans are at least 13 x 9 inches or larger. In addition, you need a slightly raised rack that elevates the meat above the pan. This prevents the meat from cooking in its drippings and allows adequate circulation. Ideally, the pan should extend 2 or 3 inches beyond the edges of the roast. If the pan is too large, meat juices will evaporate too quickly, and the drippings may burn instead of caramelizing.

**Thermometer:** Three types can be used. A *standard meat thermometer* is inserted into the thickest part of the roast prior to cooking. It stays in the oven during the process. These are inexpensive and mostly accurate.

An *instant-read thermometer* is inserted into the roast, read, and then taken out. It does not stay in the oven. It's more accurate than a basic meat thermometer, but you have to check the temperature early and more frequently. If you wait too long in the cooking time, there is a possibility of overcooking your roast.

*Our preference:* an instant-read that sits outside the oven, connected directly to the roast inside with a wire containing a stainless-steel sensor. It keeps track of the temperature without your having to open the oven. You set the end temperature for the food, and the thermometer monitors the heat. When the roast reaches the selected temperature, an alarm sounds.

---

## Honey-Cumin Roasted Pork with Caramelized Onions

You can also use a boneless veal rump roast in place of the pork.

  1  (3-pound) boned pork loin roast
  3  tablespoons honey
  1  tablespoon fresh lemon juice
  1  tablespoon ground cumin
  1½  teaspoons kosher salt
  ¼  teaspoon ground red pepper
  2  large onions (about 2 pounds), each cut into 8 wedges
  1  cup fat-free, less-sodium chicken broth, divided

**1.** Preheat oven to 375°.
**2.** Trim fat from pork; score a diamond pattern on top of pork. Combine honey and next 4 ingredients in a small bowl. Combine 2 tablespoons honey mixture and onion wedges; toss well to combine. Place pork on rack of a broiler pan or roasting pan. Arrange onion wedges around pork. Brush remaining honey mixture over pork. Insert a meat thermometer into thickest part of pork. Bake at 375° for 1 hour and 15 minutes or until thermometer registers 155° (slightly pink). Place pork on a platter, and cover with foil. Let stand 10 minutes for pork to reabsorb juices. (Temperature of roast will increase 5° upon standing.)
**3.** Remove rack from pan. Add ½ cup broth to drippings in pan, scraping pan to loosen browned bits. Combine drippings mixture and ½ cup broth in a small saucepan. Bring to a boil; reduce heat, and simmer 5 minutes. Cut pork diagonally across grain into thin slices; serve with onions and sauce. Yield: 12 servings (serving size: 3 ounces pork, about ¼ cup onions, and 1 tablespoon sauce).

CALORIES 212 (35% from fat); FAT 8.2g (sat 2.8g, mono 3.7g, poly 0.9g); PROTEIN 22.7g; CARB 11.3g; FIBER 1.5g; CHOL 62mg; IRON 1.4mg; SODIUM 403mg; CALC 28mg

## Asian Roasted Chicken

A broiler-fryer is the perfect size for serving two to four people. It cooks more quickly than a larger roasting chicken and is easier to handle.

  1  (3-pound) broiler-fryer chicken
  ¼  cup low-sodium soy sauce
  1  tablespoon grated peeled fresh ginger
  2  garlic cloves, minced
  1  (16-ounce) can fat-free, less-sodium chicken broth
  ¼  teaspoon dark sesame oil
  ½  cup (2-inch) sliced green onions

**1.** Remove and discard giblets and neck from chicken. Rinse chicken with cold water; pat dry. Trim excess fat. Starting at neck cavity, loosen skin from breast and drumsticks by inserting fingers, gently pushing between skin and meat.
**2.** Combine soy sauce, ginger, garlic, and broth in a large heavy-duty zip-top plastic bag. Add chicken; seal and marinate in refrigerator 4 to 8 hours, turning bag occasionally. Remove chicken from bag, reserving ½ cup marinade.
**3.** Preheat oven to 375°.
**4.** Place chicken, breast side up, on rack of a broiler pan or roasting pan. Insert meat thermometer into meaty part of thigh, making sure not to touch bone. Bake at 375° for 1 hour and 10 minutes or until thermometer registers 180°. Cover chicken loosely with foil; let stand 10 minutes for chicken to reabsorb juices. Discard skin.
**5.** Add ½ cup reserved marinade to drippings in pan (you'll have about ¼ cup drippings), scraping pan to loosen browned bits. Pour marinade mixture into a small saucepan; bring to a boil, and cook 5 minutes. Stir in sesame oil. Cut chicken into quarters. Drizzle with sesame mixture. Sprinkle with onions. Yield: 4 servings (serving size: about 3 ounces chicken and about 1½ tablespoons sauce).

CALORIES 226 (33% from fat); FAT 8.4g (sat 2.2g, mono 3g, poly 2g); PROTEIN 32.2g; CARB 2.3g; FIBER 0.4g; CHOL 95mg; IRON 1.5mg; SODIUM 548mg; CALC 28mg

## When Your Roast Is Done

Leaner roasts, as we've used here, will be succulent if cooked medium-rare or medium. Always place the thermometer in the thickest part of the roast, away from bone or gristle, for the most accurate readings. In general, you should pull the roast from the oven at 5° below the final recommended temperature—the roast will continue to cook slightly as it rests. (The exception to this is roast chicken, which should cook fully to 180°.) Allow about 10 minutes for the roast to rest and fully reabsorb the juices. We recommend the following degrees of doneness:
  **Beef and lamb:** medium-rare (145° internal temperature after resting) to medium (160° internal temperature after resting)
  **Pork:** medium (160° internal temperature after resting)
  **Chicken:** fully cooked (180° internal temperature)
  **About seasonings:** Cooks tend to season more today than in the past; with less fat in leaner meat and chicken, you'll get a big flavor boost from spices, herbs, chiles, seasoning pastes, and breading.

back to the best

# Creamy Four-Cheese Macaroni

*Comfort foods aren't usually heralded as being low in fat, but Creamy Four-Cheese Macaroni, which debuted in our September 1996 issue, proves that sometimes you can have it all. That's why we've included it in our salute to our all-time favorite Cooking Light recipes.*

## Creamy Four-Cheese Macaroni

(pictured on page 294)

  ⅓  cup all-purpose flour
  2⅔  cups 1% low-fat milk
  ¾  cup (3 ounces) shredded fontina or Swiss cheese
  ½  cup (2 ounces) grated fresh Parmesan cheese
  ½  cup (2 ounces) shredded extra-sharp Cheddar cheese
  3  ounces light processed cheese (such as Velveeta Light)
  6  cups cooked elbow macaroni (about 3 cups uncooked)
  ¼  teaspoon salt
  Cooking spray
  ⅓  cup crushed onion melba toasts (about 12 pieces)
  1  tablespoon butter or stick margarine, softened

**1.** Preheat oven to 375°.
**2.** Lightly spoon flour into a dry measuring cup; level with a knife. Place flour in a large saucepan. Gradually add milk, stirring with a whisk until blended. Cook over medium heat until thick (about 8 minutes), stirring constantly. Add cheeses; cook 3 minutes or until cheese melts, stirring frequently. Remove cheese mixture from heat; stir in macaroni and salt.
**3.** Spoon mixture into a 2-quart casserole coated with cooking spray. Combine crushed toasts and butter in a small bowl; stir until well-blended. Sprinkle over macaroni mixture. Bake at 375° for 30 minutes or until bubbly. Yield: 8 servings (serving size: 1 cup).

CALORIES 350 (29% from fat); FAT 11.2g (sat 6.3g, mono 2.9g, poly 0.9g); PROTEIN 18g; CARB 42.4g; FIBER 2.1g; CHOL 32mg; IRON 1.9mg; SODIUM 497mg; CALC 306mg

# november

# 5 Chefs, 5 Turkeys— 5 Great Holiday Dinners for You

## Turkey again this year? Get simple, fresh new ideas from five of America's top chefs.

We decided this year to look for the convergence of home touch and cooking skill in the perfect place—the Thanksgiving tables of some of our favorite chefs: Jimmy Bannos, George Bernas, Joe Brown, Jim Coleman, and Caprial Pence. We asked them to share the turkey recipes that will show up not at their restaurants, but in their homes—recipes guaranteed to be doable for us amateurs yet special enough for applause. Now that's something to be thankful for.

### Spice-Rubbed Smoked Turkey with Roasted-Pear Stuffing and Cranberry Syrup

This recipe is from Caprial Pence, Chef/Owner of Caprial's Bistro in Portland, Oregon. Smoking a turkey takes some of the burden off your oven, but you need to keep a few important points in mind. The turkey has to marinate eight hours, so start it a day before serving. While the turkey is smoking, closely monitor the grill to make sure the coals burn with continuous smoke. Never stuff a turkey before smoking it, because the temperature inside the grill is less stable than in an oven.

- 1 (12-pound) fresh or frozen turkey, thawed
- 3 tablespoons brown sugar
- 1 tablespoon kosher salt
- 2 teaspoons ground cumin
- 2 teaspoons dried oregano
- 2 teaspoons dried rubbed sage
- 2 teaspoons dry mustard
- 1 teaspoon dried thyme
- 1 teaspoon ground coriander
- 6 hickory wood chunks

Cooking spray
Roasted-Pear Stuffing
Cranberry Syrup

**1.** To prepare turkey, remove and discard giblets and neck. Rinse turkey with cold water, and pat dry. Trim excess fat. Starting at neck cavity, loosen skin from breast and drumsticks by inserting fingers, gently pushing between skin and meat. Lift wing tips up and over back, and tuck under turkey. Place turkey on a jelly-roll pan. Combine brown sugar and next 7 ingredients. Rub seasoning mixture over and under skin. Cover turkey with plastic wrap; refrigerate 8 hours.

**2.** Soak wood chunks in water 1 hour, and drain well. Place a large disposable aluminum-foil pan in center of bottom grill rack. Place 25 charcoal briquettes on each side of pan; ignite briquettes. Place wood chunks over hot coals. Coat top grill rack with cooking spray; place over foil pan and hot coals. Uncover turkey; remove from jelly-roll pan. Place on top rack over foil pan. Insert a meat thermometer into meaty part of thigh, making sure not to touch bone. Cover and smoke turkey 2½ hours or until meat thermometer registers 180°, adding 8 additional briquettes to each side of drip pan every hour. (Cover turkey loosely with foil if it becomes too brown. Turkey will be a deep mahogany brown when done.) Discard skin. Serve with Roasted-Pear Stuffing and Cranberry Syrup. Yield: 12 servings (serving size: 6 ounces turkey, ⅔ cup stuffing, and 2½ tablespoons syrup).

**NOTE:** Try to resist checking the turkey too often. Lifting the grill lid decreases the temperature significantly.

(Totals include Roasted-Pear Stuffing and Cranberry Syrup) CALORIES 593 (21% from fat); FAT 14.1g (sat 3.5g, mono 5.4g, poly 3.1g); PROTEIN 54.3g; CARB 61.3g; FIBER 2.6g; CHOL 166mg; IRON 4.6mg; SODIUM 511mg; CALC 104mg

### ROASTED-PEAR STUFFING:

You can substitute apples for the pears. If you have pear brandy, by all means use it in place of the sherry and brandy.

- 2 teaspoons olive oil
- 4 cups sliced peeled Bosc pear (about 3½ pounds)
- 1 cup diced onion
- 1 cup diced peeled celeriac (celery root)
- 3 garlic cloves, minced
- ½ cup dry sherry
- ½ cup brandy
- 5 cups (½-inch) cubed dense white bread (about 8 ounces)
- 1 cup fat-free, less-sodium chicken broth
- ½ cup chopped hazelnuts, toasted
- 2 teaspoons chopped fresh or ½ teaspoon dried thyme
- ½ teaspoon salt
- ¼ teaspoon freshly ground black pepper
- 2 large eggs, lightly beaten

**1.** Preheat oven to 350°.

**2.** Heat oil in a large nonstick skillet over medium-high heat. Add pear slices, and cook, without stirring, 2 minutes or until golden brown. Carefully turn pear slices; cook 2 minutes or until golden brown. Add onion, celeriac, and garlic; sauté 3 minutes or until lightly browned. Add sherry and brandy, and cook until liquid almost evaporates. Remove from heat; cool.

**3.** Combine pear mixture, bread, and remaining ingredients in a large bowl, tossing gently. Spoon bread mixture into a 2-quart casserole. Cover with lid, and bake at 350° for 45 minutes or until thoroughly heated. Yield: 12 servings (serving size: ⅔ cup).

CALORIES 167 (30% from fat); FAT 5.6g (sat 0.8g, mono 3.6g, poly 0.7g); PROTEIN 4.2g; CARB 26.4g; FIBER 2.4g; CHOL 37mg; IRON 1.2mg; SODIUM 265mg; CALC 51mg

### CRANBERRY SYRUP:

1½  cups sugar
 1  (750-milliliter) bottle ruby port or other sweet red wine
 2  cups fresh or frozen cranberries
 1  tablespoon thawed orange juice concentrate
 1  teaspoon chopped peeled fresh ginger
 3  garlic cloves, chopped

**1.** Combine sugar and port in a Dutch oven. Bring to a boil, and cook 4 minutes or until sugar dissolves. Add cranberries, orange juice, ginger, and garlic, and cook over medium heat until reduced to 3 cups (about 20 minutes). Press cranberry mixture through a fine sieve over a bowl, discarding solids. Yield: 2 cups (serving size: 2½ tablespoons).
**NOTE:** Cranberry Syrup can be stored, covered, in refrigerator up to 1 week.

CALORIES 134 (0% from fat); FAT 0g; PROTEIN 0.2g; CARB 34.3g; FIBER 0.1g; CHOL 0mg; IRON 0.2mg; SODIUM 6mg; CALC 7mg

## Herb-Roasted Turkey with Cheese Grits

(pictured on page 3)

Thanksgiving with Jim Coleman, executive chef at Rittenhouse Hotel in Philadelphia, means a stunning turkey—and also grits.

 12  thyme sprigs
  1  rosemary sprig
  1  sage sprig
  2  tablespoons minced garlic
  2  tablespoons minced shallots
  1  teaspoon freshly ground black pepper
  1  (12-pound) fresh or frozen turkey, thawed
  3  tablespoons fresh lemon juice
  2  lemons, each cut in half
     Cooking spray
     Cheese Grits

**1.** Preheat oven to 350°.
**2.** Remove leaves from thyme sprigs to measure 2 tablespoons chopped; reserve stems. Remove leaves from rosemary sprig to measure 2 tablespoons chopped; reserve stem. Remove leaves from sage sprig to measure 2 tablespoons chopped; reserve stem. Combine chopped thyme, chopped rosemary, chopped sage, garlic, shallots, and pepper in a small bowl.
**3.** Remove and discard giblets and neck from turkey. Rinse turkey with cold water, and pat dry. Trim excess fat. Starting at neck cavity, loosen skin from breast and drumsticks by inserting fingers, gently pushing between skin and meat. Rub herb mixture under loosened skin and sprinkle in body cavity. Drizzle lemon juice over skin. Place reserved stems and lemon halves in body cavity. Tie ends of legs with cord. Lift wing tips up and over back; tuck under turkey.
**4.** Place turkey on a broiler pan coated with cooking spray or on a rack set in a shallow roasting pan. Insert meat thermometer into meaty part of thigh, making sure not to touch bone. Bake at 350° for 3 hours or until thermometer registers 180°. (Cover turkey loosely with foil if it gets too brown.) Remove turkey from oven. Cover loosely with foil; let stand 10 minutes before carving. Discard skin. Serve with Cheese Grits. Yield: 12 servings (serving size: 6 ounces turkey and about ½ cup Cheese Grits).

(Totals include Cheese Grits) CALORIES 354 (29% from fat); FAT 11.3g (sat 4.5g, mono 2.5g, poly 2.5g); PROTEIN 53.5g; CARB 6.6g; FIBER 0.6g; CHOL 138mg; IRON 5.8mg; SODIUM 406mg; CALC 140mg

### CHEESE GRITS:

 4  cups water
 1  cup uncooked quick-cooking grits
 1  cup (4 ounces) shredded reduced-fat sharp Cheddar cheese
 1  tablespoon butter or stick margarine
1½  teaspoons garlic powder
 ½  teaspoon dried thyme
 ½  teaspoon salt

**1.** Bring water to a boil in a medium saucepan, and gradually add grits, stirring constantly. Cover, reduce heat to low, and simmer 5 minutes or until thick,

stirring occasionally. Remove grits from heat, and stir in shredded cheese and remaining ingredients. Yield: 12 servings (serving size: about ½ cup).

CALORIES 58 (43% from fat); FAT 2.8g (sat 1.7g, mono 0.8g, poly 0.1g); PROTEIN 3.4g; CARB 5.1g; FIBER 0.3g; CHOL 9mg; IRON 2.5mg; SODIUM 286mg; CALC 87mg

## Make-Ahead Turkey Breast with Herb Stuffing and Vanilla Sweet Potatoes

This turkey dinner from George Bernas, chef at Brandywine Inn in Dayton, Ohio, is the ultimate make-ahead meal. The turkey is poached the day before; then seasoned, and reheated in an oven the day it's served.

### STOCK:

 4  quarts water
 1  cup (2-inch-thick) slices carrot
 ½  cup (1-inch-thick) slices celery
 1  teaspoon dried thyme
 ¼  teaspoon black pepper
 3  garlic cloves
 3  bay leaves
 2  tomatoes, quartered
 1  onion, quartered
 ½  lemon
 1  (6-pound) whole turkey breast, skinned

### TURKEY:

 1  teaspoon olive oil
 ½  teaspoon dried thyme
 ¼  teaspoon salt
 ¼  teaspoon garlic powder
 ¼  teaspoon black pepper

### STUFFING:

 ¼  cup butter or stick margarine
 1  cup diced onion
 1  cup diced celery
 16  cups (1-inch) cubed stale bread (about 1½ pounds)
 2  teaspoons poultry seasoning
 1  teaspoon dried thyme
 ½  teaspoon salt
 ½  teaspoon garlic powder
 ½  teaspoon dried tarragon
 ½  teaspoon dried rubbed sage
 ¼  teaspoon black pepper

*Continued*

¼ cup butter or stick margarine
⅓ cup all-purpose flour

Vanilla Sweet Potatoes

**1.** To prepare stock, combine first 10 ingredients in a large stockpot. Bring to a boil; add turkey. Return to a boil; reduce heat, and simmer 1½ hours or until turkey reaches 170° (use an instant-read thermometer). Carefully remove turkey from stock. Cover turkey; refrigerate. Strain stock through a colander into a large bowl; discard solids, and return stock to pot. Reduce heat; continue to simmer stock until reduced to 2 quarts (about 1½ hours). Cover and chill stock 8 hours. Skim fat from surface of stock, if necessary.
**2.** Preheat oven to 250°.
**3.** To prepare turkey, rub turkey with oil. Sprinkle with ½ teaspoon thyme, ¼ teaspoon salt, ¼ teaspoon garlic powder, and ¼ teaspoon pepper. Wrap turkey in heavy-duty plastic wrap and foil. (Double-wrapping helps retain moisture when reheating.) Bake at 250° for 2 hours or until thoroughly heated.
**4.** To prepare stuffing, melt ¼ cup butter in a large Dutch oven over medium-high heat. Add diced onion and diced celery; sauté 3 minutes. Stir in bread cubes and next 7 ingredients. Stir in 2½ cups turkey stock. Place in a 13 x 9-inch baking dish. Bake simultaneously with turkey at 250° for 1 hour and 55 minutes.
**5.** While turkey and stuffing cook, prepare gravy. Melt ¼ cup butter in a large saucepan over medium heat. Stir in flour; reduce heat, and cook 15 minutes or until lightly browned. Gradually add reserved 5½ cups turkey stock, stirring with a whisk until blended. Bring to a boil; reduce heat, and simmer until reduced to 3 cups (about 2 hours).
**6.** Uncover turkey; remove turkey breast halves from bone. Slice turkey, and serve with stuffing, gravy, and Vanilla Sweet Potatoes. Yield: 6 servings (serving size: 5 ounces turkey, about 1⅓ cups stuffing, ½ cup gravy, and ⅔ cup Vanilla Sweet Potatoes).

(Totals include Vanilla Sweet Potatoes) CALORIES 945 (24% from fat); FAT 25.7g (sat 13.8g, mono 7.8g, poly 2.3g); PROTEIN 64.9g; CARB 110.5g; FIBER 8g; CHOL 197mg; IRON 7.9mg; SODIUM 1,262mg; CALC 254mg

**VANILLA SWEET POTATOES:**

2 pounds sweet potatoes
¾ cup 1% low-fat milk
¼ cup packed brown sugar
2 tablespoons vanilla extract
2 tablespoons butter or stick margarine, softened

**1.** Pierce potatoes with a fork, and arrange in a circle on paper towels in microwave oven. Microwave at HIGH 10 minutes or until tender, rearranging potatoes after 5 minutes. Wrap in a towel; let stand 5 minutes. Peel and mash potatoes. Combine potato, milk, and remaining ingredients. Place in a 1-quart casserole; cover and microwave at MEDIUM 7 minutes or until thoroughly heated. Yield: 6 servings (serving size: ⅔ cup).

CALORIES 241 (17% from fat); FAT 4.6g (sat 2.7g, mono 1.2g, poly 0.4g); PROTEIN 3.5g; CARB 44.6g; FIBER 4.5g; CHOL 12mg; IRON 1mg; SODIUM 77mg; CALC 78mg

# Jerk Turkey Cutlets with Cranberry-Habanero Salsa

From Jimmy Bannos, chef at Heaven on Seven in Chicago, here's a quicker, spicy alternative to the Thanksgiving bird—cutlets. This dish is great for a small gathering.

**MARINADE:**

½ cup (2-inch) sliced green onions
2 tablespoons ground allspice
2 tablespoons fresh or 2 teaspoons dried thyme
2 tablespoons fresh lime juice
2 tablespoons vegetable oil
1 tablespoon soy sauce
1 tablespoon honey
1½ teaspoons grated peeled fresh ginger
1½ teaspoons black pepper
¾ teaspoon salt
¾ teaspoon Worcestershire sauce
½ teaspoon ground nutmeg
½ teaspoon ground cinnamon
½ teaspoon habanero hot pepper sauce or any other hot pepper sauce
¼ teaspoon ground cloves
2 garlic cloves, minced
1 habanero pepper, seeded and chopped (optional)

**TURKEY:**

12 (2-ounce) turkey cutlets
1½ teaspoons Jamaican jerk seasoning (such as Spice Islands)
1 tablespoon vegetable oil, divided

Cranberry-Habanero Salsa

**1.** To prepare marinade, combine first 16 ingredients and habanero pepper, if desired, in a blender or food processor, and process until mixture forms a paste; divide mixture in half, reserving ¼ cup for another use.
**2.** To prepare turkey, combine ¼ cup marinade, cutlets, and jerk seasoning in a zip-top plastic bag; seal and toss well to coat. Marinate in refrigerator 4 hours or overnight, turning bag occasionally.
**3.** Remove cutlets from bag, and discard marinade. Heat 1 teaspoon oil in a nonstick skillet over medium-high heat. Add 4 cutlets, and sauté 1 minute on each side or until done. Repeat procedure with remaining oil and cutlets. Serve with Cranberry-Habanero Salsa. Yield: 4 servings (serving size: 3 cutlets and ¼ cup salsa).

(Totals include Cranberry-Habanero Salsa) CALORIES 316 (23% from fat); FAT 8g (sat 1.8g, mono 2g, poly 3.2g); PROTEIN 40.7g; CARB 19.4g; FIBER 1.2g; CHOL 102mg; IRON 2.7mg; SODIUM 731mg; CALC 47mg

**CRANBERRY-HABANERO SALSA:**

1½ cups fresh or frozen cranberries
3 tablespoons thinly sliced green onions
2 tablespoons fresh orange juice
2 tablespoons honey
1 tablespoon water
1 tablespoon finely chopped green bell pepper
1 tablespoon chopped fresh cilantro
1 teaspoon sugar
⅛ teaspoon salt
½ habanero pepper or 1 serrano chile, seeded and minced
Dash of black pepper

**1.** To prepare salsa, place cranberries in a food processor; pulse 3 or 4 times until chopped. Combine cranberries, onions, and remaining ingredients. Cover and refrigerate. Yield: 1 cup (serving size: ¼ cup).

CALORIES 60 (2% from fat); FAT 0.1g; PROTEIN 0.4g; CARB 15.8g; FIBER 0.7g; CHOL 0mg; IRON 0.3mg; SODIUM 76mg; CALC 9mg

## Cajun Turkey with Dirty-Rice Stuffing

(pictured on page 331)

This recipe is from Joe Brown, executive chef at Melange Cafe in Cherry Hill, New Jersey. Spicy Cajun-style dirty rice is a great accompaniment to turkey and cranberry sauce. Break out a commercial cranberry sauce, or try this with the Cranberry Syrup (recipe on page 311) that accompanies Caprial Pence's Spice-Rubbed Smoked Turkey with Roasted-Pear Stuffing (recipe on page 310).

1 (12-pound) fresh or frozen turkey, thawed
2 tablespoons no-salt-added Cajun seasoning (such as Spice Islands)
½ teaspoon salt
Cooking spray
Dirty-Rice Stuffing
Parsley and rosemary sprigs (optional)

**1.** Preheat oven to 350°.
**2.** Remove and discard giblets and neck from turkey. Rinse turkey with cold water; pat dry. Trim excess fat. Starting at neck cavity, loosen skin from breast and drumsticks by inserting fingers, gently pushing between skin and meat. Rub Cajun seasoning and salt under loosened skin, and sprinkle in body cavity. Tie ends of legs with cord. Lift wing tips up and over back; tuck under turkey.
**3.** Place turkey on a broiler pan coated with cooking spray or on a rack set in a shallow roasting pan. Insert meat thermometer into meaty part of thigh, making sure not to touch bone. Bake at 350° for 2½ hours or until thermometer registers 180°. (Cover turkey loosely with foil if it gets too brown.) Remove turkey from oven. Cover loosely with foil; let stand 10 minutes before carving. Discard skin. Serve with Dirty-Rice Stuffing. If desired, garnish with parsley and rosemary sprigs. Yield: 12 servings (serving size: 6 ounces turkey and ¾ cup stuffing).

(Totals include Dirty-Rice Stuffing) CALORIES 551 (30% from fat); FAT 18.3g (sat 6g, mono 6.6g, poly 3.6g); PROTEIN 62.6g; CARB 29.6g; FIBER 1.2g; CHOL 239mg; IRON 6.5mg; SODIUM 759mg; CALC 68mg

DIRTY-RICE STUFFING:
2 tablespoons olive oil
1 pound andouille sausage, chopped
½ pound chicken livers, cut into bite-size pieces
1 cup finely chopped onion
1 cup finely chopped celery
1 cup finely chopped green bell pepper
¼ cup no-salt-added Cajun seasoning (such as Spice Islands)
¼ cup chopped garlic
6 cups hot cooked long-grain rice
3 cups fat-free, less-sodium chicken broth
½ teaspoon salt

**1.** Heat oil in a large Dutch oven over medium-high heat. Add sausage and next 6 ingredients; sauté 15 minutes or until browned. Add rice, broth, and salt; cook until liquid is nearly absorbed (about 15 minutes). Yield: 12 servings (serving size: ¾ cup).

CALORIES 261 (34% from fat); FAT 9.9g (sat 3.2g, mono 4.9g, poly 1.1g); PROTEIN 12.7g; CARB 29.6g; FIBER 1.2g; CHOL 110mg; IRON 3.5mg; SODIUM 543mg; CALC 26mg

## inspired vegetarian

# Pull Out the Stops

*Here's a vegetarian menu that can take center stage at any Thanksgiving celebration.*

Come the holidays, we want to fuss a bit in the kitchen. It's the perfect time of year to pull out the stops, to take on cooking projects that are more time consuming than usual. Certainly they stand apart from the everyday meals we cobble together day in and day out. This is the time for a splurge.

**Vegetarian Thanksgiving Menu for 6**

**Belgian Endive-and-Apple Salad**

**Braised Shallots and Fall Vegetables with Red Wine Sauce**

**Lentils with Carrots**

**Celeriac Puree**

*About 727 calories (28% from fat) and 22.5 grams fat per serving*

## Belgian Endive-and-Apple Salad

You can make the dressing early in the day and toss the apples with it to keep them from browning. Wait as long as you can to cut the endive because it discolors where touched with a knife. It should be one of the last things you do before serving dinner. Walnut oil gives the dressing a rich, nutty flavor, but you can use olive oil instead.

2 tablespoons minced shallots
2 tablespoons white wine vinegar
2 tablespoons red wine vinegar
½ teaspoon salt
½ teaspoon black pepper
1 tablespoon olive oil
1 tablespoon walnut oil or olive oil
4 cups julienne-cut Golden Delicious apple (about 2 large)
3 heads Belgian endive, halved and thinly sliced lengthwise (about 4 cups)
2 tablespoons chopped fresh parsley

**1.** Combine first 5 ingredients; add oils, stirring well with a whisk. Add apple, tossing well; cover and chill.
**2.** Combine apple mixture, endive, and parsley in a large bowl; toss well to coat. Serve immediately. Yield: 6 servings (serving size: 1⅓ cups).

CALORIES 92 (47% from fat); FAT 4.8g (sat 0.5g, mono 3.3g, poly 0.7g); PROTEIN 0.5g; CARB 13g; FIBER 2.1g; CHOL 0mg; IRON 0.4mg; SODIUM 199mg; CALC 9mg

## Braised Shallots and Fall Vegetables with Red Wine Sauce

This recipe is lengthy, so you should begin with the Red Wine Sauce.

    2  tablespoons butter
    1  tablespoon olive oil
   20  large shallots, peeled and separated (about 2 pounds)
    6  carrots, cut into 2-inch-thick pieces (about ¾ pound)
  2½  cups quartered mushrooms (about ⅓ pound)
    4  large parsnips, quartered lengthwise and cut into 1-inch pieces
       Red Wine Sauce, divided
  1½  teaspoons minced fresh or ½ teaspoon dried rosemary
    ¼  teaspoon salt
    ⅛  teaspoon black pepper
    2  bay leaves
    2  thyme sprigs
    3  tablespoons chopped fresh parsley
    1  garlic clove, minced

**1.** Heat butter and oil in a large Dutch oven over medium-high heat. Add shallots and carrots; sauté 10 minutes, stirring frequently. Add mushrooms and parsnips; sauté 10 minutes. Add 1 cup Red Wine Sauce, rosemary, and next 4 ingredients; bring to a boil. Reduce heat, and simmer 20 minutes. Discard bay leaves and thyme sprigs.

**2.** Drizzle vegetables with remaining Red Wine Sauce. Combine parsley and garlic; sprinkle over each serving. Yield: 6 servings (serving size: 1½ cups braised vegetables and ¼ cup wine sauce).

(Totals include Red Wine Sauce) CALORIES 317 (32% from fat); FAT 11.1g (sat 4.4g, mono 5.1g, poly 0.9g); PROTEIN 7.1g; CARB 52.3g; FIBER 6.1g; CHOL 16mg; IRON 4.2mg; SODIUM 386mg; CALC 126mg

**RED WINE SAUCE:**

    4  cups boiling water
    ⅓  cup dried porcini mushrooms (about ½ ounce)
    1  tablespoon olive oil
    2  cups diced carrot
  1½  cups quartered button mushrooms
    1  cup diced onion
    1  cup diced celery
    1  cup chopped red bell pepper
    4  garlic cloves, minced
    2  thyme sprigs
    1  bay leaf
    1  (2-inch) rosemary sprig
    3  tablespoons tomato paste
    2  tablespoons all-purpose flour
    ¼  teaspoon salt
    ⅛  teaspoon black pepper
    2  cups Merlot or other dry red wine
    1  tablespoon low-sodium soy sauce
    1  tablespoon butter

**1.** Combine boiling water and porcini mushrooms, and set aside.
**2.** Heat oil in a large Dutch oven over medium heat; add carrot and next 8 ingredients. Cook 30 minutes or until browned, stirring frequently. Stir in tomato paste, flour, salt, and black pepper; cook 1 minute. Stir in porcini mixture and wine, scraping pan to loosen browned bits. Bring to a boil; reduce heat, and simmer 30 minutes. Strain through a colander into a large bowl. Drain well, pressing vegetable mixture with the back of a spoon to remove as much sauce as possible. Return sauce to pan, discarding solids. Bring to a boil, and cook until reduced to 2½ cups (about 5 minutes). Stir in soy sauce and butter. Yield: 2½ cups (serving size: ¼ cup).

CALORIES 42 (56% from fat); FAT 2.6g (sat 0.9g, mono 1.3g, poly 0.2g); PROTEIN 0.7g; CARB 4.4g; FIBER 0.7g; CHOL 3mg; IRON 0.6mg; SODIUM 121mg; CALC 11mg

## Lentils with Carrots

    3  cups water
    3  cups finely diced carrot
    1  cup dried small black, green, or brown lentils
    ¼  cup minced fresh onion
    ½  teaspoon salt
    1  bay leaf
    1  tablespoon butter

**1.** Combine first 6 ingredients in a saucepan; bring to a boil. Reduce heat, and simmer 25 minutes. Drain. Stir in butter. Discard bay leaf. Yield: 6 servings (serving size: ½ cup).

CALORIES 150 (14% from fat); FAT 2.3g (sat 1.3g, mono 0.6g, poly 0.3g); PROTEIN 9.5g; CARB 24.3g; FIBER 5.5g; CHOL 5mg; IRON 3.2mg; SODIUM 140mg; CALC 33mg

## Celeriac Puree

Celeriac's earthy flavor, a melding of celery and parsley, complements the flavors in this dish. If you can't find celeriac, use potatoes.

    3  cups chopped leek
    1  pound peeled baking potato, cut into 2-inch pieces (about 3 cups)
    1  pound celeriac (celery root), peeled and chopped (about 3 cups)
    2  tablespoons butter
    ¼  teaspoon salt

**1.** Place leek, potato, and celeriac in a stockpot; cover with water. Bring to a boil; cook 30 minutes or until very tender. Drain.

**2.** Place leek mixture in a blender or food processor; process until smooth. Stir in butter and salt. Yield: 6 servings (serving size: ¾ cup).

CALORIES 168 (23% from fat); FAT 4.3g (sat 2.5g, mono 1.2g, poly 0.4g); PROTEIN 3.4g; CARB 30.6g; FIBER 2.7g; CHOL 10mg; IRON 1.8mg; SODIUM 227mg; CALC 68mg

sweet talk

# Butterscotched

*Accept no substitutes: The golden, roasted flavor of melted butter and brown sugar is what you want.*

Plenty of cookbooks offer butterscotch recipes, but they often don't get it right. Although most of the imitators include brown sugar and butter—the two absolute requirements for the flavor—they call for adding them separately. For that unique, if elusive, taste, the butter and brown sugar must melt together in a saucepan before going into the mix. You should never replace butter with margarine, however. Only the real milk product makes a butterscotch worthy of the name.

### Butterscotch Bundt Cake

Cooking spray
2  tablespoons dry breadcrumbs
7  tablespoons butter, softened and divided
2  cups packed dark brown sugar
⅔  cup (6 ounces) ⅓-less-fat cream cheese
2  teaspoons vanilla extract
3  large eggs
1  large egg white
2¼  cups all-purpose flour
½  cup cornstarch
1  teaspoon baking soda
½  teaspoon salt
½  cup 1% low-fat milk
1  tablespoon powdered sugar

**1.** Preheat oven to 325°.

**2.** Coat a 12-cup Bundt pan with cooking spray; dust with breadcrumbs.

**3.** Melt 4 tablespoons butter in a large saucepan over medium heat. Add brown sugar, and cook 2 minutes, stirring constantly (sugar will not melt). Pour mixture into a large bowl; cool 20 minutes, stirring occasionally.

**4.** Add 3 tablespoons butter, cheese, and vanilla to bowl; beat at low speed of a mixer 1 minute. Beat at high speed 4 minutes (mixture will not be smooth). Add eggs and egg white, 1 at a time, beating well after each addition.

**5.** Lightly spoon flour into dry measuring cups; level with a knife. Combine flour and next 3 ingredients, stirring well with a whisk. Add flour mixture to sugar mixture alternately with milk, beginning and ending with flour mixture; mix after each addition.

**6.** Pour batter into prepared pan. Bake at 325° for 1 hour and 5 minutes or until a wooden pick inserted 1 inch from edge comes out clean. Cool in pan 10 minutes on a wire rack; remove from pan. Cool completely on wire rack. Sift powdered sugar over cake. Yield: 16 servings (serving size: 1 slice).

CALORIES 277 (29% from fat); FAT 8.8g (sat 5.1g, mono 2.6g, poly 0.5g); PROTEIN 4.5g; CARB 45.4g; FIBER 0.5g; CHOL 63mg; IRON 1.6mg; SODIUM 280mg; CALC 42mg

### Rich Butterscotch Pudding

With three egg yolks, butter, and a generous amount of brown sugar, this is the Rolls-Royce of butterscotch puddings.

2  tablespoons butter
1  cup evaporated fat-free milk, divided
¾  cup packed dark brown sugar
2  cups 1% low-fat milk
3  tablespoons cornstarch
⅛  teaspoon salt
3  large egg yolks
1½  teaspoons vanilla extract

**1.** Melt butter in a 3-quart heavy saucepan over medium heat. Add ¼ cup evaporated milk and brown sugar, stirring constantly; cook 2 minutes. Bring to a boil, and cook 30 seconds. Remove pan from heat.

**2.** Heat 1% milk in a heavy saucepan over medium-high heat; cook until tiny bubbles form around edge (do not boil). Remove from heat.

**3.** Combine ¾ cup evaporated milk, cornstarch, salt, and egg yolks in a medium bowl; stir well with a whisk. Gradually add hot milk. Stir hot milk mixture into brown sugar mixture. Cook over medium heat until mixture comes to a boil, stirring constantly; cook 1 minute. Remove from heat; stir in vanilla.

**4.** Spoon ½ cup pudding into each of 6 (6-ounce) ramekins. Cover surface of pudding with plastic wrap; chill 3 hours or until pudding is set. Yield: 6 servings.

CALORIES 254 (26% from fat); FAT 7.4g (sat 3.8g, mono 2.4g, poly 0.5g); PROTEIN 7.4g; CARB 39.4g; FIBER 0g; CHOL 124mg; IRON 1mg; SODIUM 192mg; CALC 260mg

### Raspberries with Butterscotch-Amaretto Custard Sauce

This delicate custard sauce has a subtle butterscotch flavor that pairs well with raspberries (or any kind of berry). Light brown sugar works best for this recipe.

1  tablespoon butter
½  cup packed light brown sugar
1  cup evaporated fat-free milk, divided
1⅔  cups 2% reduced-fat milk
2  tablespoons granulated sugar
2  tablespoons cornstarch
⅛  teaspoon salt
3  large egg yolks
1  tablespoon amaretto (almond-flavored liqueur) or 1 tablespoon water and a drop of almond extract
6  cups fresh raspberries or other berries

**1.** Melt butter in a medium saucepan over medium heat. Add brown sugar; cook 2 minutes, stirring constantly with a whisk. Stir in ¼ cup evaporated milk. Bring to a boil, and cook 30

*Continued*

seconds, stirring constantly. Remove from heat.

**2.** Heat 2% milk in a heavy saucepan over medium-high heat to 180° or until tiny bubbles form around edge (do not boil). Remove milk from heat.

**3.** Combine granulated sugar, cornstarch, salt, and egg yolks in a medium bowl, stirring with a whisk until smooth. Stir in hot 2% milk and ¾ cup evaporated milk. Add milk mixture to brown sugar mixture. Bring to a boil over medium heat; cook 2 minutes or until thick, stirring constantly with a whisk. Remove from heat; cool to room temperature. Stir in amaretto. Pour sauce into a bowl; cover and chill. Spoon sauce over raspberries. Yield: 6 servings (serving size: 1 cup raspberries and ½ cup sauce).

CALORIES 273 (22% from fat); FAT 6.6g (sat 2.9g, mono 2g, poly 0.9g); PROTEIN 8g; CARB 47.2g; FIBER 8.4g; CHOL 121mg; IRON 1.5mg; SODIUM 162mg; CALC 262mg

## Very Butterscotch Sauce

This thick sauce goes great over ice cream, frozen yogurt, or sliced apples.

2½ tablespoons butter
 1 cup packed dark brown sugar
 ¼ cup evaporated low-fat milk
 2 tablespoons light-colored corn syrup
 ½ cup water
 1 tablespoon cornstarch

**1.** Melt butter in a small heavy saucepan over medium-high heat; stir in sugar, milk, and syrup. Bring to a boil; reduce heat to medium, and cook 5 minutes, stirring frequently. Combine water and cornstarch; stir into milk mixture. Bring to a boil; cook 1 minute, stirring constantly. Remove from heat, and cool to room temperature. Yield: 1½ cups (serving size: 2 tablespoons).

**NOTE:** This sauce can be stored in refrigerator up to 2 weeks.

CALORIES 107 (21% from fat); FAT 2.5g (sat 1.5g, mono 0.7g, poly 0.1g); PROTEIN 0.4g; CARB 21.5g; FIBER 0g; CHOL 7mg; IRON 0.4mg; SODIUM 42mg; CALC 30mg

## Triple-Butterscotch Boston Cream Pie

Like its famous namesake, this isn't really a pie but a sponge cake with a butterscotch-custard filling and butterscotch glaze. You can make the filling in advance, and it will keep for two to three days in the refrigerator.

**FILLING:**
 2 tablespoons butter
 ½ cup packed dark brown sugar
 ¼ cup evaporated fat-free milk
 1 cup 2% reduced-fat milk
 2 tablespoons cornstarch
 ⅛ teaspoon salt
 1 large egg
 1 large egg yolk
 1 teaspoon vanilla extract

**CAKE:**
 Cooking spray
 2 teaspoons cake flour
1¼ cups sifted cake flour
 1 teaspoon baking powder
 ¼ teaspoon salt
 1 tablespoon butter
 ⅓ cup 2% reduced-fat milk
 2 large eggs
 ⅓ cup packed dark brown sugar
 ⅓ cup granulated sugar
 1 teaspoon vanilla extract

**GLAZE:**
 2 tablespoons butter
 ¼ cup packed dark brown sugar
 2 tablespoons evaporated fat-free milk
 ¼ cup sifted powdered sugar
 ½ teaspoon vanilla extract

**1.** To prepare filling, melt 2 tablespoons butter in a large heavy saucepan over medium heat. Add ½ cup brown sugar and ¼ cup evaporated milk, stirring constantly; cook 2 minutes. Bring to a boil, and cook 30 seconds. Remove from heat. Heat 1 cup 2% milk in a small heavy saucepan over medium-heat to 180° or until tiny bubbles form around edge (do not boil). Remove milk from heat.

**2.** Combine cornstarch, ⅛ teaspoon salt, 1 egg, and egg yolk in a bowl; stir well with a whisk. Gradually add hot 2% milk to egg mixture, stirring constantly.

Add milk-egg mixture to brown sugar mixture, stirring constantly. Cook over medium heat until mixture comes to a boil, stirring constantly; cook 1 minute. Stir in 1 teaspoon vanilla. Spoon filling into a bowl. Cover surface of filling with plastic wrap; chill.

**3.** Preheat oven to 350°.

**4.** To prepare cake, coat bottom of a 9-inch round cake pan with cooking spray (do not coat sides of pan); line bottom with wax paper. Coat wax paper with cooking spray, and dust with 2 teaspoons flour. Combine 1¼ cups flour, baking powder, and ¼ teaspoon salt in a bowl. Place 1 tablespoon butter and ⅓ cup 2% milk in a small heavy saucepan, and bring to a simmer over medium heat (do not boil). Remove from heat. Cover and keep warm.

**5.** Beat 2 eggs in a large bowl at high speed of a mixer 3 minutes. Gradually add ⅓ cup brown sugar and granulated sugar, beating until thick (about 3 minutes). Add flour mixture to egg mixture alternately with warm milk mixture, beginning and ending with flour mixture. Stir in 1 teaspoon vanilla. Pour batter into prepared pan. Bake at 350° for 25 minutes or until a wooden pick inserted in center comes out clean. Cool cake in pan on a wire rack 10 minutes. Remove cake from pan, and peel off wax paper. Cool cake completely on wire rack.

**6.** Split cake in half horizontally, using a serrated knife; place bottom layer, cut side up, on a plate. Spread with filling. Top with remaining cake layer.

**7.** To prepare glaze, melt 2 tablespoons butter in a small heavy saucepan over medium heat. Add ¼ cup brown sugar and 2 tablespoons evaporated milk. Bring to a boil, stirring constantly; cook 1 minute. Remove from heat; cool slightly. Add powdered sugar and ½ teaspoon vanilla, stirring with a whisk until well-blended. Spread glaze over top of cake. Cover and chill at least 1 hour. Yield: 10 servings (serving size: 1 slice).

CALORIES 292 (27% from fat); FAT 8.7g (sat 4.7g, mono 2.7g, poly 0.6g); PROTEIN 5.3g; CARB 48.3g; FIBER 0g; CHOL 107mg; IRON 1.9mg; SODIUM 253mg; CALC 129mg

# Fiber Optics

*If high-fiber foods looked good, would you eat more of them? Mother Nature thinks so.*

Let's say high-fiber foods got a makeover. You'd gobble them in all their glory—exactly what you'll do with these six tasty dishes, all of which contain at least 4 grams of fiber per serving. While that's only a start toward the 25 to 35 grams of total fiber, soluble and insoluble, you should eat every day, these fiber-rich recipes serve as a powerful incentive to get you going in the right direction.

### Barley, Corn, and Provolone Bake

Barley can boast of being higher in fiber than any other grain. That means 3 grams in a half-cup serving of cooked barley.

3½ cups water
¾ teaspoon salt, divided
1 cup uncooked pearl barley
1 teaspoon olive oil
1½ cups chopped sweet onion
1 cup fresh corn kernels (about 2 ears)
1 cup diced red bell pepper (about 1 large)
¼ cup finely chopped fresh parsley
2 teaspoons minced fresh or ½ teaspoon dried thyme
¼ teaspoon freshly ground black pepper
¾ cup (3 ounces) shredded sharp provolone, fontina, or part-skim mozzarella cheese
Cooking spray

**1.** Combine water and ¼ teaspoon salt in a large saucepan; bring to a boil. Add barley. Return to a boil; cover, reduce heat, and simmer 45 minutes. Remove from heat; let stand, covered, 5 minutes.
**2.** Preheat oven to 350°.
**3.** Heat oil in a large nonstick skillet over medium heat. Add onion and corn; sauté 6 minutes. Add bell pepper; sauté 3 minutes. Stir in cooked barley, ½ teaspoon salt, parsley, thyme, and black pepper. Remove from heat; stir in cheese. Spoon into a 2-quart casserole coated with cooking spray; cover with lid. Bake at 350° for 40 minutes. Uncover; bake an additional 5 minutes. Yield: 8 servings (serving size: ¾ cup).

CALORIES 166 (22% from fat); FAT 4.1g (sat 2g, mono 1.3g, poly 0.5g); PROTEIN 6.4g; CARB 27.3g; FIBER 5.6g; CHOL 7mg; IRON 1.3mg; SODIUM 321mg; CALC 99mg

### White Bean-Pizza Salad

White beans, high in soluble fiber, are the primary ingredient in the hummus that provides the "sauce" for the pizza.

**HUMMUS:**
1 garlic clove
2 tablespoons fresh lemon juice
2 tablespoons tahini (sesame-seed paste)
2 tablespoons water
⅛ teaspoon salt
1 (15.8-ounce) can Great Northern or other white beans, rinsed and drained

**PIZZA:**
1 (10-ounce) can refrigerated pizza crust
Cooking spray
1½ teaspoons fresh lemon juice
1½ tablespoons extra-virgin olive oil
1 tablespoon balsamic vinegar
⅛ teaspoon freshly ground black pepper
16 cherry tomatoes, halved
8 cups trimmed arugula or spinach (about 4 ounces)
⅓ cup vertically sliced red onion
¼ cup (1 ounce) crumbled feta cheese

**1.** Preheat oven to 425°.
**2.** To prepare hummus, drop garlic through food chute with food processor on; process until minced. Add 2 tablespoons lemon juice, tahini, water, salt, and beans; process until smooth.

**3.** To prepare pizza, unroll dough onto a baking sheet coated with cooking spray, and pat into a 14 x 11-inch rectangle. Bake at 425° for 8 minutes or until crisp. Remove from oven, and spread bean mixture evenly over crust. Combine 1½ teaspoons lemon juice, oil, vinegar, and pepper in a small bowl, and stir well with a whisk. Combine 1 tablespoon vinegar mixture and tomatoes in a bowl. Combine remaining vinegar mixture and arugula, tossing well to coat. Arrange arugula mixture evenly over bean mixture, and top with tomato mixture. Sprinkle onion and cheese evenly over tomato mixture. Serve immediately. Yield: 6 servings.

CALORIES 282 (30% from fat); FAT 9.3g (sat 2g, mono 4.3g, poly 2.3g); PROTEIN 11.4g; CARB 39.7g; FIBER 5.8g; CHOL 4mg; IRON 3.4mg; SODIUM 584mg; CALC 118mg

### Pear, Blue Cheese, and Walnut Salad with Smoked Turkey

Pears rank high in fiber among fresh fruits, especially when left unpeeled.

2 tablespoons cider vinegar
2 tablespoons water
1½ teaspoons olive oil
⅛ teaspoon salt
⅛ teaspoon black pepper
2 cups (2-inch) strips smoked turkey breast (about 10 ounces)
1 cup seedless red grapes, halved
½ cup chopped celery
2 large red Bartlett pears, thinly sliced
4 cups gourmet salad greens
¼ cup (1 ounce) crumbled blue cheese
2 tablespoons chopped walnuts

**1.** Combine first 5 ingredients in a large bowl, and stir with a whisk. Add turkey, grapes, celery, and pears, tossing well to coat. Arrange 1 cup greens on each of 4 plates; divide grape mixture evenly over greens. Sprinkle each serving with 1 tablespoon cheese and 1½ teaspoons walnuts. Yield: 4 servings.

CALORIES 247 (30% from fat); FAT 8.2g (sat 2.2g, mono 2.7g, poly 2.3g); PROTEIN 17.7g; CARB 26.1g; FIBER 5g; CHOL 55mg; IRON 1.6mg; SODIUM 764mg; CALC 87mg

## Wild Rice Croquettes over Mixed Greens

Long-grain brown rice and wild rice are both good sources of insoluble fiber.

3 cups water
½ teaspoon salt
½ cup uncooked wild rice
½ cup uncooked long-grain brown rice

WHITE SAUCE:
¼ cup all-purpose flour
1 cup 1% low-fat milk
1 large egg, lightly beaten
⅛ teaspoon grated whole nutmeg

REMAINING INGREDIENTS:
1 tablespoon butter or stick margarine
½ cup finely diced carrot
½ cup finely diced onion
½ cup finely diced mushrooms
¼ cup finely diced celery
¼ cup finely chopped fresh parsley
½ teaspoon freshly ground black pepper
¼ teaspoon salt
1 tablespoon olive oil, divided
8 cups mixed salad greens
⅓ cup bottled fat-free balsamic dressing (such as Girard's)

**1.** Bring water and ½ teaspoon salt to a boil in a medium saucepan; add rices. Cover, reduce heat, and simmer 45 minutes or until liquid is absorbed. Drain.
**2.** While rice is cooking, prepare white sauce. Lightly spoon flour into a dry measuring cup; level with a knife. Place flour in a medium saucepan. Gradually add milk, stirring with a whisk until blended. Bring to a boil over medium heat; cook until thick (about 1 minute), stirring constantly. Gradually stir about one-fourth of hot milk mixture into egg; add to remaining milk mixture, stirring constantly. Cook over medium heat 2 minutes or until thick, stirring frequently. Stir in nutmeg. Place white sauce in a bowl, and cover surface of sauce with plastic wrap. Refrigerate.
**3.** Melt butter in a large nonstick skillet over medium heat. Add carrot, onion,

mushrooms, and celery; cover and cook 15 minutes or until tender, stirring occasionally.
**4.** Combine rice, white sauce, vegetable mixture, parsley, pepper, and ¼ teaspoon salt in a large bowl. Divide mixture into 8 equal portions, shaping each into a 1-inch-thick patty.
**5.** Heat 1½ teaspoons oil in a large nonstick skillet over medium-high heat. Add 4 patties; cook 1 minute. Cover and cook 3 minutes. Carefully turn patties over; cook, uncovered, 3 minutes. Repeat procedure with 1½ teaspoons oil and remaining patties.
**6.** Combine greens and dressing in a large bowl, tossing well. Serve croquettes over greens. Yield: 4 servings (serving size: 2 patties and 2 cups greens).

CALORIES 338 (25% from fat); FAT 9.5g (sat 3.3g, mono 4.3g, poly 1.2g); PROTEIN 11.7g; CARB 52.7g; FIBER 5.6g; CHOL 63mg; IRON 3.1mg; SODIUM 807mg; CALC 152mg

## Fig-Swirl Coffeecake

(pictured on page 330)

This recipe received our Test Kitchens' highest rating.

1 package dry yeast (about 2¼ teaspoons)
½ teaspoon granulated sugar
¼ cup warm water (100° to 110°)
⅓ cup fat-free milk
2 teaspoons vanilla extract, divided
1 large egg
1½ cups all-purpose flour
1¼ cups whole-wheat flour
⅓ cup granulated sugar
3 tablespoons chilled butter or stick margarine, cut into small pieces
¾ teaspoon salt
Cooking spray
1½ cups dried Calimyrna or Black Mission figs (about 12 ounces)
½ cup fresh orange juice (about 1 orange)
1 cup powdered sugar
2 tablespoons fresh lemon juice

**1.** Dissolve yeast and ½ teaspoon sugar in warm water in a small bowl; let stand

5 minutes. Stir in milk, 1 teaspoon vanilla, and egg. Lightly spoon flours into dry measuring cups; level with a knife. Place flours, ⅓ cup sugar, butter, and salt in a food processor; pulse 5 times or until blended. With processor on, slowly add yeast mixture through food chute, and process until dough forms a ball. Process 1 additional minute. Turn dough out onto a floured surface; knead lightly 4 or 5 times (dough will feel tacky).
**2.** Place dough in a large bowl coated with cooking spray, turning to coat top. Cover and let rise in a warm place (85°), free from drafts, 1 hour or until dough is almost doubled in size. (Press two fingers into dough. If indentation remains, dough has risen enough.)
**3.** Trim stems off figs. Combine 1 teaspoon vanilla, figs, and orange juice in food processor; process until finely chopped. Set aside.
**4.** Punch dough down; cover and let rest 5 minutes. Roll dough into a 15 x 10-inch rectangle on a floured surface. Spread fig mixture evenly over dough, leaving a 1-inch margin along one long edge. Roll up rectangle tightly, starting with opposite long edge, pressing firmly to eliminate air pockets; pinch seam to seal. Place roll, seam side down, on floured surface; split roll in half length-wise, using a serrated knife. Working on a 12-inch pizza pan coated with cooking spray, coil one half of the dough, cut side up, around itself in a spiral pattern. Place other half of dough, cut side up, at end of first strip, pinching ends together to seal; continue coiling dough to form a circle. Cover and let rise 1 hour or until dough is doubled in size.
**5.** Preheat oven to 350°.
**6.** Bake at 350° for 30 minutes or until golden. Place cake on a serving plate. Combine powdered sugar and lemon juice in a small bowl; drizzle over hot cake. Serve warm or at room temperature. Yield: 16 servings (serving size: 1 wedge).
**NOTE:** The coffeecake dough can be made ahead of time. Follow recipe with these exceptions: In step 2, let dough rise 1½ hours at room temperature. Punch dough down; return to bowl.

Cover dough with plastic wrap; chill 8 hours. When ready to use, shape and bake according to recipe instructions.

CALORIES 208 (13% from fat); FAT 3.1g (sat 1.6g, mono 0.9g, poly 0.4g); PROTEIN 4g; CARB 43g; FIBER 4.2g; CHOL 20mg; IRON 1.5mg; SODIUM 142mg; CALC 45mg

## Quinoa Timbales

Dubbed the supergrain of the future, quinoa (KEEN-wah) is high in fiber and contains all the essential amino acids—which makes it a complete protein. You can serve the dish from a bowl if you don't want to form the timbales.

    2   cups water
    1½  cups uncooked quinoa, rinsed and
        drained
    ⅓   cup dried currants or raisins
    ¼   cup diced dried apricots
    1   tablespoon olive oil
    2   teaspoons fresh lemon juice
    ½   teaspoon salt
    ¼   teaspoon freshly ground black
        pepper
    ¼   teaspoon ground cumin
    ¼   cup chopped fresh parsley
    2   tablespoons finely chopped walnuts
    2   tablespoons minced green onions
    9   cherry tomatoes, halved
    Cooking spray

**1.** Bring water to a boil in a medium saucepan; add quinoa, currants, and apricots. Cover, reduce heat, and simmer 15 minutes or until liquid is absorbed. Remove from heat; let stand, covered, 5 minutes. Fluff with a fork.
**2.** Combine oil, lemon juice, salt, pepper, and cumin in a large bowl, and stir well with a whisk. Add parsley, walnuts, and green onions; stir well. Stir in quinoa mixture. Place 3 cherry tomato halves, cut sides down, in bottom of each of 6 (6-ounce) ramekins or custard cups coated with cooking spray. Pack about ½ cup quinoa mixture into each ramekin. Immediately invert ramekins onto individual plates. Yield: 6 servings.

CALORIES 222 (26% from fat); FAT 6.4g (sat 0.6g, mono 2.6g, poly 2.2g); PROTEIN 6.5g; CARB 36.1g; FIBER 5.7g; CHOL 0mg; IRON 4.6mg; SODIUM 207mg; CALC 59mg

# Change for the Better

*A little motivation can be a flavorful thing.*

After she shifted to healthier eating habits, Mona Elibiary of San Diego, learned how much fun it was to rework some of her favorite recipes. But nothing worked quite so well as the redo of the chicken recipe a friend had given her. Mona replaced the chicken with eggplant, changed the spices, and experimented with different flavors. The resulting Baked Eggplant with Mushroom-and-Tomato Sauce was so good that her husband, Stephen, put it on his must-have dinner list.

## Baked Eggplant with Mushroom-and-Tomato Sauce

    1   peeled eggplant, cut into ¼-inch-
        thick slices (about 1¼ pounds)
    Cooking spray
    1   cup chopped onion
    ½   teaspoon dried Italian seasoning
    ¼   teaspoon salt
    2   garlic cloves, chopped
    1   (8-ounce) package presliced
        mushrooms
    ¼   teaspoon black pepper
    1   (8-ounce) can no-salt-added
        tomato sauce
    ⅔   cup (about 3 ounces) shredded part-
        skim mozzarella cheese, divided
    ¼   cup (1 ounce) grated fresh
        Parmesan cheese

**1.** Preheat broiler.
**2.** Arrange eggplant slices on a baking sheet coated with cooking spray; broil 3 minutes on each side or until lightly browned.
**3.** Preheat oven to 375°.
**4.** Heat a large nonstick skillet coated with cooking spray over medium heat; add onion and next 4 ingredients. Cover and cook 7 minutes or until tender,

stirring occasionally. Increase heat to medium-high; uncover and cook 2 minutes or until liquid evaporates.
**5.** Spread half of mushroom mixture in bottom of a 1½-quart round baking dish coated with cooking spray. Arrange half of eggplant slices over mushroom mixture; sprinkle with ⅛ teaspoon pepper. Top with ½ cup tomato sauce and ⅓ cup mozzarella. Spread remaining mushroom mixture over mozzarella; top with remaining eggplant slices. Sprinkle with ⅛ teaspoon pepper; top with remaining tomato sauce. Cover and bake at 375° for 1 hour. Sprinkle with ⅓ cup mozzarella and Parmesan. Bake, uncovered, 5 minutes or until cheese melts. Let stand 10 minutes. Yield: 4 servings.

CALORIES 168 (30% from fat); FAT 5.6g (sat 3.2g, mono 1.5g, poly 0.5g); PROTEIN 10.9g; CARB 21g; FIBER 6.1g; CHOL 16mg; IRON 2.1mg; SODIUM 369mg; CALC 236mg

## Two-Minute, 24-Hour Casserole

"This dish takes two minutes to put together, but it needs to sit in the refrigerator overnight before you cook it so the dry pasta can soak up most of the liquid from the sauce."

—Andrea Martin, Yarmouth, Maine

    7½  cups fat-free Italian herb pasta
        sauce (such as Muir Glen)
    1   pound uncooked penne
        (tube-shaped pasta)
    1   (8-ounce) package presliced
        mushrooms
    1   (8-ounce) block ⅓-less-fat cream
        cheese, softened
    ½   cup low-fat sour cream
    Cooking spray
    1   cup (4 ounces) preshredded part-
        skim mozzarella cheese

**1.** Combine first 3 ingredients in a large bowl; stir until blended.
**2.** Beat cream cheese and sour cream at low speed of a mixer until smooth (about 2 minutes).
**3.** Spread half of pasta mixture in bottom of a 3-quart casserole coated with
*Continued*

cooking spray; spread cream cheese mixture evenly over pasta mixture. Top with remaining pasta mixture; sprinkle with mozzarella cheese.

**4.** Cover and refrigerate 24 hours.

**5.** Preheat oven to 350°.

**6.** Bake, covered, at 350° for 50 minutes. Uncover and bake an additional 10 minutes or until cheese is browned. Yield: 10 servings.

CALORIES 370 (23% from fat); FAT 9.6g (sat 5.5g, mono 2.6g, poly 0.7g); PROTEIN 14.6g; CARB 55.9g; FIBER 4.4g; CHOL 28mg; IRON 3.8mg; SODIUM 602mg; CALC 142mg

## Baked Burritos

—Leslie Sigesmund, Del Mar, California

1 cup packaged cabbage-and-carrot coleslaw mix
1 cup (4 ounces) preshredded reduced-fat Mexican blend or Cheddar cheese, divided
1 cup bottled salsa
½ cup chopped red onion
½ cup chopped green bell pepper
½ cup minced fresh cilantro
2 tablespoons fresh lime juice
1 (16-ounce) can pinto beans, drained and rinsed
1 (2.25-ounce) can sliced ripe olives, drained
6 (8-inch) fat-free flour tortillas
Cooking spray
½ cup chopped green onions

**1.** Preheat oven to 425°.

**2.** Combine coleslaw mix, ½ cup cheese, salsa, and next 6 ingredients in a large bowl; stir until blended. Spread ⅔ cup coleslaw mixture down center of each tortilla; roll up. Place burritos on a baking sheet coated with cooking spray. Sprinkle burritos with ½ cup cheese and green onions.

**3.** Bake at 425° for 13 minutes or until cheese melts. Yield: 6 servings (serving size: 1 burrito).

CALORIES 250 (10% from fat); FAT 2.7g (sat 0.9g, mono 1.2g, poly 0.6g); PROTEIN 13.4g; CARB 44g; FIBER 5g; CHOL 3mg; IRON 3.6mg; SODIUM 858mg; CALC 200mg

## Spinach Pizza Purses

"I'm a 15-year-old student with a working mother, so I have taken over most of the cooking—something I fully enjoy. I came up with this recipe a couple of years ago when I was considering making pizza but didn't want something so cheesy. "

—Elizabeth Maison, Carey, Ohio

**CRUST:**

¼ teaspoon sugar
1 package dry yeast (about 2¼ teaspoons)
¼ cup warm water (100° to 110°)
1 cup all-purpose flour
1 cup whole-wheat flour
½ cup water
1 teaspoon olive oil
¼ teaspoon salt
Cooking spray

**FILLING:**

2 cups (2-inch) red bell pepper strips
¾ cup (3 ounces) grated fresh Parmesan cheese
2 (10-ounce) packages frozen chopped spinach, thawed, drained, and squeezed dry
1 tablespoon cornmeal

**SAUCE:**

1 cup chopped tomato
1 teaspoon dried basil
1 teaspoon dried oregano
¼ teaspoon onion powder
1 garlic clove, minced
1 (15-ounce) can tomato sauce

**1.** To prepare crust, dissolve sugar and yeast in ¼ cup warm water in a large bowl; let stand 5 minutes. Lightly spoon flours into dry measuring cups; level with a knife. Stir flours, ½ cup water, oil, and salt into yeast mixture to form a soft dough. Turn dough out onto a lightly floured surface, and knead until smooth and elastic (about 5 minutes). Place dough in a large bowl coated with cooking spray, turning dough to coat top. Cover dough, and let rise in a warm place (85°), free from drafts, 40 minutes or until doubled in size. (Press two fingers into dough. If indentation remains, dough has risen enough.)

**2.** Punch dough down. Divide dough into 8 equal portions, and roll each dough portion into a 5-inch circle on a lightly floured surface.

**3.** Preheat oven to 350°.

**4.** To prepare filling, combine bell pepper, Parmesan cheese, and spinach in a medium bowl; stir until combined. Spoon ½ cup filling into center of each dough circle. Gather edges of each dough circle together, and press firmly to seal, forming a purse. Place on a baking sheet coated with cooking spray and sprinkled with cornmeal.

**5.** Bake at 350° for 25 minutes or until lightly browned.

**6.** To prepare sauce, combine chopped tomato and remaining 5 ingredients in a medium saucepan; bring to a boil. Reduce heat, and simmer 5 minutes. Serve pizza purses with sauce. Yield: 8 servings (serving size: 1 purse and ¼ cup sauce).

CALORIES 208 (19% from fat); FAT 4.4g (sat 2g, mono 1.4g, poly 0.6g); PROTEIN 11.1g; CARB 33.8g; FIBER 6.2g; CHOL 7mg; IRON 4mg; SODIUM 622mg; CALC 230mg

## Chicken Curry

"I had always enjoyed my mother's chicken curry as a child. Once I started cooking, I wanted to come up with my own version that was healthy as well. After many years of experimenting, I came up with this recipe."

—Judy Satchell, San Marcos, California

1 tablespoon olive oil
1 cup finely chopped onion
3 garlic cloves, minced
1 pound skinned, boned chicken breast, cut into bite-size pieces
1 tablespoon curry powder
1 teaspoon ground marjoram
2 cups finely chopped tomato
1 cup fat-free, less-sodium chicken broth
½ teaspoon cayenne pepper
½ cup plain fat-free yogurt
1 teaspoon all-purpose flour
2 cups cooked couscous
Raisins (optional)

**1.** Heat oil in a large nonstick skillet over medium-high heat. Add onion and garlic; cook 4 minutes or until onion is tender. Add chicken; cook 4 minutes. Add curry powder and marjoram; cook 1 minute. Add tomato, broth, and pepper; reduce heat, and simmer 15 minutes. Remove from heat.

**2.** Combine yogurt and flour; stir with a whisk, and add to chicken mixture. Cook 1 minute or until slightly thick. Serve mixture over couscous; top with raisins, if desired. Yield: 4 servings (serving size: 1 cup chicken mixture and ½ cup couscous).

CALORIES 318 (17% from fat); FAT 5.8g (sat 1g, mono 3g, poly 0.9g); PROTEIN 33.8g; CARB 32.7g; FIBER 3.4g; CHOL 66mg; IRON 2.6mg; SODIUM 229mg; CALC 97mg

## Black Bean-and-Corn Salad

"This dish is refreshing, crisp, and slightly sweet. It's great as a salad anytime or at parties as an appetizer served with tortilla chips."

—Deborah Shore, Scotch Plains, New Jersey

　¼　cup balsamic vinegar
　¼　cup cider vinegar
　2　tablespoons brown sugar
　1½　teaspoons fresh lime juice
　½　teaspoon ground cumin
　¼　teaspoon salt
　1　garlic clove, minced
　1　cup fresh or frozen whole-kernel corn, thawed
　1　cup chopped red bell pepper
　¾　cup chopped onion
　⅓　cup minced fresh cilantro
　1　(15-ounce) can black beans, rinsed and drained

**1.** Bring first 7 ingredients to a boil in a small saucepan. Reduce heat, and simmer 2 minutes or until sugar dissolves. Combine vinegar mixture, corn, and remaining ingredients in a large bowl; cover and chill. Yield: 8 servings (serving size: ½ cup).

CALORIES 82 (5% from fat); FAT 0.5g (sat 0.1g, mono 0.1g, poly 0.2g); PROTEIN 3.9g; CARB 17.3g; FIBER 2.6g; CHOL 0mg; IRON 1.4mg; SODIUM 164mg; CALC 22mg

## Tofumole

"My family loves guacamole, but they don't love all the fat. So I added tofu to cut the fat and add the health benefits of soy."

—Lorrie Paul, Ypsilanti, Michigan

　1　(12.3-ounce) package reduced-fat firm tofu, drained
　1　cup chopped seeded tomato
　¼　cup minced green onions
　2　tablespoons bottled salsa
　½　teaspoon chili powder
　¼　teaspoon salt
　¼　teaspoon black pepper
　1　small ripe peeled avocado, seeded and mashed (about ½ cup)
　48　baked tortilla chips (about 6 ounces)

**1.** Place tofu in a blender; process until smooth. Pour into a bowl; stir in tomato and next 6 ingredients. Cover and chill. Serve with chips. Yield: 12 servings (serving size: ¼ cup dip and 4 chips).

CALORIES 82 (20% from fat); FAT 1.8g (sat 0.3g, mono 0.8g, poly 0.6g); PROTEIN 3.4g; CARB 13.9g; FIBER 1.6g; CHOL 0mg; IRON 0.7mg; SODIUM 192mg; CALC 36mg

## Maple Sweet Potatoes

"Maple syrup gives these sweet potatoes a nice caramelized taste."

—Trisha Kruse, Boise, Idaho

　5　cups (½-inch-thick) slices peeled sweet potato (about 2 pounds)
　Cooking spray
　½　teaspoon salt
　¼　cup maple syrup

**1.** Preheat oven to 350°.

**2.** Arrange half of potato slices in an 11 x 7-inch baking dish coated with cooking spray; sprinkle with half of salt. Arrange remaining potato slices on top; sprinkle with remaining salt. Pour syrup over potatoes. Cover and bake at 350° for 1 hour or until tender. Yield: 8 servings (serving size: ½ cup).

CALORIES 114 (3% from fat); FAT 0.4g (sat 0.1g, mono 0g, poly 0.1g); PROTEIN 1.3g; CARB 26.8g; FIBER 2.5g; CHOL 0mg; IRON 0.6mg; SODIUM 158mg; CALC 25mg

## White Bean Enchiladas

"I once came across a lasagna recipe that called for white beans instead of cheese; that's what inspired this dish. These enchiladas are really easy to make, and you can put them together up to a day ahead. They reheat well in the microwave, too."

—Lisa Springs, San Mateo, California

　2　tablespoons fat-free sour cream
　1　(16-ounce) can cannellini beans or other white beans, rinsed and drained
　½　cup (2 ounces) preshredded reduced-fat Mexican blend or Cheddar cheese, divided
　2　tablespoons canned chopped green chiles
　1　tablespoon sliced green onions
　1　tablespoon chopped fresh cilantro
　1　teaspoon ground cumin
　1　(10-ounce) can enchilada sauce (such as Old El Paso), divided
　¼　cup water
　6　(6-inch) corn tortillas
　Cooking spray
　1　tablespoon minced fresh cilantro (optional)

**1.** Preheat oven to 350°.

**2.** Combine sour cream and beans in a food processor; process until almost smooth. Stir in ¼ cup cheese, chiles, onions, chopped cilantro, and cumin.

**3.** Combine ⅓ cup enchilada sauce and ¼ cup water in a small nonstick skillet over medium-low heat. Dip one tortilla in sauce mixture to soften; transfer to a plate. Spread ¼ cup bean mixture down center of tortilla; roll up. Place roll, seam side down, in an 11 x 7-inch baking dish coated with cooking spray. Repeat procedure with remaining tortillas and bean mixture. Add remaining sauce to pan; cook 1 minute. Spoon over enchiladas; sprinkle with ¼ cup cheese.

**4.** Bake at 350° for 30 minutes or until bubbly. Sprinkle with minced cilantro, if desired. Yield: 3 servings (serving size: 2 enchiladas).

CALORIES 372 (19% from fat); FAT 8g (sat 1.6g, mono 2.1g, poly 3.6g); PROTEIN 17.5g; CARB 60.5g; FIBER 6.2g; CHOL 3mg; IRON 3.9mg; SODIUM 1,076mg; CALC 291mg

# Cruisers Declare *Cooking Light* Recipes "a Big Hit"

*As the sixth* Cooking Light *Ship Shape Cruise Adventure set sail in the Caribbean, 300 cruisers dined on our recipes.*

Now, more than 500,000 passengers aboard Norwegian Cruise Line ships worldwide will be able to select award-winning *Cooking Light* recipes from NCL's many breakfast, lunch, and dinner menus.

### Roasted Tomato-and-Red Pepper Soup

This is one of the many *Cooking Light* recipes that are appearing aboard Norwegian Cruise Line ships worldwide.

1½ pounds red bell peppers
2 pounds tomatoes, halved and seeded
2 tablespoons olive oil
1 cup chopped onion
4 garlic cloves, minced
1½ cups tomato juice
1 tablespoon chopped fresh or 1 teaspoon dried marjoram
½ teaspoon salt
1¼ teaspoons black pepper
Marjoram sprigs (optional)

**1.** Preheat broiler.
**2.** Cut bell peppers in half lengthwise; discard seeds and membranes. Place bell peppers and tomatoes, skin sides up, on a foil-lined baking sheet; flatten peppers with hand. Broil 15 minutes or until vegetables are blackened. Place peppers in a zip-top plastic bag; seal and let stand 10 minutes. Peel peppers and tomatoes; chop. Place half of chopped peppers and half of chopped tomatoes in a blender; process until smooth. Set aside.

**3.** Heat oil in a saucepan over medium-low heat. Add onion and garlic; cover and cook 5 minutes. Add pureed vegetables, remaining chopped bell peppers and tomatoes, tomato juice, chopped marjoram, salt, and black pepper; cook over medium heat until thoroughly heated. Ladle into soup bowls, and garnish with marjoram sprigs, if desired. Yield: 5 servings (serving size: 1 cup).

CALORIES 126 (25% from fat); FAT 4g (sat 0.6g, mono 2.1g, poly 0g); PROTEIN 3.9g; CARB 22.7g; FIBER 5.6g; CHOL 0mg; IRON 3.4mg; SODIUM 521mg; CALC 42mg

## 30 minutes or less

# Fast Soups for Fast Times

*All the world loves a good soup—especially if it doesn't take an eternity to make.*

### White Bean, Chicken Noodle, and Escarole Soup

**PREPARATION TIME: 7 MINUTES**
**COOKING TIME: 12 MINUTES**

10 cups water
6 cups chopped escarole (about ¾ pound) or fresh spinach
2 teaspoons olive oil
2 garlic cloves, chopped
½ cup water
¼ teaspoon crushed red pepper
¼ teaspoon black pepper
1 (19-ounce) can cannellini beans or other white beans, drained
1 (10¾-ounce) can condensed reduced-sodium chicken noodle soup, undiluted
¼ cup (1 ounce) grated fresh Parmesan cheese

**1.** Bring 10 cups water to a boil over high heat in a large Dutch oven or stockpot. Add escarole, and reduce heat to medium. Cook 10 minutes or until tender; drain well.

**2.** Heat oil in pan over medium heat. Add garlic; cook 3 minutes or until lightly browned. Stir in ½ cup water, crushed red pepper, black pepper, cannellini beans, and soup. Bring to a boil; add cooked escarole, and cook until thoroughly heated. Ladle into individual bowls, and sprinkle with cheese. Yield: 4 servings (serving size: 1 cup soup and 1 tablespoon cheese).

**NOTE:** One (10-ounce) package of frozen chopped spinach that has been thawed, drained, and squeezed dry (about 1¼ cups) can be substituted for escarole or fresh spinach.

CALORIES 267 (27% from fat); FAT 8.1g (sat 2.2g, mono 3.4g, poly 1.8g); PROTEIN 14.5g; CARB 36.5g; FIBER 4.2g; CHOL 15mg; IRON 4.1mg; SODIUM 643mg; CALC 176mg

### Canadian Cheese Soup with Pumpernickel Croutons

**PREPARATION TIME: 5 MINUTES**
**COOKING TIME: 25 MINUTES**

3 (1-ounce) slices pumpernickel bread, cut into ½-inch cubes
1 onion, peeled and quartered
1 carrot, peeled and quartered
1 celery stalk, quartered
1 teaspoon butter or stick margarine
¾ cup all-purpose flour
2 (16-ounce) cans fat-free, less-sodium chicken broth, divided
3 cups 2% reduced-fat milk
½ teaspoon salt
½ teaspoon paprika
½ teaspoon freshly ground black pepper
1½ cups (6 ounces) shredded reduced-fat sharp Cheddar cheese

**1.** Preheat oven to 375°.
**2.** Place bread cubes on a jelly-roll pan, and bake at 375° for 15 minutes or until toasted.
**3.** While croutons bake, combine onion, carrot, and celery in a food processor, and pulse until chopped. Melt butter in a large saucepan over medium-high heat. Add vegetables; sauté 5 minutes or until tender.

4. Lightly spoon flour into a dry measuring cup; level with a knife. Gradually add 1 can of broth to flour in a medium bowl; stir well with a whisk. Add flour mixture to pan. Stir in 1 can of broth; bring to a boil. Reduce heat to medium, and cook 10 minutes or until thick. Stir in milk, salt, paprika, and pepper; cook 10 minutes. Remove from heat; add cheese, and stir until cheese melts. Ladle soup into bowls, and top with croutons. Yield: 8 servings (serving size: 1 cup soup and ¼ cup croutons).

CALORIES 203 (30% from fat); FAT 6.8g (sat 3.8g, mono 1.9g, poly 0.4g); PROTEIN 13.2g; CARB 21.9g; FIBER 1.8g; CHOL 23mg; IRON 1.1mg; SODIUM 671mg; CALC 318mg

## Provençale Shellfish Stew

PREPARATION TIME: 10 MINUTES
COOKING TIME: 20 MINUTES

  1  medium onion, peeled and quartered
  1  celery stalk, quartered
  2  garlic cloves, peeled
  1  tablespoon olive oil
  2  (8-ounce) bottles clam juice
  1  (14.5-ounce) can no-salt-added diced tomatoes, undrained
  ½  teaspoon dried thyme
  ½  teaspoon freshly ground black pepper
  ¼  teaspoon saffron threads
  1  pound medium shrimp, peeled and deveined
 12  small mussels or clams, scrubbed and debearded
  ¼  cup chopped fresh parsley
  2  teaspoons dried basil
  1  teaspoon grated orange rind
  ¼  cup orange juice

1. Place onion, celery, and garlic cloves in a food processor, and pulse to chop.
2. Heat oil in a Dutch oven over medium-high heat; add chopped vegetables. Sauté 5 minutes; stir in clam juice and tomatoes. Bring to a boil; add thyme, pepper, and saffron. Reduce heat to medium; cook 10 minutes.
3. Add shrimp and mussels; cook 3 minutes or until shrimp are done and mussels

open. Discard any unopened mussels. Remove from heat; stir in parsley and remaining ingredients. Yield: 6 servings (serving size: 1 cup).

CALORIES 217 (20% from fat); FAT 4.8g (sat 0.7g, mono 2g, poly 1g); PROTEIN 31.3g; CARB 11g; FIBER 0.8g; CHOL 155mg; IRON 18.7mg; SODIUM 355mg; CALC 143mg

## Jamaican Chicken Stew

PREPARATION TIME: 10 MINUTES
COOKING TIME: 20 MINUTES

  1  cup uncooked long-grain rice
  2  teaspoons olive oil
  1  cup chopped onion
 1½  teaspoons bottled minced garlic
  1  pound skinned, boned chicken breast, cut into bite-size pieces
  1  teaspoon curry powder
  1  teaspoon dried thyme
  ½  teaspoon ground allspice
  ½  teaspoon crushed red pepper
  ½  teaspoon cracked black pepper
  ¼  cup dry red wine
  2  tablespoons capers
  1  (15-ounce) can black beans, rinsed and drained
  1  (14.5-ounce) can diced tomatoes, undrained

1. Cook rice according to package directions, omitting salt and fat.
2. While rice cooks, heat oil in a large nonstick skillet over medium-high heat. Add onion and garlic; sauté 3 minutes or until tender. Combine chicken and next 5 ingredients in a bowl. Add chicken mixture to pan; sauté 4 minutes. Stir in wine, capers, beans, and tomatoes. Cover, reduce heat, and simmer 10 minutes or until tender. Serve over rice. Yield: 4 servings (serving size: 1½ cups stew and ¾ cup rice).

CALORIES 465 (10% from fat); FAT 5g (sat 1g, mono 2.2g, poly 1g); PROTEIN 38.5g; CARB 66g; FIBER 5.9g; CHOL 66mg; IRON 6mg; SODIUM 799mg; CALC 101mg

## Easy Fish Stew

PREPARATION TIME: 6 MINUTES
COOKING TIME: 18 MINUTES

  1  tablespoon olive oil
  1  cup chopped onion
  ¼  cup minced celery
  1  teaspoon chili powder
  2  cups water
 1½  cups frozen whole-kernel corn, thawed
  1  tablespoon Worcestershire sauce
  ¾  teaspoon salt
  1  (14.5-ounce) can no-salt-added diced tomatoes, undrained
  1  pound cod or other lean white fish fillets, cut into bite-size pieces
  ¼  cup minced fresh parsley

1. Heat oil in a Dutch oven over medium-high heat. Add onion, celery, and chili powder; sauté 3 minutes or until tender.
2. Stir in water and next 4 ingredients; cook 10 minutes. Add fish; cook 3 minutes or until fish is done. Stir in parsley. Yield: 6 servings (serving size: 1 cup).

CALORIES 143 (20% from fat); FAT 3.1g (sat 0.5g, mono 1.8g, poly 0.5g); PROTEIN 15.7g; CARB 14.6g; FIBER 1.8g; CHOL 33mg; IRON 1mg; SODIUM 380mg; CALC 51mg

## Avgolemono
*Greek Lemon Soup*

PREPARATION TIME: 5 MINUTES
COOKING TIME: 10 MINUTES

  1  cup uncooked long-grain rice
  4  large eggs, lightly beaten
  2  teaspoons grated lemon rind
  ⅓  cup fresh lemon juice
  ½  teaspoon kosher salt
  ¼  teaspoon ground red pepper
  1  (16-ounce) can fat-free, less-sodium chicken broth
  ¼  cup chopped fresh parsley
 Thin lemon slices (optional)

1. Cook rice according to package directions, omitting salt and fat.
2. While rice cooks, combine eggs, lemon rind, lemon juice, salt, and red pepper in a
*Continued*

small bowl, and set aside. Place chicken broth in a large saucepan over medium-high heat, and bring to a boil. Reduce heat to medium, and whisk in egg mixture. Cook until thick (about 5 minutes), stirring constantly (do not boil). Serve over rice; sprinkle with parsley, and garnish with lemon slices, if desired. Yield: 4 servings (serving size: ¾ cup soup, ¾ cup rice, and 1 tablespoon parsley).

CALORIES 263 (19% from fat); FAT 5.6g (sat 1.7g, mono 2.1g, poly 0.8g); PROTEIN 11.5g; CARB 40.3g; FIBER 0.9g; CHOL 221mg; IRON 3mg; SODIUM 550mg; CALC 47mg

### Roasted Red Pepper, Zucchini, and Tomato Soup with Fusilli

PREPARATION TIME: 8 MINUTES
COOKING TIME: 20 MINUTES

1½ cups uncooked fusilli (short twisted spaghetti)
1 bacon slice, chopped
½ cup chopped onion
4 garlic cloves, chopped
2 cups (¼-inch) sliced zucchini
2 (16-ounce) cans fat-free, less-sodium chicken broth
½ teaspoon cracked black pepper
1 (14.5-ounce) can no-salt-added diced tomatoes, undrained
1 (7-ounce) bottle roasted red bell peppers, undrained and chopped
¼ cup chopped fresh flat-leaf parsley
¼ cup (1 ounce) grated fresh Parmesan cheese

1. Cook pasta according to package directions, omitting salt and fat.
2. Cook bacon in a Dutch oven over medium-high heat 3 minutes. Add onion and garlic; cook 2 minutes. Stir in zucchini; cook 5 minutes. Add broth, scraping pan to loosen browned bits. Stir in black pepper, tomatoes, and bell peppers; cook 7 minutes. Stir in pasta and parsley. Ladle into bowls; sprinkle with cheese. Yield: 4 servings (serving size: 2 cups soup and 1 tablespoon cheese).

CALORIES 240 (23% from fat); FAT 6.2g (sat 2.5g, mono 2.1g, poly 0.7g); PROTEIN 12.2g; CARB 34.9g; FIBER 2.2g; CHOL 9mg; IRON 2.6mg; SODIUM 657mg; CALC 156mg

# Justice Is Served

*Thanks to his wife's plea-bargaining power, an Oakley, Kansas, attorney gets to have his cake and eat it, too.*

Throughout Katherine and Doug Spencer's 31-year marriage, Applesauce-Raisin Cake with Caramel Icing has reigned as the birthday cake of choice. But when a family history of heart disease caught up with Doug, the treat quickly lost favor with its biggest fan. Katherine turned to *Cooking Light* for help.

We reduced the amounts of shortening and nuts by more than half and cut out an almost unbelievable 1,896 calories and 240 grams of fat without sacrificing any of the sweet and sinful appeal.

### Applesauce-Raisin Cake with Caramel Icing

Even though the icing starts out with the consistency of a glaze, it sets up as it cools. If it gets stiff or begins to dry out, run your frosting spatula under hot water.

CAKE:
1 cup granulated sugar
1 cup packed brown sugar
⅓ cup vegetable shortening
2 cups unsweetened applesauce
3 cups all-purpose flour
4 teaspoons unsweetened cocoa
2 teaspoons baking soda
2 teaspoons ground cinnamon
2 teaspoons ground nutmeg
½ teaspoon salt
½ cup raisins
¼ cup chopped pecans
1 teaspoon vanilla extract
Cooking spray

ICING:
1 cup packed dark brown sugar
½ cup 1% low-fat milk
2 tablespoons butter or stick margarine
¼ teaspoon salt
1½ cups powdered sugar
1 teaspoon vanilla extract

1. Preheat oven to 350°.
2. To prepare cake, beat first 3 ingredients at low speed of a mixer until well-blended (about 5 minutes). Add applesauce; beat well. Lightly spoon flour into dry measuring cups, and level with a knife. Combine flour and next 5 ingredients, stirring well with a whisk. Add flour mixture to applesauce mixture; beat just until moist. Stir in raisins, pecans, and 1 teaspoon vanilla.
3. Spoon batter into 2 (9-inch) round cake pans coated with cooking spray. Bake at 350° for 35 minutes or until a wooden pick inserted in center comes out clean. Cool in pans 10 minutes on a wire rack; remove from pans. Cool completely on wire rack.
4. To prepare icing, combine 1 cup brown sugar, milk, butter, and ¼ teaspoon salt in a medium saucepan; bring to a boil over medium-high heat, stirring constantly. Reduce heat, and simmer until slightly thick (about 5 minutes), stirring occasionally. Remove from heat. Add powdered sugar and 1 teaspoon vanilla; beat at medium speed of a mixer until smooth and slightly warm. Cool 5 minutes (icing will thicken as it cools).
5. Place 1 cake layer on a plate; working quickly, spread with ⅓ cup icing, and top with remaining layer. Spread remaining icing over top and sides of cake. Store loosely covered in refrigerator. Yield: 18 servings (serving size: 1 slice).

CALORIES 333 (16% from fat); FAT 6g (sat 1.7g, mono 2.3g, poly 1.6g); PROTEIN 2.9g; CARB 68.5g; FIBER 1.3g; CHOL 4mg; IRON 1.8mg; SODIUM 267mg; CALC 43mg

| BEFORE | AFTER |
|---|---|
| SERVING SIZE | |
| *1 slice* | |
| CALORIES PER SERVING | |
| 494 | 333 |
| FAT | |
| 17.6g | 6g |
| PERCENT OF TOTAL CALORIES | |
| 32% | 16% |
| CHOLESTEROL | |
| 320mg | 267mg |

# Blissful Biscotti

*How do you say "cookie" in Italian?*

Biscotti. From baking to eating, these simple, naturally low-fat treats translate into any language as pure pleasure.

### Lemon Biscotti with Sour Lemon Drizzle

2¾ cups all-purpose flour
1 cup granulated sugar
2 teaspoons baking powder
1 tablespoon grated lemon rind
2 tablespoons fresh lemon juice, divided
1 tablespoon lemon extract
1 tablespoon vegetable oil
3 large eggs
Cooking spray
⅔ cup powdered sugar

**1.** Preheat oven to 350°.

**2.** Lightly spoon flour into dry measuring cups; level with a knife. Combine flour, 1 cup sugar, and baking powder in a large bowl. Combine rind, 1 tablespoon lemon juice, extract, oil, and eggs; add to flour mixture, stirring until well-blended (dough will be dry and crumbly). Turn dough out onto a lightly floured surface; knead lightly 7 or 8 times. Divide dough in half. Shape each portion into an 8-inch-long roll. Place rolls 6 inches apart on a baking sheet coated with cooking spray; flatten each roll to 1-inch thickness.

**3.** Bake at 350° for 30 minutes. Remove rolls from baking sheet; cool 10 minutes on a wire rack. Cut each roll diagonally into 15 (½-inch) slices. Place slices, cut sides down, on baking sheet. Reduce oven temperature to 325°; bake 10 minutes. Turn cookies over; bake an additional 10 minutes (cookies will be slightly soft in center but will harden as they cool). Remove from baking sheet; cool completely on wire rack.

**4.** Combine 1 tablespoon lemon juice and powdered sugar, and drizzle over biscotti. Yield: 2½ dozen (serving size: 1 biscotto).

CALORIES 91 (12% from fat); FAT 1.2g (sat 0.3g, mono 0.4g, poly 0.4g); PROTEIN 1.8g; CARB 18.4g; FIBER 0.3g; CHOL 22mg; IRON 0.6mg; SODIUM 39mg; CALC 23mg

### Power Biscotti

2½ cups all-purpose flour
1 cup sugar
¾ cup quick-cooking oats
½ cup sliced almonds
½ cup chopped dried apricots
¼ cup wheat bran
2 tablespoons flaxseed
2 teaspoons baking powder
1 tablespoon vegetable oil
2 teaspoons almond extract
1 teaspoon vanilla extract
3 large eggs
Cooking spray

**1.** Preheat oven to 350°.

**2.** Lightly spoon flour into dry measuring cups, and level with a knife. Combine flour and next 7 ingredients in a large bowl. Combine oil, extracts, and eggs; add to flour mixture, stirring until well-blended (dough will be dry and crumbly). Turn dough out onto a lightly floured surface, and knead lightly 7 or 8 times. Divide dough in half. Shape each portion into an 8-inch-long roll. Place rolls 6 inches apart on a baking sheet coated with cooking spray; flatten each roll to 1-inch thickness.

**3.** Bake at 350° for 30 minutes. Remove rolls from baking sheet; cool 10 minutes on a wire rack. Cut each roll diagonally into 15 (½-inch) slices. Place slices, cut sides down, on baking sheet. Reduce oven temperature to 325°; bake 10 minutes. Turn cookies over; bake an additional 10 minutes (cookies will be slightly soft in center but will harden as they cool). Remove from baking sheet; cool completely on wire rack. Yield: 2½ dozen (serving size: 1 biscotto).

CALORIES 104 (21% from fat); FAT 2.4g (sat 0.4g, mono 1g, poly 0.8g); PROTEIN 2.7g; CARB 18.4g; FIBER 1.1g; CHOL 22mg; IRON 1mg; SODIUM 42mg; CALC 31mg

### Snickerdoodle Biscotti

Kids will adore the flavor combination in this updated American classic. And even grown-ups will enjoy dipping them in milk.

2¾ cups all-purpose flour
1 cup sugar
2 teaspoons baking powder
¼ teaspoon salt
1 tablespoon vegetable oil
1 teaspoon vanilla extract
3 large eggs
Cooking spray
2 tablespoons sugar
1 teaspoon ground cinnamon
1 large egg white

**1.** Preheat oven to 350°.

**2.** Lightly spoon flour into dry measuring cups, and level with a knife. Combine flour, 1 cup sugar, baking powder, and salt in a large bowl. Combine oil, vanilla, and 3 eggs, and add to flour mixture, stirring until well-blended (dough will be dry and crumbly). Turn out onto a lightly floured surface, and knead lightly 7 or 8 times. Divide dough in half. Shape each portion into an 8-inch-long roll. Place rolls 6 inches apart on a baking sheet coated with cooking spray; flatten each roll to 1-inch thickness. Combine 2 tablespoons sugar and cinnamon. Gently brush tops of rolls with egg white, and sprinkle with cinnamon mixture.

**3.** Bake at 350° for 30 minutes. Remove rolls from baking sheet; cool 10 minutes on a wire rack. Cut each roll diagonally into 15 (½-inch) slices. Place slices, cut sides down, on baking sheet. Reduce oven temperature to 325°; bake 10 minutes. Turn cookies over, and bake an additional 10 minutes (cookies will be slightly soft in center but will harden as they cool). Remove from baking sheet; cool completely on wire rack. Yield: 2½ dozen (serving size: 1 biscotto).

CALORIES 84 (13% from fat); FAT 1.2g (sat 0.3g, mono 0.4g, poly 0.4g); PROTEIN 1.9g; CARB 16.5g; FIBER 0.3g; CHOL 22mg; IRON 0.7mg; SODIUM 61mg; CALC 23mg

# Biscotti Step-by-Steps

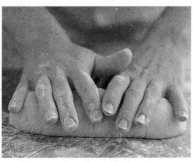

**1.** *Use your hands to gently shape dough into 8-inch rolls.*

**2.** *Careful patting and forming allows you to flatten dough to 1-inch thickness.*

**3.** *Cut each roll diagonally into 15 slices of approximately equal width.*

## Anise Biscotti

2½ cups all-purpose flour
1 cup sugar
¼ cup yellow cornmeal
1 tablespoon loose orange spice tea (about 3 tea bags)
2 teaspoons baking powder
1 teaspoon aniseed
1 tablespoon vegetable oil
1 tablespoon orange juice
2 teaspoons anise extract
1 teaspoon vanilla extract
3 large eggs
Cooking spray

**1.** Preheat oven to 350°.
**2.** Lightly spoon flour into dry measuring cups, and level with a knife. Combine flour and next 5 ingredients in a large bowl. Combine oil and next 4 ingredients; add to flour mixture, stirring until well-blended (dough will be dry and crumbly). Turn dough out onto a lightly floured surface; knead lightly 7 or 8 times. Divide dough in half. Shape each portion into an 8-inch-long roll. Place rolls 6 inches apart on a baking sheet coated with cooking spray; flatten each roll to 1-inch thickness.
**3.** Bake at 350° for 30 minutes. Remove rolls from baking sheet; cool 10 minutes on a wire rack. Cut each roll diagonally into 15 (½-inch) slices. Place slices, cut sides down, on baking sheet. Reduce oven temperature to 325°; bake 10 minutes. Turn cookies over; bake an additional 10 minutes (cookies will be slightly soft in center but will harden as they cool). Remove from baking sheet; cool completely on wire rack. Yield: 2½ dozen (serving size: 1 biscotto).

CALORIES 83 (13% from fat); FAT 1.2g (sat 0.3g, mono 0.4g, poly 0.4g); PROTEIN 1.8g; CARB 15.9g; FIBER 0.4g; CHOL 22mg; IRON 0.7mg; SODIUM 39mg; CALC 23mg

## Cranberry-Chocolate Chip Biscotti

2¾ cups all-purpose flour
1 cup sugar
½ cup dried cranberries
⅓ cup semisweet chocolate chips
2 teaspoons baking powder
⅛ teaspoon salt
1 tablespoon vegetable oil
1 teaspoon almond extract
1 teaspoon vanilla extract
3 large eggs
Cooking spray

**1.** Preheat oven to 350°.
**2.** Lightly spoon flour into dry measuring cups, and level with a knife. Combine flour and next 5 ingredients in a large bowl. Combine oil, extracts, and eggs; add to flour mixture, stirring until well-blended (dough will be dry and crumbly). Turn dough out onto a lightly floured surface; knead lightly 7 or 8 times. Divide dough in half. Shape each portion into an 8-inch-long roll. Place rolls 6 inches apart on a baking sheet coated with cooking spray; flatten each roll to 1-inch thickness.
**3.** Bake at 350° for 35 minutes. Remove rolls from baking sheet; cool 10 minutes on a wire rack. Cut each roll diagonally into 15 (½-inch) slices. Place slices, cut sides down, on baking sheet. Reduce oven temperature to 325°, and bake 10 minutes. Turn cookies over; bake an additional 10 minutes (cookies will be slightly soft in center but will harden as they cool). Remove from baking sheet; cool completely on wire rack. Yield: 2½ dozen (serving size: 1 biscotto).

CALORIES 98 (17% from fat); FAT 1.8g (sat 0.7g, mono 0.6g, poly 0.4g); PROTEIN 2g; CARB 18.6g; FIBER 0.4g; CHOL 22mg; IRON 0.7mg; SODIUM 50mg; CALC 24mg

## Chai Spice Biscotti

2¾ cups all-purpose flour
1 cup sugar
1 tablespoon loose Chai spice tea or orange spice tea (about 3 tea bags)
2 teaspoons baking powder
1½ teaspoons ground ginger
1½ teaspoons ground cinnamon
1½ teaspoons ground allspice
1 tablespoon vegetable oil
1 tablespoon triple sec (orange liqueur) or orange juice
3 large eggs
Cooking spray

**1.** Preheat oven to 350°.
**2.** Lightly spoon flour into dry measuring cups, and level with a knife. Combine flour and next 6 ingredients in a large bowl. Combine oil, liqueur, and

eggs, and add to flour mixture, stirring until well-blended (dough will be dry and crumbly). Turn dough out onto a lightly floured surface; knead lightly 7 or 8 times. Divide dough in half. Shape each portion into an 8-inch-long roll. Place rolls 6 inches apart on a baking sheet coated with cooking spray; flatten each roll to 1-inch thickness.

**3.** Bake at 350° for 30 minutes. Remove rolls from baking sheet; cool 10 minutes on a wire rack. Cut each roll diagonally into 15 (½-inch) slices. Place slices, cut sides down, on baking sheet. Reduce oven temperature to 325°; bake 10 minutes. Turn cookies over; bake an additional 10 minutes (cookies will be slightly soft in center but will harden as they cool). Remove from baking sheet; cool completely on wire rack. Yield: 2½ dozen (serving size: 1 biscotto).

CALORIES 83 (13% from fat); FAT 1.2g (sat 0.3g, mono 0.4g, poly 0.4g); PROTEIN 1.9g; CARB 16.1g; FIBER 0.4g; CHOL 22mg; IRON 0.8mg; SODIUM 40mg; CALC 27mg

### Espresso-Chocolate Chip Biscotti

2¾  cups all-purpose flour
1  cup sugar
½  cup semisweet chocolate chips
2  teaspoons baking powder
1  teaspoon ground cinnamon
⅛  teaspoon salt
¼  cup instant espresso or ½ cup instant coffee granules
2  teaspoons hot water
1  tablespoon vegetable oil
2  teaspoons vanilla extract
3  large eggs
Cooking spray

**1.** Preheat oven to 350°.
**2.** Lightly spoon flour into dry measuring cups, and level with a knife. Combine flour and next 5 ingredients in a large bowl. Combine espresso and water; stir well with a whisk. Combine oil, vanilla, and eggs, and add to flour mixture, stirring until well-blended (dough will be dry and crumbly). Turn dough out onto a lightly floured surface; knead lightly 7 or 8 times. Divide

dough in half. Shape each portion into an 8-inch-long roll. Place rolls 6 inches apart on a baking sheet coated with cooking spray, and flatten each roll to 1-inch thickness.

**3.** Bake at 350° for 35 minutes. Remove rolls from baking sheet, and cool 10 minutes on a wire rack. Cut each roll diagonally into 15 (½-inch) slices. Place slices, cut sides down, on baking sheet. Reduce oven temperature to 325°, and bake 10 minutes. Turn cookies over, and bake an additional 10 minutes (cookies will be slightly soft in center but will harden as they cool). Remove from baking sheet, and cool completely on wire rack. Yield: 2½ dozen (serving size: 1 biscotto).

CALORIES 97 (20% from fat); FAT 2.2g (sat 0.8g, mono 0.7g, poly 0.4g); PROTEIN 2g; CARB 17.6g; FIBER 0.4g; CHOL 22mg; IRON 0.8mg; SODIUM 50mg; CALC 25mg

### Toffee Biscotti

2¾  cups all-purpose flour
½  cup granulated sugar
½  cup packaged almond toffee bits
½  cup packed brown sugar
2  teaspoons baking powder
1  tablespoon vegetable oil
1  teaspoon vanilla extract
3  large eggs
Cooking spray

**1.** Preheat oven to 350°.
**2.** Lightly spoon flour into dry measuring cups, and level with a knife. Combine flour and next 4 ingredients in a large bowl. Combine vegetable oil, vanilla, and eggs; add to flour mixture, stirring until well-blended (dough will be dry and crumbly). Turn dough out onto a lightly floured surface, and knead lightly 7 or 8 times. Divide dough in half. Shape each portion into an 8-inch-long roll. Place rolls 6 inches apart on a baking sheet coated with cooking spray, and flatten each roll to 1-inch thickness.
**3.** Bake at 350° for 35 minutes. Remove rolls from baking sheet; cool 10 minutes on a wire rack. Cut each roll diagonally into 15 (½-inch) slices. Place slices, cut sides down, on baking sheet. Reduce

oven temperature to 325°; bake 10 minutes. Turn cookies over; bake an additional 10 minutes (cookies will be slightly soft in center but will harden as they cool). Remove from baking sheet; cool completely on wire rack. Yield: 2½ dozen (serving size: 1 biscotto).

CALORIES 103 (22% from fat); FAT 2.5g (sat 0.8g, mono 0.7g, poly 0.9g); PROTEIN 1.8g; CARB 18.2g; FIBER 0.3g; CHOL 23mg; IRON 0.7mg; SODIUM 62mg; CALC 25mg

### Sesame-Orange Biscotti

⅓  cup sesame seeds
2¾  cups all-purpose flour
1  cup sugar
2  teaspoons baking powder
1  tablespoon vegetable oil
1  tablespoon imitation orange extract
2  teaspoons grated orange rind
1  teaspoon vanilla extract
3  large eggs
Cooking spray
1  large egg white, lightly beaten
2  tablespoons sesame seeds

**1.** Preheat oven to 350°.
**2.** Place ⅓ cup sesame seeds in a small skillet over medium heat 3 minutes or until seeds are lightly browned, shaking pan frequently.
**3.** Lightly spoon flour into dry measuring cups, and level with a knife. Combine ⅓ cup toasted sesame seeds, flour, sugar, and baking powder in a large bowl. Combine vegetable oil and next 4 ingredients; add to flour mixture, stirring until well-blended (dough will be dry and crumbly). Turn dough out onto a lightly floured surface, and knead lightly 7 or 8 times. Divide dough in half. Shape each portion into an 8-inch-long roll. Place rolls 6 inches apart on a baking sheet coated with cooking spray; flatten each roll to 1-inch thickness. Brush tops of rolls with beaten egg white, and sprinkle with 2 tablespoons sesame seeds.
**4.** Bake at 350° for 30 minutes. Remove rolls from baking sheet; cool 10 minutes on a wire rack. Cut each roll diagonally

*Continued*

into 15 (½-inch) slices. Place slices, cut sides down, on baking sheet. Reduce oven temperature to 325°; bake 10 minutes. Turn cookies over, and bake an additional 10 minutes (cookies will be soft in center but will harden as they cool). Remove from baking sheet; cool cookies completely on wire rack. Yield: 2½ dozen (serving size: 1 biscotto).

CALORIES 96 (21% from fat); FAT 2.2g (sat 0.4g, mono 0.8g, poly 0.9g); PROTEIN 2.3g; CARB 16.1g; FIBER 0.4g; CHOL 22mg; IRON 1mg; SODIUM 41mg; CALC 44mg

## back to the best

# Fudgy Soufflé Cake with Warm Turtle Sauce

*This glamorous dessert might look fussy and complicated, but Fudgy Soufflé Cake with Warm Turtle Sauce is no prima donna.*

Making this intensely chocolaty treat couldn't be simpler. Since the recipe debuted in our January/February 1997 issue, our food editors have made it often for TV demos—despite the ease of preparation, it has a *wow* charisma that's right at home on the stage.

### Fudgy Soufflé Cake with Warm Turtle Sauce

(pictured on page 329)

Butter-flavored cooking spray
¼  teaspoon sugar
½  cup unsweetened cocoa
6  tablespoons hot water
2  tablespoons butter or stick margarine
3  tablespoons all-purpose flour
¾  cup 1% low-fat milk
¼  cup sugar
⅛  teaspoon salt
4  large egg whites
3  tablespoons sugar
Warm Turtle Sauce

**1.** Preheat oven to 375°.
**2.** Coat a 1½-quart soufflé dish with cooking spray; sprinkle with ¼ teaspoon sugar. Set aside.
**3.** Combine cocoa and hot water in a bowl; set aside.
**4.** Melt butter in a small heavy saucepan over medium heat. Add flour, and cook 1 minute, stirring constantly with a whisk. Gradually add milk, ¼ cup sugar, and salt, stirring constantly with a whisk. Cook until thick (about 3 minutes), stirring constantly. Remove from heat. Add cocoa mixture; stir well. Spoon into a large bowl; cool slightly.
**5.** Beat egg whites at high speed of a mixer until foamy. Add 3 tablespoons sugar, 1 tablespoon at a time, beating until stiff peaks form. Gently fold 1 cup egg white mixture into cocoa mixture; gently fold in remaining egg white mixture. Spoon into prepared dish.
**6.** Bake at 375° for 35 minutes or until puffy and set. Remove from oven, and serve warm or at room temperature with Warm Turtle Sauce. Yield: 6 servings (serving size: 1 wedge and about 1½ tablespoons sauce).

(Totals include Warm Turtle Sauce) CALORIES 241 (29% from fat); FAT 7.8g (sat 1.7g, mono 3.3g, poly 1.9g); PROTEIN 6.1g; CARB 58.6g; FIBER 0.4g; CHOL 2mg; IRON 1.6mg; SODIUM 182mg; CALC 54mg

#### WARM TURTLE SAUCE:

6  tablespoons fat-free caramel-flavored sundae syrup
3  tablespoons chopped pecans, toasted

**1.** Place caramel syrup in a small bowl, and microwave at HIGH 30 seconds or until warm. Stir in pecans. Yield: ½ cup (serving size: about 1½ tablespoons).

CALORIES 79 (28% from fat); FAT 2.5g (sat 0.2g, mono 1.5g, poly 0.6g); PROTEIN 0.2g; CARB 35.6g; FIBER 0.2g; CHOL 0mg; IRON 0.1mg; SODIUM 35mg; CALC 1mg

# Where the Action Is

*Three years ago, the Stewarts moved their fast-paced, health-conscious family to Concord, New Hampshire. The town hasn't been the same since.*

Mela and Jay Stewart are the kind of couple everyone wants on the social calendar. They plan last-minute get-togethers that turn into rollicking affairs. Last year, fed up that there wasn't an organized Thanksgiving Day race in their New Hampshire town, they planned the first annual Galloping Gobbler 10K.

### Olive Pizza

Jay and Mela make their own pizza dough, but we substituted store-bought to save time.

2  (10-ounce) cans refrigerated pizza crust
Cooking spray
1  tablespoon cornmeal
3  tomatoes, cut into ¼-inch-thick slices (about 1¼ pounds)
1½  cups (6 ounces) shredded part-skim mozzarella cheese
1  cup (4 ounces) crumbled feta cheese
½  cup sliced pitted kalamata olives
Freshly ground black pepper (optional)

**1.** Preheat oven to 450°.
**2.** Unroll dough portions crosswise onto a large baking sheet coated with cooking spray and sprinkled with cornmeal. Slightly overlap edges of dough, pinching edges together to seal. Pat dough into a 15 x 12-inch rectangle. Bake at 450° for 2 minutes. Top with tomato and remaining 3 ingredients. Bake an additional 12 minutes or until cheese melts. Garnish with pepper, if desired. Yield: 8 servings.

CALORIES 304 (30% from fat); FAT 10.2g (sat 5g, mono 3.2g, poly 1.6g); PROTEIN 13.9g; CARB 38.4; FIBER 1.4g; CHOL 25mg; IRON 2.4mg; SODIUM 810mg; CALC 217mg

Sautéed Green Beans and
Onions with Bacon, page 346

Fudgy Soufflé Cake with Warm
Turtle Sauce, page 328

Roasted Turnips, Sweet Potatoes,
Apples, and Dried Cranberries, page 335

Fig-Swirl Coffeecake, page 318

Cajun Turkey with Dirty-Rice
Stuffing, page 313

Apple-Glazed Pork Loin Roast with Apple-Ham Stuffing, page 345

Pumpkin Streusel Bread, page 336

# Roots

## Get back to the earth's humblest—but tastiest—of vegetables for great meals for fall and winter.

Roots are available year-round in many supermarkets, but it's most certainly during the cooler months, when their robust flavors peak, that you should seek them out. Many roots, such as potatoes, keep without refrigeration for several weeks. Place them in a cool, dry place with good ventilation. Parsnips, celeriac, turnips, and rutabagas prefer the cool of a refrigerator, but they will outlast almost anything you have in there. Select roots by weight, looking for ones that are not too large but are heavy for their size, avoiding those with hairy rootlets that indicate age. Choose regular shapes, which will make peeling easier.

## Mashed Sweet Potatoes with Pineapple

You'll need about 5 cups of mashed sweet potatoes for this recipe. To save time, substitute canned sweet potatoes.

- 3 large sweet potatoes (about 3½ pounds)
- 1 cup shredded carrot
- 1 cup fresh orange juice (about 2 oranges)
- ⅛ teaspoon ground ginger
- 2 tablespoons butter or stick margarine
- ½ teaspoon salt
- 1 (15¼-ounce) can crushed pineapple in juice, drained

**1.** Preheat oven to 350°.
**2.** Place sweet potatoes on a baking sheet. Bake at 350° for 1 hour and 25 minutes or until potatoes are tender. Cool slightly; peel.
**3.** Combine carrot, orange juice, and ginger in a small saucepan. Bring to a boil; reduce heat, and simmer 15 minutes. Drain carrot mixture in a colander over a bowl, reserving ¾ cup cooking liquid. Combine potato and carrot mixture, and mash. Stir in ¾ cup cooking liquid, butter, salt, and pineapple. Yield: 9 servings (serving size: ¾ cup).

CALORIES 219 (13% from fat); FAT 3.1g (sat 1.7g, mono 0.8g, poly 0.2g); PROTEIN 3.1g; CARB 45.9g; FIBER 5.5g; CHOL 7mg; IRON 1.2mg; SODIUM 182mg; CALC 47mg

## Harvest Stuffed Sweets

- 6 (8-ounce) sweet potatoes
- 2 cups diced peeled rutabaga or turnips
- 1 cup diced peeled carrot
- 1 cup diced peeled parsnip
- ⅓ cup low-fat buttermilk
- 1 tablespoon lemon juice
- ½ teaspoon salt
- ½ teaspoon dried thyme
- ¼ teaspoon black pepper
- 3 garlic cloves, minced

**1.** Preheat oven to 375°.
**2.** Wrap potatoes in foil; bake at 375° for 1 hour or until tender.
**3.** Place rutabaga in a large saucepan; cover with water. Bring to a boil. Cook 5 minutes. Add carrot; cook 5 minutes. Add parsnip; cook 5 minutes or until rutabaga is tender. Drain; mash vegetables to desired consistency. Stir in buttermilk and remaining 5 ingredients.
**4.** Unwrap potatoes. Cut a ¼-inch slice from top of each potato; scoop out pulp, leaving a ¼-inch-thick shell. Add pulp to rutabaga mixture; stir well. Stuff shells with potato mixture, and place on a baking sheet. Bake at 375° for 10 minutes or until thoroughly heated. Yield: 6 servings.

CALORIES 234 (4% from fat); FAT 1g (sat 0.3g, mono 0.1g, poly 0.3g); PROTEIN 4.5g; CARB 53.5g; FIBER 7g; CHOL 0mg; IRON 1.7mg; SODIUM 243mg; CALC 96mg

## Mashed Potatoes with Roasted Garlic and Rosemary

Yukon gold potatoes taste richer and whip up creamier than russets, but you can use either variety.

- 2 whole garlic heads
- 2 pounds cubed peeled Yukon gold potato
- 1 cup chopped onion
- 2 tablespoons plain fat-free yogurt
- 1 teaspoon dried rosemary, chopped
- ½ teaspoon salt
- ¼ teaspoon freshly ground black pepper

**1.** Preheat oven to 350°.
**2.** Remove white papery skin from garlic heads (do not peel or separate cloves). Wrap each head separately in foil. Bake at 350° for 1 hour; cool 10 minutes. Separate cloves; squeeze to extract garlic pulp. Discard skins.
**3.** Place potato and onion in a saucepan; cover with water, and bring to a boil. Cover, reduce heat, and simmer 15 minutes or until potato is tender. Drain in a colander over a bowl, reserving ¼ cup cooking liquid. Combine garlic, potato mixture, ¼ cup cooking liquid, yogurt,
*Continued*

and remaining ingredients; mash with a potato masher. Yield: 8 servings (serving size: ½ cup).

CALORIES 93 (2% from fat); FAT 0.2g (sat 0.1g, mono 0g, poly 0.1g); PROTEIN 2.8g; CARB 21g; FIBER 2.1g; CHOL 0mg; IRON 0.9mg; SODIUM 230mg; CALC 30mg

## Glazed Turnips with Chestnuts

Although using the bottled variety is more convenient, you can heighten the flavor of this dish with ½ pound of freshly cooked chestnuts.

    6   cups (¾-inch) cubed peeled turnips (about 2½ pounds)
1½   tablespoons butter or stick margarine
    ¼   cup dark brown sugar
    2   tablespoons water
    ¼   teaspoon salt
    1   (7.4-ounce) bottle shelled whole chestnuts, halved

**1.** Cook turnips in boiling water 3 minutes; drain. Melt butter in a large heavy skillet over medium-high heat. Add turnips and sugar; cook 10 minutes or until golden brown. Stir in water, salt, and chestnuts; cook until liquid evaporates, stirring occasionally. Yield: 6 servings (serving size: ¾ cup).

CALORIES 142 (19% from fat); FAT 3g (sat 1.8g, mono 0.8g, poly 0.2g); PROTEIN 2.2g; CARB 30g; FIBER 4.7g; CHOL 8mg; IRON 0.5mg; SODIUM 216mg; CALC 45mg

## Rutabaga-Bacon Puree

    2   bacon slices, cut crosswise into thin strips
5½   cups cubed peeled rutabaga (about 2 pounds)
    4   cups water
    2   cups cubed peeled baking potato (about ¾ pound)
    ¼   teaspoon salt
    ¼   teaspoon black pepper

**1.** Cook bacon in a Dutch oven over medium heat 5 minutes or until done

(but not crisp). Add rutabaga, water, and potato. Bring to a boil; cook 20 minutes or until tender. Drain rutabaga mixture in a colander over a bowl, reserving ¾ cup cooking liquid. Combine ¾ cup cooking liquid and rutabaga mixture in a blender, and process until smooth. Stir in salt and pepper. Yield: 8 servings (serving size: ½ cup).

CALORIES 78 (20% from fat); FAT 1.7g (sat 0.6g, mono 0.7g, poly 0.3g); PROTEIN 2.1g; CARB 14.6g; FIBER 1.7g; CHOL 2mg; IRON 0.8mg; SODIUM 112mg; CALC 48mg

## Braised Celeriac

Braising (or slow cooking) the celeriac mellows its flavor, making it an excellent partner for beef.

1½   pounds peeled celeriac (celery root), cut into wedges
    1   tablespoon butter or stick margarine
    ½   cup minced fresh onion
    1   bay leaf
    ¼   teaspoon salt
    ¼   teaspoon freshly ground black pepper
    ½   cup fat-free, less-sodium chicken broth
    ¼   cup dry white wine
    2   tablespoons minced fresh parsley

**1.** Preheat oven to 350°.
**2.** Place celeriac in a Dutch oven, and cover with water. Bring to a boil, and cook 8 minutes; drain well. Melt butter in pan over medium heat. Add onion and bay leaf; cook 5 minutes or until tender. Add celeriac, salt, and pepper. Cook 6 minutes or until lightly browned, stirring frequently. Stir in broth and wine.
**3.** Bake at 350° for 45 minutes or until tender. Discard bay leaf. Sprinkle with parsley. Yield: 8 servings (serving size: ½ cup).

CALORIES 53 (29% from fat); FAT 1.7g (sat 1g, mono 0.5g, poly 0.2g); PROTEIN 1.7g; CARB 9.1g; FIBER 1.4g; CHOL 2mg; IRON 0.8mg; SODIUM 197mg; CALC 42mg

## Potato, Fontina, and Cremini au Gratin

    3   pounds peeled baking potatoes, cut into ¼-inch-thick slices
Cooking spray
    1   tablespoon butter or stick margarine
    1   cup chopped onion
    4   cups sliced cremini mushrooms (about 10 ounces)
    ½   teaspoon salt
    ½   teaspoon dried thyme
    ⅛   teaspoon black pepper
    ¼   cup all-purpose flour
2¼   cups fat-free milk
    2   cups (8 ounces) shredded fontina cheese

**1.** Preheat oven to 350°.
**2.** Place peeled potatoes in a large saucepan, and cover with water; bring to a boil. Reduce heat, and simmer 15 minutes or until potatoes are tender. Drain well. Arrange potatoes in a 13 x 9-inch baking dish coated with cooking spray.
**3.** Melt butter in pan over medium heat. Add onion, and cook 3 minutes or until tender. Add mushrooms, salt, thyme, and pepper; cook 5 minutes, stirring occasionally. Lightly spoon flour into a dry measuring cup, and level with a knife. Sprinkle mushroom mixture with flour, and cook 1 minute, stirring constantly. Gradually add milk, stirring with a whisk until blended. Bring to a boil, and cook 3 minutes or until thick, stirring constantly. Remove from heat, and add cheese, stirring until cheese melts. Pour sauce over potatoes, tossing gently to coat. Bake at 350° for 40 minutes or until bubbly. Yield: 8 servings (serving size: 1 cup).

CALORIES 343 (29% from fat); FAT 11g (sat 6.5g, mono 3g, poly 0.8g); PROTEIN 14.3g; CARB 46.7g; FIBER 3.5g; CHOL 38mg; IRON 1.4mg; SODIUM 208mg; CALC 258mg

## Root Vegetable Gratin

The sharp, earthy taste of celeriac is tempered by the sweetness of parsnips and the buttery flavor of Yukon golds.

      1½  cups (6 ounces) shredded reduced-fat Jarlsberg or Swiss cheese
      2  tablespoons minced fresh onion
      1  tablespoon prepared horseradish
      2  garlic cloves, minced
      4  cups (¼-inch) sliced peeled Yukon gold potato
         Cooking spray
      1¾  cups (¼-inch) sliced peeled parsnip
      2½  cups shredded peeled celeriac (celery root)
      ¼  teaspoon salt
      ¼  teaspoon black pepper
      ½  cup fat-free, less-sodium chicken broth
      2  tablespoons dry breadcrumbs
      1½  tablespoons butter or stick margarine, melted

**1.** Preheat oven to 350°.
**2.** Combine first 4 ingredients in a medium bowl.
**3.** Arrange half of potato slices in a 13 x 9-inch baking dish coated with cooking spray, and sprinkle with ½ cup cheese mixture. Arrange half of parsnip over cheese mixture. Spread half of celeriac over parsnip. Repeat layers, ending with celeriac. Sprinkle with salt and pepper. Pour broth over top.
**4.** Cover and bake at 350° for 45 minutes. Uncover; sprinkle with ½ cup cheese mixture and breadcrumbs. Drizzle with butter. Bake an additional 20 minutes or until golden brown. Yield: 8 servings.

CALORIES 194 (30% from fat); FAT 6.3g (sat 3.5g, mono 1.8g, poly 0.4g); PROTEIN 10.3g; CARB 25.5g; FIBER 2.6g; CHOL 21mg; IRON 1.3mg; SODIUM 243mg; CALC 295mg

## Roasted Turnips, Sweet Potatoes, Apples, and Dried Cranberries

(pictured on page 330)

This sweet, earthy side dish is packed with nutrition. It's perfect with ham or turkey.

      3  cups (½-inch) cubed peeled turnips (about 1¼ pounds)
      3  cups (½-inch) cubed peeled sweet potato (about 1¼ pounds)
      2½  cups (¼-inch) cubed peeled Granny Smith apple (about 1½ pounds)
      1  cup dried cranberries
      ½  cup packed dark brown sugar
      1  tablespoon fresh lemon juice
         Cooking spray
      2  tablespoons butter or stick margarine, cut into small pieces

**1.** Preheat oven to 350°.
**2.** Combine first 6 ingredients in a shallow 2-quart baking dish coated with cooking spray. Top with butter. Bake at 350° for 1½ hours or until tender, stirring after 45 minutes. Yield: 7 servings (serving size: about ½ cup).

CALORIES 230 (15% from fat); FAT 3.8g (sat 2.2g, mono 1g, poly 0.3g); PROTEIN 2.2g; CARB 50g; FIBER 4.6g; CHOL 9mg; IRON 1.2mg; SODIUM 85mg; CALC 52mg

## cooking class

# How to Make Plenty of Bread

*Quick breads give it to you faster, better, and with more tasty options.*

Breads made without yeast are usually called "quick," and for good reason. Because they're leavened with baking powder, baking soda, or both, the leavening occurs in the oven while the bread bakes, rather than on your counter while the yeast rises for an hour or two. Most quick breads can be assembled in less than 20 minutes and baked in under an hour. They freeze nicely, too.

## Sun-Dried Tomato Semolina Biscuits

Semolina is durum wheat that's more coarsely ground than all-purpose flour (it's also what most dried pasta is made from). It has the consistency of fine cornmeal, which will work as a substitute. This dough is sticky, but don't add more flour; it'll make the biscuits less tender. Cut the dough with a biscuit cutter dipped in flour. Don't twist the cutter; this could seal the edges and prevent the biscuits from rising.

      2  cups boiling water
     10  sun-dried tomatoes, packed without oil
      2  cups all-purpose flour
      ¼  cup semolina flour or yellow cornmeal
      1  tablespoon sugar
      1½  teaspoons baking powder
      ¾  teaspoon salt
      ½  teaspoon baking soda
      1  teaspoon dried basil
      ¼  teaspoon ground red pepper
      ¼  cup chilled butter or stick margarine, cut into small pieces
      1  cup low-fat buttermilk
         Cooking spray

**1.** Combine boiling water and sun-dried tomatoes in a bowl; let stand 15 minutes. Drain and chop.
**2.** Preheat oven to 425°.
**3.** Lightly spoon flours into dry measuring cups; level with a knife. Combine all-purpose flour, semolina flour, and next 6 ingredients in a bowl; cut in butter with a pastry blender or 2 knives until mixture resembles coarse meal. (Flour mixture and butter can also be combined in a food processor; pulse until mixture resembles coarse meal.) Add tomatoes and buttermilk; stir just until moist.
**4.** Turn dough out onto a heavily floured surface; knead lightly 5 times. Roll to a ½-inch thickness; cut with a 2½-inch biscuit cutter. Place on a baking sheet coated with cooking spray. Bake at 425° for 15 minutes or until golden. Yield: 1 dozen (serving size: 1 biscuit).

CALORIES 140 (29% from fat); FAT 4.5g (sat 2.6g, mono 1.3g, poly 0.3g); PROTEIN 3.4g; CARB 21.3g; FIBER 0.9g; CHOL 10mg; IRON 1.4mg; SODIUM 345mg; CALC 67mg

## Quick Bread Basics

### Measuring Ingredients

The ingredient mix in quick breads is carefully balanced—especially the proportion of liquid to dry ingredients. Measure your ingredients carefully.

### Baking

Quick breads are usually baked in a preheated oven on the center rack. When the quick bread is done, there should be even browning and resistance to light finger pressure. To check quick breads, pierce them in the center with a wooden pick; it should come out with no batter attached.

### Cooling

Cooling quick breads in the pan for a few minutes will make them easier to remove. Then transfer to a rack so the bread can cool evenly on all sides. But if quick bread is left to cool in the pan completely, the heat from the pan can make the bread sweat and turn the bottom soggy.

## Pumpkin Streusel Bread

(pictured on page 332)

TOPPING:

¼ cup chopped pecans
2 tablespoons sugar
1½ tablespoons chilled butter or stick margarine, cut into small pieces
¼ teaspoon ground cinnamon

BREAD:

2 cups all-purpose flour
½ cup sugar
½ cup raisins
1 teaspoon baking soda
1 teaspoon salt
½ teaspoon ground cinnamon
½ teaspoon ground cloves
½ teaspoon ground nutmeg
1 cup canned pumpkin
½ cup plain low-fat yogurt
½ cup honey
¼ cup vegetable oil
1 teaspoon vanilla extract
2 large eggs, lightly beaten
Cooking spray

**1.** Preheat oven to 350°.

**2.** To prepare topping, combine first 4 ingredients until crumbly. Set mixture aside.

**3.** To prepare bread, lightly spoon flour into dry measuring cups; level with a knife. Combine flour and next 7 ingredients in a large bowl; stir well with a whisk. Make a well in center of mixture. Combine pumpkin and next 5 ingredients in a bowl; add to flour mixture. Stir just until moist. Spoon batter into a 9 x 5-inch loaf pan coated with cooking spray; sprinkle with topping. Bake at 350° for 1 hour or until a wooden pick inserted in center comes out clean. Cool in pan 10 minutes on a wire rack; remove from pan. Cool completely on wire rack. Yield: 16 servings (serving size: 1 slice).

CALORIES 209 (30% from fat); FAT 6.9g (sat 1.7g, mono 2.4g, poly 2.2g); PROTEIN 3.4g; CARB 34.6g; FIBER 1.4g; CHOL 31mg; IRON 1.3mg; SODIUM 252mg; CALC 29mg

## Dried Plum-and-Port Bread

This quick bread won our Test Kitchens' highest rating. It's great for dessert, a snack, or for breakfast. Prunes are actually dried plums; we use the latter name in our title because more people found it appealing. If you're using a glass baking dish, decrease the oven temperature by 25° and bake about 10 minutes less than the recipe states.

2 cups chopped pitted prunes
1¾ cups port or other sweet red wine
1½ cups all-purpose flour
½ cup whole-wheat or all-purpose flour
¾ cup packed brown sugar
2½ teaspoons baking powder
½ teaspoon salt
½ teaspoon ground cinnamon
¼ cup vegetable oil
¼ cup plain low-fat yogurt
2 teaspoons grated lemon rind
1 teaspoon vanilla extract
2 large eggs, lightly beaten
Cooking spray
1 tablespoon turbinado sugar or granulated sugar

**1.** Combine prunes and port in a small saucepan; bring to a boil. Cover and remove from heat; let stand 30 minutes.

**2.** Preheat oven to 350°.

**3.** Lightly spoon flours into dry measuring cups; level with a knife. Combine all-purpose flour and next 5 ingredients in a medium bowl; stir well with a whisk. Make a well in center of mixture. Drain prunes in a colander over a bowl, reserving liquid. Combine reserved liquid, oil, and next 4 ingredients; stir well with a whisk. Stir in prunes. Add to flour mixture, stirring just until moist.

**4.** Spoon batter into a 9 x 5-inch loaf pan coated with cooking spray; sprinkle with turbinado sugar. Bake at 350° for 1 hour and 15 minutes or until a wooden pick inserted in center comes out clean. Cool in pan 10 minutes on a wire rack; remove from pan. Cool completely on wire rack. Yield: 12 servings (serving size: 1 slice).

CALORIES 254 (21% from fat); FAT 5.9g (sat 1.2g, mono 1.8g, poly 2.5g); PROTEIN 4.5g; CARB 48g; FIBER 3.1g; CHOL 37mg; IRON 2.1mg; SODIUM 222mg; CALC 100mg

## Coffee-Nut Scones

Cut through the circle of dough, but do not separate the wedges. This allows them to bake as one large scone, and they will be much moister than scones baked separately.

⅔ cup 1% low-fat milk
2½ tablespoons instant coffee granules
1 teaspoon vanilla extract
1 large egg, lightly beaten
2¼ cups all-purpose flour
⅓ cup sugar
2½ teaspoons baking powder
¾ teaspoon salt
¼ teaspoon ground cinnamon
¼ cup chilled butter or stick margarine, cut into small pieces
3 tablespoons finely chopped walnuts
Cooking spray
2 teaspoons 1% low-fat milk
2 teaspoons sugar

**1.** Combine ⅔ cup milk and coffee granules in a microwave-safe bowl.

### Coffee-Nut Scones:

**1.** Cut the butter into the flour mixture until it resembles coarse meal. If you don't have a pastry blender, you can use two knives (although this takes considerably longer). Or you can pulse the flour mixture and butter in your food processor until mixture resembles coarse meal.

**2.** Once you add the milk mixture, turn the dough out onto a lightly floured surface. With lightly floured hands, gather the dough into a ball. Knead lightly 4 or 5 times. The secret to tender scones is handling the dough as little as possible. The dough will be sticky, but resist the temptation to add more flour because this will make the scones dry.

**3.** Pat the dough into an 8-inch round on a baking sheet coated with cooking spray. Cut the circle into 10 wedges; do not separate the pieces.

### Dried Plum-and-Port Bread:

**1.** Combine the dry ingredients, stirring with a whisk or fork. Make a well in the center, and pour the liquid ingredients into it. Stir until moist.

**2.** Stir the batter just until moistened. Overmixing at this point can make the bread tough.

**3.** Spoon mixture into a loaf pan coated with cooking spray. Sprinkle with turbinado sugar to create a crunchy topping that looks good.

Microwave at HIGH 1 minute; stir until coffee dissolves. Cover and chill completely. Stir in vanilla and egg.

**2.** Preheat oven to 425°.

**3.** Lightly spoon flour into dry measuring cups; level with a knife. Combine flour and next 4 ingredients in a bowl; cut in butter with a pastry blender or 2 knives until mixture resembles coarse meal. (Flour mixture and butter can also be combined in a food processor; pulse until mixture resembles coarse meal.) Stir in walnuts. Add milk mixture, stirring just until moist (dough will be sticky).

**4.** Turn dough out onto a lightly floured surface; knead lightly 4 times with floured hands. Pat dough into an 8-inch circle on a baking sheet coated with cooking spray. Cut dough into 10 wedges; do not separate. Brush dough with 2 teaspoons milk; sprinkle with 2 teaspoons sugar. Bake at 425° for 20 minutes or until browned. Serve warm. Yield: 10 servings (serving size: 1 wedge).

CALORIES 207 (30% from fat); FAT 7g (sat 3.3g, mono 1.9g, poly 1.3g); PROTEIN 4.9g; CARB 31g; FIBER 1g; CHOL 35mg; IRON 1.7mg; SODIUM 361mg; CALC 101mg

### Festive Fruit Soda Bread

This is similar to stollen, Germany's traditional Christmas yeast bread. But it's a lot easier and less time-consuming to make.

```
  3   cups warm water
 ¾    cup golden raisins
 ¾    cup chopped pitted dates
 ¾    cup chopped dried Calimyrna figs
  4   cups all-purpose flour
 ⅓    cup sugar
  2   teaspoons baking powder
 1½   teaspoons salt
  1   teaspoon baking soda
  3   tablespoons chilled butter or stick
      margarine, cut into small pieces
 1½   cups low-fat buttermilk
  1   teaspoon grated orange rind
  1   teaspoon grated lemon rind
  1   large egg, lightly beaten
Cooking spray
  2   teaspoons yellow cornmeal
  2   teaspoons 1% low-fat milk
  1   tablespoon sugar
```

**1.** Combine first 4 ingredients in a bowl; let stand 30 minutes. Drain and set aside.
**2.** Preheat oven to 375°.
**3.** Lightly spoon flour into dry measuring cups, and level with a knife. Combine flour and next 4 ingredients in a large bowl; cut in butter with a pastry blender or 2 knives until mixture resembles coarse meal. (Flour mixture and butter can also be combined in a food processor; pulse until mixture resembles coarse meal.) Add reserved fruit; toss well to combine. Make a well in center of mixture. Combine buttermilk, orange rind, lemon rind, and egg in a bowl, and stir with a whisk. Add to flour mixture. Stir just until moist. Let stand 2 minutes.
**4.** Turn dough out onto a lightly floured surface; knead lightly 1 minute with floured hands. Divide dough in half; shape each half into an 8 x 4-inch oval loaf. Place loaves on a baking sheet coated with cooking spray and sprinkled with cornmeal. Make 1 lengthwise cut ¾ inch deep across the top of each loaf, using a sharp knife. Brush loaves with 2 teaspoons milk; sprinkle with 1 tablespoon sugar. Bake at 375° for 30 minutes. Reduce oven temperature to 350° (do not remove bread from oven); bake an additional 25 minutes or until loaves are browned on bottom and sound hollow when tapped. Remove loaves from pan, and cool on a wire rack. Yield: 2 loaves, 12 servings per loaf (serving size: 1 slice).

CALORIES 158 (13% from fat); FAT 2.3g (sat 1.2g, mono 0.6g, poly 0.2g); PROTEIN 3.5g; CARB 32g; FIBER 1.9g; CHOL 13mg; IRON 1.3mg; SODIUM 267mg; CALC 59mg

### White Chocolate-Apricot Muffins

Combining the chopped chocolate with the dry ingredients disperses it and creates chocolate pockets throughout the muffins. To mince crystallized ginger, coat your knife blade with cooking spray to keep it from sticking. These are also good without the crystallized ginger, if you'd rather omit it.

```
 1¾   cups all-purpose flour
 ½    cup sugar
  1   tablespoon minced crystallized
      ginger
 1½   teaspoons baking powder
 ½    teaspoon salt
  2   ounces premium white baking
      chocolate, finely chopped
 ¾    cup 1% low-fat milk
  3   tablespoons butter or stick
      margarine, melted
  1   large egg, lightly beaten
Cooking spray
 ½    cup apricot preserves
  1   tablespoon sugar
```

**1.** Preheat oven to 400°.
**2.** Lightly spoon flour into dry measuring cups; level with a knife. Combine flour and next 5 ingredients in a medium bowl; stir well with a whisk. Make a well in center of mixture. Combine milk, butter, and egg; stir well with a whisk. Add to flour mixture, stirring just until moist.
**3.** Spoon about 1 tablespoon batter into each of 12 muffin cups coated with cooking spray. Spoon 2 teaspoons preserves into center of each muffin cup (do not spread over batter); top with remaining batter. Sprinkle evenly with 1 tablespoon sugar.
**4.** Bake at 400° for 22 minutes or until muffins spring back when touched lightly in center. Remove from pan. Cool completely on a wire rack. Yield: 1 dozen (serving size: 1 muffin).

CALORIES 199 (24% from fat); FAT 5.3g (sat 2.9g, mono 1.6g, poly 0.4g); PROTEIN 3.3g; CARB 35.3g; FIBER 0.7g; CHOL 27mg; IRON 1.2mg; SODIUM 212mg; CALC 72mg

### Dried Fruit-and-Walnut Loaf

Cardamom is an aromatic spice in the ginger family. If you prefer, you can substitute an equal amount of ground ginger, nutmeg, or cinnamon.

```
 2¼   cups all-purpose flour
 ½    cup sugar
 1½   teaspoons baking powder
 ¾    teaspoon salt
 ½    teaspoon baking soda
 ¼    teaspoon ground cardamom
  1   cup sweetened applesauce
 ⅓    cup low-fat sour cream
 ¼    cup honey
  3   tablespoons vegetable oil
  1   teaspoon vanilla extract
  1   large egg, lightly beaten
 ¾    cup finely chopped dried mixed
      fruit (about 5 ounces) or fruit bits
 ¼    cup finely chopped walnuts
Cooking spray
```

**1.** Preheat oven to 350°.
**2.** Lightly spoon flour into dry measuring cups; level with a knife. Combine flour and next 5 ingredients in a large bowl; make a well in center of mixture. Combine applesauce and next 5 ingredients; add to flour mixture, stirring just until moist. Fold in fruit and nuts.
**3.** Spoon batter into a 9 x 5-inch loaf pan coated with cooking spray. Bake at 350° for 1 hour or until a wooden pick inserted in center comes out clean. Cool in pan 10 minutes on a wire rack; remove from pan. Cool completely on wire rack. Yield: 14 servings (serving size: 1 slice).

CALORIES 209 (24% from fat); FAT 5.4g (sat 1.1g, mono 1.5g, poly 2.4g); PROTEIN 3.4g; CARB 37.9g; FIBER 1.7g; CHOL 17mg; IRON 1.4mg; SODIUM 205mg; CALC 38mg

## Whole-Wheat Orange Juice Muffins

1½ cups all-purpose flour
½ cup whole-wheat flour
½ cup sugar
2 teaspoons baking powder
¾ teaspoon salt
½ teaspoon ground cinnamon
1 cup orange juice
¼ cup vegetable oil
1½ teaspoons grated lemon rind
1 large egg, lightly beaten
½ cup golden raisins
Cooking spray
1 tablespoon sugar

1. Preheat oven to 400°.
2. Lightly spoon flours into dry measuring cups; level with a knife. Combine flours and next 4 ingredients in a medium bowl; stir well with a whisk. Make a well in center of mixture. Combine juice, oil, rind, and egg; add to flour mixture, stirring just until moist. Stir in raisins. Spoon batter into 12 muffin cups coated with cooking spray. Sprinkle evenly with 1 tablespoon sugar. Bake at 400° for 20 minutes or until muffins spring back when touched lightly in center. Remove from pan. Cool completely on a wire rack. Yield: 1 dozen (serving size: 1 muffin).

CALORIES 189 (26% from fat); FAT 5.5g (sat 1g, mono 1.6g, poly 2.5g); PROTEIN 3.2g; CARB 33g; FIBER 1.4g; CHOL 18mg; IRON 1.3mg; SODIUM 235mg; CALC 58mg

---

### Blending Dry and Liquid Ingredients for Muffins and Quick Breads

For quick breads and muffins, the most efficient way to blend the ingredients is to make a well in the dry ones and add the liquid mixture all at once. The ingredients can be stirred smoothly, with no more mixing than necessary to blend the batter. This way maintains tenderness. If you overmix, the flour's gluten will start to develop, which will toughen the final product. The rule of thumb is to stir ingredients about 10 times.

---

## Swedish Limpa Soda Bread

Soda bread is a quick bread that's leavened when baking soda is activated by an acidic ingredient—usually buttermilk. This is a hearty loaf perfect for soup.

3 cups all-purpose flour
½ cup whole-wheat flour
½ cup rye flour
1½ teaspoons baking powder
1¼ teaspoons salt
1 teaspoon baking soda
1 teaspoon aniseed
5 tablespoons chilled butter or stick margarine, cut into small pieces
¾ cup low-fat buttermilk
¾ cup Guinness Stout or dark beer
¼ cup honey
1 tablespoon grated orange rind
2 tablespoons molasses
1 tablespoon vegetable oil
Cooking spray
2 teaspoons cornmeal
2 teaspoons 1% low-fat milk

1. Preheat oven to 375°.
2. Lightly spoon flours into dry measuring cups; level with a knife. Combine flours and next 4 ingredients in a large bowl; cut in butter with a pastry blender or 2 knives until mixture resembles coarse meal. (Flour mixture and butter can also be combined in a food processor; pulse until mixture resembles coarse meal.) Make a well in center of mixture. Combine buttermilk and next 5 ingredients in a bowl; add to flour mixture. Stir just until moist (dough will be sticky).
3. Turn dough out onto a lightly floured surface; knead lightly 1 minute with floured hands. Divide dough in half; shape each half into a 6 x 4-inch oval loaf. Place loaves on a baking sheet coated with cooking spray and sprinkled with cornmeal. Make 1 lengthwise cut ¾ inch deep across top of each loaf, using a sharp knife. Brush loaves with 2 teaspoons milk. Bake at 375° for 30 minutes. Reduce oven temperature to 350° (do not remove bread from oven); bake an additional 25 minutes or until loaves are browned on bottom and sound hollow when tapped. Remove loaves from pan, and cool completely on a wire rack. Yield: 2 loaves, 10 servings per loaf (serving size: 1 slice).

CALORIES 139 (26% from fat); FAT 4g (sat 2.1g, mono 1.1g, poly 0.6g); PROTEIN 2.9g; CARB 23.2g; FIBER 1.2g; CHOL 8mg; IRON 1.2mg; SODIUM 248mg; CALC 36mg

---

## Tropical Fruit Coffeecake

¾ cup granulated sugar
⅔ cup packed brown sugar
½ cup (4 ounces) fat-free cream cheese, softened
¼ cup butter or stick margarine, softened
2 large egg whites
1½ teaspoons vanilla extract
2 teaspoons grated lemon rind
2¾ cups all-purpose flour
1½ teaspoons baking powder
¾ teaspoon baking soda
¾ teaspoon salt
1½ cups low-fat buttermilk
1 cup diced peeled mango
1 cup canned crushed pineapple in juice, drained
Cooking spray
⅓ cup flaked sweetened coconut

1. Preheat oven to 350°.
2. Beat sugars, cream cheese, and butter at medium speed of a mixer until well-blended (about 5 minutes). Add egg whites, 1 at a time, beating well after each addition. Beat in vanilla and rind. Lightly spoon flour into dry measuring cups; level with a knife. Combine flour, baking powder, baking soda, and salt; stir well with a whisk. Add flour mixture to sugar mixture alternately with buttermilk, beginning and ending with flour mixture. Stir in diced mango and crushed pineapple.
3. Pour batter into a 13 x 9-inch baking pan coated with cooking spray. Sprinkle coconut over batter. Bake at 350° for 50 minutes or until a wooden pick inserted in center comes out clean. Cool completely on a wire rack. Yield: 16 servings (serving size: 1 piece).

CALORIES 221 (17% from fat); FAT 4.2g (sat 2.7g, mono 1g, poly 0.3g); PROTEIN 4.7g; CARB 41.5g; FIBER 1g; CHOL 9mg; IRON 1.3mg; SODIUM 314mg; CALC 90mg

## Mango-Cardamom Muffins

2 cups all-purpose flour
⅔ cup sugar
2 teaspoons baking powder
½ teaspoon salt
¼ teaspoon baking soda
¼ teaspoon ground cardamom
1 cup chopped peeled ripe mango
¾ cup low-fat buttermilk
¼ cup butter or stick margarine, melted
1 teaspoon vanilla extract
1 large egg, lightly beaten
Cooking spray
2 tablespoons sugar

**1.** Preheat oven to 400°.
**2.** Lightly spoon flour into dry measuring cups, and level with a knife. Combine flour and next 5 ingredients in a medium bowl; stir in mango. Make a well in center of mixture. Combine buttermilk, butter, vanilla, and egg; add to flour mixture, stirring just until moist (batter will be stiff).
**3.** Spoon batter into 12 muffin cups coated with cooking spray; sprinkle evenly with 2 tablespoons sugar. Bake at 400° for 23 minutes or until muffins spring back when touched lightly in center. Remove muffins from pans, and cool on a wire rack. Yield: 1 dozen (serving size: 1 muffin).

CALORIES 187 (24% from fat); FAT 5g (sat 2.7g, mono 1.4g, poly 0.4g); PROTEIN 3.4g; CARB 32.4g; FIBER 0.8g; CHOL 29mg; IRON 1.2mg; SODIUM 259mg; CALC 72mg

## in season

# Pecan-a-Rama

*From the heart of Texas to the orchards of Georgia, pecans are falling from the trees faster than you can eat them. Let's catch up.*

While you were looking the other way, the new pecan crop came in. Pecans, like many nuts, are naturally high in fat, but it's monounsaturated, one of the "good" fats and an important part of a healthy diet.

## menu

**Sugary Spice Pecans**

(recipe below)

**Belgian Endive-and-Apple Salad**

(recipe on page 313)

**Make-Ahead Turkey Breast with Herb Stuffing and Vanilla Sweet Potatoes**

(recipe on page 311)

**Squash-Rice Casserole**

(recipe on page 348)

**Triple-Butterscotch Boston Cream Pie**

(recipe on page 316)

## Sugary Spice Pecans

Serve these pecans as a snack, or add them to mixed greens tossed in a vinaigrette and topped with goat cheese.

1 cup sugar
½ cup water
1 teaspoon ground cinnamon
Dash of ground cloves
2 cups pecan halves
1 teaspoon vanilla extract
Cooking spray

**1.** Combine first 4 ingredients in a medium saucepan. Cook over medium heat until sugar dissolves, stirring constantly (about 8 minutes). Add pecans and vanilla; cook until all syrup is absorbed and pecans are coated, stirring constantly (about 12 minutes). Spread pecan mixture on a baking sheet coated with cooking spray. (Pecans will have a sugar coating.) Separate pecans into halves. Cool completely. Yield: 3½ cups (serving size: 2 tablespoons).
**NOTE:** Store in an airtight container in a cool, dark place up to 1 month; in refrigerator up to 3 months; or in freezer up to 8 months.

CALORIES 80 (60% from fat); FAT 5.3g (sat 0.4g, mono 3.3g, poly 1.3g); PROTEIN 0.6g; CARB 8.6g; FIBER 0.5g; CHOL 0mg; IRON 0.2mg; SODIUM 0mg; CALC 4mg

## Pecan Tassies in Cream Cheese Pastry

(pictured on page 3)

**PASTRY:**

1 cup all-purpose flour
1 tablespoon granulated sugar
Dash of salt
¼ cup (2 ounces) ⅓-less-fat cream cheese, softened
2 tablespoons butter or stick margarine, softened
2 tablespoons fat-free milk
Cooking spray

**FILLING:**

⅓ cup finely chopped pecans
½ cup packed brown sugar
⅓ cup light-colored corn syrup
1 teaspoon vanilla extract
⅛ teaspoon salt
1 large egg, lightly beaten
1 large egg white

**1.** Preheat oven to 350°.
**2.** To prepare pastry, lightly spoon flour into a dry measuring cup; level with a knife. Combine flour, 1 tablespoon sugar, and dash of salt in a small bowl. Combine cream cheese, butter, and milk in a large bowl; beat at medium speed of a mixer until well-blended. Add flour mixture; beat at low speed just until blended (mixture will be crumbly). Press flour mixture into a ball.
**3.** Turn dough out onto a lightly floured surface, and knead lightly 3 or 4 times. Divide dough into 24 portions. Place 1 dough portion into each of 24 miniature muffin cups coated with cooking spray. Press dough into bottom and up sides of cups, using lightly floured fingers.
**4.** To prepare filling, divide pecans evenly among muffin cups. Combine brown sugar and remaining 5 ingredients; spoon about 2 teaspoons filling over pecans in each muffin cup.
**5.** Bake at 350° for 20 minutes or until pastry is lightly browned and filling is puffy. Cool in cups 10 minutes on a wire rack. Run a knife around outside edge of each tassie; remove from pan. Cool

completely on wire rack. Yield: 2 dozen tassies (serving size: 1 tassie).

CALORIES 77 (35% from fat); FAT 3g (sat 1.1g, mono 1.2g, poly 0.4g); PROTEIN 1.4g; CARB 11.3g; FIBER 0.2g; CHOL 14mg; IRON 0.4mg; SODIUM 50mg; CALC 9mg

## Hearty Chicken-Mushroom-Pecan Pilaf

3 cups fat-free, less-sodium chicken broth, divided
1 cup whole-grain breakfast pilaf
1 teaspoon olive oil
Cooking spray
1½ cups chopped mushrooms
1 cup chopped onion
1 cup chopped carrot
½ cup chopped celery
1 teaspoon dried thyme
1 garlic clove, minced
½ teaspoon salt
¼ teaspoon ground nutmeg
¼ teaspoon black pepper
6 (4-ounce) skinned, boned chicken breast halves
½ cup chopped pecans
½ cup chopped fresh parsley
2 tablespoons (½ ounce) grated Asiago or fresh Parmesan cheese

**1.** Bring 2 cups broth to a boil in a medium saucepan, and stir in pilaf. Cover, reduce heat to medium, and cook 30 minutes or until liquid is absorbed.
**2.** Heat oil in a large nonstick skillet coated with cooking spray over medium-high heat. Add chopped mushrooms and next 5 ingredients; sauté 5 minutes or until tender. Add 1 cup broth, salt, nutmeg, pepper, and chicken; bring to a boil. Cover, reduce heat, and simmer 25 minutes. Remove chicken from skillet, and cut into bite-size pieces.
**3.** Bring broth mixture to a boil, and cook until reduced to ½ cup (about 5 minutes). Add cooked pilaf and chicken to pan; cook 3 minutes or until thoroughly heated. Stir in pecans and parsley, and cook 1 minute. Sprinkle with cheese. Yield: 6 servings (serving size: 1⅓ cups).

CALORIES 362 (30% from fat); FAT 12.1g (sat 2g, mono 6g, poly 3g); PROTEIN 34.4g; CARB 28.6g; FIBER 6.4g; CHOL 68mg; IRON 3mg; SODIUM 567mg; CALC 83mg

## Pecan-Crusted Pork with Red Onion Marmalade and Roasted Sweet Potatoes

(pictured on page 3)

2 pounds peeled sweet potatoes, cut into ½-inch-thick slices
Cooking spray
¼ cup packed brown sugar, divided
1 bacon slice, cut into 1-inch pieces
1 teaspoon vegetable oil
1 medium red onion, sliced and separated into rings (about 1½ cups)
¼ cup water
¼ cup balsamic vinegar
1 tablespoon grated peeled fresh ginger
1 pound pork tenderloin
½ cup all-purpose flour, divided
⅓ cup ground pecans
½ teaspoon cracked black pepper
2 large egg whites, lightly beaten
1 tablespoon butter or stick margarine
4 teaspoons finely chopped pecans, toasted

**1.** Preheat oven to 400°.
**2.** Arrange potato slices in a 13 x 9-inch baking dish coated with cooking spray. Sprinkle with 2 tablespoons sugar; arrange bacon on top. Bake at 400° for 30 minutes. Turn potatoes over; bake an additional 30 minutes or until tender. Keep warm.
**3.** Heat oil in a large nonstick skillet over medium-high heat. Add onion and 2 tablespoons sugar; cook 6 minutes or until onion is tender and lightly browned, stirring frequently. Stir in water, vinegar, and ginger; bring to a boil. Cook 3 minutes, and remove from heat.
**4.** Trim fat from pork, and cut crosswise into 8 pieces. Place each piece between 2 sheets of heavy-duty plastic wrap, and flatten to ½-inch thickness, using a meat mallet or rolling pin.
**5.** Lightly spoon flour into a dry measuring cup. Place ¼ cup flour in a shallow dish. Combine ¼ cup flour, ground pecans, and pepper in a separate shallow dish. Dredge pork in flour, shaking off excess. Dip pork in egg whites; dredge in pecan mixture, coating both sides.

**6.** Melt butter in pan coated with cooking spray over medium-high heat. Arrange pork in pan in a single layer. Cook 3 minutes on each side or until browned. Top pork with onion mixture; sprinkle with chopped pecans. Serve with sweet potatoes. Yield: 4 servings (serving size: 2 cutlets, ¼ cup onion marmalade, and ¾ cup sweet potatoes).

CALORIES 685 (30% from fat); FAT 23.2g (sat 5.4g, mono 11.4g, poly 4.9g); PROTEIN 33.2g; CARB 87.3g; FIBER 9.1g; CHOL 86mg; IRON 4.5mg; SODIUM 190mg; CALC 89mg

## Oranges with Caramel Sauce and Toasted Pecans

½ cup sugar
2 tablespoons fresh orange juice
1½ teaspoons butter or stick margarine
⅓ cup evaporated fat-free milk
2 tablespoons Grand Marnier or triple sec (orange-flavored liqueur)
¼ teaspoon vanilla extract
Dash of salt
10 oranges, peeled and sliced (about 4 pounds)
½ cup chopped pecans, toasted

**1.** Combine sugar and juice in a small heavy saucepan. Place over medium-low heat; cook 5 minutes or until sugar dissolves. (Do not stir.) Cover, increase heat to medium, and boil 30 seconds (this will dissolve any sugar crystals clinging to sides of pan). Uncover and boil 2 minutes or until amber or golden. (Do not stir.)
**2.** Remove from heat; let stand 1 minute. Carefully add butter, stirring until butter melts. Gradually add milk, stirring constantly (caramel will harden and stick to spoon). Place pan over medium heat; cook 2 minutes or until caramel melts and mixture is smooth, stirring constantly. Remove from heat; stir in liqueur, vanilla, and salt. Pour caramel sauce over oranges; sprinkle with pecans. Yield: 8 servings (serving size: about ¾ cup oranges, 1 tablespoon sauce, and 1 tablespoon pecans).

*Continued*

NOTE: For a nonalcoholic version of caramel sauce, substitute 2 tablespoons orange juice for the liqueur.

CALORIES 190 (28% from fat); FAT 5.9g (sat 0.9g, mono 3.4g, poly 1.3g); PROTEIN 2.7g; CARB 32.4g; FIBER 6.4g; CHOL 2mg; IRON 0.3mg; SODIUM 37mg; CALC 88mg

## Whole-Wheat and Potato Cinnamon Rolls

    2   cups bread flour, divided
    1   cup whole-wheat flour
    2   tablespoons granulated sugar
    1   teaspoon salt
    1   package dry yeast (about 2¼ teaspoons)
    1   cup very warm water (120° to 130°)
    ½   cup mashed peeled potatoes, cooked without salt or fat
    1   tablespoon vegetable oil
Cooking spray
    2   tablespoons butter or stick margarine, melted
    ¼   cup packed brown sugar
    2   teaspoons ground cinnamon
    ¾   cup chopped pecans
    ½   cup packed brown sugar
    ½   cup evaporated fat-free milk

1. Lightly spoon flours into dry measuring cups, and level with a knife. Combine 1½ cups bread flour, whole-wheat flour, granulated sugar, salt, and yeast in a large bowl. Add water, potato, and oil; stir until a soft dough forms.
2. Turn dough out onto a lightly floured surface. Knead until smooth and elastic (about 8 minutes); add enough of remaining bread flour, 1 tablespoon at a time, to prevent dough from sticking to hands (dough will feel tacky).
3. Place dough in a large bowl coated with cooking spray, turning to coat top. Cover and let rise in a warm place (85°), free from drafts, 45 minutes or until doubled in size. (Press two fingers into dough. If indentation remains, dough has risen enough.) Punch dough down. Turn dough out onto a lightly floured surface; roll into a 20 x 7-inch rectangle. Brush butter over dough, leaving a ½-inch border; sprinkle with ¼ cup brown sugar and cinnamon. Beginning with a long side, roll up jelly-roll fashion; pinch seam to seal (do not seal ends).
4. Coat a 13 x 9-inch baking dish with cooking spray; sprinkle pecans and ½ cup brown sugar in dish.
5. Place a long piece of dental floss or string under dough 1 inch from end of roll. Cross ends of string over top of roll; slowly pull ends to cut through dough. Place roll portion, cut side up, in prepared pan. Repeat procedure with remaining dough. Carefully pour milk around roll portions. Cover and let rise 20 minutes or until doubled in size.
6. Preheat oven to 375°.
7. Uncover dough; bake at 375° for 20 minutes or until lightly browned. Cool in dish 5 minutes on a wire rack. Place a serving platter upside down on top of rolls; invert onto platter. Yield: 20 servings (serving size: 1 roll).

CALORIES 164 (30% from fat); FAT 5.5g (sat 1.3g, mono 2.5g, poly 1.3g); PROTEIN 3.6g; CARB 26.2g; FIBER 1.2g; CHOL 4mg; IRON 1.3mg; SODIUM 141mg; CALC 37mg

## Graham Cracker-and-Pecan Praline Popcorn

The brown sugar mixture heats up quickly and burns easily, so don't leave it unattended while cooking.

    10   cups popcorn (popped without salt or fat)
    2   cups honey-flavored bear-shaped graham crackers (such as Teddy Grahams)
    ½   cup coarsely chopped pecans
Cooking spray
    1   cup packed dark brown sugar
    ¼   cup light-colored corn syrup
    1½   tablespoons butter or stick margarine

1. Preheat oven to 325°.
2. Combine first 3 ingredients in a large bowl. Spread mixture onto a jelly-roll pan lined with foil and coated with cooking spray.
3. Combine brown sugar, corn syrup, and butter in a medium saucepan. Bring to a boil over medium heat, stirring constantly. Cover and cook 1 minute. Uncover and cook, without stirring, until candy thermometer registers 290° (about 5 minutes).
4. Drizzle brown sugar mixture over popcorn mixture; toss to coat. Bake at 325° for 30 minutes, stirring once. Cool completely in pan, on a wire rack and break into large pieces. Yield: 12 cups (serving size: ½ cup).

NOTE: Store in an airtight container up to 2 weeks.

CALORIES 97 (32% from fat); FAT 3.5g (sat 0.7g, mono 1.6g, poly 0.9g); PROTEIN 1g; CARB 16.4g; FIBER 0.7g; CHOL 2mg; IRON 0.5mg; SODIUM 47mg; CALC 7mg

## Asian-Spiced Pecans

Other savory pecan recipes have as much as ½ cup butter per 4 cups of nuts. Here, we use only a teaspoon of butter and add a little tomato paste to give the spice mixture enough body to cling to the pecans.

    2   tablespoons low-sodium soy sauce
    1   tablespoon tomato paste
    2   teaspoons Thai seasoning (such as Spice Islands)
    1   teaspoon butter or stick margarine, melted
Dash of black pepper
Dash of ground red pepper
    4   cups pecan halves
Cooking spray
    ⅛   teaspoon salt

1. Preheat oven to 350°.
2. Combine first 6 ingredients in a large bowl, and stir well with a whisk. Add pecan halves; toss well. Spread mixture evenly onto a jelly-roll pan coated with cooking spray.
3. Bake at 350° for 12 minutes, stirring once. Remove from oven, and sprinkle with salt. Cool completely. Yield: 4 cups (serving size: 2 tablespoons).

NOTE: Store in an airtight container in a cool, dark place up to 1 month; in refrigerator up to 3 months; or in freezer up to 8 months.

CALORIES 93 (90% from fat); FAT 9.3g (sat 0.8g, mono 5.7g, poly 2.3g); PROTEIN 1.1g; CARB 2.6g; FIBER 0.9g; CHOL 0mg; IRON 0.3mg; SODIUM 61mg; CALC 5mg

# Turning to Clay

*Clay-pot cooking is an ancient art, but there's no time like the present to try it yourself.*

Cooking in clay is practically as old as civilization itself. Though we've strayed from reliance on clay in more recent eras, favoring steel, aluminum, iron, porcelain, and even plastic, its heyday isn't quite over yet. In fact, cooking in clay (or terra-cotta) pots is enjoying a surge of popularity.

And cooking in a clay pot is just too simple not to try at home. Soak your terra-cotta pot and lid in water for 10 minutes; then pour the water out, and pat the pot dry. Put the food in the pot, cover, and slide it into the oven. The combination of high heat and moisture roasts and steams at the same time.

## Lemon-Herb Roasted Chicken

2  lemons
2  tablespoons dried oregano
1  tablespoon dried basil
2  teaspoons cracked black pepper
1  teaspoon salt
1  teaspoon olive oil
6  garlic cloves, minced
1  (5-pound) roasting chicken

**1.** Peel and section lemons, reserving peels. Combine lemon sections, oregano, and next 5 ingredients in a bowl, and mash with a fork.
**2.** Immerse top and bottom of a 2-quart clay cooking pot in water 10 minutes. Empty pot, and drain well.
**3.** Remove and discard giblets and neck from chicken. Rinse chicken with cold water; pat dry. Trim excess fat. Starting at neck cavity, loosen skin from breast and drumsticks by inserting fingers, gently pushing between skin and meat. Rub lemon mixture under and over loosened skin. Tie ends of legs together with cord. Place lemon peel in body cavity. Place

chicken, breast side up, in bottom of clay pot, and cover with top of clay pot.
**4.** Place clay pot in cold oven, and set to 450°. Bake chicken 50 minutes, and remove top. (Chicken is done when a meat thermometer registers 180°.)
**5.** Preheat broiler. (Do not move oven rack.)
**6.** Return chicken in pot to oven, and broil, uncovered, 15 minutes or until golden brown.
**7.** Carefully remove clay pot from oven. Remove chicken from clay pot. Cover chicken loosely with foil; let stand 10 minutes. Discard skin. Yield: 8 servings (serving size: 3 ounces chicken).

CALORIES 180 (36% from fat); FAT 7.1g (sat 1.9g, mono 2.7g, poly 1.6g); PROTEIN 25.1g; CARB 3.4g; FIBER 0.5g; CHOL 76mg; IRON 2mg; SODIUM 367mg; CALC 49mg

## Clay-Pot Lima Beans with Ham

1  pound dried large lima beans
5  cups water
1  cup chopped onion
1  cup diced ham
¾  cup fat-free, less-sodium chicken broth
1½  teaspoons dried basil
¾  teaspoon salt
1  (14.5-ounce) can diced tomatoes, undrained

**1.** Immerse top and bottom of a 3-quart clay cooking pot in water 10 minutes. Empty and drain well.
**2.** Sort and wash beans; place beans and 5 cups water in a large Dutch oven. Bring to a boil. Cover, reduce heat, and simmer 30 minutes or until beans are almost tender. Stir in onion and remaining ingredients; spoon into clay pot.
**3.** Place clay pot in cold oven, and set to 450°. Bake 45 minutes or until beans are tender. Carefully remove clay pot from oven; let stand 15 minutes. Yield: 8 servings (serving size: 1 cup).

CALORIES 180 (14% from fat); FAT 2.8g (sat 0.9g, mono 1.3g, poly 0.4g); PROTEIN 16.8g; CARB 40.7g; FIBER 20.3g; CHOL 14mg; IRON 3.6mg; SODIUM 708mg; CALC 24mg

## Vietnamese Caramelized Pork with Pickled Bean Sprouts

**SPROUTS:**

4  cups warm water
⅓  cup white vinegar
¾  teaspoon salt
1  pound fresh bean sprouts
½  cup (1½-inch) julienne-cut green onions
¼  cup chopped fresh cilantro
1  teaspoon dark sesame oil

**PORK:**

1  (2-pound) boned pork loin roast
⅓  cup sugar
3  tablespoons fish sauce
2  cups thinly sliced shallots
¼  teaspoon black pepper
½  cup fat-free, less-sodium chicken broth
5  (⅛-inch) slices peeled fresh ginger
2  garlic cloves, sliced
6  cups hot cooked long-grain rice

**1.** To prepare sprouts, combine first 3 ingredients. Add sprouts and onions; toss well. Cover and refrigerate 90 minutes. Drain well. Toss with cilantro and oil.
**2.** Immerse top and bottom of a 3-quart clay cooking pot in water 10 minutes. Empty and drain well.
**3.** To prepare pork, trim fat from pork; cut into ½-inch slices. Set aside. Place sugar in a small heavy saucepan over medium heat; cook until sugar dissolves, stirring as needed to dissolve sugar evenly. Cook until golden and foamy (about 5 minutes). Remove from heat; carefully stir in fish sauce (mixture will splatter). Stir in shallots and pepper. Place pan over low heat; cook 5 minutes or until shallots are soft.
**4.** Pour into a large bowl. Add pork, broth, ginger, and garlic, tossing to coat. Place pork mixture in prepared clay pot. Place clay pot in cold oven, and set to 450°. Bake 1 hour. Carefully remove clay pot from oven; remove top. Stir pork mixture. Cover, return to oven, and bake an additional 30 minutes. Place pork on a serving platter; drizzle caramel sauce
*Continued*

over pork. Serve with sprouts and rice. Yield: 6 servings (serving size: 3 ounces pork, about 1½ tablespoons sauce, 1 cup pickled sprouts, and 1 cup rice).

CALORIES 569 (19% from fat); FAT 11.9g (sat 3.9g, mono 5.2g, poly 1.6g); PROTEIN 38.1g; CARB 76.6g; FIBER 2.6g; CHOL 85mg; IRON 4.7mg; SODIUM 944mg; CALC 73mg

### Red Clay's Baked Fish

The Boston restaurant Red Clay gets a lot of requests for this dish. It's usually made with cod, but is adapted with permission here for orange roughy or other white fish.

 4 artichokes (about 2 pounds)
1½ pounds peeled baking potato, cut into ¼-inch-thick slices
 ½ cup dry white wine, divided
 1 teaspoon salt, divided
 ¼ teaspoon black pepper, divided
 4 (6-ounce) orange roughy or other firm white fish fillets
 3 cups (½-inch) sliced zucchini
 ½ cup thinly sliced fresh basil
 ½ cup chopped fresh parsley
 4 plum tomatoes, cut in half lengthwise (about ¾ pound)
 2 teaspoons olive oil
 1 (1-ounce) slice white bread
 2 teaspoons butter or stick margarine, melted
 1 tablespoon grated lemon rind
 4 lemon wedges

**1.** Cut off stems of artichokes; remove bottom leaves. Trim about ½ inch from tops of artichokes. Place artichokes, stem ends down, in a large Dutch oven filled two-thirds with water. Place potato in Dutch oven, and bring to a boil. Cover and cook 15 minutes or until just tender. Drain. Remove leaves from each artichoke, discarding tough outer leaves and reserving small inner leaves for another use. Remove fuzzy thistle from bottom with a spoon. Trim artichoke bottoms; cut each in half. Set aside.
**2.** Combine ¼ cup wine, ½ teaspoon salt, and ⅛ teaspoon pepper in a large zip-top plastic bag. Add fish; seal and marinate in refrigerator 30 minutes. Remove fish from bag, discarding marinade.

**3.** While fish is marinating, immerse top and bottom of a 3-quart clay cooking pot in water 10 minutes. Empty pot, and drain well. Add artichokes, ½ teaspoon salt, ⅛ teaspoon pepper, zucchini, basil, parsley, and tomato to clay pot, tossing well. Drizzle with ¼ cup wine, and cover with top of clay pot.
**4.** Place clay pot in cold oven, and set to 450°. Bake 25 minutes. Carefully remove clay pot from oven; remove top. Place fish and potato over vegetable mixture. Drizzle fish with oil. Cover and bake an additional 15 minutes. Place bread in a food processor; pulse 10 times or until coarse crumbs form to measure ½ cup. Combine breadcrumbs, butter, and rind.
**5.** Carefully remove clay pot from oven, and remove top. Sprinkle fish with breadcrumb mixture. Bake, uncovered, an additional 5 minutes or until golden brown. Divide vegetable mixture evenly among 4 plates. Top with fish; serve with lemon wedges. Yield: 4 servings.

CALORIES 422 (14% from fat); FAT 6.5g (sat 1.8g, mono 3.2g, poly 0.7g); PROTEIN 33.6g; CARB 59.5g; FIBER 9.5g; CHOL 39mg; IRON 4.1mg; SODIUM 702mg; CALC 155mg

### Pork Chops with Creamy Porcini Sauce

 ½ cup dried porcini mushrooms (about ½ ounce)
 ½ cup boiling water
 6 cups sliced button mushrooms (about 1 pound)
 ½ cup chopped onion
 3 tablespoons chopped fresh or 1 tablespoon dried rubbed sage
 1 garlic clove, minced
 6 (4-ounce) boned center-cut loin pork chops (about ½ inch thick)
 ½ cup evaporated low-fat milk
 ½ cup fat-free, less-sodium chicken broth
 3 tablespoons all-purpose flour
 1 tablespoon cornstarch
 1 teaspoon salt
 ⅛ teaspoon black pepper

**1.** Immerse top and bottom of a 3-quart clay cooking pot in water for 10 minutes. Empty and drain well.

**2.** Combine porcini mushrooms and boiling water in a bowl; cover and let stand 30 minutes. Drain porcini in a colander over a bowl, reserving liquid. Chop porcini. Combine reserved liquid and half of chopped porcini. Combine remaining half of porcini, button mushrooms, onion, sage, and garlic in prepared clay pot. Arrange pork chops over mushroom mixture. Combine reserved liquid, porcini, milk, broth, flour, cornstarch, salt, and pepper in a small bowl; stir with a whisk. Pour milk mixture over pork; cover with top of clay pot.
**3.** Place clay pot in cold oven, and set to 450°. Bake 1 hour. Carefully remove clay pot from oven; remove top. Stir pork mixture. Cover, return to oven, and bake an additional 30 minutes. Remove from oven; let stand 10 minutes. Yield: 6 servings (serving size: 1 pork chop and ½ cup porcini sauce).

CALORIES 251 (30% from fat); FAT 8.5g (sat 2.9g, mono 3.7g, poly 1g); PROTEIN 29.2g; CARB 13.5g; FIBER 1.7g; CHOL 72mg; IRON 2.3mg; SODIUM 534mg; CALC 82mg

### Tandoori Chicken with Curried Potatoes

 1 teaspoon vegetable oil
 1 tablespoon curry powder
 1 tablespoon paprika, divided
 1 teaspoon salt, divided
 ¾ cup plain low-fat yogurt
 2 tablespoons fresh lemon juice
 1 tablespoon chopped peeled fresh ginger
 1 medium onion, quartered (about 4 ounces)
 1 large garlic clove, peeled
 8 chicken thighs (about 2½ pounds), skinned
 3 peeled baking potatoes, cut into ¼-inch-thick slices
 1 cup sliced peeled Granny Smith apple (about 8 ounces)
 2 tablespoons chopped fresh cilantro
 2 tablespoons sliced almonds, toasted
 2 tablespoons golden raisins

**1.** Heat oil in a small nonstick skillet over medium heat. Add curry powder; cook 1 minute. Combine curry mixture,

1½ teaspoons paprika, ½ teaspoon salt, yogurt, and next 4 ingredients in a blender or food processor; process until smooth. Place in a large zip-top plastic bag. Add chicken; seal and marinate in refrigerator 24 hours. Remove chicken from bag, reserving marinade. Place marinade in a large bowl; add ½ teaspoon salt, potatoes, and apple, tossing well to coat.

**2.** Immerse top and bottom of a 3-quart clay pot in water 10 minutes. Empty pot, and drain well. Arrange potato mixture in a single layer; top with chicken thighs, and sprinkle with 1½ teaspoons paprika.

**3.** Place clay pot in cold oven, and set to 450°. Bake chicken 1 hour. Carefully remove clay pot from oven; let stand 10 minutes before serving. Serve with cilantro, almonds, and raisins. Yield: 4 servings (serving size: 2 chicken thighs, 1 cup potatoes, 1½ teaspoons cilantro, 1½ teaspoons almonds, and 1½ teaspoons raisins).

CALORIES 461 (25% from fat); FAT 12.8g (sat 3.2g, mono 4.4g, poly 3.3g); PROTEIN 49.8g; CARB 35.9g; FIBER 3.9g; CHOL 189mg; IRON 3.9mg; SODIUM 819mg; CALC 144mg

---

## Choose Your Pot

Because clay-pot cookers come in a variety of sizes and types, labeling can vary greatly among brands. Look for cookers labeled "for three to six people" or "4- to 6-pound capacity." These are best suited for all-purpose applications and work perfectly with the recipes shown here. In testing, we used both Romertopf and SchlemmerTopf bakers, as well as handmade specialty varieties. Clay pots are available in cookware shops or at Internet kitchen-supply sources.

---

# What Mom Taught Me

What do you do when Mom can't be there in person to make you those favorite holiday homecoming dishes? Learn to make them yourself.

**menu**

**Easy Fish Stew**
(recipe on page 323)

**Apple-Glazed Pork Loin Roast with Apple-Ham Stuffing**
(recipe below)

**Harvest Stuffed Sweets**
(recipe on page 333)

**Fruited Port-Cranberry Salad**
(recipe on page 346)

**Fudgy Soufflé Cake with Warm Turtle Sauce**
(recipe on page 328)

---

### Apple-Glazed Pork Loin Roast with Apple-Ham Stuffing

(pictured on page 332)

We've kept the main components of this recipe inspired by Test Kitchens staffer John Kirkpatrick's mom, but substituted lean ham for the pork sausage and added a piquant glaze and more spices.

**STUFFING:**

- 6 cups (½-inch) cubed white bread (about 8 slices)
- 1 tablespoon butter or stick margarine
- 1¼ cups diced ham (about 6 ounces)
- ½ cup chopped onion
- ⅓ cup chopped carrot
- ⅓ cup chopped celery
- ½ teaspoon dried thyme
- ½ teaspoon dried rosemary
- 1 garlic clove, minced
- 1½ cups chopped Granny Smith apple (about ½ pound)
- ¼ teaspoon salt
- ¼ teaspoon black pepper
- 1 cup apple juice

**ROAST:**

- 3 pounds boned pork loin roast
- 1 tablespoon garlic powder
- 1 teaspoon ground cinnamon
- 1 teaspoon ground cumin
- ¾ teaspoon salt
- ½ teaspoon ground allspice
- ¼ teaspoon ground ginger
- ¼ teaspoon black pepper
- Cooking spray
- ⅔ cup apple jelly
- 2 teaspoons minced peeled fresh ginger
- 1 teaspoon grated lemon rind

**1.** Preheat oven to 400°.

**2.** To prepare stuffing, arrange bread cubes in a single layer on a jelly-roll pan. Bake at 400° for 6 minutes or until toasted; set aside. Melt butter in a large nonstick skillet over medium-high heat. Add ham; sauté 4 minutes or until lightly browned. Add onion and next 5 ingredients; cook over medium-high heat 5 minutes or until tender. Add apple, ¼ teaspoon salt, and ¼ teaspoon pepper; cook 2 minutes. Add bread
*Continued*

cubes and apple juice to stuffing mixture, stir gently. Set aside.

**3.** To prepare roast, trim fat from pork. Combine garlic powder and next 6 ingredients in a small bowl; rub evenly over pork. Place pork on a broiler pan coated with cooking spray; insert meat thermometer into thickest portion of pork. Bake at 400° for 30 minutes. Combine jelly, ginger, and lemon rind in a small bowl. Brush jelly mixture over roast. Spoon stuffing onto broiler pan around pork. Cover with foil, and bake at 400° for 15 minutes; uncover and bake an additional 15 minutes or until thermometer registers 160° (slightly pink), basting pork occasionally with jelly mixture. Cover and let stand 10 minutes before slicing. Yield: 10 servings (serving size: 3 ounces pork and ½ cup stuffing).

CALORIES 396 (38% from fat); FAT 16.8g (sat 6g, mono 7.3g, poly 2.1g); PROTEIN 32g; CARB 27.9g; FIBER 1.7g; CHOL 100mg; IRON 2.5mg; SODIUM 676mg; CALC 50mg

## Orange Coconut Cake

All of the flavors in this cake inspired by Test Kitchens Director Becky Pate's mother, Rachel Brown, are the same; we cut back only on the amount of butter, coconut, and nuts.

Cooking spray
1   tablespoon all-purpose flour
1½  cups granulated sugar
10  tablespoons butter or stick margarine, softened
2   large eggs
¾   teaspoon coconut extract
3   cups all-purpose flour
½   teaspoon salt
¾   cup chopped pitted dates
¼   cup flaked sweetened coconut, toasted
¼   cup chopped pecans
1¾  cups low-fat buttermilk
1   tablespoon grated orange rind
1   teaspoon baking soda
1¼  cups powdered sugar
½   cup orange juice

**1.** Preheat oven to 350°.
**2.** Coat a 10-inch tube pan with cooking spray; dust with 1 tablespoon flour. Set aside. Beat granulated sugar and butter at medium speed of a mixer until well-blended (about 5 minutes). Add eggs, 1 at a time, beating well after each addition. Stir in extract. Lightly spoon 3 cups flour into dry measuring cups; level with a knife. Combine 3 cups flour and salt; stir well with a whisk. Add dates, coconut, and pecans to flour mixture. Combine buttermilk, rind, and baking soda. Add flour mixture to sugar mixture alternately with buttermilk mixture, beginning and ending with flour mixture. Pour batter into prepared pan. Bake at 350° for 55 minutes or until a wooden pick inserted in center comes out clean.
**3.** Combine powdered sugar and juice in a large saucepan. Bring to a boil; cook 1 minute. Pierce cake with a fork; drizzle with glaze. Cool in pan on a wire rack. Yield: 16 servings (serving size: 1 slice).

CALORIES 330 (29% from fat); FAT 10.5g (sat 5.6g, mono 3.3g, poly 0.9g); PROTEIN 4.8g; CARB 55.8g; FIBER 1.5g; CHOL 47mg; IRON 1.4mg; SODIUM 252mg; CALC 47mg

## Sautéed Green Beans and Onions with Bacon

(pictured on page 329)

This flavorful side dish from Becky Pate's mom is a great accompaniment with turkey or ham.

1    pound green beans, trimmed and halved crosswise
4    bacon slices
1    (16-ounce) bottle cocktail onions, drained
2    teaspoons sugar
½    teaspoon dried thyme
1½   tablespoons cider vinegar
¾    teaspoon salt
¼    teaspoon black pepper

**1.** Cook beans in boiling water 4 minutes or until crisp-tender. Rinse with cold water; drain and pat dry.
**2.** Cook bacon in a large nonstick skillet over medium-high heat until crisp. Remove bacon from pan, reserving 2 tablespoons drippings in pan; crumble bacon, and set aside. Add onions to drippings in pan; cook 3 minutes, stirring occasionally. Add sugar and thyme; cook 3 minutes or until onions are golden brown, stirring occasionally. Add beans; cook 2 minutes or until thoroughly heated. Add vinegar, salt, and pepper; toss to coat. Stir in crumbled bacon just before serving. Yield: 8 servings (serving size: ½ cup).

CALORIES 59 (46% from fat); FAT 3g (sat 1.1g, mono 1.4g, poly 0.4g); PROTEIN 2.2g; CARB 6.5g; FIBER 1.2g; CHOL 4mg; IRON 0.8mg; SODIUM 621mg; CALC 24mg

## Fruited Port-Cranberry Salad

We took some liberties with this recipe from Assistant Editor Stacey Strawn's Granny Prince, particularly by adding port (she didn't allow alcohol in the house).

1    envelope unflavored gelatin
½    cup port or other sweet red wine
2    (3-ounce) packages cranberry-flavored gelatin
¼    teaspoon ground ginger
¼    teaspoon ground allspice
2    cups boiling water
1    (16-ounce) can whole-berry cranberry sauce
½    cup ice water
1½   cups finely chopped Granny Smith apple (about 1 large apple)
1    (14-ounce) package frozen unsweetened raspberries, thawed
1    (8¼-ounce) can crushed pineapple in juice, drained

**1.** Sprinkle unflavored gelatin over port; set aside. Combine cranberry gelatin, ginger, and allspice in a large bowl; stir well. Stir in boiling water and port mixture. Add cranberry sauce and ice water; stir well. Chill 30 minutes.
**2.** Combine apple, raspberries, and pineapple; stir into gelatin mixture. Pour into an 8-cup gelatin mold; chill 4 hours or until set. To unmold, dip mold into hot water 5 seconds; invert onto serving platter. Yield: 12 servings (serving size: 1 slice).

CALORIES 178 (1% from fat); FAT 0.2g (sat 0g, mono 0g, poly 0.1g); PROTEIN 2.3g; CARB 41.3g; FIBER 2g; CHOL 0mg; IRON 0.4mg; SODIUM 63mg; CALC 10mg

## Mae's Apple Stack Cake

Make this cake, adapted from a recipe by Executive Editor Billy Sims's mother, Mae, at least one day ahead. This allows the apple-saucelike filling to soften the cake layers.

**APPLE FILLING:**

  3 cups water
  1 cup raisins
  1 cup apple juice
  ¼ cup sugar
  2 tablespoons lemon juice
  1 teaspoon ground cinnamon
  ½ teaspoon ground nutmeg
  3 (5-ounce) packages dried apples

**CAKE:**

5½ cups all-purpose flour
  1 tablespoon baking powder
  1 teaspoon salt
  1 cup sugar
  ¾ cup vegetable shortening
  2 teaspoons vanilla extract
  2 large eggs
  ½ cup fat-free milk
  Cooking spray
  2 tablespoons all-purpose flour, divided

**1.** To prepare filling, combine first 8 ingredients in a Dutch oven. Bring to a boil; cover, reduce heat, and simmer 1 hour or until very tender. Mash apple mixture with a potato masher, and set aside. (You should have about 4½ cups apple filling.)

**2.** Preheat oven to 375°.

**3.** To prepare cake, lightly spoon flour into dry measuring cups, and level with a knife. Combine flour, baking powder, and salt in a medium bowl; set aside.

**4.** Beat 1 cup sugar and shortening at medium speed of a heavy-duty mixer until light and fluffy. Add vanilla and eggs, 1 at a time; beat well after each addition. Add flour mixture to shortening mixture alternately with milk, beginning and ending with flour mixture; mix after each addition. Divide dough into 6 equal portions. Press 1 dough portion into a 9-inch round cake pan coated with cooking spray and dusted with 1 tablespoon flour. Repeat procedure with another dough portion and cake pan. Bake at 375° for 14 minutes or until lightly browned. Cool in pans 5 minutes on a wire rack; remove from pans. Cool completely on wire rack. Repeat procedure with remaining dough.

**5.** Spread about 1 cup apple mixture over 1 cake layer. Top with another cake layer. Repeat procedure with remaining apple mixture and cake layers, ending with a cake layer. Cover cake tightly with plastic wrap. Store at room temperature 8 hours. Yield: 20 servings (serving size: 1 wedge).

CALORIES 325 (20% from fat); FAT 7.4g (sat 1.7g, mono 2.9g, poly 3g); PROTEIN 4.9g; CARB 61.3g; FIBER 3.1g; CHOL 22mg; IRON 2.3mg; SODIUM 221mg; CALC 65mg

## Espresso Cream Puffs

Cream puffs never go out of style, but we added espresso powder to give these a new flavor. To lighten them, we decreased the butter in the puffs and used fat-free milk. *CookingLight*.com Editor Lisa Delaney thinks her grandmom, Nell Hartmann, who inspired these, would approve.

**CREAM PUFFS:**

  1 cup all-purpose flour
  2 teaspoons sugar
  ¼ teaspoon salt
  1 cup fat-free milk
  2 tablespoons butter or stick margarine
  1 tablespoon instant espresso granules or 2 tablespoons instant coffee granules
  2 large eggs
  1 large egg white
  Cooking spray

**PASTRY CREAM:**

  ½ teaspoon unflavored gelatin
  1 tablespoon water
  ¾ cup fat-free milk
  6 tablespoons sugar
  2 tablespoons cornstarch
  ½ teaspoon vanilla extract
  ⅛ teaspoon salt
  2 large egg yolks
  ¾ cup frozen fat-free whipped topping, thawed
  Powdered sugar (optional)

**1.** Preheat oven to 400°.

**2.** To prepare cream puffs, lightly spoon flour into a dry measuring cup; level with a knife. Combine flour, 2 teaspoons sugar, and ¼ teaspoon salt; set aside. Combine 1 cup milk, butter, and espresso granules in a large saucepan; bring to a boil. Reduce heat to low; add flour mixture, stirring well until mixture is smooth and pulls away from sides of pan. Remove mixture from heat. Add eggs and egg white, 1 at a time, beating well with a wooden spoon until smooth.

**3.** Drop dough by level tablespoons, 2 inches apart, onto baking sheets coated with cooking spray. Bake at 400° for 10 minutes. Reduce oven temperature to 350°; bake an additional 10 minutes or until browned and crisp. Remove from oven; pierce side of each cream puff with tip of a sharp knife. Turn oven off; let cream puffs stand in partially closed oven 20 minutes. Remove from baking sheet; cool completely on a wire rack.

**4.** To prepare pastry cream, sprinkle gelatin over water in a small bowl; set aside. Combine ¾ cup milk and next 5 ingredients in a medium saucepan. Place over low heat; cook until warm, stirring constantly. Stir in gelatin mixture; cook over medium heat until thick (about 8 minutes), stirring constantly. Remove from heat. Place pan in a large ice-filled bowl; let stand 15 minutes or until room temperature (do not allow mixture to set). Remove pan from ice. Gently whisk in whipped topping. Cover and chill 4 hours or until thick.

**5.** Cut tops off cream puffs; fill each cream puff with 1 tablespoon filling. Replace tops. Sprinkle with powdered sugar, if desired. Yield: 2 dozen (serving size: 1 cream puff).

CALORIES 67 (27% from fat); FAT 2g (sat 0.9g, mono 0.6g, poly 0.2g); PROTEIN 2.2g; CARB 9.9g; FIBER 0.2g; CHOL 40mg; IRON 0.4mg; SODIUM 77mg; CALC 28mg

## Jalapeño Corn Bread

We stayed pretty true to the corn bread recipe from Assistant Fitness Editor Melissa Ewey Johnson's mom, with the exception of canned corn and red bell pepper, which we added for texture. If you want to make it as hot as the Eweys like it, feel free to add more jalapeño.

Cooking spray
1 teaspoon vegetable oil
1¼ cups all-purpose flour
1¼ cups yellow cornmeal
2 tablespoons sugar
1 tablespoon baking powder
1 teaspoon salt
1 teaspoon ground cumin
1 cup fat-free milk
½ cup chopped red bell pepper
½ cup minced seeded jalapeño pepper (about 6 large)
3 tablespoons butter or stick margarine, melted
2 tablespoons minced fresh cilantro
2 large eggs, lightly beaten
1 (7-ounce) can whole-kernel corn, drained

**1.** Preheat oven to 425°.
**2.** Coat a 10-inch cast-iron or heavy ovenproof skillet with cooking spray, and add oil. Place pan in a 425° oven for 7 minutes.
**3.** Lightly spoon flour into dry measuring cups; level with a knife. Combine flour and next 5 ingredients in a bowl. Combine milk and remaining 6 ingredients in a bowl; add to cornmeal mixture, stirring just until moist. Pour batter into prepared pan. Bake at 425° for 25 minutes or until a wooden pick inserted in center comes out clean. Cool in pan 5 minutes on a wire rack. Remove from pan. Yield: 12 servings (serving size: 1 wedge).

CALORIES 174 (25% from fat); FAT 4.9g (sat 2.3g, mono 1.5g, poly 0.7g); PROTEIN 4.9g; CARB 28.1g; FIBER 1.4g; CHOL 45mg; IRON 1.8mg; SODIUM 416mg; CALC 105mg

## Spinach Gnocchi

Assistant Art Director Lori Bianchi Nichols grew up eating her mom's gnocchi with tomato sauce (actually inspired by her Italian dad). But because the gnocchi themselves are so good, we kept them simple, dressed with just butter and Parmesan and sparked with some spinach.

4 large peeled baking potatoes (about 2¼ pounds)
2 cups all-purpose flour, divided
1 teaspoon salt
¼ teaspoon black pepper
¼ teaspoon ground nutmeg
1 large egg, lightly beaten
1 large egg white, lightly beaten
1 (10-ounce) package frozen chopped spinach, thawed, drained, and squeezed dry
Cooking spray
14 cups water
6 tablespoons butter or stick margarine, melted
¾ cup (3 ounces) finely grated fresh Parmesan cheese

**1.** Place potatoes in a saucepan, and add water to cover. Bring to a boil; partially cover. Cook 35 minutes or until tender. Drain; cool. Place potatoes in a bowl; mash. Lightly spoon flour into dry measuring cups; level with a knife. Combine potatoes, 1½ cups flour, salt, and next 4 ingredients, stirring to form a soft dough.
**2.** Turn dough out onto a well-floured surface; knead in spinach. Add enough of remaining flour, 1 tablespoon at a time, to prevent dough from sticking to hands. Divide dough into 6 portions; shape each portion into an 18-inch-long rope. Cut each rope into 18 (1-inch) pieces; roll each piece into a ball. Drag tines of a fork through half of each ball, forming a concave shape. Place on a baking sheet coated with cooking spray.
**3.** Bring 14 cups water to a boil in a large Dutch oven. Add one-third of gnocchi; cook 1½ minutes. (Do not overcook, or gnocchi will fall apart.) Remove gnocchi with a slotted spoon; place in a colander to drain. Repeat procedure with remaining gnocchi. Toss with butter and cheese; serve immediately. Yield: 9 servings (serving size: 12 gnocchi).

CALORIES 333 (30% from fat); FAT 11.2g (sat 6.6g, mono 3.2g, poly 0.6g); PROTEIN 10.6g; CARB 47.4g; FIBER 3.4g; CHOL 52mg; IRON 2.5mg; SODIUM 533mg; CALC 163mg

## Squash-Rice Casserole

We adapted the original version of this squash casserole from the recipe book of Editorial Assistant Joyce Swisdak's mom, Elizabeth McCann, to bring down the fat and calories and update the flavor.

8 cups sliced zucchini (about 2½ pounds)
1 cup chopped onion
½ cup fat-free, less-sodium chicken broth
2 cups cooked rice
1 cup fat-free sour cream
1 cup (4 ounces) shredded reduced-fat sharp Cheddar cheese
¼ cup (1 ounce) grated fresh Parmesan cheese, divided
¼ cup Italian-seasoned breadcrumbs
1 teaspoon salt
¼ teaspoon black pepper
2 large eggs, lightly beaten
Cooking spray

**1.** Preheat oven to 350°.
**2.** Combine first 3 ingredients in a Dutch oven; bring to a boil. Cover, reduce heat, and simmer 20 minutes or until tender. Drain; partially mash with a potato masher. Combine zucchini mixture, rice, sour cream, Cheddar cheese, 2 tablespoons Parmesan cheese, breadcrumbs, salt, pepper, and eggs in a bowl; stir gently. Spoon zucchini mixture into a 13 x 9-inch baking dish coated with cooking spray; sprinkle with 2 tablespoons Parmesan cheese. Bake at 350° for 30 minutes or until bubbly.
**3.** Preheat broiler.
**4.** Broil 1 minute or until lightly browned. Yield: 8 servings (serving size: 1 cup).

CALORIES 197 (25% from fat); FAT 5.5g (sat 2.7g, mono 1.5g, poly 0.4g); PROTEIN 12.7g; CARB 24g; FIBER 1.4g; CHOL 65mg; IRON 1.5mg; SODIUM 623mg; CALC 209mg

# december

# All You Need Is Brunch

## Pull up an easy chair for a welcome dose of serenity amid the holiday storm.

If your family is going to want to eat Christmas morning after the gift-opening marathon but before the big dinner, don't forget about brunch. These eminently brunchable offerings are far from daunting; some require only one or two steps. All use minimal ingredients, most of which you already have in your pantry.

---

### menu

**Southwestern Breakfast Casserole**
*or*
**Leek-and-Bacon Tart**

**Warm Ham with Shallots and Vinegar**

**Spiced Winter Fruit**

**Almond Cake**
*or*
**Fresh Cranberry Muffins**

---

## Southwestern Breakfast Casserole

(pictured on page 367)

You can assemble this entire dish up to a week ahead. Bake the corn muffin mix ahead; store in an airtight container in the freezer for a couple of days. Assemble the casserole according to directions; cover and freeze. A day in advance, thaw it in the refrigerator 24 hours. Uncover and let stand 30 minutes at room temperature; bake as directed.

- 1 (8½-ounce) package corn muffin mix
- 3 cups (½-inch) cubed white bread
- 8 ounces hot turkey Italian sausage
- 1 cup chopped onion
- 2½ cups fat-free milk
- 1 teaspoon ground cumin
- ⅛ teaspoon black pepper
- 1 (10-ounce) can diced tomatoes and green chiles, undrained
- 1 (8-ounce) carton egg substitute
- Cooking spray
- 1 cup (4 ounces) shredded reduced-fat Monterey Jack or mild Cheddar cheese, divided

**1.** Prepare corn muffin mix according to package directions; cool. Crumble muffins into a large bowl; stir in bread. Set aside.

**2.** Remove casings from sausage. Cook sausage and onion in a large nonstick skillet over medium heat until browned, stirring to crumble. Drain.

**3.** Combine milk, cumin, pepper, tomatoes, and egg substitute; stir with a whisk until well-blended. Add sausage mixture; stir well. Stir into bread mixture. Spoon half of bread mixture into an 11 x 7-inch baking dish coated with cooking spray. Top with ½ cup cheese. Spoon remaining bread mixture over cheese. Cover and refrigerate 8 hours or overnight.

**4.** Preheat oven to 350°.

**5.** Bake at 350° for 20 minutes or until set. Top with ½ cup cheese; bake an additional 20 minutes or until set. Let stand 10 minutes. Yield: 8 servings.

CALORIES 271 (25% from fat); FAT 7.6g (sat 2.7g, mono 2.6g, poly 1.7g); PROTEIN 14.7g; CARB 33.9g; FIBER 1.6g; CHOL 22mg; IRON 2.1mg; SODIUM 700mg; CALC 290mg

## Leek-and-Bacon Tart

This is a lighter version of the traditional quiche Lorraine. The recipe calls for 7 cups of leeks, but remember they cook down considerably. The leeks, which are milder than onions, can be chopped up to two days ahead and refrigerated in an airtight container.

**CRUST:**
- 1 cup all-purpose flour
- ¼ teaspoon salt
- 2 tablespoons chilled butter or stick margarine, cut into small pieces
- 2 tablespoons vegetable shortening
- ¼ teaspoon cider vinegar
- 4 to 5 tablespoons ice water

**FILLING:**
- 3 bacon slices, cut crosswise into thin strips
- 7 cups chopped leek (about 3 large)
- ½ teaspoon salt, divided
- ¼ teaspoon black pepper, divided
- 1¼ cups egg substitute
- ⅔ cup fat-free milk

**1.** To prepare crust, lightly spoon flour into a dry measuring cup; level with a knife. Combine flour and ¼ teaspoon salt in a bowl; cut in butter and shortening with a pastry blender or 2 knives until mixture resembles coarse meal. Add vinegar and ice water, 1 tablespoon at a time; toss with a fork until moist. Gently press mixture into a 4-inch circle on heavy-duty plastic wrap; cover with additional plastic wrap. Roll dough, still covered, into a 12-inch circle; chill 10 minutes.

**2.** Preheat oven to 425°.

**3.** Remove 1 sheet of plastic wrap; let dough stand 1 minute or until pliable. Fit dough, plastic-wrap side up, into a 10-inch round removable-bottom tart pan. Remove plastic wrap. Press dough against bottom and sides of pan. Fold edges under. Line bottom of dough with a piece of foil; arrange pie weights on foil. Bake at 425° for 10 minutes or until edge is lightly browned. Remove pie weights and foil; cool on a wire rack.

**4.** To prepare filling, heat a large nonstick skillet over medium heat until hot. Add bacon; cook 4 minutes. Remove bacon from pan, reserving 2 teaspoons drippings in pan; set bacon aside. Add leek to drippings in pan; cover and cook 20 minutes, stirring occasionally. Sprinkle with ¼ teaspoon salt and ⅛ teaspoon pepper. Remove from heat. Arrange leek mixture and bacon in prepared crust.

**5.** Combine egg substitute, milk, ¼ teaspoon salt, and ⅛ teaspoon pepper; stir well with a whisk. Pour milk mixture into crust. Bake at 425° for 25 minutes or until a knife inserted near center comes out clean; let stand 10 minutes. Yield: 8 servings.

**NOTE:** You can use a commercial piecrust (such as Pillsbury) in place of the pastry crust. If you substitute a refrigerated piecrust, follow the package instructions for prebaking. It will add 15 calories and 1.4 grams of fat to the nutrition figures per serving.

CALORIES 213 (35% from fat); FAT 8.4g (sat 3.3g, mono 3.1g, poly 1.7g); PROTEIN 8.3g; CARB 26.5g; FIBER 1.5g; CHOL 12mg; IRON 3.3mg; SODIUM 379mg; CALC 95mg

## Warm Ham with Shallots and Vinegar

(pictured on page 367)

This simple dish doesn't take long to cook and is best when prepared the morning of the brunch.

  1 tablespoon olive oil
 ⅓ cup minced shallots
 ⅓ cup red wine vinegar
  2 tablespoons water
  4 (4-ounce) slices smoked ham (about ¼ inch thick), cut into thin strips
  2 tablespoons chopped fresh parsley

**1.** Heat oil in a 9-inch cast-iron or heavy skillet over medium heat. Add shallots; sauté 2 minutes. Add vinegar and water; cook until reduced by half (about 1 minute). Add ham, and cook 4 minutes or until thoroughly heated, stirring

occasionally. Remove ham mixture from pan; sprinkle with parsley. Yield: 8 servings (serving size: 2 ounces ham).

**NOTE:** You can purchase smoked ham in the deli section of the supermarket and have it cut into slices.

CALORIES 95 (43% from fat); FAT 4.5g (sat 1.2g, mono 2.6g, poly 0.4g); PROTEIN 11.2g; CARB 2.1g; FIBER 0.1g; CHOL 26mg; IRON 0.5mg; SODIUM 811mg; CALC 8mg

## Spiced Winter Fruit

(pictured on page 367)

Topped with low-fat vanilla ice cream, this also makes a simple and elegant holiday dessert. Quince, which is in season in winter, is a yellow-skinned fruit that looks and tastes like a cross between an apple and a pear but turns pink when cooked.

  1 cup packed light brown sugar
  1 teaspoon ground ginger
  1 teaspoon ground cinnamon
 ½ teaspoon ground nutmeg
  2 tablespoons butter or stick margarine
  2 quinces, each cut into 8 wedges (about ¾ pound)
  3 cups sliced peeled Bartlett or Anjou pear (about 1½ pounds)
2½ cups sliced peeled Granny Smith apple (about 1½ pounds)
 ¼ teaspoon freshly ground black pepper
Cinnamon sticks (optional)

**1.** Combine first 4 ingredients in a small bowl; set aside.

**2.** Melt butter in a large nonstick skillet over medium heat. Add quince; cover and cook 6 minutes, stirring occasionally. Add sugar mixture, pear, and apple; cover and cook 12 minutes, stirring occasionally. Stir in pepper; garnish with cinnamon sticks, if desired. Yield: 8 servings (serving size: ¾ cup).

**NOTE:** This dish will hold up to 3 days if refrigerated in an airtight container. To serve, reheat over low heat.

CALORIES 219 (15% from fat); FAT 3.6g (sat 1.9g, mono 0.9g, poly 0.3g); PROTEIN 0.7g; CARB 50.1g; FIBER 4.5g; CHOL 8mg; IRON 1.1mg; SODIUM 38mg; CALC 38mg

## Almond Cake

Since this cake is not too sweet or gooey, it is perfect for brunch. For a nonalcoholic version, omit the amaretto and substitute an equal amount of apple juice; or use ¼ cup water plus ½ teaspoon almond extract. A wire whisk and rubber spatula work fine here; you won't need your electric mixer.

1½ cups all-purpose flour
 ¾ cup sugar
  2 teaspoons baking powder
 ½ teaspoon salt
 ½ cup chopped sliced almonds, toasted and divided (about 2 ounces)
 ¼ cup fat-free milk
 ¼ cup butter or stick margarine, melted
 ¼ cup amaretto (almond-flavored liqueur)
  2 large eggs, lightly beaten
Cooking spray

**1.** Preheat oven to 350°.

**2.** Lightly spoon flour into dry measuring cups; level with a knife. Combine flour, sugar, baking powder, salt, and ¼ cup almonds in a large bowl; stir well with a whisk. Combine milk, butter, amaretto, and eggs; add to flour mixture, stirring just until moist.

**3.** Spoon batter into a 9-inch round cake pan coated with cooking spray. Sprinkle with ¼ cup almonds. Bake at 350° for 30 minutes or until a wooden pick inserted in center comes out clean. Cool 10 minutes in pan on a wire rack. Remove from pan. Cool completely on wire rack. Yield: 8 servings.

CALORIES 286 (35% from fat); FAT 11.1g (sat 4.4g, mono 4.6g, poly 1.3g); PROTEIN 5.8g; CARB 42g; FIBER 1.4g; CHOL 71mg; IRON 1.7mg; SODIUM 349mg; CALC 108mg

## Fresh Cranberry Muffins

Feel free to use your imagination with this basic muffin recipe by substituting your other favorite fruits and flavors for the cranberries and orange rind. Some options we like: blueberries and lemon rind; chopped apple, pear, or pineapple and cinnamon; or mashed banana and allspice.

  2   cups all-purpose flour
  ⅔   cup sugar
  2   teaspoons baking powder
  ¼   teaspoon salt
  1   cup chopped fresh cranberries
  ⅔   cup 2% reduced-fat milk
  ¼   cup butter or stick margarine, melted
  1   teaspoon grated orange rind
  ½   teaspoon vanilla extract
  1   large egg, lightly beaten
  Cooking spray

**1.** Preheat oven to 400°.

**2.** Lightly spoon flour into dry measuring cups; level with a knife. Combine flour, sugar, baking powder, and salt in a large bowl; stir well with a whisk. Stir in cranberries; make a well in center of mixture. Combine milk, butter, rind, vanilla, and egg; add to flour mixture, stirring just until moist. Spoon batter into 12 muffin cups coated with cooking spray. Bake at 400° for 18 minutes or until muffins spring back when touched lightly in center. Remove muffins from pan immediately; place on a wire rack. Yield: 12 servings (serving size: 1 muffin).

**NOTE:** These muffins, as well as the Almond Cake, freeze well. Bake them ahead, cool completely, and store in freezer bags. To serve, thaw at room temperature. Reheat in aluminum foil at 300° for 10 to 15 minutes or until thoroughly heated.

CALORIES 174 (26% from fat); FAT 5g (sat 2.7g, mono 1.4g, poly 0.4g); PROTEIN 3.2g; CARB 29.2g; FIBER 0.7g; CHOL 30mg; IRON 1.2mg; SODIUM 182mg; CALC 69mg

## for two

# Elegance with Ease

*Who deserves a sophisticated yet cozy romantic meal—away from the holiday hubbub? You both do.*

### menu 1

**Artichokes with Roasted-Pepper Dip**

**Bitter Greens with Tarragon Vinaigrette and Pine Nuts**

**Roasted Lobster Tails with Ginger Dipping Sauce**

**Snow Peas and Cherry Tomatoes**

## Artichokes with Roasted-Pepper Dip

You'll have some dip left over for impromptu entertaining—try it with raw vegetables, pita chips, or plain crackers.

  2    red bell peppers
  2    artichokes (1 pound)
  12   cups water
  3    lemon slices
  1    bay leaf
  2    teaspoons olive oil
  2    teaspoons Dijon mustard
  1    teaspoon red wine vinegar
  ¼    teaspoon dried fines herbes
  ⅛    teaspoon black pepper
  1    tablespoon finely crumbled feta cheese
  ½    teaspoon capers

**1.** Preheat broiler.

**2.** Cut bell peppers in half lengthwise, discarding seeds and membranes. Place pepper halves, skin sides up, on a foil-lined baking sheet; flatten with hand. Broil 10 minutes or until blackened. Place pepper halves in a zip-top plastic bag; seal. Let stand 20 minutes. Peel and set aside.

**3.** Cut off artichoke stems; remove bottom leaves. Trim about 1 inch from tops of artichokes. Bring water, lemon slices, and bay leaf to a boil in a large Dutch oven. Add artichokes; cover, reduce heat, and simmer 25 minutes or until a leaf near the center of each artichoke pulls out easily. Drain well; discard lemon and bay leaf. Set aside.

**4.** Combine bell peppers, oil, mustard, and vinegar in a blender; process until smooth. Combine bell pepper mixture, fines herbes, and black pepper. Spoon ⅔ cup into a serving bowl; sprinkle with feta and capers. Serve with artichokes. Cover and chill remaining dip. Yield: 2 servings: (serving size: 1 artichoke and ⅓ cup dip).

CALORIES 105 (30% from fat); FAT 3.5g (sat 0.9g, mono 1.9g, poly 0.4g); PROTEIN 4.2g; CARB 17.3g; FIBER 7.1g; CHOL 3mg; IRON 2.6mg; SODIUM 234mg; CALC 80mg

## Bitter Greens with Tarragon Vinaigrette and Pine Nuts

Look for loose bitter greens in bins in the produce section of your supermarket, or create your own mix with watercress, endive, arugula, radicchio, and mesclun. Just about any nut will work nicely in this salad; try hazelnuts for a holiday touch.

  2    tablespoons white wine vinegar
  2    tablespoons plain fat-free yogurt
  1    tablespoon chopped fresh or
       1 teaspoon dried tarragon
  2    teaspoons Dijon mustard
  2    teaspoons honey
  1    teaspoon olive oil
  ⅛    teaspoon salt
  ⅛    teaspoon black pepper
  5    cups mixed bitter greens
  1    tablespoon pine nuts, toasted

**1.** Combine first 8 ingredients in a small bowl; stir well with a whisk. Place greens and pine nuts in a large bowl; drizzle with vinaigrette. Yield: 2 servings (serving size: 2 cups).

CALORIES 74 (36% from fat); FAT 3g (sat 0.4g, mono 1g, poly 01.1g); PROTEIN 4g; CARB 9.2g; FIBER 2.2g; CHOL 0mg; IRON 0.8mg; SODIUM 337mg; CALC 136mg

## Roasted Lobster Tails with Ginger Dipping Sauce

**SAUCE:**

- ¾ teaspoon dry mustard
- ½ teaspoon water
- 3 tablespoons low-sodium soy sauce
- 1 tablespoon plum sauce
- 1 tablespoon dry sherry
- ¾ teaspoon minced peeled fresh ginger

**LOBSTER:**

- 2 (8-ounce) frozen lobster tails, thawed
- Cooking spray
- 1 teaspoon vegetable oil
- ¼ teaspoon dark sesame oil
- ¼ teaspoon black pepper
- Sliced green onions (optional)

**1.** Preheat oven to 425°.

**2.** To prepare sauce, combine mustard and water in a small bowl; stir well with a whisk. Stir in soy sauce, plum sauce, sherry, and ginger; set aside.

**3.** To prepare lobster, make a lengthwise cut through the top of each lobster shell using kitchen shears, cutting to, but not through, lobster meat; press shell open. Place lobster tails, cut sides up, in a shallow roasting pan coated with cooking spray. Combine oils and pepper, and spoon over lobster meat.

**4.** Bake at 425° for 13 minutes or until lobster meat turns opaque. Serve lobster with sauce; garnish with onions, if desired. Yield: 2 servings (serving size: 1 lobster tail and 2 tablespoons sauce).

CALORIES 194 (23% from fat); FAT 5g (sat 0.8g, mono 1.4g, poly 2.1g); PROTEIN 27.6g; CARB 8.3g; FIBER 0.2g; CHOL 92mg; IRON 1.2mg; SODIUM 1,263mg; CALC 86mg

## Snow Peas and Cherry Tomatoes

- 1½ cups snow peas, trimmed
- 3 tablespoons water
- ½ teaspoon butter or stick margarine
- ¼ teaspoon sugar
- 12 cherry tomatoes, halved
- ½ teaspoon dark sesame oil
- ⅛ teaspoon salt
- ⅛ teaspoon black pepper

**1.** Combine first 4 ingredients in a large nonstick skillet. Cook over medium-high heat 2 minutes or until liquid almost evaporates. Add tomatoes; cook 2 minutes or until tomatoes are thoroughly heated. Remove from heat; stir in remaining ingredients. Yield: 2 servings (serving size: 1 cup).

CALORIES 88 (28% from fat); FAT 2.7g (sat 0.9g, mono 0.8g, poly 0.8g); PROTEIN 3.8g; CARB 13.6g; FIBER 4g; CHOL 3mg; IRON 2.8mg; SODIUM 170mg; CALC 53mg

**menu 2**

**Artichokes with Roasted-Pepper Dip
(recipe on page 352)**

**Bitter Greens with Tarragon Vinaigrette and Pine Nuts
(recipe on page 352)**

**Veal Medallions with Apple-Thyme Sauce**

**Mashed Sweet Potatoes with Marsala**

## Veal Medallions with Apple-Thyme Sauce

To prevent the apple from turning brown, chop it while the sauce is cooking down. After that step, this recipe comes together rather quickly.

**SAUCE:**

- 1 cup dry sherry
- 1¾ cups fat-free, less-sodium chicken broth
- ¼ cup thawed apple juice concentrate, undiluted
- 1 tablespoon water
- 1½ teaspoons cornstarch
- ½ cup chopped Granny Smith apple
- ½ teaspoon chopped fresh or
- ⅛ teaspoon dried thyme

**VEAL:**

- 4 (2-ounce) veal medallions
- ⅛ teaspoon salt
- ⅛ teaspoon black pepper
- 2 teaspoons vegetable oil

**1.** To prepare sauce, bring sherry to a boil in a medium saucepan over medium-high heat; cook until reduced to 2 tablespoons (about 8 minutes). Add broth and apple juice concentrate; cook until reduced to 1 cup (about 12 minutes). Combine water and cornstarch in a small bowl. Add to broth mixture; bring to a boil. Cook 1 minute, stirring constantly. Remove from heat; stir in apple and thyme. Cover and keep warm.

**2.** To prepare veal, sprinkle veal with salt and pepper. Heat oil in a medium nonstick skillet over medium-high heat. Add veal; cook 3 minutes on each side or until lightly browned. Serve veal with sauce. Yield: 2 servings (serving size: 2 medallions and ½ cup sauce).

CALORIES 331 (28% from fat); FAT 10.4g (sat 2.4g, mono 3.4g, poly 2.8g); PROTEIN 30.2g; CARB 26.3g; FIBER 0.8g; CHOL 101mg; IRON 1.7mg; SODIUM 662mg; CALC 40mg

## Mashed Sweet Potatoes with Marsala

Marsala, a fortified wine often served as a dessert wine, gives the sweet potatoes a rich flavor. If you can't find Marsala, it's OK to omit it.

- 1 pound sweet potatoes
- 1½ tablespoons brown sugar
- 1½ tablespoons low-fat buttermilk
- 1 tablespoon Marsala wine
- 1 tablespoon butter or stick margarine
- ⅛ teaspoon salt
- ⅛ teaspoon black pepper
- Thyme sprigs (optional)

**1.** Preheat oven to 425°.

**2.** Bake potatoes at 425° for 1 hour and 10 minutes or until tender; cool slightly. Cut each potato in half lengthwise; scoop out pulp. Discard skins.

**3.** Place potato pulp and next 6 ingredients in a small saucepan; mash to desired consistency. Cook over low heat 2 minutes or until thoroughly heated. Garnish with thyme, if desired. Yield: 2 servings (serving size: ¾ cup).

CALORIES 322 (18% from fat); FAT 6.6g (sat 3.7g, mono 1.7g, poly 0.5g); PROTEIN 4.2g; CARB 62.6g; FIBER 6.8g; CHOL 16mg; IRON 1.5mg; SODIUM 244mg; CALC 73mg

# Tex-Mex Express

*Crossing the border just got better.*

Cooking Tex-Mex food is so fast and easy that, for many, it has become a weeknight supper solution.

## Green-Chile Ravioli

**PREPARATION TIME: 20 MINUTES**
**COOKING TIME: 10 MINUTES**

**RAVIOLI:**
- 1   cup (4 ounces) preshredded reduced-fat Mexican blend cheese
- ¼   cup minced green onions
- ½   teaspoon black pepper
- 1   (4.5-ounce) can chopped green chiles, undrained
- 1   large egg white
- 16   won ton wrappers
- 1   teaspoon cornstarch
- Cooking spray
- ⅓   cup fat-free, less-sodium chicken broth

**SAUCE:**
- ½   cup minced fresh cilantro
- 2   tablespoons balsamic vinegar
- 2   (14.5-ounce) cans diced tomatoes, drained
- 1   (15-ounce) can black beans, rinsed and drained

**1.** To prepare ravioli, combine first 5 ingredients in a bowl. Working with 1 won ton wrapper at a time (cover remaining wrappers with a damp towel to keep from drying), spoon about 1 tablespoon green chile mixture into center of each wrapper. Brush edges of wrapper with water; bring 2 opposite corners together. Press edges together firmly with fingers, forming a triangle. Place ravioli on a large baking sheet sprinkled with cornstarch. Heat a large nonstick skillet coated with cooking spray over medium-high heat. Add ravioli; cook 2 minutes on each side or until lightly browned. Add broth; cook, covered, 1 minute. Remove ravioli with a slotted spoon. Keep warm.

**2.** To prepare sauce, combine cilantro, vinegar, tomatoes, and beans in a large saucepan over medium-high heat. Cook 5 minutes or until thoroughly heated. Spoon sauce over ravioli. Yield: 4 servings (serving size: 4 ravioli and ¾ cup sauce).

CALORIES 329 (20% from fat); FAT 7.3g (sat 3.5g, mono 1.8g, poly 1g); PROTEIN 21.6g; CARB 46.6g; FIBER 5.7g; CHOL 21mg; IRON 4.7mg; SODIUM 1,341mg; CALC 331mg

---

### menu

#### Smothered Sirloin Steak with Adobo Gravy

Lemon-cilantro rice pilaf*

*Bring 1½ cups water to a boil in a large skillet; add ¾ cup long-grain rice, 1 tablespoon grated lemon rind, 1 tablespoon fresh lemon juice, ½ teaspoon ground turmeric, and ¼ teaspoon salt. Cover, reduce heat, and simmer 20 minutes. Stir in ⅓ cup sliced green onions and ¼ cup chopped fresh cilantro. Serves 4.

---

## Smothered Sirloin Steak with Adobo Gravy

**PREPARATION TIME: 9 MINUTES**
**COOKING TIME: 21 MINUTES**

- 1   pound ground sirloin
- 1   (7-ounce) can chipotle chiles in adobo sauce
- Cooking spray
- 2   cups thinly sliced onion
- ⅓   cup beef consommé
- 1   teaspoon low-sodium soy sauce
- ½   teaspoon cornstarch

**1.** Divide sirloin into 4 equal portions, shaping each into a ½-inch-thick patty.
**2.** Drain chiles in a colander over a bowl, reserving ¼ cup adobo sauce. Reserve chiles for another use.
**3.** Heat a large nonstick skillet coated with cooking spray over medium-high heat. Add patties and onion; cook 5 minutes on each side or until browned. Add adobo sauce and consommé; bring to a boil. Cover, reduce heat, and simmer 10 minutes. Combine soy sauce and cornstarch; stir until well-blended. Add to pan; bring to a boil. Cook 1 minute or until thick. Yield: 4 servings (serving size: 1 steak and 3 tablespoons sauce).

CALORIES 203 (33% from fat); FAT 7.4g (sat 2.5g, mono 3g, poly 0.6g); PROTEIN 26g; CARB 6.8g; FIBER 1.3g; CHOL 70mg; IRON 2.6mg; SODIUM 294mg; CALC 20mg

---

## Cumin-Crusted Swordfish with Cucumber-Radish Salsa

**PREPARATION TIME: 10 MINUTES**
**COOKING TIME: 12 MINUTES**

**SALSA:**
- 1   cup chopped seeded cucumber
- 1   cup coarsely chopped seeded plum tomato
- ½   cup thinly sliced radishes
- ¼   cup minced fresh cilantro
- 2   tablespoons fresh lime juice
- ¼   teaspoon sugar
- ¼   teaspoon salt
- ⅛   teaspoon black pepper

**FISH:**
- 1   tablespoon cumin seeds
- 1   tablespoon black peppercorns
- ¼   teaspoon salt
- 4   (6-ounce) swordfish steaks or other firm white fish (about ¾ inch thick)
- 1   teaspoon vegetable oil
- Cooking spray

**1.** To prepare salsa, combine first 8 ingredients in a bowl. Cover and chill.
**2.** To prepare fish, combine cumin seeds, peppercorns, and ¼ teaspoon salt in a small zip-top plastic bag. Coarsely crush cumin seed mixture using a meat mallet or rolling pin. Sprinkle cumin seed mixture on 1 side of steaks. Heat 1 teaspoon oil in a large nonstick skillet coated with cooking spray over medium-high heat. Add fish, crust sides down; cook 5 minutes on each side or until fish flakes easily when tested with a fork. Serve with salsa. Yield: 4 servings (serving size: 5 ounces fish and ½ cup salsa).

CALORIES 251 (33% from fat); FAT 9.2g (sat 2g, mono 3.3g, poly 2.6g); PROTEIN 34.9g; CARB 6.4g; FIBER 1.6g; CHOL 66mg; IRON 3.4mg; SODIUM 460mg; CALC 44mg

## Sonora Grilled Cheese

**PREPARATION TIME: 13 MINUTES**
**COOKING TIME: 4 MINUTES**

- ¼ cup low-fat mayonnaise
- ¼ teaspoon ground cumin
- ⅛ teaspoon black pepper
- 8 (1-ounce) slices hearty white bread
- 8 (¼-inch-thick) slices tomato
- ½ cup (2 ounces) shredded Monterey Jack cheese with jalapeño peppers
- ⅛ teaspoon salt
- ½ cup fat-free black bean dip
- Cooking spray

**1.** Combine first 3 ingredients; spread evenly over 4 bread slices. Top each with 2 tomato slices and 2 tablespoons cheese; sprinkle with salt. Spread bean dip evenly over remaining bread slices; place, dip sides down, on top of sandwiches. Heat a large nonstick skillet coated with cooking spray over medium heat. Coat each side of sandwiches with cooking spray. Place sandwiches in pan; cook 2 minutes on each side or until golden brown. Yield: 4 servings (serving size: 1 sandwich).

CALORIES 270 (26% from fat); FAT 7.8g (sat 2.6g, mono 2.6g, poly 1.5g); PROTEIN 10.5g; CARB 35.6g; FIBER 2.7g; CHOL 17mg; IRON 2.4mg; SODIUM 697mg; CALC 190mg

## Upside-Down Tamale Pie

**PREPARATION TIME: 5 MINUTES**
**COOKING TIME: 18 MINUTES**

- 1 pound ground round
- 1½ cups bottled salsa
- 2 teaspoons salt-free barbecue rub (such as Spice Hunter)
- 1 (15-ounce) can kidney beans, drained
- 1 (16-ounce) tube of polenta, diced
- Cooking spray
- 1 cup (4 ounces) shredded reduced-fat sharp Cheddar cheese

**1.** Place beef in a 2-quart casserole. Cover; microwave at HIGH 8 minutes, stirring after 4 minutes. Drain. Combine beef, salsa, rub, and beans in dish. Cover; microwave at HIGH 4 minutes or until hot.

**2.** Place polenta in a 9-inch pie plate coated with cooking spray. Spoon beef mixture on top of polenta; cover with plastic wrap. Microwave at HIGH 6 minutes or until thoroughly heated. Uncover; sprinkle with cheese. Yield: 6 servings (serving size: 1 wedge).

CALORIES 307 (26% from fat); FAT 8.8g (sat 3.8g, mono 3.1g, poly 0.7g); PROTEIN 28.4g; CARB 27.1g; FIBER 4.1g; CHOL 59mg; IRON 4.1mg; SODIUM 668mg; CALC 203mg

## Pork Chops Mole

**PREPARATION TIME: 4 MINUTES**
**COOKING TIME: 18 MINUTES**

Mole is a traditional sauce made with a blend of chiles, onion, and garlic. Its characteristic ingredient, chocolate, contributes richness without adding sweetness.

- Cooking spray
- 4 (4-ounce) boned pork loin chops (about ½ inch thick)
- ¼ cup water
- 1 cup chopped onion
- ½ cup yellow bell pepper strips
- ½ cup red bell pepper strips
- 1 tablespoon minced seeded jalapeño pepper
- 1 (14.5-ounce) can diced tomatoes with garlic and onion, undrained
- ½ ounce semisweet chocolate, grated
- 1 teaspoon chili powder
- 1 teaspoon dried oregano
- ½ teaspoon salt
- ¼ teaspoon cumin seeds
- ½ cup minced fresh cilantro

**1.** Heat a large nonstick skillet coated with cooking spray over medium-high heat. Cook chops 4 minutes on each side or until browned. Remove from pan. Add water to pan, scraping to loosen browned bits. Pour mixture over chops; Cover and set aside.

**2.** Reheat pan coated with cooking spray over medium-high heat. Add onion, bell pepper strips, and jalapeño; cook 4 minutes or until tender. Stir in tomatoes; cook 1 minute. Add chocolate and next 4 ingredients. Add chops; bring to a boil. Cover, reduce heat to medium-low, and cook 5 minutes, stirring occasionally. Sprinkle with cilantro. Yield: 4 servings (serving size: 1 pork chop and ⅔ cup sauce).

CALORIES 256 (38% from fat); FAT 10.8g (sat 3.7g, mono 4.4g, poly 1.7g); PROTEIN 27.2g; CARB 12.8g; FIBER 2.6g; CHOL 71mg; IRON 2.9mg; SODIUM 549mg; CALC 64mg

## Pan-Grilled Chicken with Cranberry Salsa

**PREPARATION TIME: 12 MINUTES**
**COOKING TIME: 10 MINUTES**

- 4 (4-ounce) skinned, boned chicken breast halves
- ¼ teaspoon salt
- ⅛ teaspoon black pepper
- ⅓ cup minced green onions
- 1 tablespoon minced pickled jalapeño peppers
- 2 teaspoons balsamic vinegar
- 1 (12-ounce) container cranberry-orange sauce (such as Ocean Spray)
- 2 tablespoons minced fresh cilantro, divided
- 1½ tablespoons lime juice, divided
- 2 tablespoons ⅓-less-fat cream cheese

**1.** Place each chicken breast half between 2 sheets of heavy-duty plastic wrap. Flatten to ½-inch thickness using a meat mallet or rolling pin. Sprinkle with salt and black pepper. Heat grill pan over medium-high heat; cook chicken 5 minutes on each side or until done. Keep warm.

**2.** Combine onions, jalapeños, vinegar, and cranberry sauce in a medium bowl. Stir in 1 tablespoon cilantro and 1 tablespoon lime juice.

**3.** Combine 1 tablespoon cilantro, 1½ teaspoons lime juice, and cream cheese in a small bowl; stir well to combine. Spoon cranberry salsa evenly onto individual plates. Place chicken on top of salsa; top with a dollop of cilantro cream. Serve immediately. Yield: 4 servings (serving size: 1 chicken breast half, ⅓ cup salsa, and 2 teaspoons cilantro cream).

CALORIES 292 (8% from fat); FAT 2.5g (sat 0.9g, mono 0.6g, poly 0.4g); PROTEIN 26.9g; CARB 38g; FIBER 0.3g; CHOL 69mg; IRON 1.2mg; SODIUM 397mg; CALC 26mg

# Effortless Entertaining

## This special night for special friends is way too doable not to.

Hosting a festive dinner party in the midst of the holiday rush sounds daunting—some might even say downright masochistic. But it needn't be if you follow the advice of Henry David Thoreau: "Simplify, simplify."

You can keep it simple right from the start by choosing an easy yet elegant menu, and we've got one that's just the ticket. Tantalizing as well as healthful, it provides plenty of shortcuts that will allow you to savor a special meal with friends instead of watching the action from behind the kitchen doors. And if your savoir faire leaves 'em wondering how you managed to pull it all off so effortlessly, so much the better.

As always, preparation is the key—and part of the fun. Enlist your friends to do a little shopping beforehand, or ask them to arrive an hour early to help with last-minute details. You won't need their help with the cooking, though.

---

### menu

**Kir Champagne Cocktail**

**Pea-and-Pasta Soup Sips**

**Three Kings Salad**

**Baked Fish with Roasted Potatoes, Tomatoes, and Salmoriglio Sauce**

**Onion Biscuits**

**Easy Caramel-Banana Galette**

---

## Kir Champagne Cocktail

Serve plain champagne (perhaps a more expensive brand) if you don't have time to make our recipe.

    6  sugar cubes
    6  tablespoons crème de cassis (black currant-flavored liqueur)
    3  cups champagne, chilled

**1.** Place 1 sugar cube in the bottom of each of 6 champagne glasses. Add 1 tablespoon crème de cassis and ½ cup champagne to each glass. Yield: 6 servings.

CALORIES 118 (0% from fat); FAT 0g; PROTEIN 0.4g; CARB 4.8g; FIBER 0g; CHOL 0mg; IRON 0.6mg; SODIUM 6mg; CALC 7mg

## Pea-and-Pasta Soup Sips

(pictured on page 366)

You can either dish up this soup in the kitchen or serve it from a tureen on the dining table.

    3  (16-ounce) cans fat-free, less-sodium chicken broth
 1½  cups frozen green peas
    ¾  cup small uncooked pasta (such as pastina, orzo, or ditalini)
    2  tablespoons chopped fresh parsley
    3  tablespoons Riesling or other slightly sweet white wine
    2  tablespoons grated fresh Parmesan cheese

**1.** Bring broth to a boil in a large saucepan over medium-high heat. Add peas, pasta, and parsley. Reduce heat; simmer 5 minutes or until pasta is tender. Stir in wine. Spoon soup into small cups; sprinkle with cheese. Yield: 6 servings (serving size: 1 cup soup and 1 teaspoon cheese).

CALORIES 118 (7% from fat); FAT 0.9g (sat 0.4g, mono 0.2g, poly 0.1g); PROTEIN 7.6g; CARB 16.7g; FIBER 1.7g; CHOL 2mg; IRON 1.2mg; SODIUM 562mg; CALC 40mg

## Three Kings Salad

The colorful trio of beets, oranges, and red onion represents the three wise men from the nativity story. You can section the oranges, cut the beets and onions, and make the vinaigrette ahead of time, (store them in separate containers so the colors don't bleed). Assemble up to one hour before serving. This recipe originally called for pomegranate juice (obtained by meticulously smashing pomegranate seeds and straining the juice) and fresh beets. We found most any fruit juice will work, however, and canned beets are fine, too.

    4  navel oranges
    1  (15-ounce) can whole beets, drained
    3  tablespoons balsamic vinegar
    2  tablespoons walnut oil or olive oil
    ½  teaspoon salt
    ½  teaspoon black pepper
    ¾  cup slivered red onion
       Pomegranate seeds (optional)

**1.** Peel and section oranges over a bowl; squeeze membranes to extract juice. Set sections aside; reserve 1½ tablespoons juice. Discard membranes.

**2.** Cut beets into wedges. Set aside.

**3.** Combine reserved 1½ tablespoons juice, vinegar, oil, salt, and pepper in a medium bowl; stir well with a whisk.

**4.** Divide beet wedges and orange sections evenly among 6 salad plates. Top each serving with 2 tablespoons onion slices. Drizzle with vinaigrette. Garnish with pomegranate seeds, if desired. Yield: 6 servings.

**NOTE:** To obtain pomegranate seeds, put on gloves and cut pomegranate into quarters. Coax seeds out from the base with thumbs, being careful not to break seeds. Remove and discard white membrane. Reserve ⅓ cup seeds for garnish.

CALORIES 116 (37% from fat); FAT 4.8g (sat 0.4g, mono 3.2g, poly 0.9g); PROTEIN 1.7g; CARB 18.6g; FIBER 4.8g; CHOL 0mg; IRON 0.7mg; SODIUM 363mg; CALC 53mg

## Baked Fish with Roasted Potatoes, Tomatoes, and Salmoriglio Sauce

*(pictured on page 365)*

Most any firm white fish will work here.

  6  cups peeled red potatoes, cut into
      ⅛-inch slices (about 2 pounds)
  4  cups thinly sliced fennel bulb
      (about 2 small bulbs)
  1  tablespoon olive oil, divided
  ¾  teaspoon kosher salt, divided
  ½  teaspoon black pepper, divided
  1  teaspoon fennel seeds
  3  garlic cloves, minced
  ¾  cup dry white wine
  6  tablespoons chopped fresh
      flat-leaf parsley, divided
  1  tablespoon grated orange rind
1½  teaspoons dried oregano
  1  (28-ounce) can whole tomatoes,
      drained and chopped
  6  (6-ounce) sea bass fillets or other
      firm white fish fillets
Lemon rind strips (optional)
Salmoriglio Sauce

**1.** Preheat oven to 450°.
**2.** Combine potatoes, fennel, 2 teaspoons oil, ¼ teaspoon salt, and ¼ teaspoon pepper in a 13 x 9-inch baking dish; toss gently to coat. Bake at 450° for 30 minutes.
**3.** Heat 1 teaspoon oil in a medium non-stick skillet. Add fennel seeds and garlic; sauté 1 minute. Add ¼ teaspoon salt, ⅛ teaspoon pepper, wine, 4 tablespoons parsley, rind, oregano, and tomatoes; bring to a boil. Reduce heat; simmer 8 minutes.
**4.** Sprinkle fillets with ¼ teaspoon salt and ⅛ teaspoon pepper. Arrange fillets over potato mixture; spread tomato mixture over fillets. Bake at 450° for 20 minutes or until fish flakes easily when tested with a fork. Sprinkle with 2 tablespoons parsley; garnish with lemon rind strips, if desired. Serve with Salmoriglio Sauce. Yield: 6 servings (serving size: 1 fillet, about 1 cup potato mixture, and 2 teaspoons Salmoriglio Sauce).

(Totals include Salmoriglio Sauce) CALORIES 379 (26% from fat); FAT 10.9g (sat 1.9g, mono 5.8g, poly 2g); PROTEIN 37.2g; CARB 34.2g; FIBER 3.6g; CHOL 70mg; IRON 4.6mg; SODIUM 892mg; CALC 145mg

**SALMORIGLIO SAUCE:**
Salmoriglio (sahl-moh-REE-lyee-o) is a pungent Italian sauce for drizzling over the fish. Make this sauce as close to serving time as possible.

  2  tablespoons fresh lemon juice
  2  tablespoons extra-virgin olive oil
1½  teaspoons chopped fresh or
      ½ teaspoon dried oregano
  1  teaspoon kosher salt
  1  teaspoon grated lemon rind
  2  garlic cloves, minced
Dash of freshly ground black pepper

**1.** Combine all ingredients; stir well with a whisk. Yield: ¼ cup (serving size: 2 teaspoons).

CALORIES 44 (92% from fat); FAT 4.5g (sat 0.6g, mono 3.3g, poly 0.4g); PROTEIN 0.1g; CARB 1.1g; FIBER 0.1g; CHOL 0mg; IRON 0.2mg; SODIUM 320mg; CALC 9mg

## Onion Biscuits

You can prepare the dough a day in advance and refrigerate it. Remove from food processor; cover in plastic wrap. Uncover, shape, and bake the biscuits the day of the party.

Cooking spray
  1  cup minced fresh onion
  ½  teaspoon sugar
  2  cups all-purpose flour
  2  teaspoons baking powder
  ½  teaspoon baking soda
  ½  teaspoon salt
  3  tablespoons vegetable shortening
  ¾  cup low-fat buttermilk
  1  large egg, lightly beaten
  2  teaspoons water

**1.** Preheat oven to 450°.
**2.** Heat a small nonstick skillet coated with cooking spray over medium-high heat. Add onion and sugar; sauté 8 minutes or until golden brown. Cool.
**3.** Lightly spoon flour into dry measuring cups; level with a knife. Place flour, baking powder, baking soda, and salt in a food processor; pulse 2 times or until blended. Add shortening; pulse 2 times or until combined. Sprinkle onion mixture over flour mixture. With processor on, slowly add buttermilk through food chute;

process until dough forms a ball.
**4.** Turn dough out onto a floured surface; knead lightly 4 or 5 times. Pat dough into an 8 x 6-inch rectangle; cut into 12 squares. Place on a baking sheet. Combine egg and water; brush over biscuits. Bake at 450° for 11 minutes or until golden. Yield: 1 dozen (serving size: 1 biscuit).

CALORIES 114 (25% from fat); FAT 3.2g (sat 0.7g, mono 1.1g, poly 1.1g); PROTEIN 2.9g; CARB 18.3g; FIBER 0.8g; CHOL 0mg; IRON 1.1mg; SODIUM 252mg; CALC 70mg

## Easy Caramel-Banana Galette

*(pictured on page 368)*

To make the caramel, just give the pan a swirl to dissolve the sugar, and then leave unattended for 8 minutes. Stirring the mixture can cause it to harden.

  ¼  cup golden raisins
  2  tablespoons dark rum
  ½  (15-ounce) package refrigerated
      pie crust dough (such as Pillsbury)
Cooking spray
  3  cups (¼-inch-thick) diagonally
      sliced ripe bananas (about 1½
      pounds)
  ½  cup sugar
  2  tablespoons water

**1.** Combine raisins and rum; set aside.
**2.** Preheat oven to 425°.
**3.** Roll dough into a 10½-inch circle; place on a foil-lined baking sheet coated with cooking spray. Arrange banana slices in concentric circles on crust, leaving a 1-inch border. Fold 2-inch dough border over bananas, pressing gently to seal (dough will partially cover bananas). Bake at 425° for 30 minutes.
**4.** Combine sugar and water in a saucepan; cook over medium heat until golden (about 8 minutes). Remove from heat; carefully stir in raisin mixture until combined. Cool slightly. Pour over bananas. Yield: 6 servings (serving size: 1 wedge).

CALORIES 318 (27% from fat); FAT 9.7g (sat 2.4g, mono 4g, poly 2.5g); PROTEIN 3.3g; CARB 57.3g; FIBER 2.5g; CHOL 0mg; IRON 0.9mg; SODIUM 160mg; CALC 35mg

# Fast Times, Simple Traditions

## Simplify your holiday entertaining to enjoy the true bounty of the season.

One of the best ways to move your holiday meal in a more simplified direction is to rely on the roast. Why? Because the oven does most of the work. This simple holiday menu also includes at least one make-ahead dish that can be frozen or made early the day before. Desserts are always designed that way: Cheesecakes can be made up to three days ahead; pies, crisps, and tarts the day before. And casseroles seem to have been dreamed up for advance planning, not to mention serving ease.

### menu

**Orange-Sage Roasted Turkey**

*or*

**Rosemary-and-Garlic-Studded Leg of Lamb**

**Brussels Sprouts with Browned Garlic**

*or*

**Roasted Red Onions**

**Potato and Sun-Dried Tomato au Gratin**

*or*

**Corn Bread, Cherry, and Bacon Stuffing**

**Buttermilk-Dill Rolls**

**Pumpkin Cheesecake**

### Orange-Sage Roasted Turkey

1 (15-pound) fresh or frozen turkey, thawed
Cooking spray
½ cup chopped fresh sage
2 tablespoons grated orange rind
1⅛ teaspoons salt, divided
1¼ cups fresh orange juice (about 3 oranges), divided
2 tablespoons honey, divided
1 orange, quartered
1 tablespoon cornstarch

**1.** Preheat oven to 325°.
**2.** Remove and discard giblets and neck from turkey. Rinse turkey with cold water; pat dry. Trim excess fat. Starting at neck cavity, loosen skin from breast and drumsticks by inserting fingers, gently pushing between skin and meat. Lift wing tips up and over back; tuck under turkey.
**3.** Place turkey on rack of a broiler pan or roasting pan coated with cooking spray. Combine sage, rind, and 1 teaspoon salt. Rub sage mixture under loosened skin and inside body cavity. Combine ¼ cup juice and 1 tablespoon honey; pour over turkey. Place orange quarters inside body cavity.
**4.** Insert meat thermometer into meaty part of thigh, making sure not to touch bone. Bake at 325° for 3 hours or until thermometer registers 180°. Cover turkey loosely with foil; let stand 10 minutes. Discard skin and orange wedges. Remove turkey from pan, reserving pan drippings for sauce. Place turkey on a platter; keep warm.
**5.** To make sauce, pour reserved pan drippings into a zip-top plastic bag. Seal bag; snip off 1 corner of bag. Drain drippings into a medium saucepan, stopping before fat layer reaches opening; discard fat. (You should have about ⅔ cup drippings; add enough water or fat-free, low-sodium chicken broth to make up the difference, if necessary.)

**6.** Add ⅛ teaspoon salt, ½ cup juice, and 1 tablespoon honey to drippings in pan; bring to a boil. Reduce heat, and simmer 1 minute. Combine ½ cup juice and cornstarch in a small bowl; add to drippings mixture. Bring to a boil; cook 1 minute, stirring constantly. Serve sauce with turkey. Yield: 16 servings (serving size: 5 ounces turkey and 2 tablespoons sauce).

CALORIES 261 (24% from fat); FAT 7.1g (sat 2.3g, mono 1.5g, poly 2g); PROTEIN 41.7g; CARB 5.1g; FIBER 0.1g; CHOL 108mg; IRON 2.6mg; SODIUM 264mg; CALC 44mg

### Rosemary-and-Garlic-Studded Leg of Lamb

ROAST:
1 (7-pound) leg of lamb
¼ cup minced fresh rosemary
¼ cup minced fresh garlic (about 14 cloves)
1½ teaspoons kosher salt
½ teaspoon coarsely ground black pepper

SAUCE:
1 (14½-ounce) can low-salt beef broth
1 (4-inch) rosemary sprig
¼ cup port or other sweet red wine
1 tablespoon cornstarch

**1.** Preheat oven to 400°.
**2.** To prepare roast, trim fat from lamb, and cut 16 (¾-inch-deep) slits into lamb. Combine minced rosemary and garlic. Spoon about ½ teaspoon rosemary mixture into each slit; rub lamb with any remaining rosemary mixture. Sprinkle with salt and pepper. Place roast on rack of a broiler pan or roasting pan. Insert meat thermometer into thickest part of lamb, making sure not to touch bone.
**3.** Bake at 400° for about 1½ hours or until thermometer registers 140° (medium-rare) to 155° (medium). Let stand 15 minutes before slicing. (Temperature of lamb will increase 5° upon standing.) Remove lamb from pan; scrape up browned bits with a rubber spatula. Place roast on a platter; keep

warm. To prepare sauce, pour reserved drippings into a small zip-top plastic bag. Seal bag; snip off 1 corner of bag. Drain drippings into a medium saucepan, stopping before fat layer reaches opening; discard fat. Reserve 2 tablespoons drippings in pan.

**4.** Add broth and rosemary sprig to drippings in pan; bring to a boil. Reduce heat, and simmer 1 minute. Combine port and cornstarch in a small bowl; add to broth mixture. Bring to a boil; cook 1 minute, stirring constantly. Discard rosemary sprig. Serve sauce with lamb. Yield: 16 servings (serving size: 3 ounces lamb and 2 tablespoons sauce).

CALORIES 173 (34% from fat); FAT 6.6g (sat 2.4g, mono 2.9g, poly 0.4g); PROTEIN 24.3g; CARB 2.2g; FIBER 0.2g; CHOL 76mg; IRON 2mg; SODIUM 240mg; CALC 16mg

## Brussels Sprouts with Browned Garlic

To trim Brussels sprouts, discard the tough outer leaves and trim off about ¼ inch from stems. Don't cut too much from the stems or the sprouts will fall apart.

    6   cups trimmed Brussels sprouts,
        halved (about 2 pounds)
    1   tablespoon olive oil, divided
    ½   teaspoon salt
    ⅛   teaspoon black pepper
        Cooking spray
    3   garlic cloves, thinly sliced
    1   tablespoon fresh lemon juice

**1.** Preheat oven to 425°.
**2.** Combine Brussels sprouts, 1½ teaspoons oil, salt, and pepper. Place sprouts mixture in a 13 x 9-inch baking dish coated with cooking spray. Bake at 425° for 25 minutes or until sprouts are crisp-tender. Keep warm.
**3.** Heat 1½ teaspoons oil in a small skillet over medium-low heat. Add garlic; cook 3 minutes until golden brown, stirring occasionally. Remove from heat; stir in juice. Add to sprouts mixture; toss well. Yield: 6 servings (serving size: ½ cup).

CALORIES 91 (30% from fat); FAT 3g (sat 0.4g, mono 1.7g, poly 0.4g); PROTEIN 5.2g; CARB 14.3g; FIBER 6.5g; CHOL 0mg; IRON 2.2mg; SODIUM 234mg; CALC 67mg

## Roasted Red Onions

You can place these in the oven simultaneously with the lamb.

    4   medium red onions, peeled and
        halved (about 4 pounds)
        Cooking spray
    2   teaspoons olive oil
    1   teaspoon balsamic vinegar
    ¾   teaspoon salt
    ¼   teaspoon black pepper

**1.** Preheat oven to 400°.
**2.** Arrange onions, cut sides down, in a 13 x 9-inch baking pan or on a broiler pan coated with cooking spray. Combine oil and remaining 3 ingredients in a small bowl; stir with a whisk. Drizzle onions with oil mixture. Bake at 400° for 1½ hours or until very tender. Yield: 8 servings (serving size: 1 onion half).

CALORIES 99 (15% from fat); FAT 1.7g (sat 0.3g, mono 0.9g, poly 0.4g); PROTEIN 2.6g; CARB 19.6g; FIBER 4.2g; CHOL 0mg; IRON 0.5mg; SODIUM 227mg; CALC 46mg

## Potato and Sun-Dried Tomato au Gratin

This can be assembled and refrigerated up to 24 hours ahead of time. Let stand 30 minutes at room temperature and bake as directed.

    1   cup boiling water
    ¾   cup sun-dried tomatoes, packed
        without oil (about 2 ounces)
    3   pounds peeled baking potato, cut
        into ¼-inch-thick slices
        Cooking spray
    1   tablespoon butter or stick
        margarine
    1   cup chopped onion
    ½   teaspoon dried oregano
    ¼   teaspoon salt
    ¼   teaspoon black pepper
    ¼   cup all-purpose flour
    2¼  cups fat-free milk
    2   cups (8 ounces) grated fresh
        Parmesan cheese

**1.** Combine water and sun-dried tomatoes in a bowl; cover and let stand 30

minutes or until soft. Drain and coarsely chop; set aside.
**2.** Preheat oven to 350°.
**3.** Place potato slices in a large saucepan, and cover with water; bring to a boil. Reduce heat; simmer 15 minutes or until tender. Drain well. Arrange potato slices in a 13 x 9-inch baking dish coated with cooking spray.
**4.** Melt butter in pan over medium heat. Add onion; cook 3 minutes or until tender. Add sun-dried tomatoes, oregano, salt, and pepper; cook 2 minutes. Lightly spoon flour into a dry measuring cup; level with a knife. Sprinkle tomato mixture with flour; cook 1 minute, stirring constantly. Gradually add milk, stirring with a whisk until blended. Remove from heat; add cheese, stirring until cheese melts. Pour sauce over potatoes, tossing gently to coat. Bake at 350° for 20 minutes or until bubbly and golden. Yield: 10 servings (serving size: about ¾ cup).

CALORIES 279 (25% from fat); FAT 7.6g (sat 4.6g, mono 2.1g, poly 0.4g); PROTEIN 13.7g; CARB 38g; FIBER 2.9g; CHOL 19mg; IRON 1.2mg; SODIUM 558mg; CALC 353mg

## Corn Bread, Cherry, and Bacon Stuffing

(pictured on page 367)

You can make the corn bread croutons a day ahead (place in an airtight container) or up to a week in advance (keep in the freezer).

    ⅔   cup fat-free milk
    2   large eggs
    2   (8½-ounce) packages corn muffin
        mix
        Cooking spray
    6   bacon slices
    2   cups chopped onion
    2   cups diced carrot
    2   cups diced celery
    ½   cup dried tart cherries
    1   (16-ounce) can fat-free,
        less-sodium chicken broth
    1   cup chopped fresh parsley
    1   teaspoon dried thyme
    ½   teaspoon salt
    ¼   teaspoon black pepper

*Continued*

1. Preheat oven to 400°.

2. Combine milk and eggs in a bowl; stir well with a whisk. Stir in muffin mix; let stand 2 minutes. Pour corn bread mixture into a 13 x 9-inch baking dish coated with cooking spray. Bake at 400° for 20 minutes or until a wooden pick inserted in center comes out clean. Cool and cut into ½-inch cubes. Place cubes on a baking sheet; bake at 400° for 10 minutes or until golden brown.

3. Cook bacon in a large nonstick skillet over medium heat until crisp. Remove bacon from pan, reserving 1 teaspoon drippings in pan. Crumble bacon; set aside. Add onion, carrot, and celery to pan; sauté 5 minutes over medium-high heat. Stir in cherries and broth; cook 5 minutes.

4. Combine corn bread cubes, bacon, onion mixture, parsley, thyme, salt, and pepper in a large bowl, stirring until well-blended. Spoon corn bread mixture into a 13 x 9-inch baking dish coated with cooking spray. Bake at 400° for 20 minutes or until thoroughly heated, stirring after 10 minutes. Yield: 12 servings (serving size: ¾ cup).

CALORIES 248 (28% from fat); FAT 7.6g (sat 2g, mono 3g, poly 2.1g); PROTEIN 5.7g; CARB 39g; FIBER 2.9g; CHOL 41mg; IRON 2.1mg; SODIUM 524mg; CALC 113mg

## Buttermilk-Dill Rolls

You can make the dough for these simple rolls up to two weeks ahead and freeze it in a heavy-duty zip-top plastic bag. Thaw in the refrigerator, shape, and bake as directed. These are also good without the dill, if you prefer to omit it.

1½  cups warm low-fat buttermilk
      (100° to 110°)
  2  tablespoons vegetable oil
  2  teaspoons sugar
  1  package dry yeast (about 2¼
      teaspoons)
3¼  cups all-purpose flour, divided
  2  teaspoons dried dill
  1  teaspoon kosher salt, divided
  Cooking spray
1½  teaspoons cornmeal
  1  large egg white, lightly beaten

1. Combine first 4 ingredients in a large bowl; let stand 5 minutes. Lightly spoon flour into dry measuring cups; level with a knife. Add 3 cups flour, dill, and ½ teaspoon salt to buttermilk mixture. Turn dough out onto a floured surface. Knead until smooth and elastic (about 10 minutes); add enough of remaining flour, 1 tablespoon at a time, to prevent dough from sticking to hands (dough will feel tacky).

2. Place dough in a large bowl coated with cooking spray, turning to coat top. Cover and let rise in a warm place (85°), free from drafts, 45 minutes or until doubled in size. (Press two fingers into dough. If indentation remains, dough has risen enough.) Punch dough down; cover and let rest 5 minutes. Divide in half. Working with one portion at a time (cover remaining dough to keep from drying), shape portion into 6 (2-inch-long) ovals on a floured surface. Roll up each oval tightly, starting with a long edge, pressing firmly to eliminate air pockets; pinch seam and ends to seal. Place rolls, seam sides down, on a large baking sheet sprinkled with cornmeal. Repeat with remaining dough portion.

3. Preheat oven to 375°.

4. Brush egg white over rolls; sprinkle with ½ teaspoon salt. Bake at 375° for 25 minutes or until rolls are browned on the bottom and sound hollow when tapped. Remove from pan; cool on wire racks. Yield: 12 servings (serving size: 1 roll).

CALORIES 158 (19% from fat); FAT 3.3g (sat 0.8g, mono 0.9g, poly 1.3g); PROTEIN 4.9g; CARB 26.6g; FIBER 1g; CHOL 0mg; IRON 1.6mg; SODIUM 181mg; CALC 46mg

## Pumpkin Cheesecake

Cheesecakes are best when made ahead. You can prepare this one up to three days before the party; cover and chill until time to serve.

CRUST:
  56  reduced-fat vanilla wafers (about 8
       ounces)
   1  tablespoon butter or stick
       margarine, melted
  Cooking spray

FILLING:
   3  (8-ounce) blocks fat-free cream
       cheese, softened
   2  (8-ounce) blocks ⅓-less-fat cream
       cheese, softened
  ½  cup granulated sugar
  ½  cup packed brown sugar
   3  tablespoons all-purpose flour
   1  teaspoon ground cinnamon
  ½  teaspoon ground nutmeg
  ½  teaspoon ground ginger
  ¼  teaspoon salt
  Dash of ground allspice
   2  teaspoons vanilla extract
   4  large eggs
   1  (15-ounce) can pumpkin

1. Preheat oven to 400°.

2. To prepare crust, place wafers in a food processor; pulse 2 or 3 times or until finely ground. Add butter; pulse 10 times or until mixture resembles coarse meal. Firmly press mixture into bottom of a 9-inch springform pan coated with cooking spray. Bake at 400° for 10 minutes; cool on a wire rack.

3. Reduce oven temperature to 325°.

4. To prepare filling, beat cheeses at high speed of a mixer until smooth. Add granulated sugar and next 8 ingredients; beat well. Add eggs, 1 at a time, beating well after each addition. Add pumpkin; beat well.

5. Pour cheese mixture into prepared crust; bake at 325° for 1½ hours or until almost set. (Cheesecake is done when center barely moves when pan is touched.) Remove cheesecake from oven; run a knife around outside edge. Cool to room temperature; cover and chill at least 8 hours. Yield: 16 servings (serving size: 1 slice).

CALORIES 256 (34% from fat); FAT 9.8g (sat 5.3g, mono 2.9g, poly 0.5g); PROTEIN 11.4g; CARB 29.3g; FIBER 1.4g; CHOL 86mg; IRON 1.2mg; SODIUM 479mg; CALC 172mg

# The Night Before Christmas

*A tradition of Christmas Eve tamales is a gift that one Mexican-American family hands down, each generation to the next.*

The reader: Frank Hernandez, 61, civil rights advocate, attorney, and former state judge from Dallas, Texas.

The recipe: Mama Totota's Tamales.

The back story: When Frank Hernandez's Mexican-born grandmother, Juanita Vidaurri, immigrated to Texas in 1911, so did the tamales that are central to his family's Christmas Eve tradition.

The dilemma: Solving the big problem—281 grams of fat and 3,945 calories—seemed to require a holiday miracle.

The solution: A leaner cut of pork and eliminating the 11 tablespoons of vegetable oil cut a whopping 1,882 calories and 237 grams of fat.

| BEFORE | AFTER |
|--------|-------|
| SERVING SIZE | |
| 2 tamales | |
| CALORIES PER SERVING | |
| 657 | 344 |
| FAT | |
| 46.8g | 7.4g |
| PERCENT OF TOTAL CALORIES | |
| 64% | 19% |

## Mama Totota's Tamales

14  large dried cornhusks

FILLING:
1  pound pork tenderloin
1½  teaspoons ground cumin
1½  teaspoons chili powder
1½  teaspoons dried oregano
½  teaspoon salt
½  teaspoon paprika
Cooking spray
1  cup chopped onion

DOUGH:
3  cups masa harina
1½  teaspoons paprika
1  teaspoon salt
2  cups water
2  teaspoons vegetable oil

**1.** Place cornhusks in a large bowl of hot water; weigh down husks with another bowl. Soak at least 30 minutes. Drain husks; rinse with cold water. Drain and pat dry.

**2.** Tear 2 cornhusks lengthwise into 12 (½-inch-wide) strips (6 strips per husk).

**3.** Preheat oven to 400°.

**4.** To prepare filling, trim fat from pork. Combine cumin and next 4 ingredients; rub pork with 2¼ teaspoons cumin mixture. Place pork on a broiler pan coated with cooking spray; insert meat thermometer into pork. Bake at 400° for 30 minutes or until thermometer registers 155°. Cover pork loosely with foil; let stand 10 minutes. Cut pork in half crosswise; shred with 2 forks.

**5.** Heat a small nonstick skillet coated with cooking spray over medium-high heat. Add onion; sauté 5 minutes or until tender. Combine pork, onion, and 2¼ teaspoons cumin mixture.

**6.** To prepare dough, combine masa harina, paprika, and 1 teaspoon salt in a large bowl. Add water and oil, stirring to form a soft dough. Turn dough out onto a lightly floured surface; knead lightly 4 or 5 times. Divide dough into 12 equal portions. Working with 1 portion, place dough in center of 1 husk. Press dough into a 4 x 2½-inch rectangle, leaving about a 1½-inch border at the tapered end and a 1-inch border at the broad end. Arrange about ¼ cup filling down center of dough. Take 1 long side of husk and roll dough around filling, making sure dough seals around filling. Tie 1 husk strip around tapered end of husk to secure it. Trim all but about ½ inch excess cornhusk from broad end. Repeat procedure with remaining husks, dough, and pork mixture.

**7.** Arrange 6 tamales in steamer; cover with steamer lid. Add water to a large skillet to a depth of 1 inch; bring to a boil. Place steamer in pan; steam tamales 12 minutes or until husk peels away cleanly. Remove tamales from steamer. Repeat procedure with remaining tamales. Yield: 6 servings (serving size: 2 tamales).

CALORIES 344 (19% from fat); FAT 7.4g (sat 1.7g, mono 2.5g, poly 2.5g); PROTEIN 23.1g; CARB 45.9g; FIBER 2g; CHOL 56mg; IRON 6.3mg; SODIUM 638mg; CALC 144mg

## Wrapping Tamales Step-by-Steps

**1.** *When pressing the dough, keep your fingers slightly wet to prevent the dough from sticking.*

**2.** *When rolling the tamale, make sure the cornhusk doesn't press into the filling. After tying the cornhusk strips around the tamale, you may need to press your fingers through the open end to pack the filling.*

# Throw Wide Your Doors

The holiday season might be the only time of year you bring your friends and family together—and there's no easier way than with an open house.

If you've ever been to an open house gathering—and many people like to host them during the holidays—you know that you never regret going. You end up having a better time than you ever imagined. But it's even better if your own house is the scene of the reunion. It says something about you. It says that you remembered, and that you went to the trouble to make everything happen. And that you made all that great food.

### Open House Menu

**Antipasto Bowl**

**Sun-Dried Tomato Tapenade with Crostini**

**West Indies Shrimp**

**Chipotle-Chicken Stew**

**Baked Potato-and-Bacon Soup**

**Cornmeal Cheese Twists**

**Hot Spiced Cheer**

**Coconut-Macadamia Nut Cookies**

## Antipasto Bowl

3   cups (2-inch) sliced asparagus (about ¾ pound)
3   cups quartered mushrooms (about ¾ pound)
1   cup red bell pepper strips
½   cup pitted ripe olives
3   ounces part-skim mozzarella cheese, cubed (about ⅔ cup)
1   (14-ounce) can quartered artichoke hearts, drained
1   (11.5-ounce) jar pickled pepperoncini peppers, drained
⅓   cup cider vinegar
¼   cup finely chopped fresh parsley
2   tablespoons extra-virgin olive oil
2   teaspoons dried oregano
1   teaspoon sugar
¼   teaspoon salt
¼   teaspoon black pepper
3   garlic cloves, minced

**1.** Steam asparagus, covered, 2 minutes. Drain and plunge into ice water; drain well. Combine asparagus, mushrooms, and next 5 ingredients in a large bowl.

**2.** Combine vinegar and remaining 7 ingredients in a small bowl; stir well with a whisk. Pour vinaigrette over vegetable mixture, tossing gently to coat. Cover and marinate in refrigerator 2 hours, stirring occasionally. Yield: 20 servings (serving size: ½ cup).

**NOTE:** Serve vegetables chilled or at room temperature.

CALORIES 49 (50% from fat); FAT 2.7g (sat 0.7g, mono 1.5g, poly 0.3g); PROTEIN 2.5g; CARB 5g; FIBER 1.2g; CHOL 2mg; IRON 1.2mg; SODIUM 263mg; CALC 50mg

## Sun-Dried Tomato Tapenade with Crostini

This recipe takes about 30 minutes to prepare and can be made up to two days in advance. Store the tapenade covered in the refrigerator, and garnish with parsley immediately before serving. Store toasted and cooled baguette slices in an airtight container.

2   cups boiling water
1   cup sun-dried tomatoes, packed without oil (about 3 ounces)
½   cup kalamata olives, pitted
2   tablespoons dried basil
2   tablespoons fresh lemon juice
1   garlic clove, minced
2   teaspoons olive oil
72   (½-inch-thick) slices diagonally cut French bread baguette (about 2 loaves)
Cooking spray
Chopped fresh parsley (optional)

**1.** Combine boiling water and sun-dried tomatoes; cover and let stand 15 minutes or until soft. Drain tomatoes in a colander over a bowl, reserving ¾ cup liquid. Combine tomatoes, reserved liquid, olives, basil, lemon juice, and garlic in a blender or food processor; process until smooth. Place tomato mixture in a small bowl; stir in oil. Cover and chill.

**2.** Preheat oven to 350°.

**3.** Place half of bread slices on a baking sheet coated with cooking spray. Lightly coat bread slices with cooking spray. Bake at 350° for 4 minutes. Turn bread slices over; lightly coat with cooking spray. Bake an additional 4 minutes. Repeat with remaining bread slices. Cool completely.

**4.** Garnish tapenade with parsley, if desired; serve with crostini. Yield: 24 servings (serving size: 3 crostini and 1 tablespoon tapenade).

CALORIES 77 (19% from fat); FAT 1.6g (sat 0.3g, mono 0.9g, poly 0.4g); PROTEIN 2.5g; CARB 13.6g; FIBER 1.3g; CHOL 0mg; IRON 1.1mg; SODIUM 239mg; CALC 29mg

## West Indies Shrimp

You can cook and peel the shrimp early in the day; then cover and chill. You can also make the marinade in the morning, but don't combine the two components until about 45 minutes to one hour before you expect your guests to arrive.

```
12   cups water
 2   pounds unpeeled medium shrimp
 2   teaspoons Old Bay seasoning
 1   cup chopped onion
 1   cup chopped green bell pepper
⅔    cup cider vinegar
1½   tablespoons vegetable oil
 1   teaspoon salt
¼    teaspoon black pepper
```

**1.** Bring water to a boil in a large saucepan. Add shrimp and seasoning; cook 3 minutes or until done. Drain and cool completely. Place shrimp in a large zip-top bag. Add remaining ingredients; seal and marinate in refrigerator 30 minutes, turning bag occasionally. Remove shrimp from bag, reserving marinade. Peel shrimp; place in a large bowl. Add reserved marinade; toss gently to coat. Yield: 18 servings (serving size: about 2 shrimp).

CALORIES 57 (28% from fat); FAT 1.8g (sat 0.3g, mono 0.4g, poly 0.8); PROTEIN 7.9g; CARB 2.1g; FIBER 0.3g; CHOL 57mg; IRON 1.1mg; SODIUM 260mg; CALC 23mg

---

### Simply Decorating

• Find a goldfish bowl (about $20) and fill it with those old ornaments you aren't using elsewhere. This makes an easy, low-maintenance holiday centerpiece.

• There's a reason clove-spiked oranges are an enduring tradition—they smell like holiday cheer. Set a row of them on a windowsill, tuck one in an overnight guest's linen drawer, or simply place several in a bright bowl in your kitchen.

• To dress up your mantel, arrange branches of fresh pine across the top, line up several tall white or frosted glasses, and fill them with candy canes.

---

## Chipotle-Chicken Stew

Chipotles are dried, smoked jalapeños; they give this stew a southwestern flair guaranteed to take the chill off winter. Make and store the stew in the refrigerator the day before the party. Reheat over medium-low heat, and stir in the cilantro before serving.

```
     Cooking spray
 3   pounds skinned, boned chicken
       breast, cut into bite-size pieces
 1   tablespoon olive oil
 3   cups chopped onion
 6   garlic cloves, minced
 2   cups (1-inch) cubed peeled red
       potato (about 1 pound)
1½   cups (1-inch-thick) slices carrot
¼    cup tomato paste
1½   teaspoons ground cumin
 3   (16-ounce) cans fat-free,
       less-sodium chicken broth
 3   (14.5-ounce) cans no-salt-added
       diced tomatoes, undrained
 3   drained canned chipotle chiles in
       adobo sauce, finely chopped
½    teaspoon salt
 2   tablespoons chopped fresh
       cilantro
```

**1.** Place a large Dutch oven coated with cooking spray over medium-high heat. Add chicken; sauté 7 minutes or until browned. Remove chicken from pan; keep warm.
**2.** Add oil to pan. Add onion; sauté 7 minutes or until lightly browned. Add garlic; sauté 1 minute. Add potato and next 6 ingredients; bring to a boil. Reduce heat; simmer 25 minutes or until vegetables are tender. Add chicken and salt; cover and cook 10 minutes. Stir in cilantro. Yield: 16 servings (serving size: 1 cup).

CALORIES 173 (12% from fat); FAT 2.3g (sat 0.5g, mono 1g, poly 0.5g); PROTEIN 22.7g; CARB 14.6g; FIBER 1.6g; CHOL 49mg; IRON 1.6mg; SODIUM 361mg; CALC 54mg

---

## Baked Potato-and-Bacon Soup

Bake the potatoes and shred the cheese the day before making the soup. If the soup needs to simmer awhile on the stove, you may need to add more chicken broth.

```
5¼   pounds baking potatoes
 7   bacon slices
4½   cups chopped onion
 1   teaspoon salt
 5   garlic cloves, minced
 1   bay leaf
7½   cups 1% low-fat milk
¾    teaspoon black pepper
 3   cups fat-free, less-sodium chicken
       broth
⅓    cup chopped fresh parsley
       (optional)
1¼   cups sliced green onions
1¼   cups (5 ounces) finely shredded
       reduced-fat sharp Cheddar cheese
```

**1.** Preheat oven to 400°.
**2.** Pierce potatoes with a fork; bake at 400° for 1 hour or until tender. Cool slightly. Partially mash potatoes, including skins, with a potato masher; set aside.
**3.** Cook bacon in a Dutch oven over medium heat until crisp. Remove bacon from pan; crumble. Add onion to bacon drippings in pan; sauté 5 minutes. Add salt, garlic, and bay leaf; sauté 2 minutes. Add potato, milk, pepper, and broth; bring to a boil.
**4.** Reduce heat, and simmer 10 minutes. Stir in parsley, if desired. Top individual servings with bacon, green onions, and cheese. Yield: 18 servings (serving size: 1 cup soup, about 1 teaspoon bacon, about 1 tablespoon green onions, and about 1 tablespoon cheese).

CALORIES 237 (30% from fat); FAT 7.8g (sat 3.5g, mono 3.1g, poly 0.8g); PROTEIN 10.5g; CARB 31.8g; FIBER 3.1g; CHOL 15mg; IRON 2mg; SODIUM 394mg; CALC 228mg

## Cornmeal Cheese Twists

Measure the cornmeal and grate the cheeses ahead of time.

- ¼ cup water
- 4 large egg whites
- 1 cup yellow cornmeal
- 1 cup (4 ounces) grated Asiago cheese
- 1 cup (4 ounces) grated fresh Parmesan cheese
- 1 teaspoon paprika
- Cooking spray
- 4 (11-ounce) cans refrigerated soft breadsticks (such as Pillsbury)

**1.** Preheat oven to 375°.

**2.** Combine water and egg whites in a shallow bowl. Combine cornmeal, Asiago and Parmesan cheeses, and paprika in a shallow bowl. Coat 2 baking sheets with cooking spray.

**3.** Unroll dough, separating into strips. Roll each piece into a 7-inch-long strip. Dip 2 strips in egg white mixture; dredge in cornmeal mixture. Twist strips together, pinching ends to seal; place on baking sheet. Repeat procedure with remaining dough strips, egg white mixture, and cornmeal mixture. Bake at 375° for 15 minutes or until golden brown. Yield: 2 dozen twists (serving size: 1 twist).

CALORIES 202 (24% from fat); FAT 5.3g (sat 2.2g, mono 1.6g, poly 1.2g); PROTEIN 8.3g; CARB 29.9g; FIBER 0.3g; CHOL 8mg; IRON 1.7mg; SODIUM 521mg; CALC 107mg

## Hot Spiced Cheer

If you don't have cheesecloth, remove tea leaves from an ordinary tea bag, fill the empty bag with the cloves and ginger, and tie it securely with the tea bag string; let the cinnamon sticks float separately while simmering. Serve in a decorative punch bowl alongside a small pitcher of rum marked with a label or card. You may want to have an extra sachet and more of the cider mixture handy in case you have thirsty guests.

- 10 whole cloves
- 4 (3-inch) cinnamon sticks
- 4 pieces crystallized ginger, chopped
- 1 gallon apple cider
- 4 cups pineapple juice
- 2 cups orange juice
- ¼ cup fresh lemon juice
- ⅓ cup sugar
- ¼ teaspoon salt
- White rum (optional)

**1.** Place first 3 ingredients on a double layer of cheesecloth. Gather edges of cheesecloth together; tie securely.

**2.** Combine cheesecloth bag, cider and next 5 ingredients in a large stockpot; bring to a boil. Reduce heat, and simmer 20 minutes. Discard cheesecloth bag. Serve with rum, if desired. Yield: 22 cups (serving size: 1 cup).

CALORIES 133 (1% from fat); FAT 0.2g (sat 0g, mono 0g, poly 0.1g); PROTEIN 0.4g; CARB 33g; FIBER 0.5g; CHOL 0mg; IRON 0.8mg; SODIUM 33mg; CALC 23mg

## Coconut-Macadamia Nut Cookies

You can make these cookies a day or two before the party and store in an airtight container.

- 1 cup all-purpose flour
- 1 cup regular oats
- 1 cup packed brown sugar
- ⅓ cup golden raisins
- ⅓ cup flaked sweetened coconut
- ¼ cup chopped macadamia nuts
- ½ teaspoon baking soda
- ¼ cup butter or stick margarine, melted
- 3 tablespoons water
- 2 tablespoons honey
- Cooking spray

**1.** Preheat oven to 325°.

**2.** Lightly spoon flour into a dry measuring cup, and level with a knife. Combine flour and next 6 ingredients. Combine butter, water, and honey, stirring well. Add butter mixture to flour mixture, stirring until well-blended. Drop by level tablespoons 2 inches apart onto baking sheets coated with cooking spray. Bake at 325° for 10 minutes or until almost set. Cool on pan 2 to 3 minutes or until firm. Remove from pan; cool on wire racks. Yield: 2½ dozen (serving size: 1 cookie).

CALORIES 90 (30% from fat); FAT 3g (sat 1.5g, mono 1.2g, poly 0.2g); PROTEIN 1.1g; CARB 15.4g; FIBER 0.5g; CHOL 4mg; IRON 0.5mg; SODIUM 43mg; CALC 10mg

---

## Simply Open

Hosting an open house is a great way to spend time with family and friends without adding the stress of a sit-down dinner. Here are some timesaving ideas for hosting an open house; do these early in the week, and you'll stay ahead of schedule and have more time to spend with your guests.

- Write down your shopping list.
- Buy nonperishable food items such as dried spices and canned goods, and set them aside with the recipes.
- Clean and set aside utensils, plates, bowls, cups, and serving pieces. Have extra glasses on hand—people tend to set one down, forget it, and grab a new one.
- Wrap sets of silverware in festive napkins tied with ribbon.
- Find coloring books and other toys that will keep children entertained.
- Move fragile items out of harm's way—and higher than small children can reach.
- Rearrange furniture so guests can move easily through rooms and gather in comfortable places.
- Collect enough logs to keep a fire blazing all day—or if it's more temperate where you live, position festive candles around the room to give your home a cozy feel.
- If you're serving an apéritif as your guests gather or wine with dinner, tie a piece of rosemary or pine to the bottle, and allow your friends to pour their own.

Baked Fish with Roasted
Potatoes, Tomatoes, and
Salmoriglio Sauce, page 357

Pea-and-Pasta Soup Sips,
page 356

Southwestern Breakfast
Casserole, Warm Ham
with Shallots and Vinegar,
and Spiced Winter Fruit,
pages 350 and 351

Corn Bread, Cherry, and
Bacon Stuffing, page 359

Two-Layer Caramel-Pecan
Bars, page 372

Easy Caramel-Banana
Galette, page 357

# How to Make the Ultimate Light Cookie

*Our yearlong series comes to a perfect end with holiday treats for both your hands and your mouth.*

Cookies and winter holidays belong together like children gathered around a crackling fire. But what about low-fat cookies? Do they belong to the same cozy scenario? You bet.

In fact, we've created an assortment of nine terrific recipes that includes just about every type of cookie there is: bar, drop, rolled, sliced, or cut into strips.

### Spicy Oatmeal Crisps

Pepper may sound like an odd ingredient for a cookie, but it complements the other spices well (although it can be omitted).

 ¾ cup all-purpose flour
 1 teaspoon ground cinnamon
 ½ teaspoon baking soda
 ½ teaspoon ground allspice
 ½ teaspoon grated whole nutmeg
 ¼ teaspoon salt
 ¼ teaspoon ground cloves
 ¼ teaspoon freshly ground black pepper (optional)
 1 cup packed brown sugar
 5 tablespoons butter or stick margarine, softened
 1 teaspoon vanilla extract
 1 large egg
 ½ cup regular oats
 Cooking spray

**1.** Preheat oven to 350°.
**2.** Lightly spoon flour into dry measuring cups; level with a knife. Combine flour, next 6 ingredients, and pepper, if desired, in a medium bowl. Beat sugar, butter, and vanilla in a large bowl at medium speed of a mixer until light and fluffy. Add egg; beat well. Stir in flour mixture and oats.
**3.** Drop by level tablespoons 2 inches apart onto baking sheets coated with cooking spray. Bake at 350° for 12 minutes or until crisp. Cool on pan 2 to 3 minutes or until firm. Remove cookies from pan; cool on wire racks. Yield: 2 dozen (serving size: 1 cookie).

CALORIES 81 (34% from fat); FAT 3.1g (sat 1.7g, mono 0.9g, poly 0.3g); PROTEIN 1.5g; CARB 12.2g; FIBER 0.7g; CHOL 15mg; IRON 0.6mg; SODIUM 71mg; CALC 12mg

## Spicy Oatmeal Crisps Step-by-Steps

*Measuring the exact amount of dough for each cookie can be tedious, so here's a shortcut. Measure your first few with a teaspoon or tablespoon so you can gauge the amount of dough; then increase your speed with this two-spoon technique.*

**1.** *With one spoon, pick up about the same amount of dough.*
**2.** *With the other spoon, push the dough off onto the baking sheet.*
**3.** *Keep the mounds of dough sized similarly for more uniform baking. And be sure to leave the recommended space between the cookies to allow for spreading.*

### Espresso Meringue Cookies

Be sure your bowl and beaters are completely clean; any trace of grease will prevent the egg whites from reaching maximum volume. These "kisses" are small; the whole recipe will probably fit on two large baking sheets. Parchment paper prevents sticking.

 4 large egg whites
 ¼ teaspoon cream of tartar
 ¼ teaspoon salt
 1 cup sugar
 1½ tablespoons instant espresso or 3 tablespoons instant coffee granules
 1 teaspoon vanilla extract
 36 whole coffee beans
 1 teaspoon unsweetened cocoa

**1.** Adjust oven racks to divide oven into even thirds.
**2.** Preheat oven to 250°.
**3.** Beat egg whites, cream of tartar, and salt at high speed of a mixer until foamy. Add sugar, 1 tablespoon at a time, beating until stiff peaks form. Add espresso and vanilla; beat until well-blended.
**4.** Cover 2 baking sheets with parchment paper; secure to baking sheets with masking tape. Drop batter by level tablespoons onto prepared baking sheets. Top each mound with 1 coffee bean. Sprinkle evenly with cocoa. Bake at 250° for 2 hours or until dry. (Meringues are done when the surface is dry, and meringues can be removed from paper without sticking to fingers.) Turn oven off, and partially open oven door; leave meringues in oven 1 hour. Remove from oven; carefully remove meringues from paper. Cool completely on wire racks. Yield: 3 dozen (serving size: 1 cookie).
**NOTE:** Do not use egg substitute in place of egg whites.

CALORIES 24 (0% from fat); FAT 0g; PROTEIN 0.4g; CARB 5.7g; FIBER 0g; CHOL 0mg; IRON 0mg; SODIUM 22mg; CALC 1mg

## Gingerbread Little Cakes

Many years ago, cookies were sometimes called "little cakes." This updated version is soft and spicy, with extra flavor from crystallized ginger and cardamom.

　⅓　cup finely chopped crystallized ginger
　1　tablespoon all-purpose flour
　½　cup packed brown sugar
　½　cup molasses
　1　tablespoon ground cinnamon
　2　teaspoons ground ginger
　1　teaspoon ground cardamom
　1½　teaspoons baking soda
　½　cup butter or stick margarine
　1　large egg
　2⅔　cups all-purpose flour
　　　Cooking spray

**1.** Preheat oven to 325°.
**2.** Combine crystallized ginger and 1 tablespoon flour, tossing to coat; set aside.
**3.** Combine sugar, molasses, cinnamon, ground ginger, and cardamom in a saucepan. Bring to a boil over medium heat, stirring occasionally. Stir in baking soda. (Mixture will become thick and foamy.) Remove from heat. Add butter, stirring until butter melts. Add egg; stir well with a whisk. Lightly spoon 2⅔ cups flour into dry measuring cups; level with a knife. Gradually stir 2⅔ cups flour and crystallized ginger mixture into sugar mixture.
**4.** Turn dough out onto a flat surface; knead lightly 4 or 5 times. Cool slightly. Divide dough in half. Roll each portion into ¼-inch thickness on a lightly floured surface; cut dough with a 2½-inch cutter. Place on baking sheets coated with cooking spray. Bake at 325° for 12 minutes. Cool on pans 2 minutes or until firm. Remove cookies from pans; cool on wire racks. Yield: 3 dozen (serving size: 1 cookie).

CALORIES 87 (30% from fat); FAT 2.9g (sat 1.7g, mono 0.8g, poly 0.2g); PROTEIN 1.1g; CARB 14g; FIBER 0.3g; CHOL 13mg; IRON 1mg; SODIUM 66mg; CALC 18mg

## Raspberry Strippers

Think of these as a variation of thumbprint cookies. Vanilla butter cookies are filled with fruit preserves and drizzled with a powdered sugar glaze.

　⅓　cup granulated sugar
　5　tablespoons butter or stick margarine, softened
　1½　teaspoons vanilla extract
　1　large egg white
　1　cup all-purpose flour
　2　tablespoons cornstarch
　¼　teaspoon baking powder
　¼　teaspoon salt
　　　Cooking spray
　⅓　cup raspberry or apricot preserves
　½　cup powdered sugar
　2　teaspoons fresh lemon juice
　¼　teaspoon almond or vanilla extract

**1.** Preheat oven to 375°.
**2.** Beat granulated sugar and butter at medium speed of a mixer until well-blended (about 5 minutes). Add 1½ teaspoons vanilla and egg white; beat well. Lightly spoon flour into a dry measuring cup; level with a knife. Combine flour, cornstarch, baking powder, and salt, stirring well with a whisk. Add flour mixture to sugar mixture, stirring until well-blended. (Dough will be stiff.)
**3.** Turn dough out onto a lightly floured surface. Divide dough in half. Roll each portion into a 12-inch log. Place logs 3 inches apart on a baking sheet coated with cooking spray. Form a ½-inch-deep indentation down length of each log using an index finger or end of a wooden spoon. Spoon preserves into indentation. Bake at 375° for 20 minutes or until lightly browned. Remove to a cutting board.
**4.** Combine powdered sugar, lemon juice, and almond extract; stir well with a whisk. Drizzle sugar mixture over warm logs. Immediately cut each log diagonally into 12 slices. (Do not separate slices.) Cool 10 minutes; separate slices. Transfer slices to wire racks. Cool completely. Yield: 2 dozen (serving size: 1 cookie).

CALORIES 75 (30% from fat); FAT 2.5g (sat 1.5g, mono 0.7g, poly 0.2g); PROTEIN 0.7g; CARB 12.4g; FIBER 0.2g; CHOL 6mg; IRON 0.3mg; SODIUM 56mg; CALC 4mg

## Truffle-Iced Sugar Cookies

**COOKIES:**

　1　cup all-purpose flour
　¼　teaspoon baking soda
　⅛　teaspoon salt
　4　tablespoons butter or stick margarine, softened
　⅔　cup granulated sugar
　1　teaspoon vanilla extract
　1　large egg white
　　　Cooking spray

**ICING:**

　1　cup powdered sugar
　2　teaspoons unsweetened cocoa
　1　tablespoon fat-free milk
　½　ounce semisweet chocolate
　½　ounce white chocolate

**1.** To prepare cookies, lightly spoon flour into a dry measuring cup; level with a knife. Combine flour, baking soda, and salt in a bowl, stirring well with a whisk; set aside. Beat butter at medium speed of a mixer until light and fluffy. Gradually add granulated sugar, beating until well-blended. Add vanilla and egg white; beat well. Add flour mixture; stir until well-blended. Turn dough out onto wax paper; shape into a 6-inch log. Wrap log in wax paper; freeze 3 hours or until very firm.
**2.** Preheat oven to 350°.
**3.** Cut log into 24 (¼-inch) slices; place slices 1 inch apart on a baking sheet coated with cooking spray. Bake at 350° for 8 to 10 minutes. Remove from pan; cool on wire racks.
**4.** To prepare icing, combine powdered sugar and cocoa in a small bowl; stir well. Add milk; stir well. Spread over cookies to within ¼ inch of edges. Place semisweet and white chocolate in separate heavy-duty zip-top plastic bags; seal. Microwave at HIGH 1 minute or until chocolates are soft. Knead bags until smooth. Snip a tiny hole in a corner of each bag; drizzle chocolates over frosted cookies to resemble truffles. Yield: 2 dozen (serving size: 1 cookie).

CALORIES 88 (28% from fat); FAT 2.7g (sat 1.5g, mono 0.8g, poly 0.2g); PROTEIN 1g; CARB 15.4g; FIBER 0.1g; CHOL 14mg; IRON 0.3mg; SODIUM 49mg; CALC 5mg

## Gingerbread Little Cakes:

**1.** *Working with one half of the dough at a time, roll it to a ¼-inch thickness. Try not to use too much additional flour on the countertop, since it can make the cookies dry.*

**2.** *Cut the dough into "little cakes," using a 2½-inch cutter.*

**3.** *Transfer each cut-out cookie to a baking sheet with a flat spatula.*

## Raspberry Strippers:

**1.** *Shape each portion of dough into a 12-inch log. Make a trough about ½-inch deep down the center of each log, using your index finger or the end of a wooden spoon.*

**2.** *Spoon preserves into the center.*

**3.** *Drizzle glaze over warm logs; immediately cut diagonally into 12 slices. After letting the cookies cool 10 minutes, transfer to wire racks.*

## Truffle-Iced Sugar Cookies:

**1.** *Wrap dough in wax paper. Freeze for 3 hours or until very firm.*

**2.** *Cut log into 24 (¼-inch) slices using a very sharp knife.*

## Two-Layer Caramel-Pecan Bars Step-by-Step

**1.** *Use your fingers to press the flour mixture evenly and firmly into the bottom of the pan; a compact layer holds together when cut.*

### Two-Layer Caramel-Pecan Bars

(pictured on page 368)

These bars have a crunchy brown sugar base and a gooey caramel top. Try cutting the panful into four equal strips, using firm pressure with a large, heavy knife. After removing the strips, cut each crosswise into five pieces.

⅓ cup packed brown sugar
¼ cup butter or stick margarine, softened
1 teaspoon vanilla extract
¼ teaspoon salt
¾ cup all-purpose flour
Cooking spray
2 tablespoons fat-free milk
40 small soft caramel candies
1 teaspoon vanilla extract
¼ cup finely chopped pecans

**1.** Preheat oven to 375°.
**2.** Beat first 4 ingredients at medium speed of a mixer until well-blended. Lightly spoon flour into dry measuring cups; level with a knife. Add flour to sugar mixture, stirring until well-blended. (Mixture will be crumbly.) Firmly press mixture into bottom of an 8-inch square baking pan coated with cooking spray. Bake at 375° for 15 minutes.
**3.** While crust is baking, combine milk and caramel candies in a medium saucepan. Place over low heat; cook until candies melt, stirring occasionally. Stir in 1 teaspoon vanilla; remove from heat.
**4.** Remove crust from oven. Pour caramel mixture evenly over hot crust. Sprinkle with pecans. Bake at 375° for 15 minutes. Cool completely on a wire rack. Yield: 20 bars (serving size: 1 bar).

CALORIES 123 (34% from fat); FAT 4.7g (sat 2.6g, mono 1.5g, poly 0.4g); PROTEIN 1.4g; CARB 19.6g; FIBER 0.4g; CHOL 7mg; IRON 0.3mg; SODIUM 94mg; CALC 29mg

### Lemon-Honey Drop Cookies

½ cup granulated sugar
7 tablespoons butter or stick margarine, softened
2 teaspoons grated lemon rind
⅓ cup honey
½ teaspoon lemon extract
1 large egg
1¾ cups all-purpose flour
1 teaspoon baking powder
½ teaspoon salt
¼ cup plain fat-free yogurt
Cooking spray
1 cup powdered sugar
2 tablespoons fresh lemon juice
2 teaspoons grated lemon rind

**1.** Preheat oven to 350°.
**2.** Beat first 3 ingredients at medium speed of a mixer until light and fluffy. Add honey, extract, and egg; beat until well-blended. Lightly spoon flour into dry measuring cups; level with a knife. Combine flour, baking powder, and salt, stirring well with a whisk. Add flour mixture to sugar mixture alternately with yogurt, beginning and ending with flour mixture. Drop by level tablespoons 2 inches apart onto baking sheets coated with cooking spray. Bake at 350° for 12 minutes or until lightly browned.
**3.** Combine powdered sugar and juice in a small bowl; stir with a whisk. Brush powdered sugar mixture evenly over hot cookies. Sprinkle evenly with 2 teaspoons rind. Remove cookies from pan; cool on wire racks. Yield: 32 cookies (serving size: 1 cookie).

CALORIES 89 (28% from fat); FAT 2.8g (sat 1.6g, mono 0.8g, poly 0.2g); PROTEIN 1.1g; CARB 15.3g; FIBER 0.2g; CHOL 14mg; IRON 0.4mg; SODIUM 81mg; CALC 15mg

### Chocolate-Mint Brownies

Each layer needs to cool completely before the next step; these are best served cold. Either white or green crème de menthe is OK.

**BROWNIES:**

6 tablespoons butter or stick margarine
1 cup Dutch process cocoa
3 tablespoons evaporated fat-free milk
1 cup packed brown sugar
½ cup granulated sugar
2 teaspoons vanilla extract
4 large egg whites
1 cup all-purpose flour
½ teaspoon baking powder
¼ teaspoon salt
Cooking spray

**ICING:**

1 cup powdered sugar
1 tablespoon butter or stick margarine, softened
1 tablespoon crème de menthe or ¼ teaspoon mint extract

**GLAZE:**

1 ounce unsweetened chocolate
1 tablespoon butter or stick margarine

**1.** Preheat oven to 325°.
**2.** To prepare brownies, melt 6 tablespoons butter in a medium saucepan over medium heat. Stir in cocoa and milk; cook 1 minute, stirring constantly. Add brown sugar, granulated sugar, and vanilla; cook 1 minute, stirring constantly. (Mixture will be granular.) Remove from heat; cool 5 minutes. Add egg whites, 1 at a time, stirring well after each addition. Lightly spoon flour into a dry measuring cup; level with a knife.

Combine flour, baking powder, and salt, stirring well with a whisk. Add flour mixture to cocoa mixture, stirring until well-blended. Pour batter into a 9-inch square baking pan coated with cooking spray. Bake at 325° for 25 minutes or until brownie barely springs back when touched lightly in center; cool completely on a wire rack.

**3.** To prepare icing, combine powdered sugar, 1 tablespoon butter, and liqueur. Beat at medium speed of a mixer until smooth. Spread icing evenly over brownie layer; refrigerate 30 minutes or until icing is set.

**4.** To prepare glaze, place chocolate in a small microwave-safe dish. Microwave at HIGH 45 seconds; stir in 1 tablespoon butter. Microwave at HIGH 20 seconds. Stir until smooth. Drizzle glaze over icing; refrigerate 30 minutes or until glaze is set. Yield: 25 servings (serving size: 1 brownie).

CALORIES 146 (30% from fat); FAT 4.9g (sat 2.9g, mono 1.4g, poly 0.2g); PROTEIN 2.3g; CARB 23.5g; FIBER 0.2g; CHOL 10mg; IRON 1.1mg; SODIUM 83mg; CALC 25mg

### Chewy Coconut Macaroons

    ¾  cup all-purpose flour
    2½ cups flaked sweetened coconut
    1½ teaspoons vanilla extract
    ⅛  teaspoon salt
    1  (14-ounce) can fat-free sweetened
       condensed milk

**1.** Preheat oven to 250°.

**2.** Lightly spoon flour into dry measuring cups; level with a knife. Combine flour and coconut in a medium bowl; toss well. Add vanilla, salt, and milk; stir until well-blended. (Mixture will be very thick.)

**3.** Drop batter by scant tablespoons (about 2 teaspoons) 2 inches apart onto a baking sheet lined with parchment paper. Bake at 250° for 50 minutes or until golden brown. Remove from pan; cool completely on wire racks. Yield: 32 cookies (serving size: 1 cookie).

CALORIES 82 (29% from fat); FAT 2.6g (sat 2.3g, mono 0.1g, poly 0g); PROTEIN 1.5g; CARB 13.3g; FIBER 0.5g; CHOL 2mg; IRON 0.3mg; SODIUM 41mg; CALC 33mg

### Gear for Your Goodies

Both handheld and stand mixers work fine for cookie doughs. Newer handheld electric mixers are very powerful and can handle even the thickest doughs. A stand mixer, however, frees your hands.

For even baking, use a heavy baking or cookie sheet (which has a lip on one or both ends). Baking sheets make it easier to add or remove silicon pan liners or parchment paper, both of which eliminate any need for greasing the pan and help maintain the cookies' shape during baking.

A larger baking sheet (17 x 14 inches) allows you to bake more cookies at a time than a standard 15 x 12-inch pan. Popular cushion-air pans work fine, but they're not necessarily better than a good-quality, heavy cookie sheet. You can reduce the risk of cookies burning on the bottom by using a silver-colored aluminum baking sheet rather than a dark one.

### Bakers' Secrets

Bake cookies in an oven that has been preheated for 15 minutes. Check for doneness at the earliest suggested time because opening and closing the oven too often can change baking times.

We always bake cookies on the second rack from the bottom. Be sure there is room left for air to circulate on all sides after the baking sheet is in place on the rack. An exception is the Espresso Meringue Cookies (recipe on page 369), for which two baking sheets are in the oven at the same time.

# From the Kitchen with Love

*The best gifts come from the heart, often by way of the hands.*

They say the gift of labor is the true gift of love. With these food gift ideas, you'll measure up well.

### Pumpkin-Orange Spice Loaf

Pumpkin is rich in beta carotene and vitamin C, while whole-wheat flour adds an extra dose of fiber. Wrap loaf in plastic wrap, cinch top with festive ribbon, and place decorative stickers around the top and sides.

    1½ cups all-purpose flour
    ½  cup whole-wheat flour
    2  teaspoons baking powder
    ½  teaspoon baking soda
    1½ teaspoons ground cinnamon
    ½  teaspoon salt
    ¼  teaspoon ground ginger
    ¼  teaspoon ground cloves
    1  cup sugar
    1  cup canned pumpkin
    ½  cup fat-free milk
    ¼  cup butter or stick margarine,
       softened
    1  tablespoon grated orange rind
    ¼  cup fresh orange juice
    1  large egg
    Cooking spray

**1.** Preheat oven to 350°.

**2.** Lightly spoon flours into dry measuring cups; level with a knife. Combine flours and next 6 ingredients in a large bowl; make a well in center of mixture. Combine sugar and next 6 ingredients in a bowl; stir with a whisk. Add to flour mixture; stir just until moist. Pour batter into an 8 x 4-inch loaf pan coated with
*Continued*

cooking spray. Bake at 350° for 1 hour and 10 minutes or until a wooden pick inserted in center comes out clean. Cool in pan 10 minutes on a wire rack; remove from pan. Cool completely on wire rack. Yield: 12 servings (serving size: 1 slice).

CALORIES 193 (22% from fat); FAT 4.7g (sat 2.6g, mono 1.3g, poly 0.3g); PROTEIN 3.5g; CARB 35.4g; FIBER 2g; CHOL 29mg; IRON 1.5mg; SODIUM 283mg; CALC 76mg

## Mozzarella-Ham Swirl Bread

The ham and cheese add protein, but this bread is still low in fat. Wrap the loaf in plastic wrap with red and green ribbons, and present it in a bread basket lined with a decorative napkin.

    2   tablespoons sugar, divided
    1   package dry yeast (about 2¼
        teaspoons)
    ¼   cup warm water (100° to 110°)
    2¼  cups all-purpose flour, divided
    ½   cup fat-free milk
    2   tablespoons butter or stick
        margarine, melted
    ½   teaspoon salt
    Cooking spray
    ½   cup chopped reduced-fat ham
    ½   cup (2 ounces) shredded
        part-skim mozzarella cheese
    ¼   cup chopped pimento-stuffed
        olives
    ⅛   to ¼ teaspoon crushed red pepper
    2   teaspoons Dijon mustard
    1   large egg white, lightly beaten
    1   tablespoon water
    ½   teaspoon dried Italian seasoning

**1.** Dissolve 1 tablespoon sugar and yeast in warm water in a large bowl; let stand 5 minutes. Lightly spoon flour into dry measuring cups; level with a knife. Add 1 tablespoon sugar, 1½ cups flour, milk, butter, and salt to yeast mixture; beat at medium speed of a mixer until smooth. Turn dough out onto a floured surface. Knead until smooth and elastic (about 10 minutes); add enough of remaining flour, 1 tablespoon at a time, to prevent dough from sticking to hands.

**2.** Place dough in a large bowl coated with cooking spray, turning to coat top. Cover and let rise in a warm place (85°), free from drafts, 1 hour or until doubled in size. (Press two fingers into dough. If indentations remain, the dough has risen enough.)

**3.** Combine ham, cheese, olives, and pepper. Set aside.

**4.** Uncover dough. Punch dough down; let rest 5 minutes. Roll into a 12 x 8-inch rectangle on a lightly floured surface. Brush mustard over dough leaving a ½-inch margin around edges. Spread ham mixture evenly over dough. Beginning with a short side, roll up jelly-roll fashion; pinch seam to seal (do not seal ends of roll). Place, seam side down, in an 8 x 4-inch loaf pan coated with cooking spray. Cover and let rise 30 minutes.

**5.** Preheat oven to 375°.

**6.** Uncover dough. Combine egg white and 1 tablespoon water, and brush over dough. Sprinkle dough with Italian seasoning. Bake at 375° for 30 minutes. Loosely cover with foil. Bake an additional 10 minutes or until loaf sounds hollow when tapped. Remove loaf from pan, and cool on a wire rack. Yield: 12 servings (serving size: 1 slice).

CALORIES 141 (22% from fat); FAT 3.5g (sat 1.8g, mono 1.1g, poly 0.3g); PROTEIN 5.8g; CARB 21.1g; FIBER 0.9g; CHOL 11mg; IRON 1.4mg; SODIUM 281mg; CALC 52mg

## Buckwheat Pancake Mix

Spoon the dry mix into gift bags. Attach the remainder of the recipe on a note card.

**PANCAKE MIX:**
    1½  cups whole-wheat flour
    1   cup buckwheat flour
    3   tablespoons sugar
    2½  teaspoons baking powder
    ½   teaspoon baking soda
    ¼   teaspoon salt

**REMAINING INGREDIENTS:**
    2½  cups low-fat buttermilk
    1   tablespoon stick margarine or
        butter, melted
    1   teaspoon vanilla extract
    1   large egg white

**1.** To prepare pancake mix, lightly spoon flours into dry measuring cups; level with a knife. Combine flours and next 4 ingredients in a large bowl. Store mix in an airtight container until ready to use.

**2.** To prepare pancake batter, combine buttermilk and remaining 3 ingredients; add to pancake mix, stirring until smooth.

**3.** Spoon about ¼ cup batter for each pancake onto a hot nonstick griddle or nonstick skillet. Turn pancakes when tops are covered with bubbles and edges look cooked. Cook 1 additional minute. Yield: 6 servings (serving size: 3 pancakes).

CALORIES 266 (16% from fat); FAT 4.8g (sat 2.5g, mono 1.3g, poly 0.6g); PROTEIN 11g; CARB 47.8g; FIBER 5.8g; CHOL 5mg; IRON 2.2mg; SODIUM 488mg; CALC 258mg

## Cranberry-Hazelnut Coffeecake

**STREUSEL:**
    ¼   cup sifted cake flour
    ¼   cup packed brown sugar
    ¼   cup chopped hazelnuts
    ½   teaspoon ground cinnamon
    1   tablespoon butter or stick
        margarine, melted

**CAKE:**
    1⅔  cups sifted cake flour
    1   cup granulated sugar
    1½  teaspoons baking powder
    ¼   teaspoon baking soda
    ¼   teaspoon salt
    1   teaspoon vanilla extract
    1   (8-ounce) carton fat-free sour
        cream, divided
    1   large egg
    1   large egg white
    5   tablespoons butter or stick
        margarine, softened

**REMAINING INGREDIENTS:**
    Cooking spray
    2   cups fresh cranberries, chopped

**1.** Preheat oven to 350°.

**2.** To prepare streusel, combine first 5 ingredients in a bowl, and toss well. Set aside.

**3.** To prepare cake, combine sifted cake flour and next 4 ingredients, stirring well with a whisk. Combine vanilla, ¼ cup sour cream, egg, and egg white in a small bowl; stir with a whisk. Place remaining sour cream and 5 tablespoons butter in a large bowl; beat at medium speed of a mixer until well-blended (about 2 minutes). Add flour mixture to butter mixture alternately with egg mixture, beginning and ending with flour mixture.

**4.** Spread half of batter into a 9-inch springform pan coated with cooking spray. Sprinkle cranberries over batter. Spread remaining batter over cranberries. Sprinkle streusel mixture over batter. Bake at 350° for 45 minutes or until a wooden pick inserted in center comes out clean. Cool on a wire rack. Yield: 10 servings (serving size: 1 wedge).

CALORIES 293 (30% from fat); FAT 9.8g (sat 4.7g, mono 3.9g, poly 0.6g); PROTEIN 4.9g; CARB 46.6g; FIBER 0.4g; CHOL 41mg; IRON 2mg; SODIUM 265mg; CALC 63mg

## Party Mix with Almonds and Apricots

Almonds are rich in monounsaturated fat, while apricots and cereal provide iron and fiber. Our version of party mix has half the fat and sodium of the traditional mix. Scoop party mix into clear gift bags, and secure the tops with ribbon.

    3   cups fat-free sourdough pretzel
        nuggets
    3   cups crispy corn-cereal squares
        (such as Corn Chex)
    ½   cup slivered almonds
    1   (6-ounce) bag low-sodium baked
        bagel chips, broken into 1-inch
        pieces (about 3 cups)
    2   tablespoons chili powder
    1   tablespoon ground cumin
    ¼   teaspoon salt
Butter-flavored cooking spray
    1   (6-ounce) package dried apricots,
        quartered

**1.** Preheat oven to 250°.
**2.** Combine first 4 ingredients. Spread pretzel mixture in a jelly-roll pan.

Combine chili powder, cumin, and salt. Lightly coat pretzel mixture with cooking spray; sprinkle with chili powder mixture. Bake at 250° for 15 minutes; stir in apricots. Bake an additional 30 minutes, stirring once. Yield: 11 cups (serving size: ½ cup).

CALORIES 136 (20% from fat); FAT 3g (sat 0.4g, mono 1.1g, poly 1.2g); PROTEIN 3g; CARB 19g; FIBER 1.3g; CHOL 0mg; IRON 1.5mg; SODIUM 184mg; CALC 15mg

## Sturdy Multigrain Bread

With cereal and whole-wheat and rye flours, this bread is a good source of fiber. Line a basket with a decorative napkin and fill it with assorted preserves and a loaf wrapped in plastic wrap.

    1¾  cups water
    1¼  cups multigrain hot cereal (such as
        Quaker)
    1   package dry yeast (about 2¼
        teaspoons)
    2   tablespoons honey
    1⅔  cups warm water (100° to 110°)
    ¼   cup plain low-fat yogurt
    3   tablespoons vegetable oil
    2½  cups bread flour, divided
    2   cups whole-wheat flour
    1   cup rye flour
    2   teaspoons salt
Cooking spray

**1.** Bring 1¾ cups water to a boil in a medium saucepan; stir in cereal. Cook 1 minute over medium-low heat or until liquid is nearly absorbed, stirring occasionally. Remove from heat; let stand, covered, 30 minutes or until cool.
**2.** Dissolve yeast and honey in warm water in a large bowl; let stand 5 minutes. Stir in yogurt and oil. Lightly spoon flours into dry measuring cups; level with a knife. Combine 1½ cups bread flour, whole-wheat flour, rye flour, and salt; add to yeast mixture, stirring until well-blended. Turn bread out onto a lightly floured surface; knead in cereal mixture. Knead until smooth and elastic (about 8 minutes); add enough of remaining flour, 1 tablespoon at a time, to prevent dough from sticking to hands.

**3.** Place dough in a large bowl coated with cooking spray, turning to coat top. Cover and let rise in a warm place (85°), free from drafts, 1 hour or until doubled in size. (Press two fingers into dough. If indentation remains, the dough has risen enough.) Punch dough down; roll into a 14 x 7-inch rectangle on a lightly floured surface. Roll up rectangle tightly, starting with a short edge, pressing firmly to eliminate air pockets; pinch seam and ends to seal. Place roll, seam side down, in a 9 x 5-inch loaf pan coated with cooking spray. Cover and let rise 1 hour or until doubled in size.
**4.** Preheat oven to 350°.
**5.** Uncover dough. Bake at 350° for 50 minutes or until loaf sounds hollow when tapped. Remove from pan; cool on a wire rack. Yield: 16 slices (serving size: 1 slice).

CALORIES 207 (16% from fat); FAT 3.6g (sat 0.6g, mono 0.9g, poly 1.5g); PROTEIN 6.3g; CARB 38.7g; FIBER 4.1g; CHOL 0mg; IRON 1.9mg; SODIUM 297mg; CALC 17mg

## in season

# Oh My Darlin'

*Clementines come mostly from the place where the rain falls mainly on the plain, but they've found a happy home in America.*

We should be grateful to Spain for the country's most exquisite export—the fragrant, bright-orange mandarin oranges known as clementines. The fruits were named after Father Clément, the priest who began cultivating them in Algeria at the start of the 20th century.

Like tangerines, clementines are extremely easy to work with. Their skin is loose and easy to peel, and the silky flesh inside is virtually seedless. With sugary as well as tart notes, clementines lend themselves to both savory or sweet dishes, and are especially good in sauces, whether for a soufflélike Dutch baby or for a roast chicken. There's a nutritional payoff, too. An average clementine packs up to half of the Recommended Dietary Allowance for vitamin C and is also a good source of fiber.

*Continued*

## Roasted Chicken with Clementine-and-Cranberry Sauce

If you're looking for a quick dinner solution, you can just make the sauce and serve it over sautéed chicken breasts.

  1  (4-pound) chicken
  ½  teaspoon kosher salt
  ¼  teaspoon black pepper
  1  clementine, quartered
  ½  cup fresh orange juice (about 2 oranges)
  ½  cup fresh cranberries
  2  tablespoons sugar
  ½  cup fat-free, less-sodium chicken broth
  1½ teaspoons cornstarch
  2  tablespoons Madeira wine or water
  2  cups clementine sections (about 6 clementines)

**1.** Preheat oven to 450°.
**2.** Remove and discard giblets and neck from chicken. Rinse chicken with cold water; pat dry. Trim excess fat. Starting at neck cavity, loosen skin from breast and drumsticks by inserting fingers, gently pushing between skin and meat. Rub salt and pepper under loosened skin, and sprinkle in body cavity. Place clementine quarters in cavity. Place chicken, breast side down, on a broiler pan. Insert meat thermometer into meaty part of thigh, making sure not to touch bone. Bake at 450° for 25 minutes. Reduce oven temperature to 350°. Turn chicken, breast side up; bake at 350° for 1 hour or until thermometer registers 180°. Cover chicken loosely with foil; let stand 10 minutes. Discard skin.
**3.** Place orange juice, cranberries, and sugar in a medium saucepan. Cook at medium-high 5 minutes or until cranberries pop; add broth. Combine cornstarch and wine in a small dish; stir into cranberry mixture. Bring to a boil; cook 1 minute, stirring constantly. Remove from heat; stir in clementine sections. Yield: 4 servings (serving size: 3 ounces chicken and ½ cup sauce).

CALORIES 285 (21% from fat); FAT 6.6g (sat 1.8g, mono 2.3g, poly 1.5g); PROTEIN 26.2g; CARB 28.8g; FIBER 3.6g; CHOL 76mg; IRON 1.3mg; SODIUM 275mg; CALC 38mg

## Dutch Baby with Warm Clementine Sauce

A Dutch baby is an impressive pancake that puffs up, and then collapses like a soufflé. Try it for a more elegant breakfast than plain pancakes or waffles.

  ½  cup water
  ¼  cup sugar
  1  teaspoon cornstarch
  2  cups clementine sections (about 6 clementines)
  1  tablespoon fresh lemon juice
     Cooking spray
  ½  cup 1% low-fat milk
  3  large eggs, lightly beaten
  ½  cup all-purpose flour
  ¼  teaspoon salt
  ¼  teaspoon ground nutmeg
  1  tablespoon butter or stick margarine, melted

**1.** Preheat oven to 425°.
**2.** Combine first 3 ingredients in a medium saucepan, stirring with a whisk. Bring to a boil; cook 1 minute or until thick. Remove from heat; stir in clementine sections and lemon juice. Keep sauce warm.
**3.** Wrap handle of a large nonstick skillet with foil; coat pan with cooking spray.
**4.** Combine milk and eggs in a large bowl, stirring with a whisk. Lightly spoon flour into a dry measuring cup; level with a knife. Combine flour, salt, and nutmeg; stir well with a whisk. Add flour mixture to milk mixture, stirring with a whisk until well-blended. Stir in butter until smooth. Pour batter into prepared pan.
**5.** Bake at 425° for 25 minutes. Remove from pan; cut into wedges. Top with clementine sauce. Serve immediately. Yield: 4 servings (serving size: 1 wedge and ½ cup sauce).

CALORIES 266 (27% from fat); FAT 8g (sat 3.4g, mono 2.6g, poly 1g); PROTEIN 8.3g; CARB 41.5g; FIBER 3.3g; CHOL 175mg; IRON 1.5mg; SODIUM 242mg; CALC 78mg

## Clementine-Chocolate Cream Tart

**PASTRY:**
  1  cup all-purpose flour
  2  tablespoons sugar
  ⅛  teaspoon salt
  ¼  cup chilled butter or stick margarine, cut into small pieces
  3  to 4 tablespoons ice water
     Cooking spray

**PASTRY CREAM:**
  ½  cup sugar
  ¼  cup cornstarch
  ¼  teaspoon salt
  2  cups 1% low-fat milk
  2  large egg yolks
  1  large egg
  1  teaspoon grated clementine rind
  1  teaspoon vanilla extract

**REMAINING INGREDIENTS:**
  2  ounces bittersweet chocolate, melted and divided
  9  clementines, peeled and cut crosswise into ¼-inch-thick slices
  ¼  cup apricot preserves, melted

**1.** Preheat oven to 375°.
**2.** To prepare pastry, lightly spoon flour into a dry measuring cup; level with a knife. Combine flour, 2 tablespoons sugar, and ⅛ teaspoon salt in a bowl; cut in butter with a pastry blender or 2 knives until mixture resembles coarse meal. Sprinkle surface with ice water, 1 tablespoon at a time; toss with a fork until moist and crumbly (do not form a ball).
**3.** Press mixture gently into a 4-inch circle on heavy-duty plastic wrap; cover with additional plastic wrap. Roll dough, still covered, into an 11-inch circle. Place dough in freezer 10 minutes or until plastic wrap can be easily removed. Remove 1 sheet of plastic wrap; let stand 1 minute or until pliable. Fit dough into a 9-inch round removable-bottom tart pan coated with cooking spray. Remove top sheet of plastic wrap. Press dough against bottom and sides of pan. Fold edges under. Pierce bottom and sides of dough with a fork; bake at 375° for 20 minutes. Cool on a wire rack.

**4.** To prepare pastry cream, combine ½ cup sugar, cornstarch, and ¼ teaspoon salt in a medium saucepan. Gradually stir in milk; bring to a boil over medium heat. Cook 1 minute, stirring constantly.
**5.** Combine egg yolks and egg in a small bowl; stir with a whisk until blended. Gradually stir about one-fourth of hot milk mixture into egg, and add to remaining milk mixture, stirring constantly. Cook over medium heat until mixture is thick and creamy, stirring frequently (about 5 minutes). Remove from heat; stir in rind and vanilla. Pour into a bowl, and cover surface of pastry cream with plastic wrap. Chill.
**6.** Spread half of melted chocolate over bottom of cooled crust. Spoon pastry cream into crust. Arrange clementine slices over pastry cream. Brush preserves over clementines. Drizzle remaining chocolate over tart. Chill completely; cut into 8 wedges. Yield: 8 servings (serving size: 1 wedge).

CALORIES 337 (30% from fat); FAT 11.1g (sat 5.9g, mono 3.4g, poly 0.8g); PROTEIN 6.2g; CARB 55.9g; FIBER 2.8g; CHOL 100mg; IRON 1.4mg; SODIUM 216mg; CALC 106mg

### Clementine Salad with Spiced Walnuts and Pickled Onions

**ONIONS:**
½ cup water
½ cup red wine vinegar
¼ cup sugar
1 cup vertically sliced red onion

**DRESSING:**
1 tablespoon orange juice
2 teaspoons olive oil
1 teaspoon Dijon mustard

**REMAINING INGREDIENTS:**
8 cups gourmet salad greens
2 cups clementine sections (about 6 clementines)
¾ cup Spiced Walnuts
6 tablespoons pomegranate seeds

**1.** To prepare onions, combine first 3 ingredients in a small saucepan. Bring to a boil; remove from heat. Reserve 2 tablespoons vinegar mixture. Combine remaining vinegar mixture and onion in a small bowl; cool to room temperature.
**2.** To prepare dressing, combine reserved 2 tablespoons vinegar mixture, orange juice, oil, and mustard; stir well with a whisk.
**3.** Combine dressing and salad greens in a large bowl; toss well. Divide salad greens mixture evenly among 6 salad plates. Top each with ⅓ cup clementines, about 2 tablespoons onions, 2 tablespoons Spiced Walnuts, and 1 tablespoon pomegranate seeds. Yield: 6 servings.

(Totals include Spiced Walnuts) CALORIES 175 (27% from fat); FAT 5.3g (sat 0.6g, mono 2g, poly 2.5g); PROTEIN 2.9g; CARB 31.7g; FIBER 3.9g; CHOL 0mg; IRON 1.2mg; SODIUM 58mg; CALC 49mg

**SPICED WALNUTS:**
Save the extra walnuts for the next time you make this salad, or enjoy them as a snack.

1 cup walnut halves
½ cup sugar
¼ cup water
½ teaspoon ground cinnamon
¼ teaspoon salt
Dash of ground red pepper
Cooking spray

**1.** Preheat oven to 350°.
**2.** Arrange walnuts in a single layer on a baking sheet. Bake at 350° for 10 minutes or until lightly browned.
**3.** Combine sugar and next 4 ingredients in a small saucepan. Cook, without stirring, until candy thermometer registers 238° (about 8 minutes). Remove from heat; stir in walnuts. Pour walnut mixture onto baking sheet coated with cooking spray. Cool completely; break into small pieces. Yield: 2 cups (serving size: 2 tablespoons).
**NOTE:** Store remaining walnuts in an airtight container.

CALORIES 60 (51% from fat); FAT 3.4g (sat 0.3g, mono 0.8g, poly 2.2g); PROTEIN 0.8g; CARB 7.3g; FIBER 0.3g; CHOL 0mg; IRON 0.2mg; SODIUM 37mg; CALC 6mg

### Jeweled Clementines with Vanilla Sauce

3 tablespoons sugar
¼ cup white wine vinegar
½ cup Grand Marnier (orange-flavored liqueur)
4 cups clementine sections (about 12 clementines)
1 tablespoon fat-free milk
1 (8-ounce) carton vanilla low-fat yogurt
Mint sprigs (optional)

**1.** Combine sugar and vinegar in a small, heavy saucepan. Bring to a boil; cook 6 minutes or until amber brown. Remove from heat; stir in liqueur.
**2.** Place clementine sections in a large bowl; pour sugar mixture over sections. Cover and chill 2 hours, stirring occasionally. Combine milk and yogurt; stir with a whisk. Spoon clementine mixture into individual bowls or stemmed glasses; top with yogurt mixture. Garnish with mint, if desired. Yield: 6 servings (serving size: about ½ cup clementine mixture and about 3 tablespoons sauce).

CALORIES 197 (4% from fat); FAT 0.9g (sat 0.4g, mono 0.2g, poly 0.1g); PROTEIN 3g; CARB 36.2g; FIBER 3.9g; CHOL 2mg; IRON 0.2mg; SODIUM 29mg; CALC 91mg

back to the best

# Buttermilk Pancakes

*You want meals to be special during the holidays, because the entire family is likely to gather. But making it special can mean keeping it simple.*

So it is with our Buttermilk Pancakes—easy to make, easy to eat. These light and fluffy hotcakes may be the ultimate comfort food, perfect for the whole family. In fact, since we introduced them in our March 1992 issue, Buttermilk Pancakes have been popular with many *Cooking Light* staffers' kids.

*Continued*

## Buttermilk Pancakes

To freeze any leftovers, place wax paper between pancakes, and wrap tightly in foil.

- 1 cup all-purpose flour
- 2 tablespoons sugar
- 1 teaspoon baking powder
- ½ teaspoon baking soda
- ¼ teaspoon salt
- 1 cup low-fat buttermilk
- 1 tablespoon vegetable oil
- 1 large egg, lightly beaten
- Cooking spray

**1.** Lightly spoon flour into a dry measuring cup; level with a knife. Combine flour and next 4 ingredients in a large bowl; make a well in center of mixture. Combine buttermilk, oil, and egg; add to flour mixture, stirring until smooth.
**2.** Spoon about ¼ cup batter for each pancake onto a hot nonstick griddle or nonstick skillet coated with cooking spray. Turn pancakes when tops are covered with bubbles and edges look cooked. Yield: 9 (4-inch) pancakes (serving size: 1 pancake).

CALORIES 99 (26% from fat); FAT 2.9g (sat 0.8g, mono 0.9g, poly 1g); PROTEIN 3.2g; CARB 14.9g; FIBER 0.4g; CHOL 25mg; IRON 0.8mg; SODIUM 211mg; CALC 69mg

## the cooking light profile

# Pared-Down Paradise

*This Texas couple simplified their lives by figuring out what they truly needed.*

Robert and Mimi Dopson came to the far-west Texas town of Alpine five years ago from Austin. Robert read a book, *Cashing In on the American Dream: How to Retire at 35* by Paul Terhorst, that changed their lives. It advocated living simply, and Robert and Mimi took its lessons to heart. The 50-something couple committed to serious lifestyle changes, agreeing to get rid of the trappings of success and things they didn't truly need.

## Fort Davis Apple Cake

"Orchards in Fort Davis, Texas, sell boxes of apples in September. We always buy a box and store it in the refrigerator until holiday baking time. Then we make several cakes to give as Christmas gifts."

—Mimi Dopson

**CAKE:**
- 2 cups all-purpose flour
- 1½ cups sugar
- 1 teaspoon baking soda
- 1 teaspoon ground cinnamon
- ¼ teaspoon salt
- ¼ teaspoon ground nutmeg
- ¼ teaspoon ground cloves
- ½ cup water
- ¼ cup butter or stick margarine, melted
- ¼ cup olive oil
- ½ teaspoon vanilla extract
- 3 large eggs, lightly beaten
- 3 cups chopped peeled Rome apple
- Cooking spray

**GLAZE:**
- ¾ cup sugar
- ½ cup low-fat buttermilk
- 1 tablespoon light-colored corn syrup
- ½ teaspoon baking soda
- ½ teaspoon vanilla extract

**1.** Preheat oven to 350°.
**2.** To prepare cake, lightly spoon flour into dry measuring cups; level with a knife. Combine flour and next 6 ingredients in a large bowl. Add water and next 4 ingredients; stir just until well-blended. Fold in apple. Spoon batter into a 12-cup Bundt pan coated with cooking spray. Bake at 350° for 50 minutes or until a wooden pick inserted in center comes out clean. Cool in pan 10 minutes on a wire rack; remove from pan. Cool completely on wire rack.
**3.** To prepare glaze, combine ¾ cup sugar, buttermilk, syrup, and ½ teaspoon soda in a saucepan. Cook over medium heat 6 minutes or until sugar is dissolved and mixture is light brown, stirring constantly. Stir in vanilla. Pour over cake. Yield: 16 servings (serving size: 1 slice).

CALORIES 257 (27% from fat); FAT 7.7g (sat 2.7g, mono 3.8g, poly 0.7g); PROTEIN 3.2g; CARB 44.7g; FIBER 0.9g; CHOL 49mg; IRON 1mg; SODIUM 203mg; CALC 21mg

## reader recipes

# Convenient in Alabama

*Can a tiramisu this easy to make be that good? Just ask Josh.*

Mari Chandler of Anniston, Alabama, loves convenience. That's the whole idea behind the "Made For You . . . by Mari" gift jars she sells at craft shows. "I decorate Mason jars," the Anniston, Alabama, executive assistant says, "and fill them with layers of everything you need to make brownies, cookies, muffins, breads, soups, beverages, and even pet treats.

Mari knows all about not having enough time, but she still finds time to cook. "I think about what I like to eat, then I try to come up with a light version of it. That's how I came up with this Tiramisu Anacapri." The hasty—and tasty—tiramisu clearly meets with the approval of her 25-year-old son, Josh, who has been known to eat half the entire dessert in a single sitting.

### Tiramisu Anacapri

This tiramisu was a hit with our Test Kitchens staff, who agreed it's one of the best they've come across. Ladyfingers can be found in the bakery or frozen-food section of the supermarket.

- 1 cup cold water
- 1 (14-ounce) can fat-free sweetened condensed milk
- 1 (1.4-ounce) package sugar-free vanilla instant pudding mix
- 1 (8-ounce) block ⅓-less-fat cream cheese, softened
- 1 (8-ounce) tub frozen reduced-calorie whipped topping, thawed
- 1 cup hot water
- ½ cup Kahlúa (coffee-flavored liqueur)
- 1 tablespoon instant espresso or 2 tablespoons instant coffee granules
- 24 ladyfingers (2 [3-ounce] packages)
- 3 tablespoons unsweetened cocoa

1. Combine first 3 ingredients in a large bowl; stir well with a whisk. Cover surface with plastic wrap; chill 30 minutes or until firm.

2. Remove plastic wrap; add cream cheese. Beat at medium speed of a mixer until well-blended. Gently fold in whipped topping.

3. Combine hot water, Kahlúa, and espresso. Split ladyfingers in half lengthwise. Arrange 16 ladyfinger halves, flat sides down, in a trifle bowl or large glass bowl. Drizzle with ½ cup Kahlúa mixture. Spread one-third of pudding mixture evenly over ladyfingers; sprinkle with 1 tablespoon cocoa. Repeat layers, ending with cocoa. Cover and chill at least 8 hours. Yield: 12 servings (serving size: about ⅔ cup).

CALORIES 310 (26% from fat); FAT 9.1g (sat 6g, mono 2.1g, poly 0.3g); PROTEIN 7.8g; CARB 44g; FIBER 0.2g; CHOL 95mg; IRON 1.1mg; SODIUM 265mg; CALC 124mg

## Turkey Lasagna

"The turkey gives this recipe a wonderful flavor that my husband and I really prefer over ground beef. Not having to cook the noodles saves time—and with three small children, that's a good thing. This dish also freezes well, so it's perfect for friends who have new babies or are feeling under the weather."

—Cathy Ward, Huntsville, Alabama

  1  pound ground turkey breast
Cooking spray
1½  cups water
  1  (26-ounce) bottle fat-free Italian pasta sauce (such as Healthy Choice)
  3  cups (12 ounces) shredded part-skim mozzarella cheese, divided
  2  cups 1% low-fat cottage cheese
  ½  cup (2 ounces) grated fresh Parmesan cheese
  ½  cup egg substitute
  ¼  cup chopped fresh parsley
  ¼  teaspoon black pepper
  9  uncooked lasagna noodles

1. Preheat oven to 350°.

2. Cook turkey in a large saucepan coated with cooking spray over medium heat until browned, stirring to crumble. Add water and pasta sauce; bring to a boil. Cover, reduce heat, and simmer 10 minutes. Remove from heat.

3. Combine 2 cups mozzarella, cottage cheese, and next 4 ingredients in a bowl.

4. Spread 1 cup turkey mixture in bottom of a 13 x 9-inch baking dish. Arrange 3 noodles over turkey mixture; top with 1½ cups turkey mixture. Spread half of cheese mixture over turkey mixture. Repeat layers, ending with remaining turkey mixture.

5. Cover and bake at 350° for 1 hour. Sprinkle with 1 cup mozzarella; bake, uncovered, for 10 minutes. Let stand 10 minutes before serving. Yield: 8 servings.

CALORIES 385 (24% from fat); FAT 10.4g (sat 6.2g, mono 2.8g, poly 0.7g); PROTEIN 39g; CARB 32g; FIBER 2.3g; CHOL 62mg; IRON 2.5mg; SODIUM 902mg; CALC 481mg

## Pesto Bread Rounds

"These make an excellent appetizer, meal accompaniment, or potluck contribution. The bread rounds are very versatile and go well with virtually any meal, whether it's soup, salad, or chicken. I like to garnish the rounds in fun ways, with black olives, roasted red pepper slices, or small sprigs of cilantro."

—Sher Bird Garfield, Bellevue, Washington

  1  (8-ounce) loaf French bread, cut into 20 (¾-inch) slices
  ½  cup fat-free mayonnaise
  ¼  cup (1 ounce) grated fresh Parmesan cheese
  2  tablespoons (½ ounce) grated Asiago cheese
  1  tablespoon commercial pesto
  ½  teaspoon minced garlic
  ⅛  teaspoon black pepper

1. Preheat broiler.

2. Place bread on a baking sheet; broil 1 minute or until toasted.

3. Combine mayonnaise and remaining 5 ingredients in a medium bowl. Spread 1½ teaspoons mayonnaise mixture on untoasted side of each bread slice. Place slices on baking sheet; broil 4 minutes or until cheese and edges of bread are browned. Yield: 10 servings (serving size: 2 slices).

CALORIES 99 (25% from fat); FAT 2.8g (sat 1g, mono 1.1g, poly 0.2g); PROTEIN 3.5g; CARB 14.7g; FIBER 0.7g; CHOL 3mg; IRON 0.7mg; SODIUM 395mg; CALC 68mg

---

### menu
#### Marinara Sauce over Rotini
Herbed focaccia*

*Unroll 1 (11-ounce) can refrigerated French bread dough on a jelly-roll pan coated with cooking spray; flatten slightly. Make indentations in dough about 1 inch apart with handle of a wooden spoon; brush with 1 teaspoon olive oil. Sprinkle with ½ teaspoon dried oregano, ½ teaspoon dried basil, ½ teaspoon freshly ground pepper, ¼ teaspoon kosher salt, and ¼ teaspoon dried thyme. Bake at 375° for 15 minutes or until lightly browned. Serves 4.

---

## Marinara Sauce over Rotini

"My friends and I love this sauce because of the capers. It's a flexible recipe, too, since you can use dried herbs if you don't have any fresh on hand."

—Judy Spicer, Plymouth, Michigan

  1  teaspoon olive oil
  ½  cup chopped onion
  2  garlic cloves, minced
  2  tablespoons chopped fresh or 2 teaspoons dried basil
  2  tablespoons chopped fresh or 2 teaspoons dried parsley
  1  teaspoon sugar
  ½  teaspoon dried oregano
  ¼  teaspoon salt
  ¼  teaspoon black pepper
  1  (28-ounce) can diced tomatoes, undrained
  1  tablespoon capers
  4  cups hot cooked rotini (about 4 cups uncooked corkscrew pasta)

*Continued*

**1.** Heat oil in a medium saucepan over medium heat. Add onion and garlic; sauté 2 minutes. Add basil and next 6 ingredients; bring to a boil. Reduce heat, and simmer 15 minutes, stirring occasionally. Stir in capers. Serve over pasta. Yield: 4 servings (serving size: 1 cup pasta and ¾ cup sauce).

CALORIES 277 (8% from fat); FAT 2.5g (sat 0.4g, mono 1g, poly 0.7g); PROTEIN 9.7g; CARB 54.7g; FIBER 3.3g; CHOL 0mg; IRON 3.7mg; SODIUM 531mg; CALC 77mg

## Chicken-and-Mushroom Florentine

"This recipe is the result of an experiment. I was trying to use up what I had on hand, threw some things together, and came up with this wonderful dish. The key to the great taste is shredding the chicken, which allows it to really absorb all of the different flavors."

—Donna Galloway, Fairport, New York

    1  (16-ounce) can fat-free, less-
       sodium chicken broth, divided
    4  cups sliced mushrooms
    ⅓  cup chopped onion
    1  (10-ounce) package fresh spinach
    1  (12-ounce) can evaporated fat-free
       milk, divided
    1  teaspoon garlic powder
    ½  teaspoon seasoned salt
    1  tablespoon cornstarch
    1  cup (4 ounces) shredded part-skim
       mozzarella cheese
    4  cups hot cooked ziti (about 3 cups
       uncooked short tube-shaped pasta)
  Cooking spray
    2  cups shredded cooked chicken
       breast (about ¾ pound)
    1  cup (4 ounces) shredded marbled
       Cheddar and Monterey Jack
       cheese

**1.** Preheat oven to 350°.
**2.** Bring 1 cup broth to a boil in a large nonstick skillet. Add mushrooms, onion, and spinach; reduce heat, and simmer 10 minutes.
**3.** Combine remaining broth, 1 cup milk, garlic powder, and salt in a medium saucepan; bring to a simmer. Combine remaining milk and cornstarch in a small bowl. Add cornstarch mixture and mozzarella to broth mixture in saucepan; cook 2 minutes or until thick.
**4.** Arrange pasta in bottom of a 3-quart casserole coated with cooking spray; top with spinach mixture and chicken. Spoon broth mixture over chicken; sprinkle with Cheddar. Bake at 350° for 30 minutes or until cheese melts and begins to brown. Yield: 6 servings (serving size: 1½ cups).

CALORIES 442 (25% from fat); FAT 12.4g (sat 6.7g, mono 3.5g, poly 1.3g); PROTEIN 39.5g; CARB 41.8g; FIBER 3.6g; CHOL 82mg; IRON 4.1mg; SODIUM 718mg; CALC 487mg

## Chicken Italiano

"I think this dish—which my family loves— tastes wonderful because there are so many flavors going on. I recommend leaving the tomatoes off if you're going to freeze it, and then adding them fresh before reheating."

—Sandi Osborne, Seattle, Washington

    2  (10-ounce) packages frozen
       chopped spinach, thawed and
       drained
    1  (8-ounce) block fat-free cream
       cheese
  Cooking spray
    ½  cup Italian-seasoned breadcrumbs
    4  (4-ounce) skinned, boned chicken
       breast halves
    2  teaspoons olive oil
    4  (1-ounce) slices part-skim
       mozzarella cheese, cut in half
    ¼  teaspoon dried oregano
    8  (½-inch-thick) slices tomato
    ¼  cup (1 ounce) grated fresh
       Parmesan cheese

**1.** Preheat oven to 350°.
**2.** Combine spinach and cream cheese. Press spinach mixture into bottom of a 13 x 9-inch baking dish coated with cooking spray.
**3.** Place breadcrumbs in a shallow dish. Cut each chicken breast in half horizontally to make 2 cutlets. Dredge chicken in breadcrumbs.
**4.** Heat oil in a large nonstick skillet coated with cooking spray over medium-high heat. Add chicken; cook 2 minutes on each side or until lightly browned. Arrange chicken over spinach mixture. Top with mozzarella; sprinkle with oregano. Top with tomato slices and Parmesan. Bake at 350° for 30 minutes. Spoon one-fourth spinach mixture onto each of 4 plates; arrange 2 chicken cutlets and 2 tomato slices over spinach mixture. Yield: 4 servings.

**NOTE:** Before making cutlets (see step 3), partially freeze chicken for easier slicing.

CALORIES 378 (27% from fat); FAT 11.3g (sat 5g, mono 4g, poly 1.2g); PROTEIN 49.6g; CARB 17.9g; FIBER 4.7g; CHOL 97mg; IRON 4.4mg; SODIUM 1,005mg; CALC 611mg

## Spinach Calzone

"I came up with this recipe while trying to find a use for leftover ingredients from a spinach lasagna. I like this dish because it's easy to make, tastes great, and packs in a lot of calcium."

—Ellie Hickey, Cambridge, Massachusetts

    ¾  cup 1% low-fat cottage cheese
    ½  cup low-fat sour cream
    ¼  cup (2 ounces) ⅓-less-fat cream
       cheese, softened
    3  tablespoons grated fresh Parmesan
       cheese
    1  (10-ounce) package frozen
       chopped spinach, thawed, drained,
       and squeezed dry
    1  (7-ounce) bottle roasted red bell
       peppers, drained and chopped
    1  teaspoon garlic powder
    ¼  teaspoon freshly ground black
       pepper
    1  (10-ounce) can refrigerated pizza
       crust
  Cooking spray
    ¼  cup (1 ounce) shredded part-skim
       mozzarella cheese
    ¼  cup (1 ounce) shredded reduced-
       fat sharp Cheddar cheese
    1½  cups bottled fat-free Italian herb
       pasta sauce (such as Muir Glen)

**1.** Preheat oven to 425°.
**2.** Combine first 4 ingredients; beat at medium speed of a mixer 2 minutes or

until well-blended. Stir in spinach, bell pepper, garlic powder, and black pepper.

**3.** Unroll pizza crust onto a baking sheet coated with cooking spray; pat into a 14 x 10-inch rectangle. Spread spinach mixture over half of the crust, leaving a 1-inch border. Sprinkle mozzarella and Cheddar over spinach mixture. Fold dough over filling; press edges together to seal.

**4.** Bake at 425° for 15 minutes or until browned. Cool on a wire rack 5 minutes. Heat pasta sauce in a small saucepan over medium heat. Cut calzone into 6 squares; top with sauce. Yield: 6 servings (serving size: 1 square and ¼ cup sauce).

CALORIES 289 (30% from fat); FAT 9.6g (sat 5g, mono 2.9g, poly 1.2g); PROTEIN 15.7g; CARB 35.4g; FIBER 2.8g; CHOL 24mg; IRON 3mg; SODIUM 778mg; CALC 227mg

## inspired vegetarian

# Holidays, Unplugged

*Put those fancy appliances away and get back to basics this holiday season.*

December is always a complicated month. Of course, there are Christmas, Hanukkah, and New Year's to contend with. Kids are on vacation, and family and friends come to visit. Add to this the alarming brevity of daylight and the possibility of traffic-stopping snowstorms, and you have all the ingredients for chaos.

What better reason to have recipes on hand that not only emphasize simplicity and comfort, but can also make your life more graceful and less hectic—and that don't require plugging in several appliances to get the job done? This holiday season, do yourself a favor: Save your time and energy for you and your loved ones—not for your appliances.

## Cauliflower-and-Broccoflower Salad with Sherry Vinaigrette

**VINAIGRETTE:**

- 1½ tablespoons sherry vinegar or red wine vinegar
- 2 teaspoons Dijon mustard
- 1 teaspoon extra-virgin olive oil
- ¼ teaspoon freshly ground black pepper
- ⅛ teaspoon salt
- 1 garlic clove, chopped

**SALAD:**

- 2 cups small cauliflower florets
- 2 cups small broccoflower florets
- 2 cups trimmed watercress (about 1 bunch)
- ½ cup diced celery
- ½ cup chopped green bell pepper
- ½ cup sliced green olives
- ½ cup chopped seeded cucumber
- ¼ cup sliced green onions
- ¼ cup chopped fresh parsley
- 1 tablespoon capers
- 2 hard-cooked large eggs, quartered

**1.** To prepare vinaigrette, combine first 6 ingredients in a small bowl; stir with a whisk. Set aside.

**2.** To prepare salad, steam cauliflower and broccoflower, covered, 8 minutes or until tender. Drain and place in a large bowl. Stir in watercress and next 7 ingredients. Drizzle vinaigrette over salad; toss gently to coat. Serve with egg

quarters. Yield: 8 servings (serving size: ¾ cup salad and 1 egg wedge).

CALORIES 56 (45% from fat); FAT 2.8g (sat 0.7g, mono 1.4g, poly 0.4g); PROTEIN 3.4g; CARB 4.9g; FIBER 2.2g; CHOL 53mg; IRON 1.1mg; SODIUM 233mg; CALC 51mg

## Kale, White Bean, and Savoy Cabbage Soup

**SOUP:**

- ½ cup dried cannellini beans or other white beans
- 6 cups water
- 1½ teaspoons salt, divided
- 2 teaspoons olive oil
- 3½ cups diced baking potato (about 1 pound)
- 1½ cups diced onion
- 1½ cups thinly sliced leek (about 1 large)
- 8 cups thinly sliced kale (about 1 bunch)
- 4 cups chopped Savoy cabbage (about 1½ pounds)
- ¼ cup chopped fresh parsley
- ¼ teaspoon black pepper
- 1 large garlic clove, minced

**GARLIC TOAST:**

- 8 (¾-inch-thick) slices diagonally cut Italian bread (about 12 ounces)
- 1 garlic clove, halved
- ¼ cup (1 ounce) grated fresh Parmesan cheese

**1.** To prepare soup, sort and wash beans; place in a large Dutch oven. Cover with water to 2 inches above beans; cover and let stand 8 hours. Drain beans. Return beans to pan; cover with 6 cups water. Bring to a boil; cover, reduce heat, and simmer 1 hour and 15 minutes. Add ½ teaspoon salt; simmer 15 minutes or until beans are tender. Set aside.

**2.** Heat oil in a stockpot over medium-low heat. Add potato, onion, and leek; cook 12 minutes, stirring occasionally. Stir in 1 teaspoon salt, kale, cabbage, parsley, pepper, and minced garlic. Cover, reduce heat, and cook 30 minutes. Add bean mixture; cook 30 minutes.

*Continued*

3. Preheat broiler.

4. To prepare garlic toast, place bread slices in a single layer on a jelly-roll pan. Broil 2 minutes on each side or until toasted. Rub toast with garlic halves. Ladle soup into bowls; top with garlic toast, and sprinkle with Parmesan cheese. Yield: 8 servings (serving size: 1 cup soup, 1 toast slice, and 1½ teaspoons cheese).

CALORIES 316 (11% from fat); FAT 3.7g (sat 1g, mono 1.7g, poly 0.6g); PROTEIN 12.8g; CARB 60.2g; FIBER 5.6g; CHOL 3mg; IRON 4.6mg; SODIUM 797mg; CALC 198mg

boil. Cover, reduce heat, and simmer 35 minutes or until barley is tender. Fluff with a fork; stir in parsley.

4. Melt butter in a cast-iron or heavy skillet over high heat. Add sliced button mushrooms; sauté 5 minutes or until browned. Top pilaf with sautéed mushrooms. Yield: 4 servings (serving size: 1¼ cups pilaf and about ¼ cup mushrooms).

CALORIES 322 (30% from fat); FAT 10.8g (sat 2.9g, mono 5.9g, poly 1.2g); PROTEIN 8.4g; CARB 51.7g; FIBER 10.7g; CHOL 8mg; IRON 3.2mg; SODIUM 338mg; CALC 41mg

cup reserved mushroom liquid; cover and cook 3 minutes or until carrot is crisp-tender and liquid evaporates.

4. Add bok choy; stir-fry 1 minute. Stir in noodles, remaining mushroom liquid, soy sauce, and tofu; cook 2 minutes.

5. Combine 3 tablespoons water and cornstarch; add to pan. Bring to a boil; cook 2 minutes or until slightly thick. Drizzle with sesame oil. Yield: 4 servings (serving size: 2 cups).

CALORIES 195 (29% from fat); FAT 6.4g (sat 1g, mono 1.9g, poly 2.8g); PROTEIN 10.3g; CARB 27.4g; FIBER 6.1g; CHOL 0mg; IRON 2.6mg; SODIUM 539mg; CALC 206mg

### Barley Pilaf with Sautéed Mushrooms

½ cup dried porcini mushrooms (about ½ ounce)
1 cup boiling water
2 tablespoons olive oil, divided
3 cups chopped button mushrooms (about 8 ounces)
½ cup dry white wine
⅛ teaspoon black pepper
2 garlic cloves, minced
1 cup finely chopped onion
2¼ cups water
1 cup uncooked pearl barley
½ teaspoon salt
¼ cup chopped fresh parsley
1 tablespoon butter
4 cups sliced button mushrooms (about 8 ounces)

1. Combine porcini mushrooms and boiling water in a bowl; cover and let stand 15 minutes. Drain in a sieve over a bowl, reserving mushroom liquid. Finely chop porcini mushrooms; set aside.

2. Heat 1 tablespoon oil in a large cast-iron or heavy skillet over high heat. Add chopped button mushrooms; cook 5 minutes or until browned, stirring occasionally. Reduce heat to medium. Add porcini mushrooms, wine, pepper, and garlic; cook 1 minute or until liquid almost evaporates. Remove from heat.

3. Heat 1 tablespoon oil in a large saucepan over medium heat. Add onion; cook 3 minutes. Add reserved mushroom liquid, porcini mushroom mixture, 2¼ cups water, barley, and salt; bring to a

### Asian Noodle, Tofu, and Vegetable Stir-Fry

2 ounces uncooked bean threads (cellophane noodles)
½ ounce dried wood ear mushrooms (about 6)
1 cup boiling water
2 teaspoons peanut oil or vegetable oil
1 cup coarsely chopped onion
1 tablespoon minced seeded jalapeño pepper
2 teaspoons minced peeled fresh ginger
2 garlic cloves, minced
3 cups (¼-inch) diagonally sliced carrot (about 1 pound)
¼ teaspoon salt
7 cups (1-inch) sliced bok choy
2 tablespoons low-sodium soy sauce
1 (12.3-ounce) package reduced-fat firm tofu, cubed
3 tablespoons water
2 teaspoons cornstarch
1 teaspoon dark sesame oil or chili oil

1. Place noodles in a large bowl; cover with warm water. Let stand 20 minutes. Drain; set aside.

2. Combine mushrooms and boiling water in a bowl; let stand 20 minutes. Strain through a sieve into a bowl, reserving mushroom liquid. Cut mushrooms into strips.

3. Heat peanut oil in a wok or nonstick Dutch oven over medium-high heat. Add onion, jalapeño, ginger, and garlic; stir-fry 1 minute. Add mushrooms, carrot, and salt; stir-fry 2 minutes. Stir in ¼

### Soy-Glazed Sweet Potatoes

¼ cup water
2 tablespoons brown sugar
3 tablespoons low-sodium soy sauce
2 tablespoons mirin (sweet rice wine)
1 tablespoon dark sesame oil
4 garlic cloves, minced
3 sweet potatoes, each cut lengthwise into 4 wedges (about 2 pounds)
1 tablespoon toasted sesame seeds

1. Preheat oven to 400°.

2. Combine first 6 ingredients; stir well with a whisk. Arrange potatoes in a single layer in a 13 x 9-inch baking dish. Pour soy sauce mixture over potatoes. Cover and bake at 400° for 50 minutes or until tender; baste with soy sauce mixture. Bake, uncovered, an additional 10 minutes or until liquid is absorbed. Sprinkle with sesame seeds. Yield: 4 servings (serving size: 3 wedges).

CALORIES 325 (14% from fat); FAT 5.2g (sat 0.8g, mono 1.8g, poly 2.2g); PROTEIN 4.8g; CARB 65.2g; FIBER 6.9g; CHOL 0mg; IRON 2mg; SODIUM 440mg; CALC 82mg

**HOW TO USE IT AND WHY**  Glance at the end of any *Cooking Light* recipe, and you'll see how committed we are to helping you make the best of today's light cooking. With three chefs, five registered dietitians, five home economists, and a computer system that analyzes every ingredient we use, *Cooking Light* gives you authoritive dietary detail like no other magazine. We go to such lengths so you can see how our recipes fit into your healthful eating plan. If you're trying to lose weight, the calorie and fat figures will probably help most. But if you're keeping a close eye on the sodium, cholesterol, and saturated fat in your diet, we provide those numbers, too. And because many women don't get enough iron or calcium, we can also help there, as well. Finally, there's a fiber analysis for those of us who don't get enough roughage.

**What it means and how we get there:** Besides the calories, protein, fat, fiber, iron, and sodium we list at the end of each recipe, there are a few things we abbreviate for space.

- *sat* for saturated fat
- *mono* for monounsaturated fat
- *poly* for polyunsaturated fat
- *CARB* for carbohydrates
- *CHOL* for cholesterol
- *CALC* for calcium
- *g* for gram
- *mg* for milligram

We get numbers for those categories based on a few assumptions: When we give a range for an ingredient, we calculate the lesser amount. Some alcohol calories evaporate during heating; we reflect that. And only the amount of marinade absorbed by the food is calculated.

| Your Daily Nutrition Guide | | | |
|---|---|---|---|
| | WOMEN AGES 25 TO 50 | WOMEN OVER 50 | MEN OVER 24 |
| Calories | 2,000 | 2,000 or less | 2,700 |
| Protein | 50g | 50g or less | 63g |
| Fat | 67g or less | 67g or less | 90g or less |
| Saturated Fat | 22g or less | 22g or less | 30g or less |
| Carbohydrates | 299g | 299g | 405g |
| Fiber | 25g to 35g | 25g to 35g | 25g to 35g |
| Cholesterol | 300mg or less | 300mg or less | 300mg or less |
| Iron | 15mg | 10mg | 10mg |
| Sodium | 2,400mg or less | 2,400mg or less | 2,400mg or less |
| Calcium | 1,000mg | 1,200mg | 1,000mg |

Calorie requirements vary according to your size, weight, and level of activity. This chart is a good general guide; additional nutrients are needed during some stages of life. For example, children's calorie and protein needs are based on height and vary greatly as they grow. Compared to adults, teenagers require less protein but more calcium and slightly more iron. Pregnant or breast-feeding women need more protein, calories, and calcium. Also, the need for iron increases during pregnancy but returns to normal after birth.

# Recipe Title Index

*An alphabetical listing of every recipe title that appeared*
*in the magazine in 2000. See page 399 for the General Recipe Index.*

# Month-by-Month Index

*A month-by-month listing of every food story with recipe titles that appeared in the magazine in 2000. See page 399 for the General Recipe Index.*

# General Recipe Index

*A listing by major ingredient, food category, and/or regular column
for every recipe that appeared in the magazine in 2000.*

408    General Recipe Index

Salmon *(continued)*

# Credits